FROM GENGHIS KHAN TO TAMERLANE

FROM GENGHIS KHAN TO TAMERLANE

THE REAWAKENING OF MONGOL ASIA

PETER JACKSON

YALE UNIVERSITY PRESS
NEW HAVEN AND LONDON

Frontispiece:
Chinggis Khan. Yuan Taizu, Yuan Dynasty emperor bust album, fourteenth century, National Palace Museum, 中-畫-000324-00001.
Bust of Tamerlane made from his exhumed skull. Shakko/CC BY-SA 3.0.

For information about this and other Yale University Press publications, please contact:
U.S. Office: sales.press@yale.edu yalebooks.com
Europe Office: sales@yaleup.co.uk yalebooks.co.uk

Set in Adobe Caslon Pro by IDSUK (DataConnection) Ltd
Printed in the United States of America

Library of Congress Control Number: 2023946540

ISBN 978-0-300-25112-8

A catalogue record for this book is available from the British Library.

10 9 8 7 6 5 4 3 2

In fond memory of David Orrin Morgan (1945–2019)

CONTENTS

List of Figures — *ix*
Note on Transliteration, Dating and Referencing — *x*
Abbreviations — *xiv*
Acknowledgements — *xxii*

Introduction — 1

1 Sources for the Mongol and Timurid Eras — 21

PART I: THE MONGOLS

2 The Mongol Empire: Unity, Expansion and Division, *c.* 1200–1335 — 53

3 Islamisation — 86

4 The Crisis of the Mongol World: Chinggisid Rule on the Wane — 111

5 The Crisis of the Mongol World: Economic Turbulence and Demographic Disaster — 139

PART II: GREATER IRAN AND CENTRAL ASIA BEFORE TIMUR

6 Iran and Iraq after the Ilkhans 167

7 The Central Asian Mongols: Chaghatays, Mughūls and Qara'unas 198

8 Timur's Forebears and the Elite of the Chaghadayid Realm 223

PART III: TĪMŪR-*I LANG*

9 The Making of the Great Amir and a New Ruling Cadre 251

10 The Forging of an Empire: A Career of Conquest 284

11 The Forging of an Empire: The Function and Conduct of War 313

12 The *Qarachu* Warlord and the Imperial Chinggisids 337

13 Muslim Sultan and Holy Warrior: Faith, Propaganda and Posture 361

14 The Mongol Empire Resurrected? 388

15 Aftermath: Timur's Successors 415

Conclusions 444

Glossary *454*

Chronology *458*

Genealogical Tables *463*

Endnotes *476*

Bibliography *645*

Index *685*

FIGURES

MAPS

1. The Mongol empire. 54
2. Post-Ilkhanid Iran. 162
3. The Chaghadayid realm. 196
4. The Qara'unas territories. 197
5. The regional powers in the western Chaghadayid ulus. 222
6. Timur's campaigns. 282

GENEALOGICAL TABLES

1. The Qaghans. 464
2. The khans of Chaghadai's ulus. 466
3. The Jochids. 468
4. The Ilkhans. 470
5. The Jalayirids (in Baghdad; also Tabriz and Sulṭāniyya from 1358). 471
6. The Muzaffarids (in Kirmān from 1340, Fārs from 1353 and ʿIrāq-i ʿAjam from 1356). 472
7. The Timurids. 473
8. List of rulers: Kartids (Herat) and Sarbadārs (Sabzawār). 474

NOTE ON TRANSLITERATION, DATING AND REFERENCING

TRANSLITERATION

Generally speaking, I have adopted the system for Middle Mongolian names found in J.A. Boyle's partial translation of the *Jāmiʿ al-tawārīkh* of Rashīd al-Dīn, *The Successors of Genghis Khan* (New York, 1971). However, Turkish and Mongolian proper names, notoriously, have long defied consistent transcription. To take just two examples, the name Toqa Temür, encountered in the history of the Golden Horde, can also be transcribed as Togha Temür, and the first element is identical with the name of a Chaghadayid khan that is invariably spelled Du'a (d. 1307). The name of the celebrated Ilkhan of Iran, Ghazan (d. 1304), is identical with those of the Chaghadayid khan Q̱azan (d. 1346) and the latter's antagonist, the amir Q̱azaghan (all three variant forms represent the Mongolian word for 'cauldron'). Any attempt at consistency here would result in spellings unrecognisable to historians of the Mongols and would fail to compensate by imparting any particular benefit to non-specialists.

The Iranian world figures extensively in this book, and I use the modern name Iran rather than the term Persia most often employed by nineteenth- and twentieth-century writers. For place names where an anglicised form is in common use (e.g. Aleppo, Damascus, Cairo, Herat) and for titles/ranks which have long been Europeanised (e.g. caliph, amir, sultan), these forms will be given (but 'wazir' in preference to 'vizier'); although when the word 'sultan' forms part of a proper name it appears with diacritics thus: Sulṭān. Otherwise, for Arabic and Persian, I have observed the conventions found in *The Encyclopaedia of Islam*, 2nd edn (Leiden, 1954–2009), except that I employ ch (in place of č), j (replacing d̲j̲) and q (not ḳ). Persian is transliterated as if it were Arabic: thus th rather than s̲, ḍ rather than ż, and w rather than v; though the Arabic conjunction *wa-* ('and') sometimes appears as *-u* in Persian phrases. Persian-Arabic spelling is also used for a *nisba* (e.g. Samarqandī, Ḥalabī), even where it is derived from a Turkish locality (thus Āqsarāyī, from Akseray). The Arabic definite article *al-* is omitted, however, in the *nisba*s of persons of non-Arab stock (as with Juwaynī, Āqsarāyī, Faryūmadī and Yazdī). I likewise omit the *iḍāfa* (-i) prior to the *nisba* in Persian proper names. The Arabic-Persian patronymic (*bin*, *ibn*), for which the Timurid sources frequently substitute the *iḍāfa*, is regularly abbreviated to 'b.', except when it designates an individual referred to generally by his patronymic alone – usually an author, as in the case of Ibn ʿArabshāh and Ibn Khaldūn.

Turkish, Mongol and Persian-Arabic terms that recur many times in the text (for example, *quriltai*, *noyan*, *tümen*, *malik*) are given, after the first appearance, in roman type rather than italics, and without diacritics. The names of dynasties always appear without diacritics (thus Jalayirids rather than Jalāyirids, Muzaffarids in preference to Muẓaffarids); so too do adjectives relating to place names (hence Khwarazmian rather than Khwārazmian). I have employed the form 'Mamlūk' for the regime that controlled Egypt and Syria, while using 'mamluk' (with lower-case initial letter and no macron) for the elite military slaves from whom the regime takes its name. I have called the fourteenth-century Golden Horde khan Özbeg, while retaining the more familiar form Uzbek for the people whose name was ultimately derived from his.

The Persian form of the name Mongol and its derivatives, as they appear in this book, also present inconsistencies. Although I have used 'Mughūl' and 'Mughūlistān', as found in Timurid sources, for the eastern Chaghadayid khanate and its inhabitants, the dynasty descended from Timur that ruled in India from 1525 to 1858 is referred to as 'Mughul' with no macron over the second vowel (rather than 'Moghul' or 'Mughal' as more frequently encountered in the secondary literature). Throughout, I restrict the term Mongol to the Mongolian people in general, whether domiciled in present-day Mongolia or engaged in the conquest of and rule over Asia.

The two ethnic labels Uighur and Tājīk are always used in their medieval sense, the former referring to the Turkic inhabitants of the Tarim basin (rather than to the modern population of the Chinese province of Xinjiang) and the term Tājīk applying generally to speakers of Persian or Arabic (rather than to the inhabitants of present-day Tajikistan). Perhaps the most puzzling convention I have adopted relates to Timur's Turco-Mongolian military forces. I have employed for this purpose 'Chaghatay' (the term which is also in general use for a widely spoken Central Asian dialect of the Turkish language), whereas 'Chaghadayid' refers to the polity within which Timur originated and rose to power, and to its ruling dynasty, founded by Chinggis Khan's second son Chaghadai.

Given the fact that various letters in the Arabic-Persian script differ from one another only in the placing of diacritical points, the reading of Turkish and Mongolian proper names in the primary sources (either printed or in manuscript) is frequently problematic. I have used small capitals, particularly in the notes, to transliterate an uncertain name in a text: here Č represents the double consonant ch, Ġ stands for gh, Š for sh, T̲ for th and X for kh, and the long vowels ā, ū and ī are represented by A, W and Y respectively. When diacritical points seem to be incorrect (or lacking altogether) in the manuscript original, I have transliterated the Arabic-Persian consonant as it appears there, but in italics. Thus *Ḥ* [ح, حـ] might in fact have stood for J [ج, جـ], Č [چ, چـ] or X [خ, خـ]. A mere 'tooth' without diacritical points, which could accordingly represent B, P, T, T̲, N, Y or ' (if simply the bearer of the *hamza*, ئـ), is indicated in transcription by a dot. An asterisk always precedes the hypothetical reconstruction of a name.

The spelling of Chinese names and terms conforms to the pinyin system. Russian is transliterated according to a slightly modified version of the Library of Congress system. For modern Mongolian I have adapted the system of transliteration for Russian: thus *č*, *š*, *x* and *ž*, rather than *ch*, *sh*, *kh* and *zh*.

DATING

Where dates are cited simultaneously according to both the Hijrī calendar and the Common Era, the former appears first. Thus: 807/1404–5; 25 Shaʿbān 736/8 April 1336.

REFERENCING

I have followed the same practice as I did in *The Mongols and the Islamic World*: namely, often citing together more than one version of a primary text, for instance the two English translations of Clavijo's narrative, by Markham and Le Strange respectively, or the two modern editions of Yazdī's *Ẓafar-nāma*, by ʿAbbāsī (1957) and by Ṣādiq and Nawāʾī (2008). This is designed for the benefit of readers who (like myself on so many occasions) have access to only one such version and find an author's exclusive reliance on a single alternative text deeply frustrating.

ABBREVIATIONS

TEXTS

CC	Rashīd al-Dīn, *Jāmi' al-tawārīkh*, trans. Thackston, *Compendium of Chronicles* (2012 edn)
Clavijo	Clavijo, *Embajada a Tamorlán*: (1859) trans. Markham; (1928) trans. Le Strange
CO	Ḥāfiẓ-i Abrū, *Cinq opuscules de Ḥāfiẓ-i Abrū*, ed. F. Tauer
DPT	Yazdī, Ghiyāth al-Dīn 'Alī, *Rūz-nāma-yi ghazawāt-i Hind*, trans. Semenov, *Giiāsaddīn 'Alī. Dnevnik pokhoda Tīmūra v Indiiu*
DzhT	Rashīd al-Dīn, *Jāmi' al-tawārīkh*, ed. Romaskevich et al., *Dzhāmi' at-tavārīkh*, I, part 1; ed. Alizade, *Dzhāmi' at-tavārīkh*, II, part. 1; ed. Alizade, *Dzhāmī-at-tavārīkh*, III
GW	Waṣṣāf, *Tajziyat al-amṣār*, partial trans. by Hammer-Purgstall, *Geschichte Wassaf's*
HA	Ḥāfiẓ-i Abrū
HWC	Juwaynī, *Ta'rīkh-i jahān-gushā*, trans. Boyle, *The History of the World-Conqueror*
IA	Ibn 'Arabshāh, *'Ajā'ib al-maqdūr*: (1979) ed. 'Umar; (1986) ed. al-Ḥimṣī; see also *TGA* below
IB	Ibn Baṭṭūṭa, *Tuḥfat al-nuẓẓār*

IKPI	M.Kh. Abuseitova et al. (general eds), *Istoriia Kazakhstana v persidskikh istochnikakh*, 5 vols (Almaty, 2005–7): I (Jamāl al-Qarshī, *al-Mulḥaqāt bi l-Ṣurāḥ*); III (anon., *Muʿizz al-ansāb*); V (*Izvlecheniia iz sochinenii XIII–XIX vekov*)
IKT	Ibn Khaldūn, *al-Taʿrīf bi-Ibn Khaldūn*, partial trans. by Fischel, *Ibn Khaldūn and Tamerlane*
JT	Rashīd al-Dīn, *Jāmiʿ al-tawārīkh* (the edition by Rawshan and Mūsawī, unless otherwise specified)
Khwāfī	Khwāfī, Faṣīḥ al-Dīn Aḥmad, *Mujmal-i Faṣīḥī*: (1962) ed. Farrukh; (2007) ed. Naṣrābādī
MA	anonymous, *Muʿizz al-ansāb*
Masālik	Ibn Faḍl-Allāh al-ʿUmarī, *Masālik al-abṣār* (partial edn and trans. by Lech, *Das mongolische Weltreich*, unless otherwise stated)
MFW	Rubruck, *Itinerarium*, trans. and ed. P. Jackson with D. Morgan, *The Mission of Friar William of Rubruck*
Mignanelli	Mignanelli, Beltramo di, *De ruina Damasci*: (1764) ed. Baluze; (2013) ed. Helmy in *Tra Siena*
MM	Christopher Dawson (ed.), *The Mongol Mission*
MP	Marco Polo, *Le Devisement du monde* (Ménard's edition unless otherwise specified)
Naṭanzī	Naṭanzī, *Muntakhab al-tawārīkh*: (1957) ed. Aubin; (2004) ed. Istakhrī
PC	Plano Carpini, *Ystoria Mongalorum*, ed. Menestò et al.
PSRL	*Polnoe sobranie russkikh letopisei*
RIS	L.A. Muratori (ed.), *Rerum Italicarum Scriptores*, 25 vols in 28 parts (Milan, 1723–51); 2nd series, *Raccolta degli storici italiani*, ed. Giosuè Carducci et al., 34 vols (Città di Castello and Bologna, 1900–75)
RN	Yazdī, Ghiyāth al-Dīn ʿAlī, *Rūz-nāma-yi ghazawāt-i Hind*: (1915) ed. Zimin; (2000) ed. Afshār
Sayfī	Sayfī (Sayf b. Muḥammad b. Yaʿqūb al-Harawī), *Ta'rīkh-nāma-yi Harāt*: (1944) ed. aṣ-Ṣiddíqí; (2004) ed. Ṭabāṭabā'ī Majd

SF	Van Den Wyngaert (ed.), *Sinica Franciscana*, I
SGK	Rashīd al-Dīn, *Jāmiʿ al-tawārīkh*, trans. Boyle, *The Successors of Genghis Khan*
SH	*Mongghol'un niucha tobcha'an* (The Secret History of the Mongols), trans. with commentary by De Rachewiltz
Shāmī, *ZN*	Shāmī, Niẓām al-Dīn, *Ẓafar-nāma*
SMIZO	V.G. Tizengauzen (ed.), *Sbornik materialov, otnosiashchikhsia k istorii Zolotoi Ordy*
SP	Rashīd al-Dīn, *Shuʿab-i panjgāna*
Taʿrīf	Ibn Khaldūn, *al-Taʿrīf bi-Ibn Khaldūn*: (1951) ed. al-Ṭanjī; (2008) ed. and trans. Cheddadi; see also *IKT* above
TGA	Ibn ʿArabshāh, *'Ajā'ib al-maqdūr*, trans. J.H. Sanders, *Tamerlane or Timur, the Great Amir*
TGNN	Anonymous, *Tawārīkh-i guzīda-yi nuṣrat-nāma*
TJG	Juwaynī, *Ta'rīkh-i jahān-gushā*
TN	Jūzjānī, *Ṭabaqāt-i Nāṣirī*
TR	Ḥaydar Dughlāt, *Ta'rīkh-i Rashīdī*
Waṣṣāf	Waṣṣāf, *Tajziyat al-amṣār*: (1853) Bombay lithograph edn; (2009) partial edn by Nizhād
WR	Rubruck, *Itinerarium*, ed. Chiesa
Yazdī, *ZN*	Yazdī, Sharaf al-Dīn ʿAlī, *Ẓafar-nāma*: (1957) ed. ʿAbbāsī; (1972) ed. Urunbaev; (2008) ed. Ṣādiq and Nawā'ī
Zayn al-Dīn	Zayn al-Dīn b. Ḥamd-Allāh Mustawfī Qazwīnī, *Dhayl-i Ta'rīkh-i guzīda*: (1990) ed. and trans. Kazimov and Piriiev; (1993) ed. Afshār
ZT	Ḥāfiẓ-i Abrū, *Zubdat al-tawārīkh*

PERIODICAL AND SERIES TITLES AND WORKS OF REFERENCE

AEMA	*Archivum Eurasiae Medii Aevi*
AF	Asiatische Forschungen
AHSS	*Annales. Histoire, Sciences Sociales*
AKM	Abhandlungen für die Kunde des Morgenlandes

Al-Masāq	*Al-Masāq. Islam and the Medieval Mediterranean*
ANSMN	*American Numismatic Society Museum Notes*
AOH	*Acta Orientalia Academiae Scientiarum Hungaricae*
AS	*Asiatische Studien*
BEC	*Bibliothèque de l'École des Chartes*
BEO	*Bulletin d'Études Orientales de l'Institut Français de Damas*
BHM	*Bulletin of the History of Medicine*
BI	Bibliotheca Islamica
BIAL	Brill's Inner Asian Library
BSOAS	*Bulletin of the School of Oriental and African Studies*
CAC	*Cahiers d'Asie Centrale*
CAJ	*Central Asiatic Journal*
CHC	*The Cambridge History of China*: VI: *Alien Regimes and Border States 907–1368*, ed. Herbert Franke and Denis Twitchett (Cambridge, 1994); VIII: *The Ming Dynasty, 1368–1644*, ed. Denis Twitchett and Frederick W. Mote (Cambridge, 1998), 2 parts; IX, part 2: *The Ch'ing Dynasty to 1800*, ed. Willard J. Peterson (Cambridge, 2016)
CHE	Carl F. Petry (ed.), *The Cambridge History of Egypt*, I: *Islamic Egypt, 640–1517* (Cambridge, 1998)
CHI	*The Cambridge History of Iran*: V: *The Saljuq and Mongol Periods*, ed. J.A. Boyle (Cambridge, 1968); VI: *The Timurid and Safavid Periods*, ed. Peter Jackson and Laurence Lockhart (Cambridge, 1986)
CHIA	Nicola Di Cosmo, Allen J. Frank and Peter B. Golden (eds), *The Cambridge History of Inner Asia. The Chinggisid Age* (Cambridge, 2009)
CHT	Kate Fleet (ed.), *The Cambridge History of Turkey*, I: *Byzantium to Turkey, 1071–1453* (Cambridge, 2009)
CSIC	Cambridge Studies in Islamic Civilization
CSSH	*Comparative Studies in Society and History*

CWH	*The Cambridge World History*: V: *Expanding Webs of Exchange and Conflict, 500 CE–1500 CE*, ed. Benjamin Z. Kedar and Merry E. Wiesner-Hanks (Cambridge, 2015); VI: *The Construction of a Global World, 1400–1800 CE*, ed. Jerry H. Bentley, Sanjay Subrahmanyam and Merry E. Wiesner-Hanks (Cambridge, 2015), part 1: *Foundations*; part 2: *Patterns of Change*
D&R	Documents et recherches sur l'économie des pays byzantins, islamiques et slaves et leurs relations commerciales au Moyen Age
DTS	V.M. Nadeliaev et al. (eds), *Drevnetiurkskii slovar'* (Leningrad, 1969)
EDT	Sir Gerard Clauson (ed.), *An Etymological Dictionary of Pre-Thirteenth-Century Turkish* (Oxford, 1972)
EI[2]	*Encyclopaedia of Islam*, 2nd edn, ed. Ch. Pellat, C.E. Bosworth et al., 13 vols (Leiden, 1954–2009)
EI[3]	*Encyclopaedia of Islam Three*, ed. Marc Gaborieau et al. (Leiden and Boston, MA, 2007–in progress)
EIr	*Encyclopaedia Iranica*, ed. Ehsan Yarshater (New York and Costa Mesa, CA, 1982–in progress; and https://referenceworks.brillonline.com/browse/encyclopaedia-iranica-online)
EMME	Christopher P. Atwood (ed.), *Encyclopaedia of Mongolia and the Mongol Empire* (New York, 2004)
ES	*Eurasian Studies*
EV	*Épigrafika Vostoka*
GAL	Carl Brockelmann (ed.), *Geschichte der arabischen Litteratur*, 2 vols, 2nd edn (Leiden, 1943–9), and 3 supplement vols (Leiden, 1937–42)
GMS	Gibb Memorial Series
HCCA, IV	C.E. Bosworth and M.S. Asimov (eds), *History of Civilizations of Central Asia*, IV. *A.D. 750 to the End of the Fifteenth Century*, part 1: *The Historical, Social and Economic Setting* (Paris, 1998); part 2: *The Achievements* (Paris, 2000)

HJAS	*Harvard Journal of Asiatic Studies*
HPL	Edward G. Browne, *A History of Persian Literature under Tartar Dominion (A.D. 1265–1502)*, A Literary History of Persia, III (Cambridge, 1920)
HS	Works issued by the Hakluyt Society
HT	Mirkasym Usmanov and Rafael Khakimov (eds), *The History of the Tatars since Ancient Times*, 7 vols (Kazan, 2017)
IHC	Islamic History and Civilization: Studies and Texts
Iran	*Iran. Journal of the British Institute of Persian Studies*
IrSt	*Iranian Studies*
IU	Islamkundliche Untersuchungen
IUUAS	Indiana University Uralic and Altaic Series
JA	*Journal Asiatique*
JAH	*Journal of Asian History*
JAOS	*Journal of the American Oriental Society*
JESHO	*Journal of the Economic and Social History of the Orient*
JGH	*Journal of Global History*
JNES	*Journal of Near Eastern Studies*
JPS	*Journal of Persianate Studies*
JRAS	*Journal of the Royal Asiatic Society*
JSAI	*Jerusalem Studies in Arabic and Islam*
JSYS	*Journal of Song-Yuan Studies*
JTS	*Journal of Turkish Studies*
JWH	*Journal of World History*
ME	*Medieval Encounters*
MM	The Medieval Mediterranean: Peoples, Economies and Cultures, 400–1453
MO	*Manuscripta Orientalia*
Mongolica	*Mongolica. An International Annual of Mongolian Studies*
MS	*Mongolian Studies*
MSR	*Mamlūk Studies Review*
MTB	*Memoirs of the Research Department of the Toyo Bunko*

Muqarnas	*Muqarnas: An Annual on the Visual Cultures of the Islamic World*
NCHI, III	David O. Morgan and Anthony Reid (eds), *The New Cambridge History of Islam*, III: *The Eastern Islamic World, Eleventh to Eighteenth Centuries* (Cambridge, 2010)
NZO	*Numizmatika Zolotoi Ordy*
OM	*Oriente Moderno*
Orient	*Orient. Reports of the Society for Near Eastern Studies in Japan*
PIA	Papers on Inner Asia
PL	C.A. Storey, *Persian Literature. A Bio-bibliographical Survey* (London, 1927–in progress)
PL[2]	C.A. Storey, *Persian Literature. A Bio-bibliographical Survey*, trans. and extended edn by Iu.É. Bregel′, *Persidskaia literatura. Bio-bibliograficheskii obzor*, 3 vols (Moscow, 1972)
PNAS	*Proceedings of the National Academy of Sciences of the United States of America*
QGIA	Quellen zur Geschichte des islamischen Ägyptens
REMMM	*Revue des Mondes Musulmans et de la Méditerranée*
SEA	Studies on East Asia
SOL	Sammlung Orientalischer Arbeiten
SRS	Silk Road Studies
StIr	*Studia Iranica*
StIsl	*Studia Islamica*
TDPKV	*Trudy dvadtsat′ piatogo kongressa vostokovedov Moskva 9-16 avgust a 1960*, 5 vols (Moscow, 1963)
TMEN	Gerhard Doerfer (ed.), *Türkische und mongolische Elemente im Neupersischen*, 4 vols, VOK 16, 19, 20 and 21 (Wiesbaden, 1963–75)
TP	*T'oung Pao. International Journal of Chinese Studies*
TS	*Tiurkologicheskii Sbornik*
TSCIA	Toronto Studies on Central and Inner Asia
Turcica	*Turcica. Revue d'Études Turques*

Turkestan[1]	V.V. Bartol'd, *Turkestan v épokhu mongol'kago nashestviia*, 1st edn, 2 vols (St Petersburg, 1898–1900)
Turkestan[3]	W. Barthold, *Turkestan down to the Mongol Invasion*, 3rd edn by C.E. Bosworth, with additional chapter trans. by T. Minorsky, GMS, n.s., 5 (London, 1968)
UAJ	*Ural-Altaische Jahrbücher*
VOK	Akademie der Wissenschaften und der Literatur: Veröffentlichungen der orientalischen Kommission
ZAS	*Zentralasiatische Studien*
ZDMG	*Zeitschrift der Deutschen Morgenländischen Gesellschaft*
ZOO	*Zolotoordynskoe Obozrenie*
ZOTs	*Zolotoordynskaia Tsivilizatsiia*

OTHER ABBREVIATIONS

Ar.	Arabic
b.	bin/ibn [in Arabic and Persian personal names – see above, 'Note on Transliteration']
BL	British Library
BN	Bibliothèque Nationale de France
CE	Common Era
Ch.	Chinese
Mo.	Mongolian
Pers.	Persian
RRL	Rampur Raza Library
TSM	Topkapı Sarayı Müzesi, Istanbul
Tu.	Turkish

ACKNOWLEDGEMENTS

I must begin by expressing my gratitude to Heather McCallum and Yale University Press for the enthusiastic reception they gave my book proposal; and to Heather and her colleagues Rachael Lonsdale, Lucy Buchan and Katie Urquhart for seeing the finished version through the press.

My dependence on a number of major research libraries in the UK is among the other important debts I have accumulated in writing this book, and I must record my gratitude to the staff of the British Library; the School of Oriental and African Studies (SOAS) in the University of London; the Aga Khan Library in London; the Wellcome Library; Cambridge University Library; the Needham Research Institute Library in Cambridge; the Ancient India and Iran Trust Library in Cambridge; the Bodleian Library and the Nizami Ganjevi Library in Oxford; the University of Oxford China Centre; the Kuwait Library in the Oxford Centre for Islamic Studies; the John Rylands University Library of Manchester; Birmingham University Library; Edinburgh University Library; Glasgow University Library; and the National Library of Scotland.

I am especially grateful to those institutions mentioned above from which I have been permitted to borrow books under the SCONUL scheme. In the preface to my previous book I described this as an invaluable privilege. I have had even greater reason to value it in retrospect, once the advent of Covid-19 and the suspension of

SCONUL in March 2020 seriously disrupted scholarly endeavours by apparently compelling university libraries in the UK to restrict physical access to their collections to their own staff and students for almost twenty months. I appreciated all the more the readiness of some of these institutions to reopen promptly to external visitors when SCONUL was restored to life in November 2021.

Of libraries outside the UK, the Bibliothèque Nationale de France kindly supplied digitised copies of mss. Supplément persan 1278 (Shabānkāra'ī, *Majma' al-ansāb*), Supplément persan 1651 (Naṭanzī, *Muntakhab al-tawārīkh*), Arabe 1544 (al-ʿAynī, *'Iqd al-jumān*) and Arabe 3423 (an anonymous *jung* or *safīna*, a literary anthology containing three of Timur's *fatḥ-nāma*s), and the Österreichische Nationalbibliothek a digitised version of ms. A.F. 112 (Qāyinī, *Naṣā'iḥ-i Shāhrukhī*). Several years ago the Universitätsbibliothek Graz provided me with a digitised copy of ms. 1221 (the *Libellus de notitia orbis* of Archbishop John of Sulṭāniyya). I have also made use of work I did in the more remote past in libraries outside Western Europe: the Süleymaniye Kütüphanesi, the Nuruosmaniye Kütüphanesi and the Topkapı Sarayı Müzesi, in Istanbul; and the Raza Library in Rampur, U.P., India. For the courtesy and helpfulness of the staff at all these institutions I am profoundly grateful.

I have also received invaluable help from academic colleagues. Dr. Na'ama Arom, Dr. Hannah Barker, Dr. Jonathan Brack, Dr. Konstantin Golev, Dr. Michael Hope, Dr. George Lane, Professor Charles Melville, Professor Lorenzo Pubblici, Dr. Philip Slavin, Dr. Jana Valtrová and Dr. Márton Vér kindly supplied me with references and pdf copies of articles and/or texts that were unknown or inaccessible to me. Dr. Tibor Porció was good enough to provide me with his translation of the Tibetan version of the Buddhist treatise *Sitataśastra*, which includes mention of plague in medieval Central Asia. In addition, I have benefited from corresponding with Dr. Monica H. Green, who has kindly shared references and forwarded publications that she had produced or encountered in connection with her work on the Black Death, and with Dr. Nahyan Fancy, who sent me digitised copies of a ms. of Ibn Shākir's *'Uyūn al-tawārīkh* and of a printed edition of an early section of Sibṭ Ibn al-Jawzī's *Mir'āt al-zamān*.

Thanks are also due to the anonymous readers who some years ago responded so positively to the proposal and draft introduction that I submitted to potential publishers and those who, more recently, reported on the completed text. Their encouragement has meant a great deal to me, and their comments saved me on more than one occasion from wrong or imbalanced conclusions. It goes without saying that the responsibility for any remaining errors is exclusively mine.

As so often in the past, my wife Rebecca has been a tower of strength, accepting – and even welcoming – the encroachment of Timur and his myrmidons (not to mention his numerous enemies and victims) on our daily routine. She has read the introduction and all the chapters in successive drafts and offered comments and suggestions, despite the increasingly heavy demands made of her as someone who works within the UK's beleaguered public services. For reasons which – I should emphasise – are quite unconnected with this last-mentioned circumstance, she has also shared with me the task of being my most stringent critic. I owe her an immense debt of gratitude.

This book is dedicated to the memory of a very good friend who was also a distinguished and widely respected scholar and indeed a household name for anyone working on (or even just interested in) the Mongol empire. His numerous publications comprise not merely what is still a much-quoted standard work on the Mongols more than thirty years after its first appearance (1986; second edition, 2007), and a history of medieval Persia (1988; second edition, 2016), but a pioneering article entitled 'The empire of Tamerlane: An unsuccessful re-run of the Mongol empire?' (2000), which addresses some of the themes explored in this book. His death in October 2019 was a heavy blow to a great many of us.

Madeley, Staffordshire, May 2023

INTRODUCTION

The title page is the last occasion in this book when the names of the two conquerors appear in that guise without qualification. 'Genghis' is a bastardised spelling with a convoluted pedigree that goes back to a faulty transcription of the title in the early eighteenth century. The founder of the Mongol empire (d. 1227), whose personal name was Temüjin, will appear here as 'Chinggis Khan' in accordance with the Mongolian spelling (rendered in Persian texts as 'Chingīz'). 'Tamerlane' is a European corruption of Temür-*i lang* ('Temür the Lame', in Persian; the Turkish equivalent is *Aksak Temir*). This was the usage – from wounds he had suffered to his right leg and right arm in his youth – under which he was immortalised by those writing outside his dominions. It was well embedded by the time Marlowe published his famous play in two parts, *Tamburlaine the Great* (1590; part I first performed in 1587). In preference to 'Temür', a common Turco-Mongolian name (meaning 'iron'), I have adopted 'Timur', as the spelling found in Persian and Arabic sources and more often than not reproduced in the secondary literature. My aim is to avoid confusion with the many other persons in this book who bore the name either singly or in compound form, and in relation to whom I employ the spelling Temür.

Timur (d. 807/1405), a member of the Turco-Mongol Barlās tribe, was born in Transoxiana (Ar.-Pers. *Mā warā' al-nahr*, 'what lies beyond the river [Oxus]'), within a world irreversibly shaped by the Mongols (or 'Tatars', as they were often known) and which still lay under Chinggis Khan's shadow. At one level, and particularly from an Iranian vantage point, he represented, as the Mongols had done, the forces of 'Turan' – the vast tract beyond the Oxus (Ar.-Pers. Amū-daryā) – that traditionally had long posed a threat to Iran and the Near East, a menace encapsulated in the Iranian epic *Shāh-nāma* of the eleventh-century author Firdawsī. As the last Turanian or Inner Asian conqueror at the head of a nomadic cavalry to forge a truly trans-regional empire, he did more than simply partake of the Mongols' legacy. He appears to have tried both to transcend and to perpetuate the Mongol achievement. During a series of expeditions spanning over three decades, he humbled not merely Mongol rulers descended from Chinggis Khan but the Sultan of Delhi, the Mamlūk Sultan of Egypt and Syria, the Ottoman Sultan Bayezid and a host of lesser princes. At his death, having already carved out a realm that stretched from Anatolia and Syria to the Punjab and the borders of present-day Xinjiang, he was on the point of heading an invasion of Ming China. As a commoner lacking Chinggisid ancestry, he did not reign officially over his conquests, but governed them in the name of a shadow khan of Chinggisid descent, himself accepting the Arabic-Persian title of *Amir*, 'Commander', or its Turkish equivalent, *Beg*, or sometimes 'Great *Amir*'.

Unlike Chinggis Khan, but in common with a great many of the Mongol conqueror's fourteenth-century descendants, Timur was a Muslim – one reason, perhaps, why he tends to emerge unfavourably from the almost inevitable comparisons with Chinggis Khan, who could be excused his excesses as a mere infidel.[1] Timur drew on a range of traditions, Islamic as well as Mongolian, to define and justify his rule: to exercise, as one modern author puts it, 'a cultural ambidexterity of sorts'.[2] And whether or not one sees his espousal of *jihād* as springing from sincere religious conviction, his wars against the unbeliever – and against those he denounced as 'bad' Muslims – produced a greater sensation, and had a more powerful impact, than the campaigns of any Muslim Mongol ruler before him.

TWO EMPIRES

The world in which Timur was active, well over a century after Chinggis Khan's death, had undergone significant political and social changes, of which Islamisation was only one of the most conspicuous. The unitary Mongol empire had long since ceased to be a reality. Chinggis Khan had allotted a specific territory and population (or *ulus*, to use the Mongolian term for such an amalgam; its modern meaning is 'state') to each of his sons and to other members of his family. But in the course of a civil war between rival candidates for the dignity of Great Khan (*Qaghan*) in the early 1260s, the empire had fragmented so that the principal uluses formed autonomous states. The western steppes were home to at least two such polities, ruled by the progeny of Chinggis Khan's eldest son Jochi, the foremost being the Qipchaq khanate (frequently designated as the 'Golden Horde'), centred on the Volga and the Crimea. The descendants of the second son, Chaghadai, ruled in Transoxiana and Turkestan (corresponding today to most of Uzbekistan, Tajikistan, Kyrgyzstan, south-eastern Kazakhstan and western Xinjiang). The other two principal states both came to be governed by rulers from the line of Chinggis Khan's fourth son Tolui. The Qaghan's dominions – the 'Great Khanate', or the Yuan Empire as it is known – comprised China, Mongolia, Manchuria and parts of Tibet; the Ilkhanate embraced present-day Iran, part of Afghanistan, Turkmenistan, Iraq, Azerbaijan, the Caucasus and most of Anatolia.

By Timur's day, however, the Ilkhanate had dissolved and its territories had passed into the hands of regional rulers, frequently of Iranian stock, while the Yuan dynasty was expelled from China in 1368 and supplanted by the native Ming. The Chinggisid states had already begun to follow different cultural trajectories. The majority of the nomadic populations of the western Mongol khanates – unlike the Yuan dominions – were ethnically Turks. And whereas Buddhism predominated under the Yuan, the nomads of Western and Central Asia were steadily Islamised. The Ilkhans had adopted Islam definitively in 1295; in the Jochid territories and the Chaghadayid state the khans had done so by the 1340s.

Although it now seems a trifle inappropriate to regard Timur as inaugurating the 'second phase' of the Mongol empire, as implicit in the title of a book published almost a century ago,[3] the idea that he was trying to recreate Chinggis Khan's empire is still widespread. This too is emphatically not beyond question, though it cannot be denied that Timur often acted in such a way as to evoke Chinggis Khan's memory. We might be tempted to subscribe to a recent definition of Timur's dominions as 'in effect, a neo-Mongol empire'.[4] He was of Mongol descent (although his ancestors almost certainly included Turks, and Turkish appears to have been his native language). If he did not follow, strictly speaking, a nomadic lifestyle,[5] the core of his army nevertheless comprised mounted nomad archers, just as had the Mongol forces; the khans he professed to serve were Chinggisid princes; and Mongol law and custom still played an important part in his governance. The formulation, accordingly, is by no means inapposite, provided we bear in mind two circumstances.

First, Timur's world differed geographically and spatially from that of the Mongols. His incessant military operations did not span so vast an area. Though his capture of Delhi represented a triumph that had eluded them, and his troops penetrated as deeply as theirs into Syria and Anatolia, his conquests on other fronts were less impressive. The Mongol empire has been described as 'the largest continuous land empire that has so far existed'.[6] Timur's domain encompassed only a fraction of that empire – a very large fraction, to be sure, but far from the entirety of the Chinggisid conquests.[7] Its kernel was not the original Mongolian homeland but Central Asia, and in particular the land north of the Amū-daryā (Oxus) and extending as far as, or beyond, the Sīr-daryā (Jaxartes River): Transoxiana, the western part of the territory that Chinggis Khan had bequeathed to Chaghadai. Here pasturelands were interspersed with regions centred on irrigation agriculture and wealthy towns like Samarkand and Bukhara, and Turkish nomadic groups and Persian-speaking ('Tājīk') sedentary communities, while remaining distinct, had lived in close proximity since the pre-Mongol era – a proximity reinforced by the nomads' acceptance of Islam. Even though the urban dweller and the cultivator feared the nomad's martial prowess and despised him as boorish and ignorant, while the nomad remained wary of seduction by sedentary culture and a consequential loss of military effectiveness, the relationship was one of symbiosis.[8] This was a distinctive cultural area. It is symptomatic of the well-established fissures within the Chinggisid world that Timur and his nomadic troops were known to their contemporaries – and referred to themselves – as 'Chaghatays' more commonly than as Mongols or Tatars.

Second, Timur's empire thus contrasted sharply with that of the Mongols in its ecological and cultural orientation. Although he sprang from a nomadic tribe, he drew above all on the resources of sedentary territories and did not aspire to rule over the steppelands, even those that had been subject to Chinggis Khan and his successors (with the exception of certain regions immediately east of Transoxiana).[9] Timur's principal residence, and the ultimate destination of much of the plunder he amassed on his campaigns, was the venerable city of Samarkand, and he evinced a strong attachment also to his birthplace, the town of Kish (later Shahr-i Sabz) in the valley of the Qashqa-daryā, likewise in Transoxiana. His dominions were far more homogeneous, in cultural terms, than Chinggis Khan's empire, comprising as they did territories that had not only been more or less Islamised but were in large measure coterminous with the Persianate world.[10]

TIMUR IN MODERN EUROPEAN WRITING

The reader who seeks to learn about Chinggis Khan and the empire he created is truly assailed by an *embarras de choix*. Well over twenty biographies of varying quality have appeared in English alone since the early nineteenth century,[11] and probably at least as many books on the Mongol empire. Work on Timur began to emerge rather later, and at first in studies with a different remit, like Barthold's book on Timur's grandson Ulugh Beg.[12] It was no coincidence that the earliest solid academic essay devoted to Timur in his own right, 'a short sketch' by the veteran Russian Mongolist Iakubovskii in 1946,[13] appeared in the wake of the opening of the conqueror's tomb in

Samarkand on Stalin's orders by the archaeologist M.M. Gerasimov in 1941, just a few days before the invasion of the Soviet Union by the forces of Nazi Germany. It is to the forensic reconstruction of Timur's physiognomy that we owe the familiar image found in a number of works, notably on the jacket of Hookham's *Tamburlaine the Conqueror* (see below).

Timur – or rather his triumph over the Ottoman Sultan Bayezid in 1402 – has been the subject of drama, within which Marlowe's work was both the most celebrated and the inspiration for others, and of opera, notably those by Handel (*Tamerlano*, 1724), Gasparini (*Tamerlano*, 1711; rewritten as *Bajazet*, 1713) and Vivaldi (*Bajazet*, 1735, alternatively called *Il Tamerlano*).[14] He can be said (at the risk of placing an intolerable strain on the weakest of metaphors) to have lent his name to verse by Edgar Allan Poe (in *Tamerlane and Other Poems*, 1827) – not to mention the 1970s New Zealand rock group Tamburlaine. Chinggis Khan has been denied any such tributes. Yet it is likely that fewer people know anything of the historical Timur, albeit a towering figure in his own right, than of Chinggis Khan.[15] Were it not for Marlowe, the numbers would surely have been still lower.

Additionally, Timur has attracted fewer book-length studies than has Chinggis Khan. Only three of these works have an unimpeachable claim to academic rigour, with a full scholarly apparatus of references. *The Rise and Rule of Tamerlane*, by Beatrice Manz, is a first-rate investigation, thoroughly grounded in the sources, of Timur's rise, the means by which he gained power and kept it and the administration of his far-flung conquests. My immense debt to *Rise and Rule*, as also to Manz's numerous other publications, will be apparent to anyone who reads the chapters that follow. The second book, Tilman Nagel's *Timur der Eroberer*, is an admirable attempt to situate Timur in the broadest of contexts: that of the late medieval Islamic world and its ideas, a world peopled by non-Mongol, Muslim powers like the Ottomans and the Mamlūks.[16] The third and most recent, by Michele Bernardini,[17] has unfortunately come to my notice too late for me to be able to make use of it in this book.

As Robert Irwin observed in 2005, however, Timur, 'though somewhat neglected by the academics, has long been a favourite subject for popular biography'.[18] There have been a number in English, some of them offering a significantly better treatment than the label 'popular' might seem to promise. The earliest is Hilda Hookham's *Tamburlaine the Conqueror* (1962), the, by no means negligible, work of a history schoolteacher who had access to none of the sources in the requisite original languages, Arabic and Persian. The most recent, Justin Marozzi's *Tamerlane* (2004), is written with panache and imagination and makes enjoyable reading; it is also coloured by the author's personal recollections of travel in Uzbekistan and Afghanistan in Timur's footsteps. Possibly the best of these biographies, however, are two semi-popular works in French by established scholars: Lucien Kehren, *Tamerlan, L'Empire du Seigneur de Fer* (1978), and Jean-Paul Roux, *Tamerlan* (1991). Like Hookham, both authors lacked the necessary languages,[19] although Roux poses – and answers – a good many questions not raised elsewhere and demonstrates a great deal of insight, particularly in the second part, 'L'Homme et son temps'. Lastly, mention should be made of the recent *L'Asie centrale de Tamerlan* (2022), by two scholars well versed in Islamic religious and cultural history, which *inter alia* offers an excellent introduction to Timur's homeland and embraces the era of the entire Timurid dynasty.[20]

Nomads and nomadic culture will frequently be mentioned in this book. In the literature produced by sedentary societies, nomads have long enjoyed a hostile press. Leaving relatively little in the archaeological record, and hardly more by way of textual evidence, they have traditionally been viewed as lawless, uncouth barbarians, given to predation and aggression against their settled neighbours. Only in more recent years has this image come to be modified, with the recognition that nomadic societies had no monopoly of aggression, that the pattern was frequently one of fruitful coexistence with sedentary societies and that nomads' interest in technical knowledge has been underplayed.[21] The new emphasis is especially visible in the scholarship on the Mongol empire, whose rulers can now be seen actively to have facilitated and promoted technical development and cultural exchange.[22]

It would be difficult to extrapolate this shift in perspective to Timur. He has always provoked a wide diversity of reactions, from admiration of his record of unalloyed military triumphs to condemnation of his devastating campaigns and exemplary cruelty.[23] There is much to be said for Hookham's comment that he 'could lead his hordes against all the kingdoms of the seven climes, destroying infidels because they were not Muslims and Muslims because they were not faithful'.[24] Voltaire distinguished him from Alexander the Great (whose campaigns, like Chinggis Khan's, had covered a broader geographical canvas) primarily on the basis that the Macedonian had built many cities, whereas Timur's exploits were merely destructive.[25] This judgement ignores the fact that Timur, unlike Chinggis Khan and his immediate successors, exhibited a strong interest in building magnificent structures to overawe contemporaries and posterity alike.[26] Described as 'one of the most complex, puzzling and unattractive figures in the history of Persia and Central Asia',[27] he has generally been deemed Chinggis Khan's inferior. But the contrast tends to centre less upon what has been termed his 'appalling career' – and the relative degree of humanity exhibited by the two conquerors – than on Timur's shortcomings as an administrator.[28] Particular attention has focused on his failure to leave behind a governmental structure capable of preserving the whole of his empire in the hands of his dynasty – still less of facilitating its expansion, as the Mongol empire had continued to expand for a further five decades or so following Chinggis Khan's death.[29]

Nevertheless, Timur has exerted a considerable fascination, which seems to derive in part from his image as a self-made man – in Marozzi's judgement, 'perhaps the greatest selfmade man who ever lived'.[30] Hookham clearly took the same view of one who had 'begun as a robber chief' but who had still, as 'the most able child of his period',[31] established his dominion over a vast tract. European authors have been inexorably drawn towards Timur's potential role as a saviour of Christendom, and for Hookham, contemplating the sorry state of a Europe mired in the Great Schism and under threat from the Ottoman Turks, Timur represented 'the star of hope'; he is said, with pardonable exaggeration, to have enjoyed the homage or respect of 'princes of all Asia and Europe'.[32]

Another attraction, no doubt, is Timur's chameleon-like character. He exhibits features every bit as bewilderingly ambiguous and contradictory as does the figure who struts around the stage in Marlowe's *Tamburlaine*:[33] a Mongol ('Tatar') leader whose military activity drastically curtailed the power of a major Mongol state, the Qipchaq khanate; a restlessly ambitious conqueror whose cruelty became a byword, but who could win the admiration of Muslim scholars and saints and who lavished wealth on outstanding architectural projects; a potentate who was probably illiterate but who delighted in debate with members of the intelligentsia (as well as in a complex and sophisticated version of chess); a self-conscious Muslim who nevertheless retained many attitudes and practices inherited from pre-Islamic steppe culture; and lastly, a holy warrior whose attacks were directed almost exclusively against fellow Muslims and who was courted as a potential ally both by Orthodox Christian Byzantium and by the Latin Christian West.[34] Moreover, even within Europe his image has shifted over time. It has been pointed out that renaissance writers display a better grasp of the aura that surrounded Timur than would later commentators.[35] The often favourable judgements of the fifteenth and sixteenth centuries gave way to the hostile verdicts of Gibbon and others,[36] writing when Timur began to appear as a precursor of British imperialism in India (albeit decidedly not one to be emulated).[37]

A further dimension of Timur's career, which has received scant notice until recent years, is his political legacy in relation to Islamic Western Asia as a whole. The emphasis here was perhaps adumbrated in a statement by Marshall Hodgson: 'his career is revealing not only for his own decisions and initiatives but also because it was a catalyst, releasing impulses and hopes in others of his time'.[38] However destructive Timur's military operations may have been – both within Iran and outside, in Syria, Anatolia and northern India – there can be little doubt that they exerted a catalytic effect, not least on the balance of power in several distinct regions of Western Asia. His activities ushered in an age when a number of rulers – including his Ottoman antagonists and the Türkmen potentates who had alternatively opposed or welcomed him – could establish themselves as trans-regional powers. By 1530, with the replacement of the Türkmens by the Safawids and the migration of members of Timur's own progeny from Transoxiana to India, the world from the Oxus and the Ganges to the Mediterranean was dominated by a nexus of unprecedentedly strong and durable Muslim states.

At one time historians might have chosen to concentrate on Timur as a destroyer whose operations created a *tabula rasa* for the rise of these polities, in much the same way as Mongol campaigns had inaugurated a new epoch in Islamic history by destroying the rump ʿAbbasid Caliphate. Timur's era, like the fifteenth century that succeeded it, still risks being viewed as a transition between a 'Mongol moment' and the onset of 'early modernity' with the advent of the so-called 'gunpowder empires'.[39] The effects of the Mongol sack of Baghdad in 1258 were still felt in Timur's lifetime, as Muslim scholars sought to define afresh the criteria for legitimate rule and were coming to equate legitimacy simply with political effectiveness and religious orthodoxy. But nowadays the place of Timur's career in the development of ideas concerning legitimacy is receiving greater prominence. The accent is more likely to fall on what has been termed 'a kind of matrix moment for the histories of Islamic West-Asia's main fifteenth-century polities and political elites',[40] on his rule as 'the primary point of ideological reference for all subsequent rulers of the fifteenth century'[41] and on their perception of Timur, in important respects, as foreshadowing and mentoring, as it were, their own policies and ambitions.

THE PRIMARY SOURCES

Plenty of source material exists for both Timur and Chinggis Khan (see Chapter 1 of this book), but there is a marked difference. None of the sources available for reconstructing the life of Chinggis Khan dates from before his death, although the 'Secret History of the Mongols', the only historical work of Mongol provenance for this era, may date in part from as early as 1228. Otherwise, the principal sources for the study of the Mongol empire – excluding those in Chinese, which are unfortunately inaccessible to me, and two important works in Latin by Western European visitors to the Mongol empire – were written, in Persian or Arabic, either by hostile Muslim witnesses writing outside the Mongol dominions or by Muslim officials in the employ of Chinggis Khan's Ilkhanid descendants.

Of the predominantly Persian sources on Timur, there survive two works – by Niẓām al-Dīn Shāmī and Ghiyāth al-Dīn ʿAlī Yazdī – dating from his last years, or at least begun then, and composed at his behest. A number of others were written within the next three decades under the patronage, and indeed under the supervision, of members of his dynasty, the most celebrated among them the *Ẓafar-nāma* of Sharaf al-Dīn ʿAlī Yazdī and the relevant sections of the *Zubdat al-tawārīkh* of Ḥāfiẓ-i Abrū. In other words, we have to deal here with a historiographical tradition in which both narrative and image were either crafted indirectly by Timur or were refined at the prompting of his successors. If we are to distance ourselves from how Timur wished to be seen by contemporaries and remembered by future generations, or how the various princes of his dynasty subsequently wanted to project him, we are thrown back on testimony from outside: notices in chronicles or biographical dictionaries from the rival Mamlūk empire, the memoirs of the Castilian ambassador Clavijo and other, shorter accounts by Western European authors like Archbishop John of Sulṭāniyya. One of the longest of these external sources – the 'life' of Timur, in Arabic, by Ibn ʿArabshāh, who was carried off as a child during the sack of his native Damascus in 803/1401 and transported to Timur's capital at Samarkand, returning to the Near East only after an exile of many years – appeared relatively late, towards 1440. It exhibits a pronounced antipathy towards the Great Amir that is itself problematic (if entirely understandable).

Timur left to posterity no autobiography, in contrast with his descendants Ẓahīr al-Dīn Muḥammad Bābur (d. 937/1530), the founder of the Mughul empire in India whose memoirs (*Waqāʾiʿ*, 'Events'; usually referred to as the *Bābur-nāma*) have captivated successive generations of scholars and lay folk alike,[42] and Bābur's great-grandson, the Mughul Emperor Jahāngīr (d. 1037/1627).[43] Although the seventeenth-century *Malfūẓāt* (or *Wāqiʿāt*)*-i Tīmūrī* purports to be a Persian translation of Timur's memoirs made in Mughul India in Chaghatay Turkic, there is no evidence that any such memoirs had existed at an earlier date, and they were doubtless a fabrication inspired by, and modelled on, the *Bābur-nāma*.[44] The absence of autobiographical material perhaps explains in part – though only in part – why Timur appears a less appealing figure than does Bābur.

The image we are given of Timur as a military leader is somewhat abstract: it is a striking fact that none of our Persian sources provide much detail on the military strategies to which he presumably owed some or all of his many victories; for them it was enough that God unfailingly seconded his enterprises. Timur's political pretensions can be gleaned from his diplomatic correspondence with other rulers, but a speech supposedly addressed to the Chaghatay troops on the eve of a battle with the Jochid khan Toqtamish, and incorporated in Greek translation in a Byzantine source, has come down to us, at best, at third hand and is probably not authentic.[45] So, too, the 'lives' of the conqueror, by Niẓām al-Dīn Shāmī and Sharaf al-Dīn Yazdī, offer only fitful and partial glimpses of Timur the man and afford a meagre idea of his personality. Despite the fact that Timur's every utterance was recorded by his Uighur and Persian scribes, the Persian narrative sources of the Timurid era seldom claim to be quoting the conqueror's own words;[46] even the tireless compilator Ḥāfiẓ-i Abrū, at one time a close associate, rarely does so. Depictions of Timur's grief at losing a wife or two of his sons (not to mention the deaths of other figures, where his tears are more likely to take the reader by surprise) are redolent of stereotype. However, a fuller picture can be reconstructed with the aid of independent external sources.[47] The account in the autobiography of the famous Moroccan savant Ibn Khaldūn (d. 808/1406), for instance, of his audiences with the conqueror outside Damascus offers a narrow window into Timur's thinking.

As Stephen Dale put it a few years ago, 'one of the distinguishing features of the pre-modern historiography of the Islamic world is the lack of biographies that convey individuality or at least the humanity of Muslims'.[48] What is served up in the Timurid sources amounts more to a pastiche of characteristics or 'types': a pious Muslim committed to war against the unbeliever; the friend and patron of Muslim clerics, saints and shrines; an indefatigable war leader and a highly successful general; a ruler capable of prodigious generosity to his family and followers (and of clemency and vengeful cruelty, in equal measure, towards his enemies); and one blessed from the very outset by the unstinting favour of Heaven.

THE PRESENT BOOK

My own interest in Timur, and hence this project, grew out of my previous book, *The Mongols and the Islamic World. From Conquest to Conversion* (Yale University Press, 2017), where he made a fleeting appearance in the epilogue devoted to the legacy of Chinggis Khan and the Mongol empire.[49] The present work is designed in some degree as a sequel to that book. Chapters 2 and 3 aside, it is not about Chinggis Khan and the thirteenth-century Mongol empire, the history of which is given there in little more than outline. Rather, to express it in general terms, this book is about what became of that empire in the fourteenth century, and especially in Timur's lifetime; in other words, it deals with continuity no less than with change and contrast. The focus is in part on Timur as in some sense Chinggis Khan's successor and, more broadly, on the transition between two world orders: that established by Chinggis Khan and that 'inherited', and substantially refashioned, by Timur. My concern is also with those who wrote about these two world orders – and writers, not least, who approached Timur's exploits with the celebrated conquests and achievements of his illustrious precursor in their mind's eye. At times I draw parallels with Chinggis Khan or point to differences, but I do not offer a methodical or in-depth comparison between Timur and the founder of the Mongol empire. Nor am I concerned with what might be called the 'Myth of Timur': those wishing to learn more on this should consult Bernardini's recent book, referred to earlier.

Although this book is in large part a study of Timur, his activities take up less than half the text and I have certainly not set out to construct a biography; the task of improving on the biographies that already exist appeared to me to be a highly elusive one. Nor does this book pretend to give a detailed account of Timur's career: some of his campaigns will not even receive mention. What I have sought to do is to investigate, firstly, the backdrop against which he made his appearance, by examining the fortunes of the Mongol polities in Central and Western Asia in the middle decades of the fourteenth century, though I am aware that to do so is to risk a teleological approach. Secondly, I appraise Timur's goals and policies in the light of this background, insofar as our sources render that possible. He will be set within an Islamic context, certainly, but also within a Mongol one, and specifically that of the Central Asian Mongol polity in which he originated. He is presented less as the restorer of a Chinggisid hegemony than as the champion of a renewed and remarkably extended Chaghadayid realm.

Throughout, I have tried to identify the influences under which Timur acted and to bear in mind the chief preoccupations that drove him onwards: not merely loyalty to a Chinggisid khan and reverence for the Chinggisid dynasty as a whole, but an allegiance to Mongol law and custom, 'Chinggis Khan's *Yasa*' or 'the Mongol *Töre*', as it was variously known – in other words, to a Mongol 'order'. To suggest that he was actuated by goals loftier than self-aggrandisement might appear the fruit of an over-fertile and unduly charitable imagination. Yet Timur grew up in an environment where – to judge from our sources – the nomad military had for decades cherished the Yasa/Töre as the ideal basis of governance. It is hard to believe that this did not – in part, at least – mould his aspirations.

I try to address a number of questions. Why had the Mongol world fallen apart? In what respects had the Mongol polity in Central Asia been transformed between Chinggis Khan's death and Timur's rise? To what extent did Timur model his aspirations on Chinggis Khan's achievement? How far did he manipulate Chinggis Khan's legacy? How did his methods differ from those of his illustrious exemplar? By what means did he contrive to face down the disadvantages of being a *qarachu* rather than a prince of the imperial Chinggisid blood – or 'Golden Lineage' (Mo. *Altan urugh*), as it was termed? How 'Mongol' was his empire? And how far, conversely, did his administration conform to Islamic ideals? In what ways did Timur's 'court historians' redraft history in his favour and how did his successors and their historians, in turn, further elaborate upon their efforts?

And how was he viewed by authors in territories that remained obstinately beyond his control?

Following Chapter 1 on the sources, the book falls into three parts. The first comprises four chapters. Chapter 2 is a survey of the Mongol empire founded by Chinggis Khan and bequeathed to his descendants and of the successor-states into which it fragmented after *c.* 1260. Here the reader is introduced to the institutions that characterised Mongol rule, particularly those that, for Muslims, were in conflict with the Sharīʿa: uncanonical taxation and the body of laws and customs associated with Chinggis Khan's celebrated Yasa. Chapter 3 examines the process whereby the Mongols of Central and Western Asia were brought into the Islamic fold. In Chapters 4 and 5 I am concerned with the crises that beset the Mongol world in the years preceding the advent of Timur. Historians have long been prone to identifying crises (European historians often characterising them as if they spanned an entire century), and one might cynically enquire whether any phase of human history can ever have been truly crisis-free. Yet there are solid grounds for believing that the Mongol successor-states underwent a series of major convulsions in this period. Some were of a political-ideological character, emanating from within the Mongol establishment itself, and are discussed in Chapter 4. Others sprang from wider causes, whether economic or ecological, and are the subject of Chapter 5. It is astonishing how many books on Mongol history are totally silent regarding the Black Death (1345–53) and later recurrences of plague (from 1360 onwards). Here I investigate at length the possible impact of plague, not because evidence lies to hand that links its consequences to Timur's career (none does), but from a conviction that it must have played some role in reshaping the world in which he operated. During these middle decades of the fourteenth century, two of the Mongol khanates – the Ilkhanate and the Great Khanate or Yuan Empire – ceased to exist, while two others – the Qipchaq khanate/Golden Horde and the Chaghadayid realm – collapsed into internecine strife. This was the era in which Timur grew to adulthood and rose to power in the Chaghadayid state; no less significantly, it witnessed the onset of his military operations beyond Central Asia.

South-western and Central Asia in the decades prior to Timur form the subject matter of the second part of the book, for the reason that Chaghadayid territory and the bulk of the former Ilkhanate comprised the totality of his dominions. The history of Iran under the competing dynasties that partitioned the Ilkhanid territories among them is examined in Chapter 6, where particular attention is given to their ideological pretensions and their mutual conflict. Chapter 7 concentrates on the southward expansion of the Chaghadayid realm, usually seen as the weakest and least stable of the successor-states, into Khurāsān and present-day Afghanistan. This reorientation of the Central Asian Mongols can be viewed as presaging, after a fashion, the phenomenal expansion of the Chaghadayid polity under Timur. In Chapter 8 I review what we know of the Chaghadayid aristocracy. It will be seen that the evidence for the prominence of Timur's ancestors, which of course justified in retrospect his own status as the power behind (or better, perhaps, before) the Chaghadayid throne, comes overwhelmingly from authors working under his descendants.

The third section deals essentially with Timur himself: his ascent to power and the era of his paramountcy. Timur's dealings with the tribal chiefs of the ulus, his promotion of a new ruling elite that continued to serve his descendants for much of the fifteenth century and the character of his administration are examined in Chapter 9; among the topics discussed will be the roles of his sons and grandsons and the position of Timurid royal women. In Chapter 10 I provide a survey of Timur's campaigns, while Chapter 11 is concerned with his war aims, the military resources available to him, his talents as a military commander and his notorious penchant for the macabre when punishing the resistance of urban populations. Chapter 12 studies his dealings with the Chinggisids: his relationship with his two khans and with scions of the imperial dynasty in general – topics that have attracted relatively sparse attention in the secondary literature – along with his posturing as the true heir of the Ilkhans and the fabrication of a common ancestry with Chinggis Khan. Chapter 13 moves on to Timur the Muslim potentate, examining his propaganda and efforts to legitimise his rule, particularly in Islamic terms, and his record as a warrior on behalf of the faith. Some attention is given here to his diplomatic contacts with Christian powers, particularly the rulers of Catholic (Latin) Europe, and to the impression he made on outside observers, both Christian and Muslim. In Chapter 14 we then consider how far, or indeed whether, Timur was engaged in recreating Chinggis Khan's empire, giving appropriate weight to his indebtedness to Mongol precedents and institutions and his adherence to the Yasa/Töre. Apart from the remarks in the next section of this introduction, the later history of the Timurids lies outside the scope of the book, but the final chapter traces and tries to explain the fate of Timur's empire in the two decades following his death, briefly surveys the history of his dynasty and concludes with an analysis of subsequent efforts to build empires in Inner Asia.

THE TIMURID DYNASTY

In comparison with the Mongol empire, Timur's was in some respects a transient phenomenon. After his death, the dominions he bequeathed to his sons and grandsons shrank in size and split into a number of rival principalities, developments that have traditionally been blamed on his failure to leave behind a durable and effective administrative structure for his conquests. Neither in Iran nor in Transoxiana did Timurid rule last more than two years or so beyond the centenary of his death. Notwithstanding the fate of his empire, however, his exploits had conferred on his line the kind of charisma hitherto associated only with Chinggis Khan and those of Chinggisid blood.[50] One historian was thereby led to suggest of Timur's empire that 'the only long-term upshot was a charismatic aura without institutional anchor'.[51] It may have been this new-found source of legitimacy that encouraged Timur's successors to dispense with a Chinggisid khan and assert their own sovereign status.

Alongside this, it must be conceded that the more prominent Timurids to rule in the eastern tracts of Timur's empire – his fourth son Shāhrukh (d. 850/1447), his grandson Ulugh Beg (d. 853/1449) in Samarkand and his more remote descendant Sulṭān Ḥusayn Bāyqarā (d. 911/1506) in Herat – did a great deal more than the dynasty's founder to secure it a lasting place in the cultural history of the Islamic world, and that they thereby considerably augmented the prestige they had inherited.[52] A flurry of publications over the past decade or so has thrown into relief the centrality of Central Asia in more than merely the geographical sense.[53] To quote Pamela Crossley, it 'was an early and continuous source of the integration of Eurasia as a whole, reduced to a frontier of cultural and historical study only in the early modern period'.[54] A number of recent historical works on the region have placed a strong emphasis on cultural achievement. In one, bearing the provocative title *Lost Enlightenment*, the penultimate chapter deals with Timur and his successors and the era is classed as the final epiphany in a distinguished history.[55]

TIMUR IN THE CONTEMPORARY WORLD

Like so many other prominent historical figures, Chinggis Khan and Timur both came to be endowed with an afterlife that was largely apocryphal.[56] Thus, for sixteenth-century Mongolian Buddhists, Chinggis Khan and his Yuan successors were incarnations not only of the *chakravartin*, the universal ruler who turned the wheel of the *dharma*,[57] but of the *bodhisattva* Vajrapāṇi. After being generally vilified under the Soviet regime, Chinggis Khan became the national symbol of the independent Mongolian Republic and – less predictably, perhaps – would be seen as the inspiration for many of the country's modern institutions (embracing even human rights). In China his image and the significance of his career have undergone a whole series of shifts since the Manchu/Qing epoch.

The most bizarre development in Timur's afterlife is undoubtedly the most recent. Within living memory, he has been adopted as the remote forebear and national symbol of the post-Soviet republic of Uzbekistan, which contains Shahr-i Sabz (formerly Kish), the town of Timur's birth, his beloved Samarkand and his mausoleum. Timur's appropriation in this fashion brings to mind the elan with which, six hundred years ago, many Muslims apostrophised him, despite the outrages he perpetrated, as the 'Lord of the Auspicious Conjunction' (*Ṣāḥib-Qirān*)[58] – another instance of the powerful appeal of major conquerors down the ages. Yet at the same time it is supremely paradoxical. Timur neither was nor claimed to be an Uzbek (even though Vivaldi's opera calls him 'Emperor of the Uzbek Turks') and his historians were among the first to apply that label to a completely different people, originating within the steppe territories of the Golden Horde to the north and north-west of his empire – among the very peoples, in other words, from whom he had defended Transoxiana. Indeed, the advancing Uzbeks, under their khans Abū l-Khayr (d. *c.* 1468) and his grandson Muḥammad Shībānī (d. 916/1510), descendants of Jochi, emerged as the most formidable rivals to Timur's heirs in Transoxiana and Khurāsān. It was the Uzbek Shībānī who, just over a century after Timur's death, administered the *coup de grâce* to his dynasty, driving his descendant Bābur into exile at Kabul (and ultimately to a more glorious future). In light of this humiliating episode in his career, the cult of Bābur too as an Uzbek, which is current especially in present-day Farghāna, is no less incongruous.[59]

The military–political triumph of these authentic forebears of the present-day Uzbeks entailed nothing less than the suppression of Timurid power in Central Asia and the revival of Chinggisid rule for the next two hundred years and more.[60] Given such a truly transformative achievement, one can only wonder why it has been judged necessary in our own time to recruit Timur's mixed political legacy as a nationalistic device – still less to sponsor his rehabilitation and deny the historicity of savageries that even Timurid court historians were ready to acknowledge.[61] The modern glorification of Timur can be seen, at one level, to have its roots in ideological developments of the Soviet era, when territorial considerations played a disproportionate role in the definition of nationality; at another level, it reflects the need of an emerging state to harness local cultural traditions as a means of forging a national identity virtually from scratch, a process from which the early modern Uzbeks, as nomads and – worse still – ultimately Mongols, had long been perceived as debarred.[62] The impulses behind the present-day cult of Timur may well also be connected with the political interests of Uzbekistan's then president, the late Islam Karimov, a native of Samarkand.[63] But as far as the more remote past is concerned, the answer must lie in the economic benefits that Timur's achievements brought to Transoxiana (and to Samarkand and Shahr-i Sabz/Kish in particular) and in the long-lasting prestige of his dynasty, referred to above. Otherwise, Timur's own appeal resides in his unbroken record of military victories, rather than in any service to Islam, in which he was far outshone by his progeny.

As far as I am aware, no other book-length work sets out to explore Timur's career and rule against both the backdrop of the thirteenth-century Mongol empire and the widespread collapse of Mongol rule in the fourteenth. Nobody can hope to say the last word on any subject. Inevitably, given the character of the evidence, much of what I have to say will be tentative in character; the book will pose questions at least as frequently as it offers answers. I trust, however, that it will in turn provoke fresh – and better – questions and will serve as a pathway to future research.

CHAPTER 1
SOURCES FOR THE MONGOL AND TIMURID ERAS

THE HISTORIOGRAPHY OF THE MONGOLS

A single narrative source from a Mongol author has come down to us. *Mongghol'un niucha tobcha'an*, probably compiled in the mid-thirteenth century and usually known as the 'Secret History of the Mongols', exists in a Chinese transcription dating from the early Ming era.[1] However, the Mongols' conquests brought them into contact with a great diversity of peoples whose writings are among our principal sources for Mongol history, so that the modern historian has access to a large corpus of external material. Only a small fraction of the Chinese material – notably parts of the *Yuanshi*, the annals of the dynasty compiled for the Ming after the Mongols' expulsion from China – has been translated.

Reports from mendicant friars from Western Europe who visited the Mongol world are rich in detail on Mongol culture and customs. The most important are the Franciscans John of Plano Carpini (Giovanni del Pian di Carpine), ambassador of Pope Innocent IV to the Mongol Qaghan ('Great Khan') Güyüg in 1245–7, and William of Rubruck, who described his experiences as a missionary in the Mongol empire (1253–5) in a lengthy letter to the French king Louis IX. The information these two travellers supply is of a higher quality than that found, for instance, in the more celebrated *Divisament du monde* ('Description of the World') of the Venetian

Marco Polo (*c.* 1298) or in the still more widely diffused *Flor des estoires de la terre d'Orient* ('Flower of the Histories of the East'), which the expatriate Armenian prince Hayton (Het'um) of Gorighos presented to the Pope in 1307.[2]

The majority of sources used in this book emanate from the Islamic world and a significant number were produced outside the empire. Minhāj al-Dīn b. Sirāj al-Dīn Jūzjānī, a fugitive from Ghūr (in Afghanistan) who dedicated his *Ṭabaqāt-i Nāṣirī* ('Nāṣirī Chapters') to the Sultan of Delhi, Nāṣir al-Dīn Maḥmūd, in *c.* 658/1260,[3] preserves a good deal of information not found elsewhere. So, too, authors writing in the Mamlūk empire shed plentiful light on events within the Mongol world.[4] Special mention should be made of the section on the Mongol states in *Masālik al-abṣār fī mamālik al-amṣār* ('The Paths of Observation through the Civilized Regions'), a vast encyclopaedia composed in Egypt in *c.* 738/1338 by the chancery official Ibn Faḍl-Allāh al-ʿUmarī (d. 749/1349); his administrative manual, *al-Taʿrīf bi l-muṣṭalaḥ al-sharīf* ('Instruction in the Honourable Practices'), dating from *c.* 742/1342,[5] also furnishes useful material. Of great value are two biographical dictionaries compiled by al-Ṣafadī (d. 764/1363), *al-Wāfī bi l-wafayāt* ('The Entirety of Obituaries') and *Aʿyān al-ʿaṣr* ('The Notables of the Era'), of which the second confines its scope to the seventh Hijrī century (thirteenth century CE).[6] We are also fortunate to have the memoirs of that most famous of medieval Muslim travellers, Ibn Baṭṭūṭa, who traversed the three western Mongol khanates in the course of his journeys (725–54/1325–54), though we cannot be certain what interpolations his amanuensis, Ibn Juzayy, made when editing the text in 757/1356; although the sojourn in Yuan China is almost certainly a fabrication, his visits to the ulus of Chaghadai and the Delhi Sultanate cannot be in doubt.[7]

For the early history of the empire, we are especially indebted to the Persian works of Muslim authors writing under Mongol rule.[8] When Timurid historians surveyed the reigns of Chinggis Khan and his successors, they relied especially on the *Taʾrīkh-i jahān-gushā* ('History of the World-Conqueror') of Juwaynī and Volume 1 of the *Jāmiʿ al-tawārīkh* ('Collection of Chronicles') of Rashīd al-Dīn.

These two authors, regarded today as the most indispensable internal sources for the history of the Mongol world, were both in the Ilkhans' service. ʿAlāʾ al-Dīn ʿAṭā Malik Juwaynī (d. 681/1283), who came from a family of long-standing Persian bureaucrats,[9] was the brother of Shams al-Dīn Juwaynī (d. 682/1284), chief minister, or *Ṣāḥib-dīwān*, under the first three Ilkhans, Hülegü (d. 663/1265), Abagha (663–680/1265–1282) and Tegüder-Aḥmad (681–683/1282–1284). He himself served as an official in Khurāsān from the late 1240s and rose to be governor of newly conquered Baghdad from *c.* 1259. Rashīd al-Dīn Faḍl-Allāh Hamadānī was a Jewish physician who converted to Islam, served the Ilkhanid court as a cook or steward (Mo. *ba'urchi*) and from 695/1295 to his execution in 718/1318 was joint chief minister to the Muslim Ilkhans Ghazan Maḥmūd (695–703/1295–1304), Öljeitü Khudābanda (703–716/1304–1316) and Abū Saʿīd (716–736/1316–1335).[10] He had extensive contacts. Volume 2 of *Jāmiʿ al-tawārīkh*, covering the history of the pre-Mongol Islamic world, China, India and the 'Franks' of Western Europe, has been hailed as 'the first world history' – or, as Christopher Atwood prefers, 'the first inter-ecumenical history'.[11]

Volume 1, entitled *Taʾrīkh-i mubārak-i Ghāzānī* ('The Blessed Ghazanid History') and completed in 703/1303, deals with the histories of the Turkish and Mongol tribes and of the Chinggisid dynasty. For the Mongols' early history Rashīd al-Dīn made use not only of Juwaynī's work but also, indirectly, of Mongolian material: the 'authentic chronicle' of Chinggis Khan's reign (translated into Chinese under Qubilai), other fragments now lost and oral information from a high-ranking Mongol official from Yuan China.[12] Rashīd al-Dīn's genealogical work, *Shuʿab-i panjgāna* ('The Five Branches'), produced a few years later as a supplement to *Jāmiʿ al-tawārīkh*, presents trees of the prolific Chinggisid dynasty, accompanied by lists of the khans' chief military commanders (as well as lists of Chinese Emperors, popes and western emperors). As the late Alexander Morton convincingly deduced from internal evidence, however, Rashīd al-Dīn's so-called correspondence (*mukātibāt*) dates from the early fifteenth century.[13]

Juwaynī and Rashīd al-Dīn wrote under very different conditions, which naturally coloured their approach.[14] Juwaynī, writing for a pagan monarch, faced the daunting task of explaining and justifying the violent conquest of a large part of the Islamic world by unbelievers and could view it only as God's punishment for Muslim lassitude and wrongdoing. Rashīd al-Dīn, who witnessed the triumph of Islam among the invaders, was in the happy position of dedicating his *Ta'rīkh-i mubārak-i Ghāzānī* to a Muslim convert, and the second volume of his *Jāmi' al-tawārīkh* was commissioned by another convert, Ghazan's brother Öljeitü. He was accordingly able to present the tribulations of the Mongol conquest as God's preordained means of bringing infidels to the true faith and of thereby strengthening Islam.

Albeit the most precious sources on the Mongols, down to the death of Ghazan Maḥmūd, the works of Juwaynī and Rashīd al-Dīn are not the only sources of value in the Ilkhanid historiographical tradition. Even if we discount the raft of muted, less detailed histories produced between the sack of Baghdad and 1303 – 'five decades of historiographical whispering',[15] as Judith Pfeiffer terms it – a cluster of important works date from the reign of the Ilkhan Abū Saʿīd. Shihāb al-Dīn ʿAbd-Allāh b. Faḍl-Allāh Shīrāzī, a fiscal official in Fārs known as Waṣṣāf (from his style of *Waṣṣāf al-ḥaḍrat*, 'Court panegyrist'), composed his *Tajziyat al-amṣār wa-tazjiyat al-aʿṣār* ('The Classification of Countries and the Passage of Epochs') as a continuation of Juwaynī's history, between 698/1298–9 and *c.* 728/1327–8.[16] It provides a wealth of material unavailable elsewhere both on the Ilkhans and to a lesser extent on the other Mongol states and on Muslim India (which Rashīd al-Dīn in turn copied, without acknowledgement). Regrettably, Waṣṣāf also set a new standard in verbosity – and one duly admired and emulated by later Persian historians.

Four other authors were nearly contemporary with Waṣṣāf. Jamāl al-Dīn Abū l-Qāsim ʿAbd-Allāh Qāshānī's *Ta'rīkh-i Uljāytū Sulṭān*, a history of Abū Saʿīd's father and predecessor, ends at the beginning of 717/early in 1317. *Rawḍat ūlī l-albāb fī maʿrifat al-tawārīkh wa l-ansāb* (The Garden of the Intellects in the Knowledge of Histories and Lineages), which Fakhr al-Dīn Dā'ūd Banākatī completed in 718/1318, is, for the most part, merely a digest of Rashīd al-Dīn's *Ta'rīkh-i mubārak-i Ghāzānī* down to 703/1303,[17] but contains original material on Öljeitü's reign. Ḥamd-Allāh Mustawfī Qazwīnī and

Muḥammad b. ʿAlī Shabānkāra'ī were both active in the twilight years of the Ilkhanate. Ḥamd-Allāh, like Waṣṣāf a fiscal official, was the author of a prose work, *Ta'rīkh-i guzīda* ('The Choice History', *c.* 730/1330), a long history in verse, *Ẓafar-nāma* ('Victory Despatch'), modelled on Firdawsī's epic *Shāh-nāma* and completed in 735/1334–5 and a prose continuation (*dhayl*) of *Ẓafar-nāma* down to 744/1344, usually called, misleadingly, the *Dhayl-i Ta'rīkh-i guzīda*. Ḥamd-Allāh's geography, *Nuzhat al-qulūb* ('The Hearts' Delight'), produced in *c.* 740/1340, includes historical information. In *Ta'rīkh-i guzīda* and *Ẓafar-nāma* Ḥamd-Allāh utilised *Ta'rīkh-i mubārak-i Ghāzānī* and Qāshānī's *Ta'rīkh-i Uljāytū*,[18] but his source for the period after 717/1316–17 is unknown. During the upheavals following Abū Saʿīd's death in 736/1335, he seems to have worked undisturbed. In contrast, the work of Shabānkāra'ī, closely associated with the wazir Rashīd al-Dīn's son Ghiyāth al-Dīn, testifies to the political chaos into which the Ilkhanate had descended. His *Majma' al-ansāb fī l-tawārīkh* ('A Collection of Affinities in the Chronicles') underwent three recensions: the first, destroyed after Ghiyāth al-Dīn's downfall in 736/1336 and no longer extant, the second in 738/1338 (the only version so far published) and a third in 743/1343.[19]

REGIONAL HISTORY IN THE MONGOL AND POST-MONGOL PERIODS[20]

The genre of regional history in the Ilkhanid period is well represented, notably by histories of Herat, Anatolia (Rūm) and Kirmān.[21] Given the political fragmentation of the Iranian world between the end of the Ilkhanate and Timur's campaigns, much of the Persian material from that era also has the character of local history. Apart from short fragments found in the *Majmū'a* of Ḥāfiẓ-i Abrū (see later), we have only one contemporary narrative source for the history of Khurāsān after 722/1322: the sequel (*dhayl*) to the second redaction of Shabānkāra'ī's *Majma' al-ansāb*, produced by Ghiyāth al-Dīn b. ʿAlī Nā'ib Faryūmadī in 783/1381–2,[22] whose loyalties seemed to lie chiefly with the Ilkhan Taghai Temür (d. 754/1353), his successor Amīr Walī and the Sarbadārs.

The earliest post-Ilkhanid source is Abū Bakr Ahrī's general history, *Ta'rīkh-i Shaykh Uways*, presented to the Jalayirid monarch soon after 1360 and devoted to the Jalayirids. If rather sketchy in character, it is of some value; it is, for example, the first Persian source to mention the arrival of the Black Death in north-western Iran. It was utilised by Zayn al-Dīn b. Ḥamd-Allāh Mustawfī for his *Dhayl-i Ta'rīkh-i guzīda* (again, *Dhayl-i Ẓafar-nāma*, strictly speaking),[23] which began in 742/1341–2, and continued his father's work down to 795/1393. Zayn al-Dīn is thus the first Iranian writer (discounting a fleeting allusion by Faryūmadī) to cover the military operations of Timur, to whom his *Dhayl* is dedicated. Another purported continuation of *Ta'rīkh-i guzīda* (that is, of *Ẓafar-nāma*), by an anonymous author writing under the Jalayirids in the early 1370s, has been published recently.[24]

Of the sources from southern Iran, Muʿīn al-Dīn b. Jalāl al-Dīn Muḥammad Muʿallim Yazdī finished his *Mawāhib-i ilāhī* ('Divine Gifts'), which dealt specifically with the Jalayirids' rivals, the Muzaffarid dynasty, in 767/1365–6. Also valuable for its section on the Muzaffarids is *Manāhīj al-ṭālibīn fī maʿārif al-ṣādiqīn* ('Highways for Students of the Truly Renowned'), a florid and verbose general history dedicated to the Muzaffarid ruler Shāh-i Shujāʿ by ʿAlī b. Ḥusayn, known as ʿAlā-yi Qazwīnī Hilālī (779/1377).[25] In 823/1420, during the early Timurid period, Maḥmūd Kutubī wrote his own account, *Ta'rīkh-i āl-i Muẓaffar* ('History of the Muzaffarid Lineage'), which apparently takes Muʿīn al-Dīn as its model;[26] it ends with the dynasty's destruction by Timur.

All the historical works listed above emanated from Iran. Some decades ago, Jean Aubin observed that the geographical isolation of the Chaghadayid khanate deprived us of the outside information to which we are so indebted for Jochid history (mainly Rus' chronicles), that no school of historical writing flourished in Chaghadai's ulus and that Timurid authors distorted the region's previous history.[27] And indeed the only historical work to survive from Central Asia between the Qarakhanid era and the *Ta'rīkh-i Rashīdī* of Mīrzā Ḥaydar Dughlāt (952/1546: see later) is the short sketch of Mongol history that Jamāl al-Qarshī appended to his commentary on al-Jawharī's dictionary at the dawn of the fourteenth century.[28] Yet Aubin was a trifle too dismissive of the sources composed elsewhere in the Mongol world, namely the material on Chaghadai's ulus in *Jāmi' al-tawārīkh*, *Shu'ab-i panjgāna* and in the works of Waṣṣāf and Qāshānī, and the section on Central Asia in al-ʿUmarī's *Masālik al-abṣār* – not to mention the Chinese material used in the study of Qaidu by Michal Biran, who has also deployed Mamlūk sources to illuminate the intellectual culture of Transoxiana.[29]

HISTORICAL WRITING UNDER TIMUR AND THE EARLY TIMURIDS

The rise of Timur, with his keen interest in history and his desire for his deeds to be commemorated, inaugurated a new era in historiographical enterprise. A great many historical sources were composed under him and his successors, though by authors from the Iranian world rather than from Central Asia. Of the overwhelmingly Persian literary sources, several that are known to have existed are lost.[30] A notable example is the *Rūz-nāma-yi futūḥāt-i Hindūstān* ('Journal of the Conquests in India'), written on Timur's orders by Qadi Naṣīr al-Dīn ʿUmar, who had read the khuṭba in Delhi on the victor's behalf.[31]

Two other histories composed at Timur's behest – by Niẓām al-Dīn Shāmī (or Shanbī) and Ghiyāth al-Dīn ʿAlī Yazdī – have come down to us. When Timur appeared before Baghdad in 795/1393, Shāmī was the first of its inhabitants to emerge and offer his submission.[32] In 803/1400, en route for the Hijaz, he was an eyewitness of the siege of Aleppo by the Chaghatay forces.[33] On the city's capture, he was brought before Timur and appears to have entered his service. Ordered by Timur in 804/1401–2 to write a history of his campaigns of conquest in a plain, unadorned style, Shāmī presented the first recension of the *Ẓafar-nāma* ('Victory Despatch') to Timur around Shawwāl 806/April 1404. The title figures only in a second version dedicated to Timur's grandson ʿUmar b. Amīrānshāh, to whose service Shāmī may have transferred following Timur's death a year later. According to Ḥāfiẓ-i Abrū's continuation of the *Ẓafar-nāma*, he was dead by 814/1411–12.[34] Sharaf al-Dīn 'Alī Yazdī (below) saluted Shāmī as one of the most accomplished writers of his age.[35]

Ghiyāth al-Dīn, who had served the Muzaffarids in Yazd as a qadi and secretary, based his *Rūz-nāma-yi ghazawāt-i Hindūstān* ('Journal of the Holy Wars in India') largely on Qadi Naṣīr al-Dīn ʿUmar's lost *Rūz-nāma*, though it also offers a sketch of Timur's earlier conquests and an account of his final battle with the Muzaffarid Shāh Manṣūr in 795/1393, containing details not given in other sources.[36] Mention of Shāhrukh's 'notable victories' (*futūḥāt-i arjmand*) shows that Ghiyāth al-Dīn completed the work well after Timur's death.[37]

The earliest author to continue Shāmī's history (only slightly in advance of Ḥāfiẓ-i Abrū: see later) was Tāj al-Dīn Salmānī. Formerly in the Muzaffarids' employ, he entered Timur's service as a secretary in 800/1397–8 and in 812/1409 passed from the service of the conqueror's grandson and successor in Transoxiana, Khalīl Sulṭān b. Amīrānshāh, into that of Shāhrukh, who assigned him to the staff of his own son Ulugh Beg. *Shams al-ḥusn* ('The Sun of Elegance'), which he began in 813/1410 at Shāhrukh's command, takes the story down to Khalīl Sulṭān's overthrow. As one of his chief informants was the amir Shāh Malik, based in Transoxiana, he gives greater attention to events in the eastern regions of the empire. Salmānī is devoted to the interests of Shāhrukh and his line and assures us that Shāhrukh's sons Ulugh Beg and Ibrāhīm Sulṭān were Timur's favourite grandsons.[38]

The first version of Muʿīn al-Dīn Naṭanzī's 'universal' history, *Muntakhab al-tawārīkh* ('Selection of Histories'), was presented to Timur's grandson Iskandar b. ʿUmar Shaykh, the ruler of Fārs, in 816/1413–14, and has been labelled accordingly the 'Iskandar Anonymous'; a slightly later redaction was submitted to Shāhrukh following Iskandar's downfall.[39] This second version contains synoptic tables (*jadwal*) for each dynasty, furnishing details of each ruler's character.[40] But, in a unique Istanbul manuscript, there also exists an anonymous synoptic account of Timur and his dynasty, composed at Iskandar's court in 816/1413–14,[41] of which Naṭanzī may have been the author. Iskandar had spent much of his earlier career in Farghāna and on the eastern frontiers of Transoxiana, and Naṭanzī appears to have obtained material on Timur and his campaigns from members of the Turco-Mongol officer class at Iskandar's court in Shiraz, some of whom hailed from those regions. This would account for the particular slant of Naṭanzī's work, which betrays a stronger attachment to steppe tradition and thus affords an insight into the Turco-Mongol outlook.[42] To what extent his material was in oral form is unknown.

The years immediately following Shāhrukh's conquest of Fārs, which effectively reunited the greater part of Timur's empire, witnessed a fresh burst of historical writing. Sharaf al-Dīn ʿAlī Yazdī (d. 858/1454), one of the intellectuals assembled at Iskandar's court at Shiraz, now entered the service of Ibrāhīm Sulṭān b. Shāhrukh (d. 838/1435), the new governor of the province.[43] Yazdī's work was long regarded as the most important source on Timur. In his own time this was due to its highly ornate language: unlike Shāmī, Yazdī was under no obligation to keep to a plain style and availed himself of this freedom to produce a bombastic narrative littered with flamboyant verse – eliciting (as had Waṣṣāf) the admiration of later Persian historians. In more recent centuries the *Ẓafar-nāma* owed its popularity to the fact that it has been available to scholars in French translation since the 1720s.

Designed initially, it seems, as the first section (*maqāla*) of a three-part Timurid dynastic history entitled *Taʾrīkh-i Jahāngīr* (or *Fatḥ-nāma-yi humāyūn*), it represents a considerably amplified version of Timur's biography as found in Shāmī's *Ẓafar-nāma*. Yazdī tells us that in 822/1419–20 Ibrāhīm Sulṭān ordered his scribes (*bakhshiyān*) and secretaries to read aloud the accounts of Timur produced by Turkish scribes and the prince personally checked their veracity.[44] What is now known as Yazdī's *Ẓafar-nāma*, based upon those accounts as filtered by Ibrāhīm Sulṭān, was probably completed in or soon after 832/1428–9. The *Muqaddima* ('Prologue') to the *Taʾrīkh-i Jahāngīr*, which used to be taken in error as the prologue to the *Ẓafar-nāma*, has survived independently; the two works are not found together in any *Ẓafar-nāma* manuscript from before the seventeenth century. The current year is given in the *Muqaddima* as

831 [1427–8].[45] It comprises a survey of the history of the Mongols and of the Chaghadayid ulus down to the advent of Timur. In a far-reaching analysis of Yazdī's *oeuvre* and a revision of the chronology, İlker Evrim Binbaş argues that none of the surviving compositions truly represents a finished product. Yazdī's original ideas about the project changed shape, partly under the pressure of successive crises in Shāhrukh's empire.[46] It was not until the 1440s that he produced the second *maqāla* of the *Ta'rīkh-i Jahāngīr*, on the history of Shāhrukh. The only part of this section so far discovered, embracing the period down to 810/1407–8, includes a significant quantity of information not found elsewhere regarding the struggle for power after Timur's death.[47]

Yazdī downplayed the fact that Timur was a mere commoner and suppressed most of the references to Timur's puppet Chinggisid khans (see Chapter 12). He incorporated in his *Ẓafar-nāma* a pedigree of Timur. Apparently based on the genealogy produced a few years after the conqueror's death by Ḥusayn b. ʿAlīshāh (below, pp. 225–6), it gave Timur a common ancestry with Chinggis Khan and ascribed to his Barlās forebears a pivotal role in the governance of the Chaghadayid state. But if the first *maqāla* – the *Ẓafar-nāma* proper – is a biography of Timur, it is also about Shāhrukh, whose paramountcy was assured by the time Yazdī embarked on the project. Thus he gives considerable prominence to Shāhrukh, making out that he was the favourite son and that Timur envisaged the future of his empire as lying with Shāhrukh's progeny (in the same way Rashīd al-Dīn had depicted Chinggis Khan as foreseeing the triumph of Tolui's line).[48]

Shihāb al-Dīn ʿAbd-Allāh b. Luṭf-Allāh Khwāfī, better known as Ḥāfiẓ-i Abrū (d. 833/1430), was a friend and companion of Timur who was present on the Indian, Syrian and Anatolian expeditions and is known to have been among his chess partners.[49] After Timur's death he entered the service of Shāhrukh and produced his historical writings for the most part under the sponsorship of the latter's son Bāysunghur (d. 837/1434) in Herat. He was the most prolific of all the Timurid historians,[50] composing not merely a supplement (*dhayl*) to Rashīd al-Dīn's *Jāmiʿ al-tawārīkh* down to 795/1393, commissioned by Shāhrukh,[51] but a continuation (begun in 814/1411–12) of Shāmī's *Ẓafar-nāma* down to Timur's death and a *jughrāfiyya*, an untitled work of historical geography that has not survived in its entirety. Among Ḥāfiẓ-i Abrū's collected works (*Majmūʿa*) are also to be found a number of shorter pieces devoted to pre-Timurid regimes, comprising accounts of the reign of the last significant Ilkhan, Taghai Temür, of his successor in Astarābād, Amīr Walī, of the Sarbadār state in Khurāsān, of its neighbours, the Jāʾūn-i Qurbān Mongols, of the Kartid (or Kurtid) dynasty in Herat (based on Sayfī's account until 1322) and of the Muzaffarids of southern Iran (largely indebted to Muʿīn al-Dīn Yazdī).[52] His last work was a vast general history, *Majmaʿ al-tawārīkh*, of which the fourth and final section, titled *Zubdat al-tawārīkh-i Bāysungqurī* ('The Cream of Histories for Bāysunghur'), comprises a number of his earlier contributions, including a reworking of Shāmī's chronicle with copious additions, together with a history of Timur's dominions from his death to 830/1426–7. Although much of his output was derivative, Ḥāfiẓ-i Abrū exhibited great skill in moulding a number of disparate histories into a uniform narrative. Moreover, he consulted documentary material, inserted details not found in any other known source and occasionally cited his own experience (for an example, see below, p. 332).[53] It has been proposed that he also authored the anonymous genealogical work *Muʿizz al-ansāb* ('The Reinforcement of Lineages'), dating from 830/1426–7,[54] which lifted the Chinggisid material (with modifications) from Rashīd al-Dīn's *Shuʿab*, continued it down to the fifteenth century and added the genealogy of the Barlās ruling family and their descendants the Timurids, who were by this date portrayed as agnatic kinsmen of Chinggis Khan.[55] Ḥāfiẓ-i Abrū's *Zubdat al-tawārīkh* includes a lengthy genealogy of the Barlās amirs which is almost identical with that in *Muʿizz al-ansāb*.[56]

The early fifteenth-century historians all had access to the work of at least one other Timurid writer and, in some cases, several. Ghiyāth al-Dīn Yazdī made use of the now lost *Rūz-nāma* of Qadi Naṣīr al-Dīn ʿUmar, as did Niẓām al-Dīn Shāmī in his extremely detailed account of the Indian campaign. Naṭanzī betrays some limited dependence on Shāmī, for instance in his description of the first campaign in the Qipchaq steppe in 793/1391.[57] Sharaf al-Dīn Yazdī, as we saw, utilised Shāmī's *Ẓafar-nāma* and may have had access to Qadi Naṣīr al-Dīn's account either directly or through Shāmī and Ghiyāth al-Dīn; for the final section of his own *Ẓafar-nāma* he borrowed material from Salmānī.[58] Yazdī also made use of Ḥāfiẓ-i Abrū, although the latter was seemingly unaware of Yazdī's *Ẓafar-nāma*. Ḥāfiẓ-i Abrū, in turn, drew extensively upon Shāmī and Naṭanzī in his addenda to Shāmī's work and in *Zubdat al-tawārīkh*.[59] By 1430 Shāmī's *Ẓafar-nāma* existed both in its original form and in two amplified versions drafted by Ḥāfiẓ-i Abrū and by Yazdī.[60]

The development of Timurid historiography in the four decades following Timur's death has received admirable coverage elsewhere,[61] and I shall simply add a few remarks at this juncture. For all the extensive and complex borrowings referred to above, the Timurid authors surveyed here exhibit rather divergent approaches.[62] Often these reflect the political changes within the dynasty – the declining fortunes of the branches descended from Jahāngīr, ʿUmar Shaykh and Amīrānshāh and the rise of Shāhrukh and his line – and consequential shifts in the availability of princely patronage. The partisanship of the author of the synoptic account is apparent from his treatment of two of the Timurid lines; since Jahāngīr had received no appanage and neither he nor his descendants had done anything praiseworthy, they are denied a table (*jadwal*) of their own; while the faithlessness of Amīrānshāh's sons Abā Bakr, Khalīl Sulṭān and ʿUmar emerges clearly from their careers.[63] The two recensions of Naṭanzī's work furnish another conspicuous example. As we noticed, his first version, commonly known as the 'Iskandar Anonymous', was produced for Timur's grandson Iskandar b. ʿUmar Shaykh, who governed Isfahan and Fārs, in 816/1413–14. Here – as in the synoptic account – Iskandar is presented as Timur's designated successor.[64] Naṭanzī says nothing of Iskandar's disgrace following his unauthorised expedition to Mughūlistān in 802/1399 (below, pp. 274–5). He ascribes the suppression of the revolt of the Süldüs and Jalāyir amirs against Timur to Iskandar's father ʿUmar Shaykh, whereas Shāmī and Yazdī at this point give some prominence to Jahāngīr.[65] But after Iskandar's replacement by Shāhrukh's son Ibrāhīm Sulṭān, Naṭanzī produced for Shāhrukh a new recension, *Muntakhab al-tawārīkh*, where references to Iskandar and ʿUmar Shaykh were either modified or deleted altogether.[66]

Naṭanzī was not the only Timurid court historian to display a keen sense of political expediency. Niẓām al-Dīn Shāmī cannot have been ignorant of the reported insanity of Timur's third son Amīrānshāh and his removal from the governorship of Azerbaijan in 802/1399–1400 (below, pp. 274, 275–6). Dedicating his *Ẓafar-nāma* in its final form, however, to Amīrānshāh's son ʿUmar a few years later, he passed over the episode in silence.[67] Writing under the supervision of Ibrāhīm Sulṭān from 817/1414, Sharaf al-Dīn Yazdī in turn recast Shāmī's material. Whereas Shāmī described ʿUmar Shaykh as the apple of Timur's eye and does not even record Shāhrukh's birth,[68] Yazdī consistently promotes the claims of Shāhrukh and his line over those of the descendants of Timur's older sons Jahāngīr and Amīrānshāh.[69] So, too, Ḥāfiẓ-i Abrū's continuation of Shāmī's work says nothing of Timur's nomination of his grandson Pīr Muḥammad b. Jahāngīr as his heir and suggests that the conqueror had settled on Shāhrukh.[70]

Certain authors writing under Shāhrukh had access to a limited number of the narrative sources from the Mongol and Jalayirid periods that we mentioned earlier. We know that the works of Juwaynī and Rashīd al-Dīn were available to Sharaf al-Dīn ʿAlī Yazdī, while Naṭanzī utilised both the first volume of Rashīd al-Dīn's *Jāmiʿ al-tawārīkh* and Ḥamd-Allāh Mustawfī's *Taʾrīkh-i guzīda*. In fact, the survival of so many manuscripts of Rashīd al-Dīn's history is due in no small measure to Ḥāfiẓ-i Abrū, who executed (and edited) several copies in person.[71] Ḥāfiẓ-i Abrū made extensive use not only of the *Jāmiʿ al-tawārīkh* but also of Qāshānī's *Taʾrīkh-i Uljāytū*, Ḥamd-Allāh Mustawfī's *Ẓafar-nāma*, Zayn al-Dīn b. Ḥamd-Allāh's *Dhayl* and Sayfī's history of Herat for his *Dhayl-i Jāmiʿ al-tawārīkh*, his geography and the shorter pieces listed earlier.[72] The emendations that he and other Timurid historians made, both to the Mongol-era sources and to the work of their slightly earlier contemporaries, can prove illuminating.

For Timurid writers, it is safe to say, Rashīd al-Dīn stood head and shoulders above other authors of the Mongol period. Serving the Muslim convert Ghazan Maḥmūd had enabled Rashīd al-Dīn to reassess the impact of the Mongol conquests, to reinterpret God's purposes and to depict his own day as one of renewal for Islam:

> What event or circumstance in these times has been more important than the beginning of the dynasty of Chīnggīz Khān, to be capable of defining an epoch?[73]

Sharaf al-Dīn Yazdī and Ḥāfiẓ-i Abrū, living through Shāhrukh's purported reassertion of Islamic norms (see below, pp. 407–10), duly took their cue from Rashīd al-Dīn and apostrophised their sovereign as the 'Renewer' (*mujaddid*).[74]

NON-NARRATIVE SOURCES FROM THE POST-ILKHANID AND TIMURID PERIODS

The archive of the influential Shaykhs of Jām, as found in *Farā'id-i Ghiyāthī* and compiled in the early fifteenth century by Jalāl al-Dīn Yūsuf-i Ahl, is an important source for the history of Khurāsān in the fourteenth and early fifteenth centuries. Apart from a letter collection (*inshā'*) produced in the late fifteenth century for Timur's descendant Sulṭān Ḥusayn Bāyqarā by one of his officials in Herat, ʿAbd-Allāh Marwārīd, guides to Timurid administration are lacking. It is likely that in Iran, at least, Timur's lieutenants continued the arrangements under the late Ilkhanid and Jalayirid polities. We know something of these from the chancery manual *Dastūr al-kātib fī taʿyīn al-marātib* ('A Scribe's Guide to the Determination of Ranks'), begun by Muḥammad b. Hindūshāh Nakhchiwānī under the Ilkhan Abū Saʿīd and completed under the Jalayirid Shaykh Uways, probably in *c.* 1360, and the fiscal treatise *Risāla-yi falakiyya* of ʿAbd-Allāh b. Muḥammad Māzandarānī, composed in *c.* 764/1363.[75]

Only a small quantity of documentary material relating to Timur has come down to us, including some of his correspondence with the Mamlūk and Ottoman Sultans.[76] Three victory despatches (*fatḥ-nāmahā*), penned on Timur's behalf and announcing his triumphs at Delhi (801/1398) and in northern Syria (804/1401) and his defeat of

Bayezid at Ankara (804/1402), are included in a *jung* or *safīna* (literary miscellany) in a Paris manuscript,[77] but we have nothing remotely approaching the bulk of documentary evidence available for the Mamlūk state or, *a fortiori*, for the Ottoman empire. In fact, a large fraction of Timur's surviving diplomatic correspondence, such as it is, has reached us by way of the archives of these two polities. *Ṣubḥ al-aʿshā fī ṣināʿat al-inshā'* ('Daylight for the Dim-Sighted in the Craft of Correspondence'), the voluminous chancery manual of the Egyptian official Shihāb al-Dīn Abū l-ʿAbbās Aḥmad al-Qalqashandī (d. 821/1418),[78] includes correspondence between Timur and the Mamlūk Sultan Barqūq. Important material is also found in writings in the Persian 'Mirrors for Princes' tradition: *Naṣā'iḥ-i Shāhrukhī* ('Counsels for Shāhrukh') of Jalāl al-Dīn Muḥammad Qāyinī, composed approximately ten years after Timur's death, throws a stronger light on Shāhrukh's alleged restoration of Islamic governance (and thereby, indirectly, on the character of Timur's regime) than do the narrative sources.

IBN ʿARABSHĀH AND IBN KHALDŪN

Before moving on to authors writing outside Timur's empire – in India, in the Mamlūk and Ottoman dominions and in Christian Europe – it is worth mentioning two, of major importance, who wrote within the Mamlūk Sultanate and in Arabic, but who were both in some degree outsiders and who, on other grounds, too, belong in a different class from their contemporaries in Egypt and Syria. One was the sole author based in the Mamlūk empire to have tasted life in Timur's dominions – though we should note that he had no personal contact with the conqueror and wrote at a relatively late date. Aḥmad b. Muḥammad Ibn ʿArabshāh (b. 791/1389; d. 854/1450) had been carried off from Damascus to Transoxiana in 803/1401 as a child of eleven, along with his mother and sister, and apparently did not return to Damascus until 825/1422, around eighteen years after Timur's death. The second author, the famous intellectual Walī al-Dīn ʿAbd al-Raḥmān Ibn Khaldūn (b. 732/1332; d. 808/1406), was a native of the Hafsid Caliphate of Tunisia who had spent much of his adult life in Morocco and Granada and migrated from Tunis to Egypt in 784/1382, rising to be the chief judge of the Mālikī school of law in Cairo. Accompanying the Mamlūk Sultan Faraj on his campaign into Syria, he was stranded in Damascus in Jumādā I 803/January 1401 when the Sultan and his forces beat a precipitate retreat; he then spent some weeks in Timur's encampment outside the city.[79] He and Ibn al-Shiḥna (below) are the only non-Timurid Muslim writers to have met with Timur and leave us a written memoir of their encounters.

Since Ibn ʿArabshāh did not complete his *ʿAjāʾib al-maqdūr fī nawāʾib Tīmūr* ('The Wonders of Destiny in Regard to the Disasters [Inflicted by] Timur') for another fifteen years or so after his return to Mamlūk territory, we might suspect that memory played him false. But he may have kept notes in Samarkand, where he benefited (in obscure circumstances) from a scholarly education: it has been proposed that he probably sat at the feet of luminaries like ʿAlī Jurjānī (known as 'al-Sayyid al-sharīf'; d. 816/1413) and Shams al-Dīn Muḥammad Jazarī (d. 833/1429), both of them among the many intellectuals who had been transported from their homelands to adorn Timur's capital.[80] After his return to Syria Ibn ʿArabshāh interviewed prominent figures, citing oral information from as recently as 833/1429–30, 836/1432–3 and 840/1436–7, this last being specified as the current year.[81] He also incorporated material from written sources, notably lengthy passages from the chronicle of Ibn Shiḥna (see later).[82] One of Ibn ʿArabshāh's other works is worthy of mention at this juncture: *Fākihat al-khulafāʾ wa-mufākahat al-ẓurafāʾ* ('The Fruits of the Caliphs and the Banter of the Witty'), a collection of animal fables which will be cited later in connection with the nature of Mongol law, the Yasa or Töre.

Ibn ʿArabshāh is the most hostile of the witnesses at our disposal.[83] True, the picture he draws is not uniformly damning: he devotes a chapter to Timur's estimable qualities, acknowledging his personal courage, his aversion to levity, his steadfast adherence to decisions he had taken and the uncommon perspicacity that enabled him to distinguish servile flattery from truth.[84] He further speaks in fulsome terms of the men of talent with whom Timur surrounded himself,[85] and was evidently impressed by Timur's building projects and his efforts to beautify Samarkand.[86] These sentiments might carry all the more weight for emanating from an otherwise antagonistic critic.[87] Yet the overall accent is undeniably on Timur's destructiveness, his duplicity and cruelty, and his questionable commitment to Islam. Timur was al-Dajjāl ('The Deceiver'; the counterpart to Antichrist in Islamic thought), and his followers were Yājūj and Mājūj (Gog and Magog).[88] The section headings deploy a series of opprobrious designations: 'that treacherous one' (*dhālika l-muḥtāl*), 'yon tyrant' (*dhālika l-ṭāghī*), 'yon lying impostor' (*dhālika l-khaddāʿ al-makkār*), 'yon oppressor' (*dhālika l-jabbār*), to cite but a few.[89]

Embedded in Ibn ʿArabshāh's *ʿAjāʾib* are two mentions of encounters between Timur and Ibn Khaldūn at Timur's encampment outside Damascus in 803/1400. It is possible – to judge by Ibn Khaldūn's own account of his conversations with Timur – that both exchanges relate to their initial interview rather than one of their subsequent meetings prior to Timur's withdrawal from Syria.[90] These references are problematic, however. Ibn ʿArabshāh quotes Ibn Khaldūn's words to the conqueror as if he had himself been present, and writes of the punishment of Qadi Ṣadr al-Dīn al-Munāwī as if Ibn Khaldūn had been an eyewitness, which seems doubtful inasmuch as the latter makes only a terse allusion to it.[91] Ibn ʿArabshāh is hardly likely to have met the Maghribī savant – still less to have been present at his encounters with Timur.[92] We cannot dismiss the possibility that he had access to Ibn Khaldūn's memoirs much later and second hand, through al-Maqrīzī (see below), whom he had met in 840/1436–7.[93] However, this is a matter of conjecture.

Ibn ʿArabshāh admired Ibn Khaldūn because the Maghribī scholar, he tells us, was one of only two persons ever to have outwitted Timur, namely by obtaining permission to leave the Great Amir's headquarters on the pretext of bringing back his writings from Cairo, which included an account of Timur.[94] In his own account Ibn Khaldūn says nothing of this, reporting that he offered to remain in Timur's service but was ordered to return to the Egyptian capital.[95] Even so, a Mamlūk historian cites an eyewitness account of the conversation similar to Ibn ʿArabshāh's (though referring to prized possessions rather than books alone).[96]

Whatever the truth, Ibn ʿArabshāh describes Ibn Khaldūn as 'the author of a marvellous history, who adopted therein a wonderful style' (*ṣāḥib al-taʾrīkh al-ʿajīb wa l-sālik fīhi l-uslūb al-gharīb*),[97] though he admits that he has not seen the book himself and is reliant on hearsay.[98] Ibn Khaldūn, who evidently concurred with Ibn ʿArabshāh's verdict,[99] was the author of a number of historical works. The most celebrated and most striking – the *Muqaddima*, 'Prolegomena', which Ibn ʿArabshāh had in mind here – was also the earliest to be completed; Ibn Khaldūn produced a first draft while still resident in the Maghrib.[100] Accordingly, it makes no reference to Timur and his conquests. It is in this work, however, that Ibn Khaldūn expounds his distinctive views on the rise and fall of states and the historic relationship between nomadic and sedentary civilisations (below).

The *Muqaddima* was the introduction to Ibn Khaldūn's *Kitāb al-ʿibar wa-dīwān al-mubtadaʾ wa l-khabar fī ayyām al-ʿarab wa l-ʿajam wa l-barbar wa-man ʿāṣarahum min dhawī l-sulṭān al-akbar* ('Book of Examples and Register of Subjects and Predicates in the Days of the Arabs, the Persians and the Berbers and Their Contemporaries Who Wielded the Highest Power'), a compilation of the histories of (overwhelmingly) Muslim peoples and states. It was by abridging and amending the history of the Berbers and the Maghrib given in this work that Ibn Khaldūn devised the account of the western lands which Timur demanded from him and which he completed in only a few days.[101] *Al-ʿIbar* presents fairly mechanical narrative surveys of the history of the Mongols, their successors in Iran and Anatolia and Timur's career.[102] Despite a number of egregious errors,[103] Ibn Khaldūn is known to have had access to highly reliable material. His chief source for Mongol history was al-ʿUmarī's *Masālik al-abṣār*, but he also used earlier works on Chinggis Khan's invasion.[104]

Ibn Khaldūn's encounter with Timur is related in his 'autobiography', *al-Taʿrīf bi-Ibn Khaldūn wa-riḥlatuhu gharb*[an] *wa-sharq*[an] ('Introducing Ibn Khaldūn and His Journey East and West'), where it is prefaced with a brief overview of geography and of world history, including an inaccurate sketch of Mongol history and a summary of Timur's career.[105] He also alludes here to details learned from conversations with Timur that he does not record.[106] Some of his autobiographical statements are suspect. We might doubt his assertion that when a group of notables from Damascus approached Timur to ask for quarter the conqueror enquired whether Ibn Khaldūn was still in the city or had accompanied the retreating Egyptian army.[107] Interestingly, the entry on Ibn Khaldūn in al-Maqrīzī's biographical dictionary (see below) omits to say that Timur had previously heard of him, but instead has Ibn Khaldūn take the initiative in mingling with Timur's troops and requesting permission to visit his headquarters.[108] Ibn Khaldūn's own account also gives the impression that he left for the invaders' camp from fear of an attempt on his life by those in Damascus who were opposed to surrender on the basis of Timur's oral assurances.[109] The story of Timur's enquiry may reflect nothing more than Ibn Khaldūn's desire to inflate his own importance. In the same vein is the claim that he had prevailed upon Timur to grant the Damascenes an amnesty,[110] and the statement found in al-Maqrīzī's *Durar al-ʿuqūd* (and based on oral information from Ibn Khaldūn himself?) that Timur had given him a place allotted to no other person, even seating him above his own son and telling him publicly, 'You have my regard'.[111] Yet Ibn Khaldūn could have had a different motive for alleging that Timur had asked for him. In a letter written to the Marinid Sultan of Morocco after his return to Egypt, he repeated the tale of Timur's summons, adding that this had left him no choice.[112] We could infer that he felt a need to justify waiting upon the infamous warlord.

The details concerning Timur's life in *al-Taʿrīf* are in general more accurate than those in the *ʿIbar*.[113] Here Ibn Khaldūn is fairly complimentary: he remarks more than once on the conqueror's generosity towards him,[114] though he also frankly admits having feared for his life during his stay at Timur's headquarters.[115] It is only in relation to the conduct of the Chaghatay troops, however, that he permits himself remarks that might imply criticism of their leader: for their engagement in wholesale looting and slaughter and their cruelty towards sedentary populations,[116] and particularly for the harsh treatment of the Shāfiʿī chief qadi al-Munāwī, their setting fire to the Umayyad Mosque in Damascus and their unprecedented atrocities in Aleppo, Ḥamā, Ḥimṣ and Baʿlabakk .[117]

One reason for Ibn Khaldūn's relatively positive response to Timur himself, perhaps, is that he identified him as the subject of a prophecy he had heard in the Maghrib.[118] In Fez in 761/1359–60 the preacher Abū ʿAlī Ibn Bādīs had assured him that the conjunction of the planets Jupiter and Saturn, due to occur in 766/1364–5, would presage the rise of a powerful man at the head of a nation of tent-dwellers from the north-east, who would vanquish kingdoms and become master of most of the inhabited world and whose advent could be anticipated around 784/1382–3. This prophecy was endorsed both by a Jewish physician and astrologer in the service of the King of Castile and by Ibn Khaldūn's teacher, Muḥammad b. Ibrāhīm al-Ābilī. Ibn Khaldūn repeated the prediction to Timur at their first encounter, but how far he believed it is unclear,[119] though we might note that his *ʿIbar* dates Timur's advance into Khurāsān precisely (and incorrectly) in 784.[120]

It is also conceivable that Timur's meteoric career of conquest may have furnished Ibn Khaldūn with a contemporary textbook illustration, as it were, of the historical processes that he had earlier elaborated in his *Muqaddima* concerning the relations between sedentary and nomadic societies.[121] Briefly, nomadic societies possessed *ʿaṣabiyya* (group solidarity, cohesion), born of the exigencies of their harsh steppe environment and relatively absent in settled communities, which are enervated by their access to luxury and abundance; in due course nomads who had conquered sedentary lands succumbed to the same lures. *ʿAṣabiyya* might derive additional strength from a shared religious zeal, and for Ibn Khaldūn the privations of the nomads' lifestyle and diet bred a piety more austere than that of sedentary peoples.[122] The only indication, however, that Ibn Khaldūn saw this cyclical pattern as substantiated by Timur and his armies is his claim to have told the Great Amir that the key to dominion lay in *ʿasabiyya*, and that the Turks – among whom he, like many earlier Muslim writers, classed the Mongols – possessed *ʿaṣabiyya* to a degree unrivalled by other peoples.[123]

How far Ibn Khaldūn's analysis, which was inspired above all by the history of the Arabs, the Caliphate and the Berbers in North Africa and Andalusia, generally accords with that of Inner Asian nomads need not detain us here; the cyclical model possibly fits the Iranian world and (better) China.[124] It has been pointed out that Heaven's mandate, enjoining what was virtually a 'holy war' for the reduction of the entire world, was itself a source of *'aṣabiyya*; though Ibn Khaldūn fails to make that explicit connection.[125] However, one way in which he may have accommodated the 'Tatars' Chinggis Khan and Timur within his framework was that, in order to conquer other nomadic societies and sedentary states, a nomadic group required a leader whose *'aṣabiyya* was superior to that of the rank and file. In Ibn Khaldūn's view, this was strongest where the group and the leader shared a common ancestry.[126] God had invested such leaders with many other fine qualities too: generosity, tolerance of the weak and maintenance of the needy, respect for the Sharīʿa and its scholars, observance of their prescriptions and a desire for their prayers.[127] In some measure – and regardless of his manifest faults – Timur could be deemed to satisfy these criteria.

MUSLIM AUTHORS WRITING OUTSIDE THE TIMURID DOMINIONS

Only one historical work that covers Timur's attack on India was written by a near-contemporary. Yaḥyā b. Aḥmad Sirhindī, who completed his *Ta'rīkh-i Mubārakshāhī* for the Sayyid ruler of Delhi, Mubārak Shāh b. Khiḍr Khan, in or soon after 838/1434, supplies an account of the sack of Delhi that usefully complements the Timurid sources.[128] But he is reticent about the contacts between his master and Shāhrukh and fails to mention that the Sayyids struck coins in Shāhrukh's name. We would know nothing of this relationship were it not for the slightly later author Muḥammad Bihāmadkhānī (842/1438), writing in the distant and independent Indian principality of Kalpi (see p. 435).

The great majority of early Ottoman historians wrote only several decades after Timur's death.[129] The exception is Aḥmedī (d. 815/1412), whose *Iskendernāme* contains an account of Ottoman history in the opening years of the fifteenth century that makes only a fleeting reference to Timur's invasion but exhibits, as Kastritsis has shown, a distinct ideological perspective on the catastrophe.[130] Only one other Anatolian author wrote as a contemporary of Timur. ʿAzīz b. Ardashīr Astarābādī, formerly in the service of the Jalayirid Sulṭān Aḥmad, had fled Baghdad in 795/1393, only to be taken prisoner in Karbalā by the forces of Timur's son Amīrānshāh. Escaping his captors, he took refuge in Sivas, where he dedicated his *Bazm-u razm* ('Feasting and Fighting') to its ruler, Qadi Burhān al-Dīn, in 800/1397–8.[131] At this time Timur was still a relatively remote threat. Yet Astarābādī's experience had bred a visceral loathing of the Chaghatays; his remarks about Timur and his troops may constitute the earliest denial that they were genuine Muslims.

As in the Ilkhanid era, writers in the late fourteenth- and early fifteenth-century Mamlūk Sultanate regularly paid attention to events beyond the Euphrates.[132] Some of those contemporary with Timur have left us works that end before his invasion of Syria. The Damascus chronicle of Ibn Ṣaṣrā, probably completed prior to 801/1399, survives only in a fragment covering the years 786–799/1384–1397.[133] Other partial losses are particularly regrettable: the extant portion of the annalistic chronicles by Ibn al-Furāt (d. 807/1405) and Ibn Duqmāq (d. 809/1407)[134] end prior to Timur's attack (although the latter's brief *al-Jawhar al-thamīn* supplies a few details). The two earliest surviving works that cover Timur's Syrian campaign are the *Taʾrīkh* of Ibn Ḥijjī (b. 751/1350; d. 816/1413), which extends from 796/1393–4 down to 815/1412–13 and would be one of the main sources for Ibn Qāḍī Shuhba (see later),[135] and *Rawḍat al-manāẓir fī ʿilm al-awāʾil wa l-awākhir* ('The Garden of Perspectives on the Knowledge of the First and Last Things'), by Zayn al-Dīn Muḥammd Ibn al-Shiḥna (d. 815/1412),[136] which includes an account of the invasion and his own reception, alongside other scholars, by Timur in Aleppo in the second half of Rabīʿ I 803/ early November 1400 (the version reproduced in Ibn ʿArabshāh's *ʿAjāʾib* is extensively reordered).

Otherwise, we are dependent on a group of later historians who were roughly contemporary with one another. The Egyptian Taqī al-Dīn Aḥmad b. ʿAlī al-Maqrīzī (b. 766/1364; d. 845/1442), a teacher of *ḥadīth*, was also a prolific historian, though not without his shortcomings.[137] In his annalistic chronicle, *al-Sulūk li-maʿrifat duwal al-mulūk* ('The Paths to the Knowledge of Dynasties and Kings'), written in the period 825–7/1421–3,[138] he first mentions Timur under the year 787/1385–6 when the conqueror sent an embassy to Cairo and provides a full account of his invasion of Syria and (under the wrong year 808) an extremely terse obituary.[139] Like al-Maqrīzī, Shihāb al-Dīn Abū l-Faḍl Aḥmad b. ʿAlī Ibn Ḥajar al-ʿAsqalānī (b. 773/1372; d. 852/1449),[140] whom we shall meet later as the author of a treatise on plague (below, p. 148), was a teacher of *ḥadīth* who composed an annalistic chronicle, *Inbāʾ al-ghumr fī abnāʾ al-ʿumr* ('Reports for the Uninitiated on the Men of the Age'). Timur's obituary here is much longer than that in *Sulūk*, but in general this work has been classed as inferior to *Sulūk*: Ibn Ḥajar's sources are not always clear, and his arrangement is frequently incoherent and serves to obscure the chronology.[141] The *Taʾrīkh* of the Syrian Taqī al-Dīn Abū Bakr b. Aḥmad Ibn Qāḍī Shuhba (b. 779/1377; d. 851/1448), an abridgement of his reworking of Ibn Ḥijjī's history, contains an obituary of Timur, comprising a survey of his career and his Syrian campaign, and cites exchanges between Timur and Ibn Khaldūn regarding the account of the Maghrib that the latter had composed at his behest.[142] Less useful for Timur's attack is the universal history, *ʿIqd al-jumān fī taʾrīkh ahl al-zamān* ('The Pearl Necklace in the History of Contemporaries'), of al-ʿAynī (b. 762/1360; d. 855/1451). On the other hand, Abū l-Maḥāsin Yūsuf Ibn Taghrībirdī (b. 812/1409; d. 874/1470), not yet born when Timur invaded, produced a detailed history, *al-Nujūm al-zāhira fī mulūk Miṣr wa l-Qāhira* ('The Shining Stars among the Kings of Egypt and Cairo'), which, if largely indebted to earlier authors, is still valuable for our period.[143]

In addition, some of these authors produced biographical dictionaries modelled on the thirteenth-century work of Ibn Khallikān and on al-Ṣafadī's voluminous *al-Wāfī* (see earlier).[144] Al-Maqrīzī's *Durar al-ʿuqūd al-farīda fī tarājim al-aʿyān al-mufīda* ('The Unique Pearlstrings among the Edifying Biographies of Notables'), includes a lengthy entry on Timur himself,[145] as well as briefer notices on members of his dynasty such as Khalīl Sulṭān and Shāhrukh, and enemies like the Muzaffarid Shāh Manṣūr, the Jalayirid Sulṭān Aḥmad, the Ottoman sultan Bayezid, the Jochid khan Toqtamish and the amir Edigü (or Edigei).[146] Ibn Taghrībirdī's dictionary, *al-Manhal al-ṣāfī wa l-mustawfī ba'd al-Wāfī* ('The Limpid Pool and Completion of *al-Wāfī*'), contains similar entries based on *Durar al-'uqūd*.

It is clear that Ibn 'Arabshāh's *'Ajā'ib* was the chief source utilised by these later authors based in the Mamlūk territories. In his biographical dictionary al-Maqrīzī was chiefly dependent on Ibn 'Arabshāh, whom he had met (and to whom he twice acknowledges his indebtedness for the entries on Timur and on Ibn 'Arabshāh himself);[147] Ibn Qāḍī Shuhba's obituary of Timur, too, is taken to a large extent from Ibn 'Arabshāh (though of course he also cites Ibn Ḥijjī). In some cases, however, the use of *'Ajā'ib* was indirect, through the medium of al-Maqrīzī. For the obituary of Timur in his *Inbā'* Ibn Ḥajar may have consulted *'Ajā'ib*, and he is known to have met Ibn 'Arabshāh in person four years before al-Maqrīzī did, in 836/1432–3.[148] But it certainly seems that he used *Sulūk* and that he was also indebted to it for material from Ibn Khaldūn's *'Ibar*.[149] Although Ibn Taghrībirdī's two accounts of Timur are likewise greatly indebted to Ibn 'Arabshāh, under whom he had studied and on whom his *Manhal* includes a long entry,[150] it looks as if he too, strangely, utilised *'Ajā'ib* via al-Maqrīzī.[151] His entry on Toqtamish, much shorter than al-Maqrīzī's, contains details apparently lifted from *Durar al-'uqūd* (and which cannot be from *'Ajā'ib*).[152]

Al-Maqrīzī is an exception to a general tendency to rely exclusively on the invective-laden *'Ajā'ib*. The reason, seemingly, is that he was, to quote Dale, 'in a limited sense, Ibn Khaldun's intellectual protégé',[153] and much of his information was derived from Ibn Khaldūn. He prefaced Timur's biography with a sketch of the history of the Tatars, which he may have summarised from *al-'Ibar*,[154] and further utilised oral information from Ibn Khaldūn dating, no doubt, from when the Maghribī savant was his teacher.[155] The entry on Ibn Khaldūn in *Durar*, which summarises his meetings with Timur, stresses the favourable impression he made and his high standing with the conqueror (but see earlier, p. 39).[156]

CHRISTIAN WRITERS WHO NOTICED TIMUR'S ACTIVITIES

Timur's arrival in the western Jochid territories – notably his attack in 1395 on the Venetian-held entrepôt of Tana, in the Don estuary – brought him into contact with the 'Franks', the Latin Christian powers of Europe. From a number of western authors Timur's assault on his fellow Muslims elicited a positive reaction. His victory over the Ottomans, so soon after the disastrous crusade against Bayezid at Nicopolis (1396), was bound to appear in a providential light and engendered an optimism sufficient to eclipse the fate of Tana. This is mirrored especially in the *Mémoire* (1403) of the Dominican Friar John, successively Bishop of Nakhchiwān and Archbishop of Sulṭāniyya.[157] He may have spent as long as twelve years in the conqueror's entourage before acting as envoy for Timur and his son Amīrānshāh to western Christian courts in 804/1402, in which capacity he visited the kings of France and England.[158] The *Mémoire*, which was in French, was inserted in the royal chronicle *Chronographia regum Francorum* in Latin translation in or soon after 1415.[159] John's Latin treatise, *Libellus de notitia orbis* ('Memorandum regarding Knowledge of the World', 1404),[160] based on his experience of travel in the east, is also valuable.

Ruy González de Clavijo produced a matter-of-fact and indeed often prosaic narrative of his experiences as part of an embassy from King Henry III of Castile in 1404 to Timur's headquarters in Samarkand. He is refreshingly free of the archbishop's partisan attitudes, offering a more forthright and less roseate judgement. For example, he describes frankly the adverse consequences attending the passage of the Chaghatay troops, which led to the flight of the inhabitants. So too, in the context of religious attitudes, he is the only western writer to mention that Timur was always accompanied on his travels by a portable mosque.[161] He makes no attempt to depict Timur as indulgent towards his Christian subjects and his account is spiced with digressions on the recent history of the regions he traversed – history that is regrettably often impressionistic and inaccurate. He is also less forthcoming regarding Timur himself than is John of Sulṭāniyya. Clavijo's interest is above all in the visual: what particularly caught his imagination was not some supposed sympathy for Christians but Timur's wealth, his opulent court and the magnificent buildings he had constructed.[162]

When the Chaghatay forces sacked Damascus in 803/1401, the Sienese merchant Beltramo di Mignanelli (d. 1456), a resident of the city, was fortunate enough to be absent in Jerusalem. He shortly fled to Egypt, returning to Damascus only later,[163] and it was not until 1416 that he composed his account, *De ruina Damasci*. Consequently, he was not an eyewitness of the sack but must have obtained his information from Muslims who had lived through the ordeal. Although he had little time for his fellow residents, disparaging their morality and scorning their gullibility in trusting Timur's repeated assurances, he expresses some sympathy with them in their misfortune and bitterly regrets the city's fate.[164]

The memoirs of Johann Schiltberger, a Bavarian knight taken prisoner by the Ottomans at Nicopolis in 1396 and captured in turn by Timur's victorious troops at Ankara in 1402, are not totally without value. Put together after his return to Bavaria in 1427, however, they are written in an inconsequential fashion, contain a number of chronological and geographical errors and appear to be based largely on hearsay. His lowly status also put him at a disadvantage alongside other European observers in acquiring accurate information.

The principal eastern Christian source on Timur's operations in the Near East displays the hostile reaction that might have been anticipated. The Armenian historian Tʿovma Metsobetsʿi (Thomas of Metsopʿ; d. 1446) lived through Timur's successive campaigns of devastation, in which the Christian populations of Armenia and Georgia and their churches suffered considerably. The structure is often haphazard and the chronology frequently awry, and a number of the stories concerning Timur's cunning stratagems and acts of terror are found in no other source and are patently fanciful.[165] On the other hand, Tʿovma does repeat the well-authenticated stories of the decapitations at Damascus, Timur's bad faith towards the people of Sivas and the gruesome fate of its garrison.[166] Greek authors such as Doukas and the continuator of Michaēl Panaretos (d. 1390) provide useful information, though their viewpoint is coloured by Timur's humiliation of the Ottoman Sultan Bayezid and they wrote after the fall of Constantinople to the Ottomans in 1453.[167] The fragmentary material in Syriac barely adds to our knowledge of the main events, though naturally offering greater detail regarding atrocities against local Christians.[168] Common to Christian authors – both eastern and western – are various tales that seem to have been circulating in the Near East.[169]

LATER ISLAMIC SOURCES FROM THE PERSIANATE WORLD

With three exceptions, Timurid authors after Ḥāfiẓ-i Abrū and Sharaf al-Dīn Yazdī add little to our knowledge of Timur's own epoch. *Ta'rīkh-i arba'a ulūs* ('History of the Four Uluses'), for instance, which has traditionally been attributed to Timur's grandson Ulugh Beg (d. 853/1449) and appears to have survived in abridged form as *Shajarat al-atrāk* ('The Tree of the Turks'), is lifted almost verbatim from Yazdī's *Muqaddima*.[170] Similarly, the relevant sections of *Maṭla' al-sa'dayn* ('The Rising of the Two Stars [Jupiter and Venus]') by Kamāl al-Dīn ʿAbd al-Razzāq Samarqandī (b. 816/1413; d. 887/1482) and of *Rawḍat al-ṣafā* ('The Garden of Purity') by Mīr-Khwānd (Muḥammad b. Khwāndshāh: b. 837/1433; d. 903/1498) are largely taken from Yazdī or from Ḥāfiẓ-i Abrū's *Zubdat al-tawārīkh*.[171]

The three exceptions referred to are *Mujmal-i Faṣīḥī* ('Faṣīḥ's Compendium'), a chronography down to 845/1441–2 composed under Shāhrukh and his son Bāysunghur by Faṣīḥ al-Dīn Aḥmad Khwāfī, also known as Faṣīḥ-i Khwāfī and Faṣīḥī,[172] and two general histories, *Ta'rīkh-i kabīr* ('The Great History'), down to 850/1447, by Jaʿfarī (Jaʿfar b. Muḥammad Ḥusaynī), also the author of a history of his native Yazd, and *Jāmi' al-tawārīkh-i Ḥasanī*, written by Tāj al-Dīn Ḥasan Ibn Shihāb Yazdī in eastern Iran during the years 855–7/1451–3. All three works contain details so far not traced in any earlier source;[173] Jaʿfarī and Ibn Shihāb Yazdī (who was himself active in the Timurid military in the decade or so after Timur's death)[174] are particularly important for events in southern Iran. Mention must also be made of an Arabic universal history, *al-Ta'rīkh al-Ghiyāthī*, by ʿAbd-Allāh Ibn Fatḥ-Allāh al-Baghdādī, writing in the late fifteenth century, probably under the Āq-Qūyūnlū; Part 5 covers the era of the Mongols and Turks down to 891/1486. He provides some useful detail on the later Ilkhanid period (apparently culled from an unknown source that terminated in 744/1343–4 and possibly also from Persian authors)[175] and on the Jalayirids and Muzaffarids.[176] On Timur, where his sources included Yazdī's *Ẓafar-nāma* and, indirectly, *'Ajā'ib*, he offers little or no original material.

Several later historians who utilised works from the Mongol and Timurid periods include the occasional fresh nugget. The best known today is *Ḥabīb al-siyar* ('The Friend of Biographies') by Khwānd-Amīr (Ghiyāth al-Dīn b. Humām al-Dīn), composed in Mughul India in the early sixteenth century. The *Shejere-i türk* of Abū l-Ghāzī Bahādur Khan (d. 1074/1663), Uzbek ruler of Khiva and himself a Jochid, is frequently cited for the Mongol period, though he relied greatly on memory and the work is far from reliable.[177] Not all of this late material, however, was derivative. The anonymous author of the *Tawārīkh-i guzīda nuṣrat-nāma* ('Selected Histories: The Book of Victory'), a history of the Uzbeks composed for Muḥammad Shībānī Khan in *c.* 909/1504,[178] copied (with some emendations) the Chinggisid genealogies in the *Muʿizz al-ansāb* and extended them down to his own period. And although the *Chingīz-nāma* (or *Ta'rīkh-i Dūst Sulṭān*), produced in Khiva by Ötemish Ḥājjī (965/1557–8), contains some legendary details, it yields what appears to be authentic and precious information on the Jochid territories in the obscure mid-fourteenth century.[179]

Muḥammad Ḥaydar Dughlāt (b. 905/1499–1500; d. 958/1551), better known both then and now as Mīrzā Ḥaydar, merits a lengthier mention as the first historian writing in Central Asia since Jamāl al-Qarshī (see earlier), whose work has survived and is also the first to relate the conversion of the khan Tughluq Temür in the 1350s. His family was closely associated with the region of Kāshghar and Yārkand in the eastern Chaghadayid khanate and he was a maternal grandson of the khan Yūnus (d. 892/1487), hence first cousin to the Timurid Bābur, founder of the Mughul empire. In 952/1546, in Mughul India he completed his *Ta'rīkh-i Rashīdī*, combining his memoirs with a history of Mughūlistān from the reign of Tughluq Temür (d. 764/1363) onwards.[180] Interestingly, the fragmentary information on the early Mughūl khans found in the *Bābur-nāma* tallies with Ḥaydar's account and must belong to that same oral tradition.[181] Ḥaydar's main aim was to rescue from oblivion a history preserved almost exclusively by word of mouth: when detailing Timur's attacks on Mughūlistān, he was obliged, significantly, to cite lengthy passages from Yazdī's *Ẓafar-nāma*.[182] As we shall see, he seeks to glorify his own Dughlāt ancestors, much as the Timurid court histories endeavoured to inflate the importance of Timur's forebears.

Where Timur is concerned, the voices that clamour for our attention make for a strikingly discordant chorus. Sharaf al-Dīn ʿAlī Yazdī's occasional use of allegory to offer muted criticism of Timur means we cannot altogether dismiss the image purveyed by Timurid authors as bland sycophancy.[183] Unlike other authors writing in the Mamlūk dominions, al-Maqrīzī was sufficiently influenced by Ibn Khaldūn to see Timur as one appointed to fulfil God's purposes by punishing errant Muslims. It would be a mistake, too, to write off Ibn ʿArabshāh's testimony merely on the grounds of his personal experience of exile thousands of miles from his home. Timur was certainly a ruthless and vindictive enemy, but even Ibn ʿArabshāh lists some of his more estimable qualities. And among western European authors, Mignanelli and Archbishop John each takes a very different stance regarding the conqueror.

PART I
THE MONGOLS

CHAPTER 2
THE MONGOL EMPIRE: UNITY, EXPANSION AND DIVISION, *c.* 1200–1335

EURASIAN NOMADS AND THE SEDENTARY WORLD

Over a period of several centuries in Inner Asia, groups of nomadic peoples – herders of oxen, goats, camels and especially sheep and horses, moving from lowland winter pastures along river valleys to spring and summer upland regions – had coalesced to form steppe empires. Prior to the Mongols, the most impressive was that of the Türks, sometimes called the Kök ('Blue') Türks (sixth–eighth centuries CE), which extended from the borders of present-day Manchuria to the western steppes. In time such imperial powers fragmented into their constituent tribes or spawned fresh ethnic groups. In the wake of the Türk empire, new Turkic political entities emerged: the Uighur empire (744–840) in Mongolia and the Khazar empire (seventh–late-tenth centuries) on the Volga, both of them semi-sedentarised powers ruled by a qaghan/khaqan (supreme khan, 'emperor') as the Türks had been. There were also 'stateless' nomadic confederacies, characterised by a looser political structure, like the Qarluq, the Oghuz, the Qirghiz and the Qipchaq/Qangli.

To the south-west, Turkic peoples bordered on the Islamic world (*Dār al-Islām*).[1] The Arab Muslims, following their conquest of the Sasanian Persian empire in 651 CE, had reduced Transoxiana (Mā warā' al-nahr). Over the next two centuries Transoxiana was steadily Islamised and by *c.* 1000 its steppe neighbours, the Qarluq and the

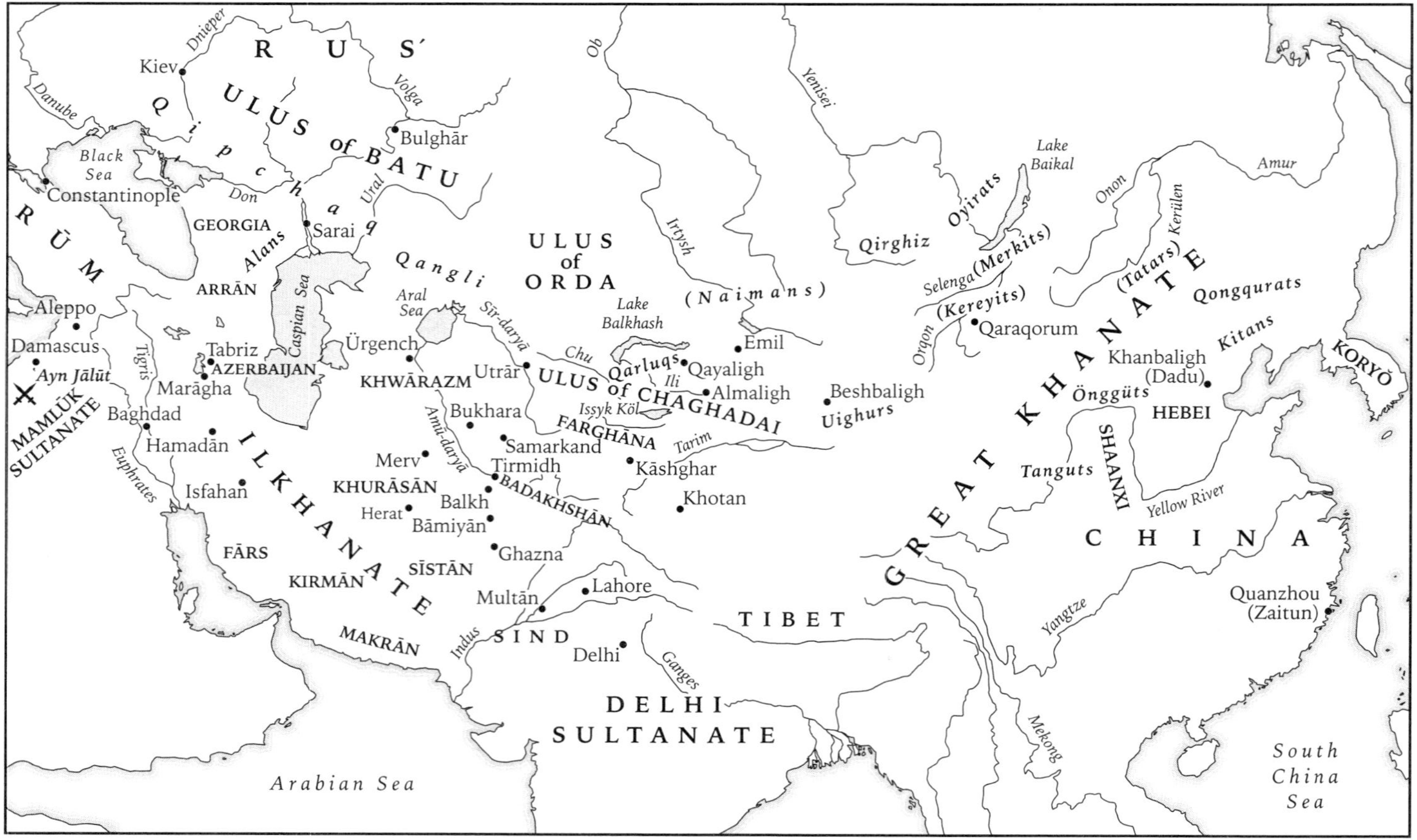

1. The Mongol empire.

Oghuz, had accepted Islam. At this time, the universal Caliphate, ruled from Baghdad by the ʿAbbasid dynasty (132–656/750–1258), was no longer a political reality and its territories were ruled by autonomous regimes that acknowledged ʿAbbasid sovereignty, forwarded to the Caliph a share of the provincial revenues and inserted his name on their coinage (*sikka*) and in the public Friday prayer (*khuṭba*), in return for honorific titles and confirmation of their status.

From the ninth century onwards several of these regional dynasties were of Turkish origin, belonging to one of two distinct categories. The first were military slaves who had entered the Islamic world as war captives and served their masters as *ghulāms* or *mamlūks* (literally 'one owned'):[2] the Ghaznawids or Yaminids (352–582/963–1186), for example, in eastern Iran and north-west India. The regime that ruled Egypt from 647/1250 and Syria from 658/1260 and is known to historians as the Mamlūk Sultanate would prove the Mongols' most redoubtable antagonist. Dynasties in the second category were founded by newly Islamised Turks entering the Dār al-Islām en masse. The Qarakhanids (*c.* 225–609/*c.* 840–1213) in Transoxiana, possibly of Qarluq origin, were the first, closely followed by the Seljuqs (431–590/1040–1194), of Oghuz stock, who conquered present-day Turkmenistan, Iran, Syria and Anatolia and took the Caliph under their protection. The Seljuqs recruited Turkish slave troops: the Khwārazmshāhs (490–628/1097–1231), who supplanted them as rulers of the eastern Islamic world, were descended from one of their Turkish slave officers.[3]

The westward migration of Turkic peoples was most probably part of a chain reaction, beginning in the east. Turkic domination of Mongolia was terminated by the Kitan, nomads from Manchuria of proto-Mongolian stock, who conquered the eastern steppe and parts of northern China and reigned there under the dynastic name of Liao (907–1125). Their name – as 'Khita' or 'Khitai' (Europeanised as 'Cathay') – came to designate northern China and even the entire country. Their overthrow by the Jurchen, a non-nomadic Manchurian people who ruled northern China as the Jin dynasty (1123–1234), sparked fresh westward migrations. Large numbers of Kitan refugees fled into Central Asia, where they reduced to subjection the Uighur principality at Beshbaligh and the Qarakhanids and decisively defeated the Seljuq Sultan Sanjar (536/1141). Their leader, a scion of the Liao dynasty, took the Inner Asian title of *Gür-khan* ('world ruler'). This new state (1125–1218), known to the Chinese as Xi Liao ('Western Liao') and to the Muslims as Qara Khitai (possibly 'Black Kitan'), brought Central Asia under non-Muslim rule for the first time since the Arab conquest.

THE RISE OF THE MONGOLS

We must briefly explore the circumstances in which nomadic empires came into being. Nicola Di Cosmo proposes that state formation among the nomads occurred in response to conditions of crisis, perhaps brought on by a succession of harsher winters, a drought or an epidemic, reducing the size of herds below a level adequate to sustain the nomads.[4] Amid the ensuing social disaggregation, tribal bonds might weaken, allowing a greater degree of social mobility and facilitating the rise of more effective leaders whose charisma did not rest on lineage and status and who, having built up their own non-tribal war-band,[5] were able to challenge the traditional tribal aristocracy. The newly fledged leadership presided over a centralised and more far-reaching militarisation of society and a rise in consumption among the ruling elite. An increase in those engaged in regular military activity, combined with the creation of a bureaucratic apparatus, adversely affected pastoral production and stimulated a need for external resources – and hence military operations against nomadic and sedentary neighbours. Although the formation of earlier steppe empires is shrouded in obscurity, this pattern fits the rise of the Mongols in the late twelfth century, since the account of the early years of Temüjin (Chinggis Khan) in the Secret History strongly suggests a time of crisis.

The Jin had jettisoned the policy of the Liao, abandoning their outposts in the steppe, and sought security by playing off the nomadic tribes against one another. The new strategy led to a power vacuum of which the Mongols would take advantage. Dwelling in the region of the Onon and the Kerülen (Kherlen) rivers to the south-east of Lake Baikal, and first mentioned in a Chinese text of the Tang era (618–907),[6] they were just one among several tribes in present-day Mongolia. Their neighbours included their principal enemies the Tatars, around the Buyur Nor and the Külün Nor, the Merkit, on the shores of Lake Baikal, the Önggüt, in the modern Ordos region, the Kereyit, along the Orqon and Selenga rivers and the Naiman, on the upper Irtysh. Of these, the Önggüt, the Kereyit and the Naiman each possessed a dynasty of hereditary khans and the rudiments of an administrative system.

Legend endowed Temüjin with a line of forebears going back to Alan Qo'a, who was impregnated by a ray of light and gave birth to a son, Bodonchar, the ancestor of the Borjighid clan to which Temüjin belonged.[7] A short-lived Mongol hegemony achieved in the mid-twelfth century was terminated by the Tatars, acting in concert with the Jurchen-Jin; the Mongol khan, Ambaghai, suffered a cruel death in the Jin capital at Zhongdu. Observations regarding the Mongols' poverty and political fragmentation thereafter are found in several thirteenth-century sources and betray the centrality of these conditions in their folk memory.[8] In *c.* 1170, Yesügei, a Borjighid chieftain descended from the earlier khans, was poisoned by the Tatars; his widow and her young offspring, abandoned by their people, spent some years fending for themselves. In time the eldest son, Temüjin, acquired a group of sworn followers (Mo. *nököt*; sing. *nökör*), from varied tribal backgrounds.[9] In alliance with his father's one-time blood-brother (Mo. *anda*), Toghril, the khan of the Kereyit, he persuaded the Jin to abandon the Tatars, who were crushed (1202). The Jin Emperor conferred on Toghril the Chinese honorific title of *wang*, 'prince' (corrupted in Mongolia to 'Ong Khan'); Temüjin received a minor title. But Temüjin soon turned against Toghril/Ong Khan and incorporated the Kereyit within the burgeoning Mongol confederacy (1203). The victor went on to subdue the Merkit and the Naiman in succession, and the 'forest tribes' (Mo. *hoi-yin irgen*) of south-eastern Siberia, such as the Qirghiz, the Oyirat and the Uriyangqat, were brought to heel in 1207–8. An assembly of tribal chiefs in 1206 had proclaimed Temüjin as Chinggis Khan (which seems to mean 'hard ruler' rather than 'world ruler', as once thought)[10] and as sovereign, in the phrasing of the Secret History, of the 'people of the felt-walled tents'.[11]

In all probability, Chinggis Khan's initial goals were, firstly, to dominate trade routes in order to obtain payment from merchants in exchange for his protection and, secondly, to exact tribute from lesser princes. In 1209 the *iduq-qut*, the Uighur prince of Beshbaligh, and not long afterwards Arslan Khan, the Muslim ruler of the Qarluq, submitted. But like previous Inner Asian nomadic rulers, Chinggis Khan coveted above all the proverbial wealth of China. He had already gained the allegiance of the Önggüt, on whom the Jin had relied to guard their northern frontier.[12] From 1211 he made war on the Jin with a view to securing regular tribute, though vengeance for Ambaghai must also have played a part. But his attention was increasingly drawn to the west, where groups of Naiman and Merkit had taken refuge among the Qipchaq-Qangli and the Qara Khitai. They posed a particular threat when the Naiman prince Güchülüg, who had wedded the Gür-khan's daughter, usurped his father-in-law's throne. In *c.* 1218 Chinggis Khan's forces conquered the Qara Khitai territories; Güchülüg was hunted down and killed in the Pamir region.

This campaign brought the Mongols in close proximity to the empire of the Khwārazmshāh ʿAlā' al-Dīn Muḥammad b. Tekish, which had recently expanded to embrace the former Qarakhanid dominions in Transoxiana and the territory of the Ghurid dynasty in present-day Afghanistan. The Khwārazmshāh prohibited trade with the Mongol territories, sanctioned the execution by his governor at Utrār of a body of merchants who represented Chinggis Khan and his kinsfolk but who were suspected of spying, and put to death the envoys whom the Mongol ruler sent to demand reparation. The Mongols, as Plano Carpini would note,[13] always exacted vengeance for the killing of their envoys and Muḥammad's action brought down upon him Chinggis Khan's seven-year expedition to Western Asia (1218–1224), in which the Khwarazmian possessions in Transoxiana, Khurāsān and Afghanistan suffered extensive devastation; cities that refused to surrender were sacked and the majority of their populations slaughtered. The Khwārazmshāh, electing not to meet the Mongols in the field, had instead divided his forces among the fortified cities of his empire and withdrawn south of the Oxus. He evaded the Mongol generals Jebe and Sübe'edei, who had been sent in pursuit, and died in 618/1221 as an abject fugitive on an island in the Caspian Sea. His son Jalāl al-Dīn spent three years in India before returning to Iran and engaging in futile operations against the Mongols and against other Muslim princes. At this stage the Mongols seem to have established an administration in Transoxiana and Khwārazm.

The maintenance of commercial contacts was clearly an important factor in Chinggis Khan's conflict with the Khwārazmshāh; so too was the desire for vengeance, just as in the war against the Jurchen-Jin, while the pressing need to pursue vanquished enemies who were still at large constituted a further strong incentive to look westwards. However, it is uncertain when the steppe imperial tradition began to figure in the Mongol leader's calculations. The concept of *translatio imperii* – the transmission of the imperial baton from one people to another – may well have been eclipsed during the era of 'stateless' nomadic confederacies like the Oghuz and Qipchaq/Qangli in the western steppes and following the downfall of the Kitan-Liao in the east, but it had not been forgotten.[14] The Mongols, at one time part of the Türk and Kitan empires, recognised a continuity with these previous steppe polities. When Chinggis Khan's son Ögödei ascended the imperial throne in 1229, he took the more exalted style of Qaghan (or Qa'an). The preamble to the ultimatums that the Mongols addressed to independent powers was, tellingly, in Turkish.[15] Like earlier steppe monarchs, the Mongol sovereigns were seen as possessing the good fortune (Tu. *qut*; Mo. *suu*) vouchsafed by Tenggeri (usually loosely translated as 'Heaven') and demonstrated in their victories.

A later tradition associated Temüjin's recognition as sovereign with a prophecy by the shaman Kököchü, known as Teb-Tenggeri, although the Secret History is ambivalent here.[16] The Mongol ruler may have been introduced to the steppe imperial tradition by the Uighurs of Beshbaligh, who were the first semi-sedentary people to submit to him and of whom many entered his service.[17] It was a Uighur, Tatar Tongga, formerly a scribe (*bitikchi*) to the Naiman khan, whom he nominated to head his chancery and tasked with teaching his sons the Uighur script, in which Mongolian would be written henceforward.[18] Chinggis Khan deliberately sited the centre of his dominions in the Orqon valley, the *Ötügen-yish*, the sacred *refugium* which had lain at the heart of the Türk and Uighur empires and possession of which was itself regarded as a source of good fortune.[19] It was from here that he set out on his great westward expedition in *c.* 1218 and here, too, that Ögödei would later build the town of Qaraqorum. Rubruck noted that the Mongols regarded the town as 'royal';[20] but it was by no means a 'capital' in the accepted sense. The Mongol Qaghans continued to practise an itinerant lifestyle, and Qaraqorum was just one halting place on their annual journeys, as well as a storehouse for treasure and other items of value.[21]

But there was an important difference from the earlier hegemonies of the Türks and Uighurs. Where they seem to have thought only in terms of dominating the steppe lands, the Mongols claimed a mandate from Tenggeri to rule the entire known world.[22] In fulfilling this aspiration they recruited numerous personnel from 'post-nomadic' societies that themselves had experience of ruling over both nomadic and sedentary subjects: not just Uighurs but also Kitans from Manchuria and Qara Khitayans. After 1220 they also employed Muslim Turks from Khwārazm and Central Asia and Persian Muslims from Khurāsān.[23] Their earliest surviving ultimatum to the Pope (see later) was written in Persian (in recognition of the fact that Europeans would be unable to read the Uighur script). These ultimatums, which are formulaic in character,[24] conveyed the simple fact that all nations were *de jure* subject to the Mongols, for just as there was one Heaven, so there was one sovereign on earth;[25] hence anyone who opposed the Qaghan was, by definition, in rebellion (Tu. *bulgha*), both against the Mongols and against Heaven itself.[26] Significantly, the term for subjection (Tu. *il* or *el*) also denoted 'peace'; to have peace with the Mongols without submission was an impossibility.[27] The first recorded Mongol ultimatum to a European monarch reached the Hungarian king in 1237–8 by the hand of the Hungarian Dominican Friar Julian. The earliest to have survived independently, however, is the letter of the Qaghan Güyüg (who is there styled *dalai qan*, 'Oceanic [i.e. universal] Ruler') to Pope Innocent IV, which the Franciscan Plano Carpini brought back in 1247:

> In the power of Heaven, all lands, from the rising of the sun to its setting, have been made subject to us ... You in person, at the head of the kings, should, in a body, with one accord come and perform obeisance to us. This is what we make known to you. If you act contrary to it, what do we know? God knows.[28]

Precisely when the Mongols' goal moved from a steppe empire to a universal state is unclear. Kim Hodong proposes that they had already adopted the style 'Great Mongol People' (or 'State': Mo. *yeke mongghol ulus*; Tu. *ulugh mongol ulush*) before the first attack on the Jin in 1211.[29] This may well be so, but it assumes that the earliest campaigns in China aimed at conquest rather than simply plunder and tribute.[30] Yet a relatively late passage in the Secret History makes Chinggis Khan claim to be ruling 'those that live in dwellings with wooden doors'.[31] For what it is worth, Friar Julian formed the impression that Chinggis Khan had begun to harbour the ambition of world-conquest at the time of his destruction of the Khwārazmshāh's empire, that is in *c.* 1221.[32] It seems that the Mongols, in Morgan's words, 'came round to the idea when they found that they were, in fact, conquering the world'.[33]

In the tradition of steppe nomadic regimes, the Mongol conquests were viewed as the joint possession of the entire imperial dynasty, to be shared out among its members. To his surviving brothers and a nephew, who together constituted the 'Left Wing' (*bara'un ghar*) of the Great Mongol ulus, Chinggis Khan granted troops and grazing lands in eastern Mongolia and Manchuria.[34] During his last years, he allotted to his sons by his chief wife, Börte, a larger territorial appanage, along with troops to the tune of a varying number of 'thousands'; such an amalgam of peoples and land is called *ulus* in Mongolian.[35]

Juwaynī tells us that the sons, who together constituted the 'Right Wing' (*je'ün ghar*) of the Great Mongol Ulus, were situated at an increasing distance from the Mongolian heartland according to seniority. Jochi, as the eldest, received the territory 'from the confines of Qayaligh and Khwārazm to the furthest parts of Saqsīn and Bulghār and as far on that side as the hooves of Tatar horses had reached', with his headquarters on the Irtysh. He died before his father, and the headship of his ulus passed to his son Batu (known posthumously as Sayin Khan, 'the Good Khan'). Jochi's other sons – including Orda, who is called the senior among them, possibly because his mother was Jochi's chief wife[36] – were subordinated to Batu. The vast Jochid lands, called by authors of the Timurid era simply *dasht*, 'the plain' par excellence, were dominated by great rivers and offered the lushest pastures. Like the empire as a whole, they comprised a Right and a Left Wing: the former headed by Batu and his heirs, and the Left – the eastern portion, now generally known as the 'Blue Horde'[37] – under Orda's line. Each of Jochi's sons had his own ulus, notably Shiban, whose ulus was part of Batu's territory, and Toqa Temür, whose pasturelands lay within Orda's domain.

Chinggis Khan's second son, Chaghadai (d. 1244–5), was given the land from the borders of the Uighur territory as far as Samarkand and Bukhara and resided in the Ili basin, near the town of Almaligh, and on the shores of the Issyk Köl. On Ögödei, the third son, were conferred the basins of the Emil and Qobuq rivers in what came to be known as Zungharia; when he later ascended the imperial throne, he would transmit his appanage to his eldest son Güyüg. It was the steppe tradition that the youngest son inherited his father's original habitat,[38] but the appanage of Chinggis Khan's fourth son, Tolui (d. 1232), is not specified. We might expect it to have been the Onon-Kerülen region, but since Juwaynī appears to say that Tolui remained at his father's side, he possibly received no territory during the conqueror's lifetime.[39] Certainly later, Jochid and Chaghadayid rulers, hostile to Tolui's line, would allege that this was so.[40] All of the aforementioned territorial dispositions primarily embraced the extensive grasslands of Inner Asia. Part of the Mongolian homeland, including Qaraqorum, and most of the sedentary territories that had so far come under Mongol rule – a large proportion of Jin China and parts of northern and eastern Iran – belonged to the 'ulus of the centre' (*qol-un ulus*), administered directly by the Qaghan's representatives.[41]

Additionally, from an early date individual Chinggisids received groups of skilled personnel or the revenues from selected cities, particularly those in whose capture they had participated. This prerogative did not convey any administrative rights: the Qaghan's officials collected the revenues and transmitted them to the agents of the respective prince or princess. A prince might thus be allocated the revenues of districts lying within a kinsman's appanage.[42] Jochid khans, for instance, were still entitled to revenue from Yuan China in the fourteenth century.[43] Some such arrangement may lie behind the seemingly bizarre assertion by Mamlūk authors that Orda's line possessed distant Ghazna and Bāmiyān in present-day Afghanistan.[44] Orda's son Quli is known to have headed a force operating in this region in the 1250s, and conceivably the Negüderis, whose leader was a Jochid commander (see later; also p. 208), were expected to forward a share of its revenues to the Blue Horde. Later, Timur would claim Kāt and Khiva in Jochid Khwārazm, on the grounds that Chinggis Khan had conferred their revenues on Chaghadai: Naṭanzī represents such arrangements as designed to reinforce concord among the dynasty's members.[45]

Chinggis Khan died in 1227 as his troops were destroying the Tangut/Xi Xia empire and was succeeded, after a two-year interval, by his son Ögödei, whom he had allegedly designated as his heir and the candidate likely to command the loyalty of the conqueror's two feuding elder sons. Under Ögödei (1229–1241) the Mongols completed the conquest of the Jin (1234) and began hostilities with the Song empire in southern China. New expeditions were despatched westwards. One, headed by the general Chormaghun, resumed operations in south-west Asia from 1229: Jalāl al-Dīn, effectively the last Khwārazmshāh, was eliminated (1231) and the remnants of the Khwarazmians were dislodged from Iraq into Syria, while the Christian kingdom of Georgia was subjected to Mongol overlordship.

A larger expedition (1236–42), headed by Chinggis Khan's grandson Batu and the veteran commander Sübe'edei, advanced through the western steppes, reduced the Volga Bulgars and the Qipchaq-Qangli, began the subjugation of Rus′ and ravaged Poland and Hungary. During the five-year interregnum preceding the enthronement of Ögödei's son Güyüg (1246–1248), Chormaghun's deputy and successor Baiju vanquished the Seljuq Sultanate in Anatolia (Rūm) and launched the first attack on Syria (1244). The next Qaghan, Möngke (1251–1259), sent out two major expeditions under his brothers: Qubilai against Song China and Hülegü against Iran and Iraq. Hülegü destroyed the Ismāʿīlī Shīʿī state (the 'Assassins') in the Elburz mountains (1256) and the ʿAbbasid Caliphate (1258), before attacking the Ayyubid principalities in Syria (1260). But this coincided with Möngke's death in China (1259) and the halting of the Mongol advance in the Near East – and took place on the very eve of the collapse of imperial unity.

THE 'GREAT MONGOL STATE'

The Mongol empire represented an advance on its predecessors, not just geographically and ideologically but at the administrative level – and especially in terms of military organisation. By this I am referring not so much to the decimal structure of the army (into *tümen*s, 10,000, *mingghan*s, thousands, and so on), which was prefigured under the Kitan and the Jurchen, as to the rigid discipline that Chinggis Khan had imposed. He issued decrees, for example, forbidding any man to leave his unit for another without permission and prohibiting his troops from abandoning pursuit of the enemy for the sake of plunder until victory was a fait accompli; the penalty in both cases was death.[46] Another innovation, in an edict issued just prior to the final campaign against the Tatars, was the sharing of booty among the rank and file as opposed to just the commanders (*noyan*s); on these grounds the late Tom Allsen termed the Mongol polity a 'redistributive empire'.[47]

The pivotal role in the regime was played by the *keshig*, the imperial guard corps, which Chinggis Khan appears to have modelled on the 'centre' (*qol*) of the Kereyit forces.[48] It comprised his sworn followers, *nökörs*, their sons and other kinsmen, along with the sons of tribal chiefs (a guarantee of their fathers' loyalty), and would later include the sons or brothers of vassal rulers. Initially totalling 1,000 men and subsequently rising to 10,000, the *keshig* was tasked with the sovereign's security, saw to his household needs and served as a nursery for recruitment for the officer class; in addition it staffed the higher levels of the central secretariat and furnished the personnel for a nascent administration.[49] Preferment in the army was based on merit and loyalty rather than on status within a tribe; those who had performed services at an especially critical juncture might be rewarded further with the conferment of the hereditary status of *tarkhan* (Mo. *darqan*), entitling them to exemption from various imposts and obligations and from punishment for up to nine offences.[50]

A crucial element in the cohesiveness of Chinggis Khan's army was the deliberate dispersal of tribal forces among new units, commanded by his *nökörs*. As each tribe came under Mongol rule, the process of detribalisation was replicated and the tribal elite replaced by a new command structure.[51] This was true, for instance, of tribes that had possessed their own ruling dynasty of khans, such as the Kereyit and the Naiman.[52] Only those tribes that had rallied to the Mongols and remained faithful, like the Oyirat and the Önggüt, were permitted to retain their tribal integrity and command structure.[53]

If the majority of tribes had ceased to exist as recognisable political entities, the new structure was far from totally obliterating tribal affiliations and individuals evidently remained conscious of their origins. The history of the tribes in Rashīd al-Dīn's *Jāmiʿ al-tawārīkh* makes it clear that members not only of the same tribe but of the same elite lineages were dispersed throughout the length and breadth of the empire as a truly trans-continental ruling stratum.[54] Thus, whereas Elgei of the Jalayir (ancestor of the Jalayirid dynasty) accompanied Hülegü to Iran and became amir of Hülegü's *orda*s,[55] the sons of his brother Qutuqdur served Chaghadai's line.[56] When Timur rose to power, the Barulas (Barlās), Jalayir and Süldüs tribes were well represented in Chaghadayid Transoxiana and a sense of tribal identity clearly still persisted, even though the tribe's 'thousands' might comprise troops from other tribes who were classed according to the tribal identity of their commander. To quote Morgan, Chinggis Khan had created what 'might be described as an artificial tribal system, in which old tribal loyalties were superseded by loyalty to the individual soldier's new military unit. Beyond that the Mongol royal house became the ultimate focus of obedience and allegiance.'[57] The tribe was no longer the vehicle of political activity.[58]

The effect of the policy of reconfiguration was twofold. Firstly, it militated against the centrifugal tendencies that had afflicted previous steppe empires. When the Mongol empire did split in the early 1260s, it did not fragment along tribal but along dynastic and geopolitical lines; and even when Turco-Mongol amirs usurped real power in the fourteenth century, they owed it not to their position in some tribal hierarchy but to their rank and role within the Chinggisid state.[59] The second result of the reconfiguration was the emergence of new political formations – 'quasi-tribes' like the Qara'unas and the Jā'ūn-i Qurbān. Some derived their name from individual commanders: the Negüderis, the Jurma'īs and Awghānīs in Kirmān and the Yasā'ūrīs in the Chaghadayid ulus on the eve of Timur's rise to power.[60]

As the empire mushroomed, the intensity of Mongol control varied from one region of the empire to another. In the early stages of expansion, bodies of troops termed *tamma* ('frontier forces') were stationed on its borders. Their task was to guard the new conquests and to conduct campaigns of devastation into adjacent territories, softening up such tracts, as it were, in preparation for a larger-scale campaign of conquest headed by fresh troops from the centre. This is the policy that Timothy May has christened the 'Tsunami strategy'.[61] At the administrative level, some sedentary territories, like Transoxiana, were subject to direct Mongol rule in the form of a governor (Tu. *basqaq*; Mo. *darugha*, *darughachi*)[62] and garrison troops. On the other hand, elsewhere in the sedentary world the Uighur *iduq-qut* and Muslim princes like those of Fārs and Kirmān in southern Iran, who submitted promptly and paid tribute, retained their thrones and enjoyed a limited degree of autonomy. The Kartid dynasty in Herat owed its very creation to Mongol patronage.[63] All these rulers – from Koryŏ (Korea) to Syria – were obliged to name the Qaghan on their coinage and (in the case of Muslim states) in the khutba and were placed under the surveillance of a resident Mongol *basqaq* or *darugha*; they had to submit population registers, furnish troops and supplies for further Mongol campaigns of expansion and instal the postal relay system within their territories.[64]

Taxation systems varied from one region of the empire to another, given the Mongols' readiness to retain the taxes inherited from vanquished regimes. Over and above these taxes, however, they levied throughout their dominions imposts of their own: the *qubchur*, a capitation-tax, traditionally paid by the nomads to their rulers and now extended to the empire's agricultural and urban populations, and the *tamgha*, a tax on commercial transactions and artisanal products. The sources also speak of the *qalan*, which perhaps embraced a variety of exactions ranging from labour services to pre-Mongol taxes.[65]

Two important developments in Ögödei's reign were the completion of the system known by the Turkish term *yam* (Mo. *dzam*) and the creation of a new fiscal structure. The *yam*, the imperial postal relay system, was based in part on communications systems found among the Türks and Uighurs and designated *ulagh*.[66] Begun in Chinggis Khan's time, it was designed primarily for use by envoys and others travelling on government business and linked up the regions of the empire in a network of stations at intervals of 33 to 45 kilometres, each staffed by approximately twenty men.[67] The new fiscal structure comprised three administrations – in China, Central Asia and Iran – termed in Chinese *xingsheng* ('branch secretariat') and labelled by Paul Buell as 'joint satellite administrations'.[68] In Central Asia the regime was headed by Masʿūd Beg; that in Iran from the mid-to-late 1240s by the Oyirat noyan Arghun Aqa. It is unclear whether any such structure existed for the Jochid territories, though it has been suggested that Möngke established one in 1254. Exercising functions hitherto performed by the *tamma*, the *xingsheng* answered directly to the central secretariat. All these institutions reflected the collegial character of imperial governance. The *tamma* were selected on a percentage basis from the armies belonging to different branches of Chinggis Khan's descendants, the *xingsheng* included officials representing each branch and a group chosen on the same basis oversaw the creation of the *yam*.[69]

The regime was characterised by a strong sense of hierarchy. Membership of the imperial dynasty (the *altan urugh*, 'Golden Lineage'),[70] and especially patrilineal descent from Chinggis Khan, long remained a source of unrivalled prestige. From the outset, the title of khan was restricted to the *altan urugh*: Chinggis Khan refused to countenance the title borne by Arslan Khan of the Qarluq and insisted that he be known simply as Arslan Sartaqtai ('Arslan the Muslim').[71] Directly below the *altan urugh* stood those noyans and foreign princes who had married into the dynasty and held the rank of imperial son-in-law (Mo. *güregen*)[72] – a status that Timur would later acquire through his two Chinggisid wives. Mongols not of the imperial line were termed *qarachu* ('commoner').[73] Those who belonged to the Qiyat, the most prestigious of the Mongol tribes because it included the Borjighid,[74] occupied a position midway between the dynasty and the generality of nomad warriors.[75]

Nomadic empires – whether the fifth-century Huns of Attila's realm or the imperial Türks of the seventh century – were multi-ethnic in character, numbering not just pastoralists but sedentary folk among their subjects. By the mid-thirteenth century, the *yeke Mongghol ulus* comprised not just nomads from Mongolia but Turkic nomads in probably even larger numbers, together with sedentary and semi-sedentary peoples well beyond the bounds of the steppe, whether Persians or Han Chinese. To such combinations of the resources of the steppe and the sown David Christian applies the Russian term *smychka* ('yoking together').[76] Thousands of skilled artisans (of both sexes) were enslaved and transported to other regions of the empire to serve the conquerors.[77] But the subject peoples as a whole were classed as *ötegü boghol*, 'slaves of long standing', that is the hereditary servants of the imperial dynasty.[78] Or, to put it another way: during the era of a supra-tribal state or empire designations like 'Türk' or 'Mongol' had a political – over and above their ethnic – significance. Friar Julian had observed of the conquered subject peoples that '[the Mongols] require them henceforth to be known as Tartars'.[79] Rashīd al-Dīn, who like earlier Muslim authors saw the Mongols as a branch of the Turks, confirms this process of changing identity when he distinguishes those peoples who have recently 'become Mongols' from those who have long been considered as such (including, incidentally, the Barulas, Timur's future tribe).[80] And he further writes:

> The peoples of Khitāy [North China], Jūrcha [Chörche, i.e. Manchuria] and Nangiyās [South China], the Uighurs, the Qipchaq, the Türkmen, the Qarluq, the Qalach [Khalaj] and all the prisoners and the Tājīk nations that have been incorporated within the Mongols' ranks are likewise termed Mongols; in their entirety they recognise it as advantageous to their reputation and status that they call themselves Mongols.[81]

MONGOL LAW AND STEPPE CUSTOM: 'CHINGGIS KHAN's *YASA*'

The Mongols observed many customs that are also to be found among earlier Inner Asian nomadic societies: the levirate, for instance, which is attested among the Uighurs and entailed the remarriage of a widow to her husband's younger brother or nephew or even his son by a different union.[82] Perhaps *the* distinctive Mongol institution was the Yasa, often called the 'Great Yasa' (*yāsā-yi buzurg*) in our Persian sources; here *buzurg*, 'great' (corresponding to Ch. *da*), has the sense of 'imperial' and maybe also 'ancestral'.[83] 'Chinggis Khan's Yasa' has been subject to controversy.[84] The idea that it was a written code issued by the Mongol conqueror on a specific occasion, the great assembly (*quriltai*) of 1206, was exploded by Morgan, who argued that no such code existed and that Juwaynī, our principal source here,[85] is speaking of a series of *ad hoc* edicts or rulings (Tu. *yasa*; Mo. *dzasagh*) which, judging from the contents of the relevant chapter, dealt primarily with the business of state, military matters, the postal relay system and the conduct of the hunt.[86]

According to Juwaynī, the rolls (*ṭūmārhā*) of the Great Book of Yasas (*yāsā-nāma-yi buzurg*) were produced whenever a new ruler was enthroned or a large army was setting out or the princes assembled to discuss the business of the realm. On all these occasions, he says, what was under consideration was 'the disposition of armies and the destruction of provinces and cities after that pattern'.[87] Rashīd al-Dīn confirms this military–administrative emphasis. On the eve of the seven-year expedition, he tells us, Chinggis Khan 'renewed the practices and the customs of the Yasa' (*az naw āyīn-u yūsūn-i yāsāq bunyād nihād*);[88] and when Ögödei convened a quriltai in 1235, as a prelude to the campaigns to the Qipchaq steppe and against the Song, he intended 'the Yasa and decrees' (*aḥkām*) to be read out to the princes and noyans.[89] In a relatively neglected passage Waṣṣāf introduces Chinggis Khan's creation of the Yasa, both singly and in its entirety (*az juzwī wa-kullī*) in the 'Great Book of Yasas' (*yāsā-nāma-yi buzurg*), and speaks – here exclusively, we might note – of the decimal structure of the army, the specification of weapons and the practice (*yusūn*) and order of advance and withdrawal on the march.[90] And when relating Qubilai's enthronement in 1260, he says that the new Qaghan sent *ilchi*s in all directions with orders to renew and enforce the 'book of *yasa*s of Chinggis Khan, comprising the mandates of world-conquest and world rulership'.[91]

We have already met with two examples of individual *yasa*s relating to military discipline (see earlier).[92] Plano Carpini furnishes other specific examples of what he terms 'laws and edicts' (*leges et statuta*) made by Chinggis Khan relating to matters of state. One stipulates that the Mongols are to bring the whole world under their sway and to make peace with no one who has not submitted to them.[93] Another prohibits any member of the dynasty from seizing the throne without the agreement of the princes (i.e. in a quriltai, comprising members of the dynasty, imperial sons-in-law and noyans).[94] The latter edict was flouted, following Ögödei's death, by Chinggis Khan's youngest brother, Temüge Ot-chigin, who was executed on Güyüg's accession.[95] Shaykh Ḥasan Jalāyir was still appealing to this *yasa* in 736/1336, during the struggles that succeeded the death of the Ilkhan Abū Saʿīd.[96]

Alongside Chinggis Khan's decrees, Plano Carpini notices traditions and customs (*consuetudines*), each presumably corresponding to the Mongol *yosun* (*yūsūn* for Muslim authors). Some, like the prohibition against spitting out a morsel of food, related to the waste of vital resources and thus had a bearing on military effectiveness.[97] Other offences – immersing oneself in running water or washing garments during spring and summer, which was thought to cause thunderstorms – obviously related to ancestral taboos. Certain offences carried the death penalty. Our Persian sources refer to these prohibitions in terms indicating that custom is being enforced by decree.[98] Beatrice Manz is surely correct in stating that 'by the fourteenth century the term *yasa* had come to signify both law and custom'.[99]

In sum, what was known as the 'Yasa of Chinggis Khan' was originally a body of ad hoc rulings which came to be viewed as having a permanent and more general application. But no source supplies a comprehensive list of the Yasa's contents, and it seems that the understanding of the Yasa varied over time and in subsequent centuries specific edicts were attributed to Chinggis Khan which represent later, and perhaps apocryphal, accretions. One example is the institution of the *qarachi* (i.e. *qarachu*) begs in the Crimea, which dates from no earlier than the fourteenth century.[100] Another is the right of a grandson whose father was dead to inherit a share in his grandfather's property on an equal basis with his uncles. In the early sixteenth century this was believed to be one of Chinggis Khan's own yasas; but there is no evidence for its existence in the thirteenth.[101]

And yet the Yasa was not some static entity that had attained its ultimate form at Chinggis Khan's death, to serve as a model and guide on later occasions. It is true that on his enthronement in 1229 Ögödei confirmed his father's enactments and decreed that they were to remain in force and were not to be altered.[102] It is also true that, according to Waṣṣāf, Chinggis Khan's ruling (he uses both Tu. *yasa* and Ar.-Pers. *qā'ida*) excluding the descendants of Jochi Qasar from the succession was still in force in his day.[103] But it appears that since Chinggis Khan's time each Qaghan had added *yasa*s of his own. Just as Ögödei had confirmed his father's *yasa*s, so Güyüg on his accession in 1246 ratified those of Ögödei and commanded that they were to remain unchanged. This indicates that the latter's *yasa*s likewise had assumed a binding authority.[104] As late as 1311 we find the newly enthroned Qaghan Buyantu (the Yuan Emperor Renzong) instigating an inquiry into the *yasa*s of his great-grandfather Qubilai and decreeing that any that had fallen into disuse should be observed afresh.[105] The pattern seems to have obtained in the regional khanates also. In Iran the Ilkhan Abagha, on his accession in 663/1265, declared the *yasa*s of his father Hülegü inviolate.[106] The Yasa was a continually evolving corpus of regulations issued by different khans; a corollary of this is that it must have come to vary in detail from one ulus to another.

The term *yasa* also had a broader meaning. Drawing on largely Persian and Chinese sources, Igor de Rachewiltz showed that it sometimes denoted 'regime', 'rule'; he pointed to the twin connotations of the English word 'rule' as both 'norm' and 'government'.[107] Thus Rashīd al-Dīn writes of a 'thousand' guarding 'the *yāsā* and *yūsūn*' of the sanctuary on Burqan Qaldun[108] – that is, maintaining the precinct in the prescribed manner. When used in this alternative sense, the term could be rendered as 'order', given that word's twofold significance in English.[109]

At this juncture it seems relevant to assess the degree to which the Chinggisids and their nomadic troops succumbed to the supposed lure of towns and cities – a danger that had been the subject of grim warnings as far back as the era of the Türks,[110] and which was portrayed on occasions as contrary to the Yasa (see, e.g., p. 136). We associate certain Mongol khans with the construction of new towns: Sulṭāniyya, for instance, founded by the Ilkhan Öljeitü (703–716/1304–1316) or Qarshī, founded by the Chaghadayid khan Köpek (*c.* 720–726/*c.* 1320–1326).[111] We also find some among the later khans taking the view that the nomadic lifestyle was antithetical to Islam (p. 203). Yet the creation of settlements is visible from an early date: Chinggis Khan's brother Jochi Qasar and his line built walled towns in Mongolia,[112] and Batu constructed the town of Sarai (Pers. *sarāī*, 'The Palace') on the lower Volga in *c.* 1250.[113] Each of these towns appears to have served not just as a storehouse but as a halting place during the ruler's seasonal migrations, as did Qaraqorum itself (see earlier). Even Orda's ulus, populated exclusively by nomads according to Marco Polo, included settlements (many walled) devoted to agriculture, if only as a subsidiary activity.[114] Sulṭāniyya lay in a region of abundant grassland and Öljeitü, who spent only forty per cent of his time there, had selected the site both as a base for his hunting expeditions and to enable his nomadic followers to pasture their livestock in the plains.[115]

In other words, the new urban settlements represented not an abandonment of the nomadic cycle but an expedient designed to serve and reinforce it. Moreover, even when the great majority of the inhabitants were not Mongols, the presence of traders, craftsmen, priests and clerics epitomised the multi-ethnic character of the Mongol khanates.[116] That the town of Andijān in Farghāna, restored by Qaidu and Du'a, contained separate quarters for each ethnic group suggests a similar complexion.[117] None of this is to deny that some of the towns built by Mongol rulers retained a symbolic significance even when their administrative or economic function had expired. This was true of Qaraqorum in the fifteenth century, while both before and during Timur's era possession of Sulṭāniyya, so closely associated with the defunct Ilkhanid dynasty, was evidently a desirable goal.

TENSION AND CONFLICT WITHIN THE DYNASTY

May has pointed to the absence of crisis, as far as we can tell, following Chinggis Khan's death.[118] But Chinggis Khan was the last sovereign of the unitary empire to be followed by his designated successor. There were no rules governing the succession to the imperial throne, other than the principle that the candidate elected – by consensus in the formal setting of a quriltai – should be the best-qualified member of the *altan urugh*, a judgement that might rest on seniority by birth, perceived wisdom, previous distinction in the military field or even familiarity with Chinggis Khan's adages (*bilig*s). This principle, to which Joseph Fletcher applied the term 'tanistry', was hardly the most effective means of avoiding strife.[119]

It is indicative of the growing strains within the imperial family that a lengthy gap separated the reigns of each of Chinggis Khan's three successors. Ögödei's death was followed by an interval of five years before the election of Güyüg. Güyüg's brief reign (1246–1248) witnessed no major military activity against external enemies but was dominated by tension with his cousin Batu, with whom he had quarrelled during the campaign in Eastern Europe in 1237–41, and he was moving against Batu with a large army at the time of his death. There followed another interval, lasting three years, before Batu procured the election of a cousin, Möngke (the son of Chinggis Khan's youngest son Tolui), as Qaghan (1251–1259). The majority of the family of Ögödei and Güyüg, who, with most of Chaghadai's line, actively opposed Möngke's succession, were executed or exiled to the Chinese front and were deprived of their territories. Chaghadai's ulus was probably diminished in size, while Ögödei's may have been dispersed among some of his heirs.[120] There were now in effect only three major uluses: the ulus of the centre and the Jochid and Toluid spheres, which dominated the map of Asia. In some degree a condominium of this kind had been foreshadowed in the administrative arrangements for Iran under Ögödei (see later), but the events of 1251 reinforced it. Rubruck, traversing the empire in 1253, concluded that the Mongol world comprised two enormous spheres of influence, those of the new Qaghan and Batu.[121] Relations between the two men seem to have been harmonious, but this would change after Batu's death and the succession of his brother Berke (*c.* 1255–6).

In order, partly, to revive a sense of common purpose, Möngke launched fresh campaigns of conquest from 1252 onwards under Qubilai and Hülegü, as we saw earlier. It is unclear whether he had appointed his brothers merely as supreme military commanders or envisaged the creation of two completely new uluses with Qubilai and Hülegü at their head. The situation regarding Iran is particularly ambiguous. According to Rashīd al-Dīn, the Qaghan's intention was that Hülegü should rule Iran (as in fact transpired), but he did not make it public.[122] Under Ögödei, Batu and his representatives had played a major role in the administration of Iran and in Anatolia, where he had extended his authority over Baiju and his troops.[123] So too the Jochids seemingly enjoyed a more impressive share of apportioned lands within Iran. According to a recently discovered source from the 1280s, the *Akhbār-i Mughūlān*, the Jochid princes who participated in Hülegü's campaign wielded authority there and occupied the richest pasturelands in Khurāsān, Iraq, Azerbaijan, Arrān and Georgia.[124]

Ibn Faḍl-Allāh al-ʿUmarī's *Masālik* presents a very different picture from Rashīd al-Dīn. Here the Jochid khans (intermittently in diplomatic contact with the Mamlūk regime) are said to deny that Hülegü had been anything more than his brother's representative. They and the other Chinggisid lines contended that the Ilkhans had acquired rulership not at the hands of Chinggis Khan or subsequent Qaghans, but in the course of time and by force.[125] For Ilkhanid authors this was evidently a sensitive matter. Under Möngke, there had already been retrospective attempts to enhance Tolui's status as a means of legitimising the new regime.[126] But Shabānkāra'ī, in the earliest extant draft of his *Majmaʿ al-ansāb* in 738/1338, developed this cultivation of Tolui further, with three bizarre statements, unsupported by Rashīd al-Dīn or any of the major Ilkhanid sources: first, that Tolui was Chinggis Khan's son not by Börte like his brothers, but by a daughter of Ong Khan of the Kereyit (here called the 'Khan of Khans') who was (allegedly) Chinggis Khan's first wife; second, that Tolui's mother was acknowledged as regent during the interregnum of 1227–9; and third, that his father had conferred upon him all the lands west of the Oxus.[127] The kindred notion that Tolui was the favourite son, entrusted with the special responsibility of reducing Khurāsān, surfaces slightly earlier, in Sayfī's history of Herat (*c.* 1322),[128] suggesting that a particular local tradition was taking root in the Iranian world. But the spurious details given by Shabānkāra'ī read like a crude bid to refute the Jochid claims by fabricating some distinctive right of Tolui and his line as a justification for the formation of the Ilkhanate.

In succession to Möngke, Qubilai, in China, and Tolui's youngest son Arigh Böke, in Mongolia, were simultaneously proclaimed Qaghan in 1260; the conflict ended in 1264 with Qubilai's victory. In Central Asia Alughu, a grandson of Chaghadai sent to rule on Arigh Böke's behalf, had declared for Qubilai. Hülegü, who came in time to support Qubilai, profited from the crisis to establish himself as ruler of Iran, slaughtering the Jochid contingents among his forces. One group, escaping to join the Jochid commander Negüder in Khurāsān, moved eastwards into the Ghazna region, where they remained independent for some decades (see pp. 208–9, 212). Hülegü's actions detonated a second war, on the Caucasus front between himself and the Jochid khan Berke, who backed Arigh Böke. Qubilai rewarded Hülegü and Alughu by recognising their rule in Central Asia and Iran.[129]

After taking Aleppo and Damascus early in 1260, Hülegü had withdrawn from Syria in the spring, doubtless to monitor events in the east, and the force he left there under the general Ked-buqa was annihilated by the Mamlūks at ʿAyn Jālūt in September. Aside from a brief occupation of Syria by the Ilkhan Ghazan in 699/1299–1300, this marked the end of Mongol expansion in the Near East. The frontier with Mamlūk territory now stabilised along the Euphrates, marking a divide also between a predominantly Persian cultural world and one where Arabic culture held sway. For more than six decades after 661/1263 Berke and later Jochid khans maintained diplomatic relations with the Mamlūk Sultans with a view to coordinating military action against the Ilkhanate; they also permitted the trade in Qipchaq slaves that was vital to the survival of the Mamlūk regime.[130] The Ilkhans, unable to avenge ʿAyn Jālūt, in turn courted western Christian rulers.[131] For the first time Mongol princes proved ready to cooperate with an external power against fellow Mongols.

THE 'FOUR ULUSES'

At Möngke's death the empire already differed considerably in size from the lands that Chinggis Khan had bequeathed to Ögödei. John Dardess has highlighted the distances separating the Qaghan's headquarters from the imperial frontiers. These distances, along with high costs of transportation, prohibited the economic integration of the princely appanages with the centre and had implications for political integration.[132] The Mongols were the first – and the last – nomadic power to rule over the entire length of the 'Silk Roads'.[133]

At their greatest extent, the Chinggisid territories extended from Korea and the South China Sea to the Carpathians and the Euphrates and from the Siberian taiga to the Hindu Kush. Yet even before these limits were reached, the unitary empire had fragmented into more or less autonomous Mongol states, principally the Qipchaq khanate, the Chaghadayid ulus, the Ilkhanate in Iran, Iraq and most of Anatolia, and the Qaghan's dominions in the Far East, centred on the city of Dadu (Mo. Khanbaligh; nowadays Beijing). The modern notion of a fourfold division of the empire was current at least by the early fifteenth century,[134] and a work ascribed to Timur's grandson Ulugh Beg bore the title *Ta'rīkh-i arba'a ulūs-i chingīzī* ('The History of the Four Chinggisid Uluses'). A century later Ḥaydar could still write of the 'four nations' (*aqwām-i arba'a*) in such a way as to suggest that they stemmed from Chinggis Khan's allocations of territory.[135]

But this was not only to disregard the events culminating in Hülegü's creation of the Ilkhanate (which had undermined the arrangements made by Chinggis Khan). It also ignored other significant political formations: the ulus of Jochi's son Orda, the Blue Horde, which embraced the lower Sīr-daryā region and part of western Siberia and which appears in practice to have been independent of Batu's successors, at least until the early fourteenth century;[136] the extensive principality created by the Jochid prince Noghai in the western reaches of the Qipchaq khanate until his overthrow in 699/1299–1300; and the appanages in Manchuria and eastern Mongolia held by the families of Chinggis Khan's brothers, which were brought more closely under Qubilai's sway, however, in 1287–8.[137]

It is doubtful whether we can speak of an 'ulus of Ögödei' in the wake of the Toluid coup of 1251. In a sense Ögödei's ulus was re-established in 670/1271, when his grandson Qaidu (d. 702/1303) was recognised by the Chaghadayids as over-khan in Central Asia in opposition to Qubilai.[138] But his empire fell apart when the Chaghadayid khan Du'a and the Qaghan Temür overthrew his son Chapar in 705/1305 (though the Chaghadayid ulus continued to be known as 'the realm of Qaidu and Du'a').[139] Although Chapar and some of his brothers sought asylum in Yuan China, several Ögödeyid princes remained in Chaghadai's ulus and their descendants would later occupy its throne. It was left to Timur to restore the Ögödeyids to a status reminiscent of the sovereignty they had lost.

The principal uluses that emerged after 1260 differed from their predecessors in important respects. In the first place, the 'joint satellite administrations' headed by Arghun Aqa in the Iranian world and by Masʿūd Beg in Central Asia passed under the control of Hülegü and Alughu, respectively (and, a few years after the latter's death in 1266, of Qaidu). These institutions, in other words, had effectively ceased to answer directly to the Qaghan. Secondly, the Qaghan no longer nominated the khans of Jochi's ulus or Chaghadai's – though until 1295 he did at least confer investiture on the candidate for the Ilkhanid throne. Thirdly, whereas the vassal Uighur principality at Beshbaligh and the kingdom of Badakhshān had originally lain outside Chaghadai's ulus and had been subject directly to the Qaghan, Qaidu and Du'a drove the *iduq-qut* eastwards and annexed much of his territory to the Chaghadayid ulus,[140] and by the end of the thirteenth century the Chaghadayids had brought Badakhshān too into their orbit.[141] Fourthly, the Ilkhan and the Chaghadayid khan each neutralised or destroyed the assets within his ulus belonging to other princes, as Hülegü did when he slaughtered the Jochid forces in Iran and as Alughu did by massacring Berke's dependants in Samarkand and Bukhara. Hülegü incorporated in his forces the *tamma* troops in Anatolia, while his son and successor Abagha in 667/1269 enforced his authority over the Chaghadayid contingent, led by the prince Tegüder, that had accompanied Hülegü to Iran. The 1260s thus saw the consolidation of geographically distinct political formations and a concentration of resources in the hands of each ruling khan.

One casualty of imperial fragmentation was the programme of world-conquest. In the Far East, Qubilai's destruction of the Song empire (1279) added considerably to his resources, as did his exaction of tribute from Annam and other regions. But Mongol expansion was checked at both ends of the Asian continent: in Syria by the fledgling Mamlūk state and on Kyushu by the Japanese. The Mamlūk occupation of Syria after ʿAyn Jālūt, shortly followed by Sultan Bāybars's enthronement of a scion of the ʿAbbasid dynasty in Cairo, legitimised the regime and enabled the Sultanate to pose as the bulwark of Islam.[142] In Western Asia, the halting of the Mongol advance greatly reduced the influx of plunder, still an important source of revenue. Where the Chinggisids' energies had been directed towards the fulfilment of Heaven's mandate, they were now focused upon their own internal disputes.

And disputes enough within the imperial dynasty lay to hand. If the Ilkhans were the first dynasty to rule over the whole of Iran since the ninth century, their right to do so was challenged. They were confronted from the outset by the territorial ambitions both of the khans of the Qipchaq steppe and of the Chaghadayids (seconded by Qaidu). An embassy from the Qipchaq khanate to the Ilkhan Ghazan in 702/1302–3 reiterated the Jochids' right to Azerbaijan and Arrān on the basis of Chinggis Khan's territorial allocations – claims echoed in the information given to Ibn Faḍl-Allāh al-ʿUmarī that Chinggis Khan had added to Jochi's possessions Hamadān, Arrān, Tabriz and Marāgha.[143] In the fourteenth century the Jochid khans Özbeg (712–742/1313–1342) and his son Janibeg (742–758/1342–1357) both invaded Azerbaijan – and Janibeg temporarily conquered it. The main reason for the conflict between Timur and the Jochid khan Toqtamish would be the latter's revival of the old claims on the lands south of the Caucasus, which Timur had subjugated on behalf of Chaghadai's ulus.

Chaghadai's realm was sometimes termed *Dumdadu Mongghol ulus* ('the Central Mongol state'), which found its way, in Latin garb, into Western European sources as *imperium medium* or *imperium de medio* (sometimes contorted, grotesquely, as *imperium Medorum*, 'the empire of the Medes', or *imperium Medie*, 'the empire of Media').[144] Its central location was a disadvantage and a source of tension. With the emergence of the Ilkhanate after 1260, Chaghadai's ulus was hemmed in by other Mongol polities on all fronts, except for a narrow corridor that gave access to the Punjab – and even here the initially independent Negüderi Mongols constituted an obstruction. The Chaghadayids thus lacked the avenues for expansion that were (theoretically) open to the Jochids in Eastern Europe, the Ilkhans in Syria and the Qaghans/Yuan Emperors in south-east Asia.[145] Rashīd al-Dīn makes the Chaghadayid khan Baraq (664–670/1266–1271 or 1272), at the quriltai convened by Qaidu in 667/1269, express a sense of constriction in relation to 'this shrunken ulus' (*hamīn mukhtaṣar ulūs*),[146] and Baraq's grandson, the khan Esen Buqa, fearful of simultaneous attacks by the Yuan and the Ilkhan, contemplated a preemptive strike on Khurāsān as his sole recourse.[147]

Khurāsān, possessing extensive pasturelands in addition to its flourishing urban centres, had long attracted nomadic invaders from beyond the Amū-daryā.[148] The Central Asian Mongols had begun to cast covetous eyes on Khurāsān in Chaghadai's own era and again in the 1240s under his son, the khan Yesü Möngke, who attempted to intervene in the affairs of the satellite Kartid kingdom of Herat.[149] One of Alughu's first actions as khan (658–664/1260–1266) had been to secure the submission of the Mongol noyans in the Indian borderlands.[150] This advance seems to have proved abortive, as would Baraq's invasion of Khurāsān in 668/1270.[151] But under Qaidu and Du'a the renewal of Chaghadayid designs on the eastern Ilkhanid territories proved markedly more fruitful, as we shall see in Chapter 7.

The inclusion of princes from different branches on distant campaigns had produced within each ulus a diverse pool of Chinggisids who were potentially a source of disaffection. A strong concentration of Ögödei's descendants from the lines of Qadan and Melik (his sons by concubines), who had backed the Toluid coup in 1251, is found in Central Asia during the era of Qaidu; most of them fought for Du'a against Chapar in 705/1305. Timur would take both of his puppet khans from Melik's line. The migration of princes between uluses, too, in search of improved prospects, was frequently a destabilising factor.[152] A few examples will suffice. Following Baraq's death Alughu's sons moved east and took service with the Yuan; by Timur's era a branch of this line ruled the principality of Hami (Qāmul).[153] After Chapar's downfall several Ögödeyid and Chaghadayid princes, along with some descendants of Arigh Böke and Jochi Qasar, settled in Ilkhanid Khurāsān: a longer-term result of this migration was that Arigh Böke's descendant Arpa and Taghai Temür, of Jochi Qasar's line, would each ascend the Ilkhanid throne in the 1330s. The most turbulent émigré of all was the Chaghadayid

Yasa'ur, who took refuge in the Ilkhan Öljeitü's territories in 716/1316, only to rebel against Öljeitü's successor Abū Saʿīd (below, p. 214).

AN ABIDING SENSE OF MONGOL UNITY?

Despite all the upheavals of the period from 1260 onwards, it is evident that the idea of the Great Mongol People – and of a single Mongol ulus presided over by the Qaghan but comprising a number of subsidiary uluses – remained alive well into the fourteenth century.[154] In 1304 Du'a allegedly referred to Qaraqorum as 'the centre of the empire' (*markaz-i dawlat*).[155] Kim has argued persuasively that the name *Da Yuan* adopted by Qubilai for his regime in 1272 was not a dynastic name in the Chinese tradition but corresponded to the Mongolian *Yeke Monggol ulus*; it did not apply only to his Chinese territories (as the Chinese literati supposed) but embraced the entire Mongol dominions.[156] Judging by the *Yuanshi* chapter on foreign lands, Qubilai and his successors retained a sense that their sovereignty extended potentially throughout the world.[157]

Nevertheless, there remained many territories yet to be subjected – lands 'in rebellion', as Rashīd al-Dīn, for one, saw it[158] – and the regional khans were conscious of their obligation to expand at the expense of independent powers. Writing to Sultan Bāybars in 661/1263, Berke paid tribute to the principle of Chinggisid harmony by complaining (with unconscious irony) that had the Mongols remained united they could have conquered the world.[159] The Ilkhan Abagha invoked the traditional mission of the Mongols in his letter to Bāybars in 667/1269 and indeed affected to believe that Bāybars was offering to recognise Mongol overlordship.[160] Öljeitü in 710/1310–11 demanded the submission of the Delhi Sultan 'Alā' al-Dīn Khaljī.[161] Even in their amicable correspondence with the Latin west, both Hülegü and Abagha alluded to the Mongols' task of world-conquest.[162] But the rhetoric did not necessarily imply respect for the duty of a rival khan to pursue the same mission. For over six decades the Jochids encouraged the Mamlūk Sultan to attack Ilkhanid territories; and Qaidu and his Chaghadayid confederates readily took advantage of Ghazan's absence on campaign in Mamlūk Syria in *c.* 699/1300 to invade his eastern provinces.[163]

That said, there were bids from time to time to restore harmony with the express aim, among others, of facilitating the dynasty's task of world-conquest. The most spectacular occurred in 1304 when, at Du'a's prompting, Chapar submitted to the Qaghan Temür and outlined a vision of coexistence that would lead to the subjugation of the Mongols' enemies.[164] A letter from the Ilkhan Öljeitü to Philip IV of France in 1305 announced the revival of the trans-regional postal relay network created by this reconciliation and spoke, significantly, of Mongol sway extending to the coasts of the Talu Sea (the ocean believed to surround the inhabited world).[165] But the peace was short-lived. As we saw, Du'a's purpose had been to emancipate the ulus of Chaghadai with Yuan assistance. Within a few years Qaidu's former dominions had been partitioned between the Chaghadayids and the Yuan.

What was the position of the Qaghan within the Mongol world thereafter? When Mongol khans appealed to their common descent from Chinggis Khan or spoke of the Qaghan as the head of the Mongol *oecumene*, were they merely paying lip-service to an ideal? There was no longer an anti-qaghan in Central Asia, and the status of the Yuan within the imperial dynasty was now unchallenged. If anything, relations between the western khanates and the Yuan were closer during the reign of the Qaghan Yesün Temür (1323–1328). In *c.* 1330 an anonymous Franciscan author wrote that the regional khans despatched regular tribute to the Yuan court.[166] For Shabānkāra'ī, writing a few years later, the Qaghans were 'Sultans of the Mongols and kings of the face of the earth', while the other khans were merely 'Sultans and kings of the outlying regions (*aṭrāf*)'; al-ʿUmarī formed a similar impression.[167] This undoubtedly represented the abiding perspective from Khanbaligh, as expressed, for instance, in the *Yuanshi* with regard to the distant Jochids.[168] Only the Ilkhans, as far as we know, had mentioned the Qaghan as their overlord on their coins, though they were by no means consistent and the custom lapsed almost totally after Ghazan Maḥmūd's accession in 1295.[169] Admittedly, the Qaghans conferred honorific titles on senior amirs within Iran, like Buqa (d. 688/1289) and Choban (d. 727/1327).[170] Our limited sources yield little indication of such patronage in relation to the other khanates,[171] but the Ilkhanate, under Toluid rule and a close ally of the Yuan, was a special case.

On the other hand, al-ʿUmarī formed the impression that the Qaghan's paramountcy was purely nominal: the regional khans kept him informed of events, but he had no influence on their policies.[172] Moreover, Shim detects a falling-off of embassies between the Yuan and the other khanates after 1332.[173] Participation in an imperial election by representatives from outside seems to have occurred only in the unusual circumstances of 1328–9, when Qoshila, for some years an exile in Chaghadai's ulus, was proclaimed Qaghan in Mongolia with the support of a military force headed by the Chaghadayid khan Eljigidei.[174]

The evidence is particularly ambivalent on the terminology relating to the Qaghan's decrees. Only his orders could properly be designated *yarligh*, as a Yuan frontier commander angrily reminded a Chaghadayid embassy in 713/1313: for the orders of other khans the term *lingchi* (Ch. *lingzhi*; Mo. *üge*) sufficed. On the contrary, the Chaghadayid envoys retorted, their khan stood in the Qaghan's place and his commands could, with equal justification, be termed *yarligh*.[175] Documents acquired in the Turfan expeditions, and dated between 1304 and 1369, reveal Chaghadayid officials observing this in practice,[176] regardless of conventional niceties. Perhaps the starkest evidence is to be found on the coinage, where the Chaghadayid khans from Köpek (d. *c.* 726/1326) to Danishmandcha (d. 749/1348–9) are styled *al-khāqān al-ʿādil*, 'the Just Qaghan', and/or *al-khāqān al-aʿẓam*, 'the Mighty Qaghan' (the exception, Tarmashirin, is usually called Sultan).[177] Nor were the Chaghadayids the only Chinggisid rulers to be described in this fashion, since the Jochid khan Janibeg is styled *khāqān* on his early coins and an inscription of 722/1322 entitles the last effective Ilkhan, Abū Saʿīd, *khāqān al-aʿẓam*.[178] The adjective *al-aʿẓam* used in these cases has more exalted connotations than the alternative *al-muʿaẓẓam*, and its use in conjunction with the title *khāqān* (as opposed to *sulṭān*, found, for example, on the coins of Abū Saʿīd's father and predecessor, Öljeitü) is especially significant.[179] Each of the designations listed above strongly implies parity with the Yuan Emperor.

The Mongol dominions still exhibited a certain homogeneity even after 1260. They shared cultural traditions, customary law, even cuisine drawn from every corner of the one-time unitary empire.[180] They inherited that empire's institutions. The first and most obvious element was the imperial Chinggisid dynasty, members of which were alone eligible to rule. Others were the *keshig*; the traditional Mongol tribunal or *yarghu*;[181] the quriltai summoned to deliberate matters of importance; the tablets (*gerege*, *paiza*) of safe-conduct conferred on *ilchi*s and merchants; and Mongol taxes, the *tamgha* and the *qubchur*. Although we may doubt whether the relay stations were consistently linked up in time of war, the *yam* bore witness to the fact that much of Asia had lain under the sway of a single power of unprecedented size and reach.

One further element was important in this context: Chinggis Khan's Yasa, to which the Mongols of each ulus certainly professed allegiance. Major considerations underlying his edicts were the Mongols' duty to conquer the world and, as a prerequisite, the preservation of their own unity – features that impart some support to Ibn Khaldūn's concept of Mongol *ʿaṣabiyya*. Juwaynī retails an anecdote in which Chinggis Khan demonstrates to his sons how one arrow can be snapped with ease but a sheaf of arrows proves unbreakable. The lesson, reinforced by a tale contrasting a snake with one head and a snake with several, is that the princes should remain united and avoid the disputes that had bedevilled so many of the Mongols' opponents.[182] On the eve of his death, Chinggis Khan is said to have recalled the tale about the snake when addressing his sons on the same theme. It is striking that the account of Chinggis Khan's appeal for harmony was still current in the early fifteenth century, when Clavijo would pick it up in a simplified form.[183] The admonition regarding consensus and harmony, observes Juwaynī, was 'the pivot of their affairs and of their Yasa'.[184] Rashīd al-Dīn quotes Chinggis Khan to the effect that if the grandees, warriors and amirs did not hold to the *yāsāq*, sovereignty would become precarious and collapse.[185] Chinggis Khan, claimed the Ilkhan Ghazan

Maḥmūd, had been able to conquer east and west by not deviating a hair's breadth from his *yasaq*, while his descendants retained these conquests by keeping the *yasaq* and custom (*āyīn*) of the realm in order.[186] When Chapar and Du'a submitted to the Qaghan Temür in 1304, they too ascribed Chinggis Khan's triumphs to his Yasa and his abolition of evil customs and cited the tale about the sheaf of arrows.[187] For the Mongols, 'Chinggis Khan's Yasa' was clearly the cornerstone of their hegemony.

The unitary empire founded by Chinggis Khan had lasted for less than six decades. It had undergone two major disjunctures: the violent transfer of supreme power from Ögödei's line to Tolui's in 1251 and the creation of a new ulus, the Ilkhanate, in 1260; we shall see in Chapter 12 how both events figured in Timur's propaganda on behalf of his Ögödeyid khan. Yet the Chinggisid tradition – 'an attractive package of institutions, ideological precepts, symbols, ceremonies and territorial claims that could be adapted to local needs and circumstances'[188] – was destined for a remarkably long life. And the survival of the successor-states that emerged around 1260 for at least seventy-five years – and considerably longer, if we take into account the eastern Chaghadayid ulus ('Mughūlistān') or the polities that emerged out of the Qipchaq khanate in the fifteenth century – is striking. Nor would the dominion of Timur's heirs in Transoxiana and Iran persist anywhere near as long as did that of its Jochid and Chaghadayid antagonists; only in India would Timurid rule outlast them.

CHAPTER 3
ISLAMISATION

Like the Qara Khitai before them, the Mongols entered the Islamic world both as conquerors and as pagans. Where earlier nomadic invaders, the Qarakhanids and the Seljuqs, were Muslim converts of recent standing, acknowledged the sovereignty of the Caliph and ruled notionally as his deputies, the Mongol Qaghans recognised no superior authority and their armies put an end to the ʿAbbasid Caliphate at Baghdad, which had lasted for over five centuries. Islamic thought made no provision for anything other than the spread of Muslim rule to embrace the whole world; the subjection of a vast Islamic territory by a non-Muslim power was not to be contemplated. It is therefore unsurprising that Muslims reacted to the Mongol invasions and conquests by interpreting them as divine chastisement and as a harbinger of the Last Things (perspectives that in some quarters would outlast Mongol paganism and survived the transformation of their khans into legitimate rulers).[1] Juwaynī makes Chinggis Khan ascend the *minbar* in the principal mosque of Bukhara in 618/1221 and announce that he was a punishment from God for Muslims' sins.[2] Jūzjānī, who had fled from his homeland when it was ravaged by the Mongols, saw them as presaging the imminent end of time and cites a tradition (*ḥadīth*) of the Prophet regarding the advent of the 'Turks'.[3]

NON-MUSLIM RULE AND THE MUSLIM PREDICAMENT

The Mongols' early operations were without doubt highly destructive. Many thousands of Muslims, including prominent shaykhs, were killed or injured during the campaigns of conquest under Chinggis Khan and Hülegü, as well as in the internecine strife that followed the fragmentation of the empire in the early 1260s.[4] But the imposition of Mongol rule had further disagreeable consequences for Muslims. It ended their privileged status by placing the representatives of all faiths on an equal footing. Symbolic of the new order was the abolition of the discriminatory tax, the *jizya*, that Islamic regimes had traditionally required from the *ahl al-dhimma* – the 'Protected Peoples', namely Christians and Jews – and the introduction of a poll-tax, the *qubchur*, on all adults regardless of religious allegiance. The Mongol era also saw an influx of 'idolators'. The Ilkhanate in particular became a magnet for Buddhist priests and monks from Tibet, China, the Uighur lands and Kashmir, and Buddhism flourished – for the first time in Iran since the ninth century.[5] Hülegü built an idol temple at Labnasagut, near his summer pastures at Alatagh, and Buddhist shrines sprang up elsewhere in Iran;[6] Abagha had his young grandson Ghazan reared by Buddhist monks.[7]

The Mongols did not merely introduce new institutions unsanctioned by the Sharīʿa, such as the *tamgha* tax and their own tribunal, the *yarghu*; they also enforced steppe customs that were in conflict with the Sharīʿa. An example is the levirate, whereby a man might marry the widows of his father (other than his own mother) or of an older brother (see p. 69). The Qur'ān expressly forbids marriage to a stepmother and marriage to a sister-in-law was at least frowned upon.[8] Although we find subject Muslim princes contracting levirate marriages,[9] the levirate was seemingly not imposed on the Muslim population at large as it was on the Muslims of China later in Qubilai's reign.[10]

The new rulers further issued *yasa*s outlawing practices that clashed with steppe custom: for example, the washing of the body or of garments in running water in the spring and summer months. The

Muslim slaughter-ritual was also prohibited and Muslims were required instead to kill animals in the steppe fashion, by cutting open the body and squeezing the vital organs.[11] These *yasa*s, which had an impact on the day-to-day practice of Islam, were seemingly enforced only for a few decades and perhaps only in the vicinity of a royal or princely encampment.[12] The implication in one of Juwaynī's anecdotes illustrating the clemency of the Qaghan Ögödei is that the prohibitions were also directed solely at offences committed in public. This is confirmed by what transpired in China in 1280, when Qubilai renewed the ban on the Muslim slaughter-ritual but a supplementary order was introduced that forbade a Muslim even to perform it within his own dwelling.[13] As Mamlūk ambassadors returning from Berke's headquarters in 661/1263 reported, it was forbidden to wash clothes there; but were this to occur, the garments should be spread out clandestinely to dry.[14] The distinction between the public and the private, also instanced in the accounts of Juwaynī and Rashīd al-Dīn, may indicate a toning-down of Mongol attitudes.

THE MONGOLS AND RELIGIOUS PLURALISM

The invaders had already encountered two major world religions even prior to their expansion.[15] Two Muslim traders were among Temüjin's earliest followers, while Christianity (in its Nestorian form) traditionally enjoyed a strong position among the Kereyit, the Naiman and the Önggüt.[16] Neither the slaughter of Muslims, their demotion to equality with the *ahl al-dhimma* nor the imposition of un-Islamic practices stemmed from consciously anti-Muslim sentiments per se; it was not the Mongols' intention to eliminate the faith. Chaghadai himself, to whom Jūzjānī imputes precisely that motive and whom he charges with making it impossible for Muslims to recite the daily prayers,[17] had a Muslim chief minister, Ḥabash ʿAmīd, and other Muslims were prominent at his court.[18]

The Mongols' own ancestral cultic practices, often inaccurately labelled 'shamanism', belong in the immanentist category – those religious systems in which ritual is centred on the empirically demonstrable and directed towards the present, whether everyday aspects of life and health, economic prosperity or political and military success. By contrast, religions that we can term transcendental are possessed of scriptural revelation and offer a system of universally applicable ethics; they focus on individual salvation in the hereafter and posit sharp boundaries with other, 'rival' faiths. Immanentist religion centres on the community rather than the individual and is inclusivist, ready to borrow from any belief-system practices and techniques that might prove as efficacious as its own traditions.[19] As Möngke put it in his final interview with Rubruck in 1254, 'Just as God has given the hand several fingers, so he has given mankind several paths'.[20] Juwaynī ascribes similar sentiments to Chinggis Khan.[21] He assures us that the Mongols were hostile towards no religion; that a *yasa* of Chinggis Khan forbade his descendants from showing partiality for any faith and that the dynasty honoured equally holy men of all religious confessions.[22]

This even-handed attitude was not a matter of accepting the validity of every religion as a form of 'celestial insurance',[23] as it were, in case any one of them might prove to be right. Rather, all faiths were seen, potentially, as offering techniques that might serve the same goals as the Mongols' own cultic practice. Much as Mongol rulers and their nomadic subjects prized the skills of the shamans and the expertise of specialists at large,[24] whether in medicine, astrology or administration, they also valued the talents and services of 'holy men', of any faith.[25] During the campaigns against Jin China, Chinggis Khan had conferred, on an ad hoc basis, the privileges of the *darqan* (*tarkhan*; see p. 65) – exemption from the *qubchur*, from military service and from forced labour – on 'religious specialists' from among the Daoists and Buddhists, and these exemptions were later extended to holy men of other faiths. An Armenian writer tells us that, although Batu's son Sartaq was a Christian, he granted such privileges not only to clergy and monks but to mosques and their personnel.[26] The purpose behind these favours was to gain the prayers of the 'religious' for the health and success of the imperial dynasty, as Rubruck confirms when he observes that 'they like one to pray for their lives'.[27] This requirement is always specified in the exemption decrees.[28]

The guarantee of freedom of worship was, at one level, a means of securing peaceful submission;[29] but there was also another dimension to the policy of even-handedness. The Mongols were well aware of the disruptive passions that could be aroused by conflicting religious allegiances because such passions played into their hands, as at Isfahan in 633/1235–6, when the element that adhered to the Shāfiʿī school of law first appealed to Ögödei for assistance against their Ḥanafī rivals and then opened the gates to his besieging forces.[30] Once established as rulers, the Mongols desired to maintain peace among the different religious communities; a vital constituent of holiness, in their eyes, was an aversion to discord. Prior to the public religious debate at Qaraqorum in 1254, the representatives of competing faiths were strictly forbidden to resort to provocation and verbal abuse.[31]

Freedom of worship and favour towards the 'religious classes' were conditional, of course, upon acceptance of Mongol rule, but the Mongols' apparent openness in religious matters requires further qualification. Not all prayers were of equal merit in the eyes of Heaven.[32] In what Atwood terms the Mongols' 'political theology', the vital distinction lay not between 'true' and 'false' religions but between individuals who prayed with a pure heart and those who did not. What rendered prayers efficacious – that is, in securing blessings for the dynasty – was not any particular doctrine or ritual but the moral uprightness of the person praying, exemplified above all in an ascetic lifestyle. Initially, under Chinggis Khan and Ögödei, clerical privileges were restricted to those who had 'left the world'; priests and monks who engaged in economic activity were subject to the appropriate imposts, the land-tax and the *tamgha*.[33] For the Mongols, since Heaven's favour manifested itself in political and military success, the 'religious classes' belonging to faiths not associated with political power were hardly worth cultivating (though the adherents of such faiths still enjoyed freedom of worship). It was doubtless for this reason that Möngke's edict confirming the immunity from taxation of the 'religious classes' within each faith excepted the Jews.[34]

If, generally speaking, Muslim religious institutions now had to share in the Chinggisids' favour towards those of other faiths, they did nevertheless benefit in some measure from Mongol patronage. Tolui's Nestorian Christian widow Sorqaqtani (d. 1251) gave alms to Muslim imams and shaykhs and endowed a *madrasa* in Bukhara.[35] So too we find Mongol noyans patronising Islamic shrines and sufi lodges and witnessing deeds of endowment.[36] The Ilkhan Abagha is known to have been present at ceremonies staged by Christians and Muslims alike and even Arghun, despite his inclination towards Buddhism and his reputation for antipathy towards Muslims, attended Muslim festivals. Both rulers visited the graves of Muslim saints in order to invoke their aid in a forthcoming military conflict.[37] In Iran this situation lasted until the conversion of Ghazan (earlier reared by Buddhists, as we saw) in 694/1295, when Buddhists were given the choice of embracing Islam or emigration.

Moreover, writing in 658/1260, Juwaynī discerned – or affected to discern – beneficial consequences of the advent of the Mongols. Their campaigns had resulted in the dispersion of Muslims over a wide area of Asia, partly through flight and through the enforced transfer of thousands of enslaved Muslims (among others) from their homelands to serve the conquerors, and partly through the readiness of Muslim traders to travel to the Mongol dominions and settle there. During Ögödei's reign, too, Islam had continued to spread into virgin territory as Muslims had reached lands, such as Uighuristan, Mongolia and China, where Islam was (allegedly) hitherto unknown.[38] Three centuries later, Mīrzā Ḥaydar Dughlāt learned that the ancestors of one of his informants had fled from Qaraqorum during the upheavals (*barhamzadagī*) there, into the Lop Nor-Katak region.[39] Even Jūzjānī could express gratification at the wide dissemination of mosques and other Islamic institutions across the Mongol empire.[40] However, while Juwaynī was cheered by the news that some among Chinggis Khan's descendants had accepted Islam,[41] he failed to name specifically Jochi's son Berke, owing to the tense relations between the Jochids and his Ilkhanid master. Jūzjānī, on the other hand, had become familiar with Berke's reputation thanks to the diplomatic contacts between that prince and the court in Delhi, and singles him out for special mention.[42] Berke is the first Chinggisid known to have embraced Islam.[43]

THE ADOPTION OF ISLAM

Let us briefly review the process of Islamisation. No doubt the experience of being uprooted from their homeland and despatched to an alien and distant setting loosened (without entirely dissolving) the ties that bound the Mongol military to the steppe traditions in which they had been reared and made them more receptive to new socio-religious influences. As early as Chinggis Khan's seven-year campaign, Mongol armies included Muslim troops. They were present in sufficient numbers during the invasion of Hungary in 1241 for Batu to demand their prayers in order to secure victory.[44] The *tamma* system involved the permanent dispersal of large numbers of Mongol troops over a considerable part of Western Asia, where they very likely constituted a minority alongside the Muslim forces in the Chinggisid armies; of these Muslims, a large proportion would have been indigenous Turks whose culture and lifestyle hardly distinguished them from the Mongols themselves.[45]

In 1247–8 the Dominican Friar Simon of Saint-Quentin, recently a member of a papal embassy to the Mongol army in the Transcaucasus, lamented that Islam had gained numerous adherents among the troops (whether they were all, or even largely, Mongols – as opposed to Turks – is not clear, however).[46] Juwaynī, too, claimed that the followers of Mongol princes had embraced Islam in such numbers as to defy computation; though this statement occurs in the course of what is patently an appeal to his readers to accept the rule of the unbeliever.[47]

There were inevitably distortions and misperceptions. Some observers saw the Mongol general Baiju and the contemporary Mongol administrator Arghun Aqa as Muslim converts.[48] Various Chinggisids gained a name for being well disposed towards Muslims and hence for accepting the faith themselves. The most obvious example is the Qaghan Ögödei, perhaps because he reputedly intervened to save Muslims when Chaghadai or their other enemies at court – usually depicted as Buddhists – sought to traduce or destroy them;[49] he was merely observing his father's *yasa* regarding the equal validity of all faiths. Batu, who, as Juwaynī acknowledges, adhered to no faith,[50] likewise gained a reputation for favour towards Muslims.

Jūzjānī says that there were portable mosques, an imam and a *mu'adhdhin* in his encampment and that the Muslims of Turkestan (presumably after 1251–2) enjoyed affluence and security under his rule; he even transmits a report that Batu had secretly become a Muslim.[51] Juwaynī also conveys the impression that the Qaghan Möngke showed greater favour to Muslims than to those of other faiths, while according to Jūzjānī, at Berke's instigation Möngke even recited the *shahāda* prior to his enthronement. Both these statements alike surely represent wishful thinking.[52]

We might, however, attach greater weight to some other early examples of Mongol khans aligning themselves with the faith: Berke (d. 665/1267) and later Töde Mengü (680–686/1281–1287) in the Qipchaq steppe; Mubārak Shāh (664/1266) and his successor Baraq (664–670/1266–1271 or 1272) in the Chaghadayid ulus; and the Ilkhan Tegüder Aḥmad (681–683/1282–1284). But these conversions appear to have had little immediate impact on the religious trajectory of their respective uluses. It is true that at least one of Berke's brothers likewise accepted Islam, that Berke's troops were reported to be overwhelmingly Muslim and that in a letter of 661/1263 to the Mamlūk Sultan, summarised by the chronicler Baybars al-Manṣūrī, the khan spoke of the conversion of numerous noyans and their troops, among them 'the forces despatched to Khurāsān and all those who went forth with Baiju'.[53] Yet Berke was followed on the throne by the non-Muslim Mengü Temür and there is no evidence for a preponderance of Muslims within the Jochid armies in the ensuing decades. Mengü Temür's brother and successor, the Muslim convert Töde Mengü, was in turn followed by the pagan khans Töle Buqa (686–690/1287–1290) and Toqto'a (690–712/1291–1312), before the enthronement of Özbeg (712–742/1312–1342) heralded the Islamisation of the ulus.

Similarly, the conversions of Mubārak Shāh and Baraq were isolated affairs. Baraq was followed by pagan rulers right down to *c.* 1330, when his grandson Tarmashirin became a Muslim. Tarmashirin clearly took his new faith seriously; al-ʿUmarī praises his character and his generosity to Muslim divines and Ibn Baṭṭūṭa describes him as regularly attending the daybreak and evening prayers at the mosque.[54] At one point, we are told, the shaykh and imam Ḥusām al-Dīn Yāghī refused to postpone the prayer while the khan performed his ablutions – an act of defiance which Tarmashirin evidently took in good part.[55] But if this conversion also appeared to lead nowhere when Tarmashirin was overthrown in what looks like a pagan reaction, only two more unbelievers briefly occupied the throne before the Ögödeyid ʿAlī Sulṭān (740–741/1339 or 1340–1341), first of an unbroken series of Muslim rulers and notorious for instigating an *émeute* in Almaligh in which Franciscan missionaries were martyred.[56] But the eastern half of the ulus, forming a distinct polity after 748/1347, remained more solidly pagan, and it was only in *c.* 754/1353, according to a Mughūl oral tradition transmitted by Mīrzā Ḥaydar, that its first khan, Tughluq Temür, accepted Islam.[57]

Tegüder Aḥmad's adoption of Islam represents another 'false dawn', though the gap before his great-nephew, the Ilkhan Ghazan Maḥmūd (695/1295), adhered to Islam was brief compared to the interval which we see in the other two western uluses. Like Tarmashirin half a century later, Tegüder Aḥmad made some effort to project his regime as Islamic. We cannot accept statements by Armenian Christian authors that he sought to destroy other faiths and should be sceptical of claims the Ilkhan himself made in his correspondence with the Mamlūk Sultan Qalāwūn. Yet Tegüder Aḥmad does seem to have attempted to satisfy Muslim grievances. For instance, he outlawed misappropriation of the revenues of Islamic charitable foundations (*awqāf*; sing. *waqf*), decreeing that the state treasury be liable instead for the stipends of physicians and other experts from the Christian and Jewish communities.[58]

It should be borne in mind that what our Muslim sources see as the conversion of a Mongol khan or prince or social grouping to the faith might have amounted, *in the first instance*, to little more than the adoption of a Muslim name alongside a Turco-Mongolian one, as in the case of both Tegüder and Ghazan. This practice would continue into later generations: thus Timur's grandson (best known as Ulugh Beg, b. 796/1394; d. 853/1449) was given at birth the twin names Muḥammad and (after Timur's father) Taraghai. But the adoption of Islam might also have entailed primarily the appropriation of new techniques and practices alongside existing ones derived from the world of the Mongols' ancestors,[59] the very eclecticism and syncretism that Rubruck observed, and deplored, in the encampment of one of Möngke's wives.[60] Clearly, neither the Chinggisids nor the ordinary Mongols viewed 'shamanistic' practices and those borrowed from other cultures as mutually incompatible; nor did those who went further, aligning themselves with one faith or another, necessarily regard such affiliations as exclusive.[61] Mongol rulers tended to display what Herbert Franke called a 'multiple personality', adopting a different stance in relation to each of the faiths over which they presided.[62] According to Rashīd al-Dīn, Qubilai's grandson Ananda (d. 1307), Prince of Anxi, converted to Islam, smashed idols and spread the faith assiduously among his troops in a conscious effort to emulate his distant cousin, the Ilkhan Ghazan Maḥmūd. But Rashīd al-Dīn was here inflating the influence of the newly converted Ilkhan. Recent research, based on non-Muslim sources, shows that Ananda retained strong links with Buddhism and protected other faiths within his territory, in the traditional Chinggisid fashion. His father Manggala had conducted himself in much the same manner.[63] What was unacceptable was for a khan to flout Chinggis Khan's *yasa* on the equality of all faiths by promoting one confession above others or seeking to enforce a particular faith on his subjects. One of the objections to Tarmashirin's rule was that he favoured Muslim noyans (for whom we must now begin to use the Arabic-Persian term *amir* or the Turkish *beg*) over non-Muslims.[64]

Certain convert khans did attempt to impose Islam with the threat of force. Özbeg is said to have made war upon the non-Muslim elements within the Qipchaq khanate,[65] while Ḥaydar alleges that the convert Chaghadayid khan Tughluq Temür slew all those amirs who refused to follow his example.[66] The effectiveness of such expedients is unclear. Later the same author admits that the majority of the Mughūls did not enter Islam until the reign of Muḥammad (d. 818/1415), who had threatened that anyone refusing to convert would have a nail driven through his head.[67] Similarly, despite Özbeg's triumph, most of the Qipchaq khanate's nomads were still reputedly unbelievers around 1400 (later, pp. 367–8).

Naturally, a number of considerations may have played a part in a khan's acceptance of Islam, and we need always to be wary of generalisation and remember that the motives for pronouncing the *shahāda* varied widely. One impulse was the desire to steal a march on a Muslim monarch outside or on a hostile Mongol ulus. Alignment with Islam rendered it possible for Berke, writing to the Mamlūk Sultan Bāybars, to depict his own conflict with the pagan Hülegü as a holy war.[68] To judge by the chronology of events, the self-portrayal as an adherent of Islam by the Jochid khan Töde Mengü to the Mamlūk Sultan in 682/1283, as I have tried to show elsewhere, could have been prompted by reports of the accession of the Ilkhan Tegüder Aḥmad, who had notified the Mamlūks of his religious allegiance and proposed a peace settlement (conditional, of course, on acknowledgement of Ilkhanid overlordship). Töde Mengü may further have intended that his own rule would be as welcome as the new Ilkhan's to the Muslims of the disputed regions south of the Caucasus.[69] Ghazan Maḥmūd, in assuming the style of 'Emperor of Islam' (*pādishāh-i Islām*) on his acceptance of the faith, possibly sought both to define a distinctive quasi-regional authority and to assert an equality of status with the other Mongol rulers (at this juncture, non-Muslims without exception).[70] But equally, the adoption of Islam might enable the convert khan to outflank a defiant Muslim enemy outside the Mongol world, and another of Ghazan's ambitions was surely to rob the Mamlūk Sultan of an advantage in his dealings with the Muslims of Anatolia, Syria and the Jazīra. In 699/1299 the Ilkhan used the atrocities committed by Mamlūk troops against the Muslim populace of Mārdīn to secure a *fatwā* denouncing the Mamlūks as infidels.[71] Ghazan's new title, lastly, may have been designed to represent him as the true heir of the defunct Caliphate; his deployment of the symbolic black flags, recalling the ʿAbbasid revolution of 132/750, was an implicit challenge to the authority of the puppet Caliph who fronted the Mamlūk regime in Cairo.[72]

Our sources tend to foster the notion that a khan's adoption of Islam prompted widespread imitation on the part of the Mongol soldiery. Thus, Rashīd al-Dīn assures us that Ghazan brought with him at his conversion all his Mongol noyans and troopers, and Waṣṣāf claims that in this fashion more than 200,000 'stubborn polytheists' (*mushrik-i mutamarrid*) entered Islam in a single day.[73] Speaking of Tughluq Temür's acceptance of Islam in the eastern Chaghadayid khanate, Mīrzā Ḥaydar Dughlāt describes how 120,000 Mongols followed the khan in embracing the faith.[74] So, too, Ḥamd-Allāh Mustawfī asserts that Tarmashirin's adoption of Islam was imitated by the majority of his people (*qawm*, presumably his nomadic subjects), while Ibn Faḍl-Allāh al-ʿUmarī depicts him as ordering his amirs and troops to embrace Islam and see to its spread throughout his territories.[75]

But al-ʿUmarī says (almost in the same breath) that there were Muslims among Tarmashirin's amirs and troops before he issued these orders,[76] and later he assures us that both the nomads (*raʿāyā*) and the settled population (*qarāriyya*) of the ulus accepted the faith while their rulers were still unbelievers.[77] Indeed, we know of individual Chaghadayid princes and amirs who were seen as Muslims by the early years of the fourteenth century.[78] Apropos of the Ilkhanate, the evidence, as Charles Melville has demonstrated, suggests that Ghazan's entry into Islam, inspired by his principal backer, the Muslim amir Nawrūz, was aimed in part at winning the support of a growing Muslim Mongol constituency against his rival, Baidu. In general, it has to be conceded that the 'top-down' model espoused in the earlier scholarship and in the primary sources does not fit the evidence.[79] We should take note of the caveat issued by Ishayahu Landa: that whereas the convert ruler might be responsible for the institutional Islamisation of the khanate, royal conversion did not play a decisive role in bringing most of the non-Muslim nomad population to Islam – rather, the reverse was the case.[80]

THE AGENTS OF ISLAMISATION AND THEIR TACTICS

Regarding the agents of Islamisation, we can only speculate. Muslim traders have been suggested as possible vectors, and Reuven Amitai pointed to evidence for their instrumentality in the spread of Islam among steppe-dwellers in the pre-Mongol period.[81] But more intimate relationships might certainly also engender an allegiance to

Islam. Mongols intermarried with the Muslim population and Chinggisid khans and princes took wives from the subject Muslim dynasties. It was by no means inevitable that the offspring would choose their mother's faith (the Ilkhans Tegüder Aḥmad and Öljeitü were both born of Christian mothers),[82] but the Chaghadayid khan Naliqo'a (*c.* 707–708/*c.* 1308–1309), whose mother belonged to the Qutlughkhanid dynasty in Kirmān, was a zealous Muslim.[83] The importance of the foster-brother (*kökeltash*) in Mongol society, combined with the relationship between the adult Mongol prince or noyan and the family of his Muslim wet-nurse, could also play a part, as suggested by Rashīd al-Dīn's account of the foster-family of Prince Ananda.[84]

We know also of close cooperation and even friendships between Mongol commanders and officials, on the one hand, and Muslim bureaucrats and princely dynasties on the other, from as early as the mid-thirteenth century. A case in point is the extensive connections of the Oyirat noyan Arghun Aqa (d. 673/1275). They included Bahā' al-Dīn, father of the two Juwaynīs and at one time Arghun Aqa's deputy, and the brothers themselves.[85] The unsubstantiated claim in an Armenian source that Arghun Aqa was a Muslim could reflect his social contacts with Muslims,[86] which in turn may help to explain the fact that his son Nawrūz displayed a strong commitment to Islam by the 1290s.[87]

There were noticeably strong links between some Mongol leaders and leading sufi shaykhs. The most prominent example is Shaykh Sayf al-Dīn Bākharzī, at whose hands, according to a widely reported tradition, Berke accepted Islam.[88] The life of the shaykh in the biographical dictionary of al-Dhahabī (d. 748/1348) credits him with having already brought to the faith a Mongol amir in Bukhara. Known in Turco-Mongol circles as Ulugh Shaykh ('The Great Shaykh'), Bākharzī even enjoyed the esteem of the pagan Batu, who was gratified to learn that Berke had become the shaykh's disciple (*murīd*),[89] and was nominated to administer the charitable foundation (*waqf*) that Sorqaqtani had financed in Bukhara.[90]

At one time it was believed that sufis mediated the faith, both in earlier steppe polities and in the Mongol world, on the specific grounds that the conduct and practices of the more antinomian among Muslim mystics closely resembled those of the shamans. Reuven Amitai has challenged this supposed affinity, pointing out that, whereas the shamans dealt exclusively with good fortune and material prosperity in the present world, sufis were overwhelmingly concerned with other-worldly matters.[91] However, this does not in itself preclude a role for sufis in the Islamisation process, given the favour and patronage that the Chinggisids and their noyans extended to 'holy men' from the faiths that they encountered in Central and Western Asia.[92] For what it is worth, a contemporary Latin Christian visitor to the Near East, the Dominican Guillaume Adam, Archbishop of Sulṭāniyya, pointed to the role of *faqīr*s in the conversion of the Jochid Mongols.[93] Islamic sources too furnish some limited evidence of the importance of sufis in the context of bringing Mongols to Islam. The prominent sufi Saʿd al-Dīn Muḥammad Ḥamuwayī (d. 651/1253–4), father of the Ṣadr al-Dīn at whose hands the Ilkhan Ghazan would receive Islam in 694/1295, is credited with the conversion of more than one Mongol amir in Khurāsān.[94] Amitai draws attention to another sufi who acquired a Mongol following later in the century.[95] The strong ties of Saʿd al-Dīn and his son with Khurāsān, moreover, and their proximity to Arghun Aqa's estates, render it very likely that they were among the close Muslim associates of Arghun Aqa's family, including Nawrūz.[96]

THE APPEAL OF ISLAM

We should consider certain inherent advantages that Islam might have been seen to possess. In the first place, Islam claims to stand in a distinctive relationship with Christianity and Judaism, which were represented as earlier, incomplete stages in a process of divine revelation fulfilled in Islam. Islam therefore appeared more 'inclusive', inasmuch as it could be deemed to subsume both the other two faiths. Buddhist rhetoric furnishes a parallel here in its quest to bring local deities and cults within its own world-picture. When a Buddhist source cites Möngke as likening Buddhism to the palm of the hand

and other religions to the fingers,[97] it matters less whether the Qaghan enunciated this view than what it tells us about the way in which Buddhist missionaries portrayed their faith.[98] Secondly, as we saw earlier, the Mongols' approach to matters of religion was coloured by perceptions of holy living and the consequential bestowal of Heaven's favour – favour, it is important to recall, that was measured by political or military success. In that context, by the end of the thirteenth century the record of the Muslim Mamlūk rulers – the elimination of the Frankish strongholds on the Syrian coast, as well as the repulse of the Mongols themselves – could undeniably be interpreted as demonstrating the good will of Heaven. We might therefore extrapolate from Strathern's thesis of regarding the 'empirical demonstration of immanent power'[99] and see Mamlūk victories as crucial elements in the Ilkhanid acceptance of Islam.

We know virtually nothing directly of the arguments that clerics or sufis may have employed to win converts among 'ordinary' Mongols, but in the aftermath of Ghazan's acceptance of Islam, Muslim authors adopted a providential narrative in place of the penitential, apocalyptic discourse that had hitherto dominated; and their writings can perhaps yield clues to the way in which Islam was at least presented to Mongol rulers. The conversion of Öljeitü, who – unusually – embraced Twelver Shiʿism and had the names of the Twelve Imams included in the khutba and on the coinage (though he later reverted to Sunnī Islam),[100] furnishes us with a ready-made rationale. Shīʿīs drew an analogy between the status of the Prophet's descendants (*Ahl al-bayt*) and that of the *altan urugh* and reasoned that Sunnī Muslims, in recognising the Umayyad Caliphs and even the ʿAbbasids (descended not from the Prophet but from his uncle), had chosen to give their allegiance to the equivalent of a mere noyan.[101] This played upon Mongol veneration of the imperial dynasty and we shall encounter the same coupling of allegiances in Timur's thinking, no doubt for the same reason. There are signs that the analogy with the *altan urugh* was presented to Ghazan Maḥmūd, who expressed the desire to right the wrongs done to the *Ahl al-bayt* and made use of Shīʿī symbolism, but he had probably stopped short of becoming a Twelver Shīʿī.[102]

This may not have been the only way in which concepts at the heart of Mongol political theology were exploited. As noted in Chapter 2, the Mongol programme of world-conquest was predicated on the duty to bring all peoples into submission to Tenggeri and an insight of the late Igor de Rachewiltz is especially relevant in this context. In an article that deserves to be far more widely known, he pointed to the fact that the very term Islam means 'submission': for the Mongols this may well have resonated with their own submission to the will of Heaven and their summons to other peoples to obey Heaven's mandate.[103] We find the Sufi Shaykh Sulṭān Walad, grandson of Jalāl al-Dīn Rūmī, drawing a parallel between the one God and the supreme khan, as the sole ruler on earth – a parallel already explicit in the Mongols' own orders of submission to independent powers.[104]

Mongol reverence, specifically for the person of Chinggis Khan and belief in his Heaven-conferred good fortune, was also, it seems, harnessed to the process of Ilkhanid Islamisation. Over a generation earlier, Juwaynī had asserted that God endowed Chinggis Khan with the wisdom and intelligence to accomplish his conquests, and with the intuitive knowledge enabling him to rule without recourse to learning; had Alexander lived in that age, we are told, he would have elected to be the Mongol conqueror's pupil.[105] Rashīd al-Dīn – under both Ghazan Maḥmūd and Öljeitü and in his historical and theological works alike – credited the two Ilkhans with a supernatural perspicacity and ability to see into men's hearts and to predict the future; they were not merely divinely ordained rulers but divinely enlightened.[106] The ascription of functions of this nature to the Ilkhan harmonised well with assumptions that were already current in Mongol circles. The late Ilkhanid historian Shabānkāra'ī, contending that Chinggis Khan possessed such a degree of wisdom that had he only been a Muslim he could undoubtedly have been regarded as a prophet,[107] was drawing on a long-standing pagan Mongol tradition regarding the conqueror's gifts. In 690/1291 the Jewish wazir Saʿd al-Dawla had assured Ghazan's pagan father Arghun that the qualities of prophethood had descended to him from Chinggis Khan.[108]

The project in which Muslim writers were engaged was nothing less than to infuse the political theology of the pagan Mongols with unimpeachably Islamic themes. Thus the pagan prophecy uttered by Teb-Tenggeri in Chinggis Khan's favour (p. 59 above) came to be superseded by Muslim prophetic traditions that foretold the appearance of Ghazan Maḥmūd and the strengthening of Islam through his conversion to the faith.[109] Rashīd al-Dīn even rewrote Mongol history by retrospectively portraying Ghazan's Mongol forebears and their followers at large as monotheists.[110] There is already a hint of this, again, in the doxology with which Juwaynī opens his history, where he declares that God 'is . . . loved alike by the lovers of truth and by depraved idolators' and writes of Islam and infidelity alike 'treading His path' and expressing His Oneness.[111] There is a striking affinity between the tactics employed by Muslims and by Buddhists, and a parallel exercise was under way in the Yuan empire.[112] Here Confucian *literati* depicted the Qaghans' ancestors as practising the very virtues advocated by Confucius,[113] while prominent Buddhists, led by Qubilai's adviser, the Pʿags-pa Lama (d. 1280), sought to incorporate Chinggis Khan and his successors within the sequence of Buddhist universal emperors, the *chakravartins*.[114] Buddhist inscriptions from beyond the eastern borders of Chaghadai's ulus similarly speak of the Chaghadayids quartered there (descendants of Alughu) as belonging to 'the lineage of the *bodhisattvas*'.[115]

Those who sought to bring Islam to the conquerors surely deployed precisely such appeals to an imagined past, seeking, in Weiers's words, to 'Quranize and Muslimize the history of Chinggis Khan and the Mongols'.[116] Far from representing a subversive expedient, the programme fitted very neatly into – and profited from – the Mongols' own practice of adapting ideas and techniques lifted from the cultures of the subject peoples to their own imperial agenda.[117] In good measure it served its purpose. Not only did Ghazan Maḥmūd, in taking the style of *Pādishāh-i Islām*, arrogate to himself the position of paramount Muslim king, he also seems to have been viewed as an imam and as the Mahdī.[118] Ghazan and Öljeitü thus derived a new legitimacy from their status as Muslim sovereigns. What had ultimately made this possible was Hülegü's destruction of the Caliphate, which meant that Mongol rulers who accepted Islam were spared the inconvenience of recognising a higher authority.

Stimulating work by Jonathan Brack has highlighted these efforts by Muslim scholars in the Ilkhanate, notably Rashīd al-Dīn, to reconceptualise the Chinggisid claim to divinely ordained rulership by relocating it within an Islamic framework. He explains the success of Muslims (as also of Buddhists) in winning over Mongol rulers by their 'ability to harness, or fashion and fit, their own models of sacral kingship', which he contrasts with Christian proselytism, 'far less inclined, or equipped, to accommodate the supernatural pretensions of potential royal converts'.[119] The result, he shows, was a new synthesis of Mongol and Islamic conceptions of sacral kingship, to be carried still further in the Timurid era.

The impact of Hülegü's destruction of the Caliphate is a matter for debate, in relation both to the sentiments of ordinary Muslims and to the implications for Muslim rulers. Something should be said regarding the latter, although this book is not the place for an extended discussion. For Muslim princes, who had been accustomed to obtaining sanction for their rule from Baghdad, the overthrow of the Caliphate was potentially disastrous. Certain rulers, of course, stood in greater need of caliphal sanction than others. As a usurper who had treacherously murdered his predecessor, and as the representative of an upstart regime that was hardly more than ten years old, the Mamlūk Sultan Bāybars hit upon his own solution – an ʿAbbasid as Caliph who would provide him in return with the necessary legitimation.[120] But during its admittedly long life (659–923/1261–1517) the Caliphate in Cairo found relatively few Muslim princes outside Mamlūk territory who would recognise its authority.[121] It appears that, as a consequence of the debacle in 1258, Muslim monarchs came to be seen as inheriting the authority of the ʿAbbasids – as themselves possessing, in other words, *khilāfat*, the status of God's deputy and (in a legislative context) the Prophet's successor. In the 1420s the Timurid historian Sharaf al-Dīn ʿAlī Yazdī precisely expressed this equation with respect to Timur (below, p. 413).

Of course, Muslim Chinggisid rulers continued to draw on their descent from the thirteenth-century Mongol conqueror as a major source of legitimacy. For Yazdī they too could claim to possess *khilāfat*.[122]

THE OBSERVANCE OF ISLAM

Certain Islamic norms were taken on board at a strikingly early date. According to Juwaynī, in preparation for the feasting that accompanied Möngke's enthronement the animals were slaughtered in the Muslim fashion out of deference to Berke, who was present on Batu's behalf.[123] (This measure – a flagrant infringement of an ancestral taboo and of a *yasa* of Chinggis Khan – is unlikely to have been implemented apropos of the dishes served up to the whole assembly; rather, it must have applied solely to the meat destined for Berke and his entourage.) Rubruck, crossing the Qipchaq steppe in 1253, heard that Berke did not allow pork to be eaten in his camp,[124] and Jūzjānī claims that not one among Berke's troops partook of intoxicating drink.[125] Berke is also said to have obeyed Bākharzī's instruction that he retain only four of his sixty (*sic*) wives.[126] His letter to Bāybars claimed that the converted Mongols of his *ulus* were paying the alms-tax (*zakāt*) and partaking in the holy war (*al-ghazāh wa l-jihād fī sabīl Allāh*).[127] For Waṣṣāf, who had no doubt that Tegüder Aḥmad was a genuine Muslim, it was symptomatic that the Ilkhan abstained from wine;[128] he further tells us that the edict issued by Nawrūz upon Ghazan's enthronement, ordering pagan Mongols and Uighurs to embrace Islam and recite the *shahāda*, refers to them as those who had hitherto regarded as licit the consumption of pork and other forbidden food.[129]

Rubruck's testimony as to Berke's diet, Bākharzī's injunction to the neophyte Jochid prince and Berke's letter to Bāybars remind us that the first stage in the adoption of Islam involved a change of practice, rather than a shift in conviction, and adhesion to a community, as opposed to a profound inner experience.[130] Describing the conversion of a group of Mongols by a shaykh named al-Hawwārī, the early fourteenth-century author Ibn al-Fuwaṭī says that 'they repented at his hand and began to pay *zakāt* and to perform their prayers diligently'.[131] What was required, above all, was external indications of the new faith.

Treatment of the *ahl al-dhimma*, too, might change, if only temporarily. In Chaghadai's *ulus*, the fact that Buzan granted permission for Christians and Jews to rebuild their places of worship, according to Ibn Baṭṭūṭa, suggests that Tarmashirin had either destroyed these edifices or at the very least withheld permission for their restoration.[132] In the immediate wake of his adoption of Islam, Ghazan had presided over a persecution of Christians and Jews, not simply subjecting them to the *jizya* but ordering them to wear distinctive apparel (*ghiyār*); according to a report that reached Damascus, they were even required to pay the arrears of *jizya* due since the end of the Caliphate in 656/1258.[133] In all likelihood these actions are to be attributed to the prompting of Nawrūz, since after the amir's downfall in 697/1297 the Ilkhan reverted to the more traditional even-handed policy and ceased to levy the *jizya*, though the clampdown on Buddhists remained in place.[134] It was only under Ghazan's successors Öljeitü and – to a greater extent – Abū Saʿīd that the *dhimmī*s were again subjected to discriminatory measures.

On the whole, however, adoption of Islam did not prevent Mongol rulers from continuing to display an interest in the holy men of other religious confessions. The Tibetan *Blue Annals* reveal that the Karma-pa Lama Rol-pa'i rDo-rǰe (d. 1383) declined an invitation from the eastern Chaghadayid Tughluq Temür to visit his court.[135] This seems to have occurred in the early 1360s, some years, that is, after the khan's conversion. Presumably Tughluq Temür, like earlier Chinggisids, was concerned with making use of the Lama's talents, which – if we can believe the *Blue Annals* – included the ability to put an end to epidemics.[136]

Nor did steppe usages that lacked Islamic sanction necessarily cease on a khan's decision to align himself with the faith; we have seen how the prohibition of washing clothes persisted at Berke's headquarters. Some pre-Islamic practices continued for many decades and two in particular come to mind. The burial of grave goods with the dead, practised among the Islamised Seljuqs, is still found in the Qipchaq khanate following the conversion;[137] it would be observed at Timur's interment (see later, pp. 407, 412). Mongol khans also retained levirate marriage. Ghazan Maḥmūd insisted on his right to wed Bulughan Khatun, who had been the wife of his father Arghun, despite the objections of the ʿulama; and a Mamlūk author assures us that the Ilkhan would have abandoned his new faith had he not found a compliant jurist.[138] The Jochid khan Özbeg, destined for an undying reputation as the monarch who brought the Golden Horde into the Islamic fold, is the subject of a similar tale.[139] Mīrzā Ḥaydar tells us how, five generations after the conversion of the eastern Chaghadayids, the khan Dūst Muḥammad (d. 873/1468–9) sought authorisation to marry one of his father's widows. He secured a favourable verdict after executing seven ʿulama who refused; the eighth gave his assent, but only on the grounds that the union was licit because the khan was an infidel. Ḥaydar then makes the khan's father appear in a dream and charge him with apostasy.[140] There are other instances from the fifteenth century, by no means confined to Chinggisids.[141] Some of Timur's sons and grandsons, whose Islamic credentials are commonly viewed as impeccable, contracted such marriages (see later, p. 412). Ḥaydar's grandfather, the Dughlāt amir Muḥammad Ḥaydar, married a widow of Dūst Muḥammad who had earlier been the wife of his own half-brother Sāniz;[142] a son of this union, Ḥaydar's uncle Sayyid Muḥammad Mīrzā, married the widow of his half-brother, Sāniz's son Abā Bakr.[143] The practice still met with condemnation. Recounting how Timur's grandson and successor, Khalīl Sulṭān, gave his widowed mother to a (half-) brother, the hostile Salmānī describes the union as 'invalid' (*bāṭil*).[144]

None of this should encourage us to write off the Islamisation of Mongol khans as hollow or skin-deep, and it would be facile to classify khans into 'authentic' and 'spurious' Muslims.[145] We have no means of penetrating the thoughts and emotions of the 'convert', any more than we can gain an insight into the impulses behind the change of religious allegiance. Religion, moreover, has never been a static commodity, stubbornly resistant to external influences. At the microcosmic level, new adherents have always brought to the faith their own distinctive experiences, which have left an imprint on belief and observance. On the macrocosmic plane, too, religions, like individuals, 'travel' – not just in the geographical sense, over vast distances, but culturally, inasmuch as they penetrate regions of the world very different from the social and cultural context in which they were born, and undergo at least some modification.[146] If we might hesitate to speak of the Turkicisation or Mongolisation of medieval Islam (as we are learning to think of the Germanisation of medieval Christianity),[147] there is nevertheless a case for associating marked shifts in practice with the Chinggisid era. And who is to judge what is 'authentic' Islam and what is not?[148] In Islam, authority in matters of faith lay with the ʿulama, that vaguely defined universal body of scholars and jurists to whom the faithful looked (frequently in vain) for a consensus.

Undeniably, contemporary authors did on occasion express views about the authenticity of individual professions of Islam,[149] dismissing the commitment of this or that convert Mongol khan as in some way substandard. On closer examination, however, such verdicts can appear rather predictable. Ibn Baṭṭūṭa describes the Chaghadayid khan Buzan, whose revolt brought down Tarmashirin, as a Muslim but one 'tainted in faith and of evil conduct' who oppressed Muslims.[150] Yet by this point the Moroccan traveller had moved on to the Delhi Sultanate, where his informants concerning Buzan's coup were almost certainly among the Muslim refugees who had flocked into India from Transoxiana (including members of Tarmashirin's own family).[151] Yazdī's testimony that Buzan 'lacked the outward semblance of Islam'[152] should perhaps carry more weight. So too we should note that when Ḥamd-Allāh Mustawfī was told that Tegüder Aḥmad had little knowledge of Islam,[153] his informant was the son of an amir killed by that monarch.[154] Rashīd al-Dīn casts doubt on Tegüder Aḥmad's faith with an ambiguous phrase meaning either that he prayed in the Muslim fashion or merely that he claimed to be a Muslim.[155] But Tegüder Aḥmad had been laid low by Arghun, the father of the historian's patron Ghazan Maḥmūd, and Rashīd al-Dīn was eager, moreover, to portray Ghazan as the first truly Muslim Ilkhan – the one who 'compelled the people to practise good conduct and . . . avoid evil'.[156] Rashīd al-Dīn neglects to call Baidu, whom Ghazan Maḥmūd supplanted in 695/1295, a Muslim or even to recognise him as a reigning Ilkhan. By contrast, the continuator of the history by the Monophysite Christian Bar Hebraeus – writing in *c.* 1296 – says that Baidu, having converted to Islam under pressure from his amirs, was only half-hearted and never observed the ablutions or the fasts. This confirms, at least, that Baidu was ready to identify himself with the faith.[157]

Hostile outsiders certainly portrayed the Islamisation of the Ilkhanid Mongols as a sham. The Ḥanbalī theologian and jurist Ibn Taymiyya (d. 728/1328), who met Ghazan and his lieutenants in Syria in 699/1299–1300,[158] issued three *fatwā*s over the next decade or so, launching an uncompromising attack on the un-Islamic practices that the Mongols had carried over from their pagan past. They might pronounce the *shahāda*, exalt the Prophet's name and observe the Ramaḍān fast, but they were seldom seen to pray and no *mu'adhdhin* was to be found in the Mongol host. They did not pay the *zakāt*, nor did the Ilkhan exact the *jizya* from his *dhimmī* subjects and require their abasement (this charge, of course, dates from after Ghazan rescinded his discriminatory measures against them). In fact, Ibn Taymiyya noted, the Mongols showed equal favour to the Peoples of the Book and to idolators and failed to distinguish between the learned men of different confessions. Freethinkers (*zindiq*s), heterodox Muslims (Bāṭinīs, Rāfiḍīs) and Jews were prominent within the Ilkhanid establishment and merely masqueraded as Muslims; Ibn Taymiyya singles out Rashīd al-Dīn, a convert from Judaism, for special obloquy. The Mongols called Chinggis Khan the son of God and saw him as the Seal of the Prophets and gave precedence to his injunctions (*amr*), rooted in his own opinions and his own whim (*bi-ẓannihi wa-hawāhi*), over the Qur'ān. Their prime commitment was not to Islam but to the growth of their empire: those who submitted – even pagans – became their friends; those who defied them – even the best of Muslims – were their enemies. If some of these judgements are valid, others are questionable. In the accounts of his interview with the Mongol noyan Qutlughshāh – all derived ultimately from what Ibn Taymiyya later told the historian al-Birzālī – Qutlughshāh's most objectionable remark was that Chinggis Khan had been a Muslim.[159]

RESISTANCE TO ISLAMISATION

The conversion of Ghazan Maḥmūd, less than forty years after the end of the Caliphate, undoubtedly marked a turning point – a new beginning – in the eyes of Muslim historians such as Rashīd al-Dīn and indeed in the historiographical tradition itself.[160] But there was opposition to Muslim convert khans in some quarters, even if we cannot always ascertain whether it was directed at Islamisation per se. Generally, our sources merely show hostile amirs claiming that the khan had flouted Chinggis Khan's Yasa, a charge previously levelled at khans by rebel noyans.[161] In Tarmashirin's case, the specific *yasa* in question related to the summoning of an annual quriltai, according to Ibn Baṭṭūṭa, who links this with the khan's failure to visit the eastern tracts of the Chaghadayid ulus.[162] Both Tegüder Aḥmad and Tarmashirin were accused of promoting Muslim amirs at the expense of non-Muslims,[163] which could certainly be construed as disregard of Chinggis Khan's *yasa* on the equal treatment of all faiths. In 697/1297 Ghazan Maḥmūd was confronted by a group of rebel princes whose aim, Waṣṣāf tells us, was to turn 'all the mosques of the land of Islam back (*bāz*) into places of [pagan] worship and cells for bishops and monks'.[164] The word *bāz* is significant: they desired a reversion to the pluralistic stance that had hitherto obtained.

Our sources reveal other reservations concerning the new faith. Qāshānī recounts a religious debate among different Muslim schools of law (*madhhab*s) at the court of the Ilkhan Öljeitü, when Qutlughshāh was provoked into questioning why the Mongols in Iran had jettisoned Chinggis Khan's Yasa for a faith in which some schools permitted marriage to a daughter and others to a sister.[165] As Morgan observes, this betrays a decidedly imperfect understanding of Islam.[166] Qutlughshāh's misapprehension may have been less glaring, however, than it appears at first sight. Possibly he was bowdlerising the Muslim practice of endogamy, which was at variance with long-standing Mongol tradition (and which Qubilai had temporarily prohibited among Muslims in China in 1280).[167] But it is also worth noting that in the same episode Qutlughshāh contrasted the 'old (*kuhna*) religion of the Arabs' with the 'new Yasa and custom (*yusūn*)' of Chinggis Khan, and denounced Islam for its division into many sects (*qism*, i.e. schools)[168] – no doubt an affront to those who ascribed the Mongols' spectacular conquests above all to their unity (above, p. 84) and were reluctant to jeopardise it. Interestingly, Qāshānī makes Özbeg's chief amir voice similar objections to the rejection of Chinggis Khan's Yasa and custom in favour of 'the old Sharīʿa of the Arabs' – a sentiment which earned him execution.[169] Yet, even if these views were commonly voiced at the time of the adoption of Islam, they clearly did not constitute insuperable obstacles: Rashīd al-Dīn, who knew and worked with Qutlughshāh, classed him as a Muslim.[170] Islamisation had come to stay; but it was a gradual and fitful process, and one in which Islamic practice itself had been subtly modified.

CHAPTER 4
THE CRISIS OF THE MONGOL WORLD: CHINGGISID RULE ON THE WANE

Introducing the Chaghadayid khan Tarmashirin, Ibn Baṭṭūṭa speaks of his realm as a vast one, surrounded by the territories of four of the world's seven great kings, namely the 'King of China' (the Qaghan/Yuan Emperor), the 'King of India' (the Delhi Sultan), the 'King of al-ʿIrāq' (the Ilkhan) and 'King Ūzbak' (Özbeg, the khan of the Golden Horde).[1] Like Tarmashirin, three of these four rulers were Mongols and descendants of Chinggis Khan and, at the time of Ibn Baṭṭūṭa's sojourn in Central Asia, each presided over a formidable power. Within a few decades, however, two of these five states had ceased to exist, while in two others authority was fragmented. Only the 'King of India' – no Chinggisid but, as Ibn Baṭṭūṭa was told,[2] of Qara'unas Mongol stock – might still have merited the accolade of a great king.

THE COLLAPSE OF MONGOL RULE AND THE RISE OF THE 'GREAT AMIRS'

In the middle decades of the fourteenth century, all the Mongol khanates entered a period of crisis. Yuan China experienced a series of upheavals, which included revolts by the subject Han Chinese, and the Mongols were expelled in 1368 by a rebel commander, Zhu Yuanzhang, the founder of the Ming dynasty (as Emperor Taizu). The Qaghan Toghan Temür (Emperor Shundi) withdrew into the Mongolian steppes, where he and his successors would reign as the Northern Yuan until the Manchu conquest in the 1630s.[3] But the years from 1388 onwards witnessed a bewildering succession of Qaghans. In 1406 the Ming Emperor, writing to the Qaghan Gülichi, observed that seven rulers had occupied the throne since the Mongols had abandoned China; two years later, in a letter to a Yuan prince who had designs on Gülichi's throne, he gave the figure as six, but added that none had died a natural death.[4] On various occasions the throne was occupied by descendants of Arigh Böke or of Ögödei,[5] as princes from these branches, presumably domiciled in Mongolia since the thirteenth or early fourteenth century, now seized their opportunity to challenge Toluid Qaghans who possessed depleted resources and were hard pressed by the Ming.

By that stage disputed succession, and a resulting attenuation of the khan's power, had been the pattern in the other khanates for many years. The collapse in the most westerly Mongol states – the Ilkhanate and the Jochid territories – was sparked by genealogical failure. It is perhaps immaterial whether we attribute this to the effects on royal fertility of excessive eating and drinking,[6] or to the consequences of inbreeding through consanguineous marriage policies,[7] or to both. In Iran, the death of the Ilkhan Abū Saʿīd (13 Rabīʿ II 736/30 November 1335) with no male heir meant the end of Arghun's line. The absence of consensus regarding the succession threw open the field to claimants not only from Hülegü's descendants, but also from the progeny of Arigh Böke and of one of Chinggis Khan's brothers.[8] In the Qipchaq khanate the line of Batu seems to have died out around 1360.[9] Thereafter the throne was disputed by descendants of Batu's younger brothers, particularly Shiban and Toqa Temür. We now also find Toqa Temür's descendants ruling the Blue Horde (the 'Left Wing'), the ulus of Orda; thus Orda's line too may have become extinct.[10]

By contrast, genealogical failure played no part in the crisis in the Chaghadayid khanate. Here the overthrow of Tarmashirin (735/1334), the last of Du'a's sons to reign, introduced a period of almost three decades in which the throne was contested among Du'a's grandsons and (later) their offspring, other descendants of

Chaghadai and princes from Ögödei's line. Relative stability returned to Transoxiana only with Timur's paramountcy from 1370, but in the interim the ulus had split, with a separate line of khans in the eastern Chaghadayid territories (known as Mughūlistān or Jata) since 748/1347.

A second feature common to all four Chinggisid polities in the mid-to-late fourteenth century was the transfer of effective power to a prominent Turco-Mongol amir, not a member of the Chinggisid dynasty but a commoner (*qarachu*), who ruled in the name of a titular Chinggisid khan. In Ilkhanid history, at least, this was not altogether unprecedented: Buqa, under Arghun, and Nawrūz, in the first two years of Ghazan's reign, had each dominated the government until his own overthrow, while Abū Saʿīd's accession at the age of twelve had necessitated that a Mongol noyan – first Sevinch, the young Ilkhan's guardian (*atabeg*),[11] and then Choban, of the Süldüs tribe – serve as regent in everything but name.[12] Nevertheless, apart from Choban's dominance, which lasted for several years,[13] these periods had been brief. What was new in the mid-fourteenth century was the virtual institutionalisation of power for a significant period in the hands of the 'Great Amir', the phenomenon that Timothy May has christened 'The rise of the *qarachu*'.[14] The analogy that comes to mind is with the *maior domus* ('Mayor of the Palace') in the early medieval Merovingian realms. A more apposite parallel, from steppe history, is the Beg or Shad in the Khazar empire,[15] while the contemporary Islamic world offered the spectacle of a Mamlūk Sultan whose rule was sanctioned by an ʿAbbasid shadow Caliph and who was notionally the Caliph's deputy.

Of all the 'Great Amirs', Timur, who rose to power in the western Chaghadayid state, would enjoy by far the longest and most spectacular career, but he was just one example among several. The phenomenon of the 'Great Amir' surfaced in the Ilkhanate from 1336 and in the western Chaghadayid territories from 1347, in Batu's ulus and in that of Orda from about 1360 and in the eastern Chaghadayid lands from *c.* 1369. In the Northern Yuan territories the era of puppet Qaghans began later, in 1388, though in the years immediately following the Mongols' expulsion from China a warlord named Naqachu had exercised independent control of Liaoyang, without formally recognising Yuan authority, until his surrender to the Ming in 1386.[16] In both the eastern Chaghadayid khanate and Batu's ulus, the *qarachu* amir in question – Qamar al-Dīn and Mamai, respectively – is said to have gone so far as to usurp the dignity of khan for himself; but such experiments were infrequent and were in any case frustrated by widespread opposition. Here I shall examine the partial eclipse of the khans within each of the three Mongol states in Western Asia in turn.

THE END OF THE ILKHANATE IN IRAN

In the Iranian world the ruling dynasty was overshadowed by regional strong men earlier than in the other Mongol states; and here, in contrast with the Jochid and Chaghadayid polities, indigenous sources enable us to reconstruct a detailed narrative of events.[17] Five days after Abū Saʿīd's death, the wazir Ghiyāth al-Dīn, in conjunction with his son-in-law, the powerful amir Sharaf al-Dīn Maḥmūdshāh 'Īnjū',[18] proclaimed as khan Arpa Ke'ün (Mo. *ke'ün*, 'prince'), a descendant of Arigh Böke whom the wazir made out to be the late monarch's designated successor. The new ruler displayed some energy, moving north to repulse the invading forces of Özbeg, khan of the Golden Horde, who retreated at his approach. On his return Arpa married Abū Saʿīd's widowed sister Satibeg, but also made efforts to cultivate amirs who had fallen from favour under his predecessor. Arpa's position was rendered less secure because Abū Saʿīd's favourite wife Dilshād Khatun was pregnant, although three days after Arpa's own death she would give birth to a daughter, thereby ending any residual hopes of a universally recognised male heir.[19]

Arpa forfeited support by executing not only Sharaf al-Dīn Maḥmūdshāh but also some Hülegüid princes and Abū Saʿīd's senior wife, Baghdād Khatun, who was accused of poisoning the late Ilkhan and of corresponding with Özbeg.[20] Abū Saʿīd's maternal uncle, ʿAlī Pādishāh of the Oyirat, the governor of Iraq, reacted by setting up as Ilkhan Mūsā, grandson of Baidu. Arpa, deserted by amirs he had restored to favour, was defeated, captured and put to death on 3 Shawwāl 736/15 May 1336;[21] the wazir had been seized and executed not long before.

ʿAlī Pādishāh and his puppet sovereign rapidly faced opposition. The governor of Anatolia, Shaykh Ḥasan of the Jalāyir tribe (known as Ḥasan-*i Buzurg*, 'the Greater'), recognised Muḥammad, a descendant of Hülegü's son Mengü Temür, as khan. In an engagement near Alatagh on 14 Dhū l-Ḥijja 736/24 July 1336, ʿAlī Pādishāh in turn was defeated and killed. In Muḥammad's name Shaykh Ḥasan occupied Tabriz and Baghdad, marrying Dilshād Khatun. But Mūsā was still at large. Moreover, not long afterwards the governor of Khurāsān, Shaykh ʿAlī Qūshchī, came out against Shaykh Ḥasan and convened an assembly of the notables of the province, who elected as Ilkhan Taghai Temür, from the branch of Chinggis Khan's brother Jochi Qasar.[22] The decision to enthrone a non-Toluid prince may well have outraged some observers. We saw in Chapter 2 how, in 738/1338, the late Ilkhanid chronicler Shabānkāra'ī advanced bogus claims on behalf of Tolui and his line. His primary aim was doubtless to counter the view of the other Chinggisid lines that the Ilkhanate was a secondary creation which did not derive from Chinggis Khan's own territorial dispositions, but his version of events was perhaps also designed as a counterblast to the pretensions of Taghai Temür.[23]

There were now three competing Ilkhans. When Taghai Temür advanced westwards from Khurāsān in Shaʿbān 737/March 1337, Mūsā made common cause with him against Muḥammad; but in an encounter with the forces of Shaykh Ḥasan and Muḥammad near Marāgha in mid-Dhū l-Qaʿda/late May, Taghai Temür precipitately left the field. Mūsā was compelled to take flight and was captured and put to death on 10 Dhū l-Ḥijja/10 July 1337. On his return to Khurāsān, Taghai Temür was seized by Arghūnshāh, leader of the Jā'ūn-i Qurbān Mongols, who executed the khan's chief supporter Shaykh ʿAlī Qūshchī, though Arghūnshāh shortly released his prisoner and took over Shaykh ʿAlī's role as the pillar of Taghai Temür's throne.

Shaykh Ḥasan had meanwhile been confronted by a new antagonist, Choban's grandson Ḥasan (-*i Kūchak*) b. Temürtash, who defeated him in the vicinity of Alatagh on 17 Dhū l-Ḥijja 738/16 July 1338, capturing and executing the Ilkhan Muḥammad. The Chobanid Ḥasan took the unprecedented step of proclaiming as Ilkhan a woman – Abū Saʿīd's sister Satibeg, at one time married to his grandfather Choban and now the widow of Arpa – and occupied Sulṭāniyya in her name. Shaykh Ḥasan saw no alternative but to appeal to Taghai Temür for assistance, but when Taghai Temür once more advanced westwards in Rajab 739/February–March 1339, Ḥasan-i Kūchak drove a wedge between the allies by divulging a letter in which Taghai Temür expressed his readiness to break with Shaykh Ḥasan and to marry Satibeg. With both Ḥasans ranged against him, Taghai Temür was forced to withdraw.[24]

Shaykh Ḥasan now chose as Ilkhan Jahan Temür, a grandson of the Ilkhan Gaikhatu, and fell back on Iraq, where he occupied Baghdad. His Chobanid rival and namesake reacted by discarding Satibeg towards the end of 739/June or July 1339 after a reign of nine months,[25] and forcing her, against her will, to marry his new protégé Sulaymān, a descendant of Hülegü's son Yoshmut. Sulaymān survived for somewhat longer than most of the other shadow khans in the western half of the Ilkhanate, reigning for at least four years.[26] These years saw repeated skirmishing between the forces of Shaykh Ḥasan, centred on Iraq, and those of Ḥasan-i Kūchak, whose power base lay in Azerbaijan. A third and final attempt by Taghai Temür to extend his authority to the west ended in defeat at the hands of Ḥasan-i Kūchak's brother, Malik Ashraf. Thereafter Taghai Temür confined his attention to Khurāsān and Māzandarān, where he was soon embroiled in conflict with the rebel Sarbadārs, a complex alliance of representatives of the traditional ruling class of Khurāsān, petty rural landowners and Shīʿī dervishes of the Bayhaq/Sabzawār region.[27] At length, he fell victim to assassination by a group of Sarbadārs in 754/1353.

In the west, when Ḥasan-i Kūchak was murdered by one of his wives in Rajab 744/December 1343, Malik Ashraf took over the leadership of the Chobanid party. He jettisoned Sulaymān, instead nominating in 745/1344–5 an obscure figure named Anūshīrwān (Nūshīrwān) as Ilkhan, who reigned until 757/1356.[28] Shaykh

Ḥasan in turn, having abandoned Jahan Temür, probably at the very onset of 741/June–July 1340, and struck coins in Taghai Temür's name in Iraq and Khūzistān until 743/1342–3,[29] now transferred his allegiance to Sulaymān. Sulaymān was also accepted by local amirs in Diyār Bakr and had coins issued in his name until 746/1345–6.[30] We also find coins still struck in the name of his wife Satibeg in eastern Anatolia in 743/1342–3 and 745/1344–5.[31]

The Mamlūk Sultan al-Nāṣir Muḥammad profited from these shifting and fractious conditions and from the readiness of the chief protagonists in the struggle to turn to him for confirmation of their position and for support against their rivals. We learn of this fraternisation, about which the Ilkhanid sources are largely silent, from contemporary Mamlūk authors, notably al-Yūsufī (d. 756/1355) and al-Shujāʿī (writing after that date),[32] while we know from manuals of Mamlūk chancery practice that the new balance of forces was reflected in diplomatic protocol.[33] At different points ʿAlī Pādishāh, Shaykh Ḥasan-i Buzurg and the latter's one-time lieutenant Aratna all sought the Sultan's assistance at the price of including his name on the coinage and in the khuṭba. The Sultan's death in 741/1341, and the onset of political instability under the rule of his sons and grandsons, made appeals to Egypt somewhat less attractive or realistic, but a number of rulers in Anatolia and the Jazīra (notably the Artuqid prince of Mārdīn and the chief of the Qarā-Qūyūnlū Türkmen) continued intermittently to recognise Mamlūk overlordship.[34] Egypt was not the only magnet for the opportunistic or discontented. The Ilkhan Mūsā's brother Ḥājjī Ke'ün sought refuge at the court of the Delhi Sultan, from where, if Ibn Baṭṭūṭa can be trusted, he made an unsuccessful attempt to take the Ilkhanid throne in succession to Mūsā in the late 1330s.[35]

These struggles mask an almost imperceptible drift from nominal Chinggisid sovereignty to the fragmentation of the western Ilkhanid provinces into independent kingdoms under non-Chinggisid rulers. Initially the most important of these rulers were the two surviving kingmakers:[36] the Chobanid Ashraf, who controlled Azerbaijan until 758/1357, and Shaykh Ḥasan, the founder of the Jalayirid dynasty (down to 835/1432), which ruled in Baghdad and also in Azerbaijan from 759/1358. The others included Aratna, first of a dynasty that ruled over Sivas, Kayseri, Arzinjān (Erzincan) and adjacent towns in eastern Anatolia until 783/1381; Mubāriz al-Dīn Muḥammad b. Muẓaffar, of Arab origin and founder of the Muzaffarid dynasty (until 795/1393) in Yazd, Kirmān and Isfahan and later in Fārs and Shabānkāra; the Injuids, an indigenous sayyid family, in Fārs until their elimination by Mubāriz al-Dīn in 754/1353; a number of Turkish amirs in Anatolia, including the rising Ottoman leader; and lastly, to the east, the Kartid kings of Herat (down to 785/1383), the Sarbadār state in western Khurāsān (down to 788/1386) and three other polities headed by Mongol amirs, including Amīr Walī (son of one of Taghai Temür's lieutenants) in Astarābād and Māzandarān.

In 758/1357 elements in Azerbaijan, weary of Malik Ashraf's tyranny, invited in Özbeg's son Janibeg, khan of the Golden Horde.[37] Ashraf had begun striking coins in his own name in 756/1355, styling himself Sultan, but he changed policy in the following year, acknowledging Janibeg. He finally switched his allegiance to a figurehead Ilkhan, Ghazan (II), a son of Taghai Temür, presumably as an alternative source of legitimacy to the formidable Janibeg, since at the time of the Jochid invasion he defiantly claimed to be ruling on Ghazan's behalf.[38] Ashraf was shortly captured and put to death by Jochid troops. To the best of our knowledge, Ghazan (II) was the last of these puppet monarchs in Mongol Iran. The date given for his death, 9 Jumādā II 758/31 May 1357, suggests that he was killed during the Jochid attack since the battle between Janibeg and Ashraf fell on the following day.[39] Now there was no longer even a nominal Ilkhan awaiting recognition.

The Jochid invasion prompted one or two among the rival potentates briefly to recognise Janibeg's sovereignty. Early in his reign, in 759/1358, Amīr Walī appears to have added Janibeg's name to his coins;[40] for a short period in 758–9/1357–8 Shaykh Ḥasan struck coins at Baghdad in Janibeg's name. However, some were less inhibited about asserting their own sovereignty. Aratna, after flirting first with the Mamlūk Sultan and then with Taghai Temür, took the step of having coins minted in his own name as early as 742/1341–2.[41] To judge from their coins issued at Ṭūs, the Jā'ūn-i Qurbān Mongols in

Khurāsān ceased to acknowledge Taghai Temür in or soon after 745/1344–5.[42] Shaykh Abū Isḥāq Īnjū took the title of Sultan and issued coins in his own name at Shiraz from 745/1344–5.[43] The Muzaffarid Mubāriz al-Dīn Muḥammad accepted as his sovereign first Taghai Temür and then Sulaymān,[44] but from 755/1354 his coins too bore his own name. Shaykh Ḥasan, once he had abandoned Jahān Temür, struck coins in his own name from 745/1344–5, apart from a brief interval in 758–9/1357–8. Initially, at least, he retained the modest title of *amīr-i ulūs* (Tu. *ulusbegi*); there is some doubt whether he ever assumed sovereign status.[45]

The subsequent history of the one-time Ilkhanate will be traced in Chapter 6, but we should mention at this point further developments that would have appeared far from welcome in Mongol eyes. Neither Shaykh Abū Isḥāq nor Muḥammad b. Muẓaffar felt able to dispense altogether with external legitimation. From the moment of issuing coins in their own right both secured sanction for their rule from a quite different quarter, namely al-Muʿtaḍid billāh, the phantom ʿAbbasid Caliph in Cairo;[46] Muḥammad b. Muẓaffar may have negotiated earlier with a scion of the ʿAbbasid dynasty in India, with a similar end in view.[47] Moreover, the second Muzaffarid ruler, Shāh-i Shujāʿ, was hailed by his historians as *Pādishāh-i Islām* (see later, p. 193), the title assumed by the Ilkhan Ghazan Maḥmūd on his accession in 694/1295. Muʿizz al-Dīn Pīr Ḥusayn of Herat was more explicit than the Injuids or Muzaffarids in his rejection of the recent past. At the same time as assuming the title of Sultan (750/1349), he announced that he was abolishing the customs of the infidels (*kuffār*) and that henceforth only the Sharīʿa would be valid.[48] In some measure, this rash move helps to explain the invasion of his territories by the Chaghadayid army under Qazaghan (see later). Recognition of caliphal authority and claims of independent rulership alike were tantamount to rejection of Mongol law and custom, the Yasa or (as it was also known) Töre,[49] closely bound up as it was with the sovereignty of the *altan urugh*. It was with good reason that Muʿizz al-Dīn's son and successor was accused before Timur of neglecting to abide by the Töre.[50] When Timur himself claimed the right to appoint the Caliph (below, p. 368), he was doubtless seeking to plug a yawning gap in the ramparts of Chinggisid legitimation.

THE KHANSHIP IN THE JOCHID DOMINIONS

The Qipchaq khanate (the White Horde) gives the impression of being the strongest of the three political formations discussed in this chapter and its khans undeniably retained real power for longer than their counterparts in Iran or Transoxiana. Özbeg had cemented his authority by executing a large number of his kinsmen on his accession. Dying in Shawwāl 742/March–April 1342, he was succeeded by his son Tinibeg, who was soon murdered by a half-brother, Janibeg, at the instigation of his mother, the khatun Taidoghli (Taidula); Janibeg shortly put to death another brother, Khiḍrbeg.[51] Janibeg's reign appears as the apogee of the Qipchaq khanate, inasmuch as it witnessed the first successful occupation of Azerbaijan, a former Ilkhanid territory long coveted by the Jochids and wrested from the Chobanid Malik Ashraf in 758/1357. This triumph was admittedly evanescent and doubtless owed more, as Vásáry suggests, to the weakness of the opposition than to Jochid strength.[52] Yet Janibeg had also taken territory from the Chaghadayids and thus boasted, in his ultimatum to Ashraf, of ruling over three uluses.[53]

Janibeg died later in 758/1357 and his son Berdibeg, who ruled for a mere two years, put to death a great many of his brothers and kinsmen.[54] In 761/1360, there then ensued what a Persian author refers to as 'strife and discord' (*fitna-u āshūb*)[55] and Rus' chroniclers call the 'Great Troubles' (*velikaia zamiatnia*), as a series of often ephemeral khans, based in various parts of the sprawling Jochid territories, struggled with one another.[56] We have far less material on these rulers than we do for the Ilkhanid contestants three decades earlier. Some of them are hardly more than names; some are known only from the coins they struck. The Timurid authors Shāmī and Yazdī supply a list of khans which appears incomplete.[57] Rus' chronicles furnish a good deal of material, though the Muslim and Rus' sources are often at variance and certain khans are ignored by the latter.[58]

That the murders perpetrated in turn by Özbeg, Janibeg and Berdibeg brought Batu's line to an end is suggested by the fact that Berdibeg's first three successors were pretenders who do not appear to have been descendants of Özbeg: Kulnā (760–761/1359), Nawrūz (761/1359–1360) and Kildibeg (762–763/1361–1362), of whom the last was almost certainly an impostor and may have passed himself off initially as Janibeg's homonymous nephew.[59] In addition, from 761/1360 onwards we find representatives of other Jochid branches assuming the rank of khan in Batu's ulus. Most of the khans can be identified in the relatively full Chinggisid genealogies found in *Muʿizz al-ansāb* and the Turkish *Tawārīkh-i guzīda-yi Nuṣrat-nāma* (*c.* 909/1504), which continues the lines of descent down to its own time. Whereas *Muʿizz* is biased towards the Toqatimurids, *Tawārīkh-i guzīda* exhibits a partisanship for the Shibanid Uzbeks, attaching the title of khan to Ming Temür, a proximate ancestor of the Uzbek rulers (and indeed to Shiban himself).[60]

Princes descended from Shiban appear first: Khiḍr, whom a Rus′ chronicle describes as coming from the east and 'beyond the Yaik' (Yayiq; that is, the Ural River) in 1360,[61] his son Temür Khwāja and his brother Murād Khwāja,[62] and ʿAzīz Shaykh.[63] Two of the khans in the early 1360s belonged to the line of Toqa Temür, namely Ordu Melik,[64] then ʿAbd-Allāh.[65] At one point Bazarchi – descended from another of Jochi's sons, Tangut – was briefly khan.[66] Shibanids appear intermittently as khans down to *c.* 1380, when the Shibanid ʿArabshāh yielded Sarai to Timur's protégé, the Toqatimurid Toqtamish.[67] But many of the khans since 1362 had been descendants of Toqa Temür,[68] and it was this line which ruled the major part of the ulus far into the fifteenth century and, in the Kazan, Astrakhan and Crimean khanates, well beyond that. Only in the easternmost reaches of the Jochid realm did the Shibanids come to dominate, under the leadership of ʿArabshāh's grandson Abū l-Khayr, founder of the Uzbek khanate from the mid-fifteenth century onwards.[69]

The extent of the chaos in the 1360s and 1370s can be gauged from numismatic evidence. Coins were struck in the names of rival khans at a variety of mints in a bewildering sequence. In 762/1360–1 no fewer than four khans – Khiḍr, his son (and murderer) Temür

Khwāja, Ordu Melik and Kildibeg – were named on coins at New Sarai; in the same year three of them – Khiḍr, Ordu Melik and Kildibeg – received numismatic recognition in Azāq (Azov), while Sarai changed allegiance six times.[70] Some khans – Murād and ʿAbd-Allāh, for instance – were sufficiently strong for Rus′ princes to seek at their hands the office of Grand Prince of Vladimir,[71] suggesting that they enjoyed significant support within the Mongol elite (although possession of Sarai may also have been an important criterion).

The history of the Qipchaq khanate during the 'Great Troubles' resembles, in some ways, that of the Ilkhanate a few decades earlier. There were khans who, unable to maintain themselves in one of the principal centres like Sarai, New Sarai or Azāq, contented themselves with outlying regions. An example is the Shibanid Bolod (Pūlād) Temür (also called Khayr Pūlād), who was briefly recognised in Sarai and New Sarai in 764/1363 but was soon obliged to withdraw,[72] although his son ʿArabshāh would reappear from Blue Horde territory and hold Sarai from 1377–8 to 1380.[73] Some regions appear to have fallen into the grasp of non-Chinggisid rulers whom the Rus′ chronicles term 'nobles of the Horde' (*kniazi ordin'skii*).[74] In Astrakhan the amir Ḥājjī Cherkes was virtually autonomous until his expulsion by Toqtamish.[75] Since 762/1361 Khwārazm, too, had become independent of the competing Jochids under the so-called Ṣūfī dynasty of amirs from the Qongqurat tribe, whose coins omitted any mention of a khan.[76] The upheavals in the Qipchaq khanate seemingly weakened the commercial link between Bulghār and the fur-producing regions to its north, a trade that was gradually taken over by Moscow.[77]

Certain amirs emerged as kingmakers. It is as ʿAbd-Allāh's principal backer that we first encounter the most celebrated strong man of the Qipchaq khanate, the amir Mamai, who, according to Rus′ sources, had installed him after overthrowing Khiḍr's son Temür Khwāja in 1361. Coin evidence reveals that, prior to this, Mamai had briefly struck coins in his own name in 762/1361, possibly on the grounds that he belonged to the Qiyat, as did the entire Borjighid clan (and hence the Chinggisids themselves: see above, p. 57).[78] The support of this amir, whose power base was the Crimea and the tracts west of the Volga, explains why ʿAbd-Allāh was generally the sole khan recognised in Azāq from 763/1361–2 onwards, was able to occupy Sarai on more than one occasion and enjoyed a relatively long reign until 771/1369–70.[79] His successor as Mamai's khan, the young Muḥammad Bulaq, similarly retained the title of khan for several years, with coins struck in his name from 771/1370 to 780/1379,[80] although Mamai eventually had him put to death (see later). Relations were sometimes strained: in 773/1371–2, in a gesture reminiscent of the Chobanids in Iran four decades earlier, Mamai minted coins in the name of Tulunbeg, allegedly his wife and a daughter of Berdibeg.[81]

Pochekaev suggests that Mamai was encouraged to intervene in the politics of the Qipchaq khanate by the emergence of his kinsman, the Qiyat amir Tengiz Buqa, as power-broker in the Blue Horde and thus a potential source of support.[82] The history of the Blue Horde, centred now at Sighnāq on the lower Sīr-daryā, is shrouded in mist. It seems that Orda's line in turn had died out by *c.* 761/1360, since the sixteenth-century writer Ötemish Ḥājjī indicates that Tengiz Buqa raised up as khan a Toqatimurid, Qara Noghai, in the very same month that Khiḍr was enthroned in Sarai.[83] After the brief reigns of Qara Noghai and his two brothers, their cousin and successor, Mubārak Khwāja, profited from the conflicts further west to affirm his independence of the Golden Horde khans by minting at Sighnāq in 768–9/1366–8 the first coins to bear the name of a khan of the Blue Horde.[84] The next ruler of the Blue Horde, Orus Khan (d. 779/1377–8), encroached upon the Qipchaq khanate's own territories, occupying Sarai itself for two brief intervals in 774/1372–3 and 776/1374–5.[85]

At this juncture a new contender for the throne of Orda's ulus appeared in the form of another descendant of Toqa Temür, Toqtamish, who had taken refuge at Timur's court in the western Chaghadayid realm. With Timur's backing he engaged in a protracted conflict with Orus and his sons and was established as khan of the Blue Horde in 780/1378–9. He then moved west, occupied Sarai and overthrew Mamai, who was killed after taking refuge in Genoese Kaffa. Toqtamish had achieved more than Orus by uniting the two Jochid uluses under his own rule. His triumph proved to be illusory, however, when his subsequent defiance of his benefactor Timur provoked two invasions, in 793/1391 and 797/1395, the latter of which wrecked the cities of the Qipchaq khanate.[86] The situation thereafter recalls that prior to 1380, since the amir Edigü (or Edigei) now emerged as kingmaker and Toqtamish was merely one of several contestants until his death in exile in Siberia in 809/1406–7.[87]

KHANS AND WARLORDS IN CENTRAL ASIA

As we have seen, Janibeg also claimed to have extended his rule over Chaghadayid territory. When this occurred, we cannot know.[88] The rapid changes of ruler in the Chaghadayid khanate would certainly have afforded its neighbours ample opportunity for territorial aggrandisement. We can only sketch these upheavals in outline. Apropos of the tumultuous events in Iran following Abū Saʿīd's death, the encyclopaedist Shams al-Dīn Muḥammad Āmulī opined that, had he attempted to recount them, he would surely have run out of time before his death.[89] Happily, he had contemporaries who shouldered the task (and the attendant risk), but in response to events in Chaghadai's ulus, nobody did. We lack even outside information of the kind furnished for the Jochid ulus by Rus′ chronicles. What little we learn of events and rulers has to be pieced together from the numismatic record and from later narrative sources, the work of Timurid authors or Mīrzā Ḥaydar Dughlāt.

After a reign of six years Tarmashirin had been brought down in 735/1334 by a rising in the eastern regions ('Jata') of the Chaghadayid ulus, headed by a nephew, Buzan.[90] Numismatic evidence shows that Buzan reigned for only a short time (he is not listed as khan by either Shāmī or Yazdī) and was succeeded by another of Du'a's grandsons, Changshi, who is known to have been enthroned towards the end of 1335.[91] According to Ibn Baṭṭūṭa, however, Buzan was overthrown by Khalīl, son of Yasa'ur, with military assistance from the Kartid king of Herat.[92] It is conceivable that Khalīl, who certainly ruled during the following decade (see later), had made an unsuccessful bid for the throne at this earlier stage, but Ibn Baṭṭūṭa, whose account of his reign includes some fantastic elements, may be unreliable here.

Naṭanzī, on the other hand, makes Tarmashirin's insane brother Dorji succeed him and wrongly places Buzan (likewise described as completely unhinged) after Changshi. Buzan's efforts to hold the throne were unavailing and merely resulted in the deaths of many Chaghadayid princes and amirs; indeed Naṭanzī asserts that Buzan killed his entire family (*urugh*).[93]

If insanity seems to figure disproportionately within the Chaghadayids' ranks at this juncture and if, overall, the discrepancies between the sources are intractable, the conflicting versions of events nevertheless serve to reinforce al-ʿUmarī's characterisation of the Chaghadayid ulus after Tarmashirin's downfall as 'chaotic' (*muta-khabbaṭ^{an}*).[94] During this time a great many Muslim Mongols abandoned the ulus and made for India (see later, p. 217). Sharaf al-Dīn Yazdī asserts that eight khans ruled Chaghadai's ulus in the interval separating Tarmashirin's death from Tughluq Temür's first invasion of Transoxiana (which he computes at thirty-three years on the basis of his faulty chronology, but which was in fact only twenty-six).[95] Naṭanzī, calling the crisis in the ulus 'historically a watershed' (*ibtidā-yi ta'rīkhī*), says that in his day the Mughūls still regarded the upheavals of Buzan's reign as a turning point and a byword (*ḍarb al-mathal*).[96]

Changshi, an unbeliever who sought to reverse Tarmashirin's promotion of Islam, was displaced and killed in 737/1336–7 by his brother Yesün Temür; the new khan subsequently repented and atoned, we are told, by cutting off his mother's breasts for having prompted his fratricide.[97] He in turn was overthrown in 740/1339–40 by an Ögödeyid prince named ʿAlī Sulṭān, a Muslim, who likewise enjoyed a brief reign. Numismatic evidence suggests that ʿAlī Sulṭān ruled only in the northern and eastern parts of the khanate, minting coins in Almaligh and Utrār; in Transoxiana he was confronted by a rival khan, Muḥammad b. Pūlād (Bolod), a great-grandson of Du'a, who struck coins at Tirmidh but was recognised in Almaligh itself in Shaʿbān 741/January 1341.[98]

Muḥammad's fate is unknown, but from 742/1341–2 we find two khans, Khalīl Sulṭān and Qazan (or Qazan Temür) Sulṭān, sons of Yasa'ur and members of a senior Chaghadayid line, reigning jointly,[99] and Ibn Baṭṭūṭa's perplexing account mentions a campaign by Khalīl against Almaligh,[100] of which Muḥammad was presumably the victim. Their father Yasa'ur had quarrelled with Du'a's line and migrated in 716/1316 into Ilkhanid Khurāsān, where he was defeated and killed by the future Chaghadayid khan Köpek in 720/1320.[101] What had then befallen his family is unclear. Possibly Khalīl Sulṭān (who was evidently the senior of the two co-rulers)[102] was identical with Yasa'ur's eldest son, Juki.[103] There were close links between Herat and Khalīl, who according to Ibn Baṭṭūṭa obtained the Chaghadayid throne (but at Buzan's expense) with the aid of its king, Muʿizz al-Dīn Pīr Ḥusayn Muḥammad.[104] That author describes how he subsequently defied his benefactor, was defeated and captured by the army of Herat and was still a prisoner when Ibn Baṭṭūṭa, as he alleges, left India in the latter part of 747/early in 1347.[105] Whether or not this testimony is to be trusted, Qazan ruled alone from 745/1344–5; the brothers may have fallen out in the previous year.[106]

Qazan, whom the Timurid sources depict as a ruthless tyrant bent on destroying the princes and amirs, was the last khan to reign over the entire Chaghadayid ulus and also the last effective khan in Transoxiana. The coinage indicates that during his joint reign with his brother his sphere of influence may have been centred on Tirmidh and Badakhshān.[107] If this is indeed the case, it might help to explain the fact that resistance to his rule originated in that southern region and that he was overthrown in 747/1346–7 by the Qara'unas Amir Qazaghan, whose territorial base lay close by, in Arhang, Mūnk and Sali Sarai.[108] The Timurid historian Naṭanzī characterised this development with the words 'authority in the sultanate passed to the amirs'.[109] For the next eleven years the western half of Chaghadai's ulus was under the sway of Qazaghan, who nominated as khan first the Ögödeyid prince Danishmandcha (747–748/1346 or 1347–1348) and then Bayan Quli (748–*c.* 759/1348–*c.* 1358), a grandson of Du'a.[110] We know little of events in this period, except for a Jochid invasion of the ulus and a loss of territory to Janibeg, mentioned only by Ahrī.[111]

At a date given in Mīrzā Ḥaydar's *Ta'rīkh-i Rashīdī* as 748 [1347–8], the eastern part of the ulus – the tract called Mughūlistān

('Mongol territory') in the sources and known to its western neighbours as Jata (*chete*, 'bandits')[112] – enthroned its own khan, a grandson of Du'a named Tughluq Temür, the candidate of Ḥaydar's ancestor Bolodchi (Pūlādchī). Whether this represented another rising against Qazan,[113] a rejection of Amir Qazaghan's phantom khan Danishmandcha (in which case it might explain the amir's sudden decision to dispose of his protégé), or indeed whether Tughluq Temür's election in the east preceded Qazaghan's installation of Danishmandcha, is unknown. Ḥaydar is the sole author to recount the emergence of a separate khan in Mughūlistān, and then only briefly.

Tughluq Temür's ancestry is questionable. Ḥaydar, who at one point says that he was brought to Āqsū from the Qalmāq territory (i.e. western Mongolia),[114] calls him a son of the khan Esen Buqa (d. *c.* 1320) and says that his mother, a concubine, had been married off by the khan's jealous wife to the amir Dukhtui and had then given birth to Tughluq Temür.[115] Timurid sources, by contrast, claim that Tughluq Temür's father was another of Du'a's sons, Emil Khwāja, and *Muʿizz al-ansāb* goes so far as to allege that the boy was rumoured to be Dukhtui's son;[116] this may, of course, be merely propaganda on behalf of the Timurid dynasty, which had an interest in disparaging the legitimacy of the rival Chaghadayid line. It is worth noting, however, that in the 1360s Tughluq Temür had been accepted as an authentic descendant of Chaghadai by elements in the western part of the ulus, including Timur himself (see pp. 234, 254–5).[117]

The division of the khanate was not as yet definitive.[118] Qazaghan's death was followed by the short-lived paramountcy of his son ʿAbd-Allāh, who murdered Bayan Quli and replaced him with a titular khan of his own, another of Du'a's grandsons named Temür Shāh, only to be overthrown by a group of rebel amirs. For the next year or two, as far as we are aware, there was no khan,[119] and each of the amirs, labelled by Timurid authors 'the factional princes' (*mulūk al-ṭawā'if*),[120] became autonomous within his own locality. Shāmī and Yazdī employ the same phrase, 'strife and discord' (*fitna-u āshūb*), for this situation as had been used for the 'Great Troubles' in the Jochid ulus.[121]

Tughluq Temür took advantage of these conditions to invade Transoxiana twice, in 761/1360 and 762/1361, securing his own recognition as khan by the majority of the western amirs. On the second occasion he left his son Ilyās Khwāja as his lieutenant, but after being recalled to Mughūlistān to succeed his dead father (764/1362–3)[122] the prince only returned once to Transoxiana in an unsuccessful attempt to recover the region. Ilyās Khwāja was killed in or soon after 1369, along with many other members of the dynasty, by the Dughlāt amir Qamar al-Dīn, who provoked vigorous opposition from other amirs in Mughūlistān by arrogating to himself the title of khan.[123] Qamar al-Dīn's provocation of Timur exposed the ulus to a series of attacks from the west and eventually he was brought down; Khiḍr Khwāja, purportedly another son of Tughluq Temür, was raised up as khan in *c.* 1388. From the mid-1360s, the two halves of the ulus followed separate destinies, though well into the next century the eastern khans persisted in regarding Transoxiana as rightfully their own possession, usurped by Timur and his dynasty.[124]

The ulus of Chaghadai differed from the Ilkhanate and the Qipchaq khanate. Firstly, the contest here involved only two khans, in Transoxiana and in Mughūlistān, rather than many, with shifting spheres of influence, as in the Jochid lands. Secondly, local non-Chinggisid dynasts did not profit from the crisis to secure their own independence as they did in the former Ilkhanate and in Jochid Khwārazm. In Transoxiana there are signs that some of the *mulūk al-ṭawā'if* aspired to autonomous status: Kaykhusraw of Khuttalān, for example, and the shah of Badakhshān, whose coins omitted the khan's name from 769/1367–8.[125] But here both processes – fragmentation and the emancipation of non-Mongol principalities – were arrested by Timur. In the eastern Chaghadayid dominions, the absence of similar attempts at self-assertion may simply be due to the fact that (to the best of our knowledge) no local Muslim client dynasties had survived far into the fourteenth century.[126] A line of Buddhist Uighur *iduq-qut*s had apparently ruled in Qarākhwāja and Beshbaligh as Chaghadayid vassals,[127] but for how long is unknown. True, the power of the Dughlāt in Kāshghar may date from this era, particularly given the pivotal role of Dughlāt amirs in enthroning

Tughluq Temür and his putative son Khiḍr Khwāja – if, that is, we can trust the later testimony of Ḥaydar, hardly inclined to minimise his ancestors' role in events (see pp. 235–6). Yet the Dughlāt lands remained an integral part of the eastern khanate; there was no counterpart to the Ṣūfī amirs in Khwārazm, the Kartids at Herat or even the Jalayirids. This perhaps indicates the resilience of the Chaghadayid central power, for all its general air of instability.

THE ROOTS OF UPHEAVAL

How can we account for the upheavals that racked the three western Mongol polities between 1335 and *c.* 1370? This question is the subject of a stimulating discussion by Melville. He proposes that the Ilkhanate had 'lost its way and its sense of identity in the turbulence of acculturation' and forfeited the loyalty of the amirs: the abandonment of various elements of the Chinggisid dispensation had left the Mongol elite comparatively rudderless and encouraged them to pursue their own sectional interests rather than those of the dynasty.[128] The following remarks are meant to amplify and further develop these ideas.

Naturally, we are in no position to judge how far self-interest dictated the actions of the amirs during earlier reigns, and it does not seem facile to observe that the intervention of the overmighty amir was almost by definition infectious, and the fragmentation of power thus self-perpetuating, once one such figure had acted as kingmaker and demonstrated to his rivals that it was feasible. Yet Melville is right to point to an important difference from earlier conflicts over the Ilkhanid throne: that whereas these had involved princes with administrative experience who staked their claims in person, after 1336 amirs plucked candidates from the shadows with a view primarily to legitimising their own actions;[129] and on occasion, we might add, discarded them when they had outlived their usefulness.

According to Naṭanzī, the Chobanid Ashraf was assured by his advisers in the early 1340s that the Chinggisid dynasty had forfeited its time-honoured good fortune (*ughūr*).[130] Niẓām al-Dīn Yaḥyā Ibn al-Ḥakīm, one of al-ʿUmarī's informants, possibly furnishes an illustration of this, alleging that in Iran princes of the blood were the object of the ruler's fear and mistrust, with the result that many courted invisibility and adopted some lowly calling like weaver or tanner as a means of disclaiming any ambition. He further impugns the origins of any of Hülegü's current descendants, given the tendency of their womenfolk to play their husbands false and of the fathers to consort with commoners.[131] A few years later, in his *Ta'rīf*, al-ʿUmarī alleges that Sulaymān's lineage and his precise claim to the throne were uncertain; he acknowledges the authenticity of Taghai Temür's ancestry, but says that the names of his forebears were unknown.[132] The remark about royal women may illustrate little more than a taste for scurrility on Ibn al-Ḥakīm's part; but in any event the proliferation of Chinggisid princes would naturally have fostered doubt as to the genuineness of royal blood. According to the contemporary source used by the later author Ibn Fatḥ-Allāh, ʿAlī Pādishāh only alleged (*za'ama*) that Mūsā was descended from Baidu.[133] The belief in some quarters that Muḥammad Khan – as al-ʿUmarī was told – was the only living Hülegüid whose antecedents were sure (though even this was disputed in many quarters) probably reflects the obscurity of so many Chinggisids.[134]

The Chinggisid dynasty adhered to the idea of collective sovereignty, whereby every male member of the *altan urugh* was entitled to a share of territory and was eligible for succession to the dignity of khan. But since the centralising measures in Ghazan's reign,[135] many of Hülegü's line no longer possessed independent resources as their birthright; they might not even possess military experience, something of a handicap in the current situation. It is no accident that the Ilkhan who enjoyed the longest reign after 1335 – Taghai Temür – was born into a branch of the imperial dynasty that had entered Iran from outside with its military retinue a generation or two previously (see p. 80); he had inherited from his father pasturelands in the vicinity of Sarakhs, along with a body of dependants, followers and troops (*atbā'-u ashiyā'-u ḥasham-u lashgariyān*).[136] Ibn Baṭṭūṭa credits him, as Ilkhan, with an army totalling 50,000.[137] By contrast, prior to his accession, Arpa is said to have fallen on hard times as a day-guard (*muyāwama*) in Abū Saʿīd's reign.[138] He put to death an

Ögödeyid prince, Tükel Qutlugh, and his two sons, almost at the very moment of their arrival as refugees from Transoxiana, from fear that they might be deemed more eligible for the throne than himself.[139] Perhaps they had come at the head of a respectable military force (or just possibly, as descendants of Chinggis Khan's designated successor, they benefited from a prestige that the Toluid Ilkhan lacked).

Arpa's successors were similarly without resources of their own. Mūsā – grandson of an Ilkhan whom Ghazan had dethroned and executed – had been earning his bread in obscurity as a weaver (*nassāj*) in Baghdad until his 'discovery' by ʿAlī Pādishāh, to whose attention he had been brought by a silk-weaver (*shaʿrbāfī*) from that city.[140] According to al-Dhahabī, Muḥammad had been living as an ordinary member of the populace in Tabriz.[141] One of the last shadow Ilkhans, Anūshīrwān, was keeper of the wardrobe (*qubchachi*) to Malik Ashraf, although if, as the manuscript of Zayn al-Dīn's work suggests, he was 'of the stock of the *ke'ün*s' (meaning, presumably, that he had Chinggisid blood),[142] this would explain an otherwise puzzling choice. Moreover, it is striking that contemporary observers regarded some of these monarchs as remarkably youthful. In Shabānkāra'ī's account, Mūsā is called a young man (although authors writing in the Mamlūk empire say that he was forty).[143] Al-Shujāʿī describes both Muḥammad and Sulaymān as hardly more than boys, while al-Dhahabī alleges that Muḥammad was aged only ten.[144]

On the other hand, shadow khans were not necessarily selected for their lack of energy and might not fulfil expectations even if they were. Arpa, a military man, was hardly a puppet,[145] though Āmulī regarded him as lacking in judgement.[146] Shabānkāra'ī tells us that ʿAlī Pādishāh had initially selected another prince in opposition to Arpa, but that when Mūsā was brought to his attention he discerned in him greater signs of royal birth.[147] Mūsā showed himself capable of invigorating his supporters in time of adversity,[148] and even Sulaymān exhibited a certain initiative once he was free of Ashraf's tutelage. Taghai Temür, who did not strike contemporaries as overly intelligent and is characterised by Aubin as 'an odd and limited personality',[149] may have been envisaged by his backers as a marionette. Yet although Ḥāfiẓ-i Abrū would later describe him as having little freedom of action and lacking in resolution,[150] and although Faryūmadī concedes that the scope of his sway was restricted and that his reign was a period of instability and unrest for Khurāsān, the latter also praises Taghai Temür for his sense of justice and other laudable qualities, judging him worthy of the throne of Chinggis Khan.[151] Taghai Temür thus appears to have proved less of a cipher than some of his competitors. It is perhaps significant that in al-Shujāʿī's narrative Abū Saʿīd's former amirs in 739/1339 rallied to Taghai Temür and his (temporary) ally Shaykh Ḥasan against Ḥasan-i Kūchak and Satibeg, whose support is said to have comprised, rather, 'empty-headed youths' (*shabāb jahala*).[152] This might indicate the persistence of a party among the amirs who favoured a return to stronger rule and an end to conflict.

Nevertheless, the tendency to promote relatively impotent figures to the dignity of khan may have been more pronounced in the Ilkhanate than elsewhere in the Mongol world. In the enormous Jochid territories, the different branches of the imperial line had retained their grazing grounds, and numerous princes possessed lands, revenues and a military following,[153] enjoying a status more analogous to powerful amirs. In 787/1385–6 the army that Toqtamish sent to devastate Azerbaijan would include no less than twelve Jochid princes.[154] There is indeed a striking contrast with late Ilkhanid Iran – and possibly with the Northern Yuan after 1388, where the Qaghans, it has been suggested, lacked their own independent bases of support and were reliant on a powerful backer.[155] Not that the Jochid khans during the 'Great Troubles' necessarily enjoyed extensive power. A Rus′ chronicler was under the impression that Muḥammad, Mamai's khan in the 1370s, was no more than a figurehead and that Mamai put him to death, assuming the style of khan himself only a short time before his defeat by the Muscovite army at Kulikovo Pol′e (1380).[156] We have no evidence, however, that any of the rival candidates in Batu's ulus was a private individual lacking the resources to mount his own bid for the throne.

We know less about the khans of Chaghadai's ulus. It undoubtedly furnishes one example of a mere cipher. Kābul (or Qabūl) Shāh, who was propelled onto the throne by Timur's then ally, Amīr Ḥusayn in 765/1363–4, is expressly said to have been living as a recluse with a view to keeping at bay the perils of the age – an assertion that echoes al-ʿUmarī's description of the predicament of Ilkhanid princes a little earlier.[157] As we shall see (pp. 339–40), however, khans on occasion grew restive under the tutelage of a *qarachu* amir. It is also evident from the narratives of Timur's early career that the Chaghadayid ulus, like the Qipchaq khanate, contained princes at the head of their own military retinues; they included the Ögödeyid Soyurghatmish, whom Shāmī describes as one of the great amirs before his nomination as khan.[158] Neither of Timur's two khans was a passive nonentity, and both would play a prominent role in military affairs.[159]

With the passage of the generations, then, the number of eligible candidates for the dignity of khan had mushroomed enormously, which may have contributed to a devaluation of Chinggisid descent.[160] But a marked characteristic of the period immediately preceding the fourteenth-century crises in the Chinggisid world was that the succession had come to be concentrated within one sub-branch of the imperial line,[161] at the expense of the pattern which Fletcher termed 'tanistry' (see p. 73) and which seems to have held sway in the early decades after Chinggis Khan's death. Thus the choice of Qaghan after 1294 was confined to the descendants of Qubilai's second son Jimgim. In the Ilkhanate and the Qipchaq steppe the transition was certainly eased by the actions of both Ghazan in 696–7/1296–7 and Özbeg in 712/1312–13, respectively, in executing a number of princes who might otherwise have claimed the throne when the occasion offered.[162] As a result, Ghazan (whose own offspring had died in infancy) was able to transmit the kingship to his brother Öljeitü, and the latter to pass it on to his young son Abū Saʿīd. Özbeg was succeeded by two of his sons and then by his grandson Berdibeg; Janibeg and Berdibeg had followed Özbeg's example by killing kinsmen.[163] But even in Chaghadai's ulus, where Du'a – to the best of our knowledge – had not resorted to such drastic measures as Ghazan or Özbeg and his successors, six of his numerous sons were able to monopolise the succession for the period from

706/1307 to 735/1334, save for a brief interval (708–709/1308–1309 or 1310). During that interval the throne was occupied by a distant, and possibly senior, relative,[164] to whom Yasa'ur and his sons Khalīl Sulṭān and Qazan, khans in the 1340s, would be closely related, so that we may be witnessing here opposition between two rival Chaghadayid lines.[165]

Now we know that in the thirteenth and early fourteenth centuries voices had been raised in favour of the older tradition of lateral succession and seniority. In the Blue Horde in 701/1301–2, for instance, Bayan's right to succeed his father Qonichi had been challenged by a cousin, who rested his claim on the fact that his own father had ruled the ulus at an earlier date.[166] Some decades later, even credentials of this kind had become dispensable. In the Qipchaq khanate, right down into the fifteenth century, we are confronted by a baffling sequence of rulers whose kinship with a previous sovereign was remote, to say the least, most obviously Bazarchi (see earlier). In Chaghadai's ulus descendants of Ögödei, and in the Ilkhanate, both Arpa, of the line of Arigh Böke, and Taghai Temür, a descendant of Chinggis Khan's brother Jochi Qasar, could now be considered as candidates; while in the Yuan dominions an Ögödeyid named Alughui Temür made an unsuccessful attempt to take the imperial throne in 1360–1.[167] What facilitated the opening-up of the succession in the Ilkhanate, of course, was the fact that the branch descended from Arghun had become extinct in the male line. But the disputes we have examined in this chapter possibly involved the rejection of primogeniture as an alien practice borrowed from outside Mongol culture; and perhaps in all three western khanates we see the emergence of a conservative element bent on reasserting an older, more quintessentially Chinggisid pattern of succession. The advocacy of Arpa's candidature by the wazir Ghiyāth al-Dīn – not otherwise known as a diehard proponent of conservative steppe tradition – may have sprung from recognition of the strength of this feeling within Iran.[168]

It is certainly conceivable that the ties that bound the Ilkhanid Mongol elite to steppe tradition were loosening. Both the enthronement of Arpa and then ʿAlī Pādishāh's proclamation of Mūsā as

Ilkhan had taken place without the usual quriltai, while the assembly in Khurāsān which chose Taghai Temür, though termed a quriltai by Faryūmadī, was merely a gathering of amirs, officials and shaykhs.[169] We can also discern a growing tension in the Ilkhanate between the centralising Persian bureaucratic tradition and the conservative instincts of many Mongol noyans intent on limiting the power of the centre. Melville sees the appointment of the wazir Ghiyāth al-Dīn to command the army during Abū Saʿīd's last months as symptomatic of the breakdown of distinctions between the Mongol ruling elite and Tājīk officials – and hence an affront to Mongol sensibilities.[170]

But reverence for Chinggis Khan's line (as opposed to its individual members, perhaps) was a different matter. As McChesney points out, the 'Chinggisid principle remained sacrosanct in political thought' into the sixteenth century and beyond, if until then 'dormant in political life'.[171] Just as Janibeg dismissed Ashraf's entitlement to rule in Azerbaijan,[172] in the western Chaghadayid ulus Qazaghan's swift reaction to the adoption of the title Sultan by the *malik* Muʿīzz al-Dīn Pīr Ḥusayn of Herat (see later, pp. 181–2, 218–19) also indicates an abiding sense of the exclusive qualification of Chinggisids – rather than upstart Tājīk princes – for sovereignty.[173]

Attachment to the dynasty persisted even longer elsewhere. Naṭanzī testifies to its strength among the amirs of Mughūlistān. 'Nobody', he assures us, 'while the line (*urugh*) of Chinggis Khan existed, would think of subjecting himself to a *qarachu*.'[174] When Ilyās Khwāja was taken prisoner by the forces of Timur and his ally Amīr Ḥusayn in 765/1363–4, without consulting their leaders some of his captors set him free, out of what Yazdī calls 'the loyalty to the khan that is ingrained in the Turks' nature'.[175] In that part of the Qipchaq khanate where Mamai was master, we learn from a Rus′ source that extensive devotion to his khan provoked him into killing not merely the khan but also numerous amirs.[176] The brevity of Mamai's own 'reign' as khan, and the strong opposition in Mughūlistān to Qamar al-Dīn's usurpation, attest to a widespread readiness to champion the rights of the *altan urugh*. All this has implications for the question of the dynasty's prestige. Regardless of the sentiments expressed by Ashraf's entourage in the 1340s, one has only to observe

Timurid interest in Chinggisid marriage connections to see that the legitimising properties of Chinggisid blood had scarcely diminished – even if Timur's own stance, by 1405, on the maintenance of a Chinggisid khan is not easy to fathom.

Let us turn to the dilution of Mongol identity. At the highest level, whereas the Ilkhan Arghun had been unfamiliar with the Persian script, his grandson Abū Saʿīd wrote a fine Persian hand and composed Persian verse.[177] During the several decades that had elapsed since the arrival of Mongol noyans and garrison troops in Afghanistan, Iran, Iraq and Anatolia, they had been undergoing a process of acculturation. Ibn Faḍl-Allāh al-ʿUmarī bears witness to this, telling us that by his day (*c.* 738/1337–8) the Mongols in the Pontic steppe had become increasingly intermingled with, and absorbed by, the subject nomad population of Qipchaq tribesmen. He also writes of social intercourse and intermarriage between Mongol and Persian notables.[178] Moreover, we know from Waṣṣāf that the Jurma'ī Mongols settled on the borders of Kirmān were intermarrying with the local population by the late 1270s.[179] Coexistence of this kind raised the spectre of the abandonment of the pastoralist lifestyle, for so long seen as the backbone of nomad power. In 744/1343–4 Ashraf felt the need to remind his supporters that it was not customary for the Mongols to reside in towns and that this was contrary to Chinggis Khan's Yasa.[180]

It is unthinkable that the process of acculturation – piecemeal as it was and doubtless varying in speed from one region of Western Asia to another – did not involve limited acceptance of Islamic norms and sometimes the profession of the Islamic faith. What now offended Muslim sentiment was probably not so much Mongol paganism as the combination of Islamic credo and practice with a continued allegiance to steppe custom and the Yasa. In the vassal kingdom of Herat, for instance, Ibn Baṭṭūṭa speaks of a clash between Mongol elements and a Muslim jurist, an advocate of rigorous adherence to the Sharīʿa who condemned the laxity engendered by Chinggis Khan's Yasa and was killed by the Mongols in 737/1337.[181] We saw earlier how Herat's malik Muʿizz al-Dīn proclaimed in 750/1349 that the practices of the infidels were at an end. Back in the late 1330s word had reached the Mamlūk territories that the Ilkhan Arpa was a Christian (a claim corroborated by an Armenian chronicler, though hardly borne out by Arpa's assumption of the regnal style Muʿizz al-Dunyā wa l-Dīn Maḥmūd), and that he had obliged the Mongols to wear the traditional headgear (*al-sarāqūjāt*), denounced the grandees for having made peace with the Muslims (that is, the Mamlūks), and entertained designs on Syria.[182] Shabānkāra'ī depicts Arpa as living in the 'Mongol style' and observing the usages of Chinggis Khan, while Ahrī says that he ruled in accordance with the Yasa, disregarded the edicts of Öljeitü and Abū Saʿīd and spent all the revenues on the troops (*cherig*).[183]

At the opposite pole, Janibeg in the Qipchaq khanate appears to have proceeded further along the path of Islamisation than had his father Özbeg, compelling his troops to don turban and cloak (and thus to discard traditional Mongol attire).[184] In Chaghadai's ulus, according to sources from the Mamlūk empire, the convert khan Tarmashirin abrogated the Yasa and promoted the Sharīʿa.[185] But within only a few years Changshi, allegedly at the prompting of Buddhist monks (*bakhshī*s), was installing transportable pagodas in his camp and causing images to be painted on the walls of mosques.[186] Then, after another brief interval, Muslim amirs, if Ibn Baṭṭūṭa can be trusted, seem to have rallied in support of Khalīl Sulṭān's bid for the throne in what they perceived as a jihad.[187] Evidently this was an era characterised by spasmodic – and sometimes rapid and enforced – cultural change.

A manifest volte-face in foreign policy could equally take on the complexion of an unwelcome cultural shift, as the aforementioned testimony regarding Arpa's antipathy towards peace with Egypt reminds us. The treaty between Abū Saʿīd and the Mamlūk Sultan al-Nāṣir Muḥammad in 1323 closed the door on an era that had promised (intermittently) booty and other perquisites of service in the field.[188] A parallel situation arose in the Chaghadayid ulus – more conspicuously, in fact, since by 1335 the khans had made peace with enemies on two fronts. In the east, Köpek's termination of conflict with the Yuan in 1323 appears to have provoked resentment among the Chaghadayid elite.[189] Following his invasion of India in 730/1329

Tarmashirin seems to have entered into a more amicable relationship with the Delhi Sultan Muḥammad b. Tughluq (724–752/1324–1351), reflected in the exchange of letters and gifts.[190] The only major avenue of plunder and expansion open to Chaghadai's ulus was now Ilkhanid Khurāsān. These rapprochements entailed the jettisoning of what had been a constant element in Mongol foreign relations from the outset – and the flouting of one of Chinggis Khan's most memorable *yasa*s, forbidding his descendants to make peace with any outside power in the absence of submission. Such flagrant disregard for Chinggisid canon was not just acutely disorientating. It may also have seemed tantamount to abject political failure – though no failure could match that of the hapless Qaghan Toghan Temür, whose loss of territory in China to insurgent groups by 1360 enabled the rebel Ögödeyid prince Alughui Temür (see earlier) to challenge his very right to rule on the basis that he manifestly no longer enjoyed Heaven's favour.[191]

This chapter has drawn attention to developments which could be seen as conducive to a growing disequilibrium in the Mongol world between the 1320s and *c.* 1350 – developments that administered a shock to the political ideology underlying the Chinggisid empire or that provoked a reaction on the part of conservative-minded elements. But during this period the Mongol states were also assailed by economic difficulties and by the major demographic convulsion known as the Black Death. These will be the subject of the following chapter.

CHAPTER 5
THE CRISIS OF THE MONGOL WORLD: ECONOMIC TURBULENCE AND DEMOGRAPHIC DISASTER

When Timur first emerged into prominence within Chaghadai's ulus, the Chinggisid states had not merely been beset by crises of a dynastic or sociocultural nature but had been affected by developments that lay outside the sphere of politics or religious change and that embraced a wider area of Asia. The conquests of Chinggis Khan and his successors had led to the emergence of what we might call a 'global' network, but which might more accurately be termed a trans-continental one. The economic developments we are about to examine involved, in part, disruption of that network and undermined the stability of the Mongol khanates and their trading partners. But alongside them we must also consider climatic fluctuations and a general shift to harsher weather, possible outbreaks of livestock disease, and (certainly) the spread of plague far beyond its reservoir regions in eastern Central Asia and its invasion of human populations for the first time since the eleventh century.[1] The aim will be to assess whether these events contributed to Timur's rise and conquests.

COMMERCIAL AND MONETARY MALAISE

The cost of Mongol imperial expansion and inter-Mongol warfare to the subjugated peoples was undeniably high. It is too easy to discount these ordeals in view of the benefits of greatly extended commercial contacts, or a marked efflorescence of historical writing in Persian, or unprecedented cultural exchange across the breadth of Asia. But Mongol rule, once the conquest process had come to a halt, had introduced some degree of order into a world hitherto split among a host of lesser powers. The existence of a *Pax Mongolica* has surely been overstated.[2] Yet the Mongols, who like earlier nomadic powers manifested a strong interest in the growth of trade, reduced transaction costs by eliminating many of the competing polities that had previously levied dues on commercial activity; the khans and the elite protected commerce and engaged in transactions themselves, using the prodigious quantities of plunder they had acquired to pay inflated prices for goods.[3] The commercial contacts generated by their enormous empire extended over vast distances. An important consequence of the creation of the Chinggisid polity – even after its fragmentation into separate khanates in the 1260s – was thus a growing 'interconnectedness'[4] between regions of Asia as diverse as the Pontic–Caspian steppes, China, south-east Asia, the Indian subcontinent, Iran and the Near East. This was reflected in the geographical expansion of long-distance trade and travel; much of it passed overland, although a growing proportion went by the sea route. In sections of his work written by 702/1303, Waṣṣāf describes the island of Qays (Kīsh) in the Persian Gulf as a magnet for the products of India, the furthest parts of China, Turkestan, Egypt, Syria and distant Qayrawān in Tunisia, a situation he clearly viewed as without precedent.[5] Fifty years later the papal envoy John of Marignolli wrote of Hurmuz as a place where merchants gathered from all over the world.[6]

There was also a marked growth in the links between Asia and Christian Europe, marked by the establishment of the Genoese in Kaffa from 1266 and the Venetians in Tana, at the mouth of the River Don, some years later. These ports became the north-western termini of the trans-Asiatic trade routes (the so-called Silk Roads) linking Europe with Central Asia and China, and Italian traders began to travel further east than ever before in quest of silk, spices and other precious commodities. Western European merchants, predominantly Genoese, were to be found in China from the 1290s.[7]

Among westerners who entered the Mongols' service was the Qaghan Qubilai's celebrated agent, Marco Polo.

Mongol expansion also contributed to an economic quickening through the dethesaurisation of precious metals. From an early date the Mongols had manifested a concern to secure tribute, at least in part, in specie, as they did, for example, from China, from the Koryŏ kingdom and from the Seljuq Sultanate of Anatolia;[8] and a great proportion of this gold and silver was melted down and converted into ingots, called in the sources *bālish* or *yastuq* (Rubruck's *iascot* or, more correctly, *iastoc*).[9] It is evident both from Rubruck's narrative and from Juwaynī's anecdotes regarding the generosity of the Qaghan Ögödei that great quantities of silver ingots were bestowed as largesse.[10] In northern China the Mongols continued to rely on the use of paper notes as the Jin had done, and from 1260 Qubilai instituted a single monetary system based on a paper currency (*chao*) backed by adequate bullion reserves and redeemable, in principle, for silver.[11] Having acquired the treasury of the vanquished Song empire in the late 1270s,[12] however, the Yuan paid for the heavy cost of the campaign by issuing an unprecedented volume of paper currency that was no longer redeemable for silver.[13] As a result, abundant quantities of uncoined silver were exported from China to Western Asia, where silver commanded a much higher price. The commercial handbook of the Florentine banker Pegolotti (*c.* 1330) bears witness to the widespread use of the silver ingot, known as *sommo* (or *somo*), in transactions from the Qipchaq khanate to the borders of the Yuan empire.[14] The *sommo* came to serve as a money of account, expressed in terms of a certain weight of silver. The late thirteenth and mid-fourteenth centuries witnessed greatly increased outputs of silver coinage across Western Europe, Egypt, the Delhi Sultanate and Bengal.[15]

So much for the general pattern. What is less clear is the mutual interplay between regional developments and the wider interconnected economic system. Let us begin with northern India, which had witnessed a decline in the value of gold thanks to the accumulation of enormous stocks of the metal, as both plunder and tribute, in the course of campaigns against the Hindu states of the Deccan and the far south by the armies of the Khaljī Sultans of Delhi in the years 695–718/1296–1318.[16] The early years of the Delhi Sultan Muḥammad b. Tughluq (724–752/1324–1351) saw a problematic shortage of silver and a disturbance in the gold–silver ratio. The sultan, who at this stage was seeking to raise troops in unprecedented numbers in support of his ambitious anti-Chaghadayid foreign policy, was led first to issue debased silver *tanga*s in 727/1326–7 and then to embark on an ill-starred token currency of bronze (*muhr-i mis*) in the years 730–2/1330–2 (allegedly in imitation of Chinese paper money).[17] Precisely what economic impact these developments had further west is uncertain, but both Egypt and the Ilkhanate experienced monetary turbulence in the 1330s. The continued depreciation of gold is referred to by Ḥamd-Allāh Mustawfī, who tells us in his *Nuzhat al-qulūb* (*c.* 1340) that the sharp increase in Muḥammad's expenditure had led to a fall in the value of gold in India (that is, a shift in the gold–silver ratio in favour of the cheaper metal): it was therefore no longer advantageous to export gold to India and the direction of this traffic was now reversed.[18]

For some decades, the Ilkhans, as a matter of policy, had manipulated bullion flows with a view to capitalising on, and accentuating, fluctuations in the gold–silver rate. From *c.* 690/1291, they did so to considerable effect, with the result that the Mamlūk empire was excluded from the bullion trade and its capacity to mint gold and silver coinage greatly diminished.[19] Throughout the ensuing three decades Egypt suffered from a scarcity of silver.[20] (This is not to deny that local circumstances contributed to a fall in the value of gold in Egypt.)[21] The disintegration of central authority in the Ilkhanate after Abū Saʿīd's death, however, caused a (partial) withdrawal of international merchants, a diminution of the transit trade along the east–west route through Iran and a decline in Ilkhanid bullion stocks, which can be seen to have peaked shortly before, in 734/1333–4.[22] The resulting demonetisation of the Ilkhanid economy coincided with a tail-off in the bullion trade, since the gold–silver ratios in both the European and Asiatic zones had reached parity and it was no longer profitable to exchange one metal for another.[23] In addition, the Ilkhans' revenue declined by over 50 per cent between

Ghazan's reign and *c.* 1340, owing to political in-fighting and disorder in the provinces.[24]

It should be noted that the economic situation in Central Asia may present a contrast with that in the Ilkhanate. Seemingly the silver mines in the Talās (Ṭarāz) region, which had flourished a few centuries earlier, were being exploited once more by *c.* 1250 by a group of German miners whom the Mongols had enslaved, most probably, in Transylvania in 1241–2.[25] The Talās mint is strongly represented in a hoard of coins dated from 671/1272–3 onwards, and the nearby mint at Kenjek was producing a plentiful coinage by the early fourteenth century.[26] It may be that the increased availability of silver was one circumstance underlying the monetary reforms of Masʿūd Beg around this time. Standardisation of coinage is among the reforms associated with the Chaghadayid khan Köpek (*c.* 1320–1326). Ibn Faḍl-Allāh al-ʿUmarī tells us that by his own day the Chaghadayid dinar enjoyed a high reputation for fineness,[27] and that the accession of the Muslim convert Tarmashirin (*c.* 1330), followed by his abolition of *mukūs* (taxes not sanctioned by the Sharīʿa), had made the Chaghadayid territories a magnet for traders from Egypt and Syria.[28] Here the political chaos that followed Tarmashirin's overthrow may have had a similar impact to the economic and political conditions in the Ilkhanate after Abū Saʿīd's death.

In an article on the origins of the Black Death, John Norris proposed that the conversion of the westerly Mongol khanates to Islam had impeded commerce and caused 'breaks between them . . . and the Christians of the West', and that 'communication along the Central Asian tracks through the khanates was very difficult for Western, or even Persian, traders, and after about 1340 virtually impossible'. He further argued that 'in the fifteen years before the outbreak, there was no warfare and very little communication between the Khanate of the Golden Horde and any of the states to the east of it'.[29] Benedictow writes of 'fulminating anti-Christian attitudes', so that 'the presence of Christian merchants was considered increasingly intolerable', citing as illustration Janibeg's attack on Kaffa in 1343.[30]

These assumptions risk exaggerating the duration and geographical scope of such commercial disruption as occurred. It is certainly true that, as Pegolotti asserts, merchants could fall victim to the upheavals unleashed by a ruler's death,[31] and a few years later the Franciscan missionary Paschal de Vittoria reports that the caravan in which he travelled was held up in 'the cities of the Saracens' from fear of war and pillage consequent upon the murder of the Chaghadayid khan Changshi by his brother Yesün Temür (1337).[32] On the other hand, ʿAlī Sulṭān's oppression of Christian missionaries in the Chaghadayid dominions in 1339/40 (when an Italian merchant shared their fate) had been brief.[33] There were indeed instances of Muslim princes plundering the goods of western traders, as the Chobanids Ḥasan (-i Kūchak) and Ashraf did in Azerbaijan during the late 1330s and the 1340s.[34] Yet the impulse behind this was hardly religious. Ashraf acted in this predatory fashion towards his own subjects;[35] and by 753/1352 Persian merchants who had suffered at the Chobanids' hands had allegedly been emigrating for some years in great numbers into Mamlūk territory and were unwilling to go back.[36] Nor was Janibeg waging some kind of jihad. He was reacting, rather, to the killing of a Mongol by a Venetian in Tana in 1343 and was further intent on curbing the efforts of the Genoese to establish their autonomy at the expense of his sovereignty over Kaffa. He restored the Venetians' rights as early as December 1347, and thereafter Italian traders were able to resume commercial activity in the Black Sea region.[37]

Moreover, neither Chobanid depredations nor Janibeg's brief reprisals against the Italians had implications for the trade routes east of the Ural River, through Turkestan. This too was admittedly subject to interruption. Marignolli was ordered to return from China by sea in 1344–5, owing to fighting in Central Asia.[38] In March 1345 word reached Kaffa that the road through the 'Middle Empire' (*caminum Inperii* [sic] *de medio*, *llo chamin de llo Imperio de Meço*; namely, the Chaghadayid territories), which had been reportedly open in the previous October, was now 'entirely blocked'[39] for reasons unknown. In the short term, the 'War of the Straits' between Genoa and Venice in the years 1350–5 certainly prevented traders from either city capitalising on such opportunities as existed.[40] One circumstance that had a major long-term impact on trans-Asiatic trade at this time – and on the participation of western merchants in particular – was the resumption of commerce between the Italian mercantile cities and the Mamlūk empire in 1345.[41] By 1400 the volume of spices reaching Venice by way of Alexandria or Beirut dwarfed the quantity that arrived on the overland route via Tana.[42] This was a gradual development (though Barbaro links the diversion of the silk and spice trade to Syria with Timur's sack of Astrakhan).[43] But the picture of sustained commercial paralysis immediately preceding the Black Death, as outlined by Norris and Benedictow, is not fully borne out by the evidence.

Commercial activity and government revenues within the Mongol world can hardly have remained untouched by a combination of monetary fluctuation and a (limited) slackening of trans-Asiatic commerce, reducing the resources of a khan and the wherewithal to retain the loyalty of his amirs and hence eroding the solidarity of the elite. Conceivably, therefore, the onset of political instability in the three western Mongol khanates came about in part through economic difficulties that they shared with their principal neighbours and trading partners,[44] but we lack sufficient evidence to be sure.

THE SECOND PANDEMIC

What role did a changing environment play in the Mongol world of the late thirteenth and early fourteenth centuries? One important question relates to the role of climatic variation,[45] to which thirteenth-century volcanic activity – and perhaps chiefly the massive eruption of the Samalas volcano in Indonesia (1258)[46] – may have contributed. That severe climatic change over two decades or so could prompt tribal migration and engender the collapse of a political system has been convincingly argued apropos of the fall of the Liao in China (1123–5).[47] It is a strong possibility that the end of the Medieval Climate Anomaly around the turn of the thirteenth century had far-reaching effects in Eurasia, introducing a sequence of climatic extremes – decidedly colder weather and increased precipitation – that have been identified by means of proxy data such as tree-ring density.[48] Certainly the Timurid sources yield evidence of the harshest winter conditions in Transoxiana and the territories to the north and east, which inflicted heavy losses in men and livestock during Timur's campaigns in Mughūlistān and the Qipchaq steppes and sometimes obliged him to suspend operations for many weeks, as on his very last campaign. On at least two occasions, in 778/1376–7 and 807/1404, at the onset of the China expedition, the Sīr-daryā was frozen over.[49]

No less important may have been the role of plague, which was in all likelihood linked with climatic change.[50] One symptom of the growing interconnectedness between hitherto comparatively segregated regions during the Mongol period was the emergence of what Emmanuel Le Roy Ladurie christened a 'common market' of microbes and Samuel Adshead called 'a single uniform disease structure'.[51] In the middle years of the fourteenth century, Eurasia experienced the second of the three great plague pandemics in world history. Generally known in European historiography as the Black Death, the second pandemic went on to effect a considerable reduction in the populations of Europe, where the death toll probably exceeded 45 per cent in some regions, and of the Near East, where the mortality in the Mamlūk dominions in 748–50/1347–9 may have been at least as high as one-third.[52] Recurrent strikes in the Near East and Europe, beginning in the early 1360s and the mid-1370s, continued beyond 1500. We have a more or less clear idea of the socio-economic consequences of plague for the predominantly agrarian societies of Western Europe and the agrarian regimes of Muslim Egypt and Syria.[53] Regrettably, for the Black Death in the Islamic world – even in the Mamlūk empire – we have nothing like the rich trove of sources available for the progress of plague in Western Europe (although even those sources fail to provide unequivocal answers to many questions).[54] The Iranian world and the Mongol khanates to the north yield less material still. The Black Death therefore tends to appear only fleetingly in the secondary literature on these regions or to be ignored altogether.

At this juncture, a few words are in order concerning the trend of scholarship on the Black Death. Research on human remains at various European sites has left no room for doubt that this was plague, by identifying the DNA of the plague bacillus, *Yersinia pestis*.[55] Moreover, recent palaeogenetic investigation of material from two Nestorian Christian graveyards in present-day Kyrgyzstan (see later) has likewise uncovered incontrovertible evidence of *Yersinia pestis*.[56] Palaeogenetic research by a team of scholars headed by Cui Yujun established that the plague bacillus had previously undergone a 'Big Bang', a process of polytomy – genetic divergence – into four distinct lineages, of which Branch 1 is associated with the European Black Death and Branch 2 was spread over an area that extended from the Caucasus through Central Asia and Tibet to China.[57] The team located the remote origins of the polytomy in the third or fourth quarter of the thirteenth century, in the north-eastern regions of the Qinghai–Tibet plateau, on the grounds that it had the largest variation in strains of the bacillus.[58] More recent work suggests that the polytomy occurred in the Tien Shan region of Kyrgyzstan, which contains a still greater diversity.[59]

It is inherently probable that Mongol military activity was ultimately responsible for seeding plague in a number of distinct localities in Eurasia. A pioneering study by the late Ronnie Ellenblum linked the widespread plague outbreak of the years 447–9/1055–7 with the inroads of the Seljuqs' nomadic Oghuz Turkish forces.[60] The Mongols' diet and that of their Turkic auxiliaries included (though as a supplementary rather than a basic component) the marmot,[61] known to have been among the vectors of fleas carrying *Yersinia pestis*. Allsen suggested that the Mongol practice of dispersing or transferring subject populations in large numbers, sometimes across ecological frontiers and in harsh climatic conditions, had lowered their resistance to disease at a local level.[62]

Many scholars are inclined to move the remote origins of the second pandemic back into the thirteenth century. Robert Hymes has highlighted the incidence of plague in northern China from 1211 and in the south after 1241, coinciding with the onset of Mongol attacks on Xi Xia, the Jin and, later, the Song.[63] Monica Green has pointed to outbreaks of disease associated with Hülegü's operations in Western Asia, notably the attack on Baghdad in 656/1258. She identifies this as plague, made possible by the Mongols' practice of stockpiling bags of millet at stages along their route, an attraction to flea-bearing rodents.[64] In what follows it is important to be aware of the terminology employed by our Arabic and Persian sources. In Arabic *ṭāʿūn* denotes plague (though not invariably so), whereas the term *wabā* has a broader application and subsumes typhus, smallpox and cholera.[65] But since the two words are not used with any rigour or consistency, we cannot be certain in any particular case that the visitation reported is plague. For instance, although the Baghdad outbreak is always termed *wabā*, a pestilence in Syria in 656/1258 perhaps carried by refugees from Baghdad is called *ṭāʿūn* in some early sources.[66] Nor, given the impossibility of conducting palaeogenetic research on any relevant site, is it clear how the thirteenth-century outbreaks were related to the Black Death and later attacks.

GEOGRAPHIC ORIGINS AND CHRONOLOGY OF THE PLAGUE

The study of plague by Ibn Ḥajar al-ʿAsqalānī (d. 852/1449), and its abridged and annotated version by al-Suyūṭī (d. 911/1505),[67] distinguished earlier visitations (seen as localised affairs) in Egypt or Iraq, for example, from that of the mid-fourteenth century, which they term 'the universal plague' (*al-ṭāʿūn al-ʿāmm*).[68] It would make a profound impression on Ibn Khaldūn, then in his teens (though writing a few decades later). Recalling in his autobiography how he lost both his parents and several of his teachers, he terms it 'the winnowing plague' (*al-ṭāʿūn al-jārif*).[69] In *al-Muqaddima* he claims that plague had 'devastated nations and caused populations to vanish . . . Cities and buildings were laid waste, . . . dynasties and tribes grew weak. The entire inhabited world changed. It was as if the voice of existence in the world had called out for oblivion'.[70]

Two issues arise: the geographic origins of the Black Death (which has implications for the extent of the regions affected) and the chronology and scope of its spread (including subsequent outbreaks). There is now widespread agreement that the Black Death emanated from the steppes.[71] European observers first notice the pandemic, and its transmission to Europe, in the context of Janibeg's assault in 1346 on the Genoese settlement at Kaffa in the Crimea. The disease was rife among his troops and, according to the Florentine Gabriele de' Mussi, the khan, in an early recourse to biological warfare, had Mongol corpses catapulted into the besieged city and hence the plague spread to the Mediterranean. But this account (emanating from an author who was never in the east) has now been discredited; rather, plague crossed the Black Sea from the Crimea only *after* Janibeg and the Italians made peace.[72] Yet it is true that when the Arab historian Ibn al-Wardī first mentions the disease he suggests that it came from 'Özbeg's territories';[73] that the Byzantine historian Nicephorus Gregoras, writing in the 1350s, says that it had originated in the 'Marshes of Maeotis' (the Sea of Azov) and the estuary of the Don;[74] and that the Venetian chancellor Rafaino Caresini says that it had begun in 'the Tartar regions'.[75] Other Italian chroniclers similarly locate its origins in the 'northern regions' (*in partibus aquilonaribus*), namely the tracts north of the Black Sea.[76] The Pontic–Caspian steppes evidently served as the springboard – or perhaps we should say *a* springboard – for the transmission of the disease both to the Mamlūk territories and to Western Europe. In the spring of 748/1347 it spread from the Crimea to Baghdad, Sicily, Egypt, Syria and Anatolia.[77] What is easily ignored, however, is the likelihood that observers were merely reporting the quarter from which the pandemic had first come to their attention and that they were ignorant of its earlier presence in more remote parts.

To what extent was plague present east of the Jochid lands? Some of the contemporary testimony is admittedly too vague, or even too fanciful, to be of use. Ibn al-Wardī was told that the pandemic had arisen in the 'Land of Darkness' (*al-ẓulamāt*), a semi-legendary tract to be equated, in all likelihood, with the fur-bearing regions occupied by the Yugra people in Siberia.[78] The claim found in European sources that the disease had come from 'India'[79] is of little value, given the widespread use of that term in Europe to indicate China or Central Asia as often as the subcontinent, and even, albeit more rarely, Iran.[80] The Florentine chronicler Matteo Villani (who would perish in the outbreak of 1363) says that the disease originated 'towards Cathay and Upper India' (*in verso il Cattai e l'India superiore*), a phrase probably denoting northern and southern China.[81]

Likewise, amid a lurid account of plagues of worms and snakes, accompanied by fire from Heaven and a noxious mist, a Bolognese chronicle tradition specifically mentions Cathay and Persia, while a Prague chronicler locates similar phenomena in the territory between them.[82]

Gabriele de' Mussi lists among the peoples affected 'the Chinese, Indians, Persians, Medes. . .';[83] the last-named are possibly the inhabitants of the Chaghadayid khanate, sometimes misnamed *imperium Medorum*, 'the empire of the Medes', or *imperium Medie*, 'the empire of Media' (see Chapter 2, p. 79; thus John of Sulṭāniyya in the early fifteenth century would call Timur a 'Mede').[84] Ibn al-Wardī (d. 749/1349), who fell victim to the disease in Aleppo and who has left us both a treatise on the subject and a detailed account in his chronicle, supplies a comparatively precise list of the territories affected: southern China (*Ṣīn*), India, Sind, Özbeg's dominions (*bilād Uzbak*), Transoxiana (*Mā warā' al-nahr*), Iran (*'Ajam*), northern China (*Khiṭā*), the Crimea (*Qirim*), Anatolia (*Rūm*) and so on.[85] This author rather saps confidence with his remorselessly rhyming word-play, but his account would be admired and quoted by later authors.[86] A defect common to all such reports is the failure to indicate any sequential order; though Ibn al-Wardī dates its arrival in the Qipchaq khanate ('Özbeg's territories') precisely in Rajab 747/ October–November 1346.[87]

The year is supported by the Rus' chronicles, which list those lands and peoples struck by the pandemic nearer at hand:

> In that year [6854 = 1346] a punishment from God befell the peoples of the eastern regions, at the *orda*, and in Ornach, in Sarai, in Bezhdezh and in the neighbouring cities and districts, and there was a heavy mortality among the peoples, [namely] the Bessermens, the Tatars, the Armenians, the Abkhazians. . .[88]

Now 'Ornach' is Ürgench in Khwārazm, and the 'Bessermens' are the Muslims of Khwārazm and the lower to middle Sīr-daryā region in what is now southern Kazakhstan.[89] And here we have valuable corroboration from a Muslim source, for the fifteenth-century compilator Khwāfī tells us that an epidemic (*wabā*) broke out in Ürgench ('Jurjāniyya') in 746/1345, carrying off the vast majority of the populace, so that possibly fewer than one in a hundred (*sic*) survived; it abated only after an act of communal supplication on 28 Rajab [24 November 1345].[90] This transpired some months prior to the arrival of the disease in the Crimea. Independent voices, then, encourage a belief that the pestilence, far from originating in the Pontic steppes and thence radiating outwards, had arrived there from the east.

Can we date the arrival of the second pandemic in the ulus of Chaghadai? Out of 439 dated gravestones from the abovementioned Nestorian cemeteries in Kyrgyzstan, 114 indicate an extraordinary leap in mortality in 1337–8 and 1338–9 and another, lesser peak in 1341–2; and a few of the inscriptions from these years refer expressly to pestilence (*mawtānā* in Syriac).[91] Philip Slavin estimates that three-quarters of the Christian community represented in one of these cemeteries, at Kara-Dzhigach (near Bishkek), fell victim to plague in 1338–9 and that the community died out by 1345.[92] Plague has been proposed as the reason for the closure of the routes through Chaghadai's ulus in late 1344/early 1345 (see earlier), but nowhere do our Genoese informants specify the cause.[93]

At this time a well-frequented commercial route linked western Eurasia with China. Ibn ʿArabshāh writes of it as once flourishing but by his day a thing of the past;[94] and Pegolotti and a slightly earlier commercial handbook from Florence alike name Tana (at the mouth of the Don) and Ürgench as halting points on this route, which led on to Utrār, Almaligh and Gansu.[95] The presence of both Tana and Ürgench among those localities where the pestilence struck, combined with the date given by Khwāfī, would support the view that it had spread westwards along the trans-Asiatic trade routes. Norris and Benedictow dismissed this possibility, as we saw, on the grounds of an alleged termination of trade between the western Mongol khanates and Christian Europe; we also noticed that none of the evidence they adduced had any bearing on traffic through the lands to the east of the Ural.

Of the two Andalusian Muslims who each devoted a treatise to the plague, Ibn Khātima thought that it had originated in northern China. The other, Ibn al-Khaṭīb, cites trustworthy travellers to the effect that it had begun in 'al-Khiṭā and al-Ṣīn' (northern and southern China, respectively).[96] It is unfortunate that among his informants Ibn al-Khaṭīb names Ibn Baṭṭūṭa,[97] who claims to have visited China but almost certainly did not – although naturally this does not preclude the possibility that Ibn Baṭṭūṭa had obtained trustworthy information on the subject at some point during his travels.

The Egyptian historian al-Maqrīzī (d. 845/1442) learned that the pestilence had originated in the Qaghan's dominions, which he specifies as the lands of the Chinese (*Khiṭā*) and the Mongols, and describes the heavy mortality among the nomads (though he also heard a baseless rumour that the Qaghan himself and his six sons had fallen victim to the disease). He further cites a report from the Qipchaq khanate that this outbreak had transpired in the year 742/1341–2.[98] Al-Maqrīzī is hardly the most methodical or the most thorough of the Mamlūk historians, but the fact that he – or more probably an earlier author whose now lost work he utilised (al-Yūsufī?) – derived some of his information from the Jochid territories at the western end of the Eurasian steppes may lend his account greater authority. For what it is worth (which is doubtless very little), his date corresponds to that offered by Geoffrey Le Baker, who says that the plague reached England (1348) in the seventh year since it had begun.[99] More importantly, it is also roughly in harmony with the heightened mortality rate among the Christians of Kyrgyzstan (see earlier).

Among the several tribulations that befell China in the last decades of the Yuan was a series of virulent epidemics,[100] occurring in 1331, 1333, 1340, 1344–6, 1351–4 and 1356–62.[101] Some or all of these were conceivably outbreaks of plague; but doubts persist in the complete absence of any descriptions of symptoms and Paul Buell has argued vigorously that there was 'no demonstrable mass outbreak' of plague in Yuan China.[102] It is noteworthy that Marignolli, who was resident in Khanbaligh from 1342 until 1344 and then travelled southwards to take ship from Quanzhou (known to Europeans as

Zayton), says nothing of pestilence amid his admittedly sketchy recollections.[103] On the other hand, a contemporary Chinese author speaks of an epidemic in 1340 in Shaanxi,[104] towards the eastern end of the trans-Asiatic trade routes. But at what date had the pandemic first exploded in eastern Inner Asia? Reporting its arrival at Aleppo in Rajab 749/September–October 1348, Ibn al-Wardī claims that it had begun fifteen years earlier, and Ibn al-Khaṭīb independently corroborates this by furnishing the precise date 734/1333–4.[105] It may be no coincidence that 1333 is the very year in which southern China suffered one of its major epidemics. The problem is that the mid-fourteenth-century outbreaks seem to have had a less catastrophic impact in China than in Europe and the Near East,[106] partly because disease at any one time affected only a single province or a few provinces. But the incidence of epidemic disease in China might combine with the existence of a well-established maritime commerce between those regions, peninsular India and the Persian Gulf,[107] to suggest an additional route by which plague reached southern and south-western Asia. Ibn Khātima cites two alternative avenues for the plague: from China through the 'lands of the Turks' and Persian Iraq, and from 'Abyssinia' to Egypt and Syria,[108] presumably through the Red Sea. The sea route has indeed been proposed as one avenue by which plague reached the Middle East.[109]

We should have been glad to learn something of the chronology of the Black Death from the one Muslim traveller who is known to have been at large during this same period and who witnessed its ravages in Syria. When Ibn Baṭṭūṭa left for India in 733/1333, plague had evidently not yet broken out in the Chaghadayid dominions; nor does he mention hearing of its arrival there while he was resident in the Delhi Sultanate.[110] He does, however, speak of two outbreaks of pestilence in the Indian subcontinent. The first, referred to also by Indo-Muslim sources, occurred in *c.* 735/1334–5, during a campaign by the Delhi Sultan Muḥammad b. Tughluq in Tilang (Telingana), and carried off half his officers and a third of his troops – proportions that certainly call to mind the subsequent death toll in Europe and the Near East.[111] The second, which is mentioned by Ibn Baṭṭūṭa alone, struck Maʿbar (the Coromandel coast) in 744/1343–4 or

745/1344–5 and killed, among many others, its Sultan, Ghiyāth al-Dīn Dāmghānī.[112] This latter epidemic could have been transmitted to Maʿbar by ship from one of the four officially sponsored ports through which most Yuan trade with the Indian Ocean passed and which lay close to the regions affected by the 1344 outbreak in China. When plague reached Western Asia, however, Ibn Baṭṭūṭa was either in the Maldives or on the south Indian littoral. He claims to have landed in Ẓafār from Qāliqūṭ in Muḥarram 748/April–May 1347 and to have arrived in Baghdad in Shawwāl 748/January 1348 (neither date is necessarily reliable, and the second is surely suspect, given that although the plague had by then reached Baghdad Ibn Baṭṭūṭa makes no reference to it there).[113]

The plague made markedly swifter progress by sea – as, for instance, in 1347 from the Crimea to Egypt and to the western Mediterranean.[114] If, therefore, we possessed reliable evidence linking the abovementioned outbreaks in Kyrgyzstan and India with the pandemic that struck the Crimea, the Near East and Western Europe, we should be able to construct a plausible chronology. We might see the pestilence in Kyrgyzstan as an earlier phase of the disease, transmitted by the land route and due to strike the Qipchaq khanate a few years later, and might relate that in Maʿbar to a more recent outbreak in China, diffused more rapidly, in all likelihood by the maritime route. But regrettably no such reliable evidence lies to hand.

One difficulty is that the language of our sources is inconsistent and fails to conform strictly to the meanings given earlier in this chapter. In his great general history the Damascene Ibn Kathīr (d. 774/1373) speaks regularly of the Black Death as *ṭāʿūn*; but Ibn al-Wardī uses *ṭāʿūn* and *wabā* alike for the plague, while Ibn Baṭṭūṭa refers both to the epidemics in Tilang and Maʿbar and to the Black Death, which he witnessed personally in Syria in 749/1349, exclusively as *wabā*.[115] So too we might have reservations about the disease (*wabā*) that struck the Khwāf region in Khurāsān following an earthquake in 737/1336–7, which could have been an isolated outbreak of cholera.[116] Equally, however, it is not inconceivable that these outbreaks in southern India and at Khwāf were plague.

THE IMPACT OF THE PLAGUE ON THE MONGOL WORLD

If there is general agreement that the Mongols inadvertently created the conditions for the emergence and spread of the plague, it is harder to ascertain how far the Mongol dominions were subject to its visitations. The main problem is the dearth of indigenous sources from the Jochid and Chaghadayid polities. We depend almost exclusively on Rus′ chronicles for information about plague in the Qipchaq khanate,[117] and we would know nothing of the Kaffa episode but for Italian chroniclers.

Yet the contemporary narrative sources from the sedentary Ilkhanid lands are hardly more forthcoming. As Morgan observes, there is little evidence relating to the plague's impact on Persia.[118] The information we do have is as follows: Ahrī and, following him, Zayn al-Dīn b. Ḥamd-Allāh Mustawfī interrupt a depressing litany of battles and executions to make passing mention of 'a mighty epidemic' (*wabā-yi ʿaẓīm*) that had broken out in 747/1346–7 in Azerbaijan, obliging the Chobanid Malik Ashraf to leave Tabriz.[119] In 748/1347, when Ashraf was besieging his rival Shaykh Ḥasan-i Buzurg in Baghdad, he lost six of his commanders and twelve hundred men to pestilence.[120] (These figures would be more useful if we had some idea of the original size of Ashraf's force.) Faryūmadī alludes in passing to the loss by the Ilkhan Taghai Temür (based in Astarābād) of two of his sons and the majority of his amirs, owing to the putridity of the atmosphere and the onset of pestilence (*ʿufūnat-i hawā'-u ḥudūth-i wabā*).[121] We learn, too, that pestilence (*wabā*) carried off so many members of the local Bawandid dynasty at Āmul in neighbouring Māzandarān that only the king, Fakhr al-Dawla Ḥasan, and two of his sons survived.[122] Undoubtedly, therefore, the Caspian region was severely affected. There is limited evidence that plague also struck parts of eastern Iran, where in 747/1346–7 disease (referred to as *wabā-yi ʿamīm*, 'a widespread epidemic') ravaged Sīstān and removed its king, Quṭb al-Dīn Muḥammad.[123] On the other hand, the late fifteenth-century historian ʿAbd al-Razzāq Samarqandī provides the important negative testimony that prior to 838/1435 the city of Herat had never been visited by the plague.[124]

The gravity of the attacks after the late 1340s is unclear. Plague (*wabā-u ṭā'ūn*) hit Azerbaijan in the winter of 761/1360, obliging the Jalayirid Shaykh Uways to leave Tabriz for Qarābāgh,[125] and a plague (*ṭā'ūn*) or great pestilence (*wabā-yi 'aẓīm*) again convulsed Azerbaijan in the autumn of 771/1369, when fatalities in Tabriz allegedly totalled around 300,000 (clearly an inflated figure).[126] In 782/1380 plague (*ṭā'ūn*) struck down the ruler of Sivas, Aratna's grandson ʿAlī Beg, and also hit Trebizond during the latter half of 1382.[127] It was probably the same outbreak that afflicted Kalāt in Sīstān in the summer of 784/1382–3 and is mentioned in unequivocal terms by Ḥāfiẓ-i Abrū as an attack of plague (*balā-yi ṭā'ūn-u 'anā-yi wabā*) in which half the populace perished.[128] Another outbreak in 794/1392 (again called *ṭā'ūn*) carried off the governor of Sulṭāniyya,[129] and a 'mighty epidemic' (*wabā kabīr*) killed a large number of Baghdad's inhabitants in 797/1394–5.[130] Some outbreaks may have been localised, like that which killed 200,000 in Isfahan in *c.* 810–11/1408,[131] an event of which the highly detailed *Zubdat al-tawārīkh* of Ḥāfiẓ-i Abrū makes no mention.

We should note in particular that for the period from 1346 down to Timur's era plague is not mentioned either in the sources from southern Iran – the various local histories of Yazd and the histories of the Muzaffarid dynasty by Muʿīn al-Dīn Yazdī and Maḥmūd Kutubī – or in Ḥāfiẓ-i Abrū's survey of the Kartid dynasty of Herat (or indeed, for that matter, in his accounts of the Sarbadārs, Amīr Walī and Taghai Temür, whose territory, as we saw earlier, undoubtedly suffered from plague). Nor does the Black Death seem to have struck the Persian Gulf.[132] The sources do not suggest that the former Ilkhanid territories as a whole suffered the series of attacks that afflicted the Mamlūk empire and Europe in the late fourteenth century.[133] Zayn al-Dīn is even able to assure us that in 768/1366–7 the Jalayirids' subjects in Iraq and Azerbaijan – the latter a region struck twice by pestilence within the previous twenty years – were enjoying unprecedented prosperity.[134]

Admittedly, the mortality rates are likely to have varied quite sharply from one region to another, just as they did in Europe.[135] But the silence of so many authors in the Iranian world suggests either that the ravages of the disease there were patchy and less severe than in Europe and the Mamlūk empire, or that contemporary Iranian Muslim authors were too inured to catastrophe of every kind to spare it their attention;[136] and such attitudes may have been widespread among populations denied the benefits of Mongol rule. Whatever the reasons why the plague attracted so little notice, one easily gains the impression that the activities in which contemporary historians took most interest – military campaigns and political intrigue – continued unabated. We have a single shred of external information relating broadly to south-west Asia. A report received by Pope Clement VI early in 1349 reveals that the Latin Archbishop of Sulṭāniyya (whose province embraced the Ilkhanid and Chaghadayid lands, India and Ethiopia) had died of disease, and that of the Western European religious personnel in the fifteen Dominican houses in 'the whole of Persia', only three survived.[137]

Regarding the impact of the disease upon the largely pastoralist Mongols en masse, we are far from well informed.[138] Although some of the detail Giovanni Villani supplies about the lands contiguous with Golden Horde territory is plainly fantastic – his assertion that in Tana and in Trebizond only one in five persons survived, for instance – he also states that mortality among the 'Tartars' themselves was especially heavy.[139] Uli Schamiloglu has hypothesised that the end of Volga Bulgarian as the language of funerary inscriptions, and the rise of Standard Turkic, in the upper Volga region bear witness to the impact of plague upon a literate urban population within the Jochid dominions.[140] According to a merchant with whom Ibn al-Wardī spoke, a qadi in the Crimea had estimated the number of deaths from the epidemic (in 747/1346–7, that is) at 85,000.[141] It is uncertain, however, whether this figure applied to the Crimea alone and what proportion of the victims were nomads, as opposed to the urban populace in the peninsula (including Western European settlers and merchants), or how many were among Janibeg's besieging troops at Kaffa. The Franciscan János of Eger, confessor to King Louis of Hungary, learned that 300,000 Tartars (presumably in Janibeg's realm) had died of the plague within a few months in 1346.[142]

McNeill posed the question whether 'intensified exposure to disease, and especially to bubonic plague, was not a real factor in undermining Mongol military might', and suggested that it hastened the end of their hegemony over their sedentary subjects.[143] This hypothesis suffers from the drawback that urban/agrarian populations were themselves afflicted and their capacity to dislodge their nomadic overlords would have been reduced more or less in proportion. The Black Death does not in itself, for example, explain the weakening of Mongol authority over Rus′, which was also convulsed by the pandemic.

Conversely, it is sometimes suggested that the disease spread less rapidly, and had a lesser impact, among dispersed nomadic groupings than within the dense ranks of urban dwellers.[144] Belich writes of a 'partial exemption' of nomads, giving them a temporary military advantage over their sedentary neighbours that was eroded once they themselves gathered in larger formations for conflict.[145] Expressed in these terms, however, the dichotomy hardly takes into account the size and density of a khan's *orda*; and the vital distinction is not necessarily between nomadic and sedentary societies, but between large-scale concentrations of people (whether pastoralists or urban dwellers), on the one hand, and small, relatively isolated communities on the other. Nobody reading Rubruck's awestruck reaction on first sighting Batu's encampment in 1253, or Ibn Baṭṭūṭa's description of Özbeg's encampment eight decades later, can be in any doubt that these observers were confronted by a vast tent-city, containing a large agglomeration of people in close proximity to one another and served by portable mosques and bazaars.[146] The potential for the rapid communication of plague within the headquarters of a khan or an amir was thus hardly less than it was among more conventional urban societies. As we saw, in the late 1340s the Ilkhan Taghai Temür's amirs and nomadic followers – presumably, that is, around his own *orda* – were badly hit. In the final analysis there is no sure way of knowing whether the mortality was generally lower within pastoralist than within sedentary societies (recall that the city of Herat was untouched by the Black Death). We should bear in mind, in any event, that the two categories no longer coincided with

Mongols and non-Mongols, respectively, since some of the Mongol elite had adopted a more or less sedentary lifestyle.[147]

There is a further important consideration. Byzantine authors refer to widespread casualties among domestic animals.[148] Al-Maqrīzī, too, mentions in particular the deaths of livestock and draught animals in 'Khitā' and in the territories of Qaraman and Kayserı in Anatolia and the heavy loss of baggage animals suffered by Ashraf's army outside Baghdad.[149] It may have been a suspicion that the affliction had originated among the animal population that caused the governor of Damascus to order the city's dogs to be killed.[150] There are indications that disease recurred among the livestock of the Chaghadayid khanate during the decades associated with the plague: the overthrow of the khan Qazan Sulṭān in 747/1346 came about, we are told, because he had lost the majority of his beasts during the intense cold of the previous winter. Another outbreak, which cost the troops of Jata more than a quarter of their mounts in 766/1365, obliged them to raise their siege of Samarkand and retire.[151] It is possible that some of these instances involved a phenomenon that arose from harsh weather conditions rather than being linked directly with the plague, namely *yut* (Mo. *dzhud*), a murrain that afflicts horses and other animals when their hooves are unable to penetrate an ice-covering in search of grass.[152] It is first mentioned in the early 1290s[153] and must have grown more frequent with the climatic extremes of the early fourteenth century (see earlier). The fact that livestock numbers were also badly affected would have dealt a still heavier blow to a pastoralist society dependent especially on sheep, horses and camels.

At the very least, we can conclude that in the course of the Black Death the mortality figures within the Mongols' ranks, combined with heavy losses among their animals, were of a significant order, sufficient to deter them temporarily from military action. Faryūmadī says that the deaths from plague gave rise to 'total despondency' (*inkisār-i tamām*) in Khurāsān among Taghai Temür's leading men and induced them to seek peace with their Sarbadār enemies;[154] the disarray may explain why Taghai Temür apparently struck no coins in the years 747–51/1346–51.[155] The picture from the Jochid lands is similar. Thanks to the Tartar deaths from plague, we are told, King Louis of Hungary was able to leave his realm with equanimity on his first expedition to Naples in 1347,[156] and the Qipchaq khanate was apparently in no condition in 1349 to prevent his father-in-law, Casimir III of Poland, from absorbing the principality of Galicia, which had been tributary to the khans for several decades.[157] The suspension of major campaigns, with a concomitant falling-off in tribute and plunder (Janibeg's conquest of Azerbaijan was relatively brief, and we know virtually nothing about his appropriation of Chaghadayid territory), would have exerted pressure on the Jochid Mongols' resources and undoubtedly have intensified internal rivalries.

How far were the Pontic–Caspian steppes affected by any of the later attacks? Rus′ chronicles show that the Qipchaq khanate almost certainly suffered two outbreaks within thirty years of the Black Death. The first, which struck the Near East in 764/1362–3, must have also spread to the Jochid lands by 1364, when it was raging in Rus′ after travelling northwards from Bezhdezh.[158] The second occurred in 1374, when plague also struck Armenia.[159] Khaidarov and Dolbin argue that the 1364 outbreak had even more devastating consequences for the Qipchaq khanate than that of 1346–7 because it seemingly arrested the growth of the urban centres.[160] Whatever the case, both the 1364 and 1374 irruptions beset the khanate when it had already slid into a state of prolonged disunity and disorder. These successive outbreaks may also have led to depopulation that prompted the intervention of princes from the less urbanised Jochid territories in the east, beginning with the Shibanid Khiḍr in 1360 and continuing with the khans of the Blue Horde during the mid-to-late 1370s.[161] It has been proposed that the Blue Horde suffered less from the plague than did the Qipchaq khanate;[162] and certainly Mamai's 'horde' in particular was struck hard in 1374.[163] This will have impaired his capacity to withstand Toqtamish a few years later and have exerted a longer-term effect on Jochid strength in the face of Timur's attacks.

There is some evidence, then, that northern Iran and the Qipchaq steppe, at least, were hit by plague in the late 1340s and intermittently thereafter. That Timur was able to profit from its earlier ravages in the territories he attacked, however, is more easily assumed than demonstrated.[164] The supposition begs a large question: what impact did disease have on Timur's own homeland, his power base in Transoxiana? In the absence of any information on Central Asia in this era from narrative sources composed prior to 1404, we simply cannot know how badly the Chaghadayid dominions themselves were affected by the pandemic.[165] The Nestorian gravestones confirm that it struck the ulus. Otherwise, the evidence is vague: the inclusion of Transoxiana in Ibn al-Wardī's list of regions affected, Ibn Khātima's mention of the 'land of the Turks' and (just possibly) Gabriele de' Mussi's allusion to the 'Medes'.[166] After *c.* 1340 we lack even reports from Europeans in Chaghadai's ulus; though that in itself could be significant, given the effects of the Black Death on the archiepiscopal province of Sulṭāniyya (see earlier). Like the Qipchaq khanate, Chaghadayid Transoxiana proved vulnerable to invasion by its pastoralist eastern neighbours in the early 1360s, but there is no certainty that this was related to the effects of plague. We have no knowledge of plague in Mughūlistān itself (but see p. 105 above), though the Buddhist treatise *Sitataśastra* makes unspecific references to epidemics in Central Asia,[167] and the *Blue Annals*, a Tibetan compilation from 1476, mentions epidemics in the 1360s, notably in nearby Gansu.[168] The impact of plague on the two halves of the ulus remains obscure. Whatever the case, it was the Mughūl invasion, as we shall see later, that furnished Timur with his first foothold on the ladder to prominence.

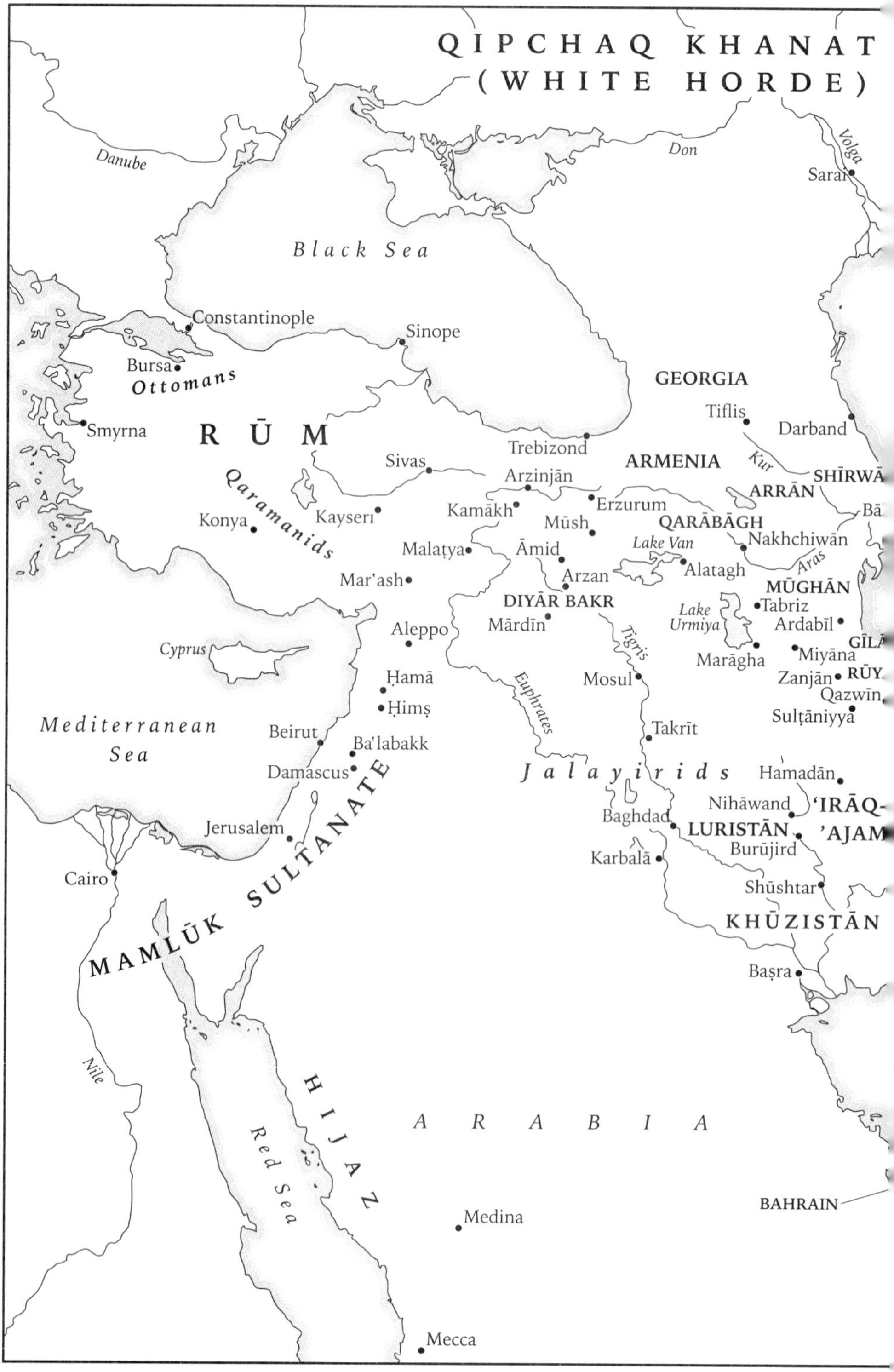

2. Post-Ilkhanid Iran.

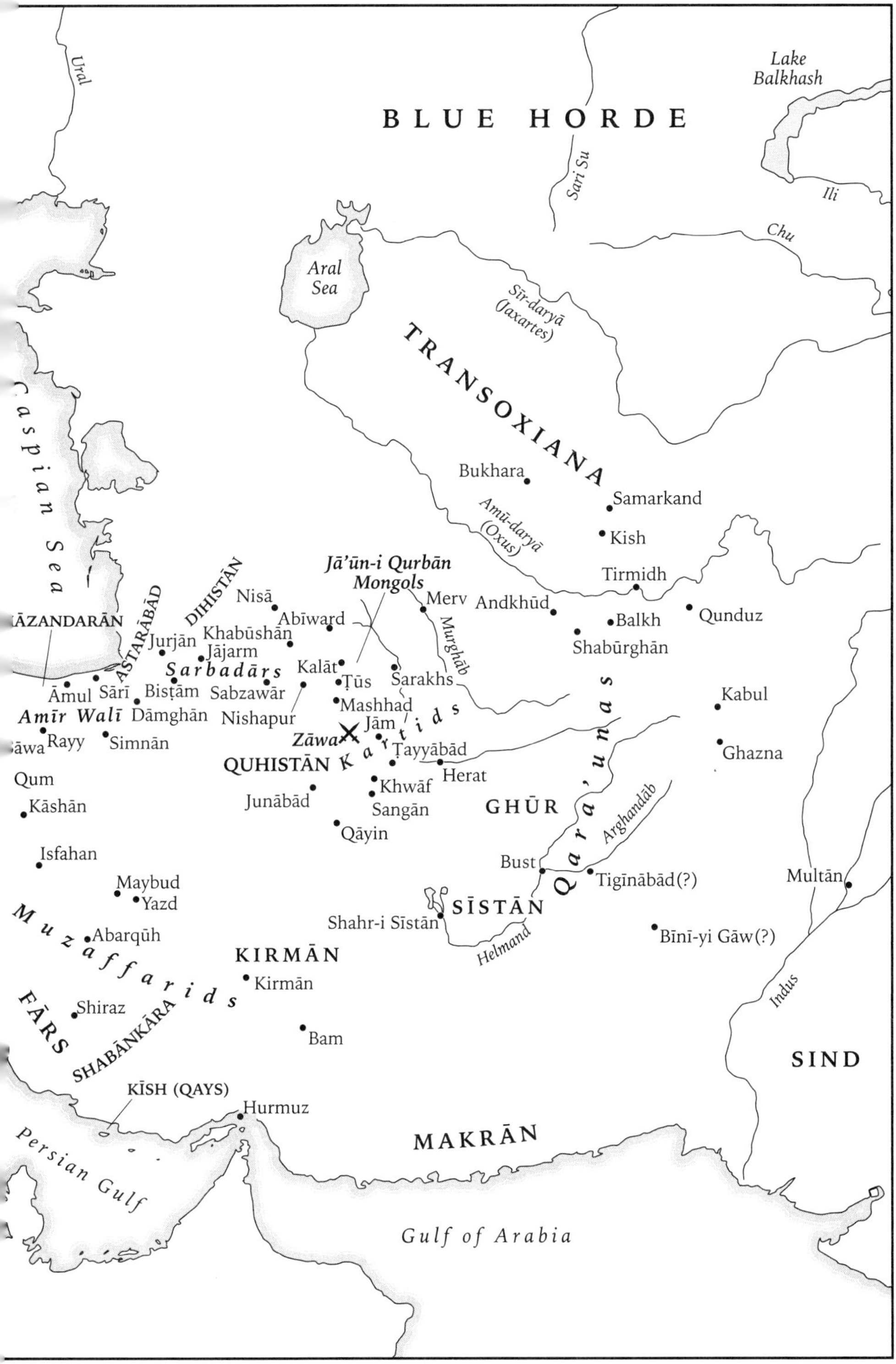
BLUE HORDE
Lake Balkhash
Ural
Sari Su
Ili
Chu
Aral Sea
Sīr-daryā (Jaxartes)
TRANSOXIANA
Caspian Sea
Bukhara
Samarkand
Amū-daryā (Oxus)
Kish
Tirmidh
Jā'ūn-i Qurbān Mongols
Merv
Andkhūd
Balkh
Qunduz
Shabūrghān
Murghāb
DIHISTĀN
ASTARĀBĀD
ĀZANDARĀN
Nisā
Abīward
Khabūshān
Jurjān
Jājarm
Sarbadārs
Kalāt
Ṭūs
Sarakhs
Āmul
Sārī
Bisṭām
Sabzawār
Nishapur
Mashhad
Amīr Walī
Dāmghān
Jām
Kabul
Sāwa
Rayy
Simnān
Zāwa
Kartids
Ṭayyābād
Ghazna
QUHISTĀN
Herat
Qum
Khwāf
Junābād
Sangān
GHŪR
Qara'unas
Kāshān
Qāyin
Arghandāb
Isfahan
Bust
Maybud
Tigīnābād(?)
Multān
Yazd
SĪSTĀN
Muzaffarids
Shahr-i Sīstān
Bīnī-yi Gāw(?)
Abarqūh
Helmand
KIRMĀN
Kirmān
Indus
FĀRS
Shiraz
SHABĀNKĀRA
Bam
SIND
KĪSH (QAYS)
Hurmuz
MAKRĀN
Persian Gulf
Gulf of Arabia

PART II
GREATER IRAN AND CENTRAL ASIA BEFORE TIMUR

CHAPTER 6
IRAN AND IRAQ AFTER THE ILKHANS

The fate of the Ilkhanate presents a sharp contrast with that of the neighbouring Mongol states. The Jochid and Chaghadayid realms continued to exist as recognisable political formations, although neither was spared upheaval. In Iran and Iraq there were efforts for nearly twenty years to preserve the fiction of Chinggisid sovereignty. But here, unlike the Jochid and Chaghadayid polities, Chinggisid rule dissolved altogether and the Ilkhanate was sundered into a number of regional states governed by non-Chinggisid – and, in several cases, non-Mongol – princes. Their conflicts would make the country an easy prey for Timur's invasions, when the most prominent of these principalities were suppressed.

ORIENTATIONS: MONGOLS AND TĀJĪKS

Writing in the Caspian region in or shortly after *c.* 763/1362, Awliyā'-Allāh Āmulī describes how the territorial rulers and landholders (*mulūk-u wilāyāt-u ṭarafdārān*) each became independent in his own realm after the death of the Ilkhan Abū Sa'īd.[1] A few years later, Faryūmadī specified no less than twelve such elements in western Iran and another dozen in Khurāsān and Māzandarān, the greater number of them petty dynasts whose rule was confined to a single town or fortress and its hinterland – Qum, Kāshān, Rayy, Ṭūs, Taftāzān and so on.[2] Some were swiftly dispossessed by stronger neighbours such as the Ilkhan Taghai Temür, Amīr Walī, the Jalayirids and the Muzaffarids. Āmulī's statement applied chiefly to the local princes on the periphery of Iran who had been prominent among the Ilkhans' vassals: the Kartids of Herat, the maliks in the Caspian territories of Gīlān and Māzandarān and the Türkmen chiefs in Anatolia. The more significant among the vassal dynasties that predated the Mongol conquest in the central Iranian lands – those of Fārs, Kirmān and Yazd, for instance – had been swept away decades previously by Arghun, Ghazan, Öljeitü and Abū Saʿīd and their territories had come under direct Ilkhanid administration. The majority of the independent rulers who emerged in the Iranian lands after Abū Saʿīd's death owed their position to their military or administrative role during his reign. Even those who lacked Mongol ancestry were linked to the Chinggisids by ties of patronage, service and sometimes intermarriage.

The post-Ilkhanid period has been termed an 'Iranian interlude', by analogy with the pre-Seljuq era, when dynasties of Iranian stock had ruled much of the country.[3] There is much to be said for this perspective. Of the leading successor-states that arose from the debris of the Ilkhanate, four were of 'Tājīk' extraction: the Injuids, the Muzaffarids (of Arab descent), the Sarbadārs (a dynasty only in the loosest sense) and the Kartids of Herat.[4] Lesser actors in this category were the Mihrabanids of Sīstān and the rulers of the fragmented Caspian lands. Some dynasties advanced bogus claims to be Iranian: the Hazaraspids of Greater Luristān, who boasted descent from Iran's (mythical) ancient kings but were probably of Syrian Kurdish origin, and the Kurdish maliks of Shabānkāra.[5] The post-Ilkhanid Iranian interlude was certainly a brief one, since the foremost Iranian dynasties lasted for sixty years – fewer decades than their pre-Seljuq counterparts. Then Timur – arguably a Mongol amir, at the head of Mongol forces – destroyed the Kartid, Muzaffarid and Sarbadār polities, and only minor regional princes survived, under Timurid overlordship. By the dawn of the fifteenth century, virtually all of Greater Iran lay under Turco-Mongol or Türkmen rule.

Yet for much of the pre-Timurid period this was still a world that bore the strong imprint of Mongol culture and Mongol statecraft. In the first place, Mongol rule persisted in several regions of the former Ilkhanate after 1340, particularly in Azerbaijan and Khurāsān, where the two main regions of pasturage in the Mongol era were located.[6] The Jalayirid Shaykh Ḥasan, the Chobanids Ḥasan and Ashraf, Amīr Walī, Aratna and the leaders of the Jā'ūn-i Qurbān were all of Mongol extraction. The Jalayirids, the Chobanids and Amīr Walī were among the chief powers in Iran. If the Chobanids, at least, increasingly resorted to non-Mongol sources of military support (and to elements of political symbolism other than Chinggisid charisma),[7] Aratna and the Jalayirids minted coins bearing legends in the Uighur script, as had the Ilkhans.[8] Both Shaykh Ḥasan and Ashraf were closely linked to the Ilkhans by marriage. Moreover, Shaykh Ḥasan's mother was Arghun's daughter Öljetei,[9] and he is sometimes called 'Shaykh Ḥasan-i Ūljatāy' in the sources; his successor, Shaykh Uways, was also of Ilkhanid descent through his mother, the Chobanid Dilshād Khātūn.[10] The Jalayirid authors Ahrī and Nakhchiwānī exploited this august pedigree (along with Jalayirid possession of Tabriz after 759/1358) in order to present the dynasty as the true heirs of the Ilkhans and proponents of Mongol tradition.[11] For the anonymous author of the *Dhayl-i Ta'rīkh-i guzīda*, writing in the 1370s and applauding the end of Ashraf's rule in Azerbaijan, Shaykh Uways was 'the pick (*khulāṣat*) of the house of Chinggis Khan'.[12] Uways went so far as to take the title 'Bahādur Khan' earlier borne by Abū Sa'īd.[13] Even external observers shared this perspective; Mamlūk authors often referred to the Jalayirid ruler as 'the Khan' (*qān*).[14] Moreover, under the Ilkhans a good deal of intermarriage had occurred between the families of Mongol commanders and local Tājīk notables. It is easy to ignore the diffusion of Mongol – and sometimes Chinggisid – blood among the new and indigenous dynasties. To take just a few examples: the mother of the Muzaffarid ruler Mubāriz al-Dīn was almost certainly a Mongol,[15] while the mother of the last Kartid malik, Ghiyāth al-Dīn, was a daughter of the Ilkhan Taghai Temür, and Ghiyāth al-Dīn's half-brother, Shams al-Dīn Muḥammad, was born of a woman from the Mongol tribe of the Arlāt.[16]

Secondly, and no less importantly, far from negligible concentrations of Mongol troops still existed in many regions of the Ilkhanate.

To illustrate just how dispersed were Mongol amirs from the same family, the descendants of Ked-buqa, Hülegü's general killed at ʿAyn Jālūt in 658/1260, were to be found in Herat, Māzandarān and Tabriz.[17] Eastern Iran was home to Mongol forces in significant numbers. The Ilkhan Taghai Temür had at his disposal in Māzandarān and Astarābād a large Mongol contingent which Ibn Baṭṭūṭa sets at 50,000.[18] After his murder, one element among these troops, the Jā'ūn-i Qurbān, remained masters of the regions of Nishapur and Ṭūs. Another Mongol division was quartered in Quhistān, but there were also Mongols in the armies of Tājīk rulers such as the malik of Herat and Mubāriz al-Dīn Muḥammad b. Muẓaffar.[19] After Taghai Temür's murder the Sarbadārs were able to station a force comprising both Tājīks and Mongols within his territory.[20]

The older Mongol groupings were among the more disruptive elements in eastern Iran. As we shall see in Chapter 7, eastern Khurāsān was dominated by the Negüderis or Qara'unas, who had been brought within the Chaghadayid orbit well before Abū Saʿīd's death. After the exiled malik of Herat, Muʿizz al-Dīn, returned to Herat from Transoxiana in 755/1354, the Qara'unas amirs and some local Mongol commanders who accompanied them subjected western Khurāsān to the utmost devastation.[21] The Kartids seem on occasion to have found the Negüderis serviceable allies.[22] As rulers of Kirmān from 741/1340, the Muzaffarids enjoyed the loyal support of another Mongol grouping, the Nawrūzīs, who nomadised within the province.[23] However, the dynasty would be called upon time and again to check the Jurma'ī and Awghānī Mongols. Ḥāfiẓ-i Abrū says that these elements, installed on the fringes of Kirmān by the Ilkhan Abagha to guard the province, had served as loyal auxiliaries until they revolted in 755/1354. But elsewhere he depicts them, as do the local historians, as consistently insubordinate.[24] In the wake of Timur's conquest of Kirmān, his governor Edigü would have to quash a rebellion by the Jurma'īs and Awghānīs.[25]

The Mongols were strongly represented, too, in the western tracts of the Ilkhanate, but there they were perhaps less of a menace to stability and in Anatolia the memory and heritage of the Seljuq Sultanate were generally almost as strong as were Mongol traditions.[26] The Oyirat in Iraq and the Jazīra, whom Shaykh Ḥasan had brought under his authority in 736/1336 and whose adhesion had contributed greatly to Jalayirid strength,[27] were still a force to be reckoned with in the later Jalayirid decades. In eastern Anatolia the presence of Mongol troops distinguished Aratna's principality from the various neighbouring Türkmen *beylik*s;[28] many of these Mongols were strongly attached to his dynasty.[29] In his successful efforts to detach the 'Qara Tatars' there from the Ottoman Sultan Bayezid in 804/1402, Timur would play on their loyalty to the memory of Aratna, described erroneously by Ibn ʿArabshāh as 'their last king'.[30]

It has been suggested that the Ottomans (ʿOsmanli) in the far north-western extremity of Anatolia had originated as Mongol fugitives from the Jochid lands towards the end of the thirteenth century;[31] and in support of this hypothesis it is interesting that Astarābādī writes of the Ottoman Sultan (Murad I) as 'a simple Mongol' (*mughūlī-yi sāda*).[32] Ottoman historians made no allusion to such a background, locating ʿOsman's antecedents within the Seljuq Sultanate. When writing of Ottoman beginnings, they focused on the Mongols' destructive impact; yet when narrating the Mongols' own history, they were influenced by contemporary Persian historiography and wrote admiringly of them.[33] Whatever the truth, as one-time Ilkhanid vassals the Ottomans partook of the Mongol legacy and Meḥmed II styled himself Khan as well as Sultan.[34]

We saw evidence in the previous chapter that the Mongols of the Ilkhan Taghai Temür, at least, were severely affected by the advent of plague in the late 1340s. Yet it is striking that, in the immediately post-Ilkhanid period, only two native Iranian rulers made significant headway against Mongol groupings. One was the Kartid Muʿizz al-Dīn Pīr Ḥusayn Muḥammad of Herat (d. 771/1370), who wrested control of Quhistān from the local Mongol garrison forces (see later), but a few years later his ambitions suffered a check at the hands of the Chaghadayid Mongols of Transoxiana. The other was the *ustundār* of Rūyān, Jalāl al-Dawla Iskandar (d. 761/1359–60), who in the late 1340s occupied Qazwīn, Simnān and Rayy; though after his death they passed into the hands of the Mongol Amīr Walī.[35] And if the Sarbadārs in 754/1353 eliminated the last Ilkhan of any significance, they still had to withstand attacks by formidable Mongol elements over the next few decades. Clearly, the Iranian complexion of the post-Ilkhanid world can be overstated.

THE INJUIDS AND THE CHOBANIDS

Let us begin with the two most ephemeral of the successor-dynasties. Fārs and Isfahan were at first under the rule of the Injuids, who claimed descent from the eleventh-century Herati scholar ʿAbd-Allāh Anṣārī. They derived their name from the appointment of Sharaf al-Dīn Maḥmūdshāh by Choban as comptroller of the Ilkhans' personal estates (Mo. *injü*) in the region. Maḥmūdshāh had come to wield considerable power both at court and in Fārs.[36] He played a central role in the enthronement of Arpa in 736/1335; nevertheless, the new Ilkhan shortly had him executed. During the ensuing struggle for the Ilkhanate, Fārs was disputed between various members of the Chobanid dynasty and Maḥmūdshāh's sons until 744/1343, when the youngest, Shaykh Abū Isḥāq, who had been ruling Isfahan for some years, secured control of the province. However, he soon developed designs on Kirmān, now in the hands of the Muzaffarid Mubāriz al-Dīn Muḥammad, who had intermittently been allied with the Chobanids, and this proved to be Abū Isḥāq's undoing. After several failed offensives against Yazd and Kirmān, he was ousted from Shiraz in 754/1353 by Muzaffarid forces, which went on to take Isfahan, and he was executed in 757/1356.[37]

The Injuids' Chobanid rivals were the other relatively short-lived power.[38] Since abandoning the struggle with the Injuids, Choban's grandsons Ḥasan-i Kūchak and Ashraf had been confined to their core territory in Azerbaijan, from where they engaged in frequent conflict with the Jalayirid Shaykh Ḥasan. Ashraf's particularly oppressive and rapacious regime led many prominent folk to emigrate from Azerbaijan to the Qipchaq khanate. If we can believe the anonymous continuation of Ḥamd-Allāh Mustawfī's *Taʾrīkh-i guzīda* (or rather his *Ẓafar-nāma*), composed under Ashraf's Jalayirid rivals, the invasion of Azerbaijan by Janibeg, khan of the Golden Horde, in 758/1357 was a response to appeals from the Chobanids' subjects.[39]

Ashraf, unable to withstand the attack, fled, only to be captured and put to death. But Jochid rule in Azerbaijan did not last. Janibeg's son Berdibeg, left to govern the territory, soon withdrew on his father's death. The vacuum was filled first by Ashraf's former lieutenant, Akhīchuq, who now struck out on his own. Briefly expelled by the Jalayirid Shaykh Uways, he returned on the enemy's withdrawal but was eliminated within a year by the Muzaffarid ruler Mubāriz al-Dīn. The latter in turn retired just before Shaykh Uways reoccupied Azerbaijan in Shaʿbān–Ramaḍān 759/July–August 1358;[40] with one more brief interval, the territory remained in Jalayirid hands until Timur's invasion.

THE JALAYIRIDS

The Jalayirids, who already ruled Iraq from Baghdad, henceforth also dominated north-western Iran. They held the wealthy commercial entrepôt of Tabriz – the 'great residence' (*takhtgāh-i buzurg*: 'great' doubtless in the Mongol sense of 'imperial'),[41] as Faryūmadī termed it – and Sulṭāniyya, the principal centres of power under the Ilkhans. The dynasty's earliest known ancestor was Elgei, a Mongol commander who had accompanied Hülegü to Iran and acted as chief amir in the newly created Ilkhanate. His sons served the Ilkhans, and his grandson Ḥusayn was chief amir to Öljeitü and Abū Saʿīd and governor of Khurāsān in the 1320s.[42] Ḥusayn's son Shaykh Ḥasan, the real founder of the family's fortunes, took part in the struggles for the Ilkhanid throne after Abū Saʿīd's death, supporting a series of Chinggisid candidates until the mid-1340s. His son and successor, Shaykh Uways (757–776/1356–1374), was the first independent monarch of the dynasty.

Shaykh Uways is generally regarded as the most successful and most humane of the Jalayirid rulers. He conquered Azerbaijan within a short space (759/1358) and reduced the Shīrwānshāh to vassal status. Thereafter, apart from a dangerous revolt (765/1364) by his governor in Baghdad, Khwāja Mīrjān, the reign represents an era of consolidation. An important element in Uways's policy, it seems, was his clemency, as instanced in the reinstatement of Khwāja Mīrjān in

Baghdad in 769/1367–8.[43] Timur would later comment on the Jalayirid monarch's just government. Shaykh Uways died on 2 Jumādā I 776/9 October 1374 when preparing an assault on his eastern neighbour and fellow Mongol, Amīr Walī, who had earlier made inroads into Jalayirid territory (see later).

Like Timur subsequently, the Jalayirids were drawn into the fractious relationships of the Muzaffarid princes. In 770/1368–9 Shāh Maḥmūd b. Muḥammad b. al-Muẓaffar, who governed Isfahan on behalf of his brother and rival Shāh-i Shujāʿ, sought Shaykh Uways's daughter in marriage and requested military assistance. In response Shaykh Uways despatched an army to support him, which expelled Shāh-i Shujāʿ from his capital, Shiraz. But when the brothers were reconciled after a few years, the Jalayirid troops returned home.[44] The death of Shaykh Uways, shortly followed by that of Shāh Maḥmūd in 776/1375, freed up Shāh-i Shujāʿ to take his revenge, and the divisions among Uways's sons provided him with the opportunity.

Jalayirid officers had put to death Uways's eldest son, Ḥasan, prior to enthroning the second, Sulṭān Husayn, whom the late monarch had designated as his heir. Sulṭān Husayn was dominated by the amir Sāriq ʿĀdil, better known as ʿĀdil Āqā, whom Uways had appointed as governor of Rayy around 772/1370–1 and whose unpopularity had provoked the formation of an opposition party among the amirs.[45] His short reign witnessed a marked decline in the central power. Challenged by his brothers, Sulṭān Bāyazīd and Shaykh ʿAlī,[46] he was forced to preside over a threefold division of the Jalayirid lands, with Sulṭān Bāyazīd ensconced in Sulṭāniyya and Shaykh ʿAlī in Baghdad. In 778/1376–7 Sulṭān Husayn's forces were defeated by Shāh-i Shujāʿ, who advanced as far as Tabriz and took up residence there for four months. When Sulṭān Ḥusayn moved on the city from Baghdad, where he had taken refuge, the Muzaffarid made haste to withdraw from Tabriz to Shiraz.[47] He returned in 781/1379–80 to besiege ʿĀdil Āqā in Sulṭāniyya. Although the Muzaffarids suffered an initial defeat, the arrival of reinforcements secured ʿĀdil Āqā's submission and a large quantity of treasure.[48]

In 784/1382 Sulṭān Ḥusayn was overthrown and executed by yet another brother, Sulṭān Aḥmad. From the outset the new monarch was beset by crises. In 780/1378–9, during Sulṭān Ḥusayn's reign, a Jalayirid amir, Pīr Bādik, had defected to the Muzaffarids, and with Shāh-i Shujāʿ's backing occupied Shūshtar. In Baghdad he had the khutba made and the coinage struck in Shāh-i Shujāʿ's name, while at the same time joining forces with Shaykh ʿAlī, who was nominally governor of the city. Sulṭān Ḥusayn had moved against them and they fled to Khūzistān, returning to Baghdad after his withdrawal. On learning of Sulṭān Aḥmad's accession, Shaykh ʿAlī and Pīr Bādik advanced on Tabriz. Sulṭān Aḥmad was reduced to calling upon his western neighbours, the Qarā-Qūyūnlū Türkmen, who did him the signal service of defeating his adversaries; both Shaykh ʿAlī and Pīr Bādik fell in the engagement and Baghdad came under Sulṭān Aḥmad's rule.[49] Meanwhile, ʿĀdil Āqā had proclaimed Sulṭān Bāyazīd b. Uways as ruler in Sulṭāniyya and in the autumn of 784/1382 they advanced northwards in pursuit of Sulṭān Aḥmad. A settlement was reached, however, whereby Sulṭān Aḥmad would govern Azerbaijan, Arrān, Mūghān and the Türkmen territory, while ʿIrāq-i ʿAjam was to be Sulṭān Bāyazīd's share, and the brothers would divide the revenues of Iraq (-i ʿArab).[50]

At this point Jalayirid politics were further complicated by the advent of Shāh-i Shujāʿ's nephew Shāh Manṣūr, during an especially volatile phase of his career. Sent in 779/1377–8 by his uncle to secure Yazd, he had absconded (see later) and made first for Jalayirid territory, where he spent some time as a guest of ʿĀdil Āqā and was made governor of Hamadān. He then departed to Amīr Walī's dominions, where in 781/1379 he participated in the expedition to restore the Sarbadār leader ʿAlī-yi Mu'ayyad in Sabzawār,[51] but after a time came back once more to rejoin ʿĀdil Āqā, who was by now on good terms with Shāh-i Shujāʿ and placed Shāh Manṣūr in confinement. Released by well-wishers in Sulṭāniyya, the prince headed for Tabriz, where Sulṭān Aḥmad welcomed him and deputed him to recover Shūshtar on his behalf, a task Shāh Manṣūr duly fulfilled.[52]

In 785/1383–4 Shāh-i Shujāʿ profited from the struggle between Sulṭān Aḥmad Jalāyir and ʿĀdil Āqā to enter Jalayirid territory once more. ʿĀdil Āqā, along with Sulṭān Aḥmad's brother Sulṭān Bāyazīd, joined him at Hamadān and the allies offered Sulṭān Aḥmad terms which he accepted. According to Kutubī, Sulṭān Aḥmad had complained to the Muzaffarid ruler regarding ʿĀdil Āqā's promotion of Sulṭān Bāyazīd and had appealed to him to engineer a reconciliation between himself and his brother. Whether through Shāh-i Shujāʿ's good offices or not, a settlement was reached on the same terms as before, namely that Sulṭān Bāyazīd should rule in ʿIrāq-i ʿAjam; ʿĀdil Āqā accompanied Shāh-i Shujāʿ back to Shiraz. In 786/1384 Sulṭān Aḥmad moved from Baghdad to Sulṭāniyya, where Bāyazīd resided; Bāyazīd surrendered the town and the brothers made peace.[53] With the passing of Shāh-i Shujāʿ in that year, the Muzaffarid threat came to an end. This did not mean, however, that Sulṭān Aḥmad's rule was secure. His murder of his brother Sulṭān Ḥusayn had outraged public opinion. Unable to trust his amirs, he removed a great many of them and relied instead on persons of lower social origins – at least according to Astarābādī, a former subject and admittedly a hostile witness.[54] Not unexpectedly, there were elements within Sulṭān Aḥmad's territories, ʿĀdil Āqā included, who would desert him to serve Timur.

TÜRKMEN AND MONGOLS IN THE JAZĪRA AND ANATOLIA

In addition to maintaining intermittent hostilities with the Muzaffarids and Amīr Walī, the Jalayirids could ill afford to lose sight of their western frontier. The Seljuq Sultanate of Rūm, which had disappeared around the beginning of the fourteenth century, had been replaced by numerous principalities (usually termed *beylik*s in the historiography). The most important were the Qaramanids, who held the old Seljuq capital of Konya, the Dulghadir (Dhū l-Qadr) around Marʿash and the Ottomans in the far north-west. The rulers were, for the most part, Türkmen chiefs; the exception was Aratna (d. 753/1352) in eastern Anatolia.[55]

Immediately to the west of the Jalayirid dominions, by mid-century there had emerged two nomadic Türkmen confederacies of obscure origin: the Āq-Qūyūnlū ('White Sheep': Mo. *qoyun*, 'sheep'), centred on the town of Āmid in Diyār Bakr, and the Qarā-Qūyūnlū ('Black Sheep') in the territory stretching from Erzurum to Mosul.[56]

To the Jalayirids the Qarā-Qūyūnlū posed the greater threat. We first hear of them in 767/1365–6, when Shaykh Uways attacked and defeated their chief, Bayrām Khwāja, in the vicinity of Mūsh and exacted tribute from him. Yet within a few years Bayrām Khwāja had occupied Mosul. Qarā Muḥammad (either his son or his nephew), who succeeded him in 782/1380, proved a more dangerous neighbour, owing in part to his decisive intervention on Sulṭān Aḥmad's behalf in the conflict for the Jalayirid throne. Relations between Qarā Muḥammad and Sulṭān Aḥmad, cemented by marriage, grew closer over the years that followed but were always potentially fraught.

Aratna had governed the province of Anatolia for Abū Saʿīd and subsequently for Shaykh Ḥasan. Residing first at Sivas and later at Kayserı, he adopted the style of Sultan ʿAlā' al-Dīn. If Faryūmadī is to be believed, his government was exemplary, to the extent that the people nicknamed him 'the Prophet with Sparse Beard' (*kūsa-yi payghambar*).[57] He was succeeded in turn by his son Ghiyāth al-Dīn Muḥammad (d. 767/1366) and the latter's son ʿAlā' al-Dīn ʿAlī Beg (d. 782/1380), each of whom forfeited territory to the Qaramanids and the Āq-Qūyūnlū; Kayserı appears to have passed into the hands of an independent amir.[58] After ʿAlī Beg's death, his deputy (*nā'ib*) Burhān al-Dīn, who belonged to the line of qadis of Kayserı and claimed descent from the Seljuq Sultans, supplanted his master's young son or perhaps maintained the boy for a time as a mere figurehead.[59] Qadi Burhān al-Dīn, who as a Tājīk (and usurper of Aratna's throne) experienced some difficulty in imposing his lordship on the Mongols in his dominions, presided from Sivas over a fragmented polity that was no more than a 'network of mutual obligations, of alliances and vassalities'.[60] Despite his efforts to stem the Ottoman advance, he was ousted from Sivas in 801/1398 and captured and put to death by Timur's ally, the chief of the Āq-Qūyūnlū.

Anybody contemplating Anatolia in 1340 could have been excused for thinking that the future lay with the Qaramanids. But by 1400 the political map had been drastically redrawn and the Ottomans had emerged by far as the strongest among the local powers. Having crossed the Straits in 1354, they reduced Serbia to vassalage in 1389. Their Sultan, Bayezid I Yildirim ('the Thunderbolt'), who occupied the Bulgarian kingdom by 1393 and destroyed a crusading army at Nicopolis in 1396, threatened the very survival of the Byzantine empire. He had subjected or eliminated the majority of the other Türkmen *beylik*s, conquered Qaraman (800/1397) and Sivas (801/1398) and menaced the principality of Arzinjān (Erzincan).[61] His military successes rendered him the greatest challenge to Timur in the Near East and one which the Central Asian conqueror could not afford to ignore.

THE MUZAFFARIDS

The Jalayirid dynasty's most formidable rivals within the Ilkhanate – before the advent of Timur – were the Muzaffarids, whose dominions lay to the south of the Dasht-i Kabīr. They claimed descent from a member of an Arab family that had migrated from Khwāf in Khurāsān to Yazd at the time of the Mongol invasions.[62] His grandson Sharaf al-Dīn al-Muẓaffar (d. 713/1314) was entrusted by the atabeg of Yazd with the governorship of the town of Maybud, and al-Muẓaffar's son and successor, Mubāriz al-Dīn Muḥammad, was instrumental in the suppression of the ruling dynasty of Yazd and appointed governor of that city in 719/1319–20 by the Ilkhan Abū Saʿīd. Ten years later he married a princess who sprang from the Qutlughkhanid dynasty that had ruled Kirmān until 704/1305.[63] When Kirmān's ruler was expelled by a group of amirs, he appealed to the Kartid king of Herat, who despatched one of his own amirs to take over the province. But shortly afterwards, possibly in 741/1340, the Chobanid Pīr Ḥusayn sent a force to reduce Kirmān, rewarding Mubāriz al-Dīn for his previous support by making him its governor.[64]

From this point onwards Mubāriz al-Dīn enjoyed unchallenged authority over Kirmān. He went on to annex the principality of Shabānkāra (*c.* 755/1354), to wrest first Shiraz (754/1353) and then Isfahan (757/1356) from his Injuid rival Shaykh Abū Isḥāq and to replace the atabeg of Luristān with a cousin who would serve the Muzaffarids as a dutiful subordinate.[65] These achievements established him as by far the most impressive potentate in southern Iran. In 755/1354 the Caliph in Cairo conferred on him the title of Sultan (see later). Jaʿfarī lists among his territories Shiraz, Yazd, Kirmān, Isfahan, Shūshtar, Khurramābād, Qum, Kāshān, Sāwa, Qazwīn, Sulṭāniyya and Tabriz.[66] But Mubāriz al-Dīn's hold on some of these towns, notably Tabriz, was brief. Invading Azerbaijan in the wake of the Jochid withdrawal and defeating its ruler, Akhīchuq, at Miyāna (759/1358), he swiftly retired on the approach of a superior Jalayirid force.[67]

Mubāriz al-Dīn was a harsh and dourly moralistic ruler, whom the poet Ḥāfiẓ contrasts with the easy-going Shaykh Abū Isḥāq,[68] and his unpopularity among his allegedly hedonistic subjects offered a temptation to his relatives to replace him. But what eventually brought him down was his favouritism towards a grandson, Shāḥ Yaḥyā. In mid-Ramaḍān 759/late August 1358, following his return from Azerbaijan, he was deposed, imprisoned and blinded and replaced by his eldest son, Shāh-i Shujāʿ, who had held Kirmān as his appanage since 754/1353. Released a month later, he was imprisoned afresh for conspiring to have Shāh-i Shujāʿ murdered and died towards the end of Rabīʿ I 765/in the last days of 1363.[69]

The reign of Shāh-i Shujāʿ, who generally resided in Shiraz, was bedevilled by conflicts with his kinsmen, and it is no accident that Hilālī was concerned to stress his status as his father's acknowledged heir since 755/1354.[70] On his accession Shāh-i Shujāʿ granted Abarqūh and ʿIrāq-i ʿAjam to his brother Shāh Maḥmūd, Kirmān to another brother, Sulṭān Aḥmad, and Yazd to a nephew, Shāḥ Yaḥyā.[71] This neat partition of the Muzaffarid dominions was destined to be the exception in the dynasty's history rather than the rule. Shāh-i Shujāʿ and Shāh Maḥmūd engaged in frequent hostilities, the latter usually in alliance with the Jalayirid Shaykh Uways. In 765/1363–4 a coalition of Shāh Maḥmūd, Sulṭān Aḥmad and Shāḥ Yaḥyā ousted Shāh-i Shujāʿ from Shiraz and he withdrew to Abarqūh.[72] In returning to the struggle, he ultimately benefited from the same fickleness on the part of his relatives that had reduced him to straits. First, he was reconciled with Shāḥ Yaḥyā, who married his daughter; then he was joined by another nephew, Shāh Manṣūr;[73] and finally, after an indecisive battle between Shāh-i Shujāʿ and Shāh Maḥmūd outside Shiraz on 16 Dhū l-Qaʿda 767/25 July

1366,[74] Sulṭān Aḥmad came over to him. Shāh-i Shujāʿ was able to re-enter Shiraz a week or two later and the brothers made peace, but it was short-lived.[75]

The conflict between Shāh-i Shujāʿ and Shāh Maḥmūd lasted almost until the latter's death on 9 Shawwāl 776/13 March 1375, when Shāh-i Shujāʿ took over Isfahan unopposed.[76] Not long afterwards he had learned, too, of the death of the Jalayirid Shaykh Uways, and this, together with the acquisition of Isfahan, encouraged him in a bid to occupy Tabriz (777/1375) as his father had done;[77] but he enjoyed only brief success, returning to his own territories after less than two months. In 770/1368–9 he had, like his father, secured a diploma of investiture from the ʿAbbasid Caliph in Cairo,[78] but he was still confronted by recalcitrant kinsmen, notably Shāḥ Yaḥyā. When an expedition against Yazd met with defeat, Shāh-i Shujāʿ formed the intention of heading another campaign there in person, but was persuaded by a nephew, Shāḥ Yaḥyā's brother Shāh Manṣūr, to put him in command instead. Shāh Manṣūr might have seemed an excellent choice for such a mission, as he had served his uncle with distinction and had married another of Shāh-i Shujāʿ's daughters.[79] Arriving before Yazd, however, he was won over by his mother and induced to join forces with his brother Shāḥ Yaḥyā, whereupon his troops deserted and fell back on Shiraz. Shāḥ Yaḥyā then acted in characteristically duplicitous fashion: he proposed that Shāh Manṣūr secure reinforcements from Amīr Walī in Astarābād but omitted to fit him out with a military escort. In the event, Shāh Manṣūr left for Māzandarān in the hope of repairing his fortunes.[80] Later, from Jalayirid Shūshtar, he would obstruct his uncle's enterprises once again (see earlier).

Shāh-i Shujāʿ's last years were clouded by personal tragedy. A son, Sulṭān Uways, who had earlier taken refuge with Shāh Maḥmūd in Isfahan and had been reconciled with his father only after the latter's entry into the city, fell ill and died; and during his return march from Sulṭāniyya to Shiraz Shāh-i Shujāʿ also lost his chief wife.[81] Then in 785/1383, mindful, so Kutubī says, of how he had treated his own father and prone to listen to informers, he had another son, suspected of designs on his throne, imprisoned and blinded, an action of which he soon repented bitterly.[82] His health declined thereafter and he died on 22 Shaʿbān 786/9 October 1384, following a vain attempt to wrest Shūshtar from Shāh Manṣūr.[83] One of his last acts was to divide his lands: his young son Zayn al-ʿĀbidīn ʿAlī was to have Shiraz, Kirmān passed again to Sulṭān Aḥmad and Yazd went to Shāh Yaḥyā.

Like those made on Shāh-i Shujāʿ's accession, these arrangements were swiftly overturned. First, Shāh Yaḥyā was invited to take over Isfahan by its populace, whom Zayn al-ʿĀbidīn had alienated. He then moved on Shiraz, whence Zayn al-ʿĀbidīn advanced to meet him. Peace was mediated between the two cousins, who each returned home. Soon, however, the inhabitants of Isfahan, acting on what Kutubī calls 'the perversity that is ingrained in their character', expelled Shāh Yaḥyā, who withdrew to Yazd, and Zayn al-ʿĀbidīn despatched his maternal uncle, Muẓaffar Kāshī, to govern Isfahan on his behalf.[84] These rapid shifts of fortune attracted the attention of Timur. Before his death, Shāh-i Shujāʿ had written to the Central Asian conqueror, recognising him as the executor of his will and as guardian to Zayn al-ʿĀbidīn.[85] In 789/1387 the latter, required to attend Timur's court, rashly ignored the summons,[86] thereby provoking Timur's attack on the Muzaffarid territories.

THE KARTIDS OF HERAT

Let us now turn to the regions that lay adjacent to Transoxiana and on which the Chaghadayid khans had evinced designs since the middle decades of the thirteenth century. Eastern Iran was divided among four polities (discounting Sīstān, since the local history ends in 725/1325 and we know relatively little about the kingdom thereafter).[87] The Kartid ruler Muʿizz al-Dīn Pīr Ḥusayn Muḥammad, who dominated eastern Khurāsān from his capital at Herat and had been the Ilkhans' most important vassal in the region, played an increasingly prominent role. His victory at Zāwa in 743/1342 over his Sarbadār neighbours (see later) and a subsequent triumph over the invading troops of the Arlāt and Apardī amirs from the Chaghadayid Qara'unas territories in *c*. 1349 induced hubris.[88] By

750/1349 he felt strong enough to repudiate his dynasty's client status and to assume the style of Sultan.[89] This brought down upon him a sharp reaction from the Chaghadayid ulus headed by Amir Qazaghan (see pp. 218–19). Thanks to this humiliation, Muʿizz al-Dīn was expelled from Herat in favour of a brother, Malik Bāqir. He failed to secure Qazaghan's help but retrieved his throne in 755/1354; Bāqir went into exile.

Like Timur a generation later, Qazaghan had allegedly been incited to invade Kartid territory by the shaykhs of Jām.[90] Aubin has thrown into relief the enormous influence wielded by this family, who combined the management of the prestigious shrine of Shaykh Aḥmad Jāmī with possession of an ample agricultural base and who carried weight with Tājīk and Mongol alike.[91] Shaykh Quṭb al-Dīn of Jām played a part in the election of Taghai Temür as Ilkhan in 737/1337 and was among those whose approval Arghūnshāh secured for Taghai Temür's second enthronement, in Nishapur, two years later.[92] Members of the family had intermarried with the Kartids. Muʿīn al-Dīn Muḥammad Jāmī, Muʿizz al-Dīn's wazir, was the son of Muʿizz al-Dīn's sister or aunt and was himself the malik's son-in-law.[93] The appeal to Qazaghan emanated from Muʿīn al-Dīn's uncle, Raḍī' al-Dīn, the administrator (*mutawallī*) of the shrine at Jām. Aubin suggests that the motive was resentment at the malik's authoritarian tendencies rather than some family feud.[94]

Muʿizz al-Dīn subsequently showed himself ready to intervene in the affairs of the Chaghadayid ulus. When Timur took refuge in Mākhān in 767/1368, he entered into negotiations with the malik that are obscured in the sources but that apparently resulted in a compact enabling him to attempt to re-establish himself in Transoxiana in opposition to Amīr Ḥusayn, now his rival. In the event, however, Timur was initially unsuccessful and fled northwards, appealing for assistance to the Mughūls, a gesture that induced Ḥusayn and his other enemies to make peace with him (see pp. 255–6). Muʿizz al-Dīn, having duly launched a campaign into the Balkh region, retired on hearing of the reconciliation.[95]

Muʿizz al-Dīn, who died on 7 Dhū l-Qaʿda 771/2 June 1370,[96] was succeeded by his elder son, Ghiyāth al-Dīn Pīr ʿAlī; the younger,

Shams al-Dīn Muḥammad, received an appanage at Sarakhs. Conflict arose between the brothers and eventually Pīr ʿAlī expelled Muḥammad from Sarakhs. But a far greater problem confronted him in the form of the Sarbadārs in western Khurāsān. Muʿīn al-Dīn Jāmī may in time have become dissatisfied with Muʿizz al-Dīn's external policy. He had urged him in 754/1353 to profit from Taghai Temür's murder by moving against the Sarbadārs;[97] as far as we know, Muʿizz al-Dīn had failed to comply. It was left to Pīr ʿAlī, perhaps from a desire to avenge his grandfather Taghai Temür, to secure in 773/1371–2 a fatwa from jurists in Herat and to embark on all-out war against the Sarbadārs – a policy that would propel them into the arms of Timur.[98]

THE MONGOLS OF NORTHERN AND EASTERN IRAN

Amīr Walī was the son of Shaykh ʿAlī-yi Hindū, a Mongol amir from the Besüt tribe who had perished along with his master, the Ilkhan Taghai Temür, at the hands of the Sarbadārs in Dhū l-Qaʿda 754/December 1353. At some point before 757/1356 Amīr Walī, who had fled to Nasā, returned north to seize power in Astarābād and expelled the Sarbadārs from Taghai Temür's territories in Māzandarān. Initially he claimed to be acting for the late Ilkhan's son Luqmān, but after a few years he dropped this pretence and banished Luqmān from his dominions.[99] Amīr Walī engaged in conflict on a number of different fronts. Under the year 772/1370–1 Zayn al-Dīn calls him ruler not only of Astarābād but of Simnān, Dāmghān and Rayy.[100] In that year he moved against the Jalayirids and fought with Shaykh Uways. Faryūmadī hails this as a victory for Amīr Walī that cost the lives of several Iraqi amirs and won him widespread renown.[101] The next year Uways gathered an army for another campaign against Amīr Walī, but the death of a brother necessitated his return to Tabriz. He died (776/1374) when preparing to march against Walī for yet a third time.[102] Amīr Walī was subsequently induced to attack the Jalayirids by the renegade Muzaffarid prince Shāh Manṣūr, on the grounds that Sulṭān Ḥusayn b. Uways was a nonentity and his amirs were bitterly at odds.[103] But Faryūmadī, writing in 783/1381–2, confirms that Amīr Walī and Sulṭān Ḥusayn were at that time on friendly terms. He also defines Amīr Walī's dominions as Khurāsān, Māzandarān, Dihistān, *Talikhān, Rayy and Qūmis.[104] In 786/1384, however, the forces of Sulṭān Ḥusayn's successor, Sulṭān Aḥmad, overran much of Walī's territory, obliging him to fall back on Gīlān and Māzandarān.[105] This was a severe blow to Amīr Walī's strength and standing on the very eve of his confrontation with Timur.

There were two distinct bodies of Mongol troops in Khurāsān who formed a loosely structured polity: the Jā'ūn-i Qurbān and the Mongols of Quhistān; Jürgen Paul defines the former as a 'regional state' which on occasion formed part of the larger polity ruled by the Ilkhan Taghai Temür, and which comprised Nasā, Kalāt, Ṭūs and Abīward and, on occasion, Nishapur.[106] Both groups initially recognised Taghai Temür as their lord. The name of the Jā'ūn-i Qurbān ('Three per Cent') betrays their origins as a force recruited proportionately from other Mongol divisions. According to Naṭanzī,[107] this force was created at the Ilkhan Ghazan's behest, entrusted to a son of the Ilkhanid general and kingmaker, Nawrūz b. Arghun Aqa, after the latter's execution in Herat in 697/1297 and despatched to Kalāt, near Ṭūs. Its history is summarised by Faryūmadī, who asserts instead, however, that the unit – which he terms the 'mini-thousand (*hazāracha*) of the Jā'ūn-i Qurbān and the Nawrūzīs' – was assigned by Ghazan's successor Öljeitü to Nawrūz's brothers, Oyiratai Ghazan and Ḥājjī.[108] Although often called Oyirats in the secondary literature, the Jā'ūn-i Qurbān, like all Mongol forces assembled on a proportionate basis, comprised diverse tribal elements; only the leadership certainly belonged to the Oyirat.[109]

The headship of the Jā'ūn-i Qurbān was subsequently disputed between Oyiratai Ghazan's son Arghūnshāh and a cousin, Ḥiya Taghai, but from 737/1336–7 the former, now chief amir to the Ilkhan Taghai Temür, enjoyed undisputed authority. He was constantly at odds, however, with Muʿizz al-Dīn, the Kartid malik of Herat, and in 741/1340–1 he suffered a defeat by the Sarbadārs, to whom he lost Nishapur.[110] On his death (746/1345–6), his brother Tükel Buqa was nominated by Taghai Temür but was shortly killed by a relative, Ḥiya Taghai's son Ḥasan Baṣrī. After 745/1344–5 the Jā'ūn-i Qurbān apparently ceased to recognise Taghai Temür;[111] but when Ḥasan Baṣrī met his end at the hands of Arghūnshāh's amirs, the Ilkhan nominated Arghūnshāh's son Muḥammad Beg to command the Jā'ūn-i Qurbān and gave him a daughter in marriage. Muḥammad Beg soon had to face a rebellion by the governor of Mashhad and Ṭūs, a Mongol amir named ʿAlī-yi Ramaḍān. This gave rise to a series of splits, from which the Sarbadār leader Yaḥyā Karābī profited to occupy Ṭūs.[112]

After ʿAlī-yi Ramaḍān's murder, Muḥammad Beg presided over a somewhat truncated domain until his death in 774/1373.[113] He was succeeded (if we can use the term, since by this time, if not before, the Jā'ūn-i Qurbān seem no longer to have acknowledged a single head)[114] by his brother ʿAlī Beg, who had earlier acquired the unenviable distinction of offending the young Timur. When in the 1360s the latter and his then confederate, Amīr Ḥusayn, sought shelter in Khurāsān from their enemies and fell into ʿAlī Beg's hands, he had them chained and confined in the stronghold of Mākhān, near Merv, releasing them only at Muḥammad Beg's instigation.[115] This was a lapse of hospitality that Timur would not forget.

The Mongol troops in Quhistān, with their headquarters at Junābād, were at first commanded by ʿAbd-Allāh b. Ma'ulai, who belonged to a line of noyans of the Küyin Tatar in the later Ilkhans' service.[116] He engaged in conflict with the malik of Herat, but was eventually killed fighting for Taghai Temür against the Sarbadārs. His sons Muḥammad Beg (not to be confused with the Jā'ūn-i Qurbān amir above) and Satilmish Beg succeeded him in turn. The latter regained the territory that Malik Muʿizz al-Dīn had wrested from his father and headed a campaign against Herat in alliance with dissident Kartid commanders and the Qara'unas amirs Muḥammad Khwāja and Choban; but in an engagement with Muʿizz al-Dīn's forces in 759/1359 Satilmish Beg and the two Qara'unas amirs were killed. The arbitrary conduct of Jaʿfar Beg (son of Ḥasan Baṣrī and thus from the Jā'ūn-i Qurbān ruling dynasty), whom Satilmish Beg's followers had recognised as leader in view of his son's youth, alienated his amirs: they handed Junābād over to

Muʿizz al-Dīn and Jaʿfar Beg withdrew to Iraq.[117] This marked a significant Kartid advance in the region.

THE SARBADĀRS

The Sarbadār state, centred on the cities of Sabzawār and Nishapur, was a highly unusual political formation. It rested on a fitful and uneasy alliance between local landowners, religiously conservative urban elements and dervishes of a radical Shīʿī bent, a cocktail that rendered it prey to considerable instability.[118] Lacking any pattern of hereditary leadership or ethos of legitimacy, it has variously been labelled a 'republic' and a 'kingdom without kings'.[119] There was constant tension between the Sarbadār military and the Shaykhiyya – charismatic/messianic dervishes – and the locus of power shifted to and fro between the two elements; there were further divisions within the ranks of the Sabzawārī populace, among the landowners and members of the urban craft guilds. The regime was marked by a series of violent *coups d'état*, and scarcely any of the rulers died a natural death.

The rising of the Sarbadārs (the most plausible etymology is Pers. *sar ba-dār*, roughly 'gallows-birds') had begun on 12 Ṣafar 737/9 September 1337, when a local notable, ʿAbd al-Razzāq, who had killed a tax-collector in the town of Bāshtīn some months earlier and gathered a band of sympathisers, took over nearby Sabzawār.[120] But in effect the first leaders were ʿAbd al-Razzāq's brother and successor Wajīh al-Dīn Masʿūd, who had murdered him in Dhū l-Qaʿda 738/May–June 1338 (or possibly late in 739/spring of 1339), and Ḥasan Jūrī, a peripatetic radical preacher of Twelver Shīʿī (Athnāʿashariyya) doctrines who drew much of his support from Sabzawār and who proclaimed the imminent appearance of the Mahdī. Although Masʿūd had initially acknowledged Taghai Temür's sovereignty and minted coins in his name, the Ilkhan was roused by Sarbadār attacks on the Jā'ūn-i Qurbān and their capture of Nishapur in 741/1340 to send an army against them under his brother ʿAlī Ke'ün, who was defeated and killed (742/1341–2). Masʿūd's forces occupied a wide area formerly under Taghai Temür's rule, including Jājarm, Jurjān,

Dāmghān, Sāwa and Simnān, and he now struck coins in the name of the Chobanids' protégé, the Ilkhan Sulaymān.

But relations between Masʿūd and Ḥasan Jūrī, whose methods and aims differed sharply, were strained; and when the allies advanced against Herat and confronted Muʿizz al-Dīn's troops at Zāwa on 13 Ṣafar 743/18 July 1342, Masʿūd had Ḥasan Jūrī struck down in the heat of the battle. With the resulting demoralisation of Ḥasan's followers, however, the Sarbadārs were defeated. Although they were victorious over Mongol forces in Māzandarān in Rajab 743/ December 1342, when several high-ranking Mongol noyans were killed,[121] a bid by Masʿūd to extend his power over that region in 745/1344 was thwarted by the local princes of Āmul and Rustamdār, who were loyal to Taghai Temür. Masʿūd was captured and executed, and the Sarbadārs once more acknowledged Taghai Temür's overlordship.[122]

Yet neither military reverses like Zāwa and the disastrous Māzandarān campaign nor a strikingly mercurial internal history spelled the end for the Sarbadārs. Masʿūd's first three successors, who included his brother (or nephew, according to Faryūmadī), belonged to the Sarbadār military; but in 748/1347 power passed to one of Ḥasan Jūrī's former adherents, Tāj al-Dīn ʿAlī Chishumī,[123] who acquired a good name through his administrative reforms and his personal integrity. Although presumably a Shīʿī, he refrained from attempting to impose Shiʿism on the military and thereby preserved some kind of unity within the movement for the few years he ruled. Following his murder in 752/1351–2 by a disgruntled Sabzawārī artisan, Ḥaydar Qaṣṣāb, the leadership passed to a member of the Sabzawārī aristocracy, Yaḥyā Karābī (or Karāwī), who treacherously killed the Ilkhan Taghai Temür under pretence of offering homage (754/1353). Karābī's own murder (756/1355–6) introduced a series of short-lived rulers – his nephew (or, according to Faryūmadī, his brother) Ẓahīr al-Dīn Karābī, Ḥaydar Qaṣṣāb and Masʿūd's son Luṭf-Allāh. Ḥaydar's murderer, Ḥasan Dāmghānī, ruled for a brief space, during which he was able to wrest Ṭūs from the Jā'ūn-i Qurbān (*c.* 759/1357–8). The throne then passed to a moderate Shīʿī, ʿAlī-yi Mu'ayyad,[124] acting at first in concert with Darwīsh ʿAzīz, a radical who had briefly established a theocratic state in Mashhad but had been expelled from there by Ḥasan Dāmghānī. This duumvirate mirrored that of Wajīh al-Dīn Masʿūd and Ḥasan Jūrī in the earliest stage of the movement; in similar fashion its termination coincided with a campaign against Herat, except that ʿAlī-yi Mu'ayyad disposed of Darwīsh ʿAzīz and his followers without waiting for the onset of battle.[125] In 767/1365–6 he achieved the sweet triumph of wresting Taghai Temür's old residence of Astarābād from Amīr Walī, retaining it for some years.[126]

The Sarbadārs enjoyed a bad press. Their military activities in Khurāsān were highly disruptive; they were responsible for the deaths of a number of Mongol commanders and civil administrators and their treacherous assassination of Taghai Temür caused a widespread sensation.[127] For Faryūmadī, they were 'vile non-dervishes' (*makhdhūlān-i nā-darwīsh*) and the very term dervish was a misnomer for a gang of highway robbers (*quṭṭāʿ al-ṭarīq*).[128] Ibn Baṭṭūṭa, who passed through the region in the 1340s, transmits the same charge, condemning them as exclusively Shīʿīs who aimed to eradicate Sunnī Islam from Khurāsān.[129] But he was misled by the Shīʿī proclivities of Ḥasan Jūrī and his followers, which were uncharacteristic of the Sarbadārs as a whole.[130] Mahendrarajah has shown that the image of the Sarbadār state as Shīʿī-dominated, in these early years, is at odds with the evidence. Before 763/1362 the rulers were sometimes Sunnī and usually issued, either on their own authority or on behalf of Sunnī overlords, coins that bore the names of the four Orthodox Caliphs. Only thereafter do Sarbadār coins consistently bear the names of the Twelve Imams; the work of ʿAlī-yi Mu'ayyad, this in fact represents a reaction against the extreme beliefs of the Shaykhiyya.[131]

In Aubin's view the Sarbadār polity owed its survival to the desire of its neighbours to maintain a buffer-state between them.[132] Despite a perceived lack of social or doctrinal respectability, the Sarbadārs fitted readily into the multi-faceted power structure in Khurāsān and exhibited the diplomatic suppleness to profit from it. Their flexibility meant that their assistance was solicited on numerous occasions by various prominent figures in the Iranian world. A rebel amir in

Māzandarān named Abū Bakr, whose atrocities would earn him an unsavoury reputation, called on them for aid in his conflict with Taghai Temür.[133] Driven from Shiraz in 754/1353, Shaykh Abū Isḥāq 'Īnjū' tried to induce Yaḥyā Karābī to launch a diversion against Muzaffarid Yazd or Kirmān.[134] So too, when Malik Bāqir was obliged to yield Herat to his brother Muʿizz al-Dīn in 755/1354, his first recourse was to make for Sabzawār.[135] Of the Jā'ūn-i Qurbān Mongols, the brothers and son of Ḥasan Baṣrī reacted to his murder by seeking refuge in Sabzawār, and the rebel ʿAlī-yi Ramaḍān and the 'official' ruler, Muḥammad Beg, would shortly both in turn appeal for help to Karābī.[136] Later, the Muzaffarid Shāh Yaḥyā asked the Sarbadārs for help against his kinsmen: although ʿAlī-yi Mu'ayyad, revealingly, could spare only one hundred horsemen, his response was enough to inspire Shāh-i Shujāʿ with a desire for revenge.[137] And lastly, the Kartid prince Shams al-Dīn Muḥammad, the younger brother and rival of Ghiyāth al-Dīn Pīr ʿAlī, likewise received a warm welcome from ʿAlī-yi Mu'ayyad when dislodged from his appanage at Sarakhs, though he subsequently moved on to seek his fortunes at Timur's headquarters.[138]

In the quarter-century preceding ʿAlī-yi Mu'ayyad's accession the Sarbadār state had been governed by a total of twelve rulers. His relatively long reign (763/1361 or 1362–783/1381, with a three-year interruption), coupled with his moderate doctrinal stance, easily presents the semblance of stability alongside the survival rates of his predecessors and their relative extremism.[139] But in fact the latter phase of his reign was marked by crises born of his policy towards the dervishes and of their contacts with neighbouring states. In 778/1376–7 the supporters of Darwīsh ʿAzīz, who had taken refuge with Shāh-i Shujāʿ in Shiraz, returned with Muzaffarid military assistance and expelled ʿAlī-yi Mu'ayyad from Sabzawār; he was reduced to seeking asylum with his old rival Amīr Walī. The excesses of the dervish regime played into their hands and a lengthy campaign by Walī restored ʿAlī-yi Mu'ayyad in Sabzawār in Rajab 781/October 1379.[140] Meanwhile, in 777/1376, Ghiyāth al-Dīn Pīr ʿAlī, with the encouragement of a different group from among the exiled dervishes, seized Nishapur.[141] The Sarbadār alliance with Amīr Walī, moreover, was brief. He and Pīr ʿAlī, despite their mutual antipathy, were each soon threatening Sabzawār, driving ʿAlī-yi Mu'ayyad to offer his submission to Timur and to appeal for the conqueror's assistance.

THE IMPACT OF MUTUAL STRIFE

The degree to which Iran was affected by the conflicts of these various belligerents can perhaps best be gauged by considering the vicissitudes of certain towns in northern and eastern Iran. Simnān, at one time under the rule of the Sarbadarid Masʿūd, may have passed into the hands of the *ustundār* of Rūyān, Jalāl al-Dawla Iskandar (d. 761/1359–60), one of the princes who crushed Masʿūd's invasion of Māzandarān two years later. He is described as holding sway from the borders of Qazwīn as far as Simnān and occupying Rayy.[142] Thereafter the town was seized by Amīr Walī and was caught up in his conflicts with the Jalayirids. Rayy was an object of contention between Amīr Walī and the Jalayirids, changing hands a number of times.[143] To the east, Nishapur, wrested by Masʿūd from the Jā'ūn-i Qurbān in 741/1340–1, was part of the region extensively ravaged in 755/1354 by the Qara'unas amirs in concert with Muḥammad Beg of the Jā'ūn-i Qurbān and Satilmish Beg from Quhistān,[144] but nevertheless remained a Sarbadār possession until its capture by the Kartid Malik Ghiyāth al-Dīn Pīr ʿAlī in 777/1376. It would take several years to recover from the annual campaigns of devastation conducted by his troops.[145]

Many shifts in sovereignty during this period can only be detected from numismatic evidence. The change of name on the coinage could simply signify a transfer of allegiance by the town authorities rather than forcible occupation, but it is hard to resist the conclusion that, amid a plethora of rivalries, the towns in Khurāsān and Māzandarān, especially, were a prey to violent competition. The Sarbadār regime could be viewed as the least stable element in the region, on account both of its associations with heterodoxy and of the adventurous policies of leaders like Masʿūd, Yaḥyā Karābī, Ḥasan Dāmghānī and ʿAlī-yi Mu'ayyad. It may accordingly have engendered conflict to a greater extent than did its neighbours.

The struggles between the successor-states, and within the respective dynasties, defy accommodation within any category other than 'grim and unedifying' (to borrow Roemer's phrasing);[146] indeed, they could readily be dismissed as an exhausting sequence of meaningless events. We might ascribe them in part to the mobility of military men and their retinues, looking for opportunities to enhance their status and influence, or the readiness of local populations to seek the intervention of an outside ruler.[147] Whatever the cause, the turbulence surely underlies the tendency of post-Ilkhanid authors to eulogise the era of Mongol rule or to apostrophise Abū Saʿīd's reign as its happiest phase.[148]

Even so, it is necessary to be aware of these recurrent shifts in power and fortune, for two reasons. First, they obviously weakened the feuding rulers on the eve of Timur's advance into Iran. Sharaf al-Dīn Yazdī tells us that in 779–80/1378 one of Timur's trusted amirs, Ḥājjī Sayf al-Dīn, freshly back from pilgrimage to the Hijaz, acquainted the Great Amir with the doings of the *mulūk al-ṭawā'if* in Iran.[149] Sayf al-Dīn's return journey must have taken him through Khurāsān. We are told nothing of Timur's reaction, but it seems highly likely that the report whetted his appetite for campaigns south of the Oxus. As an example of the impact of mutual strife, Pīr ʿAlī's repeated operations against the Sarbadārs weakened his own position as well as ʿAlī-yi Mu'ayyad's, and the need to maintain a strong garrison in Nishapur meant that his resources were perilously overstretched, a circumstance that Timur was to exploit.[150] The Sarbadār chief, at least, had evidently been justified in seeing Timur's advent as his salvation. Curiously enough, when Timur in 788/1386 put an end to the Sarbadār state, possessed of less claim to legitimacy than any of the other post-Ilkhanid principalities, he treated its leaders with marked forbearance (possibly in part for that very reason) and their followers would play a significant role in his campaigns.

But secondly, the conflicts that racked the one-time Ilkhanate may have prompted many to accept, or even welcome, rule by Timur's representatives. His denunciations of so many regional and local powers – other than the Sarbadārs, we might note – as mere highway robbers may amount to nothing more than propaganda; his anger at the harm they inflicted on Muslim populations could have been mere affectation. Of the upheavals undergone by numerous regions since the death of the Ilkhan Abū Saʿīd, however, there can be no doubt. Timur's record of victories – and his known concern to promote commerce – may have led many of the propertied classes in Iran to see him in the same light in which he appeared to the sedentary population of Transoxiana, where he was a welcome alternative to local despotisms and a defender against other external predators like the Mughūls and the nomads of the Qipchaq steppe.[151] Even submission to the formidable Great Amir seemed to promise ʿIrāq-i ʿAjam, Fārs and, perhaps above all, Khurāsān and Azerbaijan greater peace and prosperity than they had enjoyed for some decades.

THE 'IDEA OF IRAN'

The characterisation of the fourteenth century as an 'Iranian interlude' (see earlier) may be due, in some measure, to two circumstances. Firstly, under Mongol hegemony Persian had largely replaced Arabic as the language of historiography in the region. Secondly, the rule of the Ilkhans had witnessed the resurgence – for the first time since the Arab conquest of the Sasanian empire in the seventh century – of the concept of a unitary Iran (as an ideal, at least, espoused by the Persian authors and ministers who served them, and referenced in the depictions of episodes from Firdawsī's *Shāh-nāma* that adorned Abagha's palace at Takht-i Sulaymān).[152] It is doubtful that the Ilkhans themselves understood this as an essential element in their legitimation,[153] although in presenting his puppet Ilkhan as 'Anūshīrwān the Just' (*al-ʿādil*) the Chobanid Ashraf clearly hoped to evoke memories of the celebrated Sasanian monarch.[154]

With the collapse of the Ilkhanate the concept of a unitary Iran ceased to be a reality. The assumption has been made that the stronger among the successor-states were endeavouring to reunite the country.[155] Some indeed aspired to the Ilkhanid mantle. Taghai Temür surely anticipated ruling over the entire Ilkhanate when he entered Sulṭāniyya in Shaʿbān 737/March–April 1337 and again in late 739/the summer of 1339,[156] or even within the next few years, when coins were struck in his name as far afield as Anatolia; but setbacks in the west (see above, pp. 115–16) and the rise of the Sarbadārs put paid to any chance he might have had. Azerbaijan was the 'axis (*quṭb*) of the land of Iran and the location of the throne of its kings from Chinggis Khan's line', as a contemporary noted when it was in Chobanid hands;[157] and of those who may have aimed to recreate the Ilkhanate, if under a different name, the Jalayirids – descended from Hülegü and masters of Tabriz as well as of the other Ilkhanid chief residences of Sulṭāniyya and Baghdad – might seem the most plausible candidates.

But in this context we should not ignore the Muzaffarids. Although they strove to wrest the two former Ilkhanid capitals from Jalayirid hands on various occasions, their territorial ambitions embraced a still broader canvas.[158] Bearing in mind the activities of Pīr Bādik between 780/1378–9 and 782/1380–1, Shāh-i Shujāʿ's name figured fleetingly in the khutba and on the coinage in Baghdad and also, presumably, in Shūshtar. Around this time we witness Muzaffarid intervention in the tangled politics of the Sarbadār realm, and when listing the many tracts under Shāh-i Shujāʿ's sway, Faryūmadī claims that he also received tribute (*kharāj*) from Hurmuz, Kīsh (Qays), Bahrain and other lands 'beyond the sea' (possibly coastal regions of western India)[159] – all territories that derived great wealth from commercial traffic. Hilālī's history, which climaxes with the Muzaffarids, treats Mubāriz al-Dīn as the direct successor of Abū Saʿīd, while both here and in Muʿīn al-Dīn Yazdī's history of the dynasty Shāh-i Shujāʿ is given Ghazan Maḥmūd's title, *Pādishāh-i Islām*.[160] Despite the many obstacles Shāh-i Shujāʿ experienced in uniting the Muzaffarid dominions, suggests Aubin, he 'cherished the dream of bringing the whole of Iran under his authority'.[161]

The Muzaffarids had another claim to distinction, however – and one enjoyed by none of their competitors. Noteworthy is the reaction of contemporaries to Mubāriz al-Dīn's recognition in 755/1354 of the ʿAbbasid Caliph al-Muʿtaḍid billāh in Cairo. In the eyes of Muʿīn al-Dīn Yazdī, and later of Kutubī, the restoration of the khutba for the Caliph in "ʿIrāq [-i ʿAjam]' after an interval of almost a hundred years since the Mongol sack of Baghdad, was clearly an event that signalled the transition to a new epoch. Jaʿfarī writes that the diploma conferring the title of Sultan on Mubāriz al-Dīn was widely reported (*shuhrat yāft*), that he suppressed every innovation (*bidʿat*) in ʿIrāq [-i ʿAjam] and Fārs and that he was spoken of as the one promised (*mawʿūd*) in the seventh (Hijrī) century.[162] The founder of the Muzaffarid dynasty was now the lieutenant (*nā'ib-u qā'im-i maqām*) of the Commander of the Faithful,[163] and Hilālī alludes repeatedly to Shāh-i Shujāʿ's viceregency (*khilāfat*).[164]

We cannot know what ʿAbbasid sanction – obtained (and indeed sought) by none of their Ilkhanid predecessors – meant to Muzaffarid rulers.[165] But there is a parallel, of sorts, in the programmatic announcement by the self-styled Sultan, the Kartid ruler Muʿizz al-Dīn Pīr Ḥusayn of Herat (750/1349), that the customs of the infidels (*kuffār*) were being abolished and that henceforth only the prescriptions of the Sharīʿa would be observed.[166] However formal these developments, and however limited their consequences, they had a bearing on legitimacy in Islamic terms and were redolent of the past glories of ʿAbbasid sovereignty. At the time they may have possessed a significance that outweighed some abstract notion of Iranian unity. In their implicit assault on Mongol and Ilkhanid legitimacy, too, they may have presented a challenge to which Timur felt compelled to respond. The Muzaffarids and the Kartids were admittedly among the strongest powers in the former Ilkhanate, but their ideological pretensions additionally raised them above their neighbours and rivals.

In any event, the task of reducing the whole of Iran exceeded the resources and abilities of any of the possible contestants. They were too evenly matched for one to triumph over the rest;[167] and the obstacles, moreover, were as likely to manifest themselves in the shape of recalcitrant kinsmen or overmighty subordinates (or, in the Sarbadār case, proponents of a competing ideology) as to take the form of a rival dynasty. As for the concept of Iranian unity, the most we can say is that occupation of the one-time Ilkhanid residences, to which considerable prestige was attached,[168] was a desideratum both for the

Jalayirids and for the Muzaffarids who sought to supplant them in Azerbaijan, and perhaps too for Amīr Walī, who exhibited designs of his own on Sulṭāniyya.[169] Timur certainly aspired to reduce the whole of the former Ilkhanate – and almost succeeded. But the Iranian world he conquered would be ruled from Samarkand – from Turan – and in the name of the khan of Chaghadai's ulus.

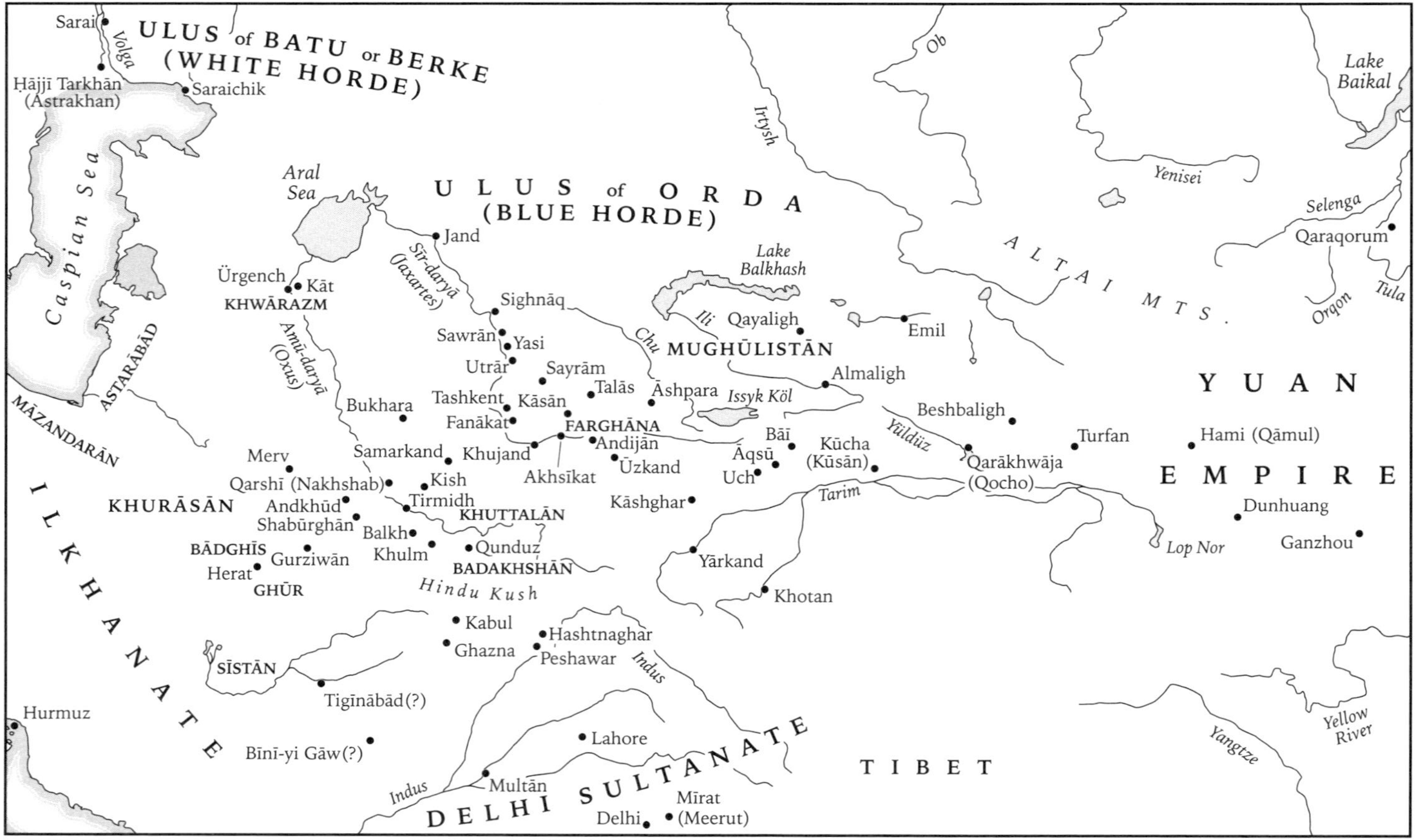

3. The Chaghadayid realm.

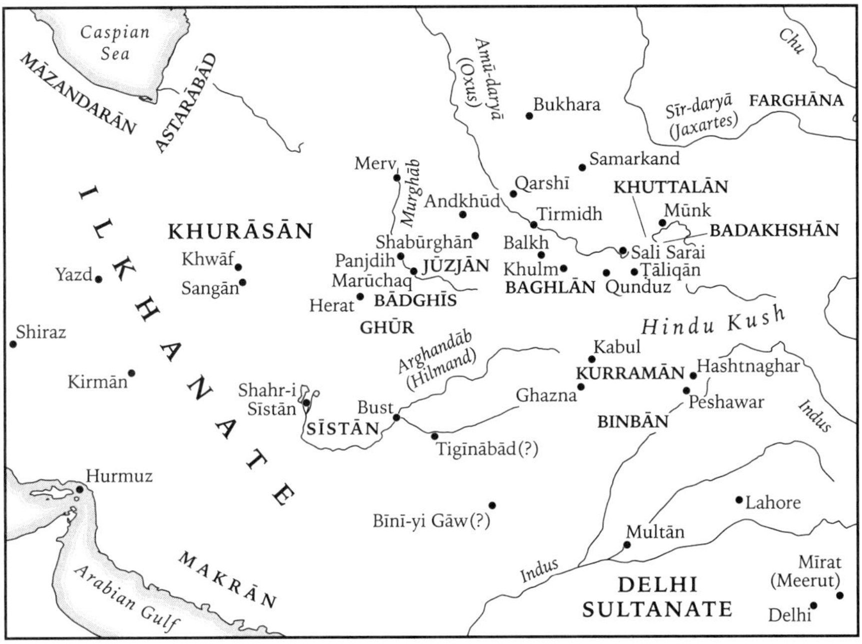

4. The Qara'unas territories.

CHAPTER 7
THE CENTRAL ASIAN MONGOLS: CHAGHATAYS, MUGHŪLS AND QARA'UNAS

Let us now focus more closely on the ulus of Chaghadai – the polity in which Timur originated. Amīr Ḥusayn, successively Timur's ally and rival, and the dynasty of amirs to which he belonged are described as Qara'unas – a problematic term that applied originally to Mongol elements in eastern Khurāsān and present-day Afghanistan and to which we must give some attention. Despite Aubin's verdict on the quality of historical material from the ulus (cited earlier, pp. 26–7), writers in Ilkhanid Iran, and Waṣṣāf in particular,[1] are highly informative concerning relations between the Chaghadayids and the Ilkhans and the southward expansion of the former into Khurāsān and Afghanistan, which will be dealt with in the latter part of this chapter.

NOMADS, MUSLIMS AND TWO KHANATES

The ulus of Chaghadai is sometimes seen, along with the Jochid dominions, as the most conservative of the khanates that emerged from the unitary Mongol empire after 1260: less urbanised, characterised to a greater degree by pastoral nomadism and adhering more tenaciously to the customary law of the steppe. This image derives support from a number of quarters: Chaghadai's reputation for strict enforcement of the Yasa, for instance; Ibn Faḍl-Allāh al-ʿUmarī's assertion that the Chaghadayid Mongols of his day, along with those of the Far East, still observed the Yasa more rigorously than did the Jochid or Ilkhanid Mongols;[2] and Ibn Khaldūn's belief that, in contrast with their counterparts elsewhere, they had preserved their nomadic lifestyle, resisting the allures of luxury, and had thereby retained their pristine military strength – this last a dubious proposition for which there is no hard evidence.[3]

Chaghadai's ulus was a hybrid, ecologically speaking: it embraced alike agrarian and urbanised Transoxiana and Kashgharia and the extensive pasturelands of the Semirech'e (Yeti su). Al-ʿUmarī writes that in the Ilkhanate the Mongol soldiery, while remaining nomads, had agricultural land assigned to them for their upkeep.[4] By the mid-fourteenth century Chaghadai's ulus may well have presented a similar picture. A *waqf* endowment drawn up in the Bukhara region in 726/1326 reveals that amirs bearing Mongol names like Negübei and Duladai owned gardens and vineyards in or near the city.[5] It has been pointed out that Qarshī ('The Palace'), founded by Köpek Khan close to the town of Nakhshab, was the first Chaghadayid centre to be located among the river valleys and oases of Transoxiana rather than in the open steppes.[6] By Timur's emergence on the political scene, the various tribes in the western regions of the ulus controlled the towns – Kish and Khujand, for instance – adjacent to their pasturelands.

At a date usually taken to be 748/1347, on the authority of Mīrzā Ḥaydar Dughlāt, the ulus split in two: a western khanate, embracing Transoxiana and incorporating much of what is now northern Afghanistan,[7] and an eastern khanate, known as Mughūlistān ('Mongol territory') and centred on the Semirech'e and the long-standing Chaghadayid headquarters at Almaligh. The boundaries of Mughūlistān supplied by Ḥaydar are vague and presumably relate to his own era,[8] and the 'frontier' between the eastern and western khanates before Timur's era is difficult to ascertain. Ghiyāth al-Dīn Yazdī, writing in or not long after 1404, says that Mughūl territory extended as far as the borders of Yangī-Talās (Ṭarāz), a town that in Ḥaydar's time would be reckoned as part of Mughūlistān.[9] The further limits of Mughūlistān are harder to establish. Ḥaydar writes of the Yüldüz region as its eastern frontier,[10] but the Chaghadayid khans had wrested Qarākhwāja (Qaraqocho) from the Uighur principality by the early decades of the fourteenth century.[11] Ḥāfiẓ-i Abrū says that Qazan Sulṭān ruled 'as far as the confines of Qarākhwāja' and we are also told that in 773/1371–2 Timur appointed Köpek Temür to govern the eastern Chaghadayid lands 'as far as Qarākhwāja'.[12] In a subsequent attack on Mughūl territory, Timur himself raided the town.[13] Beyond Qarākhwāja, the town of Hami (Qāmul) was ruled by a branch of the Chaghadayids who had gone over to the Qaghan/Yuan Emperor in the late thirteenth century (see p. 80).[14] Sharaf al-Dīn Yazdī locates the frontier of China at the military outpost (*totqa'ul*) where the Ming had constructed continuous walls;[15] precisely where this lay is uncertain.

The scholarly consensus is that the eastern khanate contrasted markedly with the western Chaghadayid territories. The two halves of the ulus can certainly be distinguished on religious grounds. By the time Timur came to prominence in Transoxiana, the khans and the amirs alike were Muslims. A number of the khans seem to have been attracted to a sufi lifestyle. ʿAlī Sulṭān (*c.* 740–741/*c.* 1339 or 1340–1341), notorious for having presided over the martyrdom of a party of Franciscan missionaries in the Almaligh region, is described in Western European sources as 'a Saracen religious' and as a *faqīr*.[16] Qazaghan's second nominee as khan, Bayan Quli (749–*c.* 759/1348 or 1349–*c.* 1358), was buried close to the mausoleum of Sayf al-Dīn Bākharzī at Fatḥābād near Bukhara, which Ibn Baṭṭūṭa had visited and would describe in glowing terms; the location of the khan's grave suggests that he had been a devotee of the shaykh and his descendants.[17] One of Bayan Quli's successors, Kābul (or Qabūl) Shāh, whom Qazaghan's grandson Amīr Ḥusayn enthroned in 765/1363–4, is described as 'a saint by nature and a *qalandar* by temperament'[18] who had been wrenched from the life of a sufi.[19] Perhaps the most obscure and problematic of the early Muslim khans of Chaghadai's ulus is Khalīl Sulṭān b. Yasa'ur (*c.* 742–745/*c.* 1342–1345: see pp. 124–6), to whom Ibn Baṭṭūṭa attributes some improbable military exploits on behalf of the faith, but who would also figure in hagiographical literature as a dervish associated with the early career of Shaykh Bahā' al-Dīn Naqshband (d. 791/1389).[20]

In Transoxiana, the amirs too appear to have been solidly Muslim; we have seen in Chapter 3 that the process of Islamisation was already well under way before Tarmashirin's reign. Authors writing in the Mamlūk territories heard that Tarmashirin had favoured and promoted Muslim amirs and shunned those who remained infidels.[21] Ibn Baṭṭūṭa, who met the khan's chief amir, Boroldai, at Parwān, found him surrounded by shaykhs and says that he had constructed as many as forty hospices in Ghazna.[22]

Yet Islam had made markedly less progress among the elite and rank-and-file of the nomads of Mughūlistān than it had further west. This may well be the significance of al-ʿUmarī's comment (see earlier) that the Yasa was observed more rigorously in Chaghadai's ulus and in the Yuan empire, bearing in mind that in the late 1330s neither polity was ruled by a Muslim (the contemporary Chaghadayid khan was Changshi and the ulus had witnessed a reaction against Tarmashirin's Islamising measures). Mīrzā Ḥaydar says that the Dughlāt amir Tülek – older brother of Ḥaydar's ancestor Bolodchi (Pūlādchī), who had been instrumental in Tughluq Temür's enthronement in 748/1347 – became a Muslim in secret only three years before that khan accepted the faith (i.e. *c.* 751/1350–1).[23] Ḥaydar assures us that 120,000 Mughūls followed Tughluq Temür's example,[24] but at a subsequent juncture he admits that the majority of the Mughūls did not become Muslims until the reign of Tughluq Temür's grandson Muḥammad Khan (*c.* 811–818/*c.* 1408–1415)[25] – namely, after Timur's death. It has been proposed that the attempt to enthrone a prince (whose name bears no imprint of Islam) in the eastern khanate from a rival Chaghadayid branch in *c.* 1390 reflects the persistence of strong non-Muslim elements.[26] Later still in his narrative, Ḥaydar alleges that even at the accession of Yūnus Khan (873/1468–9) the majority of the Mughūls were Muslims in name only – if that.[27]

Whatever the truth, the early Timurid historians Shāmī, Salmānī, Naṭanzī and Sharaf al-Dīn ʿAlī Yazdī all stigmatise the Mughūls as infidels; Ghiyāth al-Dīn Yazdī calls them 'enemies of the faith' and Sharaf al-Dīn describes Jata as 'for the most part lacking the felicity of the appearance of Islam'.[28] In the first half of the fifteenth century the Mughūls were constantly raiding towns like Turkistān, Shāsh (Tashkent) and Andijān and carrying Muslims off into captivity,[29] just as they had done annually in the fourteenth,[30] while down to the reign of Yūnus the Muslims of Transoxiana, for their part, would sell Mughūl prisoners as if they were unbelievers.[31] What legitimised Timur's rule, in part, was his capacity to keep the pagan Mughūls at bay.

One reason for the tardiness of the eastern half of the ulus in adopting Islam was that it embraced an extensive tract where Buddhism had long held sway.[32] The Chaghadayid khans had habitually patronised Buddhist foundations (though much of our evidence comes from slightly further east, where a rival branch of the dynasty ruled on behalf of the Yuan).[33] There was certainly an Islamic presence within the Buddhist-dominated regions. From a story transmitted by Mīrzā Ḥaydar, it seems that Katak, in the Lop Nor region, already had a mosque by the mid-fourteenth century,[34] but according to the same author, Qarākhwāja and Turfan were brought into the Islamic fold only in the last years of that century, thanks to the holy wars (*ghazāt*) undertaken by the khan Khiḍr Khwāja.[35] Even so, the Timurid envoy Ghiyāth al-Dīn Naqqāsh, who passed through Turfan in 823/1420, says that most of the town's populace was still Buddhist and makes no mention of a mosque.[36]

The differences between the western and eastern Chaghadayid territories are easily overstated, however. At the time of Timur's rise many Mongol amirs in the west continued to practise transhumance, at the very least; and according to Clavijo, just a few decades later, the Chaghatay nomads just south of the Amū-daryā, while still living in the open throughout the year, sowed crops of corn, cotton and millet.[37] In Ḥamd-Allāh Mustawfī's geographical work, *Nuzhat al-qulūb*, dating from *c.* 740/1340, Farghāna, which lay along the upper reaches of the Sīr-daryā and would straddle the border between the two khanates, is said to contain numerous districts with extensive cultivation.[38] The impression is confirmed almost two centuries later by Bābur's nostalgic description of Farghāna as abounding in grain and fruit; he adds that its mountains afford excellent summer pastures.[39] Well to the east of Farghāna, Sharaf al-Dīn ʿAlī Yazdī's reference to Bāī as summer quarters (*yailaq*) and to Kūsān (Kūcha) as winter quarters (*qishlaq*) suggests that the nomads dwelt in the vicinity of towns here, just as they did in Transoxiana.[40]

It is true that in the eastern khanate the economy as a whole was characterised by horse-breeding and traditional pastoral nomadism. Most of the large towns in the Semirech'e had been destroyed in the thirteenth century to increase the available grazing lands,[41] and Mīrzā Ḥaydar writes that Mughūlistān in his own day contained many ruined towns.[42] Ḥaydar represents the Mughūl amirs and their troops as averse to city life even in the 1470s, to the frustration of their khan, Yūnus, who tried repeatedly to make Kāshghar his residence and who seemingly equated Islam with dwelling in towns.[43] Ḥaydar differentiates the towns south of the Tian Shan – Āqsū, Kāshghar, Yārkand, Khotan, Kūcha (Kūsān) and Ūch (*Altı shahr*, 'The Six Towns', as the region would later be known) – from Mughūlistān.[44] In part, this reflects the political conditions nearer his own time, when the oasis towns of the Tarim basin formed part of *Manghalai Sübe* ('Advance Strategic Point'?),[45] formerly the domain of Ḥaydar's Dughlāt forebears and depicted in his book as virtually an autonomous region until its reduction by the Chaghadayid Sulṭān Saʿīd Khan in 920/1514. But on the ecological level, too, Kāshghar and the other urbanised regions south of the Tian Shan were distinct from Mughūlistān and would doubtless have presented some affinities with Transoxiana.[46]

Nevertheless, this is not to deny that antipathy between town-dweller and nomad persisted. Much as Tarmashirin, over a century earlier, had apparently pressurised the Mongols of Transoxiana to turn to agriculture, Yūnus Khan endeavoured to impress upon his Mughūl amirs that they would never count as real Muslims if they did not settle in towns.[47] As a young man he had spent twenty-eight years in exile in the cities of Timurid Iran (of which twelve had been passed in the care of Sharaf al-Dīn ʿAlī Yazdī, the scholar and historian).[48] A Muslim divine from Transoxiana, expecting Yūnus to prove a typical 'steppe Turk', was amazed to meet a cultured and urbane prince.[49] We encounter evidence that in the early sixteenth century the sedentary, urbanised Turk still held the nomad in contempt.

Bābur dismisses steppe-dwellers in general – not just his enemy, the Uzbek khan Muḥammad Shībānī (for all his punctiliousness in Islamic observance), but even his own maternal uncle, the eastern Chaghadayid Sulṭān Aḥmad Khan (d. 909/1504) – as uncouth and illiterate; while Bābur's cousin Mīrzā Ḥaydar, who almost at the beginning of his book thanks God that he has ceased to be part of the Mughūl ulus, voices disdain for the ignorant Mughūl herdsmen.[50]

MONGOLS AND TURKS

On one level, Islamisation was symptomatic of a growing acculturation within the Mongols' ranks. Another symptom was the Turkicisation of the khans and the elite. We cannot know how far this represents a borrowing of Turkish custom and cuisine by ethnic Mongols and their adoption of Turkic dialects,[51] or how far it resulted simply from the fact that the greater number of the nomadic troops were Turks either recruited, or implanted, in Chinggis Khan's day – Uighurs, Qipchaq, Qangli and Qarluq, for example (we find amirs from the two last-named tribes participating in Tughluq Temür's invasions in the early 1360s).[52] The Chaghadayid Mongols doubtless underwent the same process that al-ʿUmarī describes in his account of the Jochid territories, where the conquerors were absorbed by, and assimilated to, the non-Mongol majority among their nomadic subjects (the Qipchaq, in the Jochids' case).[53] Yet it should be borne in mind that the ethnicon 'Turk' embraced a range of peoples who lacked a sense of common identity or a shared historical consciousness.[54] It was employed by Muslim authors of the fourteenth and later centuries to denote the nomadic inhabitants of the Eurasian steppes in general as distinct from the sedentary Iranian ('Tājīk') populations: accordingly the Mongols themselves were often categorised as a branch of the Turks.[55]

Both Köpek and Tarmashirin spoke Turkish, according to Ibn Baṭṭūṭa,[56] who further tells us that Tarmashirin recited the litany (*dhikr*) in that language.[57] If we can believe the Moroccan traveller, Tarmashirin in conversation referred to himself as the 'Sultan of the Turks'.[58] But the nomads in Timur's army appear still to have manifested at least the outward characteristics of Mongols: when the conqueror's grandson Sulṭān Ḥusayn defected to the Mamlūk enemy in 803/1400, we are told that they required him to cut off the traditional hair braids and to alter his attire.[59] To judge from the material unearthed in Turfan, Mongolian continued to be employed as the official language of documents issued in the second half of the fourteenth century by the khans or their officers – certainly in the eastern regions of the Chaghadayid ulus, the one-time Uighur territories where Buddhist culture predominated.[60] Here only local documents relating to more parochial matters were written in Uighur Turkish,[61] though we have an earlier edict from Du'a's reign which is written not just in the Uighur script but in the Uighur language.[62] When Clavijo asserts that Mongolian was spoken in Transoxiana, however, and when Ibn Khaldūn says that his account of the Maghrib was translated into that language on Timur's orders, they must both mean Turkish; the confusion possibly arose from the fact that, as Clavijo proceeds to say, documents were drawn up in the Mongolian (i.e. Uighur) script.[63] Timur's son Amīrānshāh issued a bilingual document in 800/1398 in Turkish in the Uighur script and in Persian, and another document – a *soyurghal* dated 825/1422 in Turkish and in the Uighur script – has survived from the reign of Shāhrukh.[64]

MUGHŪLS/JATA AND QARA'UNAS

To historians writing in Mamlūk Egypt and other regions of the Near East, Timur's invading armies would usually be known – just as the Mongols of Chinggis Khan and his successors had been known – as 'Tatars'.[65] But the Timurid historians and European visitors such as Clavijo commonly designate Timur's military forces as 'Chaghatays'. Timurid authors distinguish the Chaghatays from the sedentary, 'Tājīk' populations of Transoxiana and Khurāsān, who were numerically significant within Timur's armies but deemed to be of lesser importance. The distinction is neatly brought out in Shāmī's description of a group of seven men in Amīr Ḥusayn's following: of those seven, he says, one was a Chaghatay, two were Khurāsānīs and the other four were 'men of Mā warā' al-nahr'.[66]

The label 'Chaghatay', which transcended tribal affiliations and the conflicts of the 1360s within the tribal aristocracy, was confined to the Turco-Mongol inhabitants of the western polity that had emerged following the division of the ulus of Chaghadai into two distinct realms in 748/1347.[67] The term came to encapsulate a special corporate cultural identity, in which the pivotal elements were a shared nomadic culture, loyalty to the Chinggisid political tradition (not least the Yasa) and to Chaghadai's dynasty within it, and allegiance to Islam.[68] By contrast, Timurid authors termed the eastern khanate 'the Mongol territory' (*wilāyat-i Mughūl* or *Mughūlistān*);[69] they called its nomadic inhabitants 'Mughūls', or 'Jata' (*chete*, 'robbers'), and, as we saw, wrote them off as infidels. The term Jata possibly first surfaces in a text from the very beginning of the fourteenth century,[70] but it is interesting to find it also applied to the forces of the Ilkhan Taghai Temür by the later author Sayyid Ẓahīr al-Dīn Marʿashī (d. 892/1487), who makes the pejorative sense of the word explicit by defining them as 'a body of villainous Turks' (*ṭā'ifa-yi ashrār-i atrāk*).[71] The term is perhaps semantically akin to *qazaq*,[72] which first appears in the early decades of the fifteenth century when Naṭanzī reports that one of Toqtamish's sons was roaming the Qipchaq steppe like a *qazaq* and that a crowd of 'ruffians (*awbāsh*) and *qazaq*s' had rallied to him.[73] And even after *qazaq*, like *jata*, had become associated with a specific group of Mongols, now more familiar to us in the spelling Kazakh, it was still used in the sense of 'freebooter' by Mīrzā Ḥaydar Dughlāt in the sixteenth century when writing of the careers of the eastern Chaghadayid khans Ways (d. *c.* 832/1428–9) and his own cousin Sulṭān Saʿīd.[74]

Evidently, by Timur's era new terminology had come into use to differentiate the nomad populations of the various uluses. Like the Mughūls, the Jochid Mongols were regarded as a separate 'ethnicity' and as early as *c.* 1400 were being designated as 'Uzbeks' and their territory as 'Uzbek's territory'[75] (much as it had once been known as 'Berke's territory'), after Özbeg, the khan who had contributed to the establishment of the Muslim faith in the Qipchaq steppe; Ḥāfiẓ-i Abrū regularly speaks of the head of Jochi's ulus as 'the Uzbek monarch' (*pādishāh-i Ūzbak*). Timurid authors were also beginning to speak of the original Mongolian homeland, and its inhabitants, as *Qalmāq* ('those left behind [in Mongolia?]'),[76] a designation not met with in the pre-Timurid epoch; this term (Europeanised in a later age as 'Kalmuck') would come to be restricted to the Oyirat of Zungharia.

Now according to Mīrzā Ḥaydar Dughlāt the Mongols of the eastern Chaghadayid khanate habitually referred to the inhabitants of the western parts of Chaghadai's ulus as Qara'unas.[77] Like the label Jata, this was presumably intended as a term of disparagement, but the rationale is unclear. Relying on Marco Polo's description of the 'Caraunas' as the product of union between Mongol fathers and Indian mothers,[78] some historians have assumed that the term cited by Mīrzā Ḥaydar denoted 'mongrel', 'half-breed', and was attached contemptuously by 'pure' Mongols to the more sophisticated (or more effete, depending on one's standpoint) Persianised Mongols of Transoxiana. In a verse celebrating the execution of a large number of captured raiders by the Delhi Sultan ʿAlā' al-Dīn Khaljī in *c.* 1306, the poet Amīr Khusraw certainly appears to distinguish Qara'unas from Mongols (though perhaps just for the sake of rhyme).[79] Scholarly opinion as to the implications of Ḥaydar's statement, however, has differed widely.[80]

The term Qara'unas had originated in a rather different context. Over the previous hundred years it had applied to the Mongol groupings whose arrival in the territory between the Oxus and the Indus Rivers predated the advent of Hülegü and his forces. Together with the other Mongol armies in the category of *tamma* – those, that is, despatched to garrison fresh conquests – they were selected on a percentage basis from the entire military establishment and individual contingents each represented a different branch of the imperial dynasty.[81] There is nothing inherently implausible, therefore, in the notion that the Qara'unas were of mixed stock, since we know that some of the *tamma* contingents were hybrid in a quite distinct sense, inasmuch as they comprised members of different tribes: Rashīd al-Dīn tells us, for instance, that one military unit despatched to Iran with Chormaghun was made up of Uighurs, Qarluq, Türkmen and men from Kāshghar and Kūcha.[82]

One of Ibn Baṭṭūṭa's informants, a shaykh resident at Multān, described the Qara'unas as 'the Turks who inhabit the highlands between Sind and the land of the Turks'.[83] If the detachments in what is now Afghanistan included Turkish elements of the kind listed by Rashīd al-Dīn, the Qara'unas could indeed be described as of mixed blood.[84] Aubin proposed that the term Qara'unas had been extended from the mixed nomadic population of present-day Afghanistan to embrace the Turco-Mongol clans on both sides of the middle Oxus and even in Transoxiana proper.[85] A tentative hypothesis will be offered later in this chapter.

QARA'UNAS AND NEGÜDERIS

A further, and closely related, problem is the relationship between the Qara'unas and the Negüderis, a body of Mongol troops based in the southern part of the region. They took their name from their commander, Negüder, who had originally represented the Jochids. Joined by fugitives from western Iran when Hülegü attacked the Jochid contingents in his army in *c.* 1261, they had withdrawn eastwards towards the Indian borderlands, where, according to Rashīd al-Dīn, they seized 'the mountains of Ghazna and Bīnī-yi Gāw as far as Multān and Lahore'.[86] Marco Polo describes Negüder as making war on 'all the Tartars who dwell round about his kingdom';[87] and certainly until the late thirteenth century the Negüderi territories were a no-man's-land, obstructing any ambitions on the part of Ilkhans or Chaghadayids alike to expand towards India. When the Chaghadayid khan Baraq invaded Khurāsān in 668/1270 and Hülegü's son and successor, the Ilkhan Abagha (663–680/1265–1282), proposed to surrender to him Ghazna, Kurramān and Binbān 'as far as the Indus',[88] the offer was an empty one; the region was not in his gift.

Abagha in turn attempted to exert indirect authority over the Negüderis through refugee Chaghadayid princes such as the former khan Mubārak Shāh and Böjei, who had both entered his service on Baraq's retreat.[89] This reliance on renegade Chaghadayids was a failure. Mubārak Shāh proved a fickle subordinate, meeting his death in an attack on Kirmān in 674/1275–6;[90] and when Böjei's son ʿAbd-Allāh, in command of the Negüderis in the Ghazna region a few years later, attacked in response to an overture from the rebel sultan of Kirmān, he did so on behalf of Qaidu and the Chaghadayids. Abagha retaliated in 677–8/1278–9 with a punitive campaign against the Negüderis in eastern Khurāsān.[91]

Some confusion has arisen from a failure to notice that after 677–8/1278–9 there existed two quite distinct groups of Qara'unas, one in Afghanistan and the other in the Ilkhanid lands. During his campaign Abagha obtained the submission of some of the enemy chiefs and brought back, to form part of his personal property (*injü*) and to serve his dynasty, a significant body of Negüderis who were henceforward stationed in western Iran.[92] These troops, nominally totalling a tümen and usually called Qara'unas in the sources,[93] played a prominent, if not always constructive, role in Ilkhanid politics over the following years, notably in the civil war between Tegüder-Aḥmad and Abagha's son Arghun, when they supported the latter. Waṣṣāf, describing them as 'like demons rather than humans and the most brazen of the Mongols', says that plundering was their habitual activity.[94]

It is entirely possible that, as May suggests, Negüder did not extend his authority over the entirety of the Qara'unas, if by that we mean the *tamma* troops in the region.[95] But for a number of our sources the two terms Qara'unas and Negüderis appear to be interchangeable. Take Rashīd al-Dīn's allusions to the attack on Fārs in 677/1278–9 and Abagha's punitive expedition. He frequently refers to the enemy on this occasion as Qara'unas;[96] yet in relating how Abagha, during this same campaign, sent Arghun ahead into the Ghūr and Ghazna region, he speaks of the target at one point as Qara'unas and at another as Negüderis.[97] Waṣṣāf often writes of the Mongols in Sīstān who attacked Kirmān and Fārs as Negüderis.[98] But he also mentions how, at the height of the struggle between Du'a and Chapar in 705/1305, the Chaghadayid commander Taraghai, finding his route to India blocked, joined the Qara'unas.[99] Waṣṣāf writes in addition of Qara'unas troops accompanying Qaidu's son Sarban and other Central Asian princes into Khurāsān in 706/1306.[100]

At one point the two terms are used interchangeably even of the Qara'unas in Ilkhanid service further west. In 698/1299, a group of them, led by a certain Buqa, absconded from Ṭārum in ʿIrāq-i ʿAjam with the aim of joining the Negüderis in Bīnī-yi Gāw, but failed to reach their destination and entered the service of the malik of Herat. The local chronicler Sayfī calls the deserters themselves Negüderis, whereas Rashīd al-Dīn terms them Qara'unas.[101]

Certain authors, however, confine themselves to one or the other label. Sources for the history of the Muzaffarids describe Negüderi bands raiding as far west as the Yazd region in the later Ilkhanid era. In 713/1314 the young Mubāriz al-Dīn Muḥammad b. al-Muẓaffar, en route for the Ilkhanid court to claim the governorship of Maybud, had to fight off a Negüderi attack;[102] once in power in Yazd, he engaged in a protracted conflict with the Negüderis, which lasted for thirteen or fourteen years (i.e., presumably, until *c.* 733/1332–3).[103] The early fourteenth-century *Ta'rīkh-i Sīstān*, which makes only a single reference to the Negüderis, in the context of a raid in 694/1294, does not employ the term Qara'unas at all. The Indian sources, on the other hand, do not refer to Negüderis and always speak of Qara'unas:[104] thus Ibn Baṭṭūṭa's informant at Multān, cited earlier. It has been proposed that the Negüderis were only one element among the Qara'unas in Afghanistan,[105] and although by no means totally convinced I shall proceed on that assumption here.

Let us briefly return to the designation of the Mongols of the western Chaghadayid realm as Qara'unas and to Polo's definition of Qara'unas as 'half-breeds'. The reliability of Polo's information is open to question.[106] From the context, his narrow escape from capture by Negüderi marauders is more likely to have fallen during his outward journey – that is, in *c.* 1272/3, almost a quarter of a century before his book was written.[107] Now Ibn Baṭṭūṭa describes Ghāzī Malik, the future Delhi Sultan Ghiyāth al-Dīn Tughluq (720–724/1320–1324), as a Qara'unas,[108] and more than one author writing in Delhi has Tughluq arriving in the Sultanate from Khurāsān during the reign of ʿAlā' al-Dīn Khaljī (695–715/1296–1316). The fact that the early seventeenth-century Indian historian Firishta makes Ghāzī Malik/Tughluq the son of a Turkish mamluk by a woman of the Jat tribe in the Punjab might lend support to Polo's definition, although we surely require more than an isolated reference to a single individual by a late, and not unduly trustworthy, source.[109] Nevertheless, the application of the label Qara'unas to the Mongols of the western Chaghadayid khanate may well have a different rationale, as we shall see, from that given by Polo.

THE CHAGHADAYID ADVANCE SOUTH OF THE OXUS

The Central Asian Mongols appear to have been, if anything, weaker numerically than their Jochid neighbours, for example: Ibn Faḍl-Allāh al-ʿUmarī says that the Golden Horde's forces greatly outnumbered those of the Chaghadayids, while the Armenian Hayton attributes only 400,000 men to Chapar and 600,000 to the Jochid khan Toqto'a.[110] But on the other hand, according to one of al-ʿUmarī's Persian informants, a single Chaghadayid trooper was worth a hundred from the Qipchaq steppe and attacks from beyond the Caucasus provoked less alarm in the Ilkhanate than did those by the Chaghadayids in the east.[111] The reason for this was surely, in part at least, topography. In the 1260s the Ilkhan Abagha had constructed a barrier (*sibe*, *sübe*) and a deep ditch beyond the northern bank of the Kura River,[112] and though this did not totally obstruct Jochid invasions it may have meant that the Jochids could advance only on an even narrower front than the natural topography of the Caucasus region permitted, thus limiting the damage they could inflict on the provinces of Azerbaijan and Arrān. No such barrier faced Chaghadayid armies once they crossed the Oxus and advanced into Ilkhanid territories on a far broader front.

Rashīd al-Dīn refers to the links between the 'Qara'unas' – those, that is, of the Iranian–Indian borderlands – and the ulus of Chaghadai as 'of long standing'.[113] Yet the forces of the Chaghadayids and their ally Qaidu were not stationed south of the Oxus permanently, it appears, until almost the final decade of the thirteenth century. In 687/1288 Du'a's noyan Yasa'ur raided the region of Balkh, Shabūrghān and Merv, penetrating as far as Khwāf and Sangān.[114] Not long afterwards we find Yasa'ur based in Balkh and Bādghīs, while Qaidu's son

Sarban had his quarters in Shabūrghān and in the upper Oxus region.[115] And it was only at the very end of the century that Du'a and Qaidu were able to bring at least a large proportion of the Negüderi Mongols under their control. In their first attempt they were no more successful than Abagha had been. It involved the renegade Ilkhanid amir Nawrūz, who sought asylum at Qaidu's headquarters, was put in charge of a division of Chaghadayid troops south of the Oxus and participated in an attack on Khurāsān in 690/1291;[116] operating in the region Waṣṣāf calls 'Sīstān' (meaning Ghūr and Gharchistān), he is more than once described as commander of the Negüderis.[117] He struck coins in Badakhshān on behalf of Qaidu and Du'a.[118]

The fate of Badakhshān is instructive. For much of the thirteenth century it had lain within the Qaghan's sphere of influence.[119] But according to Rashīd al-Dīn it had been repeatedly attacked by Qaidu and Du'a, and when Bayan, khan of the Blue Horde, was endeavouring to build a coalition against them in 702/1303 and seeking to involve the Qaghan Temür, he spoke of the malik of Badakhshān as potentially a willing partner in the alliance.[120] By that date, however, the kingdom was already being listed among the territories of the Chaghadayid Qutlugh Khwāja; and in 716/1316 a contingent from Badakhshān would accompany the Chaghadayid forces on an invasion of Khurāsān.[121] Ibn Faḍl-Allāh al-ʿUmarī, writing in 738/1338, at one point classes it as part of the Chaghadayid khanate.[122]

In 694/1294 Nawrūz abandoned the Central Asian Mongols and made his peace with the Ilkhanid prince Ghazan, whom he persuaded to embrace Islam and under whom he would enjoy a glittering but brief career as viceroy.[123] Qaidu and Du'a reacted sharply to his desertion. At a date between 1294 and 1298 Qutlugh Khwāja, Du'a's eldest son, was installed south of the Oxus in overall command of an army of five tümens (notionally 50,000), including two supplied by Qaidu.[124] According to Waṣṣāf, Qutlugh Khwāja held sway over a vast area, comprising Badakhshān, Balkh and its dependencies, Shabūrghān, Jūzjān, Kishm, Andkhūd, Ṭāyaqān, Ṭāliqān, Fāryāb, Marūchaq, Panjdih and even Merv.[125] Rashīd al-Dīn says that he spent the summer in the regions of Ghūr and Gharchistān and that he wintered in Ghazna, while Qāshānī locates his headquarters at Bīnī-yi Gāw and Waṣṣāf in the valley of the Arghandāb,[126] all regions that a few decades previously had been Negüderi territory. Qutlugh Khwāja's chief amir, Taraghai, was possibly himself a Qara'unas chief. He joined the Qara'unas in the Indian borderlands in 705/1305, and his father, Qutlugh Temür of the Qongqurat tribe, who, according to *Shuʿab-i panjgāna* married a Chaghadayid princess, Yesünjin (a sister of the abovementioned Böjei), may be identical with a homonymous noyan in the Tigīnābād region in the 1260s, who had submitted to Baraq.[127]

Qutlugh Khwāja's troops launched a series of forays into India,[128] notably in 699/1299–1300 and 703/1303, during the reign of the Delhi Sultan ʿAlā' al-Dīn Khaljī, when they threatened Delhi itself. Qutlugh Khwāja, who headed the first of these attacks, died of his wounds during the return journey, but in *c.* 703/1303 his lieutenant Taraghai, who appears then to have assumed the leadership of Qutlugh Khwāja's forces,[129] subjected Delhi to a two-month siege which the Sultanate's historians describe as a still greater menace.[130] In addition to attacking India, both Qutlugh Khwāja and Sarban launched regular plundering expeditions against the Ilkhan's eastern territories, where Herat was a principal target.[131] In 700/1300–1 Qutlugh Khwāja's forces penetrated still further, to Kirmān, Fārs and Hurmuz. Waṣṣāf says that Ilkhanid troops had defected to him, both under compulsion and of their own volition (perhaps lured by the prospect of rich plunder from India).[132]

Chaghadayid interest in the tracts to the south was no passing phenomenon. When Chapar offered his submission to the Qaghan Temür in 1304 and listed the external frontiers of the Mongol world on which Chinggis Khan's descendants might now concentrate their energies, it was with good reason that he specified as the focus of the Central Asian Mongols 'Sind and Hindūstān'.[133] In 705/1305 Du'a conferred the troops and pasturelands of Qutlugh Khwāja on another of his sons, the future khan Esen Buqa,[134] but the strife in Central Asia during the next five years appears to have checked Chaghadayid ambitions in this region. There is evidence of conflict within the ranks of Qutlugh Khwāja's forces in *c.* 1305/6, in which Taraghai was killed, and of opposition to Esen Buqa.[135] A document purportedly addressed to ʿAlāʾ al-Dīn Khaljī's son Khiḍr Khan describes how the chaos had spread to the Mongol army at Hashtnaghar and Peshawar, and claims that the Delhi Sultan's army had profited from it to occupy Ghazna;[136] but we cannot be certain how reliable this testimony is. The future Sultan Ghiyāth al-Dīn Tughluq is credited with numerous victories over Mongol invaders, which were commemorated in an inscription at Multān seen by Ibn Baṭṭūṭa, and in consequence they allegedly did not dare to attack India during his reign.[137]

On Esen Buqa's departure northwards in *c.* 709/1309 to be enthroned as khan, the command in Afghanistan passed to his younger brother, It-qul.[138] Shortly afterwards, in 712/1312, we find Dāʾūd Khwāja, a son of Qutlugh Khwāja, as ruler of the Negüderi territories, wintering in the region of Bust and Tigīnābād and spending the summer on the upper Oxus. He was attacked and ousted by an Ilkhanid army at the instigation of two noyans, Temür and *Lakchir, described as 'heading the remnants of the Qaraʾunas of Negüder'.[139] Since their father Abachi had been among the commanders of Qutlugh Khwāja's troops who invaded Fārs,[140] we have here an indication that some Negüderi elements, at least, may have escaped from the Chaghadayid orbit. Whether the Chaghadayid invasion launched by Esen Buqa late in Ramaḍān 713/early in January 1314 to avenge Dāʾūd Khwāja's humiliation succeeded in reinstating him, we are not told.[141] The readiness of the Ilkhan Öljeitü to intervene may be linked with designs on the Indian borderlands, since as recently as 710/1310–11 he had sent an embassy to Delhi requiring the submission of its Sultan.[142] But the Mongols of Iran were again unable, apparently, to impose their authority on this region. Within a few years much of it was subject to another Chaghadayid, the prince Yasaʾur, who in 716/1316 had quarrelled with Esen Buqa and his brother Köpek and had migrated into Khurāsān, where Öljeitü granted him asylum with his following. Here he crowned three years of turbulent activity at the expense of local rulers by rebelling against Öljeitü's young successor, Abū Saʿīd. He was defeated and killed in 720/1320 by Chaghadayid forces from Transoxiana headed by Köpek, to whom the malik of Herat had appealed for assistance.[143]

The split of 748/1347 within Chaghadai's ulus was foreshadowed in periods of condominium during earlier decades. Rashīd al-Dīn writes of Qutlugh Khwāja in terms that suggest he was co-ruler of the ulus of Chaghadai with his father Du'a.[144] We meet with joint rule again, perhaps, in the 1320s, when Esen Buqa entrusted Köpek with Farghāna and Transoxiana.[145] At this juncture the nucleus of the khanate still seems to have lain in the east. Mīrzā Ḥaydar claims – whether correctly or not, we cannot be sure – that Du'a's grave was in Yārkand.[146] Whereas the winter quarters of his successor Könchek (706/1306–7 to 708/1308–9) were in the vicinity of Yüldüz,[147] and Esen Buqa made his summer quarters at Talās and wintered in the vicinity of the Issyk Köl,[148] Köpek, succeeding his brother as khan (*c.* 720–726/1320–1326), retained a marked preference for the western regions. He established a new centre at Qarshī in Transoxiana, possibly intended to serve as a second capital.[149] According to Ḥāfiẓ-i Abrū, he was buried in Kish (later Shahr-i Sabz).[150] Köpek had also rebuilt Balkh, which had lain in ruins since Chinggis Khan's time.[151] His brother and successor, Eljigidei (*c.* 727–*c.* 730/ *c.* 1326–*c.* 1330), once more had his headquarters in the east, but during the reign of a fourth brother, Tarmashirin (*c.* 730–735/*c.* 1330–1334), the focus was again directed south of the Oxus.

It was perhaps as a follow-up to the removal of Yasa'ur, or possibly to an invasion of Khurāsān by Köpek in 722/1322,[152] that in 724/1324 Tarmashirin crossed the Oxus and established himself in the Kabul–Ghazna region, from where he mounted a profitable raid into India.[153] In 726/1326 he was attacked at Ghazna by the Ilkhan's forces under Ḥasan b. Choban, who subjected the city to a horrific sack, drawing no distinction between the soldiery and the civilian populace and even demolishing the tomb of Maḥmūd of Ghazna.[154] At the time of Tarmashirin's second – and larger-scale – invasion of India in 730/1329–30 (see later), Indian sources describe Tirmidh as his residence (*dār al-mulk*),[155] while Ibn Baṭṭūṭa in *c.* 733/1333 found him encamped not far from Nakhshab.[156] Nevertheless, Ghazna seems to have been his power base, since Ibn Baṭṭūṭa says that it was the seat of his chief amir, Boroldai, and that he made for Ghazna when confronted by a formidable rebellion under his nephew

Buzan.[157] By Timur's era, Boroldai's tümen was seen as part of the Qara'unas.[158]

In some degree, the southerly orientation of the Chaghadayid khans balanced the loss of territory elsewhere. During Esen Buqa's reign the Chaghadayids forfeited some of their eastern lands to the Yuan forces,[159] and the abiding peace with the Yuan from 1323 onwards closed off the eastern frontier as an arena for raids and plunder. Similarly, by 1320 Chaghadai's ulus had lost part of the lower Sīr-daryā region to the Jochids of the Blue Horde. In other words, well before the rise of Timur the centre of gravity of the ulus had shifted markedly to the south and south-west. Köpek's foundation of Qarshī very probably reflects the new orientation of the Chaghadayid state.[160] Not for nothing did Mamlūk authors who recorded Tarmashirin Khan's obituary call him 'ruler of Balkh, Bukhara, Samarkand and Merv'.[161] In his geographical work Ḥāfiẓ-i Abrū would describe north-eastern Khurāsān (defined as 'Balkh, Ṭāliqān, Andkhūd and Shabūrghān as far as the borders of Badakhshān and Bāmiyān') as under the rule of the amirs of Transoxiana at the death of the Ilkhan Abū Saʿīd (736/1335).[162] The Ilkhanate's drift into internecine conflict at that juncture ensured that no Mongol power, at least, would challenge Chaghadayid authority in these tracts.

Insofar as any challenge materialised, it came from Delhi. Early in the reign of the Sultan Muḥammad b. Tughluq (724–752/1324–1351), his forces occupied Peshawar and Hashtnaghar. Our sole source for this campaign says that they were soon forced to retreat due to the lack of grain and fodder,[163] but Ibn Baṭṭūṭa, who arrived in the Sultanate in 734/1333, found Muḥammad's officers again quartered in Hashtnaghar, where they levied a tax on the traffic in horses.[164] Tarmashirin's invasion of India in 730/1329–30 – the last major attack on the Delhi Sultanate from Central Asia prior to that of Timur – may have been intended as retaliation for the Sultan's initiative. The Chaghadayid forces ravaged the Punjab and penetrated beyond the Ganges, unsuccessfully investing Mīrat (Meerut); possibly Muḥammad bribed Tarmashirin to withdraw.[165] If so, this may lie behind the reconciliation between the two men, as referred to by Ibn Baṭṭūṭa (above, pp. 137–8).

Thereafter, Muḥammad changed tactics, using the proverbial wealth at his disposal to win over Mongol chiefs and other grandees in the lands beyond the Indus, particularly in the aftermath of Tarmashirin's downfall in 735/1334 and the onset of conflict within the Chaghadayid realm.[166] He had already addressed a proclamation to the sayyids, shaykhs, ʿulama, artisans and military men of Transoxiana in 734/1333–4, inviting them to migrate to India and sending an enormous sum to defray their travelling expenses;[167] a group that included the qadi of Tirmidh arrived in Delhi with, or soon after, Ibn Baṭṭūṭa.[168] Tarmashirin's son and daughter and her husband Nawrūz Güregen, accompanied by a great many followers, took refuge in the Sultanate and were welcomed in Delhi.[169]

By the mid-1340s Mongol amirs were wintering in the Punjab annually with the aim of benefiting from Muḥammad's celebrated munificence.[170] Ibn Baṭṭūṭa sets the number of Mongols in the Sultanate at 40,000.[171] The contemporary Indian author Baranī goes so far as to describe 'the whole of Mongol territory (*Mughulistān*) this side of Transoxiana' as the Sultan's 'obedient client' (*banda-yi parwarda*).[172] The fact that Muḥammad, as the son of Ghiyāth al-Dīn Tughluq, was himself of Qara'unas origin (see earlier) may have facilitated these cordial relations. There are even indications that Muʿizz al-Dīn Pīr Ḥusayn Muḥammad, the Kartid malik of Herat, acknowledged his overlordship and was concerned not to offend him when he himself assumed the style of sultan in 750/1349.[173]

Qazan Sulṭān, the last effective Chaghadayid khan and the last, too, to rule over the entire ulus, was overthrown and killed in 747/1346–7 by the amir Qazaghan, who assumed the rulership of the western regions of the khanate for the next eleven years. According to the early fifteenth-century historian Naṭanzī, Qazaghan too belonged to the Qara'unas people (*qawm*).[174] The Indian author Bihāmadkhānī (842/1438) speaks of him as 'opening the path of friendship and clientage' (*mu'ākhat-u muwālat*) with the Delhi Sultan.[175] At some point during Muḥammad's last years, Qazaghan sent a Mongol force of 4,000 or 5,000 men, under a commander named Altun Bahādur, to aid the Sultan in suppressing a revolt in Gujarat.[176] In view of the harmonious relations at this time between Muḥammad and Mongol amirs beyond the Indus, it does not seem implausible to suggest that Qazaghan's rising and Qazan Sulṭān's overthrow had been bankrolled ultimately (if perhaps unintentionally) from Delhi.

However, this new-found cooperation did not last. When Muḥammad fell ill and died on the banks of the Indus on 21 Muḥarram 752/20 March 1351, his cousin and future successor, Fīrūz Shāh, gave the Mongol auxiliaries leave to withdraw. Thus released from any duty to cooperate with the Delhi forces, the Mongols were seduced by Tarmashirin's son-in-law Nawrūz Güregen into profiting from the uncertain situation: they attacked and looted the Sultan's encampment, but were eventually repulsed and retired to their own country.[177]

QARA'UNAS PARAMOUNTCY IN THE WESTERN CHAGHADAYID REALM

The Qara'unas were as far from being monolithic in the mid-fourteenth century as they had been in 1313 (see earlier). Qazaghan would be killed in 759/1358 by the Qara'unas Qutlugh Temür of the Orona'ut tribe, an amir of a thousand and the son of Tarmashirin's chief amir Boroldai, in reprisal for having denied him his paternal inheritance.[178] By this date Qara'unas amirs were playing a far more prominent role in the politics of the western Chaghadayid realm. As effective head of the ulus, Qazaghan had continued to reside in his own lands in Arhang, Mūnk and Sali Sarai, close to the upper Oxus.[179] From the middle of the century we find the western khanate closely involved once more in present-day Afghanistan. Most notably, Qazaghan in 752/1351 administered a decisive check to the aspirations of Muʿizz al-Dīn, the Kartid malik of Herat. In the wake of victories over the Sarbadārs and the Apardī amirs of the Qara'unas, Muʿizz al-Dīn had launched a number of attacks on Andkhūd and Shabūrghān;[180] if we can trust the confused account of Ibn Baṭṭūṭa, he had defeated and taken prisoner the former Chaghadayid khan Khalīl Sulṭān.[181] He had then proclaimed himself Sultan, in defiance of the canons of Chinggisid sovereignty (above, pp. 181–2). Muʿizz al-Dīn was forced into a submissive treaty by Qazaghan's campaign.

Expelled soon afterwards from Herat and replaced by one of his brothers, he was reduced to crossing the Oxus in 753/1352 to seek Qazaghan's aid; though in the event he regained his throne without external assistance.[182] But he is known to have struck coins in the name of Qazaghan's puppet Chaghadayid khan Bayan Quli.[183]

Qazaghan's son ʿAbd-Allāh briefly succeeded him, but his downfall in 760/1359 introduced an era of confusion in which the 'factional princes' (*mulūk al-ṭawāʾif*: see p. 127 and n.120) exercised autonomous rule in their territories. Qazaghan's line remained closely linked with northern Afghanistan. Yazdī has ʿAbd-Allāh, following his expulsion from Transoxiana, take refuge in Andarāb, 'above Baghlān', where he perished,[184] while Naṭanzī says that his progeny fled to the region of Kabul and Ghazna on their father's assassination.[185] Subsequently, in the context of the military activity of Qazaghan's grandson (and Timur's close ally) Amīr Ḥusayn, Naṭanzī speaks of the Qara'unas (or a group of them, at least) as being the dependants of Ḥusayn's dynasty;[186] and he and other Timurid authors credit Ḥusayn with having large Qara'unas forces at his disposal.[187] Amīr Ḥusayn is first listed among the *mulūk al-ṭawāʾif* as controlling Balkh.[188] When the khan of Mughūlistān, Tughluq Temür, having overrun Transoxiana for the second time, sought to eliminate Ḥusayn, his troops devastated the entire region of Qunduz and Baghlān as far as the passes of the Hindu Kush.[189] It was from Kabul that Ḥusayn himself had begun his revolt against the amir Buyan Süldüs, the current 'strong man' in the ulus, shortly before in 761/1360.[190] On the temporary split between Timur and Ḥusayn in 764/1362–3, the latter made for the *garmsīr* of Hīrman (Hilmand), which was to be the rendezvous, and joined a Negüderi amir named Tümen.[191] When Ḥusayn seized power in Samarkand for the second time, in the spring of 767/1366, he did so at the head of 'the troops of Balkh, Badakhshān, Qunduz, Quttalān [Khuttalān], Ḥiṣār-i Shādmān, Andkh[ū]y and Shabulghān [Shabūrghān]'.[192] An extensive tract south of the Oxus formed the hereditary power base of the man who was first Timur's ally and subsequently his principal opponent within the western Chaghadayid state and whose overthrow in 771/1370 finally sealed Timur's hegemony.

The rise to power of the Qara'unas amirs signalled a cleavage between the western parts of the Chaghadayid ulus and Mughūlistān. Increasingly, the khans and the principal tribal amirs in the west were becoming identified with the Qara'unas/Negüderis, a development which underlay the fragmentation of the khanate into two states in *c.* 1347 and which that division in turn would only accentuate. Buzan's revolt against his uncle Tarmashirin had begun in Mughūlistān (see above, p. 124). If it is true, as Ibn Baṭṭūṭa asserts, that Tarmashirin was overthrown because he had consistently failed to visit that part of his dominions,[193] we can surely infer that this represented a reaction on the part of the Mongol elite in the east against the khans' southward-oriented policy.

But the Qara'unas amirs did not confine their ambitions to the upper Oxus region. In his father's lifetime, ʿAbd-Allāh b. Qazaghan had already invested Ürgench in Jochid Khwārazm and extracted an enormous sum from the populace.[194] His decision, when head of the ulus, to move north of the Oxus and take up residence in Samarkand in 760/1359 elicited protests from his followers and earned the enmity of amirs in that region.[195] So too, the plan in 770/1369 of Qazaghan's grandson Amīr Ḥusayn, himself now master of the ulus, to transfer his headquarters from the upper Oxus to Balkh, over which he had extended his control some years previously,[196] would provoke the hostility of a number of amirs based not far to the north who felt threatened by this step, not least his former ally Timur.[197]

The relatively transient hegemony of the Qara'unas amirs within the western khanate may itself have justified the application of the term to that part of the ulus by the Mughūls in the east. Timur's advent to power marked – or he and his dynasty wanted it to mark – a pronounced break with the Qara'unas era, although the forces now at his disposal, paradoxically, were for the most part Qara'unas. In Beatrice Manz's view the strength of his position lay in his command of non-tribal forces, among whom the Qara'unas constituted the largest element.[198] She has drawn attention to the silence of Timurid authors, other than Naṭanzī, regarding the Qara'unas. Michele Bernardini, for his part, goes further and writes of the 'later Timurid *damnatio memoriae*' of all Qara'unas history as Timur came to identify himself, and his eulogists sought to reconstruct him, as a Mongol (see also later, p. 256);[199] from this point onwards, the Qara'unas and their amirs are referred to simply as 'Turks'.[200] For Manz, 'Temür's victory . . . represents a victory of the northern and older part of the Ulus Chaghatay over the southern coalition, led by the emirs of the Qara'unas, who had succeeded in gaining power over the Ulus with Qazaghan's victory in 747/1346–7'.[201] Though it has not won universal acceptance,[202] this perspective has much to commend it. We are undoubtedly entitled to see the rising by Ḥājjī Barlās and Buyan Süldüs against ʿAbd-Allāh as a reaction against Qara'unas hegemony by the older military elite, prefiguring Timur's eventual contest with Amīr Ḥusayn.

Both the recent history of the ulus and episodes in his early career predisposed Timur to resume the process of expansion begun by the Chaghadayid khans into both eastern Iran and India. But he can be also seen as having continued and developed a 'Qara'unas' foreign policy, inasmuch as from an early date, like ʿAbd-Allāh b. Qazaghan, he harboured designs on Khwārazm. We might equally view him as looking beyond the predominantly southward orientation of the previous half-century and seeking to exploit the central location of the ulus, by embarking on an ambitious programme of asserting his khan's authority well beyond eastern Iran.

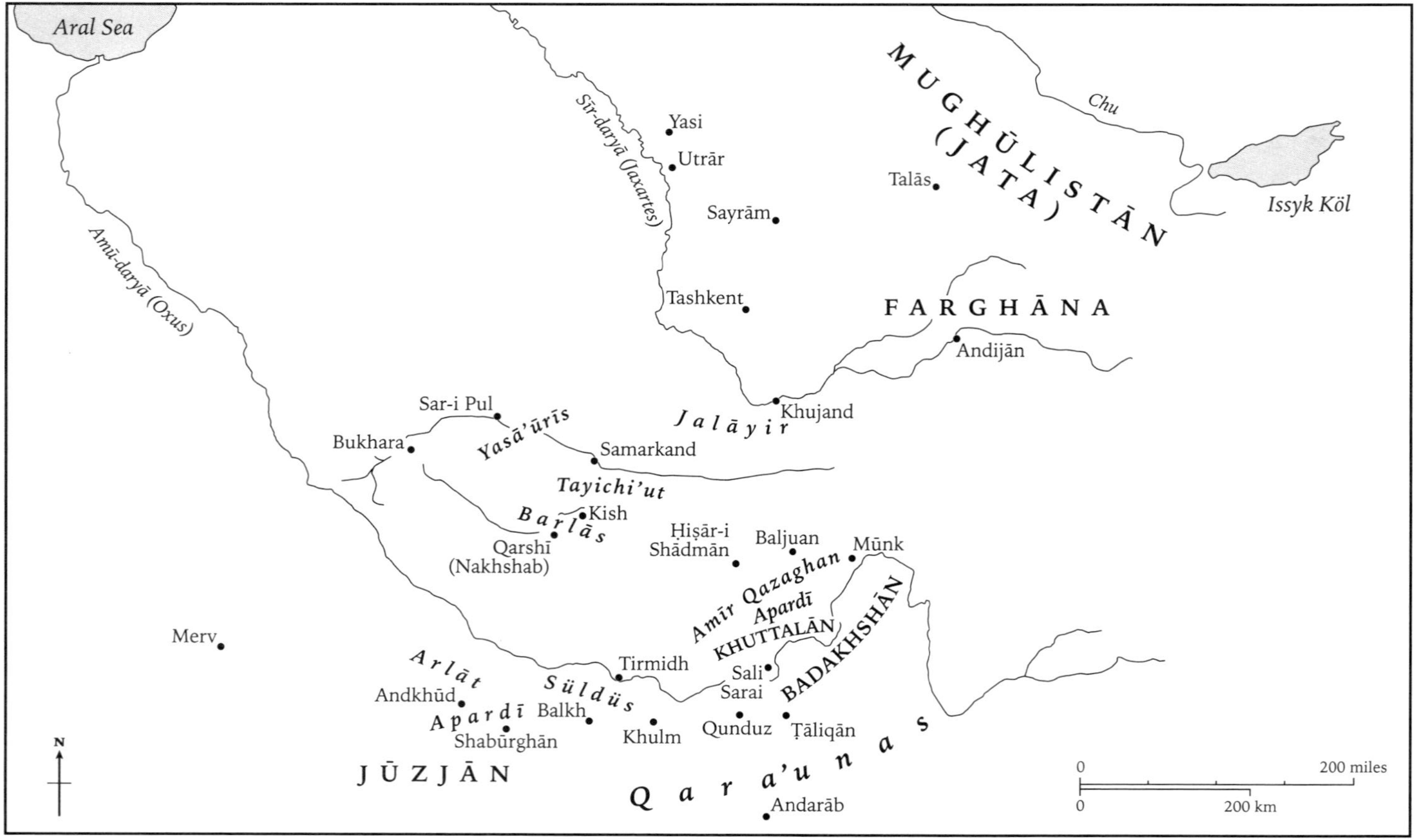

5. The regional powers in the western Chaghadayid ulus.

CHAPTER 8
TIMUR'S FOREBEARS AND THE ELITE OF THE CHAGHADAYID REALM

Whatever qualification might be made to Aubin's verdict on the dearth of sources for the Chaghadayids (above, pp. 26–7), he was certainly justified in the context of the Mongol ruling elite in Central Asia, for which our information is meagre. In the *Jāmiʿ al-tawārīkh* Rashīd al-Dīn says that Chinggis Khan allocated a number of noyans to Chaghadai, each commanding a 'thousand', and names two of them: Qarachar of the Barlās (Barulas) tribe and Möge of the Jalayir.[1] In his *Shuʿab-i panjgāna* he gives a longer list, naming not merely Qarachar and Möge but also two noyans of the Süldüs tribe, *Turchiyan and Qishliq, Chaghadai 'the Lesser' of the Sönit (later renamed Sönitei) and Buqa Dūqalāt of the *Utar tribe.[2] Thereafter the sources for the Mongol epoch make only spasmodic reference to Chaghadayid amirs, whose tribal affiliation is usually not given. In this chapter I shall scrutinise the claims made later by Timurid historians for the status of the Barlās amirs, review what we know of the elite of the Chaghadayid state preceding Timur's rise to power and reassess the position of his ancestors within their ranks.

TIMUR'S BACKGROUND AND DESCENT

The son of Taraghai of the Barlās and thus a descendant of Qarachar,[3] Timur was born in a village in Chaghadayid Transoxiana named Khwāja Īlghār, a dependency of the tümen and town of Kish (later known as Shahr-i Sabz),[4] which lay within Barlās territory. Timur's father died in 761/1360 or possibly in the following year.[5] Of his mother, *Tekine Khatun, nothing is known for certain.[6] Timur himself would later claim, according to Archbishop John of Sulṭāniyya, that she was of lowly origins,[7] but we might hesitate to take this too seriously in view of the conqueror's propensity to brag about the disadvantages of his youth in conversation.[8] This is not the last occasion on which we shall discern a gulf between Timur's own discourse and the Persian literary sources. Ibn ʿArabshāh cites the appendix to a work in Persian which he calls *Muntakhab* (almost certainly not Naṭanzī's history of that title) and which he had seen, claiming that it included a genealogy linking Timur to Chinggis Khan through the female line.[9] This testimony could indicate that *Tekine came of relatively good stock, but if so it is puzzling that we hear so little about her when we might have expected Timurid historians to underscore her exalted descent. *Muʿizz al-ansāb* specifies that the Yasāʾūrī amir Ḥājjī Maḥmūdshāh was the son of Timur's maternal aunt (*khālazāda*);[10] though since we do not know to what family or tribe this lady belonged, we are regrettably none the wiser.

As to other members of Timur's family, a stepmother, Taraghai's widow Qadaq Khatun, survived until 791/1389.[11] Timur had two sisters. The elder, Qutlugh Terken Āghā, who married in succession two amirs of the Dughlāt tribe, had sheltered him for forty-eight days at her home in Samarkand in 764/1362–3;[12] she comforted him when he lost his daughter and Timur appears to have been greatly attached to her, judging by his reaction to her death (785/1383–4).[13] Ḥāfiẓ-i Abrū's *Zubdat al-tawārīkh* and *Muʿizz al-ansāb* name three brothers of Timur: ʿĀlim Shaykh, Soyurghatmish and Juki.[14] The first is possibly the ʿĀlim Shaykh whom Yazdī lists among those appointed as military commanders and *tovachi*s (inspectors of troops) following Timur's 'enthronement' as head of the ulus in 771/1369–70.[15] The other two surface nowhere in the narrative sources; they possibly died young.[16]

The society into which Timur was born was well advanced along the path of Islamisation. Tarmashirin Khan, as we noticed, made strenuous efforts to impose the faith on his Mongol subjects and

Taraghai lived through the era when the Mongols of Chaghadai's ulus – or at least those in Transoxiana – were already accepting the faith in significant numbers. In the extensive genealogy of Qarachar's descendants presented in *Mu'izz al-ansāb*, the great majority of individuals in the two generations above Timur bear Muslim names (admittedly a far from infallible guide to religious allegiance).[17] Sharaf al-Dīn Yazdī links Taraghai with a spiritual mentor, a Suhrawardī shaykh named Shams al-Dīn Kulāl, to whose shrine in Kish Timur later had his father's body removed, and who had given Timur himself valuable support at the outset of his career.[18]

Timur's unimpeachable Mongol ancestry as a descendant of Qarachar has been generally accepted. To the best of my knowledge, the most recent scholar to question his Mongol extraction was the late Hans Robert Roemer, who concluded that he was in all likelihood of Turkish descent, though conceding that he may have had one or two Mongol forebears.[19] Undeniably, Timur's everyday language was Turkish, but this seems to have been true of other members of tribes of Mongol origin in the Chaghadayid territories, as well as of the khans themselves (see earlier, pp. 204–5). The point might well be considered otiose, given what we know of the complex elements that make up ethnic identity, and in particular what Rashīd al-Dīn tells us regarding the extension of the name Mongol to a diversity of peoples (see earlier, p. 69) – not to mention intermarriage during the thirteenth to fourteenth centuries between Mongol tribal dynasties and Turkish women. More important, as we shall see later, is Timur's attachment to Mongol tradition and institutions.

What concerns us in this chapter, however, is the status both of Qarachar and of his progeny, because there is good reason to suspect that the Timurid period witnessed far-reaching embellishment of the record. After Timur's death an author named Ḥusayn b. 'Alīshāh produced a genealogy (extant in a single manuscript and as yet unpublished), in which he grafted Qarachar onto Chinggis Khan's family tree, making him descend in the direct male line from Qachulai, the son of the Mongol khan Tümenei and brother of Chinggis Khan's great-grandfather Qabul Khan.[20] Since the tree also emphasises the Jochid ancestry of Timur's grandson Khalīl Sulṭān b. Amīrānshāh, it was in all likelihood composed during his brief reign in Samarkand (807–811/1405–1409).[21] Sharaf al-Dīn ʿAlī Yazdī went further. He tells how Qachulai had a dream which he reported to his father and which presaged that he himself would be the ancestor of a great conqueror, just as would Qabul Khan. Tümenei, the story continues, thereupon drew up a compact written in the Uighur script and impressed with his red seal (*āl-i tamgha*), whereby after his death sovereignty was to pass to Qabul Khan and administrative and military responsibilities to Qachulai.[22]

In Yazdī's account of Temüjin/Chinggis Khan's career, Qarachar is introduced at intervals in such a way as to enhance his prominence from an early date. Temüjin is represented as consulting him at critical junctures and during the final battle with the Kereyit, Qarachar is made to engage in combat with Ong Khan and to unhorse him.[23] We are even told that when the young Temüjin, his mother and his brothers were cast adrift after Yesügei's death, Qarachar was a child and his father Sughu Sechen (said to have been a pillar of Yesügei's rule) had himself died some days previously,[24] as if Yazdī thought it important to absolve the two men of any responsibility for their failure to rescue the future Chinggis Khan from the predicament in which he found himself. Yazdī also assures us that, some decades after the drafting of Tümenei's covenant, when Chinggis Khan apportioned the Mongol tribes among his kinsfolk, Qarachar, as one of his cousins (*az abnā-yi aʿmām*), received a share along with the conqueror's sons and brothers.[25] And when Chinggis Khan was nearing death, he is said to have summoned not merely his sons and his brothers but Qarachar also; he then had Tümenei's covenant produced from the treasury, where it had been housed for three generations, and confirmed it with a fresh enactment. He further entrusted his son Chaghadai to the guardianship of Qarachar, who had (allegedly) wielded administrative and military authority during Chinggis Khan's lifetime and was henceforth to do so within Chaghadai's ulus.[26] Thereafter, while Chaghadai occupied himself with the hunt and other pleasures, we are told, Qarachar duly saw to the business of government and the military.[27] He allegedly played a part in the suppression of the popular revolt of Maḥmūd Tārābī against the Mongols in Bukhara in 636/1238–9.[28]

Tragically (but perhaps not inconveniently), Yazdī tells us, Tümenei's covenant was destroyed at the time of the usurpation of the Ögödeyid ʿAlī Sulṭān (*c.* 740/1339–40).[29] When narrating Timur's birth, Yazdī emphasises that the significance of Qachulai's dream and Tümenei's interpretation had thereby been made clear,[30] and he reiterates Qarachar's common ancestry with Chinggis Khan and the descent from Tümenei both in the *Muqaddima* and in the main part of his *Ẓafar-nāma*.[31] The genealogy is found also in *Muʿizz al-ansāb* and Ḥāfiẓ-i Abrū's *Zubdat al-tawārīkh* (830/1426–7).[32] In this fashion Timur was turned into a kinsman of Chinggis Khan and (remotely) a member of the Mongol imperial dynasty.

Now we know that the Mongols were unfamiliar with a written script prior to 1204, when Mongolian began to be written in the Uighur alphabet. Hence it is far from obvious how the covenant described by Yazdī could have existed for several decades. Moreover, we have no written evidence from Timur's lifetime for belief in his descent from Tümenei; nor does any pre-Timurid source substantiate Yazdī's extraordinary claims. Ultimately they may have rested on the fact that the Secret History and Rashīd al-Dīn, reproducing one of the characteristic fictions by which medieval nomads used the idiom of blood kinship to express shared political interests and loyalties,[33] had given the Barulas people *as a whole* a common ancestor with Chinggis Khan. In his *Jāmiʿ al-tawārīkh* Rashīd al-Dīn traced the tribe's lineage back to Tümenei's son Qachulai,[34] whereas in the Secret History Tümenei's great-grandfather is given two brothers, Qachula [*sic*] and Qachi'u, and the Barulas are made to descend from both.[35] Neither work, however, included Sughu Sechen or Qarachar in the genealogy.[36] We might also note that, although Rashīd al-Dīn on occasion mentions Barulas noyans, the section on the Barulas in his history of the tribes is strikingly brief.[37] In his *Shuʿab-i panjgāna* he likewise omits Qarachar from Qachulai's progeny but describes him in the list of Chaghadai's amirs as being 'of the stock (*ūrūq*) of Būzūnchār' (namely, Bodonchar, Chinggis Khan's ancestor in the ninth degree); though he muddies the waters by listing him twice, as

'Barulatai Qarachar' and 'Qarachar of the Barulas'.[38] Unless this is just a restatement of Barulas tribal origins (as I suspect), it constitutes the only pre-Timurid evidence for Qarachar's descent from the Mongol khans.[39]

Outsiders writing in and after Timur's era imbibed conflicting traditions regarding his pedigree. The early sixteenth-century *al-Ta'rīkh al-Ghiyāthī* reproduces the genealogy linking Timur to Chinggis Khan's ancestor Tümenei, but says below that his father (Taraghai) was a peasant (*min al-fallāḥīn*) and that Timur's early life was passed in obscurity.[40] Ibn Khaldūn, writing before the dissemination of Timurid propaganda regarding Timur's ancestry (see earlier; also below, p. 359), exhibits considerable uncertainty. If he was confident of Chinggis Khan's descent from a line of Mongol khans,[41] that of Timur was a more doubtful matter. At one juncture in the *'Ibar* Ibn Khaldūn states that Timur belongs to the line (*nasab*) of Chaghadai; at another, he similarly terms him a descendant of Chaghadai (*min banī jaqaṭāī*), expressly called Chinggis Khan's son;[42] at still another, however, he describes Timur and his people (*qawm*) alike as related to Chaghadai, but admits to being unaware whether this was Chinggis Khan's son or some other Mongol of the same name;[43] lastly, he asserts that Timur's precise connection to the Chaghadayid dynasty was unknown but that he was believed to be of a different lineage.[44]

It is only with Ibn 'Arabshāh, a Syrian writing well after his enforced sojourn in Timur's empire, that Taraghai has greatness briefly thrust upon him. Curiously, while transmitting yet more variant accounts, this otherwise hostile witness regards as the most genuine (*al-aṣaḥḥu*) a tradition that made Timur's father one of the nobility (*arkān dawla*) or at least an amir of a hundred; he is here relying on the Persian work he calls *Muntakhab* (see earlier). Alongside this, however, he cites alternative reports that describe Taraghai as an impoverished shoemaker (*iskāf^an^ faqīr^an^ jidd^an^*), that characterise him and his son, somewhat damningly, as part of the generality lacking in sense or religion (*min . . . ṭā'ifat awshāb lā 'aql lahum wa-lā dīn*), and that relegate them to the rabble of worthless nomads (*min al-ḥasham al-raḥḥāla wa l-awbāsh al-baṭāla*).[45] These other accounts seem incongruous in view of the fact that Taraghai was a kinsman of Ḥājjī Barlās, the head of the tribe. It is also worth noting that, according to the Timurid sources, Taraghai had been a friend of the eastern Chaghadayid amir Ḥamīd.[46] But Clavijo heard that Taraghai, though of noble stock, had a mere three or four men under his command, and this is of a piece with the statement of John of Sulṭāniyya that Timur's own followers initially totalled only seven or ten.[47]

Timur's concern to marry into the imperial dynasty and his use of the title *güregen* do not in themselves undermine the claim to Mongol ancestry, as Roemer suggested.[48] Marriage links with the Chinggisids were highly valued, and many an amir listed by Rashīd al-Dīn some decades earlier as belonging to an authentic Mongol tribe is given the style of *güregen*. The use of that title in Timur's case implies, rather, that he needed it, precisely because he was *not* born into the imperial line and his descent from Tümenei is spurious.

THE STATUS OF QARACHAR

There is no doubt that Qarachar was among Chinggis Khan's most valued lieutenants.[49] Like Rashīd al-Dīn, the author of the Secret History had named him as one of three commanders of a thousand allotted to Chaghadai; though he made Chinggis Khan place his son in the care of a completely different noyan called Kököchös.[50] Naṭanzī mentions Qarachar only briefly, saying that he was appointed as amir (presumably chief amir) by Chaghadai's grandson and successor, Qara Hülegü (d. *c.* 649/1252).[51] Even Yazdī's principal source, Timur's historian Niẓām al-Dīn Shāmī (806/1404), had stopped short of portraying Qarachar in such terms as would Yazdī. While asserting that Chinggis Khan had entrusted Chaghadai to Qarachar (and the current role of Qarachar's descendant Timur, he says, had demonstrated the farsightedness of this act), he merely emphasised Qarachar's high rank within the ulus. For example, he depicts Qarachar as the guardian of the Yasa, a function that Rashīd al-Dīn had attributed to Chaghadai himself.[52] In the *Mu'izz al-ansāb* Qarachar is called 'the drafter (*wāḍi'*) of the binding oath (*möchelge*) in Chinggis Khan's *Töre*'.[53]

A meticulously researched article by Samuel Grupper, published over twenty years ago, presented evidence from the *Yuanshi*, the dynastic history compiled under the Ming from earlier documentation soon after the Mongol rulers' expulsion in 1368. The biographical section of the *Yuanshi* includes notices on the Barulas noyans Qurumshi and his son Ebülün, revealing that their ancestors had played a significant role in military affairs under the Yuan.[54] The founder of the line, Bulughan Qalja, like Qarachar, had joined Chinggis Khan at an early stage, had been admitted to the imperial guard (*keshig*) and had thence been promoted by the conqueror to command a tümen;[55] and successive generations of his descendants likewise served in the imperial guard and operated on various fronts as commanders of a thousand. Grupper sees in this evidence, which antedates the Timurid sources by more than a quarter of a century, a parallel that helps to explain how Timur came to achieve a position of dominance in Chaghadayid affairs.[56] 'The records of Buluğan Qalja and his aristocratic descendants and of Qaračar Noyan and his offspring', he suggests, 'illustrate a certain episodic similarity.'[57] And, he continues, 'this account [the history of the Barulas noyans in the *Yuanshi*], as it now stands, independently corroborates Timurid claims for a similar set of alignments in the Čağatai Qanate'.[58]

That I rather doubt. Grupper's findings indicate no more than that another noyan from the Barulas rose to high military office in Chinggis Khan's time. The question here is not whether Qarachar had been a high-ranking military officer under Chaghadai and had thereby enjoyed a position of authority at a broader administrative level, much as did Bulughan Qalja under the Yuan. Maria Subtelny's surmise, on the strength of information in *Mu'izz al-ansāb*, that he was both the commander of Chaghadai's *keshig* and his chief judge (*yarghuchi*) is persuasive.[59] The probability that Qarachar served as *yarghuchi*, in particular, receives support from a source, importantly, which is untainted by pro-Timurid sympathies. Writing of the privileges conferred by the khan Tughluq Temür on his own Dughlāt forebears (see later), Mīrzā Ḥaydar tells us of the procedure to be followed in the event that one of them had committed nine offences: the accused would be subjected to a court of inquiry (*yarghū wa-pursish*), and any statement he might make was to be reported to the khan by the Barlās.[60] Later, Ḥaydar speaks of aged amirs from the Barlās in contemporary Mughūlistān who were consulted about 'the Töre and regulation' (*tüzük*, presumably rules governing military matters).[61] This association of the Barlās tribe with the *yarghu* (though not necessarily with the office of *yarghuchi*) and with prescribed order may well throw genuine light on Qarachar's career; it could also, as Subtelny observes, have imbued Timur with a commitment to upholding the Yasa (or Töre, as it was known by his day).[62]

What is at issue is whether the evidence from the *Yuanshi* has implications for the status of Qarachar's descendants. The ongoing prominence of a dynasty of Barulas noyans within the Yuan empire has no necessary bearing at all on the situation in Central Asia, since the particular configuration of military command and political influence naturally varied both from one ulus to another and over time. In general, Rashīd al-Dīn shows that, although a military command in many cases passed on an officer's death to his son or brother, it was also not uncommon to be succeeded by someone from a completely different tribe.[63] The position of a lineage within each ulus was not determined simply by the promotion of an ancestor under Chinggis Khan or by the allocation of noyans to each of his sons. It was further influenced by the services of those individuals and their descendants (or others who might rise to supplant them). Khans would favour, for instance, the families of their principal wives; or following a disputed succession the victor might confer high rank on his supporters, who perhaps included 'new men' from hitherto less prominent tribes. This is likely to have been true of Chaghadai's ulus, considering the chequered history of the khanship after 1334.

It is also important to note the variation in institutional development within the different uluses, as highlighted by Atwood.[64] From Qubilai's time the dignity of *keshig* chief under the Yuan tended to be monopolised by particular families, but this did not transpire, for example, in the Ilkhanate. Nor did the headship of *keshig* guards in the regional khanates necessarily reflect, in terms of tribal affiliation, the assignment of such ranks at the centre by the Qaghan. We lack any evidence for the policy of the Chaghadayid khans in this respect.

THE BARLĀS AMIRS FROM QARACHAR TO TIMUR

Regarding the activities of Qarachar's descendants in the ulus of Chaghadai,[65] we have barely any information, even taking into account the limitations of the source material.[66] Qarachar's son Ijil, who figures among Timur's forebears and is said to have served the khans Alughu and Mubārak Shāh in turn,[67] is indeed mentioned twice in a single manuscript of the *Jāmiʿ al-tawārīkh*, copied in Baghdad in 717/1317, where we are told that he was in attendance on Prince Tegüder and that he was 'a great amir in the service of Abagha'.[68] In other words, this amir formed part of the Chaghadayid contingent that had participated, as we saw, in Hülegü's campaigns in Iran (p. 78), and had then been transferred into the Ilkhan's service following Tegüder's abortive revolt in 1267. John Woods has suggested that these phrases in the Baghdad manuscript – not found in any other manuscript of the work – may have been interpolated by someone other than the original copyist.[69] Nothing further is known of Ijil, but this is hardly a promising career move for one of Timur's direct ancestors in Transoxiana. Nevertheless, Sharaf al-Dīn Yazdī skirts around the problem by stating that after Ijil left for Iran he was succeeded by his son Ailangir, who was allegedly exercising his functions towards the end of the century, in Du'a's reign, and caused the ulus to flourish.[70]

Can any of the material supplied by Yazdī be reconciled with the scanty details we possess on the internal history of the Chaghadayid ulus in the thirteenth and early fourteenth centuries? It is indeed possible that Qarachar's son Ilder is identical with a Mongol commander of that name, one of the two men said to have suppressed the vestiges of the Tarābī revolt in 636/1238.[71] Yet the only other members of the Barlās ruling clan to make an appearance in the late thirteenth–early fourteenth centuries (and then only fleetingly) are *Temülei (alternatively *Nemülei or *Nambulai) and his son Dā'ūd, who figure in *Muʿizz al-ansāb* as descendants of Qarachar's son *Yesünte Möngke and thus members of a different branch. In the 1290s *Temülei commanded one of the two tümens sent by Du'a to garrison the territories south of the Oxus alongside Qaidu's forces

(Du'a's own son Qutlugh Khwāja headed the other: see p. 213).[72] As a lieutenant of Du'a, Dā'ūd was active in the internecine conflicts of 1305–6 in Transoxiana.[73] None of the other Chaghadayid noyans named by Waṣṣāf or Qāshānī as participants in this struggle appears in the Barlās genealogy,[74] while Barlās amirs other than *Temülei and Dā'ūd are invisible in the narrative accounts for the thirteenth- and early fourteenth-century khanate. We might imagine that we have to do with a completely different polity from the one of which Yazdī is writing.

At the outset of Timur's career, the head of the Barlās tribe was Dā'ūd's nephew, Ḥājjī Barlās,[75] whose hereditary territory lay around the town of Kish (Shahr-i Sabz). According to *Mu'izz al-ansāb*, he commanded the *ulugh ming* ('great thousand'), which is slightly later called the *ulugh tümen*.[76] Manz and Woods have identified this unit with the force originally allotted to Qarachar by Chinggis Khan, and Ando too has equated it with the 'tümen of Qarachar' and the 'tümen of Shahr-i Sabz' (which Ḥāfiẓ-i Abrū calls the hereditary possession of the Barlās), as mentioned in other Timurid sources.[77] The problem, again, is why the regiment once commanded by Qarachar should be termed 'great'. Did the term apply to all the units that Chinggis Khan conferred on Chaghadai, or is the information in *Mu'izz al-ansāb* merely a device to inflate the standing of Qarachar and his descendants?[78]

We should note that, even if Grupper is right about the status of Barlās amirs, Timur himself was only a minor figure within the Barlās tribal hierarchy; and the predicament facing Timurid authors was how to explain away the fact that this figure, who did not belong directly to the line that presided over the Barlās tribe, had somehow become its head. Shāmī and Yazdī ignore the difficulty by stating that, prior to the khan's invasion, Timur and Ḥājjī Barlās had ruled jointly over Kish, which is patently false.[79] But on the basis of the genealogy given for him by the Timurid historians, his relationship to Ḥājjī Barlās was fairly remote. His grandfather, Ailangir's son *Borogul, and his father Taraghai seem to have been private individuals with no share in events at the centre.[80] This did not prevent Yazdī from writing of Taraghai, somewhat incongruously, as Timur's 'renowned (*nāmdār*) father'.[81] In his *Muqaddima*, Yazdī has remarkably little to say about Timur's father and grandfather, other than that Taraghai's energies were entirely devoted to the advancement of Islam and the protection of Muslims, that his home supplied the needs of men of learning and was a meeting place for the religious and the pious, and that he was a disciple of Shaykh Shams al-Dīn Kulāl (see earlier).[82] And in the main part of his work Yazdī makes out that *Borogul and Taraghai deliberately chose to renounce their territory and their tümen to their kinsfolk.[83]

Following the attack on Transoxiana by the eastern Chaghadayid khan Tughluq Temür in 761/1360 and Ḥājjī's flight before the invaders, what enabled Timur to obtain 'the territory of his illustrious forebears', as Niẓām-i Shāmī puts it, was not hereditary right but his readiness to abandon Ḥājjī Barlās and his prompt submission to the khan, purportedly with Ḥājjī's consent and with the aim of preserving the Kish region from devastation.[84] When Yazdī tells us that Tughluq Temür left Ilyās Khwāja as regent of Transoxiana but entrusted the administration to Timur's sound judgement,[85] this is surely designed in part to echo the supposed role of Qarachar at an earlier date.

Even if Qarachar transmitted his military command to his heirs, and even if the details of his role as furnished in *Mu'izz al-ansāb* are totally accurate, we are still left with a question: if members of the Barlās tribe's ruling family had been as prominent as Timurid authors claim, why do we hear so little about them in the pre-Timurid material? Although Rashīd al-Dīn, Waṣṣāf and Qāshānī name a number of noyans active within Chaghadai's ulus from the 1280s to *c.* 1320, they do not include any of those of Qarachar's line who will later be listed among Timur's forebears. Arguments from silence are hazardous, and it could be objected that our picture of the Mongol aristocracy in the thirteenth- and early fourteenth-century Chaghadayid dominions is distorted by the vantage point of our sources, which largely come from the Ilkhanate. But the activities of Barlās amirs, centred on their camping grounds around Kish, were presumably played out not far from the Oxus; these were not backwoods amirs in Mughūlistān operating beyond the horizon of Ilkhanid authors.

We cannot dismiss the possibility that the Barlās amirs, as prominent figures in the western regions of the ulus, returned to the forefront of affairs when Köpek Khan took up residence in Transoxiana at nearby Qarshī, and when Ilkhanid authors had virtually ceased to report events within Chaghadai's ulus. There is no evidence either way, however. Ibn Baṭṭūṭa furnishes a little information, and as we have seen (pp. 201, 218) the chief amir under Tarmashirin, who was likewise based in the west, was Boroldai of the Orona'ut tribe.[86] The nearest counterpart, in fact, to the line of Barlās commanders named in the *Yuanshi*, and whose careers have been examined by Grupper, may well be those of Qarachar's progeny in Central Asia who were descended from *Yesünte Möngke and hence *not* among Timur's direct ancestors. And we are still, in any case, a long way from sworn compacts between the Chaghadayid khans and Qarachar's 'successors' or from some far-reaching executive authority based thereon that was the sole preserve of Barlās amirs.

A SECOND REWRITING OF HISTORY? MĪRZĀ ḤAYDAR ON HIS DUGHLĀT ANCESTORS

The way that Yazdī presents Qarachar finds a parallel (of sorts) in the role vouchsafed to Mīrzā Ḥaydar's Dughlāt forebears in his *Ta'rīkh-i Rashīdī* (952/1546). Ḥaydar does not refer to the 'Buqa Dūqalāt' of Rashīd al-Dīn (see p. 223). Instead, at the time of 'the division of his territories' Chinggis Khan is said to have given the Dughlāt amir Örtü (or Örte) Bora, unmentioned by any previous author, an extensive tract known as Manghalai Sübe, which included the towns of Kāshghar, Yārkand, Khotan, Ūzkand, Akhsīkat, Kāsān, Andijān, Āqsū, Atbāsh and Kūsān; he also conferred on him numerous privileges, tantamount to the award of *tarkhan* (Mo. *darqan*) status.[87] Örtü Bora and his line are said to have held the hereditary office of chief amir (*ulusbegi*).[88] Later, Ḥaydar says that the grant was made by Chaghadai, rather, and names the first of the Dughlāt to exercise power over the region as *Baidughan.[89]

It is highly improbable that the Dughlāt dominated such an extensive tract in the eastern khanate – including, allegedly, parts of

Farghāna – during the thirteenth century. In the *Jāmiʿ al-tawārīkh* Rashīd al-Dīn mentions the descent of the Dughlāt tribe, like the Barlās, from Tümenei. Yet he treats them, as he does the Barlās, very cursorily, with the revealing comment that none of their amirs was known to have attained status or fame either in Chinggis Khan's era or in his own.[90] More probably, the rise to power of the Dughlāt in Mughūlistān transpired during the interregnum following Tughluq Temür's death and certainly no earlier than the 1330s.[91] It was at this point that Tarmashirin's neglect of the eastern part of his dominions afforded ambitious noyans there the opportunity to act as power-brokers when it appears there was a dearth of Chaghadayid candidates.[92] Ḥaydar recounts two such episodes: the enthronement in 748/1347 of the young Tughluq Temür, whose descent was questionable,[93] by Örtü Bora's descendant Bolodchi (Pūlādchi); and the enthronement of Khiḍr Khwāja, a supposititious son of Tughluq Temür, by Bolodchi's son Khudāydād in *c.* 1388,[94] seemingly in opposition to elements that favoured the claims of Gunashiri[n], member of a rival, Buddhist branch of the Chaghadayid dynasty based in Gansu.[95] Ḥaydar tells us that Bolodchi and Khudāydād both received additional privileges for their services.[96]

It is, of course, conceivable that some of the information provided by the Timurid authors and by Mīrzā Ḥaydar embodies authentic oral traditions from the thirteenth and fourteenth centuries (in much the same way as histories written in the Kazan, Kasimov and Crimean khanates during the sixteenth–eighteenth centuries can be shown to have preserved reliable material from the era of the unitary Golden Horde).[97] Yet the often tendentious nature of such late evidence, reflecting as it does the need of Timur's dynasty for legitimation or the family and clan pride of Ḥaydar and his Dughlāt kinsfolk, inspires caution. And while authors in those later Jochid histories yield valuable information on that region,[98] they too adopt a quite distinctive stance of their own, displaying a marked interest in contemporary elite families, as for example does ʿAbd al-Ghaffār Qirimī in the Shirin beys[99] – a focus that corresponds to the partisanship of the Timurid sources and of Mīrzā Ḥaydar.[100]

PRINCIPAL MONGOL LINEAGES OF CHAGHADAI'S ULUS IN THE PRE-TIMURID ERA

Let us then fall back on the historical reality in Central Asia during the century preceding Timur's era, insofar as it can be illuminated from the contemporary Ilkhanid sources. Who were the military commanders on whom the Chaghadayid khans relied? The noyans who appear to have enjoyed the highest rank belonged not to the Barlās (or, for that matter, to the Dughlāt) but to the Süldüs and Jalayir tribes. Jalayirtai of the Süldüs,[101] a leading noyan at the time of Baraq's invasion of Iran in 668/1270, may have been the son or grandson of either Turchiyan or Qishliq, who (as we noticed earlier) are both listed in *Shuʿab-i panjgāna* (here fuller than *Jāmiʿ al-tawārīkh*) among the commanders of a thousand allotted to Chaghadai. For his services to Chinggis Khan, Qishliq had been granted *darqan/tarkhan* status and his progeny enjoyed great honour;[102] his descendant Ghiyāth al-Dīn Tarkhān, a prominent supporter of Timur, would inherit that status.[103] Of Köpek of the Süldüs tribe, Rashīd al-Dīn tells us that he was Du'a's chief amir (*muqaddam-i umarā'*) and commanded the Chaghadayid troops south of the Oxus; he perished in an invasion of India in *c*. 1306.[104]

A second line of prominent amirs originated with another of Chaghadai's commanders of a thousand, Möge of the Jalayir. His son Ulugh Yasa'ur ('Yasa'ur the Greater'; Yasa'ur-*i Buzurg*) participated in Baraq's invasion of Iran, and soon afterwards was among those who deserted the khan and submitted to Qaidu.[105] On Du'a's behalf he headed an army which devastated Balkh, Shabūrghān and Merv early in 687/1288,[106] and the khan put him in command of the Chaghadayid forces around Balkh and Bādghīs, in which capacity he was among the amirs (as was Köpek) who led reinforcements to aid the insurgent Ilkhanid amir Nawrūz on his return from Turkestan to Khurāsān in 690/1291.[107] Yasa'ur is last heard of among the generals who accompanied Du'a on his invasion of eastern Iran in 695/1295.[108] According to Rashīd al-Dīn, his numerous sons were still to be found in the region.[109] One of them, Changshi Güregen, played a leading role both as a military commander in campaigns against the Ilkhans and as a close associate of the Chaghadayid prince Yasa'ur, who was his sister's son, from 705/1305 until that prince's departure for the Ilkhanate in 716/1316; Changshi, who remained in Transoxiana, died a year later.[110] Like the Jalayir amirs at the time of Timur's rise to power, he had his principal base in the region of Khujand and Farghāna.[111] But in what blood relationship he stood to them is unknown. We know of other Jalayir amirs also who served the Chaghadayids.[112] They included two brothers of Changshi, Qaban and Buqa, and a nephew of Ulugh Yasa'ur named Orus Buqa, who was active on Du'a's behalf in 1305–6.[113]

We learn hardly anything regarding the wives of Chaghadayid khans from our sources, but Rashīd al-Dīn names a number of amirs from Chaghadai's ulus who married into the imperial family and thereby attained the status of *güregen*, imperial son-in-law. Both Jalayirtai and Ulugh Yasa'ur were deemed of sufficiently high status to be given princesses of Ögödei's line in marriage;[114] Yesü Buqa of the Jalayir, described as 'a great amir' (possibly therefore head of the tribe?), married a niece of Baraq;[115] Ḥasan, a son of Köpek of the Süldüs (see earlier), took to wife Il-Qutluq, a granddaughter of Arigh Böke;[116] and Mengü Temür of the Süldüs was married to a sister of the Chaghadayid khan Mubārak Shāh.[117] In addition, of the ubiquitous Qongqurat tribe ʿAlī Beg was given a granddaughter of Ögödei's son Qadan,[118] and Qutlugh Temür wedded Yesünjin, a daughter or granddaughter of Chaghadai's youngest son Baiju.[119]

What little we know of intermarriage in the decades immediately before Timur's rise to power suggests a similar picture. Qazan Sulṭān's daughter Sarai Mulk Khanim was married to Amīr Ḥusayn (and, after his overthrow, to Timur);[120] her mother was a sister of Mūsā of the Tayichi'ut.[121] A daughter of Tarmashirin was the wife of Bāyazīd Jalāyir and thus the mother of ʿAlī Darwīsh;[122] she is probably identical with Sevinch Qutlugh Āghā, who became Amīr Ḥusayn's chief wife (and would later be married to Bahrām Jalāyir).[123] In short, of those amirs known to have intermarried with Chaghadai's line,[124] none is from the Barlās (and had there been any, *Muʿizz al-ansāb* would surely have mentioned the fact).[125] We are left with the dominant impression that the Barlās were no longer a tribe of the first rank; though it should be remembered that the data we have are sparse.

THE NON-MONGOL ELITE OF TRANSOXIANA

It will be as well to mention at this juncture those of the elite in Chaghadai's ulus who were neither Mongol (or Turco-Mongol) amirs nor military commanders. Local Muslim Turkish dynasties are known to have retained power after the Chinggisid conquest, under Chaghadayid overlordship: at Kāshghar, Khotan, Talās, Shāsh (Tashkent) and Almaligh itself, for instance.[126] But with one exception there exists no evidence for the survival of such Muslim princes beyond the end of the thirteenth century. The exception is the shahs of Badakhshān, rulers of Iranian stock who claimed descent from Alexander the Great and who were subject to the Chaghadayids by 1300 (above, p. 212). On the eve of Timur's rise to power, these local dynasts were still active in the politics of the ulus, participating, for example, in Qazaghan's expedition against Herat in 752/1351.[127]

Turning now to Tājīk officials who straddled the boundary between civil and military, the sayyids of Tirmidh occupied a prominent place. Ibn Baṭṭūṭa tells us that when Khalīl Sulṭān b. Yasa'ur made a bid for the Chaghadayid throne one of the first to join him, at the head of 4,000 men, was ʿAlā' al-Mulk Khudāwandzāda, described not only as a *sharīf* (that is, a sayyid, descended from the Prophet's grandson al-Ḥusayn) but as a 'great amir' and as the lord (*ṣāḥib*) of Tirmidh. The Moroccan traveller claims to have met this figure some years earlier, when passing through Transoxiana. Following his victory and accession as khan, if we can believe Ibn Baṭṭūṭa, Khalīl Sulṭān made ʿAlā' al-Mulk his wazir and later sent him to govern Almaligh.[128] ʿAlā' al-Mulk had a distinguished pedigree: an ancestor or kinsman, also titled ʿAlā' al-Mulk, had been sufficiently important to be proclaimed anti-caliph by the Khwārazmshāh Muḥammad b. Tekish at the peak of his bitter quarrel with the ʿAbbasid Caliph in 614/1217.[129] But Khalīl Sulṭān allegedly grew to suspect the wazir ʿAlā' al-Mulk of harbouring designs on the sovereignty and had him executed, an act which cost him crucial Muslim support.[130] No member of the dynasty subsequently rose to such exalted heights as either of these two ʿAlāʾ al-Mulks. A third person with this style governed Tirmidh in 801/1399 and 807/1404, when he played host to Timur on his return from India and during his final journey to Samarkand near the end of the seven-year expedition.[131] Other sayyids of Tirmidh ('*khānzāda*s', as they are termed) are found in the conqueror's entourage and even participated in his military campaigns.[132]

How much power or influence did other such non-Mongol Muslim grandees – whether Turks or Tājīks – wield within the Chaghadayid polity? Masʿūd Beg had served Baraq, Qaidu and Du'a as finance minister (*ṣāḥib-dīwān*), and according to Jamāl al-Qarshī he was succeeded by each of his sons in turn; but how far into the fourteenth century they continued in office is unknown.[133] The finance ministers of the later Chaghadayid khans do not figure in the sources. Similarly, we learn little of the Maḥbūbī family, who had supplanted the prestigious dynasty of the Āl-i Burhān as *ṣadr*s of Bukhara following the Tārābī rising in 636/1238 and who are attested well into the fourteenth century. Scions of the Āl-i Burhān still possessed some importance in 726/1326, when they were among the witnesses listed in a *waqf* endowment at Bukhara.[134] Yet both lineages seem to have disappeared by the time Timur came onto the stage, and the office of *ṣadr* had forfeited much of its political clout.[135] It is not inconceivable that for both families – and for Masʿūd Beg's descendants – the upheavals of the 1330s and 1340s had proved to some degree catastrophic.

It remains to consider a group that can be classed among the elite primarily in the spiritual sense: shaykhs and their sufi followers. The term 'shaykh' can embrace a whole gamut of individuals ranging from jurists (*fuqahāʾ*, sing. *faqīh*) to ascetics and mystics. In the first half of the fourteenth century it is too early for us to speak of organized sufi orders. The Naqshbandiyya, for instance, who derived their name and prestige from Shaykh Bahāʾ al-Dīn Naqshband (d. 791/1389), were only just emerging. But the progeny of the celebrated saint Sayf al-Dīn Saʿīd b. al-Muṭahhar Bākharzī (d. 659/1261) and their dependants form one already identifiable group. Ibn Baṭṭūṭa alludes to the vast endowments that had accrued to the saint's tomb foundation at Fatḥābād, near Bukhara; and three *waqf-nāma*s drawn up in the period 726–734/1326–1333 on behalf of Bākharzī's grandson Shaykh Yaḥyā, the administrator (*mutawallī*) of the hospice attached to the tomb, have come down to us.[136] The imam and jurist Shaykh Ḥusām al-Dīn Yāghī, one of Tarmashirin's entourage, has already been mentioned (p. 94).[137] Ibn Baṭṭūṭa describes the jurist Badr al-Dīn Maydānī as having been on good terms with the infidel khan Köpek. Maydānī was responsible for bringing Köpek's distant cousin Yasa'ur to accept Islam, and is alleged later, in 716/1316, to have deflected the prince from plundering Khujand and Bukhara.[138] Ibn ʿArabshāh describes Shaykh Shams al-Dīn Fākhūrī (seemingly identical with Shams al-Dīn Kulāl, the spiritual mentor of Timur's father: see earlier), whom Timur in his youth is said to have visited in Kish, as the cornerstone (*maʿqid*) of the country and wielding extensive influence.[139] We know relatively little about such figures in Chaghadai's ulus; but their activities and status no doubt paralleled those of shaykhs in the Ilkhanate, about whom we are better informed.

Lesser figures, including shaykhs, might come to the fore and exercise authority, especially in conditions of crisis. When Ilyās Khwāja's troops tried to take Samarkand in 766/1365, the response was a popular uprising led by three men of whom two are titled *mawlānāzāda* in the sources and were in all likelihood ʿulama or sufi masters. Named as Mawlānāzāda Samarqandī, Mawlānā (or Mawlānāzāda) *Khurdak Bukhārī and Abū Bakr *Kalawī 'the cotton-dresser' (*naddāf*), they are said to have become 'Sarbadārs' and prevented the Mughūl forces from entering the city; on the Mughūl withdrawal, they allegedly subjected the populace to tyrannical rule for some months. Having occupied Samarkand, Amīr Ḥusayn lured the Sarbadār leaders to his camp but then treacherously seized and executed them, with the exception of Samarqandī, who was spared at Timur's intercession.[140] The episode reflects the fear inspired by a grass-roots *émeute* that might have produced a regime akin to the Sarbadār state in Khurāsān; though there is no evidence that the two movements were connected. It also illustrates Timur's regard for sufi shaykhs.

THE TRIBAL ARISTOCRACY AT THE ADVENT OF TIMUR

Since the defeat and death of Qazan Sulṭān at the hands of Amīr Qazaghan in 747/1346–7, the Chaghadayid khans in Transoxiana had ceased to exercise effective power. At the time of Timur's first emergence in the sources, authority was shared among a number of amirs and tribal leaders, termed *mulūk al-ṭawā'if* ('factional princes') in the Timurid sources. Each presided over what has been defined, in the different geographical contexts of eastern Anatolia and Khurāsān, as 'a complex including at least one town (or fortress or both), an expanse of agricultural hinterland, and sufficient pasture'.[141] The absence of adequate source material for the three decades separating Ibn Baṭṭūṭa's visit from the rise of Timur renders it difficult to assess what, if any, continuity existed in the ranks of the tribal elite. The fact that Qazan Sulṭān is accused of uprooting a number of important families and putting several amirs to death testifies to considerable upheaval.[142]

The elite included amirs from the same tribal groups as had been represented in Chaghadai's time. Timur's distant kinsman Ḥājjī Barlās ruled the Kish (Shahr-i Sabz) region. Bāyazīd Jalāyir held the territory around Khujand. The Süldüs formed two branches, at Balkh under Öljei Bugha and at Ḥiṣār-i Shādmān under Buyan.[143] But other elements were possibly of more recent origin. We know nothing of the provenance of the Qipchāq who were present in the ulus by Timur's day, but Manz adduces evidence to suggest that they may have been subordinate to the Jalāyir.[144] The lineage of the amir Mūsā of the Tayichi'ut, whose territory lay in the vicinity of Kish, must have enjoyed some standing, since his sister had married Qazan Sulṭān (see earlier); but the Tayichi'ut are not mentioned in connection with the early Chaghadayid ulus.[145] The amir Khiḍr, whose original camping grounds lay around Sar-i Pul and Pāykand, in the vicinity of Samarkand, commanded the grouping known as the Yasā'ūrīs. Power in Khuttalān and Arhang, lying immediately north of the Oxus, was shared between Öljeitü of the Apardī and Kaykhusraw, who is always called the ruler of Khuttalān but whom Ando has identified as belonging to another branch of the Barlās and as a descendant of Qarachar's uncle.[146]

To the south-west, a member of the Naiman, Muḥammad Khwāja Apardī, ruled over Shabūrghān;[147] his son Zinda Ḥasham is later described by Naṭanzī as heading 'the Naiman troops'.[148] Faryūmadī numbers Öljeitü and Muḥammad Khwāja (who he says were brothers) among the Qara'unas amirs. It appears that the Naiman (not mentioned among the tribal groups allotted to Chaghadai) were now a significant element in the khanate,[149] perhaps since the extension of the khans' authority south of the Oxus. Qazaghan, who is similarly ascribed to the Qara'unas and who possibly belonged to the Besüt tribe, dominated the upper Oxus from the towns of Mūnk and Sali Sarai and had become the leading figure in the ulus; Manz suggests that he may have gained his position by appointment rather than inheritance,[150] rather like Timur later. The Arlāt chiefs, Bayrāmshāh and his son Tilenchi, were based around Andkhūd,[151] and in *c.* 1375 the *yurt* of another Arlāt chief, *Turkān, lay south of the Oxus, towards Gurziwān.[152] As both regions were very close to Apardī territory, Manz proposes that the Arlāt were subject to the Apardī amirs.[153]

Whatever their rights and resources in the thirteenth-century Chaghadayid ulus, by Timur's time the principal tribal leaders commanded not just the troops who bore the name of their own tribe, and sometimes other, smaller tribal groupings in addition, but also non-tribal forces drawn from within their region, so that we read, for example, of 'the thousand of Khulm';[154] they also exercised authority over the local sedentary and urban populations, on whom they levied taxes.[155] Yet probably few tribal leaders enjoyed an unchallenged position within what might be termed their own tribal constituency. Among the Süldüs, the amir Buyan took the initiative in bringing down Qazaghan's son ʿAbd-Allāh and may have been practically independent of Öljei Bugha. In the wake of ʿAbd-Allāh b. Qazaghan's overthrow and during Buyan's feeble ascendancy, Öljei Bugha went his own way, out of a desire, we are told, for the headship (*sardārī*: either that of his tribe or the dignity of *amīr al-umarā*, 'chief amir') that had at one time been in his family (*khānadān*).[156] Within the Jalāyir tribe, Bahrām Jalāyir would later ally with Timur and wrest the headship and territory of the tribe from Bāyazīd's sons;

although this did not prevent him from seeking military assistance from the Mughūls.[157] As we saw in Chapter 7, Qazaghan had been killed in 759/1358 by another Qara'unas amir, Qutlugh Temür.[158] Rivals for the tribal leadership might back competing claimants for the headship of the ulus, or these in turn promoted rival candidates within the tribal hierarchy, with a view to obtaining support for their own pretensions.[159]

The situation was further complicated by the presence of various other elements which could be termed quasi-tribal. We have seen that the Mongol territories contained a number of groupings that had often originated in *tamma* dispositions and came to take their name from a former commander, as had the Negüderis for instance. Thus in the formerly Ilkhanid lands we encounter the Jurma'īs, Awghānīs and Nawrūzīs (a Negüderi group) in mid-fourteenth-century Kirmān, the Jā'ūn-i Qurbān in Khurāsān and the Samāghār and the Bārambāy in Anatolia.[160] A similar development occurred within Chaghadai's ulus. An obvious example is the Yasā'ūrīs, who may have derived their name from the amir active on Du'a's behalf in the 1290s (see earlier)[161] but who are usually taken to be the one-time followers of his maternal grandson, the renegade Chaghadayid prince Yasa'ur (d. 720/1320);[162] if the latter assumption is correct, they had perhaps been associated more recently with his sons Khalīl and Qazan, joint khans in the 1340s. Manz makes the plausible suggestion that the Apardī too had originated as the contingent of an individual leader, since Apardī appears at one juncture as the name of Öljeitü's (and Muḥammad Khwāja's) father.[163]

Ibn ʿArabshāh speaks of four tribes in Transoxiana at the time of Timur's emergence, each of which allegedly provided one of the khan's four 'wazirs': these tribes were the Arlāt, the Jalāyir, the Qauchin and the Barlās.[164] Since Rashīd al-Dīn classes the Arlāt as one of the three branches of the Orona'ut,[165] it is possible that the abovementioned Qutlugh Temür, Qazaghan's murderer, was connected with the Arlāt. Ibn ʿArabshāh's list is obviously not exhaustive: the Süldüs, for instance, who were undeniably important, are omitted. The coincidence of the number four, however, might suggest that he is referring here not to tribal leaders but to *keshig* chiefs and indicating, too, that they were selected on a hereditary basis.[166] Whether or not he was right is uncertain: it should be kept in mind that he might not have been well placed to obtain accurate information on administrative matters.

The name Qauchin is particularly problematic, since it does not figure as a tribal designation in any other source. Perhaps Ibn ʿArabshāh was simply misled by the attachment of the surname Qauchin to numerous individuals: for example, ʿAlī Qauchin, mentioned by Shāmī, and Temüge Qauchin, mentioned more than once by Sharaf al-Dīn Yazdī.[167] The latter writes of 'the *qauchins*', a category in which he proceeds to class a number of officers, evidently of diverse tribal origins.[168] By Mīrzā Ḥaydar's day *qauchin* would have become a general designation for the military, as distinct from the cultivators and the religious class.[169]

Now the Mongolian word *quchin* has the connotation of 'veteran'.[170] According to Shāmī, 'the original personal detachment' (*qushūn-i khāṣṣa-yi aṣlī*) was known to the Turks as *qauchin*. Yazdī's phrasing in the corresponding passage differs slightly (*qūshūn-i būī-yi hazāra-yi khāṣṣa*, 'the detachment of guards of the personal thousand'), and he specifies that these constituted the army's centre (*qalb*).[171] Beatrice Manz suggests that the Qauchin 'began either as personal troops attached to the Chaghadayid khans, or as a land-based, standing army within the Chaghadayid khanate'.[172] We know that in the unitary Mongol empire of the thirteenth century a Qaghan's guard corps was neither taken over by his successor nor completely disbanded, but partly maintained to keep watch over his burial place.[173] Since a khan's personal guard continued to exist as a distinct unit after his death,[174] Shāmī's use of the word 'original' (*aṣlī*) in the above quotation might indicate that he is alluding to the guard detachments of earlier Chaghadayid khans. These would doubtless have included the groups referred to in the Timurid sources as the 'people (*qawm*)' or the 'troops (*yāsāqiyān*)' of Eljigidei.[175] Naṭanzī supplies a brief account of the genesis of the elements who prided themselves on being 'Köpek's *injü*', presumably identical with the 'tümen of Köpek Khan', and indicates that their origins stemmed from a privilege bestowed upon Köpek by his brother Esen Buqa.[176]

Köpek's tümen appears to have been located in the vicinity of Balkh, with which his son Yangi was at one point associated.[177] It seems most likely that the *qauchin* in the late fourteenth-century ulus of Chaghadai overlaps with the *keshig* elsewhere in the Mongol world – although in a number of instances the term denotes Timur's own personal guard rather than that of a former khan.[178] In any event, the tümen of Köpek Khan certainly appears to have been at Timur's disposal from an early juncture.[179]

It must be admitted that our knowledge of the Chaghadayid elite in the period before Timur's seizure of power is sketchy. We can reasonably assume that the amirs of the Jalāyir, the Süldüs and the Barlās were descended from the noyans allotted to Chaghadai by his father and that the troops commanded by those noyans would have multiplied in the course of several generations. But we cannot be certain how elements like the Arlāt, for instance, came to be present in the ulus; Manz, again, points out that Arlāt are to be numbered among the troops of Qaidu some decades earlier.[180] The very fact that the sources narrating Timur's rise to power reveal the presence in Transoxiana and Turkestan of individuals from so many different tribes highlights the magnitude of the problem. The late thirteenth to early fourteenth centuries may have seen the migration into Chaghadai's ulus of noyans from tribes not already represented there, or their contingents may have joined Qaidu and have been absorbed in the wake of Chapar's defeat. Again, they may have been incorporated within the ulus as Du'a and his successors extended their sway south of the Oxus. This last development may well account for the presence of the Arlāt and the Naiman Apardī at least.

The list of amirs and their respective power bases, as furnished by the Timurid sources, combines with mention of the Qara'unas to remind us that the Chaghadayid ulus of the mid-fourteenth century differed significantly from the ulus which Chinggis Khan had bestowed on his second son. It extended much further to the south, beyond the Oxus into present-day Afghanistan and Turkmenistan, and incorporated military contingents possessed of a distinctive history and particularist interests that marked them off from those in traditional Chaghadayid territory. A corollary of this development, as we noticed, had been the growing ascendancy of the more southerly tribal (or, rather, quasi-tribal) elements, among which the Qara'unas were apparently the strongest and the most influential.

The rise of the Qara'unas amirs came at the expense of those who headed older, 'established' tribes based in Transoxiana – in particular, the Barlās, the Jalāyir and the Süldüs – dating back to Chinggis Khan's own military and territorial dispositions.[181] By Timur's day we no longer find prominent amirs from these older tribes conducting operations south of the Oxus, as Yasa'ur of the Jalāyir or Köpek of the Süldüs, for instance, had done during Du'a's reign (an exception is the participation of Buyan Süldüs in Qazaghan's campaign against Herat).[182] As far as we can tell, the descendants of these men were now largely confined to their traditional camping grounds further north. As we saw earlier, the situation had given rise to fresh tensions, in this case within the ranks of the nomadic aristocracy of the western khanate. It was such tensions, rather than any advantages accruing from his birth and background, that furnished the opportunities from which Timur was able to profit.

PART III

TĪMŪR-*I LANG*

CHAPTER 9
THE MAKING OF THE GREAT AMIR AND A NEW RULING CADRE

'It was ever the habit and practice of the fortunate Ṣāḥib-Qirān, in furtherance of the affairs and needs of the realm and the faith,' writes Sharaf al-Dīn Yazdī, 'to give them his personal attention'[1] – or, to adopt the less ponderous phrasing of a more recent biographer, 'Timur's empire was a one-man show'.[2] He maintained 'a government', to quote Manz, 'which was highly personal but not, I believe, without system'.[3] It has to be said that the sources – mesmerised as they are by Timur's spectacular career of conquest – are less than informative regarding what that governmental system was. We should probably attribute the numerous overlaps in responsibility among Timur's subordinates, and their ill-defined functions, to the conqueror's own tendency to guard his power jealously.[4] But in any event, spending much of his career on campaign, Timur lacked the opportunity, and probably the inclination, to forge a new administrative structure. He governed through individuals, whether Turco-Mongol military personnel or representatives of the Persian-speaking bureaucratic class. In the early years of his ascendancy he depended closely on members of his personal following, and not least (though far from exclusively) on members of the prolific Barlās ruling family. Latterly, he entrusted the administration of large tracts of territory to his sons and grandsons. By his death not only had a new ruling dynasty emerged but an entirely new governing class that would last well into the era of Timur's successors and in many cases beyond, to the end of the dynasty.

TIMUR'S EARLY LIFE AND RISE TO POWER

The date given in Timurid sources for Timur's birth is 25 Shaʿbān 736/8 April 1336 – chosen, apparently, because it coincided with the conjunction of Jupiter and Saturn and possessed a profound astrological significance (see further pp. 356, 386 below). Yet authors writing in his lifetime, some of whom met the conqueror, show a striking degree of unanimity in favour of an earlier date. Ibn Khaldūn, writing in 804/1401–2, says vaguely that Timur was between sixty and seventy years old.[5] The more precise estimates furnished by Ibn ʿArabshāh and Archbishop John of Sulṭāniyya suggest that he was born around 728/1327–8;[6] this is in fact the exact year supplied by al-Maqrīzī, possibly by inference from Ibn ʿArabshāh's testimony.[7] It is further confirmed by others who derived their information from Timur's headquarters. According to Ibn al-Shiḥna (and hence Ibn ʿArabshāh) Timur himself told a group of scholars from Aleppo in 803/1401 that he was seventy-five,[8] while Mignanelli says that Timur's people had given his age as seventy-four in 1401.[9] If all this is more or less correct, then Timur would have witnessed, as a child of seven or so, the upheavals after Tarmashirin's downfall; he would have reached fighting age (say, fifteen to sixteen, the age at which he later appointed his sons and grandsons to their first administrative posts) during the joint reign of the brothers Khalīl and Qazan; and he would have been about twenty when Qazan was overthrown by Amīr Qazaghan, the eastern regions of the khanate seceded and the central authority in Transoxiana began to atrophy. For all we know, these last developments may have exerted a formative influence upon him.

We have relatively little in the way of a physical description of Timur (other than the modern reconstruction of his facial features: see Introduction, p. 6). The fullest comes from Ibn ʿArabshāh, who is unlikely to have met him but may have seen him from afar during his youth in Samarkand. Timur, he says, was tall and lofty in stature, with a broad brow and head, strong and vigorous, . . . of light colouring with a tendency to ruddiness, possessing broad shoulders . . . and a flowing beard; he had a loud voice.[10] Confidence in the details of this description is somewhat sapped by Ibn ʿArabshāh's use of the rhyming prose to which he was all too addicted. Those who certainly did meet the conqueror refer to his lameness, his need for assistance in mounting a horse and his use of a litter. Clavijo tells us only how Timur was dressed, but we do have the briefest sketch of the Great Amir's appearance from the pen of Archbishop John: 'He is of middling build and has the Tartar countenance and a white beard *à l'espagnol*'. This was expanded in the Latin version of John's report by a contemporary French annalist, who added (on grounds that are as obscure as the sense) 'and short, fair hair like a leopard'.[11]

As we observed in Chapter 8, a question mark hangs over the status of Timur's ancestors; his own background seems to have been undistinguished. Certainly contemporary external authors – Ibn ʿArabshāh, Clavijo, John of Sulṭāniyya and the Sienese merchant Mignanelli – depict him in his youth as a sheep-stealer and brigand.[12] This image of a bandit, doubtless fostered by Timur's enemies (and encountered even in the Rus′ chronicle tradition),[13] is all the more seductive in that the Timurid sources are noticeably reticent concerning the first thirty years or so of his life. He surely acquired the traditional skills of the nomad warrior; Ibn ʿArabshāh mentions his ability to judge the points of a horse.[14] His early career may well have resembled that of Temüjin, the future Chinggis Khan, falling within the category of *qazaqliq* ('freebooting')[15] – in Timur's case, much of it spent south of the Oxus, in Khurāsān. Like Temüjin, Timur gradually amassed a warband comprising personal followers (*nökörs*) from a variety of tribes – from very small beginnings, to judge by the figures supplied for the 1360s by the Timurid sources.[16] We know a little about Timur's intellectual attainments. Ibn Khaldūn judged him to be highly perspicacious and intelligent (*shadīd al-fiṭna wa l-dhakā'*),[17] while Ibn ʿArabshāh mentions his profound interest in history and his impressive capacity to memorise past events, but hints that his understanding of written Persian, Turkish and Mongolian (presumably meaning here the Uighur script) was limited, if adequate, and that he was quite ignorant of Arabic. Indeed, the phrasing suggests that Timur required even Persian historical accounts to be read aloud to him.[18]

Timur's first opportunity for advancement arose in 761/1360. At this date the eastern Chaghadayid khan, Tughluq Temür, invaded Transoxiana, encouraged by the recent overthrow of ʿAbd-Allāh b. Qazaghan, the failure to instal a khan in succession to ʿAbd-Allāh's nominee, the transfer of the headship of the ulus to the weak and indolent Buyan Süldüs and the fragmentation of real power among the *mulūk al-ṭawāʾif*. The invaders were joined by Bāyazīd Jalāyir, who was left to govern the ulus alongside some Mughūl amirs.[19] Rather than accept Tughluq Temür's sovereignty, Buyan's ally Ḥājjī Barlās took refuge in Khurāsān. Timur had no compunction in offering his submission to Tughluq Temür's lieutenants, though Shāmī and Naṭanzī make out that he did so in order to preserve the Kish region from devastation and that he had secured Ḥājjī's prior consent. Timur may have been encouraged to join the Mughūls by the fact that his cousin, Ḥājjī Maḥmūdshāh Yasāʾūrī (see earlier, p. 224), had done so and was acting as guide (*ghajarji*) to Tughluq Temür's forces.[20] The khan's amirs, struck by Timur's bearing, duly entrusted him with the tümen of Kish.[21] Given the remoteness of his relationship to Ḥājjī Barlās, this might have argued something akin to desperation on the Mughūls' part; possibly the many Barlās candidates closer by blood to Ḥājjī remained aloof and refused to cooperate – or to pledge their support to a potentially stronger regime. We have to assume, on the other hand, that Timur had already acquired a sufficiently impressive warband (though we have no solid information at this juncture) to render his support desirable.

In any event, Tughluq Temür soon withdrew to his own territories. Timur had meanwhile joined forces with Khiḍr Yasāʾūrī and with Qazaghan's grandson Amīr Ḥusayn, leader of the Qaraʾunas forces in the ulus, against Buyan Süldüs, who was held responsible for the murder of Ḥusayn's uncle ʿAbd-Allāh. Buyan was obliged to flee to Badakhshān and Amīr Ḥusayn emerged as the head of the ulus, with Timur, now married to Ḥusayn's sister, as his second-in-command. Ḥājjī Barlās, who allied with Bāyazīd Jalāyir in order to recover his patrimony, reappeared and detached various Barlās amirs from Timur's following; it seems that Bāyazīd Jalāyir was now briefly established as head of the ulus.[22] This prompted Timur to jettison

Khiḍr, who was routed, and to relinquish his position to Ḥājjī. Not long afterwards, however, Timur and Khiḍr, once more in Amīr Ḥusayn's service, were attacked by Ḥājjī Barlās and Bāyazīd Jalāyir. Deserted by Khiḍr, who suspected that Timur would again reach an accommodation with Ḥājjī, Timur joined forces with the latter and Bāyazīd Jalāyir, and the coalition put Khiḍr to flight.

When Tughluq Temür invaded Transoxiana a second time in 762/1361, advancing as far as Samarkand, Timur did not oppose him and was again rewarded with the grant of the tümen of Kish.[23] Having inadvertently done Timur a service by dislodging Ḥājjī Barlās (who was killed as a fugitive in Khurāsān) and by executing both Buyan Süldüs and Bāyazīd Jalāyir, two former heads of the ulus, the khan again withdrew to Mughūlistān, and left his son Ilyās Khwāja to govern the western part of the ulus under the supervision of the amir Bekichuk. Bekichuk's arbitrary and tyrannical conduct alienated Timur,[24] who once more aligned himself with Amīr Ḥusayn. For an uncertain period the confederates wandered with relatively few followers in the regions south of the Oxus. At one point they were seized and incarcerated for two months by ʿAlī Beg, a leader of the Jā'ūn-i Qurbān Mongols in Khurāsān (see p. 185 above). At another, they aided ʿIzz al-Dīn, malik of Sīstān, to overcome a rival, but the malik broke his promise to reward them and they clashed with a squadron of his troops – the occasion when Timur received the wounds to his right arm and right leg from which he derived his sobriquet 'the Lame'.[25] At an uncertain date Timur himself also engaged in negotiations with Muʿizz al-Dīn Pīr Ḥusayn, the Kartid malik of Herat, who for a time hosted his son Jahāngīr.[26]

In time Amīr Ḥusayn and Timur returned to Transoxiana and expelled the Mughūl army. Restored as head of the ulus, Ḥusayn marked his victory by convening a quriltai at which Kābul (or Qabūl) Shāh was enthroned as khan (765/1363–4). But Timur had not finally broken with the Mughūls. Within a few years, having fallen out with Amīr Ḥusayn and the Qara'unas elements, he allied with Kaykhusraw of Khuttalān, who had returned from Jata with Bahrām Jalāyir and Mughūl reinforcements; he himself additionally sought military aid from the khan of Mughūlistān.[27] This in turn alarmed

Ḥusayn into asking the shaykhs of Khujand and Tashkent to mediate. Timur had been disgusted at the treatment of Muslims by Mughūl troops and, we are further told, was inclined, as the result of a dream, towards reconciliation with Ḥusayn and ending his collaboration with the Mughūls. Bahrām and his Mughūl allies were obliged to withdraw.[28] Bernardini dates from this point the use of the term Jata ('robbers') for the Mughūl polity, whose khan had earlier been the repository of legitimacy but which now embodied a threat to the 'authentic' Mongol, Timur.[29]

Harmonious cooperation between Timur and Amīr Ḥusayn did not last. Their growing estrangement, facilitated by the death of Timur's wife (who was Ḥusayn's sister), was further spurred on by Ḥusayn's failure to support Timur at a critical juncture during an engagement on the River Chirchik near Tashkent (the so-called 'Battle of the Mire') with Ilyās Khwāja's forces. Yet the two men continued for a time to cooperate, notably against a popular outbreak in Samarkand, led by religious figures, which Niẓām al-Dīn Shāmī termed a Sarbadār rising, presumably likening it to the more widespread movement in Khurāsān.[30] When the final confrontation came in 771/1370, Timur defeated and captured Amīr Ḥusayn and permitted his former ally to be killed by Kaykhusraw of Khuttalān, who thereby avenged his own brother's death at Ḥusayn's hands. Timur celebrated his triumph by marrying Ḥusayn's chief wife, Sarai Mulk Khanim, daughter of the former khan Qazan Sulṭān. Even in advance of moving against Ḥusayn, he had convened a quriltai which elected as Chaghadayid khan one of his confederates, the Ögödeyid prince Soyurghatmish.[31]

Timur had risen to be the effective ruler of the western Chaghadayid ulus by dint of a succession of short-lived alliances, each discarded once it had become a liability or no longer served its purpose. This readiness to turn his back on agreements, which is discernible on subsequent occasions, gave rise to the charge of treachery that was to be levelled at him by outside observers such as Qadi Burhān al-Dīn of Sivas and Ibn ʿArabshāh. But Timur's shifts of allegiance doubtless appear more reprehensible today when political actors are required to demonstrate ideological consistency and loyalty (and may even do so). In the Chaghadayid milieu personal affections or animosities and calculations of self-interest may have been viewed as perfectly respectable grounds for political alignment. In any case, Timur was not the only leader in Transoxiana who acted in this fashion. At a critical juncture during Tughluq Temür's second invasion, Kaykhusraw of Khuttalān had abandoned his ally Amīr Ḥusayn and gone over to the Mughūl khan.[32] The Timurid sources, as Bernardini observes, depict Timur's tergiversations in a positive light as the quest for partners in order to ensure success for his military ventures and justify his moves by the duplicitous or reprehensible conduct of others – Ḥusayn's bad faith or his greed for the wealth of his subjects.[33] They naturally show Timur as affirming his strong belief in the sworn oath as a pillar of sound rulership.[34]

THE TRIBAL SYSTEM AND THE TRIBAL CHIEFS

His victory over Amīr Ḥusayn did not bring Timur undisputed authority within the ulus. Over the next decade – and even thereafter – he was confronted by numerous risings.

In order to vanquish his rival he had relied on the aid of a few tribal chiefs and amirs who had at one time been Ḥusayn's allies: Shaykh Muḥammad of the Süldüs; the Apardī leaders Öljeitü and his nephew, Muḥammad Khwāja's son Zinda Ḥasham; Kaykhusraw of Khuttalān; and Ḥājjī Maḥmūdshāh Yasā'ūrī.[35] Although Timur had ceased to hold the Barlās territory and the *ulugh ming* ('great thousand'), which had reverted to the line of Ḥājjī Barlās,[36] he had more or less established his authority over the tribe. But the Jalāyir, whose leader, Bahrām, was in Mughūlistān and would shortly die there, had played no part in Amīr Ḥusayn's overthrow. At some point following his victory, Timur recognised Bahrām's son ʿĀdilshāh as head of the tribe.[37] The continued support of these amirs was by no means guaranteed.

Timur took steps gradually to reduce the power and resources of the tribal chiefs; it must be said that some of them rendered it all the easier for him to justify these actions by their efforts to challenge him even after they had submitted. The allegiance of the Yasā'ūrīs seems to have been secured with less difficulty than that of the other elements. After the death of Khiḍr Yasā'ūrī, the leadership of this grouping was shared between his brother 'Alī, Ilyās and Ḥājjī Maḥmūdshāh, all three of whom joined Timur.[38] 'Alī Yasā'ūrī was put to death, however, for opposing Timur's final break with Amīr Ḥusayn,[39] and thereafter we hear nothing of Ilyās. Ḥājjī Maḥmūdshāh, Timur's cousin, appears henceforth as one of his trusted supporters, save for a brief intrigue with the ruler of Khwārazm. He may have gained sole command of the Yasā'ūrīs, rendering it likely that Timur felt able to rely on them.[40]

The most problematic leaders of all were Mūsā of the Tayichi'ut and Zinda Ḥasham of the Apardī. Mūsā had deserted Timur just before the final collision with Amīr Ḥusayn;[41] Zinda Ḥasham defied Timur virtually from the outset in his stronghold of Shabūrghān. He ordered the killing of the Arlāt chiefs Bayrāmshāh and Tilenchi, who were well disposed towards Timur, and gave shelter to Mūsā, whom Timur had summoned to account for his desertion. Zinda Ḥasham and Mūsā declined to attend a quriltai, and surrendered only when Timur in person moved on Shabūrghān. Timur permitted Zinda Ḥasham to retain the town, but the Apardī amir soon fomented another rising and had to be brought to heel by a second expedition, under Timur's amir Chekü, in 773/1371–2. Deprived of Shabūrghān, he conspired with Mūsā, Abū Isḥāq, son of Khiḍr Yasā'ūrī, and a number of other amirs to take Timur prisoner. Mūsā, as the uncle of Timur's chief wife Sarai Mulk Khanim, was forgiven; his sons Ḥamza, Rustam and Muḥammad Beg (who was married to Timur's daughter) are found in the conqueror's service.[42] Zinda Ḥasham was incarcerated in Samarkand, where he died. His lands were now conferred on Timur's officer Buyan Temür b. Aq Bugha, who like the Apardī amirs belonged to the Naiman.[43] But by 790/1388 Timur's lieutenant Jahānshāh Barlās, who had succeeded his father Chekü in command of a considerable area south of the Oxus (see later), is described as heading 'the whole of the troops of Boroldai, of Ṭāyikhān and of the Apardī'.[44] The Apardīs of Khuttalān remained under the rule of Öljeitü's descendants;[45] his son Khwāja Yūsuf appears among Timur's officers, as does his grandson Khwāja 'Alī.[46] We also find the Apardī amir *Malash and his son serving Timur's son ʿUmar Shaykh in Farghāna in 792/1390 and another son was active in the same region in 802/1399.[47]

Unlike some of Timur's other rivals within the ulus, Kaykhusraw of Khuttalān, who had supported the Mughūl khan Tughluq Temür in 1361–2, was an inveterate enemy of Amīr Ḥusayn, who had killed his brother. He was therefore ready to join forces with Timur when the latter and Ḥusayn eventually fell out.[48] But having abandoned Timur during his first invasion of Khwārazm and secretly encouraged Ḥusayn Ṣūfī to resist, Kaykhusraw was charged with treachery in 774/1372 after Timur returned to Samarkand. He was tried in a court of inquiry (*yarghu*) and delivered over to the *nökör*s of Amīr Ḥusayn, who took vengeance for their former master's death at Kaykhusraw's hands three years previously. The tümen of Khuttalān was entrusted to a relative of Kaykhusraw, Shīr Bahrām's son Muḥammad Mīraka.[49] Kaykhusraw's son Sulṭān Maḥmūd took refuge in Khwārazm and later acted as guide to the invading forces of the Jochid khan Toqtamish in 789/1387.[50]

Like the Yasā'ūrīs and Apardīs, the Süldüs and the Jalāyir also survived. As noticed earlier (p. 242), the Süldüs comprised two branches. Öljei Bugha, whose territory lay around Balkh, had been succeeded by his son Mingli Bugha, who was executed in 765/1364 for his opposition to Amīr Ḥusayn and Timur. Mingli Bugha's infant son Pīr ʿAlī does not appear to have succeeded to his position, but Timur later allowed him to inherit his father's property and he remained loyal until after Timur's death.[51] In 776/1374–5 Shaykh Muḥammad b. Buyan Süldüs, the head of the other branch at Ḥiṣār-i Shādmān, conspired with ʿĀdilshāh Jalāyir and the Arlāt chief Turkān to seize Timur while he was on campaign against Jata, but ʿĀdilshāh divulged the conspiracy. Shaykh Muḥammad, found guilty in a *yarghu*, was handed over to the brother of a Süldüs kinsman whom he had killed, and was put to death; Bāyazīd Jalāyir's two sons, ʿAlī Darwīsh and Muḥammad Darwīsh, were also executed, for reasons that are not made clear but which were probably linked with their father's role as head of the ulus some years previously (see earlier). The '*īl* and *tümen* of the Süldüs' were conferred on Timur's follower Aq Temür. ʿĀdilshāh Jalāyir was forgiven and restored to favour.[52] Despatched at the head of a force to invade Jata, however, he then made a bid to seize Samarkand during Timur's absence in Khwārazm and fled into Jochid territory when thwarted by a force under Timur's son Jahāngīr. On this occasion Timur's response was to render the Jalāyir impotent by dividing them up among amirs from other tribes;[53] though a few years later he conferred the tribe on one of his own men, Sari Bugha (see later), a Jalāyir but not a member of the tribe's ruling clan – this despite Sari Bugha's earlier collaboration with ʿĀdilshāh.[54] The latter had meanwhile been captured and executed in 777/1375–6.[55]

In this fashion the major groupings in the western Chaghadayid khanate – the Yasā'ūrīs, the Apardīs, the rulers of Khuttalān, the Süldüs and the Jalāyir – were subjected to Timur's authority. Ando asserts that by 1376 Timur had sidelined virtually all the rebellious tribal elements, while Manz regards the reduction of the Jalāyir to obedience a few years later as the watershed.[56] Timur's ascent to power by no means put an end to revolts, though revolts grew markedly less frequent. In 790/1388, for instance, the commanders of 'Boroldai's *īl* and tribe' (*qabīla*) in present-day northern Afghanistan mutinied and Muḥammad Mīraka in Khuttalān was swift to follow their example. Both risings were put down by Timur's lieutenant Jahānshāh.[57] Nor did Timur's triumph mark the final suppression of rivalries among and within the ruling clans of the different tribes. When he handed Amīr Ḥusayn over to Kaykhusraw of Khuttalān for execution (breaking a promise of safe conduct), then Kaykhusraw himself to be killed by Ḥusayn's *nökör*s and finally Shaykh Muḥammad Süldüs to meet his death at the hands of a vengeful kinsman, Timur was simply making use of the blood-feud in order to remain above it. Yet he had undeniably transformed the character of politics in the Chaghadayid ulus. If the conflicts after 1405 reveal the limitations of his political vision, they also highlight the extent of his achievement. The principal actors in the succession struggle were not resurgent tribal chiefs, but members of the new elite that he had created: princes of his dynasty and his personal followers or their descendants.[58]

TIMUR'S LIEUTENANTS, OFFICERS AND ADMINISTRATORS

In the early stages of his career Timur benefited from the loyal service of a warband – a group of henchmen who have been identified by Manz and Ando. We are not told explicitly that they were bound to him by a sworn oath, like some of Temüjin's early adherents.[59] They were drawn from a number of tribes: Chekü and Ḥusayn (not to be confused with Timur's Qara'unas rival of that name), both from the Barlās; Dā'ūd of the Dughlāt and Mu'ayyad of the Arlāt, who each married a sister of Timur; Ḥājjī Maḥmūdshāh Yasā'ūrī, Timur's cousin; ʿAbbās of the Qipchaq; Aq Bugha of the Naiman; Sayf al-Dīn of the Nüküz (later known as Ḥājjī Sayf al-Dīn); Sari Bugha of the Jalāyir; three men, Khiṭāy Bahādur of the Qipchaq, Shaykh ʿAlī Bahādur of the Barlās and Aq Temür Bahādur of the Dörben, who are all said to belong to Eljigidei's 'people' (*qawm*) or tümen (above, p. 245); Ilchi Bahādur, of the *Belgüt,[60] and two men, Taban (likewise from the *Belgüt) and Qumārī Inaq, who are both called *qauchin* (see above, pp. 245–6). In addition, Manz surmises that Üch Qara, *Eyegü Temür of the *Belgüt, Ghiyāth al-Dīn Tarkhān and Timur's second cousin, Taghai Bugha Barlās, were probably early supporters.[61] Of these, Üch Qara in 768/1366–7 had been among Amīr Mūsā's (and hence Ḥusayn's) commanders opposing Timur's forces, but he was one of Timur's officers by 776/1374–5.[62] Qumārī's brother Temüge Qauchin and Mubashshir, both found in Timur's service at an early date,[63] could also be added to the list.

These personal adherents varied considerably also in social status. Some of them already commanded bodies of troops, perhaps tribal contingents as in the case of Sari Bugha; and in the context of the conflict with Amīr Ḥusayn, Shāmī calls Dā'ūd, Chekü, Sari Bugha, Ḥusayn, Sayf al-Dīn, ʿAbbās and Aq Bugha 'great amirs'.[64] Ghiyāth al-Dīn Tarkhān undoubtedly sprang from an illustrious lineage that went back to Chinggis Khan's time (see above, p. 237). By contrast, Salmānī says of Üch Qara that Timur had purchased him from Ghiyāth al-Dīn Tarkhān, who had inherited him from his forebears and made him his mamluk,[65] while Taban is described merely as

Timur's *nökör*.[66] But regardless of their antecedents, they all owed their standing in Timur's favour ultimately to the fact that they had rallied to him and rendered faithful service. The majority of the men named in this and the preceding paragraph are found fighting alongside him in the 1360s, and they figure among the appointments listed by Sharaf al-Dīn ʿAlī Yazdī under Timur's 'enthronement'.[67]

Timur drew adherents from his tribe, the Barlās, and these individuals mostly occupied a rung on the ladder between his own family and his personal followers.[68] Among them, however, as an early supporter Chekü enjoyed an especially privileged position. Descended in the fifth generation from Qarachar's son Shirgha and hence a distant cousin of Timur,[69] he alone had stayed at Timur's side when the troops of Kish abandoned him to rejoin Ḥājjī Barlās in 762/1361.[70] Having been sent against Zinda Ḥasham, Chekü was entrusted with the government of Shabūrghān when Timur confiscated it from Zinda Ḥasham in 773/1371–2, and then, in the following spring, he was given Qunduz, Baghlān and Kabul and 'the *īl* of Boroldai', a grant that, in the aggregate, was tantamount to command not only of the Apardīs but of all the Qara'unas troops formerly under Amīr Ḥusayn's banner.[71]

Numerous other figures from the Barlās appear in Timur's service, and some rose to a high station. A certain number of them undoubtedly belonged to the ruling clan, descended from one or other of the sons of Qarachar or from the latter's forebears;[72] the remainder were perhaps drawn from the rank and file of the tribe. The *Muʿizz al-ansāb* includes thirteen of the Barlās among Timur's commanders.[73] Yādgār Barlās, who heads the list, was *darugha* of Balkh in 802/1399.[74] Another of the thirteen, Timur's close kinsman Taghai Bugha, was one of three amirs who defended Bukhara when it was besieged by Toqtamish's forces in 789/1387.[75] Those Barlās amirs who appear in the narrative sources but are not listed at this juncture by the *Muʿizz* include Jahāngīr, Ḥājjī Barlās's brother; Pīr Ḥusayn Barlās;[76] Sayfal Barlās, who was made governor of Qandahār on its capture in 785/1383–4;[77] Ismāʿīl Barlās;[78] Mazīd Barlās, later governor (*wālī*) of Nihāwand and treacherously killed by one of his own *nökör*s in 798/1396;[79] Yūsuf Barlās;[80] Qumārshāh Barlās;[81] Saʿīd Barlās;[82]

and Shāh Malik, Edigü and Nūr Malik, the sons of Chekü's elder brother Ghiyāth al-Dīn Barlās.[83] Khudāydād, son of Ḥusayn Barlās (see earlier) and hence usually known as Khudāydād Ḥusaynī,[84] rose to prominence and played a central role in events in Transoxiana following Timur's death.

Some of Timur's early supporters enjoyed major long-term administrative responsibilities.[85] Following his rise to power he nominated Sari Bugha, Ḥusayn Barlās, Aq Bugha, Ḥājjī Maḥmūdshāh, Ilchi and Dawlatshāh Bakhshī to be amirs of the *dīwān*: this body seems to be distinct from the *dīwān-i a'lā* (the finance ministry) and to be identical with the *dīwān-i buzurg*, the 'chief *dīwān*', which functioned as both a council of state and the highest tribunal in Timur's dominions.[86] Yazdī lists several figures, headed by Chekü, who were made army commanders and assigned the rank of *tuwāchīgarī*, which entailed the recruitment and inspection of troops (Mo. *tovachi*, 'inspector'). Khiṭāy, Shaykh 'Alī and Aq Temür are specifically said to have been made not merely army chiefs but 'leaders of the *bahādur*s': this term (Tu. *batur*: 'hero', 'champion') apparently denotes the next rank below that of amir.[87] In addition, command (*ayālat*) of the tümen of the Süldüs was conferred on Aq Temür in 776/1374–5,[88] and later on his son Shaykh Temür.[89] Taban became *darugha* of the Sabzawār territory in 783/1381–2, with a view to keeping the Sarbadār leaders under surveillance.[90]

The sons, brothers and other kinsmen of many of Timur's initial adherents likewise served him. We cannot always be sure which of these had entered his service at an even earlier juncture or which, conversely, joined him only after he gained ascendancy over the ulus. In the latter category, for instance, were four sons of 'Abbās,[91] and four sons of Ḥājjī Sayf al-Dīn,[92] all of whom were among Timur's officers at a later date. Whereas the early personal followers seem on the whole to have remained just military commanders without administrative responsibilities, their sons or other close relatives were on occasion entrusted with such tasks. Aq Bugha's son Temür Khwāja was in command at Ṣabrān (Ṣawrān) on the Sīr-daryā at the time of the Jochid invasion in 789/1387.[93] Another son, Buyan Temür, followed Chekü as governor of Shabūrghān.[94] Temürtash, Aq Bugha's nephew, was *darugha* of Tirmidh in the years 783–90/1381–88 and later, in 804/1401–2, *darugha* of Ḥuwayza in Khūzistān.[95] But most of those who governed Timur's conquests were either *qauchins* like Temüge, who was made *darugha* of Yazd, or Barlās amirs like Jahāngīr, who became *darugha* of Bākharz.[96]

It is especially instructive to identify those personal followers who had the crucial task of guarding Samarkand and Transoxiana during Timur's frequent and lengthy absences between 1370 and 1405. Timur's brother-in-law Amīr Dā'ūd Dughlāt was the first: we are told that in 771/1369–70 he was given the administration (*ḍabṭ*) of Samarkand and the office of governor (*darūghagī*).[97] When Timur set out against Khwārazm in 773/1371–2, the custody of Samarkand was entrusted to Amīr Sayf al-Dīn;[98] and on his departure for Khwārazm again in the spring of 777/1376, Aq Bugha was left in charge of the city.[99] In 778/1377, during the campaign against Orus Khan of the Blue Horde, Chekü governed Samarkand.[100] At the onset of the three-year campaign in 788/1386, it was the turn of Sulaymānshāh b. Dā'ūd and Amīr ʿAbbās to guard Transoxiana.[101] Timur presumably had particular confidence in these men, but none of them, as far as we know, governed Samarkand for a prolonged period or on more than one occasion, which may illustrate the limits of his trust;[102] alternatively, he perhaps had pressing need of their services elsewhere.

Like his Mongol precursors Timur sought to ensure the loyalty of his new military elite through matrimonial ties. Sulaymānshāh, son of Dā'ūd Dughlāt and thus himself Timur's nephew, married the conqueror's daughter Āghā Beki, and his son Yūsuf married a daughter of Timur's grandson Muḥammad Sulṭān b. Jahāngīr.[103] Ghiyāth al-Dīn Tarkhān's daughter Gawhar Shād would later wield great influence as Shāhrukh's wife, and two other daughters married ʿUmar Shaykh's sons Pīr Muḥammad and Rustam.[104] Two of Ḥājjī Sayf al-Dīn's daughters married Amīrak Aḥmad b. ʿUmar Shaykh and Abā Bakr b. Amīrānshāh.[105]

It has been suggested that Timur restricted the very highest ranks to members of the leading tribes like the Dughlāt, the Jalāyir and of course the Barlās. He also tended to grant office to men related by blood to the previous holders (not necessarily their sons or brothers).[106] As a result, several founded aristocratic dynasties that would serve Shāhrukh and later rulers – and in some cases were closely related to the Timurids.[107] Just a few examples can be detailed here, of whom Chekü Barlās is the most conspicuous.[108] When he died in the winter of 785/1383–4, his extensive command south of the Oxus was conferred upon his son Jahānshāh.[109] Timur was hardly the most trusting of men, and it is a testimony to their place in his esteem that he permitted father and son to occupy such a significant power base for so many decades and to head such substantial forces – forces, moreover, whose allegiance could have proved tenuous, given their earlier attachment to Qazaghan and Amīr Ḥusayn. Jahānshāh twice accompanied Timur to the Qipchaq steppe, participated in the Indian and Syrian campaigns and fought at Ankara.[110] His son Burunduq appears frequently as an amir during Timur's last years and was tasked in 807/1404 with assessing the total number of troops gathered from all over Timur's dominions for the expedition to China.[111] Jahānshāh's brother Miḍrāb (d. 817/1414–15), one of the amirs allotted to Shāhrukh in 799/1397 on his appointment as governor of Khurāsān, served in India,[112] would later rise to be amir of the *dīwān* to Shāhrukh and would in turn govern Qunduz and Baghlān.[113] A third son of Chekü, Zīrak, is mentioned among Timur's officers.[114] Timur appointed yet another scion of this family, Edigü, son of Chekü's brother Ghiyāth al-Dīn, to the government (*ḥukūmat*) of Kirmān in 795/1393.[115] *Mu'izz al-ansāb* calls both Chekü and Jahānshāh chief amir (*amīr al-umarā*) to Timur,[116] suggesting that these Barlās relatives occupied a loftier position than any of Timur's other henchmen; and Clavijo speaks of Jahānshāh as the most favoured among the conqueror's amirs and commander of the entire army.[117]

Sari Bugha's descendants, too, form a recognisable dynasty. His son Shaykh Nūr al-Dīn Bahādur first appears as a commander in the engagement with the Muzaffarid Shāh Manṣūr in 795/1393.[118] Two years later he distinguished himself in battle against Toqtamish's forces and was singled out by Timur for especial honours. In 798/1395–6 he was despatched to Shiraz to replace Sevinchek as governor of Fārs, and as *darugha* of Fārs he waited on Timur in Dhū l-Ḥijja 800/August 1398 with a splendid array of gifts.[119] The following month he was with Timur's army on the Indian expedition. During the Syrian campaign in 803/1400–1 he was among the amirs deputed to secure Damascus and in the attack on Baghdad he was the first of Timur's commanders to ascend the walls.[120] He also fought at Ankara and at Smyrna in 804/1402.[121] Shaykh Nūr al-Dīn would have a significant role in the crisis that followed Timur's death. Of the other members of this family who achieved prominence, his brother Berdibeg commanded his own tümen by 793/1391, when he took part in the first campaign against Toqtamish; two years later we find him among Timur's amirs in the final conflict with the Muzaffarids and in 799/1396–7 he was active on the frontier with Mughūlistān, where he was still serving in 803/1400–1.[122] A third son of Sari Bugha, Ḥājjī Beg, was left in charge of Isfahan in 789/1387,[123] and a cousin, Shaykh Ḥasan, was entrusted with the fortresses of Īryāb and Shanūzān when Timur was on his homeward march from India.[124]

Timur demanded faithful service from his officers and many of them paid a heavy price for participating in his constant military operations or governing his conquests. Ilchi Bahādur drowned during the first invasion of Khwārazm in 773/1371–2.[125] Ḥusayn Barlās drowned in the Ili in 776/1375 during an invasion of Jata.[126] Khiṭāy Bahādur fell in battle against Orus Khan in 778/1376–7;[127] his son Muḥammad was killed in the uprising at Isfahan in 789/1387.[128] Taban was murdered in a revolt at Sabzawār in 785/1383.[129] In the campaign in Luristān in 788/1386, Aq Temür and ʿUmar b. ʿAbbās succumbed to disease and died.[130] Eyegü Temür, Harī Malik b. Yādgār Barlās and Ramaḍān Khwāja were all killed in the course of the first invasion of the Qipchaq steppe in 793/1391.[131] Anūshīrwān b. Aq Bugha was fatally wounded in 781/1379–80 during Timur's fourth campaign against Khwārazm,[132] and his brother Buyan Temür fell in the Chaghatay assault on rebel Isfahan.[133] Amīr ʿAbbās, one of those left to guard Transoxiana when Timur returned to Iran in 788/1386, suffered a mortal wound the next year while resisting Toqtamish's invading forces.[134]

On the other hand, a few among the new elite – even members of Timur's personal retinue – proved disloyal and some incurred the ultimate penalty. In 805/1402–3 Ṣayin Temür and his brother Murād were put to death for various offences and the son and other brothers of Ṣayin Temür followed them to the scaffold.[135] ʿUthmān b. ʿAbbās was executed on an unspecified charge that Sharaf al-Dīn Yazdī dismisses as baseless.[136] Sari Bugha collaborated with ʿĀdilshāh Jalāyir's bid to seize Samarkand and fled with him into Blue Horde territory, whence they joined Qamar al-Dīn.[137] Sari Bugha returned two years later, however, in 779/1377–8 to seek Timur's pardon. He was not merely restored to favour but entrusted with the command over his people (*qawm*), namely the Jalāyir tribe.[138]

Timur's frequent forbearance towards disaffected amirs, whether tribal leaders (with the notable exceptions of ʿAlī Yasā'ūrī, Kaykhusraw and ʿĀdilshāh) or members of his personal entourage, is striking. Manz suggests that executions were traditionally frowned upon in the ulus (although if there was such a convention, it had apparently escaped the notice of the khans Buzan and Qazan Sulṭān). In all probability, Timur was influenced by his experience of the short-lived hegemony of Tughluq Temür in the year 762/1361, when the Mughūls had alienated the majority of amirs in Transoxiana by their harshness and their execution of prominent figures such as Bāyazīd Jalāyir, as also by Amīr Ḥusayn's rashness in putting to death Kayqubād of Khuttalān. He may therefore have deemed it advisable to govern with a light hand, at least until his rule was more securely entrenched.[139]

Once engaged in his conquests outside Transoxiana, Timur added to the ranks of his commanders several amirs who had cooperated with him, notably in Iran: Muḥammad b. Sulṭānshāh Khurāsānī, for instance, who fled from the Kartid kingdom to join him by 778/1376–7 but whose background is obscure.[140] ʿĀdil Āqā, who had governed Sulṭāniyya for the Jalayirids but had submitted to Timur, was allowed to remain as governor (*ba-ayālat*) in 787/1385, but Muḥammad b. Sulṭānshāh was left alongside him with a force to control (*ḍabṭ*) the region.[141] As we shall see in Chapter 10, Timur recruited into his service the Sarbadār leader ʿAlī-yi Mu'ayyad and the latter's nephew ʿImād al-Dīn Masʿūd, who was appointed to a governorship outside his native Khurāsān. In moving such men around his dominions, Timur sought to ensure their loyalty by planting them in regions where they had no pre-existing power base. These allies did not invariably prove satisfactory when left *in situ.* ʿĀdil Āqā's agents, unable to extract any more revenue from Tabriz in 788/1386, were tortured and executed, and he himself was put to death soon afterwards.[142] Alongside the many prominent figures taken from their homes and obliged to accompany the Chaghatay army back to Transoxiana, there were individuals who joined Timur voluntarily, like the Syrian ʿAbd al-Malik Ibn al-Takrītī in 803/1401, later to be governor of Sayrām.[143]

Turning now to the bureaucracy, some of the staff of Timur's chancery were of Turco-Mongol origin, like the 'personal scribe' (*dabīr-i khāṣṣ*) Yul Qutlugh;[144] he is not mentioned in *Muʿizz al-ansāb*, however, which names three Turks in its list of Timur's scribes (*nawīsandagān*), each entitled *bakhshī*. The same work lists over twenty Tājīk scribes,[145] but we know relatively little about these figures. Nor, given our ignorance vis-à-vis their counterparts in pre-Timurid Transoxiana, are we in any position to identify 'new men' among them who owed their promotion to Timur himself. The first person who comes to our notice as chief finance minister (*ṣāḥib-dīwān*) under Timur is Khwāja Masʿūd Simnānī, listed by *Muʿizz* as a scribe along with his father Yaḥyā and ʿAlī, another of Yaḥyā's descendants. The juxtaposition suggests that family connections were important in admission to Timur's bureaucracy just as to the ranks of the amirs. Khwāja Masʿūd died of an arrow wound during the siege of Baghdad in 803/1401, and Jalāl-i Islām Ṭabasī seems briefly to have succeeded him. The fact that both men participated in Timur's campaigns – Jalāl-i Islām, who is first heard of as a scribe (*bitikchi*), certainly also held military office and himself perished on the Anatolian expedition in 805/1402 – may explain why we hear of them at all.[146]

Although officials of the provincial *dīwān*s make fleeting appearances in the sources, we never learn of their origins or family relationships, in contrast with the Turco-Mongol amirs. They did not even enjoy a monopoly of the collection of indemnity payments (*māl-i amānī*) from towns that had capitulated, or the registering of tribute payments or the levying of taxes, often sharing these tasks with members of the Chaghatay military elite. The fortunes of this scribal class have been scrutinised by Beatrice Manz, who has highlighted the contempt that Timur and the military evinced towards Persian officials. One manifestation of this was the fact that they lacked the power and prestige enjoyed by their precursors under the Seljuqs or even the Ilkhans. Timur usually blamed a prince's insubordination on members of the Persian bureaucratic establishment in the province; the punishments they incurred, moreover, were significantly harsher than those meted out to Turco-Mongol amirs.[147] Similarly, Tājīk architects in his service could expect no mercy if their work fell short of his expectations: on his return from the seven-year campaign, the newly completed Friday mosque at Samarkand was found wanting and the two men responsible were hanged.[148]

Timur manifested some concern that his amirs should not engage in acts of tyranny. During his progress through Khurāsān in 788/1386, and again on his arrival in Transoxiana, he instituted an inquiry (*pizhūhish*) in every province through which he passed, making an example of oppressors; in recognition of the wrongs they had suffered, the inhabitants of Transoxiana were exempted from the land-tax (*kharāj*) for three years.[149] While halted at Baylaqān in Arrān in 806/1404, he held a general assembly of grandees from Iran and Turan and required the ʿulama present to report acts of injustice and oppression by his governors and fiscal officers.[150] That the expedient was no mere window-dressing is clear, inasmuch as in this same year Apaq, *darugha* of Chechektü, was severely punished for oppression,[151] while the head of the provincial *dīwān* at Shiraz was imprisoned and tortured for extortion. The next year investigations at Herat and Samarkand led to the execution of members of the *dīwān* in both cities. According to Clavijo, one of the victims was the chief magistrate of Samarkand, hanged for abusing the Great Amir's trust during Timur's six-year absence.[152]

TIMUR'S PROGENY

Timur founded an imperial dynasty. In time he came to rely on his sons, three of whom received major territorial appanages, and later in turn upon his grandsons. ʿUmar Shaykh, who was born in *c.* 755 or 756/1355 or 1356 and was most probably Timur's eldest son, first appears in 771/1369–70, when he displayed great courage in the final engagement with Amīr Ḥusayn.[153] He was despatched in 777/1375–6 as governor (*ḥākim*) to Andijān in Farghāna,[154] where he assumed responsibility for defending Transoxiana against the attacks of Qamar al-Dīn. During his father's first campaign to the Qipchaq steppe in 793/1391, he distinguished himself by his bravery in the battle on the Qundurcha.[155] In 795/1393, after eighteen years' service in Farghāna, he was moved to Fārs and ʿIrāq-i ʿAjam on their conquest from the Muzaffarids, but was killed while besieging the fortress of Khurmātū in the following year.

Jahāngīr, Timur's second son, was the only one born of a lawful wife rather than a concubine. He is first mentioned in 768/1366–7, when Timur sent him to Herat as his representative in negotiations with the Kartids.[156] We hear relatively little of his activities; he appears most prominently in the context of his marriage in 775/1374 to Khānzāda, a niece of the Ṣūfī ruler of Khwārazm and a granddaughter, through her mother, of Özbeg Khan of the Golden Horde. Jahāngīr distinguished himself during Timur's third invasion of Jata, in 776/1375, when he commanded the vanguard.[157] Having foiled the attempt by the rebel amirs ʿĀdilshāh and Sari Bugha to capture Samarkand in 777/1375–6, he fell ill and died later that year at the age of twenty,[158] without having received an appanage.

Timur's two remaining sons, who were too young to play any part in his rise to power or his early rule, survived him. He entrusted the third, Amīrānshāh, with the government of Khurāsān in 782/1380–1, at the age of fourteen.[159] In 795/1393 Amīrānshāh was transferred to another large appanage in north-western Iran, comprising Azerbaijan, Darband, Bākū, Shīrwān, Gīlān and Rayy;[160] and in 798/1396, with the successful campaign against the Jalayirids, the grant was extended to cover the territory 'from Darband-i Bākū to Baghdad and from

Hamadān to Anatolia (Rūm)'.[161] In 802/1398–9 Timur deprived him of this appanage for misconduct (on which see later). The fourth son, Shāhrukh, born in 779/1377 and destined to emerge eventually as Timur's effective successor, seemingly had his first experience of campaigning in 795/1393 against Muzaffarid Shiraz.[162] On him were conferred Khurāsān, Sīstān, Māzandarān and Rayy in 799/1397.[163]

With Timur's two eldest sons having both died by 1395, the conqueror needed to make provision for their offspring and it was from the ranks of his grandsons that he chose his heir – the senior among them, Jahāngīr's elder son Muḥammad Sulṭān – at some point prior to the Indian expedition.[164] But seniority was not the sole criterion. Muḥammad Sulṭān was nominated because his mother, as the maternal granddaughter of the Jochid khan Özbeg, was of Chinggisid descent, a circumstance by which Timur, a mere *qarachu*, set great store. The prince first surfaces during the campaign against Toqtamish in 793/1391, when he delighted his grandfather by requesting command of the vanguard.[165] Having held Transoxiana from 800/1397–8, he seems to have been moved to the Iranian conquests in 803/1401, though he was often absent, acquitting himself with distinction in Timur's campaigns. His death at Akshehir in Anatolia on 18 Shaʿbān 805/13 March 1403,[166] at the age of twenty-nine, was both a source of grief to Timur and a serious political setback. Neither of Muḥammad Sulṭān's two sons was old enough to inherit his position and it was some time before Timur acknowledged as his heir Jahāngīr's younger son Pīr Muḥammad, who had held an appanage stretching from Ghazna and Kabul to Qandahār and the Indus River (a territory described as 'the throne of Maḥmūd of Ghazna') since 794/1391–2.[167] The delay may reflect the fact that, unlike Muḥammad Sulṭān, Pīr Muḥammad lacked Chinggisid blood. As it transpired, the territories of Jahāngīr's line were geographically peripheral and inferior to those of any other branch of the dynasty, two circumstances that would affect the outcome of the succession after 1405.

ʿUmar Shaykh's firstborn son, also (confusingly) named Pīr Muḥammad, was made governor of Fārs and its dependencies at the age of sixteen, following his father's death.[168] After a period of demotion, during which his brother Rustam governed in Shiraz, the city was returned to Pīr Muḥammad in 805/1402–3 and Rustam was allocated Isfahan instead.[169] Their brother Iskandar b. ʿUmar Shaykh had been sent in 802/1399, at the age of fifteen, to Andijān in Farghāna to guard that frontier.[170] Having disgraced himself (see later), he was restored to favour in 806/1403–4 and given the administration (*ayālat*) of Hamadān, Nihāwand, Wurūjird (Burūjird) and the territory of the Lesser Lur.[171] In this way central and southern Iran – roughly the former Muzaffarid dominions – emerged as the sphere of influence of ʿUmar Shaykh's sons, though Iskandar, like his father, retained links with distant Farghāna.

Of Amīrānshāh's sons, Khalīl Sulṭān, following the Ankara engagement, had been sent to guard the border facing the Mughūls.[172] But soon afterwards, in 806/1403–4, he received Baylaqān, Bardaʿa, Ganja, Arrān, Armenia and Georgia.[173] In 805/1402–3 Timur had allotted to another of Amīrānshāh's sons, Abā Bakr, 'ʿIraq-i ʿArab as far as Wāsiṭ and Baṣra, Kurdistan, Mārdīn and the rest of Diyār Bakr'.[174] But in the latter part of Shaʿbān 806/early April 1404 he conferred a much larger appanage, which encompassed 'the whole of Azerbaijan, Rūm as far as Constantinople, and Syria as far as Egypt' (termed 'the ulus of Hülegü' by Sharaf al-Dīn Yazdī), on their brother ʿUmar.[175] The document registering this grant, which is reproduced in Ḥāfiẓ-i Abrū's continuation of Shāmī's *Ẓafar-nāma*, adds not only ʿIrāq-i ʿAjam 'from Rayy to Azerbaijan' but also ʿIrāq-i ʿArab 'as far as the Hijaz' and 'Fārs and Kirmān as far as Hurmuz'.[176] This suggests that ʿUmar was being designated as ruler over the entire western half of Timur's dominions, including Abā Bakr's territory, and even the tracts held by the sons of ʿUmar Shaykh; Timur thereby risked stoking tension among his grandsons. At any rate Amīrānshāh's line had thus come to be closely associated with the western reaches of Timur's empire, with the qualified exception of Khalīl Sulṭān, who had links of recent origin with Transoxiana – and, as we shall see, he was one of the few princes present in Transoxiana at the time of his grandfather's death.

Shāhrukh's tenure of the government of Khurāsān was relatively lengthy. It is hardly surprising that once he became master of

Transoxiana in 813/1410 he preferred to continue residing in Herat rather than moving to Timur's capital at Samarkand. His sons had received appanages in the easternmost tracts of the empire – and both at a relatively young age. In 807/1404 Ulugh Beg, then only ten, was granted Tashkent, Sayrām, Yangī, Āshpara and 'the Jata territory as far as Khitai', while his half-brother Ibrāhīm Sulṭān, a few months his junior, was appointed to Andijān, Akhsīkat, Talās and 'Kāshghar as far as Khotan'.[177]

It is noteworthy that during his later absences from Transoxiana Timur tended to entrust the government of Samarkand to members of his dynasty rather than to his officers. Thus Shāhrukh was sent to govern the city in Dhū l-Qaʿda 796/September 1394.[178] When Timur departed for India in 800/1398, it was the turn of Amīrānshāh's son ʿUmar.[179] At the beginning of the seven-year campaign in 802/1399, Timur left his heir Muḥammad Sulṭān in Samarkand, with overall responsibility for Transoxiana.[180] ʿUmar was once more in charge of the capital in 804–5/1401–3, since Timur commissioned a group of amirs to wait on him and assist in its administration;[181] but in 806/1403 he was transferred to Azerbaijan (see earlier).

Timur was reportedly so affected by Jahāngīr's premature death, by the loss of his daughter Āghā Beki in 783/1381–2 and by the successive deaths of his wife Dilshād Āghā and his sister Qutlugh Terken in 785/1383–4 that on each occasion he lost interest in affairs of state and had to be persuaded to give them his attention.[182] The descriptions, too, given by Sharaf al-Dīn Yazdī of the conqueror's joyful reunions with the various princes of his dynasty during his far-flung campaigns, and the celebrations that welcomed the birth of each of his grandsons, suggest that he was genuinely fond of his progeny and he appears to have taken a close interest in their upbringing.[183] In the engagement outside Delhi he is said to have shed tears of joy on witnessing the fortitude of his grandsons.[184] The princes' wives were for the most part taken from the families of tribal amirs or from the ranks of the new Timurid aristocracy: Jahāngīr married a daughter of Kaykhusraw of Khuttalān, for instance, and Shāhrukh's chief wife, Gawhar Shād, who would play a prominent role in events following his death, was the daughter of Ghiyāth al-Dīn Tarkhān.[185] But Timur also secured Chinggisid wives for certain of his sons and grandsons (below, p. 358).

Notwithstanding, any members of Timur's family who proved unreliable were demoted. The most notorious example is Amīrānshāh, but the precise circumstances are unclear. According to the sources written under Timur's successors, the prince had been injured in a fall from his horse while hunting in the autumn of 798/1395 and suffered some kind of mental breakdown. His behaviour grew highly erratic, as he took to demolishing buildings in Tabriz and Sulṭāniyya (including the tomb of the Ilkhan Öljeitü); Clavijo was told that Amīrānshāh was trying thereby to secure a lasting reputation for himself, since he was unable to do so by more conventional and creative means.[186] When Amīrānshāh's wife Khānzāda appeared at his father's court in 802/1399–1400 and informed him of her husband's excesses, Timur summoned the prince and had his close associates executed; Amīrānshāh himself was merely deprived of his appanage.[187] He spent the next few years in close attendance on his father until, in 806/1404, Timur permitted him to reside in Baghdad with his son Abā Bakr. His earlier misconduct did not prevent some from regarding him as his father's rightful heir after Timur's death.

Three other princes who sullied their record were Timur's grandsons Pīr Muḥammad and Iskandar, sons of ʿUmar Shaykh, and Sulṭān Ḥusayn, born to the conqueror's daughter Āghā Beki by her marriage to Muḥammad Beg, a son of Amīr Mūsā of the Tayichi'ut. Pīr Muḥammad defied Timur in 802/1400, disobeying his order to lead a campaign against Luristān and Baghdad by feigning illness; and he and his entourage in Shiraz went on to perpetrate various outrages. Saʿīd Barlās, one of the amirs nominated to govern Shiraz during his absence, imprisoned him in the fortress of Quhandiz and notified Timur, who sent instructions for the execution of the prince's advisers and the transfer of Shiraz to his brother Rustam b. ʿUmar Shaykh;[188] three years would elapse before Pīr Muḥammad was reinstated. Pīr Muḥammad's other brother Iskandar, appointed to govern Farghāna but officially subordinated to Muḥammad Sulṭān, swiftly disgraced himself by heading an unauthorised plundering raid deep into Mughūl territory and was arrested on Muḥammad Sulṭān's orders. Timur executed Iskandar's *atabeg*, Buyan Temür, son of the Jata amir Bekichuk, along with twenty-six companions (*nökör*s); the prince himself was bastinadoed.[189] Lastly, Sulṭān Ḥusayn was guilty of a more heinous offence. During the campaign against Damascus in 803/1400–1, he went over to the Mamlūks and fought for the Egyptian Sultan in an ensuing engagement, only to be captured by Timur's troops. Timur executed Sulṭān Ḥusayn's advisers but spared his grandson and allowed him to participate in later military operations.[190] Sulṭān Ḥusayn, in whose nature, says Yazdī, mischief and disloyalty were ingrained,[191] would rebel again after Timur's death (see below, pp. 419–20).

On these occasions Timur treated the princes in question surprisingly leniently, reserving the harshest penalty for their Persian advisers or attendants.[192] Anne Broadbridge is surely right in her surmise that Amīrānshāh, Pīr Muḥammad and Sulṭān Ḥusayn were all alike chafing at their exclusion from the succession.[193] For Timur the succession was determined by particularly stringent criteria. As we saw, he made Muḥammad Sulṭān his heir on the grounds of his birth (and that of his father Jahāngīr). Since Sulṭān Ḥusayn's mother was a full sister of Jahāngīr,[194] he may have thought himself entitled to a more eminent station. Timur's forbearance towards all three princes perhaps indicates that he understood – if he could not overlook – such frustration among members of his dynasty.

It is worth looking in greater depth at the offence of Amīrānshāh. With the death of ʿUmar Shaykh in 796/1394 he had become the most senior member of the dynasty below Timur; in addition, his marriage to Jahāngīr's widow Khānzāda made him the stepfather of the young heir-apparent Muḥammad Sulṭān, and his marriage to a daughter of the khan Soyurghatmish enabled him to style himself Güregen[195] – the first member of the dynasty, and the only one, it seems, to adopt the title since Timur had done so in 771/1369–70.[196] Evidently conscious of his exalted status, Amīrānshāh began to stake a claim to autonomy. Documents he issued in 796/1394 (nine months after ʿUmar Shaykh's death) and in 798/1396 omitted the names of both Timur and the heir-apparent – but not, interestingly, that of the Chaghadayid khan Sulṭān Maḥmūd, Amīrānshāh's own brother-in-law.[197] In a document of

800/1398, however, the khan's name too was absent.[198] From the first of the three dates we can deduce that Amīrānshāh harboured aspirations to independence even before his hunting accident, and the story of his breakdown may be merely a camouflage for outright defiance. In addition, Timur's new-found claims to be the heir of the Ilkhans (below, pp. 355–7) may have whetted Amīrānshāh's ambitions, since his appanage comprised the Ilkhanid heartlands.[199] The destruction of Öljeitü's tomb, it has been suggested, could have been inspired by Amīrānshāh's desire to assert his own superior 'Chinggisid' claim over the shrine and also, perhaps, his championship of Sunnī Islam.[200]

The appointment of a prince to govern a large territory meant the commitment of sizeable forces under his command. When Amīrānshāh took up his post as governor of Khurāsān in 782/1380–1, he was assigned no fewer than thirteen named amirs, among others, together with fifty companies (*qūshūn*s) of cavalry, all picked out on a proportional basis from the army as a whole,[201] as had been the practice under the thirteenth-century Mongol Qaghans. Eleven amirs, together with a large army, accompanied Pīr Muḥammad b. Jahāngīr to Kabul and Ghazna in 794/1391–2, and Yazdī adds that the sons and brothers of other amirs went with them.[202] Lastly, Shāhrukh, appointed to govern Khurāsān in 799/1397, took with him sixteen named amirs, among others, together with a squadron drawn from every tümen; and again the amirs were each required to contribute a son or brother to this august cavalcade.[203] In both the latter two cases, Timur was seeking to guarantee the amirs' loyalty by despatching members of their families to different locations. In addition, each prince had his personal retinue of officers, dating from before his nomination to a provincial governorship. Describing the appointment of ʿUmar Shaykh as governor of Fārs in 795/1393, Sharaf al-Dīn Yazdī distinguishes between the prince's personal amirs (*umarā-yi khāṣṣa*), all of whom had presumably accompanied him from Farghāna, and those whom Timur deputed to keep watch (*ba-tūsqāl*) over him in his new post for one year.[204]

Timur was capable of resentment at a prince's success. Naṭanzī expressly attributes his despatch of a fresh army to Jata in 780/1378–9 to jealousy (*rashk*) at a victory by ʿUmar Shaykh over Qamar al-Dīn;[205]

and Pīr Muḥammad's triumphs in Sind appear to have provoked the conqueror into invading India in person (below, pp. 298–9). The circumstances surrounding ʿUmar Shaykh's appointment to Fārs constitute possibly the earliest hint that Timur, for all his affection towards his sons and grandsons, did not wholly trust them. If we can believe Clavijo, Timur twice circulated rumours of his own death in order to flush out anybody disposed to challenge his arrangements for the succession.[206]

He employed other expedients as a means of restraining members of his family. Firstly, princes were at intervals moved from one provincial governorship to another, and the intention was very possibly to prevent them forming too close a link with any particular region. Admittedly, such transfers can be open to misinterpretation: when Timur reallocated ʿUmar Shaykh to Fārs and Amīrānshāh to north-western Iran in 795/1393, he could simply have been entrusting newly subjected provinces to experienced princes on whom he could particularly depend. Secondly, it seems that princes were not given full authority over all the troops within their appanages.[207] Thirdly, during his own campaigns Timur might also borrow the armies allotted to the princes, temporarily substituting other troops so as to weaken any possible bonds and to reinforce the loyalty of his soldiers to himself.[208] And fourthly, he habitually appointed loyal officers to the staff of each appanaged prince, in order to watch over his own interests and guard against insubordination.

We cannot be certain whether this fourth expedient dated from the earliest such appointment, that of ʿUmar Shaykh to Farghāna. Possibly Amīrānshāh's defiance rendered Timur more circumspect when making territorial grants to his grandsons, but whatever reservations he may have harboured did not deter him, when he appointed ʿUmar b. Amīrānshāh to govern 'Hülegü's ulus' in 806/1404, from assigning to the prince his father's amirs and troops – potentially a hazardous gesture that could be justified only by Timurid vulnerability in these westerly tracts to the attacks of the Qarā-Qūyūnlū. On the other hand, ʿUmar was accompanied on his westward journey by several amirs, including Rustam-i Mūsā, Tükel-i Yādgār Barlās, Junayd-i Boroldai and one of Timur's most trusted lieutenants, the *amīr al-umarā* Jahānshāh.[209] In that same year, when Timur set out from Māzandarān for Samarkand, he placed Saʿīd Barlās (who had already proved his worth by checking the excesses of Pīr Muḥammad b. ʿUmar Shaykh and his men) in attendance on Pīr Muḥammad's brother Rustam and Sevinchek in attendance on Abā Bakr b. Amīrānshāh.[210] We can see here the traditional Turkish institution of the atabegate, first deployed during the Seljuq era and also in evidence, as Michael Hope has demonstrated, under the Ilkhans.[211] The amir Yaḥyā, for instance, is expressly described in 796/1393–4 as *atābak* to Khalīl Sulṭān b. Amīrānshāh (then aged about ten and yet to receive an appanage),[212] and ʿUthmān-i ʿAbbās is called Shāhrukh's *atābak*.[213] Such appointments could prove a poisoned chalice. As atabeg to Iskandar b. ʿUmar Shaykh in 802/1399–1400 Buyan Temür-i Bekichuk was held responsible for that prince's wayward conduct and executed.[214] At intervals Timur took the further precaution of changing the amirs in question, but once his overarching authority was withdrawn, as we shall see, each officer was free to choose where to transfer his allegiance – whether to the prince whose conduct he had been monitoring (and to whom he might not feel firmly attached) or to one of this prince's rivals.

TIMURID WOMEN

Something has already been said in Chapter 8 concerning Timur's sisters (p. 224). The most important of his spouses were his chief wife,[215] Sarai Mulk Khanim, daughter of the khan Qazan Sulṭān, whom he had wed following the overthrow of her previous husband, Amīr Ḥusayn (hence his right to the title *Güregen*, 'royal son-in-law'), and her first cousin Tümen Āghā, whose father was Mūsā of the Tayichi'ut and whom Timur married in 780/1378–9.[216] The two princesses, titled the 'Greater' and the 'Lesser' Khanim, respectively, are often found travelling together and at the head of 'the rest of the ladies'.[217] Sarai Mulk Khanim's birth guaranteed her an especially exalted status, as shown by Timur's readiness to erect a mosque in memory of her mother, Qazan Sulṭān's widow.[218] But even these two women are shadowy figures, of whom the Timurid sources tell us relatively little, rather as the Ilkhanid sources do regarding royal women.[219] Still less conspicuous are the few other wives mentioned by name, Tükel Khanim (daughter of the eastern Chaghadayid khan Khiḍr Khwāja) and Cholpan Mulk Āghā (daughter of a Mughūl amir),[220] both of whom he married at a relatively late date.

The women of Timur's family seem to have observed the proprieties. Clavijo noted that Sarai Mulk Khanim was escorted by eunuchs and wore a thin veil; though he could see that her face was completely covered with some white unguent – reminiscent of Mongol women in the mid-thirteenth century.[221] Mongol princesses had participated in political decision-making.[222] We should not expect a less prominent role for Timurid women just on account of Islamisation. Royal ladies had been important in earlier Islamised dynasties of steppe origin such as the Seljuqs and the Khwārazmshāhs;[223] and although Ilkhanid wives and princesses lost some of their property through Ghazan's reforms, they remained influential, particularly if they had exalted ancestry or had borne male heirs.[224] Timurid wives are found presiding over the pitching of camp or transport of booty and organising banquets,[225] yet we do not see them attending quriltais, as had the women of the Chinggisid dynasty.[226] Exceptions were the quriltai summoned for the marriages of Timur's grandsons in 1404,[227] and that following Timur's death, when 'the amirs, khatuns and princes' deliberated where to deploy the force mobilised for the assault on the Ming.[228]

The women of Timur's family, usually those who were more junior,[229] are seen accompanying him on campaign. Alternatively, they might be summoned to join him at his headquarters and then be sent back to Sulṭāniyya or to Samarkand; or they came to meet him and offer felicitations on some military triumph. Even when they were with him on campaign, Timur's principal wives, Sarai Mulk Khanim and Tümen Āghā, were not necessarily always in his company. On leaving Māzandarān for Iraq early in 795/towards the end of 1392, for instance, Timur left them with the heavy baggage, and took with him Cholpan Mulk Āghā and two of his concubines, Durr Sulṭān Āghā and Nigār Āghā.[230] Given the scope of his campaigning, the journeys made by his womenfolk at his behest were sometimes on a grand scale: in 789/1387 Sarai Mulk Khanim, and in 804/1401–2 Tümen Āghā, travelled all the way from Samarkand to his encampment in Azerbaijan.[231]

On occasion we glimpse Timur's feelings for a wife to whom he was particularly devoted. When Dilshād Khatun died in 785/1383–4, we are told, the conqueror was so prostrated by grief that it was difficult for him to be brought back to a sense of his duties as a ruler.[232] The sources sometimes offer other human touches, as when following the victory outside Delhi Cholpan Mulk Āghā 'with the other ladies' entered the city for the purpose of a sightseeing visit (*tamāshā*) to the palace of Hazār Sutūn ('The Thousand Pillars'), one of the architectural glories dating from the Khaljī era.[233]

We might be tempted to assume that the political importance of Timurid royal ladies resided for the most part in their birth – in other words, their qualification for transmitting the right to succeed him.[234] Yet in fact neither Sarai Mulk Khanim nor Tümen Āghā bore Timur any children. Remarkably few of his eighteen lawful wives did so; his three sons other than Jahāngīr were all born to concubines, of whom Timur likewise had a great number.[235] Timurid womenfolk nevertheless performed significant roles. As we saw, Timur's daughters and granddaughters were sometimes married off to members of the new military elite. Like the wives and daughters of Mongol khans, his wives and daughters-in-law presided over their own establishments and they played their part in entertaining foreign envoys such as Clavijo. Timurid women made grants to pious foundations: we know of a *madrasa* in Samarkand founded by Sarai Mulk Khanim and located directly opposite Timur's mosque, and a *khānaqāh* there founded by Tümen Āghā;[236] while Timur's sister Qutlugh Terken used her private wealth to construct *madrasa*s and hospices (*khawāniq*).[237] At times, grandsons accompanied Timur's wives on their travels, and it was Sarai Mulk Khanim who sent Timur news of the births of Shāhrukh's sons Ulugh Beg and Ibrāhīm Sulṭān.[238] Some royal ladies were given the important task of rearing infant princes who were not their own sons. Sarai Mulk Khanim, for instance, was responsible for the upbringing of both Khalīl Sulṭān and Ulugh Beg.[239] She and Tümen Āghā each had charge of one of the two sons of Muḥammad Sulṭān b. Jahāngīr (who had himself been brought up by Timur's sister Qutlugh Terken Āghā).[240] Tümen Āghā reared Shāhrukh's son (and Yazdī's later patron) Ibrāhīm Sulṭān.[241]

There are few known instances of a Timurid princess actively intervening in a political matter. One was Khānzāda's journey to Timur's headquarters in 802/1398–9 to complain of Amīrānshāh's conduct (see earlier).[242] The impulse behind this, perhaps, was a perception that Amīrānshāh was challenging the rights of her son by her first marriage, the heir-apparent Muḥammad Sulṭān. Sarai Mulk Khanim is found twice fulfilling an intercessory role. In 806/1404, in concert with the amir Shaykh Nūr al-Dīn, she acted as the intermediary for Abā Bakr's request that Amīrānshāh be allowed to accompany him to Baghdad. Towards the end of Timur's life, in 807/1404–5, she intervened on behalf of Amīrānshāh's son Khalīl Sulṭān when he fell foul of his grandfather on account of his clandestine marriage to the ineligible Shād Mulk, a former concubine of Amir Ḥājjī Sayf al-Dīn, and a furious Timur had decreed the woman's execution.[243] On all three occasions, Timur allowed himself to be won over. Otherwise, there is no suggestion that his womenfolk enjoyed an influential role in his administration or even any reference to their offering him informal advice. This does not mean that such advice was not given. But Clavijo noted the esteem in which the Great Amir held Khānzāda in view of her ancestry,[244] and it may be significant that the two women whose appeals are known to have swayed Timur, Sarai Mulk Khanim and Khānzāda, were both of Chinggisid descent. In all likelihood their counsel carried greater weight with him for that reason.

In view of the initial difficulty of asserting and maintaining his authority over the tribal elements in Transoxiana, Timur, like Chinggis Khan before him, was mindful of the need for profitable warfare outside the ulus, whereby he could harness and divert the energies of subordinates and potential rivals, foster his own image as a highly successful war leader and ensure loyalty by rewarding faithful service in the style of a munificent lord.[245] The next chapter will survey his conquests beyond the bounds of the western Chaghadayid polity.

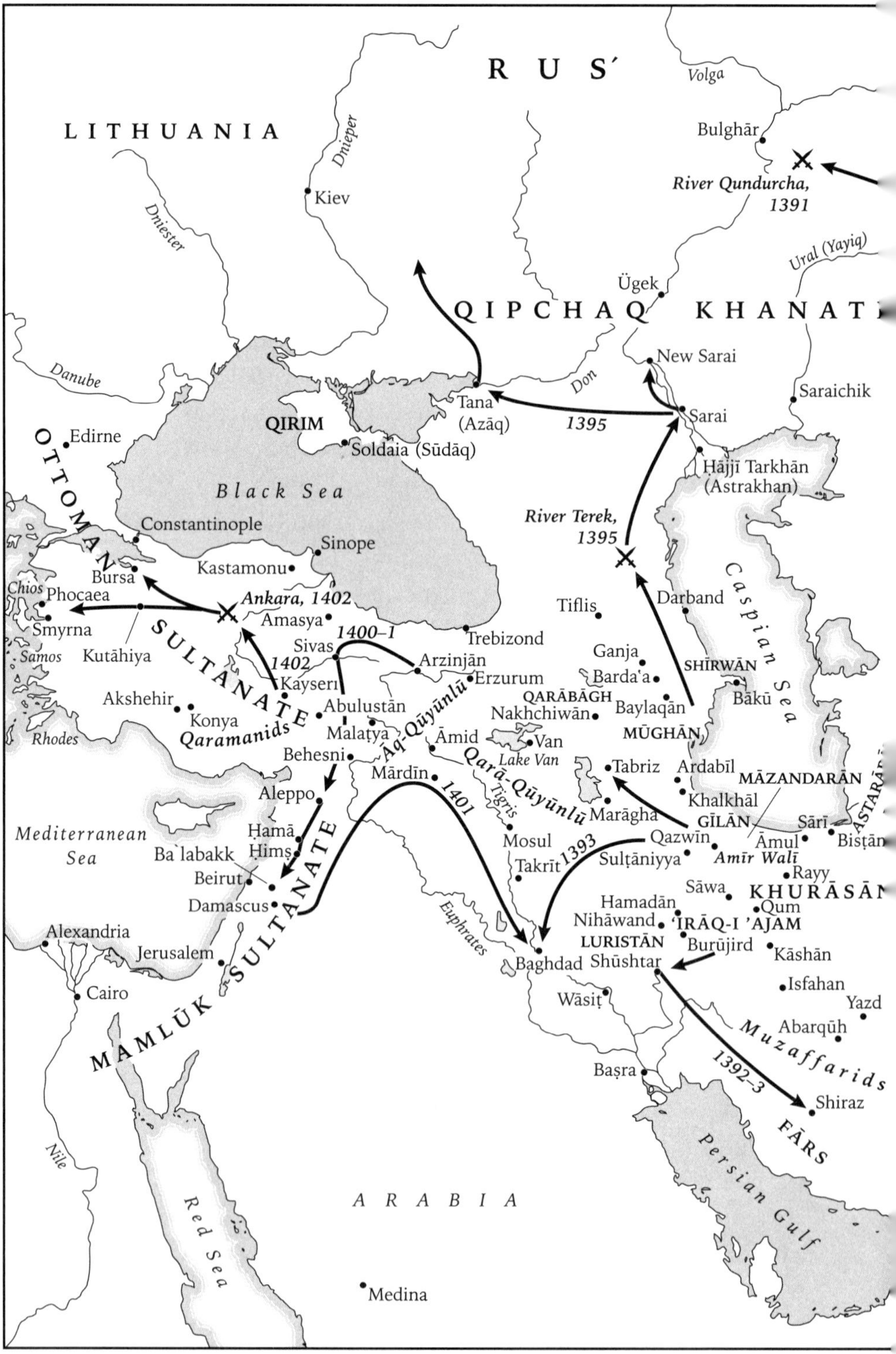

6. Timur's campaigns.

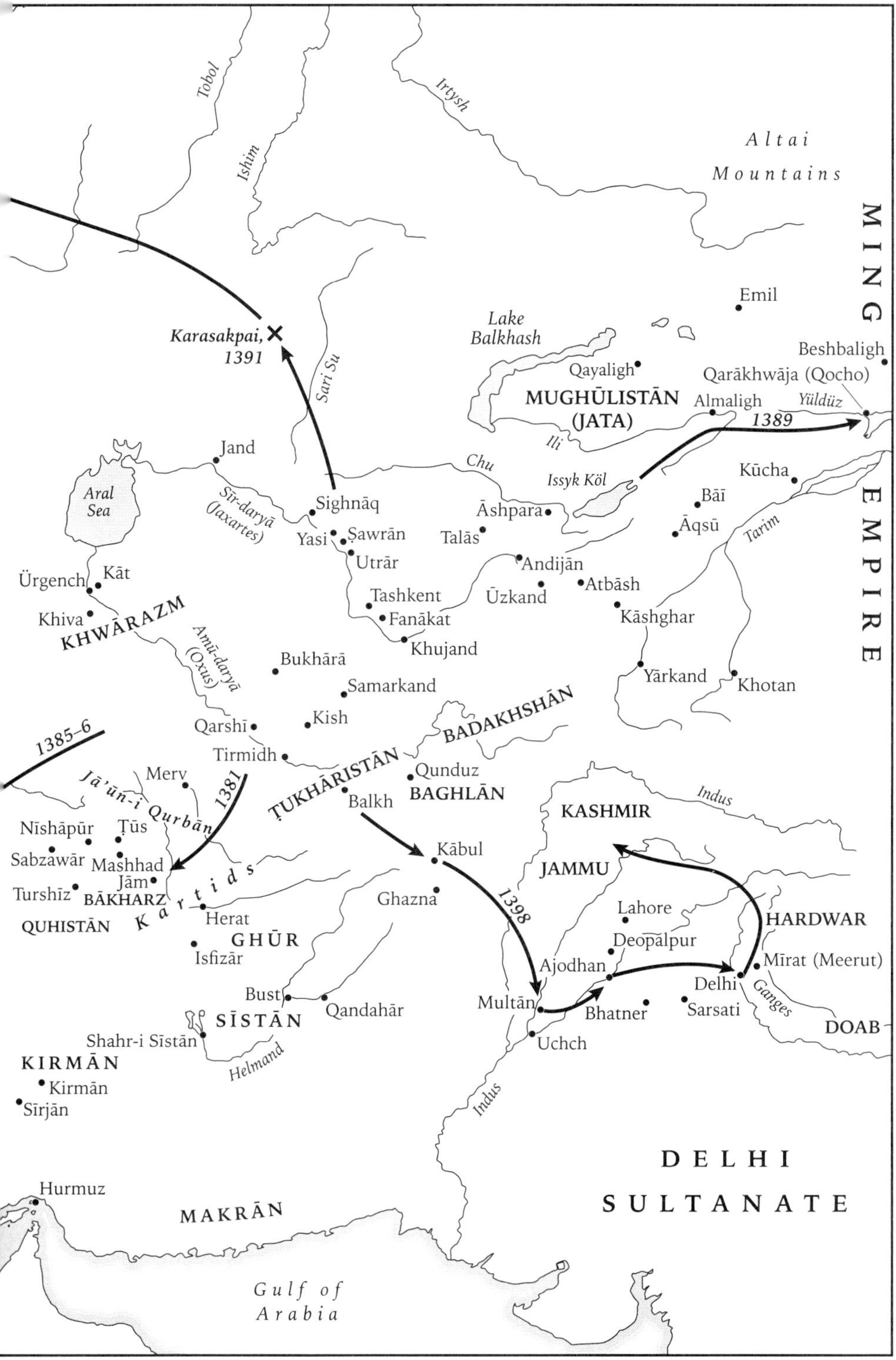
Tobol
Irtysh
Ishim
Altai Mountains
MING EMPIRE
Emil
Karasakpai, 1391
Lake Balkhash
Sari Su
Beshbaligh
Qayaligh
Qarākhwāja (Qocho)
MUGHŪLISTĀN (JATA)
Almaligh
Yūldūz
1389
Ili
Jand
Chu
Issyk Köl
Kūcha
Aral Sea
Sīr-daryā (Jaxartes)
Sighnāq
Āshpara
Bāī
Yasi
Ṣawrān
Talās
Āqsū
Tarim
Utrār
Andijān
Ürgench
Kāt
Tashkent
Ūzkand
Atbāsh
Khiva
KHWĀRAZM
Fanākat
Kāshghar
Amū-daryā (Oxus)
Khujand
Bukhārā
Yārkand
Khotan
Samarkand
Kish
BADAKHSHĀN
Qarshī
1385–6
Tirmidh
ṬUKHĀRISTĀN
Merv
Jā'ūn-i Qurbān
1381
Qunduz
BAGHLĀN
Balkh
Indus
Nīshāpūr
Ṭūs
KASHMIR
Sabzawār
Mashhad
Kābul
Jām
Kartids
JAMMU
Turshīz
BĀKHARZ
Ghazna
1398
QUHISTĀN
Herat
Lahore
HARDWAR
GHŪR
Deopālpur
Isfizār
Ajodhan
Mīrat (Meerut)
Delhi
Bust
Multān
Ganges
Qandahār
Bhatner
Sarsati
SĪSTĀN
DOAB
Shahr-i Sīstān
Uchch
KIRMĀN
Helmand
Kirmān
Sīrjān
Indus
DELHI SULTANATE
Hurmuz
MAKRĀN
Gulf of Arabia

CHAPTER 10
THE FORGING OF AN EMPIRE: A CAREER OF CONQUEST

This chapter is concerned with the frequency and scope of military operations against external powers, which more than anything else defined Timur's rule;[1] their impact on Western Asia and the means whereby they were achieved will be the subject of Chapter 11. The question of his long-term aims – and whether or not a certain consistency emerges on closer examination – will be explored both there and in Chapter 14.

THE REDUCTION OF KHWĀRAZM AND THE WAR AGAINST JATA

Timur's first twelve years as leader of the Chaghatays were spent in campaigns against Mughūlistān and Khwārazm. By the time Timur supplanted Amīr Ḥusayn, Ilyās Khwāja, the khan of Mughūlistān, had been murdered, together with (allegedly) his entire dynasty, by the Dughlāt amir Qamar al-Dīn, who arrogated to himself the title of khan.[2] This outrage aroused a good deal of opposition among Qamar al-Dīn's fellow amirs, from which Timur hoped to profit. As for Khwārazm, it had been subdued temporarily by Alughu's forces in the early 1260s and more recently by ʿAbd-Allāh b. Qazaghan, as we saw, but by 762/1361 it was under the Qongqurat amir Ḥusayn Ṣūfī and free of both Jochids and Chaghadayids.[3]

Timur turned his attention to Khwārazm in the spring of 773/1372. He required Ḥusayn Ṣūfī to surrender the two cities of Kāt and Khiva, which he claimed as an integral part of Chaghadai's ulus on the grounds that their revenues had traditionally been allotted to Chaghadai's line,[4] though we might note that the Ilkhanid historian Shabānkāra'ī had listed Khwārazm as a whole among the lands allotted to Chaghadai by Chinggis Khan.[5] Ḥusayn Ṣūfī rejected the demand but yielded when Timur headed a campaign against him. A reassertion of Khwarazmian autonomy incurred a second attack, during which Ḥusayn Ṣūfī died. His brother and successor, Yūsuf Ṣūfī, at first defied Timur but then, confronted by yet another invasion, bought him off towards the end of 775/in the spring of 1374 with a fresh submission and the bestowal of a niece as the wife of Timur's son Jahāngīr.[6] Yūsuf's failure in turn to keep faith with the conqueror, however, and his temerity in launching a plundering raid against Bukhara in 778/1377 when Timur was distracted by an expedition against the Blue Horde (see later), brought down upon him a final invasion. He died of chagrin in the course of a three-month siege of his capital, Ürgench, which was ruthlessly sacked, and Khwārazm was annexed to the Chaghatay dominions in 781/1379.[7] Even thereafter, collaboration between members of the Ṣūfī dynasty and the Jochid khan Toqtamish obliged Timur in 790/1388 to head a fourth expedition to Khwārazm. With his enemies having fled the province and taken refuge in the Qipchaq steppe, he withdrew, ordering that the population of both the capital and its hinterland be conveyed to Samarkand.[8]

Between 772/1371 and 792/1390, Timur launched at least eight expeditions against Mughūlistān,[9] of which he headed five in person. Unlike Khwārazm's rulers, Qamar al-Dīn neglected to reach even a temporary accommodation with him. The third expedition to Jata, which began on 1 Shawwāl 776/5 March 1375, defeated Qamar al-Dīn's forces but served only to drive him momentarily from his territories and to ravage them.[10] When, encouraged by some dissident Chaghatay amirs, Qamar al-Dīn attacked Andijān and Ūzkand, Timur set out on his fourth campaign in Jata. At one point, left alone in the vicinity of Atbāsh with only 200 men while his troops were mostly dispersed on plundering forays, he narrowly avoided ambush by a greatly superior army of 4,000. The Chaghatays inflicted two defeats on Qamar al-Dīn's forces.[11] That same year, Timur headed a fifth campaign against Jata, in which the commanders of an advance force again worsted Qamar al-Dīn.[12] Still later, in 785/1383, he despatched a division to Jata in search of Qamar al-Dīn, but it was discomfited by the enemy and withdrew; another expedition sent to avenge this humiliation was unable to locate the Dughlāt amir.[13] Qamar al-Dīn was still at large in 792/1390, when Timur's forces pursued him beyond the Irtysh.[14] According to Ḥaydar, he at length went to ground and died of his wounds; his body was never found.[15] His downfall had brought about the restoration, in *c*. 1388, of the Chaghadayid line in the east in the form of Khiḍr Khwāja, a putative son of Tughluq Temür (see above, p. 236) who sent envoys as a propitiatory gesture on various occasions, though his loyalty could by no means be taken for granted.

Timur made more sustained and strenuous efforts to subjugate Mughūlistān than any other recalcitrant territory. This was doubtless from a desire to reunite the Chaghadayid lands under his own khan, but other relevant considerations were that the Mughūls launched annual raids on Transoxiana and enslaved its Muslim inhabitants,[16] and that Jata's rulers on occasion timed their attacks on Transoxiana to coincide with an invasion by the Jochid forces, as they did in 789/1387.[17] The aim of Timur's expedition of 791/1389, when a number of Chaghatay armies were detailed to traverse Mughūlistān by different routes, was 'to eradicate (*ba-isti'ṣāl*) the ulus of Jata'.[18] The distances involved were enormous. The operations that year took Timur's forces well beyond the Ili, to the Irtysh and Yüldüz rivers and even as far as Qarakhwāja.[19] In 802/1399–1400 Timur's grandson Iskandar, seeking to profit from the death of Khiḍr Khwāja and the dissension among his sons, would head a campaign that embraced Yārkand, Ūch, Āqsū, Bāī, Kūsān, Tārim and Khotan.[20]

Generally speaking, none of these campaigns might appear to have brought Timur anything more than prodigious quantities of loot, yet his first attack expelled the Mughūls from Farghāna;[21] he then incorporated some of the 'thousands' of Jata in his own army.[22] We read of the subjects (*īl*) of the Chaghadayid prince Sālār being conferred in 776/1375 on Timur's officer Khudāydād Ḥusaynī.[23] Timur also secured the allegiance and service of some of the Jata amirs, notably Bekichuk's son Buyan Temür, who served as guide to the Chaghatay forces in Jata in 791/1389 and would later be *atābak* to Iskandar.[24] Although Timur's attempt in 772/1371 to rule the Jata region through a Mughūl amir, Köpek Temür of the Kereyit, miscarried,[25] thereafter he appointed lieutenants for the eastern territories from the Chaghatay establishment who did not merely seek to keep the Mughūls at bay but extended Timurid rule there. In 791 or 792/1389 or 1390 ʿUmar Shaykh occupied Kāshghar.[26] Sharaf al-Dīn Yazdī names a number of amirs who were already in Jata on Timur's orders when they joined Iskandar's invading army near Kāshghar in 802/1399.[27] Fortresses were built beyond the Sīr-daryā, notably at Āshpara, on the river of that name and 120 kilometres north-east of Talās, where troops under Timur's grandson Muḥammad Sulṭān were fostering cultivation and establishing irrigation works from 799/1396–7.[28] Yazdī writes as if Āshpara was the frontier (*sarḥadd*) with Jata.[29] Near the end of his life, while preparing to attack China, Timur made further provision for agricultural development in the regions between Samarkand and Āshpara.[30] For Salmānī, writing only a few years later, one purpose of the campaign against the Ming was the subjugation of Mughūlistān.[31] Significantly, Timur at this juncture allocated Tashkent, Sayrām, Yangī, Āshpara and 'the Jata territory as far as Khitai' to his grandson Ulugh Beg, and Andijān, Akhsīkat, Talās and 'Kāshghar as far as Khotan' to Ulugh Beg's brother Ibrāhīm Sulṭān.[32] It is clear, therefore, that he envisaged the extension of more direct rule over a significant part of the eastern Chaghadayid khanate.

CONFRONTATION WITH THE JOCHIDS

In 778/1377, during his fifth expedition to Jata, Timur had received an appeal from Toqtamish, a fugitive prince from the Blue Horde, for assistance against its khan, Orus. The marked growth in the power of Orus, who had seized Sarai, and not least his manifest designs on Khwārazm, encouraged Timur to lend Toqtamish his support. He responded warmly, conferring on Toqtamish the territories of Ṣawrān (Ṣabrān) and Sighnāq, and when Toqtamish twice suffered a crushing defeat by the forces of the Blue Horde Timur rejected Orus Khan's demand for the prince's surrender, led his army to Sighnāq and inflicted a major reverse on the khan. Orus shortly died, and after the brief reign of his son Toqta Qaya the throne passed to another son, Temür Malik. On the news of Orus Khan's death, Timur had bestowed on Toqtamish the rulership not simply of the Blue Horde but of the whole of Jochi's ulus. After a further reverse, Toqtamish finally defeated Temür Malik in the region which Yazdī calls Qaratal (probably in error for the Qaratau) in the winter of 780/1379. The next spring he moved against the Qipchaq khanate, where he took Sarai and vanquished the kingmaker Mamai, thus extending his rule over the entire ulus of Jochi.[33]

Timur was reportedly delighted when news arrived of his protégé's final triumph over Temür Malik.[34] Within a few years, however, any hopes he entertained that the new khan would prove a dutiful subordinate once securely in command of the Jochid lands were disappointed. From Dhū l-Ḥijja 786/January–February 1385 Toqtamish, in a bid to cultivate alternative allies, revived the earlier Jochid policy of friendship with the Mamlūk Sultanate,[35] which had lapsed during the 'Great Troubles'; he also entered into friendly relations with the Jalayirid Sulṭān Aḥmad. It is possible that he had begun to harbour the same designs on Azerbaijan and Arrān as his predecessors Özbeg and Janibeg; and Janibeg had been acknowledged as suzerain in several other regions of Iran during the 1350s (above, p. 118). But Toqtamish may have been spurred on primarily by Timur's own expansionist policy: the reduction of Khwārazm, the advance through northern Iran, threatening the economic interests of the Qipchaq khanate, and the capture of Sulṭāniyya.[36] His mistake lay in defying his benefactor only after lucrative campaigns in Iran had greatly increased Timur's resources and his capacity to react effectively.

Toqtamish began by sacking Tabriz and other towns in Azerbaijan in 787/1385–6.[37] In 789/1387 he had the audacity to invade Transoxiana and lay siege to Bukhara in Timur's absence on campaign in Iran. Timur, invading Jochid territory, was victorious on the

Qundurcha River (near modern Orenburg) in mid-Rajab 793/mid-June 1391, thanks to the desertion of Beg Bolod, one of Toqtamish's kinsmen.[38] The reverse did not check the ambitions of Toqtamish, who proposed a formal alliance to the Mamlūk Sultan and secured his other frontier by making peace with Lithuania. Then, at the onset of 797/in the autumn of 1394 he launched raids against Darband and Shīrwān, compelling Timur to break off a projected attack on Syria and move northwards. Following a crushing victory on the River Terek on 23 Jumādā II 797/15 April 1395 over Toqtamish, who fled into the Būlar (Bulghār) region, he pushed west into the Qipchaq khanate. An advance on Moscow, described laconically by Timurid authors as entailing the devastation of its territory and the humiliation of its leaders (*umarā*),[39] was in fact aborted – the reason, if we believe Rus′ sources, being a nocturnal visitation by the Virgin Mary; but possibly Timur had calculated that richer targets lay to the south. After sacking the wealthy commercial towns of the khanate, Sarai, Qirim, Tana, Astrakhan, Ügek and Saraichik, he returned to Azerbaijan in the spring of 798/1396. Sharaf al-Dīn Yazdī expressly calls the fate of Sarai revenge for Toqtamish's demolition in 789/1387 of the palace of Zanjīr Sarai in Transoxiana, built by Timur's father-in-law, the Chaghadayid khan Qazan Sulṭān.[40] As Timur himself had recently spent at least three winters there,[41] Toqtamish may have singled it out for attention. Timur's campaign of destruction gravely undermined the economic foundations of the Golden Horde.[42] Venetian representatives visiting Tana in 1396 had found it desolate and in ruins, and nothing had been done to restore it even by 1411.[43] More than four decades after its sack, Barbaro would lament the dilapidated condition of Astrakhan, which had evidently still not recovered.[44]

At first, Timur recognised as khan of Jochi's ulus Qoyurichaq, a son of Orus who had accompanied him on campaign but who reigned only briefly.[45] Although he had removed his most formidable rival within the Mongol world (and a greater threat, Clavijo heard, than the Ottoman Sultan: see below, p. 323), the Jochid princes, headed by Temür Qutlugh, who had rallied to him against Toqtamish soon deserted him; Temür Qutlugh himself became khan of the Jochid lands. The amir Edigü, who had submitted to Timur and acted as his agent, likewise abandoned him and established his own mastery over the Golden Horde, where he enthroned his candidates at will.[46] By the time Timur died, he and Toqtamish may have allied against Edigü (below, p. 349). Toqtamish would perish in battle with the Jochid khan Shadibeg in Siberia in 809/1407, and it was his sons who overthrew Edigü.[47]

Timur's aims regarding the Jochid ulus differed from his policy towards Mughūlistān. Although Sharaf al-Dīn Yazdī writes of the 'conquest and control' (*taskhīr-u taṣarruf*) of the Qipchaq khanate in 797–8/1395–6, in the very next breath he is more realistic, employing the language of annihilation (*mustaʾṣal sāzad*), and describes those of the enemy who had survived as wandering and scattered and without property.[48] One result of Timur's assault was the flight of a large number of the Jochids' Mongol subjects headed by an amir of Toqtamish named Aqtau; we know from other sources that they were shortly defeated again by Timur's forces and emigrated into Bayezid's territories south of the Danube.[49] A further consequence – and probably the chief purpose of Timur's second campaign – was the diversion of the lucrative trans-Asiatic trade through his own dominions, especially his capital at Samarkand; or, to put it another way, the replacement of the northerly 'steppe' route by a more southerly one that passed through Transoxiana and Iran.[50] But whereas in Jata he had a number of fortresses built to keep the Mughūl nomads at bay and nominated loyal subordinates to command them, Timur at no point established his own rule within any part of the Qipchaq khanate except Khwārazm. Temür Qutlugh seems to have ruled without reference to him; evidence is lacking even for a diplomatic intervention there on Timur's part when the news of Temür Qutlugh's death reached him in 802/1399.[51] He merely left the Jochid princes and amirs to fend for themselves against one another and against the now greatly weakened Toqtamish.

THE CONQUEST OF KHURĀSĀN, SĪSTĀN AND MĀZANDARĀN

Khurāsān was a natural target for the new master of Transoxiana. Political authority there, as in Māzandarān, was highly fragmented.

And Khurāsān, like Sīstān, was the stamping ground of the Qara'unas and had been the object of Chaghadayid interest for many decades. Qara'unas amirs had attacked Khurāsān on at least two occasions, in *c.* 1349 and in 759/1358. So too, when Luqmān, son of the late Ilkhan Taghai Temür, had fled to Transoxiana after his dispossession by Amīr Walī, he had secured the help of Timur's enemy, the Apardī amir Zinda Ḥasham; but the allies had been defeated and retired across the Oxus.[52] Qazaghan's campaign against Herat in 752/1351, together with the subsequent appeal for aid from Muʿizz al-Dīn Pīr Ḥusayn Muḥammad (above, p. 219), furnished adequate grounds for regarding the kingdom as subject to the Chaghadayid state of which Timur was now the effective head.

In his youth, as we saw, Timur himself had been on amicable terms with Muʿizz al-Dīn. In fact, Ghiyāth al-Dīn Yazdī claims that Timur postponed an attack on Herat until after Muʿizz al-Dīn's death, in view of their past friendship.[53] But according to other authors, even when negotiating with the malik earlier in his career Timur had recalled the fate of Ilkhanid noyans like Nawrūz and Choban who, to their cost, had sought asylum at Herat and trusted Kartid promises.[54] He would have been aware, too, that Muʿizz al-Dīn had tried to establish his authority in Kirmān and had intervened in the affairs of the Chaghadayid ulus itself, profiting from Amīr Ḥusayn's conflict with Badakhshān in order to ravage the Balkh region.[55]

Muʿizz al-Dīn's son and successor, Ghiyāth al-Dīn Pīr Shāh, temporised when summoned to submit in 781/1379–80, having surrounded Herat with a new wall the year before; but he eventually yielded and accompanied Timur back to Transoxiana, where he was given a daughter of Timur in marriage before returning to his capital. When he nurtured plans of defiance, a party headed by the malik's wazir, Muʿīn al-Dīn Jāmī, a member of the family of the shaykhs of Jām, grew anxious to avoid the carnage that would inevitably follow; they incited Timur to take the city.[56] Timur reacted in the autumn of 782/1380 by first sending a force under his son Amīrānshāh against Herat and then following himself with a larger army. With Herat under siege, Ghiyāth al-Dīn had no choice but to surrender. In

Muḥarram 783/April 1381 he and his brother Muḥammad, the ruler of Sarakhs, who had taken the initiative in submitting to Timur,[57] were despatched to Samarkand and later to Andijān, where towards the end of 784/early in 1383 they were put to death after Muḥammad was implicated in a conspiracy.[58] In 791/1389 Amīrānshāh, whom Timur had appointed to govern Khurāsān, massacred the remaining Kartids in a fit of drunkenness.[59]

In 783/1381 the Sarbadār ruler, Najm al-Dīn Khwāja ʿAlī-yi Mu'ayyad, enmeshed in a struggle with Amīr Walī, joined Timur's invading forces and offered his submission, henceforward acting as the conqueror's lieutenant in Sabzawār.[60] The Jā'ūn-i Qurbān leader, ʿAlī Beg, against whom Timur bore a grudge for treating him harshly in his youth (above, p. 185),[61] had similarly visited Timur's headquarters to perform obeisance as early as 781/1379–80, and had offered to act as guide to Amīrānshāh's troops.[62] Now, however, when Timur withdrew from Khurāsān, ʿAlī Beg joined forces with Amīr Walī. The allies laid siege to Sabzawār, which had to be relieved by Timur's army. In Rabīʿ I 784/May 1382 Timur duly moved against ʿAlī Beg, who after repeated breaches of faith was at length obliged to surrender; he was put to death in Samarkand around the same time as Ghiyāth al-Dīn of Herat. In Dhū l-Ḥijja 784/February–March 1383 Timur subjected Māzandarān, a region that, Ghiyāth al-Dīn Yazdī proudly announces, no previous 'Khaqan' or *Ṣāḥib-Qirān* had ever conquered.[63] A campaign against Amīr Walī reduced his territories, but Amīr Walī himself took refuge with the Jalayirid Sulṭān Aḥmad b. Shaykh Uways. He later made for Khalkhāl, whose ruler handed him over to Timur's forces; he was put to death in 788/1386.[64]

In the autumn of 785/1383 Timur had turned his attention to Sīstān. Its malik, Quṭb al-Dīn, had agreed to pay him tribute, but Timur was perhaps still smarting from the failure of the malik's father to reward him for his help two decades or so earlier (above, p. 255). The details of the invasion given in the local history, the seventeenth-century *Iḥyā' al-mulūk* of Malik Shāh Ḥusayn, differ from those supplied by the Timurid sources, each side accusing the other of bad faith, particularly apropos of the surrender of the citadel (in which context Ibn ʿArabshāh corroborates the Sīstānī charge, and accuses

Timur of avenging the injury he had suffered in the region in his youth). The campaign culminated in the sack and burning of Shahr-i Sīstān in Shawwāl/November–December and the devastation of the town and region of Bust. Quṭb al-Dīn was later put to death in Samarkand. His kinsman Tāj al-Dīn Shāh-i Shāhān, who had won Timur's favour, was made malik of Sīstān in his place.[65]

Khurāsān was conferred on Amīrānshāh; Astarābād was entrusted to Luqmān as Timur's subordinate; the Jā'ūn-i Qurbān troops were distributed among various amirs and transported first to Transoxiana and later to Tashkent. Alone among the previous powers in Khurāsān, the Sarbadār leaders were recruited into Timur's service and repaid his trust. ʿAlī-yi Mu'ayyad, who had fought for him in Sīstān, died on campaign with Timur in Luristān in 788/1386, and his nephew ʿImād al-Dīn Masʿūd, who succeeded him in Nishapur, was appointed governor of Shūshtar in 795/1393 and then of Baghdad in the following year.[66]

By 786/1384–5 Timur had brought eastern Iran entirely under his authority. He would subjugate most of the remainder of Iran in the course of three expeditions. The three-year campaign of 788–90/1386–8 entailed the first attacks on Jalayirid Azerbaijan and Christian Georgia but was directed primarily against the Muzaffarids; Timur also secured the submission of Shīrwān and the petty principalities in Gīlān.[67] During the five-year campaign of 794–8/1392–6 he subdued Māzandarān, again ravaged Georgia, took Baghdad and other cities from the Jalayirids, confronted the Mamlūk army for the first time, launched a third invasion of Georgia and had the final reckoning with Toqtamish. The seven-year campaign, which began in 802/1399 and witnessed the invasion of Mamlūk Syria and the overthrow of the Ottoman Sultan, was cut short by Timur's plans to invade China and by his death.

SOUTHERN AND CENTRAL IRAN: THE OVERTHROW OF THE MUZAFFARIDS

The Muzaffarid dynasty, ruling Fārs and Kirmān in southern Iran and Isfahan and Yazd in ʿIrāq-i ʿAjam, was headed by Shāh-i Shujāʿ.

An ambitious ruler who had intervened in the tangled politics of the Sarbadār state in *c.* 777/1376 and had more than once attempted to seize the old Ilkhanid residences of Sulṭāniyya and Tabriz and the grazing grounds of Azerbaijan and Arrān in the north-west, Shāh-i Shujāʿ was nevertheless ready to conciliate Timur. He submitted when summoned to do so and paid tribute, and he rejected an appeal from Amīr Walī to ally with him against the Central Asian conqueror.[68] We have seen how, on his deathbed, he commended his young son Zayn al-ʿĀbidīn to Timur and how Zayn al-ʿĀbidīn's heedlessness provoked the Chaghatay warlord's intervention in southern Iran, where in any case the tempestuous nature of Muzaffarid politics afforded him a further pretext to intervene. When Timur advanced on Isfahan in 789/1387, Zayn al-ʿĀbidīn's lieutenant Muẓaffar Kāshī promptly surrendered the city to him, though the populace revolted soon afterwards, killing Timur's representatives, and in reprisal was subjected to a horrific massacre on 6 Dhū l-Qaʿda/18 November.[69] From Yazd Shāh Yaḥyā came to offer his submission to Timur and was entrusted with Shiraz, which had surrendered to the conqueror without a fight; Isfahan was conferred on Shāh Yaḥyā's son Sulṭān Muḥammad, while Sulṭān Abū Isḥāq, a grandson of Shāh-i Shujāʿ, was confirmed as ruler of Sīrjān. Sulṭān Aḥmad likewise arrived from Kirmān to wait on Timur:[70] if we can trust Kutubī, he had responded to an embassy from the conqueror as early as 787/1385–6 by inserting Timur's name in the khutba and on the coinage.[71] Having asserted his overlordship in southern Iran, Timur withdrew to Transoxiana to deal with Toqtamish's incursion (see earlier, p. 288).

Of the Muzaffarid rulers, only Zayn al-ʿĀbidīn had neglected to visit Timur's headquarters. Fleeing from Shiraz in the direction of Baghdad, he was intercepted at Shūshtar and imprisoned by his cousin, Shāh Manṣūr, who then moved on Shiraz and ousted Shāh Yaḥyā.[72] In 792/1390 the latter made a bid to wrest Kirmān from his uncle Sulṭān Aḥmad, but suffered a crushing defeat.[73] Meanwhile Zayn al-ʿĀbidīn was released from confinement by supporters in Shūshtar and established himself in Isfahan.[74] But his attempt, in concert with Sulṭān Aḥmad and Shāh Yaḥyā, to take revenge on

Shāh Manṣūr miscarried badly and the allies were routed. Shāh Manṣūr followed up his victory by occupying Isfahan; Zayn al-ʿĀbidīn was captured in flight, imprisoned once more and this time also blinded.[75]

Shāh Manṣūr's repeated triumphs demanded Timur's attention. When the Great Amir advanced on the Muzaffarid dominions early in 795/at the end of 1392 and entered Fārs, Shāh Manṣūr, who had spent the previous few years warring against his kinsmen and devastating their territories, naturally found no ally; despite a spirited resistance, he was eventually routed in battle near Shiraz and killed.[76] Weary of Muzaffarid fractiousness and reportedly angered by the harm their subjects had suffered during their quarrels, Timur in Rajab 795/February 1393 had all the remaining members of the dynasty executed except the hapless brothers Zayn al-ʿĀbidīn and Sulṭān Shiblī, who were sent to Samarkand.[77] Fārs and ʿIrāq-i ʿAjam were allotted to Timur's son ʿUmar Shaykh and Kirmān to Edigü Barlās.

The wealthy principality of Hurmuz in the Gulf, tributary to the Muzaffarids for some decades, had profited from the strife among the dynasty's princes to withhold payments for the past four years. In 798/1396, therefore, Timur sent an army under his grandson Muḥammad Sulṭān to claim the arrears on his behalf. The prince of Hurmuz submitted and undertook to pay four years' tribute, offering partial payment in kind as an interim measure. But according to Naṭanzī the campaign achieved only limited success. Aubin suggests that it highlighted the Chaghatays' lack of naval power.[78]

INTERMITTENT AND PARTIAL SUCCESS IN WESTERN IRAN: JALAYIRIDS AND QARĀ-QŪYŪNLŪ

It was not to be expected that Timur would long defer any designs on the Jalayirid territories, which were centred on the two cities of Tabriz and Sulṭāniyya, the heartlands of the Ilkhanate; indeed the Jalayirid monarchs posed as the true successors of the Ilkhans. The situation here certainly invited his intervention. The Jalayirids' western territories were contested with the rising Qarā-Qūyūnlū

Türkmen, based in Diyār Bakr, and the current Jalayirid ruler, the indolent and dissolute Sulṭān Aḥmad b. Shaykh Uways, faced further disaffection provoked by his violent seizure of the throne in 784/1382 and by his arbitrary proceedings against his amirs. After 1385 Toqtamish's ambitions south of the Caucasus gave Timur an additional incentive to subject the Jalayirid lands to his own rule.

Here, however, Timur enjoyed less success than elsewhere. In 786/1384, following his invasion of Māzandarān, he occupied Sulṭāniyya, but the Jalayirid monarch fled. Sulṭān Aḥmad's attempt to recover the city was thwarted by his former amir, ʿĀdil Āqā, to whom Timur had entrusted the governorship.[79] Timur once again invaded the Jalayirid lands during his three-year campaign, in 788/1386, occupying Tabriz, installing ʿĀdil Āqā there as his representative and wintering in Qarābāgh. After an incursion into Georgia, when he captured King Bagrat V, he resumed his westward advance in 789/1387, this time against the Qarā-Qūyūnlū leader Qarā Muḥammad, taking a number of towns in Armenia, notably Erzurum, and securing the submission of Ṭahartan (or Muṭahhartan), the ruler of Arzinjān (Erzincan).[80] Although Chaghatay control over Tabriz remained tenuous, the expulsion of the Jalayirids from the former Ilkhanid residence was a highly symbolic triumph.[81] But Timur failed to bring the Qarā-Qūyūnlū under his authority before he was distracted by the Muzaffarids' disputes. He had, however, at least obtained the submission of the Qarā-Qūyūnlū's rival, Qarā Yulūk of the Āq-Qūyūnlū, who would render valuable service during Timur's Anatolian campaign in 802–4/1400–1 and to whom he entrusted Malaṭiya.[82] The Āq-Qūyūnlū, ironically, proved to be the nemesis of Timur's dynasty in western Iran several decades later.

Timur returned to the attack in the course of his five-year campaign, in 795/1393, following the overthrow of the Muzaffarids. Sulṭān Aḥmad Jalāyir, who had sent gifts but excused himself from waiting upon Timur, abandoned Baghdad and sought asylum in the Mamlūk empire. Timur's future biographer, Niẓām al-Dīn Shāmī, claims to have been the first inhabitant of Baghdad to perform obeisance to the conqueror, though it was not until some eight years later that he entered Timur's service.[83] Timur, who had installed the

Sarbadār ʿImād al-Dīn Masʿūd as governor in Baghdad, did not pursue Sulṭān Aḥmad, but passed two months in the city. He then busied himself with the capture of Takrīt, Mārdīn and Āmid, before moving north on his second major campaign against Toqtamish. Masʿūd was obliged to withdraw from Baghdad in the following year. Sulṭān Aḥmad, who had obtained reinforcements from the Mamlūk Sultan, in the event recovered his capital with the aid of Qarā Yūsuf, Qarā Muḥammad's successor at the head of the Qarā-Qūyūnlū.

Timur's third assault on the Jalayirid dominions occurred in Dhū l-Qaʿda 803/July 1401.[84] Baghdad suffered a horrific sack, in which only shaykhs and dervishes were exempt from the slaughter. On this occasion, Timur left no representative to govern the city, and Sulṭān Aḥmad, who had taken refuge with the Ottoman Sultan, returned to his capital after Timur's withdrawal, only to be expelled again in 804/1402 by the conqueror's grandson Abā Bakr. If Chaghatay attacks failed to eliminate the Jalayirid polity completely, they had fatally weakened it, to the advantage of enemies closer at hand – the Qarā-Qūyūnlū, against whom Timur had made less headway. Recovering Baghdad, Sulṭān Aḥmad found himself obliged to yield the city to Qarā Yūsuf. He then withdrew once more into Mamlūk Syria, where Qarā Yūsuf, expelled from Baghdad by Timurid forces, soon joined him and the two men for a time served in the retinue of the governor of Damascus. Sulṭān Aḥmad's final return to Baghdad was brief; he again had to surrender it to Qarā Yūsuf, who had meanwhile occupied Tabriz. Sulṭān Aḥmad survived Timur by six years, falling victim in 813/1410 not to the Timurids but to the Qarā-Qūyūnlū. A year later Qarā Yūsuf wrested Baghdad from Sulṭān Aḥmad's great-nephew and successor, Sulṭān Maḥmūd b. Shāh Walad. Scions of the Jalayirid dynasty lingered on in Khūzistān, as vassals of Shāhrukh, until 835/1432.[85]

THE INVASION OF INDIA

India had been a target of attacks from the ulus of Chaghadai since the late thirteenth century; the most recent major incursion, in 730/1329–30, had been that of Tarmashirin. The Delhi Sultanate had also often served as a refuge for princes or amirs displaced from Central Asia. In the latter stages of the war between Du'a and Chapar, it is possible that some of the Mongol inroads into the subcontinent had been the work of fugitives, rather than invasions organised formally like those of Qutlugh Khwāja and Taraghai in 1300–3.[86] We have seen, too, how the Delhi Sultan Muḥammad b. Tughluq had made efforts to attract to India, and enlist in his service, grandees and clerics from Transoxiana during the upheavals following Tarmashirin's downfall (above, p. 217). In *c.* 764/1361–2 Bahrām Jalāyir had briefly taken refuge in the direction of India.[87] Timur's ally Amīr Ḥusayn at one point contemplated doing so, and his two surviving sons fled there following his overthrow in 771/1370 (only to perish, Sharaf al-Dīn Yazdī assures us).[88] As recently as 790/1388 two rebel amirs from the Qara'unas territories had sought safety in Delhi.[89] Very probably Timur was mindful of these events when he first conceived of invading the Delhi Sultanate.

But Timur also received direct encouragement to intervene in Indian affairs. We know nothing of the contents of the letters which, according to the Indian author Bihāmadkhānī, he had exchanged with the Delhi Sultan Fīrūz Shāh (d. 790/1388).[90] In *c.* 1389 Fīrūz Shāh's youngest son, Nāṣir al-Dīn Muḥammad Shāh, expelled by a rival, despaired of recovering his throne and set out for Samarkand to solicit Timur's assistance, but in the event was recalled to Delhi to take the throne in 792/1390.[91] He died in 796/1394 and his elder son and successor, ʿAlā' al-Dīn Sikandar Shāh, survived him by only six weeks. The next Sultan, Muḥammad Shāh's younger son Ghiyāth al-Dīn Maḥmūd Shāh, was a mere cipher in the hands of the amir Mallū Khan, whose power was challenged by his brother Sārang Khan, the governor of Multān. The great officers of state monopolised authority within the truncated Sultanate; provincial revenues were misappropriated by local amirs.[92] Ibn Khaldūn confirms that Timur had received a request for help from an émigré (perhaps a reference to the earlier appeal by Muḥammad Shāh);[93] other sources give the impression simply that he had sensed an opportunity with Fīrūz Shāh's death and the onset of factionalism.[94] A more immediate stimulus was the capture of Uchch and investment of Multān by Pīr Muḥammad b. Jahāngīr,[95] on whom in 794/1392 Timur had conferred an extensive territory, comprising Qunduz, Baghlān, Ghazna, Kabul and Qandahār as far as the Indus.[96] The campaign may have been undertaken purely on the prince's initiative,[97] and Shāmī's total reticence on the episode may betray a sensitive awareness that Timur felt the need to prevent his grandson from acquiring too much kudos.

The ostensible justification for the Indian expedition, whether expressed as the need to restore Fīrūz Shāh's heirs to their rightful position or (later) couched in terms of the spread of Islam and the elimination of paganism,[98] was in all probability a façade. Timur is equally likely to have been actuated by the Chaghadayid tradition of attacking and plundering India, while harbouring a determination to achieve greater success. The most we can say, in the religious context, is that he was aware, firstly, of the resurgence of Hindu chiefs profiting from the weakness of the regime in Delhi,[99] and that he saw it as his duty, secondly, to punish Delhi's Muslim rulers for the fact that their Hindu subjects enjoyed freedom of worship and may have been largely exempt from the poll-tax (*jizya*) required from unbelievers elsewhere; Ghiyāth al-Dīn Yazdī accuses the Sultans of levying only 'tribute and the land tax' (*bāj-u kharāj*).[100]

By the time Pīr Muḥammad entered Sind early in Rabīʿ I 800/ towards the end of 1397, the condition of the Sultanate had deteriorated further. It now had two sovereigns, since three years earlier a group of amirs had set up at Fīrūzābād, in opposition to Maḥmūd Shāh in Delhi, a great-grandson of Fīrūz Shāh as Sultan Nāṣir al-Dīn Nuṣrat Shāh.[101] Pīr Muḥammad, who took Multān from Sārang Khan on 19 Ramaḍān 800/5 June 1398, was closely followed by the main army under Timur, which sacked Bhatner and Sarsati. Nuṣrat Shāh fled into the Doab. Maḥmūd Shāh and Mallū Khan, meeting Timur with their forces outside Delhi on 7 Rabīʿ II 801/16 December 1398, suffered a crushing defeat. Despite the promise of quarter for its citizens, the city was subjected to a horrific sack, as a result, most probably, of disorders that had erupted and perhaps without Timur's authorisation.[102] According to Sharaf al-Dīn Yazdī, news of the capture of Delhi – a formidably fortified complex, it should be emphasised, that had not fallen to an outside conqueror for over two centuries and had defied even major Mongol attacks – reverberated throughout the world.[103]

Timur took Mīrat (Meerut), before withdrawing by way of Hardwar and Jammu across the Indus, ravaging the lands of the Khokhars and other Hindu territories as he went.[104] He entrusted Multān to its former governor, Khiḍr Khan, who had waited upon him and offered his submission;[105] this officer claimed the additional merit of sayyid ancestry, a qualification for which Timur evinced considerable respect (below, pp. 377–80). After Maḥmūd Shāh's death in 815/1412, Khiḍr Khan would take over Delhi and found the Sayyid dynasty (817–855/1414–1451), paying tribute to the Timurids and having the khutba read in Shāhrukh's name. But the story that Timur had conferred Delhi upon him is doubtless a fiction concocted by Sirhindī, writing under the Sayyids, in a bid to lend them greater legitimacy.[106] The late (and unreliable) Indian author Firishta asserts that even the Deccan acknowledged Timur's overlordship;[107] but this may be another fiction.

THE ASSAULT ON THE MAMLŪK AND OTTOMAN SULTANATES

Ibn ʿArabshāh asserts that Timur broke off his Indian campaign after receiving news of the deaths of Qadi Burhān al-Dīn, the ruler of Sivas, and the Egyptian Mamlūk Sultan al-Ẓāhir Barqūq in 800/1398 and 801/1399, respectively.[108] Burhān al-Dīn's domain, which he had taken over from the dynasty of the Mongol amir Aratna, lay squarely within the one-time Ilkhanate, and after his death his lands were appropriated by the Ottomans, who had likewise once been subject to the Ilkhans. The Mamlūk empire had never been in Mongol hands; but the Ilkhan Hülegü's forces had occupied Mamlūk Syria for some months in 658/1260, and his successors, notably Ghazan Maḥmūd, had made fresh efforts to conquer the country. Since Ilkhanid power had atrophied in the late 1330s, moreover, the Mamlūk Sultan had been acknowledged as their suzerain by various princes hitherto under Ilkhanid overlordship, notably the Artuqids of Mārdīn.[109] As the ruler of a large part of the Iranian world, Timur could claim to have inherited the traditional Ilkhanid rivalry with the Mamlūks. An officer of Timur who had been captured in Rabīʿ I 796/January 1394 divulged (admittedly under torture) the presence in Cairo of Persian (*ʿajamī*) spies, of whom seven, among them merchants, were arrested;[110] whether they had been sent for this specific purpose by Timur himself, or merely planned to render themselves useful to him, is unclear. By this time there was no little anxiety at the Mamlūk Sultan's court regarding Timur's movements.

Timur had first entered into diplomatic contact with the Sultan in Dhū l-Ḥijja 787/January 1386, with what purpose we are not told.[111] Barqūq is known to have rejected in arrogant terms an invitation from Timur to make a commercial agreement, and a number of princes in eastern Anatolia and the Jazīra, alarmed at Timur's progress, turned to the Egyptian Sultan for protection. They included Qarā Yūsuf, the Qarā-Qūyūnlū chief, and Barqūq would shortly enter into friendly relations also with Burhān al-Dīn and Bayezid.[112] Over and above these provocations, his execution at al-Raḥba in 795/1393–4 of Timur's envoys who had brought a demand for submission, his warm reception in Cairo in 796/1394 of the exiled Jalayirid Sulṭān Aḥmad and his detention of Timur's foster-brother (*kökeltash*) *Atlamish, who had been captured by Qarā Yūsuf and sent to Barqūq,[113] more than satisfied the necessary *casus belli*. According to Yazdī, Timur had announced his intention of moving on Egypt and Syria to the ruler of Mārdīn as early as Ṣafar 796/December 1393–January 1394.[114]

With Barqūq's death and the accession of his young son, al-Nāṣir Faraj, the Mamlūk regime jettisoned its policy of support for rulers under threat from Timur and indeed began to manifest a certain hostility towards them.[115] Nevertheless, Faraj continued to keep *Atlamish in captivity. Having written from Malaṭiya to the chief cities of Syria and listed his grievances against both Barqūq and Faraj, Timur invaded the country in the autumn of 803/1400. He first captured Aleppo (where Shāmī was among the prisoners) and proceeded to take Ḥamā, Ḥimṣ and Baʿlabakk. Then he moved on

Damascus, whose governor had executed the envoy bearing Timur's letter. The Mamlūk army, under the nominal leadership of Sultan Faraj, moved to the defence of the city, but a false rumour of a coup in Cairo induced panic among the amirs, who hurried the young sultan back to his capital; the troops thereupon withdrew to Egypt in disarray. Damascus held out for a short time, but was taken in mid-803/early in 1401 and was subjected to a sack in which many of the populace perished and the Umayyad Mosque was largely burned down.

Timur remained encamped outside the city for three months. During this time he received Ibn Khaldūn, the Maghribī jurist and savant, who had accompanied Faraj from Cairo but had then found himself stranded in Damascus, and who would shortly include his encounters with the Great Amir in his autobiography. It was here too that Ibn ʿArabshāh was enslaved with his family as a child, to be transported, with numerous other inhabitants of Damascus, to Samarkand. Then, in the early spring of 803/1401, Timur withdrew from Syria in order to deal for the last time with Baghdad and then to prepare for the confrontation with Bayezid. According to Sharaf al-Dīn Yazdī, when news arrived of Timur's victory over the Ottomans Faraj released *Atlamish and undertook also to have the khutba and the coinage in Timur's name. The Sultan thus effectively became Timur's governor for Egypt and Syria.[116] In a subsequent letter to the Marinid Sultan of Morocco, who (possibly on the basis of information from Ibn Khaldūn) had hinted at his inadequacy in the face of the Chaghatay invasion, Faraj justified his conduct on the specious grounds that Timur had sought a reconciliation and that it had been his duty to accept.[117]

Timur's relations with Bayezid had at first been ostensibly friendly. But like the Jalayirid, Kartid and Muzaffarid rulers and Burhān al-Dīn, the late fourteenth-century Ottoman monarchs could be deemed to have usurped the status properly reserved for Mongol khans; Bayezid's father Murad I (d. 791/1389) had styled himself not merely Sultan but also Khāqān (Qaghan), while Bayezid himself had requested confirmation of his title of Sultan from the ʿAbbasid Caliph in Cairo.[118] Moreover, his dominions had grown spectacularly, not only in Anatolia but in south-eastern Europe, with the annexation of Bulgaria, the reduction of Serbia to tributary status and sustained pressure on the rump of the Byzantine empire at Constantinople. There were also more immediate motives for confrontation with the Ottomans. In their correspondence, Bayezid hinted that he might invade the Crimea and could easily recruit reinforcements from among the Tatars of the Qipchaq steppe, who now had good reason to hate Timur.[119] Conversely, Turkish princes dispossessed by the Ottomans had made for Timur's court in the hope of assistance.[120] The death of Burhān al-Dīn, moreover, drew the attention of both potentates to his lands in eastern Anatolia, where Bayezid was quick to seize Sivas. The most recent sources of tension were the shelter given by Bayezid to the Jalayirid Sulṭān Aḥmad and his attack on Timur's protégé Ṭahartan, ruler of Arzinjān.[121] In 803/1400 Timur opened the war by storming Sivas. Bayezid's encroachments on the Mamlūk sphere of influence in eastern Anatolia, incidentally, had ended any chances of cooperation with Egypt which he had mooted in an embassy to Cairo in 802/1400.[122]

In 804/1402 Timur resumed his westward advance and met Bayezid in battle near Ankara on 27 Dhū l-Ḥijja/28 July.[123] Despite the valiant resistance of his forces, not least his Christian Serb auxiliaries under the vassal prince Stepan Lazarovich,[124] Bayezid suffered a crushing defeat. Timur had suborned a significant number of Tatars in the Ottoman forces ('Qara Tatars', as the sources sometimes call them) by appealing to a common ethnicity. Formerly in the service of Aratna's dynasty and until 1398, therefore, subject to Qadi Burhān al-Dīn, they were recent recruits to the Ottoman army, and their desertion in the heat of battle assured the Chaghatay victory.[125] For the remaining eleven months of his life Bayezid was a prisoner, carried in the victor's train and witnessing the destruction of his capital, Bursa; though Sharaf al-Dīn Yazdī assures us that he was treated kindly (the tale that he was kept in an iron cage is probably apocryphal), as were his family after his death.[126] The same author says that when the Sultan fell ill and died in the following year Timur wept.[127] The conqueror restored some of Bayezid's territories to the dynasties that had previously held them and conferred what was left of the empire on the fallen ruler's sons. The Ottoman province of Rumeli, centred on Edirne (Adrianople), beyond the Bosphorus, was assigned to Süleyman; Bursa to İsa Beg; and Rūm proper to Meḥmed, who struck coins in Timur's name at Ankara in 805/1402–3 and Amasya in 806/1403–4.[128] Timur sacked Smyrna (now Izmir), a stronghold of the Knights Hospitallers, in Jumādā I 805/December 1402.[129] But he proceeded no further, perhaps because he lacked the naval power to cross the Straits and anticipated a dearth of pasturage for his army in the Balkans,[130] and withdrew towards Iran.

DIPLOMATIC RELATIONS WITH CHRISTIAN POWERS

It is perhaps appropriate to discuss at this point Timur's dealings with Bayezid's Christian enemies. These diplomatic contacts served a number of purposes. One aim was to obtain tribute from Christian rulers, which Timurid authors designate as *jizya*. He numbered among his vassals the Christian Georgian Kings Bagrat V and Giorgi VII, who intermittently paid tribute.[131] The Emperor Manuel III Comnenus of Trebizond, whose sister was Bagrat's consort, yielded to a punitive expedition and supplied the conqueror with twenty galleys.[132] He seems also to have acted as intermediary between Timur and the Byzantine imperial government at Constantinople; though he also paid tribute to the neighbouring Turks.[133] The Byzantines likewise played a double game.[134] In the absence of Emperor Manuel II Palaeologus (1391–1425), seeking aid from Western Europe against the Ottomans, his nephew John VII acted as regent on his behalf. Clavijo says that John had made an agreement with Bayezid to surrender Constantinople and act as the Sultan's lieutenant should the Ottomans defeat Timur.[135] Yet by 1401 John too was exchanging embassies with the Central Asian conqueror. It was presumably John who yielded him tribute, as Timur himself confirmed in a letter to John dated May 1402.[136]

If we can trust a report that reached France, the conqueror offered the Byzantine government (no doubt in exchange for the promise of tribute) the return of all territory taken from the empire by Bayezid.[137] This was assuredly incompatible with Timur's self-conscious posture as a Muslim *ghāzī* and the depiction of his campaigns against Christians as holy war (*ghazw*).[138] But it is noteworthy that he proved less generous to the Christian Emperor than to some of the Muslim Anatolian princes who had been dispossessed by the Ottoman Sultan and who now found their territory not merely restored but augmented: the Qaramanid amir, for instance, received Akshehir over and above his ancestral lands.[139]

Timur also engaged in diplomatic relations with the Latin Christian world. Sharaf al-Dīn Yazdī first mentions envoys from the 'Franks' under the year 802/1399–1400; they brought with them a 'son of Amir Murād' (and therefore a brother of Bayezid?) who had been taken prisoner.[140] These must have been based in the Aegean region. The Genoese colonists at Pera are alleged to have hoisted Timur's banner in the wake of his first embassy to Constantinople in August 1401, and Clavijo tells us that a sum of money was sent to Timur.[141] Although Smyrna, under its Hospitaller garrison, defiantly rejected his demand for *jizya*, some of the local Franks whose petty lordships peppered the Aegean region offered tribute: for instance the Genoese colony at Phocaea (Fūcha) and the Genoese lord of Chios (Sāquz, as Shāmī and Yazdī call it).[142]

A second aim was to elicit the cooperation of Bayezid's enemies. In August 1401 Timur despatched to Constantinople two envoys, the Dominican Friar Francis and a Muslim, to deter the Byzantine government and the western colonists there from making peace with Bayezid and to inform them of his impending campaign.[143] This was probably the occasion on which the Byzantines, along with the Genoese at Pera, wrote to Timur promising to prevent Ottoman forces in the Balkans from crossing the Straits to aid Bayezid.[144] After Ankara, however, while some of the Genoese profited from the Turks' predicament, others flouted the agreement and helped Bayezid's fleeing troops to escape.[145] The Venetians too gave Turkish refugees asylum on the island of Samos.[146] Possibly the Italians, wary of Timur and reluctant to assist in the total elimination of the more familiar enemy, aimed to preserve a balance of power.[147] Clavijo dates Timur's hatred of Christians from the Genoese volte-face, while an Italian chronicler blames it for the attack on Smyrna.[148]

Timur's contacts with Christian monarchs in Western Europe are more fully documented.[149] The initiative appears to have come from his son Amīrānshāh, who in 1401 sent the Dominican Friar John, Archbishop of Sulṭāniyya, to Venice and Genoa. Possibly Amīrānshāh, who had been removed from the government of Azerbaijan by his father (see p. 274 above), was seeking a path back into Timur's favour by engineering the despatch of friendly embassies from Europe. John of Sulṭāniyya appears on this first occasion to have travelled onwards to the courts of France and England.[150] In 1402 he was despatched once more to the courts of western rulers, this time with his fellow Dominican, Francis, who had been Timur's envoy to John VII in 1401.[151] They carried a letter purportedly from Timur himself, dated 1 Muḥarram 805/1 August 1402 and announcing his triumph at Ankara; the letter to Charles VI of France and a contemporary Latin translation survive in the Archives Nationales. A French chronicler confirms the envoys' arrival in Paris in May 1403, and the replies of Charles VI and of Henry IV of England have come down to us.[152] Although the authenticity of Timur's letter has been questioned, it will be treated here as genuine.[153]

The most celebrated of the diplomatic exchanges between Timur and the west was initiated by Henry III of Castile, who in 1402 sent his agents to the Levant to ascertain the relative strength of Timur and Bayezid. They joined Timur at some point prior to the battle at Ankara, and he sent back with them his own envoy, Ḥājjī Muḥammad. In response, in May 1403 the Castilian king despatched to Timur the embassy that included Clavijo.[154] Yazdī notices the arrival of an *ilchi* from 'the ruler (*farmāndih*) of the Frankish lands' and his presence at the feast (*toy*) and quriltai that marked the marriages of Timur's grandsons.[155] But by his departure in November 1404 Clavijo had failed to obtain a reply to Henry's letter or a final audience with the Great Amir, now intent on his preparations for the invasion of China and in any case seriously ailing.[156] Clavijo's narrative suggests that the arrival of the Castilian party, coinciding as it did with the presence of an embassy from China, had offered an opportunity for Timur to boast to his entourage of the diplomatic attentions of 'the greatest of the kings of the Franks', doubtless in order to face down the perceived snub by the Ming Emperor (see later), whose envoys were demoted to a less honourable station at court.[157]

There seems to have been no question of demanding tribute from these distant powers, but a third purpose behind Timur's overtures to western Christendom was to foster commercial activity from which he and his subjects might benefit, a concern he shared with his Mongol predecessors. Archbishop John mentioned this on his arrival in Paris,[158] and when speaking of Timur's readiness to allow freedom of worship to Christians he added the telling phrase 'especially merchants'.[159] Much as Timur had proposed to Barqūq the renewal of trade between their territories in 796/1394,[160] so too his correspondence with Western European rulers stresses the desirability of trading links.[161] John even listed in his *Mémoire* commodities that Timur especially prized.[162]

TIMUR'S LAST CAMPAIGN

Initially Timur's dealings with the fledgling Ming dynasty in China had been amicable.[163] The Ming, however, in line with time-honoured Chinese diplomacy in relation to foreign powers, interpreted his despatch of embassies and gifts as the due attentions of a tributary prince; a purported letter from Timur to Taizu (the Hongwu Emperor; Zhu Yuanzhang) in 1394 appears in such guise in the *Mingshi*, the official annals of the dynasty.[164] When Timur became aware of this conflict of perspectives, he was inevitably angry; Clavijo witnessed the hostile reception given to the Chinese embassy that had brought the unpalatable message.[165] According to the *Mingshi*, Timur executed Chinese envoys both on this occasion and five years later when they were sent to announce Yongle's accession.[166] Taizu, who died in 1398, was known derisively at Timur's court as Tonguz Khan ('Fat Pig Khan') – a pun on the first element in his original name, Zhu Yuanzhang (a homophone of the word for pig, though represented in writing by a different character).[167] The Ming were rebels who had expelled the Mongol rulers from China, and in 1388 they had inflicted a humiliating defeat on the Qaghan Toghus Temür in Mongolia itself.[168] For all their ostensible rejection of Mongolian culture, they further had the effrontery to pose, in some respects, as the heirs of the Yuan.[169] Timur must have known of Taizu's diplomatic attempts to draw Mughūlistān into the Ming orbit, and probably also of the Ming attack in 1391 on Gunashiri[n], the Chaghadayid prince of Hami (Qāmul).[170]

The subjection of the Middle Kingdom, from which the Mongols had been driven ignominiously little more than thirty years before, represented a natural climax to Timur's career. It would have brought him control of the eastern reaches of the 'Silk Roads', though it is uncertain whether this played a part in his calculations. In any event, the one-time Yuan dominions were the only part of the Chinggisid empire against which he had yet to try his strength. He had already acquired a potential Qaghan, a Mongol prince who had sought refuge at his headquarters (see below, pp. 349–50); though whether he was aware of the precedent of 1328–9, when the Chaghadayid khan Eljigidei had assisted the Yuan prince Qoshila to become Qaghan (see p. 83), we cannot know. Possibly Timur anticipated sufficient support from the eastern Mongols in enthroning his candidate and additional assistance, when he moved on into China, from the numerous Mongols who had hitherto elected to serve the Ming. As the only part of the former Mongol empire whose rulers had not embraced Islam, moreover, the Ming territories presented an obvious target for holy war. Indeed, Taizu was believed to have eradicated Islam in China; though the charge that he had slaughtered large numbers of Muslims was almost certainly specious.[171]

According to the Timurid sources, the Great Amir had envisaged an expedition to China as early as 800/1398, only to switch his plans to the invasion of India on learning of Pīr Muḥammad's operations in Sind.[172] It was not until the end of winter in 806/1404 that he embarked on a war against the Ming.[173] An enormous army was mustered for the campaign and advanced to Utrār, on the Sīr-daryā, where Timur died of a fever, however, on the evening of 18 Shaʿbān 807/18 or 19 February 1405.[174] The initial goal, if we can believe Salmānī, had been the subjugation of Mughūlistān 'as far as the frontier of China' (*Khiṭā*),[175] and the amirs were for continuing the campaign, which was certain, in their view, to be crowned with success in view of the fact that Timur's death was still a secret. While Timur's body was taken to Samarkand to be buried in the Gūr-i Mīr, the splendid mausoleum he had commissioned, the centre of his army, under the nominal leadership of Shāhrukh's son Ibrāhīm Sulṭān, duly began to move east from Utrār. But news of the revolt of Timur's grandson Sulṭān Ḥusayn put paid to the plan, and they fell back on Samarkand.[176]

Timur's demise brought relief to the Mughūls (and, possibly, to the Qalmāq Mongols and the Ming). Mīrzā Ḥaydar Dughlāt transmits a story that he had repeatedly heard from his father: a man clad in white and riding a black horse appeared and announced the conqueror's death to the eastern Chaghadayid khan Khiḍr Khwāja, who, to his consternation, had recently been ordered to provide grain for the Chaghatay army en route to China; the mysterious rider then galloped off, ignoring the pleas of the bystanders to tell them more. This transpired, says Ḥaydar, forty-five days before official confirmation of the news arrived.[177] Given what we know of Timur's plans, the tale is surely apocryphal, and the khan concerned was emphatically not Khiḍr Khwāja, who had died in 802/1399 (see below, p. 319).[178] But even had the Mughūls opted for prompt compliance, they would still have endured all the tribulations accompanying the passage of a large army which would have bled dry both the grazing grounds and the agricultural regions, while resistance would have meant bloody subjugation.[179] Although the Ming were evidently aware of Chaghatay preparations to attack China,[180] the Yongle Emperor would later claim, in a letter to Shāhrukh, that Timur had acted as a loyal subordinate;[181] but this was surely a diplomatic posture designed to preserve Ming imperial dignity.

THE DIMENSIONS OF EMPIRE

Al-Maqrīzī's short obituary of Timur describes him as the conqueror of the whole of Iraq, Khurāsān, Samarkand, India (*al-Hind*), Diyār Bakr, Anatolia (*bilād al-Rūm*), Aleppo and Damascus.[182] This is far from a comprehensive list of the regions that Timur attacked. His campaigns had taken him north into the Qipchaq steppe and east to Yüldüz in Mughūlistān. But equally al-Maqrīzī is not including all the territories that Timur ruled. He conquered Khwārazm, Farghāna and parts of the eastern Chaghadayid khanate as far as Kāshghar; he reduced most of the former Ilkhanate, only Azerbaijan, the Jazīra and Iraq remaining imperfectly subdued (and lost within a short interval of his death).

Abrupt shifts in Timur's attention while on campaign could indicate a constant readiness to respond swiftly to events – but perhaps signal the absence of any coherent or long-term strategy. Thus he left India on learning of Barqūq's death in distant Egypt in 801/1399 and broke off his operations in Syria in 803/1401 in order to deal with Jalayirid *revanchisme* in Baghdad. Nor did his triumphs mark the absorption within his dominions of each of the sedentary lands that al-Maqrīzī specifies. For all that 'Rūm as far as Constantinople' and 'Syria as far as Egypt' are listed among the territories conferred on his grandson ʿUmar b. Amīrānshāh in 806/1404,[183] Timur's expeditions against Mamlūk Syria, the Delhi Sultanate and the Ottoman state were not followed by any attempt to incorporate them directly into his empire.[184] He appears to have been satisfied with humbling these competitors and establishing his unquestioned superiority, as he did in the form of tribute and other expressions of submission from the Mamlūk Sultan Faraj. As I shall argue in Chapter 11, one of his principal aims was to amass plunder.

Some regions Timur subjected to a markedly indirect overlordship. In both India and Anatolia he sought to bolster the power of local princes in order to impede the resurgence of a major antagonist. This preoccupation helps to account for his lenient treatment of the Sultan of Kashmir;[185] he was content, too, with securing a tributary ruler in the Punjab. In Anatolia, he chose to adjust the clock by fifty years, promoting strife among Bayezid's sons, reinstating the Ottomans' rivals and distributing among them much of the fallen Sultan's territory. Even in the Iranian lands, he did not favour direct control any more than had the Mongols. Where prompt surrender and cooperation were offered, he retained the existing rulers as his lieutenants. On occasion he reinstated princes who had earlier been dispossessed by his defeated rivals, as he did the rulers of Lur-i Buzurg, ousted earlier by the Muzaffarids;[186] alternatively, an uncooperative prince could be replaced by some disgruntled kinsman, as in Sīstān, or by a local rival, as at Āmul in Māzandarān both in 794/1392 and in 806/1403–4.[187] Only the stronger and more ambitious among the regional dynasties – the Kartids and the Muzaffarids – were completely extinguished; though even in the former case a compliant cousin of the last Kartid monarch was entrusted with the government of Ghūr.[188]

As for the steppe lands, Timur could not realistically expect to establish direct rule over the Jochid dominions or the bulk of Mughūlistān. He may well have harboured the design of reducing Mughūlistān in order to reunite the Chaghadayid ulus, and there is evidence, as we saw, that his final expedition, in 1404–5, was designed to achieve this before proceeding against China (p. 287). But when Ghiyāth al-Dīn Yazdī writes of Timur's conquest of 'all the limits and tribes of Mughūlistān' and the submission of 'the entirety of the Mughūls' as a fait accompli, and claims that Timur's writ (following his victory in 1395) extended over the whole of what had been Toqtamish's dominions,[189] he exaggerates grossly; Timur achieved this, if at all, for no more than a brief interval. Sharaf al-Dīn Yazdī's statement, too, that Timur embarked upon the reduction of Iran in 782/1380–1 because he had completed the conquest of Turan and thus the entire uluses of Chaghadai and Jochi were firmly under the control of his appointees,[190] is equally simplistic.

In these northerly latitudes, especially, the phenomenal pace and scope of Timur's military operations tend to mask the problems that he encountered. On his two Qipchaq campaigns the Chaghatay forces endured severe trials in the wilderness, particularly in the winter of 797–8/1395–6, when they lost the greater part of their livestock.[191] To read the narratives of Timur's wars in the steppes of Jata against Qamar al-Dīn, or in the Qipchaq plains against Toqtamish, is to recognise the difficulties. Albeit the leader of forces in which nomad horse-archers constituted the elite, Timur also commanded Tājīk troops in addition to Turks and Mongols and foot as well as cavalry (see below, pp. 321–2); they also comprised heavy cavalry, complete with horse-armour (*bar-gustuwān*), even on campaign in the steppe against Toqtamish.[192] He therefore faced the same disadvantages that confronted sedentary armies in dealing with a highly mobile and frequently elusive nomadic enemy, and that would face his descendants in turn – outlined, for instance, in Ḥaydar Dughlāt's litany of the obstacles that Timur's great-grandson Sultan Abū Saʿīd (d. 873/1469) met with when trying to curb the depredations of his Mughūl neighbours by dint of force.[193] If Timur's record in his conflict with Jata looks impressive alongside Abū Saʿīd's, he was also more successful there than in the Pontic–Caspian steppes, where he settled for demolishing the economic basis of the Qipchaq khanate and left the field to Toqtamish's enemies.[194]

We shall never know whether Timur could have achieved against the Ming anything like the success he enjoyed elsewhere in Eurasia, or even whether he could have imposed his candidate on the throne of the Northern Yuan. Still less can we be confident that victory over the Ming would have spelled the end of Chinese civilisation.[195] Timur's previous successes had nevertheless established him as a colossus bestriding the central and eastern Islamic world and John of Sulṭāniyya assured his readers that Timur had never suffered defeat in person.[196] Ibn ʿArabshāh conjures up the names of three obscure figures who are said to have defied the conqueror,[197] but John's claim is largely true, especially of Timur's years as head of the ulus. Even if the sources play down – or maybe even ignore – engagements where his lieutenants were worsted in his absence,[198] he achieved an astounding number of victories in the field. The next chapter will try to analyse the causes, and assess the limitations, of this unalloyed sequence of triumphs.

CHAPTER 11
THE FORGING OF AN EMPIRE: THE FUNCTION AND CONDUCT OF WAR

We must now appraise Timur's war aims. The chronology of the military operations which he mounted over a period of three decades or more does not readily suggest a coherent strategy. Generally speaking, they were designed to focus and absorb the energies of the unruly nomads of Transoxiana, but they undoubtedly arose also from more sophisticated impulses. Timur's first campaigns, against Khwārazm and Mughūlistān, suggest that his initial goal was the restoration and consolidation of Chaghadai's ulus. At some point he began to conceive of his task as greater, although when is unclear. Whether he aimed to revive the Mongol empire, as often claimed, is a question deferred to Chapter 14.

TRIBUTE, RANSOM AND PLUNDER

A major imperative behind Timur's restless campaigning was the acquisition of great quantities of loot. Golden speaks of him as engaged in 'a kind of plundering "tourism" of his neighbours', while Morgan summarises Timur's career as 'really a series of plundering expeditions on a massive scale'.[1] According to Christian, 'Timur's hybrid army of pastoralists, infantry, and artillery was much more expensive than traditional steppe armies'; hence he 'treated conquered regions beyond his Chagatay [*sic*] *ulus* as looting zones'.[2] It should be recalled, however, that Chinggis Khan's forces had likewise been heterogeneous in character, and thus no less costly, by the time he brought Transoxiana and Khwārazm under direct Mongol control; yet this did not prevent the Mongols from establishing their rule over a vast area. But in any event the priority given to plundering militated against the creation of a Timurid empire in any real sense. The administration of an extensive swathe of territory is a liability; it involves heavy expenditure on the maintenance of garrisons and the annual transportation and accounting of revenues. Nor could land envisaged as a permanent acquisition be treated in the rapacious manner that characterised raids into enemy territory. This is why Timur's military operations have the semblance of near-ludicrous inefficiency, inasmuch as he often had to 'conquer' the same region more than once. There was greater profit in simply looting cities and mulcting their populations, withdrawing, and repeating the process a few years later. In Baumer's words, Timur's conquests were 'not so much an empire as a zone of war and influence'.[3]

Conversely, the enormous riches acquired as plunder fuelled Timur's campaigns and served to maintain the momentum of his imperial project, which could never have relied solely on the tax-yield of his dominions. The treasuries of the Kartids of Herat, the kings of Sīstān, the Muzaffarids and the Sayyid rulers of Māzandarān all went to swell his coffers.[4] According to Ḥāfiẓ-i Abrū, he obtained 700 camel-loads of silver from the fortress of Māhāna in Māzandarān.[5] Any ruler, moreover, who capitulated to Timur's troops was required henceforth to pay regular tribute. The sums involved have seldom come down to us. Although the annual tribute from Hurmuz, at the time of the expedition under Timur's grandson Muḥammad Sulṭān in 798/1396, amounted to 300,000 dinars, and its malik offered four years' arrears in a single payment, it is doubtful whether much of this was in fact paid.[6] From the 'Gīlānāt' in 806/1404 Timur received as tribute 10,000 *mann*s (perhaps 30,000 kilograms) of silk, 7,000 horses and 3,000 oxen.[7] At a less exalted level, the 'Alavari', Kurdish nomads near Nishapur, contributed annually 3,000 camels and 15,000 sheep in return for grazing rights.[8]

Even cities that capitulated readily were subjected to a crippling ransom – the 'security payment (*māl-i amānī*) by way of horseshoe money (*na'l-bahā*) for the victorious host', as Sharaf al-Dīn Yazdī puts it when recounting the surrender of Isfahan – that was systematically collected by the officials of Timur's supreme *dīwān*.[9] The means employed were usually violent but there was the odd exception: the conqueror was so delighted by news of the birth in 796/1394 of his grandson Muḥammad Taraghai (Ulugh Beg), we are told, that he overlooked the resistance of Mārdīn and dispensed with the ransom.[10] But a variety of torments obliged the citizens of Baghdad in 795/1393 to disgorge a total of 135 million dirhams.[11] Following Delhi's surrender an indemnity had been determined, but its collection by the Chaghatay troops provoked strong resistance, with the result that they ran riot and took to widespread looting. Yazdī lists the objects collected: rubies, diamonds, different kinds of luxury textiles, precious vessels, gold and silver vases and quantities of coin beyond computation. All this was redistributed after Timur's return to Samarkand.[12]

Mignanelli's account of Timur's unscrupulous measures to extort wealth from the Damascene populace conveys a sufficiently damning image of the conqueror's greed and disingenuousness to be worthy of Ibn ʿArabshāh's pen. Initially, in his dealings with the four qadis who had been sent out to negotiate with him, Timur professed to be interested only in confiscating the goods of Sultan Faraj and those who had fled prior to the invaders' arrival; his agents also compiled inventories of the citizens' property, purportedly as a precaution against looting by his men. But once the citadel had fallen Timur claimed to be disappointed by the amount of the Sultan's wealth unearthed there and demanded monetary compensation for the exertions of his troops. A large quantity of money having been produced, he found fault with the coins, which were of debased silver (in sharp contrast with the Chaghadayid issues), and required a still bigger sum. When this was agreed, he raised two fresh issues in succession: the need to compensate the Khurāsānī troops in his army and the expenses he would incur in leaving the city and marching home to Samarkand. Spurred on by the expectation of seeing Timur depart at last, the qadis collected a further contribution, only to be confronted with a sudden and unexpected change of tactic. The conqueror handed the city over to his troops, who entered Damascus armed with the inventories and proceeded to extort wealth from the citizens by means of various torments.[13]

These details are sufficiently corroborated in the Arabic sources, notably al-Maqrīzī's *Sulūk*,[14] for us to regard Mignanelli's narrative as trustworthy in its essentials. Timurid authors further tell us that the alloyed silver was melted down in Timur's camp and reminted in purer metal for ease of transportation back from Syria,[15] an expedient not encountered in the context of the conqueror's other sieges. Whether we can take Timur's conduct on this occasion as otherwise typical, however, is hard to judge. It was rare, certainly, for a city that had surrendered peaceably and offered an indemnity to then suffer a violent sack.[16] Perhaps we need to entertain the possibility that Damascus received harsher treatment in view of Timur's marked antipathy towards its people, which will be dealt with below (see pp. 333, 379–80).

Nor could the inhabitants of a city that yielded necessarily expect to be left *in situ*. Booty importantly comprised a human element, and Timur's troops uprooted conquered populations just as the Mongols had done; Toqtamish acted similarly in Azerbaijan in 787/1385, when some 200,000 people were deported to the Qipchaq steppe.[17] When ʿUmar Shaykh took Kāshghar in 779/1377–8, he removed its population to his own urban base at Andijān.[18] On the surrender of the garrison of Turshīz, in Quhistān, Timur treated them generously but, in appreciation of their military prowess, despatched them to man strongpoints on the borders of Turkestan.[19] In 806/1403–4 we find bodies of Khalaj (from present-day Afghanistan) and Arabs stationed in the vicinity of Sāwa, Qum and Kāshān.[20] Entire tribal groupings, like the Qara Tatars from Anatolia and the Jāʾūn-i Qurbān Mongols from Khurāsān, were conveyed to Transoxiana;[21] in the former case, Ḥāfiẓ-i Abrū notes that Timur took care to handle them diplomatically until his departure from Anatolia.[22]

Among the more specific goals of Timur's looting campaigns was the embellishment of cities in Transoxiana and the creation of a court distinguished for its cultural and economic splendour.[23] Clavijo testifies to Timur's desire to make Samarkand more populous, claiming that the conqueror had increased its population by 100,000 or more,[24] and we saw earlier how the inhabitants of Ürgench and its hinterland were removed to Samarkand in 790/1388. Skilled personnel of various categories, of which Clavijo supplies a list, were carried off to Samarkand: from Tabriz in 788/1386, for instance, from Fārs in 790/1388 and 795/1393, from Iraq in the latter year and from Damascus in 803/1401.[25] Clavijo mentions enslaved artisans who produced large amounts of armour for Timur's troops.[26] The 200 masons engaged in building Timur's new mosque in Samarkand were drafted from Azerbaijan, Fārs and India, among other lands.[27] The conqueror's love of the hunt even prompted him to collect falconers from Damascus.[28] Muslim divines were also removed from captured cities, though not necessarily to Samarkand: 'all the learned, administrators and Qur'ān-readers' from Khwārazm, for example, were deported to Kish in 781/1379–80, as were 200 from Herat in 783/1381.[29] On occasion Timur's actions had a primarily symbolic purpose, much like the naming of palaces in Samarkand after illustrious cities taken in Iran. Following the capture of Herat in 783/1381, he removed its gates and installed them at the entrance to Kish.[30]

It is clear from our sources that not just enslaved personnel but livestock formed an important element of the booty. Jahāngīr, returning from Mughūlistān in 776/1375, presented his father with an abundant booty in captives, horses and sheep, and Timur's own expedition to the eastern khanate in 791/1389 gained countless prisoners, horses, sheep and camels.[31] Sharaf al-Dīn Yazdī tells us that after the engagement on the Qundurcha in 793/1391 ordinary troopers acquired horses and sheep in such numbers that they had to leave many behind; Shāmī says that on this occasion each infantryman returned with ten to twenty horses, while a cavalryman brought back 100 or more.[32] 'Innumerable flocks and herds' fell into Chaghatay hands during Timur's second invasion of the Qipchaq khanate in 797/1395.[33] Fresh mounts were particularly vital, given the heavy casualties among the horses, for instance in bad weather during the operations in the Qipchaq steppes: as Timur pointedly reminded his one-time protégé Toqtamish, he had lost a great many horses on campaign against Orus Khan in 778/1376–7.[34]

Livestock were not acquired just from major nomadic powers. Campaigns in Diyār Bakr against the Türkmen in 789/1387, 795/1392–3 and 796/1394 brought in horses, camels, sheep and oxen in prodigious numbers, as did a campaign in the Shūshtar region in 795/1393 and operations around Abulustān in 803/1401.[35] During the withdrawal from Syria, roughly 200,000 sheep were taken in the vicinity of Aleppo and more than 800,000 sheep from the Türkmen in the region of Qalʿat al-Rūm, so that in Timur's encampment a sheep sold for as little as one dinar.[36] Manz suggests that the booty 'may not have done much more than make up his losses in livestock'.[37] But Timur often had the animals distributed among the rank and file, as at Aleppo, where the booty, livestock and mounts acquired, he claimed, exceeded whatever had fallen into his hands in the Sīstān, Hindūstān, Māzandarān, Khwārazm, Shiraz, Toghmaq (Qipchaq steppe) and Mughūl campaigns.[38] Rewarding the Chaghatay nomads in this fashion, both as a matter of campaign logistics and as a guarantee of loyalty, was vital.

TRIUMPH IN A FRACTURED WORLD

The hyperbole of Timurid authors aside, the tracts under Timur's direct rule embraced an impressively vast area and the geographical span of his campaigns was truly extraordinary. We must now try to explain his success. In his biography of Timur, al-Maqrīzī observed that the conqueror's appearance coincided with an era of division and disunity (*ḥāl ikhtilāf wa-iftirāq*) and specifies some of the conflicts from which Timur profited, in particular the strife within the Qipchaq khanate.[39] Ibn ʿArabshāh, too, makes the Ottoman Sultan Bayezid ascribe Timur's triumphs to the disharmony among his opponents.[40] Qamar al-Dīn's actions in Mughūlistān facilitated Timur's success in both halves of the Chaghadayid ulus,[41] and the internecine struggles within the Jalayirid and the Muzaffarid dynasties, together with the hostilities between the Kartids of Herat, Amīr Walī and the Sarbadārs, which we noticed in Chapter 6, all contributed to undermine resistance in Iran. Although some of his enemies had earlier cooperated against a mutual rival, there is no indication that any of them were ready to unite against Timur. In addition, this incessant conflict generated support for his invasion among those who sought security that their current rulers could not provide. Moreover, until only a few years before his death Timur continued to benefit from circumstances over a wide expanse of Eurasia, such as the political crises that the deaths of a cluster of monarchs in 801–2/1398–9 – Temür Qutlugh, Khiḍr Khwāja, Barqūq and Ming Taizu (Hongwu) – unleashed upon the Jochid polity, Mughūlistān and the Mamlūk and Chinese empires respectively.[42]

It is always easy to identify periods of acute internal division in order to explain the triumph of the unifier from outside. Chinggis Khan and his successors too had exploited the internal factionalism or external rivalries of many of the states against which they waged war. Where half a century previously Timur would have been confronted by a unitary khanate embracing the whole of Iran or by a strong and aggressive power in the Qipchaq steppe, he now faced a number of competing states in Iran and a Qipchaq khanate where (until its conquest by Toqtamish) authority was fragmented at the centre and challenged at the peripheries – not to mention the enfeebled condition of the Delhi Sultanate, to which al-Maqrīzī makes no reference.[43] Local conflicts and tensions also played directly into Timur's hands, as he profited from the adhesion of those who welcomed his arrival and actively sought his intervention to displace an unpopular ruler. According to Mamlūk authors, Sulṭān Aḥmad's subjects, estranged by his tyrannical conduct, twice invited Timur to take their city.[44] So too the Sarbadārs, the Āq-Qūyūnlū and Anatolian princes ousted by the Ottomans all solicited his aid.

TIMUR AND HIS TROOPS ON CAMPAIGN

We are given relatively little idea of the tactics Timur employed on the battlefield, which seem to have included the feigned retreats and flank attacks practised by the Mongols (and naturally many others before them).[45] Mignanelli heard that when attacked by the forces of the Mamlūk governor of Aleppo, Timur's army deliberately opened up a path for the Syrian troops to penetrate their lines and then surrounded them,[46] a tactic known to have been adopted by the Mongols at Mohi in 1241. Ghiyāth al-Dīn Yazdī furnishes a brief account of the final conflict with Shāh Manṣūr near Shiraz, when the Chaghatay left wing maintained dense arrow fire and rolled up Shāh Manṣūr's right wing behind his centre, while the Chaghatay right succeeded in taking the enemy's left wing from the rear.[47] When Amīrānshāh was sent by his father to Khurāsān in 791/1389 to suppress a rising by the Jā'ūn-i Qurbān and a body of Sarbadārs, his right and left wings are said to have enveloped the enemy troops 'in the style of the hunt' (*shikārī-wār*) – namely, by encircling them within a contracting ring (*nerge*, *jirge*), a manoeuvre regularly employed by the Mongols in the past.[48] Timur used a similar tactic against Bayezid at Ankara,[49] and he may have done so when engaging the forces of Sultan Maḥmūd Shāh and Mallū Khan outside Delhi in 801/1398.[50] But this was by no means typical of the engagements that his troops fought, and here one of the principal reasons for the Chaghatay victory was the precautions Timur took against the Sultan's elephants, a major threat of which his men had no previous experience. Sharaf al-Dīn Yazdī says that Timur ordered the erection of a palisade and the excavation of a trench in front of his army and had a line of buffaloes drawn up beyond the trench; the foot soldiers further scattered caltrops in the elephants' path to impede their formidable charge. Ibn ʿArabshāh mentions the caltrops, but both he and Clavijo add that the Chaghatay forces panicked the beasts by sending forward camels loaded with burning reeds.[51] Such detail as this is rare, however.

Many of the claims made for the size of Timur's armies are surely exaggerated. John of Sulṭāniyya, for example, gives a total of a million men and 1,500,000 for the force that Timur took across the Euphrates to attack Aleppo. Ibn Khaldūn assured the Sultan of Morocco that the forces at Timur's command were without limit and probably exceeded a million. A report from a Genoese to the Venetians in Crete in 1401 alleged that Timur had 700,000 men (not counting others who manned his siege engines). And indeed all the numbers supplied by Schiltberger – a million men at the siege of Sivas, 1,600,000 at Ankara, and 1,800,000 on the China expedition – are ludicrously high.[52] At the opposite extreme, a report from the governor of Aleppo to Sultan Barqūq in 796/1393–4 says that 240,000 troops accompanied Timur, but that only 30,000 were warriors and the rest a rabble (*bawsh*),[53] which certainly smacks of Mamlūk chauvinism. Ibn al-Shiḥna, followed by Ibn ʿArabshāh, states that there were 800,000 men on Timur's muster-roll.[54] Mignanelli, rejecting this same total of 800,000, estimated that without cooks, stone-cutters and other labourers they numbered only 300,000; he set those in attendance on Timur at 30,000.[55] Both the figures of 30,000 quoted in this paragraph might refer to Timur's personal guard.

Some of the numbers we are given for particular campaigns have an authentic ring. Early in 807/towards the end of 1404 Amir Burunduq reported to Timur that the forces mustered for the campaign against China totalled 200,000 horse and foot.[56] The chronicler of Saint-Denis reports that Timur's army at Ankara comprised 100,000 men. An Italian annalist heard that Timur had attacked Damascus with eleven tümens (110,000), while Timur himself in 793/1391 left an inscription in present-day Kazakhstan stating that he had moved against Toqtamish with 200,000 men.[57] When confronted by figures expressed as tümens, we should recall that they are notional: at any one time the tümen is unlikely to have been at full strength owing to casualties of warfare (or to disease and adverse weather).[58]

But Chaghatay armies as a whole were clearly large. They were not simply made up of nomadic cavalry from Central Asia. Mongol armies had ceased, at an early juncture, to comprise exclusively steppe cavalry: years of campaigning against the Jin empire had enabled Chinggis Khan to add Chinese infantry and siege engineers, for instance, to the forces with which he attacked the Khwārazmshāh. Similarly, Timur's armies included contingents from conquered sedentary territories governed by Timurid princes or those supplied by satellite rulers or by urban centres: horsemen and infantry, like the 'foot-soldiers of Khurāsān' who participated in the Indian campaign.[59] There was an inspector (*tovachi*) specifically for the infantry.[60] Some contingents were highly specialised. During the campaigns of 797/1395 in the Elburz range and 806/1404 against the Georgians a contingent from the Mekrit (Bekrin?), skilled in mountain warfare, performed an important role.[61]

Certain rulers appear to have contributed only to operations adjacent to their own dominions: Pīr Pādishāh b. Luqmān, ruler of Astarābād, for example, accompanied Timur's expeditions against Gīlān and Māzandarān;[62] the Shīrwānshāh Shaykh Ibrāhīm, Ṭahartan of Arzinjān and Qarā ʿUthmān of the Āq-Qūyūnlū were all present at Ankara.[63] But others fought on occasion at an enormous distance from their homeland.[64] In 796/1394, for instance, we find the loyal king of Sīstān, Shāh-i Shāhān, with Timur's forces in the Muzaffarid territories, where he subsequently played a prominent role in the three-year investment of Sīrjān, and still later he accompanied Timur against the Jalayirids, Mamlūks and Ottomans.[65] The troops of Fārs, under the conqueror's grandson Rustam, joined Timur for the siege of the citadel of Behesni early in 803/in the autumn of 1400.[66] The forces for the China expedition came from Mā warāʾ al-nahr, Turkestan, Khwārazm, Balkh, Badakhshān, Khurāsān, Sīstān, Māzandarān, Azerbaijan and Iraq, and included the Qara Tatars who had been brought from Anatolia.[67]

Admittedly, a modern historian estimates that Timur's army before Delhi was at least twice the size of the enemy host,[68] and the Timurid sources set the latter at merely 10,000 horse and 20,000 foot,[69] although this is difficult to reconcile with the claim by Shāmī and Ghiyāth al-Dīn that the number of 'Hindu' dead cast into the shade the slaughter at Isfahan or in Sīstān.[70] At Ankara the Chaghatay forces appear to have outnumbered those of Bayezid, of which, moreover, the majority were infantry.[71] On the other hand, Sharaf al-Dīn Yazdī says that Toqtamish's army on the Qundurcha in 793/1391 surpassed Timur's by several *qoshuns*, and Clavijo learned that the cavalry whom Timur led against Toqtamish in 797/1395 were fewer than the enemy.[72] Both statements are certainly plausible. We have seen testimony (above, p. 211) that earlier in the fourteenth century the forces available to the Jochid khans may have exceeded those of the Chaghadayids – and although Timur's army was swollen by troops from parts of the Iranian world, the manpower of the eastern Chaghadayid lands, conversely, was largely beyond his control. It was perhaps for this reason that the Castilian envoy judged Toqtamish to have been a far more formidable antagonist than even Bayezid and the engagement on the Terek as eclipsing the victory at Ankara.[73]

It was more than a matter of numbers, however. No less important than the size of Timur's armies were his talents as a general,[74] his willingness to take risks, the discipline he maintained among his troops and his capacity to inspire their loyalty, which elicits appreciative comment even from the hostile Ibn ʿArabshāh.[75] During his first advance into the Qipchaq steppe, rather than cross the Ural (Yayiq) at recognised fording points, Timur had his entire army swim across the river, thereby frustrating Toqtamish's plan of ambush.[76] Shāmī speaks of him as observing 'the usages of the *tūra* and *yāsāq* of past monarchs in the stations of battle'.[77] It is unclear what precisely this entailed. Timur was not, however, averse to innovation. Sharaf al-Dīn Yazdī was impressed by his unprecedented disposal of his forces into seven divisions (*qul*s) prior to the battle on the Qundurcha; though from what he says the advantages of this arrangement seem to have lain primarily in the miraculous associations of the number seven, signalling the conqueror's divine inspiration.[78]

For the China campaign, according to Ḥaydar Dughlāt, two milk cows and two milk goats were allotted to each individual over and above the existing (unspecified) body of provisions.[79] Ḥāfiẓ-i Abrū tells us that late in 792/1390, prior to the first Qipchaq expedition, a written oath (*möchelge*) was taken from the *tovachi*s that they would require every man without exception, whether Turk or Tājīk, horseman or foot soldier, to bring provisions and equipment for one year. There follows a highly specific list of arms, equipment and implements (including pickaxes, spades, rope and even a hundred needles per man), to be presented for inspection when required. It was expressly forbidden for anyone to bake his own bread or *tutmaj*.[80] Yazdī appears to be speaking of this oath in the context of a dire shortage of provisions that arose in the course of this same campaign. Here the troops are expressly ordered to refrain from cooking their own food and to be satisfied with porridge (*bulamāq*) from the kitchens (*maṭbūkh*),[81] a dish which Clavijo seemingly describes as made from thin cakes of flour mixed with sour milk.[82] The measure proved ineffective, but Timur's purpose, no doubt, had been to eradicate inequalities rather than to maximise readiness for battle. When campaigning in the steppes in winter, he replenished the army's stock of provisions by means of the hunt, to which he was addicted. It is likely that when operating in more populous tracts his forces lived mainly off the land – and its population.[83] In Ḥaydar's account of the preparations for the attack on China, the Mughūl khan Khiḍr Khwāja was told to see to the maximum quantity of cultivation with a view to the army's passage through his territories.[84]

Timur imposed a firm discipline upon his armies, exacting an oath from all the amirs of a thousand and a hundred in 786/1384 not to leave their companies (*qoshun*s) on pain of death (a stipulation reminiscent of one of Chinggis Khan's *yasa*s); an order to the same effect was issued during the first Qipchaq campaign in 793/1391.[85] Troopers who looted or took slaves prior to receiving Timur's authorisation were punished with death.[86] Ibn Khaldūn told al-Maqrīzī of a group of sappers at Damascus who were executed for fleeing – one reason why his troops tended to stand their ground.[87] Even Timur's grandson Iskandar b. ʿUmar Shaykh was bastinadoed for heading an unauthorised campaign into Jata in 802/1400.[88]

Sharaf al-Dīn Yazdī writes of Timur's restlessness and reluctance to abandon any project he had embarked upon, and observes that restraint (*iʿtidāl*) was foreign to his temperament.[89] There is evidence that his commanders were reluctant to participate in some of his enterprises. Objections were possibly voiced to war with the Mamlūks, and Ḥāfiẓ-i Abrū recalls that the amirs sought to dissuade Timur from attacking Bayezid.[90] Timur's armies, moreover, were often required to cover enormous distances in a remarkably short time, as in the march from Yüldüz to Samarkand, accomplished in three weeks in 791/1388,[91] or in their first advance on Baghdad in 795/1393.[92] They were also forced to campaign in extraordinarily severe winter conditions, particularly in the Qipchaq steppes.[93] In Syria one of Ibn ʿArabshāh's informants encountered two of Timur's soldiers, who professed contrition for their crimes but told him of their conscription into the conqueror's army and of the harsh discipline and other hardships to which they were subject.[94] So determined was the Great Amir to move swiftly and strike when the enemy was unprepared that he sometimes neglected to allow his men much-needed rest, provoking fruitless remonstrations from his amirs before and during the Syrian campaign.[95]

Yet still they followed him. One reason was that he shared their privations on the march and took part in battle alongside them. And while we should not discount impulses such as loyalty, a powerful incentive, no doubt, was Timur's frequent practice of distributing the proceeds of victory among his troops – the plunder from Mughūlistān in 791/1389, for instance, the indemnity (*amān*) from Baghdad (795/1393), Malaṭiya and other cities, the plunder from the citadel of Aleppo and the treasury at Kutāhiya.[96] At Delhi each of Timur's troopers acquired some 150 captives – men, women and children – as his personal slaves, the humblest soldier gaining twenty.[97] On losing most of his livestock at Astrakhan in the harsh winter of 797/1395 Timur took pity on his men and distributed all the grain and other booty from Astrakhan and Sarai.[98] During the retreat from India, he ordered those who had gained a share of the plunder to relinquish half their gains to anyone with none.[99]

MILITARY INTELLIGENCE

Like the Mongols before him, Timur had access to excellent intelligence. The courier system within his dominions enabled news to be transmitted extremely rapidly. Clavijo writes of the relays of horses at intervals of one day's or half a day's journey between Tabriz and Samarkand, as also throughout his dominions, as if this was Timur's own creation. But it must represent a revival of the *yam*, which had decayed after the end of the Ilkhanate and to which Timur had made modifications.[100] In 789/1387 an *ilchi* bringing news of Toqtamish's invasion covered the distance from Samarkand to Shiraz in a mere seventeen days.[101]

It is clear that the Great Amir, again like his Mongol precursors, took pains to acquire information regarding political conditions in regions which he planned to invade.[102] He repeatedly sought to learn the size of Qadi Burhān al-Dīn's forces and to ascertain who were his allies and his rivals.[103] According to Ibn ʿArabshāh, he had stationed spies within his own territories and throughout other realms, and drew on the reports of merchants, craftsmen, physicians, seasoned travellers and others, among whom this author lists – in a taxonomy that is more exhaustive than poetic – 'vicious wrestlers and dissolute acrobats' (*maṣāriʿ sharīr wa-bahlawān fājir*), 'voluble *qalandar*s and roving mystics' (*qalandarī qawwāl wa-ḥaydarī jawwāl*) and 'charming water-carriers and genial cobblers' (*saqqā' ẓarīf wa-ḥidhā laṭīf*).[104] There were merchants among those arrested in Cairo in 796/1394 on suspicion of espionage (see above, p. 301).

Not all Timur's intelligence reached him through such lowly individuals. We saw (p. 191) how Amīr Ḥājjī Sayf al-Dīn reported to him on the *mulūk al-ṭawā'if* in Iran in 780/1379. Regarding the situation in the Delhi Sultanate Timur was briefed by the Khokhar chief Shaykhā in 800/1398.[105] He interrogated members of the Ming embassy, as well as the leaders of a merchant caravan that had come from China, about the wealth and manpower of that country;[106] and according to Ibn ʿArabshāh, he sent word from Rūm to Allāhdād, his lieutenant at Āshpara, requiring a report on the terrain, routes and landmarks in the eastern regions as far as the Ming territories, evidently in preparation for his invasion.[107] While quartered outside Damascus, Timur made use, too, of Ibn Khaldūn, whom he ordered to describe in writing the tracts between Egypt and Morocco.[108] Some authors have assumed that he envisaged a military expedition along the North African coast,[109] and this is possibly what underlay Ibn Khaldūn's later sense of the need to justify his presence at Timur's court to the Moroccan Sultan (see above, p. 39). But Timur could simply have been contemplating commercial opportunities rather than plans of conquest.

The other arm of Timur's policy – deliberate disinformation regarding his own movements – could prove highly effective, and he acquired a reputation for guile. Roux commented that the ruses attributed to Timur in the sources would appear to us infantile or 'worthy of a Western' but for the fact that they proved successful.[110] He might have added that they were hardly novel either. Thus during the advance on Diyār Bakr in 796/1394 Timur spread rumours of his retreat so that his opponents were unprepared for his attack.[111] Ibn Khaldūn learned from Timur's imam ʿAbd al-Jabbār that it was the conqueror's practice to head his army in the wrong direction in order to mislead the opposition;[112] and Clavijo heard that during a campaign in the Qipchaq steppe Timur had the troops' womenfolk disguised as men and left to guard his camp, to deceive the foe while he and his forces secretly moved off to attack Toqtamish from a different quarter.[113] He also employed ruses to undermine an enemy's credibility, as in 803/1400, when in a letter sent to Aleppo he mentioned that its governor had invited him to invade Syria; clearly he anticipated that the letter would be read in the presence of other Mamlūk amirs and would sow suspicion and dissension among his opponents.[114]

ARMAMENTS

If the military resources which fuelled Timur's conquests did not differ appreciably from those of his Mongol precursors, his armies certainly came to include one element that Chinggis Khan had not possessed. His military arsenal after 1398 included 120 war-elephants appropriated from the Delhi Sultan's elephant stable (*pīl-khāna*). Although this has been questioned and the suggestion made that they failed to reach Samarkand and perished on the return march,[115] their arrival in the city is recorded by Sharaf al-Dīn, who tells us that ninety-five elephants were drafted to carry materials for the construction of Timur's new mosque there.[116] In any case a number were detached and distributed to various cities or client rulers in Iran and Anatolia,[117] and these, probably with some from Samarkand, were then deployed in further campaigns. Clavijo describes how they had swords affixed to their tusks and aimed blows at the enemy.[118] There were elephants in Timur's army in Syria in 803/1401 (when Ibn ʿArabshāh reports that they were used to trample to death captured enemy soldiers) and on the Baghdad and Anatolian campaigns of 804/1401–2; at the battle of Ankara they carried archers and naphtha-throwers.[119] Schiltberger tells us that the conqueror had thirty-two elephants at Ankara; the *Chronographia regum Francorum* at one point specifies twenty-six; and John of Sulṭāniyya says that Timur possessed a total of forty.[120] Harsh weather, however, deterred Timur from taking elephants with him to China.[121] Given the prestige associated with possession of such beasts at that time, contemporary authors perhaps had fewer reservations regarding the value of elephants in warfare than do modern scholars.[122] Clavijo voices the opinion that one elephant was worth a thousand foot soldiers in battle.[123]

The leitmotiv of Timur's campaigns was the investment of fortified cities and towns. His sieges were on the whole highly successful affairs (the exception is the stronghold of Alinjaq in Siwnikʿ, which held out against a Chaghatay division for ten years with Georgian aid),[124] and Clavijo lists skilled engineers (*maestros de yngenios*) among the artisans carried off by Timur's armies and assembled at Samarkand.[125] A problematic question is his access to gunpowder weaponry. A later Mamlūk author contrasts the successful invasion of the Mamlūk empire by the Ottomans in 1517 with Timur's attack over a century earlier, on the grounds that the Ottomans used cannon and Timur did not; but this has now been refuted.[126] The Mongols had acquired gunpowder from the Chinese in the early thirteenth century and were deploying it in Western Asia by the 1250s, perhaps primarily in the form of incendiary devices;[127] although it has been pointed out that there is no evidence for the use of gunpowder in Mongol sieges of Mamlūk fortifications in Syria.[128]

Timur certainly employed Greek Fire, that is naphtha (*nafṭ*, *ātish-u nafṭ*), in his campaigns, for example against Georgian strongholds and the Damascus citadel and in the battle of Ankara.[129] There is evidence, however, that his arsenal included gunpowder weaponry. The issue hinges on the sense of the term *raʿd*, which in modern Persian means 'gun', 'cannon'.[130] One of the earliest uses of the word occurs in relation to the siege of Yazd in 751/1350–1, when the Injuid army had fired a projectile (*yak tīr raʿd andākhtand*) into the city.[131] Naṭanzī refers to Timur's use of *raʿd* against Ürgench (781/1379) and Baghdad (803/1401).[132] Shāmī and Yazdī first mention *raʿd* in Chaghatay siege warfare at Awnīk in 796/1394,[133] and say that the

Chaghatay forces employed naphtha and *ra'd* in naval operations off the coast of Māzandarān in 794/1392.[134] Ḥāfiẓ-i Abrū speaks of a *kamān-i ra'd* ('explosive bow') used by Amīrānshāh when investing Herat in 791/1389.[135] Yazdī has Timur's troops using explosives (*ra'd*, *ra'd-andāzī*) against Smyrna, against the citadel of Damascus and against Fīrūzkūh in 806/1404.[136]

Gunpowder weaponry was available to some of Timur's opponents. Yazdī says that during Timur's investment of the citadel of Aleppo and the siege of Kamākh by Muḥammad Sulṭān in 804/1402 *ra'd* was deployed by both sides.[137] The army that confronted him outside Delhi in 801/1398 included warriors armed with explosive devices (*ra'd-andāzān*).[138] Shāmī lists *ra'd* among the armaments deployed against Timur's army by the garrisons of Aleppo and Damascus, and Ḥāfiẓ-i Abrū mentions a *kamān-i ra'd* among the weaponry of the Frankish defenders of Smyrna.[139] But at one juncture Yazdī, commenting how Syrian armies habitually used flame-throwers and explosive devices (*ātish-bāzī-u ra'd-andāzī*) and set some store by them,[140] seems to imply that the Chaghatay forces made little or no use of this kind of armament. It is noteworthy that when describing Timur's sieges of Turshīz (784/1382), Van (789/1387), Takrīt (796/1393) and Sivas (803/1400), he refers only to stone-hurling catapults (*manjanīq-u 'arrāda*) alongside siege towers and sapping.[141]

When Yazdī alludes to the din made by *ra'd*, which terrified the ruler of Hurmuz into submission, and to the clamour of the 'explosive bow' (*kamān-i ra'd-fighān*) at Damascus, the association with thunderous noise evidently indicates something quite distinct from naphtha.[142] According to Ibn Shihāb Yazdī, among the forces of Kirmān sent against Azerbaijan in 808/1406, only a year after Timur's death, were 150 rocket-firers (? *takhsh-andāz*) and gunpowder operatives (*ra'd-andāz*), a hundred of them mounted: this last detail must exclude the possibility that they were deploying stone-throwing catapults. When the same author describes how forces from Yazd and Abarqūh attacking the city of Kirmān in 819/1416 included 450 of such troops, his tone betrays surprise at their relative lack of progress.[143] But in any event we should recall that at this time gunpowder-based weaponry was still far from superseding stone-throwing engines in effectiveness,[144] and even a relative lack of it is unlikely to have put Timur's forces at a significant disadvantage.

CLEMENCY, PERFIDY AND THE CALCULATED USE OF TERROR

The accounts of many of Timur's campaigns make grim reading and have gained him a truly unenviable reputation. Inevitably, parallels with the Mongol campaigns of conquest come to mind. Like Chinggis Khan – and many other conquerors, among them his antagonist Bayezid Yildirim – Timur preferred prompt submission to a campaign which brought with it a heavy cost in money or men.[145] Princes who yielded outright generally benefited from his clemency and even generosity; resistance invited acts of savage violence.[146] His initial overtures stressed both his good will and (pointedly) his reluctance to sanction massacres. His indulgent response to the Artuqid Sultan al-Ẓāhir ʿĪsā of Mārdīn, who more than once reneged on an earlier submission, is a striking exception in this context.[147]

Vengeance had long played an important role in steppe society,[148] and Timur had an inconveniently long memory when it came to personal grudges. If he was slow to take revenge on ʿAlī Beg of the Jā'ūn-i Qurbān (above, p. 292), a local malik in Sīstān, who had fired an arrow at him when he and Amīr Ḥusayn were leaving that region not long afterwards, was recognised and put to death when he brought gifts to the conqueror in 785/1383–4.[149] Two years previously the inhabitants of the village of Khūrāsha, in the Juwayn district, were massacred in retaliation for having killed Timur's kinsmen Ḥājjī Barlās and his brother, another offence dating back more than twenty years.[150]

The slaughter was especially extensive when defiance had led to the death of someone of high status in Timur's army. When ʿUmar Shaykh was killed by an arrow at Khurmātū in Kurdistan in Rabīʿ I 796/January–February 1394, his death spelled annihilation for the local populace.[151] Five hundred of the inhabitants of Deopalpur in the Punjab paid with their lives for the treacherous killing of Timur's officer Musāfir Kābulī, and their wives and offspring were carried off into captivity.[152] Timur took harsh measures, as had Chinggis Khan's forces, against cities where his representatives and negotiators had been killed or which had reneged on an earlier submission. At Shahr-i Sīstān (785/1383), Isfahan (789/1387), Ṭūs (790/1388), Ḥamā and Baghdad (803/1401), for example, his army conducted a general massacre (*qatl-i 'āmm*). At Herat (785/1383), on the other hand, Timur rescinded his original intention of sacking the town and enslaving its population when he ascertained that they had played no part in the insurrection, and was content with the imposition of a ransom, which was extorted from them by his agents, however, with ruthless violence.[153] A notable exception to these practices is Yazd, which rebelled in 798/1396 but which, on Timur's express orders, not only escaped massacre or looting but was spared the customary ransom; as a result, the city within a short interval had grown more splendid and more populous than before. Timur's forbearance might be linked with Yazd's importance as a centre of luxury cloth production; but he may also have taken into account that 30,000 of its inhabitants had already perished of starvation.[154]

Timur's assurances to a city's inhabitants could not invariably be trusted. The Venetian colonists in Tana, who were lulled by his protestations of friendship, discovered to their cost that the high-ranking representative of Timur who accompanied their envoys back to the town had been tasked with spying out its defences in preparation for the Chaghatay assault.[155] Mamlūk authors describe how the populace of Damascus were beguiled by the professions of admiration for the city that he made to their delegate Ibn Mufliḥ, and his claim that he required simply a large present of food, drink and valuables, only to find their successive gifts of such commodities furiously spurned as inadequate.[156] Timur is also accused – though in each case by hostile witnesses – of having broken a specific guarantee of quarter, as at Shahr-i Sīstān, Takrīt, Āmid, Awnīk, Sivas and Aleppo.[157] He may have gone back on his word in fury at the duration of the investment, much as the Mongols had on occasion broken faith following a protracted siege.[158] Several authors by no means ill-disposed towards Timur, however, including Clavijo and John of Sulṭāniyya, tell how at Sivas he undertook not to shed the blood of the defenders and, once the city had surrendered, cynically had them buried alive, claiming to have kept his promise.[159] Significantly, Timurid authors who are uninhibited about reporting the action are silent regarding the breach of faith.

Figures for those slaughtered vary widely, and were undoubtedly – like the extent of physical destruction – subject to exaggeration.[160] It is clear that in some cases a populace was by no means totally annihilated: as Aubin points out, enough denizens of Isfahan survived to pay another ransom a few years later.[161] The number buried alive at Sivas, where Burhān al-Dīn had executed Timur's envoys and the siege had proved costly in men, ranges from 3,000 to 5,000, indicating that the victims comprised just the garrison,[162] to the entire population of 36,000 (the Greek Christians alone supposedly exempted) according to John of Sulṭāniyya.[163] On occasion, the figures rival those of the Mongols' victims (in many instances grossly inflated). Prior to the battle outside Delhi, Timur gave orders for the massacre of thousands of Hindus (set at 100,000 by Timurid authors but probably half that number) who had been taken prisoner during the march through the Punjab, as a precaution against their aiding the Delhi army;[164] though the purpose may also have been to strike terror into the enemy host. At Baghdad in 804/1401, allegedly, 100,000 or so of the population perished (over and above those killed during the siege and on the day of the city's capture).[165]

Undeniably, Timur's massacres were a more spectacular affair than those of the Mongols. Chinggis Khan had simply ordered the severance of thousands of heads (which were then counted as a means of gauging the numbers killed).[166] Timur had towers of heads constructed, as at Zirih in Sīstān in 785/1383–4, at Isfahan in 789/1387, at Takrīt in 795/1393, at Delhi in 801/1398, at Aleppo in 803/1400, at Baghdad in 803/1401 (120 towers here, according to Ibn ʿArabshāh) and at Smyrna in 805/1402.[167] The number of heads at Isfahan totalled 70,000; Ḥāfiẓ-i Abrū, who made a circuit of the stricken city, estimated that there were twenty-eight towers, each averaging 1,500 skulls, on either side.[168] Those at Aleppo presented an especially grisly spectacle, since the heads were deliberately positioned to face outwards; the Byzantine historian Doukas gives a similar report regarding the tower at Smyrna.[169] Sharaf al-Dīn Yazdī observes that at Isfahan some of the troops shrank from the work of killing and purchased heads from others, so that a brisk traffic developed, a severed head initially fetching twenty *köpeki* dinars.[170] Towers of heads were by no means a novelty. Amīrānshāh had earlier raised one at Ṭūs in 781/1389 and he built another in 784/1383 after suppressing a revolt in Herat.[171] In *c.* 1349 the Kartid Muʿizz al-Dīn had erected in Herat two towers with the heads of slaughtered Qara'unas Mongols,[172] a precedent doubtless not far from the minds of Timur and his son. We know also of towers of Mongol heads constructed in 753/1352 by the Muzaffarids and still earlier by the Delhi Sultan ʿAlā' al-Dīn Khiljī.[173]

Authors such as Shāmī and Yazdī faced a difficult task. Whereas those who wrote of the slaughter of Muslims in Chinggis Khan's day had been recounting the actions of infidels, Timurid historians had to reconcile Timur's conduct with the fact that he was a Muslim. They justify the atrocities on the grounds that the cities concerned had been guilty of defiance or duplicity but they betray no embarrassment at the carnage; Timur's destructiveness is treated as simply one manifestation of the irresistible power conferred upon him by God.[174]

On two occasions, however, Timurid authors absolve the conqueror of immediate responsibility for the fate of a city. They explain the sack of Delhi as the result of 'Hindu' resistance (although Muslims must have comprised at least a significant minority of the populace), so that the troops reacted with violence, but Timur himself, engaged in feasting and celebration of his victory, was not informed rapidly enough.[175] And the rape of Damascus is depicted as arising indirectly from Timur's antipathy towards Syrians, who over seven centuries earlier had backed the Umayyads against the Prophet's cousin and son-in-law ʿAlī. His sentiments, we are told, somehow communicated themselves to his troops, who ran amok, with the result that Damascus caught fire. But the conflagration, says Yazdī, arose through nobody's choice or design: a shocked Timur took pity on the people, ordered the release of all the prisoners taken both there and elsewhere in Syria (a blatant untruth) and resolved to depart within two days.[176] Shāmī's longer account likewise assigns no blame for the fire, but gives no indication, significantly, that Timur sought to make amends.[177]

It is perfectly likely, of course, that in the aftermath of a city's fall Timur temporarily forfeited control over his troops, as appears to have occurred prior to the massacres at Delhi and Damascus. Ibn al-Shiḥna says that when he complained to one of Timur's henchmen that the Chaghatay troops at Aleppo were severing the heads of live Muslims, the man reported this to Timur and brought back word that the towers were intended to comprise only the skulls of the slain but that the Great Amir's orders had been misconstrued.[178] We know, too, that at Ṭūs in 791/1389 Amīrānshāh's troops, required to furnish a specific number of heads, resorted to cutting off the heads of women, old folk and children to swell the total.[179] It may have been in part to prevent such episodes that Timur often evacuated the inhabitants of a city before allowing the Chaghatay soldiery to enter and pillage at will.

There is no question, even so, that Timur's acts of reprisal exceeded those of Chinggis Khan in macabre ingenuity. At Isfizār in 784/1383 he had 2,000 live inhabitants enveloped in clay and piled up to form a brick tower – an act reminiscent of the Sarbadārs' ally Abū Bakr, who in the 1350s had inserted captured Mongols, alive and covered with clay, in the walls of a fortress he was building at Shāsmān.[180] A Byzantine author details an especially vindictive fate devised by Timur for the notables of Sivas, trussed up in such a way that their heads were between their thighs and thrown alive into pits that were then filled in with earth.[181] Timur's aim, like that of the Mongols, was to send an unequivocal message to other cities lest they be tempted to resist or to reject his authority – that the punishment, as Shāmī put it, 'might for centuries be a cautionary tale (*'ibra*) to mankind'.[182] Yet there was a difference of degree. The Mongols had devised a gruesome end for princes who had broken faith with them, such as the ruler of Mosul in 660/1262; they had massacred an entire populace to punish prolonged defiance or revolt or, as in 618/1221–2 at Bāmiyān and Nishapur, to avenge the death of a Mongol prince or general during the siege.[183] But where they engaged in mass killing in a single locality, one looks in vain for the studied inhumanity that would render Timur notorious.[184] In Aubin's view, 'the barbarism natural to the Chaghatay warriors would not have left such a horrific memory in the history of the east, subjected to so many other ordeals, had the Great Amir not imprinted on it the most characteristic qualities of his temperament – a taste for order and for the colossal'. And he observes later that Timur 'viewed terror as the means of government par excellence'.[185]

THE WORK OF REHABILITATION

Nevertheless, the violence of Timur's campaigns can easily overshadow his attempts to rehabilitate the conquered territories. It must be acknowledged, moreover, that some of these attempts took place within a shorter interval of the initial destruction than had the corresponding efforts of thirteenth-century Mongol rulers,[186] while in certain cases Timur was reviving towns whose destruction dated as far back as the Mongol conquest. Fanākat had been in such a ruined state since the passage of Chinggis Khan's forces that no trace remained of cultivation (*'imārat*), and Timur in 794/ the Year of the Monkey/1392 gave orders for its restoration (and renamed it Shāhrukhiyya); the inhabitants were gathered together and transported back.[187] Timur had Ürgench (partly) repopulated and rebuilt in the latter part of 793/late 1391, only three years after its destruction.[188] He had a 5-*farsakh* (16-kilometre) canal dug from the River Ghuriyān in 800/1398, and a number of villages along its course grew to flourish.[189] According to Ḥāfiẓ-i Abrū, most of the villages in the Murghāb region dated from Timur's conquest, since when his amirs had excavated canals and inaugurated cultivation.[190] Sharaf al-Dīn Yazdī says that in the course of his travels Timur was constantly on the alert for improvements he might bring to localities in which he halted, however briefly, with a view to permanently enhancing his reputation.[191] This, of course, is to ignore the strong economic incentives. He was concerned to foster trade, and Aubin proposed that the primary aim was to sustain the pastoral economy by revitalising urban markets.[192]

Nor were such efforts confined to Khwārazm, Transoxiana and neighbouring Khurāsān. The local historian of Sīstān ascribes the rehabilitation of Shahr-i Sīstān in 788/1386 to Shāh-i Shāhān, the new malik, but since this followed closely upon his return from Timur's headquarters it is likely that the work was begun on the conqueror's authority.[193] Amir Sevinchek, rebuilding in 796/1393–4 the fortress of Quhandiz in Fārs, which had been demolished by the Muzaffarid ruler Shāh-i Shujāʿ, was certainly acting on Timur's orders.[194] Following his campaign of 806/1403–4 in Georgia and Armenia, Timur conceived of the restoration and refortification of Baylaqān, which was in a completely ruined state; he enclosed the suburbs with a new wall, added numerous houses, shops and baths, and linked the town to the Araxes River with a canal.[195] Clavijo, who did not see Baylaqān, appears to refer to it when he tells us that a city in Qarābāgh built by Timur already contained 20,000 or more houses.[196] Soon afterwards Timur had the abandoned stronghold of Gil-Khandān near Damāwand refortified.[197] During his lifetime members of his dynasty, too, likewise presided over the rehabilitation of conquered cities. Having punished Baghdad severely for its resistance, Timur had already determined on its restoration two years later, in 806/1403–4, when he conferred its government on his grandson Abā Bakr, and the prince appears duly to have embarked on the task.[198] Measures of this kind were probably as near as Timur came to the constructive enhancement of his empire's tax base.

If military superiority did not translate everywhere into direct rule (see also Chapter 14), Timur's conquests had gained him a widespread and lasting renown evocative of Chinggis Khan. The two leaders differed in status, however, since Timur was a commoner (*qarachu*). The next chapter will explore his relationship with the two khans whose reigns encompassed almost his entire period as head of the ulus of Chaghadai, their status in his extensive conquests and Timur's dealings with other scions of the prolific imperial dynasty.

CHAPTER 12
THE *QARACHU* WARLORD AND THE IMPERIAL CHINGGISIDS

Timur ruled but did not reign.[1] The world in which he moved was accustomed to the notion that sovereignty could reside only in the *altan urugh*, the 'Golden Lineage' – Chinggis Khan's agnatic descendants. No commoner (*qarachu*), however prestigious or powerful, could dream of equality with the imperial family. Mīrzā Ḥaydar Dughlāt relates how the eastern Chaghadayid khan Ways (d. *c.* 832/1429), taken prisoner by the Oyirat chief Esen Tayishi, averted his face from his captor and refused to offer him his hand, thereby winning the warlord's respect.[2] The restriction of the succession to Chinggisids was seen as one of the stipulations of Chinggis Khan's Yasa (or Töre, as it was now generally known). When Tughluq Temür's lieutenants asked Timur in 761/1360 why he had chosen to submit, in contrast with his kinsman and the head of his tribe, Ḥājjī Barlās, Naṭanzī makes him reply: 'Since the land belongs to the sovereign on the grounds of lineage and conquest, . . . what business has the *qarachu* to meddle? It is obligatory to obey and follow the command of Heaven and Chinggis Khan's Töre.'[3] And once in power in Transoxiana, Timur contented himself with the official style of 'Amir' or, later, 'Great Amir' (*amīr-i buzurg*), and ruled – as had his predecessors Qazaghan, ʿAbd-Allāh and Amīr Ḥusayn – in the name of a member of the Chinggisid dynasty. His sons and grandsons are duly given no title higher than *Amīrzāda* ('son of the Amir'; later contracted to *Mīrzā*) in the sources.

TIMUR'S ROYAL MASTERS

In this chapter I shall address a number of questions regarding Timur's two khans. What roles did they fulfil – other, that is, than providing a notional embodiment of Chinggisid legitimacy and thus, as Astarābādī acidly observes,[4] a camouflage for his actions? What was his personal relationship with them? And how did other Chinggisids figure in his plans and policy? These questions have attracted scant attention in the secondary literature; the khans whom Timur enthroned in Samarkand tend to be almost totally ignored, perhaps because he himself always appears so much larger than life (as was no doubt his aim).

Both Timur's khans were descendants of Ögödei: Soyurghatmish (771–790/1370–1388) was a son of Qazaghan's puppet khan Danishmandcha, and Sulṭān Maḥmūd (790–805/1388–1402) was Soyurghatmish's son.[5] Despite this, when describing Timur's enthronement of Soyurghatmish the sources speak of 'the renewal (*aḥyā*) of the house of Chaghadai'.[6] Why Ögödeyids? Chinggis Khan's first two successors had been Ögödei and his son Güyüg, and it had been contended, at the time of the Toluid coup in 1251–2, that the princes had undertaken to keep the office of Qaghan in Ögödei's line.[7] This has accordingly prompted the suggestion that Timur's choice of Ögödeyids to reign over Chaghadai's ulus was linked to some design of resurrecting the universal Chinggisid empire as it had existed prior to that coup;[8] or that Timur was seeking to reassert Chinggis Khan's will by restoring the Ögödeyid patrimony.[9] We shall consider these questions in Chapter 14. Undoubtedly, the dispossession of Ögödei's progeny by the Toluids was to prove of use to Timur at an ideological level, in his correspondence with independent monarchs (see later). But it would be somewhat paradoxical if the hypothesis were correct, since Soyurghatmish was descended from Ögödei's son Melik, who in 1251–2 had supported the Toluids against his own close kinsfolk.[10] For all its vicissitudes, the line of Ögödei, as Chinggis Khan's successor, might have retained in some quarters a greater prestige, and we should further recall that Ögödei's grandson Qaidu had created a powerful – if relatively short-lived – empire in Central Asia, incorporating the whole of the Chaghadayid territories.[11]

Bernardini proposes that Timur's choice of Ögödeyid princes represented a deliberate departure from the policy of his Qara'unas predecessors, whose khans, with the fleeting exception of Danishmandcha, had been descendants of Chaghadai. This is certainly plausible, but he also connects it with Timur's hostility towards the Chaghadayids of Jata.[12] The difficulty here is that when Soyurghatmish was enthroned there was probably no longer a khan in Mughūlistān, Ilyās Khwāja having been killed and supplanted by Qamar al-Dīn – a circumstance that in fact enabled Timur to avoid the charge of defying a legitimate Chaghadayid khan.[13] For that matter, Timur's choice may have been due simply to a dearth of suitable Chaghadayids in Transoxiana.[14] Although *Mu'izz al-ansāb* lists a great many Chaghadayid princes, some of whom must have been living at this time, it tells us nothing about them; possibly several of them were in Jata. Indeed Ḥāfiẓ-i Abrū attributes the acceptance of Danishmandcha in 747/1346–7 to the amirs' inability to find a Chaghadayid with the requisite aptitude (*ahliyat*) or to agree on one candidate.[15] It has been proposed that by Timur's time the ranks of Chaghadai's progeny had been thinned by plague.[16] Buzan seems to have killed many of them (see p. 125), and possibly some, too, had fallen victim to the tyranny of Qazan Sulṭān. Small wonder that Amīr Ḥusayn's puppet khan Kābul Shāh (whose father Dorji had been put to death by Buzan) had earlier sought safety in the guise of a *qalandar* 'from fear of the afflictions of the age'.[17]

Khans were kept on a tight rein, an elementary precaution – and perhaps a necessary one, given the fact that they had occasionally reacted against an amir's tutelage. Qazaghan had stationed informers in Danishmandcha's *orda* in the guise of attendants and guards (*kashīktān*), so that troublemakers might have no opportunity to speak with the khan.[18] Bayan Quli (749–*c.* 759/1348 or 1349–*c.* 1358), the second of Qazaghan's nominal sovereigns, had accompanied him on the expedition against Herat,[19] and ʿAbd-Allāh b. Qazaghan in turn had taken the khan with him to Samarkand;[20] though this did not deter Bayan Quli from intrigues that aroused the apprehensions of ʿAbd-Allāh, who duly put him to death.[21] Amīr Ḥusayn had been accompanied on campaign by his khan, the erstwhile recluse Kābul Shāh (765–769/1363 or 1364–1367 or 1368),[22] but Kābul Shāh found Ḥusayn's tyranny intolerable and made attempts to check him both in private and in public, with the result that Ḥusayn had him killed. Amīr Ḥusayn's next khan, ʿĀdil Sulṭān, whom Naṭanzī characterises as a very proud (*mukhtāl*) man, repeatedly conspired against Ḥusayn, at one point fomenting a rebellion and gathering large numbers to his side. Ḥusayn is said to have turned a blind eye to these activities, since he had already incurred obloquy by putting one khan to death and was reluctant to kill another.[23] According to Yazdī, when ʿĀdil Sulṭān warned Timur of Ḥusayn's treacherous intentions, Timur refused to believe him; and when the khan subsequently took fright and broke free from Ḥusayn, Timur, presumably reluctant to compromise his alliance with Ḥusayn, intercepted him near Kish and sent him back.[24] ʿĀdil Sulṭān was still with Amīr Ḥusayn in Balkh when he was despatched, along with Ḥusayn's eldest son, to seek terms from Timur in 771/1369–70.[25]

What was Timur's relationship with his khans? Contemporaries who had lived under the sovereigns enthroned by Qazaghan and his line might well have expected Timur's nominees to be equally short-lived. Yet in marked contrast with his Qara'unas predecessors (and with Great Amirs in the final decades of the Ilkhanate), Timur did not find it necessary to dispose of either of his khans – as Qazaghan had killed Soyurghatmish's father Danishmandcha, as ʿAbd-Allāh had put to death Bayan Quli, as Amīr Ḥusayn had eliminated Kābul Shāh or as Timur himself, in 771/1370, had executed Ḥusayn's last khan, ʿĀdil Sulṭān.[26] Both Soyurghatmish and Sulṭān Maḥmūd died a natural death; their successive reigns covered thirty-four lunar years, a period exceeding the aggregate reigns of the nominal Ilkhans after 1335; and each occupied the Chaghadayid throne for longer than any khan since Du'a (681–706/1282–1307).

The explanation might simply be that Timur had chosen protégés who were too feeble to pose a threat to him. Admittedly, Ibn ʿArabshāh draws an analogy with the relationship between the Mamlūk Sultan and the ʿAbbasid Caliph in Cairo (possibly inspired in part by the fact that Timur was being referred to as 'Sultan') and says that Soyurghatmish was caught in Timur's clutches 'like an ass in the mire'; while the Syrian chronicler Ibn Ḥijjī describes Sulṭān Maḥmūd as wielding no authority at all.[27] Whatever the truth, the statement in the *Mémoire* of Archbishop John of Sulṭāniyya that Timur visited the khan once a year to do homage, otherwise paying him no heed but merely maintaining him in state,[28] is at variance with other contemporary sources. So too is Mīrzā Ḥaydar's comment that Timur had kept his khans locked up and under guard in Samarkand; although later he quotes the Timurid Sultan Abū Saʿīd (d. 873/1469) to the effect that this had been the policy only in more recent years.[29] According to the Latin version of John's report, Sulṭān Maḥmūd was constantly present in Timur's entourage;[30] as we shall see, he took part in many of Timur's campaigns.

Neither of Timur's khans was a mere cipher whose role as spectator in some remote sanctum was relieved only by intermittent ceremony. Whereas no evidence exists that the few previous khans had personally participated in military combat, Soyurghatmish seems to have been an active warrior. Himself the son of a khan, he must have had his own military retinue in the years prior to his enthronement, since Shāmī describes him as at that time one of the great amirs.[31] He was stationed in the van of Timur's army in the final engagement with Amīr Ḥusayn,[32] and as khan he took part in other military operations of Timur's.[33] It was only during the campaign against Khwārazm in 790/1388 that in view of his illness he was left behind in Bukhara, where he died.[34] As for Sulṭān Maḥmūd, we might be tempted to discount Ghiyāth al-Dīn Yazdī's statement that Timur recognised the khan's talent for administration,[35] but he clearly headed his own division; at one point reference is made to his tümen, though it is possible that effective command (*bāshlāmīshī*) was vested in an amir.[36] Sulṭān Maḥmūd did not merely accompany Timur's armies as his father had done – he was present, for example, on both the major expeditions against Toqtamish, on an excursion against Baṣra in 795/1393 (with Timur's grandson Muḥammad Sulṭān), on the Indian expedition and on the campaigns in Syria and against Baghdad[37] – but enjoyed the personal distinction of capturing the Ottoman Sultan at the battle of Ankara in 804/1402.[38]

This was a partnership of sorts, if not necessarily an equal one, and the Great Amir and his khans may have been bound by ties of affection. The fact that Shāmī devotes some lines to the widespread mourning that followed the death in 790/1388 of Soyurghatmish, an old comrade-in-arms of Timur's,[39] suggests (if nothing else) that his patron was attached to the khan's memory. According to Ḥāfiẓ-i Abrū, when Soyurghatmish fell ill Timur left Mawlānā ʿIzz al-Dīn Shīrāzī, whose skill and experience in healing were unequalled, to tend him.[40] Naṭanzī too refers to the past friendship (*sawābiq-i ikhlāṣ*) of Timur and the khan. But although he says that for this reason Timur retained Soyurghatmish's name in the khutba and on the coinage for a further three years,[41] this certainly did not transpire in Samarkand, for coins struck there in the name of Sulṭān Maḥmūd have come down to us from the year 790.[42] Naṭanzī and Ibn Khaldūn both appear to suggest that Timur, who had married Sulṭān Maḥmūd's mother, reared his stepson,[43] which could indicate that the new khan was only a boy at Soyurghatmish's death. Ibn Khaldūn recounts how, during his first audience with the conqueror, Timur, who was reclining, turned around expecting to find Sulṭān Maḥmūd among a group of amirs standing behind him,[44] which might imply, at best, a dubious privilege of being second among equals. But it could just betoken a relatively informal relationship. When the khan fell ill and died on a raiding expedition in Anatolia in the autumn of 805/1402,[45] Sharaf al-Dīn Yazdī assures us that Timur wept.[46] This may, however, be no more than a literary conceit, since Yazdī also claims – less plausibly – that Timur shed tears when told of the death of his prisoner Bayezid (see above, p. 303).

Timur himself told Ibn Khaldūn that he was merely one among the lieutenants of the sovereign (*ṣāḥib al-takht*),[47] and until the death of 'Ghiyāth al-Ḥaqq wa l-Dīn Sulṭān Maḥmūd Khan, the Emperor of Mankind, the Sultan of the world's Sultans, the worthiest of Kings by land or by sea', to borrow the sonorous phrasing of the *Rūz-nāma*,[48] the Chaghatay establishment (if we except the restive Amīrānshāh in 800/1398) was punctilious in maintaining his sovereign rights[49] – just as Timur, Shāmī says, had respected the rights of Soyurghatmish.[50] The khan was styled 'Sovereign of Islam' (*Pādishāh-i Islām*), a title that evoked memories of the convert Ilkhan Ghazan Maḥmūd. Documents were issued in Sulṭān Maḥmūd's name.[51] Ibn Ḥijjī called him 'the king and sultan of the Tatars', of whose realm Timur was the administrator (*mudabbir*).[52] For the Egyptian historian Ibn al-Furāt, Timur was 'the *atābak* of the Tatars'[53] (possibly an allusion to the fact that, like the atabegs of the Seljuq era, he had married the sovereign's mother and had been his guardian) and Sulṭān Maḥmūd Khan was Timur's 'master' (*ustād*).[54]

Timur's campaigns were purportedly launched on the khan's behalf and the princes he attacked were required to acknowledge the khan's sovereignty. According to Shāmī, as Timur set out on his first expedition against Toqtamish in the Qipchaq steppe, he announced that he was doing so in accordance with the *yarligh* of the *Pādishāh-i Islām*, in this case Sulṭān Maḥmūd;[55] and the same appeal to the khan's authority appears in a letter to Sayyid ʿAlī Kiyā, the ruler of Gīlān.[56] In accepting subjection to Timur in 787/1385–6, the Marʿashī Sayyid rulers of Māzandarān agreed to strike coins and have the khutba given for Soyurghatmish.[57] When the Chaghatay armies summoned enemy cities and strongholds to submit, they did so in the joint names of the khan and of Timur.[58] Ibn ʿArabshāh cites Timur's instructions to Qadi Burhān al-Dīn, the ruler of Sivas, Isfandiyār, the ruler of Sinope and Kastamonu, and other Anatolian princes to insert his and the khan's names in the khutba and on the coinage, and his demand, too, that the cities of Syria have the Friday prayers pronounced in both the khan's name and his own.[59] On the capture of Delhi in 801/1398, the khutba there was made for Sulṭān Maḥmūd Khan, Timur and the latter's grandson and heir-apparent, Muḥammad Sulṭān b. Jahāngīr (in that order).[60] The same procedure was observed when Damascus yielded in 803/1401, and the coins minted at Timur's headquarters during the siege had named all three men.[61] Their names likewise head a document issued in 804/1401.[62] When Sultan Faraj submitted (805/1402–3), he duly struck coins bearing the names of the *Pādishāh-i Islām* and Timur (Muḥammad Sulṭān having died by this point) and had the khutba made for them throughout Egypt and Syria.[63] This may be why Ibn Ḥijjī and other Mamlūk authors accord Sulṭān Maḥmūd a brief obituary.[64]

To the best of our knowledge, Timur did not nominate a khan following Sulṭān Maḥmūd's death in 805/1402. Ultimately it is unclear how strongly he was attached to the idea of maintaining a khan. According to Naṭanzī the late khan's son Abū Saʿīd was still alive in his own day.[65] In these circumstances, and given this author's dismissive contrast between khan and *qarachu*,[66] we might readily infer that he disapproved of the failure to appoint Abū Saʿīd. Alternatively, of course, he may have been hinting obliquely at Abū Saʿīd's ineligibility. Perhaps the prince was too young to be enthroned in 1402; or perhaps Timur himself deemed him unsuitable on other grounds.

Regrettably, the evidence is far from unequivocal.[67] Naṭanzī also says that Timur retained Sulṭān Maḥmūd's name in the khutba and on the coinage for a year after the khan's death,[68] rather as he had done earlier with Soyurghatmish's name (see earlier), or so Naṭanzī tells us. The fact that Sulṭān Maḥmūd is named on some coins minted in Samarkand as late as 807/1404–5, the very year of Timur's own demise, would support this.[69] (Although we find vassal rulers in Anatolia striking coins after 805 in Timur's name alone,[70] they would surely have been unaware of the Great Amir's sentiments in this regard.) Of course, Timur may have envisaged dispensing altogether with a khan in Samarkand.[71] Yet there are other possibilities. One is that he postponed naming a new khan out of respect for the late sovereign (who had died, we should recall, 3,000 kilometres from Transoxiana). Perhaps first the preparations for the invasion of China, and then Timur's own death, pre-empted his choice of the dead man's successor. But one aim of that campaign seems to have been the installation in the Far East of a client Qaghan, Bunyashirin or Tāīzī Oghlan, a Muslim convert and possibly, like Sulṭān Maḥmūd, an Ögödeyid (see pp. 349–50). The reason for the postponement, then, may have been that Timur intended this prince to replace Sulṭān Maḥmūd throughout his dominions and not in the Northern Yuan territories alone.

THE KHANSHIP AFTER TIMUR

Timur's heirs in general discontinued the practice of appointing a Chinggisid khan. Why, we can only speculate. It might be that the conqueror's considerable prestige was now sufficient to afford his dynasty the legitimation it required – or his heirs could simply have been determined that it should so suffice. But equally, given the rapid disintegration of his empire into so many rival principalities – some as remote as Fārs and Azerbaijan – the maintenance of Ögödeyid khans (from what can only have been, in any case, an extremely limited pool) perhaps appeared all the more difficult and impractical – and even incongruous.

Links with the Mongol imperial dynasty retained their importance, certainly, for several decades to come; but the accent henceforward was on a (spurious) common ancestry with Chinggis Khan rather than on rule through a Chinggisid. The brief reign of Timur's immediate successor in Samarkand, his grandson Khalīl Sulṭān, represents an intermediate stage in this process. He endeavoured to bolster his position by nominating as khan a fellow Timurid with Chinggisid ancestry: his eight-year-old half-nephew Muḥammad Jahāngīr, the son of Timur's heir-apparent Muḥammad Sulṭān, whose mother was a granddaughter of the Jochid khan Özbeg.[72] As we shall see in Chapter 15, Khalīl Sulṭān may have seen this expedient as the best means of countering the claims of his principal rival, the new heir-apparent Pīr Muḥammad b. Jahāngīr, who was the boy's uncle but lacked Chinggisid ancestry. It is possibly significant, too, that the location was Samarkand, where Timur's two khans had been enthroned. But what was deemed appropriate or even desirable in Chaghadayid Transoxiana might not have appeared so elsewhere in Timur's vast conquests as autonomy beckoned temptingly to his sons and grandsons. In 807/1405, when Pīr Muḥammad b. ʿUmar Shaykh was looking to secure his position in Fārs, some recommended that he jettison the Chinggisid dispensation (*yāsāq*) by following Muzaffarid precedent and acknowledging the authority of the ʿAbbasid Caliph in Cairo, a blatant contravention of Mongol law and tradition.[73] Subsequently Timurid rulers, beginning with Shāhrukh in Herat, did not bother with khans at all – or with any other form of legitimation. On Shāhrukh's triumphal entry into Samarkand in 811/1409, Khalīl Sulṭān's 'khan' Muḥammad Jahāngīr was relegated to the governorship of Ṭukhāristān.[74] Shāhrukh assumed the titles of qaghan and sultan and was even styled *Pādishāh-i Islām*;[75] his coins in Herat in 819–20/1416–18 go so far as to style him Caliph.[76]

Although Mīrzā Ḥaydar Dughlāt represents the Timurids in Transoxiana as continuing to appoint khans down to the reign of Shāhrukh's son Ulugh Beg (d. 853/1449),[77] no coins struck during this period bear a khan's name in addition to that of the Timurid ruler.[78] Considering his position as governor of Transoxiana and his image as a keen devotee of Mongol tradition,[79] we might have expected Ulugh Beg, in particular, to have enthroned a Chinggisid khan in Samarkand. It seems he did not. Granted, we read of a khan named Sātūq, whom Ulugh Beg discarded in favour of an alternative candidate and despatched with an army against the eastern Chaghadayid khan Ways (Uways) in *c.* 1429; both Ways and Sātūq were killed within a very short interval. The story has been challenged on the grounds that Ḥaydar is its sole source;[80] but it is his presentation of the episode that is questionable rather than its historicity. Sātūq, in all likelihood the son of Ways's predecessor Muḥammad Khan who bore this name, was surely no shadow khan in Samarkand but an exile whom Ulugh Beg had welcomed at his court and whom he saw at this juncture as a potentially useful client in Mughūlistān.[81] Ulugh Beg had similarly despatched the eastern Chaghadayid Shīr Muḥammad to rule Mughūlistān in 823/1420;[82] he was following a policy that he had pursued on previous occasions in relation both to Mughūlistān and to the Qipchaq khanate. In terms of its accuracy, and doubtless also its object, Ḥaydar's version of the Sātūq Khan episode probably corresponds to his later claim that the Timurid ruler Abū Saʿīd shared his throne with the Chaghadayid Yūnus prior to sending him in 860/1456 to wrest Mughūlistān from his brother, Esen Buqa II, as a means of stemming Mughūl raids.[83] On both occasions, Ḥaydar alleges that a Timurid had acknowledged the sovereignty of an eastern Chaghadayid (though when bidding Yūnus farewell Abū Saʿīd is said to make his own autonomy explicit).

In this respect we might see the eastern Timurid dominions under Shāhrukh and Ulugh Beg as analogous to the Jalayirid realm from the mid-fourteenth century onwards, when Chinggisid figureheads had likewise been discarded after serving their purpose for a rather shorter time. The sole reliable allusion we have to a puppet khan in the half-century after Timur's death, in fact, involves an unnamed Chinggisid enthroned in Samarkand at the time of Ulugh Beg's overthrow in 853/1449 by his son ʿAbd al-Laṭīf, specifically in order to judge the vanquished ruler.[84] Significantly, Khwānd-Amīr, who dismisses this khan as 'a poor wretch' (*maflūkī*), writes of ʿAbd al-Laṭīf's action as an emulation of Timur's practice,[85] rather than based on more recent precedent. At any rate, this is the last mention of such a figurehead. Once more we should note the possibility that the idea of a Chinggisid khan remained viable for longer in Transoxiana than elsewhere in the Timurid world.

Within less than a generation of Timur's death, Chinggisid khans had also become dispensable in the historiographical context. Whereas Shāmī's *Ẓafar-nāma*, completed a year or so following Sulṭān Maḥmūd's demise, consistently alludes to Chinggisid sovereignty, authors writing later, beginning with Ghiyāth al-Dīn Yazdī, who completed the *Rūz-nāma* perhaps a few years after 1405, and continuing with Tāj al-Dīn Salmānī and Sharaf al-Dīn Yazdī, refer to Timur himself as 'the Khāqān'.[86] The preface of *Muʿizz al-ansāb* (830/1426–7) attaches the title of khan to both Timur and his effective successor, Shāhrukh.[87] Admittedly Ghiyāth al-Dīn Yazdī retained his references to Timur's two Chinggisid khans; but Sharaf al-Dīn ʿAlī Yazdī, who utilised the works of both Shāmī and Ghiyāth al-Dīn, went some way to expunge the khans from the record. He neglected to call Soyurghatmish or Sulṭān Maḥmūd *Pādishāh-i Islām*, deleted several references in his predecessors' works to either man and sought to elevate Timur to the rank of sovereign *de jure*.[88]

Thus, for Yazdī, Timur himself ascended the royal throne following the capture of Balkh in 771/1369–70, having been recognised and acclaimed by the amirs as supremely qualified to do so and having received their written oaths of allegiance.[89] It was just Timur's name that was added to the coinage and mentioned in the khutba in Māzandarān from 787/1385–6;[90] when recounting the capture of Delhi and the fall of Damascus, too, Yazdī makes out that the khutba in the occupied cities was given in Timur's name alone;[91] and he also has the submissive Mamlūk Sultan Faraj, lastly, striking coins and making the khutba only for Timur in 805/1402–3.[92] Writing of the review of the Chaghatay army on the first Qipchaq campaign in 793/1391, Yazdī contrived to give the impression that Sulṭān Maḥmūd Khan paid his respects to Timur just as did the other commanders.[93] Nor was Yazdī above tampering with documentary evidence: in reproducing a letter from Timur to Barqūq of 796/1393–4, he elided a reference to the khan as the new ruler of Iran and substituted Timur himself.[94] Curiously, however, Yazdī was neither thorough nor consistent, since he mentions Timur's nomination of Soyurghatmish as khan, the installation of Sulṭān Maḥmūd as Soyurghatmish's successor and Sulṭān Maḥmūd's own death.[95] The presence of a Chinggisid khan alongside Timur proved less easy to suppress than we might imagine.

SUPPORT FOR REFUGEE CHINGGISID PRINCES

As the protagonist of a Chinggisid world order, Timur also lent his assistance to Chinggisid princes from regions outside the Chaghadayid ulus, who were expected to show their gratitude by recognising his authority and contributing troops to his campaigns. At different times his headquarters hosted various princes who had turned to him for support. In Iran he installed Luqmān, a son of the Ilkhan Taghai Temür and brother of the last phantom Ilkhan Ghazan II (above, p. 118), as ruler of Astarābād in 786/1384 with the royal title of *pādishāh*, and later appointed Luqmān's son Pīr Pādishāh to succeed his father.[96]

The most celebrated – and undoubtedly the most problematic – of these client princes was the Jochid Toqtamish, whom Timur welcomed at his court in 778/1377 and whom he aided in his efforts to wrest the throne of the Blue Horde from Orus Khan and his sons. Toqtamish, having succeeded in taking over not only the Blue Horde but the Qipchaq khanate for good measure, repaid his benefactor by resurrecting the old Jochid claims to the Transcaucasus and invading Azerbaijan. A punitive campaign by Timur in 793/1391 put him to flight. When Toqtamish persisted in his aggressive stance, Timur finally inflicted on him a crushing defeat (797/1395), nominating as khan of the Jochid ulus Orus Khan's son Qoyurichaq, who was then present in his entourage (above, p. 289).[97] In 1404 Clavijo was told (probably correctly) that Toqtamish and Timur were now reconciled and that Toqtamish and his son were guests in Timur's dominions; he claims, moreover, to have seen the son at Timur's court.[98] Yazdī informs us that during Timur's final days at Utrār an embassy from Toqtamish sought his forgiveness and promised loyalty, presumably in the hope of joint operations against Edigü; Timur promised to restore Toqtamish to his throne after his Chinese campaign,[99] but nothing came of this as a result of his death.

Two other Jochids – Kunacha and Temür Qutlugh – and the noyan Edigü had earlier entered Timur's service out of long-standing hostility towards Toqtamish. The princes rose high in Timur's favour and were numbered among his intimates; Kunacha frequently played chess with him.[100] But Temür Qutlugh and Edigü deserted Timur after the victory on the Qundurcha and appear to have overthrown Timur's nominee Qoyurichaq.[101] Kunacha also defected shortly afterwards, seemingly on the news of Temür Qutlugh's proclamation as khan.[102] Other Jochids, however, remained loyal and would participate in Timur's campaigns: Ibaj Oghlan (a son or grandson of the former khan Ordu Melik) and Burhān Oghlan, for instance (the latter eventually executed for dereliction of duty).[103] We also learn of the presence of the Jochid princes Yaruq and Bash (or Tash) Temür (the latter, from whom descended the khans of the Crimea, briefly became khan in 797/1395).[104]

Lastly, Timur gave asylum to at least one prince from Mongolia. In the last months of 800/summer of 1398, during the Indian expedition, a certain 'Tāīzī Oghlan' arrived at the conqueror's headquarters in Kabul from 'Qalmāq' in the wake of a failed rising against the Qaghan of the Northern Yuan.[105] We are also told, however, of another prince, named Öljei Temür (known alternatively as Bunyashiri[n]), with whom Niẓām al-Dīn Shāmī ends his list of Qaghans in the east.[106] Sharaf al-Dīn Yazdī, on the other hand, places Tāīzī immediately after Öljei Temür in his list of Qaghans, adding that he embraced Islam while at Timur's court and after the latter died he left for Qalmāq, where he briefly reigned as Qaghan before being killed.[107] This suggests that Öljei Temür/Bunyashiri[n] and Tāīzī were identical. The fact that Tāīzī, according to Yazdī, was from Ögödei's line, while the *Mingshi* describes Bunyashiri[n] as a descendant of the Yuan, is not necessarily problematic, since the Ming possibly used the term Yuan here in the looser sense of the entire Chinggisid dynasty.[108] As Manz pointed out, 'Tāīzī' represents Öljei Temür's Chinese title ('heir-apparent').[109]

Writing in advance of Timur's China campaign, Shāmī expresses the pious hope that God would help Öljei Temür to obtain the throne, since it was his by right,[110] which might well indicate that Timur had assured the prince of his backing. The Great Amir doubtless planned to bestow on him the rulership of the Mongolian homeland and even, conceivably, the throne of China following a successful campaign against the Ming.[111] Nagel thinks this unlikely, on the grounds that Timur's world-rulership claims were advanced exclusively on behalf of Chaghadai's line,[112] or rather, strictly speaking, Ögödei's. But that does not preclude the possibility that Timur aimed to instal a client Chinggisid khan in the Far East – much as the Chaghadayid khan Eljigidei had sought to put another exile, Qoshila, on the Yuan throne in 1328–9 (above, p. 83). Since the invasion of China was projected, at least by Timurid authors, as a holy war, Timur would surely have been under an obligation to enthrone a Muslim; as noted earlier, Tāīzī had allegedly embraced Islam. In the event, by 1407 Öljei Temür/Bunyashiri[n] had moved to Beshbaligh, where he sought the assistance of the Mughūl khan before returning to Mongolia and supplanting Gülichi (see p. 112) as Qaghan in 1408; after a reign of four years, he was overthrown and killed by the Oyirat chief Maḥmūd in 1412.[113]

Clearly, the presence of Chinggisid dependants at Timur's court contributed to his enormous prestige; and they duly enjoyed the place of greatest honour at his headquarters. When he received Toqtamish's emissary at Aqsulat in 807/1404–5, the Ögödeyid Tāīzī Oghlan and the Jochids Chekire (Schiltberger's 'Zegre', a future contestant for the throne of the Qipchaq khanate) and Bash Temür (see above) were seated on his right; Timurid princes had the lowlier position on his left.[114] A miniature in the Diez Album in Berlin, probably dating from the reign of Khalīl Sulṭān and within two or three years of Timur's death, depicts an enthroned monarch, with a number of (named) princes and amirs below him.[115] Again in the place of greatest honour, on Khalīl Sulṭān's right, are four Chinggisids: Tāīzī Oghlan (alias Öljei Temür); Chinggis Oghlan (alias Chekire); another Jochid, Yādgār Oghlan (a son of the late khan Temür Qutlugh); and Ajashirin, one of the eastern branch of the Chaghadayids resident in Gansu that governed the principality of Hami. It is striking that the two last-named princes do not even appear in the Timurid narrative sources.[116] In all likelihood, the number of Chinggisids who looked to Timur to enhance or redress their fortunes was greater than those sources indicate.

THE KHANS AND A GREATER CHAGHADAYID ULUS

Under Timur's paramountcy, the Chaghadayid ulus was conceived of as immeasurably larger than the polity over which Tarmashirin and Qazan Sulṭān had held sway. Sometimes this is indicated only vaguely. Timur announced to Sultan Barqūq in 796/1393–4 that a descendant of Chinggis Khan had appeared, to claim the throne of Iran and to wrest Muslim territories from the wicked.[117] But we soon see the emergence of an extraordinary ideology. According to Astarābādī, the conqueror's letter to Burhān al-Dīn in 796/1394 (now lost) asserted that 'that country' (namely, eastern Anatolia) had passed from Chinggis Khan via Hülegü down to Sulṭān Maḥmūd Khan by hereditary right.[118] Timur's letter of the same year to Sultan Bayezid contended that Chinggis Khan had conferred the land of Iran upon Chaghadai but that it had been usurped by Hülegü and his progeny, and that since the Ilkhanid line was now extinct it had been proposed to the *Pādishāh-i Islām* (Sulṭān Maḥmūd Khan) that he should reclaim what was rightly his ancestral territory.[119]

There is a more explicit elaboration of the claims on behalf of the Chaghadayids in an undated letter (possibly just a draft) to the Egyptian Sultan. Chinggis Khan had allocated to Chaghadai, wrote Timur, not merely the territory from the Altai to Samarkand and

Bukhara and from Ghazna to the borders of Hindūstān, but also Herat, Rayy, Fārs, Azerbaijan, Baghdad and 'as much of the cultivated land as he had conquered'. Since Chaghadai, he continues, had failed to make good his title to this enormous tract, Möngke sent Hülegü to reduce what remained unsubdued, thus giving rise to a prolonged feud between the Ilkhans and Chaghadai's line.[120] This, of course, was to disregard completely the rights that the Jochids had long claimed in north-western Iran. If Timur was seeking to re-establish a Mongol world order, it was not one with which Chinggis Khan or the thirteenth-century Mongols would have felt in all respects readily familiar. In a further rewriting of history he even pointed to past (and genuine) diplomatic contacts between the Mamlūk Sultanate and the Chaghadayids, in which al-Malik al-Nāṣir (Sultan al-Nāṣir Muḥammad; d. 741/1341) had supposedly expressed his submission to them and recognised their rights over Iran,[121] a truly absurd reconstruction, since the Mamlūk Sultan's own overlordship, rather, had been recognised by certain Mongol grandees in the Ilkhanate during the conflicts following Abū Sa'īd's death (see p. 117 above). In the light of such grotesque distortions, it is noteworthy that Sharaf al-Dīn Yazdī, writing for a Timurid who had no interest in trumpeting claims – authentic or spurious – on behalf of the Chaghadayids and Ögödeyids, purveys at one point the traditional line that Chaghadai had received only the lands beyond the Oxus.[122]

It was logical, therefore, that Timur should proclaim the sovereignty of his two Chinggisid nominees in the former Ilkhanid lands. Admittedly, when the ruler of Māzandarān submitted in 787/1385–6, Timur subordinated him directly to Luqmān Pādishāh.[123] But the reason for this, presumably, was that Luqmān now ruled neighbouring Astarābād as the heir of the Ilkhan Taghai Temür; there is nothing to suggest that he embodied a restored Ilkhanate. On the contrary: in this very year, as we saw earlier, Māzandarān's rulers were required to name on their coins not Luqmān but Sulṭān Maḥmūd. In the Ilkhanid territories entrusted to him, Amīrānshāh named Sulṭān Maḥmūd on documents he issued during his bid for autonomy in the mid-1390s (above, pp. 275–6).[124] The style 'Light of the Ilkhanid Garden' (*nūr-i ḥadīqa-yi īlqānī*), by which Timur refers to Sulṭān Maḥmūd in his letter of 796/1394 to the Ottoman Sultan Bayezid, is further corroboration that Greater Iran was regarded as part of the khan's dominions, as is the long list of Iranian regions said to have been conquered on his behalf.[125] We have seen, too, that the khan's name was inserted in the khutba in Syria and Egypt by Sultan Faraj in 805/1403.

Timur's definitions of Chaghadai's original appanage were undeniably false; yet his victories had turned them into contemporary reality. It is worth reflecting at this juncture on the dramatic shift in the fortunes of the 'Central Mongol state' (*Dumdadu Mongghol ulus*: see p. 79 above) since the 1320s – still more since the 1260s when Baraq had complained of the constriction of its territories. The ulus of Chaghadai now extended, in the south-west, almost as far as the limits of the unitary Mongol empire. From the vantage point of the Chaghatays, the years 781/1380 to 807/1405 must have appeared as the apogee of the ulus.

Nowhere do we receive any direct indication of the status of Soyurghatmish or Sulṭān Maḥmūd in relation to the Chinggisid khans whom Timur installed elsewhere, such as Qoyurichaq and Temür Qutlugh. Just how broadly Timur defined the rights of his two Ögödeyid protégés therefore remains uncertain. Did this *qarachu* warlord-writ-large envisage installing a raft of satellite khans of equal status in the different constituent parts of the former Mongol empire, while himself satisfied with a more immediate executive authority in Transoxiana and Iran?[126] Or did his own khan take precedence over the rest?

Before the late 1380s, at least, while the non-Chaghadayid usurper Qamar al-Dīn was at large and there was no recognised Chinggisid khan in Mughūlistān, it is unthinkable that Soyurghatmish would have been projected as anything other than khan of the entire ulus of Chaghadai. This probably continued to be the case even after the restoration of the eastern Chaghadayid line in the person of Khiḍr Khwāja (*c.* 1388). Significantly, Sharaf al-Dīn Yazdī, speaking of Khiḍr Khwāja, only once gives him the title of khan; more often he refers to him as Khiḍr Khwāja Oghlan and not as khan of

Mughūlistān/Jata but merely as 'governor' (*ḥākim*).[127] In Delhi, a time-honoured objective of Chaghadayid khans from Du'a to Tarmashirin, it was only natural that the khutba should be read in Sulṭān Maḥmūd's name (and confusing, since the ousted Tughluqid sultan bore the same name!).

The situation of the one-time Ilkhanid lands – and in those Near Eastern territories that the Ilkhans had sought unsuccessfully to reduce – was distinctive, inasmuch as Hülegü's line had died out. This was not true of the dominions of the Jochids or the Northern Yuan. Toqtamish, Qoyurichaq and Temür Qutlugh are each in turn described as khan in the Timurid sources. It is also significant that Shāmī and Sharaf al-Dīn Yazdī, listing Qubilai's successors in the Far East down to the early fifteenth century, continue to style them Qa'an and that the former, as we have seen, voices the hope that Öljei Temür will occupy the throne in Mongolia.[128] In any event, Ibn ʿArabshāh's inclusion of the rulers of the Qipchaq steppe, China (*Khitā*) and Turkestan among those who obeyed Timur and retained only the trappings of sovereignty is of questionable value.[129]

Yet both Soyurghatmish and Sulṭān Maḥmūd are most commonly referred to, in documents or in Timur's correspondence, as *Pādishāh-i Islām*.[130] We should pause to consider the possible connotations of this title. Given the dubious circumstances in which the Ilkhanate had come into existence and Hülegü's lack of any sanction for his rule that derived from Chinggis Khan, Ghazan's assumption of the style *Pādishāh-i Islām* had perhaps been designed in part to assert parity of rank with the infidel Jochid and Chaghadayid khans, whose title to their lands was of longer standing (see above, p. 96). When applied to Sulṭān Maḥmūd Khan almost a century later, *Pādishāh-i Islām* may have signified something greater, at least in relation to the (now Muslim) khans of the Golden Horde and Mughūlistān.

The two earliest Timurid sources imply that Sulṭān Maḥmūd was indeed deemed to be the paramount Chinggisid khan. Ghiyāth al-Dīn ʿAlī Yazdī tells us that in every Muslim territory he conquered Timur adorned the khutba and the coinage with Sulṭān Maḥmūd's name and titles.[131] The assertion might be predicated, of course, on a perception of Jochid and eastern Chaghadayid lands as infidel territory (see pp. 201–2, 367–8), but on occasion Shāmī and Ghiyāth al-Dīn give Sulṭān Maḥmūd a more exalted title: *Pādishāh-i jahān*, 'Sovereign of the world', or *Pādishāh-i 'ahd-u zamān*, 'Sovereign of the world and the age', respectively.[132] For Shāmī, the khan was 'the protector of the greater part of the Seven Climes' (*ḥāmī-yi ḥawma-yi haft iqlīm*),[133] and Timur had 'established the august line (*ūrūgh*) of Chaghadai in the state of sovereignty over Iran and Turan, nay over the greater part of the inhabited world'.[134] Unless this was nothing more than hollow verbiage (and Shāmī conveniently overlooks the fact that the sovereigns whom Timur thus exalted were Ögödeyids), the phrasing could signify that client Mongol khans were seen as subordinate to Sulṭān Maḥmūd. The logic of Timur's stance surely requires this, since, as he reminded the Mamlūk Sultan, the Ögödeyids had been deprived of the imperial throne by an illicit coup.[135] We might therefore distinguish the status of the two men he enthroned as khans of Chaghadai's ulus (interpreted broadly) from a more exalted role on a still larger stage. But this must remain a matter of surmise.

TIMUR AS THE LEGATEE OF THE ILKHANS

As has been noted, the Jalayirid rulers, notably Shaykh Uways, posed, and were portrayed by those at their court, as the heirs of the Ilkhans, with whom they were connected by blood. Timur, possibly conscious of a need to quash such claims, was presented on very different grounds as the executor of Ilkhanid expansionist policy, an avocation he appears to have embraced in his later years. His biographers' accounts of his conduct occasionally evoke memories of Ghazan Khan, as when Sharaf al-Dīn Yazdī has him enacting the role of commander among his boyhood peers: we are evidently meant to recall Rashīd al-Dīn's account of Ghazan's childhood.[136] We saw how Timur depicted his khan as the heir of the extinct Ilkhanid line. Qarā Yūsuf Qarā-Qūyūnlū alluded to Timur's own 'Ilkhanid pretensions' (*da'wā-yi īlkhānī*).[137] Timur even spoke of himself in his diplomatic correspondence as belonging to the Ilkhanid house (*az dūdmān-i īlkhāniyya*),[138] and he was styled Ilkhan in a letter from Barqūq's chancery which has survived in various chronicles (notably that of Ibn Ṣaṣrā) and which Ibn ʿArabshāh claims to have seen.[139] It was doubtless for the same reason that another missive, in 796/1394, which demanded Barqūq's submission was an abridged reissue of Hülegü's ultimatum to the Ayyubid Sultan of Syria, al-Nāṣir Yūsuf.[140] Broadbridge suggests that this was designed as an intimidating reminder to the Mamlūks of Ilkhanid victory; Aigle, that Timur was seeking to project himself as a second Hülegü.[141] Whatever the truth, it proved counterproductive, since Barqūq responded with a message of defiance that incorporated phrases from al-Nāṣir Yūsuf's reply to Hülegü.[142]

No less significant is the myth that grew up surrounding the date of 736/1336 for Timur's birth.[143] The 'official' historians writing prior to 1405 supply no date for this event. Later writers under Timur's successors, however, beginning with Sharaf al-Dīn Yazdī and Ḥāfiẓ-i Abrū, would allege that he had been born in 736, the year of the death of the last effective Ilkhan, Abū Saʿīd. Timur's precise birth date was specified as 25 Shaʿbān [8 April 1336], which had been chosen, seemingly, because it coincided with a conjunction of the two superior planets, Jupiter and Saturn, and thus would have qualified Timur as *Ṣāḥib-Qirān*, 'Lord of the Auspicious Conjunction' (see below, pp. 386–7).[144] The implication is clear. Divine providence had intervened to remedy the collapse of the Ilkhanate, and Timur, as the instrument of that providence, was the Ilkhans' true successor. Alone among the sources from the Islamic world composed before 1405, the *waqf-nāma* for the shrine of Shaykh Aḥmad Yasawī, which he had commissioned, gives this more recent date for his birth.[145] Since Timur himself gave his age in 803/1401 as seventy-five (above, p. 252), he can have endorsed the revised date of 736 – if indeed he did – only at a late juncture.

The propaganda mounted by Timur and his servitors was by no means consistent.[146] For all that he denounced the Toluids for their usurpation of the rights of Chaghadai's line and of the dignity of Qaghan from the Ögödeyids, his court may have been ready on occasion to resort to the Toluids' own claims as part of his ideological armoury. The fiction that Chinggis Khan had granted Tolui the Iranian lands whose conquest was subsequently completed by Tolui's son Hülegü, had first been articulated by the Ilkhanid historian Shabānkāra'ī in the late 1330s (see p. 75).[147] It duly found its way into Ibn Khaldūn's *al-Ta'rīf* and Ibn 'Arabshāh's *Fākihat al-khulafā'*,[148] and is likely to have reached these authors ultimately (if perhaps indirectly, in Ibn 'Arabshāh's case) from Timur's own court circle. Endowing the rights of the defunct Ilkhanid line with Chinggis Khan's sanction, it afforded a justification (of sorts) for Timur's posture as the heir of the Ilkhanid tradition; but a further rationale, possibly, was that it served as a backstop, placing beyond question rights that (to draw on just one of Timur's redraftings of history) with the extinction of Hülegü's line had supposedly been transferred to the Chaghadayids.

BLOOD LINKS WITH THE CHINGGISIDS

In addition to ruling in the name of Chinggisid khans, Timur forged marital links with the Chinggisid dynasty. His first Chinggisid wife was a daughter of the Chaghadayid khan Qazan Sulṭān, Sarai Mulk Khanim, who had previously been married to Amīr Ḥusayn and whom Timur inherited from his vanquished rival in 771/1370. Much later, in 800/1397, he married Tükel Khanim, a daughter of the eastern Chaghadayid khan, Khiḍr Khwāja.[149] These unions entitled Timur to be styled a *güregen* ('imperial son-in-law'), and he is frequently called 'Amīr Timur Güregen' in the sources. It is possible that he was encouraged to wed Dilshād Āghā, the captured daughter of the Dughlāt amir Shams al-Dīn, in 776/1375 because her mother was a daughter of the Chaghadayid khan Yesün Temür (d. 740/1339–40).[150] Various non-Timurid authors mention that he also married Soyurghatmish's widow and thereby became stepfather to Sulṭān Maḥmūd Khan – although the implication that this occurred early in the era of Timur's hegemony is clearly incorrect and that Sulṭān Maḥmūd was then still a boy is also open to question (but see p. 342).[151]

Neither of Timur's Chinggisid wives bore him any offspring (see above, p. 280), and perhaps in part for this reason he took steps to connect his family with the imperial dynasty by securing Chinggisid wives for his sons and grandsons. Of his sons, the eldest, ʿUmar Shaykh, married Malikat Āghā, whose father Khiḍr, member of a minor branch descended from the Chaghadayid khan Baraq, had formerly held an appanage centred on Ūzkand; possibly ʿUmar Shaykh was seeking to cement his hold on Farghāna. After his death she was married to Shāhrukh.[152] Amīrānshāh married Ūrūn Sulṭān Khānīka, a daughter of the khan Soyurghatmish.[153] Well before this, in *c.* 768/1366–7, when Timur lacked the status to merit direct links with the Chinggisids, his son Jahāngīr had married Ruqiyya Khānīka, the offspring of Kaykhusraw of Khuttalān by another daughter of the Chaghadayid khan Yesün Temür,[154] and a further marriage late in 775/early in 1374 to Sevin Beg Khānzāda, a member of the Ṣūfī dynasty in Khwārazm, connected Jahāngīr to her maternal grandfather, the Jochid khan Özbeg.[155] Clavijo writes of Timur's esteem for Khānzāda thanks to her ancestry.[156] Jahāngīr's son by this union, Timur's heir-apparent Muḥammad Sulṭān, married a granddaughter of Bayan Quli Khan; hence we sometimes find him styled Güregen.[157]

In contrast with the enthronement of Chinggisid khans, such marriages were still being contracted some generations after Timur's death.[158] The importance of these links is clear from the fact that Chinggisid ancestry was a vital element behind Timur's choice of Jahāngīr's son Muḥammad Sulṭān, whose mother Khānzāda was of Jochid descent, as his successor.[159] And when Khalīl Sulṭān took power in Transoxiana after Timur's death he nominated as khan Muḥammad Sulṭān's son Muḥammad Jahāngīr, who was thus similarly descended from Chinggis Khan (see earlier). The fact that Khalīl Sulṭān, himself Khānzāda's son by her second marriage, attracted relatively scant support and was overthrown within a few years in favour of Shāhrukh, who lacked Chinggisid ancestry, might indicate that this attribute was ceasing to matter. Although Shāhrukh's son Ulugh Beg was married in 807/1404 to Āghā Beki, a daughter of Muḥammad Sulṭān, at Timur's behest, Shāhrukh himself married certain of his children and grandchildren to descendants of Muḥammad Sulṭān,[160] while one of Ulugh Beg's wives was the daughter of Timur's khan Sulṭān Maḥmūd.[161] And in the following century Khwānd-Amīr would devote no little space to the distinguished ancestry of the Timurid Sulṭān Ḥusayn Bāyqarā (d. 911/1506), descended through both parents from ʿUmar Shaykh and from the Mongol imperial line.[162]

These marital connections, significant as they appear, pale alongside the claims that came to be made for Timur's own ancestry. As we saw (p. 224), Ibn ʿArabshāh cites a genealogy linking Timur to Chinggis Khan on the distaff side; but agnatic kinship was guaranteed to be more impressive. In the thirteenth century the Secret History had asserted that the Barulas tribe shared a common ancestry with the Mongols, and this was repeated some decades later by Rashīd al-Dīn (pp. 227–8). Ibn Khaldūn's statement that Timur and his khan were related through common male ancestors (but to Chaghadai, wrongly)[163] might echo this relationship between the Barulas and the imperial dynasty, rather than indicating that Timur was claiming Chinggisid descent as early as 803/1401.[164]

Timur's blood relationship to Chinggis Khan first appears in writing several years after his death. Whereas Shāmī in 806/1404 had asserted merely that Timur's ancestor Qarachar had been entrusted with the administration of Chaghadai's ulus,[165] the genealogies drafted by Ḥusayn b. ʿAlīshāh, by Ḥāfiẓ-i Abrū in his *Zubdat al-tawārīkh* (830/1426–7) and by Yazdī in his *Muqaddima* (831/1427–8) went further. They made Qarachar descend from Qachulai, Tümenei's son and the brother of Chinggis Khan's great-grandfather Qabul Khan, and Yazdī wrote of a compact whereby sovereignty was to reside in Qabul Khan's line and executive power with Qachulai's descendants – creating a formal precedent and model for the relationship between Timur and the khans on whose behalf he ruled. But earlier circumstances may have a bearing on the question. Among the names chosen for Timur's grandsons born between 796/1394 and 807/1405 were not only those of his Barlās ancestors but some – Qaidu, Baisonqur, Buzunchar – that figure in the generations above Chinggis Khan.[166] This could signal that in the last decade or so of his life Timur was already attracted by a pedigree linking him with Chinggis Khan's ancestors through an unbroken male line.

At the beginning of this chapter, we noticed that the sources employ the styles *amīr* and *amīrzāda* when speaking of Timur and his progeny. Yet these same sources frequently refer to Timur as 'Sultan' – a title borne by the Seljuq monarchs, as by many others since, and applied to the Muslim Ilkhans.[167] He is hailed as 'the Great Sultan' on the entrance portal of the Bibi Khanim mosque, while the inscription left at Karasakpai in the eastern Qipchaq steppe during the campaign of 793/1391 against Toqtamish combines both forms, referring to 'Timur Beg, Sultan of Turan'.[168] All this indicates that the conqueror countenanced the appropriation of the title for himself.[169] We shall consider its implications in Chapter 13.

CHAPTER 13
MUSLIM SULTAN AND HOLY WARRIOR: FAITH, PROPAGANDA AND POSTURE

In seeking to understand how Timur projected himself and his regime to contemporaries, we have at our disposal four categories of sources. The first is his diplomatic correspondence with other monarchs, such as the Mamlūk Sultans Barqūq and Faraj and the Ottoman Sultan Bayezid, and (with a somewhat different tenor) the kings of France and England. In second place is what might be termed 'court history' – the accounts of his career that Timur commissioned, namely Shāmī's *Ẓafar-nāma* and the *Rūz-nāma* of Ghiyāth al-Dīn ʿAlī Yazdī (begun before Timur's death). Also valuable is a third group, sources composed under Timur's successors: Naṭanzī's *Muntakhab al-tawārīkh*; Sharaf al-Dīn ʿAlī Yazdī's *Ẓafar-nāma*; and the works of Ḥāfiẓ-i Abrū, a member of Timur's entourage since the 1380s. It is important to notice, however, that authors in this last group sometimes embellish earlier accounts in line with developing legend (and myth) about the conqueror and as required by the members of his dynasty.[1] We also depend, therefore, on a fourth category, 'unofficial' sources: the testimony of outsiders who either visited his headquarters and met him, such as the Castilian envoy Clavijo and the Maghribī philosopher Ibn Khaldūn, or who perforce spent time in his dominions, as did Ibn ʿArabshāh and Schiltberger. It should be stressed that observers in this fourth category may supply us with material that indeed emanates from Timur's entourage but is unrefracted by the 'court historians' (although Ibn

ʿArabshāh is as hostile as they are eulogistic).[2] In the next two chapters, we must distinguish between authors likely to reflect Timur's own sentiments and aspirations and those working several years later, who express the standpoint of his descendants. While Timur's claims can hardly be described as modest, in some respects they stopped short of those advanced on his behalf by his successors.

THE CHAMPION OF ISLAM

Timur took with him on all his campaigns a portable wooden mosque in which he performed his devotions.[3] Shāmī and Sharaf al-Dīn Yazdī attest to his observance of Ramaḍān and the ʿĪd, and stress that it was his practice not to rely upon the size or equipment of his army but to prostrate himself in prayer before or during battle and to implore God for victory.[4] For Naṭanzī, he was the *Sulṭān-i ghāzī*, and Yazdī stresses that Timur had desired to wage war against the enemies of the faith from the very outset of his career.[5] Stating how Timur first contemplated an attack on China in 800/1398, Shāmī depicts his goal as the extirpation of idolatry (*butparastī*).[6] He was so eager for holy war (*ghazw-u jihād*) against the Ming in 807/1404–5, we are told, that he was in no way deterred by the harsh winter conditions.[7]

The invasion of India, where Timur's chief opponent was a Muslim (albeit one with a large number of Hindu subjects), had been less easy to justify, although Shāmī, Ghiyāth al-Dīn and Sharaf al-Dīn Yazdī attempt to portray it as *ghazw* and *jihād* and write of his army as 'the army of Islam'.[8] 'The lofty purpose of His Majesty during this expedition', writes Sharaf al-Dīn of Timur's decision to punish the infidels of Kator for their attacks on Muslims, 'was ever directed in particular towards the triumph of the faith, the strengthening of Islam, the holy war against the unbeliever and the demolition of idols.'[9] After the capture of Mīrat (Meerut) in 801/1399, when Timur's leg had grown inflamed and painful, he was allegedly so enthusiastic at the prospect of combat with an approaching Hindu force that his pain abated and he mounted to play his part.[10] Yazdī justifies the slaughter of Hindus in the Siwālik region during the return march on the grounds that they had once paid the jizya but had latterly withheld it, and their lives and property were the lawful object of holy war.[11]

Timur's last operations were directed against a major non-Muslim state, Ming China, and were further justified, as we saw, on the spurious grounds that the Hongwu Emperor had been responsible for the massacre of Muslims. Yet if we discount the sack of Venetian-held Tana (an integral part of his onslaught on the economic foundations of the Qipchaq khanate, rather than a specifically anti-Christian action), the campaigns that he in fact carried through against the unbeliever were confined to the populations of the Hindu Kush, of the Punjab, of Jammu and of Kashmir (ruled, like the Delhi Sultanate, by a Muslim, who had offered submission but had neglected to wait on Timur[12]); the Georgians, whom he attacked no less than six times; the Rus′ (if briefly and almost incidentally, in 1395); the Orthodox Christian Alans (Ās) and other Christian elements like the Kaitak in Daghestan;[13] and the outpost of Smyrna (now Izmir), held by the Hospitallers of St John.

It is an incontrovertible fact that, for all the stress Timur and his panegyrists laid upon his services to Islam,[14] and notwithstanding his destruction of Hindu temples in India and numerous churches in Georgia and Armenia,[15] or his massacres of the Jewish population in Damascus, and perhaps also in Aleppo and Bursa,[16] the great majority of the rulers and peoples he attacked were Muslim. It was, on balance, Muslim states that suffered the greatest damage at his hands – 'as if', writes Roux, 'his sole legitimate theatre of action was Islam'.[17] Unlike the Ottoman state that Timur dismembered, the Delhi Sultanate had already undergone a marked decline in the half-century or so prior to 1398, forfeiting distant provinces like Bengal and Maʿbar; but Timur's invasion accelerated the fragmentation of its more central territories, as governors in Jaunpur, Gujarat, Malwa, Khandesh and Kalpi proclaimed their independence within a few years of his sack of Delhi.[18] Indeed, in two instances Timur's military operations were indirectly of considerable benefit to Christian powers. By removing Bayezid in 804/1402, and then fostering conflict among the fallen Sultan's sons with the result that they were forced to make concessions to the Byzantine empire, he afforded the beleaguered

Greeks a half-century's respite.[19] In the longer term, his victories over Toqtamish emancipated the grand principality of Moscow (ironically, since Timur himself had briefly menaced the city); in the more immediate term, his attacks on the Qipchaq khanate aided the rise of the newly Christianised grand duchy of Lithuania.[20] Naṭanzī's account of the raid on Ürgench by ʿAbd-Allāh b. Qazaghan in 754/1353–4 (see above, p. 220) reports Qazaghan's outrage at this attack on a Muslim populace:[21] we might see here an implicit criticism of Timur's actions.

Despite his condemnation of the latitude afforded by Delhi's rulers to their Hindu subjects, moreover, Timur himself did not consistently require non-Muslim princes or garrisons to accept Islam. Admittedly, we are told that the raja of Jammu, taken captive in 801/1399, professed Islam and took to eating beef.[22] The investment of Christian Smyrna began with a formal summons to embrace Islam.[23] The Georgian king, Bagrat V, was prevailed upon to accept the faith while Timur's prisoner in 788/1386.[24] But there is no indication that conversion was demanded of Constantine, Bagrat's son and the brother and rival of the new Georgian king, Giorgi VII, when he waited on the Great Amir with gifts in 805/1402–3.[25]

Authors who wrote of Timur's exploits may have been sensitive to the inherent contradictions. Stating that the conqueror delayed attacking the Kartid realm until his old ally Malik Muʿizz al-Dīn was dead (but cf. p. 291 above), Ghiyāth al-Dīn Yazdī also describes the late ruler as the most Muslim of Muslim kings,[26] as if to stress Timur's sense of duty towards an eminently worthy coreligionist. Niẓām al-Dīn Shāmī and Sharaf al-Dīn Yazdī mention that at the capture of Azāq (Tana) in 797/1395 the Muslim inhabitants were separated from the rest of the populace, who were put to 'the sword of jihad' (though in fact we know that many Christians were taken prisoner and some were later ransomed).[27] So also the Muslim inhabitants of Loni, near Delhi, were exempted from massacre in 801/1398.[28] At Sivas and Malaṭiya, the Muslims were able to buy their immunity when the Armenians and other Christians were made captive.[29]

There were those who denied that Timur was truly a Muslim. In Astarābādī's view, Timur's conduct deviated from the path of law and religion and from the ways of integrity and piety; he was given to rape, bloodshed, looting and the like.[30] His Tatars were 'demons' (*ʿafārīt*; sing. *ʿifrīt*) and 'fiends' (*shayāṭīn*), 'accursed infidels' (*malāʿīn-i kuffār*), 'Mongol unbelievers and Chaghatay and Tatar oppressors'.[31] Ibn ʿArabshāh strikes a similar note, lambasting Timur's closest followers as 'fiends' (*al-shayāṭīn*), men lacking in either property or piety (*lā dunyā lahum wa-lā dīn*).[32] He caricatures the devotion of Timur's adherents in terminology customarily used of the spiritual bond between the sufi adept and his master.[33] He transmits the verdict of scholars that Timur and all who observed Chinggis Khan's law were unbelievers.

Astarābādī's master Burhān al-Dīn and the Mamlūk and Ottoman Sultans all impugned the authenticity of Timur's Islamic faith and accused him of slaughtering and otherwise mistreating Muslims.[34] Such denunciations were by no means unfounded. It was symptomatic that eight out of a group of nine mamluks who were among Timur's gifts to Sultan Barqūq in 796/1393–4 were ascertained to be freeborn Muslims, the sons of prominent dignitaries in Baghdad; they had therefore been enslaved contrary to Islamic law and the Sultan released them. Their presence may have constituted a veiled warning of the fate of Barqūq's subjects if he did not submit.[35] Timur's armies regularly enslaved Muslims, scholars and craftsmen in particular, who were then conveyed to Transoxiana. It was not until after his death that these captives were released on the orders of Shāhrukh and allowed to return to their homes; they included Ibn ʿArabshāh. A letter from Barqūq that Ibn ʿArabshāh claims to have seen (see above, p. 356)[36] was a reply to a missive from Timur which states, 'You maintain that we are infidels, but it is our belief that you are depraved',[37] and which may well betray Timur's sensitivity to the charge.

Mamlūk historians, who frequently speak of Timur in dismissive terms as *al-lang* ('the Lame One'), diverge somewhat in their estimations of him. We have seen in Chapter 1 that they were influenced overwhelmingly by Ibn ʿArabshāh, with one exception. Al-Maqrīzī's indebtedness to Ibn ʿArabshāh did not deter him from expressing his own judgement, and there is a marked difference between *Sulūk* and *Durar* in their handling of Timur.[38] Although al-Maqrīzī, in contrast with Ibn ʿArabshāh,[39] is silent regarding the arrival in Samarkand of envoys from Sultan Faraj bearing tribute and – unlike Ibn Qāḍī Shuhba and Ibn Ḥajar – could not bring himself to describe the humiliation of the young Sultan by Timur's envoys in 806/1403,[40] the treatment of the Syrian campaign in *Sulūk* approximates to the conventional standpoint of Egyptian observers. Here the obituary of the conqueror says that he had wrecked and burned the world's cities, destroyed Baghdad and transported whole populations, and calls him – in an unconscious echo of Timur's own categorisation of his enemies (see later, pp. 399–400) – 'a highway robber' (*qāṭiʿ al-ṭarīq*).[41] The entry on Timur in *Durar*, on the other hand, ends by describing him as 'one of the peerless of the world (*fard*[an] *min afrād al-ʿālam*), whom God had sent to ravage countries and ruin [His] servants in requital for their deeds'.[42] There is a paradox here: why did al-Maqrīzī offer a providential (and even largely neutral) verdict on Timur after reading, and hearing at first hand, the censorious judgements of Ibn ʿArabshāh?[43] The most plausible explanation is that al-Maqrīzī was still strongly influenced by his earlier contact with Ibn Khaldūn, for whom, and for whose work, he had a great admiration,[44] and by *al-Taʿrīf*, to which he had access when he wrote his entry on Ibn Khaldūn and which describes Timur as one favoured by God.[45]

Other authors were less ready to grant the conqueror a place in the divine plan. For Ibn Qāḍī Shuhba, Timur was simply 'the leader of the depraved, destroyer of the cities of the Muslims and shedder of the blood of monotheists'.[46] Ibn Ḥijjī calls him a 'Kharijite',[47] indicating that his religious views placed him beyond the pale. At another juncture, he is called *al-ṭāghī al-bāghī*, 'the oppressive tyrant' (*al-ṭāghī* also carried connotations of pagan deities and their worship).[48] So too the fact that Ibn Taghrībirdī, several years later, borrows Ibn ʿArabshāh's list of Timur's admirable qualities does not prevent him from appending to Timur's name the term *al-ṭāghiya* or other unflattering epithets.[49] Occasionally in the *Manhal* biography he follows Timur's name with the phrase *laʿanahu llāh*, 'God curse him' (twice within the final sentence), which was traditionally used in relation to infidels;[50] in the *Nujūm* obituary Timur merits malediction only once.[51] And although Ibn Taghrībirdī echoes in *Manhal* the phrase from al-Maqrīzī's *Durar* regarding Timur's peerlessness (*fard*^{an} *min afrād*), he does not repeat the earlier author's verdict that God had sent Timur to fulfil His purposes. The biography concludes with the assertion that Hell (*al-jaḥīm*) has become Timur's abode.[52]

Al-Maqrīzī was not alone in casting Timur as God's instrument; Timur himself had done so. Mignanelli, returning to Damascus in 1402, was told that the conqueror had responded to the obsequious speech of a Damascene captive by claiming to be God's scourge.[53] This may be apocryphal, like Juwaynī's account of Chinggis Khan mounting the steps of the pulpit in the principal mosque of Bukhara and announcing to the city's inhabitants that God had sent him as a punishment for their sins (above, p. 86).[54] Both stories doubtless owed more to contemporary Muslim perception than to reality. For Timur's own view of his role, however, we have the testimony of his correspondence. One of his letters to Barqūq, which was in fact a selective abridgement of Hülegü's ultimatum of 658/1260 to the Ayyubid Sultan al-Nāṣir Yūsuf (above, p. 356), opened with the announcement that Timur's troops were the army of God, given dominion over those on whom the divine wrath had fallen.[55] In a letter to the citizens of Aleppo in 803/1400 Timur declared that the eternal God had tasked him with conquering the world.[56] As we shall see, he ascribed his triumphs to divine favour. Both claims can be seen as echoing those advanced on behalf of the pagan Chinggis Khan (see Chapter 14). For Timur God was at least as much the Inner Asian Tenggeri as the God of Islam[57].

On occasion Timurid historians identified the forces of Timur's Mongol antagonists as non-Muslims. As we have seen, the Mughūls of Jata were viewed as infidels. So too a group of Negüderi Mongols with whom Timur's forces clashed in the Hilmand region are said to have lacked the blessings of Islam.[58] Shāmī and Yazdī, describing how Toqtamish sent approximately nine tümens against Tabriz in 787/1385–6, claim that the majority were not Muslims, and Zayn al-Dīn's earlier account speaks of 100,000 infidels sacking the city.[59] These verdicts may well be justified. The Venetian traveller Barbaro, visiting Jochid territory in 1436, was told that it was the great amir Edigü (d. 822/1419) who had established the faith there, and Clavijo cites the same verdict.[60] But Barbaro learned also of 'idolators' who performed their rites in secret, and Ibn ʿArabshāh asserts that the majority of the nomads of the Qipchaq steppe were still idolators in his day.[61] Moreover, Yazdī stigmatises Toqtamish's allies among the Qāytāgh (Kaitak) in Daghestan, many of them Christian, as infidels,[62] and says that he recruited Rus′, Alans and men from Kaffa for war with Timur.[63] The charge (repeated by Timur) is plausible: in 1380 Mamai had augmented his forces for the campaign against Moscow by hiring 'Franks', Circassians and Alans.[64]

Timur's correspondence employs the language of holy war (*ghazā*) of his campaigns against his Muslim adversaries no less than against unbelievers.[65] He had a leading member of his entourage, a Ḥanafī scholar from Samarkand named ʿAbd al-Jabbār b. al-Nuʿmān Khwārazmī, interrogate a group of ʿulama in captured Aleppo regarding those slain on both sides the previous day: 'Who were the martyrs, our dead or yours?' Knowing Timur's reputation for posing captious questions and punishing unpalatable answers, the ʿulama were in a fearful quandary, but Ibn al-Shiḥna, as their spokesman, defused the situation and impressed Timur by quoting the Prophet's answer to a similar question.[66]

During his negotiations with the Mamlūk Sultan Faraj in 802/1400 Timur appears to have asserted his own right, as the paramount ruler within the *Dār al-Islām*, to appoint the Caliph.[67] It is difficult to judge how this might have played out. Would the appointee have lent additional legitimacy to Timur (and his khan), or would the Great Amir have been affronted by the very suggestion? His claim might betray a feeling of unease that Barqūq and Faraj enjoyed the prerogative of nominating the Caliph, and perhaps also an uncharacteristic sense of inferiority, arising in addition from their charge that he was an infidel.

In 803/1401, Ibn Khaldūn tells us, a scion of the ʿAbbasid line presented himself to Timur at Damascus and claimed for himself a better right to the Caliphate than al-Mutawakkil ʿalā Allāh, the figurehead in Cairo. His argument rested primarily on a tradition (*ḥadīth*) of the Prophet whereby (he alleged) the office of Caliph was to remain with the ʿAbbasids. When Timur delegated the case to a committee of jurists, including Ibn Khaldūn, they were in an uncomfortable position. But at the instance of ʿAbd al-Jabbār Khwārazmī, they found against the claimant on the pretext that the tradition was spurious, rather than by weighing his right against that of the incumbent.[68] Given Timur's known views on the history of the Caliphate (see later), it is hard to imagine that he would have found any ʿAbbasid acceptable. Perhaps he wished to keep his options open; or alternatively he was reluctant to jeopardise the chances of success against the Mamlūks by challenging the highly popular al-Mutawakkil. In a letter to Bayezid, he drew attention to the fact that the Caliph had suffered at Barqūq's hands.[69] It may be that he thought al-Mutawakkil, banished, imprisoned and twice deposed,[70] might be ready to accept his protection. This would by no means have been an unrealistic hope, since Sharaf al-Dīn Yazdī tells us that early in Muḥarram 801/late in September 1398 Timur received an embassy from the rulers of Mecca and Medina (hitherto under the Mamlūk Sultan's protection) expressing the desire to be brought under his guardianship.[71] The fact that in recent decades a wider circle of Muslim monarchs (among them the Muzaffarid Shāh-i Shujāʿ, the Jalayirid Sulṭān Aḥmad and the Ottoman Bayezid) had sought the Caliph's recognition may have furnished another disincentive to antagonise al-Mutawakkil.[72] But even had Timur contemplated taking al-Mutawakkil under his protection, we might well doubt whether he would have let the Caliph reciprocate with confirmation of his rulership.

Timur was an avid builder and the majority of his constructions were secular in purpose, like the fortifications at Samarkand or the palaces there, named after cities he had taken elsewhere, or the buildings with which he adorned Kish (Shahr-i Sabz), notably the Aqsarai palace, which so impressed Clavijo.[73] But there were also religious edifices: the shrine of Shaykh Kulāl in Kish; the mausoleum erected in 800/1397 over the tomb of Shaykh Aḥmad Yasawī in Yasi (the town later known as Turkistān); the opulent Bibi Khanim mosque in Samarkand; and the Gūr-i Mīr, originally built in honour of Timur's grandson and heir, Muḥammad Sulṭān b. Jahāngīr, and subsequently the burial place of Timur himself and of Sayyid Baraka (see later).[74] The author of *Qandiyya* mentions the tombs of Timur's sisters Qutlugh Terken Āghā (built in 773/1371–2) and Shīrīn Bīka Āghā (built in 787/1385–6), but does not say explicitly that these structures had been commissioned by Timur.[75] The conqueror is known to have founded a sufi hospice (*khānaqāh*) in the Dimashq quarter of Samarkand and to have commissioned two hospices at Turbat-i Shaykh Jām.[76] Although he hardly earned the reputation for cultural patronage that his descendants have enjoyed, the claim that he did not build a single *madrasa* but 'instead created colossal domed shrines for his patron saints and Sufi mentors'[77] may be a trifle unfair, since the *madrasa* associated with his chief wife, Sarai Mulk Khanim (above, p. 280), was presumably built with his approval and authority.[78]

What all Timur's constructions shared was their massive scale and a common visual vocabulary that impressed upon the viewer Timur's greatness and power, reinforced by the inscriptions they bore.[79] Sharaf al-Dīn Yazdī hit the mark when describing restraint as foreign to his nature (see above, p. 324). Several anecdotes report Timur's initial dissatisfaction with the size or height of his architects' creations and his furious insistence on larger proportions (as in the case of the Bibi Khanim mosque).[80] An early seventeenth-century author transmits a comparable tale in which Timur rejected the gift of a Qur'ān skilfully written in minuscule characters but was delighted with one made up of lines at least a cubit (*dhirā'*: probably over 50 centimetres) in length.[81]

A HOLY WARRIOR WITHOUT EQUAL

In his dealings with the Mamlūk empire, Timur could, and did, evoke parallels with the activities of Ghazan Maḥmūd (see p. 355), viewed as the first truly Muslim Ilkhan; and the style *Pādishāh-i Islām*, used regularly of Timur's two khans, had been the very title assumed by Ghazan on his conversion. One of his last acts was to despatch a caravan to the holy cities in the Hijaz with a view to measuring the Kaʿba for a cover that he planned to instal – as Ghazan had done in 702/1303.[82] But Timur's operations covered a far larger area than Ghazan's and he sought to locate himself also in the tradition of earlier, non-Mongol Muslim conquerors. Chief among them was Maḥmūd of Ghazna (d. 421/1030), of the Turkish Yaminid dynasty, whose campaigns against unbelievers and heterodox Muslims had secured him an abiding reputation as a warrior for the faith.[83] Timur associated himself with this celebrated figure in 794/1392 when conferring on his grandson Pīr Muḥammad b. Jahāngīr an appanage stretching from Qandahār, Kabul and Ghazna to the Indus, a grant described as 'the throne of Maḥmūd of Ghazna'.[84]

It was highly desirable, of course, for Timur to emerge from any comparison as greater than earlier Muslim warriors, much as he could be depicted as surpassing Chinggis Khan (see later, p. 390). In his account of the Indian expedition, Ghiyāth al-Dīn Yazdī, who was evidently acquainted with ʿUtbī's history of Maḥmūd's campaigns, the *Taʾrīkh-i Yamīnī*, compared Maḥmūd's empire with Timur's and found it wanting.[85] For Shāmī, writing of a campaign against Christian Georgia, Timur's exploits there had 'drawn the line of oblivion through the holy wars (*ghazawāt*) of Maḥmūd of Ghazna'; while Sharaf al-Dīn Yazdī contrasts Timur's triumphant campaign of 806/1403 in Georgia with the meagre achievements of all previous Muslim sovereigns in that region.[86] In the entire course of world history, he assures us, only two men – Alexander (Dhū l-Qarnayn) and Timur – had been privileged, through their conquests, to strengthen Islam and promote its commandments: of these, Timur's achievement, Yazdī hints, was the greater.[87]

Of all the princes whom Timur brought low, one stands out above all as a doughty protagonist of Islam. The Ottoman Bayezid had continued the advance begun by his forebears at the expense of Christian powers in the Balkans; his own operations had reduced Serbia to vassal status, eliminated the Bulgarian kingdom and brought the Byzantine empire to the very brink of annihilation. Regardless of character deficiencies that did not endear him to his Muslim subjects,[88] his spectacular record of conquest thus promised to match Timur's own. Timur's unwillingness to tolerate the existence of such a formidable competitor on the western margins of the one-time Ilkhanate may well have been tinged with admiration for the Ottoman Sultan. In his early correspondence with Bayezid, he felicitated him on his holy wars against 'the accursed Frankish infidels' (*kuffār-i mulā'īn-i farang*), expressed a desire that this struggle should not be compromised by Timur's activities, and drew the parallel with his own campaigns against infidels in the east; he even hinted at the possibility that he might send Bayezid assistance in his holy wars.[89] He further pointed to the presence of infidels – Christian Poles and Lithuanians – among the confederates of Toqtamish, who had thereby become a legitimate target of jihad and against whom Timur was then seeking Bayezid's cooperation.[90] Shāmī and Yazdī allege that later, in the wake of his defeat and capture of Bayezid, Timur intended to reinstate him in his Anatolian territories, thereby providing him with the means to wage holy war still more effectively than in the past, and had promised the Sultan that he would do so.[91] An Ottoman author writes of negotiations for the ransom of Bayezid, which were nullified by the fallen Sultan's death.[92]

Anooshahr argues that the mounting confrontation with Bayezid rendered Timur acutely aware of the Ottoman Sultan's credentials as a holy warrior, leading him both to lay greater stress on his own motivation as a *ghāzī* and to aspire to superiority over all other *ghāzī*s.[93] Bernardini sees the Indian campaign as a watershed in this context, inasmuch as it enabled Timur to see himself as a holy warrior (and Bayezid's equal).[94] Ironically, Bayezid's own record of warfare against Muslim rulers would earn condemnation from the Ottoman chronicler Aḥmedī, for whom his humiliation by Timur was due punishment from God.[95]

Timur's biographers took care to mention that Bayezid's forces at Ankara included Frankish contingents, notably Serbs,[96] and Yazdī makes the smug assertion that when Bayezid's wife, the Serbian prince Lazar's daughter, who had until that point remained a Christian, was captured and restored to her husband she had the good fortune, under Timur's aegis, to become a Muslim.[97] In these circumstances, we might suppose that one purpose behind Timur's capture of Hospitaller Smyrna, as one western author suspected, was to throw into sharp relief the limited character of Bayezid's successes against the infidel.[98] And indeed the Timurid sources stress that Smyrna's Christian garrison had never paid the *jizya* or the *kharāj* to any Muslim ruler, Yazdī adding that both Bayezid and his father Murad I had repeatedly striven to take the stronghold and that Timur had accomplished it in a fortnight when Bayezid had spent seven fruitless years on the enterprise.[99]

Timur's own career would have made him all the more conscious of the inadequacy of his credentials as a *ghāzī*.[100] This was partly a question of his inconsistency, as illustrated in his diplomatic flirtations with Christian princes (see pp. 304–7), and in part of his violence towards Muslim populations. When he first mentions the plan to march against China, Sharaf al-Dīn Yazdī gives the impression that Timur had fulfilled his other obligations – suppressing the lawless, bringing to heel the *mulūk al-ṭawā'if* and restoring order in the Islamic world – and was thrashing around, as it were, for a new enterprise.[101] But he also has Timur recognise that his many campaigns had inflicted distress on ordinary Muslims and conceive the desire to turn his attention to holy war. Writing some years earlier, Tāj al-Dīn Salmānī had hinted at just such a desire on Timur's part to use *ghazā* as a means of reparation.[102] While speaking to Maḥmūd Khwārazmī of how God had enabled him to conquer so many territories, Timur began to weep.[103] Did these tears in some measure signify remorse? We can discern a certain moral *gravitas* surrounding the preliminaries of the campaign against the Ming, since following the quriltai and the feasting in 807/1404 Timur issued an order prohibiting the consumption of alcohol and other illicit acts,[104] a precaution absent, as far as we know, from his earlier operations against non-Muslims. This must have reflected in part the formidable character of the China project, but one impulse behind it, perhaps, was that Timur was conscious of his failing health and the prospect of death.[105] Fresh from his victory over the Muslim *ghāzī* Bayezid, he was possibly actuated by a concern for his profile as a Muslim warrior who had spent remarkably little of his career fighting the infidel – and perhaps by anxiety regarding his ultimate fate.

TIMUR AND THE CHRISTIAN WORLD

We should consider here how Timur's stance as a holy warrior influenced his attitude towards Christians and how they in turn regarded him. It is at first sight somewhat surprising to find in his entourage two Dominican friars from Western Europe whom we have already encountered in Chapter 10. Archbishop John of Sulṭāniyya, the more prominent, may well have been in attendance on Timur for as long as twelve years. The second Dominican, Francis, seems to have been John's successor as Bishop of Nakhchiwān.[106] Conceivably they were the two figures whom a Venetian envoy from Tana found in Timur's company in 1395.[107] It is not necessary to assume that his view of Christians had modified.[108] As Bernardini observes, Timur's conduct towards Latin Christians differed sharply from his treatment of their eastern confrères.[109] It was no accident that he employed John and Francis as his emissaries to the Latin West; Mongol rulers (even Muslim converts) had used Nestorians or Italian merchants in a similar fashion.[110]

During his campaigns against the Ottomans and the Mamlūks, Timur's forces committed numerous atrocities against the subject Christian communities. Syriac sources speak of monasteries being sacked and all their inhabitants massacred; of a bishop being strangled; of a bishop, his monks and other companions, who had taken refuge in caves, being asphyxiated by smoke from fires deliberately kindled by the invaders. Amīrānshāh, too, campaigning on his father's behalf, is accused of slaughtering the monks of Qartamīn.[111] The Armenian Tʿovma Metsobetsʿi mentions the demolition of Christian villages and churches and of the cathedral at Arzinjān (Erzincan), but also says that there were Chaghatays who revered the Vardapet Yovhannēs as a holy man and that some Chaghatays assisted in the construction of the church at Arjīsh; one of Timur's amirs, who in 1397 restored the Metsopʿ region so that it enjoyed eleven years' prosperity, is credited with pro-Christian sentiments.[112]

If eastern Christian writers in general took a realistic view of Timur, Latin Christian reactions to his operations are more diverse. His victory at Ankara inclined not just Byzantine authors but some in the west to look upon him as a potential ally. The timing of his appearance was certainly appropriate, though fortuitously so. If the attack on Tana – albeit not a specifically anti-Christian gesture – had furnished a shocking instance of his bad faith (see above, p. 331), Bayezid's victory at Nicopolis the very next year had thrown the Ottoman menace into sharper relief.[113] Reports of the sufferings of Muslim populations at Chaghatay hands, moreover, surely helped to promote a more positive impression of the new power that had arisen in Western Asia. Such reactions belonged in a tradition that went back as far as the thirteenth century.[114] For, in much the same way, Christians in both Europe and the Near East had initially hoped that Chinggis Khan's victorious Mongols were a Christian host, or at least that the Mongol advance offered a Heaven-sent opportunity to attack the Muslim world.[115] Later, diplomatic exchanges between the western powers and the Ilkhan Ghazan had been preceded by the disastrous Mamlūk conquest of Latin Palestine; now, at the dawn of the fifteenth century, Timur's overtures to the west followed hard on Nicopolis. Rumours reached England that he and his army had captured Jerusalem and had embraced Christianity – in terms reminiscent of the exuberant reports spawned in the west by Ghazan's fleeting conquest of Syria in 1299.[116] It is just possible that Frankish raids on the Syrian coast and on Alexandria in Muḥarram-Ṣafar 806/ July–September 1403 were a belated response to the Mamlūks' predicament.[117]

The role of John of Sulṭāniyya in promoting a favourable image of Timur and his son in Western Europe was pivotal; he effectively became a propagandist on their behalf.[118] Yet despite this advocacy, he acknowledged in his *Mémoire* the conqueror's cruelty, surmising that he had destroyed as much as a quarter of the world's Muslim population,[119] and admitted that the violence was directed at Christians as well as Muslims.[120] In the *Libellus*, however, he was largely silent about the disastrous impact of Timur's campaigns on eastern Christians.[121] Although he referred to the devastation of Georgia and the destruction of its churches, he portrayed the onslaught as God's punishment for the Georgians' alleged addiction to sodomy.[122] The archbishop went so far as to ascribe Timur's hatred of Christians in general to his loathing of sodomy; though he also claimed here that he and Francis had been instrumental in correcting Timur's misapprehensions and softening his antipathy, so that he now permitted Christians freely to practise their faith and to retain their churches.[123] Ascribing Timur's attack on Bayezid to affection for his Christian allies,[124] John reported the release of any Christian captives of Bayezid's that Timur had taken;[125] though the contemporary cleric Dietrich von Nyem gave the credit here not to Timur but to the assistance of Genoese ships from Pera.[126] In any case, John's departure from Timur's headquarters probably occurred too soon after Ankara for him to have obtained reliable information on this head. That he deleted from Henry IV's reply an exhortation to Timur to embrace Christianity affords an insight into his private view of realities.[127]

The archbishop took a more sanguine view of Amīrānshāh, in whose service he had spent some time.[128] In the *Mémoire* he describes the prince as 'entirely Christian',[129] while Henry IV expressed warm appreciation of Amīrānshāh's Christian sympathies, of which John had told him.[130] John's verdict may rest on nothing more than the prince's supposedly insane conduct, which included the demolition of the mosques at Tabriz and Sulṭāniyya.[131] The Armenian T'ovma Metsobets'i – certainly no friend of Timur – also speaks of Amīrānshāh's good will to Christians and even has him worship in the church at Arjīsh.[132] This is hard to reconcile with his slaughter of monks at Qartamīn, as attested by Syriac sources (see earlier), or T'ovma's statement that he forced three Armenian princes to apostatise.[133]

Was there any reason for John's enthusiasm beyond the recent overthrow of the Ottoman Sultan? The answer appears to lie in an Armenian prophecy cited in his *Libellus*. It predicted the rise of a formidable chieftain who would advance westwards at the head of a nation of archers (the common Armenian term for the Mongols), vanquishing all kings and princes. For a time he would persecute Christians, but on reaching 'Canaan' he would despatch envoys to Frankish rulers and – where he was unable to advance further – would make peace with them. His envoy would engage in negotiations with Christian princes that would profit the faith and, on his return, he would bring about the conversion of some of his kinsfolk.[134] This was an updated (and appropriately modified) version of a fourth-century prophecy by St Nerses the Great that Rubruck had heard in Armenia in 1255; Armenian manuscript colophons confirm its resilience during the fourteenth and fifteenth centuries.[135] John seemingly accepted the prophecy as already in part fulfilled and as the best hope for the faltering Catholic mission in the east, neglected, in his eyes, by the Roman Popes.[136]

Optimism of this sort, however, was far from universal. What is especially arresting is the degree of reservation expressed regarding Timur. Welcomed though his triumph over Bayezid undoubtedly was, there was little or no attempt to transmute him into a manifestation of the long-awaited Prester John.[137] One reason, perhaps, was the fact that earlier diplomatic contacts with 'Tartars' had led nowhere; another was that Timur made no attempt to conceal his Islamic allegiance.[138] Although we lack any evidence that the west knew the tenor of his early correspondence with the Sultan (expressing approval of Ottoman strikes against the Franks: see earlier), the sense was growing that he and Bayezid posed an equal menace to the Christian world. Already his devastation of the lands of the Christian Kaitak had led the Roman Pope Boniface IX in 1401 to authorise a crusade against him – within a few years of launching one against Bayezid.[139] Two decades or so later the Milanese Andrea Biglia (d. 1435) could depict Timur simply as part of an abiding Mongol threat.[140]

TIMUR'S REVERENCE FOR THE FAMILY OF THE PROPHET

Whatever the charges levelled against him by his Muslim opponents, and however he saw his role in relation to Christian powers, Timur undeniably comported himself in some respects like a conventional Muslim ruler. He is credited with devotion to the *Ahl al-bayt* ('People of the House', that is descendants of the Prophet, *sādāt*; sing. *sayyid*).[141] Sayyids were among his intimates and chess partners.[142] The most illustrious were those of Tirmidh (see pp. 239–40), and in 773/1371–2 the Khwāndzāda of Tirmidh, implicated in a conspiracy against Timur, was spared on the grounds that he was a sayyid and was simply sent on pilgrimage to the Hijaz.[143] It was out of regard for their status that Timur at first excused the resistance of the Sayyid rulers of Māzandarān in 794/1392; though he is said to have undergone a change of heart later on learning that many of their followers were heretics (*fidā'ī*).[144] In 806/1404, the kinship of one of the princes of Gīlān, Sayyid Riḍā Kiyā, with the Prophet's line would earn him a significant remission of tribute payments.[145] For Sharaf al-Dīn Yazdī, Timur's love for the Prophet's descendants was a source of his good fortune.[146]

Of the various sayyids in his entourage, Timur was particularly attached to Sayyid Baraka, whose fame and influence over the Great Amir would earn him an entry in al-Maqrīzī's biographical dictionary. According to Yazdī, Sayyid Baraka belonged to the most important line of the Sharīfs of Mecca,[147] but al-Maqrīzī says that his origins were a matter of dispute, some alleging that he was from Cairo, others from Mecca and still others from Medina.[148] It now seems most likely that he hailed from Nakhshab (Nasaf).[149] Sayyid Baraka's motive for joining Timur, in Naṭanzī's account, was that Amīr Ḥusayn had refused to grant him certain *waqf* properties. He appeared before Timur on the eve of the final battle with Ḥusayn and presented him with a drum and a standard, symbols which were interpreted as a propitious omen and determined Timur to move against his rival without delay; the two men became firm friends and the Sayyid duly received the desired *waqf*s.[150] Sayyid Baraka, who is occasionally given the title of Amir in the sources, remained almost constantly in Timur's entourage.[151] Yazdī, describing him as one of those who had predicted Timur's glorious career, tells how during the battle on the Qundurcha the Sayyid intervened with a fervent prayer and secured his patron's victory (the whole account reads suspiciously like a version of how Sayyid Baraka first joined Timur). The tale is repeated by Ibn ʿArabshāh, who heard that Timur used to give Shams al-Dīn Fākhūrī, Shaykh Zayn al-Dīn Khwāfī and Sayyid Baraka the credit for all his good fortune (the pun on *baraka* is lost in translation).[152] When Timur was prostrated by grief at the deaths of his wife Dilshād Āghā and his sister Qutlugh Terken in 785/1383–4, Sayyid Baraka was one of a delegation of shaykhs who brought him to a sense of his responsibilities as a ruler.[153] Baraka's own death at Timur's winter quarters in Qarābāgh in 806/1403–4 dealt the conqueror a grave blow.[154] A few years after Timur's death, Shāhrukh had the Sayyid's body removed from his tomb at Andkhūd to the Gūr-i Mīr in Samarkand; the story that Timur himself had expressed a wish to be buried at Baraka's feet was probably a fiction devised by Shāhrukh for political reasons.[155]

Timur professed veneration for the fourth Caliph, the Prophet's cousin and son-in-law, ʿAlī b. Abī Ṭālib.[156] On more than one occasion he is said to have voiced anger at the usurpation of the Caliphate by the Umayyad Muʿāwiya in 40/661 and the killing of the Prophet's grandson al-Ḥusayn b. ʿAlī by the representatives of the Caliph Yazīd at Karbalā in 60/680.[157] Timur had broached these matters in discussion with the ʿulama at Aleppo, where he had been mollified by the response of Ibn al-Shiḥna.[158] But his sentiments on the subject of the Prophet's family had dire consequences for Damascus, whose history was more intimately bound up with the Umayyads. Falling gravely ill shortly after the city's surrender, he denounced the people of Syria for supporting the Umayyads against ʿAlī and others of the Prophet's family.[159] This is a striking echo here of the hostility expressed towards Yazīd and the Syrians by Ghazan Maḥmūd's noyan Ma'ulai, in conversation with Ibn Taymiyya following the Mongol capture of Damascus just over a century earlier,[160] and with Ghazan's own avowed partisanship of the *Ahl al-bayt* (see above, p. 100).

Yazdī says that Timur's loathing for the Umayyads and their Syrian supporters was thereupon transferred, by some kind of contagion (*sirāyat*), as it were, to his troops and sparked off the wholesale looting and burning of the city, in which the Umayyad Great Mosque caught fire and suffered considerable damage.[161] Ibn ʿArabshāh blames the fire specifically on 'the Refusers (*rawāfiḍ*) of Khurāsān' (i.e. Shīʿīs), seeking revenge for al-Ḥusayn's death.[162] Indeed, the desecration of the Umayyad tombs at Damascus is known to have been the work of a contingent from Khurāsān under Shīʿī Sarbadār leadership, who hailed Timur as al-Ḥusayn's avenger.[163] Ibn ʿArabshāh says that Timur executed those responsible for the city's sack, but Mignanelli (or his Damascene informants) put a different construction on the episode, alleging that those executed were Muslim peasants, dressed up as Chaghatay troopers to fool the populace into believing in Timur's justice.[164] In Shāmī's account, which says nothing of Timur's illness, the conqueror merely expresses disgust that the Damascenes had neglected the tombs of the Prophet's wives, and unidentified persons are blamed for the conflagration.[165]

Disagreement with Timur concerning the Prophet's family could prove hazardous even for respected ʿulama. At Damascus, a group of Syrian scholars, headed by the Ḥanbalī chief qadi, Taqī al-Dīn Ibrāhīm Ibn Mufliḥ, were first grilled about the martyrdom of al-Ḥusayn b. ʿAlī at the hands of Umayyad forces and were told that as Syrians they were of the same persuasion as the perpetrators. When Timur next put to them the question whether knowledge or birth was the more important, they sensed that they were being drawn still further onto dangerous terrain and fell silent. Only the Ḥanbalī Qadi Shams al-Dīn Muḥammad b. Aḥmad al-Nābulusī had the courage to stand his ground, asserting the superiority of the Caliph Abū Bakr over ʿAlī. He further declared that Timur's forces included Shīʿīs and those who 'contrived innovations' (*ibtadaʿū bidaʿā*) and voiced his readiness to suffer death and martyrdom at the hands of those who were in reality Shīʿīs. Timur ordered that al-Nābulusī be excluded from his presence henceforward.[166]

Ibn Khaldūn confirms that the Great Amir's views regarding al-Ḥusayn and the Umayyads gave rise to the imputation of Shīʿī leanings (*rafḍ*);[167] and Timur had been taken for a Shīʿī by one of the group from Aleppo whom he received in audience along with Ibn al-Shiḥna.[168] Yet Timur was no Shīʿī. Given the Mongol view of the analogy between the Prophet's family and the Chinggisid dynasty, his championship of ʿAlī and al-Ḥusayn is surely the devotional counterpart, as it were, of his political allegiance to the *altan urugh*.[169]

Timur's reverence for the *Ahl al-bayt* was surely one circumstance underlying the posthumous fabrication of his descent from ʿAlī. Three inscriptions in the Gūr-i Mīr (one of them on Timur's tomb) and another in the Shāh-i Zinda complex link ʿAlī to the Mongol origin legend, in which the Chinggisids' remote ancestress, Alan

Qo'a, had given birth to Bodonchar after being impregnated by a ray of light (see p. 57). The inscriptions in the Gūr-i Mīr, equating that light with a perfect mortal who was reputedly one of ʿAlī's descendants,[170] date from more than two decades after Timur's death and were doubtless a response to the contemporary messianic challenges confronting the dynasty.[171] In time the details grew more specific. Dawlatshāh alleges that Alan Qo'a's husband was a grandson of the Fourth Shīʿī Imam, al-Ḥusayn's son ʿAlī Zayn al-ʿĀbidīn (d. 94 or 95/712–13 or 713–14);[172] while the genealogy incorporated in a late fifteenth-century manuscript that has recently come to light (and that also gives Timur Qarakhanid ancestry) traces his descent to ʿAlī's son (by a woman other than the Prophet's daughter) Muḥammad b. al-Ḥanafiyya.[173]

Within a few decades, therefore, Timur was no longer merely being endowed with forebears whom he supposedly shared with Chinggis Khan. He had acquired in addition an ancestor from outside the Mongol world who was widely viewed as a repository of spiritual and esoteric wisdom and as Islam's earliest saint and whose prestige in the Islamic world was second only to that of the Prophet.[174] Indeed, we might see ʿAlī almost as having supplanted Chinggis Khan in Timur's genealogy, whether on a biological or a spiritual plane.[175] The coupling of Alan Qo'a with a descendant of ʿAlī represents a new stage in the long-drawn process whereby the lore of the pagan Mongols was harnessed to an Islamic framework (see above, pp. 102–3).

TIMUR AND MUSLIM DIVINES

Muslim theologians, jurists and sufis were prominent among the audience before whom Timur pursued his goals, and the sources – particularly the Timurid sources – portray Muslim clerics as not merely approving his rise to power in Transoxiana but predicting and sanctioning his wider conquests.[176] Partly, no doubt, with this support in mind, he relied to some extent on Muslim spiritual advisers and frequented the company of Muslim saints.[177] The Mongol era had engendered in particular a proliferation of sufis, who appeared to offer consolation for its upheavals and insecurities and frequently also interceded with the conquerors.[178] At the very beginning of his career, Timur had benefited greatly from the backing of Shaykh Shams al-Dīn Kulāl, his father's adviser.[179] There were ʿulama in his army outside Delhi in 801/1398. They included the historian Mawlānā Naṣīr al-Dīn ʿUmar (above, pp. 27–8), who in his entire life had never even slaughtered a sheep but who found himself called upon, nevertheless, to kill fifteen Hindu prisoners.[180] The Mamlūk governor of Aleppo, vainly seeking the agreement of his fellow amirs to ask for quarter in 804/1400, is said to have observed that only sayyids, imams and ʿulama carried any weight with the conqueror.[181] As we have noticed, Timur enlisted the help of ʿulama in identifying acts of oppression by his officers. Scholars and saints were among the few spared when Timur's army conducted a massacre in a captured city, as in the suppression of the rising at Isfahan (789/1387) or at the final sack of Baghdad (804/1401).[182] Sayyids and ʿulama at *Talmīna were exempt from contribution towards the indemnity (*māl-i amānī*) imposed on their fellow inhabitants.[183] Captured scholars appear to have been presented to Timur and recruited into his service. Ṣāʾin al-Dīn ʿAlī b. Muḥammad Ibn Turka Iṣfahānī (Yazdī's future teacher; d. 835/1431), for instance, was deported from Isfahan to Samarkand in 789/1387. The Damascene Shams al-Dīn Muḥammad al-Jazarī (d. 833/1429), formerly in Bayezid's employ and captured at Bursa, gave the Qurʾān reading at the marriages of Timur's grandsons in 807/1404;[184] later, he may have taught Ibn ʿArabshāh (above, p. 36).

Ibn Khaldūn asserts that Timur especially relished taking part in debate; although whether the rider 'both about what he knows and what he does not' constituted wry humour or mordant irony, we cannot be sure.[185] In any event, such meetings differed from the public disputations staged in the Mongol era: the audience was confined to Timur's court, and whereas the Mongol sovereigns limited their role to chairmanship Timur was a direct participant, although his purpose was no doubt identical – to enhance the prestige of his court and empire and to express his own God-given role as an 'untutored, *sui generis* genius' on the model of Chinggis Khan.[186]

We are told that Timur enjoyed hearing tales from history,[187] and Ibn Khaldūn's conversations with him encompassed illustrious kings of the past, Chosroes (the Sasanian Khusraw Anūshīrwān, d. 579 CE), Caesar, Alexander the Great and Nebuchadnezzar; though when Ibn Khaldūn appealed to the ninth-century *Ta'rīkh* of al-Ṭabarī, Timur retorted dismissively, 'What is al-Ṭabarī to us?'[188] Such a cavalier attitude towards the most authoritative of early Muslim historians looks rather like evasion: a cloak, perhaps, for the gaps in Timur's own grasp of history, which – in contrast with Ibn Khaldūn – he is unlikely to have owed to literary sources (see above, p. 253).

Despite Timur's appetite for the company of the learned, men of this class were by no means exempt from brutal treatment; and on the occasion mentioned earlier Shams al-Dīn al-Nābulusī might appear fortunate merely to have been forbidden the precincts of Timur's court. Ibn ʿArabshāh describes the cruel beating, in Timur's presence and on his orders, of the Shāfiʿī Qadi Ṣadr al-Dīn al-Munāwī, apprehended while attempting to follow Sultan Faraj in flight to Egypt.[189] The same author names Ibn Mufliḥ as one of those slain during the crisis in Damascus, but adds that he was killed in error.[190] Persuaded by Timur's professions of good will to work for a negotiated settlement, Ibn Mufliḥ had continued to travel back and forth between the city and Timur's encampment, and Ibn Ḥajar pays tribute to his unsuccessful efforts, drawing a parallel with Ibn Taymiyya's visits to Ghazan's headquarters in 1299.[191] Ibn Ḥijjī names several lawyers and scholars in Damascus who were tortured or killed during the occupation and furnishes a list of those who were later found to be missing.[192] We learn, too, of others who died during the journey east as captives in the conqueror's train. Ibn ʿArabshāh lists in the latter category al-Nābulusī and al-Munāwī,[193] each of whom had offended Timur but whose lives had been temporarily spared. Al-Munāwī drowned in the Zāb River during the march,[194] but it seems that Ibn ʿArabshāh was mistaken regarding al-Nābulusī, who escaped from Timur's troops after the sack of Baghdad and returned to Damascus late in Muḥarram 804/early in September 1401 to report his colleague's fate.[195] The Ḥanafī qadi Taqī al-Dīn ʿAbd-Allāh Ibn al-Kafrī died after suffering injuries.[196] On leaving

Syria, Timur is said to have ordered the release of some of his prisoners in Shaʿbān 803/March–April 1401, among them the qadi of Aleppo, Mūsā b. Muḥammad al-Anṣārī, who was in poor health, however, and died the following month.[197] According to al-Maqrīzī, a number for whom Ibn Khaldūn had interceded accompanied the Maghribī scholar back to Egypt in Shaʿbān.[198]

An instrumental role in the debates at Timur's headquarters was played by his imam, the distinguished scholar and jurist ʿAbd al-Jabbār b. al-Nuʿmān (or Nuʿmān al-Dīn) b. Thābit Khwārazmī (see earlier, p. 368), the son of the Ḥanafī chief qadi of Samarkand and one of the Great Amir's principal advisers.[199] Fluent in Arabic, Persian and Turkish, he served as interpreter in discussions between Timur and Muslim savants, Ibn Khaldūn included.[200] Debate at Timur's court, as we saw, could provoke scholars into utterances that might imperil their lives, and Ibn ʿArabshāh charges ʿAbd al-Jabbār with weltering in the blood of Muslims.[201] Yet Mamlūk authors not only pay tribute to his accomplishments but allege that he was of service to Muslims and that he found Timur's company irksome.[202] ʿAbd al-Jabbār fell sick and died at Güzel Ḥiṣār in Anatolia in the summer of 805/1403.[203]

Timur also spent time with religious personnel who had little or no claim to intellectual renown, and he took care to solicit their support and prayers in advance of his military campaigns.[204] Although he is known to have passed through Ardabīl in 802/1399,[205] the tale of his meeting with Khwāja ʿAlī, the head of a religious community at Ardabīl and a successor of Shaykh Ṣafī al-Dīn, the ancestor of the Safawid dynasty, is late and probably apocryphal.[206] But on invading Khurāsān in 782/1381, he halted in Andkhūd to consult the mystic Bābā Sangū (who unaccountably predicted a successful outcome by throwing a piece of meat at him) and visited the learned Shaykh Zayn al-Dīn at Tāyyabād; later in the campaign, he waited on Shaykh Zayn al-Dīn at Khwāf and was assured that he had been appointed over all kings.[207] Clavijo was told that Timur had lodged with the leading dervish of a village near Erzurum.[208] Ghiyāth al-Dīn Yazdī believed that support of this kind contributed more to Timur's triumphs than his troops, for all their numbers.[209] Such luminaries could also mediate the capitulation of strongpoints to Timur's besieging armies.

The Great Amir's cultivation of saints was not confined to those who were still alive. Mahendrarajah has demonstrated, for instance, how the Kartid wazir Muʿīn al-Dīn Jāmī (see p. 291) successfully appealed to Timur on behalf of Shaykh Aḥmad (d. 536/1141), the 'guardian of kings' since the days of the Seljuq Sultan Sanjar, and secured his patronage and protection for the foundation at Jām.[210] In the course of his Indian campaign Timur made the pilgrimage to the shrine of Shaykh Farīd al-Dīn at Ajodhan to ask for aid;[211] and once back in Samarkand he visited the shrine of Qutham b. 'Abbās.[212] Both after his return and at his departure on the seven-year campaign in 802/1399, he stopped at Kish, distributed alms to the needy and visited the tomb of Shams al-Dīn Kulāl; on the latter occasion, he also visited the shrines of other saints along his route, notably that of Shaykh Aḥmad at Jām, and sought their blessing on his enterprise.[213] During his final march back to Samarkand in 806–7/1404, he halted at Jām yet again, at Bisṭām to pray for the assistance of Shaykh Bāyazīd Bisṭāmī and at the tomb of Kulāl in Kish.[214]

TIMUR AND THE SUPERNATURAL: 'LORD OF THE AUSPICIOUS CONJUNCTION'

According to Mignanelli, Timur had around him men skilled inter alia in astronomy and magic,[215] although Ibn Khaldūn, who heard that he was fascinated by magic (*siḥr*), expressly denied that this was true.[216] For his first Qipchaq expedition in 793/1391 Timur set out on a date approved by the astrologers, and he secured favourable auguries in advance of his five-year expedition in 794/1392.[217] It is noteworthy that prior to the engagement outside Delhi he rejected the astrologers' findings in favour of an augury taken from the Qur'ān.[218] Yet astrological prediction continued to figure in his plans, as in the decision to invade the Ottoman empire despite his amirs' misgivings, or in the choice of the date 23 Jumādā I 807 (27 November 1404) for departing Samarkand on what was to prove his last campaign.[219]

Timur himself became the subject of astrological prophecy at a relatively early stage. He was hailed as 'Lord of the Auspicious Conjunction' (*Ṣāḥib-Qirān*) – an allusion to the conjunction (*qirān*) of the two 'superior' planets (that is, the two furthest from the earth while still visible to the naked eye), Saturn and Jupiter. Astrologers had for centuries appealed to the alignment of the planets to forecast historical events or attribute retrospective importance to them.[220] With a pedigree reaching back into the pre-Islamic era, though with no basis in the Islamic scriptural tradition,[221] the idea of the Lord of the Auspicious Conjunction played a substantial role in Islamic astrological literature and in popular religious thought. The concept embraced the ideal sovereign, the victorious ruler and the messianic figure. As some dated the Prophet's birth in 571 CE to a conjunction of Saturn and Jupiter in the sign of Scorpio, he was regarded, by implication, as a *Ṣāḥib-Qirān*.[222] The fourth Caliph, ʿAlī, could be viewed as another.[223] The title, which had been applied to Ghaznawid and Seljuqid Sultans,[224] was used of Ghazan by Rashīd al-Dīn (for whom Ghazan, by virtue of his many gifts, outstripped all others who merited it) and of Öljeitü by both Rashīd al-Dīn and Qāshānī.[225] Muslim authors had even applied it to the infidels Chinggis Khan, Ögödei and Hülegü, while Arghun's Jewish wazir, Saʿd al-Dawla, had urged him so to style himself.[226]

Ibn Khaldūn had learned from a preacher in Morocco as far back as 761/1359–60 that the conjunction of Jupiter and Saturn in 766/1364–5 (in Scorpio, for the first time since the Prophet's birth)[227] would presage the rise of a new conqueror at the head of a nation of tent-dwellers in *c.* 784/1382–3. One of those who endorsed the prophecy was Ibn Khaldūn's own teacher (see above, p. 40). Albeit dismissive of the credulity of the masses apropos of the advent of the Mahdī, Ibn Khaldūn evidently had an absorbing interest in conjunction astrology.[228] At their first encounter, he assured Timur that his appearance had been foretold for some decades and spoke of anticipating this moment for more than thirty years.[229] The prediction would have furnished just the material Timur prized for its value as propaganda. Among Timurid authors, the first to use the title of *Ṣāḥib-Qirān* of him was Shāmī; this might indicate that, as Maria

Subtelny argues, Timur himself accepted it.[230] He would become known to posterity as *the* Lord of the Auspicious Conjunction par excellence.

Whatever the image purveyed by his court historians and the arguments advanced on his behalf, Timur did not think exclusively in Islamic terms. It would have been foreign to his instincts – and impolitic – for him to do so. He also saw himself as emulating the feats of Chinggis Khan and upholding the Mongol traditions of his ulus; his victories were (in theory) not accomplished in his own name but in the name of the khan of that ulus. The following chapter will consider how 'Mongol' his regime was.

CHAPTER 14
THE MONGOL EMPIRE RESURRECTED?

Timur's conquests have been equated with the second phase of the Mongol empire; and historians have even gone beyond this to identify a programme of restoring that empire in the aftermath of the collapse of Mongol rule over major regions of Asia. In this chapter, I shall examine similarities between Timur's operations and those of the Mongols and the claims he made that evoke the memory of Chinggis Khan; compare his empire with Chinggis Khan's; ascertain whether he indeed saw himself – or contemporaries saw him – as restoring the Mongol empire; and assess his attachment to Mongol traditions and institutions, especially the Yasa or Töre, the body of customary law associated with his great precursor.

MONGOL ECHOES

Timur seems consciously, at times, to have modelled his own actions on those of Chinggis Khan, though not in every respect. Like Chinggis Khan, he took steps to foster discipline among the military and he bypassed the existing tribal leadership and appointed to the command of military units men he could trust, in many cases detached from their tribal background.[1] But whereas the Mongol conqueror had split up many of the steppe tribes, Timur stopped short of doing so, and had been content to place tribes in Transoxiana under the command of his own officers and to transfer nomadic groupings elsewhere from one part of his dominions to the other. In general he and, in some measure, his Turco-Mongol political opponents acted out their lives on a stage dominated by the figure of Chinggis Khan. We have seen how on occasion he claimed, as Chinggis Khan was thought to have done, that his armies embodied God's punishment for those who erred (p. 367 above). No less significantly, he was known to point to his relatively humble origins, his initial hardships and his early career as a stealer of livestock as proof that his subsequent triumphs were due to the special favour of God.[2] It is significant that we learn of his early career from outsiders and not from the 'court' historians whose works he commissioned and to whom such details would have appeared demeaning and thus foreign to the Persian ideal of rulership. Manz suggests that Timur's readiness to speak of his background sprang from an impulse to emulate Chinggis Khan, who, though descended from a line of illustrious khans, had similarly lived through years of privation in his youth.[3]

Timur was not alone in utilising (or fabricating) parallels with Chinggis Khan. We see his contemporary, Taizu (the Hongwu Emperor), likening his own obscure beginnings to those of Temüjin, as part of the appeal to his Mongol neighbours in the north, and other foreign powers, to acknowledge the transfer of Heaven's mandate from the weak and corrupt Yuan to the fledgling Ming dynasty.[4] Naturally there can be no question here of reciprocal influence: the congruence in ideological tactics simply reflects the widespread sense that Chinggis Khan had risen to power in the face of extremely daunting obstacles.

The resemblance between Timur's and Chinggis Khan's lives sometimes emerges in a subtle fashion in the Timurid sources. One might point to the fact that they contrast Timur's generosity with the avarice of his one-time confederate and lord (and later adversary), Amīr Ḥusayn,[5] just as Temüjin's munificence had been set against the tightfistedness of Ong Khan, successively his patron, ally and rival.[6] Ibn ʿArabshāh transmits a story that at Timur's birth his hands were seen to be covered in blood, presaging his career as a mighty conqueror. This is strikingly reminiscent of the claim in the

Secret History that Temüjin had been born grasping in his fist a clot of blood.[7]

Timurid historians drew appropriately flattering comparisons. Ghiyāth al-Dīn Yazdī contrasts Timur's Indian expedition more than once with the invasion of the Delhi Sultanate by the Muslim convert khan Tarmashirin seven decades previously, in 730/1329. Thus Timur crossed the River Chenab early in 801/in the autumn of 1398 by dint of constructing a bridge – no mean feat – where Tarmashirin had been content to ford it;[8] and Timur's forces took Mīrat, which Tarmashirin had unsuccessfully invested,[9] though oddly enough Ghiyāth al-Dīn says nothing of Tarmashirin's failure to capture Delhi. But the comparisons with Chinggis Khan are particularly frequent. For Sharaf al-Dīn Yazdī, the army that Timur reviewed in 797/1395, prior to his second campaign against Toqtamish, was more numerous and better equipped than any since the time of Chinggis Khan.[10] On occasion Yazdī went further. His purpose in detailing the history of Chinggis Khan and his descendants was to demonstrate that Timur and his dynasty had no peers at any time in the past. Whereas Chinggis Khan's armies had comprised the entirety of the Turks and Mongols, who were subsequently to be distributed among a total of four uluses, Timur's conquests were accomplished with the troops of a single ulus (a judgement that glossed over the subjugation of much of the former Ilkhanate).[11] Yazdī might have added that, whereas the Mongol empire had been the creation of three generations of rulers, Timur's was the achievement of one man. But even without this, the superlatives and the contrasts continue to mount up. Timur had traversed the Indus, when Chinggis Khan in 1221 had refrained from venturing across the river in pursuit of the Khwārazmshāh Jalāl al-Dīn.[12] Yazdī does not scruple to claim that any city taken by Chinggis Khan had been obliterated, while those conquered by Timur had been restored to a state superior to their previous condition.[13] Ḥāfiẓ-i Abrū flatly opined that Timur had relegated Chinggis Khan to the rubbish heap of history.[14]

If our own age thinks of Timur as a self-made man (see Introduction, p. 8), the concept would have meant nothing to him, his followers or his admirers. They attributed his spectacular success to Heaven, as he did, for just as Chinggis Khan had claimed to be one specially blessed with good fortune (*qut*) by Heaven, so too did Timur. In this connection he seems almost to have taken pride in his disability. At Aleppo in 803/1400 he allegedly told Ibn al-Shiḥna's party that he was only 'half a man', but then proceeded to list the territories he had conquered as evidence that he enjoyed God's aid.[15] The savant Maḥmūd Khwārazmī (*'al-Ḥāfiẓ al-muḥraq'*) later told Ibn ʿArabshāh of a conversation in which Timur drew attention to his physical infirmity but observed that God had nevertheless subjected to him many peoples and territories, bringing low kings and despots and filling the world with terror of him.[16] His claims to divine favour figure in his correspondence with other rulers.[17] Timurid authors readily ascribed his subordinates' successes, too, to the Great Amir's own good fortune (*farr-i iqbāl*, *iqbāl*, *dawlat-i qāhira*).[18] There was, of course, an Islamic dimension to all this which is absent from Chinggis Khan's rhetoric.

Timur's missives to rival potentates shared some characteristics with those of his great precursor. He invited these princes to make peace with him. At the height of the engagement at Ankara in 804/1402, says Shāmī, he prayed for victory, calling God to witness that he had summoned Bayezid to make peace (*ṣulḥ*), which would have been pleasing to God, but that the Ottoman Sultan had refused and flouted the divine command.[19] This is strikingly evocative of the 'orders of God', the ultimatums despatched by the thirteenth-century Mongols. It is a reasonable inference that for Timur 'peace' meant submission and acceptance of his authority, just as it had to the Mongol qaghans. Not for the first time we can discern an affinity between Timur's God and the Tenggeri of the steppe peoples.

Yet Timur's correspondence did not invariably demand submission; sometimes the tone was disarmingly amicable. Much as Chinggis Khan had addressed the Khwārazmshāh Muḥammad as the dearest of his sons, Timur affected to regard his protégé Toqtamish, the Mamlūk Sultan Faraj and Henry III of Castile alike as his sons also.[20] And as Chinggis Khan had allegedly spoken of the Khwārazmshāh ruling in the west and himself in the east, so Timur, in an early letter to Bayezid dating from the first months of 1395, appeared to offer him all Toqtamish's territory west of the Dnieper.[21]

It has been proposed that Timur's division of his territories among the lines of his four sons was a conscious imitation of Chinggis Khan's own distribution of appanages to Jochi, Chaghadai, Ögödei and Tolui.[22] I am now less convinced of this than I was.[23] Any likeness to be detected here can only be of the loosest sort. Chinggis Khan, as we saw, divided his peoples and lands not just among his four sons by his chief wife Börte, but among other kinsfolk as well – his mother and brothers and a nephew, in the Mongolian–Manchurian borderlands. The emergence of the 'Four Uluses' was a later development, which served, in fact, to obscure the settlement made by the Mongol conqueror and the disruption it suffered between 1251 and the 1260s. In the mid-sixteenth century Mīrzā Ḥaydar Dughlāt could write as if the four major khanates originated directly in Chinggis Khan's apportionment of his territories among four sons,[24] ignoring not just the allocations in the Far East but the disappearance of Ögödei's ulus and the subsequent creation of the Ilkhanate. The idea of 'Four Uluses' would naturally have gained support from the misapprehension that Chinggis Khan had conferred Iran on Tolui, which was possibly among the mutually contradictory claims that Timur advanced (see above, pp. 356–7), and we have seen that a good deal of uncertainty surrounds the question of Tolui's appanage (p. 62). Possibly, of course, neither Timur – for all his interest in history – nor his apologists knew anything of the territorial dispositions in the Far East, where Qubilai had deprived the descendants of Chinggis Khan's brothers of their appanages as far back as the late thirteenth century.[25]

The resemblance to Chinggis Khan in this context is problematic on other grounds. Given the premature deaths of his two older sons, who had each left male offspring of their own, Timur's territorial allocations resulted in far more than four principalities, and the process was a piecemeal one. If he did indeed contemplate a systematic allocation of territories on the Chinggisid model, it was not until his very last years; but even then it is hazardous to claim that he 'divided his realm into four main regions'.[26] Timur does not appear to have imitated the Mongol conqueror by distributing appanages among his sons at an increasing distance from his original homeland according to their seniority. He granted his youngest son, Shāhrukh, Khurāsān rather than his original core territory of Transoxiana (which was presumably intended to form the base of his eventual heir, Pīr Muḥammad b. Jahāngīr, just as it had earlier been allotted to Muḥammad Sulṭān); and the grants of lands straddling the Mughūl frontier to Shāhrukh's sons Ulugh Beg and Ibrāhīm Sulṭān also sit oddly with the received idea of a fourfold partition along strictly geographical lines. In any case, the idea that in dividing his lands Timur had taken Chinggis Khan as his exemplar conflicts, to some extent, with his practice of transferring princes between appanages, to prevent them forming strong links with any particular region and occasionally, too, in order to play them off against each other,[27] expedients that differed sharply from Chinggis Khan's modus operandi. Perhaps this particular parallel with Chinggis Khan rests on nothing more than the coincidence that Timur fathered four sons; though here he undoubtedly neglected to tread in Chinggis Khan's footsteps, as each son was born to a different mother.

TIMUR'S IMPERIAL PROGRAMME

Conscious echoes of Mongol history and the propagation of bogus genealogical links with the Chinggisid dynasty were one matter; aspiring to recreate the Mongol empire was quite another. Was Timur intent on rebuilding Chinggis Khan's empire? And if so, was he conscious of a duty to see to its continued extension, a mission of which the early fourteenth-century Mongols had remained mindful? Now our principal Persian sources do not allude explicitly to the revival of Chinggis Khan's empire. Shāmī, for instance, linked Timur and Chinggis Khan on a twofold basis. The tree of Timur's rule, he says, had taken root and thrived in 'the gardens of the good fortune and august *urugh* of Chinggis Khan'; indeed, in remote times and more recently Timur's efforts 'had watered the gardens and villas of that illustrious lineage, and the customs and practices of that sovereign [Chinggis Khan] had refreshed the *Ṣāḥib-Qirān* and in particular had regenerated the august progeny of Chaghadai . . . '.[28] Were this not vague enough, Sharaf al-Dīn Yazdī tells us merely that Timur never rested from adding to his dominions and all the kingdoms of the earth appeared too small for him, so that he would not be satisfied until the whole of the inhabited world had come under his control; he had often been heard to remark that the world was not of a size to accommodate two sovereigns.[29] These are common literary tropes,[30] on the same plane as Ghiyāth al-Dīn Yazdī's frequent allusions to world-rulership and both authors' salutation of Timur as a second Alexander.[31]

Timur's two biographers describe a letter he had written to the people of Aleppo, in which he had declared that God had commissioned him to reduce the entire world;[32] while Ibn ʿArabshāh makes him announce, as he emerged from his interview with Shaykh Zayn al-Dīn Khwāfī, that he had been made ruler of the world.[33] If any of these statements faithfully represent Timur's own words, they might constitute evidence that he planned to resurrect the Mongol empire. Indeed, in Ibn al-Shiḥna's account of the reception of the party from Aleppo in 803/1400, Timur claimed to have conquered all the territories in Iran, Iraq, India and 'the rest of the Tatar lands'[34] – something of an overstatement. In a letter to Barqūq, Timur refers to Chinggis Khan's conquest of 'Iran and Turan', and his victory despatch from northern Syria calls his own forces 'the army of Turan and Iran'.[35] Timurid writers seem to have conceived of his dominions in those same terms,[36] even though much of 'Turan' lay outside his control. His inscription of 793/1391 in the Qipchaq steppe calls him Sultan of Turan (above, p. 360). But the implications of all these phrases are hardly conclusive.

The sources, then, provide little warrant for the assertions that permeate the secondary literature – that Timur either aimed to reduce the whole of the former Mongol empire or that he projected himself as its restorer.[37] That he saw his task in these terms is hardly more than an inference from the enormous geographical scope of his campaigns – and perhaps, too, from his deliberate attempts to echo the career of the Mongol conqueror. Even had he articulated the aim of recreating the Mongol empire, this might of course have been just a rhetorical ploy, a conveniently potent rallying cry, rather than expressing a deep-rooted ambition. As we have noticed, much of his campaigning was designed to assert control over lucrative trade routes, to keep his followers occupied and reward them with enormous quantities of loot, or to adorn cities in Transoxiana like Kish and Samarkand. We have also to take into account Timur's final, abortive expedition against China, the sole part of the one-time Chinggisid dominions that had not hitherto claimed his attention.[38] But the China campaign is the oddity among Timur's projects. We have no inkling of his precise plans in the event of victory over the Ming; and the justification for attacking the Ming – ostensibly, at least – was to wage holy war against the unbeliever rather than to restore the Mongol empire. As we saw in Chapter 12, Timur conceivably envisaged a global role for his Ögödeyid khan, but it is unclear how he might have defined the authority of his candidate for the throne of the (Northern) Yuan – likewise an Ögödeyid.

Whatever Timur's initial goal, the misappropriation of Chinggisid territories and sovereignty beyond the bounds of Chaghadai's ulus by non-Chinggisid, and often non-Mongol, rulers over the previous few decades furnished a pretext to embrace a more far-reaching programme. As Qazaghan in the 1350s had been roused to quash the pretensions of the Kartid malik of Herat, so Timur, who had inherited Qazaghan's mantle, could hardly be satisfied with doing less. At any rate, to judge from the scope of his operations, by 803/1401 his ambitions had grown prodigiously.

The expansion of those ambitions, I suspect, was contingent and opportunistic. Timur may have begun to conceive of a reconstituted Ilkhanate (subject, of course, to his Chaghadayid khan) only after capturing Sulṭāniyya, which strongly implied a claim to the former Ilkhanid territories; it was also necessary to issue a counterblast to Jalayirid pretensions and to establish a *glacis* in Azerbaijan against Toqtamish. We do not have to accept his claim, in a letter to Barqūq, that he had refrained from attacking the Jalayirids during the lifetime of Shaykh Uways, out of respect for that prince's just rule;[39] Uways had died in 776/1374, when Timur had yet to advance even into Khurāsān.

Clearly, Timur's military enterprises were in some cases a response to external requests for assistance. It is reasonable to assume that the appeal from Toqtamish in 778/1377, and the latter's successful installation as khan of the Blue Horde, marked an important stage in the broadening of Timur's mental horizons beyond the recurrent defiance of Ṣūfī Khwārazm and the constant menace from Qamar al-Dīn; Toqtamish's debt to Timur seemed to offer enhanced security in the north and thus the first opportunity to make conquests in Iran.[40] There is evidence that Timur had received an appeal for help from the deposed Delhi Sultan Muḥammad b. Fīrūz Shāh a few years before he entered India. And it may be no accident that he began to think of a campaign against the Ming around the time that he gave asylum to the Yuan prince Öljei Temür/Tāīzī Oghlan (above, pp. 349–50).

Equally, Timur was compelled at times to react to threatening territorial advances by other rulers. According to Yazdī, it was the shocking news of Toqtamish's devastation of Azerbaijan in 787/1385–6, and the sufferings of its Muslim population, that first inspired Timur with the conviction that it was his duty to take over rulership of Iran;[41] we should recall that barely thirty years had passed since Janibeg's sovereignty had been recognised in Azerbaijan and other parts of Iran (see p. 118). Timur's two assaults on the Qipchaq khanate were reprisals for Toqtamish's attacks – 'to chastise him anew', in Yazdī's words, 'that he might not again presume to overstep his authority and power'.[42]

But even before this, Timur had been lured into external involvements by the flight of rebels from Transoxiana into other polities. The insurgent amirs ʿĀdilshāh of the Jalāyir and Sari Bugha of the Qipchāq, for example, had taken refuge first with Orus Khan of the Blue Horde and then with Qamar al-Dīn in Mughūlistān.[43] In the course of Timur's campaigns in Khurāsān, too, new opponents were dislodged and fled into as yet unsubdued territories. And in the same way that Chinggis Khan had been drawn further afield by a desire for vengeance on those who harboured his rivals or killed his envoys, so Timur ultimately found a *casus belli* in the welcome that the Ottoman and Mamlūk Sultans had given the refugee Jalayirid

Sulṭān Aḥmad, in the assistance given by the Mamlūks to both Sulṭān Aḥmad and the Qarā-Qūyūnlū chieftain and in the fate of the ambassadors Timur had sent to protest at this succour to his enemies. His historians would draw a parallel between Barqūq's execution of Timur's envoys in 795/1393–4 and the detention of his amir *Atlamish, on the one hand, and the murder of Chinggis Khan's envoys at the Khwārazmshāh's instigation, on the other.[44]

Timur's achievement, and perhaps his aspirations, fell short of his supposed model in two important respects: in the total acreage of his empire and in its ecological complexion. As Morgan put it, 'theories that seek to explain his activities as an attempt to refound the Mongol empire under his own aegis fail to account for his apparent lack of interest in the occupation of the steppes of Mughulistān and the Golden Horde'.[45] This does not do justice to the fact that, as Salmānī indicates, one aim of the campaign against China in 1405 was the subjugation of Mughūlistān.[46] But apropos of the Qipchaq khanate, the point is well made. Moreover, if Timur's conquests equated to a significant proportion of the Mongol dominions, they did not include the Mongolian homeland and the sacred *ötügen-yish* of the Türks in the Orqon valley, the site of Qaraqorum. Nor did he control the entire length of the Silk Roads (a deficiency that his China expedition may have been partly designed to remedy), or the 'forest peoples' (Mo. *hoi-yin irgen*) in the Siberian taiga, from whom the Mongols had extracted valuable furs as tribute. Although the fur trade may have been partly diverted through his dominions, he does not seem to have enjoyed direct access to its source.

It is easy – and tempting – to identify commonalities with Chinggis Khan and his initial successors. Yet Timur's was no 'empire of the steppes', despite rubbing shoulders, in Grousset's well-known book of that title, with every nomad-ruled polity from the Scythians onwards.[47] Although he originated in a nomadic confederacy, his rule was based essentially on the resources of the sown; and his conquests comprised sedentary territories, or territories that included pasturelands but where the majority of the population were settled: lands, in other words, that could be made to yield greater economic benefits.[48] Thus within Mughūl territory Farghāna and the Kāshghar region, for instance, were brought within the empire. May offers the ingenious suggestion that there was also an ideological, if practical, distinction at work: that Timur confined his direct control to tracts which were accustomed to the authority of a *qarachu* amir and a Chinggisid puppet, as opposed to the Jochid territories and Mughūlistān, where Mongol tradition and the power and prestige of Chinggisid khans were more firmly entrenched.[49] But Timur was not consistent. Even if this distinction shaped his calculations, it did not prevent him from planning to bring Mughūlistān under tighter control (p. 287 above).

At whatever date Timur took the decision(s) to limit the scope of his conquests,[50] there is a sharp contrast with Chinggis Khan, who had built a steppe empire and thence extended his sovereignty outwards with the reduction of a number of sedentary states. And whereas Chinggis Khan had remained strongly attached to his bases in the steppe, from the outset Timur's principal residences lay in sedentary Transoxiana, in Samarkand and in Kash/Shahr-i Sabz – although his military operations hardly allowed him to spend prolonged periods in the region.[51] He had not, of course, totally jettisoned the nomadic lifestyle. The sources specify his summer and winter quarters each year when on campaign. In Samarkand, he wintered in the citadel and in the summer pitched his tent-pavilions in the city's gardens.[52] And if he himself cannot strictly be labelled a nomad, nomadic cavalry, travelling with their families (*khāna-kūch*),[53] formed the kernel of his army. Like the Mongol operations of the thirteenth century, his involved the migration – often involuntary – of sizeable bodies of nomads from one end of his dominions to the other.

Whatever his goals at their most ambitious, the empire over which Timur presided was emphatically not a restoration of Chinggis Khan's. In this context there is one final consideration, of no little importance. Timurid historians certainly perceived some kind of continuity with the Mongol era, but we should not forget that Timur conducted his campaigns in the name of the khan of the Chaghadayid ulus; if he was endeavouring to revive a 'Mongol order', it was an order centred on his khan. Manz may be understating the case when she describes what Timur bequeathed to his heirs as 'a limited realm around his own homeland'.[54] True, the security and prosperity of Transoxiana seem to have been his main priority.[55] Yet the territorial claims advanced on Sulṭān Maḥmūd's behalf rested on a boldly inflated conception of Chaghadai's original inheritance. The seizure of Herat could be viewed as a reprise of the policy of Qazaghan towards the Kartids; the sack of Delhi had long been a goal of the Chaghadayid khans. Not so Timur's ambitions vis-à-vis the Jalayirid and Muzaffarid lands. His conquests embraced Khwārazm and the majority of the one-time Ilkhanate – both territories that Timur alleged had been allotted to Chaghadai by Chinggis Khan. As suggested in Chapter 12, his dominions are most aptly characterised, not as a revived Chinggisid empire but as a greatly extended Chaghadayid one (albeit excluding much of Mughūlistān). In all likelihood this was the extent of his project.

THE RESTORER OF ORDER

In relation to the thirteenth-century Mongol empire, the most that can be said with certainty is that Timur sought to recreate, in some measure, the world order over which the Mongols had presided,[56] and there can be no doubt that the restoration of some degree of order was one of his principal objectives. He conceded that certain (and conveniently deceased) rulers such as the Jalayirid Shaykh Uways and the Delhi Sultan Fīrūz Shāh had governed well and justly.[57] Such approval did not extend, however, to these monarchs' successors, and in general Timur affected a view of independent princes as perpetuators of *disorder*. He spoke of the oppression and tyranny practised by local rulers and of their killing of pilgrims and merchants.[58] On hearing that the atabeg of Lesser Luristān had been despoiling the pilgrim caravans that passed through his territory en route for the Hijaz, Timur was allegedly so incensed that he personally headed an impromptu expedition against the offender.[59] On these grounds the Qarā-Qūyūnlū Türkmen were attacked in 789/1387 and Bedouins in Iraq in 796/1393–4,[60] as was the city of Takrīt in the latter year for hosting a band of ruffians who preyed on merchants and travellers.[61] Clavijo mentions Timur's seizure of the fortress of Igdir and the execution of its lord for banditry.[62] In the context of the attack on the Jats of Tohana in the Punjab, too, Sharaf al-Dīn Yazdī stresses his resolve to secure the safety of the roads.[63] In 795/1393 his grandson Muḥammad Sulṭān was deputed to extirpate highway robbers (*quṭṭāʿ al-ṭarīq*) in northern Iraq;[64] and when Timur in 806/1404 issued a diploma conferring on ʿUmar b. Amīrānshāh an enormous appanage in the western half of the empire, the suppression of highway robbery was among the duties he enjoined on his grandson.[65]

Given the importance that Timur ascribed to trade (see earlier, pp. 307, 335–6), it does not seem unduly cynical to infer that one impulse behind his preoccupation with banditry was to ensure that the tolls on mercantile traffic reached his rather than other hands. He drew considerable revenue from the two localities known as the Iron Gates, just north of the Oxus and at Darband.[66] According to Shāmī, security did indeed prevail throughout Timur's dominions and trade accordingly flourished.[67] We should make due allowance for flattery, but Archbishop John of Sulṭāniyya emphasises how Timur had abolished numerous tariffs and other exactions, except in the larger cities, with a view to promoting commerce. The local populace sometimes paid the penalty when a merchant was despoiled by robbers, being obliged to pay him twice what his goods were worth and additionally subjected by Timur to a fine of five times the value;[68] such measures are known to have been in force during the early Mongol empire.[69] On balance, however, Timur's campaigns, amid the devastation and slaughter they inflicted, probably also curbed or eliminated numerous local predatory and disruptive elements.[70] Both in his correspondence and in the narrative sources his lesser opponents are frequently characterised as *quṭṭāʿ al-ṭarīq* ('highway robbers'), a term that he applied not just to Hindu tribes or to Sultan Fīrūz Shāh's feuding grandsons and their slave officers in India, or to the Afghans, Kurds and Lurs, but to the Qarā-Qūyūnlū chief Qarā Yūsuf and to the garrison of Takrīt.[71]

Timur's more prominent antagonists were spared this particular stricture; though they in turn could be accused, as was the Jalayirid Sulṭān Aḥmad, of being little better, in view of their failure to suppress such instruments of chaos.[72] Much like Transoxiana before Timur's seizure of power, the Ilkhanid world could be seen as divided among a number of factional princes – *mulūk al-ṭawā'if*, as he himself termed them in a letter to Barqūq.[73] Some of these dynasts, governing lands at one time under Mongol rule (the Jalayirid and Ottoman monarchs, for instance), had the temerity to style themselves Sultan.[74] This, it will be recalled, had been the offence of the Kartid Muʿizz al-Dīn Ḥusayn back in 750/1349; although both in his proclamation of sovereignty and in his correspondence with the Delhi Sultan the Kartid malik had himself justified his actions, as would Timur, by pointing to the rise of *mulūk al-ṭawā'if* and of infidels and other disorderly elements (in this case the Sarbadārs).[75] The chief offence of some rulers was their failure (in the case of Ḥusayn Ṣūfī) to govern justly or (in the case of the Mughūl Qamar al-Dīn) their annual attacks on Mā warā' al-nahr, their bloodshed and pillaging and their carrying off Muslims into captivity.[76]

Where the Mamlūks were concerned, Timur drew upon the Ilkhanid rhetoric that had dismissed them as slaves (and the Mongols' 'runaway' Qipchaq slaves at that) and thus unqualified to rule.[77] He could do so all the more plausibly since Barqūq, a Circassian slave, had supplanted the dynasty founded more than a century before by the Qipchaq slave Qalāwūn (d. 689/1290).[78] Timur frequently expressed his contempt for the slave rulers in Cairo in his correspondence with other princes.[79] We see this same prejudice reflected in his attitude towards Fīrūz Shāh's slave officers who were now the effective masters of the Delhi Sultanate.[80] Yet for Timur and his panegyrists, independent princes – not just those who had usurped Chinggisid territory or sovereignty, but the Mamlūk Sultan and the Sultan of Delhi – merit no title higher than *wālī* ('prince', 'governor').[81] We might readily assume that the mere act of ruling sufficed to damn them. They lacked the legitimising sanction of a Chinggisid khan that Timur enjoyed; their sole recourse was to acknowledge his supremacy.

THE PRESERVATION OF MONGOL INSTITUTIONS

If Timur's empire fails to measure up to Chinggis Khan's, it nevertheless displayed characteristics that entitle it to be regarded as in large measure a Mongol state. To summarise Chapter 12, it was nominally headed by a scion of the Chinggisid dynasty almost until Timur's death, and the Great Amir took steps to link himself and, latterly, his descendants with the dynasty through marriage. In time he also claimed – or it was claimed on his behalf – that he shared a common ancestry with Chinggis Khan. His correspondence with rival potentates carried echoes of the ultimatums sent out by the Mongol qaghans. We might add that in the eyes of its early historians it came to be viewed as part of a 'Mongol commonwealth'.[82]

The armies were based on a decimal system and were recruited for fresh campaigns on a proportional basis from forces deployed elsewhere, just as under the Mongols. Thus when preparing for the expedition against China towards the end of winter in 806/1403–4 Timur issued orders that each of the amirs and commanders in 'the ulus of Hülegü Khan' who were stationed in Azerbaijan and Iraq should despatch a son or brother with troops to Samarkand; certain of them were instructed to head such contingents in person.[83] We see no sign of the 'tsunami strategy' that May identified as the hallmark of Mongol expansionism – the establishment of regions of more or less immediate authority fronting onto zones of penetration that would in turn be subjected to more immediate control at the next forward push. The reason for this, presumably, is that Timur's primary aim was so often plunder rather than the imposition of direct rule. But the resemblance to the Mongols' operations extended to the conduct of battle (above, pp. 319–20) and even to the hunt.[84]

Timur's regime preserved certain administrative institutions and terminology from the era of the unitary Mongol empire. As indicated in Chapter 1 (p. 34), we have to assume that his administrators in Iran continued the system in operation under the previous regimes. The governors installed in conquered cities bore the title of *darugha*, as in the Mongol period, although their functions probably differed somewhat.[85] The titles of other military-administrative offices – *qorchi* (quiver-bearer), *yurtchi* (quartermaster in charge of the imperial encampment), and so on – were taken over from the Mongols.[86] Servitors who distinguished themselves by acts of outstanding bravery in battle, or by other services, were granted *tarkhan* status, affording them unimpeded access to the Great Amir and exempting them and their descendants (as it had in the Mongol epoch) from investigation into as many as nine offences.[87]

In what respects taxation followed Mongol tradition we cannot be completely certain. According to Ḥāfiẓ-i Abrū, Qazaghan's justice had been such that no amir or collector had been able to exact one dinar in excess of 'the *'ushr* in kind (*ba-jins*) and the customary *qubchur*'.[88] We can probably assume, therefore, that Timur's administration too levied these taxes. The implication of Ḥāfiẓ-i Abrū's statement is that Qazaghan had not imposed the *tamgha*, the impost on commercial transactions and artisanal activity traditionally levied by the Mongols. But one of the uncanonical taxes that Timur maintained, and which Qāyinī would claim Shāhrukh had abolished (see later), may well have been the *tamgha*. Although it is not mentioned in the sources on Timur, we do encounter *tamghachi*s, whose duties very probably included its collection.[89]

Some institutional terminology was relatively new, however. Timur and his successors issued grants known as *soyurghal*, a term that in the Mongol imperial era may have denoted merely 'favour'/'reward' and still had that meaning, among others. It is not used, however, in the Ilkhanid sources but only in Timurid sources with reference to that period.[90] The *soyurghal* had developed into a specific institution under the Jalayirids and was adapted by Timur, though it seems to have had a variety of meanings, encompassing the grant of extensive domains to members of Timur's dynasty, his conferment of a territory on its previous rulers and sometimes the grant of tax-exempt land to his amirs.[91]

THE YASA OR TÖRE

We saw how contemporaries had viewed Mongol sovereignty as anchored in Chinggis Khan's Yasa. Some Mongol customs and edicts may have been discarded in the course of Islamisation, but the sources fail to inform us which they were. How great a part did Mongol law play in Timur's administration? It is possible that to boast an allegiance to the Yasa was indispensable for the *qarachu* amir – an essential element in his efforts to rally support from the Mongol military.[92] By the mid-fourteenth century, admittedly, Islam too could serve a similar purpose. But the 'strong man' who sought to secure his domination of the ulus needed to appeal both to the faith and to traditional Mongol law – rather as Rashīd al-Dīn had depicted Ghazan as at once a true Muslim and a Mongol prince who had been thoroughly acquainted with the Yasa since childhood and still upheld it.[93] For Timur, as a *qarachu*, this twofold appeal to the faith and the Yasa was all the more necessary.[94]

Let me briefly recapitulate what was said of Mongol law in Chapter 2. The term Yasa (Turkish *yasaq*; Mongolian *dzasagh*) had come to be used collectively of the edicts of Chinggis Khan and his successors. The standard Persian sources for the Mongol epoch have remarkably little to say about the individual provisions of the Yasa and give the impression that they related above all to the conduct of military affairs and to governance. But with the aid of external sources such as Plano Carpini we can be sure that *yasa*s were also promulgated that enforced some steppe customs. In addition, as De Rachewiltz showed, the word *yasa* meant not just 'decree' but sometimes 'regime' or 'rule' or even '[good] order'.

During the Timurid period we hear less of the Yasa than of the *Töre* (or *törü*), a word that had a much older history, going back to the seventh-century Kök Türks,[95] and embraced a wider range of meanings, though the original sense appears to have been 'customary law'.[96] Since the sources speak both of 'Chinggis Khan's Yasa' and of 'the Ṣāḥib-Qirān's Töre', it seems likely, as Subtelny proposes, that the Töre represented a version of Turco-Mongolian custom which overlapped with and complemented the Yasa;[97] it related, presumably, to aspects of nomadic life such as the hunt, raiding, military discipline and ceremonial.[98] But it has to be said that Timurid authors are no more forthcoming in this context than are those writing during the Mongol era; and to review the references to Yasa and Töre in the Timurid sources is to lose confidence in our ability to assess the content of either.[99]

On occasion Töre, like Yasa, seems to designate the corpus of Mongol law, as when Naṭanzī describes how Timur was informed that Malik Ghiyāth al-Dīn of Herat was failing to live in accordance with 'the triumphant *tūra*'.[100] Sharaf al-Dīn Yazdī remarks that Shams al-Dīn Almālighī, Timur's envoy to Toqtamish in 797/1395, was well versed in the 'customs and practices of the *tūra*'.[101] Referring to the proposal that Timur's grandson Pīr Muḥammad b. ʿUmar Shaykh seek recognition from the ʿAbbasid Caliph in Cairo, as the Muzaffarids had done, Ḥāfiẓ-i Abrū describes it as a 'deviation (*taghayyur*) from the Mongol *yāsāq* and the triumphant *tūra*' – evidently because it clashed with the notion that sovereignty could be vested solely in a member of the *altan urugh*.[102] But both *töre* and *yasaq* are certainly used in the sense of an individual edict or regulation. Thus in the Qipchaq khanate the amir Edigü is said to have devised 'precise *töre*s and great *yasaq*s'.[103] Mughūl historians allegedly viewed the Chaghadayid khan Baraq's *yasaq* as analogous to Chinggis Khan's *yasaq*s (N.B. the plural).[104] When Shāmī says that Timur 'set the path of the *yūsūn* and *yāsāq* once more on its former foundations' by enthroning Soyurghatmish in 771/1370,[105] the allusion, we might assume, is to Chinggis Khan's specific enactment that the throne be occupied by Ögödei and his line.[106] But Naṭanzī uses *yasaq* for Timur's own *farmān*,[107] and at one point terms even the command of the ruler of Lesser Luristān *yāsāq*.[108]

Yet the words *yasaq* and *Töre* in the Timurid narrative sources are often employed in a more general sense of law, rule or good practice, as when Timur is said to have observed 'the usages of the *tūra* and *yāsāq* of sovereigns of old in the stations of battle'.[109] Naṭanzī and Ḥāfiẓ-i Abrū write of recording Timur's deeds, character and *yāsāq*.[110] Shāmī speaks of the conqueror's 'justice and *yāsāq*',[111] and has Timur assert that the killing of envoys has no place in his rule and procedures (*yāsāq-u qawāʿid*).[112] He and Yazdī quote a statement by Timur that it is not the practice (*tūra-u yāsāq*) to leave an enemy at large in a territory and move off elsewhere.[113] Because the Ottoman Sultan Meḥmed I had eliminated his brothers rather than share his dominions with them, Shāhrukh would charge him in 818/1416 with jettisoning the Ilkhanid *tūra* in favour of an Ottoman one.[114] The general massacre at Baghdad (1401) is said to have occurred in accordance with the *yāsāq* (that is, the rule when a city refused to surrender?).[115]

Naṭanzī describes a quriltai which Timur summoned in 773/1371–2 as based on Chinggis Khan's *tūra*.[116] We read of the '*tūra* and custom' (*rasm*) in connection with the feasting at the quriltai of 807/1404,[117] much as Bābur, over two centuries later, commented on habitual Timurid observance of the Töre when his kinsman Badīʿ al-Zamān gave a feast in his honour at Herat.[118] Naṭanzī alleges that under Amīr Ḥusayn the muster-masters conducted the review and ordering (*yāsāq*) of the troops in line with the custom (*ba-yūsūn*) of the old registers.[119] He uses the phrase 'the carpet of the *tūrā* and *yāsāq* was rolled up' to indicate the onset of instability.[120] When the addiction of the Blue Horde khan Temür Malik to drink and pleasure led to disorder, the 'practices (*qawāʿid*) of the triumphant *tūrā* were obstructed and disregarded'; while Ilyās Khwāja's incapacity and inexperience brought about 'complete modification and alteration in the triumphant *tūrā*'.[121]

The term *yasa*[*q*] evidently still had the abstract meaning 'authority' or 'regime' as well. Thus Naṭanzī refers to the 'lack of authority' (*bī-yāsāqī*) of Buyan Süldüs,[122] and later announces his intention to describe Timur's actions (*awḍāʿ*), *yāsāq*, equity, sagacity and so on;[123] and in 763/1361–2 Timur, confronted by the tyranny of Tughluq Temür's chief military commander in Transoxiana, perceived that the khan's *yasaq*, as Sharaf al-Dīn Yazdī puts it, was no longer effective.[124] So too Yazdī has Amīrānshāh's wife Khānzāda complaining to Timur in 802/1399 that her husband had completely repudiated his father's *yasaq*.[125]

TÖRE AND SHARĪʿA

As Vásáry has pointed out, Mongol customary law and the Sharīʿa were not incompatible in every respect. Yet the view that they were was widespread, not only among Muslims – some of whom, Ibn ʿArabshāh tells us, based their judgement that Timur was an infidel upon his adherence to Chinggis Khan's Yasa (see later) – but for pagan Mongols who found themselves required to adopt Islam.[126] Mīrzā Ḥaydar tells how his ancestor, the Dughlāt amir Khudāydād, asked by Timur's grandson Ulugh Beg to instruct him on the provisions of the 'Chinggisid Töre', pointed out that he himself had rejected the Töre for the Sharīʿa; if, however, Ulugh Beg were to abandon the Sharīʿa and study the Töre, he [Khudāydād] would instruct him.[127] Sharaf al-Dīn Yazdī uses *yāsā*[*q*] and *tūra* less frequently than do Shāmī and Naṭanzī.[128] Ḥāfiẓ-i Abrū, as Woods has shown, elided all but one of the references to the Yasa/Töre that he found in Naṭanzī's work.[129] The latter used the word *tūra* frequently, doubtless because his informants were Turco-Mongol officers.[130]

These writers may have seen it as politically inexpedient to employ these terms in the era of Shāhrukh, who acquired a name for himself as the restorer of Islamic norms; and we might learn something of Timur's adherence to the Töre by looking at his son's reign. At Timur's death, his grave was adorned in the pagan nomadic tradition, with weapons, clothing and jewellery – items which Shāhrukh, in a gesture that emphasised his own allegiance to the Sharīʿa and must have risked offending the nomad military, took care to remove when he entered Samarkand a few years later.[131] In a letter to the Ming Emperor Yongle in 815/1412–13 which is preserved in Ḥāfiẓ-i Abrū's *Zubdat al-tawārīkh*, Shāhrukh claimed to be enforcing the Sharīʿa.[132] A contemporary Mirror for Princes, *Naṣā'iḥ-i Shāhrukhī* ('Counsels for Shāhrukh'), by the preacher and traditionist Jalāl al-Dīn Abū Muḥammad Qāyinī (820/1417), confirms that Shāhrukh had replaced the Yasa with the Sharīʿa, and dates this in 813/1411.[133] In 814/1411–12, at Shāhrukh's command, Ulugh Beg issued orders that the Muslim intellectuals and artisans transported to Samarkand by Timur's troops be allowed to return to their homes: this measure was expressly linked with the restoration of the Sharīʿa (which forbade the enslavement of Muslims).[134]

Authors like Qāyinī, Sharaf al-Dīn Yazdī and Ḥāfiẓ-i Abrū projected Shāhrukh as the 'Renewer' (*mujaddid*) sent by God, according to Muslim tradition (*ḥadīth*), to revive the faith at the onset of each new Hijrī century; this appellation, hitherto confined to intellectuals like al-Ghazālī (d. 505/1111), was now being used of a monarch.[135] Shāhrukh, who adopted the title *Pādishāh-i Islām* borne by the Ilkhan Ghazan Maḥmūd (and more recently by Timur's two khans), modelled his rule in some measure on that of Ghazan, under whom the Islamic faith and Mongol rule alike had attained the new beginning celebrated so enthusiastically by Rashīd al-Dīn.[136] This emphasis on canonical Islamic practice may have been prompted by the rise of messianic movements like the Ḥurūfīs, who made strident demands for a return to authentic Islam, and should be linked with Shāhrukh's prohibition of the consumption of wine, which was vigorously enforced in Herat, according to a Ming envoy to the Timurid court in 1414–15.[137]

The emphasis placed by Qāyinī and others – as well as by Shāhrukh himself in his letter to Yongle – on the revival of the Sharīʿa can mislead us into thinking that the Timurid ruler was turning his back on Mongol tradition, an impression strengthened by the failure to appoint a khan. But Manz drew attention some years ago to the way in which Timur's heirs persistently displayed an interest in their Chinggisid heritage and Chinggisid connections.[138] More recently, as a nuanced way of approaching Shāhrukh's stance, Jonathan Brack has argued cogently that the Timurid monarch and his publicists were following in the footsteps of Ilkhanid writers who had taken up the idea of Chinggis Khan's Heaven-sanctioned rulership and embedded it within an essentially Islamic discourse (see pp. 101–3). Evidently, in this context, Timur's own image had developed during the years since his death. Thus what Shāmī calls 'the signs of felicity in his bearing' that allegedly so impressed the amirs of Mughūlistān when they met him in 761/1360 had become in Yazdī's account of this same episode 'the flash of divine splendour (*farr-i īzadī*) on his brow'.[139] By adopting titles such as *mujaddid* and Mahdī, Shāhrukh in turn was not discarding the Chinggisid model of divinely ordained rule but instead, in part, rebranding and elaborating it. And in the process a new type of Muslim kingship was being fashioned, on foundations that were less restrictive than the older criteria of hereditary succession to the Prophet or the sanction of Muslim scholars and jurists, on the one hand, and the Mongols' association of divine favour with empirical success, on the other.[140]

But what precisely, then, did Shāhrukh abolish? Qāyinī speaks of 'casting off the *yarghu* and the customs (*rusūm*) of the Töre'. We shall turn to the *yarghu*, the traditional Mongol tribunal, shortly. But it is to be noted that Qāyinī's treatise also devotes some space to uncanonical taxation, here termed *qalānāt* (for *qalan*, see above, p. 67) and defined as embracing any impost other than the tithe (*ʿushr*), the land-tax (*kharāj*), alms (*zakāh*) and the *jizya*.[141] It must therefore have included the *tamgha*, the tax on commercial transactions, for many a symbol of the incompatibility of the traditional Mongol system with the Sharīʿa.[142] This levy was not peculiar to the Timurids. Early in the sixteenth century Faḍl-Allāh Rūzbihān Khunjī lamented that under the Āq-Qūyūnlū Sultan Yaʿqūb (d. 896/1490) 'the limpid water of the commandments of Islam had become sullied by the turbidity of the Chinggisid Yasa', so that it had fallen to the minister Qāḍī ʿĪsā to restore the Sharīʿa to its rightful place, specifically by engineering the abolition of the *tamghāwāt*.[143]

Let us now consider the *yarghu*. In his letter to Yongle Shāhrukh says that the Sharīʿa is being upheld throughout Khurāsān and Mā warāʾ al-nahr and that he has abolished the *yarghu* and regulations (*qawāʿid*) of Chinggis Khan. This is almost incidental to his main purposes: to assure Yongle of Shāhrukh's protection for Chinese merchants, to refute the claim that Timur had acknowledged the overlordship of the Hongwu Emperor (see pp. 307, 309) and, by way of riposte, to urge him to accept Islam and implement Islamic law throughout his dominions.[144] Mention of the *yarghu* is as specific as Shāhrukh's letter gets.

Morgan called attention to the centrality of the *yarghu* in the judicial machinery operative under the Mongols;[145] and it was still prominent in Timur's epoch. A *yarghu* might be a court of inquiry into military failure (as in 790/1388 when Timur, on his return to Samarkand, investigated the conduct of his amirs during the recent invasion by Toqtamish)[146] or a process of interrogation regarding suspected conspiracy or mutiny. Indeed, according to Sharaf al-Dīn Yazdī, Timur, as a child playing with other boys and posing as their leader, had judged in a *yarghu* those who flouted his orders.[147] Amīr Ḥusayn had ordered a *yarghu* to investigate charges against Timur himself;[148] the conqueror's grandson Muḥammad Sulṭān would hold a *yarghu* in Samarkand 802/1399–1400 to investigate the charge of insubordination against his cousin Iskandar b. ʿUmar Shaykh;[149] and Timur subjected Amīrānshāh's amirs in that year and Pīr Muḥammad b. ʿUmar Shaykh in 803/1400 to such an inquiry.[150] It is possible that in Timur's day the *yarghu* was known more commonly as the *dīwān-i buzurg*, or at least that it was conducted by the members of that body.[151] The Mongols' Muslim subjects saw these tribunals as contrary to Islamic law, not least because there was a tendency to assume guilt in the absence of proof and torture was frequently used to extract a confession.[152] Under Timur, the *yarghu* tried not just Turco-Mongol amirs like Kaykhusraw of Khuttalān and Shaykh Muḥammad b. Buyan Süldüs,[153] but also Tājīks – just as in the Ilkhanate. Thus one *yarghu* tried both a Mongol amir and a sayyid of Tirmidh.[154]

What Shāhrukh had in mind, perhaps, was a reassertion of the authority of the qadis and his own exercise of *maẓālim* jurisdiction along lines more in keeping with Islamic law. A contemporary, Sharaf al-Dīn Yazdī's teacher Ibn Turka Iṣfahānī, claimed that thanks to Shāhrukh no trace of the *yarghu* remained and nobody resorted to it except in secret.[155] The problem with such testimony, as with that of Qāyinī, is twofold. On the one hand, authors intent on extolling Shāhrukh's return to orthodoxy had little interest in depicting Timur as a protagonist of canonical Islam; on the other, Shāhrukh was clearly concerned not to dissociate himself either from Timur's legacy or from his broader Turco-Mongolian heritage.[156] His self-conscious espousal of Islamic law must be set alongside his assumption of the title of Khāqān/khan. At any rate, it is doubtful that he did abolish the *yarghu*, which still existed in Herat under Sulṭān Ḥusayn Bāyqarā in the late fifteenth century.[157]

In this context of the survival of Mongol institutions, it is interesting to observe how Sharaf al-Dīn Yazdī handles the conduct of that grim enforcer of the Yasa, Chaghadai. Describing Chinggis Khan's attribution of specific areas of competence to his sons, he speaks of Chaghadai as being given responsibility for enforcing the Yasa and the *yarghu* and for ordering military affairs, whereas in the corresponding passage of Juwaynī the phrase is simply 'the Yasa and law [enforcement]' (*yāsā-u siyāsat*).[158] Elsewhere Yazdī says:

> In observing the usages of the *yarghu* and the *yasaq* he exercised the utmost diligence, recognising that care was necessary in attending to the least detail. He did not overlook a single point in relation to what he had commanded: that in spring and summer nobody should sit in water, nor wash his hands in a stream, nor lift water from a stream in vessels of gold or silver, nor spread out on the plain a garment that has been washed . . .[159]

In this passage Yazdī again parts company with Juwaynī, who gives precisely the same details regarding the offences and the climatic repercussions,[160] but says nothing of the *yarghu* at that juncture. We might infer that by Yazdī's day the most conspicuous (and objectionable) survival from the pagan Mongol regime was not particular *yasa*s that were at variance with Islam, but the *yarghu* – closely followed, perhaps, by taxes not sanctioned in Islamic law.[161]

If Timur's stance regarding Chinggisid sovereignty, by the time of his death, is open to question, his commitment to Mongol law and custom cannot be in doubt. But the two sources that yield express testimony in this context are both markedly hostile: ʿAzīz b. Ardashīr Astarābādī, who cites a declaration by Burhān al-Dīn of Sivas that Timur was opposed to the Sharīʿa,[162] and more particularly Ibn ʿArabshāh, who lays considerable stress on the fact that Timur observed Chinggis Khan's Töre rather than the Sharīʿa. Timur is said to 'believe in' Chinggis Khan's law, to prefer it to the prescriptions of Islam and to be bringing the foundations of his government totally into harmony with the Töre. Indeed, at one point Ibn ʿArabshāh speaks of the Töre as Timur's religion (*milla*), no less than the religion of his enemies in Jata.[163] He asserts, in a lengthy verse obituary on the conqueror, that Timur had striven to extinguish the light of God and of the pure faith by means of the tenets of Chinggis Khan, 'that ill-omened infidel tyrant (*dhāka l-ẓālim al-naḥs al-kufūr*)'.[164] He cites the verdict of the ʿulama whom he had encountered in the Jochid territories: that Timur and all who followed Chinggis Khan's law were to be accounted unbelievers.[165] He is also, incidentally, sceptical regarding Shāhrukh's abolition of the Töre and of Chinggis Khan's regulations (*qawāʿid*), on the grounds that the resistance of the Timurid military and religious elite must have proved an insuperable obstacle.[166] Nowhere in his *'Ajā'ib al-maqdūr*, however, are any provisions of the Töre specified. Where he does list prescriptions of the Yasa, in his Mirror for Princes, *Fākihat al-khulafā'*, they are apocryphal – and in some cases nothing but ludicrous.[167] These distortions apart, Ibn 'Arabshāh echoes in some degree the fulminations of Ibn Taymiyya a century before (see p. 108).

Equally, of course, the efforts of Shāmī and Yazdī to depict Timur as one who fulfilled the requirements of Muslim law (*shar'*, *sharī'at*) might be taken as supererogatory protest. It is significant that they tend to invoke his devotion to Islam primarily in connection with his fulfilment of the duty of holy war: against Indian infidels, the Georgians and the Knights of St John at Smyrna.[168] And the truth probably lies somewhere between the roseate picture they construct and the fulminations of Ibn 'Arabshāh. Timur observed customs practised for some centuries by steppe peoples: for instance, levirate marriage, whereby his son Amīrānshāh was married to the widow of an older brother, Jahāngīr, and 'Umar Shaykh's widow became the wife of Shāhrukh. He evidently still subscribed to beliefs long held by the steppe peoples – or at least had not renounced a willingness to play to such beliefs. This need not surprise us: the Ilkhan Ghazan had retained pre-Islamic practices after his acceptance of Islam.[169] In 795/1393 Timur ascended a hill with the princes and noyans to give thanks to Heaven for his victory over the Muzaffarid Shāh Manṣūr, in a clear echo of the practice of the pagans Chinggis Khan and Batu over a century and a half previously.[170] He would be buried with grave goods in the time-honoured steppe fashion and contrary to Islamic practice.[171]

The pre-Islamic elements of Timur's heritage are nowhere more vividly apparent than in the claims of a quasi-spiritual nature that he made or that were made on his behalf. Perhaps in part to compensate for his lack of sovereign status, he credited himself with extraordinary powers. If we can believe rumours that reached Western Europe, he declared that an angel revealed to him men's thoughts so that nobody dared to conspire against him, and that he had climbed forty rungs on a ladder to Heaven at an angel's prompting, the number of rungs signifying that he was destined to rule the world for forty years.[172]

The contemporary Timurid sources, presumably inhibited about ascribing pre-Islamic sentiment and practice to their patron, are silent in this context, and our information comes either from later authors like Sharaf al-Dīn Yazdī or from western Christian observers who are probably citing current oral tradition. Even Ibn ʿArabshāh credits Timur with the special insight that could distinguish honest counsel from mere sycophancy.[173] The claims made for Timur's supernatural powers were not without precedent. The Heavenward climb is an old theme, found, for example, in the Turkish epic *Qutadghu bilig* (dated 1069).[174] More loosely, it recalls, too, the capacity of Chinggis Khan's chief shaman, Teb-Tenggeri (Kököchü), to ascend to Heaven on horseback, as transmitted by both Rashīd al-Dīn (who dismissed it as the invention of common folk) and the Armenian Hayton.[175] Rashīd al-Dīn had also written of Ghazan's great perspicacity and his ability to read men's hearts and foretell the future (above, p. 101). Among Timur's Chaghatay nomadic soldiery ideas imbued with a quasi-shamanistic theme evidently still resonated. But Yazdī, for whom Timur's mind was 'the place of the illumination of hidden secrets' (*maṭraḥ-i anwār-i asrār-i ghaybī*),[176] contrived to clothe the Great Amir's experiences in Muslim garb. On occasion Timur had dreams that guided his course of action, a miraculous gift vouchsafed to the Prophet and one that the greatest sultans, kings and khaqans, Yazdī tells us, had inherited through being vested with the 'external (or formal) Caliphate' (*khilāfat-i ṣūrī*).[177]

To return to Timur's regard for the Yasa/Töre: I wonder whether Ibn ʿArabshāh made such strenuous efforts to advance the specific argument about Mongol law for polemical purposes – as part of his broader repertoire that Timur was an infidel leading an army of infidels. In much the same way, Ibn ʿArabshāh's contemporary and contact, al-Maqrīzī, was disingenuous when he charged Mamlūk amirs with enforcing the Mongol Yasa; he based the accusation merely on the similarity between the words *yāsa* and *siyāsat* (and, no less importantly, in their usage).[178] Just as disregard for the Yasa had been a useful pretext for Mongol amirs bent on challenging a khan's power, so the charge of adherence to it could have a role in controversy within the ranks of the Mongols' antagonists.

It should be mentioned that respect for the Töre in a more restricted sense survived right down into the sixteenth century. We have already noted Bābur's association of the Töre with the proper conduct of a feast. The Töre surfaces in other formal contexts also. Mīrzā Ḥaydar writes of the amir Muḥammad Burunduq, who had served Shāhrukh and had later entered the employ of Sulṭān Ḥusayn Bāyqarā. He excelled his contemporaries in his knowledge of the 'Chinggisid Töre'; but when Ḥaydar's father arrived at Sulṭān Ḥusayn's court the amir merely coached him in the correct manner of performing obeisance on one knee,[179] as if this formed a vital part of the Töre. It seems that the Chinggisid 'system' had dwindled to matters of ceremonial and protocol. One example is the enthronement of khans by raising them up on a carpet of white felt.[180] If this ceremony still had the power to offend Muslim sensibilities, it could nevertheless be accommodated by the time the Uzbek khan ʿAbd-Allāh ascended the throne in 990/1582, when Muslim dignitaries sprinkled over the felt water from the well of Zamzam, near Mecca.[181] Islamising non-Muslim etiquette was one way of coping with its survival. Another was simply to discard it. Bābur denied that the Töre was a 'definitive text' (*naṣṣ qāṭiʿ*) and envisaged the abandonment of customs that had lost their usefulness,[182] an attitude that would have been unthinkable two centuries previously and would almost certainly have outraged Timur's Chaghatay followers.

In Chapters 9–14 we have been examining the career of a virtually parvenu *condottiere* who combined outstanding military talents with a relatively shrewd feel for legitimacy and a highly eclectic sense of historical reality. Timur's mission, it seems, was to extend Chaghadayid sovereignty over the former Ilkhanate, to restore to the Chinggisid world some kind of order and to bring to heel those who had reduced it to chaos. The final chapter will be concerned with the fate of his empire after his death.

CHAPTER 15
AFTERMATH: TIMUR'S SUCCESSORS

Timur's death unleashed a power struggle within his family that lasted for almost fifteen years. By the end of that period, his westernmost territories had been lost; but the greater part of his empire – Transoxiana and southern and central Iran – was still in Timurid hands and acknowledged the paramount authority of his youngest son, Shāhrukh. This chapter will examine the conflicts from which Shāhrukh emerged victorious and will then survey more briefly the rest of the Timurid era down to the dynasty's end in 912–13/1506–7 and Timur's longer-term legacy to the Islamic east. It will conclude by attempting to address the question why later would-be empire-builders at the head of nomadic armies in Inner Asia achieved nothing like the success that had attended Timur.

EMPIRE AND SUCCESSION

Some years before his death – possibly around 1398 – Timur had named as his heir his grandson Muḥammad Sulṭān, the son of Jahāngīr by a freeborn wife of Jochid descent and thus a prince blest with Chinggisid ancestry. The choice was in keeping with Timur's well-authenticated concern regarding high birth – a major reason, presumably, why he did not nominate either of his two surviving sons, Amīrānshāh and Shāhrukh, both born of concubines. The heir-apparent seems to have been an able and energetic prince; though we have no way of knowing whether he would have proved fully equal to the task had he not died in 805/1403. It is unclear when Timur settled on Muḥammad Sulṭān's half-brother Pīr Muḥammad as his successor. Salmānī's account suggests that he did so only on his deathbed, and Yazdī appears to confirm this, since he says that the grieving amirs had to send word to the prince of his designation.[1] If Timur had indeed procrastinated in naming a new heir, the most probable reason is that Pīr Muḥammad b. Jahāngīr, unlike his brother, had no Chinggisid blood. But Clavijo, who heard that Timur loved Pīr Muḥammad dearly for his father's sake, writes of the foreign embassies being escorted to the prince's pavilion to perform obeisance;[2] this might indicate that Pīr Muḥammad was already being groomed for the succession in 1404. Whatever the truth, Pīr Muḥammad, governing Ghazna, Kabul and Qandahār in the remote south-eastern reaches of the Timurid empire, and having attained less distinction in his grandfather's service than had Muḥammad Sulṭān, was not ideally placed to hold together what Timur had left.

And the question we might ask at this juncture is what precisely Timur had left. An agglomeration of far-flung territories that had required almost incessant campaigning during Timur's lifetime was perhaps only too likely to disintegrate once his charisma and ever dominant presence were removed. Or, to put it another way, the fate of Timur's empire was a consequence of its very nature: based essentially on serial plundering expeditions that ceased with its founder's death, it was bound to shrink once this particular source of income was closed off. The rapid sundering and contraction of Timur's dominions has also been attributed to the highly personal nature of his rule and his failure to create an adequate administrative framework for his lands – contrasted always with Chinggis Khan's achievement in bequeathing an empire which both preserved its unity for over three decades and continued to expand at a prodigious rate. Svat Soucek, for instance, blames the lack of solidity of the Timurid empire specifically on the nature of the land grants to individual princes, who thereby possessed 'too much administrative, fiscal, and hereditary independence' and whose appanages were not integrated into an overall structure.[3] And it is certainly true that the Timurid dominions displayed nothing like the intricate arrangements that had characterised the unitary Mongol empire, requiring as they did that the Qaghan, as head of the dynasty, should receive a portion of the revenue from each subordinate ulus and, conversely, binding (at least for a few decades) the interests of the regional khans to his own by distributing to each a share of the revenue from the centre (*qol-un ulus*).

We should also notice other differences, however. Like their Chinggisid precursors, the Timurids adhered to the principle that each member of the dynasty was eligible to succeed to the sovereignty, a circumstance that likewise contributed to the disorder following his death.[4] His restrictive criteria for the succession may have given rise to profound dissatisfaction among certain members of his family (see above, p. 275). By contrast, Chinggis Khan had been able to secure the agreement of his other sons to the succession of Ögödei; and the subsequent transmission of power to Ögödei's progeny appears not to have been challenged – apart from Temüge Otchigin's failed coup in the 1240s – at any point prior to 1250. In addition, whereas all Chinggis Khan's sons and most of his grandsons had been born and grown to adulthood in the Mongolian homeland, the several grandsons of Timur who were politically prominent after 1405 had formed links from an early stage with regional appanages lying at some considerable distance from Samarkand. In consequence, their consciousness of the empire as a totality was weaker than that of their Mongol precursors. For Timur, Transoxiana had remained the kernel of his extensive dominions; but for Timurid princes ('*mīrzā*s'), and especially those of the third generation (with a few notable exceptions), it was liable to have a more peripheral significance (as it would even for Shāhrukh after he had reduced it). The most attractive option was to focus on the preservation and extension of their own appanages and to maximise their autonomy.[5]

We saw in Chapter 12, moreover, how Timur secured marriages for some of his progeny with Chinggisid princesses. One outcome of these various unions was the emergence of a tier of Timurid princes whose Chinggisid blood might have appeared to raise them above their fellows in the years after Timur's death – and to raise them, more significantly, above both his designated heir, Pīr Muḥammad b. Jahāngīr, and his eventual successor, Shāhrukh. The most obvious examples were ʿUmar Shaykh's sons Pīr Muḥammad, Iskandar and Amīrak Aḥmad (all three born of the Chaghadayid princess Malikat Āghā); and Amīrānshāh's sons Khalīl Sulṭān (born of Sevin Beg Khānzāda, whom Amīrānshāh had married after Jahāngīr's death), Abā Bakr and ʿUmar (both born of Soyurghatmish Khan's daughter Ūrūn Sulṭān Khānīka, marriage to whom had entitled their father to take the title Güregen: see p. 275).[6] It is no accident that among these princes were numbered all those who played a leading role in the regional struggles that followed the conqueror's death. Certain of them aimed still higher. Khalīl Sulṭān would usurp power in Samarkand in 807/1405 in contravention of his grandfather's will. Clavijo heard a rumour that ʿUmar b. Amīrānshāh (to whom, as we saw, Timur had granted an enormous appanage in the west: p. 272) had designs on the throne, and the prince is said in 809/1407 briefly to have meditated wresting power in Samarkand from Khalīl Sulṭān.[7] Abā Bakr b. Amīrānshāh clearly harboured ambitions in parts of the empire well beyond the borders of his father's appanage. And in time Iskandar, lastly, would prove a formidable competitor to Shāhrukh.

It is also necessary to take into account the attitudes and conduct of Timur's amirs, which present a striking contrast to the fidelity of Chinggis Khan's noyans to his provisions for the empire after his death. Not that the Timurid commanders felt no devotion to Timur's memory. They surely did; but that devotion was transmitted only conditionally to his progeny.[8] Just as Timur had moved princes between appanages, so he had often transferred amirs from one princely entourage to another, thus preventing them from forming strong ties to any particular prince. Nor is there any reason to believe that loyalty would have led the majority of the amirs to adhere to his arrangements for the succession. In fact, we know of only two amirs by name – Khudāydād Ḥusaynī and Shaykh Nūr al-Dīn (see later) – who remained more or less unshaken in their advocacy of the claims of Jahāngīr's line. Such was the prestige that had accrued in the wake of Timur's unalloyed military successes, and so opulent the rewards which had thereby cascaded down to his amirs, that a great many of them must have been demoralised by his death. Their chief preoccupation would not have been allegiance to Timur's testament – still less to light upon the paragon of administrative genius calculated to win the plaudits of modern-day historians. It would have been to serve a ruler, rather, who could maintain the flow of benefits that Timur had continued to confer right down until his death. Indeed, a pronounced feature of the next few years was the readiness of amirs to switch allegiance from one prince to another.

THE REIGN OF KHALĪL SULṬĀN IN SAMARKAND

The first prince to make a bid for the succession was Timur's maternal grandson Sulṭān Ḥusayn, then with the left wing of Timur's army at Ṣawrān. Guilty of treachery on an earlier occasion in Syria in 803/1401 (above, p. 275), he now disbanded the majority of the army of the left wing and marched on Samarkand with a small force. Timur's governor in Samarkand, Arghūnshāh, refused to admit him and he made his way to Herat. In the event, it was another grandson who seized power in Samarkand: Khalīl Sulṭān b. Amīrānshāh, who commanded the right wing of Timur's army at Tashkent but whose appanage comprised Arrān, Armenia and Georgia (see above, p. 272). He may have believed that his Chinggisid ancestry gave him a better right than the heir-apparent Pīr Muḥammad. Salmānī gives us to understand that the amirs of the right wing, alarmed at the threatened usurpation of Sulṭān Ḥusayn, were 'beguiled' (*nīrang kashīda*) into choosing Khalīl Sulṭān as Timur's successor; though when they subsequently learned of Timur's testament, Salmānī tells us, they regretted their decision.[9] Arghūnshāh opted to hand over Samarkand to Khalīl Sulṭān, who entered the city on 16 Ramaḍān 807/18 March 1405.[10]

Once in power at Samarkand, Khalīl Sulṭān saw Pīr Muḥammad b. Jahāngīr and his supporters as the principal threat, and this would explain why he installed as khan the infant Muḥammad Jahāngīr and claimed to be ruling in the boy's name. As the son of his half-brother, the late heir-apparent Muḥammad Sulṭān, Muḥammad Jahāngīr had the advantage of Chinggisid descent, which his uncle Pīr Muḥammad lacked, and his enthronement might tap into memories of his popular father.[11] As a further means of boosting support, Khalīl Sulṭān gave the widows of Timur in marriage to amirs whom the sources (written, of course, for Shāhrukh) depict as mostly men of low birth and questionable character. He even despatched Khān Sulṭān Khānīka, widow of his half-brother Muḥammad Sulṭān, with a large sum of gold, to Pīr Muḥammad in an attempt to buy him off with her hand (despite the fact that their marriage would have been contrary to Islamic law).[12] Salmānī, who acquired much of his information from the amir Shāh Malik, an enemy of Khalīl Sulṭān,[13] attributes the policy towards Timurid royal womenfolk to the prompting of Khalīl Sulṭān's wife Shād Mulk – 'that procuress (*dallāla*)' and 'that hussy (*salīṭa*) . . . who calls herself his wife'. He clearly regarded her influence as pernicious; no doubt she was seeking to avenge herself on those khatuns who had earlier treated her with contempt.[14] The policy alienated support, however, and the gift of the 'Lesser Khanim', Tümen Āghā, who had cared for Shād Mulk during her pregnancy,[15] certainly failed to secure the backing of her new husband, the veteran amir Shaykh Nūr al-Dīn.

Whether Pīr Muḥammad b. Jahāngīr would have acceded to Khalīl Sulṭān's overture, we cannot know. Khān Sulṭān Khānīka's escort included Sulṭān Ḥusayn, who had meanwhile left Herat to join Khalīl Sulṭān and who now, true to form, conspired against the latter with the amir Pīr ʿAlī Tāz. Two of the amirs who were escorting the princess were put to death, and the rest bullied into collaborating with Sulṭān Ḥusayn, who then forced Khān Sulṭān Khānīka to marry him and once more advanced on Samarkand with the intention of seizing power. When Khalīl Sulṭān moved against him in Dhū l-Ḥijja 807/June 1405, the amirs who were accompanying Sulṭān Ḥusayn under duress mutinied and he fled to Balkh, where the amir Sulaymānshāh arrested him. In defiance of Pīr Muḥammad's demand that Sulṭān Ḥusayn be handed over, Sulaymānshāh took him to Shāhrukh in Herat. At the prompting of his amirs, who pointed to Sulṭān Ḥusayn's unequalled record for faithlessness, Shāhrukh had this inveterate intriguer executed and sent his head, stuffed with straw, to Pīr Muḥammad.[16] Since the latter is styled Güregen on the coins he struck at Balkh in 807–8/1405–6, he may have married Khān Sulṭān Khānīka at this time, thereby enhancing his status.[17]

Relieved of the challenge from Sulṭān Ḥusayn, Khalīl Sulṭān gained a vital breathing space. It was several months before Pīr Muḥammad b. Jahāngīr invaded Transoxiana with reinforcements from Shāhrukh, headed by Ulugh Beg and Shāh Malik. Defeated, however, by Khalīl Sulṭān's forces in an engagement on the Qarshī River on 4 Ramaḍān 808/23 February 1406,[18] he fell back on Ḥiṣār-i Shādmān (or Balkh, according to Salmānī), and later, in Ramaḍān 809/February–March 1407, he was assassinated by Pīr ʿAlī Tāz. The murder was instigated, Salmānī tells us, by Khalīl Sulṭān, who had allegedly promised the killer the whole of Pīr Muḥammad's territory; but no other author substantiates this charge.[19]

Despite the defeat and elimination of his chief rival, Khalīl Sulṭān suffered from one major disadvantage, over and above hostility towards his wife and a perception that he was in thrall to her.[20] His troops – the army of the right wing – were, as Jürgen Paul has shown, a motley assemblage comprising 'displaced tribes' from outside the ulus of Chaghadai, who had been transported far from their own regions and appear to have desired above all to return home. They comprised principally Jā'ūn-i Qurbān Mongols from western Khurāsān and Māzandarān, Qara Tatars from Anatolia and some Jalayirid troops from Iraq.[21] Having fought for him against Pīr Muḥammad b. Jahāngīr, these elements subsequently deserted him.

Although he benefited from being on the spot in Transoxiana, Khalīl Sulṭān had been there for only two or three years and lacked strong local support. He won the allegiance of only a few of his grandfather's leading henchmen: Burunduq b. Jahānshāh Barlās (who disappears from the record, however, as early as 1406), Allāhdād (brother of Ḥājjī Sayf al-Dīn), Shams al-Dīn b. ʿAbbās and Arghūnshāh; two other supporters, the amirs Temür Khwāja and Khwāja Yūsuf, had been put to death by Sulṭān Ḥusayn.[22] No less importantly, Khalīl Sulṭān failed to obtain recognition from any of his kinsmen other than Shāhrukh – and that only temporarily in the wake of Pīr Muḥammad's defeat.

In particular, Khalīl Sulṭān was faced with the opposition of three of the most prominent amirs almost from the outset. Shaykh Nūr al-Dīn of the Jalāyir and Shāh Malik, who were with Timur's main army, had been close to the conqueror, and their names are often linked in the sources for Timur's career.[23] Following Timur's death they had sent word to Arghūnshāh, ordering him to put Samarkand in a state of defence and to arrest Sulṭān Ḥusayn should he enter. But they were not prepared to countenance the succession of Khalīl Sulṭān either; instead they made public their adherence to Timur's will and championed the claims of Pīr Muḥammad b. Jahāngīr. Shāh Malik shortly left Transoxiana to enter Shāhrukh's service, whereas Shaykh Nūr al-Dīn entered into cooperation with another long-standing associate and an early follower of Timur, the Barlās amir Khudāydād Ḥusaynī, who had encouraged the Mughūls to attack Khalīl Sulṭān.[24] With power bases in northern Transoxiana, the two amirs effectively obstructed Khalīl Sulṭān's efforts to consolidate his hold over the territory for the next three years.[25] In 811/1409, having invited Shāhrukh to attack Transoxiana, they defeated Khalīl Sulṭān and took him prisoner.[26] Salmānī observes sardonically that by the end of Khalīl Sulṭān's short reign the dimensions of his territory were modest indeed: it extended (outward from Samarkand, that is) no further in the direction of the Amū-daryā (Oxus) than Kish and, in the vicinity of the Sīr-daryā, only as far as Dīzak.[27]

Khudāydād and Shaykh Nūr al-Dīn had consistently advocated the rights of Jahāngīr's line and expected Shāhrukh to recognise Khalīl Sulṭān's nominal 'khan', Muḥammad Jahāngīr b. Muḥammad Sulṭān, as head of the Timurid empire and ruler of Transoxiana; Jaʿfarī says that they now proclaimed him sovereign. When it became clear that this was no part of Shāhrukh's plan, Khudāydād retreated northwards with his prisoner Khalīl Sulṭān and sought assistance from the eastern Chaghadayid khan Muḥammad against Shāhrukh; but he swiftly fell out with the Mughūls, who killed him, whereupon Khalīl Sulṭān was released and made for Shāhrukh's headquarters.[28] Shāhrukh assumed authority in Transoxiana and appointed his own son Ulugh Beg as its governor.

THE CONFLICTS IN WESTERN AND CENTRAL IRAN

Both John of Sulṭāniyya and Clavijo allege that Amīrānshāh, as the elder of Timur's two surviving sons, was regarded in some quarters as the conqueror's rightful heir.[29] According to Ḥāfiẓ-i Abrū, Pīr Muḥammad b. ʿUmar Shaykh in Fārs was urged by some of his advisers to recognise Amīrānshāh as his sovereign.[30] This westernmost branch of the Timurids, however, was confronted by formidable enemies, the Jalayirid Sulṭān Aḥmad and Qarā Yūsuf Qarā-Qūyūnlū. Released from captivity by the Mamlūk governor of Aleppo on Timur's death, they immediately returned eastwards. Amīrānshāh's son Abā Bakr was driven from Baghdad by Sulṭān Aḥmad. The ruler of Shakkī and the hitherto loyal Shīrwānshāh Shaykh Ibrāhīm both jettisoned their allegiance to Timur's heirs and rallied to Qarā Yūsuf.

Abā Bakr took refuge in Azerbaijan with his brother ʿUmar, who soon grew suspicious of him and incarcerated him in Sulṭāniyya. But Abā Bakr escaped and joined Amīrānshāh, who had feared that ʿUmar might also imprison him and had withdrawn in the direction of Khurāsān.[31] Father and son halted at Kālpūsh for some time, corresponding with Shāhrukh; eventually, in response to his urgings, they retired westwards. According to Salmānī, Khalīl Sulṭān had called upon them to harass Khurāsān and assured an amir that their goal was to conquer it, while Shāhrukh for his part suspected that the two princes were bringing Khalīl Sulṭān reinforcements.[32] Clavijo, who heard (after his return to Spain) that on obtaining control of Samarkand Khalīl Sulṭān sent a message to his father to join him and to be acclaimed as Timur's successor,[33] may simply have misunderstood the motive behind Amīrānshāh's eastward advance. It is difficult to know what to make of this whole episode. Certainly Amīrānshāh had been under a cloud since Timur had deprived him of his appanage in north-western Iran, and his candidature is unlikely to have been widely acceptable.

By Timur's death the territories of ʿUmar Shaykh were partitioned among his three sons, Pīr Muḥammad, Rustam and Iskandar, based at Shiraz, Isfahan and Hamadān, respectively.[34] They were now drawn into the conflicts of Amīrānshāh's line. When Abā Bakr and Amīrānshāh returned to Azerbaijan, they ousted ʿUmar, who sought asylum with his cousins in southern Iran. They rallied to his support, only to be worsted by Abā Bakr and Amīrānshāh in Dhū l-Ḥijja 808/May–June 1406, when each withdrew to his own city; ʿUmar now took refuge in Khurāsān with Shāhrukh, who granted him Māzandarān.[35] Here ʿUmar, who harboured designs on the throne himself (as Clavijo tells us), spent no more than six months before rising in revolt against Shāhrukh. The latter's remonstrations were unavailing, and in an engagement near Jām the turbulent prince was defeated. He headed for Transoxiana, with the aim, we are told, of displacing and even killing his brother Khalīl Sulṭān, but was intercepted near the Murghāb. Brought before Shāhrukh in a gravely wounded condition, he was treated kindly and despatched to Herat for medical care, but died en route in Dhū l-Qaʿda 809/May 1407.[36]

ʿUmar's displacement did not put an end to conflict in ʿIrāq-i ʿAjam. According to Jaʿfarī, in Muḥarram 809/June–July 1406 Abā Bakr followed up his victory with an unsuccessful bid to take Isfahan from Rustam b. ʿUmar Shaykh before retiring to Azerbaijan.[37] For his part, Pīr Muḥammad b. ʿUmar Shaykh, angry at an unauthorised attack on Kirmān by his brother Iskandar (who seems to have made a habit of unauthorised campaigns), wrested Yazd from him and sent him under guard to Shāhrukh in Herat. On the journey, however, the prince was freed and joined Rustam in Isfahan.[38] Together they made war on Pīr Muḥammad and besieged him in Shiraz for a month, but had to rest content with devastating the province before withdrawing to Isfahan. Pīr Muḥammad thereupon drove them from Isfahan and forced them to flee to Khurāsān.[39]

Until this juncture Amīrānshāh's line still held out in Azerbaijan; but Timurid rule there was brought to an abrupt end in 810/1408 when Amīrānshāh and Abā Bakr suffered a crushing defeat by the Qarā-Qūyūnlū and Amīrānshāh was killed, with the result that the territory was forfeited to the Türkmen Qarā Yūsuf. It was around this time that Abā Bakr received an appeal for help from Pīr Muḥammad b. ʿUmar Shaykh, then in conflict with his two brothers. But on reaching Yazd with his forces, he learned that Pīr Muḥammad had succeeded in taking Isfahan and he made instead for Kirmān. Here he was briefly recognised as ruler by its governor Uways (the son and successor of Edigü Barlās). When Uways turned against him and drove him out, Abā Bakr moved to Sīstān in quest of reinforcements, but on learning of Shāhrukh's advance into Sīstān to subdue its recalcitrant malik (see later) he fell back on Kirmān, where he was killed in Ramaḍān 811/February 1409.[40]

THE RISE OF SHĀHRUKH

According to Salmānī, when the amirs Shaykh Nūr al-Dīn and Shāh Malik escorted the royal ladies as far as the Sīr-daryā on their way to Samarkand following Timur's death, they had consulted them about the situation, pointing out that Pīr Muḥammad b. Jahāngīr was far away and might well be distracted by a campaign in the Indian borderlands; were his arrival thus delayed, it would be necessary to consider the claims of Shāhrukh,[41] who was closer at hand.[42] Shortly after this, Salmānī makes Shāh Malik protest to supporters of Khalīl Sulṭān that Shāhrukh was Timur's true successor.[43] These sentiments may, of course, represent simply partisan testimony from an author writing *ex post facto* and in Shāhrukh's service; but they hint already at an awareness of the impracticality of Timur's arrangement for the succession.

Another author who likewise appears to anticipate Shāhrukh's eventual triumph is Ḥāfiẓ-i Abrū. His statement that on the news of Timur's death Shāhrukh's name was inserted in the khutba and on the coinage in Khurāsān and ʿIrāq-i ʿAjam is surely premature.[44] It should be borne in mind that Ḥāfiẓ-i Abrū, writing for Shāhrukh's line, makes no mention of Timur's nomination of Pīr Muḥammad b. Jahāngīr as his successor, but claims instead that his choice fell on Shāhrukh (see above, p. 33). Thus, when recounting how Shaykh Nūr al-Dīn and Shāh Malik moved on Samarkand after the conqueror's death, Ḥāfiẓ-i Abrū asserts, in the vaguest terms, that their intention was to choose 'one of the princes' (*yakī az farzandān*) to rule the territory,[45] as though Timur had inadvertently neglected to select one himself. He claims, lastly, that Shāhrukh's sovereignty was recognised by Pīr Muḥammad b. ʿUmar Shaykh on the grounds that Shāhrukh had inherited the 'ancestral domain' (*yurt-i buzurg*; that is, Transoxiana);[46] this assertion is also suspect (see p. 393). Nevertheless, the fact that Pīr Muḥammad, after taking Yazd in 809 or 810/1406 or 1407, sent off his brother Iskandar under guard to Herat admittedly points to some kind of amicable understanding with Shāhrukh,[47] who was stepfather to both brothers.[48]

In Salmānī's account Shāhrukh staunchly upholds Timur's will. He seeks to conciliate Pīr Muḥammad b. Jahāngīr by delivering Sulṭān Ḥusayn to justice;[49] he writes to Amīrānshāh, advocating Pīr Muḥammad's rights and attempting to convince Amīrānshāh that Khalīl Sulṭān should stand aside, abandon Transoxiana and rest content with his appanage in north-western Iran.[50] As we have seen, Shāhrukh would abandon this legitimist stance in 811/1409, but whatever his attitude in 1405 regarding the succession in Samarkand, he currently had his hands full south of the Oxus. The local rulers permitted to retain their lands under Timur's overlordship now found themselves, with his removal, in a position to sell their support to Timurid claimants or restless amirs; a number seized the opportunity to throw off the Timurid yoke altogether. One of the first to rebel was Pīr Pādishāh b. Luqmān, the grandson of the Ilkhan Taghai Temür, whom Timur had appointed to succeed his father in Astarābād and who, as a Chinggisid, now felt entitled to assert his independence.[51] The former Sarbadār leaders had been steadfast in their loyalty to Timur; but Sulṭān Alī, the son of ʿImād al-Dīn Masʿūd, now rose in revolt in Sabzawār in an attempt to revive the Sarbadār polity. He joined forces with Pīr Pādishāh, but the confederates were defeated by Shāhrukh's troops and Sulṭān Alī took refuge with Amīrānshāh, who handed him over to Shāhrukh.[52] Shāhrukh was also required to bring to heel Quṭb al-Dīn, who had succeeded Timur's loyal client Shāh-i Shāhān as malik of Sīstān, had given shelter to the turbulent Abā Bakr and had taken the opportunity to have the khutba read and coins struck in his own name alone; Quṭb al-Dīn submitted in 812/1409 and once more recognised Timurid sovereignty over his kingdom.[53]

The need to suppress the disturbances in Khurāsān and Māzandarān prevented Shāhrukh from taking a more active part in the conflict over the succession had he so desired. By largely abstaining from the dispute over the succession in Transoxiana, he did, however, conserve his fiscal resources, unlike his nephews.[54] He despatched troops under his son Ulugh Beg and the amir Shāh Malik to aid Pīr Muḥammad, but in the wake of the latter's defeat and death he was obliged temporarily to recognise Khalīl Sulṭān as ruler in Samarkand. It was the stout resistance offered to Khalīl Sulṭān by Shaykh Nūr al-Dīn and Khudāydād Ḥusaynī and the prince's capture by the latter, rather than any manoeuvres on Shāhrukh's own part, that delivered Transoxiana into his hands.

The headship of the empire was another matter. Although Shaykh Nūr al-Dīn initially submitted to Shāhrukh and Ulugh Beg, he soon reverted to supporting Jahāngīr's line. He secured the person of the somewhat reluctant Muḥammad Jahāngīr, made war on Shāhrukh's supporters in the prince's name and obtained help from the Mughūls until they decided to make their peace once more with Shāhrukh and abandoned him. When he persisted in his opposition, Shaykh Nūr al-Dīn was killed by his former confederate, Shāh Malik, acting on Shāhrukh's behalf, in 814/1411.[55] Even after the acquisition of Transoxiana, the subjection of the Timurid inheritance took some years and was destined to remain incomplete. As a consequence of the death of Amīrānshāh in 810/1408, Shāhrukh was now Timur's only surviving son and unquestionably the senior member of the dynasty. But his path to supremacy was still far from smooth.

THE AMBITIONS OF ISKANDAR B. ʿUMAR SHAYKH

In the years immediately following Timur's death, southern Iran under Pīr Muḥammad b. ʿUmar Shaykh and his brothers has the semblance of a parallel universe, embroiled in the conflict between Amīrānshāh's sons but divorced from the struggle taking place in Khurāsān and Transoxiana. Following their defeat by Pīr Muḥammad, however, both Rustam and Iskandar fled into Khurāsān. Rustam took refuge with Shāhrukh; but Iskandar, unwilling to follow his example, first made for Kabul and then crossed the Amū-daryā; he seems briefly to have envisaged heading for Ūzkand in Farghāna, his father's one-time base. But his entourage urged him instead to throw himself on Pīr Muḥammad's mercy and in Ramaḍān 811/ January 1409 he duly returned to Fārs.[56] With the assassination of Pīr Muḥammad b. ʿUmar Shaykh on 3 Muḥarram 812/18 May 1409,[57] Iskandar succeeded in asserting his own authority over Shiraz and Yazd.

Iskandar made three successive attempts to take Isfahan, which properly belonged to his brother Rustam, still absent in Khurāsān. The first challenge confronting him came from Sulṭān Muʿtaṣim, a son of the Muzaffarid Zayn al-ʿĀbidīn (and also a grandson, through his mother, of the Jalayirid Shaykh Uways). Having fled to Syria on the overthrow of his dynasty, this prince returned eastwards on the news of Timur's death and enlisted the aid of Qarā Yūsuf Qarā-Qūyūnlū. Then, invited to take over Isfahan by its qadi and other elements, he made a bid in 812/1409 to occupy the city with a Türkmen force, only to be defeated and killed by Iskandar's troops.[58] In 813/1410–11 Shāhrukh sent Rustam back to resume his position as ruler of Isfahan, and subsequently despatched a force under Khalīl Sulṭān to support him (but see later). This did not prevent Iskandar from continuing to strive for control of Isfahan. Rustam fled to Qarā Yūsuf, with whose military assistance he returned to the city, but was defeated by Iskandar and took refuge in Khurāsān.[59] In 814/1411 Iskandar attacked Kirmān and obtained its submission, and in 815/1412–13 his troops also occupied Qum.[60]

Iskandar had begun to comport himself as an independent prince, adopting the style of Sultan perhaps as early as 812/1409–10. He is regularly given the title in an anonymous synoptic account of the Timurids produced at his court in 816/1413–14 (which may have been Naṭanzī's work). His growing power posed a direct challenge to Shāhrukh. Affiliated with Farghāna through both his father and his Chinggisid mother (see p. 358), Iskandar evidently still felt drawn to the region in 811/1409, when he was driven from Isfahan and briefly envisaged establishing himself at Ūzkand (see earlier). The fulsome references to Iskandar as master of 'the Mughūl people and ulus' (*īl-u ulūs-i mughūl*), which occur from 806/1403–4 onwards, harked back to his audacious invasion of Kashgharia in 802–3/1399–1400 at the age of only sixteen.[61] The synoptic account goes so far as to allege that Iskandar's forces were still obstructing the Mughūl advance at the time of writing.[62]

Like Naṭanzī's first recension, the synoptic account presents Iskandar as Timur's designated heir. Iskandar's history is also partially rewritten. Here Muḥammad Sulṭān – the genuine heir-apparent until his death (and possibly an object of Iskandar's resentment) – is alleged to have rebelled against Timur. In further flights of fancy, Iskandar is depicted as taking over Fārs with the laudable motive of preventing his brothers disgracing themselves and as conquering the entire region as far as the gates of Tabriz, from Mecca and Medina to Kīsh and Makrān and from Khurāsān to Darband, appointing his own governors throughout. Not only do the Jalayirid Sulṭān Aḥmad and other local dynasts recognise his overlordship but even (less plausibly) the Chinese Emperor, with whom he has exchanged embassies, is his tributary. Just as Timur and ʿUmar Shaykh had outshone all previous sultans by their deeds, we are told, so had Iskandar eclipsed even his father and grandfather.[63]

The confrontation between uncle and nephew was played out on an ideological as well as a geopolitical level. We have noticed already, in Chapter 14, that intellectuals in Herat and elsewhere in Shāhrukh's dominions, among them Sharaf al-Dīn Yazdī, promoted the idea that Shāhrukh was the *mujaddid*, the 'Renewer', and that he had abolished the Töre in favour of the Sharīʿa. At Isfahan Iskandar presided over the development of a sophisticated ideology of sacral kingship centred on himself. Both Naṭanzī's work and the synoptic account incorporate elements of the ideology current at his court. Naṭanzī hails the prince as the 'Mahdī of the last days' (*mahdī-yi ākhir al-zamān*) and it has been proposed that the terms in which he recounts Iskandar's supposed nomination by Timur were an implicit allusion to the Shīʿī doctrine of *naṣṣ* – designation by an imam of his successor.[64] Iskandar, Shāhrukh and their respective publicists were seeking to capitalise on the aura that had come to surround Timur as *Ṣāḥib-Qirān*, 'Lord of the Auspicious Conjunction', and on his enormous prestige. In the process, both courts were formulating a new conception of Muslim kingship.

In 816/1414 Shāhrukh finally moved against Iskandar, most of whose amirs had been estranged by his harshness and deserted to the enemy; Isfahan fell to Shāhrukh's forces, and the defeated prince was handed over to his brother Rustam, who blinded him. Iskandar was placed in the custody of his brother Bāyqarā, on whom Shāhrukh conferred the government of Hamadān and Luristān, but the two princes shortly rebelled and made a bid to occupy Shiraz. Iskandar was captured and put to death;[65] Bāyqarā held out in Shiraz until 818/1415, when Fārs was entrusted to Shāhrukh's son Ibrāhīm Sulṭān. Rustam, who had proved less of an obstacle to Shāhrukh's ambitions, was allowed to remain in Isfahan as Shāhrukh's governor until his death in 827/1424.[66]

SHĀHRUKH'S PARAMOUNTCY

In the wake of his acquisition of Transoxiana Shāhrukh acted as the master of Timur's empire, endowing members of the dynasty with grants of land. Ṭukhāristān, for instance, was conferred on the deposed 'khan' Muḥammad Jahāngīr (above, p. 345). In 810/1407 Shāhrukh bestowed Balkh on Qaidu,[67] who had succeeded his murdered father Pīr Muḥammad b. Jahāngīr in the south-eastern marches. The hapless Khalīl Sulṭān was tasked in Dhū l-Qaʿda 812/ March 1410 with bringing under control ʿIrāq-i ʿAjam and Azerbaijan. But opposition by Iskandar's forces prevented him from establishing himself in Isfahan and he was obliged to take up residence in Rayy, where he shortly died on 16 Rajab 814/3 November 1411.[68] In his account of this episode, Ḥāfiẓ-i Abrū expressly mentions that ʿIrāq-i ʿAjam and Azerbaijan had been subject to the administration of Khalīl Sulṭān's late father, and further asserts that Shāhrukh was now committing these lands to the prince in full sovereignty (though elsewhere he indicates that Khalīl Sulṭān was being sent to reinforce Rustam against his brother Iskandar). Shāhrukh is even made to assure Khalīl Sulṭān that he will later follow him in person.[69] It is difficult to avoid the impression that the scheme was designed to get a problematic former rival – and one-time sovereign – out of the way.

A number of Shāhrukh's territorial allocations to his kinsmen were far removed from the geographical sphere of influence of their respective branches and ran counter to Timur's own division of his territories. Examples are the grant of Shabūrghān in 810/1407–8 as *soyurghal* to Sayyid Aḥmad b. ʿUmar Shaykh,[70] and of Ūzkand and Andijān in 812/1409–10 as *soyurghal* to Amīrak Aḥmad b. ʿUmar Shaykh.[71] Following Iskandar's overthrow Shāhrukh conferred Qum on Muḥammad Sulṭān's son Saʿd-i Waqqāṣ, who soon rebelled and allied with the Qarā-Qūyūnlū, however, and was deprived of the territory in 818/1415.[72]

Qaidu suppressed the maliks of Badakhshān, who had backed the rebel amir Pīr ʿAlī Tāz,[73] and initially acted as a loyal subordinate. Like Iskandar, however, he was not slow to display aspirations to autonomy and emerged as the last of Shāhrukh's relatives to challenge his supremacy. Khiḍr Khan, whom Timur had appointed as his governor in Multān and who took control of Delhi in 817/1414, acknowledged Shāhrukh's overlordship and had his name recited in the khutba (see p. 300). In 819/1416–17, however, Qaidu sent envoys to Khiḍr Khan, requiring him to insert his (Qaidu's) name in the khutba and on the coinage. Khiḍr Khan thereupon appealed to Herat and was granted permission to insert his own name in the khutba immediately after Shāhrukh's.[74] Qaidu, who was obliged to abandon his pretensions, subsequently rebelled, possibly encouraged by his cousin Bāyqarā b. ʿUmar Shaykh, who had taken shelter with him in Qandahār. In 821/1418–19 Shāhrukh headed an expedition to the south-east, deprived Qaidu of his principality and imprisoned him; his principality was entrusted to Shāhrukh's own son Soyurghatmish.[75]

Within only fifteen years of Timur's death, then, his empire had both contracted and been reconfigured. With the successive deaths of ʿUmar, Abā Bakr and Khalīl Sulṭān the foremost members of the second generation of Amīrānshāh's line had left the stage. Iskandar's downfall had greatly diminished the sphere of influence of ʿUmar Shaykh's offspring. Shāhrukh no longer faced any rivals among his brothers' descendants. He ruled Khurāsān directly; his son Ulugh Beg deputised for him in Transoxiana, his sons Ibrāhīm Sulṭān, Soyurghatmish and Bāysunghur administered Fārs, Kabul and

Māzandarān, respectively, and other sons or amirs of Shāhrukh governed on his behalf in Kirmān and much of ʿIrāq-i ʿAjam. His empire thus appears like a replica of Timur's, with the important differences that it was significantly reduced in size, the conqueror's territorial allocations had been largely dispensed with and its centre was Herat rather than Samarkand. The choice, of course, reflected the fact that Khurāsān was the domain conferred on Shāhrukh by his father; but Herat was also by this date a more logical site for the centre of the Timurid empire.

If I have devoted so much space to this series of internecine conflicts and rapid shifts of power, it is in order to highlight the utter absence of any sense of common endeavour among Timur's progeny or any respect for his will once he was dead. As Stephen Dale observes, Timurid princes, despatched to govern a territory at a relatively early age, isolated from their families, their brothers and half-brothers and presiding over miniature courts that might be dominated by their father's loyalists only in the initial stages, soon developed their own independent political ambitions.[76] His comments relate to the later Timurid decades but they apply equally well to the years following Timur's death. Salmānī quotes at length a letter from Shāhrukh to Amīrānshāh, then in the act of advancing from Azerbaijan towards Khurāsān (in *c.* 808/1405–6). According to Shāhrukh, in dividing up his territories Timur had expressed a desire that every one of the princes be satisfied with his lot and avoid conflict, so as to afford the dynasty's enemies no opportunity for gain.[77] There is nothing unduly surprising here. Chinggis Khan had supposedly addressed a similar plea for unity to his sons (see pp. 84–5). And if the conflicts among Chinggis Khan's grandsons did not constitute a sufficiently grim warning to Timurid princes, the dissension that had rent the Jalayirid and Muzaffarid dynasties, and from which Timur himself had profited so greatly, certainly offered a cautionary tale. Salmānī says that Amīrānshāh's withdrawal was in response to his brother's letter.[78] The impression left by events of the years following Timur's death, however, is that otherwise the admonition went largely unheeded. The ensuing upheavals were due less to the efforts of dynasts whom Timur had displaced to retrieve their ancestral territories – although the Jalayirids and the Qarā-Qūyūnlū enjoyed far greater success in this regard than did the Sarbadārs or the Muzaffarids – than to the irrepressible tendency of his descendants to encroach on each other's appanages and the reluctance of most of them to acknowledge any superior authority. The synoptic account is unjust to blame Abā Bakr's activities alone for the dynasty's loss to outsiders of an enormous stretch of territory 'from Sāwa to the borders of the Franks and Syria';[79] he was far from being the sole agent of upheaval.

FOREIGN RELATIONS AFTER TIMUR

It is noteworthy – and, in the circumstances, unsurprising – that Shāhrukh and his successors followed a less ambitious policy towards foreign powers than had the dynasty's founder. During the early decades, for the most part, they relinquished far-flung campaigns and large-scale plundering expeditions and devoted greater attention to developing the fiscal resources of their own territories and to asserting an ideological superiority over neighbours and rivals. Timur's heirs benefited less from his military operations in the west than they did in the east. The Ottoman Sultanate recovered remarkably swiftly from his onslaught, and the Qarā-Qūyūnlū were strong enough to terminate Timurid rule in Azerbaijan and then to supplant the Jalayirids. Even in Shāhrukh's day, the Timurid possessions continued to be threatened in the west by the Qarā-Qūyūnlū. If Shāhrukh avenged Amīrānshāh in 823/1420 by regaining Azerbaijan and temporarily imposed his overlordship on the Qarā-Qūyūnlū ruler Jahānshāh b. Qarā Yūsuf in 838/1435, he was still obliged to head a series of expeditions to the region.

Although the Mamlūk Sultanate underwent internal upheavals in the years following Timur's death, its vassal status had not outlasted Timur himself and it had regained its position as the major power in the Near East by the reign of Bārsbāy (825–841/1422–1438). Timurid princes retained their forebear's antipathy towards the Mamlūks, but mainly insofar as they were in competition with the Egyptian Sultan for influence in the Holy Cities of Mecca and

Medina.[80] From 828/1424–5 Shāhrukh, as the paramount ruler in the eastern Islamic world, vigorously advanced a claim to provide the ceremonial cushion for the Kaʿba, a right hitherto monopolised by the Mamlūk Sultan.[81] In the confrontation between the two powers, the Mamlūk Sultan came out better, gaining the allegiance of the Āq-Qūyūnlū, who had collaborated with Timur but now, bereft of his patronage, sought protection from Cairo.[82]

Although Khwārazm had been recovered for the Jochids by Edigü soon after Timur's death, it was reconquered on Shāhrukh's behalf in 815/1413, after a failed first attempt, by Shāh Malik.[83] Ulugh Beg regained Kāshghar from the Mughūls, only to lose it once more in *c.* 838/1434–5. Military activity tended on the whole, however, to be confined to self-defence against the threat of raids on Transoxiana by the Jochids north of the Sīr-daryā and the Mughūls to the east. In an effort to neutralise these troublesome neighbours, Timurid rulers continued the founder's practice of assisting displaced Chinggisid princes to return to the Qipchaq khanate or Mughūlistān and to rule there (ideally) as clients and allies. In *c.* 1408 Abā Bakr b. Amīrānshāh had allegedly sent Chekire Oghlan (see above, pp. 350–1) back to the Qipchaq steppe with an escort that included Schiltberger.[84] Ulugh Beg would likewise encourage refugee Chinggisids to re-establish themselves in their homelands: in the Qipchaq khanate, Baraq (son of Qoyurichaq and grandson of Orus Khan) in 822/1419; and in Mughūlistān, first Shīr Muḥammad in 823/1420 and then Sātūq in *c.* 1429 (both of them grandsons of Khiḍr Khwāja).[85] The expedient cannot be said to have met with success. Baraq raised claims to the Sighnāq region, which had at one time been Blue Horde territory; Ulugh Beg reacted by heading a disastrous expedition against him in 830/1426–7, in defiance of Shāhrukh's instructions. Although Shīr Muḥammad refrained from raiding Timurid territory, he ceased to show gratitude for Ulugh Beg's support once he was enthroned,[86] while Sātūq failed to make any headway in Jata against the reigning khan, Ways.

The notion of attacking the Ming having been abandoned soon after Timur's death, diplomatic relations with China undeniably improved. Khalīl Sulṭān released the Ming envoys whom his grandfather had incarcerated and sent them back to China with an embassy of his own. A return Ming embassy is said (with no hint of irony) to have been tasked with condoling the prince on Timur's death.[87] In 1407, when the Mughūl khan, Khiḍr Khwāja's son and successor Shamʿ-i Jahān, requested Chinese aid in recovering Samarkand from the Timurids, Zhu Di (the Yongle Emperor) gave a discouraging response and urged restraint.[88] Regular diplomatic exchanges between the Ming and the Timurids continued during Shāhrukh's reign.[89] Undoubtedly, however, they still reflected at first the same strongly dissonant viewpoints as had characterised correspondence with Timur, whereby the Ming court interpreted sumptuous gifts as tribute from a subject prince (see p. 307). In 815/1412, in reply to a letter from Shāhrukh, Zhu Di claimed to rule the entire earth and counselled Shāhrukh and Khalīl Sulṭān (who by this juncture had not merely lost his throne but had died) to settle their differences.[90] Shāhrukh responded to another mission from Zhu Di, which reached Herat in 820/1417, with an embassy which was the largest to reach China from the western regions during this period and was absent from Herat for a total of three years (822/1419 to 825/1422); the account of this mission – written by a participant, Ghiyāth al-Dīn Naqqāsh – was incorporated in Ḥāfiẓ-i Abrū's *Zubdat al-tawārīkh*.[91]

The truncated Delhi Sultanate continued to acknowledge Timurid suzerainty under Khiḍr Khan's successors, who are known as the Sayyid dynasty.[92] The Indian historian Bihāmadkhānī asserts that at the time of writing (842/1438–9) Shāhrukh's orders had been received in Delhi for almost forty years and that the contemporary Delhi ruler, Khiḍr Khan's grandson Muḥammad b. Mubārak Shāh (837–849/1434–1445), was still obedient to him.[93] Interestingly, of those regions that had suffered a visitation from Timur without experiencing more than a brief occupation, the Delhi polity was the only one to remain in a long-term subordinate relation to his successors.

THE LATER TIMURIDS

In the event, the paramountcy of Shāhrukh's line did not long outlive him.[94] His death (850/1447) and that of his son and successor Ulugh

Beg (853/1449) were followed by a few years of mutual strife among the Timurids, reminiscent of that from 1405 to 1420. In 855/1451 the throne of Transoxiana was seized by Abū Saʿīd,[95] a grandson of Amīrānshāh who further extended his sway over Khurāsān in 862/1458; a casualty of this conflict was Shāhrukh's widow, Gawhar Shād, whom Abū Saʿīd executed on suspicion of collaborating with one of Shāhrukh's grandsons. At his death (873/1469) Abū Saʿīd was able to transmit power beyond the Oxus to his sons; but Khurāsān fell under the rule of Sulṭān Ḥusayn Bāyqarā (873–911/1469–1506), who belonged to the branch of ʿUmar Shaykh. Over a period of nearly seven decades following Timur's death, possession of the principal Timurid territories – Khurāsān and Transoxiana – had thus passed among the branches of three of his four sons. Ironically, as Manz observes, Jahāngīr's descendants – designated by the conqueror himself to succeed him – were 'the only line that had not produced a major ruler'.[96]

The Timurid possessions continued to be threatened in the west by the Qarā-Qūyūnlū, who reoccupied Azerbaijan and advanced their power into Iran. Jahānshāh, having seized Isfahan in 856/1452 and Fārs and Kirmān in the following year, was even able to wrest Herat from Shāhrukh's squabbling grandsons for a few months in 862/1458, before Abū Saʿīd occupied the city. But by this point the Qarā-Qūyūnlū faced a burgeoning menace to their rear, in the person of the Āq-Qūyūnlū ruler Uzun Ḥasan, who defeated and killed Jahānshāh in 872/1467; and in 873/1468–9 Abū Saʿīd took the ill-judged decision to aid the Qarā-Qūyūnlū against this new rival, hoping thereby to recover lost Timurid territory. He allowed himself to be lured into Azerbaijan, where he suffered a crushing defeat, was captured and handed over to a Timurid prince who had entered Uzun Ḥasan's service and who put him to death in revenge for the execution of his great-grandmother Gawhar Shād. As a consequence, Uzun Ḥasan took over the Qarā-Qūyūnlū (and formerly Timurid) provinces of ʿIrāq-i ʿAjam, Fārs and Kirmān.[97] The Timurids had for some decades ceased to rule over any tracts west of Khurāsān.

In their eastern territories the Timurids were confronted by another rising power, the Uzbeks, under the dynasty founded by Abū l-Khayr (d. *c.* 1468), a descendant of Jochi's son Shiban, in the former lands of the Blue Horde. Abū l-Khayr's death temporarily halted the Uzbek advance but it revived under his grandson Muḥammad Shībānī, who proved a redoubtable enemy to the Timurids. In 906/1501 the Uzbeks took Samarkand from Ẓahīr al-Dīn Muḥammad Bābur, Abū Saʿīd's grandson and fifth in descent from Timur, and in 912–13/1506–7 swept away the bickering sons of Sulṭān Ḥusayn Bāyqarā in Herat. Timurid Khwārazm was occupied in *c.* 1510 by a second Uzbek grouping, led by another Shibanid prince, who founded the khanate of Khiva. Following the death of Muḥammad Shībānī in battle with the Safawid Shah Ismāʿīl near Merv in 916/1510 and the Uzbeks' loss of Khurāsān to the Safawids, Bābur, who had retreated from his appanage of Farghāna to Kabul in 910/1504, was able to re-establish himself in Transoxiana for a few years, but in 920/1514 he was obliged to fall back on Kabul for the last time. Here, from 1519, he developed ambitions in a totally different direction, one that echoed the operations of his ancestor Timur in 1398. Successive military probings in the Punjab culminated in Bābur's victory at Panipat over the Delhi Sultan Ibrāhīm Lodi in 932/1526 and his conquest of northern India.

TIMUR'S LONG-TERM LEGACY

If Timur had failed to leave behind an empire possessed of a robust institutional framework, it is nevertheless a striking fact that his descendants – and his enemies, for that matter – saw him as worthy of emulation. Whatever still remained of the Chinggisid ideology was now distinctly tempered; in Allsen's words, the 'common historical memory' had gone, to be replaced by 'alternative political myths and models'.[98] Of these alternatives, the most widespread was that centred on Timur. He had extended his authority over an enormous swathe of territory, had acquired a reputation for never having suffered defeat and had vanquished the most powerful Muslim princes of his day; and – unlike Chinggis Khan's – his triumphs had been achieved under the banner of Islam.

The growth of Timurid kudos would derive additional momentum from the spectacular career of Bābur (d. 937/1530), who retrieved the dynasty's fortunes by conquering the Delhi Sultanate and founding the Mughul empire. The new power was known by this appellation, not because the invaders originated from the khanate of Mughūlistān but because the populations of northern India readily accommodated them within a long tradition of Mongol incursions from beyond the Oxus, beginning in the thirteenth century. True enough, the Mughul Emperors traced their descent to Chinggis Khan (through Bābur's mother, a Chaghadayid Mughūl princess, daughter of the Mughūl khan Yūnus) as well as to Timur; but they came to prize their Timurid ancestry and heritage more highly. Significantly, the erstwhile Timurid dominions in Transoxiana retained a place in Bābur's ambitions; he even willed that he be buried not in Delhi or Agra but in Kabul. Successive emperors contributed to the upkeep of Timur's tomb in Samarkand down to the eighteenth century and the recovery of the Timurid homeland in Transoxiana remained a distant ideal in Mughul India during that period.[99] Shāh Jahān (1037–1068/1628–1658), the only Mughul sovereign to attempt its reconquest, certainly took Timur as a model.[100]

Nor was the cultivation of Timurid prestige confined to the Mughul Emperors – 'true Timurids', in Dale's words, 'who enthusiastically embraced Timurid legitimacy and consciously presided over a Timurid renaissance'.[101] Chroniclers of the contemporary Safawid dynasty in Iran likewise invoked Timur as a means of legitimising the dynasty's rule, particularly under Shah ʿAbbās I (995–1038/1587–1629).[102] In the 1740s we find the Safawids' successor Nādir Shāh Afshār modelling himself on Timur.[103] The Ottomans too sought to associate themselves with Timurid cultural accomplishments; some Ottoman historians even justified Timur's crushing victory over their Sultan Bayezid at Ankara on the grounds that he was the more legitimate ruler of the two.[104] It is true that a universal history written for the founder of the Uzbek state, Abū l-Khayr, covered the Timurid era only briefly and includes no illustrations that depict Timur; at this initial stage, Chinggisid descent trumped any conceivable link with the Timurid dispensation. But even the Uzbeks came in time consciously to adopt aspects of late Timurid culture with a view to rendering their rule more acceptable to their subjects in Transoxiana.[105]

Lastly, early in the nineteenth century the rulers of the *parvenu* state of Khokand in Farghāna would contrive for themselves a genealogy that linked them to Timur through the Mughul Emperor Bābur (as the last Timurid prince of Farghāna), while also seeking to replicate at their court the cultural efflorescence of fifteenth-century Timurid Herat.[106]

LATER INNER ASIAN CONQUERORS

Timur, in the words of John Darwin, was 'a transitional figure in Eurasian history'.[107] He commanded an army of which the kernel was nomadic troops and he sought to dominate the commercial land routes across Eurasia, as Chinggis Khan had done. Though drawing both economic and military resources from the sedentary world, and evidently ready, at intervals, to embrace a semi-sedentary existence in his capital, Samarkand, he can still claim to have been the last in a series of nomadic Turkic or Turco-Mongol conquerors to emerge from Inner Asia and impose their sway over Greater Iran – and in Timur's case even beyond (if briefly).

Why did no more Timurs burst upon the Eurasian scene? Certainly, there was no dearth of aspiring conquerors thereafter. But from the sixteenth century onwards the great powers of Eurasia were located not in Inner Asia but on its periphery. They occupied the regions that Timur had either invaded or had planned to attack: the resurgent Ottomans in Anatolia, the Near East and (eventually) North Africa; the Safawids in Iran; Muscovy in the north-west; the Mughuls throughout most of the Indian subcontinent; and the Ming (and after 1644 their successors, the Qing) in China.

The Uzbek khan Muḥammad Shībānī, having ousted the Timurids from Transoxiana, defeated their allies, the khans of Mughūlistān, and overthrown the Timurid state in Khurāsān, might have seemed to be on the verge of establishing another world empire ruled from Samarkand. But his defeat and death at Safawid hands in 916/1510 put paid to this possibility. Nor was the political structure of the Uzbek dominions – involving a revival of the appanage system that placed strong limits on the khan's power – conducive to a common effort to extend the dynasty's lands,[108] any more than the parallel structure that the Timurids had maintained after 1405. Although in the wake of their defeat by the Safawids the Uzbeks still harboured expansionist designs to the south, they were soon further stymied by the creation of the Mughul empire under the Timurid Bābur, whose territory extended from Kabul to the borders of Bengal, blocking their path. They were additionally called upon to devote much of their energy to fighting the Kazakhs, nomadic tribes to the north and north-east. The Kazakhs, having originally formed part of the Uzbek confederacy, had seceded in the late 1450s under descendants of Jochi's son Toqa Temür.[109] In the early sixteenth century they were a formidable power, occupying the entire region to which they have given their name. Yet neither the Uzbeks nor the Kazakhs ever amounted to more than a loose confederacy for any significant period; and in any case both Uzbek and Kazakh alike would be neutralised by the Oyirat threat.

The Oyirat confederacy arose amid the Mongol tribes known to their western Muslim neighbours as Qalmāq (on the possible etymology, see above, pp. 206–7), and first appears towards the close of the fourteenth century, when it challenged the power of the Qaghans of the Northern Yuan in western Mongolia. At various times the Oyirat leaders, Maḥmūd (d. 1416), Toghan (d. 1438) and then the latter's son and successor Esen (d. 1454), intervened in the Northern Yuan succession and attempted to rule through a Qaghan of their own choice.[110] Like Timur half a century earlier, Esen is sometimes said (doubtless wrongly) to have aimed to restore the Mongol empire.[111] His military accomplishments included the defeat and capture of the Mughūl khan Ways and even of the Ming Emperor (1449). But when in 1452 he assumed the title of khan – to which, as a *qarachu*, he was not entitled – many of his commanders deserted him and he was killed. Over the next few decades the Oyirat launched periodic attacks on their Uzbek and Kazakh neighbours, but they were increasingly a prey to debilitating internal conflict and in the middle decades of the sixteenth century they were obliged to acknowledge the authority of Dayan Khan and his grandson Altan Khan, descendants of the Northern Yuan who ruled the Khalkha Mongols.[112]

In the early seventeenth century, however, a chief named Erdeni Baatur Khongtaiji (d. 1653) reunited the Oyirat, who were coming to be known as the Zunghars. His successor Galdan (d. 1697) first took the title of khan (conferred on him by the Dalai Lama in 1678), even though he lacked Chinggisid descent. Under Galdan the Zunghars annexed the wealthy cities of the Tarim basin, putting an end to the rule of the eastern Chaghadayids. Galdan suffered a disastrous defeat by the Qing Chinese army, however; and although his nephew Tsewang Arabdan (d. 1727) was able to revive Zunghar power to some extent, the Qing Emperors Kangxi (reigned 1661–1722) and Qianlong (reigned 1735–1795) each proved an implacable enemy to the Zunghars. Qianlong's forces eventually destroyed the Zunghar confederacy in 1757–8, massacring a great many of the adult males.[113]

The Zunghars represent the last of the steppe empires in Inner Asian history but if we are to search for the most successful Inner Asian leader in the two or three centuries after Timur's death, we must look elsewhere – further east, in fact, at the forerunner and founder of China's Qing dynasty: the leader of the Manchurian Jurchen, who practised a 'semi-nomadic'[114] economy, combining horse-breeding with hunting and agriculture. It was the Manchu Hung Taiji (d. 1643) who from 1627 onwards reduced the eastern Mongol Khalkha tribes to submission and overthrew Lighdan, khan of the Chakhars and a direct descendant of the Northern Yuan (1634). In 1636 Hung Taiji assumed the title of Emperor for himself and the name Qing for his new dynasty and embarked on the conquest of Ming China, completed in 1644, just after his death.[115] In time his Qing successors brought under their rule much of Inner Asia, overwhelming the Zunghars and turning Muslim Kashgharia into the province of Xinjiang. The juxtaposition of the Manchu military machine (drawing as it did both on the steppe resources of Mongolia and the mixed/sedentary resources of the Manchurian borderlands) with the economic and institutional strength of China proved more than a match for the nomads of Inner Asia. The Zunghars, confronted by the formidable power of the Qing, were ultimately unable to withstand it.

THE DEMISE OF NOMAD POWER

The termination of the threat from nomadic confederacies has frequently been attributed to the advent of firearms, against which (it is claimed) the traditional horse-archer proved less effective.[116] But the matter is by no means so simple. The Zunghars had access to cannon, if not in the quantities available to their Qing and Russian antagonists. Gunpowder weaponry, in any case, was slow to make a difference. Robert Irwin has argued persuasively that in the fifteenth and sixteenth centuries, at least, firearms conferred no decisive advantage. Bābur's possession of firearms seems to have played no part in the Mughul victory at Panipat in 932/1526.[117] Indeed, in terms of range and rate of fire (not to mention mobility) the Crimean Tatar cavalry was still more than a match for Polish and Russian musketeers in the seventeenth century.[118]

Nor was the fact that Timur was the last great nomadic conqueror to emerge from Inner Asia due, as often supposed, to the penetration of western European Christians into the Indian Ocean from 1497 onwards, which nurtured long-distance seaborne trade and presaged a very different world where the nomadic conqueror was an anachronism. As Darwin argues, that world would begin to manifest itself only when another three centuries had passed.[119] In the meantime, the European impact on Asian societies was rather more limited than the impact of the latter on Europe.[120] Overland commerce on a significant scale, both across northern Eurasia and between Central Asia and India, operated alongside, and in a complementary fashion to, the maritime trade and persisted at least down into the eighteenth century, fed by India's continuing need of Central Asian horses and Central Asian demand for Indian cotton, cotton textiles and dyestuffs.[121] Furthermore, the expansion of Muscovy into Siberia fostered new opportunities for trade and new northerly routes between steppe and sown.[122]

Arguably, it was not until the eighteenth century that nomadic hegemony ceased to be a possibility.[123] And what really spelled the end for steppe empires was not the challenge from seaborne commerce, but rather the loss of tribute in kind (notably in furs) and the reduction of the nomads' profitable share in the proceeds of long-distance overland trade, as the sedentary powers of Muscovite Russia and Qing China extended their own authority over northern Inner Asia and the Siberian taiga. The intensive methods of government employed by these two empires enabled them in addition to amass much larger bodies of cavalry than previously and to deprive the pastoralists of their advantage in numbers of mounts.[124] As Allsen put it: 'In the thirteenth century, the Mongols mobilised resources from steppe and sown to subjugate most of Eurasia. In the eighteenth century, the Russians and Manchus used the same formula to subjugate the nomads.'[125]

CONCLUSIONS

By the time Timur was acclaimed as head of the ulus of Chaghadai in Transoxiana, the Mongol world had been in crisis for some decades. The Ilkhanate had collapsed amid internecine strife following the death of Abū Sa'īd in 1335. Much of its territory had passed into the hands of non-Mongol rulers. Certain of them, moreover, defied the canons of legitimacy framed by the Mongols, by arrogating to themselves sovereign titles and seeking an alternative basis of authority from outside the Mongol world in the form of investiture by the 'Abbasid Caliph in Cairo. To the north, with the extinction of Batu's line, the Qipchaq khanate was disputed among a number of rival khans of Jochid descent, and their kinsmen, the khans of the Blue Horde, had gained autonomy and were on the point of asserting their own rule over Sarai and other centres. In China, a mere two years before Timur rose to power, Mongol rule had come to an end and the Qaghan, routed by the Ming, had fallen back on the Mongolian homeland. Chaghadai's ulus itself had split two decades or so previously, and the eastern region, known as Mughūlistān, was now governed by its own line of Chaghadayid khans. Even in the western part of the ulus, in Transoxiana, tribal amirs now wielded real power, notably those from the Qara'unas, who made and unmade khans at will.

Timur himself was not a tribal amir and we cannot rely on the prehistory of his dynasty as furnished by Timurid authors. If his ancestor Qarachar had indeed held a position of the highest prominence within Chaghadai's ulus, it seems that the ruling clan of the Barlās tribe had forfeited it well before Timur's era, and earlier sources – insofar as they mention the internal affairs of the ulus – are largely silent about the Barlās. Timur himself, moreover, was only a junior member of that clan, whatever claims Timurid writers make for his father and grandfather. He was essentially a *parvenu* who rose to be chief of his tribe (temporarily) by joining the invading 'Mughūl' forces of the eastern Chaghadayid khan Tughluq Temür. He then jettisoned the Mughūls to join Amīr Ḥusayn, heir to the Qara'unas amirs. Having undergone the exile and hardships of an adventurer (*qazaq*) as a member of Ḥusayn's following (apart from a brief flirtation once more with the Mughūls), he assisted him to become head of the ulus. From an uncertain date (surely prior to his submission to Tughluq Temür) he had been building up a warband of his own; and when the opportunity offered as Ḥusayn increasingly alienated support, he finally broke with his ally – much as he had earlier thrown over the Mughūls – to establish his own paramountcy.

What distinguishes Timur from the other Turco-Mongol 'Great Amirs', whether his predecessors in Transoxiana and the Ilkhanate or contemporaries like Mamai and Edigü in the Jochid territories, is above all the duration of his rule and the magnitude of his military successes outside the ulus. Within Transoxiana he eliminated or faced down every antagonist; beyond it, he either eliminated all rival potentates from Mughūlistān as far as Syria and Anatolia or reduced them to submission and obedience. Granted that his dominions fell significantly short of the extensive conquests of the thirteenth-century Mongols; that he did not impose direct rule over many of his conquests; that on occasion he was obliged to revisit conquered territories to reassert his authority; that he often did so by dint of terror tactics alongside which those of the Mongols paled; and that he neglected, unlike Chinggis Khan and his heirs, to create a framework that would underpin the survival of his empire. Yet he also manifested a concern to rehabilitate certain of the lands he had devastated, fostering the extension of cultivation and a resumption of trade – efforts, we should notice, by no means confined to his own homeland. It is hard to be comprehensively dismissive of his achievements.

The purposes behind Timur's almost incessant military activity – other than to funnel the ambitions and to absorb the energies of Chaghatay amirs and their followers and to win himself fame and glory – are unclear. Taking into account the chronology of his conquests, it seems reasonable to assume that his ambitions grew with the advent of opportunity such as appeals for his assistance or with the manifestation of external challenges. But it is easier to assert that he was engaged in recreating the Mongol empire than to demonstrate it on the basis of hard textual evidence. Indeed, it is perhaps also too easy to draw parallels with Chinggis Khan. That Timur himself consciously sought to evoke memories of the Mongol conqueror does not mean that he simply aspired to emulate him. His panegyrists, at least, betray a greater concern to portray him as surpassing Chinggis Khan's exploits (not to mention those of earlier paladins like Maḥmūd of Ghazna) than to cast the two conquerors in an identical mould.

What we can say with more confidence is that Timur was reviving, though on a much grander scale, an expansionist policy that Chaghadayid rulers had followed for some decades. He affected, inter alia, to be remedying wrongs done to the Chaghadayids (and the Ögödeyids). His expeditions were launched, and his territorial claims were articulated, on behalf of the nominal khan of Chaghadai's ulus. The campaigns into Mughūlistān seemingly aimed at restoring unity to the ulus in the longer term; the assault on the Punjab and the rape of Delhi fulfilled, after a lapse of several decades, an ambition of the early fourteenth-century Chaghadayid khans. If Timur truly envisaged the reassertion of Mongol rule throughout the former Chinggisid territories, it was not until his very last year or so, when he prepared to challenge the Ming in eastern Asia. Insofar as we can identify a broad aim from a relatively early stage in his career of conquest, it is that of restoring some kind of 'Chinggisid order' at all levels: suppressing local elements that disrupted peace by preying upon merchants and pilgrims and displacing those princes who had usurped control over one-time Chinggisid territories and – like the Kartids of

Herat and the Muzaffarids of southern and central Iran – had misappropriated the trappings of sovereignty. For Timur, that Chinggisid order, and that sovereignty, were embodied in the khan he served.

Timur's rise to power coincided with an era when khans of Chinggisid lineage no longer exercised de facto rule in the Qipchaq steppe (prior, that is, to the accession of Toqtamish) or in Transoxiana; in Iran they had ceased to rule altogether, and in the Far East the Qaghan had forfeited authority over China. Yet there is evidence that loyalty and devotion continued to attach to the imperial dynasty, not least in the more northerly territories of the one-time Mongol empire; and Timur's own concern to ally himself and his progeny with the Chinggisids by marriage bears witness to it (as does his possible readiness, later, to acquiesce in a genealogy that linked him to Chinggis Khan's ancestors through the male line).

As descendants of Chinggis Khan's designated successor Ögödei, the two khans whom Timur nominated in turn may have enjoyed a greater prestige than has commonly been supposed. Even the attempts by later Timurid authors to suppress the references to them as found in Shāmī's contemporary work were far from exhaustive. On occasion his khans fought alongside him – indeed Sulṭān Maḥmūd Khan appears to have participated actively in a number of the conqueror's major campaigns – and Timur may have had strong personal ties with them. Timur stands out from other Great Amirs, too, in his respectful and humane treatment of his two sovereigns. Although we lack evidence that he appointed a successor to Sulṭān Maḥmūd, and although his heirs (with the short-lived and qualified example of Khalīl Sulṭān) did without a Chinggisid khan altogether, it is by no means certain that Timur himself had intended permanently to dispense with one. He retained Sulṭān Maḥmūd's name on the coinage as a temporary measure, and alternative possibilities suggest themselves. His own death may have occurred too soon thereafter; or conceivably he envisaged the enthronement of another Ögödeyid candidate – a fugitive from the Northern Yuan territory – in the course of a successful expedition against the Ming.

In addition to maintaining a Chinggisid sovereign and forging links between the imperial dynasty and his own family, Timur cultivated the image of a world-conqueror and made assiduous use of appeals to a Chinggisid dispensation by propounding versions of Mongol history that were at variance with historical fact – and sometimes even with one another. The effectiveness of this propaganda is by no means certain; it is a better indication of the continuing importance of the Chinggisid past than of the conqueror's political and diplomatic sophistication. There was greater mileage in the claims that he made to supernatural experiences and to the gift from Heaven of a special insight, which echoed tales current in the pre-Islamic Mongol era and would certainly have resonated with Timur's nomadic Chaghatay troops. Overall, the historical distortion and the claims to Heaven's favour were alike deployed in the service of Chaghadai's ulus (even though the sovereigns Timur installed were not of Chaghadai's line). Viewed through the Chaghatay prism, the years from 1370 to 1405 surely represented the high water-mark of that ulus.

Timur was reputedly an inventive and resourceful general in the field but we learn little of his military tactics. His numerous triumphs rested in large degree on his authority over his disciplined troops, who appear to have been devoted to him (despite the excessive demands he sometimes made on them) and with whom he often generously shared the spoils of war. He was also fortunate in his opponents. Contemporary observers notice that he profited by living in an era of disunity. In Greater Iran he faced several polities on hostile terms with one another; in addition, the leading powers among them – notably the Jalayirids and the Muzaffarids – were riven by fraternal conflict. The damage done by these struggles served to endow Timur with the aura of a restorer of peace and good order and may have fostered acceptance of his rule at least as much as did his notorious cruelty. Some local elements, like the Sarbadārs in western Khurāsān, hard pressed by their neighbours, yielded readily. There is no sign, in Iran at least, that any of the rulers who did not so yield made any solid attempt to forge alliances against him; he was accordingly able to pick them off one by one.

If the wider environment – economic upheaval, climatic instability and repeated outbreaks of plague – had contributed to the collapse of Mongol rule in much of Asia, however, it is far from clear that it contributed at a later date to Timur's successes. Plague undoubtedly visited the Jochid territories at least three times in the four decades preceding his attacks but all we can say with some certainty is that the outbreaks seem to have made it possible for his client and later antagonist, Toqtamish of the Blue Horde, to vanquish Mamai and extend his rule over the Qipchaq khanate. And although plague also attacked the Jalayirid dominions twice within the same period, its impact on the wider Iranian world – indeed the very question of its incidence and range – is obscure. Contrary to the view expressed in some of the secondary literature, we are in no position to claim that in this context Timur enjoyed any advantage over his opponents, particularly given the lack of evidence regarding plague in his home territory of Central Asia.

As Manz has shown, in governing his empire (if we can so term it, given its loose structure and the fact that its official sovereign was a member of the imperial Chinggisid dynasty) Timur made use of his body of loyal followers, men he had recruited into his warband and promoted during the conflicts of the 1360s in Transoxiana and at the time of his rise to power. They constituted a new ruling cadre as the tribal chiefs were progressively sidelined or removed; and since their descendants went on to serve Timur's successors this new elite lasted down into the sixteenth century. As the decades progressed, Timur also employed his sons and grandsons in the highest levels of administration. Not that his innate caution enabled him to trust them. Young Timurid princes despatched to govern enormous territories on his behalf were accompanied by reliable amirs to keep watch over them and (presumably) to report on their conduct should need arise. Even so, the long-term result of these gubernatorial appointments was to forge strong links between a number of princes and particular regions – and thereby to undermine princely consciousness of being part of a single, united dynastic enterprise.

Timur's caution is evident, too, in his arrangements for the succession. He nominated as his heir his grandson Muḥammad Sulṭān, in whom he may well have reposed the greatest confidence, at a relatively late stage (when he himself was about seventy years of age), primarily on the twin grounds that the prince's mother was of Chinggisid descent and that his father Jahāngīr had been the only one of Timur's sons born to a legitimate wife. After Muḥammad Sulṭān died prematurely, however, no new heir seems to have been selected until Timur was close to death; and there is widespread agreement among scholars that his choice – Jahāngīr's other son, Pīr Muḥammad – was a poor one. Once having complicated the matter by his stress on birth and lineage, Timur may unintentionally have introduced a sense of hierarchy among his progeny that militated against the acceptance of Pīr Muḥammad. There is a sharp contrast with Chinggis Khan's ability to settle the succession on the most suitable candidate in advance and to secure the commitment of his other sons.

Despite the common perception that Timur was a less humane man than Chinggis Khan and more prone to wanton and far-sought acts of cruelty, it is also paradoxically easier to discern in the sources, on occasion, signs of his humanity. Various authors portray him as weeping, not merely on the death of one of his wives or his sons, but on being informed of the deaths of his khan Sulṭān Maḥmūd and his prisoner Bayezid – and even when witnessing the prowess of his grandsons outside Delhi or reciting God's favour in granting him so many triumphs. If we can believe Sharaf al-Dīn Yazdī, he seems also to have experienced some degree of repentance for the sufferings that those triumphs had inflicted on Muslim populations.

One respect in which Timur differed markedly from Chinggis Khan and the majority of thirteenth- and early fourteenth-century Mongol rulers relates to his religious convictions. He was a self-conscious Muslim. Like his Ilkhanid precursor, the convert Ghazan Maḥmūd, he was extolled by his servitors and his historians for the genuineness of his Islamic faith and denounced by his enemies as an infidel to whom Islamic teaching and practice were foreign. He may have been deeply sensitive to this charge, especially when it emanated from the Ottoman Sultan, himself a proven holy warrior on behalf of the faith. Ultimately, we are in no position to judge how much truth underlay the accusation, any more than when assessing the whole-heartedness of Mongol convert rulers such as Ghazan or Tarmashirin.

If Timur's frequent wars in the name of Islam were far from exclusively directed against non-Muslims, this had also been true of Muslim princes in earlier centuries. The same qualification could be made equally in the context of his diplomatic dealings with Christian rulers; though the illusions that surrounded these were fostered almost entirely by the much-travelled Archbishop John of Sulṭāniyya. In Timur's case, however, no formal alliances resulted and we have good reason to believe that the priority on his side was to nurture trade.

Central to the issue of religious allegiance is that Timur's governance was based in part on the Töre or Yasa. The corpus of customary law associated with Chinggis Khan and his successors was revered by the Turco-Mongol nomads but seen by Muslims as in conflict with the Sharīʿa; though it is less certain what precisely it entailed in Timur's day than in the thirteenth century. If by the time of his descendant Bābur the Töre had come to be associated with aspects of court etiquette, we do not know that this was yet the case under Timur. It seems that he retained the tax on commercial and artisanal activity, the *tamgha*. Law was enforced through the traditional procedures of the Mongol *yarghu*, and Shāhrukh's claim subsequently to have abolished this particular institution (whether or not the claim was justified) confirms that it had continued to function under his father. Given Timur's origins in the ulus of Chaghadai – viewed in his own lifetime as the guardian of the Yasa – it could not have been otherwise. Timur also continued a number of pre-Islamic practices, observing certain rituals, for instance, that dated from the era of pagan Mongol rule and promoting levirate marriage on the part of his sons; his burial along with grave goods is a telling indication of his attachment to steppe *mores*.

Our image of Timur derives from a great variety of source material, a significant proportion of it hostile. But we need to remain alive to the possibility that he came across to the majority of his followers as a generous lord; to many of those who met him, Ibn Khaldūn included, as an impressive and magnetic figure; and to the majority of his subjects as a devout and uncompromising protagonist of Islam. Not a few Muslim observers will have seen his duplicity and his shocking acts of cruelty primarily as the means to two highly desirable ends – the triumph of the faith and the suppression of disorder. Against this background, it is not altogether fanciful to see his activities as a partial remedy for the crisis that had beset the Chinggisid world in the middle decades of the fourteenth century.

In this book we have been confronted repeatedly by a process of synthesis: between the Turco-Mongolian world and the Persianate *oecumene* extending from Kabul and the cities of Khurāsān to Azerbaijan and Fārs; of orthodox Islamic practice and the customs of the pagan steppe; and (with some reservation, perhaps) of the time-honoured imperial ideology of the Eurasian nomads with traditional patterns and images of Muslim kingship that emphasised the duty, inter alia, of extending Muslim rule. Synthesis is no less clearly visible than elsewhere in the dual character of Timur's political persona as presented in our disparate sources. Let us take, firstly, his origins and early career. He appears to have spoken with pride of his humble beginnings and even of the physical disability that had nevertheless not debarred him (with divine aid) from attaining a position of extraordinary power. Yet we gain insights into his early background only from outside observers: it is conspicuously absent from the Persian sources that he commissioned or that were produced under his successors – sources following a tradition of historical writing to which mention of such unpromising antecedents was alien. Secondly, his title to rule rested not simply on an unbroken sequence of far-flung military victories but on the quasi-spiritual – we might almost say 'shamanistic' – gifts that he claimed to have received from Heaven, marking him out as one endowed with unique qualities even among celebrated Muslim conquerors. The duality is revealed, thirdly, in the range of his titulature, epitomised by the phrase 'Timur Beg, Sultan of Turan' in the inscription dating from his first campaign in the Qipchaq steppe in 1391. As a *qarachu* Mongol captain, he was subordinate to the khan of Chaghadai's ulus and accordingly assumed the lesser title of amir/beg; as a Muslim potentate, on the other hand, he enjoyed all the attributes traditionally vouchsafed to Muslim monarchs (apparently going so far as to claim even the right to nominate the Caliph) and allowed himself to be styled Sultan.

Neither the relatively limited extent of Timur's sway when set against that of the Mongol empire, nor the scepticism expressed during his lifetime as to his political ethics and his commitment to the faith, nor the fate of his dominions after his death, prevented him from serving as a model in subsequent decades for Muslim monarchs from the Balkans to the Ganges and the Sīr-daryā. His widespread victories; his claims, in the Chinggisid tradition, to divine backing for his enterprises; his assiduous deployment of Islamic legitimation; and his image as a holy warrior on an unprecedented scale – all combined to win him a posthumous reputation that was nothing less than paradigmatic. His exploits had, it seems, transformed the very nature and parameters of political authority in the central and eastern Islamic world.

GLOSSARY

ahl al-bayt	(Ar.) descendants of the Prophet Muḥammad (lit. 'The People of the House'); see also *sayyid*
ahl al-dhimma	(Ar.) 'Protected Peoples', i.e. other monotheistic religious communities living under Muslim rule (notably Christians and Jews)
altan urugh	(Mo.) the imperial Chinggisid dynasty (lit. 'the Golden Kin')
amān	see *māl-i amān(ī)*
amīr al-umarā	(Ar.) chief amir; see also *ulusbegi*
atabeg	(Tu.) guardian (lit. 'father commander'); the Ar. form is *atābak*
bahādur	(Pers., from Tu. *batur*) champion, 'hero'
bakhshī	(Tu.) Buddhist monk or scholar; hence scribe
basqaq	(Tu.) governor; see also *darugha*
beg	(Tu.) tribal military commander
bilig	(Mo.) saying (usually of Chinggis Khan)
bitikchi	(Tu.-Mo.) scribe, secretary
cherig	(Mo.) troops; auxiliary forces
darqan	see *tarkhan*
darugha	(Mo.) governor; see also *basqaq*
*dhimmī*s	see *ahl al-dhimma*
dīwān	(Ar.-Pers.) financial administration

faqīh	(Ar.) jurist
faqīr	(Ar.-Pers.) ascetic
farmān	(Pers.) order, decree
fatḥ-nāma	(Pers.) victory despatch
ghazā	(Ar.-Pers.) Islamic holy war; see also *jihād*
ghāzī	(Ar.-Pers.) holy warrior
ghulām	(Ar.-Pers.) slave, page
güregen	(Mo.) imperial son-in-law
ḥājj	(Ar.-Pers.) the annual pilgrimage to Mecca
ḥakīm	(Ar.-Pers.) governor
iduq-qut	(Tu.) 'holy majesty', the title of the Uighur ruler of Beshbaligh
īl	(Tu.-Mo.) peace; submission
imām	(Ar.-Pers.) prayer leader
injü	(Mo.) personal property
jerge/nerge	(Tu.-Mo.) encirclement tactic employed in the hunt
jihād	(Ar.-Pers.) holy war
jizya	(Ar.-Pers.) poll-tax payable by non-Muslim subjects of the Islamic state
keshig	(Mo.) guard corps (of a ruler)
ke'ün	(Mo.) prince (lit. 'son', 'boy')
khānaqāh	(Ar.-Pers.) sufi hospice
kharāj	(Ar.-Pers.) tax on land/crops
khatun	(Tu.-Mo.) princess, lady
khuṭba	(Ar.-Pers.) sermon given at the Friday prayers
kökeltash	(Mo.) foster-brother
madrasa	(Ar.-Pers.) college, school of theology
māl-i amān(ī)	(Ar.-Pers.) indemnity paid by conquered urban population
malik	(Ar.-Pers.) king
mamlūk	(Ar.) military slave; see also *ghulām*
möchelge	(Mo.) binding oath
mukūs	(Ar.-Pers.) taxes not sanctioned by the *Sharī'a*

mulūk al-ṭawā'if	(Ar.-Pers.) 'factional princes'; label applied to the autonomous amirs in the Chaghadayid *ulus* prior to Timur's rise, and to the post Ilkhanid rulers in Iran
nā'ib	(Ar.-Pers.) lieutenant, deputy
nökör	(Mo.) follower, comrade
noyan	(Mo.) commander
orda	(Mo.) encampment
pādishāh	(Pers.) emperor
qāḍī	(Ar.-Pers.) judge within the Islamic legal system
Qaghan	(Tu.-Mo.) emperor; also arabicised as *Khāqān*
qalan	(Tu.-Mo.) tax(es) [significance debatable]
qalandar	(Ar.-Pers.) mystic, sufi, dervish; see also *faqīr*
qarachu	(Mo.) commoner, Mongol of non-Chinggisid lineage
qawm	(Ar.-Pers.) people
qishlaq	(Tu.-Mo.) winter quarters
qol-un ulus	(Mo.) '*ulus* of the centre'
qoshun	(Mo.) military division, company
qubchur	(Mo.) poll-tax imposed on the Mongols' subjects
quriltai	(Mo.) assembly
ṣadr	(Ar.-Pers.) principal religious dignitary
sayyid (pl. *sādāt*)	(Ar.-Pers.) descendant of the Prophet
Sharī'a	(Ar.-Pers.) Islamic law
shaykh	(Ar.-Pers.) Muslim religious notable
shiḥna	(Ar.-Pers.) governor
soyurghal	(Tu.-Mo.) grant of land or income (lit. 'favour')
tamgha	(Tu.-Mo.) tax on commercial or artisanal activity; originally 'seal'
tamma	(Mo.) frontier forces
tarkhan	(Tu.) privileged person enjoying certain fiscal and other exemptions; Mo. form *darqan*
ṭā'ūn	(Ar.-Pers.) plague
Töre	(Tu.) steppe custom and customary law; see also *yasa*

tümen	(Mo.) military unit of 10,000; also a district capable of raising that number of troops
'ulamā (sing. *'ālim*)	(Ar.-Pers.) 'the learned', scholars
ulus	(Mo.) people/territory ruled by a particular khan or prince; 'state'
ulusbegi	(Tu.-Mo.) chief commander
'ushr	(Ar.-Pers.) tithe; tax on irrigated land
wabā	(Ar.-Pers.) epidemic
waqf (pl. *awqāf*)	(Ar.-Pers.) charitable foundation
walī	(Ar.-Pers.) governor
yailaq	(Tu.-Mo.) summer quarters
yam	(Tu.) postal relay station; network of such stations
yarghu	(Tu.-Mo.) tribunal
yarghuchi	(Tu.-Mo.) judge
yarligh	(Tu.-Mo.) order, command
yasa(q)	(Tu.) edict, regulation; Mo. form *dzasagh*; often used of the corpus of Chinggis Khan's edicts or of Mongol law generally
yosun	(Mo.) custom
yurt	(Tu.-Mo.) camping grounds, pasturelands

CHRONOLOGY

624/1227	Death of Chinggis Khan
626–639/1229–1241	Reign of the Qaghan Ögödei
644–646/1246–1248	Reign of the Qaghan Güyüg
649/1251	Toluid seizure of the imperial throne
649–657/1251–1259	Reign of the Qaghan Möngke
658/1260	Hülegü's general Ked-buqa defeated by the Mamlūks at ʿAyn Jālūt
658–662/1260–1264	Civil war in Mongolia between Qubilai and Arigh Böke
c. 658/1260	Mongol defeat at ʿAyn Jālūt; foundation of the Ilkhanate by Hülegü
663–680/1265–1282	Reign of the Ilkhan Abagha
668/1269–70	Invasion of Khurāsān by the Chaghadayid khan Baraq
670/1271	Ögödei's grandson Qaidu established as over-khan in Central Asia
681–683/1282–1284	Reign of the Ilkhan Tegüder Aḥmad
c. 681–706/1282–1307	Reign of the Chaghadayid khan Du'a
683–690/1284–1291	Reign of the Ilkhan Arghun
694/1295	Ghazan's conversion to Islam and his accession as Ilkhan

late 1290s	Qaidu and Du'a bring the Qara'unas under their aegis
702/1303	Death of Qaidu and succession of Chapar
703–716/1304–1316	Reign of the Ilkhan Öljeitü
705/1305	Outbreak of war between Du'a's and Chapar's supporters
716–736/1316–1335	Reign of the Ilkhan Abū Saʿīd
727 or 728/1327–8	Birth of Timur (cf. the fabricated date 736)
730/1329–30	Invasion of India by the Chaghadayid khan Tarmashirin
735/1334	Tarmashirin's overthrow
736–758/1335–1357	Era of puppet Ilkhans
741/1340	The Muzaffarid Mubāriz al-Dīn Muḥammad takes over Kirmān
747/1346–7	Overthrow of the Chaghadayid khan Qazan Sulṭān; beginning of the paramountcy of Qara'unas amirs in Transoxiana
748/1347–8	Split in the Chaghadayid khanate with the emergence of an eastern polity ('Mughūlistān', 'Jata')
754/1353	Ilkhan Taghai Temür assassinated by the Sarbadārs; the Muzaffarids wrest Shiraz from the Injuids
758/1357	The Jochid khan Janibeg conquers Azerbaijan, putting an end to the Chobanid dynasty
759/1358	Murder of the Qara'unas Amir Qazaghan The Jalayirid Shaykh Uways occupies Tabriz
761–762/1360–1361	Two invasions of Transoxiana by the Mughūl khan Tughluq Temür
764/1362–3	Death of Tughluq Temür and succession of his son Ilyās Khwāja
765/1363–4	The Qara'unas Amīr Ḥusayn, seconded by Timur, expels the Mughūl forces and becomes effective head of the *ulus* of Chaghadai in Transoxiana

1368	Expulsion of the Mongol Yuan dynasty from China by the Ming
c. 1369	Ilyās Khwāja murdered by Qamar al-Dīn
771/1369–70	Timur supplants Amir Ḥusayn, enthrones Soyurghatmish as khan and marries the Chaghadayid princess Sarai Mulk Khanim
777/1375	Death of Timur's son Jahāngīr
778/1377	Toqtamish appeals to Timur for help
780/1379	Toqtamish asserts his rule over the Qipchaq khanate
781/1379	Timur annexes Khwārazm
782/1380–1	Timur's third son Amīrānshāh made governor of Khurāsān
783/1381	Submission of the Sarbadārs; annexation of Herat
785/1383	Sīstān reduced to vassal status
786/1384	Timur occupies Sulṭāniyya
787/1385–6	Toqtamish ravages Azerbaijan
788/1386	Amīr Walī captured and put to death
788–790/1386–1388	Timur's three-year campaign in north-western Iran and the Caucasus
789/1387	Toqtamish invades Transoxiana and besieges Bukhara
790/1388	Death of Soyurghatmish and enthronement of Sulṭān Maḥmūd as khan; Timur transfers the populace of Ürgench to Samarkand
791/1389	Surviving members of the Kartid dynasty put to death
793/1391	Timur's first campaign in the Qipchaq steppe; defeat of Toqtamish on the Qundurcha River
794/1391–2	Pīr Muḥammad b. Jahāngīr nominated governor of Kabul
794–798/1392–1396	Timur's five-year campaign

795/1392–3	Destruction of the Muzaffarids; Timur's eldest son ʿUmar Shaykh appointed governor of Fārs; Timur's first occupation of Baghdad
796/1394	Death of ʿUmar Shaykh; Amīrānshāh begins to display signs of insubordination
797/1395	Timur's second campaign in the Qipchaq steppe; defeat of Toqtamish on the Terek River and sack of major Jochid urban centres
799/1397	Timur's youngest son Shāhrukh appointed governor of Khurāsān
800–801/1398–1399	Timur's invasion of India and sack of Delhi
801/1399	Death of the Mamlūk Sultan Barqūq and accession of his son Faraj
802/1399–1400	Amīrānshāh deprived of his appanage
802/1399	Beginning of Timur's seven-year campaign in the far west
803/1400–1	Timur's invasion of Mamlūk Syria; sack of Aleppo and Damascus; Ibn Khaldūn received at Timur's headquarters
803/1401	Sack of Baghdad
1401	First diplomatic contacts with Western Europe
804/1402	Victory over the Ottoman Sultan Bayezid near Ankara
805/1402–3	Deaths in Anatolia of Sulṭān Maḥmūd Khan and Timur's grandson and heir-apparent Muḥammad Sulṭān b. Jahāngīr
1403	Archbishop John of Sulṭāniyya arrives in Western Europe as Timur's envoy
1404	Castilian envoy Clavijo at Timur's headquarters
807/1405	Death of Timur at Utrār while preparing to attack Ming China; Khalīl Sulṭān occupies Samarkand; the Jalayirid Sulṭān Aḥmad returns to Baghdad

808/1406	Khalīl Sulṭān defeats Pīr Muḥammad b. Jahāngīr
809/1407	Assassination of Pīr Muḥammad b. Jahāngīr
810/1408	Amīrānshāh defeated and killed by the Qarā-Qūyūnlū; loss of Azerbaijan
811/1409	Khalīl Sulṭān defeated and captured; Shāhrukh recognised as ruler in Transoxiana and entrusts its government to his son Ulugh Beg
812/1409	Assassination of Pīr Muḥammad b. ʿUmar Shaykh; his brother Iskandar accepted as ruler of Fārs
813/1410	Qarā Yūsuf of the Qarā-Qūyūnlū defeats and kills the Jalayirid Sulṭān Aḥmad
816/1414	Overthrow of Iskandar by Shāhrukh, who extends his rule over Fārs
821/1418–19	Shāhrukh deprives Qaidu b. Pīr Muḥammad of Kabul, thereby reuniting the remnants of Timur's empire under his own sovereignty

GENEALOGICAL TABLES

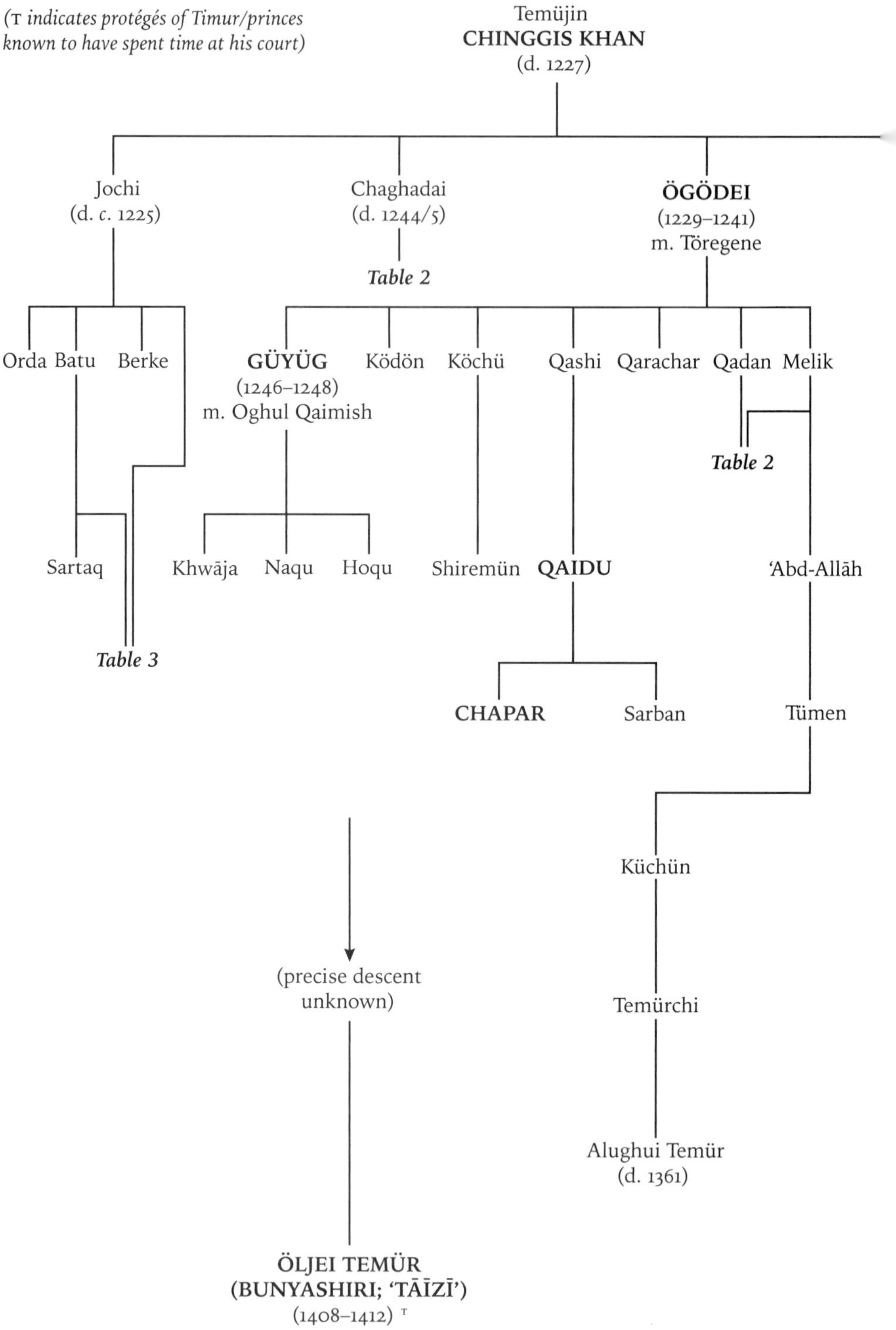

Table 1. The Qaghans.

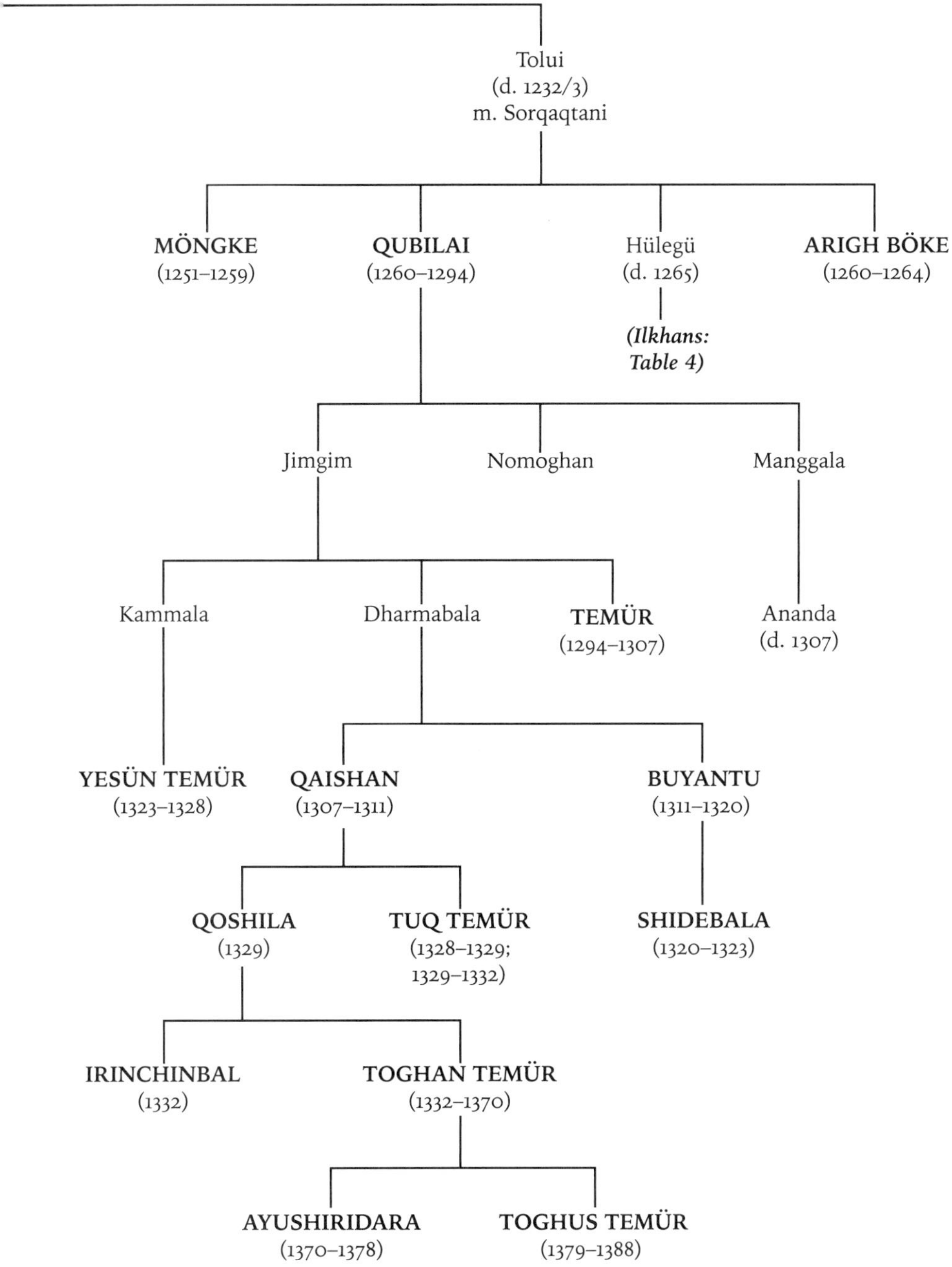
Tolui
(d. 1232/3)
m. Sorqaqtani
MÖNGKE
(1251–1259)
QUBILAI
(1260–1294)
Hülegü
(d. 1265)
(Ilkhans: Table 4)
ARIGH BÖKE
(1260–1264)
Jimgim
Nomoghan
Manggala
Kammala
Dharmabala
TEMÜR
(1294–1307)
Ananda
(d. 1307)
YESÜN TEMÜR
(1323–1328)
QAISHAN
(1307–1311)
BUYANTU
(1311–1320)
QOSHILA
(1329)
TUQ TEMÜR
(1328–1329; 1329–1332)
SHIDEBALA
(1320–1323)
IRINCHINBAL
(1332)
TOGHAN TEMÜR
(1332–1370)
AYUSHIRIDARA
(1370–1378)
TOGHUS TEMÜR
(1379–1388)

2A

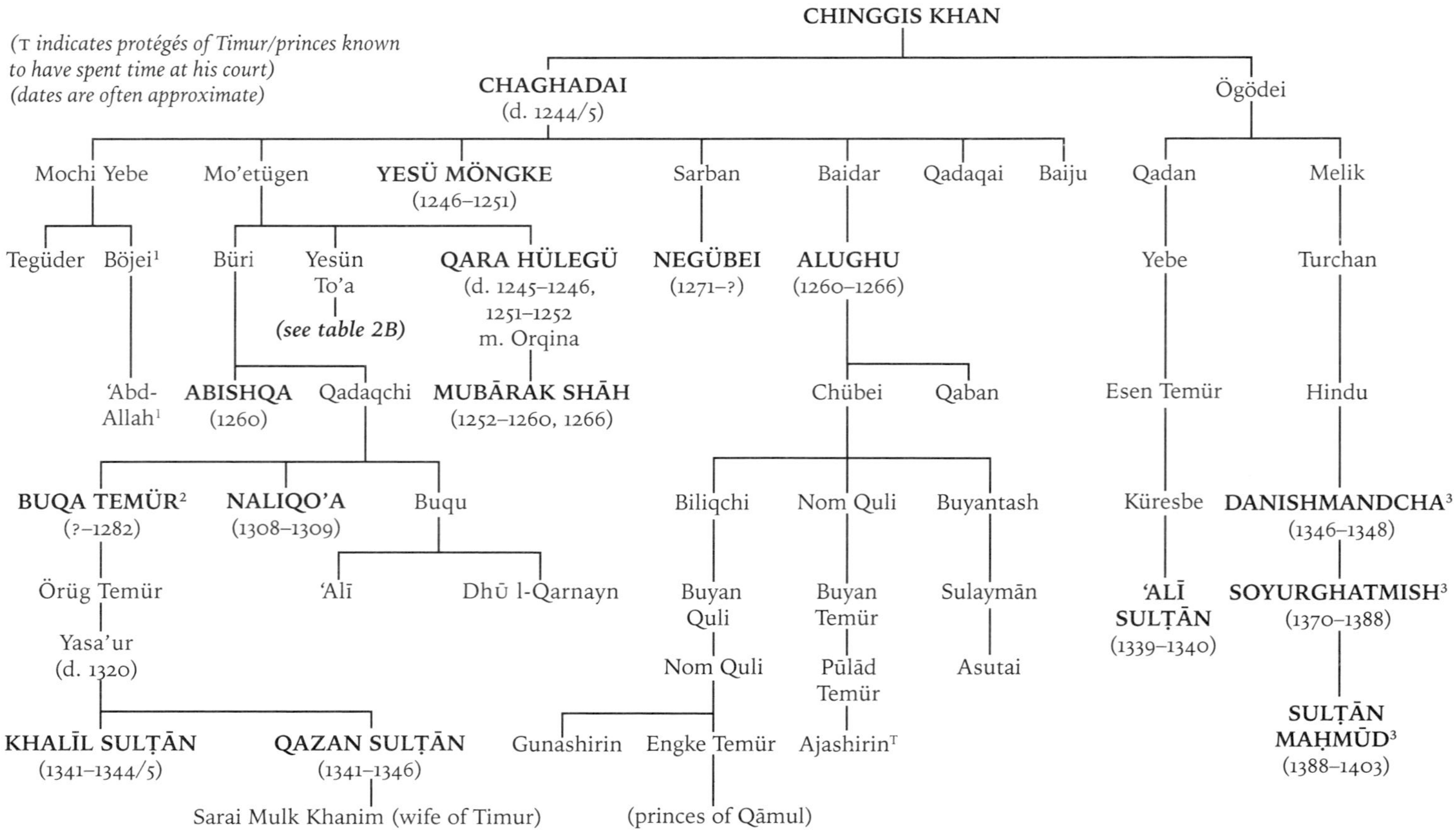
(T indicates protégés of Timur/princes known to have spent time at his court)
(dates are often approximate)
CHINGGIS KHAN
CHAGHADAI
(d. 1244/5)
Ögödei
Mochi Yebe
Mo'etügen
YESÜ MÖNGKE
(1246–1251)
Sarban
Baidar
Qadaqai
Baiju
Qadan
Melik
Tegüder
Böjei[1]
Büri
Yesün To'a
(see table 2B)
QARA HÜLEGÜ
(d. 1245–1246, 1251–1252
m. Orqina
NEGÜBEI
(1271–?)
ALUGHU
(1260–1266)
Yebe
Turchan
'Abd-Allah[1]
ABISHQA
(1260)
Qadaqchi
MUBĀRAK SHĀH
(1252–1260, 1266)
Chübei
Qaban
Esen Temür
Hindu
BUQA TEMÜR[2]
(?–1282)
NALIQO'A
(1308–1309)
Buqu
Biliqchi
Nom Quli
Buyantash
Küresbe
DANISHMANDCHA[3]
(1346–1348)
Örüg Temür
'Alī
Dhū l-Qarnayn
Buyan Quli
Buyan Temür
Sulaymān
'ALĪ SULṬĀN
(1339–1340)
SOYURGHATMISH[3]
(1370–1388)
Yasa'ur
(d. 1320)
Nom Quli
Pūlād Temür
Asutai
KHALĪL SULṬĀN
(1341–1344/5)
QAZAN SULṬĀN
(1341–1346)
Gunashirin
Engke Temür
Ajashirin[T]
SULṬĀN MAḤMŪD[3]
(1388–1403)
Sarai Mulk Khanim (wife of Timur)
(princes of Qāmul)

2B

(dates are often approximate)

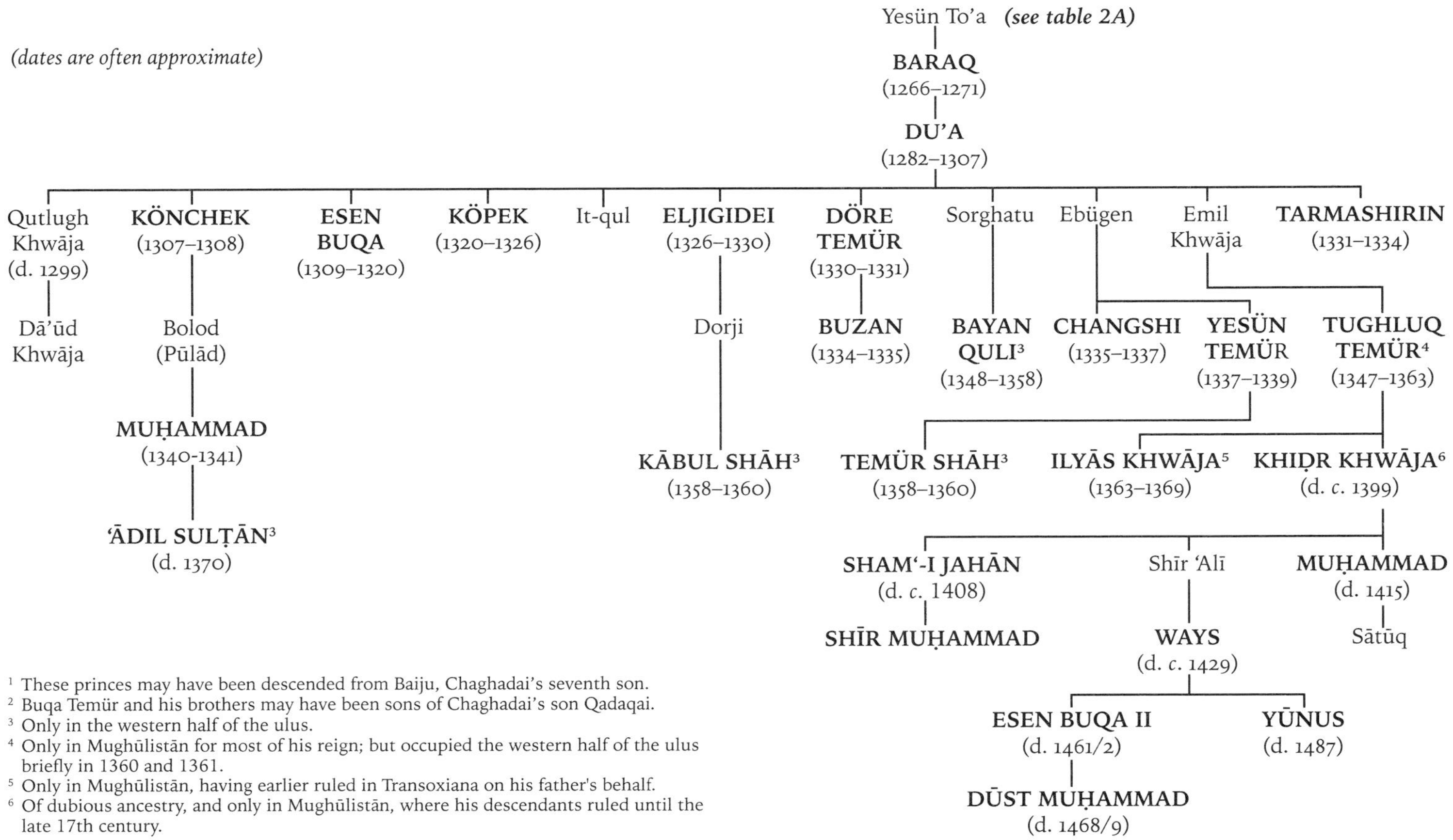

1 These princes may have been descended from Baiju, Chaghadai's seventh son.
2 Buqa Temür and his brothers may have been sons of Chaghadai's son Qadaqai.
3 Only in the western half of the ulus.
4 Only in Mughūlistān for most of his reign; but occupied the western half of the ulus briefly in 1360 and 1361.
5 Only in Mughūlistān, having earlier ruled in Transoxiana on his father's behalf.
6 Of dubious ancestry, and only in Mughūlistān, where his descendants ruled until the late 17th century.

Table 2. The khans of Chaghadai's ulus.

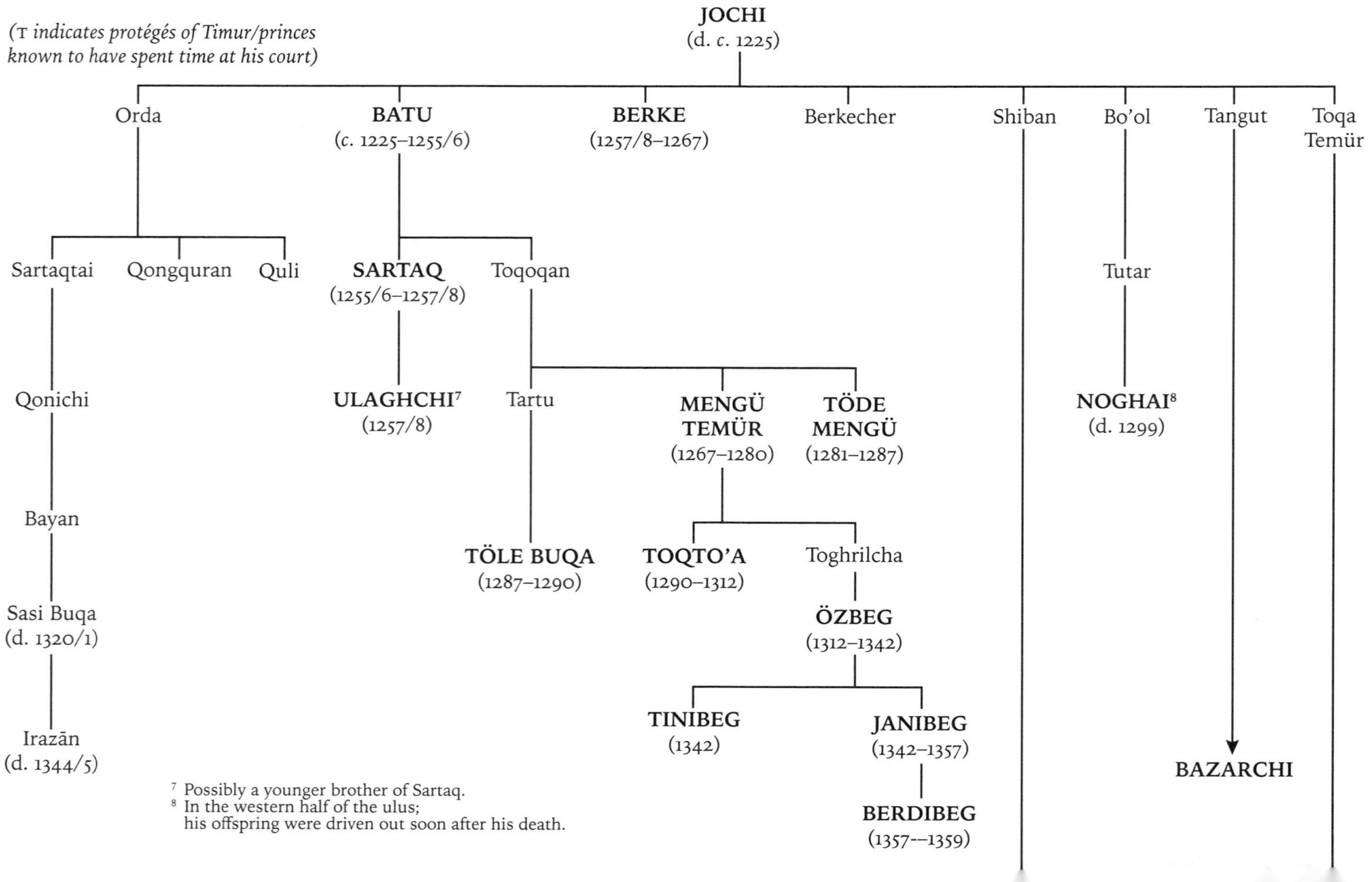

7 Possibly a younger brother of Sartaq.
8 In the western half of the ulus; his offspring were driven out soon after his death.

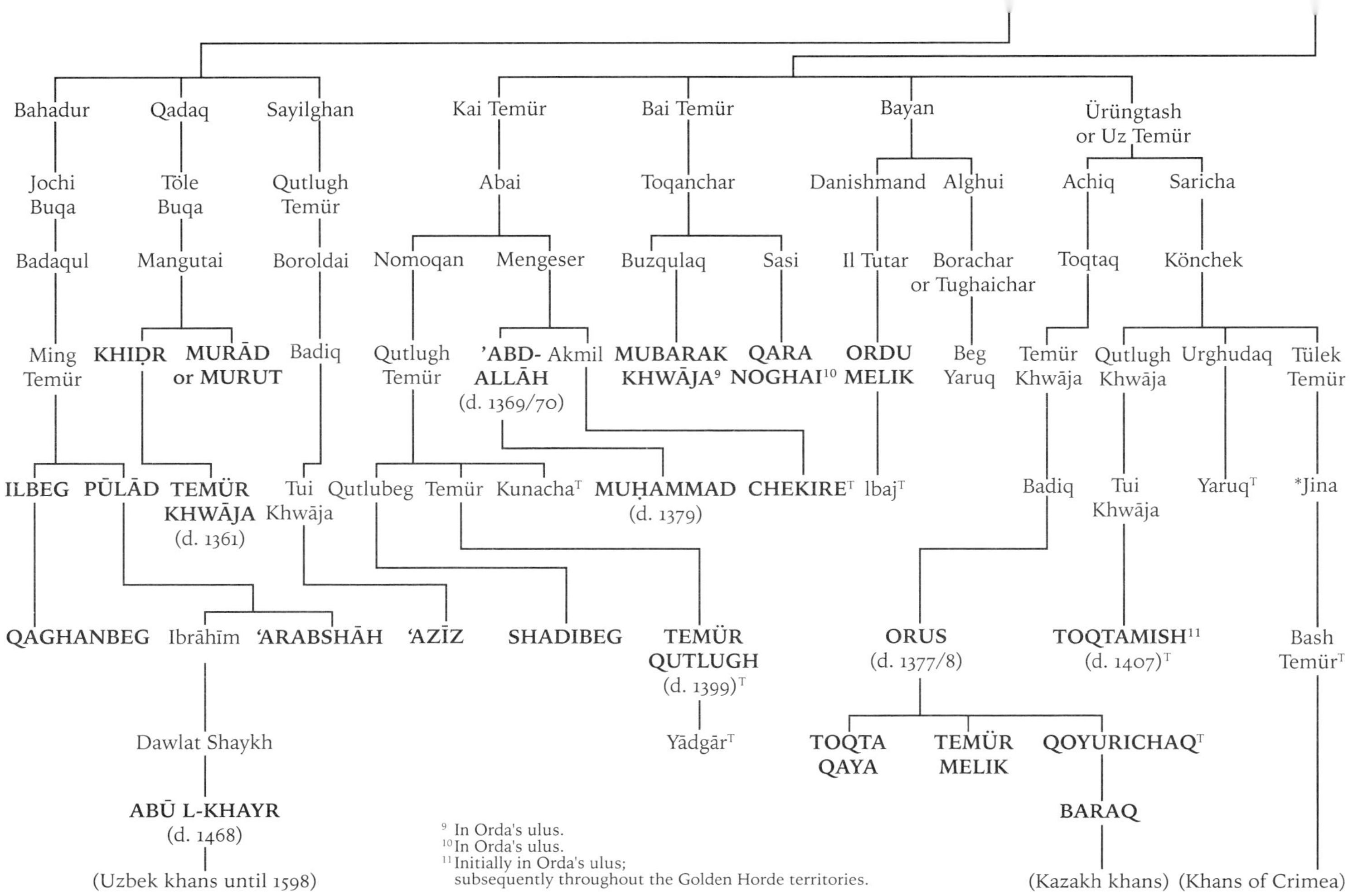

[9] In Orda's ulus.
[10] In Orda's ulus.
[11] Initially in Orda's ulus; subsequently throughout the Golden Horde territories.

Table 3. The Jochids.

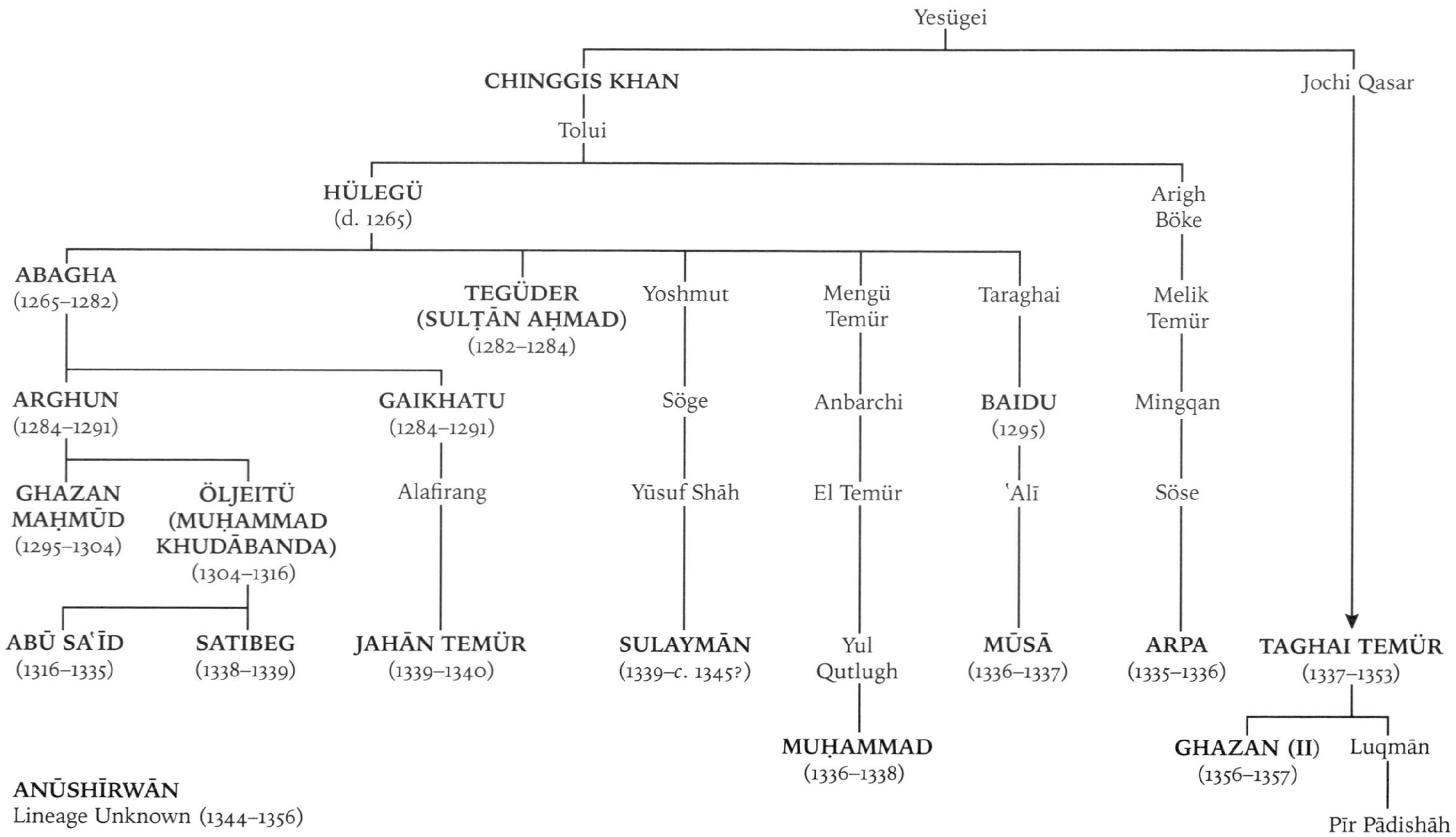

Table 4. The Ilkhans.

(In Baghdad; also Tabriz and Sulṭāniyya from 1358)
(Dates signify headship of the dynasty, with possession of Baghdad)

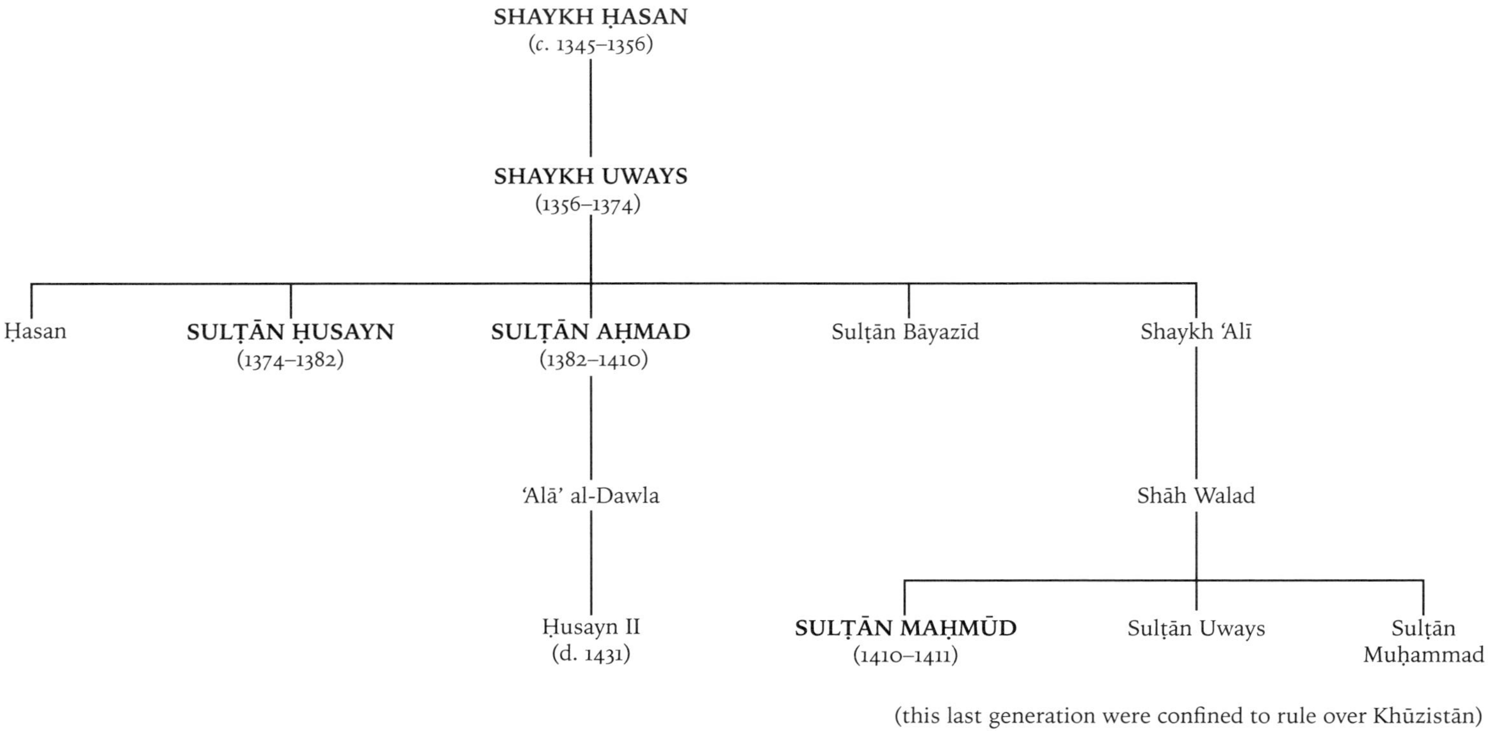

Table 5. The Jalayirids (in Baghdad; also Tabriz and Sultāniyya from 1358).

(In Kirmān from 1340, Fārs from 1353 and ʿIrāq-i ʿAjam from 1356)
(Dates signify headship of the dynasty, with possession of Shiraz; other placenames indicate appanage)

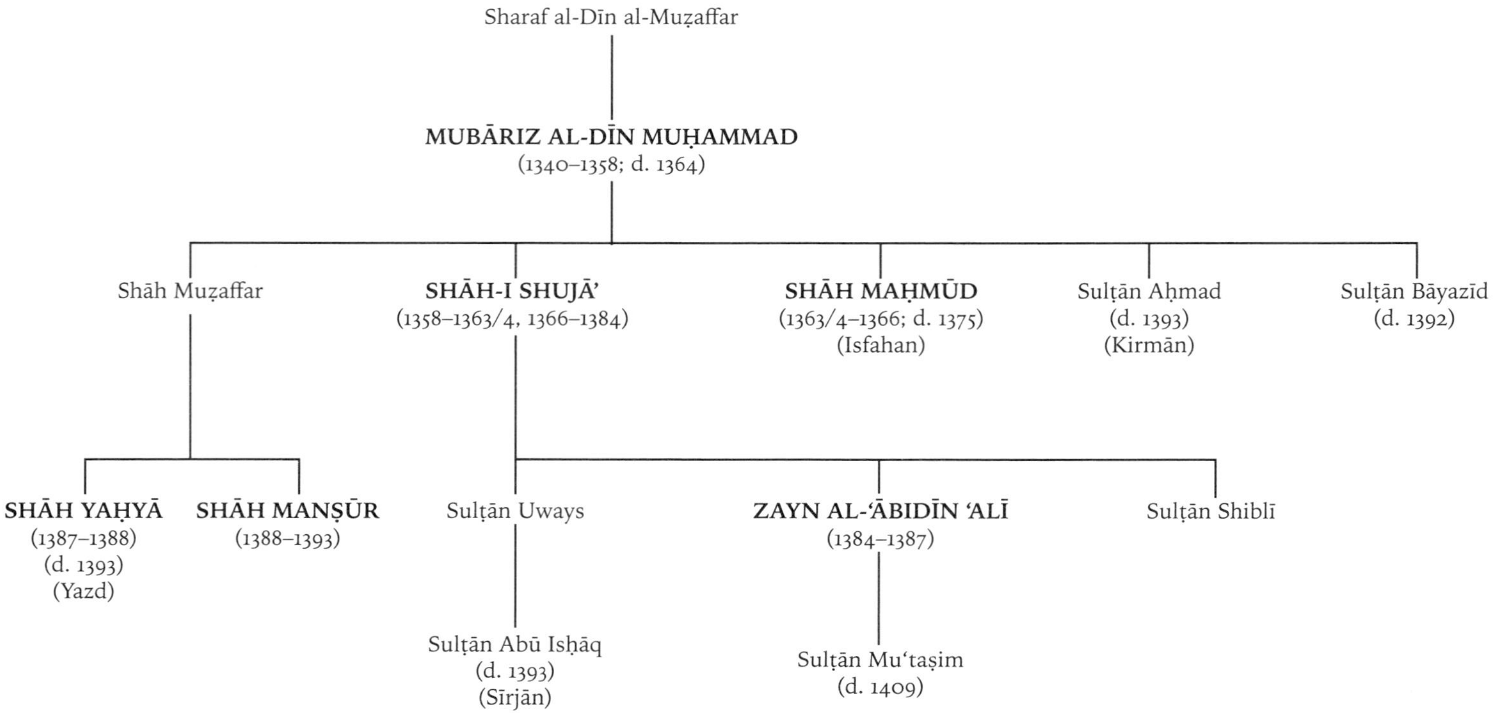

Table 6. The Muzaffarids (in Kirmān from 1340, Fārs from 1353 and ʿIrāq-i ʿAjam from 1356).

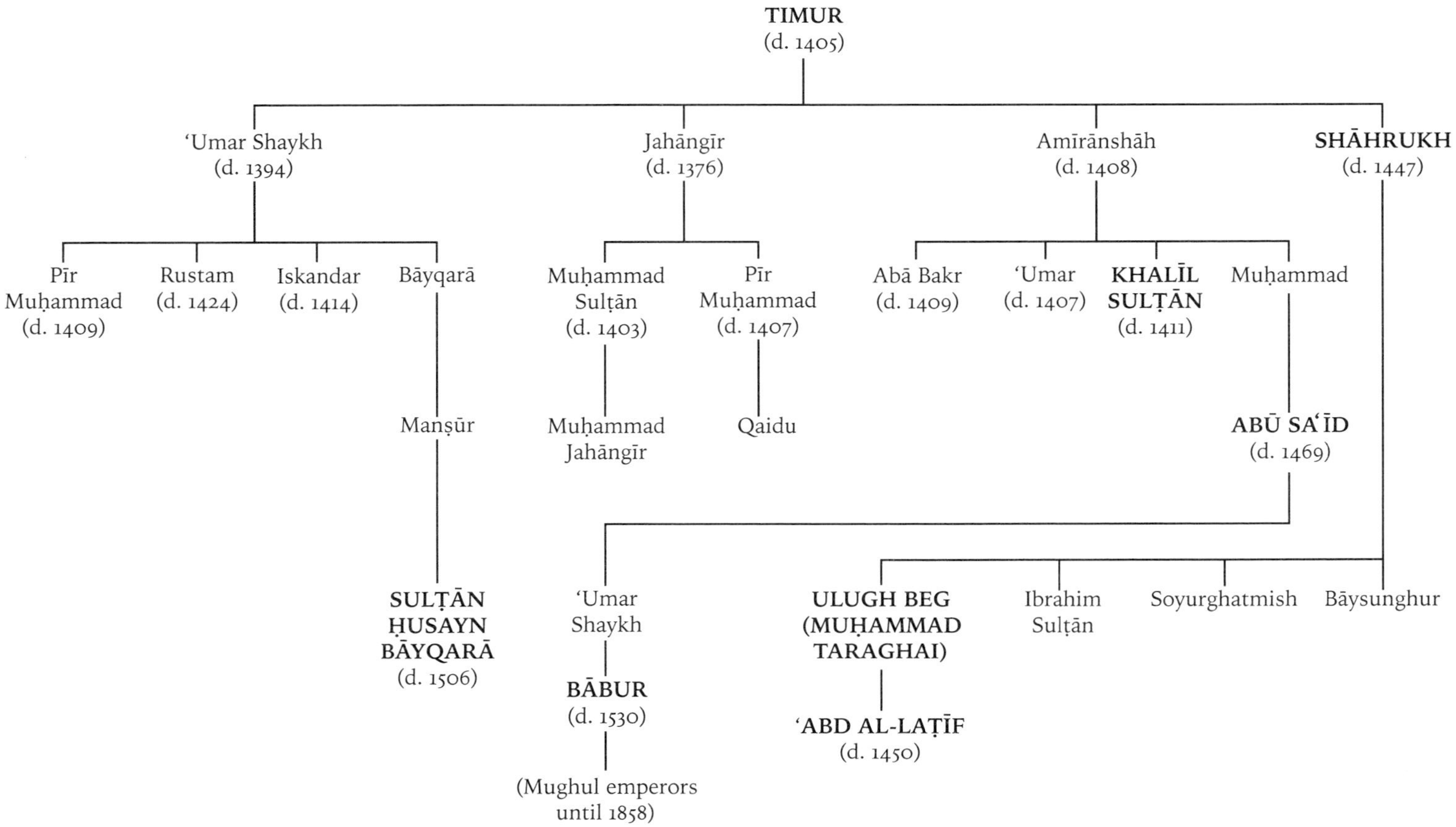

Table 7. The Timurids.

KARTIDS (Herat)

Muʿizz al-Dīn Pīr Ḥusayn Muḥammad
1332–1351 *and* 1354–1370

Malik Bāqir
1351–1354

Ghīyath al-Dīn Pīr Shāh
1370–1381

Muḥammad
[Sarakhs 1370–1381]

SARBADĀRS (Sabzawār)

[only the principal rulers are listed]

Wajīh al-Dīn Masʿūd
1338/9–1344

Tāj al-Dīn ʿAlī Chishumī
1347–1351/2

Yaḥyā Karābī
1351/2–1355/6

Khwāja ʿAlī-yi Mu'ayyad
1361–1381

Table 8. List of rulers: Kartids (Herat) and Sarbadārs (Sabzawār).

ENDNOTES

INTRODUCTION

1. David O. Morgan, *The Mongols*, 2nd edn (Oxford, 2007), 176. Idem, *Medieval Persia 1040–1797*, 2nd edn (London, 2016), 92.
2. Chase F. Robinson, *Islamic Civilization in Thirty Lives. The First 1,000 Years* (London, 2018), 216. See also Christopher Markiewicz, *The Crisis of Kingship in Late Medieval Islam. Persian Emigres and the Making of Ottoman Sovereignty*, CSIC (Cambridge, 2019), 156–8.
3. Lucien Bouvat, *L'Empire mongol (2ème phase)*, Cavaignac Histoire du Monde, VIII[3] (Paris, 1927): the book embraces not just Timur and his descendants in Iran and Central Asia but also the Mughul dynasty in India.
4. Richard M. Eaton, *India in the Persianate Age 1000–1765* (London, 2019), 101. This designation was first used, to the best of my knowledge, by Maria E. Subtelny, 'Tamerlane and his descendants: From paladins to patrons', in *NCHI*, III, 169–200 (here 170).
5. Christopher I. Beckwith, *Empires of the Silk Road. A History of Central Eurasia from the Bronze Age to the Present* (Princeton, NJ, 2009), 197; though in n. 44 ibid., Beckwith somewhat overstates the case.
6. Morgan, *The Mongols*, 5.
7. As pointed out unequivocally by Svat Soucek, *A History of Inner Asia* (Cambridge, 2000), 125.
8. Beatrice F. Manz, *The Rise and Rule of Tamerlane* (Cambridge, 1989), 21–2, 36–7, 109. Idem, 'Historical introduction', in Manz (ed.), *Central Asia in Historical Perspective* (Boulder, CO, San Francisco and Oxford, 1994), 4–24 (here 5). Maria E. Subtelny, 'The symbiosis of Turk and Tajik', ibid., 45–61 (here 46–7).
9. A point well made by Morgan, *Medieval Persia*, 88.
10. I use 'Persianate' here in a geographically narrower sense than is found in the preface to Nile Green (ed.), *The Persianate World. The Frontiers of a Eurasian Lingua Franca* (Oakland, CA, 2019), xiii–xv; see also his 'Introduction: The frontiers of the Persianate world (ca. 800–1900)', ibid., 1–71 (here 1–9, 23–5).

11. Pride of place must go to one that did not begin life in Anglophone guise: Paul Ratchnevsky, *Činggis-Khan. Sein Leben und Wirken* (Wiesbaden, 1983), more recently available as *Genghis Khan. His Life and Legacy* (Oxford, 1991), a splendid translation by the late Thomas Nivison Haining, who enhanced its value still further by reworking important material from the notes into the text and adding further notes of his own. Michal Biran, *Chinggis Khan* (Oxford, 2007), however, comes a close second. Appearing in a series entitled 'Makers of the Muslim World', it exhibits a distinctive slant of its own, not found in earlier biographies of the conqueror, and includes a chapter on 'Changing Images of Chinggis Khan in the Muslim World'.
12. W. Barthold, *Four Studies on the History of Central Asia*, trans. V. and T. Minorsky, 3 vols in 4 parts (Leiden, 1956–62), II: *Ulugh-Beg*, 12–55 for Timur; original Russian text (*Ulugbek i ego vremia*, first published in 1918) repr. in V.V. Bartol'd, *Sochineniia*, ed. B.G. Gafurov, 9 vols in 10 parts (Moscow, 1963–77), II, part 2, 37–73.
13. A.Iu. Iakubovskii, 'Timur (opyt kratkoi kharakteristiki)', *Voprosy Istorii* 8–9 (1946), 42–74.
14. See Kristiaan Aerke, 'Au miroir des peurs occidentales', in Vincent Fourniau (ed.), *Samarcande 1400–1500. La Cité-oasis de Tamerlan: cœur d'un Empire et d'une Renaissance* (Paris, 1995), 55–72 (here 61–3, for plays; 66–8, for operas); for plays, see also Adam Knobler, 'Timur the (Terrible/Tartar) trope: A case of repositioning in popular literature and history', *ME* 7 (2001), 101–12 (here 105–7).
15. Though there are possibly signs of change. Timur merited a notice in Michael Prestwich, *Medieval People. Vivid Lives in a Distant Landscape from Charlemagne to Piero della Francesca* (London, 2014), 236–9: here he heads the figures who represent 'An Age of Transition 1400–1500' and who include Joan of Arc, Gutenberg and Margaret of Anjou. He is thus undoubtedly keeping more exalted company.
16. Tilman Nagel, *Timur der Eroberer und die islamische Welt des späten Mittelalters* (Munich, 1993).
17. *Tamerlano* (Rome, 2022).
18. In a review of Marozzi's *Tamerlane* (see below): Robert Irwin, 'Quite the gentleman', *London Review of Books* 27, no. 10 (19 May 2005), 9–10.
19. See the frank avowal in Jean-Paul Roux, *Tamerlan* (Paris, 1991), 16.
20. Alexandre Papas and Marc Toutant, *L'Asie centrale de Tamerlan* (Paris, 2022).
21. Denis Sinor, 'The greed of the northern barbarian', in Larry V. Clark and Paul A. Draghi (eds), *Aspects of Altaic Civilization II: Proceedings of the XVIII PIAC* (Bloomington, IN, 1978), 171–82; repr. in Sinor, *Studies in Medieval Inner Asia* (Aldershot, 1997). For more recent correctives, see Beckwith, *Empires of the Silk Road*, intro., xxi–xxv and 320–55; Ruth I. Meserve, 'On medieval and early modern science and technology in Central Eurasia', in Michael Gervers and Wayne Schlepp (eds), *Cultural Contact, History and Ethnicity in Inner Asia*, TSCIA 2 (Toronto, 1997), 49–70; Beatrice F. Manz, *Nomads in the Middle East* (Cambridge, 2021), 16–17; and, most recent of all, Warwick Ball, *The Eurasian Steppe: People, Movements, Ideas* (Edinburgh, 2021), esp. chap. 1.
22. See esp. Thomas T. Allsen, *Culture and Conquest in Mongol Eurasia*, CSIC (Cambridge, 2001); idem, 'The Mongols as vectors for cultural transmission', in *CHIA*, 135–54; the comments of David Morgan, 'The Mongol empire in

world history', in Linda Komaroff (ed.), *Beyond the Legacy of Genghis Khan*, IHC 64 (Leiden, 2006), 425–37; and Marie Favereau, 'The Mongol Peace and global medieval Eurasia', *Comparativ: Zeitschrift für Globalgeschichte und vergleichende Gesellschaftsforschung* 28 (2018), part 4, 49–70.

23. See, for example, Toynbee's verdicts, as quoted by Adam Knobler, 'The rise of Tīmūr and Western diplomatic response, 1390–1405', *JRAS*, 3rd series, 5 (1995), 341–9 (here 341, n.1), and in Robinson, *Islamic Civilization in Thirty Lives*, 212.
24. Hilda Hookham, *Tamburlaine the Conqueror* (London, 1962), 79.
25. Aerke, 'Au miroir des peurs occidentales', 56–7, 65.
26. See Lisa Golombek, 'Tamerlane, Scourge of God', *Asian Art* 2, part 2 (Spring 1989), 30–61 (here 32–53). The contrast is noted by Justin Marozzi, *Tamerlane. Sword of Islam, Conqueror of the World* (Hammersmith, 2004), 168.
27. Morgan, *Medieval Persia*, 92.
28. The phrase is Morgan's: ibid., 97.
29. See, for instance, René Grousset, *The Empire of the Steppes. A History of Central Asia*, tr. Naomi Walford (New Brunswick, NJ, 1970), 431; Morgan, *The Mongols*, 81; Morgan, *Medieval Persia*, 86.
30. Marozzi, *Tamerlane*, 84.
31. Hookham, *Tamburlaine*, 3, 5, for the phrases quoted.
32. Ibid., 2, 3; cf. also 6.
33. See Jerry Brotton, *This Orient Isle: Elizabethan England and the Islamic World* (London, 2016), 161–5; also the comments of Marozzi, *Tamerlane*, 54–63.
34. For alternative catalogues of paradoxes, compare Lucien Kehren, *Tamerlan. L'Empire du Seigneur de fer* (Neuchâtel, 1978), 13; Roux, *Tamerlan*, 22; and Beatrice F. Manz, 'Tamerlane's career and its uses', *JWH* 13 (2002), 1–25 (here 2, 5).
35. Maria E. Subtelny, *Timurids in Transition. Turko-Persian Politics and Acculturation in Medieval Iran* (Leiden, 2007), 12.
36. Tilman Nagel, 'Tamerlan im Verständnis der Renaissance', in Michele Bernardini (ed.), *La civiltà Timuride come fenomeno internazionale* (Rome, 1996 = *OM* 76/n.s., 15), I, 203–12.
37. Knobler, 'Timur the (Terrible/Tartar) trope', 107–11. For quotations from Gibbon, see David Morgan, 'The empire of Tamerlane: An unsuccessful re-run of the Mongol empire?', in J.R. Maddicott and D.M. Palliser (eds), *The Medieval State: Essays Presented to James Campbell* (London and Rio Grande, 2000), 233–41 (here 233). But compare the brief analysis of Gibbon's more positive judgements on Timur, in Aerke, 'Le miroir des peurs occidentales', 65–6.
38. Marshall G.S. Hodgson, *The Venture of Islam. Conscience and History in a World Civilization*, 3 vols (Chicago, IL, 1974), II: *The Expansion of Islam in the Middle Periods*, 430.
39. See İlker Evrim Binbaş, *Intellectual Networks in Timurid Iran. Sharaf al-Dīn 'Alī Yazdī and the Islamicate Republic of Letters* (Cambridge, 2016), 290–1; Jo Van Steenbergen, 'Introduction: State formation in the fifteenth century and the Western Eurasian canvas: Problems and opportunities', in Van Steenbergen (ed.), *Trajectories of State Formation across Fifteenth-Century Islamic West-Asia. Eurasian Parallels, Connections and Divergences*, Rulers and Elites: Comparative Studies in Governance 18 (Leiden and Boston, MA, 2020), 1–20 (here 5–6).

40. Jo Van Steenbergen, 'From Temür to Selim: Trajectories of Turko-Mongol state formation in Islamic West-Asia's long fifteenth century', in Van Steenbergen (ed.), *Trajectories of State Formation*, 27–87 (the phrase quoted is at 29).
41. Markiewicz, *The Crisis of Kingship*, 3; see also ibid., 20–1 and chap. 4 ('The Timurid Vocabulary of Sovereignty').
42. Stephen F. Dale, *The Garden of the Eight Paradises. Bābur and the Culture of Empire in Central Asia, Afghanistan and India (1483–1530)* (Leiden and Boston, MA, 2004), introduction (esp. 12–13), 23–7, 36–66. Dale, *Babur. Timurid Prince and Mughal Emperor, 1483–1530* (Cambridge and Delhi, 2018), 3–9.
43. See Stephen Dale, 'Autobiography and biography: The Turco-Mongol case: Bābur, Ḥaydar Mīrzā, Gulbadan Begim and Jahāngīr', in L. Marlow (ed.), *The Rhetoric of Biography. Narrating Lives in Persianate Societies* (Boston and Cambridge, MA, 2011), 89–105 (here 97–102).
44. Maria Szuppe, 'Historiography, v. Timurid period', *EIr*, XII, 356–63 (here 360). Nagel, *Timur der Eroberer*, 11. For the view that the work was not dictated by Timur himself but nevertheless is possibly based on genuine documentary evidence compiled after his death, see Irfan Habib, 'Timur in the political tradition and historiography of Mughal India', in Maria Szuppe (ed.), *L'Héritage Timouride. Iran-Asie Centrale-Inde, XVe-XVIIIe siècles* (Tashkent and Aix-en-Provence, 1997 = *CAC* 3–4), 297–312 (here 305–9).
45. M. Treu, 'Eine Ansprache Tamerlans', *Byzantinische Zeitschrift* 19 (1910), 15–28; a partial trans. in Karl Dieterich (ed.), *Byzantinische Quellen zur Länder- und Völkerkunde (5.-15. Jhd.)*, Quellen und Forschungen zur Erd- und Kulturkunde 5, 2 vols (Leipzig, 1912), II, 28–9. See further Ed. Kurtz, 'Zu der Ansprache Tamerlans', *Byzantinisch-Neugriechische Jahrbücher* 3 (1922), 77–9.
46. With the notable exception of what purport to be deathbed pronouncements, cited by Yazdī, *ZN*, (1957), II, 465–6, 467–8/(2008), II, 1290–1, 1292–3.
47. See, for example, the comment of Beatrice F. Manz, 'Tamerlane and the symbolism of sovereignty', *IrSt* 21 (1988), 105–22 (here 107–8). For a 'brief sketch of his personality', see Hans R. Roemer, 'Tīmūr in Iran', in *CHI*, VI, 42–97 (here 83–91); there is a longer survey in Roux, *Tamerlan*, 165–85.
48. Dale, 'Autobiography and biography', 89. See too his caveat regarding the narrative sources in Dale, *The Garden of the Eight Paradises*, 10–11.
49. Peter Jackson, *The Mongols and the Islamic World. From Conquest to Conversion* (New Haven, CT, and London, 2017), 384–7.
50. A. Azfar Moin, *The Millennial Sovereign. Sacred Kingship and Sainthood in Islam* (New York, 2012), 33–5.
51. Johann P. Arnason, 'State formation and empire building', in *CWH*, V, 483–512 (here 493).
52. For an overview of the cultural achievements of this era, see Soucek, *A History of Inner Asia*, 128– 36; *HCCA*, IV, part 2, chaps 16–18; and Sheila S. Blair and Jonathan M. Bloom, *The Art and Architecture of Islam, 1250–1800* (New Haven, CT, and London, 1994), 41–50, 55–69. Maria E. Subtelny, 'The Timurid legacy: A reaffirmation and a reassessment', in Szuppe (ed.), *L'Héritage Timouride*, 9–19 (here 10–14), looks at some less well-known fields in which Timurid patronage left its mark. More briefly, see David J. Roxburgh, 'The Timurids and Turkmen', in Roxburgh (ed.), *Turks. A Journey of a Thousand Years, 600–1600* (London, 2005), 190–260 (here 198–200) and Lisa

Balabanlilar, *Imperial Identity in the Mughal Empire. Memory and Dynastic Politics in Early Modern South and Central Asia* (London and New York, 2012), 13–17.

53. Notably Peter B. Golden, *Central Asia in World History* (Oxford, 2011); Christopher I. Beckwith, *Warriors of the Cloisters. The Central Asian Origins of Science in the Medieval World* (Princeton, NJ, 2012); Christoph Baumer, *The History of Central Asia*, III: *The Age of Islam and the Mongols* (London and New York, 2016); and David Christian, *A History of Russia, Central Asia and Mongolia*, II: *Inner Eurasia from the Mongol Empire to Today, 1260–2000* (Hoboken, NJ, and Chichester, 2018). See also David Christian, 'Inner Eurasia as a unit of world history', *JWH* 5 (1994), 173–213.
54. Pamela K. Crossley, *Hammer and Anvil. Nomad Rulers at the Forge of the Modern World* (Lanham, MD, 2019), 3.
55. S. Frederick Starr, *Lost Enlightenment. Central Asia's Golden Age from the Arab Conquest to Tamerlane* (Princeton, NJ, 2013).
56. Chinggis Khan: see Biran, *Chinggis Khan*, 139, 142–5, 148–53. Timur: see generally Ron Sela, *The Legendary Biographies of Tamerlane. Islam and Heroic Apocrypha in Central Asia* (Cambridge, 2011).
57. Veronika Veit, 'The eastern steppe: Mongol regimes after the Yuan (1368–1636)', in *CHIA*, 157–81 (here 171). And see more generally Johan Elverskog, *Our Great Qing. The Mongols, Buddhism, and the State in Late Imperial China* (Honolulu, HI, 2006).
58. See Moin, *The Millennial Sovereign*, chap. 2.
59. Dale, *The Garden of the Eight Paradises*, 470, and *Babur*, 215–16.
60. R.D. McChesney, 'The Chinggisid restoration in Central Asia: 1500–1785', in *CHIA*, 277–302. McChesney, 'Islamic culture and the Chinggisid restoration: Central Asia in the sixteenth and seventeenth centuries', in *NCHI*, III, 239–65.
61. Stephen Kinzer, 'A kinder, gentler Tamerlane inspires Uzbekistan', *New York Times*, 10 Nov. 1997. Marozzi, *Tamerlane*, 169–73. For the forthrightness of Timurid historians regarding Timur's atrocities, see Roux, *Tamerlan*, 191–2, and Beatrice F. Manz, 'Unacceptable violence as legitimation in Mongol and Timurid Iran', in Robert Gleave and István T. Kristó-Nagy (eds), *Violence in Islamic Thought from the Mongols to European Imperialism* (Edinburgh, 2018), 79–103 (here 98–101).
62. Manz, 'Tamerlane's career and its uses', 15–24. Subtelny, 'The Timurid legacy', 15–17.
63. See Paul G. Geiss, *Pre-Tsarist and Tsarist Central Asia. Communal Commitment and Political Order in Change* (London and New York, 2003), 247–8; also Marozzi, *Tamerlane*, 169–73.

1: SOURCES FOR THE MONGOL AND TIMURID ERAS

1. Christopher P. Atwood, 'The date of the "Secret History of the Mongols" reconsidered', *JSYS* 37 (2007), 1–48; but compare Igor de Rachewiltz, 'The dating of the *Secret History of the Mongols* – a reinterpretation', *UAJ*, n.F., 22 (2008), 150–84. See also Atwood, 'Informants and sources for the Secret History of the Mongols', *MS* 29 (2007), 27–39.
2. For all these western sources and others, see Peter Jackson, 'Western European sources', in Michal Biran and Kim Hodong (eds), *The Cambridge History of the Mongol Empire* (Cambridge, 2023), II, 194–237.

3. On Jūzjānī, see D.O. Morgan, 'Persian historians on the Mongols', in Morgan (ed.), *Medieval Historical Writing in the Christian and Islamic Worlds* (London, 1982), 109–24 (here 110–13).
4. See Ulrich Haarmann, *Quellenstudien zur frühen Mamlukenzeit*, IU 1 (Freiburg im Breisgau, 1970); and Donald P. Little, 'Historiography of the Ayyūbid and Mamlūk epochs', in *CHE*, 412–44 (here 418–32).
5. He mentions that he believes Tinibeg (who reigned briefly in 742/1342: see p. 120) to be the current khan of the Golden Horde: Ibn Faḍl-Allāh al-ʿUmarī, *al-Taʿrīf bi l-muṣṭalaḥ al-sharīf* (Cairo, 1312/1894), 47/ed. Samīr al-Durūbī (al-Karak, 1413/1992), 62.
6. Donald P. Little, 'Al-Ṣafadī as a biographer of his contemporaries', in Little (ed.), *Essays on Islamic Civilization Presented to Niyazi Berkes* (Leiden, 1976), 190–210; repr. in Little, *History and Historiography of the Mamluks* (London, 1986).
7. A. Miquel, 'Ibn Baṭṭūṭa', *EI*[2], III, 735-6, with incorrect date of completion: compare IB, IV, 448–9, 451 (tr. Gibb, 977, 978). See D.O. Morgan, 'Ibn Baṭṭūṭa and the Mongols', *JRAS*, 3rd series, 11 (2001), 1–11 (esp. 2–3, 9, 10). I am preparing an article on the problems posed by IB's narrative, particularly the alleged visit to China.
8. For the Persian sources surveyed here, see generally Charles Melville, 'The Mongol and Timurid periods, 1250–1500', in Melville (ed.), *A History of Persian Literature*, X: *Persian Historiography* (London and New York, 2012), 155–208. On Mongol-era sources, Charles Melville, 'Historiography, iv. Mongol period', *EIr*, XII, 348–56, and my *The Mongols and the Islamic World*, chap. 1. On the Timurid sources, John E. Woods, 'The rise of Tīmūrid historiography', *JNES* 46 (1987), no. 2, 81–108; Michele Bernardini, 'The historiography concerning Timur-i Lang: A bibliographical survey', in Samuela Pagani (ed.), *Italo-Uzbek Scientific Cooperation in Archaeology and Islamic Studies: An Overview, Rome, January 30, 2001* (Rome, 2003), 137–96 (this piece goes into less depth than Woods, but embraces an exhaustive range of sources, non-Muslim and post-medieval authors included); and Szuppe, 'Historiography, v. Timurid period'.
9. George Lane, *Early Mongol Rule in Thirteenth-Century Iran. A Persian Renaissance* (London and New York, 2003), 178–81.
10. On this major historian, see the excellent book by Stefan Kamola, *Making Mongol History. Rashid al-Din and the Jami' al-Tawarikh* (Edinburgh, 2019).
11. Christopher P. Atwood, 'Rashīd al-Dīn's Ghazanid Chronicle and its Mongolian sources', in Timothy May, Dashdondog Bayarsaikhan and Christopher P. Atwood (eds), *New Approaches to Ilkhanid History* (Leiden, 2020), 53–121 (here 53). For the older label, compare *Turkestan*[3], 46.
12. On the sources of *Taʾrīkh-i mubārak-i ghāzānī*, see Kazuhiko Shiraiwa, 'Rashīd al-Dīn's primary sources in compiling the *Jāmiʿ al-tawārīkh*: A tentative survey', in Anna Akasoy, Charles Burnett and Ronit Yoeli-Tlalim (eds), *Rashīd al-Dīn. Agent and Mediator of Cultural Exchanges in Ilkhanid Iran*, Warburg Institute Colloquia 24 (London and Turin, 2013), 39–56 (here 40–52); more detail in Atwood, 'Rashīd al-Dīn's Ghazanid Chronicle', 62–112.
13. A.H. Morton, 'The letters of Rashīd al-Dīn: Īlkhānid fact or Timurid fiction?' in Reuven Amitai-Preiss and David Morgan (eds), *The Mongol Empire and Its Legacy*, IHC 24 (Leiden, 1999), 155–99.

14. For a comparison, see Morgan, 'Persian historians on the Mongols', 113–21. On Juwaynī, see Lane, *Early Mongol Rule*, chap. 6.
15. Judith Pfeiffer, 'The canonization of cultural memory: Ghāzān Khan, Rashīd al-Dīn, and the construction of the Mongol past', in Akasoy, Burnett and Yoeli-Tlalim (eds), *Rashīd al-Dīn. Agent and Mediator*, 57–70 (here 59).
16. Judith Pfeiffer, '"A turgid history of the Mongol empire in Persia": Epistemological reflections concerning a critical edition of Vaṣṣāf's *Tajziyat al-amṣār va tazjiyat al-a'ṣār*', in Judith Pfeiffer and Manfred Kropp (eds), *Theoretical Approaches to the Transmission and Edition of Oriental Manuscripts. Proceedings of a Symposium Held in Istanbul March 28–30, 2001*, Beiruter Texte und Studien 111 (Berlin and Würzburg, 2007), 107–29.
17. Ron Sela, 'Rashīd al-Dīn's historiographical legacy in the Muslim world', in Akasoy, Burnett and Yoeli-Tlalim (eds), *Rashīd al-Dīn. Agent and Mediator*, 213–22 (here 216).
18. Ibid., 217.
19. See A.M. Muginov, 'Istoricheskii trud Mukhammeda Shebāngāra'ī', *Uchenye Zapiski Instituta Vostokovedeniia* 9 (1954), 220–40; Jean Aubin, 'Un chroniqueur méconnu, Šabānkāra'ī', *StIr* 10 (1981), 213–24 (here 218–21), and repr. in Aubin, *Études sur l'Iran médiéval. Géographie historique et société*, ed. Denise Aigle, StIr Cahier 60 (Paris, 2018), 143–54 (here 148–50). For the 1343 text I have used BN ms. Supplément persan 1278.
20. See generally Charles Melville, 'Persian local histories: Views from the wings', *IrSt* 33 (2000), 7–14.
21. Especially Herat: Sayfī (Sayf b. Muḥammad b. Ya'qūb Harawī), *Ta'rīkh-nāma-yi Harāt* (to *c.* 722/1322). Full bibliographical details of other local sources will be given when they are first cited in the notes.
22. Given as the current year in Faryūmadī, *Dhayl-i Majma' al-ansāb*, ed. (along with Shabānkāra'ī's text) Mīr Hāshim Muḥaddith (Tehran, 1363 sh./1984), 313–14. Muḥaddith has the *Dhayl* beginning at 337, but this seems to be far too late, in view of the mention of events in the 1360s and 1370s prior to that point. Charles Melville, *The Fall of Amir Chupan and the Decline of the Ilkhanate, 1327–37: A Decade of Discord in Mongol Iran*, PIA 30 (Bloomington, IN, 1999), 9, n.14, takes Shabānkāra'ī's text as ending at 305, and I have followed his judgement.
23. As pointed out by Charles Melville, 'Ḥamd Allāh Mustawfī's *Ẓafarnāmah* and the historiography of the late Ilkhanid period', in Kambiz Eslami (ed.), *Iran and Iranian Studies: Essays in Honor of Iraj Afshar* (Princeton, NJ, 1998), 1–12 (here 2).
24. See Osamu Otsuka, 'Research on the continuations of the *Tārīkh-i Guzīda* with a special reference to the newly discovered "Continuation" concerning Jalayerid history', *Ajia Afurika gengo bunka kenkyū* [*Journal of Asian and African Studies*] 85 (March 2013), 171–205: the text is edited (from BN ms. Supplément persan 172, fos 334b–344b) at 194–205.
25. *Mawāhib*: PL^2, II, 784–5. *Manāhij*: *PL*, I, 85; *HPL*, 360.
26. This work was appended to a copy of Ḥamd-Allāh Mustawfī Qazwīnī's *Ta'rīkh-i guzīda*. See Maḥmūd Kutubī, *Ta'rīkh-i āl-i Muẓaffar*, ed. 'Abd al-Ḥusayn Nawā'ī (Tehran, 1335 sh./1956), 33; and 127 for the statement regarding *Ta'rīkh-i guzīda*.

27. Jean Aubin, 'Le khanat de Čaġatai et le Khorassan (1334–1380)', *Turcica* 8 (1976), part 2, 16–60 (here 16). On the difficulty of writing Chaghadayid history, see also Woods, 'The rise of Tīmūrid historiography', 81.
28. P. Jackson, 'Djamāl Ḳarshī', *EI*², XII, 240.
29. Michal Biran, 'The mental maps of Mongol Central Asia as seen from the Mamluk Sultanate', in *Chinese and Asian Geographical and Cartographical Views on Central Asia and Its Adjacent Regions* (Wiesbaden, 2015 = *JAH* 49), 31–51. Biran, 'The Mamluks and Mongol Central Asia', in Reuven Amitai and Stephan Conermann (eds), *The Mamluk Sultanate from the Perspective of Regional and World History*, Mamluk Studies 17 (Göttingen, 2019), 367–89 (here 376–85).
30. They are listed by Woods, 'The rise of Tīmūrid historiography', 83, and by Binbaş, *Intellectual Networks*, 166–9. On *Malfūẓāt* (or *Wāqi'āt*)-*i Tīmūrī*, Timur's supposed memoirs, see earlier, pp. 11–12.
31. Shāmī, *ZN*, I, 192.
32. Ibid., I, 139.
33. Ibid., I, 227.
34. HA, *Dhayl-i Ẓafar-nāma*, ed. Felix Tauer, 'Continuation du Ẓafarnāma de Niẓāmuddīn Šāmī par Ḥāfiẓ-i Abrū', *Archiv Orientální* 6 (1934), 429–65 (here 430).
35. Yazdī, *ZN* (1957), II, 403/(2008), II, 1236.
36. *RN* (1915), 35–7/(2000), 47–9 (*DPT*, 51–2). Woods, 'The rise of Tīmūrid historiography', 93–5.
37. *RN* (1915), 207/(2000), 188 (*DPT*, 191). Compare also (1915), 36/(2000), 47 (*DPT*, 51), where Shāhrukh is singled out for praise. The phrase quoted does not necessarily allude to the reduction of Fārs in 817/1414, as Woods proposed: Shāhrukh's acquisition of Transoxiana and Timur's capital Samarkand in 811/1409 would alone justify it.
38. Tāj al-Dīn Salmānī, *Shams al-ḥusn*, ed. and tr. Hans Robert Roemer, *Šams al-Ḥusn, eine Chronik vom Tode Timurs bis zum Jahre 1409*, VOK 8 (Wiesbaden, 1956), facsimile text, fos 24a, 51b (abridged German trans., 22, 38). See Woods, 'The rise of Tīmūrid historiography', 88–9; also *PL*², II, 815–17.
39. Those passages found only in the 'Iskandar Anonymous' are printed in Naṭanzī (1957) at 409–35; the later recension is at 1–407.
40. Denise Aigle, 'Les tableaux du Muntaḫab al-tavārīḫ-i Muʿīnī: une originalité dans la tradition historiographique persane', *StIr* 21 (1992), 67–83; also her 'The historical *taqwīm* in Muslim East', in Aigle, *The Mongol Empire between Myth and Reality. Studies in Anthropological History* (Leiden and Boston, MA, 2015), 89–104 (here 97–100).
41. Ed. and tr. as 'Anonymous synoptic account of the Timurid house', in Wheeler M. Thackston (ed.), *Album Prefaces and Other Documents on the History of Calligraphers and Painters* (Leiden, Boston, MA, and Cologne, 2001), 88–98 (previously published, in translation only, in Thackston [ed.], *A Century of Princes. Sources on Timurid History and Art* [Cambridge, MA, 1989], 237–46). See Shiro Ando, 'Die timuridische Historiographie II – Šaraf al-Dīn ʿAlī Yazdī', *StIr* 24 (1995), 219–46 (here 232–3). If Naṭanzī was indeed the author, this short piece may represent an elementary version of the *jadwal* included in the second recension.
42. Jean Aubin, 'Le mécénat timouride à Chiraz', *StIsl* 8 (1957), 71–88 (here 76–7); repr. in Aubin, *Études*, 155–68 (here 159). Woods, 'The rise of Tīmūrid

historiography', 90, 92–3. For Naṭanzī, see also Priscilla P. Soucek, 'Eskandar b. ʿOmar Šayx b. Timur: A biography', in Bernardini (ed.), *La civiltà Timuride*, I, 73–87 (here 82).

43. For his membership of the circle of scholars at Iskandar's court and his service with Ibrāhīm Sulṭān, see Binbaş, *Intellectual Networks*, 89 ff., and 42–50, respectively.
44. Ibid. (1972), fos 7b–8a/(2008), I, 21–2. Binbaş, *Intellectual Networks*, 205–6.
45. Yazdī, *ZN* (1972), fo. 66b/(2008), I, 182. On the date, see Binbaş, *Intellectual Networks*, 239, 244.
46. Binbaş, *Intellectual Networks*, 203–12, 214–16, 244–6. See also his 'The histories of Sharaf al-Dīn ʿAlī Yazdī: A formal analysis', *AOH* 65 (2012), 391–417.
47. Binbaş, *Intellectual Networks*, 229–34. The unique ms., used by Binbaş, is in Mashhad and is inaccessible to me; but see Ando, 'Die timuridische Historiographie II', 223–34.
48. See Yazdī, *ZN* (1957), I, 416, 573, and II, 479/(2008), I, 695, 849, and II, 1304. For Chinggis Khan's prescience regarding the Toluids, see *JT*, I, 618, and II, 785 (*SGK*, 17, 164; *CC*, 215, 272); Jackson, *The Mongols and the Islamic World*, 100.
49. Autobiographical statements regarding his presence on these expeditions are collected in *ZT*, I, editor's introduction, pp. *pānzdah-hafdah*.
50. For surveys and evaluation of his works, see Woods, 'The rise of Tīmūrid historiography', 96–9; F. Tauer, 'Ḥāfiẓ-i Abrū', *EI*², III, 57–8; and Maria Eva Subtelny and Charles Melville, 'Ḥāfeẓ-e Abru', *EIr*, XI, 507–9.
51. Sela, 'Rashīd al-Dīn's historiographical legacy', 217–18.
52. These shorter pieces, other than that on the Muzaffarids, are all conveniently available in *CO*.
53. For example, *ZT*, I, 234–7, includes an isolated account of events in the Delhi Sultanate in the years 751–2/1350–2.
54. Binbaş, *Intellectual Networks*, 246–7.
55. See generally Sholeh A. Quinn, 'The *Muʿizz al-Ansāb* and the *Shuʿab-i Panjgānah* as sources for the Chaghatayid period of history: A comparative analysis', *CAJ* 33 (1989), 229–53; İlker Evrim Binbaş, 'Structure and function of the genealogical tree in Islamic historiography (1200–1500)', in İlker Evrim Binbaş and Nurten Kılıç-Schubel (eds), *Horizons of the World: Festschrift for İsenbike Togan / Hudûdü'l-Âlem: İsenbike Togan'a Armağan* (Istanbul, 2011), 465–544 (here 517–21); Aigle, 'The historical *taqwīm* in Muslim East', 94–7. Some of the material indicates that *MA* assumed its final form in the latter half of the century. The differences between the two principal mss. (of which the older, in the BN, has been edited by Vokhidov in *IKPI*, III) regarding Chinggisid genealogy are well brought out by Shiro Ando, *Timuridische Emire nach dem Muʿizz al-ansāb. Untersuchung zur Stammesaristokratie Zentralasiens im 14. und 15. Jahrhundert*, IU 153 (Berlin, 1992), 21–31.
56. *ZT*, I, 36–44.
57. Woods, 'The rise of Tīmūrid historiography', 91–2.
58. Ibid., 95. Binbaş, *Intellectual Networks*, 226.
59. Felix Tauer, 'Analyse des matières de la première moitié du Zubdat-u-tawārīḫ de Ḥāfiẓ-i Abrū', in Felix Tauer, Věra Kubičková and Ivan Hrbek (eds), *Charisteria Orientalia praecipue ad Persiam pertinentia* (Prague, 1956), 345–73. On the relationship between Yazdī and HA, see Binbaş, *Intellectual Networks*, 234–6.

60. Woods, 'The rise of Tīmūrid historiography', 106.
61. See Binbaş, *Intellectual Networks*, and his briefer remarks in 'The Timurids and the Mongol empire', in Timothy May and Michael Hope (eds), *The Mongol World* (London and New York, 2022), 936–52 (here 945–6).
62. For a survey of these divergences, see Beatrice F. Manz, 'Family and ruler in Timurid historiography', in Devin DeWeese (ed.), *Studies on Central Asian History in Honor of Yuri Bregel*, IUUAS 167 (Bloomington, IN, 2001), 57–78.
63. 'Anonymous synoptic account', in Thackston (ed.), *Album Prefaces*, 92, 93.
64. Naṭanzī (1957), 433/(2004), 316. 'Anonymous synoptic account', 90. Soucek, 'Eskandar b. ʿOmar Šeyx', 76–7. Binbaş, *Intellectual Networks*, 195–7, and his 'Condominial sovereignty and condominial messianism in the Timurid empire: Historiographical and numismatic evidence', *JESHO* 61 (2018), 172–202 (here 179–80).
65. Naṭanzī (1957), 414/(2004), 303. Compare Shāmī, *ZN*, I, 71, and Yazdī, *ZN* (1957), I, 196/(2008), I, 452.
66. Woods, 'The rise of Tīmūrid historiography', 89–90. Binbaş, 'Condominial sovereignty', 182–3, questions the traditional interpretation of the process whereby Naṭanzī produced the work.
67. John E. Woods, 'Turco-Iranica II: Notes on a Timurid decree of 1396/798', *JNES* 43 (1984), 331–7 (here 334–5). Woods, 'The rise of Tīmūrid historiography', 92.
68. For example, Shāmī, *ZN*, I, 147; compare also ibid., I, 74.
69. Woods, 'The rise of Tīmūrid historiography', 103–4.
70. Manz, 'Family and ruler', 59. Interestingly, a similar partisanship even surfaces later in the sphere of manuscript illustration, so that a text of Yazdī's *ZN* prepared in the 1480s for Sulṭān Ḥusayn Bāyqarā, who was descended from ʿUmar Shaykh, contains two illustrations commemorating that prince: Charles Melville, 'Visualising Tamerlane: History and its image', *Iran* 57 (2019), 83–106 (here 86).
71. See Kamola, *Making Mongol History*, 179–81; also his 'A sensational and unique novelty: The reception of Rashid al-Din's World History', *Iran* 58 (2020), 50–61 (here 57–8). On HA's emendations to the Chaghadayid genealogy in the text, see Kamola, 'Untangling the Chaghadaids: Why we should and should not trust Rashīd al-Dīn', *CAJ* 62 (2019), 69–90 (here 80).
72. Melville, 'Ḥamd Allāh Mustawfī's *Ẓafarnāmah*', 1–5.
73. *JT*, I, 32 (*DzhT*, I, part 1, 59–60); my translation: compare *CC*, 12, and the trans. in *JT*, III, ed. Quatremère, 61, 63.
74. Beatrice F. Manz, 'Mongol history rewritten and relived', in Denise Aigle (ed.), *Figures mythiques des mondes musulmans* (Aix-en-Provence, 2000 = *REMMM* 89–90), 129–49 (here 143–5).
75. Patrick Wing, *The Jalayirids: Dynastic State Formation in the Mongol Middle East* (Edinburgh, 2016), 14–15.
76. Assembled in ʿAbd al-Ḥusayn Nawāʾī (ed.), *Asnād-u mukātabāt-i taʾrīkhī-yi Īrān az Taymūr tā Shāh Ismāʿīl* (Tehran, 1341 sh./1962).
77. BN ms. arabe 3423: Delhi, fos 391b–392b (dated 1 Rajab 801/9 March 1399; also in Nawāʾī [ed.], *Asnād*, 69–73); Syria, fos 398a–400a (dated 8 Rabīʿ I 803/27 Oct. 1400); Ankara, fos 400b–402a (dated 1 Muḥarram 805/1 Aug. 1402). As far as I am aware, only Jean Aubin, 'Comment Tamerlan prenait les villes', *StIsl* 19 (1963), 83–122, consulted this material.

78. C.E. Bosworth, 'al-Ḳalḳashandī', *EI*[2], IV, 509–11.
79. For his career down to the meeting with Timur, see Allen J. Fromherz, *Ibn Khaldun, Life and Times* (Edinburgh, 2010), 39–106; Walter J. Fischel, *Ibn Khaldūn in Egypt. His Public Functions and His Historical Research (1382–1406): A Study in Islamic Historiography* (Berkeley and Los Angeles, 1967), 15–44; CA, more briefly, M. Talbi, 'Ibn Khaldūn, Walī al-Dīn ʿAbd al-Raḥ mān', *EI*[2], III, 825–31 (here 825–8), and Abdesselam Cheddadi, 'Ibn Khaldūn, ʿAbd al-Raḥmān', *EI*[3] (2018), fasc. 4, 83–100 (here 83–6).
80. R.D. McChesney, 'A note on the life and works of Ibn ʿArabshāh', in Pfeiffer and Quinn (eds), *History and Historiography of Post-Mongol Central Asia*, 205–49 (here 209–23, for Ibn ʿArabshāh's life down to his departure from Samarkand). On al-Jazarī, see İlker Evrim Binbaş, 'A Damascene eyewitness to the Battle of Nicopolis: Shams al-Dīn Ibn [*sic*] al-Jazarī (d. 833/1429)', in Nikolaos G. Chrissis and Mike Carr (eds), *Contact and Conflict in Frankish Greece and the Aegean, 1204–1453. Crusade, Religion and Trade between Latins, Greeks and Turks*, Crusades Subsidia 5 (Farnham and Burlington, VT, 2014), 153–75 (here 156–64). On both men, see Binbaş, *Intellectual Networks*, 92–3.
81. IA (1979), 9, 25, 83, 204, 314, 351/(1986), 48–9, 72, 139, 336, 450, 481 (*TGA*, 6, 23, 78, 187, 294, 324–5). McChesney, 'A note', 237–9 and n.103. For the probable date of composition, see Ito Takao, 'Al-Maqrīzī's biography of Tīmūr', *Arabica* 62 (2015), 308–27 (here 313–14).
82. IA (1979), 136–44/(1986), 211–22 (*TGA*, 125–32); for another example of citation from a written source, see (1979), 44/(1986), 96 (*TGA*, 42).
83. See the remarks of McChesney, 'A note', 206–7.
84. IA (1979), 315/(1986), 451–2 (*TGA*, 295–6).
85. Ibid. (1979), 333–5, 338, 349/(1986), 466–8, 470, 479 (*TGA*, 311–13, 314, 322).
86. Ibid. (1979), 330–2/(1986), 465 (*TGA*, 309–10).
87. Compare the observations of Marozzi, *Tamerlane*, 85–8.
88. IA (1979), 128/(1986), 195 (*TGA*, 118). For Timur as al-Dajjāl, see also Aḥmad b. Muḥammad Ibn ʿArabshāh, *Fākihat al-khulafāʾ wa-mufākahat al-ẓurafāʾ*, ed. Muḥammad Rajab al-Najjār (al-Kuwayt, 1997), 364/ed. Ayman ʿAbd al-Jābir al-Buḥayrī (Cairo, 1421/2001), 355.
89. IA (1979), 102, 184, 194, 252/(1986), 165, 306 (reading *ṭāgh*), 320, 391 (cf. *TGA*, 97, 169, 178, 231).
90. Ibid. (1979), 155–7, 316–18/(1986), 252–5, 452–4 (*TGA*, 143–5, 296–8).
91. Ibid. (1979), 157–8/(1986), 256–7 (*TGA*, 145). Cf. *Taʿrīf* (1951), 370–1/(2008), 243 (*IKT*, 35); and see also Fischel's n.81 at 79).
92. As Robert Irwin, *Ibn Khaldun. An Intellectual Biography* (Princeton, NJ, and Oxford, 2018), 100, points out. On the suspect character of Ibn ʿArabshāh's testimony regarding Ibn Khaldūn's encounters with Timur, compare also *IKT*, 2–3.
93. McChesney, 'A note', 240. Ito, 'Al-Maqrīzī's biography of Tīmūr', 312.
94. For Ibn Khaldūn's successful ploy, see IA (1979), 317–18/(1986), 453–4 (*TGA*, 297–8); and the comments of Muhsin Mahdi, *Ibn Khaldûn's Philosophy of History. A Study in the Philosophic Foundation of the Science of Culture* (London, 1957), 59–60. Fischel, *Ibn Khaldūn in Egypt*, 61–5, dismisses Ibn ʿArabshāh's version of events. The other person credited with duping Timur was the Jochid amir Edigü: IA (1979), 89/(1986), 147 (*TGA*, 83–4); see further Shāmī, *ZN*, I, 125; Yazdī, *ZN* (1957), I, 393–4/(2008), I, 671–2; John

of Sulṭāniyya, *Mémoire*, ed. H. Moranvillé, 'Mémoire sur Tamerlan et sa cour par un Dominicain, en 1403', *BEC* 55 (1894), 441–64 (here 458).

95. As pointed out by Hookham, *Tamburlaine*, 238. See *Ta'rīf* (1951), 378–9/(2008), 252 (*IKT*, 43).
96. Taqī al-Dīn Abū Bakr b. Aḥmad Ibn Qāḍī Shuhba, *Ta'rīkh*, ed. ʿAdnān Darwīsh, 4 vols (Damascus, 1977–97), IV, 182.
97. IA (1979), 316/(1986), 452 (cf. *TGA*, 296). In his *Fākihat al-khulafā'*, Ibn ʿArabshāh further calls Ibn Khaldūn 'the pillar of historians' (*'umdat al-mu'arrikhīn*): ed. al-Buḥayrī, 357, cited by Irwin, *Ibn Khaldun*, 100 and n.40 at 217; see also the edn by al-Najjār, 365.
98. IA (1979), 316/(1986), 452 (*TGA*, 296).
99. *Ta'rīf* (1951), 229/(2008), 145. Idem, *al-Muqaddima*, tr. Franz Rosenthal, *Ibn Khaldûn. The Muqaddimah: An Introduction to History*, 2nd edn, 3 vols (Princeton, NJ, 1967; repr. London and Henley, 1986), I, 77–8, 82. See Irwin, *Ibn Khaldun*, 40–1, on these passages.
100. Irwin, *Ibn Khaldun*, 62, raises the possibility ('only a possibility') that Ibn Khaldūn might have written those sections of *'Ibar* dealing with North Africa before beginning work on the *Muqaddima*.
101. *Ta'rīf* (1951), 370, 374/(2008), 243, 246 (*IKT*, 35, 38). Ibn Qāḍī Shuhba, *Ta'rīkh*, IV, 182.
102. See Ibn Khaldūn, *Kitāb al-'ibar wa-dīwān al-mubtada' wa l-khabar fī ayyām al-'arab wa l-'ajam wa l-barbar wa-man 'āṣarahum min dhawī l-sulṭān al-akbar*, ed. Yūsuf Asʿad Dāghir, *Ta'rīkh al-'allāma Ibn Khaldūn*, 7 vols (Beirut, 1956–61), V, 1098–1191. Reuven Amitai, 'Ibn Khaldūn on the Mongols and their military might', in Kurt Franz and Wolfgang Holzwarth (eds), *Nomad Military Power in Iran and Adjacent Areas in the Islamic Period* (Wiesbaden, 2015), 193–208 (here 195), tentatively concludes that the Mongol sections of the *'Ibar* contain no information unavailable in earlier sources.
103. Ibn Khaldūn, *Kitāb al-'Ibar*, V, 258, 262, 1121 (Tolui's death in battle with the forces of the Khwārazmshāh Jalāl al-Dīn); 362 (his succeeding his father as Qaghan; though this may derive from Tolui's two-year regency prior to the enthronement of Chinggis Khan's successor Ögödei). Ibn Khaldūn almost certainly borrowed the first error from the Mamlūk encyclopaedist Shihāb al-Dīn Aḥmad b. ʿAbd al-Wahhāb al-Nuwayrī (d. 733/1333), *Nihāyat al-arab fī funūn al-adab*, XXVII, ed. Saʿīd ʿĀshūr with Muḥammad Muṣṭafā Ziyāda and Fu'ād ʿAbd al-Muʿṭī al-Ṣayyād (Cairo, 1405/1985), 328; Reuven Amitai, 'Al-Nuwayrī as a historian of the Mongols', in Hugh Kennedy (ed.), *The Historiography of Islamic Egypt (c. 950–1800)* (Leiden, 2001), 23–36 (here 30–1); repr. in Amitai, *The Mongols in the Islamic Lands* (Aldershot, 2007). The source of the second misconception is obscure. Ibn Khaldūn's ascription of Ghazna and Bāmiyān to Orda's ulus, in *Kitāb al-ʿIbar*, V, 1146, must have been taken from either Baybars al-Manṣūrī or al-Nuwayrī: for a possible reason why their statements may have been correct, see above, p. 63.
104. Walter J. Fischel, 'Ibn Khaldūn's sources for the history of Jenghiz Khān and the Tatars', *JAOS* 76 (1956), 91–9 (here 96–7).
105. *Ta'rīf* (1951), 351–65/(2008), 228–38; the account of the Mongols begins at (1951), 360/(2008), 235.
106. Ibid. (1951), 383/(2008), 255 (*IKT*, 47 and n.239 at 118). Brief exchanges have been preserved by Ibn Qāḍī Shuhba, as referred to later.

107. *Ta'rīf* (1951), 368/(2008), 239 (*IKT*, 31). In *IKT*, n.41 at 68–9, Fischel points out that this is at variance with the account in IA, but thought that Timur might have learned of Ibn Khaldūn's presence in Damascus through his spies; hence also Fischel, *Ibn Khaldūn in Egypt*, 45, and Mahdi, *Ibn Khaldûn's Philosophy of History*, 58–9. Doris Behrens-Abouseif, *Practising Diplomacy in the Mamluk Sultanate. Gifts and Material Culture in the Medieval Islamic World* (London, 2014), 72, likewise accepts Ibn Khaldūn's claim.
108. Taqī al-Dīn Aḥmad b. ʿAlī al-Maqrīzī, *Durar al-'uqūd al-farīda fī tarājim a'yān al-mufīda*, ed. Maḥmūd al-Jalīlī, 4 vols (Beirut, 1423/2002), II, 397: *khālaṭa l-'asākir wa-ṭalaba minhum anna yūṣilūhu bi l-amīr Tīmūr fa-sārū bihi wa-sta'dhanū 'alayhi fa-adhina lahu wa-amara bi-iḥḍārihi* . . .. Ibn Taghrībirdī, *al-Manhal al-ṣāfī*, ed. Muḥammad Muḥammad Amīn, Saʿīd ʿAbd al-Fatḥ ʿĀshūr et al., 9 vols so far (Cairo, 1984–1423/2002), VII, 208, makes a similar but briefer statement. Compare also Taqī al-Dīn Aḥmad b. ʿAlī al-Maqrīzī, *al-Sulūk li-ma'rifat duwal al-mulūk*, ed. Muṣṭafā Ziyāda and Saʿīd ʿAbd al-Fattāḥ ʿĀshūr, 4 vols in 12 parts (Cairo, 1934–72), III, part 3, 1052.
109. *Ta'rīf* (1951), 368/(2008), 239 (*IKT*, 31). The point is made by Fischel, *Ibn Khaldūn in Egypt*, 45.
110. *Ta'rīf* (1951), 381/(2008), 254 (*IKT*, 45). He may be referring just to the amnesty for the administrators and officials: ibid. (1951), 378/(2008), 250 (*IKT*, 42).
111. al-Maqrīzī, *Durar al-'uqūd*, II, 397–8: *anta 'aynī* (literally 'you are my eye'; the phrase also exists in Persian, the language that Timur presumably employed here).
112. *Ta'rīf* (1951), 380, *sami'tu an sulṭānahum Tamur sa'ala 'annī fa-lam yasa'u illā liqāwahi*/(2008), 253 (*IKT*, 45).
113. On the character of this work, see Walter J. Fischel, 'Ibn Khaldūn's *Autobiography* in the light of external Arabic sources', in *Studi orientalistici in onore di Giorgio Levi della Vida* (Rome, 1956), I, 287–308.
114. *Ta'rīf* (1951), 378, 381/(2008), 252, 254 (*IKT*, 43, 45).
115. Ibid. (1951), 370–1, 372/(2008), 243, 244 (*IKT*, 35, 36).
116. Ibid. (1951), 382/(2008), 255 (*IKT*, 46): the passage contains some obscure phrasing: see Fischel's commentary (*IKT*, nn.230–2 at 116–17).
117. Ibid. (1951), 370–1, 374, 380/(2008), 243, 247, 253 (*IKT*, 35, 39, 45); for Aleppo, see also ibid. (1951), 365/(2008), 238. Josephine Van den Bent, '"None of the kings on Earth is their equal in *'aṣabiyya*": The Mongols in Ibn Khaldūn's works', *Al-Masāq* 28 (2016), 171–86 (here 181).
118. For what follows, see Irwin, *Ibn Khaldun*, 98–9; compare also his 'Al-Maqrīzī and Ibn Khaldūn, historians of the unseen', *MSR* 7 (2003), 217–30 (here 219), and repr. in Irwin, *Mamlūks and Crusaders. Men of the Sword and Men of the Pen* (Farnham and Burlington, VT, 2010).
119. *Ta'rīf* (1951), 371, 372/(2008), 244, 245 (*IKT*, 35–6, 37). On al-Ābilī, see Irwin, *Ibn Khaldun*, 26–7.
120. Ibn Khaldūn, *Kitāb al-'Ibar*, V, 1143–4. The true date was 782/1380–1.
121. As suggested by Talbi, 'Ibn Khaldūn', *EI*[2], III, 827–8. Mahdi, *Ibn Khaldûn's Philosophy of History*, n.7 at 193–4, argued that the phrase *'umrān badawī* should be translated 'primitive society'. But see Irwin, *Ibn Khaldun*, 185; also Stephen Frederic Dale, *The Orange Trees of Marrakesh. Ibn Khaldun and the Science of Man* (Cambridge, MA, 2015), 27–8.

122. Ibn Khaldūn, *al-Muqaddima*, tr. Rosenthal, I, 179–80, 320–1. Dale, *The Orange Trees of Marrakesh*, 173, 180–1. Stephen F. Dale, 'Ibn Khaldun, the Yüan and Îl-khân dynasties', in Peter B. Golden et al. (eds), *Festschrift for Thomas T. Allsen in Celebration of His 75th Birthday* (Wiesbaden, 2015 = *AEMA* 21 [2014–15]), 43–52 (here 45–6).
123. *Ta'rīf* (1951), 372/(2008), 245 (*IKT*, 36–7). Dale, *The Orange Trees of Marrakesh*, 149–50.
124. For the limitations of the model, even for those regions, see Dale, 'Ibn Khaldun, the Yüan and Îl-khân dynasties', 49–52. Marie Favereau, *The Horde. How the Mongols Changed the World* (Cambridge, MA, 2021), 305–6, argues strongly that Ibn Khaldūn's model does not fit the Mongols; and see also André Wink, 'Post-nomadic empires: From the Mongols to the Mughals', in Peter Fibiger Bang and C.A. Bayly (eds), *Tributary Empires in Global History* (Basingstoke, 2011), 120–31 (here 121–2); Dale, *The Orange Trees of Marrakesh*, 204; Jos Gommans, 'The warband in the making of Eurasian empires', in Maaike Van Berkel and Jeroen Duindam (eds), *Prince, Pen, and Sword: Eurasian Perspectives* (Leiden, 2018), 297–383 (here 306–7, 322–5); and the remarks of Manz, *Nomads in the Middle East*, 17–18.
125. Amitai, 'Ibn Khaldūn on the Mongols', 197–201.
126. Or at least where the lack of common ancestry had become obscured and forgotten in the course of time. Ibn Khaldūn, *al-Muqaddima*, tr. Rosenthal, I, 264–78, 284.
127. Ibid., I, 292–3.
128. Habib, 'Timur in the political tradition and historiography of Mughal India', 297–9.
129. See V.L. Ménage, 'The beginnings of Ottoman historiography', in Bernard Lewis and P.M. Holt (eds), *Historians of the Middle East* (Oxford and London, 1962), 168–79. Wing, *The Jalayirids*, 11–12, provides a succinct but useful overview of these late-fifteenth, sixteenth-century Ottoman sources.
130. Dimitri Kastritsis, 'The Alexander Romance and the rise of the Ottoman empire', in A.C.S. Peacock and Sara Nur Yıldız (eds), *Islamic Literature and Intellectual Life in Fourteenth- and Fifteenth-Century Anatolia*, Istanbuler Texte und Studien 34 (Würzburg, 2016), 243–83 (here 258–60). Kemal Salay, 'Aḥmedī's history of the Ottoman dynasty', in *Richard Nelson Frye Festschrift I. Essays Presented to Richard Nelson Frye on His Seventieth Birthday by His Colleagues and Students* (Cambridge, MA, 1992 = *JTS* 16), 129–200.
131. For a full analysis of this work, see Heinz Helmut Giesecke, *Das Werk des 'Azīz ibn Ārdašīr Āstarābāḏī. Eine Quelle zur Geschichte des Spätmittelalters in Kleinasien*, SOL 2 (Leipzig, 1940).
132. These and later fifteenth-century authors are surveyed on the basis of their treatment of events in selected years (none coinciding directly with Timur's Syrian campaign), by Sami G. Massoud, *The Chronicles and Annalistic Sources of the Early Mamluk Circassian Period*, IHC 67 (Leiden and Boston, MA, 2007). Some of them are covered in Little, 'Historiography of the Ayyūbid and Mamlūk epochs', 432–42.
133. See Brinner's introduction to his edition and translation, I (trans.), xiii–xiv.
134. Ibn Qāḍī Shuhba borrowed a short section from Ibn Duqmāq embracing the years 804 and 805: Massoud, *The Chronicles and Annalistic Sources*, 153.

135. Ibid., 81–3, 167–72, 183–9, for Ibn Ḥijjī's work and for the relationship with the various recensions of it produced later by Ibn Qāḍī Shuhba.
136. See *GAL, Supplement*, III, 177.
137. On which see Irwin, 'Al-Maqrīzī and Ibn Khaldūn', 225–30. A specific example is given at p. 413. For a survey of al-Maqrīzī's career, see Nasser Rabbat, 'Who was al-Maqrīzī? A biographical sketch', *MSR* 7 (2003), part 2, 1–19.
138. For this date, see Massoud, *The Chronicles and Annalistic Sources*, 160.
139. al-Maqrīzī, *al-Sulūk*, III, part 2, 537. For the obituary, see ibid., IV, part 1, 26.
140. F. Rosenthal, 'Ibn Ḥadjar al-ʿAsḳalānī', *EI²*, III, 776–8.
141. Massoud, *The Chronicles and Annalistic Sources*, 54–60, 116–19, 162–7.
142. Ibn Qāḍī Shuhba, *Ta'rīkh*, IV, 428–42. The citation from Ibn Ḥijjī (but adding the date of Timur's death as 4 Ramaḍān): ibid., IV, 437. The conversation about the Maghrib: ibid., IV, 182, saying that he owed the account to the Qadi Shihāb al-Dīn Ibn al-'Izz, who had been present.
143. Ibn Taghrībirdī, *al-Nujūm al-zāhira fī mulūk Miṣr wa l-Qāhira*, 16 vols (Cairo, 1348–92/1929–72), XII, 253–70; tr. William Popper, *History of Egypt 1382–1469 A.D.*, 8 vols, University of California Publications in Semitic Philology 13–14, 17–19, 22–24 (Berkeley and Los Angeles, CA, 1954–63), II, 54–63; obituary in *al-Nujūm al-zāhira*, XIII, 160–3 (tr. Popper, II, 203–6).
144. Jacqueline Sublet & Muriel Rouabah, 'Une famille de textes autour d'Ibn Ḫallikān entre VIIᵉ/XIIIᵉ et XIᵉ/XVIIᵉ siècle. Documents historiques et biographiques arabes conservés à l'IRHT', *BEO* 58 (2008–9), 69–86. I have omitted in this paragraph the celebrated biographical dictionary of Ibn Ḥajar al-ʿAsqalānī, *al-Durar al-kāmina fī aʿyān al-mi'at al-thāmina*, since it excludes those who died after the ninth Hijrī century and hence lacks an entry on Timur; the entries are also often relatively brief.
145. al-Maqrīzī, *Durar al-ʿuqūd*, I, 501–59 (no. 377). I have used the text edited by al-Jalīlī (Beirut, 1423/2002), which is fuller than the two earlier editions and is the only one to include the entry on Timur: see Ito, 'Al-Maqrīzī's biography of Tīmūr', 309–11.
146. Khalīl Sulṭān: al-Maqrīzī, *Durar al-ʿuqūd*, II, 66–77 (no. 452). Shāhrukh: II, 120–2 (no. 510). Sulṭān Aḥmad: I, 228–43 (no. 156; the biography proper begins at 233). Edigü: I, 432–6 (no. 353). Bayezid: I, 439–53 (no. 358). Toqtamish: I, 495–501 (no. 376). Shāh Manṣūr: III, 427–9 (no. 1366).
147. al-Maqrīzī, *Durar al-ʿuqūd*, I, 287, 558. Joseph Drory, 'Maqrīzī in *Durar al-ʿuqūd* with regard to Timur Leng', in U. Vermeulen, K. D'Hulster and J. Van Steenbergen (eds), *Egypt and Syria in the Fatimid, Ayyubid and Mamluk Eras*, VII. *Proceedings of the 16th, 17th and 18th International Colloquium Organized at Ghent University in May 2007, 2008 and 2009* (Leuven, Paris and Walpole, MA, 2013), 393–401. Ito, 'Al-Maqrīzī's biography of Tīmūr', 312.
148. McChesney, 'A note', 238.
149. Shihāb al-Dīn Abū l-Faḍl Aḥmad b. ʿAlī Ibn Ḥajar al-ʿAsqalānī, *Inbā' al-ghumr bi-ibnā' al-ʿumr fī l-ta'rīkh*, ed. Ḥasan Ḥabashī, 3 vols (Cairo, 1389–92/1969–72), II, 301–4/ed. Muḥammad ʿAbd al-Muʿīd Khān, 9 vols (Hyderabad, A.P., 1387–96/1967–76), V, 231–6. For his confusion of Timur's puppet khan Soyurghatmish with the Jochid Toqtamish, which is found also in *ʿIbar*, see below, p. 615, n.151.
150. Ibn Taghrībirdī, *al-Manhal al-ṣāfī*, II, 131–45.

151. Ito, 'Al-Maqrīzī's biography of Tīmūr', 321–2. But the biography of Ibn Khaldūn in *Manhal*, though certainly based on that in *Durar*, is considerably abridged: see Anne F. Broadbridge, 'Royal authority, justice and order in society: The influence of Ibn Khaldūn on the writings of al-Maqrīzī and Ibn Taghrībirdī', *MSR* 7 (2003), part 2, 231–45 (here 240).
152. Compare Ibn Taghrībirdī, *al-Manhal al-ṣāfī*, IV, 80, with *Durar al-'uqūd*, I, 498, regarding Toqtamish being Berdibeg's son and his sister Mamai's wife.
153. Dale, *The Orange Trees of Marrakesh*, 256–7; also Broadbridge, 'Royal authority', 234–40.
154. See the extracts juxtaposed by Ito, 'Al-Maqrīzī's biography of Tīmūr', 324–5, appendix.
155. al-Maqrīzī, *Durar al-'uqūd*, I, 551–3, 555. Ito, 'Al-Maqrīzī's biography of Tīmūr', 314–15.
156. al-Maqrīzī, *Durar al-'uqūd*, II, 397–8.
157. He claimed to be an Italian: anonymous, *Chronographia regum Francorum*, ed. H. Moranvillé, 3 vols (Paris, 1891–7), III, 205. Hence it is clear that he was not, as once thought, the Frenchman 'John of Galonifontibus', who perhaps preceded him as Bishop of Nakhchiwān: R. Loenertz, 'Evêques dominicains des deux Arménies', *Archivum Fratrum Praedicatorum* 10 (1940), 258–81 (here 258–9).
158. Anthony Luttrell, 'Timur's Dominican envoy', in Colin Heywood and Colin Imber (eds), *Studies in Ottoman History in Honour of Professor V.L. Ménage* (Istanbul, 1994), 209–29 (here 211–13, 215–17). For John and his colleague Francis, see pp. 305–6, 374.
159. *Chronographia regum Francorum*, III, 206–23.
160. Extensive extracts were edited by Anton Kern, 'Der "de notitia orbis" Iohannes' III. (de Galonifontibus?) O.P. Erzbischofs von Sultanyeh [*sic*]', *Archivum Fratrum Praedicatorum* 8 (1938), 82–123; for sections he omitted or abridged, I have used the text of Universitätsbibliothek Graz ms. 1221 (fos 41a–127a).
161. Clavijo (1859), 97, 108–9, 162/(1928), 165, 184, 272.
162. David J. Roxburgh, 'Ruy Gonzalez de Clavijo's narrative of courtly life and ceremony in Timur's Samarqand, 1404', in Palmira Brummett (ed.), *The "Book" of Travels: Genre, Ethnology, and Pilgrimage, 1250–1700* (Leiden, 2009), 113–58. More generally, see Beatrice F. Manz and Margaret L. Dunaway, 'Clavijo', *EIr*, V, 692–3.
163. Mignanelli (1764), 139a/(2013), 334–5; partially tr. in Walter J. Fischel, 'A new Latin source on Tamerlane's conquest of Damascus (1400/1401) (B. de Mignanelli's "Vita Tamerlani" 1416)', *Oriens* 9 (1956), 201–32 (here 230). On the author, see Angelo M. Piemontese, 'Beltramo Mignanelli senese biografo di Tamerlano', in Bernardini (ed.), *La civiltà Timuride*, I, 213–26; also the lengthy biographical notice in Mignanelli (2013), 3–87.
164. Mignanelli (1764), 136a–b, 137a, 138a/(2013), 323–4, 325, 326, 331, 332 (tr. in Fischel, 'A new Latin source', 218–19, 220, 221, 225, 226).
165. See T'ovma Metsobets'i, *Patmut'iwn lank-T'amuray ew yajordats' iwrots'*, tr. Robert Bedrosian, *T'ovma Metsobet'si's History of Tamerlane and His Successors* (New York, 1987), 1–6, 15–23, 34–5, 37, 49–56.
166. Ibid., 51, 52–3.
167. See generally N. Nicoloudis, 'Byzantine historians on the wars of Timur (Tamerlane) in Central Asia and the Middle East', *Journal of Oriental and African Studies* (Athens), 8 (1996), 83–94.

168. Jean M. Fiey, 'Sources syriaques sur Tamerlan', *Le Muséon* 101 (1988), 13–20. Three such fragments, in Bodleian ms. Hunt. 52 of the *Chronography* of Bar Hebraeus, are translated by E.A. Wallis Budge in his edition of the Syriac text of Bar Hebraeus, *The Chronography of Gregory Abû'l Faraj . . . Commonly Known as Bar Hebraeus* (London and Oxford, 1932), II, appendices, xxx–liii.
169. Beatrice F. Manz, 'Johannes Schiltberger and other outside sources on the Timurids', in Encarnación Sánchez García, Pablo Martín Asuero and Michele Bernardini (eds), *España y el Oriente islámico entre los siglos XV y XVI (Imperio Ottomano, Persia y Asia central). Actas del congreso Università degli Studi di Napoli 'l'Orientale' Nápoles 30 de septiembre-2 de octubre de 2004* (Istanbul, 2007), 53–62.
170. Binbaş, *Intellectual Networks*, 211–12.
171. For these historians, see Beatrice F. Manz, *Power, Politics and Religion in Timurid Iran* (Cambridge, 2007), 56–62 (though with particular reference to Shāhrukh's reign).
172. On Khwāfī, see ibid., 64–7.
173. For the latter two works, see *PL*, I, 90–1, where Ibn Shihāb's, however, is dismissed as unimportant.
174. For his career, see Beatrice F. Manz, 'Nomad and settled in the Timurid military', in Reuven Amitai and Michal Biran (eds), *Mongols, Turks, and Others: Eurasian Nomads and the Sedentary World*, BIAL 11 (Leiden and Boston, MA, 2005), 425–57 (here 448).
175. Ibn Fatḥ-Allāh al-Baghdādī, *al-Ta'rīkh al-Ghiyāthī*, ed. Ṭāriq Nāfiʿ al-Ḥamdānī (Baghdad, 1975), 76. Melville, *The Fall of Amir Chupan*, 10.
176. As we might expect from an author based in Baghdad, the Jalayirid section (*al-Ta'rīkh al-Ghiyāthī*, 81–144) is markedly more detailed than that on the Muzaffarids (ibid., 147–65).
177. B. Spuler, 'Abū'l-Ghāzī Bahādur Khān', *EI²*, I, 120–1.
178. For the date of *TGNN*, see Akramov's introduction to his edn (Tashkent, 1967), 24–5.
179. See István Vásáry, 'The beginnings of coinage in the Blue Horde', *AOH* 62 (2009), 371–85 (here 381, n.13); also Uli Schamiloglu, 'The *Umdet ül-ahbar* and the Turkic narrative sources for the Golden Horde and the later Golden Horde', in Hasan B. Paksoy (ed.), *Central Asian Monuments* (Istanbul, 1992), 81–93 (here 88).
180. For a biographical sketch, see W. Barthold, 'Ḥaydar Mīrzā', *EI²*, III, 317. I have used the 1996 edition and translation by W.M. Thackston, since his translation as reissued in 2012 (*Classical Writings of the Medieval Islamic World: Persian Histories of the Mongol Dynasties*, I) is not accompanied by the Persian text.
181. For a brief comparison of the two works, see Eiji Mano, 'The *Baburnama* and the *Tarikh-i Rashidi*: Their mutual relationship', in Lisa Golombek and Maria Subtelny (eds), *Timurid Art and Culture. Iran and Central Asia in the Fifteenth Century*, Studies in Islamic Art and Architecture (Supplements to *Muqarnas*, 6) (Leiden, 1992), 44–7.
182. *TR*, I (text), 4–5, 106, 109–10, II (trans.), 3, 85, 89.
183. E.A. Polyakova, 'Timur as described by the 15th century court historiographers', *IrSt* 21 (1988), nos 1–2, 31–44 (here 36–43).

2: THE MONGOL EMPIRE: UNITY, EXPANSION AND DIVISION, *c.* 1200–1335

1. For what follows, see Manz, *Nomads in the Middle East*, 82–108.
2. D. Sourdel, 'Ghulām, i. – The Caliphate', *EI2*, III, 1079–81; C.E. Bosworth, '. . . ., ii. – Persia', ibid., 1081–4; P. Hardy, '. . . ., iii. – India', ibid., 1084–5. D. Ayalon, 'Mamlūk', *EI*², VI, 314–21.
3. See generally C. Edmund Bosworth, 'The steppe peoples in the Islamic world', in *NCHI*, III, 21–77; Bosworth, 'The political and dynastic history of the Iranian world (A.D. 1000–1217)', in *CHI*, V, 1–202.
4. The following hypothesis is taken from Nicola Di Cosmo, 'State formation and periodization in Inner Asian history', *JWH* 10 (1999), 1–40 (here 8–26).
5. On the importance of the war-band, as opposed to the tribal host, in the forging of nomadic statehood, see Jürgen Paul, 'The state and the military – a nomadic perspective', in Irene Schneider (ed.), *Militär und Staatlichkeit. Beiträge des Kolloquiums am 29. und 30.04.2002*, Orientwissenschaftliche Hefte 12 (Halle, 2003), 25–68 (here 40–4).
6. Kam Tak-sing, 'The term Mongγol revisited', *CAJ* 60 (2017), 183–206, offers the latest theory on the origin of the tribal name.
7. For this tale and for the line of descent, see SH, §§ 17–18, 20–21, 43–50 (tr. De Rachewiltz, I, 3–5, 8–10), and *JT*, I, 223–5 (*CC*, 82–3); but ibid., I, 293 (*CC*, 102), Rashīd al-Dīn makes Chinggis Khan eighth in descent from Bodonchar.
8. SH, § 254 (tr. De Rachewiltz, I, 183). *TJG*, I, 15–16, 26 (*HWC*, 21–3, 36). WR, 84 (*MFW*, 124). *TN*, II, 99 (tr. Raverty, 937–42). Other references in Thomas T. Allsen, *Commodity and Exchange in the Mongol Empire. A Cultural History of Islamic Textiles* (Cambridge, 1997), 12–13.
9. For his career, see Ratchnevsky, *Genghis Khan*; Biran, *Chinggis Khan*; and for a fine but briefer summary, Thomas T. Allsen, 'The rise of the Mongolian empire and Mongolian rule in north China', in *CHC*, VI, 321–413 (here 333–43).
10. Igor de Rachewiltz, 'The title Činggis Qan/Qaγan re-examined', in Walther Heissig and Klaus Sagaster (eds), *Gedanke und Wirkung. Festschrift zum 90. Geburtstag von Nikolaus Poppe*, AF 108 (Wiesbaden, 1989), 281–9. Jackson, *The Mongols and the Islamic World*, 64.
11. SH, §§ 202, 203 (tr. De Rachewiltz, I, 133, 135).
12. Paul D. Buell, 'The role of the Sino-Mongolian frontier zone in the rise of Cinggis-Qan', in Henry G. Schwarz (ed.), *Studies on Mongolia: Proceedings of the first North American Conference on Mongolian Studies*, SEA 13 (Bellingham, WA, 1979), 63–76.
13. PC, 328 (*MM*, 68).
14. See Peter B. Golden, 'The Türk imperial tradition in the pre-Chinggisid era', in David Sneath (ed.), *Imperial Statecraft: Political Forms and Techniques of Governance in Inner Asia, Sixth–Twentieth Centuries*, SEA 26 (Bellingham, WA, 2006), 23–61 (here 27 ff.).
15. Peter B. Golden, 'Imperial ideology and the sources of political unity amongst the pre-Činggisid nomads of western Eurasia', *AEMA* 2 (1982), 37–76 (here 72), and repr. in Golden, *Nomads and Their Neighbours in the Russian Steppe: Turks, Khazars and Qipchaqs* (Aldershot and Burlington, VT, 2003).
16. *TJG*, I, 28 (*HWC*, 39). Thus also Hülegü to Louis IX of France (1262), cited in Peter Jackson, *The Mongols and the West, 1221–1410*, 2nd edn (London and New York, 2018), 220. SH, § 244 (tr. De Rachewiltz, I, 168), however, says

nothing of this (see De Rachewiltz's note ibid., II, 761). For Kököchü's career, see Ratchnevsky, *Genghis Khan*, 98–100.

17. Golden, 'Imperial ideology',40–72.
18. Thus according to *TJG*, I, 17 (*HWC*, 25), for example. See *EMME*, 530.
19. Thomas T. Allsen, 'Spiritual geography and political legitimacy in the eastern steppe', in Henri J.M. Claessen and Jarich G. Oosten (eds), *Ideology and the Formation of Early States* (Leiden, 1996), 116–35 (here 124–8). Allsen, 'A note on Mongol imperial ideology', in Volker Rybatzki, Alessandra Pozzi, Peter W. Geier and John R. Krueger (eds), *The Early Mongols: Language, Culture and History. Studies in Honor of Igor de Rachewiltz on the Occasion of His 80th Birthday*, IUUAS 173 (Bloomington, IN, 2009), 1–8 (here 2). Timothy May, 'Nökhöd to noyad: Chinggis Khan's social revolution', *Mongolica* 19 (40) (2006), 296–308 (here 298–300). On the *ötügen-yish* in earlier steppe polities, see Allsen, 'Spiritual geography', and Golden, 'The Türk imperial tradition', 48–50.
20. WR, 86, *habent pro regali* (*MFW*, 125).
21. John W. Dardess, 'From Mongol empire to Yüan dynasty: Changing forms of imperial rule in Mongolia and Central Asia', *Monumenta Serica* 30 (1972–3), 117–65 (here 118–21). Christopher P. Atwood, 'Imperial itinerance and mobile pastoralism: The state and mobility in medieval Inner Asia', *Inner Asia* 17 (2015), 293–349.
22. Michal Biran, 'The Mongol transformation: From the steppe to Eurasian empire', in Johann P. Arnason and Björn Wittrock (eds), *Eurasian Transformations, Tenth to Thirteenth Centuries. Crystallizations, Divergences, Renaissances* (Leiden and Boston, MA, 2004 = *ME* 10), 339–61 (here 342, 347).
23. Ibid., 345–6, 349.
24. See Eric Voegelin, 'The Mongol orders of submission to European powers, 1245–1255', *Byzantion* 15 (1940–1), 378–413 (esp. texts at 386–9); revised version in Ellis Sandoz (ed.), *Collected Works of Eric Voegelin*, X: *1940–1952* (Columbia, MO, 2000), 76–125 (here 91, 96–7); Igor de Rachewiltz, 'Some remarks on the ideological foundations of Chinggis Khan's empire', *Papers on Far Eastern History* 7 (1973), 21–36.
25. See the ultimatum from Güyüg handed to the papal envoy Ascelin in 1247: Simon of Saint-Quentin, *Historia Tartarorum*, ed. Jean Richard, *Simon de Saint-Quentin. Histoire des Tartares* (Paris, 1965), 115–16 (excerpted from Vincent of Beauvais, *Speculum historiale*, xxxii, 52); and Möngke's ultimatum to Louis IX, in WR, 274 (*MFW*, 248). Both texts are conveniently reproduced in Voegelin, 'The Mongol orders of submission', 389, 391 (and see also 409). The formula is quoted also (but naming Güyüg rather than Chinggis Khan) by PC, 293 (*MM*, 43).
26. The 'spiritual' aspect of the Chinggisid programme is well brought out by Antti Ruotsala, *Europeans and Mongols in the Middle of the Thirteenth Century: Encountering the Other* (Helsinki, 2001), 105–6, and Sh. Bira, 'Mongolian Tenggerism and modern globalism: A retrospective outlook on globalisation', *JRAS*, 3rd series, 14 (2004), 1–12; and see most recently Jonathan Brack, 'Chinggisid pluralism and religious competition: Buddhists, Muslims, and the question of violence and sovereignty in Ilkhanid Iran', *Modern Asian Studies* 56 (2022), 815–39 (here 821–3).
27. On these two terms, see Paul Pelliot, 'Les Mongols et la papauté', *Revue de l'Orient Chrétien* 23, 24 and 28 (1922–3, 1924 and 1931–2), 26, 126–7

(references are to the pagination of the separatum); Antoine Mostaert and Francis W. Cleaves, 'Trois documents mongols des archives secrètes vaticanes', *HJAS* 15 (1952), 419–506 (here 485, 492–3); and De Rachewiltz's commentary in SH, I, 550, 551.

28. From the Persian original, edited by Pelliot in 'Les Mongols et la papauté', 15–16 (French trans., 21); compare the English trans. in Igor de Rachewiltz, *Papal Envoys to the Great Khans* (London and Stanford, CA, 1971), 214.
29. Kim Hodong, 'Was "Da Yuan" a Chinese dynasty?', *JSYS* 45 (2015), 279–305 (here 286–7). Kim, 'Formation and changes of *ulus*es in the Mongol empire', in Michal Biran (ed.), *Mobility Transformations and Cultural Exchange in Mongol Eurasia* (Leiden, 2019 = *JESHO* 62, nos 2–3), 269–317 (here 271–2, 274–5).
30. By contrast, Allsen, 'The rise of the Mongolian empire', 351–2, concludes that the campaign of 1211–12 was designed purely to gain plunder and dates the establishment of Mongol garrisons in Jin territory no earlier than 1215.
31. SH, § 203 (tr. De Rachewiltz, I, 135; and see his commentary ibid., II, 770–1).
32. Julian, 'Epistula de vita Tartarorum', in Heinrich Dörrie (ed.), 'Drei Texte zur Geschichte der Ungarn und Mongolen: die Missionsreisen des fr. Iulianus O.P. ins Ural-Gebiet (1234/5) und nach Rußland (1237) und der Bericht des Erzbischofs Peter über die Tartaren', *Nachrichten der Akademie der Wissenschaften in Göttingen, phil.-hist. Klasse* (1956), no. 6, 125–202 (here 172).
33. David O. Morgan, 'The Mongols and the eastern Mediterranean', in Benjamin Arbel, Bernard Hamilton and David Jacoby (eds), *Latins and Greeks in the Eastern Mediterranean after 1204* (London, 1989 = *Mediterranean Historical Review* 4, no. 1), 198–211 (here 200). See also Morgan, *Medieval Persia*, 61; and compare too Biran, *Chinggis Khan*, 73.
34. For what follows, see *TJG*, I, 31–2 (*HWC*, 42–3).
35. *TMEN*, I, 175–8 (no. 54: 'Inbegriff der Untertanen eines Herrschers').
36. See Anne F. Broadbridge, *Women and the Making of the Mongol Empire*, CSIC (Cambridge, 2018), 230–1.
37. Some scholars term it the 'White Horde', for example K.Z. Ashrafyan, 'Central Asia under Timur from 1370 to the early fifteenth century', in *HCCA*, IV, part 1, 319–45 (here 328).
38. Thus *TJG*, III, 3 (*HWC*, 549), and WR, 42 (*MFW*, 92).
39. *TJG*, I, 31–2, 146 (*HWC*, 43, where the rendering 'Toli's territory . . . lay adjacent thereto' is not warranted by the text, and 186). See Jackson, *The Mongols and the Islamic World*, 102.
40. *Masālik*, text, 1, 15 (German trans., 91, 100).
41. See SH, §§ 269–70 (tr. De Rachewiltz, I, 200–1; and see commentary at II, 988).
42. Peter Jackson, 'From *ulus* to khanate: The making of the Mongol states, c. 1220-c. 1290', in Amitai-Preiss and Morgan (eds), *The Mongol Empire and Its Legacy*, 12–38 (here 21–3). For a fuller survey, see Thomas T. Allsen, 'Sharing out the empire: Apportioned lands under the Mongols', in Anatoly M. Khazanov and André Wink (eds), *Nomads in the Sedentary World* (Richmond, Surrey, 2001), 172–90.
43. Qiu Yihao, 'Independent ruler, indefinable role: Understanding the history of the Golden Horde from the perspectives of the Yuan dynasty', in Marie Favereau (ed.), *La Horde d'Or et l'islamisation des steppes euroasiatiques* (Aix-en-Provence, 2018 = *REMMM* 143, part 1), 29–48 (here 33–8).

44. Rukn al-Dīn Baybars al-Manṣūrī al-Dawādār (d. 725/1325), *Zubdat al-fikra fī ta'rīkh al-hijra*, ed. D.S. Richards, BI 42 (Beirut, 1998), 365; al-Nuwayrī, XXVII, 377–8 (in greater detail). Peter Jackson, 'The dissolution of the Mongol empire', *CAJ* 22 (1978), 186–244 (here 244).
45. Naṭanzī (1957), 427/(2004), 311.
46. *TJG*, I, 24 (*HWC*, 32). SH, § 153 (tr. De Rachewiltz, I, 76; for the Mongolian term, see the commentary, ibid., I, 567). PC, 298 (*MM*, 47), confirms that the punishment for halting prematurely for the sake of plunder was death.
47. Thomas T. Allsen, 'Preliminary remarks on redistribution in the Mongolian empire', *Mongolica* 18 (39) (2006), 35–48 (esp. 36–7). On this measure, see SH, § 153 (tr. De Rachewiltz, I, 76); İsenbike Togan, *Flexibility and Limitation in Steppe Formations. The Kerait Khanate and Chinggis Khan* (Leiden, New York and Cologne, 1998), 90–1, 99.
48. Togan, *Flexibility and Limitation in Steppe Formations*, 111–12, 118, 124–5.
49. On the *keshig*, see generally Ch'i-ch'ing Hsiao, *The Military Establishment of the Yüan Dynasty* (Cambridge, MA, 1978), 34–8; Thomas T. Allsen, 'Guard and government in the reign of the Grand Qan Möngke, 1251–59', *HJAS* 46 (1986), 495–521 (here 514–15); S.M. Grupper, 'A Barulas family narrative in the *Yuan Shih*: Some neglected prosopographical and institutional sources on Timurid origins', *AEMA* 8 (1992–4), 11–97 (here 38–52); Charles Melville, 'The *keshig* in Iran: The survival of the royal Mongol household', in Komaroff (ed.), *Beyond the Legacy of Genghis Khan*, 135–64; and Michael Hope, 'The *Keshig*', in May and Hope (eds), *The Mongol World*, 370–81. There is also a useful discussion in Gommans, 'The warband', 316–21, where the continued extension of the *keshig* is viewed as key to Chinggis Khan's success, particularly in ensuring that the incorporation of sedentary peoples did not undermine the strength of the nomadic warrior element.
50. See *TMEN*, II, 460–74 (no. 879); *EMME*, 133; Marie Favereau, '*Tarkhan*: A nomad institution in an Islamic context', in Favereau (ed.), *La Horde d'Or et l'islamisation*, 165–89.
51. Peter B. Golden, '"I will give the people unto thee": The Činggisid conquests and their aftermath in the Turkic world', *JRAS*, 3rd series, 10 (2000), 21–41 (here 22–6). Thomas T. Allsen, 'Technologies of governance in the Mongolian empire: A geographic overview', in Sneath (ed.), *Imperial Statecraft*, 117–40 (here 134–5). See also May, 'Nökhöd to noyad', 300–7, who sees the creation of this new élite as a counterweight to Chinggis Khan's own family.
52. SH, §§ 186–187 (tr. De Rachewiltz, I, 108–9).
53. Ratchnevsky, *Genghis Khan*, 93.
54. As is apparent, for example, from the diverse allegiances of noyans from the Qongqurat tribe: *JT*, I, 159–60 (*DzhT*, I, part 1, 395; *CC*, 60). See also the comment on the Ilkhanid military aristocracy, ibid., II, 975 (*DzhT*, III, 22; *CC*, 340); and Wing, *The Jalayirids*, 39–42, on the 'Jalayir diaspora'; more generally, Michal Biran, 'Introduction', in Biran (ed.), *In the Service of the Khans: Elites in Transition in Mongol Eurasia* (Bern, 2017 = *AS* 71, part 4), 1051–7 (here 1054).
55. Mo. *orda*/Tu. *ordu*, 'camp': see *TMEN*, II, 32–9 (no. 452: 'Palastzelt, Heerlager').
56. *JT*, I, 67–8 (*DzhT*, I, part 1, 134–6; *CC*, 27–8).
57. Morgan, *The Mongols*, 79.
58. On this question, see the discussion in Wing, *The Jalayirids*, 34–5; also Joseph Fletcher, 'The Mongols: Ecological and social perspectives', *HJAS* 46 (1986), 11–50 (here 37).

59. As stressed by Wing, *The Jalayirids*, 3–4, 17, 39–43.
60. Golden, 'I will give the people unto thee', 38–9.
61. Timothy May, 'Mongol conquest strategy in the Middle East', in Bruno De Nicola and Charles Melville (eds), *The Mongols' Middle East. Continuity and Transformation in Ilkhanid Iran* (Leiden, 2016), 13–37 (esp. 13–14, 22–3). Biran, *Chinggis Khan*, 64.
62. I am not convinced by the arguments of Donald Ostrowski, 'The *tamma* and the dual-administrative structure of the Mongol empire', *BSOAS* 61 (1998), 262–77, that the *basqaq* was a military governor and the *darugha*(*chi*) a civilian one. For the equivalence of the two officers, see István Vásáry, 'The origin of the institution of *basqaqs*', *AOH* 32 (1978), 201–6; repr. in Vásáry, *Turks, Tatars and Russians in the 13th–16th Centuries* (Aldershot and Burlington, VT, 2007).
63. On the local dynasties in Fārs, Kirmān and Herat, see Lane, *Early Mongol Rule*, chap. 5.
64. W.E. Henthorn, *Korea: The Mongol Invasions* (Leiden, 1963), 194. Thomas T. Allsen, 'The Yüan dynasty and the Uighurs of Turfan in the 13th century', in Morris Rossabi (ed.), *China among Equals. The Middle Kingdom and Its Neighbors, 10th–14th Centuries* (Berkeley and Los Angeles, CA, 1983), 243–80 (here 261). Reuven Amitai, 'Mongol provincial administration: Syria in 1260 as a case study', in Iris Shagrir, Ronnie Ellenblum and Jonathan Riley-Smith (eds), *In laudem Hierosolymitani. Studies in Crusades and Medieval Culture in Honour of Benjamin Z. Kedar*, Crusades, Subsidia 1 (Aldershot, 2007), 117–43 (here 139).
65. Differing interpretations in I.P. Petrushevsky, 'The socio-economic condition of Iran under the Īl-Khāns', in *CHI*, V, 483–537 (here 529–30), and John Masson Smith, Jr, 'Mongol and nomadic taxation', *HJAS* 30 (1970), 46–85 (here 50–60). For the *qubchur*, see Thomas T. Allsen, *Mongol Imperialism. The Policies of the Grand Qan Möngke in China, Russia, and the Islamic Lands, 1251–1259* (Berkeley and Los Angeles, CA, 1987), 163–70. On taxation in the Mongol and post-Mongol eras, see Bert G. Fragner, 'Social and internal economic affairs', in *CHI*, VI, 491–567 (here 533 ff.).
66. Márton Vér, 'The origins of the postal system of the Mongol Empire', *AEMA* 22 (2016), 227–39.
67. David Morgan, 'Reflections on Mongol communications in the Ilkhanate', in Carole Hillenbrand (ed.), *Studies in Honour of Clifford Edmund Bosworth*, II: *The Sultan's Turret. Studies in Persian and Turkish Culture* (Leiden, 2000), 375–85. Adam J. Silverstein, *Postal Systems in the Pre-Modern Islamic World* (Cambridge, 2007), chap. 4 (esp. 144–8). Hosung Shim, 'The *jam* system: The Mongol institution for communication and transportation', in May and Hope (eds), *The Mongol World*, 382–93. For the routes, see Hosung Shim, 'The postal roads of the Great Khans in Central Asia under the Mongol-Yuan empire', *JSYS* 44 (2014), 405–69.
68. Paul D. Buell, 'Sino-Khitan administration in Mongol Bukhara', *JAH* 13 (1979), 121–51 (here 141–7).
69. *JT*, I, 665 (*SGK*, 55–6; *CC*, 230).
70. On this designation, see Henry Serruys, 'Mongol *altan* "gold" = "imperial"', *Monumenta Serica* 21 (1962), 357–78 (here 359–60); and on *altan* more broadly, Allsen, *Commodity and Exchange*, 61–3.
71. *JT*, I, 144 (*DzhT*, I, part 1, 350–1; *CC*, 55).

72. On the status of *güregen*, see Ishayahu Landa, 'Imperial sons-in-law on the move: Oyirad and Qonggirad dispersion in Mongol Eurasia', *AEMA* 22 (2016), 161–97; *TMEN*, I, 475–7 (no. 340).
73. For *qarachu*, see *TMEN*, I, 397–8 (no. 274: 'Nichtadliger,. . .').
74. *Masālik*, text, 6–7 (German trans., 95).
75. Thus the Jochid envoy Aq Buqa, of Qiyat stock, reviled the Jalayir amir Ḥusayn (father of Shaykh Ḥasan-i Buzurg, the founder of the Jalayirid dynasty) in Tabriz in 715/1315 for his disrespect in passing the cup to him while himself remaining seated: Jamāl al-Dīn Abū l-Qāsim ʿAbd-Allāh Qāshānī, *Ta'rīkh-i Uljāytū Sulṭān*, ed. Mahin Hambly (Tehran, 1348 sh./1969), 175.
76. David Christian, *A History of Russia, Central Asia and Mongolia*, II: *Inner Eurasia from the Mongol Empire to Today, 1260–2000* (Malden, MA, and Oxford, 2018), 15–18.
77. Allsen, *Mongol Imperialism*, 213–16.
78. Golden, 'I will give the people unto thee', 24–5.
79. Dörrie (ed.), 'Drei Texte', 177.
80. For this distinction, see *JT*, I, 16, 40, 43, 65, 145 (*DzhT*, I, part 1, 30, 76, 82, 129–30, 352; *CC*, 7, 18, 27, 56). The Barulas are briefly noticed ibid., I, 201 (*DzhT*, I, part 1, 530–1; *CC*, 74).
81. Ibid., I, 78 (*DzhT*, I, part 1, 163–4; compare trans. in *CC*, 32, which I have considerably modified). See also the remarks of Kim, 'Formation and changes of *uluses*', 273–4.
82. J. Holmgren, 'Observations on marriage and inheritance practices in early Mongol and Yüan society, with particular reference to the levirate': *JAH* 20 (1986), 127–92. Louis Hambis, 'Une coutume matrimoniale chez les Mongols et les peuples de Haute-Asie', in *Mélanges offerts à Jean Dauvillier* (Toulouse, 1979), 385–93. Alice Sárközi, 'Levirate among the Mongols', in Elena V. Boikova and Rostislav B. Rybakov (eds), *Kinship in the Altaic World: Proceedings of the 48th Permanent Altaistic Conference, Moscow, 10–15 July 2005* (Wiesbaden, 2006), 259–67.
83. See Igor de Rachewiltz, 'Some reflections on Činggis Qan's ǰasaγ', *East Asian History* 6 (1993), 91–104 (here 97); István Vásáry, '*Yāsā* and *Sharī'a*: Islamic attitudes towards the Mongol law in the Turco-Mongolian world (from the Golden Horde to Timur's time)', in Gleave and Kristó-Nagy (eds), *Violence in Islamic Thought*, 58–78 (here 69). In the same way, the sacred precinct near the mountain Burqan Qaldun in Mongolia, where Chinggis Khan and others of his dynasty were buried, was known as 'the great [i.e. imperial] sanctuary' (*ghuruq-i buzurg*): Vásáry, '*Yāsā* and *Sharī'a*', 72; for Tu. *ghoruq*/*qoruq*, see *TMEN*, III, 444–50 (no. 1462: 'Reservat, tabu, Verbotenes . . .', esp. examples at 446).
84. The most recent survey is Denise Aigle, 'The Yasa', in May and Hope (eds), *The Mongol World*, 319–30.
85. David Ayalon, 'The Great *Yāsa* of Chingiz Khān: A re-examination (A)', *StIsl* 33 (1971), 99–140; repr. in Ayalon, *Outsiders in the Lands of Islam. Mamluks, Mongols and Eunuchs* (London, 1988).
86. D.O. Morgan, 'The "Great *Yāsā* of Chingiz Khān" and Mongol law in the Īlkhānate', *BSOAS* 49 (1986), 163–76 (here 167–8); repr. in G.R. Hawting (ed.), *Muslims, Mongols and Crusaders* (London and New York, 2005), 198–211 (here 202–3).
87. *TJG*, I, 17–18 (*HWC*, 25). Morgan, 'The Great *Yāsā* of Chingiz Khān', 166; repr. in Hawting (ed.), *Muslims, Mongols and Crusaders*, 201.

88. *JT*, I, 488 (*CC*, 10, 'laid down new regulations'). Compare too the trans. in Morgan, 'The Great *Yāsā* of Chingiz Khān', 165; repr. in Hawting (ed.), *Muslims, Mongols and Crusaders*, 200.
89. *JT*, I, 663 (*SGK*, 54; *CC*, 230).
90. Waṣṣāf (1853), 560, lines 2–5/(2009), 378 (omitting a phrase).
91. Ibid. (1853), 17, lines 21–22 (*GW*, I, text, 35, trans., 35). Morgan, 'The Great *Yāsā* of Chingiz Khān', 169; repr. in Hawting (ed.), *Muslims, Mongols and Crusaders*, 204.
92. PC, 263–4 (*MM*, 25), also mentions an edict (*statutum*), issued following an acute dearth of provisions on campaign, that no soldier was to discard any part of an animal that could be ingested, including the blood and the entrails.
93. Ibid., 264, 284–5, 293 (*MM*, 25, 38, 43). *TJG*, I, 17 (cf. *HWC*, 24), must allude to this injunction when it states that Chinggis Khan annihilated any ruler who opposed him, along with his dependants, family and troops, 'in accordance with the requisite *yasa* and ruling that he had made' (*bar ḥasb-i yāsā wa-ḥukmī ki lāzim kardast*).
94. PC, 264 (*MM*, 25). For the quriltai, see Florence Hodous, 'The *Quriltai* as a legal institution in the Mongol empire', *CAJ* 56 (2012–13), 87–102.
95. PC, 264 (*MM*, 25), mistakenly calling Ot-chigin Chinggis Khan's nephew. *TJG*, I, 199, 210 (*HWC*, 244, 255).
96. Muḥammad b. ʿAlī Shabānkāra'ī, *Majmaʿ al-ansāb*, ed. Mīr Hāshim Muḥaddith (Tehran, 1363 sh./1984), 303. Wing, *The Jalayirids*, 82.
97. For the list, see PC, 239–40 (*MM*, 11). With respect to the prohibition of spitting out food, compare the edict above (n. 92), against discarding any edible part of an animal.
98. *TJG*, I, 161, *yāsā-u ādhin*; I, 227, *yāsā-u āyīn* (*HWC*, 204, 272). Compare Denise Aigle, 'Mongol law *versus* Islamic law: Myth and reality', in her *The Mongol Empire between Myth and Reality*, 134–56 (here 134, 137–40), and 'Le Grand *Jasaq* de Gengis-Khan, l'empire, la culture mongole et le Shariʿa', *JESHO* 47 (2004), 31–79 (here 33, 41–2, 47–8), who argues that external observers from sedentary cultures failed to distinguish law and custom. Certainly PC, 250 (*MM*, 17), was occasionally unsure of the distinction, but in all likelihood for the reason I propose here.
99. Manz, *Nomads in the Middle East*, 135.
100. Christopher P. Atwood, '*Ulus* emirs, *keshig* elders, signatures, and marriage partners: The evolution of a classic Mongol institution', in Sneath (ed.), *Imperial Statecraft*, 141–73. Jackson, *The Mongols and the Islamic World*, 115. See more generally İsenbike Togan, 'Variations in the perception of jasagh', in D.A. Alimova (ed.), *Markazii Osiyo tarikhi zamonavii medievistika talkinida (Professor Roziia Mukminova khotirasiga bagishlanadi) / History of Central Asia in Modern Medieval Studies (In Memoriam of Professor Roziya Mukminova)* (Tashkent, 2013), 67–101.
101. Ken'ichi Isogai, '*Yasa* and *Shari'a* in early 16th century Central Asia', in Szuppe (ed.), *L'Héritage timouride*, 91–103.
102. *TJG*, I, 149, 155 (*HWC*, 189–90, 196). Morgan, 'The Great *Yāsā* of Chingiz Khān', 171; repr. in Hawting (ed.), *Muslims, Mongols and Crusaders*, 206.
103. Waṣṣāf (1853), 561, lines 12–18/(2009), 378–9.
104. *TJG*, I, 211 (*HWC*, 256). David Morgan, 'The "Great *Yasa* of Chinggis Khan" revisited', in Amitai and Biran (eds), *Mongols, Turks, and Others*, 291–308 (here 302–3).

105. Waṣṣāf (1853), 504, lines 15–16/(2009), 254 (*GW*, IV, 282).
106. *JT*, II, 1060 (*DzhT*, III, 102; *CC*, 368).
107. De Rachewiltz, 'Some reflections on Činggis Qan's ǰasaγ', 97, 98, for the broader meaning, as instanced in SH, § 189; and see too his commentary in SH, II, 683.
108. *JT*, I, 602–3 (*CC*, 211). For the sanctuary, see above, n.83.
109. Jackson, *The Mongols and the Islamic World*, 114. See also Togan, 'Variations in the perception of jasagh', 67, where she uses the phrase 'new order'.
110. Peter B. Golden, 'Courts and court culture in the proto-urban and urban developments among the pre-Chinggisid Turkic peoples', in David Durand-Guédy (ed.), *Turko-Mongol Rulers, Cities and City Life* (Leiden, 2013), 21–73 (here 41–2).
111. I have adopted this spelling rather than the usual 'Kebek', in view of the readings KWPAK in *SP*, fo. 120a, and KWBK in Qāshānī. *Ta'rīkh-i Uljāytū Sulṭān*, 148 (the reading found also in the fourteenth-century Istanbul ms. Ayasofya 3019, fo. 65b).
112. Dardess, 'From Mongol empire to Yüan dynasty', 119.
113. On the uncertain location of Sarai, see Daniel C. Waugh, 'Archaeology and the material culture of the Ulus Jochi (Golden Horde)', in May and Hope (eds), *The Mongol World*, 588–621 (here 597).
114. Thomas T. Allsen, 'The Princes of the Left Hand: An introduction to the history of the *ulus* of Orda in the thirteenth and early fourteenth centuries', *AEMA* 5 (1985–7), 5–40 (here 27–8).
115. Charles Melville, 'The itineraries of Sultan Öljeitü, 1304–16', *Iran* 28 (1990), 55–70. Bernard O'Kane, 'From tents to pavilions: Royal mobility and Persian palace design', *Ars Orientalis* 23 (1993), 249–68 (here 249–50).
116. Anatoly M. Khazanov, 'Nomads and cities in the Eurasian steppe region and adjacent countries: A historical overview', in Stefan Leder and Bernhard Streck (eds), *Shifts and Drifts in Nomad–Sedentary Relations*, Nomaden und Sesshafte 2 (Wiesbaden, 2005), 163–78 (here 171–3).
117. Naṭanzī (1957), 106/(2004), 86–7. Compare also Ḥamd-Allāh Mustawfī Qazwīnī, *Nuzhat al-qulūb*, partial edn and trans. by Guy Le Strange, *The Geographical Part of the Nuzhat al-Qulūb*, GMS 23 (Leiden and London, 1915–19), I (text), 246, II (trans.), 239. Jackson, *The Mongols and the Islamic World*, 207 and n.188.
118. Timothy May, *The Mongol Empire* (Edinburgh, 2018), 76–7.
119. Fletcher, 'The Mongols: Ecological and social perspectives', 17; and on the succession, 24–8. See also the analysis in Marie Favereau Doumenjou and Liesbeth Geevers, 'The Golden Horde, the Spanish Habsburg monarchy, and the construction of ruling dynasties', in Van Berkel and Duindam (eds), *Prince, Pen, and Sword*, 452–512 (here 463–5).
120. Kim, 'Formation and changes of *ulus*es', 305–6.
121. On the condominium down to 1259, see V.V. Trepavlov, 'Sopravitel'stvo v mongol'skoi imperii (XIII v.)', *AEMA* 7 (1987–91), 249–78 (here 253–9); B. Akhmedov, 'Central Asia under the rule of Chinggis Khan's successors' (revised by D. Sinor), in *HCCA*, IV, part 1, 261–8 (here 263–4).
122. *JT*, II, 977 (*DzhT*, III, 24; cf. *CC*, 340–1). Allsen, 'Sharing out the empire', 173–4, is inclined to accept this as evidence for a Toluid takeover of northern China and the Iranian lands; see also his *Mongol Imperialism*, 47–51, for the idea that Möngke was in effect creating two new khanates.

123. Jackson, 'The dissolution of the Mongol empire', 212–20, and *The Mongols and the Islamic World*, 120–3.
124. Anonymous, *Akhbār-i mughūlān dar anbāna-yi Quṭb*, ed. Īraj Afshār (Qum, 1389 sh./2009), 40; tr. George Lane, *The Mongols in Iran. Quṭb al-Dīn Shīrāzī's Akhbār-i Moghūlān* (London and New York, 2018), 60.
125. *Masālik*, text, 2, 20 (German trans., 91, 103–4). Thomas T. Allsen, 'Changing forms of legitimation in Mongol Iran', in Gary Seaman and Daniel Marks (eds), *Rulers from the Steppe: State Formation on the Eurasian Periphery* (Los Angeles, CA, 1991), 223–41 (here 234).
126. Allsen, *Mongol Imperialism*, 37–42.
127. Shabānkāra'ī, *Majma' al-ansāb*, 247, *mamālik-i gharbī ki ān mamlikat-i Īrān-zamīn ast az āb-i Āmūya tā ḥadd-i Shām-u Miṣr wa-takhtgāh-i khalīfa*; ibid., 259, the 'western lands' are described again as Tolui's inheritance; on Tolui's mother, see ibid., 244–5, 247, 256. Compare also *Majma' al-ansāb*, BL ms. Add. 16696, fos 107b–108a: on this text, an abridged version of Shabānkāra'ī's later recension of 743/1343, see Aubin, 'Un chroniqueur méconnu', 221 (repr. in his *Études*, 150–1).
128. Sayfī (1944), 49, 50–1/(2004), 87, 89.
129. For these developments, see Jackson, *The Mongols and the Islamic World*, 142–7.
130. For recent surveys, see Marie Favereau, *La Horde d'Or et le sultanat mamelouk. Naissance d'une alliance* (Cairo, 2018), and her 'The Golden Horde and the Mamluks: The birth of a diplomatic set-up (660–5/1261–7)', in Frédéric Bauden and Malika Dekkiche (eds), *Mamluk Cairo, a Crossroads for Embassies. Studies on Diplomacy and Diplomatics*, IHC 161 (Leiden and Boston, MA, 2019), 302–26. On the trade in mamluks, see Reuven Amitai, 'Diplomacy and the slave trade in the eastern Mediterranean: A re-examination of the Mamluk-Byzantine-Genoese triangle in the late thirteenth century in light of the existing early correspondence', *OM* 88 (2008), 349–68.
131. Jackson, *The Mongols and the West*, 203–4.
132. Dardess, 'From Mongol empire to Yüan dynasty', 124–6.
133. Szilvia Kovács and Márton Vér, 'Mongols and the Silk Roads: An overview', in *The Mongols and the Silk Roads* (Budapest, 2021 = *AOH* 74, part 1), 1–10 (here 5).
134. When Clavijo (1859), 128/(1928), 213–14, heard a particularly inaccurate version of it. The modern misapprehension is strongly criticized in Kim, 'The unity of the Mongol empire', 33–4.
135. *TR*, I (text), 106, 248, II (trans.), 85, 194; compare also I (text), 241, II (trans.), 187–8.
136. Allsen, 'The Princes of the Left Hand', esp. 18–26. See also the discussion in Trepavlov, 'Sopravitel'stvo v mongol'skoi imperii', 263–5, and Kanat Uskenbay, 'Left Wing of the Ulus of Jochi in the 13th–the beginning of the 15th centuries', in Rafael Khakimov, Vadim Trepavlov and Marie Favereau (eds), *Zolotaia Orda v mirovoi istorii* (Kazan, 2016), English translation as *The Golden Horde in World History* (Oxford and Kazan, 2017), 203–12 (here 205, 207).
137. Kim, 'Formation and changes of *ulus*es', 308–10, offers a more nuanced account than that in Jackson, 'From *ulus* to khanate', 32–5.
138. For a fine study of Qaidu's empire, see Michal Biran, *Qaidu and the Rise of the Independent Mongol State in Central Asia* (Richmond, Surrey, 1997).

139. References in Jackson, *The Mongols and the Islamic World*, 182–3 and n.4 at 485.
140. Allsen, 'The Yüan dynasty and the Uighurs', 254–60.
141. P.N. Petrov, 'Khronologiia pravleniia khanov v Chagataiskom gosudarstve v 1271–1368 gg. (po materialam numizmaticheskikh pamiatnikov)', in S.G. Kliashtornyi, T.I. Sultanov and V.V. Trepavlov (eds), *Istoriia i kul'tura tiurkskikh narodov Rossii i sopredel'nykh stran* (Moscow, 2009 = *TS* 2007–8), 294–319 (here 302–3), dates its subjection to Köpek's reign. But see p. 212.
142. Mona Hassan, *Longing for the Lost Caliphate. A Transregional History* (Princeton, NJ, 2016), 71–4.
143. Waṣṣāf (1853), 398/(2009), 10 (*GW*, IV, 12–13). *Masālik*, text, 15 (German trans., 100); ibid., text, 78 (German trans., 143–4), al-ʿUmarī mentions only Tabriz and Marāgha, but specifies that these regions were allocated for the maintenance of the Jochid troops who participated in Hülegü's expedition.
144. Dai Matsui, '*Dumdadu Mongɣol Ulus* "The Middle Mongolian Empire"', in Rybatzki et al. (eds), *The Early Mongols*, 111–19, with examples also from European sources. For its history down to the 1360s, see Michal Biran, 'The Mongols in Central Asia from Chinggis Khan's invasion to the rise of Temür: The Ögödeid and Chaghadaid realms', in *CHIA*, 46–66, and Michael Hope, 'The Middle Empire', in May and Hope (eds), *The Mongol World*, 298–316.
145. Michal Biran, 'The Battle of Herat (1270): a case of inter-Mongol warfare', in Nicola Di Cosmo (ed.), *Warfare in Inner Asian History (500–1800)* (Leiden, 2002), 175–219 (here 211).
146. *JT*, II, 1067, 1068–9 (*DzhT*, III, 110; *CC*, 370). Ibid., I, 770 (*SGK*, 152; *CC*, 267), Baraq says that the number of his troops exceeds the capacity of his ulus to support them.
147. Qāshānī, *Ta'rīkh-i Uljāytū Sulṭān*, 203–4, 208. Liu Yingsheng, 'War and peace between the Yuan dynasty and the Chaghadaid khanate (1312–1323)', in Amitai and Biran (eds), *Mongols, Turks, and Others*, 339–58 (here 344, 349).
148. Maria Szuppe, 'Le Khorassan aux XIVe–XVIe siècles: la littérature savante comme expression de l'unité avec la Transoxiane', in *La Persia e l'Asia centrale da Alessandro al X secolo*, Atti dei Convegni Lincei 127 (Rome, 1996), 149–64 (here 152–3).
149. Sayfī (1944), 127–8/(2004),164. The year 639/1241–2, like many of those Sayfī gives for these earlier decades, is unreliable.
150. Waṣṣāf (1853), 12, lines 17–22 (*GW*, I, text, 23–4, trans., 25).
151. Biran, 'The Battle of Herat (1270)', 201–2.
152. See Biran, *Qaidu*, 41, 50, 82, for princes who joined or deserted Qaidu at different times; also O. Karaev, *Chagataiskii ulus. Gosudarstvo Khaidu. Mogulistan. Obrazovanie Kyrgyzskogo naroda* (Bishkek, 1995), 30.
153. See Kim, 'Formation and changes of *ulus*es', 303–5.
154. Kim Hodong, 'Unity and continuity of the Mongol empire', *Mongolica* 18 (39) (2006), 57–65. Kim, 'The unity of the Mongol empire'. Kim, 'Formation and changes of *ulus*es', passim. Favereau, 'The Mongol Peace'.
155. Qāshānī, *Ta'rīkh-i Uljāytū Sulṭān*, 34; cited by Allsen, 'Spiritual geography', 128.
156. Kim, 'The unity of the Mongol empire', 32. Kim, 'Was "Da Yuan" a Chinese dynasty?', 287–9. Kim, 'Unity and continuity', 57–8.

157. Francesca Fiaschetti, 'The borders of rebellion: The Yuan dynasty and the rhetoric of empire', in Francesca Fiaschetti and Julia Schneider (eds), *Political Strategies of Identity Building in Non-Han Empires in China*, AF 157 (Wiesbaden, 2014), 127–45 (esp. 129–30, 133, 138–41). See also Fiaschetti, 'The Six Duties: Yuan diplomatic interactions with East and Southeast Asia', *AEMA* 23 (2017), 81–101; and Michael C. Brose, 'Realism and idealism in the *Yuanshi* chapters on foreign relations', in Daniel Boucher, Neil Schmid and Tansen Sen (eds), *China at the Crossroads: A Festschrift in Honor of Victor H. Mair* (Taipei, 2006 = *Asia Major*, 3rd series, 19), 327–47.
158. Hungary: *JT*, I, 667 (*CC*, 231). Japan, 'Lūchak' and 'Khaynām' (Hainan?): ibid., I, 911–12 (*CC*, 316). The latter two names appear to refer to the principal islands S and SE of China. Lūchak probably represents Liuqiu (Taiwan): Fiaschetti, 'The borders of rebellion', 138, n.88; Pelliot, *Notes on Marco Polo* (Paris, 1959–73), II, 767–70, however, looked for it elsewhere in SE Asia.
159. Qaraṭāy al-ʿIzzī al-Khaznadārī, *Taʾrīkh majmūʿ al-nawādir mimmā jarā li l-awāʾl wa l-awākhir* (*c.* 1330), ed. Horst Hein and Muḥammad al-Ḥuğayrī, BI 46 (Beirut and Berlin, 2005), 128 (also excerpted in *SMIZO*, I, Ar. text, 72, Russian trans., 75, but there wrongly attributed to Ibn Wāṣil).
160. Reuven Amitai-Preiss, 'An exchange of letters in Arabic between Abaγa Īlkhān and Sultan Baybars (A.H. 667/A.D. 1268)', *CAJ* 38 (1994), 11–33 (here 17–18, 20), and repr. in Amitai, *The Mongols in the Islamic Lands*. See more generally Amitai-Preiss, 'Mongol imperial ideology and the Ilkhanid war against the Mamluks', in Amitai-Preiss and Morgan (eds), *The Mongol Empire and Its Legacy*, 57–72 (here 62–72), and repr. in Amitai, *The Mongols in the Islamic Lands*; Jackson, *The Mongols and the West*, 219–21.
161. Waṣṣāf (1853), 528. Peter Jackson, *The Delhi Sultanate. A Political and Military History*, CSIC (Cambridge, 1999), 225.
162. Reuven Amitai, *Holy War and Rapprochement. Studies in the Relationship between the Mamluk Sultanate and the Mongol Ilkhanate (1260–1335)* (Turnhout, 2013), 50–3. Na'ama O. Arom, '"In-*ger*" and "outer" diplomacy – Ilkhanid contacts with the Mongols and the outside world, 1260–1282', in Francesca Fiaschetti (ed.), *Diplomacy in the Age of Mongol Globalization* (Leiden, 2019 = *ES* 17), 286–309 (here 295–8). Arom, 'Arrowheads of Hülegü Khan: Envoys and diplomacy in his invasion of the Middle East, 1255–1262', in May et al. (eds), *New Approaches to Ilkhanid History*, 249–71 (here 259–66).
163. Biran, 'The Mamluks and Mongol Central Asia', 369–70.
164. Waṣṣāf (1853), 454, lines 10–15/(2009), 137–8 (*GW*, IV, 150–1).
165. Antoine Mostaert and Francis Woodman Cleaves (eds), *Les Lettres de 1289 et 1305 des ilkhan Aryun et Öljeitü à Philippe le Bel*, Harvard-Yenching Institute, Scripta Mongolica Monograph series 1 (Cambridge, MA, 1962), 56–7. See Shim, 'The postal roads of the Great Khans', 440–4, for details; and for the Talu Sea, Denis Sinor, 'The mysterious "Talu Sea" in Öljeitü's letter to Philip the Fair of France' (1972), repr. in his *Inner Asia and Its Contacts with Medieval Europe* (London, 1977).
166. Anonymous, *De statu, conditione ac regimine magni canis*, ed. Christine Gadrat, '*De statu, conditione ac regimine magni canis*: l'original latin du «Livre de l'estat du grant can» et la question de l'auteur', *BEC* 165 (2007), 355–71 (here 366); fourteenth-century French translation, ed. M. Jacquet, 'Le Livre du Grant

Caan, extrait d'un manuscrit de la Bibliothèque du Roi', *JA* 6 (1830), 57–72 (here 59), and tr. in Sir Henry Yule, *Cathay and the Way Thither: Being a Collection of Medieval Notices of China*, new edn by Henri Cordier, 4 vols, HS, 2nd series, 33, 37, 38 and 41 (London, 1913–16), III, 89–103 (here 89). Köpek was sending tribute to Khanbaligh after the peace of 1323: Liu, 'War and peace', 352–3. 'Tribute', of course, might refer merely to gifts as seen through the prism of Chinese diplomatic protocol; or it could represent the Qaghan's traditional share of the revenues from Central Asia and hence a *quid pro quo* for the despatch of Chinese revenues due to the regional khanates.

167. Shabānkāra'ī, *Majma' al-ansāb*, 221. Ibn Faḍl-Allāh al-ʿUmarī, *al-Taʿrīf*, Cairo edn, 46/ed. al-Durūbī, 62.
168. See, for example, Zhào Zhū Chén, 'The Golden Horde and the Yuan dynasty', in Khakimov et al. (eds), *The Golden Horde in World History*, 352–6 (here 355); Qiu, 'Independent ruler, indefinable role', 41–3.
169. Allsen, 'Changing forms of legitimation in Mongol Iran', 226–32.
170. Thomas T. Allsen, 'Notes on Chinese titles in Mongol Iran', *MS* 14 (1991), 27–39.
171. But see Liu, 'War and peace', 352 for the conferment of the rank of marshal on Köpek's envoy Baiju by Emperor Yingzong (Shidebala, 1321–1323).
172. *Masālik*, text, 26 (German trans., 109).
173. Shim, 'The postal roads of the Great Khans', 454; he attributes this, however, to the onset of plague in China, on which see Chap. 5.
174. John W. Dardess, *Conquerors and Confucians. Aspects of Political Change in Late Yüan China* (New York and London, 1973), 19–20, 26–30, describing this (27) as 'one last case of major political interaction between two major realms of the Mongol empire'. Liu, 'War and peace', 350.
175. Qāshānī, *Ta'rīkh-i Uljāytū Sulṭān*, 203. Kim, 'Unity and continuity', 63–4 (here citing al-ʿUmarī in error). Michal Biran, 'Diplomacy and chancellery practices in the Chagataid khanate: Some preliminary remarks', *OM* 88 (2008), 369–93 (here 389). Liu, 'War and peace', 342.
176. Dai Matsui, 'A Mongolian decree from the Chaghataid Khanate discovered at Dunhuang', in Peter Zieme (ed.), *Aspects of Research into Central Asian Buddhism. In Memoriam Kōgi Kudara*, SRS 16 (Turnhout, 2008), 159–78 (here 160–1). Matsui, 'An Uigur decree of tax exemption in the name of Duwa-Khan', *Šinžlex Uxvany Akademiin Mebee* [*Proceedings of the Mongolian Academy of Sciences*] (2007), no. 4, 60–8 (here 61–2). Herbert Franke, 'Ein mongolischer Freibrief aus dem Jahre 1369', *UAJ* 47 (1975), 64–71 (here 64). But for exceptions compare György Kara, 'Mediaeval Mongol documents from Khara Khoto and East Turkestan in the St. Petersburg branch of the Institute of Oriental Studies', *MO* 9 (2003), part 2, 3–40 (here 28, citing a decree of Yesün Temür dated 1339); and Márton Vér, 'Chancellery and diplomatic practices in Central Asia during the Mongol period as shown in Old Uyghur and Middle Mongolian documents', in Fiaschetti (ed.), *Diplomacy in the Age of Mongol Globalization*, 182–201 (here 186, n.16, citing doc. MongHT 72). We find *lingchi* used by an official of the Chaghadayid Asutai, prince of Xining (1350s), who was subject to the Yuan: Peter Zieme and György Kara (ed. and trans.), *Ein uigurisches Totenbuch*, AF 63 (Wiesbaden, 1979), 162–3.
177. P.N. Petrov, 'Nakhodki monet XIV v. bliz Khorgosa', in *Monety i medali (Sbornik statei po materialam kollektsii otdela numizmatiki)*, II (Moscow, 2004),

168–238 (esp. 174–7, 181–3). Petrov, 'Khronologiia', 301–2, 305, 308, 311, 314.

178. Janibeg: Bertold Spuler, *Die Goldene Horde. Die Mongolen in Rußland 1223–1502*, 2nd edn (Wiesbaden, 1965), 261 (coin of 743/1342–3); Broadbridge, *Kingship and Ideology*, 161. Abū Sa'īd: Reuven Amitai, 'Political legitimation in the Ilkhanate: More thoughts on the Mongol imperial ideology, the introduction of Muslim justifications, and the revival of Iranian ideals', in May et al. (eds), *New Approaches to Ilkhanid History*, 209–48 (here 223–4).
179. I suggest that it is therefore misleading to state that the rulers of the other uluses never aspired to the title of *qa'an*/*qaghan*/Great Khan: compare Kim, The unity of the Mongol empire', 33, and Favereau, 'The Mongol Peace', 52.
180. Paul D. Buell and Eugene N. Anderson, *A Soup for the Qan: Chinese Dietary Medicine of the Mongol Era as Seen in Hu Szu-hui's* Yin-shan Cheng-yao (London and New York, 2000), 6.
181. Morgan, 'The Great *Yāsā* of Chingiz Khān', 173–6; repr. in Hawting (ed.), *Muslims, Mongols and Crusaders*, 208–11.
182. *TJG*, I, 30 (*HWC*, 41–2).
183. Clavijo (1859), 128–9/(1928), 214.
184. *TJG*, I, 143, *madār-i kār-u yāsā-yi īshān* (trans. in *HWC*, 181–2, modified).
185. *JT*, I, 582 (*CC*, 201); compare also I, 581 (*CC*, 200).
186. Ibid., II, 1479 (*DzhT*, III, 511; *CC*, 512). Compare also Morgan, 'The Great *Yāsā* of Chingiz Khān', 172; repr. in Hawting (ed.), *Muslims, Mongols and Crusaders*, 207.
187. Waṣṣāf (1853), 452, line 20–453, line 6/(2009), 134–5 (*GW*, IV, 147–8); and compare also (1853), 454, lines 21–24/(2009), 138 (*GW*, IV, 150).
188. Thomas T. Allsen, 'Eurasia after the Mongols', in *CWH*, VI, part 1, 159–81 (here 161).

3: ISLAMISATION

1. David Cook, 'Apocalyptic incidents during the Mongol invasions', in Wolfram Brandes and Felicitas Schmieder (eds), *Endzeiten. Eschatologie in den monotheistischen Weltreligionen* (Berlin, 2008), 293–312. Devin DeWeese, '"Stuck in the throat of Chingīz Khān": Envisioning the Mongol conquests in some Sufi accounts from the 14th to 17th centuries', in Judith Pfeiffer and Sholeh A. Quinn (eds, with Ernest Tucker), *History and Historiography of Post-Mongol Central Asia and the Middle East. Studies in Honor of John E. Woods* (Wiesbaden, 2006), 23–60 (here 25–7). John Dechant, 'Depictions of the Islamization of the Mongols in the *Manāqib al-'ārifīn* and the foundation of the Mawlawī community', *Mawlana Rumi Review* 2 (2011), 135–64 (here 143). Jackson, *The Mongols and the Islamic World*, 322 (citing Jamāl al-Qarshī). A.C.S. Peacock, *Islam, Literature and Society in Mongol Anatolia*, CSIC (Cambridge, 2019), 81–2 (Abū Bakr Rūmī), 224 (Najm al-Dīn Rāzī). Leonard Lewisohn, 'Sufism in late Mongol and early Timurid Persia, from 'Ala' al-Dawla Simnānī (d. 736/1326 [*sic*]) to Shāh Qāsim Anvār (d. 837/1434)', in Sussan Babaie (ed.), *Iran after the Mongols*, The Idea of Iran 8 (London and New York, 2019), 177–209 (here 181–2).
2. *TJG*, I, 81 (*HWC*, 105). Timothy May, 'The Mongols as the Scourge of God in the Islamic world', in Gleave and Kristó-Nagy (eds), *Violence in Islamic Thought*,

32–57 (here 32–3, 47, 52), is rightly sceptical that Chinggis Khan uttered this speech.

3. *TN*, II, 92–4, 97–8 (passages omitted from Raverty's trans., 869, 935, on the grounds that the world had not yet ended); also the long *qaṣīda* at II, 205–10 (partial trans. in Cook, 'Apocalyptic incidents', 308–9). For Jūzjānī's thinking, see May, 'The Mongols as the Scourge of God', 44–7.
4. Jackson, *The Mongols and the Islamic World*, chaps 6–7.
5. *JT*, II, 1332 (*DzhT*, III, 373; *CC*, 463).
6. Samuel M. Grupper, 'The Buddhist sanctuary-vihāra of Labnasagut and the Il-qan Hülegü: An overview of Il-qanid Buddhism and related matters', *AEMA* 13 (2004), 5–77. Arezou Azad, 'Three rock-cut cave sites in Iran and their Ilkhanid Buddhist aspects reconsidered', in Anna Akasoy, Charles Burnett & Ronit Yoeli-Tlalim (eds), *Islam and Tibet – Interactions along the Musk Routes* (Farnham & Burlington, VT, 2011), 209–30. See more generally Roxann Prazniak, 'Ilkhanid Buddhism: Traces of a passage in Eurasian history', *CSSH* 56 (2014), 650–80; Jonathan Brack, 'Rashīd al-Dīn: Buddhism in Iran and the Mongol Silk Roads', in Michal Biran, Jonathan Brack and Francesca Fiaschetti (eds), *Along the Silk Roads in Mongol Eurasia: Generals, Merchants, and Intellectuals* (Oakland, CA, 2020), 215–37; and Jonathan Z. Brack, *An Afterlife for the Khan. Muslims, Buddhists, and Sacred Kingship in Mongol Iran and Eurasia* (Oakland, CA, 2023), 19–24.
7. *JT*, III, 1210, 1211, 1253–4 (*DzhT*, III, 252, 253, 295; *CC*, 417, 418, 437, reading at this last juncture 'Arghun' in error for Abagha).
8. Qur'ān, iv, 26. J. Schacht, 'Nikāḥ, 1. In Classical Islamic law', *EI*², VIII, 27.
9. Jackson, *The Mongols and the Islamic World*, 305–6. PC, 239 (*MM*, 11) writes of the enforced marriage of a Christian Rus′ prince with his widowed sister-in-law.
10. Paul Ratchnevsky, 'The levirate in the legislation of the Yuan dynasty', in *Asiatic Studies in Honour of Dr. Jitsuzō Tamura on the Occasion of His Sixty-Fourth Birthday* (Kyoto, 1968), 45–62.
11. See generally Peter Jackson, 'The Mongols and the faith of the conquered', in Amitai and Biran (eds), *Mongols, Turks, and Others*, 245–90 (here 260–2). That these practices were the subject of *yasa*s is clear from *TJG*, I, 161, 163, 227 (*HWC*, 204, 206, 272).
12. Togan, 'Variations in the perception of jasagh', 72–3. Jackson, *The Mongols and the Islamic World*, 309–10. Aigle, 'Mongol law *versus* Islamic law', 152–5, points out that had steppe customs been enforced on the Muslim population at large our Muslim sources would certainly have said more on the subject; see also Aigle, 'Le Grand *Jasaq*', 67–70.
13. *JT*, II, 921 (*SGK*, 294; *CC*, 319). See Francis Woodman Cleaves, 'The rescript of Qubilai prohibiting the slaughtering of animals by slitting the throat', in *Richard Nelson Frye Festschrift I*, 67–89 (here 72).
14. Abū Bakr b. ʿAbd-Allāh Ibn al-Dawādārī (fl. *c.* 1330), *Kanz al-durar wa-jāmiʿ al-ghurar*, VIII, ed. Ulrich Haarmann, *Der Bericht über die frühen Mamluken* (Cairo, 1391/1971), 99. Ibn Abī l-Faḍā'il (al-Mufaḍḍal), *al-Nahj al-sadīd wa l-durr al-farīd* (759/1358), ed. Edgar Blochet, 'Moufazzal Ibn Abil-Fazaïl. Histoire des Sultans Mamlouks', Part 1, *Patrologia Orientalis* 12 (1919), 343–550 (here 459).
15. For a fuller analysis of Mongol religious attitudes than is given here, see my 'The Mongols and religion: Ancestral pluralism, selective appropriation – and

cynical manipulation?', forthcoming in *CAJ*; and for the Mongols' Islamisation, Jackson, *The Mongols and the Islamic World*, chaps 12–13.

16. Qiu Yihao, 'Jaʿfar Khwāja: Sayyid, merchant, spy, and military commander of Chinggis Khan', in Biran, Brack and Fiaschetti (eds), *Along the Silk Roads*, 143–59.
17. *TN*, II, 152, 167 (tr. Raverty, 1107, 1146). See Jackson, *The Mongols and the Islamic World*, 306–7, 319.
18. *Turkestan*³, 468. Biran, 'The Mongols in Central Asia', 63–4. Hope, 'The Middle Empire', 299.
19. See the analysis in Devin DeWeese, *Islamization and Native Religion in the Golden Horde. Baba Tükles and Conversion to Islam in Historical and Epic Tradition* (University Park, PA, 1994), 27–8, 33–5; and for the terminology, Alan Strathern, 'Global patterns of ruler conversion to Islam and the logic of empirical religiosity', in A.C.S. Peacock (ed.), *Islamisation. Comparative Perspectives from History* (Edinburgh, 2017), 21–55 (here 25–6); more fully developed in Strathern, *Unearthly Powers. Religious and Political Change in World History* (Cambridge, 2019), chap. 1; Jonathan Brack, 'Disenchanting Heaven: Interfaith debate, sacral kingship, and conversion to Islam in the Mongol empire, 1260–1335', *Past and Present* 250 (2021), 11–53 (here 17–25); and Brack, 'Chinggisid pluralism', 817–18.
20. WR, 256 (*MFW*, 236).
21. *TJG*, I, 18: *'ulamā-u zuhhād-i har ṭā'ifarā ikrām-u i'zāz-u tabjīl mīkardast wa-dar ḥaḍrat-i ḥaqq-i ta'ālā ānrā wasīlatī mīdānist* ('he used to honour, respect and revere the learned and ascetics of every sect and recognised this as a means of access to the court of Almighty God'; cf. trans. in *HWC*, 26).
22. Ibid., I, 11, 18–19 (*HWC*, 15–16, 26); hence *Masālik*, text, 10 (German trans., 97).
23. The term employed by Morgan, *The Mongols*, 40.
24. See Elizabeth Endicott-West, 'Notes on shamans, fortune-tellers and *yin-yang* practitioners and civil administration in Yuan China', in Amitai-Preiss and Morgan (eds), *The Mongol Empire and Its Legacy*, 224–39.
25. Allsen, *Culture and Conquest in Mongol Eurasia*, 200–1.
26. Kirakos Ganjaketsʿi, *Patmut'iwn Hayots'*, tr. Robert Bedrosian, *Kirakos Ganjakets'i's History of the Armenians* (New York, 1986), 295; tr. L.A. Khanlarian, *Kirakos Gandzaketsi. Istoriia Armenii*, Pamiatniki Pis'mennosti Vostoka 53 (Moscow, 1976), 219.
27. WR, 158, 170, 172 (*MFW*, 179, 187); compare also 108, 140 (*MFW*, 141, 167–8).
28. See Christopher P. Atwood, 'Buddhists as natives: Changing positions in the religious ecology of the Mongol Yuan dynasty', in Thomas Jülch (ed.), *The Middle Kingdom and the Dharma Wheel. Aspects of the Relationship between the Buddhist Saṃgha and the State in Chinese History* (Leiden, 2016), 278–321 (here 279); Jackson, 'The Mongols and the faith of the conquered', 275–7.
29. As Chinggis Khan's commanders allegedly promised Güchülüg's subjects freedom of worship: *TJG*, I, 50 (*HWC*, 66–7). But Michal Biran, *The Empire of the Qara Khitai in Eurasian History. Between China and the Islamic World*, CSIC (Cambridge, 2005), 195, doubts that Güchülüg had forced Muslims to renounce their faith.
30. Ibn Abī l-Ḥadīd ('Izz al-Dīn Abū Ḥāmid ʿAbd al-Ḥamīd b. Hibat-Allāh), *Sharḥ Nahj al-bilāgha*, partial edn and trans. by Moktar Djebli, *Les Invasions*

mongoles en Orient vécues par un savant médiéval arabe (Paris, 1994), Ar. text, 56–7 (trans., 60–2). David Durand-Guédy, *Iranian Elites and Turkish Rulers. A History of Iṣfahān in the Saljūq Period* (London and New York, 2010), 295–7. Khwānd-Āmīr describes a similar course of events at Rayy in 1221; quoted in Richard Foltz, 'Ecumenical mischief under the Mongols', *CAJ* 43 (1999), 42–69 (here 44).

31. WR, 248 (*MFW*, 231).
32. For what follows, see Christopher P. Atwood, 'Validation by holiness or sovereignty: Religious toleration as political theology in the Mongol world empire of the thirteenth century', *International History Review* 26 (2004), 237–56 (here 252–3).
33. Jackson, 'The Mongols and the faith of the conquered', 266–8.
34. For example, Atwood, 'Validation by holiness or sovereignty', 255; Michal Biran, 'The Mongol Empire and inter-civilizational exchange', in *CWH*, V, 534–58 (here 546); May, *The Mongol Empire*, 156–7, similarly suggests that Jews, Zoroastrians and Manichaeans were all excepted 'largely as they did not have sufficient political clout'.
35. *TJG*, III, 8–9 (*HWC*, 552–3).
36. Judith Pfeiffer, 'Confessional ambiguity vs. confessional polarization: Politics in the negotiation of religious boundaries in the Ilkhanate', in Pfeiffer (ed.), *Politics, Patronage and the Transmission of Knowledge in 13th–15th Century Tabriz* (Leiden and Boston, 2014), 129–68 (here 136–7); also Pfeiffer, 'Reflections on a "double rapprochement": Conversion to Islam among the Mongol elite during the early Ilkhanate', in Komaroff (ed.), *Beyond the Legacy of Genghis Khan*, 369–89 (here 376–8).
37. Jackson, *The Mongols and the Islamic World*, 314–15.
38. *TJG*, I, 9, 159 (*HWC*, 13–14, 201).
39. *TR*, I (text), 10, II (trans.), 8. Kim Hodong, 'Muslim saints in the 14th to the 16th centuries of eastern Turkestan', *International Journal of Central Asian Studies* 1 (1996), 295–322 (here 288–9). Possibly Ḥaydar's informant was referring to the occupation of the city by the would-be Qaghan Qoshila in 1328–9 (see above, p. 83), but other conceivable contexts are the war between Qubilai and Arigh Böke in the early 1260s and Qaidu's assault on Qaraqorum in 1289.
40. *TN*, II, 151 (tr. Raverty, 1106–7).
41. *TJG*, I, 11 (*HWC*, 16).
42. *TN*, II, 212–18 (tr. Raverty, 1282–93).
43. See Jean Richard, 'La conversion de Berke et les débuts de l'islamisation de la Horde d'Or', *REI* 35 (1967), 173–84, and repr. in Richard, *Orient et Occident au moyen age: contacts et relations (XIIe-XVe s.)* (London, 1976); István Vásáry, 'History and legend in Berke Khan's conversion to Islam', in Denis Sinor (ed.), *Aspects of Altaic Civilization III* (Bloomington, IN, 1990), 230–52, and repr. in Vásáry, *Turks, Tatars and Russians*; and Devin DeWeese, 'Problems of Islamization in the Volga-Ural region: Traditions about Berke Khan', in Ali Çaksu and Radik Mukhammetshin (eds), *Proceedings of the International Symposium on Islamic Civilisation in the Volga-Ural Region, Kazan, 8–11 June 2001* (Istanbul, 2004), 3–13.
44. *TJG*, I, 226 (*HWC*, 270–1).
45. Amitai, *Holy War and Rapprochement*, 63–4.

46. Simon of Saint-Quentin, *Historia Tartarorum*, ed. Richard, 47 (excerpted from Vincent of Beauvais, xxx, 84); see Richard's n.5 at 47–8. Amitai, *Holy War and Rapprochement*, 66, suggests that these converts were Turks in the Mongols' service.
47. *TJG*, I, 11 (*HWC*, 16).
48. Sara Nur Yıldız, 'Baiju: The Mongol conqueror at the crossfire of dynastic struggle', in Biran, Brack and Fiaschetti (eds), *Along the Silk Roads*, 44–63 (here 55–6). Ishayahu Landa, 'New light on early Mongol Islamisation: The case of Arghun Aqa's family', *JRAS*, 3rd series, 28 (2018), 77–100 (here 82–4).
49. *TN*, II, 153 (tr. Raverty, 1109).
50. *TJG*, I, 222 (*HWC*, 267).
51. *TN*, II, 176 (tr. Raverty, 1171–2). See also p. 98, regarding Batu's esteem for Sayf al-Dīn Bākharzī.
52. *TJG*, III, 79 (*HWC*, 600); compare also I, 11 (*HWC*, 16). *TN*, II, 179 (tr. Raverty, 1181). See Rubruck's scornful remarks on Nestorian Christian optimism about Chinggisid conversion: WR, 82, 172 (*MFW*, 122, 187).
53. Baybars al-Manṣūrī, *Zubdat al-fikra*, 82 (also excerpted in *SMIZO*, I, Ar. text, 77, Russian trans., 99).
54. Ibn Faḍl-Allāh al-ʿUmarī, *al-Taʿrīf*, Cairo edn, 47/ed. al-Durūbī, 63.
55. IB, III, 36–8 (tr. Gibb, 558–9). Michal Biran, 'The Chaghadaids and Islam: The conversion of Tarmashirin Khan (1331–34)', *JAOS* 122 (2002), 742–52 (here 746–7 and n.43), proposing an identification for Ḥusām al-Dīn.
56. On this episode, see Jean Richard, *La Papauté et les missions d'Orient au Moyen Age (XIIIe-XVe siècles)* (Rome, 1977), 163–4; S. Maureen Burke, 'The *Martyrdom of the Franciscans* by Ambrogio Lorenzetti', *Zeitschrift für Kulturgeschichte* 65 (2002), 460–92.
57. For the date, see *TR*, I (text), 18–19, II (trans.), 14.
58. Judith Pfeiffer, 'Aḥmad Tegüder's second letter to Qalā'ūn (682/1283)', in Pfeiffer and Quinn (eds), *History and Historiography of Post-Mongol Central Asia*, 167–202 (here 173–4). Jackson, *The Mongols and the Islamic World*, 366–7.
59. As suggested by Pfeiffer, 'Reflections on a "double rapprochement"', 371–2.
60. WR, 194 (*MFW*, 199).
61. Jonathan Brack, 'Theologies of auspicious kingship: The Islamization of Chinggisid sacral kingship in the Islamic world', *CSSH* 60 (2018), 1141–71 (here 1151). Brack, 'Disenchanting Heaven', 24. Ishayahu Landa, 'The Islamization of the Mongols', in May and Hope (eds), *The Mongol World*, 642–61 (here 645, 647).
62. Herbert Franke, *From Tribal Chieftain to Universal Emperor and God. The Legitimation of the Yüan Dynasty* (Munich, 1978 = *Sitzungsberichte der bayerischen Akademie der Wissenschaften, philosophisch-historische Klasse*, 2), 79.
63. See Liu Haiwei, 'Rulership and representations: Reconsidering the religious identity of Prince Ananda', *CAJ* 64 (2021), 165–81, and Vered Shurany, 'Prince Manggala – the forgotten Prince of Anxi', in Biran (ed.), *In the Service of the Khans*, 1169–88 (here 1177–81).
64. Shams al-Dīn Abū ʿAbd-Allāh Muḥammad b. ʿUthmān al-Dhahabī, *Taʾrīkh al-Islām wa-wafayāt al-mashāhīr wa l-aʿlām*, ed. ʿUmar ʿAbd al-Salām Tadmurī, 53 vols (Beirut, 1415–24/1995–2004), LIII, 330. Hence Ṣalāḥ al-Dīn Khalīl b. Aybak al-Ṣafadī, *al-Wāfī bi l-wafayāt*, ed. Helmut Ritter et al., *Das biographische Lexikon des Ṣalāḥaddīn Ḫalīl b. Aybak aṣ-Ṣafadī*, 32 vols, BI 6

(Istanbul, Leipzig, Wiesbaden and Beirut, 1931–2013), X, 382–3; and idem, *A'yān al-'aṣr wa-a'wān al-naṣr*, ed. Fāliḥ Aḥmad al-Bakkūr, 4 vols (Beirut, 1419/1998), I, 523.
65. DeWeese, *Islamization and Native Religion*, 108–13, with a survey of the data in the various sources. Favereau, *The Horde*, 217–18. Roman Hautala warns against taking the accounts of Muslim chroniclers too seriously here: see his 'Comparing the Islamisation of the Jochid and Hülegüid *uluses*: Muslim and Christian perspectives', in Favereau (ed.), *La Horde d'Or et l'islamisation*, 65–79 (here 73–6).
66. *TR*, I (text), 12, II (trans.), 10.
67. Ibid., I (text), 36, II (trans.), 31. On him, see p. 201.
68. Baybars al-Manṣūrī, *Zubdat al-fikra*, 82 (also excerpted in *SMIZO*, I, Ar. text, 77, Russian trans., 99).
69. Jackson, *The Mongols and the Islamic World*, 343–4.
70. I agree, however, with Allsen, 'Changing forms of legitimation in Mongol Iran', 234–5, that in projecting themselves as Muslim monarchs Ghazan and his successors certainly had an eye to their own Muslim subjects.
71. *JT*, II, 1289–90 (*DzhT*, III, 332–3; *CC*, 449–50). Waṣṣāf (1853), 372, line 20–373, line 11 (*GW*, III, 273–4).
72. Anne F. Broadbridge, *Kingship and Ideology in the Islamic and Mongol Worlds*, CSIC (Cambridge, 2008), 65–6.
73. Troopers: *JT*, I, 29 (*DzhT*, I, part 1, 56; *CC*, 12). Noyans: ibid., II, 1255 (*DzhT*, III, 297; *CC*, 438). Waṣṣāf (1853), 317, line 3 (*GW*, III, 141).
74. *TR*, I (text), 13, II (trans.), 11.
75. Ḥamd-Allāh Mustawfī Qazwīnī, *Ta'rīkh-i guzīda*, ed. ʿAbd al-Ḥusayn Nawā'ī (Tehran, 1339 sh./1960), 586. *Masālik*, text, 38, 41 (German trans., 117, 119).
76. *Masālik*, text, 38–9, *fa-minhum man kāna qad sabaqa islāmahu* (German trans., 117, misleadingly renders this as 'manche von ihnen. . . .').
77. Ibid., text, 41 (German trans., 119).
78. John E. Woods, *The Timurid Dynasty*, PIA 14 (Bloomington, IN, 1990), 12. Biran, 'The Chaghadaids and Islam', 751, citing Waṣṣāf. See further Devin DeWeese, 'Islamization in the Mongol empire', in *CHIA*, 120–34 (here 131).
79. Charles Melville, '*Pādishāh-i Islām*: The conversion of Sultan Maḥmūd Ghāzān Khān', in Melville (ed.), *Persian and Islamic Studies in Honour of P.W. Avery* (Cambridge, 1990 = *Pembroke Papers* 1), 159–77 (esp. 171). Amitai, *Holy War and Rapprochement*, 64–9. See also the comments of DeWeese, 'Problems of Islamization', 10–11, regarding Berke's conversion.
80. Landa, 'The Islamization of the Mongols', 653.
81. Reuven Amitai, 'Towards a pre-history of the Islamization of the Turks: A re-reading of Ibn Faḍlān's *Riḥla*', in Étienne de la Vaissière (ed.), *Islamisation de l'Asie centrale. Processus locaux d'acculturation du VIIe au XIe siècle*, StIr cahier 39 (Paris, 2008), 277–96. See too Gerald Mako, 'The Islamization of the Volga Bulgars: A question reconsidered', *AEMA* 18 (2011), 199–223.
82. Bruno De Nicola, 'The role of the domestic sphere in the Islamisation of the Mongols', in Peacock (ed.), *Islamisation*, 353–76 (esp. 357–64).
83. Waṣṣāf (1853), 518, lines 13–16 (BALYĠW in error)/(2009), 285 (*GW*, IV, 315). Qāshānī, *Ta'rīkh-i Uljāytū Sulṭān*, 147. For his mother, see also *SP*, fo. 118b.

84. István Vásáry, 'The institution of foster-brothers (*emildāš* and *kökeldāš*) in the Chingisid states', *AOH* 36 (1982), 549–62; repr. in Vásáry, *Turks, Tatars and Russians*. Jackson, *The Mongols and the Islamic World*, 349–50.
85. Landa, 'New light on early Mongol Islamisation', 90–3.
86. Kirakos, tr. Bedrosian, 327/tr. Khanlarian, 235.
87. See Landa, 'New light on early Mongol Islamisation', 98–9.
88. *TN*, II, 195 (tr. Raverty, 1247). Jamāl al-Qarshī, *al-Mulḥaqāt bi l-Ṣurāḥ*, ed. and trans. Sh.Kh. Vokhidov and B.B. Aminov, in *IKPI*, I (Almaty, 2005), Ar. text, 165 (Russian trans., 120); also in *Turkestan*[1], I, 136. *Masālik*, text, 16 (German trans., 101). al-Dhahabī, *Ta'rīkh al-Islām*, XLVIII, 387; and see next note.
89. al-Dhahabī, *Siyar a'lām al-nubalā'*, ed. Bashshār 'Awwād Ma'rūf and Muḥyī Halāl al-Sirḥān (Beirut, 1405/1985), XXIII, 366. For other Chinggisids who respected Bākharzī, see Biran, 'The Mamluks and Mongol Central Asia', 384.
90. *TJG*, III, 9 (*HWC*, 552–3).
91. Reuven Amitai-Preiss, 'Sufis and shamans: Some remarks on the Islamization of the Mongols in the Ilkhanate', *JESHO* 42 (1999), 27–46; repr. in Amitai, *The Mongols in the Islamic Lands*. See also Devin DeWeese, 'Khwaja Ahmad Yasavi as an Islamising saint: Rethinking the role of sufis in the Islamisation of the Turks of Central Asia', in Peacock (ed.), *Islamisation*, 336–52.
92. See Pfeiffer, 'Reflections on a "double rapprochement"', 377–88.
93. DeWeese, *Islamization and Native Religion*, 140–2.
94. Amitai, *Holy War and Rapprochement*, 65, citing Baybars al-Manṣūrī, *Zubdat al-fikra*, 11. Landa, 'New light on early Mongol Islamisation', 97–8, citing al-Dhahabī, *Ta'rīkh al-Islām*, LV [XLVII in my numbering], 454–5.
95. Amitai, *Holy War and Rapprochement*, 66–7.
96. Landa, 'New light on early Mongol Islamisation', 99.
97. Xiangmai, *Zhiyuan bianweilu*, tr. in P.Y. Saeki, *The Nestorian Documents and Relics in China*, 2nd edn (Tokyo, 1951), appendix XV(A).
98. For a fuller argument, see Jackson, *The Mongols and the West*, 314–16.
99. Strathern, 'Global patterns of ruler conversion', 26–7 and passim.
100. Judith Pfeiffer, 'Conversion versions: Sultan Öljeytü's conversion to Shi'ism (709/1309) in Muslim narrative sources', *MS* 22 (1999), 35–67.
101. Qāshānī, *Ta'rīkh-i Uljāytū Sulṭān*, 99. Pfeiffer, 'Confessional ambiguity', 145, 159, and 'Conversion versions', 40, 41. Nagel, *Timur der Eroberer*, 71–3.
102. Qāshānī, *Ta'rīkh-i Uljāytū Sulṭān*, 93; ibid., 99, Öljeitü is told that Ghazan had chosen Shi'ism. Pfeiffer, 'Confessional ambiguity', 143–8 and 'Conversion versions', 40. On Ghazan's views, see Michael Hope, *Power, Politics, and Tradition in the Mongol Empire and the Īlkhānate of Iran* (Oxford, 2016), 174–7.
103. Igor de Rachewiltz, 'Heaven, Earth and the Mongols in the time of Činggis Qan and his immediate successors (*c*. 1160–1260) – a preliminary investigation', in Noël Golvers and Sara Lievens (eds), *A Lifelong Dedication to the China Mission. Essays Presented in Honor of Father Jeroom Heyndrickx, C.I.C.M., on the Occasion of His 75th Birthday and the 25th Anniversary of the F. Verbiest Institute K.U. Leuven*, Leuven Chinese Studies 17 (Leuven, 2007), 107–44 (here 127). See Brack, 'Chinggisid pluralism', 832, 837–8, on the manner in which 'Alā' al-Dawla Simnānī and Rashīd al-Dīn handled the analogy.

104. Dechant, 'Depictions of the Islamization of the Mongols', 151–2.
105. *TJG*, I, 16–17 (*HWC*, 23–4). Brack, 'Theologies of auspicious kingship', 1149–50.
106. *JT*, II, 1345, 1348 (*DzhT*, III, 386, 389; *CC*, 467–9). Hope, *Power, Politics, and Tradition*, 179–80. Pfeiffer, 'Confessional ambiguity', 154–5. Brack, 'Theologies of auspicious kingship', 1163–4.
107. Shabānkāra'ī, *Majma' al-ansāb*, 223.
108. Waṣṣāf (1853), 241, lines 3–4 (*GW*, II, 214–15). For other indications that Mongol rulers were credited with prophetic gifts, see Brack, 'Theologies of auspicious kingship', 1164–5.
109. Brack, 'Theologies of auspicious kingship', esp. 1152–60.
110. See especially *JT*, I, 27, and II, 951–2 (*DzhT*, I, part 1, 51; *SGK*, 324; *CC*, 11, 330); Jackson, *The Mongols and the Islamic World*, 374–5, for other references in *JT*, and 376 for similar depictions by later historians.
111. *TJG*, I, 1 (trans. in *HWC*, 3, modified). See also Dechant, 'Depictions of the Islamization of the Mongols', 147–51.
112. As Brack, 'Theologies of auspicious kingship', 1167, points out.
113. Christopher P. Atwood, 'Explaining rituals and writing history: Tactics against the intermediate class', in Isabelle Charleux et al. (eds), *Representing Power in Ancient Inner Asia: Legitimacy, Transmission and the Sacred*, SEA 30 (Bellingham, WA, 2010), 95–129.
114. Franke, *From Tribal Chieftain*, esp. 52, 54–7; for later developments in Buddhist thought on this subject, see ibid., 64 ff.; Elverskog, *Our Great Qing*. Brack, 'Theologies of auspicious kingship', 1167.
115. Jens Wilkens, 'Buddhism in the West Uyghur kingdom and beyond', in Carmen Meinert (ed.), *Transfer of Buddhism across Central Asian Networks (7th to 13th Centuries)* (Leiden and Boston, MA, 2016), 191–249 (here 240–2). A *bodhisattva* was one who had attained enlightenment but remained in the world.
116. Michael Weiers, 'Die Mongolen und der Koran', in Rybatzki et al. (eds), *The Early Mongols*, 209–17 (here 215).
117. Brack, 'Theologies of auspicious kingship', 1167–8.
118. Hope, *Power, Politics, and Tradition*, 176–80. Peacock, *Islam, Literature and Society*, 221. Brack, 'Theologies of auspicious kingship', 1159.
119. Brack, 'Theologies of auspicious kingship', 1168; and see also his 'Chinggisid pluralism', 830–8, and now *An Afterlife for the Khan*, chaps 3–4.
120. Mustafa Banister, '"Nought remains to the Caliph but his title": Revisiting Abbasid authority in Mamluk Cairo', *MSR* 18 (2014–15), 219–45, and his *The Abbasid Caliphate of Cairo, 1261–1517* (Edinburgh, 2021). Hassan, *Longing for the Lost Caliphate*, chap. 2.
121. John E. Woods, *The Aqquyunlu: Clan, Confederation, Empire*, revised edn (Salt Lake City, UT, 1999), 7. But see p. 369 and n.72 at p. 619, for some late fourteenth-century examples.
122. Yazdī, *ZN* (1957), I, 69–9/(2008), I, 302.
123. *TJG*, III, 38 (*HWC*, 573).
124. WR, 86 (*MFW*, 127).
125. *TN*, II, 214 (tr. Raverty, 1285).
126. al-Dhahabī, *Siyar al-a'lām al-nubalā'*, XXIII, 366.
127. Baybars al-Manṣūrī, *Zubdat al-fikra*, 82 (also excerpted in *SMIZO*, I, Ar. text, 77, Russian trans., 99).

128. Waṣṣāf (1853), 110, line 5 (*GW*, I, text, 225, trans., 209).
129. Ibid. (1853), 324, lines 10–13 (GW, III, 159).
130. See the comment of DeWeese, 'Problems of Islamization', 13.
131. Devin DeWeese, 'Cultural transmission and exchange in the Mongol empire: Notes from the biographical dictionary of Ibn al-Fuwaṭī', in Komaroff (ed.), *Beyond the Legacy of Genghis Khan*, 11–29 (here 21).
132. IB, III, 47–8 (tr. Gibb, 565). Biran, 'The Chaghadaids and Islam', 748. Hautala, 'Comparing the Islamisation', 72, proposes that Tarmashirin 'had significantly restricted the religious autonomy of local Christians and Buddhists'.
133. Shams al-Dīn Abū ʿAbd-Allāh Muḥammad al-Jazarī, *Ḥawādith al-zamān wa-anbāʾihi wa-wafayāt al-akābir wa l-aʿyān min abnāʾihi*, ed. ʿUmar ʿAbd al-Salām Tadmurī, 3 vols (Ṣaydā, 1419/1998), I, 286.
134. Jackson, *The Mongols and the Islamic World*, 369–70.
135. ʾGos lo-tsā-ba gZon-nu-dpal, *Debther sṅon-po*, tr. George N. Roerich, *The Blue Annals*, 2 vols (Calcutta, 1949; repr. in 1 vol., Delhi, 1979), 504.
136. Ibid., 501, 502, 504.
137. Irina Shingiray, 'An Islamicate body: A case study of a nomadic burial from the core territory of the Golden Horde', in Favereau (ed.), *La Horde d'Or et l'islamisation*, 83–105. For the Seljuqs, see Nicholas Morton, 'The Saljuq Turks' conversion to Islam: The Crusading sources', *Al-Masāq* 27 (2015), 109–18 (here 112).
138. al-Ṣafadī, *al-Wāfī bi l-wafayāt*, XXV, 229–30. Reuven Amitai-Preiss, 'Ghazan, Islam and Mongol tradition: A view from the Mamlūk Sultanate', *BSOAS* 59 (1996), 1–10 (here 2–3); repr. in Hawting (ed.), *Muslims, Mongols and Crusaders*, 253–62 (here 254–5), and in Amitai, *The Mongols and the Islamic Lands*. For other examples of levirate marriage by Muslim Ilkhans, see Jackson, *The Mongols and the Islamic World*, 364.
139. DeWeese, *Islamization and Native Religion*, 118–21.
140. *TR*, I (text), 56, II (trans.), 47–8; cited by James Millward, 'Eastern Central Asia (Xinjiang): 1300–1800', in *CHIA*, 260–76 (here 264). Dūst Muḥammad died not long afterwards.
141. Interestingly, a Ming envoy who visited the Timurid lands in 1414–15 comments (in the context of Herat?) that marriage between a younger brother and the elder brother's widow was common: Morris Rossabi, 'A translation of Ch'en Ch'eng's *Hsi-yü fan-kuo chih*', *Ming Studies* 17 (1983), 49–59 (here 51).
142. *TR*, I (text), 55, 65–6, II (trans.), 47, 54–5.
143. Ibid., I (text), 267, II (trans.), 207. This is expressly said to be in accordance with the custom of *yengelik*, for which see *TMEN*, IV, 206–7 (no. 1907: *yengä*, 'Stiefmutter: Gattin des älteren Bruders bzw. des Vaters . . .'), and *EDT*, 950.
144. Salmānī, *Shams al-ḥusn*, text, fo. 164b (German trans., 120).
145. See the salutary comments of Devin DeWeese, 'Muslims and infidel nomads in Timurid Central Asia: Four stories from the religious frontiers of Mawarannahr in the 14th and 15th centuries', in István Zimonyi and Osman Karatay (eds), *Central Eurasia in the Middle Ages. Studies in Honour of Peter B. Golden*, Turcologica 104 (Wiesbaden, 2016), 91–102 (here 91–2).
146. See, for example, 'Introduction', in Arietta Papaconstantinou (ed., with Neil McLynn and Daniel L. Schwartz), *Conversion in Late Antiquity: Christianity, Islam, and Beyond* (Farnham and Burlington, VT, 2015), xvi–xvii.

147. Thus James C. Russell, *The Germanization of Early Medieval Christianity. A Sociohistorical Approach to Religious Transformation* (Oxford, 1994).
148. DeWeese, *Islamization and Native Religion*, 51–9, includes a cogent discussion of this issue.
149. For examples, see Peacock, *Islam, Literature and Society*, 66–7.
150. IB, III, 39–40 (tr. Gibb, 560, 565).
151. See Jackson, *The Delhi Sultanate*, 234.
152. Yazdī, *ZN* (1972), fo. 81a/(2008), I, 217: *az ḥulya-yi islām ʿārī būd*. In the early fifteenth century Buzan's reign was still a byword (*ḍarb al-mathal*) for upheaval: Naṭanzī (1957), 112–13/(2004), 91.
153. Ḥamd-Allāh Mustawfī Qazwīnī, *Ẓafar-nāma*, facsimile edn by Naṣr-Allāh Pūrjawādī and Nuṣrat-Allāh Rastagār, *Ẓafar-nāma von Ḥamdallāh Mustaufī und Šāhnāma von Abu'l-Qāsim Firdausī*, 2 vols (Tehran, 1377 sh., and Vienna, 1999), II, 1292, line 12; partial trans. by Leonard J. Ward, 'The Ẓafar-Nāmah of Ḥamdallāh Mustaufī and the Il-Khan Dynasty of Iran', unpublished Ph.D. thesis, University of Manchester, 1983, 3 vols, II, 269.
154. Buqa, whose father *Yula Temür had been killed by Tegüder Aḥmad: ibid., II, 1165 (Ward trans., II, 4, calls the son 'Baqā'ī' and his father 'Bolād Timūr'). On *Yula Temür, see *SP*, fo. 146b; Ḥamd-Allāh Mustawfī Qazwīnī, *Ta'rīkh-i guzīda*, 595, 814.
155. *JT*, II, 1176 (*DzhT*, III, 170; *CC*, 389). Reuven Amitai, 'The conversion of Tegüder Ilkhan to Islam', *JSAI* 25 (2001), 15–43 (here 17), and repr. in Amitai, *The Mongols in the Islamic Lands*, adopts the first of these meanings.
156. Not in the Rawshan and Mūsawī edn of *JT* or in *CC*; but see *DzhT*, III, 616 (from the mss. in BN and the Institut Vostokovedeniia, Leningrad).
157. Budge, *The Chronography of Gregory Abû'l Faraj*, I (trans.), 505. See also Stepʿanos Orbelian, *Patmutʿiwn nahangin Sisakan*, tr. M.-F. Brosset, *Histoire de la Siounie* (St Petersburg, 1864–6), I, 260. But compare Karīm al-Dīn Maḥmūd b. Muḥammad Āqsarā'ī, *Musāmarat al-akhbār*, ed. Osman Turan, *Müsâmeret ül-ahbâr. Mogollar zamanında türkiye Selçukluları tarihi* (Ankara, 1944), 185–6, quoted by Peacock, *Islam, Literature and Society in Mongol Anatolia*, 67, on Baidu's antipathy towards Islam.
158. For what follows, see Denise Aigle, 'A religious response to Ghazan Khan's invasions of Syria: The three "Anti-Mongol" *fatwā*s of Ibn Taymiyya', in Aigle, *The Mongol Empire between Myth and Reality*, 283–305; Aigle, 'Ghazan Khan's invasions of Syria: Polemics on his conversion to Islam and the Christian troops in his army', ibid., 255–82; also Pfeiffer, 'Confessional ambiguity', 158–9.
159. Ibn al-Dawādārī, *Kanz al-durar*, IX, ed. Hans Robert Roemer, *Der Bericht über den Sultan al-Malik an-Nāṣir Muḥammad ibn Qala'un* (Cairo, 1379/1960), 32. Quṭb al-Dīn Mūsā b. Muḥammad al-Yūnīnī (d. 726/1326), *Dhayl Mir'āt al-zamān*, partial edn and trans. by Li Guo, *Early Mamluk Syrian Historiography*, 2 vols, IHC 21 (Leiden, Boston, MA, and Cologne, 1998), I (trans.), 158, II (text), 119; also the complete edn by ʿAbbās Hānī Jarrākh, in Sibṭ Ibn al-Jawzī, *Mir'āt al-zamān*, and al-Yūnīnī, *Dhayl Mir'āt al-zamān* (Beirut, 1434/2013), XXI, 120. K.V. Zetterstéen (ed.), *Beiträge zur Geschichte der Mamlūkensultane in den Jahren 690–741 der Hiğra nach arabischen Handschriften* (Leiden, 1919), 76. Brack, 'Chinggisid pluralism', 838. Aigle, 'A religious response', 301, states that Qutlughshāh described Chinggis Khan as the seal of the prophets, but this is not borne out by the sources.

160. See Pfeiffer's comments in 'The canonization of cultural memory', 58–62.
161. For example, the Ilkhan Gaikhatu: Morgan, 'The Great *Yāsā* of Chingiz Khān', 171; repr. in Hawting (ed.), *Muslims, Mongols and Crusaders*, 206. The theme surfaces also in the account of an apocryphal rebellion against the Yuan Emperor given in IB, IV, 300 (tr. Gibb and Beckingham, 908).
162. IB, III, 40–1 (tr. Gibb, 560–1).
163. Tegüder Aḥmad: Waṣṣāf (1853), 132, lines 14–15 (*GW*, I, text, 270, trans., 252): the charge is here put into the mouth of the amir Aruq. Tarmashirin: al-Dhahabī, *Ta'rīkh al-Islām*, LIII, 330; al-Ṣafadī, *al-Wāfī bi l-wafayāt*, X, 382-3, and *A'yān al-'aṣr*, I, 523.
164. Waṣṣāf (1853), 327, lines 18–19 (cf. *GW*, III, 167).
165. Qāshānī, *Ta'rīkh-i Uljāytū Sulṭān*, 98.
166. Morgan, *The Mongols*, 142, and *Medieval Persia*, 73. See Qur'ān, iv, 27; Schacht, 'Nikāḥ, 1', *EI*².
167. Cleaves, 'The rescript of Qubilai', 73 and n.116 at 88.
168. Qāshānī, *Ta'rīkh-i Uljāytū Sulṭān*, 98. The ms. Ayasofya 3019 of Qāshānī's work here reads *yāsāq-u yusūn-i naw* (fo. 43b), but the adjective *naw* is omitted in the printed text: Morgan, 'The "Great *Yasa* of Chinggis Khan" revisited', 304, n.38.
169. Qāshānī, *Ta'rīkh-i Uljāytū Sulṭān*, 145; cited by Vásáry, '*Yāsā* and *Sharī'a*', 67.
170. *JT*, II, 1278 (*DzhT*, III, 320; *CC*, 446). On the other hand, in his notices on Qutlughshāh, al-Ṣafadī, *al-Wāfī bi l-wafayāt*, XIII, 348, and *A'yān al-'aṣr*, II, 666–7, labels him an infidel.

4: THE CRISIS OF THE MONGOL WORLD: CHINGGISID RULE ON THE WANE

1. IB, III, 31 (tr. Gibb, 556). For the other two 'great kings', that is the Sultans of Morocco and of Egypt, see ibid., II, 382 (tr. Gibb, 482–3).
2. Ibid., III, 201 (tr. Gibb, 648–9): his informant was the Suhrawardī shaykh Rukn al-Dīn, whom he met in Multān. See further p. 208.
3. On the uncertain titulature of the dynasty, particularly after 1388, see David M. Robinson, *In the Shadow of the Mongol Empire. Ming China and Eurasia* (Cambridge, 2020), 49–52.
4. David M. Robinson, *Ming China and Its Allies. Imperial Rule in Eurasia* (Cambridge, 2020), 29, 31.
5. The list of Qaghans given by Khwānd-Amīr includes three from Arigh Böke's line after 1412: *Ḥabīb al-siyar fī akhbār afrād al-bashar*, ed. Jalāl Humā'ī, 4 vols (Tehran, 1333 sh./1954), III, 73–4; tr. Wheeler M. Thackston, *Classical Writings of the Medieval Islamic World. Persian Histories of the Mongol Dynasties*, II (London and New York, 2012), 41. But Yesüder, who usurped the throne in 1388, may also have belonged to that branch. See M. Honda, 'On the genealogy of the early Northern Yüan', *UAJ* 30 (1958), 232–48 (here 236–47); and for a fuller discussion, Robinson, *In the Shadow of the Mongol Empire*, 82–4.
6. John Masson Smith, Jr, 'Dietary decadence and dynastic decline in the Mongol empire', *JAH* 34 (2000), 35–52. But compare Charles Melville, 'The end of the Ilkhanate and after: Observations on the collapse of the Mongol world empire', in De Nicola and Melville (eds), *The Mongols' Middle East*, 309–35 (here 318–19), arguing that such excess did not have the same effect in other

Chinggisid states as in the Ilkhanate but conceding that nevertheless 'something seems to have been wrong with the genetic composition of the ruling family'.

7. George Qingzhi Zhao, 'Population decadence and dynastic decline in the Mongol Empire', in Michael Gervers and Wayne Schlepp (eds), *Continuity and Change in Central and Inner Asia* (Toronto, 2002), 21–33. Broadbridge, *Women and the Making of the Mongol Empire*, 227, however, cites medical opinion to the contrary.
8. See David O. Morgan, 'The decline and fall of the Mongol empire', *JRAS*, 3rd series, 19 (2009), 427–37 (here 433). But for the view that the succession to Abū Saʿīd was not the sole reason for the collapse of the Ilkhanate, see Melville, 'The end of the Ilkhanate', esp. 312–13, 318–22.
9. Ötemish Ḥājjī, *Chingīz-nāma*, ed. and transcribed by Takushi Kawaguchi, Hiroyuki Nagamine and Mutsumi Sugahara, *Ötämiš Ḥājī. Čingīz-nāma* (Tokyo, 2008), text, 32, says expressly that nobody from the line of Sayin Khan (as Batu was known posthumously) remained. Naṭanzī (1957), 85/(2004), 70, appears to say this also. See Ilnur Mirgaleev, 'The Time of Troubles in the 1360s and 1370s', in Khakimov et al. (eds), *The Golden Horde in World History*, 689–92 (here 690).
10. Favereau, *The Horde*, 275.
11. Michael Hope, 'The *atābak*s in the Mongol empire and the Ilkhanate of Iran (602–736/1206–1335)', in May et al. (eds), *New Approaches to Ilkhanid History*, 321–45 (here 338–40). For the early history of the style *atabeg* ('father beg/amir', i.e. guardian to a young prince), which had first emerged under the Seljuqs, see Cl. Cahen, 'Atabak', *EI²*, I, 731–2.
12. Jean Aubin, *Émirs mongols et vizirs persans dans les remous de l'acculturation*, StIr Cahier 15 (Paris, 1995), 85, therefore sees Abū Saʿīd, during his minority, as 'le premier des Ilkhâns-fantoches'.
13. See Hope, *Power, Politics, and Tradition*, 190–4, 196.
14. In chapter 13 of his *The Mongol Empire*, entitled 'Conclusion: End of the Chinggisids and the rise of the Qarachu'. See also the remarks of Woods, *The Aqquyunlu*, 7–8.
15. Peter B. Golden, *An Introduction to the History of the Turkic Peoples. Ethnogenesis and State-Formation in Medieval and Early Modern Eurasia and the Middle East*, Turcologica 9 (Wiesbaden, 1992), 240.
16. Veit, 'The eastern steppe', 161–3. May, *The Mongol Empire*, 344–6. Hok-lam Chan, 'Naqaču the Grand Marshall, a Mongol warlord in Manchuria during the Yuan-Ming transition', in Rybatzki et al. (eds), *The Early Mongols*, 31–46.
17. For a survey of the vicissitudes of the period 1335–1357, see Bertold Spuler, *Die Mongolen in Iran: Politik, Verwaltung und Kultur der Ilchanzeit 1220–1350*, 4th edn (Leiden, 1985), 107–15; Wing, *The Jalayirids*, chap. 5. Melville, *The Fall of Amir Chupan*, 45–59, covers the months down to the end of 1337 in greater detail.
18. Naṭanzī (1957), 170/(2004), 140, for his marriage to the wazir's daughter.
19. Only Ḥamd-Allāh Mustawfī Qazwīnī, *Dhayl-i Taʾrīkh-i guzīda*, ed. V.Z. Piriiev (Baku, 1978), text, 440, and tr. M.D. Kazimov and V.Z. Piriiev (Baku, 1986), 98, specifies the date of the birth. Shabānkāraʾī, *Majmaʿ al-ansāb*, 293, simply places it seven months after Abū Saʿīd's death.
20. Ḥamd-Allāh Mustawfī Qazwīnī, *Dhayl*, ed. Piriiev, text, 436, 437; tr. Kazimov and Piriiev, 92, 93–4.

21. The date given ibid., ed. Piriiev, text, 440; tr. Kazimov and Piriiev, 97. P. Jackson, 'Arpā Khan', *EIr*, II, 518–19.
22. Jean Aubin, 'Le *quriltai* de Sultân-Maydân (1336)', *JA* 279 (1991), 175–97, and repr. in Aubin, *Études*, 279–97. He is frequently called Togha Temür in the secondary literature, but I have adopted the spelling as established by John Masson Smith, Jr, *The History of the Sarbadār Dynasty 1336–1381 A.D. and Its Sources* (The Hague and Paris, 1970), 181–2. Ḥamd-Allāh Mustawfī Qazwīnī, *Dhayl*, ed. Piriiev, text, 443/tr. Kazimov and Piriiev, 101, makes it clear that Shaykh ʿAlī was opposed to Shaykh Ḥasan. Wing, *The Jalayirids*, 85, incorrectly calls Taghai Temür a descendant of Otchigin (Temüge).
23. One wonders whether similar considerations underlie the assertion by Waṣṣāf (1853), 561, lines 12–18/(2009), 378–9, that Chinggis Khan, angered by Jochi Qasar's late arrival at a rendezvous, issued a *yasa* prohibiting any of Qasar's descendants from obtaining the dignity of khan, and that in view of the demotion of his line they were classed as equal in status to *qarachu* amirs. But Waṣṣāf, as far as we know, completed his work in 727/1326–7 or 728/1327–8, well before Abū Saʿīd's death. For a lost source documenting Qasar's offences, see Atwood, 'Rashīd al-Dīn's Ghazanid Chronicle', 100–2. I have preferred Waṣṣāf's version (despite his statement that Qasar was younger than Temüge Otchigin) to the directly contrary but briefer statement in *JT*, I, 275 (*CC*, 97), that Qasar's progeny were the only descendants of any of Chinggis Khan's brothers who were permitted to sit among the princes, whereas the rest were ranked among the amirs.
24. See Michael Hope, 'The political configuration of late Ilkhanid Iran: A case study of the Chubanid Amirate (738–758/1337–1357)', *Iran*, DOI: 10.1080/05786967.2021.1889930 (I am very grateful to Dr. Hope for forwarding his article), 1–17 (here 10).
25. As specified by Abū Bakr Quṭbī Ahrī, *Taʾrīkh-i Shaykh Uways*, ed. and tr. J.B. Van Loon, *Taʾrīkh-i Shaikh Uwais. An Important Source for the History of Ādharbaijān in the Fourteenth Century* (The Hague, 1954), text, 166, trans., 67.
26. The figure given ibid., text, 167, trans., 68; but coins were issued in Sulaymān's name for a longer period (see later).
27. See Hans R. Roemer, 'The Jalayirids, Muzaffarids and Sarbadārs', in *CHI*, VI, 1–41 (here 22–4); also C.P. Melville, 'Sarbadārids', *EI*², IX, 47–8.
28. See the anonymous *Dhayl-i Taʾrīkh-i guzīda*, ed. Otsuka, text, 194; his death is dated in Muḥarram 757 [Jan.–Feb. 1356], ibid., 195. For his coins, which go down to 756/1355, see Alexander V. Akopyan and Farbod Mosanef, 'Between Jūjīds [*sic*] and Jalāyirids: The coinage of the Chopānids, Akhījūq and their contemporaries, 754–759/1353–1358', *Der Islam* 92 (2015), 197–246 (here 210–11).
29. Stephen Album, 'Studies in Ilkhanid history and numismatics, I. A late Ilkhanid hoard (743/1342)', *StIr* 13 (1984), 49–116 (here 84, 95). Ḥamd-Allāh Mustawfī Qazwīnī, *Dhayl*, ed. Piriiev, text, 462/tr. Kazimov and Piriiev, 125, indicates that Jahān Temür was discarded prior to the spring of 1341. On his brief reign, see Charles Melville, 'Jahān Timūr', *EIr*, XIV, 385–6.
30. Album, 'Studies in Ilkhanid history and numismatics, I', 100.
31. Ibid., 80.
32. For what follows, see Broadbridge, *Kingship and Ideology*, 139–45; Patrick Wing, 'The decline of the Ilkhanate and the Mamluk Sultanate's eastern

frontier', *MSR* 11, part 2 (2007), 77–88; also Wing, *The Jalayirids*, 89–91. For the Mamlūk perspective he relies on the fifteenth-century author al-Maqrīzī. But al-Yūsufī and al-Shujāʿī, at least, furnish more detail than does al-Maqrīzī. On al-Yūsufī's vast general history down to 755/1354, of which only the years 733–8 survive, see Donald Presgrave Little, 'The recovery of a lost source for Baḥrī Mamlūk history: Al-Yūsufī's *Nuzhat al-nāẓir fī sīrat al-Malik al-Nāṣir*', *JAOS* 94 (1974), 42–54; for the date of composition of al-Shujāʿī's *Ta'rīkh al-Malik al-Nāṣir Muḥammad b. Qalāwūn al-Ṣāliḥī wa-awlādihi*, see the edn and trans. by Barbara Schäfer (Wiesbaden, 1977–85), II (trans.), 5. al-Yūsufī was al-Shujāʿī's chief source.

33. Anne F. Broadbridge, 'Diplomatic conventions in the Mamluk Sultanate', *Annales Islamologiques* 41 (2007), 97–118 (here 108). More briefly in Broadbridge, *Kingship and Ideology*, 139.
34. Broadbridge, *Kingship and Ideology*, 148–56. On al-Nāṣir Muḥammad's successors, see generally Carl F. Petry, *The Mamluk Sultanate: A History* (Cambridge, 2022), 20–3.
35. IB, III, 256–8 (tr. Gibb, 677–9). Ḥājjī Ke'ün is otherwise unknown and does not appear in *MA*.
36. For a more complete list, see Roemer, 'The Jalayirids, Muzaffarids and Sarbadārs', 4.
37. Zayn al-Dīn (1990), text, 481 (Russian trans., 108)/(1993), 57–8.
38. Ahrī, *Ta'rīkh-i Shaykh Uways*, text, 177, trans., 77: Ashraf's response is cited by Wing, *The Jalayirids*, 104. For Ghazan (II), see Akopyan and Mosanef, 'Between Jūjīds and Jalāyirids', 209, 213–16, 218–19. The anonymous *Dhayl-i Ta'rīkh-i guzīda*, ed. Otsuka, text, 195, makes Ghazan a son of Anūshīrwān Khan; but this is probably an error, since he appears (significantly, as 'Qazān Pādishāh') among Taghai Temür's sons in *MA*, fo. 12a, ed. Vokhidov, text, 25 (Russian trans., 28); Faryūmadī, *Dhayl-i Majma' al-ansāb*, 328–9, says that this prince had been captured by the Sarbadārs when they defeated Taghai Temür's brother ʿAlī Ke'ün at Zāwa (743/1342). The assumption by Aubin, 'Le khanat de Čaġatai', 38–9, that Ghazan disappeared thereafter is thus presumably wrong.
39. Anonymous *Dhayl-i Ta'rīkh-i guzīda*, ed. Otsuka, text, 195; and for the date of the invasion, ibid., 196. Woods, *The Aqquyunlu*, 8, mistakenly makes Anūshīrwān the khan killed during the Jochid invasion.
40. A.I. Grachev, 'O «pravlenii» khana Dzhanibeka v Dzhurdzhane', *NZO* 1 (2011), 94–102.
41. Philip Remler, 'Ottoman, Isfandiyarid, and Eretnid coinage: A currency community in fourteenth century Anatolia', *ANSMN* 25 (1980), 169–188 (here 171–2). Jürgen Paul, 'Mongol aristocrats and beyliks in Anatolia: A study of Astarābādī's *Bazm va Razm*', in Johann Büssow, David Durand-Guédy and Jürgen Paul (eds), *Nomads in the Political Field* (Rome, 2011 = *ES* 9, parts 1–2), 105–58 (here 118–19). Peacock, *Islam, Literature and Society*, 61–2.
42. Jürgen Paul, 'Zerfall und Bestehen: Die Ǧaun-i Qurban im 14. Jahrhundert', *AS* 65 (2011), 695–733 (here 707). But compare Faryūmadī, *Dhayl-i Majma' al-ansāb*, 323, as quoted at p. 185.
43. Stephen Album, 'Power and legitimacy: The coinage of Mubāriz al-Dīn Muḥammad ibn al-Muẓaffar at Yazd and Kirman', *Le Monde Iranien et l'Islam* 2 (1974), 157–71 (here 159).

44. Ibid., 161. Melville, 'The end of the Ilkhanate', 326.
45. Broadbridge, *Kingship and Ideology*, 156–7 and n.89. Akopyan and Mosanef, 'Between Jūjīds and Jalāyirids', 219. Wing, *The Jalayirids*, 94, contends that Shaykh Ḥasan did not issue coins in his own name; but compare Michael Weiers, 'Münzaufschriften auf Münzen mongolischer Il-Khane aus dem Iran, Teil drei', *UAJ*, n.F., 5 (1985), 168–86 (here 181–2).
46. Jaʿfarī (Jaʿfar b. Muḥammad Ḥusaynī), *Taʾrīkh-i Yazd*, ed. Īraj Afshār (Tehran, 1338 sh./1960), 35. Muʿīn al-Dīn Yazdī, *Mawāhib-i ilāhī dar taʾrīkh-i āl-i Muẓaffar*, BL ms. Add. 7632, fo. 133b, and hence Kutubī, *Taʾrīkh-i āl-i Muẓaffar*, 45, date this in 755/1354. Album, 'Power and legitimacy', 167–8. Ahrī, *Taʾrīkh-i Shaykh Uways*, text, 176 (trans., 76), states that Mubāriz al-Dīn himself assumed the caliphal title al-Muʿtaḍid billāh, an error which misled Wing, *The Jalayirids*, 103.
47. Faryūmadī, *Dhayl-i Majmaʿ al-ansāb*, 316.
48. Aubin, 'Le khanat de Čaġatai', 31. Shivan Mahendrarajah, *A History of Herat from Chingiz Khan to Tamerlane* (Edinburgh, 2022), 137–43. On this, see further p. 194.
49. See the comment in *ZT*, III, 44, apropos of the suggestion that Timur's grandson Pīr Muḥammad b. ʿUmar Shaykh might seek confirmation from the Caliph at Cairo.
50. Naṭanzī (1957), 318–19/(2004), 244.
51. These details are given by al-Shujāʿī, I (text), 214, 234, II (trans.), 249, 267–8. For Khiḍrbeg's murder, see Ahrī, *Taʾrīkh-i Shaykh Uways*, text, 176, trans., 76.
52. István Vásáry, 'The Jochid realm: The western steppe and Eastern Europe', in *CHIA*, 67–85 (here 79).
53. Ahrī, *Taʾrīkh-i Shaykh Uways*, text, 173, trans., 76; cited in Wing, *The Jalayirids*, 103.
54. *MA*, fo. 22a, ed. Vokhidov, text, 45 (Russian trans., 42). Rus′ sources specify twelve brothers. Kutubī, *Taʾrīkh-i āl-i Muẓaffar*, 57, says 'several' (*chand*). See also Naṭanzī (1957), 85/(2004), 70.
55. Zayn al-Dīn (1990), text, 486 (Russian trans., 114)/(1993), 71. News of the confusion (which Rus′ sources link with the advent of Khiḍr: see later) had reached Azerbaijan by the onset of spring 761/1360. For valuable chronology from two Venetian documents, see S.P. Karpov, 'Nachalo smuty v Zolotoi Orde i perevorot Navruza', *ZOO* 6 (2018), 528–36.
56. See Spuler, *Die Goldene Horde*, 109–21; M.G. Safargaliev, *Raspad Zolotoi Ordy* (Saransk, 1960), 111–36. For the term 'Great Troubles', see Charles J. Halperin, *Russia and the Golden Horde. The Mongol Impact on Medieval Russian History* (Bloomington, IN, 1985), 54.
57. Shāmī, *ZN*, I, 13. Yazdī, *ZN* (1972), fo. 66b/(2008), I, 182.
58. For a detailed survey of the various khans, see R.Iu. Pochekaev, *Tsari ordynskie. Biografii khanov i pravitelei Zolotoi Ordy*, 2nd edn (St Petersburg, 2012), 140–88. Safargaliev, *Raspad*, 111–12 and n.1, calculates the total number of khans from the death of Berdibeg down to Toqtamish at more than 25; Baumer, *The History of Central Asia*, III, 269, counts 19 between Berdibeg and Toqtamish's accession.
59. Pochekaev, *Tsari ordynskie*, 142–3, surmises that Kulna was descended from Batu but was not of Özbeg's line, and ibid., 146–7, argues that Nawrūz is to be identified with Bazarchi (see n.66); hence his genealogy as given in Table 1,

ibid., 402. Christian, *A History of Russia, Central Asia and Mongolia*, II, 53, regards Nawrūz, whom he calls Berdibeg's brother, as the last of the Batuids. But a Venetian source calls Nawrūz an impostor: Karpov, 'Nachalo smuty', 531. According to Naṭanzī (1957), 85–6/(2004), 70, Kildibeg's lineage was unknown. Rus' sources say that he claimed to be a son of Janibeg: *Patriarshaia ili Nikonovskaia letopis'*, in *PSRL*, X, 189; tr. Serge A. and Betty Jean Zenkovsky, *The Nikonian Chronicle*, III. *From the Year 1241 to the Year 1381* (Princeton, NJ, 1986), 188–9; Ötemish Ḥājjī, *Chingīz-nāma*, ed. Kawaguchi et al., text, 38, says that he was taken for an impostor. Hence R.Iu. Pochekaev, 'K voprosu o perekhode vlasti v gosudarstvakh Chingizidov (4). Zolotaia Orda v 1358–1362 gg.: dinasticheskii krizis i fenomen samozvanstva', *ZOTs* 2 (2009), 39–49 (here 45–6), and *Tsari ordynskie*, 151, where he is called 'Pseudo-Kildibeg'. For the nephew, see *MA*, fo. 22a–b, ed. Vokhidov, text, 45–6 (Russian trans., 42; extract also in *SMIZO*, II, 51–2). A.P. Grigor'ev, 'Zolotoordynskie khany 60–70-kh godov XIV v.: khronologiia pravlenii', *Istoriografiia i Istochnikovedenie Istorii Stran Azii i Afriki* 7 (1983), 9–54 (here 50), claims that coins were minted in Kildibeg's name as late as 767/1365–6; but compare Iu.E. Varvarovskii, *Ulus Dzhuchi v 60–70-e gody XIV veka* (Kazan, 2008), 81.

60. See Zhaksylyk Sabitov and Roman Reva, 'Sravnenie svedenii «Muizz al-ansab» i «Tavarikh-i guzida-yi Nusrat-nama» o khanakh ulusa Dzhuchi s dannymi numizmatikh', *ZOO* 4 (2016), 102–14. For Ming Temür, see *TGNN*, text, 162 (fo. 69b); tr. in S.K. Ibragimov (ed.), *Materialy po istorii kazakhskikh khanstv XV–XVIII vekov (izvlecheniia iz persidskikh i tiurkskikh sochinenii)* (Alma-Ata, 1969), 34. I have largely ignored the genealogical data on the Jochids in *Shajarat al-atrāk*, tr. M.Kh. Abuseitova, in *IKPI*, V, 101–5, and those given by Naṭanzī, which are generally at variance with *MA*: for Naṭanzī's unreliability, see Safargaliev, *Raspad*, 114–16, and Zh.M. Sabitov, 'Anonim Iskendera kak genealogicheskii istochnik', *ZOTs* 1 (2008), 117–21. The Jochid genealogies from *MA* are themselves sometimes faultily reproduced in *SMIZO*, II, as noticed by T.I. Sultanov, '*Mu'izz al-ansāb* and spurious Chingīzids', *MO* 2, no. 3 (Sept. 1996), 3–7 (here 5); there are additional errors in Vokhidov's Russian translation. For reliable genealogies, see Pochekaev, *Tsari ordynskie*, tables 1–3.

61. *Patriarshaia ili Nikonovskaia letopis'*, in *PSRL*, X, 232 (tr. Zenkovsky, III, 186).

62. Khiḍr and Temür Khwāja appear in *TGNN*, text, 165 (fo. 71a; tr. in Ibragimov, *Materialy*, 37). However, Khiḍr's father Mangqutai, a grandson of Shiban's son Qadaq, is given without issue in *MA*, fo. 23a, ed. Vokhidov, text, 47 (Russian trans., 43); and see also Ötemish Ḥājjī, *Chingīz-nāma*, cited in Vásáry, 'The beginnings of coinage', 381, n.16. Since *Patriarshaia ili Nikonovskaia letopis'*, in *PSRL*, X, 233, and XI, 2 (tr. Zenkovsky, III, 189, 191), calls Murād ('Amurat') Khiḍr's brother, he must be the 'Murūt' named as such in *TGNN* and the 'Murūd' of Shāmī and Yazdī.

63. Very probably the ʿAzīz Baba who appears only in *TGNN*, text, 166 (fo. 71b; tr. in Ibragimov, *Materialy*, 37–8), as a descendant of Shiban's son *Sayilghan; thus Pochekaev, *Tsari ordynskie*, Table 2 at 403. He struck coins at New Sarai and Azāq between 765/1363–4 and 768/1366–7: B.D. Grekov and A.Iu. Iakubovskii, *Zolotaia Orda i ee padenie* (Moscow and Leningrad, 1950), 278–9; Grigor'ev, 'Zolotoordynskie khany', 50.

64. *MA*, fo. 27a, ed. Vokhidov, text, 55 (Russian trans., 44; also extract in *SMIZO*, II, 60). *TGNN*, text, 174 (fo. 75b; tr. in Ibragimov, *Materialy*, 43). Grigor'ev,

'Zolotoordynskie khany', 29, 31, is mistaken in suggesting that he was probably a brother of Temür Khwāja and thus a son of Khiḍr.

65. *MA*, fo. 28a, ed. Vokhidov, text, 57 (trans., 46), calling him ʿAbdal: the extract in *SMIZO*, II, 62, is in error regarding his paternity; compare *TGNN*, fo. 74a (tr. in Ibragimov, *Materialy*, 41: ʿAbdul). ʿAbd-Allāh is made a descendant of Özbeg by Spuler, *Die Goldene Horde*, 112; Golden, *An Introduction*, 300; Pochekaev, 'K voprosu', 46–7, and *Tsari ordynskie*, 159, 179, and Table 1 at 402; and Mirgaleev, 'The Time of Troubles', 690.
66. The ancestry of Bazarchi, who is omitted in *MA*, is given in *TGNN*, text, 166 (fo. 71b; tr. in Ibragimov, *Materialy*, 38). Ötemish Ḥājjī, *Chingīz-nāma*, ed. Kawaguchi et al., text, 38, calls him a descendant of Jochi's son Bo'al. Shāmī, *ZN*, I, 13, Yazdī, *ZN* (1972), fo. 66b/(2008), I, 181, and hence Khwānd-Amīr, *Ḥabīb al-siyar*, III, 76 (tr. Thackston, 43), list him among the Jochid khans. Safargaliev, *Raspad*, 112, n.1, regards Bazarchi and others who left no coins and are not mentioned in the Rus′ sources as 'highly questionable'. For the proposed identification of Bazarchi with Nawrūz, see n.59.
67. Pochekaev, *Tsari ordynskie*, 194. ʿArabshāh in turn had ousted a fellow Shibanid, Qaghanbeg: ibid., 185.
68. I.M. Mirgaleev, 'Succession to the throne in the Golden Horde: Replacement of the Batuids by the Tuqai-Timurids', *ZOO* (2017), no. 5, 344–51, is flawed, in my opinion, by a failure to take account of the data in *MA*, as is apparent, for example, at 345, n.1.
69. Allen J. Frank, 'The western steppe: Volga-Ural region, Siberia and the Crimea', in *CHIA*, 237–59 (here 240–1).
70. Table II in Grigor′ev, 'Zolotoordynskie khany', 34; Vásáry, 'The Jochid realm', 80, adds, for New Sarai, ʿAbd-Allāh and Murād. For Sarai, see Vásáry, 'Golden Horde', *EI*[3] (2016), fasc. 3, 110.
71. George Vernadsky, *The Mongols and Russia* (New Haven, CT, 1953), 251, 253. Robert O. Crummey, *The Formation of Muscovy 1304–1613* (Harlow, 1987), 45.
72. Grigor′ev, 'Zolotoordynskie khany', 33, 38–9. See Pochekaev, *Tsari ordynskie*, 174–80, who establishes the identity of this Pūlād and distinguishes him from other contemporary local rulers of the name. He was descended from Shiban's son Bahādur: *MA*, fo. 23a, ed. Vokhidov, text, 47 (Russian trans., 42; also extract in *SMIZO*, II, 54–5); *TGNN*, text, 162 (fo. 69b; tr. in Ibragimov, *Materialy*, 35). Varvarovskii, *Ulus Dzhuchi*, 86–7, assumes that Pūlād was not a Chinggisid.
73. Grigor′ev, 'Zolotoordynskie khany', 45–6, 50, and Pochekaev, *Tsari ordynskie*, 185–7. For his arrival from the Blue Horde in 1377, see *Patriarshaia ili Nikonovskaia letopis′*, in *PSRL*, XI, 27 (tr. Zenkovsky, III, 233).
74. For example, Taghai (or Toghai) in the Naruchat′ region (Mokhsha, i.e. the Mordvin territories), of whom we cannot be certain that he was a Chinggisid and whose coins do not bear the title of sultan or khan: *Patriarshaia ili Nikonovskaia letopis′*, in *PSRL*, X, 233, and XI, 5 (tr. Zenkovsky, III, 189, 196–7); V.L. Egorov, *Istoricheskaia geografiia Zolotoi Ordy v XIII–XIV vv.* (Moscow, 1985), 208; A.V. Pachkalov, 'K voprosu ob imennykh monetakh Mamaia', *NZO* 2 (2012), 117–19 (here 118). From *c.* 1370 Bulghār was ruled by an amir named Ḥasan: *Patriarshaia ili Nikonovskaia letopis′*, in *PSRL*, XI, 12, 25 (tr. Zenkovsky, III, 208, 229); Egorov, *Istoricheskaia geografiia*, 102–5.

75. Spuler, *Die Goldene Horde*, 120, 121, 123. Varvarovskii, *Ulus Dzhuchi*, 90–1. Compare Safargaliev, *Raspad*, 125–7. Authors disagree on the date of his expulsion.
76. See Safargaliev, *Raspad*, 120–1; Varvarovskii, *Ulus Dzhuchi*, 108–16; Devin DeWeese, 'Mapping Khwārazmian connections in the history of Sufi traditions: Local embeddedness, regional networks, and global ties of the Sufi communities of Khwārazm', *ES* 14 (2016), 37–97 (here 70–1). For the earlier history of the dynasty, see Isayahu Landa, 'From Mongolia to Khwārazm: The Qonggirad migrations in the Jochid *ulus* (13th–15th c.)', in Favereau (ed.), *La Horde d'Or et l'islamisation*, 215–31 (here 216–18). The appellation 'Ṣūfī' has yet to be explained.
77. Janet Martin, *Treasure of the Land of Darkness. The Fur Trade and Its Significance for Medieval Russia* (Cambridge, 1986), 32–3.
78. Pachkalov, 'K voprosu ob imennykh monetakh Mamaia'.
79. See Tables II and IV in Grigor'ev, 'Zolotoordynskie khany', 34, 50.
80. Ibid., Table IV, at 50–1. His installation by Mamai is dated 6878 [1370] in *PSRL*, XI, 12 (tr. Zenkovsky, III, 207). He is probably the Muḥammad who appears in *MA*, fo. 28a, ed. Vokhidov, text, 57 (Russian trans., 46), and *TGNN*, fo. 74b (tr. in Ibragimov, *Materialy*, 41), as ʿAbdal's son. Pochekaev, *Tsari ordynskie*, 163 and Table 1 at 402, following Safargaliev, makes him a son of Tinibeg.
81. Mirgaleev, 'The Time of Troubles', 691. See the discussion in Varvarovskii, *Ulus Dzhuchi*, 89, and Pochekaev, *Tsari ordynskie*, 163. The source for the marriage is Ibn Khaldūn, *Kitāb al-ʿIbar*, V, 1141 (extract also in *SMIZO*, I, text, 373, Russian trans., 389), though he does not give the princess's name and incorrectly makes Toqtamish her brother.
82. Pochekaev, *Tsari ordynskie*, 156, 157.
83. Ötemish Ḥājjī, *Chingīz-nāma*, ed. Kawaguchi et al., text, 37. See Vásáry, 'The beginnings of coinage', 382. *Shajarat al-atrāk*, in *IKPI*, V, 103, makes Noghai (here called 'Tukai') the son of 'Shahi' (Sasi?).
84. Vásáry, 'The beginnings of coinage', 378–80, corrects previous readings of these dates. Mubārak Khwāja appears in *MA*, fo. 25b, ed. Vokhidov, text, 52 (Russian trans., 44), and *TGNN*, text, 173 (fo. 75a; tr. in Ibragimov, *Materialy*, 42; see also extract in *SMIZO*, II, 60), as a descendant of Toqa Temür's eldest son Bai Temür. See further Uskenbay, 'Left Wing of the Ulus of Jochi', 208. I cannot accept the counter-argument of Pochekaev, *Tsari ordynskie*, 111 and n.265 at 327, that the khan Mubārak Khwāja was a different person from the Toqatimurid of this name and was a descendant of Orda who ruled the Blue Horde from *c.* 1329. For a coin struck in Blue Horde territory, in 753/1352–3 at Bārchin, that is, Barchinlighkent on the Sīr-daryā, but in the name of the Qipchaq khan Janibeg, see George M. Mellinger, 'The silver coinage of the Golden Horde: 1310–1358', *AEMA* 7 (1987–91), 152–211 (here 183–4); Spuler, *Die Goldene Horde*, 102, n.7, wrongly locating the town in Khurāsān.
85. Pochekaev, *Tsari ordynskie*, 165, 182–3. Varvarovskii, *Ulus Dzhuchi*, 91 (citing al-Qalqashandī). Favereau, *The Horde*, 275, 278. It was long assumed that Orus belonged to Orda's line, but Vásáry, 'The beginnings of coinage', showed this to be incorrect. According to *MA*, fos 25b–26b, ed. Vokhidov, text, 52–3 (Russian trans., 44, 45; extract in *SMIZO*, II, 61, 62), Orus and Toqtamish were both fifth in descent from Toqa Temür's son Ürüngtash, though *TGNN*, text, 172 (fo. 74b; tr. in Ibragimov, *Materialy*, 41–2), makes them respectively

third and fourth in descent from Toqa Temür's son Uz Temür (presumably identical with *MA*'s Ürüngtash). See DeWeese, 'Toḳtamis͟h', *EI*², X, 560–3 (here 560–1); R.Iu. Reva, 'Saiid-Akhmad I i Giias ad-Din I (istoriografiia otkrytiia, genealogiia, novoobnaruzhennye monetnye vypuski', *NZO* 4 (2014), 48–60 (table at 55), gives the generations slightly differently. Coins of Orus at Sighnāq date from 770 [1368–9] onwards: Vásáry, 'The beginnings of coinage', 379.

86. Spuler, *Die Goldene Horde*, 129–30, 133–5. Roemer, 'Tīmūr in Iran', 72–3.
87. On the turbulent history of the Jochids and Edigü's career, see Frank, 'The western steppe', 237–41.
88. It may have dated back to a major attack that Özbeg had launched just before his death in 742/1342 (but which seems to have proved abortive), on which see al-Shujāʿī, I (text), 214, 234, II (trans.), 249, 268.
89. Shams al-Dīn Muḥammad b. Maḥmūd Āmulī, *Nafāʾis al-funūn fī ʿarāʾis al-ʿuyūn*, ed. Abū l-Ḥasan Shaʿrānī and Sayyid Ibrāhīm Miyānajī, 3 vols (Tehran, 1377–9/1958–60), II, 263.
90. I have adopted the spelling implied in *MA*, fo. 32a, ed. Vokhidov, text, 65 (BWRAN; cf. Russian trans., 50), and confirmed by *TGNN*, text, 191 (fo. 83a). Yazdī, *ZN* (1972), fo. 81a, line 4/(2008), I, 217, specifies that he came from Jata (on which see pp. 127, 206). The date of Tarmashirin's downfall and the duration of his reign are given only in Mamlūk sources, beginning with al-Dhahabī, *Taʾrīkh al-Islām*, LIII, 329; hence al-Ṣafadī, *al-Wāfī bi l-wafayāt*, X, 383, and *Aʿyān al-ʿaṣr*, I, 523.
91. So according to a Nestorian inscription published by Četin Džumagulov, 'Die syrisch-türkischen (nestorianischen) Denkmäler in Kirgisien' (tr. Peter Zieme), *Mitteilungen des Instituts für Orientforschung* 14 (1968), 470–80 (here 478): regarding the date, see the correction in Aubin, 'Le khanat de Čaġatai', n.34 at 24–5.
92. IB, III, 48–9 (tr. Gibb, 565).
93. Naṭanzī (1957), 102, 112/(2004), 83, 91. *Shajarat al-atrāk*, Harvard University, Houghton Library ms. 6F, fo. 113b, introduces as Tarmashirin's successor a son of the Ilkhan Öljeitü named ʿRJΓAM(?); but this is probably an error based on the bizarre statement in Yazdī's *Muqaddima*, in *ZN* (1972), fo. 81a/(2008), I, 217, that Tarmashirin was the uncle (reading *khāl* for *khān*) of Öljeitü. In fact, he had a daughter of that name: *MA*, fo. 32a, ed. Vokhidov, text, 65 (Russian trans., 50). Alternatively, there is perhaps some confusion here between the Ilkhan and the amir Öljeitü Apardī. Examination of *Shajarat* and Yazdī's *ZN* (which mentions Buzan's killing of Dorji) suggests that a line or more is missing here in both texts.
94. *Masālik*, text, 22 (German trans., 105).
95. Yazdī, *ZN* (1957), I, 33/(2008), I, 262. The figure eight can be reached only by excluding Buzan and Khalīl Sulṭān (or perhaps ʿAlī Sulṭān).
96. Naṭanzī (1957), 112–13/(2004), 91. Cf. Aubin, 'Le khanat de Čaġatai', 17.
97. For the dates of Changshi and Yesün Temür, see Michael Fedorov, 'On the exact date of Yesün Temür's accession to the throne, according to numismatic data', *Iran* 39 (2001), 301–2; Kara, 'Mediaeval Mongol documents from Khara Khoto', 28–30; Michael Fedorov, 'A hoard of fourteenth century Chaghatayid silver coins from North Kirghizstan', *Numismatic Chronicle* 162 (2002), 404–19 (here 416). Petrov, 'Khronologiia', 308.

98. Petrov, 'Khronologiia', 309. Pūlād was Muḥammad's father and not an alternative name for Muḥammad himself, as once thought: see Shāmī, *ZN*, I, 13; Yazdī, *ZN* (1972), fo. 81a, 81b/(2008), I, 218, 220; *MA*, fo. 32b, ed. Vokhidov, text, 66 (Russian trans., 52); and *TGNN*, text, 188–9 (fos 81b–82a). For ʿAlī Sulṭān's ancestry, see *MA*, fos 42b–43a, ed. Vokhidov, text, 86–7 (Russian trans., 59).
99. Petrov, 'Khronologiia', 310–11, has now disproved the notion that these two khans were one and the same man. The early fifteenth-century hagiographical work by Ṣalāḥ al-Dīn b. Mubārak Bukhārī, *Anīs al-ṭālibīn wa-ʿuddat al-sālikīn*, ed. Tawfīq Subḥānī (Tehran, 1371 sh./1992), 85, makes Khalīl a dervish and links him with Shaykh Bahāʾ al-Dīn Naqshband; here he is said to have reigned six years.
100. IB, III, 49–50 (tr. Gibb, 566).
101. See Kazuhide Katō, 'Kebek and Yasawr – the establishment of the Chaghatai khanate', *MTB* 49 (1991), 97–118 (here 104–11); Mahendrarajah, *A History of Herat*, 105–11; more detail at p. 214.
102. Petrov, 'Khronologiia', 311.
103. Sayfī (1944), 768/(2004), 762, says that Juki was killed along with his father, but later authors claim that both Juki and Qazan fell alive into Köpek's hands: HA, *Dhayl-i Jāmiʿ al-tawārīkh*, ed. Khān-bābā Bayānī, 2nd edn (Tehran, 1350 sh./1971), 159; Mīr-Khwānd, *Taʾrīkh Rawḍat al-ṣafā* (Tehran, 1338–9 sh./1959–60), V, 503. Possibly, therefore, Juki, like Qazan, survived. We should note that *TGNN*, text, 187 (fo. 81a), gives Yasaʾur a total of five sons, though none is there called Khalīl. Hope, 'The Middle Empire', 310, suggests that one of the sons may have adopted a Muslim name.
104. Usually called Muʿizz al-Dīn Ḥusayn. For the correct form of his name, see Aubin, 'Le khanat de Čaġatai', 19 and n.17.
105. IB, III, 48–9, 51 (tr. Gibb, 565, 567). This statement raises questions regarding IB's itinerary, since later, IV, 4 (tr. Gibb and Beckingham, 775), he claims to have left India for China in Ṣafar 743/July 1342, and nowhere else does he suggest that he returned to the Sultanate – or that he visited Herat.
106. Petrov, 'Khronologiia', 312–13.
107. Ibid., 311.
108. Shāmī, *ZN*, I, 14. Cf. Yazdī, *ZN* (1957), I, 29/(2008), I, 257. Naṭanzī (1957), 197, 200, 261/(2004), 162, 164, 205; ibid. (1957), 197/(2004), 162, he calls Qazaghan a Qaraʾunas. See pp. 217, 219.
109. Naṭanzī (1957), 113/(2004), 92; and also compare ibid. (1957), 117/(2004), 96.
110. The date of Danishmandcha's death is given as late in 748 [early 1348] in *ZT*, I, 210, and in HA's additions to Shāmī, *ZN*, II, 9. I have adopted 'Bayan', as ibid., II, 9–10 (see also *ZT*, I, 211, variant ms. reading), in preference to the form 'Buyan' usually given.
111. Ahrī, *Taʾrīkh-i Shaykh Uways*, text, 177, trans., 76.
112. For the putative sense of *Jata*, see *TMEN*, III, 55–6 (no. 1071).
113. *ZT*, I, 185, speaks in vague terms of 'most' (*akthar*) of Qazan's territories slipping from his grasp prior to Amīr Qazaghan's second bid to overthrow him in 747/1346–7.
114. *TR*, I (text), 18, II (trans.), 14.
115. Ibid., I (text), 8–9, II (trans.), 6–7. Bābur, *Bābur-nāma* or *Waqāʾi*, tr. Annette Susannah Beveridge, *The Bābur-nāma in English* (London, 1921–2; repr. in 1

vol., 1969), 19/tr. Wheeler M. Thackston, *The Baburnama. The Memoirs of Babur, Prince and Emperor* (New York, 2002), similarly makes Tughluq Temür the son of Esen Buqa.

116. Shāmī, *ZN*, I, 13 (in the earlier redaction). Yazdī, *ZN* (1972), fo. 81b, and (1957), I, 33/(2008), I, 219, 262. *MA*, fo. 32b, ed. Vokhidov, text, 66 (Russian trans., 51), mentioning no other child of Dukhtui. Barthold, *Four Studies*, I, 138, and *Zwölf Vorlesungen*, 208–9 (= Bartol′d, *Sochineniia*, II, part 1, 79–80, and V, 165–6, respectively), commented on Tughluq Temür's questionable ancestry. See also DeWeese, 'Islamization in the Mongol empire', 132.
117. Thus Timurid authors list Tughluq Temür and his son and successor Ilyās Khwāja among the Chaghadayid khans, between Temür Shāh and Kābul Shāh: Shāmī, *ZN*, I, 13; Yazdī, *ZN* (1972), fo. 81b/(2008), I, 219.
118. A point argued strongly by Kim Hodong, 'The early history of the Moghul nomads: The legacy of the Chaghatai khanate', in Amitai-Preiss and Morgan (eds), *The Mongol Empire and Its Legacy*, 290–318 (here 314–18).
119. Michele Bernardini, 'The Mongol puppet lords and the Qarawnas', in Robert Hillenbrand, A.C.S. Peacock and Firuza Abdullaeva (eds), *Ferdowsi, the Mongols and the History of Iran: Art, Literature and Culture from Early Islam to Qajar Persia. Studies in Honour of Charles Melville* (London and New York, 2013), 169–76 (here 172).
120. I have followed the rendering in Michele Bernardini, *Mémoire et propagande à l'époque timouride*, *StIr* cahier 37 (Paris, 2008), 51, 61. For the original use of the term, applied to the regional rulers of the Arsacid era, see M. Morony, 'Mulūk al-ṭawā'if', *EI*[2], VII, 551–2.
121. Shāmī, *ZN*, I, 15 (the phrase is employed in addition at I, 10); Yazdī, *ZN* (1957), I, 33/(2008), I, 262; compare also Naṭanzī (1957), 197, 204/(2004), 162, 167. Michele Bernardini, 'La prise du pouvoir par Tamerlan dans l'ulus Chaghatay', in Marie-France Auzépy and Guillaume Saint-Guillain (eds), *Oralité et lien social au Moyen Âge: Occident, Byzance, Islam: parole donnée, foi jurée, serment. Actes du colloque international organisé à Paris du 10 au 12 mai 2007* (Paris, 2008), 137–45 (here 139).
122. Yazdī, *ZN* (1957), I, 67/(2008), I, 299. On the date of Tughluq Temür's death, see Naṭanzī (1957), 125/(2004), 101; Bernard O'Kane, 'Chaghatai architecture and the tomb of Tughluq Temür at Almaliq', *Muqarnas* 21 (2004), 277–87. But Petrov, 'Khronologiia', 316, proposes 765/1363–4 on numismatic grounds.
123. *TR*, I (text), 28, II (trans.), 20. Kim, 'The early history of the Moghul nomads', 299–300, 303–7. *TR* gives no date. Naṭanzī (1957), 125/(2004), 102, dates Ilyās Khwāja's murder in 765/1363–4, but the eastern Chaghadayid chancery issued a document in his name in the Year of the Rooster, corresponding to 1369: Herbert Franke, 'Zur Datierung der mongolischen Schreiben aus Turfan', *Oriens* 15 (1962), 399–410 (here 408–10).
124. Kim, 'The early history of the Moghul nomads', 315.
125. P.N. Petrov, 'Badakhshan XIII–XIV vv. pod vlast′iu mongol′skikh khanov', *Zapiski Vostochnogo Otdeleniia Rossiiskogo Arkheologicheskogo Obshchestva*, n.s., 2 (2006), 496–540 (here 518–19, 536); Petrov, 'Khronologiia', 317.
126. See the brief discussion in Jackson, *The Mongols and the Islamic World*, 243.
127. Allsen, 'The Yüan dynasty and the Uighurs of Turfan' 260. Peter Zieme, *Religion und Gesellschaft im uigurischen Königreich von Qočo. Kolophone*

und Stifter des alttürkischen buddhistischen Schrifttums aus Zentralasien, Abhandlungen der rheinisch-westfälischen Akademie der Wissenschaften 88 (Opladen, 1992), 52–3.

128. Melville, 'The end of the Ilkhanate', esp. 319–22, 328–30 (the phrase quoted is at 330): he largely confines his attention to Iran.
129. Ibid., 319, 323.
130. Naṭanzī (1957), 158. Woods, *The Aqquyunlu*, 7–8. There is some doubt concerning the reading, which appears in Naṭanzī (2004), 127, as *ughul* (Mo. *oghul*, 'son', 'prince'): see Broadbridge, *Kingship and Ideology*, 160 and n.101. For Tu. *ughur*, see *TMEN*, II, 152–3 (no. 604: 'Glück'); Jonathan Brack, 'A Mongol Mahdi in medieval Anatolia: Rebellion, reform, and divine right in the post-Mongol Islamic world', *JAOS* 139 (2019), 611–29 (here 625), translates the term as 'charisma'.
131. *Masālik*, text, 20 (German trans., 104).
132. Ibn Faḍl-Allāh al-ʿUmarī, *al-Taʿrīf*, Cairo edn, 44/ed. al-Durūbī, 58.
133. Ibn Fatḥ-Allāh al-Baghdādī, *al-Taʾrīkh al-Ghiyāthī*, 69.
134. *Masālik*, text, 20 (German trans., 104).
135. See Hope, *Power, Politics, and Tradition*, 172–4; also Bruno De Nicola, *Women in Mongol Iran. The* Khātūns, *1206–1335* (Edinburgh, 2017), 164–5.
136. Shabānkāraʾī, *Majmaʿ al-ansāb*, 306.
137. IB, III, 70 (tr. Gibb, 578). See P. Jackson, 'Ṭog͟ha Temür', *EI*[2], X, 552–3; Paul, 'Zerfall und Bestehen', 707, n.55.
138. Shabānkāraʾī, *Majmaʿ al-ansāb*, 294. I prefer this interpretation to the 'day labourer' in Wing, *The Jalayirids*, 75.
139. Ḥamd-Allāh Mustawfī Qazwīnī, *Dhayl*, ed. Piriiev, text, 437–8/tr. Kazimov and Piriiev, 94. Tükel Qutlugh is otherwise unknown and does not appear in *MA*.
140. Thus according to Shabānkāraʾī, *Majmaʿ al-ansāb*, 301. al-Dhahabī, *Taʾrīkh al-Islām*, LIII, 331 (no. 1000), calls Mūsā himself a weaver and says that he had been living in Daqūqā; hence al-Ṣafadī, *al-Wāfī bi l-wafayāt*, XXVI, 534–5 (no. 370), where it is confirmed that he had been learning weaving (*al-ḥiyāka*), and *Aʿyān al-ʿaṣr*, IV, 2107 (with the misreading *kāna nassākh*[an], 'he was a scribe'); also Ibn Fatḥ-Allāh al-Baghdādī, *al-Taʾrīkh al-Ghiyāthī*, 69 (*ḥāʾik*[an]). See Melville, *The Fall of Amir Chupan*, 46 and n.135.
141. al-Dhahabī, *Taʾrīkh al-Islām*, LIII, 353 (no. 1062); hence al-Ṣafadī, *al-Wāfī bi l-wafayāt*, IV, 293 (no. 1823), and *Aʿyān al-ʿaṣr*, IV, 1826. *al-Wāfī* reads as if he was born to a concubine of Abū Saʿīd after the latter's death. The fuller text in *Aʿyān* says that the mother was a concubine of Anbarjī who was pregnant at that prince's death; but Anbarjī was in fact Muḥammad's great-grandfather.
142. Zayn al-Dīn (1993), 35; hence HA, *Dhayl-i Jāmiʿ al-tawārīkh*, 224. I have doubts concerning the acceptance of 'Kāvīyān' by Wing, *The Jalayirids*, 92, as an allusion to the *Shāh-nāma* and hence an appeal to the tradition of pre-Islamic Iranian kingship. Zayn al-Dīn (1993) reads *kāwiyān* but supplies the ms. reading *kāʾūnān*, which appears clearly in Zayn al-Dīn (1990), text, 473, and is adopted by Woods, *The Aqquyunlu*, 8, and Broadbridge, *Kingship and Ideology*, 159. In the (1990) Russian trans., 98, *qubchachi* is misread as 'Qipchaq': for *qubchachi*, see *TMEN*, I, 385–6 (no. 263: 'Kleidungskämmerer'). Ahrī, *Taʾrīkh-i Shaykh Uways*, text, 171, trans., 71, says that Anūshīrwān was

'of the tribe (*īl*) of the Turklīs'. An obscure line in Yazdī, *ZN* (1972), fo. 74b/ (2008), I, 200, appears to suggest that he was not descended from Chinggis Khan; and Melville, 'The end of the Ilkhanate', 324, n.54, and Hope, 'The political configuration', 13, do not regard him as a Chinggisid. Note that the name Nūshīrwān, if hardly common within the Mongol imperial dynasty, was borne by a near-contemporary Ögödeyid prince: *MA*, fo. 44a, ed. Vokhidov, text, 89 (Russian trans., 60).

143. Shabānkāra'ī, *Majma' al-ansāb*, 301. But compare al-Dhahabī, *Ta'rīkh al-Islām*, LIII, 331 (no. 1000); hence al-Ṣafadī, *al-Wāfī bi l-wafayāt*, XXVI, 535, and *A'yān al-'aṣr*, IV, 2107.

144. Muḥammad: al-Dhahabī, *Ta'rīkh al-Islām*, LIII, 353 (no. 1062), followed in the fifteenth century by Ibn Ḥajar, as quoted in Melville, *The Fall of Amir Chupan*, 51, n.153 (also ibid., for a citation from Aḥmad Tabrīzī); al-Ṣafadī, *al-Wāfī bi l-wafayāt*, IV, 293 (*kāna ṣabī*[an] *min abnā' al-'ishrīn*), and *A'yān al-'aṣr*, IV, 1826 (similar reading), but the number twenty probably results from a copyist's conflation of *'ashara* and *sinīn*; al-Shujā'ī, I (text), 17 (*ṣaghīr*), II (trans.), 33; Ibn Fatḥ-Allāh al-Baghdādī, *al-Ta'rīkh al-Ghiyāthī*, 73-4 (*kāna ṭifl*[an]). Sulaymān: al-Shujā'ī, I (text), 57 (*ṣabī*), 100 (*ṣabī wa-ṣaghīr*), II (trans.), 81, 130.

145. al-Dhahabī, *Ta'rīkh al-Islām*, LIII, 324 (no. 974, *nasha'a fī ghumār al-nās jundiyy*[an]); hence al-Ṣafadī, *al-Wāfī bi l-wafayāt*, VIII, 334 (no. 3760), and *A'yān al-'aṣr*, I, 269 (reading simply *nasha'a fī ghumār al-nās*). Roemer, 'The Jalayirids, Muzaffarids and Sarbadārs', 2, views Arpa as the last Ilkhan possessed of any competence. See also Melville, *The Fall of Amir Chupan*, 61–2.

146. Muḥammad b. Maḥmūd Āmulī, *Nafā'is al-funūn*, II, 263.

147. Shabānkāra'ī, *Majma' al-ansāb*, 301–2.

148. See also Melville, *The Fall of Amir Chupan*, 63 ('appears to have been vigorous').

149. Aubin, 'Le *quriltai* de Sultân-Maydân', 191 (repr. in his *Études*, 292): 'personnalité falote et bornée'. See also Roemer, 'The Jalayirids, Muzaffarids and Sarbadārs', 20: 'not a strong personality'.

150. *CO*, text, 17: *ū dar ḥukūmat istiqlālī nadāsht wa-dar umūr-i pādishāhī ḍa'f-u wahnī paydā gashta*. See the translation in Paul, 'Zerfall und Bestehen', 706, n.51.

151. Faryūmadī, *Dhayl-i Majma' al-ansāb*, 320, 327. We can discount the many laudatory verses in Ibn Yamīn (d. 769/1368), *Dīwān-i ash'ār*, ed. Ḥusayn 'Alī Bāstānī-Rād ([Tehran, 1344 sh./1965]), index, *s.v.* Ṭaghāītimūr, since the poet abandoned Taghai Temür for the Sarbadārs' service in 742/1341: see J. Rypka, 'Ibn-i Yamīn', *EI*², III, 968–9; idem, *History of Iranian Literature* (Dordrecht, 1968), 261.

152. al-Shujā'ī, I (text), 49, II (trans.), 72.

153. Barthold, *Zwölf Vorlesungen*, 172 (= Bartol'd, *Sochineniia*, V, 139), though he is speaking of the period around 1300. For examples from the 1380s and 1390s, see Shāmī, *ZN*, I, 161, and Yazdī, *ZN* (1957), I, 208, 286, 393–4, 541/ (2008), I, 466, 557, 671–2, 816.

154. Yazdī, *ZN* (1957), I, 286/(2008), I, 557.

155. Robinson, *In the Shadow of the Mongol Empire*, 86–8.

156. *Patriarshaia ili Nikonovskaia letopis'*, in *PSRL*, XI, 43, 44, 46, 47–9 (tr. Zenkovsky, III, 259, 261, 265–6, 267–70). But this may be an error: see Pochekaev, *Tsari ordynskie*, n.481 at 351–2.

157. Yazdī, *ZN* (1957), I, 73–4/(2008), I, 307. Compare also Naṭanzī (1957), 129/(2004), 104. DeWeese, 'Islamization in the Mongol empire', 132. For the spelling of the name on his coins, see Petrov, 'Khronologiia', 317.
158. Shāmī, *ZN*, I, 38.
159. Bernardini, 'The Mongol puppet lords', 173–4. See further Chap. 12, pp. 339–40.
160. As noticed, for instance, by Russian witnesses: Allsen, 'Eurasia after the Mongols', 160. Compare also Jackson, *The Mongols and the Islamic World*, 118. For a parallel situation earlier, among the Seljuqids of Anatolia, see Peacock, *Islam, Literature and Society*, 60.
161. See the model outlined by Woods, *The Aqquyunlu*, 20–3. This pattern is compatible with the remarks of May, *The Mongol Empire*, 338, concerning lateral succession, which on his definition embraces the transition from brother to brother.
162. Ghazan executed seven princes within his first few years, five of them within a single month: Waṣṣāf (1853), 329, lines 3–4 (*GW*, III, 170). For Özbeg, see Qāshānī, *Ta'rīkh-i Uljāytū Sulṭān*, 144–5; ʿAlam al-Dīn Abū Muḥammad al-Qāsim b. Muḥammad al-Birzālī, *al-Muqtafā li-ta'rīkh al-shaykh Shihāb al-Dīn Abū Shāma*, ed. ʿUmar ʿAbd al-Salām Tadmurī, 4 vols (Ṣaydā, 1427/2006), IV, 93 (also in *SMIZO*, I, text, 173, Russian trans., 174).
163. Favereau, *The Horde*, 262–3.
164. Naliqo'a. See Barthold, *Four Studies*, I, 131 and n.3 (= Bartol'd, *Sochineniia*, II, part 1, 74 and n.60), who suggested that Naliqo'a may have been a grandson of Chaghadai himself; but he is made a grandson of Büri in *JT*, I, 753 (*SGK*, 139; *CC*, 261), and in *SP*, fo. 118b; see also *MA*, fos 29b–30a, ed. Vokhidov, text, 60–1 (Russian trans., 48). This version represents a later emendation by Rashīd al-Dīn: Kamola, 'Untangling the Chaghadaids', 76, 82, 85; hence Barthold was possibly right. Even so, an adherent of Du'a's sons had articulated the priority of their claims over those of Naliqo'a: Qāshānī, *Ta'rīkh-i Uljāytū Sulṭān*, 147; Waṣṣāf (1853), 518/(2009), 286 (*GW*, IV, 315).
165. On the rival line, see the discussion in Russell G. Kempiners, 'Vaṣṣāf's *Tajziyat al-amṣār wa Tazjiyat al-a'ṣār* as a source for the history of the Chaghadayid khanate', *JAH* 22 (1988), 160–87 (here 176–80); he accepts the descent of Naliqo'a and his close kin from Büri, however.
166. *JT*, I, 713 (*SGK*, 102; *CC*, 247, with the transcription 'Nayan'). On this conflict, see Barthold, *Four Studies*, I, 127 (= Bartol'd, *Sochineniia*, II, part 1, 70). The date is given by al-ʿAynī, *'Iqd al-jumān*, in *SMIZO*, I, text, 483 (Russian trans., 512–13).
167. Kim, 'Formation and changes of *ulus*es', 307–8. David M. Robinson, *Empire's Twilight. Northeast Asia under the Mongols*, Harvard-Yenching Institute Monograph Series 68 (Cambridge, MA, 2009), 96–7. Alughu Temür's ancestry is given in Song Lian et al., *Yuanshi*, chap. 108, ed. and tr. Louis Hambis, *Le Chapitre CVIII du Yuan che. Les fiefs attribués aux membres de la famille impériale et aux ministres de la cour mongole d'après l'histoire chinoise officielle de la dynastie mongole*, Monographies du *TP* 3 (Leiden, 1954), 92 and nn.2–6; to be corrected from *SP*, fo. 127b, and *MA*, fo. 43b, ed. Vokhidov, text, 88 (Russian trans., 60); he was descended from Ögödei's son Melik.
168. See the discussion in Melville, *The Fall of Amir Chupan*, 61–2.
169. Listed by Faryūmadī, *Dhayl-i Majma' al-ansāb*, 306–7. See Aubin's comment: 'Le *quriltai* de Sultân-Maydân', 181 (repr. in his *Études*, 283–4).

170. Melville, *The Fall of Amir Chupan*, 44.
171. McChesney, 'The Chinggisid restoration in Central Asia', 279.
172. Wing, *The Jalayirids*, 103–4.
173. HA, *Ta'rīkh-i salāṭīn-i Kart*, ed. Mīr Hāshim Muḥaddith (Tehran, 1389 sh./2010), 179–80; quoted by Woods, *The Aqquyunlu*, 8, from *CO*, text, 38.
174. Naṭanzī (1957), 125/(2004), 102; and compare also the sentiments put into Timur's mouth ibid., (1957), 206/(2004), 168 and cited at p. 337. For the continued importance of the dynasty in Transoxiana, see Bernardini, 'La prise du pouvoir par Tamerlan', 141.
175. Yazdī, *ZN* (1957), I, 71/(2008), I, 305, *khānrā wafādārī ki dar jibillat-i atrāk markūz ast*. In his account of the same engagement, however, Shāmī, *ZN*, I, 26–7, says that Ilyās Khwāja had avoided capture.
176. *Patriarshaia ili Nikonovskaia letopis'*, in *PSRL*, XI, 46 (tr. Zenkovsky, III, 265–6). But compare n. 156.
177. Arghun: *JT*, II, 1135 (*DzhT*, III, 179; *CC*, 392). Abū Saʿīd: Shabānkāra'ī, *Majma' al-ansāb*, 286–7; Ibn al-Wardī, *Tatimmat al-Mukhtaṣar fī akhbār al-bashar*, ed. Aḥmad Rifʿat al-Badrāwī (Beirut, 1389/1970), II, 444; al-Ṣafadī, *al-Wāfī bi l-wafayāt*, X, 323, and *A'yān al-'aṣr*, I, 497; Melville, 'The end of the Ilkhanate', 329 and n.68. See Ahrī, *Ta'rīkh-i Shaykh Uways*, text, 155–6, trans., 57, for specimens of Abū Saʿīd's verse.
178. *Masālik*, text, 73, 102 (German trans., 141, 159). On the assimilation of the Mongols to the subject Turkish population in the Ilkhanate, see Reuven Amitai, 'Where have all the Mongols gone? On the arrival and disappearance of Mongolian speakers in southwest Asia during the thirteenth and fourteenth centuries', in Anne Dunlop (ed.), *The Mongol Empire in Global History and Art History*, I Tatti Research Series 5 (Firenze, 2023), 33–71.
179. Waṣṣāf (1853), 202, ll. 11–12 (*GW*, II, 127, omitting the name Jurma); cited by Ann K.S. Lambton, *Continuity and Change in Medieval Persia. Aspects of Economic, Administrative and Social History, 11th–14th Century* (London, 1988), 25.
180. Zayn al-Dīn (1990), text, 472 (Russian trans., 97)/(1993), 33. See also Woods, *The Aqquyunlu*, 17; Monika Gronke, 'The Persian court between palace and tent: From Timur to ʿAbbas I', in Golombek and Subtelny (eds), *Timurid Art and Culture*, 18–22 (here 18).
181. IB, III, 69–73 (tr. Gibb, 577–9). On this episode, see Aubin, 'Le khanat de Čaġatai', 21–2, 25; Mahendrarajah, *A History of Herat*, 254.
182. al-Ṣafadī, *al-Wāfī bi l-wafayāt*, VIII, 334, and *A'yān al-'aṣr*, I, 269. On Arpa's alleged Christian faith, see also A.G. Galstian (trans.), *Armianskie istochniki o Mongolakh* (Moscow, 1962), 81; and for his regnal style, Shabānkāra'ī, *Majma' al-ansāb*, 294.
183. Shabānkāra'ī, *Majma' al-ansāb*, 294. Ahrī, *Ta'rīkh-i Shaykh Uways*, text, 158, trans., 59.
184. al-Shujāʿī, I (text), 214, 234, II (trans.), 249, 268. DeWeese, *Islamization and Native Religion*, n.57 at 95–6. Jackson, *The Mongols and the Islamic World*, 332.
185. al-Dhahabī, *Ta'rīkh al-Islām*, LIII, 330. al-Ṣafadī, *al-Wāfī bi l-wafayāt*, X, 382–3. Idem, *A'yān al-'aṣr*, I, 523.
186. Idol-temples: anonymous *Dhayl-i Jāmi' al-tawārīkh*, BL ms. Or. 2885, fo. 422a. Images: Naṭanzī (1957), 112/(2004), 90–1.
187. IB, III, 48 (tr. Gibb, 565).

188. Reuven Amitai, 'The resolution of the Mongol–Mamluk war', in Amitai and Biran (eds), *Mongols, Turks, and Others*, 359–90 (esp. 373–84); and see his remarks in *Holy War and Rapprochement*, 82. Melville, 'The end of the Ilkhanate', 322, hints at the possible relevance of the peace of 1323 to the demise of the Mongol polity in Iran.
189. Liu, 'War and peace', 351–3.
190. IB, III, 43 (tr. Gibb, 562). *Masālik*, text, 40, says merely that the Mongols fell into dispute with their rulers and ceased [their attacks on India] both from fear of Muḥammad b. Tughluq and because of their own internal conflicts (*wa-ikhtalafat kalimat ahl hādhihi l-bilād 'alā mulūkihā fa-nkaffū li-ba's dhālika l-sulṭān wa-ikhtilāf dhāt al-bayn*: Lech's German trans., 118, incorrectly reads 'Die Inder waren mit ihren Fürsten uneins', when the subject of the sentence is in fact the Chaghadayid Mongols). For the date of Muḥammad b. Tughluq's accession, see Jackson, *The Delhi Sultanate*, 330–1 (appendix V).
191. Quanheng, *Gengshen waishi*, tr. Helmut Schulte-Uffelage, *Das Keng-shen Wai-shih. Eine Quelle zur späten Mongolenzeit*, Ostasiatische Forschungen: Monographien 2 (Berlin, 1963), 86–7. See also Kim, 'Formation and changes of *ulus*es', 307–8.

5: THE CRISIS OF THE MONGOL WORLD: ECONOMIC TURBULENCE AND DEMOGRAPHIC DISASTER

1. The conventional view is that the first plague pandemic ended in *c*. 740 CE and the second began in the fourteenth century, but it is clear that an enormous tract from Central Asia to the Near East (but not, on this occasion, Europe) was struck by plague midway between these dates, in the 1050s: see later (and n.68).
2. See now Jong Kuk Nam, 'Rethinking trade between Europe and the Mongol realm during the *Pax Mongolica*', in Dunlop (ed.), *The Mongol Empire in Global History and Art History*, 167–83. I sought to qualify the concept in *The Mongols and the Islamic World*, chap. 8.
3. See, for instance, Janet Lippman Abu-Lughod, *Before European Hegemony. The World System A.D. 1250–1350* (Oxford, 1989), esp. 158, 177, 182, and her 'The world system in the thirteenth century: Dead-end or precursor?', in Michael Adas (ed.), *Islamic and European Expansion. The Forging of a Global Order* (Philadelphia, PA, 1993), 75–102.
4. I use this term rather than something like 'proto-globalisation', which seems anachronistic.
5. Waṣṣāf (1853), 169–70, 303 (*GW*, II, 53, and III, 110).
6. John of Marignolli, *Relatio*, in *SF*, I, 546; new edn in Irene Malfatto, 'Le digressioni sull'Oriente nel *Chronicon Bohemorum* di Giovanni de' Marignolli' (Firenze, 2013), 20, http://ecodicibus.sismelfirenze.it/index.php/iohannes-de-marignollis-chronicon-bohemorum-excerpta-de-rebus-orientalibus;dc; (I am indebted to Dr Jana Valtrová for kindly bringing this edition to my attention); passage translated in Yule, *Cathay*, III, 256.
7. Roberto S. Lopez, 'Trafegando in partibus Catagii: altri Genovesi in Cina nel Trecento', in his *Su e giù per la storia di Genova* (Genoa, 1975), 171–86. Michel Balard, 'Precursori di Cristoforo Colombo: i Genovesi in estremo Oriente nel XIV secolo', 149–64; repr. (with addenda) in his *La Mer Noire et la*

Romanie génoise (XIIIe-XVe siècles) (London, 1989). Gabriella Airaldi, 'I Genovesi in Cina all'epoca Yuan', in Franco Cardini and Maria Luisa Ceccarelli Lemut (eds), *Quel mar che la terra inghirlanda. In ricordo di Marco Tangheroni* (Pisa, 2007), I, 59–65.

8. China: WR, 132 (*MFW*, 162); Richard von Glahn, *Fountain of Fortune. Money and Monetary Policy in China, 1000–1700* (Berkeley and Los Angeles, CA, 1996), 56–7. Korea: WR, 200 (*MFW*, 203). Anatolia: Āqsarā'ī, *Musāmarat al-akhbār*, 73, 82; cited by A.P. Martinez, 'Bullionistic imperialism: The Īl-Xānid mint's exploitation of the Rūm-Saljūqid currency, 654–695 H./1256–1296 A.D.', in E. Halasi-Kun and Gy. Hazai (eds), *Tibor Halasi-Kun Memorial Volume* (Wiesbaden, 1994 = *Archivum Ottomanicum* 13 [1993–4]), 169–276 (here 169).
9. For example, *JT*, I, 123, and II, 1022 (*DzhT*, I, part 1, 285, and III, 65; *CC*, 47, 356). On these terms, see Paul Pelliot, 'Le prétendu mot "*iascot*" chez Guillaume de Rubrouck', *TP* 27 (1930), 190–2; Larry V. Clark, 'The Turkic and Mongol words in William of Rubruck's *Journey* (1253–1255)', *JAOS* 93 (1973), 181–9 (here 186); and on the ingots, Allsen, *Mongol Imperialism*, 180–2.
10. *TJG*, I, 162–3, 165–84, 186–9 (*HWC*, 205–6, 208–28, 230–1, 233). See also WR, 178, 192, 226, 234 (*MFW*, 190, 198, 218, 224).
11. Von Glahn, *Fountain of Fortune*, 57–8.
12. For the enormous quantity of silver stockpiled by the Song, see Kuroda Akinobu, 'The Eurasian silver century, 1276–1359: Commensurability and multiplicity', *JGH* 4 (2009), 245–69 (here 258–9).
13. Von Glahn, *Fountain of Fortune*, 60–2.
14. Francesco Balducci Pegolotti, *La pratica della mercatura*, ed. Allan Evans (Cambridge, MA, 1936), 22–3.
15. Kuroda, 'The Eurasian silver century', 249–63.
16. Jackson, *The Delhi Sultanate*, 201–8. For the fall in the value of gold, see Martinez, 'Bullionistic imperialism', 178.
17. Simon Digby, 'The currency system', in Tapan Raychaudhuri and Irfan Habib (eds), *The Cambridge Economic History of India, I:* c.*1200*–c.*1750* (Cambridge, 1982), 96–100. For the debased silver issue and the token currency, see H. Nelson Wright, *The Coinage and Metrology of the Sulṭāns of Delhī* (Delhi, 1936), 162–7; Jackson, *The Delhi Sultanate*, 261–2. The Delhi historian Ḍiyā' al-Dīn Baranī, *Ta'rīkh-i Fīrūzshāhī* (*c.* 758/1357), ed. Saiyid Ahmad Khán (Calcutta, 1862), 475, and tr. Ishtiyaq Ahmad Zilli (Delhi, 2015), 292, implicitly links the token coinage with the need to pay the troops. See also the earlier recension of Baranī's work, in RRL Persian ms. 2053, 302, and in Bodleian mss. Elliott 353, fo. 201b, and S. Digby Or. 54, fo. 167b. On this variant text, see Iqtidar Husain Siddiqui, *Perso-Arabic Sources of Information on the Life and Conditions in the Sultanate of Delhi* (New Delhi, 1992), 151–66.
18. Ḥamd-Allāh Mustawfī Qazwīnī, *Nuzhat al-qulūb*, ed. and tr. Le Strange, I (text), 230, II (trans.), 222. The context is the export of gold to India from the islands of Wāqwāq, which Le Strange identifies with Japan (for other possible locations, see F. Viré, 'Wāḳwāḳ', *EI*[2], XI, 103–9); but the statement must have geographically wider implications.
19. See Martinez, 'Bullionistic imperialism', 177 and n.42 at 236–7.
20. Hassanein Rabie, *The Financial System of Egypt A.H. 564–741/A.D. 1169–1341* (Oxford, 1972), 193–4. Jere Bacharach, 'Monetary movements in medieval

Egypt, 1171–1517', in J.F. Richards (ed.), *Precious Metals in the Later Medieval and Early Modern Worlds* (Durham, NC, 1984), 159–81 (here 167).

21. For example, the phenomenal disbursement of gold in 724/1324 by the visiting Sultan of Mali: Warren Schultz, 'Mansa Mūsā's gold in Mamluk Cairo: A reappraisal of a World Civilizations anecdote', in Pfeiffer and Quinn (eds), *History and Historiography of Post-Mongol Central Asia*, 428–47.
22. A.P. Martinez, 'Regional mint outputs and the dynamics of bullion flows through the Īl-Khānate', in Pierre Oberling (ed., with Geraldine Cecilia Butash), *Turks, Hungarians and Kipchaks. A Festschrift in Honor of Tibor Halasi-Kun* (Cambridge, MA, 1984 = *JTS* 8), 121–73 (here 139).
23. A.P. Martinez, 'The wealth of Ormus and of Ind: The Levant trade in bullion, intergovernmental arbitrage, and currency manipulations in the Il-Xanate, 704–751/1304–1350', *AEMA* 9 (1995–7), 123–251 (here 134–6).
24. Ḥamd-Allāh Mustawfī Qazwīnī, *Nuzhat al-qulūb*, ed. and tr. Le Strange, I (text), 27, II (trans.), 33.
25. For the Germans, who were moved to Bolad in Zungharia in or soon after 1251 and were mining gold, see WR, 110, 112 (*MFW*, 144–6).
26. Michael Fedorov, 'The newly discovered Chaghatayid mint of Kenjek (Kenchek)', *Revue Numismatique* 158 (2002), 367–74 (esp. 373). E.A. Davidovich, *Klady drevnikh i srednevekovykh monet Tadzhikistana* (Moscow, 1979), 241–2.
27. *Masālik*, text, 47 (German trans., 123). On Chaghadayid monetary reforms, see Biran, 'The Mongols in Central Asia', 61–2.
28. *Masālik*, text, 41 (German trans., 119). For his abolition of *mukūs*, see also al-Dhahabī, LIII, 330; al-Ṣafadī, *al-Wāfī bi l-wafayāt*, X, 383; idem, *A'yān al-'aṣr*, I, 523.
29. John Norris, 'East or west? The geographic origin of the Black Death', *BHM* 51 (1977), 1–24 (here 13–14). Views of this sort go back to C.R. Beazeley, *The Dawn of Modern Geography* (London, 1897–1900), III, 376. Virgil Ciocîltan, *The Mongols and the Black Sea Trade in the Thirteenth and Fourteenth Centuries*, tr. Samuel Willcocks (Leiden, 2012), 111–12, likewise sees Janibeg's attack as provoking commercial stagnation.
30. Ole J. Benedictow, *The Black Death 1346–1353. The Complete History* (Woodbridge, 2004), 49–50. The rationale for this scenario is in part the need to explain why the pandemic did not arrive in Rus' until 1352, a chronology questioned by John T. Alexander, *Bubonic Plague in Early Modern Russia. Public Health and Urban Disaster* (Oxford, 2003), 13.
31. Pegolotti, *La pratica della mercatura*, 22.
32. Paschal de Vittoria, 'Epistola', in *SF*, 504 (tr. in Yule, *Cathay*, III, 86).
33. Richard, *La Papauté et les missions d'Orient*, 162–4.
34. Jackson, *The Mongols and the West*, 271.
35. Anonymous *Dhayl-i Ta'rīkh-i guzīda*, ed. Otsuka, text, 195–6.
36. al-Maqrīzī, *al-Sulūk*, II, part 3, 863.
37. See Șerban Papacostea, 'Les Génois et la Horde d'Or: le tournant de 1313', in Damien Coulon, Catherine Otten-Froux, Paule Pagès and Dominique Valérian (eds), *Chemins d'Outre-mer. Études d'histoire sur la Méditerranée médiévale offertes à Michel Balard* (Paris, 2004), II, 651–9 (here 651–2); the comments of Nicola Di Cosmo, 'Black Sea emporia and the Mongol empire: A reassessment of the Pax Mongolica', *JESHO* 53 (2010), 83–108 (here 97–8); and Favereau, *The Horde*, 248.

38. Marignolli, *Relatio*, in *SF*, I, 536/ed. Malfatto, 8 (tr. in Yule, *Cathay*, III, 228). He has previously said that his party had stayed in Khanbaligh (where they had arrived in 1342) for almost three years and that they set sail on St Stephen's day (26 Dec. [1344]): *SF*, I, 530/ed. Malfatto, 4 (tr. in Yule, *Cathay*, III, 216). Shim, 'The postal roads of the Great Khans', 457, appears to date his departure from China in 1346–7: Shim's citation of Ibn Baṭṭūṭa's departure in the same period is highly risky, given the doubts that attach to IB's visit to China.
39. Raimondo Morozzo della Rocca, 'Notizie da Caffa', in G. Barbieri (ed.), *Studi in onore di Amintore Fanfani* (Milan, 1962), III: *Medioevo*, 265–95 (here 279, 286).
40. Benjamin Z. Kedar, *Merchants in Crisis. Genoese and Venetian Men of Affairs and the Fourteenth-Century Depression* (New Haven, CT, and London, 1976), 15 and n.45 at 173.
41. Eliyahu Ashtor, *Levant Trade in the Later Middle Ages* (Princeton, NJ, 1983), 65–70. There was opposition, however, to the renewal of trade with the Mamlūks.
42. Robert-Henri Bautier, 'Les relations économiques des Occidentaux avec les pays d'Orient au Moyen Âge: points de vue et documents', in M. Mollat du Jourdain (ed.), *Sociétés et compagnies de commerce en Orient et dans l'Océan indien. Actes du VIIIe colloque international d'histoire maritime, Beyrouth 5–10 septembre 1966* (Paris, 1970), 263–331 (here 295–7).
43. Giosafa Barbaro, *Viaggi*, § 52, ed. and tr. E.Ch. Skrzhinskaia, *Barbaro i Kontarini o Rossii. K istorii italo-russkikh sviazei v XV v.* (Leningrad, 1971), text, 132 (Russian trans., 157); tr. William Thomas, in Henry Edward John Stanley, Baron Stanley of Alderley (ed.), *Travels to Tana and Persia by Josafa Barbaro and Ambrogio Contarini*, HS, 1st series, [49a] (London, 1873), 31.
44. See the remarks of R.S. Humphreys, 'Egypt in the world system of the later Middle Ages', in *CHE*, 445–61 (here 456); also Jackson, *The Delhi Sultanate*, 255–6.
45. Nils Chr. Stenseth et al., 'Plague dynamics are driven by climate variation', *PNAS* 103, no. 35 (29 August 2006), 13110–15. Boris V. Schmid et al., 'Climate-driven introduction of the Black Death and successive plague reintroductions into Europe', *PNAS* 112, no. 10 (10 March 2015), 3020–5. For a broad survey of developments in the field, see Monica H. Green, 'Editor's introduction', in Green (ed.), *Pandemic Disease in the Medieval World. Rethinking the Black Death* (Kalamazoo, MI, 2015 = *The Medieval Globe* 1 [Fall 2014]), 9–25 (here 10–15); also Green, 'Taking pandemic seriously: Making the Black Death global', ibid., 27–61; and most recently James Belich, *The World the Plague Made. The Black Death and the Rise of Europe* (Princeton, NJ, and Oxford, 2022), 33–78. On climate change in the western steppe in particular, see Uli Schamiloglu, 'Climate change in Central Eurasia and the Golden Horde', *ZOO* 4 (2016), 6–25.
46. Richard Stothers, 'Volcanic dry fogs, climate cooling, and plague pandemics in Europe and the Middle East', *Climatic Change* 42 (1999), 713–23 (here 719–20). Clive Oppenheimer, 'Ice core and palaeoclimatic evidence for the timing and nature of the great mid-13th century volcanic eruption', *International Journal of Climatology* 23 (2003), 417–26. Franck Lavigne et al., 'Source of the great AD 1257 mystery eruption unveiled, Samalas volcano, Rinjani volcanic complex, Indonesia', *PNAS* 110, no. 42 (15 Oct. 2013), 16742–7. But note the

cautious comments of Bruce M.S. Campbell, *The Great Transition. Climate, Disease and Society in the Late-Medieval World* (Cambridge, 2016), 55–8.

47. Yali Li, Gideon Shelach-Lavi and Ronnie Ellenblum, 'Short-term climatic catastrophes and the collapse of the Liao dynasty (907–1125): Textual evidence', *JIH* 49, no. 4 (Spring 2019), 591–610.
48. On these developments, see generally Campbell, *The Great Transition*, esp. 198–252.
49. See Shāmī, *ZN*, I, 69, 75–6, 112–14, 117, 123; Yazdī, *ZN* (1957), I, 188–9, 415, 551, 553, and II, 452, 457/(2008), I, 441, 694, 825–6, and II, 1279–80, 1283. For the river, ibid. (1957), I, 206–7, and II, 458/(2008), I, 465, and II, 1284.
50. See Campbell, *The Great Transition*, 249–51; also Philip Slavin, 'Death by the lake: Mortality crisis in early fourteenth-century Central Asia', *Journal of Interdisciplinary History* 50, no. 1 (Summer 2019), 59–90 (here 70–3).
51. Emmanuel Le Roy Ladurie, 'A concept: The unification of the globe by disease (fourteenth to seventeenth centuries)', in his *The Mind and Method of the Historian*, tr. Siân and Ben Reynolds (Brighton and Chicago, IL, 1981), 28–83 (phrase quoted at 30). S.A.M. Adshead, *Central Asia in World History* (Basingstoke, 1993), 95.
52. W. Europe: Rosemary Horrox, *The Black Death* (Manchester, 1994), Introduction, 3 ('a probable average mortality of around 47% or 48%' in England); and see also the more localised percentages, for the outbreaks of 1348–9 and the early 1360s combined, presented by Le Roy Ladurie, 'A concept', 44% (Provence) and 54% (Savoy). Near East: Michael W. Dols, *The Black Death in the Middle East* (Princeton, NJ, 1977), 212–23; idem, 'The general mortality of the Black Death in the Mamluk empire', in A.L. Udovitch (ed.), *The Islamic Middle East, 700–1900. Studies in Economic and Social History* (Princeton, NJ, 1981), 397–428 (here 411–17).
53. See David Herlihy, *The Black Death and the Transformation of the West*, ed. Samuel K. Cohn, Jr (Cambridge, MA, 1997), esp. 46–9; and Stuart J. Borsch, *The Black Death in Egypt and England. A Comparative Study* (Austin, TX, 2005), 113–17.
54. On the Islamic Near East, see the brief remarks concerning sources in Dols, *The Black Death*, 40–2, and more particularly the detailed discussion at 320–9 (appendix 3); there is also a useful survey by Stuart Borsch, 'Black Death', *EI*[3] (2014), fasc. 3, 57–60.
55. Stephanie Haensch et al., 'Distinct clones of *Yersinia pestis* caused the Black Death', *Public Library of Science, Pathogens* 6, no. 10 (7 Oct. 2010): www.doi.org/10.1371/journal.ppat.1001134 [last accessed 14 November 2018]. Kirsten I. Bos et al., 'A draft genome of *Yersinia pestis* from victims of the Black Death', *Nature* 478 (27 Oct. 2011), 506–10. Pierre Toubert, 'La Peste Noire (1348), entre histoire et biologie moléculaire', *Journal des Savants* (2016), 17–31 (here 19–20). Green, 'Editor's introduction', 14. For a survey of the successive investigations identifying *Yersinia pestis* DNA in historic burial sites, see Lester K. Little, 'Plague historians in lab coats', *Past and Present* 213 (Nov. 2011), 267–90.
56. Maria Spyrou et al., 'The source of the Black Death in fourteenth-century Central Eurasia', *Nature* 606, no. 7915 (23 June 2022), 718–24. Philip Slavin, 'A rise and fall of a Chaghadaid community: Demographic growth and crisis in "late-medieval" Semirech'ye (Zhetysu), *circa* 1248–1345', *JRAS*, 3rd series, 33 (2023), 513–44 (here 521); in 'Death by the lake', 63 ff., Slavin had already argued vigorously that the pestilence in question was plague.

57. Cui Yujun et al., 'Historical variations in mutation rate in an epidemic pathogen, *Yersinia pestis*', *PNAS* 110, no. 2 (8 Jan. 2013), 577–82. Green, 'Taking pandemic seriously', 38–9, and her 'Climate and disease in medieval Eurasia', in *Oxford Research Encyclopedia of Asian History* (Oxford, 2018): https://doi.org/10.1093/acrefore/9780190277727.013.6.
58. Cui et al., 'Historical variations', 578–9. Campbell, *The Great Transition*, 244–52. Green, 'Taking pandemic seriously', 37. See also Hymes, quoted below (n. 63).
59. Galina Eroshenko et al., '*Yersinia pestis* strains of ancient phylogenetic branch o.ANT are widely spread in the high-mountain plague foci of Kyrgyzstan', *Public Library of Science ONE* 12 (2017) [accessed 18 January 2021]. Slavin, 'Death by the lake', 61–2, 82–3. For a helpful introduction to scientific research on the Black Death, see Monica H. Green, 'The four Black Deaths', *American Historical Review* 125 (2020), 1601–31 (here 1607–15).
60. Ronnie Ellenblum, *The Collapse of the Eastern Mediterranean. Climate Change and the Decline of the East, 950–1072* (Cambridge, 2012), 68–9, 100–2.
61. WR, 34 (*MFW*, 84). John Masson Smith, Jr, 'Mongol campaign rations: Milk, marmots, and blood?', in Oberling (ed.), *Turks, Hungarians and Kipchaks*, 223–8 (esp. 227). Slavin, 'Death by the lake', 74.
62. Thomas T. Allsen, 'Population movements in Mongol Eurasia', in Reuven Amitai and Michal Biran (eds), *Nomads as Agents of Cultural Change. The Mongols and Their Eurasian Predecessors* (Honolulu, HI, 2015), 119–51 (here 136).
63. Robert Hymes, 'Epilogue: A hypothesis on the East Asian beginnings of the *Yersinia Pestis* polytomy', in Green (ed.), *Pandemic Disease in the Medieval World*, 285–308 (here 289–93).
64. Green, 'The four Black Deaths', 1621–3.
65. Lawrence I. Conrad, '*Ṭāʿūn* and *wabāʾ*: Conceptions of plague and pestilence in early Islam', *JESHO* 25 (1982), 268–307.
66. Nahyan Fancy and Monica H. Green, 'Plague and the fall of Baghdad (1258)', *Medical History* 65 (2021), 157–77.
67. On Suyūṭī's work, see Yaron Ayalon, *Natural Disasters in the Ottoman Empire. Plague, Famine, and Other Misfortunes* (Cambridge, 2015), 26–7.
68. Shihāb al-Dīn Abū l-Faḍl Aḥmad b. ʿAlī Ibn Ḥajar al-ʿAsqalānī, *Badhl al-māʿūn fī faḍl al-ṭāʿūn*, ed. Aḥmad ʿIṣām ʿAbd al-Qādir al-Kātib (al-Riyāḍ, 1411/1991), 368. Jalāl al-Dīn Abū l-Faḍl ʿAbd al-Raḥmān al-Suyūṭī, *Mā rawāhu l-wāʿūn fī akhbār al-ṭāʿūn*, BL ms. Or. 3053, fo. 21a. See also Ibn Abī Ḥajala (third quarter of the fourteenth cent.), quoted in Lawrence I. Conrad, 'Arabic plague chronologies and treatises: Social and historical factors in the formation of a literary genre', *StIsl* 54 (1981), 51–93 (here 74). But the pestilence that struck Transoxiana, Khurāsān, Azerbaijan, ʿIrāq-i ʿAjam, Khūzistān, Baghdad and Egypt in the mid-1050s (similarly termed *wabā ʿaẓīm*) had been regarded as afflicting the whole world: see ʿAbd al-Raḥmān Ibn al-Jawzī (d. 597/1201), *al-Muntaẓam fī taʾrīkh al-mulūk wa l-umam*, ed. F. Krenkow (Hyderabad, Deccan, 1357–9/1938–40), VIII, 179–80, and the other sources cited in Ellenblum, *The Collapse of the Eastern Mediterranean*, 101–2.
69. *Taʿrīf* (1951), 15, 19, 55/(2008), 26, 31, 57 (rendering the phrase as 'la grande peste'). Fromherz, *Ibn Khaldun*, 40–1, 49.
70. Ibn Khaldūn, *al-Muqaddima*, tr. Rosenthal, I, 64.

71. For example, Benedictow, *The Black Death*, 50–1. Dols, *The Black Death*, 35–8, locates its origin in Central Asia. William H. McNeill, *Plagues and Peoples* (Oxford, 1977), 151–2, 160–2, proposed that the plague originated in Yunnan, where it had become endemic since the Mongol conquest in 1252–3, and that the emergence of the more northerly route from China to the Pontic–Caspian steppes introduced the bacillus *Pasteurella pestis* (i.e. *Yersinia pestis*) into the steppe rodent populations. See Nükhet Varlık, *Plague and Empire in the Early Modern Mediterranean World. The Ottoman Experience, 1347–1600* (Cambridge, 2015), 94–7, for an overview of the conflicting arguments regarding origins.
72. Hannah Barker, 'Laying the corpses to rest: Grain, embargoes and *Yersinia pestis* in the Black Sea, 1346–48', *Speculum* 96 (2021), 97–126.
73. Ibn al-Wardī, *Tatimmat al-Mukhtaṣar*, II, 489.
74. Nikephoros Gregoras, *Rhomaïkē historia*, xvi, 1.5, tr. Jan Louis Van Dieten, *Nikephoros Gregoras. Rhomäische Geschichte* (Stuttgart, 1973–2007), III, 175; extract also tr. in Christos S. Bartsocas, 'Two fourteenth century Greek descriptions of the "Black Death"', *Journal of the History of Medicine and Allied Sciences* 21 (1966), 394–400 (here 395).
75. Rafaino Caresini, *Chronica* [to 1388], ed. Ester Pastorello, 'Raphayni de Caresinis cancellarii Venetiarum Chronica', in *RIS*, n.s., XII, part 2 (Bologna, 1938–58), 4: *inguinaria pestis incipiens in partibus Tartarorum.*
76. See the references at 68, n.6, in Sergei Karpov, 'Black Sea and the crisis of the mid XIVth century: An underestimated turning point', *Thesaurismata. Bollettino dell'Istituto ellenico di studi bizantini e postbizantini di Venezia* 27 (1997), 65–77.
77. For the dates, see Dols, *The Black Death*, 57–63. The progress of the plague through Anatolia is discussed by Varlık, *Plague and Empire*, 99–107.
78. Ibn al-Wardī, *Risālat al-naba' 'an al-wabā*, tr. Michael Dols, 'Ibn al-Wardī's *Risālah al-naba' 'an al-waba'*: A translation of a major source for the history of the Black Death in the Middle East', in Dickran K. Kouymjian (ed.), *Near Eastern Numismatics, Iconography, Epigraphy and History. Studies in Honor of George C. Miles* (Beirut, 1974), 443–55 (here 448). Ibn al-Wardī, *Tatimmat al-Mukhtaṣar*, II, 497. On the Land of Darkness, see IB, II, 399–402 (tr. Gibb, 491–2); MP, tr. Ricci, 387–8/tr. Latham, 305–6/tr. Kinoshita, 211–12 (not in Ménard's edn); Martin, *Treasure of the Land of Darkness*, 21–2. Yazdī, *ZN* (1957), I, 539/(2008), I, 814, indicates that Būlar (in Volga Bulgaria: see Egorov, *Istoricheskaia geografiia*, 96) lay near the *ẓulamāt*.
79. *Historia Roffensis*, tr. in Horrox, *The Black Death*, 70. Henry Knighton, *Chronica de eventibus Angliae a tempore regis Edgari usque mortem regis Ricardi Secundi*, ed. G.H. Martin, *Knighton's Chronicle 1337–1396* (Oxford, 1995), 94–5. *Pskovskie letopisi*, ed. A. Nasonov, I (Moscow and Leningrad, 1941; repr. The Hague, 1967), 22; *Patriarshaia ili Nikonovskaia letopis'*, in *PSRL*, X, 224 (tr. Zenkovsky, III, 169); Lawrence N. Langer, 'The Black Death in Russia: Its effects upon urban labor', *Russian History* 2 (1975), 53–67 (here 56). Compare also the assertion by Geoffrey le Baker, *Chronicon*, tr. David Preest, *The Chronicle of Geoffrey le Baker of Swinbrook* (Woodbridge, 2012), 86 (also tr. in Horrox, *The Black Death*, 80), that the pandemic had begun among 'the Indians and the Turks'.
80. Thus the papal envoy Marignolli, en route from the Qaghan's court at this time, describes China, along with Malabar and Maʿbar, as the three regions of

India: Marignolli, *Relatio*, in *SF*, I, 543/ed. Malfatto, 17 (tr. in Yule, *Cathay*, III, 248). The Florentine chronicler Giovanni Villani, *Nuova cronica*, xiii, 84, ed. Giuseppe Porta (Parma, 1990–1), III, 486, thought of the dominions of the Ilkhan Ghazan as 'India'.

81. Matteo Villani, *Cronica*, i, 2, ed. Giuseppe Porta (Parma, 1995), I, 9. Matteo's brother (who died of the plague in 1348) likewise mentions Cathay but does not claim that the epidemic began there: Giovanni Villani, *Nuova cronica*, xiii, 84, ed. Porta, III, 486. On rumours current in Western Europe, and involving distant territories such as China or 'India', see Philip Ziegler, *The Black Death* (London, 1969), 13–15; Samuel K. Cohn, Jr, *The Black Death Transformed. Disease and Culture in Early Renaissance Europe* (London, 2002), 101–2. For southern China as 'Upper India', see Folker E. Reichert, *Begegnungen mit China. Die Entdeckung Ostasiens im Mittelalter* (Sigmaringen, 1992), 97 and n.200, citing their identification by Odoric of Pordenone; also ibid., 227.
82. 'Corpus chronicorum Bononiensium III: Cronaca A', in *RIS*, n.s., XVIII, part 1, 583–4 (tr. in Klaus Bergdolt, ed., *Die Pest 1348 in Italien. Fünfzig zeitgenössische Quellen* [Heidelberg, 1989], 95); 'Cronaca B', ibid., 584–5. František of Prague, *Chronica Pragensis*, ed. as 'Kronika Františka Pražského', in Josef Emler (ed.), *Prameny dějin českých. Fontes rerum Bohemicarum*, IV (Prague, 1884), 449–50/new edn by Jana Zachová, *Chronicon Francisci Pragensis/Kronika Františka Pražského*, Prameny dějin českých/Fontes rerum Bohemicarum, nová řada, I (Prague, 1997), 203–4; similar details in *Chronicon Estense*, in *RIS*, n.s., XV, part 3, 160 (tr. in Bergdolt, *Die Pest 1348*, 89). For a hail of snakes and toads in Cathay and fire falling from Heaven in 'the Indies', see Gabriele de' Mussi, *De morbo*, ed. A.G. Tononi, 'La peste dell'anno 1348', *Giornale Ligustico di Archeologia, Storia e Letteratura* 11 (1884), 139–52 (here 151; tr. in Horrox, *The Black Death*, 25), and compare also 'Continuatio Novimontensis', ed. Wilhelm Wattenbach, in *MGHS*, IX (Hannover, 1851), 674 (tr. in Horrox, 59); for a plague of worms, see Giovanni Villani, *Nuova cronica*, xiii, 84, ed. Porta, III, 486–7. Such tales are found also in Islamic sources: Sarah Kate Raphael, *Climate and Political Climate. Environmental Disasters in the Medieval Levant* (Leiden, 2013), 106–11.
83. Gabriele de' Mussi, *De morbo*, 145 (tr. in Horrox, *The Black Death*, 18).
84. Matsui, '*Dumdadu Mongyol Ulus*', 114–15. In addition to the examples cited there from Western European sources, see Paschal de Vittoria, 'Epistola', 504, 506 (tr. in Yule, *Cathay*, III, 85, 87, 88). But an older equation of the term with Khurāsān and adjacent regions persisted, as found for instance in Clavijo's account. For Timur as a Mede, see John of Sulṭāniyya, *Libellus de notitia orbis*, Universitätsbibliothek Graz ms. 1221, fos 57a (*mediusque homo*), 58a (*medio homine*); partial edn by Kern, 'Der "Libellus de notitia orbis" Iohannes' III.', 99.
85. Ibn al-Wardī, *Risālat al-naba'*, tr. Dols, here 448 (but with the misleading translation 'the land of the Uzbeks', found also in Dols, *The Black Death*, 38 and n.4). Ibn al-Wardī, *Tatimmat al-Mukhtaṣar*, II, 497–8.
86. Notably Ibn Ḥajar, *Badhl*, 371 ff., and al-Suyūṭī, *Mā rawāhu l-wā'ūn*, fos 21a ff.
87. Ibn al-Wardī, *Tatimmat al-Mukhtaṣar*, II, 489.
88. *Troitskaia letopis'*, ed. M.D. Priselkov (Moscow, 1950), 368. See also *Ermolinskaia letopis'*, in *PSRL*, XXIII, 108; *Moskovskii letopisnyi svod kontsa XV veka*, in *PSRL*, XXV, 175; *Patriarshaia ili Nikonovskaia letopis'*, in *PSRL*, X, 217 (tr. Zenkovsky, III, 157).

89. Benedictow, *The Black Death*, 50, quoting this passage (from another Rus′ chronicle), misidentifies place- and ethnic names (ibid., n.44). 'Ornach': this does not lie at the mouth of the Don (as also stated in Zenkovsky, III, 157, n.86) but is the Rus′ name for Ürgench, as is clear from the 'Hornach' of the Dominican Friar Julian (surely derived from his Rus′ informants) in 1237: Dörrie, 'Drei Texte', 169–71, 174. Compare also the 'Ornac' of the Rus′ prelate Peter in his statements to the Papal Curia in 1244/5: ibid., 189, 190. The name is found in the *Historia Tartarorum* (1247) of C. de Bridia (a member of Carpini's party) and is correctly identified by George D. Painter, in Painter et al. (eds), *The Vinland Map and the Tartar Relation*, new edn (New Haven, CT, and London, 1995), 102–4. Bessermens: see T.I. Tepliashina, 'Étnonim *besermiane*', in V.A. Nikonov (ed.), *Étnonimy* (Moscow, 1970), 177–88. PC, 270, 314, 331 (*MM*, 28–9, 59, 70–1), associates *terra Biserminorum* both with 'Ornas' (= Ornach/Ürgench) and with towns along the Sīr-daryā such as Yangikent and Barchinlighkent.
90. Khwāfī (1962), II, 71/(2007), II, 935 (tr. Iusupova, 73–4, as 'cholera'): the weekday specified (Thursday) is correct. For Jurjāniyya as the old Arabic name for Gurganj/Ürgench, see B. Spuler, 'Gurgandj', *EI²*, II, 1141–2.
91. D. Chwolson, *Syrisch-Nestorianische Grabinschriften aus Semirjetschie* (St Petersburg, 1890 = *Mémoires de l'Académie Impériale de St.-Pétersbourg*, 7ᵉ série, XXXVII, no. 8), 129–30. Chwolson, *Syrisch-Nestorianische Grabinschriften aus Semirjetschie, neue Folge* (St Petersburg, 1897), 31–2, 35–8; for the gravestones dated 1341–2, see ibid., 39–40. Wassilios Klein, *Das nestorianische Christentum an den Handelswegen durch Kyrgyzstan bis zum 14. Jh.*, SRS 3 (Turnhout, 2000), 287–9; on the three sites, see ibid., 110–11, and Slavin, 'Death by the lake', 62–4.
92. Slavin, 'A rise and fall of a Chaghadaid community', 540, 541.
93. Barker, 'Laying the corpses to rest', 116.
94. IA (1979), 82/(1986), 138–9 (*TGA*, 77).
95. Bautier, 'Les relations économiques des Occidentaux', 315. Pegolotti, *La pratica della mercatura*, 21. This route passed through Sarai and Saraichik ('Saracanco'): see also Paschal de Vittoria, 'Epistola', 502, 503–4 (tr. in Yule, *Cathay*, III, 82, 84–5).
96. Ibn Khātima, *Taḥṣīl al-gharaḍ al-ḥāṣid fī tafsīl al-maraḍ al-wāfid*, tr. Taha Dinānah, 'Die Schrift von Abī [*sic*] Ja'far Aḥmed ibn 'Alī ibn Muḥammed ibn 'Alī ibn Ḫātimah aus Almeriah über die Pest', *Archiv für Geschichte der Medizin* 19 (1927), 27–81 (here 41). Ibn al-Khaṭīb, *Muqni'at al-sa'īl 'an al-maraḍ al-hā'il*, ed. and tr. M.J. Müller, 'Ibnulkhatīb's Bericht über die Pest', *Sitzungsberichte der königlich bayerischen Akademie der Wissenschaften, philosophisch-philologische Classe* (1863), part 2, 1–34 (text at 8–9, trans. at 22).
97. The text of IB contains no such statement that the plague had begun in China; we may therefore be dealing with oral testimony. The two men could have coincided in Granada in 750/1349: IB lists those whom he met there at IV, 370–3 (tr. Gibb and Beckingham, 942–4), though they do not include Ibn al-Khaṭīb. The latter was one of the sources of the notice on IB found in the *Durar al-kāmina* of Ibn Ḥajar (see Gibb's trans., I, ix).
98. al-Maqrīzī, *al-Sulūk*, II, part 3, 773, and mentioning its arrival in southern China (Ṣīn) ibid., 774: these passages tr. in G. Wiet, 'La grande peste Noire en Syrie et en Égypte', in *Études d'orientalisme dédiées à la mémoire de Lévi-*

Provençal (Paris, 1962), I, 367–84 (here 368, 369). Norris, 'East or west?', 8, assumes that 'Khitā' could refer at this time only to the former Qara Khitai dominions; but the association with the Kitan-Liao was much older and strongly suggests northern China and perhaps also Mongolia. Compare also Dols, *The Black Death*, 38, n.3. Shim, 'The postal roads of the Great Khan', 454–6, opines that the Black Death began in Mongolia in 1331–2.

99. Geoffrey Le Baker, *Chronicon*, tr. Preest, 86 (also tr. in Horrox, *Black Death*, 80–1); though the paragraph starts, erroneously, by dating the onset of plague in Asia in 1349.
100. On which see Tana Li, 'The Mongol Yuan dynasty and the climate, 1260–1360', in Martin Bauch and Gerrit Jasper Schenk (eds), *The Crisis of the 14th Century. Teleconnections between Environmental and Societal Change?* (Berlin and Boston, MA, 2020), 153–68.
101. George D. Sussman, 'Was the Black Death in India and China?', *BHM* 85 (2011), 319–55 (here 347–8). The material, as he acknowledges, must be approached with caution, since the source is an eighteenth-century list 'compiled centuries after the events from provincial summaries of local events recorded unevenly in different parts of the country' (ibid., 346–7). Campbell, *The Great Transition*, 247, believes that the 1331 outbreak in Hebei province should probably be ruled out as plague. For 1340, see below and n. 104.
102. Paul D. Buell, 'Qubilai and the rats', *Sudhoffs Archiv* 96 (2012), no. 2, 127–44 (129 for the phrase cited). For other doubts, see Timothy Brook, *The Troubled Empire. China in the Yuan and Ming Dynasties* (Cambridge, MA, 2010), 64–5; Abu-Lughod, *Before European Hegemony*, 341–2; and Sussman, 'Was the Black Death in India and China?', 352–5. In the opinion of Richard Smith, 'Trade and commerce across Afro-Eurasia', in *CWH*, V, 233–56 (here 248), the Black Death 'appears to have largely bypassed China and India'. Belich, *The World the Plague Made*, 47, 56–60, like Sussman, argues that India escaped altogether.
103. Zachová, however, in the introduction to her edition of František's *Chronicon*, iii, believes that the chronicler obtained his information on improbable natural phenomena in China (see earlier) from Marignolli. For the chronology of Marignolli's return journey, see n. 38.
104. Herbert Franke (trans.), *Beiträge zur Kulturgeschichte Chinas unter der Mongolenherrschaft. Das* Shan-kü sin-hua *des Yang Yü*, AKM 32/2 (Wiesbaden, 1956), 58.
105. Ibn al-Wardī, *Risālat al-naba'*, tr. Dols, 448; see also his *Tatimmat al-Mukhtaṣar*, II, 497, for the figure of fifteen years. Ibn al-Khaṭīb, *Muqni'at al-sa'il,* text, 9, trans., 22.
106. See the comments of Li Bozhong, 'Was there a "fourteenth-century turning point"? Population, land, technology, and farm management', in Paul Jakov Smith and Richard von Glahn (eds), *The Song-Yuan-Ming Transition in Chinese History* (Cambridge, MA, 2003), 135–75 (here 138).
107. John Chaffee, 'Muslim merchants and Quanzhou in the late Yuan–early Ming: Conjectures on the ending of the medieval Muslim trade diaspora', in Angela Schottenhammer (ed.), *The East Asian 'Mediterranean'. Maritime Crossroads of Culture, Commerce and Human Migration* (Wiesbaden, 2008), 115–32. Tansen Sen, 'The formation of Chinese maritime networks to Southern Asia, 1200–1450', *JESHO* 49 (2006), 421–53. Idem, *Buddhism,*

Diplomacy, and Trade. The Realignment of India-China Relations, 600–1400 (Lanham, MD, 2016), 234–8. See also earlier.

108. Ibn Khātima, *Taḥṣīl*, tr. Dinānah, 41.
109. Hymes, 'Epilogue: A hypothesis', 299–300. Buell, 'Qubilai and the rats', 142–3, dismisses the possibility, on the grounds that fleas and the plague bacillus could not survive the protracted ocean voyage. Yet this is by no means certain.
110. I am assuming that the date 1 Muḥarram 734 [12 Sept. 1333] in IB, III, 92, 93 (tr. Gibb, 592, 593), for his arrival on the Indus is correct, as envisaged by Gibb in his trans. (IB, II, 529), and argued in his 'Notes sur les voyages d'Ibn Baṭṭūṭa en Asie mineure et en Russie', in *Études d'orientalisme*, I, 125–33, and as accepted by other authors. It was challenged by Ivan Hrbek, 'The chronology of Ibn Baṭṭūṭa's travels', *Archiv Orientální* 30 (1962), 409–86 (here 411; and see also 453, 485), which was unfortunately never completed and hence adduces no evidence to support his contention.
111. ʿAbd al-Malik ʿIṣāmī, *Futūḥ al-salāṭīn* (*c.* 1350), ed. A.S. Usha (Madras, 1948), 469, 471, for the casualties. Baranī, *Taʾrīkh-i Fīrūzshāhī*, 481 (tr. Zilli, 296); his first recension, RRL Persian ms. 2053, 290–1, and Bodleian mss. Elliott 353, fo. 194a and S. Digby Or. 54, fo. 162a, confirms that many of Muḥammad's amirs too fell sick and died. IB, III, 333–4, 443 (tr. Gibb, 717, 765). The fifteenth-century historian Yaḥyā b. Aḥmad Sirhindī, *Taʾrīkh-i Mubārakshāhī*, ed. S.M. Hidayat Husain (Calcutta, 1931), 106, says merely that Muḥammad fell ill and withdrew. For the probable date of the Tilang campaign, see Stephan Conermann, *Die Beschreibung Indiens in der „Riḥla" des Ibn Baṭṭūṭa. Aspekte einer herrschaftssoziologischen Einordnung des Delhi-Sultanates unter Muḥammad Ibn Tuġluq*, IU 165 (Berlin, 1993), 86; Jackson, *The Delhi Sultanate*, 268. Sussman, 'Was the Black Death in India and China?', 335, believes that this epidemic 'is unlikely to have been plague'. For other epidemics in the period 1329–39, of which one appears to have come from China, see Simon Digby, 'Before Timur came: Provincialization of the Delhi Sultanate through the fourteenth century', *JESHO* 47 (2004), 298–356 (here 326 and n.48).
112. IB, IV, 200–1 (tr. Gibb and Beckingham, 863). Numismatic evidence shows that Ghiyāth al-Dīn died in 744 or 745: S.A.Q. Husaini, 'The history of Madura Sultanate', *Journal of the Asiatic Society of Pakistan* 2 (1957), 90–130 (here 105, 128–9). But Conermann, *Die Beschreibung Indiens*, 9–10, dates IB's arrival in Maʿbar over a year later, in Jumādā I 746/Sept. 1345; compare also ibid., 90–1.
113. Ẓafār: IB, IV, 310 (tr. Gibb and Beckingham, 913); Shiraz: ibid., II, 63 (tr. Gibb, 306); Baghdad: ibid., IV, 313 (tr. Gibb and Beckingham, 915). Nevertheless, Ross E. Dunn, *The Adventures of Ibn Battuta. A Muslim Traveler of the Fourteenth Century*, 2nd edn, repr. with new preface (Berkeley and Los Angeles, CA, 2012), 288, n.4, asserts that the dates given for IB's visits in Syria and Egypt are corroborated by others' testimony regarding the progress of the Black Death.
114. That is, once peace had been made between Janibeg and the Italians and the grain trade had resumed, as convincingly demonstrated by Barker, 'Laying the corpses to rest'.
115. Ibn al-Wardī, *Tatimmat al-Mukhtaṣar*, II, 497, 502. IB, III, 334, and IV, 319–24; also 200–1, for the outbreak in Maʿbar. Ahmad Fazlinejad and Farajollah Ahmadi, 'The Black Death in Iran, according to Iranian historical

accounts from the fourteenth through the fifteenth centuries', *JPS* 11 (2018), 56–71, persistently translate *wabā* as 'cholera'.

116. Khwāfī (1962), II, 52–3/(2007), II, 918–19 (Iusupova trans., 62, thus renders the word).
117. For a survey of this information, see T.F. Khaidarov, 'Russkie letopisi kak istochnik po épidemii chumy v Zolotoi Orde', *ZOTs* 9 (2016), 96–101.
118. Morgan, *Medieval Persia*, 83. Compare also Lambton, *Continuity and Change*, 25; and James L.A. Webb, Jr, 'Globalization of disease, 1300–1900', in *CWH*, VI, part 1, 54–75 (here 61).
119. Ahrī, *Ta'rīkh-i Shaykh Uways*, text, 173, trans., 73. Zayn al-Dīn (1990), text, 475 (Russian trans., 100)/(1993), 41. Hence HA, *Dhayl-i Jāmi' al-tawārīkh*, 226, and Khwāfī (1962), II, 73/(2007), II, 936 (tr. Iusupova, 74–5). Fazlinejad and Ahmadi, 'The Black Death in Iran', 64–6.
120. al-Maqrīzī, *al-Sulūk*, II, part 3, 774 (tr. in Wiet, 'La grande peste Noire', 369), telling us that Shaykh Ḥasan reported the episode in a letter to the Mamlūk Sultan. Jean-Noël Biraben, *Les Hommes et la peste en France et dans les pays européens et méditerranéans* (Paris and The Hague, 1975–6), I, 53, claiming that the plague is not mentioned at Baghdad in 1347, was clearly unaware of this evidence. Ahrī, *Ta'rīkh-i Shaykh Uways*, text, 173, trans., 73, places Ashraf's campaign in spring 748/1347; hence Zayn al-Dīn (1990), text, 475 (Russian trans., 100)/(1993), 42; HA, *Dhayl-i Jāmi' al-tawārīkh*, 226; and Khwāfī (1962), II, 74/(2007), II, 937 (tr. Iusupova, 75). Fazlinejad and Ahmadi, 'The Black Death in Iran', 66, assume that Ashraf's army had brought the plague to Baghdad.
121. Faryūmadī, *Dhayl-i Majma' al-ansāb*, 327–8 (no year specified). Aubin, 'Le khanat de Čaġatai', 38. For Taghai Temür's two sons, 'Abd al-'Azīz and Abū Sa'īd, see *MA*, fo. 14a, ed. Vokhidov, text, 25 (Russian trans., 28).
122. Sayyid Ẓahīr al-Dīn Mar'ashī, *Ta'rīkh-i Ṭabaristān-u Rūyān-u Māzandarān*, ed. Muḥammad Ḥusayn Tasbīḥī (Tehran, 1345 sh./1966), 120. Khwānd-Amīr, *Ḥabīb al-siyar*, III, 336–7 (tr. Thackston, 189–90), says that disease struck during Fakhr al-Dawla's reign, but wrongly dates the king's death as early as 745/1344. Local sources are clear that he died in 750/1349: continuation of Ibn Isfandiyār, *Ta'rīkh-i Ṭabaristān*, abridged trans. by Edward G. Browne, GMS 2 (Leiden and London, 1905), 269; Awliyā'-Allāh Āmulī, *Ta'rīkh-i Rūyān*, ed. Manūchihr Sutūda (Tehran, 1348 sh./1969), 205; Mar'ashī, *Ta'rīkh-i Ṭabaristān-u Rūyān-u Māzandarān*, 121. H.L. Rabino, *Mázandarán and Astarábád*, GMS, n.s., 7 (London, 1928), 35, was misled into thinking that plague hit the region twice, in 743/1342–3 and 750/1349–50; hence Fazlinejad and Ahmadi, 'The Black Death in Iran', 66.
123. Malik Shāh Ḥusayn Sīstānī, *Iḥyā' al-mulūk*, ed. Minūchihr Sutūda (Tehran, 1344 sh./1966), 95. Clifford Edmund Bosworth, *The History of the Saffarids of Sistan and the Maliks of Nimruz (247/861 to 949/1542–3)* (Costa Mesa, CA, and New York, 1994), 443.
124. Cited by Fazlinejad and Ahmadi, 'The Black Death in Iran', 68.
125. Zayn al-Dīn (1990), text, 487 (Russian trans., 115: *po prichine kholery i chumy*)/(1993), 72. Hence HA, *Dhayl-i Jāmi' al-tawārīkh*, 239; and compare also Khwāfī (1962), II, 93/(2007), II, 956 (tr. Iusupova, 88).
126. Zayn al-Dīn (1990), text, 490 (Russian trans., 119, again rendering *wabā* as 'cholera')/(1993), 86, cited by Wing, *The Jalayirids*, 117. Hence HA, *Dhayl-i*

Jāmiʿ al-tawārīkh, 243, and Khwāfī (1962), II, 103/(2007), II, 966 (tr. Iusupova, 95).

127. ʿAzīz b. Ardashīr Astarābādī, *Bazm-u razm*, ed. Kilisli Rıfat Beg, with introduction by Mehmet Fuat Köprülüzade (Istanbul, 1928), 174, 175, 180. R.M. Shukurov, *Velikie Komniny i vostok (1204–1461)* (St Petersburg, 2001), 203. Michaēl Panaretos, *Peri tōn tēs Trapezountos basileōn*, ed. and tr. Scott Kennedy, in *Two Works on Trebizond. Michael Panaretos. Bessarion* (Cambridge, MA, 2019), trans., 53.
128. *ZT*, II, 578 (also HA's additions in Shāmī, *ZN*, II, 49).
129. Zayn al-Dīn (1993), 149, from the Tehran University ms.; not in the Leningrad mss. used in Zayn al-Dīn (1990).
130. al-Maqrīzī, *Durar al-ʿuqūd*, I, 239, and *al-Sulūk*, III, part 2, 829. Ibn Qāḍī Shuhba, *Taʾrīkh*, I, 542.
131. Jaʿfarī (Jaʿfar b. Muḥammad Ḥusaynī), *Taʾrīkh-i kabīr*, partial trans. by Abbas Zaryab, 'Der Bericht über die Nachfolger Timurs aus dem Ta'rīḫ-i kabīr des Ǧaʿfarī ibn Muḥammad al-Ḥusainī', unpublished doctoral dissertation, Johannes Gutenberg-Universität Mainz, 1960, 47.
132. Ahmad Fazlinejad and Farajollah Ahmadi, 'The impact of the Black Death on Iranian trade (1340s–1450s A.D.)', *Iran and the Caucasus* 23 (2019), 221–32 (here 229).
133. For the incidence of plague in the Mamlūk dominions, see Michael W. Dols, 'The Second Plague Pandemic and its recurrences in the Middle East: 1347–1894', *JESHO* 22 (1979), 162–89 (here 168–9).
134. Zayn al-Dīn (1990), text, 489 (Russian trans., 118)/(1993) 82. Hence HA, *Dhayl-i Jāmiʿ al-tawārīkh*, 242.
135. Uli Schamiloglu, 'Preliminary remarks on the role of disease in the history of the Golden Horde', *Central Asian Survey* 12 (1993), 447–57 (esp. 451–2); compare also 453. For Europe, see, for example, David Mengel, 'A plague on Bohemia? Mapping the Black Death', *Past and Present* 211 (May 2011), 3–34 (esp. 31–3).
136. For an analysis of the contrasting reactions in the Christian West and the Muslim Near East to plague and other tribulations, see Ayalon, *Natural Disasters*, 40–8; at 46, he describes the plague as 'just another natural occurrence'. As an outsider who wrote a plague treatise, Ibn Abī Ḥajala (d. 776/1375) ranked the Mongol invasions and the recent pandemic as comparable afflictions: Conrad, 'Arabic plague chronologies and treatises', 74. Roux, *Tamerlan*, 212, classes the two episodes together as 'deux grandes cataclysmes'; also compare ibid., 305.
137. The report is printed in R. Loenertz, 'La première restauration de la Société des Frères Pérégrinants (1373–1375)', *Archivum Fratrum Praedicatorum* 3 (1933), 5–55 (here 46). Loenertz, *La Société des Frères Pérégrinants, Étude sur l'Orient dominicain* (Rome, 1937), 194–6, has reservations, however, concerning the significance of the phrasing (n.82 ibid.). Richard, *La Papauté et les missions d'Orient*, 181; for the dimensions of the province of Sulṭāniyya, see ibid., 171–5.
138. See, for instance, Soucek, *A History of Inner Asia*, 116: 'It seems that the disease was indeed affecting the Mongols but stayed at a low endemic level among them'.

139. Giovanni Villani, *Nuova cronica*, xiii, 84, ed. Porta, III, 486. Compare too Gabriele de' Mussi, *De morbo*, 144 (tr. in Horrox, *The Black Death*, 16), who claims that 'countless Tartars and Saracens' died of the plague in 1346.
140. Uli Schamiloglu, 'The end of Volga Bulgarian', in *Varia Eurasiatica. Festschrift für Professor András Róna-Tas* (Szeged, 1991), 157–63.
141. Ibn al-Wardī, *Tatimmat al-Mukhtaṣar*, II, 489.
142. 'Chronicon Dubnicense', in Flórián Mátyás (ed.), *Historiae Hungaricae fontes domestici*, III (Leipzig, 1884), 148.
143. McNeill, *Plagues and Peoples*, 191. Similarly, Abu-Lughod, 'The world system in the thirteenth century', 87, suggests that the timing of the Mongols' expulsion from China 'was not unrelated to the high plague casualties among the "foreign" military troops that enforced Yuan rule'.
144. Schamiloglu, 'Preliminary remarks', 450–1. In his 'The rise of the Ottoman Empire: The Black Death in medieval Anatolia and its impact on Turkish civilization', in Neguin Yavari, Lawrence G. Potter and Jean-Marc Ran Oppenheim (eds), *Views from the Edge. Essays in Honor of Richard W. Bulliet* (New York, 2004), 255–79 (here 271), Schamiloglu deploys this same argument in relation to Ottoman expansion and Byzantine decline; see also Ayalon, *Natural Disasters*, 48–53, and Machiel Kiel, 'The incorporation of the Balkans into the Ottoman Empire, 1353–1453', in *CHT*, I, 138–91 (here 145). But compare Peacock, *Islam, Literature and Society*, 239–40 and n.88, who is sceptical; also Paul, 'Mongol aristocrats and beyliks in Anatolia', 110 and n.19, citing al-Maqrīzī, *al-Sulūk*, II, part 3, 774. Varlık, *Plague and Empire*, 107–18, gives a detailed analysis of the arguments.
145. See Belich, *The World the Plague Made*, 41–2, 79.
146. WR, 92 (*MFW*, 131); and see also 22 (*MFW*, 74). IB, II, 381 (tr. Gibb, 482).
147. As pointed out by Janet Martin, *Medieval Russia 980–1584*, 2nd edn (Cambridge, 2007), 223.
148. Nikephoros Gregoras, xvi, 1.5, tr. Van Dieten, III, 176, and in Bartsocas, 'Two fourteenth century Greek descriptions', 395; Emperor John Cantacuzenos, ibid., 396.
149. al-Maqrīzī, *al-Sulūk*, II, part 3, 773, 774 (tr. in Wiet, 'La grande peste Noire', 368, 369).
150. ʿImād al-Dīn Abū l-Fidā Ismāʿīl b. ʿUmar Ibn Kathīr (d. 774/1373), *al-Bidāya wa l-nihāya fī l-taʾrīkh* (Cairo, 1351/1932–[no final date]), XIV, 226 (tr. in Wiet, 'La grande peste Noire', 383).
151. 1346: Yazdī, *ZN* (1957), I, 21–2/(2008), I, 250. 1365: Shāmī, *ZN*, I, 31. Yazdī, *ZN* (1957), I, 84/(2008), I, 319. Compare also Naṭanzī (1957), 127/(2004), 103.
152. *TMEN*, IV, 209–11 (no. 1911: 'Epizootie, Viehsterben im Winter durch Unzugänglichkeit des Futters'). For thirteenth- and fourteenth-century examples, see Lambton, *Continuity and Change*, 166 and n.39.
153. Waṣṣāf, 271 (*GW*, III, 33).
154. Faryūmadī, *Dhayl-i Majmaʿ al-ansāb*, 328.
155. Smith, *The History of the Sarbadār Dynasty*, 75; though he attributes this to the khan's defeat at Sarbadār hands (743/1342).
156. 'Chronicon Dubnicense', 148.
157. Paul W. Knoll, *The Rise of the Polish Monarchy. Piast Poland in East Central Europe, 1320–1370* (Chicago, IL, 1972), 138, 140.

158. *Troitskaia letopis'*, 380. *Patriarshaia ili Nikonovskaia letopis'*, in *PSRL*, XI, 3 (tr. Zenkovsky, III, 192).
159. *PSRL*, XI, 21 (tr. Zenkovsky, III, 222); and Avedis K. Sanjian (trans. and ed.), *Colophons of Armenian Manuscripts, 1301–1480. A Source for Middle Eastern History* (Cambridge, MA, 1969), 99, for Armenia. On these two epidemics, see Langer, 'The Black Death in Russia', 57 (though his assertion that the disease arrived from Sarai in 1364 seems to be based on a misreading of *PSRL*, XI, which lists the Sura [Sara] River, a right-hand tributary of the Volga, among the tracts affected). For the arrival of plague in Rus' from the Jochid lands in the fourteenth century, see Alexander, *Bubonic Plague in Early Modern Russia*, 12–15. On both epidemics in the Near East, see Michael Dols, 'Al-Manbijī's "Report of the Plague": A treatise on the plague of 764–65/1362–64 in the Middle East', in Daniel Williman (ed.), *The Black Death: The Impact of the Fourteenth-Century Plague. Papers of the Eleventh Annual Conference of the Center for Medieval & Early Renaissance Studies* (Binghampton, NY, 1982), 65–75 (here 67); Varlık, *Plague and Empire*, 119.
160. T.F. Khaidarov and D.A. Dolbin, 'Vtoraia pandemiia chumy v Zolotoi Orde i ee posledstviia', *ZOO* (2014), no. 4, 96–112 (here 102–6).
161. Schamiloglu, 'Preliminary remarks', 453–4; also his 'The impact of the Black Death on the Golden Horde: Politics, economy, society, civilization', *ZOO* 5 (2017), no. 2, 325–43 (here 335–6).
162. Iskander Izmaylov, 'Great Troubles', in *HT*, III, 726.
163. *Patriarshaia ili Nikonovskaia letopis'*, in *PSRL*, XI, 21 (tr. Zenkovsky, III, 222).
164. See, for example, Starr, *Lost Enlightenment*, 478–9; Belich, *The World the Plague Made*, 81.
165. Uli Schamiloglu, 'Beautés du mélange', in Fourniau (ed.), *Samarcande 1400–1500*, 191–204 (here 197), assumes that it decimated the ruling dynasty there. Aubin, 'Le khanat de Čaġatai', 38, speculates that plague may explain Chaghadayid sluggishness ('atonie') under Qazaghan, apparently alluding to their failure to react to the attack on the Qara'unas by the malik of Herat: see ibid., 29; also p. 181.
166. The statement by Biraben, *Les hommes et la peste*, I, 52, that according to one of Ibn Khātima's sources the plague struck Samarkand in 1341 is baseless: Ibn Khātima (tr. Dinānah, 41) merely cites an informant *from* Samarkand regarding the significance of the term *Khiṭā*. Adshead, *Central Asia in World History*, 98, repeats the error, and also claims, misleadingly, that it is confirmed by Geoffrey Le Baker (see n. 79). The citation from Ibn Shākir al-Kutubī (d. 764/1363) by Fancy and Green, 'Plague and the fall of Baghdad', 176, n.96, regarding plague in Samarkand in 749/1349 is irrelevant, since Ibn Shākir is in reality reproducing the account of plague in Transoxiana in 449/1057–8 by the mid-thirteenth-century author Sibṭ Ibn al-Jawzī. Fancy and Green have requested *Medical History* to issue an erratum notice (personal communication from Monica Green, dated 18 August 2022).
167. I owe this information to the kindness of Dr. Tibor Porció, who sent me his translation of the Tibetan version of the treatise.
168. 'Gos lo-tsā-ba gŽon-nu-dpal, *Debther sṅon-po*, tr. Roerich, *The Blue Annals*, 500–1, 504.

6: IRAN AND IRAQ AFTER THE ILKHANS

1. Awliyā'-Allāh Āmulī, *Ta'rīkh-i Rūyān*, 179. For the date of writing, see Melville, 'The Caspian provinces', 47, 51.
2. Faryūmadī, *Dhayl-i Majma' al-ansāb*, 341–7. Beatrice F. Manz, 'Iranian elites under the Timurids', in Van Steenbergen (ed.), *Trajectories of State Formation*, 257–82 (here 267).
3. Shivan Mahendrarajah, 'The Iranian interlude: From Mongol decline to Timur's invasion', in Babaie (ed.), *Iran after the Mongols*, 159–76.
4. Manz, 'Iranian elites under the Timurids', 266.
5. Osamu Otsuka, 'The Hazaraspid dynasty's legendary Kayanid ancestry: The flowering of Persian literature under the patronage of local rulers in the late Il-khanid period', *JPS* 12 (2019), 181–205 (esp. 183–4, 192–3, 198–9).
6. As pointed out by Beatrice Forbes Manz, 'The local and the universal in Turko-Iranian ideology', in Charles Melville (ed.), *The Timurid Century*, The Idea of Iran 9 (London and New York, 2020), 25–43 (here 30–1).
7. Hope, 'The political configuration', 2–7, 9–14, is particularly good on these themes.
8. Peacock, *Islam, Literature and Society*, 63. Wing, *The Jalayirids*, 132 and n.15 at 143. H.L. Rabino, 'Coins of the Jalā'ir, Ḳarā Ḳoyūnlū, Musha'sha' and Āḳ Ḳoyūnlū dynasties', *Numismatic Chronicle*, 6th series, 10 (1950), 94–139 (here 105, for a coin of 771 naming Shaykh Uways in Uighur characters).
9. See Melville, *The Fall of Amir Chupan*, 17 (Table 2), 56, for Shaykh Ḥasan's marital connections with the Ilkhanid line; also Wing, *The Jalayirids*, 18.
10. Wing, *The Jalayirids*, 101.
11. Ibid., 15, 129–34. Charles Melville, 'History and myth: The Persianization of Ghazan Khan', in Éva M. Jeremiás (ed.), *Irano-Turkic Cultural Contacts in the 11th–17th Centuries* (Piliscsaba, [2002] 2003), 133–60 (here 142, on the verse history by Azhdarī).
12. Anonymous *Dhayl-i Ta'rīkh-i guzīda*, ed. Otsuka, text, 197.
13. Broadbridge, *Kingship and Ideology*, 162. Daniel Zakrzewski, 'An idea of Iran on Mongol foundations: Territory, dynasties and Tabriz as royal city (seventh/thirteenth to ninth/fifteenth century)', in Melville (ed.), *The Timurid Century*, 45–76 (here 59).
14. For example, Nāṣir al-Dīn Muḥammad b. 'Abd al-Raḥīm Ibn al-Furāt, *Ta'rīkh al-duwal wa l-mulūk*, IX, part 2, ed. Costi K. Zurayk and Nadjla Izzeddin (Beirut, 1938), 344–6 and passim (Sulṭān Aḥmad). Shihāb al-Dīn Abū l-'Abbās Aḥmad Ibn Ḥijjī, *Ta'rīkh*, ed. Abū Yaḥyā 'Abd-Allāh al-Kandarī, 2 vols (Beirut, 1424/2003), I, 65, 70 (Sulṭān Aḥmad). al-Maqrīzī, *al-Sulūk*, III, part 3, 1020 (Sulṭān Aḥmad). al-Maqrīzī, *Durar al-'uqūd*, I, 438 (no. 357, Shaykh Uways). al-'Aynī, *'Iqd al-jumān*, partial edn by Aymān 'Umar Shukrī as *al-Sulṭān Barqūq mu'assis Dawlat al-mamālīk al-jarākisa 784–801 H./1382–1398 min khilāl makhṭūṭ 'Iqd al-jumān fī ta'rīkh ahl al-zamān li-Badr al-'Aynī* (Cairo, 2002), 367, 440 (Sulṭān Aḥmad); also 376 (both rulers). Ibn Taghrībirdī, *al-Nujūm al-zāhira*, XIII, 181, 182 (tr. Popper, II, 216; Sulṭān Aḥmad). On one occasion, even HA refers to Uways as 'Sulṭān Uways Khān': *ZT*, II, 766.
15. Faryūmadī, *Dhayl-i Majma' al-ansāb*, 325–6, says that she was the maternal aunt of the amir Ordu Buqa, who is himself called a nephew of the Mongol amir Nikruz by Ahrī, *Ta'rīkh-i Shaykh Uways*, text, 166, trans., 67. Kutubī,

Ta'rīkh-i āl-i Muẓaffar, 7, simply calls her a Turk; but this term was frequently applied to Mongols by contemporaries.

16. *CO*, text, 32, 49, 65 (the first two references also in HA, *Ta'rīkh-i salāṭīn-i Kart*, 172, 192). Aubin, 'Le khanat de Čaġatai', 32, 49. Other examples of Mongol marriages among the Kartids are given by Lawrence Goddard Potter, 'The Kart dynasty of Herat: Religion and politics in medieval Iran', unpublished PhD thesis, Columbia University, 1992, 145.
17. Faryūmadī, *Dhayl-i Majma' al-ansāb*, 324–5.
18. IB, III, 70 (tr. Gibb, 578).
19. Faryūmadī, *Dhayl-i Majma' al-ansāb*, 324, 325–6. HA, *Ta'rīkh-i salāṭīn-i Kart*, 173 (also in *CO*, text, 32). Kutubī, *Ta'rīkh-i āl-i Muẓaffar*, 65. Aubin, 'Le khanat de Čaġatai', 50. Beatrice Forbes Manz, 'Military manpower in late Mongol and Timurid Iran', in Szuppe (ed.), *L'Héritage Timouride*, 43–55 (here 50–1).
20. Faryūmadī, *Dhayl-i Majma' al-ansāb*, 330.
21. Ibid., 320. He makes out that Malik Muʿizz al-Dīn himself accompanied them, but compare Aubin, 'Le khanat de Čaġatai', 39, n.169, on the improbability of this claim.
22. Lawrence Goddard Potter, 'Herat under the Karts: Social and political forces', in Yavari, Potter and Oppenheim (eds), *Views from the Edge*, 184–207 (here 195).
23. See Yazdī (Muʿīn al-Dīn), *Mawāhib-i ilāhī dar ta'rīkh-i āl-i Muẓaffar*, ed. Saʿīd Nafīsī (Tehran, 1326 sh./1947), 207; Kutubī, *Ta'rīkh-i āl-i Muẓaffar*, 32–3. Kutubī, ibid., 9–10, and HA, *Jughrāfiyya*, partial edn by Ṣādiq Sajjādī (Tehran, 1377–8 sh./1997–9), II, 200, write of a Negüderi commander named Nawrūz who was killed in battle with Mubāriz al-Dīn in *c.*718/1318–19. Alternatively, they could have taken their name from a Mongol amir in Isfahan in the 1340s, mentioned by Faryūmadī, *Dhayl-i Majma' al-ansāb*, 342. Yet another possibility is that these elements originated as the followers of the Ilkhanid amir Nawrūz (d. 697/1297): see later.
24. Their origins: HA, *Jughrāfiyya*, ed. Sajjādī, III, 129–30. Their insubordination: ibid., 113–22.
25. Ibid., III, 187–8. HA's detailed narrative is used in Jean Aubin, *Deux sayyids de Bam au XVe siècle. Contribution à l'histoire de l'Iran timouride*, Akademie der Wissenschaften und der Literatur in Mainz, Abhandlungden der geistes- und sozialwissenschaftlichen Klasse 7 (Wiesbaden, 1956), 20–1.
26. Manz, *Nomads in the Middle East*, 147.
27. Wing, *The Jalayirids*, 88, 93.
28. Charles Melville, 'Anatolia under the Mongols', in *CHT*, 51–101 (here 94–7). There is a good survey of the beyliks in N.E. Anatolia in Shukurov, *Velikie Komniny*, 201–27.
29. Paul, 'Mongol aristocrats and beyliks in Anatolia', 121–32 passim (esp. 125, 128, 129).
30. IA (1979), 194/(1986), 321 (*TGA*, 178). Peacock, *Islam, Literature and Society*, 51.
31. Colin J. Heywood, 'Filling the black hole: The emergence of the Bithynian atamanates', in Kemal Çiçek *et al.* (eds), *The Great Ottoman-Turkish Civilisation*, 4 vols (Ankara, 2000), I: *Politics*, 107–15; repr. in Heywood, *Ottomanica and Meta-Ottomanica. Studies in and around Ottoman History, 13th–18th Centuries* (Istanbul, 2013), 91–105. Compare Rudi P. Lindner, 'The settlement of the

Ottomans', in Jürgen Paul (ed.), *Nomad Aristocrats in a World of Empires*, Nomaden und Sesshafte 17 (Wiesbaden, 2013), 131–42 (here 132).

32. Astarābādī, *Bazm-u razm*, 382. Jackson, *The Mongols and the Islamic World*, 404–5. But Ali Anooshahr, *The Ghazi Sultans and the Frontiers of Islam. A Comparative Study of the Late Medieval and Early Modern Periods* (London and New York, 2009), 134, assumes that the label 'Mongol' is being used here loosely, as a term of abuse.
33. Hiroyuki Ogasawara, 'The Chingizids in the Ottoman historiography', in Ekrem Čaušević, Nenad Moačanin and Vjeran Kursar (eds), *Perspectives on Ottoman Studies* (Münster, 2010), 865–72. Baki Tezcan, 'The memory of the Mongols in early Ottoman historiography', in H. Erdem Çıpa and Emine Fetvacı (eds), *Writing History at the Ottoman Court. Editing the Past, Fashioning the Future* (Bloomington, IN, 2013), 23–38.
34. Rudi P. Lindner, 'How Mongol were the early Ottomans?', in Amitai-Preiss and Morgan (eds), *The Mongol Empire and Its Legacy*, 282–9. Linda T. Darling, 'Persianate sources on Anatolia and the early history of the Ottomans', *Studies on Persianate Societies/Parūhash dar jawāmi'-i fārsī-zabān* 2 (1383 sh./2004), 126–44 (here 139–42). For Meḥmed II's titles, see, for example, Marc D. Baer, *The Ottomans. Khans, Caesars and Caliphs* (London, 2021), 92–4.
35. And according to Jaʿfarī, *Ta'rīkh-i Yazd*, 35, Qazwīn was also conquered for a time by the Muzaffarid Mubāriz al-Dīn Muḥammad.
36. Described at length by Shabānkāra'ī, *Majma' al-ansāb*, 296–9.
37. See John Limbert, 'Inju dynasty', *EIr*, XIII, 143–7.
38. For a thorough survey of the dynasty's history, see Charles Melville and ʿAbbas Zaryāb, 'Chobanids', *EIr*, V, 496–502, and Hope, 'The political configuration'.
39. Ahrī, *Ta'rīkh-i Shaykh Uways*, text, 176–7 (trans., 76). Anonymous *Dhayl-i Ta'rīkh-i guzīda*, ed. Otsuka, text, 195.
40. For this rapid series of events, see Wing, *The Jalayirids*, 104–6. The dates of Uways's arrival in Marāgha, 29 Shaʿbān [8 Aug.], and of his enthronement in Tabriz, 24 Ramaḍān [31 Aug.], are supplied in the anonymous *Dhayl-i Ta'rīkh-i guzīda*, ed. Otsuka, text, 198, 199.
41. Faryūmadī, *Dhayl-i Majma' al-ansāb*, 318. For the ongoing centrality of Tabriz as *dār al-mulk* of Iran in the post Ilkhanid era, see Zakrzewski, 'An idea of Iran on Mongol foundations', 46–59. For its commercial prosperity, see Sheila S. Blair, 'Tabriz: International entrepôt under the Mongols', in Pfeiffer (ed.), *Politics, Patronage and the Transmission of Knowledge*, 321–56; and Patrick Wing, '"Rich in goods and abounding in wealth": The Ilkhanid and post-Ilkhanid ruling elite and the politics of commercial life at Tabriz, 1250–1400', ibid., 301–20.
42. For the genealogy, see *JT*, I, 68 (*DzhT*, I, part 1, 135–8; *CC*, 28); Wing, *The Jalayirids*, chap. 3 *passim*, calling him 'Īlgā'.
43. On Khwāja Mīrjān's revolt and subsequent career, see Wing, *The Jalayirids*, 108–10.
44. Zayn al-Dīn (1990), text, 489–90 (Russian trans., 119)/(1993), 85.
45. On Sulṭān Ḥusayn's reign, see Wing, *The Jalayirids*, 148–51.
46. Faryūmadī, *Dhayl-i Majma' al-ansāb*, 313, calls the latter Uways's eldest son.
47. Zayn al-Dīn (1990), text, 491–2 (Russian trans., 121–2)/(1993), 95–6. Kutubī, *Ta'rīkh-i āl-i Muẓaffar*, 92–4.
48. This campaign is described in some detail by Kutubī, *Ta'rīkh-i āl-i Muẓaffar*, 96–7.

49. Zayn al-Dīn (1990), text, 493, 494, 496 (Russian trans., 123, 124–5, 127)/(1993), 100, 102–3, 108–9. A briefer account in Kutubī, *Ta'rīkh-i āl-i Muẓaffar*, 98. Wing, *The Jalayirids*, 153–6, illuminates this episode.
50. Zayn al-Dīn (1990), text, 496–7 (Russian trans., 127–8)/(1993), 109.
51. Jean Aubin, 'La fin de l'état sarbadâr du Khorassan', *JA* 262 (1974), 95–118 (here 102), and repr. in his *Études*, 311–30 (here 317).
52. Zayn al-Dīn (1990), text, 497 (Russian trans., 128)/(1993), 109, 111. Kutubī, *Ta'rīkh-i āl-i Muẓaffar*, 98, 99.
53. Zayn al-Dīn (1990), text, 497–8 (Russian trans., 129)/(1993), 112–13. For Sulṭān Aḥmad's appeal, compare Kutubī, *Ta'rīkh-i āl-i Muẓaffar*, 99.
54. Astarābādī, *Bazm-u razm*, 16–17; citied by Wing, *The Jalayirids*, 151.
55. For a useful survey of the more important *beylik*s, see Manz, *Nomads in the Middle East*, 142–4.
56. On the earlier history of these two confederacies, see Hans R. Roemer, 'The Türkmen dynasties', in *CHI*, VI, 147–88 (here 150–5, 159–60); and Sara Nur Yıldız, 'Post-Mongol pastoral polities in eastern Anatolia during the late Middle Ages', in Deniz Beyazit (ed.), *At the Crossroads of Empires. 14th–15th Century Eastern Anatolia. Proceedings of the International Symposium Held in Istanbul, 4th–6th May 2007* (Paris, 2012), 27–48 (here 36–8).
57. Faryūmadī, *Dhayl-i Majma' al-ansāb*, 314. See Cl. Cahen, 'Eretna', *EI*[2], II, 705–7.
58. See Paul, 'Mongol aristocrats and beyliks in Anatolia', 137–47.
59. The precise situation is uncertain: ibid., 128, n.90, and 132–3. For his ancestry, see A.C.S. Peacock, 'Metaphysics and rulership in late fourteenth-century central Anatolia: Qadi Burhān al-Dīn of Sivas and his *Iksīr al-sa'ādāt*', in Peacock and Yıldız (eds), *Islamic Literature and Intellectual Life*, 101–36 (here 101–2, citing Astarābādī, *Bazm-u razm*, 41–7). His career is summarised in J. Rypka, 'Burhān al-Dīn, Ḳāḍī Aḥmad', *EI*[2], I, 1327–8.
60. Paul, 'Mongol aristocrats and beyliks in Anatolia', 151–3; for the phrase quoted, see 147.
61. For the rise of the Ottoman state, see Rudi P. Lindner, 'Anatolia, 1300–1451', in *CHT*, 102–37. There is a useful *aperçu* of the Ottoman conquests down to 1402 in Colin Imber, *The Ottoman Empire, 1300–1650. The Structure of Power*, 2nd edn (Basingstoke, 2009), 7–16; and greater detail in Ernst Werner, *Die Geburt einer Großmacht – Die Osmanen (1300–1481). Ein Beitrag zur Genesis des türkischen Feudalismus* (Vienna, Cologne and Graz, 1985), 163–82.
62. P. Jackson, 'Muẓaffarids', *EI*[2], VII, 820–2, for a brief survey of the dynasty. Its prehistory is detailed by Kutubī, *Ta'rīkh-i āl-i Muẓaffar*, 3–5.
63. Kutubī, *Ta'rīkh-i āl-i Muẓaffar*, 11. HA, *Jughrāfiyya*, ed. Sajjādī, III, 95.
64. This is the (dateless) sequence of events given by Faryūmadī, *Dhayl-i Majma' al-ansāb*, 343. Kutubī, *Ta'rīkh-i āl-i Muẓaffar*, 17–18, states that Kirmān's ruler had been driven out in 740/1339–40 by Mubāriz al-Dīn, acting on Pīr Ḥusayn's behalf, but was restored by troops from Herat before the Muzaffarid again reduced Kirmān: he specifies Jumādā II 741 [Nov.–Dec. 1341] for this second conquest, but later, at 48, supplies the date 742 [1341–2].
65. Kutubī, *Ta'rīkh-i āl-i Muẓaffar*, 50–2.
66. Ja'farī, *Ta'rīkh-i Yazd*, 35. His list also includes two obscure localities, Kūh-i Kiyā and Rūd-i Garm. But in the similar list given by Aḥmad b. Ḥusayn b. 'Alī Kātib, *Ta'rīkh-i jadīd-i Yazd*, ed. Īraj Afshār, 2nd edn (Tehran, 2537

shāhanshāhī/1978), 85–6, these are substituted by Abarqūh and Wurūjird (Burūjird).

67. The fullest account is to be found in Kutubī, *Ta'rīkh-i āl-i Muẓaffar*, 57–9. There is a brief notice in Ahrī, *Ta'rīkh-i Shaykh Uways*, text, 182 (trans., 82), who dates the battle between Akhījuq and Mubāriz al-Dīn on 2 Shawwāl 860 (*recte* 759, corresponding to 8 Sept. 1358, though this is almost certainly too late: compare n. 40, and see later for the date of Mubāriz al-Dīn's deposition) and makes out that the Muzaffarid army remained in Tabriz for only one day.
68. See the poems translated in *HPL*, 276–8; also a verse by Shāh-i Shujāʿ, ibid., 164.
69. For Mubāriz al-Dīn's deposition and final years, see Kutubī, *Ta'rīkh-i āl-i Muẓaffar*, 59–63. The correct form of Shāh-i Shujāʿ's name was established by Aubin, 'La fin de l'état sarbadâr', n.32 at 101–2 (repr. in his *Études*, 316, n.32).
70. ʿAlā-yi Qazwīnī Hilālī (ʿAlī b. al-Ḥusayn b. ʿAlī), *Manāhīj al-ṭālibīn fī maʿārif al-ṣādiqīn*, BL ms. IO Islamic 1660, fo. 653b. The reign is surveyed in P. Jackson, 'Shāh-i Shudjāʿ', *EI*², IX, 198–9.
71. Kutubī, *Ta'rīkh-i āl-i Muẓaffar*, 65, 66–7.
72. These events are detailed ibid., 68–71, 73–5. But Hilālī, *Manāhīj al-ṭālibīn*, fo. 657a, dates them in 766 and says that Shāh Maḥmūd took up residence in Shiraz on 15 Rabī II [10 Jan. 1365].
73. Kutubī, *Ta'rīkh-i āl-i Muẓaffar*, 79; for the marriage, see also 49.
74. Date given by Yazdī (Muʿīn al-Dīn), *Mawāhib-i ilāhī*, BL ms. Add. 7632, fos 215b–216a, and Kutubī, *Ta'rīkh-i āl-i Muẓaffar*, 80.
75. Kutubī, *Ta'rīkh-i āl-i Muẓaffar*, 78–84.
76. Ibid., 91–2: the date is given at 91.
77. The date given by Hilālī, *Manāhīj al-ṭālibīn*, fo. 660a, is Jumādā I [Sept.–Oct.].
78. Kutubī, *Ta'rīkh-i āl-i Muẓaffar*, 82. Roemer, 'The Jalayirids, Muzaffarids and Sarbadārs', 16.
79. Kutubī, *Ta'rīkh-i āl-i Muẓaffar*, 79, 84, 88, 92. Faryūmadī, *Dhayl-i Majmaʿ al-ansāb*, 319, alone mentions the marriage.
80. Kutubī, *Ta'rīkh-i āl-i Muẓaffar*, 94–6. A brief summary of this episode is found in Faryūmadī, *Dhayl-i Majmaʿ al-ansāb*, 319.
81. Kutubī, *Ta'rīkh-i āl-i Muẓaffar*, 87, 92, 98, 100.
82. Ibid., 100.
83. Ibid., 101; the date of Shāh-i Shujāʿ's death is given at 108.
84. Ibid., 108–9. For the reputation of Isfahan's populace, see also ibid., 113; and Roemer, 'The Jalayirids, Muzaffarids and Sarbadārs', 15.
85. IA (1979), 29–31, 37–8/(1986), 79–81, 88–9 (*TGA*, 27–30, 36). Versions of the letter are reproduced by Kutubī, *Ta'rīkh-i āl-i Muẓaffar*, 104–8; by Yazdī, *ZN* (1957), I, 308–11/(2008), I, 582–5; and by Yūsuf-i Ahl, *Farā'id-i Ghiyāthī*, partial edn by Hishmat Mu'ayyad, 2 vols (Tehran, 2536 shāhanshāhī/1977 and 1358 sh./1979), I, 66–70.
86. Yazdī, *ZN* (1957), I, 311/(2008), I, 585.
87. By the Ilkhan Ghazan's reign, in any case, Sīstān had moved beyond the limits of Ilkhanid suzerainty: Bosworth, *The History of the Saffarids of Sistan*, 436; Jaʿfarī, *Ta'rīkh-i Yazd*, 27; Aḥmad b. Ḥusayn, *Ta'rīkh-i jadīd-i Yazd*, 76.
88. HA, *Ta'rīkh-i salāṭīn-i Kart*, 179, cited from *CO*, text, 38 by Aubin, 'Le khanat de Čaġatai', 29 and n.53.

89. Faryūmadī, *Dhayl-i Majma' al-ansāb*, 320, is clearly wrong in stating that Muʿizz al-Dīn delayed his assumption of sovereignty as long as the Ilkhan Taghai Temür (d. 754/1353) was alive. According to HA, *Ta'rīkh-i salāṭīn-i Kart*, 172 (also in *CO*, text, 32), the malik had consistently refused to acknowledge Taghai Temür as his overlord, though he did marry the Ilkhan's daughter.
90. HA, *Ta'rīkh-i salāṭīn-i Kart*, 179 (also in *CO*, text, 38). Shivan Mahendrarajah, *The Sufi Saint of Jam. History, Religion, and Politics of a Sunni Shrine in Shi'i Iran*, CSIC (Cambridge, 2021), 64–5.
91. Aubin, 'Le khanat de Čaġatai', 34. See now also Shivan Mahendrarajah, 'A revised history of Mongol, Kart, and Timurid patronage of the shrine of Shaykh al-Islam Ahmad-i Jam', *Iran* 54 (2016), part 2, 107–28.
92. Faryūmadī, *Dhayl-i Majma' al-ansāb*, 306, 310.
93. Aubin, 'Le khanat de Čaġatai', 30, 32, 34–5.
94. Ibid., 35.
95. Ibid., 45–7. The main primary sources are Yazdī, *ZN* (1957), I, 112–14, 130/(2008), I, 351–3, 371, and Naṭanzī (1957), 253–4, 271–2/(2004), 200, 212–13.
96. The date in HA, *Ta'rīkh-i salāṭīn-i Kart*, 193, and adopted by Mahendrarajah, *The Sufi Saint of Jam*, 65. *CO*, text, 50, has 3 Dhū l-Qaʿda.
97. Yūsuf-i Ahl, *Farā'id-i Ghiyāthī*, I, 354–8, cited by Shivan Mahendrarajah, 'The Sarbadars of Sabzavar: Re-examining their "Shiʿa" roots and alleged goal to "destroy Khurasanian Sunnism"', *Journal of Shi'a Islamic Studies* 5 (2012), 379–402 (here 392–3).
98. HA, *Ta'rīkh-i salāṭīn-i Kart*, 196 (also in *CO*, text, 52). Mahendrarajah, 'The Sarbadars of Sabzavar', 393–4. Smith, *The History of the Sarbadār Dynasty*, 150, for the possible revenge motive.
99. On Amīr Walī's antecedents, see Faryūmadī, *Dhayl-i Majma' al-ansāb*, 330, where his father is said to have been killed alongside Taghai Temür; also *CO*, text, 9. Only Yazdī, *ZN*, (1957), I, 282/(2008), I, 553, locates Shaykh ʿAlī's death at Nasā.
100. Zayn al-Dīn (1990), text, 490 (Russian trans., 119)/(1993), 87. Hence *CO*, text, 11.
101. Faryūmadī, *Dhayl-i Majma' al-ansāb*, 330–1: he calls Amīr Walī 'Ghiyāth al-Dunyā wa l-Dīn Shāh Walī' and sometimes 'Sulṭān Walī'.
102. For the conflict between Shaykh Uways and Amīr Walī, see Wing, *The Jalayirids*, 114–15.
103. Zayn al-Dīn (1990), text, 492 (Russian trans., 122–3)/(1993), 97–8.
104. Faryūmadī, *Dhayl-i Majma' al-ansāb*, 331; for their friendship, see also 313–14.
105. Zayn al-Dīn (1990), text, 498 (Russian trans., 129)/(1993), 113.
106. See the discussion in Paul, 'Zerfall und Bestehen', 721–6; ibid., 701–2, for their territory.
107. Naṭanzī (1957), 154/(2004), 124.
108. For the early history of the Jā'ūn-i Qurbān, see Faryūmadī, *Dhayl-i Majma' al-ansāb*, 323–4; Paul, 'Zerfall und Bestehen', 704–12. Aubin, 'Le khanat de Čaġatai', 60, for a genealogy of their amirs.
109. Paul, 'Zerfall und Bestehen', 700.
110. *CO*, text, 19. Smith, *The History of the Sarbadār Dynasty*, 114.
111. Smith, *The History of the Sarbadār Dynasty*, 125, on the basis of numismatic evidence. Paul, 'Zerfall und Bestehen', 707.

112. The sequence of events (dateless) is found in Faryūmadī, *Dhayl-i Majma' al-ansāb*, 323–4. For 'Alī-yi Ramaḍān, see Paul, 'Zerfall und Bestehen', 709–11.
113. On the date, see Paul, 'Zerfall und Bestehen', 713.
114. Ibid., 712.
115. Shāmī, *ZN*, I, 20–1. Yazdī, *ZN* (1957), I, 51–2/(2008), I, 282–3. Naṭanzī (1957), 121 (naming their captor as Ḥājjī Beg), 211–13/(2004), 98–9, 171–2. Aubin, 'Le khanat de Čaġatai', 43.
116. *JT* I, 89 (*DzhT*, I, part 1, 192; *CC*, 35), for Ma'ulai's tribal affiliation. Having earlier served in Khurāsān, he was appointed governor of Diyār Bakr by Ghazan in 694/1295: ibid., II, 1260 (*DzhT*, III, 301; *CC*, 439).
117. The account given by Faryūmadī, *Dhayl-i Majma' al-ansāb*, 321–2. There is a less detailed account in HA, *Ta'rīkh-i salāṭīn-i Kart*, 188–90 (also in *CO*, text, 46–7). See Aubin, 'Le khanat de Čaġatai', 42, and Mahendrarajah, *A History of Herat*, 156–7, who gives the precise date of the Kartid victory.
118. For the best discussion of the distinct elements within the movement, see Jean Aubin, 'Aux origines d'un mouvement populaire médiéval: le chekhisme du Bayhaq et du Nishâpour', *StIr* 5 (1976), 213–24 (repr. in his *Études*, 299–309).
119. See Aubin, 'La fin de l'état sarbadâr', 95, 96 (repr. in his *Études*, 311, 312); Roemer, 'The Jalayirids, Muzaffarids and Sarbadārs', 39.
120. What follows draws on the clear and succinct survey of the history of the Sarbadārs in Roemer, 'The Jalayirids, Muzaffarids and Sarbadārs', 16–39. The standard work is still Smith, *The History of the Sarbadār Dynasty*, though his analysis has been challenged in various respects. The dates for 'Abd al-Razzāq's rising and his murder are taken from the skeletal chronology of the Sarbadār rulers (only down to Luṭf-Allāh b. Mas'ūd, 757–759/1356–1358) in Faryūmadī, *Dhayl-i Majma' al-ansāb*, 347–9.
121. Mentioned only by Faryūmadī, ibid., 325: in view of the precise month he supplies, I have assumed that this was different from the engagement in which 'Alī Ke'ün was killed.
122. Smith, *The History of the Sarbadār Dynasty*, 120.
123. Frequently called Shams al-Dīn in error: see Aubin, 'Le khanat de Čaġatai', 33, n.75.
124. Aubin, 'La fin de l'état sarbadâr', 96 and n.4 (repr. in his *Études*, 312), shows that Mu'ayyad was his patronymic.
125. Roemer, 'The Jalayirids, Muzaffarids and Sarbadārs', 32.
126. Smith, *The History of the Sarbadār Dynasty*, 83–4, 148–9, 152. Walī was back in Astarābād by 775/1373–4.
127. *CO*, text, 8.
128. Faryūmadī, *Dhayl-i Majma' al-ansāb*, 332. Compare Aubin, 'La fin de l'état sarbadâr', 102 (repr. in his *Études*, 317).
129. IB, III, 64–6 (tr. Gibb, 574–5).
130. Smith, *The History of the Sarbadār Dynasty*, 77–80.
131. Mahendrarajah, 'The Sarbadars of Sabzavar', 394. See Faryūmadī, *Dhayl-i Majma' al-ansāb*, 334.
132. Aubin, 'La fin de l'état sarbadâr', 95 (repr. in his *Études*, 311).
133. Faryūmadī, *Dhayl-i Majma' al-ansāb*, 346–7.
134. Aubin, 'Le khanat de Čaġatai', 38 and n.106.

135. Faryūmadī, *Dhayl-i Majma' al-ansāb*, 321.
136. Ibid., 323. Paul, 'Zerfall und Bestehen', 711.
137. Kutubī, *Ta'rīkh-i āl-i Muẓaffar*, 89. Aubin, 'La fin de l'état sarbadâr', 102 (repr. in his *Études*, 316–17).
138. Faryūmadī, *Dhayl-i Majma' al-ansāb*, 321. Aubin, 'Le khanat de Čaġatai', 50.
139. See the comments of Smith, *The History of the Sarbadār Dynasty*, 147; and Roemer, 'The Jalayirids, Muzaffarids and Sarbadārs', 32–3.
140. The date given by Faryūmadī, *Dhayl-i Majma' al-ansāb*, 333, 334.
141. For a detailed account, see Aubin, 'La fin de l'état sarbadâr', 99–103 (repr. in his *Études*, 314–18).
142. Awliyā'-Allāh Āmulī, *Ta'rīkh-i Rūyān*, 179. Mar'ashī, *Ta'rīkh-i Ṭabaristān-u Rūyān-u Māzandarān*, 41. He certainly took Qazwīn: ibid., 48. For Iskandar's role in the conflict with Mas'ūd, see Smith, *The History of the Sarbadār Dynasty*, 120.
143. Zayn al-Dīn (1990), text, 494, 498 (Russian trans., 125, 129)/(1993), 104, 113. See earlier.
144. Faryūmadī, *Dhayl-i Majma' al-ansāb*, 320; on this attack, see earlier and n. 21.
145. *CO*, text, 54. Mahendrarajah, 'The Sarbadars of Sabzavar', 394.
146. Roemer, 'The Jalayirids, Muzaffarids and Sarbadārs', 3. See Shāmī, *ZN*, I, 135, on the effects of the Muzaffarids' internal rivalries; though he is admittedly a hostile witness.
147. Manz, 'Military manpower in late Mongol and Timurid Iran', 46–53.
148. Ahrī, *Ta'rīkh-i Shaykh Uways*, text, 149 (trans., 51). Muḥammad b. Maḥmūd Āmulī, *Nafā'is al-funūn*, II, 262–3. Awliyā'-Allāh Āmulī, *Ta'rīkh-i Rūyān*, 178–81, 204. Compare the reference to Abū Sa'īd's passing in the anonymous *Dhayl-i Ta'rīkh-i guzīda*, ed. Otsuka, text, 194; and the comments of David Morgan, 'Iran's Mongol experience', in Morris Rossabi (ed.), *How Mongolia Matters: War, Law, and Society*, BIAL 36 (Leiden, 2017), 57–68 (here 68), and Hope, 'The political configuration', 9–10. For a different view of Abū Sa'īd's reign, particularly following Choban's removal, see Melville, *The Fall of Amir Chupan*, esp. 6–7 and 29–42 ('Disintegration of the Ilkhanate').
149. Yazdī, *ZN* (1957), I, 215/(2008), I, 476. Aubin, 'Le khanat de Čaġatai', 50–1 and n.159. He had left in 778/1376–7, after the death of Timur's son Jahāngīr: Yazdī, *ZN* (1957), I, 201/(2008), I, 457.
150. Mahendrarajah, 'The Sarbadars of Sabzavar', 394.
151. Morgan, *Medieval Persia*, 85, and 'The decline and fall of the Mongol empire', 435. See also Aubin, 'Comment Tamerlan', 89–92; Roemer, 'Tīmūr in Iran', 48; and Roux, *Tamerlan*, 285.
152. Dorothea Krawulsky, 'The revival of the name Īrān under the Mongol Īlkhāns', in her *The Mongol Īlkhāns and Their Vizier Rashīd al-Dīn* (Frankfurt am Main, 2011), 43–51. Bert G. Fragner, 'Ilkhanid rule and its contributions to Iranian political culture', in Komaroff (ed.), *Beyond the Legacy of Genghis Khan*, 68–80 (esp. 72–4). Fragner, 'Iran under Ilkhanid rule in a world history perspective', in Denise Aigle (ed.), *L'Iran face à la domination mongole* (Tehran, 1997), 121–31, and repr. in Fragner, *Selected Writings*, ed. Velizar Sadovski and Antonio Panaino (with Sara Circassia and Bettina Hofleitner), Indo-Iranica, Series Purpurea 1–2 ([Milan], 2009–10; reissued as 1 vol., 2014), 149–59. Assadullah Souren Melikian-Chirvani, 'Conscience du passé et résistance culturelle dans l'Iran mongol', in Aigle (ed.), *L'Iran face à la domination*

mongole, 135–77. Charles Melville, 'The royal image in Mongol Iran', in Lynette Mitchell and Charles Melville (eds), *Every Inch a King. Comparative Studies on Kings and Kingship in the Ancient and Medieval Worlds* (Leiden and Boston, MA, 2013), 343–69 (here 347–9). Jackson, *The Mongols and the Islamic World*, 325–7. The most recent discussion is by Melville, 'Concepts of government and state formation in Mongol Iran', in Babaie (ed.), *Iran after the Mongols*, 33–54 (here 42–7).

153. See Amitai, 'Political legitimation in the Ilkhanate', esp. 210–24, 232–5. Tomoko Masuya, 'Images of Iranian kingship on secular Ilkhanid tiles', in Babaie (ed.), *Iran after the Mongols*, 95–113 (here 110), suggests that the scenes depicted at Takht-i Sulaymān meant nothing to the Ilkhans.
154. Broadbridge, *Kingship and Ideology*, 159.
155. See, for example, J.M. Smith, Jr, 'D̲jalāyir, D̲jalāyirids', *EI*², II, 401 (Shaykh Ḥasan-i Buzurg); Smith, *The History of the Sarbadār Dynasty*, 121 (Chobanids); Roemer, 'The Jalayirids, Muzaffarids and Sarbadārs', 5 (Shaykh Ḥasan-i Buzurg), 14, 15 (Muzaffarids); Aubin, as cited later and n. 161 (Shāh-i Shujāʿ).
156. 1337: Ḥamd-Allāh Mustawfī, *Dhayl*, ed. Piriiev, text, 443/tr. Kazimov and Piriiev, 101. 1339: Faryūmadī, *Dhayl-i Majmaʿ al-ansāb*, 310–11. Roemer, 'The Jalayirids, Muzaffarids and Sarbadārs', 17, 21, is almost certainly right to assume that this was among Taghai Temür's objectives.
157. Ibn Faḍl-Allāh al-ʿUmarī, *al-Taʿrīf*, Cairo edn, 44/ed. al-Durūbī, 58. A few years earlier, in *Masālik*, text, 88, he had described Tabriz as the 'navel (*umm*) of the whole of Iran' (German trans., 150, rendering *umm* as 'Mutter').
158. See Roemer's comment: 'The Jalayirids, Muzaffarids and Sarbadārs', 11.
159. Faryūmadī, *Dhayl-i Majmaʿ al-ansāb*, 319. On the Gulf region in this period, see Jean Aubin, 'Les princes d'Ormuz du XIIIᵉ au XVᵉ siècle', *JA* 241 (1953), 77–138 (here 108–9).
160. Hilālī, *Manāhij al-ṭālibīn*, fos 648b, 653b. Yazdī (Muʿīn al-Dīn), *Mawāhib-i ilāhī*, passim.
161. Aubin, 'La fin de l'état sarbadâr', 101–2 (repr. in his *Études*, 316).
162. Jaʿfarī, *Taʾrīkh-i Yazd*, 35. See also Aḥmad b. Ḥusayn, *Taʾrīkh-i jadīd-i Yazd*, 86. The 'promise' presumably refers to the *mujaddid*, the 'Renewer' expected at the beginning of each Hijrī century: see E. Van Donzel, 'Mud̲jaddid', *EI*², VII, 290. Mubāriz al-Dīn was born in Jumādā II 700/Feb.–March 1301: Kutubī, *Taʾrīkh-i āl-i Muẓaffar*, 5.
163. Yazdī (Muʿīn al-Dīn), *Mawāhib-i ilāhī*, fo. 133a–b. Kutubī, *Taʾrīkh-i āl-i Muẓaffar*, 45.
164. Hilālī, *Manāhij al-ṭālibīn*, fos 649a ff.
165. Although the authors who celebrate Mubāriz al-Dīn's diploma from the Caliph are all local, Kutubī and Jaʿfarī, writing well after the Muzaffarids' downfall, were under no pressure to exaggerate the event's significance. It is noteworthy that their contemporary HA, a Timurid court historian, makes only the briefest reference to the caliphal grant – and does so in the quite different chronological context of advice given to Pīr Muḥammad in 1405 (see pp. 345, 405).
166. Mahendrarajah, *A History of Herat*, 139–42. The malik's edict is found in Yūsuf-i Ahl, *Farāʾid-i Ghiyāthī*, ms. Fâtih 4012, fo. 447a–b. Aubin, 'Le khanat de Čaġatai', 32–3, proposes that by 'infidels' Muʿizz al-Dīn meant the

heretical Sarbadārs rather than pagan Mongols, whatever his audience may have thought; Woods, *The Aqquyunlu*, 8, believes that he had both in mind.

167. See the remarks of Subtelny, 'Tamerlane and his descendants', 169–70.
168. As stressed by Wing, *The Jalayirids*, 93, 105.
169. Paul, 'Zerfall und Bestehen', 704, imputes imperial ambitions to Amīr Walī.

7: THE CENTRAL ASIAN MONGOLS: CHAGHATAYS, MUGHŪLS AND QARA'UNAS

1. For the data he supplies, see Kempiners, 'Vaṣṣāf's *Tajziyat al-amṣār*'.
2. *Masālik*, text, 41 (German trans., 118–19). Slightly later, however, al-ʿUmarī alleges that all the Mongol states observe the Yasa: ibid., text, 47 (German trans., 123).
3. *Ta'rīf* (1951), 363/(2008), 237. See the doubts of Amitai, 'Ibn Khaldūn on the Mongols', 197.
4. *Masālik*, text, 95 (German trans., 154–5). Amitai, 'Ibn Khaldūn on the Mongols', 202.
5. See especially O.D. Chekhovich (ed.), *Bukharskie dokumenty XIV veka* (Tashkent, 1965), 72, 75, 76, 77, 84, 85, 87 (trans, 150–1, 154, 155, 156, 163, 164, 165); other references are cited in Biran, 'The Mongols in Central Asia', 61 and n.34.
6. Michal Biran, 'Rulers and city life in Mongol Central Asia (1220–1370)', in Durand-Guédy (ed.), *Turko-Mongol Rulers, Cities and City Life*, 257–83 (here 271).
7. Beatrice F. Manz adopted the designation 'Ulus Chaghatay' for the western khanate, in 'The ulus Chaghatay before and after Temür's rise to power: The transformation from tribal confederation to army of conquest', *CAJ* 27 (1983), 79–100, and her *Rise and Rule*, and has been followed by other authors. I have avoided this usage, since it seems to me that the Mongols of the eastern khanate would equally have considered themselves part of Chaghadai's ulus.
8. *TR*, I (text), 301, II (trans.), 226–7. There is a discussion of this question in K.A. Pishchulina, *Iugo-vostochnyi Kazakhstan v seredine XIV–nachale XVI veka (voprosy politicheskoi i sotsial'no-ėkonomicheskoi istorii)* (Alma-Ata, 1977), 12–13.
9. *RN* (1915), 17/(2000), 22 (*DPT*, 29). *TR*, I (text), 300, II (trans.), 226.
10. *TR*, I (text), 53, II (trans.), 45: the context is the reign of Esen Buqa II (d. 866/1461–2).
11. Qāshānī, *Ta'rīkh-i Uljāytū Sulṭān*, 34. For the Chaghadayid advance in this region, see Allsen, 'The Yüan dynasty and the Uighurs of Turfan', 258–60; also Baumer, *The History of Central Asia*, III, 245.
12. Naṭanzī (1957), 296/(2004), 229–30. *ZT*, I, 182, 461 (also in Shāmī, *ZN*, II, 6, 30).
13. Shāmī, *ZN*, I, 115. Yazdī, *ZN* (1957), I, 342/(2009), I, 622.
14. For the history of this principality, see Paul Pelliot, 'Le Ḫōǰa et le Sayyid Ḥusain de l'Histoire des Ming', *TP* 38 (1948), 81–292 (here n.103 at 134–8).
15. Yazdī, *ZN* (1957), II, 160/(2008), II, 1004. For *totqa'ul*, see *TMEN*, I, 251–3 (no. 124, *totqāvul*: 'Straßenwächter, Feldgendarm').
16. *Chronica XXIV generalium ordinis Minorum* [early 1370s], in *Analecta Franciscana*, III (Quaracchi, 1897), 531, *quidam religiosus saracenus Alisoldani nomine*. Bartolomeo da Pisa, *De conformitate vitae beati Francisci ad vitam domini Iesu* [1385/90], in *Analecta Franciscana*, IV (Quaracchi, 1906), 335,

quidam pessimus falcherius saracenus . . . nomine Alisolda; tr. Yule, *Cathay and the Way Thither*, III, 32 (rendering *falcherius* wrongly as 'falconer').

17. Yazdī, *ZN* (1957), I, 30/(2008), I, 259–60. Bakhtiyar Babajanov, 'Monuments épigraphiques de l'ensemble de Fatḥâbâd à Boukhara', *CAC* 7 (1999), 195–210. DeWeese, 'Islamization in the Mongol empire', 131–2. Biran, 'Rulers and city life', 277. For the description, see IB, III, 27–8 (tr. Gibb, 554).
18. Naṭanzī (1957), 129/(2004), 104, *mardī-yi abdāl-nihād qalandar-mizāj*.
19. Yazdī, *ZN* (1957), I, 73–4/(2008), I, 307.
20. IB, III, 48–51 (tr. Gibb, 565–7). The association between the two men is recorded in Bukhārī, *Anīṣ al-ṭālibīn*, 84–5. See Devin DeWeese, 'The *Mashā'ikh-i Turk* and the *Khojagān*: Rethinking the links between the Yasavī and Naqshbandī Sufi traditions', *Journal of Islamic Studies* 7 (1996), part 2, 180–207 (here 195–6); repr. in DeWeese, *Studies on Sufism in Central Asia* (Farnham and Burlington, VT, 2012).
21. al-Dhahabī, *Ta'rīkh al-Islām*, LIII, 330. Hence al-Ṣafadī, *al-Wāfī*, X, 382–3, and *A'yān al-'aṣr*, I, 523.
22. IB, III, 42, 87–8 (tr. Gibb, 561–2, 589).
23. *TR*, I (text), 12–13, II (trans.), 10.
24. Ibid., I (text), 13, II (trans.), 11.
25. Ibid., I (text), 36, II (trans.), 31, calling Muḥammad Khan Khiḍr Khwāja's son, as do *ZT*, III, 413, *TGNN*, text, 189 (fo. 82a–b), and Bābur, *Bābur-nāma*, tr. Beveridge, 19/tr. Thackston, 12; and compare also Yazdī, *ZN* (1957), 159/(2008), II, 1003. But *MA*, fo. 33b, ed. Vokhidov, text, 68 (Russian trans., 51), seems to make him a grandson (without naming his father). The date of Muḥammad's accession is found in the Ming annals: Emil Bretschneider, *Mediaeval Researches from Eastern Asiatic Sources. Fragments towards the Knowledge of the Geography and History of Central and Western Asia from the 13th to the 17th Century*, 2 vols (London, 1888; repr. 1910), II, 239–40. News of his death reached Shāhrukh in Fārs in Jumādā II 818/Aug.–Sept. 1415: *ZT*, III, 599.
26. Landa, 'The Islamization of the Mongols', 650. On this episode, see Kim, 'The early history of the Moghul nomads'; also p. 236.
27. *TR*, I (text), 114, II (trans.), 93.
28. *RN* (1915), 18/(2000), 22, *a'dā-yi dīn* (*DPT*, 30). Salmānī, *Shams al-ḥusn*, text, fos 24a, 132b (German trans., 22, 94). Naṭanzī (1957), 127, 228, 411/(2004), 103, 182, 299. Yazdī, *ZN* (1957), I, 122, 261/(2008), I, 363, 530; it is noteworthy that one of these strictures relates to the period when Timur was in the Mughūls' service. See also ibid. (1957), I, 189/(2008), I, 442, where Qamar al-Dīn's army is described as *bī-dīn*. The invading forces of the Mughūl amir Engke Tura too are termed infidels and are said to have withdrawn from Transoxiana back to infidel territory (*kāfiristān*): ibid. (1957), I, 319, 322, 339/(2008), I, 594, 599, 619; compare also Shāmī, *ZN*, I, 107.
29. *TR*, I (text), 42, II (trans.), 37.
30. *RN* (1915), 17/(2000), 22 (*DPT*, 29–30).
31. *TR*, I (text), 63, 114, II (trans.), 52, 93.
32. The point is made by Landa, 'The Islamization of the Mongols', 650. See the analysis in Johan Elverskog, *Buddhism and Islam on the Silk Road* (Philadelphia, PA, 2010), 191–2.
33. Wilkens, 'Buddhism in the West Uyghur kingdom and beyond', 228–30, 233–4.

34. *TR*, I (text), 10, II (trans.), 8.
35. Ibid., I (text), 32, II (trans.), 28.
36. *ZT*, IV, 821; extract also in K.M. Maitra (ed. and trans.), *A Persian Embassy to China* (Lahore, 1934; repr. New York, 1970), 12–13. S. Soucek, 'Turfan', *EI*[2], X, 676–7. James A. Millward, *Eurasian Crossroads. A History of Xinjiang* (London, 2007), 69.
37. Clavijo (1859), 112/(1928), 190; compare also (1928), 195 (not in Markham's 1859 trans.).
38. Ḥamd-Allāh Mustawfī Qazwīnī, *Nuzhat al-qulūb*, ed. and tr. Le Strange, I (text), 247, II (trans.), 239.
39. Bābur, *Bābur-nāma*, tr. Beveridge, 1–12/tr. Thackston, 3–7. Scott C. Levi, *The Rise and Fall of Khoqand, 1709–1876. Central Asia in the Global Age* (Pittsburgh, PA, 2017), 12.
40. Yazdī, *ZN* (1957), II, 160/(2008), II, 1004: the names are spelled PAY and KWSN.
41. WR, 114 (*MFW*, 147). Biran, 'Rulers and city life', 264. Slavin, 'Death by the lake', 68–70.
42. *TR*, I (text), 110, 301, II (trans.), 89, 226.
43. Ibid., I (text), 57, 60–1, 114, II (trans.), 48, 51, 93. Dale, *The Garden of the Eight Paradises*, 165–6. Compare also *TR*, I (text), 111, II (trans.), 90, where the majority of the Mughūls are said never to have lived in villages or beheld cultivation. Millward, 'Eastern Central Asia', 265.
44. Yüldüz: *TR*, I (text), 53, II (trans.), 45. Āqsū: ibid., I (text), 12, 57, 58, II (trans.), 10, 48, 49. Kāshghar: ibid., I (text), 46, 247, II (trans.), 39, 193. Both the latter two towns: ibid., I (text), 119, 301, II (trans.), 96, 227.
45. Ibid., I (text), 9, II (trans.), 7 (Thackston reads *sūya* for *sūba*). For *sübe/sïba*, see *TMEN*, I, 349–51 (no. 227: 'Wall, umwallter Platz, ... Grenze'). Ḥaydar's explanation of the phrase *Manghalai Sübe*, 'facing the sun', is incorrect. I have followed the rendering adopted by Kim, 'The early history of the Moghul nomads', 300, n.42. Cf. Barthold, *Four Studies*, I, 138 ('vanguard province'), and Millward, 'Eastern Central Asia', 262, n. 3 ('strategic point to the front').
46. See the outline in Millward, 'Eastern Central Asia', 260.
47. *TR*, I (text), 114, II (trans.), 93. For Tarmashirin, see Biran, 'The Chaghadaids and Islam', 749; also above, Chap. 3, passim.
48. *TR*, I (text), 46–7, 52–3, II (trans.), 40, 45. Binbaş, *Intellectual Networks*, 49–50.
49. *TR*, I (text), 62–3, II (trans.), 52.
50. Bābur, *Bābur-nāma*, tr. Beveridge, 329/tr. Thackston, 249; and see also Beveridge trans., 105/Thackston trans., 77. *TR*, I (text), 5, 110, II (trans.), 4, 89. Dale, *The Garden of the Eight Paradises*, 161–5.
51. On this, see Buell and Anderson, *A Soup for the Qan*, passim.
52. Yazdī, *ZN* (1957), I, 33, 44–5/(2008), I, 262, 274–5. I have tentatively identified Yazdī's KRLKWT with the Qarluq, though the latter name is normally spelled with a *qāf*.
53. See *Masālik*, text, 73 (German trans., 141); also the comments of Schamiloglu, 'Beautés du mélange', 192–4.
54. Joo-Yup Lee, 'Some remarks on the Turkicisation of the Mongols in post-Mongol Central Asia and the Qipchaq steppe', *AOH* 71 (2018), 121–44 (here 124–37).

55. David Ayalon, 'The European–Asiatic steppe: A major reservoir of power for the Islamic world', in *TDPKV*, II, 47–52; repr. in Ayalon, *The Mamlūk Military Society* (London, 1979). Mihály Dobrovits, 'The Turco-Mongolian tradition of common origin and the historiography in fifteenth century Central Asia', *AOH* 47 (1994), 269–77. And see now Joo-Yup Lee, 'The historical meaning of the term *Turk* and the nature of the Turkic identity of the Chinggisid and Timurid elites in post-Mongol Central Asia', *CAJ* 59 (2016), 101–32 (esp. 118–21). 'Ethnic' labels could be extremely fluid. The use of terms such as 'Mongol', 'Tatar' and 'Turk' within the Mamlūk Sultanate changed over the decades, according to whether the individual's place of origin enjoyed friendly relations with the Sultan or was deemed to have accepted Islam: Koby Yosef, 'Cross-boundary hatred: (Changing) attitudes towards Mongol and "Christian" *mamlūk*s in the Mamluk Sultanate', in Amitai and Conermann (eds), *The Mamluk Sultanate from the Perspective of Regional and World History*, 149–214 (esp. 156–87).
56. IB, III, 32, 33 (tr. Gibb, 556, 557).
57. Ibid., III, 36 (tr. Gibb, 558).
58. Ibid., III, 37 (tr. Gibb, 559).
59. IA (1979), 152/(1986), 243 (*TGA*, 140). I follow the interpretation of Anne F. Broadbridge, 'Spy or rebel? The curious incident of the Temürid Sulṭān-Ḥusayn's defection to the Mamluks at Damascus in 803/1400–1', *MSR* 14 (2010), 29–42 (here 31), and Barthold, *Zwölf Vorlesungen*, 217 (= Bartol'd, *Sochineniia*, V, 171).
60. See, for example, Franke, 'Zur Datierung'; idem, 'Ein mongolisches Brieffragment aus Turfan', *ZAS* 5 (1971), 17–26; idem, 'Ein mongolischer Freibrief aus dem Jahre 1369'; Matsui, 'A Mongolian decree from the Chaghataid Khanate'. The question is discussed by Manz, *The Rise and Rule*, 7 and n.11. Nagel, *Timur der Eroberer*, 99, thinks that Mongolian may have been the dominant language (spoken?) in Mughūlistān.
61. I owe this information to a paper by Dr. Márton Vér, 'Interregional mobility in Eastern Central Asia as seen in the Old Uyghur and Middle Mongolian sources and the mid-fourteenth century crisis', read to the Mongol zoominar on 10 July 2020.
62. Matsui, 'An Uigur decree of tax exemption'. Biran, 'Diplomacy and chancellery practices in the Chagataid khanate', 388–9.
63. Clavijo (1859), 120/(1928), 201; and also compare IA (1979), 346, 348/(1986), 477, 479 (*TGA*, 321–2). *Ta'rīf* (1951), 374/(2008), 246 (*IKT*, 38; and for the language of the report, see Fischel's commentary, n.120 at 89–90, and McChesney, 'A note', 222). Yet Ibn Qāḍī Shuhba, *Ta'rīkh*, IV, 182, says that it was read to Timur in Persian (*bi l-'ajamī*). See István Vásáry, 'Bemerkungen zum uigurischen Schrifttum in der Goldenen Horde und bei den Timuriden', *UAJ* 7 (1987), 115–26 (here 123); repr. in Vásáry, *Turks, Tatars and Russians*.
64. Dai Matsui, Ryoko Watabe and Hiroshi Ono, 'A Turkic-Persian decree of Timurid Mīrān Šāh of 800 AH/1398 CE', *Orient* 50 (2015), 53–75. J. Deny, 'Un *soyurgal* du Timouride Šāhruḫ en écriture ouigoure', *JA* 245 (1957), 253–66.
65. Much of the remainder of this chapter formed the basis for my 'The Mongols of Central Asia and the Qara'unas', *Iran* 56 (2018), 91–103; though I have slightly modified the conclusion found there.

66. Shāmī, *ZN*, I, 20. *ZT*, I, 327 (also in Shāmī, *ZN*, II, 16). Beatrice F. Manz, 'The development and meaning of Chaghatay identity', in Jo-Ann Gross (ed.), *Muslims in Central Asia. Expressions of Identity and Change* (Durham, NC, and London, 1992), 27–45 (here 37). Jean-Louis Bacqué-Grammont, 'Le tchaghataï, une nouvelle identité', in Fourniau (ed.), *Samarcande 1400–1500*, 161–5.
67. Thus Naṭanzī (1957), 124–5/(2004), 101, distinguishes 'the army of Jaqaṭāī' from 'the Mughūls'.
68. Manz, 'The development and meaning of Chaghatay identity', esp. 31–6, 42. Manz, 'The empire of Tamerlane as an adaptation of the Mongol empire: An answer to David Morgan, "The empire of Tamerlane: An unsuccessful re-run of the Mongol empire?"', in Timothy May (ed.), *The Mongols and Post-Mongol Asia. Studies in Honour of David O. Morgan* (Cambridge, 2016 = *JRAS*, 3rd series, 26, nos 1–2), 281–91 (here 286).
69. Shāmī, *ZN*, I, 15. Shāmī uses the term Jata less frequently than later authors.
70. Jamāl al-Qarshī, *al-Mulḥaqāt bi l-Ṣurāḥ*, Ar. text, 193 (Russian trans., 143); this edition reads JBA'YH and interprets it as 'collectors of taxes'; in *Turkestan*[1], I, 146, and in *Four Studies*, II, 11 and n.6 (= *Sochineniia*, II, part 2, 36 and n.47), Barthold read the word as JTA'YH.
71. Marʿashī, *Taʾrīkh-i Ṭabaristān-u Rūyān-u Māzandarān*, 41.
72. *TR*, I (text), 106, II (trans.), 85. For the equation with *Qazaq*, Barthold, *Zwölf Vorlesungen*, 215 (= *Sochineniia*, V, 170), and Peter B. Golden, 'Migrations, ethnogenesis', in *CHIA*, 109–19 (here 117); and on Tu. *qazaq* (possibly from *qaz-*, 'to wander') and the related abstract noun *qazaqliq*, Subtelny, *Timurids in Transition*, 29–30 and n.73; Yuri Bregel, 'Uzbeks, Qazaqs and Turkmens', in *CHIA*, 221–36 (here 225 and n.16); Joo-Yup Lee, Qazaqlïq, *or* Ambitious Brigandage, *and the Formation of the Qazaqs. State and Identity in Post-Mongol Central Eurasia* (Leiden, 2016), esp. 21–36, and his 'The political vagabondage of the Chinggisid and Timurid contenders to the throne and others in post-Mongol Central Asia and the Qipchaq steppe: A comprehensive study of *qazaqlïq*, or the *qazaq* way of life', *CAJ* 60 (2017), 59–95 (here 59–62).
73. Naṭanzī (1957), 87, 102/(2004), 72, 82. See also Yazdī, *ZN* (1957), II, 482/(2008), II, 1306, where Timur's grandson Sulṭān Ḥusayn is said to have moved on Samarkand 'in the manner of a *qazaq*'.
74. *TR*, I (text), 36–7, 39, 91, II (trans.), 32–3, 34, 73.
75. Beatrice F. Manz, 'Multi-ethnic empires and the formulation of identity', *Ethnic and Racial Studies* 26 (2003), 70–101 (here 87 and n.16). Sometimes the term is used anachronistically, as in Yazdī, *ZN* (1972), fo. 68b/(2008), I, 186–7, where the label is applied to a Jochid force in 690/1291, well before Özbeg's reign, and in Naṭanzī (1957), 104/(2004), 85.
76. Yazdī, *ZN* (1972), fo. 65b, and (1957), II, 32, 33, 477, 513/(2008), I, 279, 878, 879, and II, 1301, 1333. For Tu. *qal-* ('to remain behind'), see *EDT*, 615–16. Golden, *An Introduction*, 315, following Bartol'd, interprets the term as meaning 'those who have remained pagan'; and for a detailed discussion, see Joo-Yup Lee, 'Were the historical Oirats "Western Mongols"? An examination of their uniqueness in relation to the Mongols', *EM* 47 (2016), 1–24 (here 6–8).
77. *TR*, I (text), 106, II (trans.), 85.
78. MP, I, 158 (tr. Ricci, 42, 43; tr. Latham, 34; tr. Kinoshita, 29).

79. Amīr Khusraw Dihlawī, *Khazā'in al-futūḥ*, ed. Mohammad Wahid Mirza (Calcutta, 1953), 46. See Jackson, *The Delhi Sultanate*, 328 (appendix III).
80. There is a brief review of the principal theses in Ando, *Timuridische Emire*, 52–3.
81. Jean Aubin, 'L'ethnogénèse des Qaraunas', *Turcica* 1 (1969), 65–94 (here 66–78), and repr. in Aubin, *Études*, 251–77 (here 252–63), is the essential starting point for any discussion.
82. *JT*, I, 74 (*DzhT*, I, part 1, 154; *CC*, 30).
83. IB, III, 201 (tr. Gibb, 649).
84. A.P. Martinez, 'Some notes on the Īl-xānid army', *AEMA* 6 (1986 [1988]), 129–242 (here 230–2), argues that the term is unlikely to signify 'half-breed' and means, rather, 'coarse', 'brutish'.
85. Aubin, 'Le khanat de Čaġatai', 17, 18–19, followed by Roemer, 'Tīmūr in Iran', 43 and n.1, and Roux, *Tamerlan*, 53. But Manz, *The Rise and Rule*, 161 (appendix A), is rightly doubtful.
86. *JT*, I, 738–9 (*SGK*, 123; *CC*, 256). See Aubin, 'L'ethnogénèse', 80–1 (repr. in his *Études*, 264–5); Jackson, *The Delhi Sultanate*, 115. Bīnī-yi Gāw is believed to have lain near modern Quetta. For a full discussion of Negüder and the Negüderis, see Timothy May, 'The Ilkhanate and Afghanistan', in May et al. (eds), *New Approaches to Ilkhanid History*, 272–320 (here 285–91).
87. MP, I, 159 (tr. Ricci, 43; tr. Latham, 34; tr. Kinoshita, 30). Polo confuses Negüder with the Chaghadayid prince Tegüder, who likewise commanded a division in Iran in the 1260s (above, p. 78), an equation often replicated in the secondary literature, on which see Pelliot, *Notes on Marco Polo*, I, 190–6. Hirotoshi Shimo, 'The Qarāūnās in the historical materials of the Īlkhanate', *MTB* 35 (1977), 131–81 (here 161–2), distinguishes the two men but further compounds the problem by suggesting, on obscure grounds, that Tegüder's troops joined the Negüderis. Similarly, Martinez, 'Some notes', 236–40, muddies the waters by saying that Tegüder (whom he calls 'Negüder') was sent by the Chaghadayids to command the Qara'unas and raising the possibility that the term Negüderi was derived not from a proper name but from Mo. *negüdel*, 'to nomadise'.
88. *JT*, II, 1080 (*DzhT*, III, 122; Thackston, *CC*, 374, fails to recognise 'Binbān').
89. Ibid., I, 759, 772 (*SGK*, 153–4; *CC*, 263, 268). Arom, '"In-*ger*" and "outer" diplomacy', 301–2. Böjei had submitted after the defeat of the khan Baraq near Herat: *MA*, fo. 29b, ed. Vokhidov, text, 60 (Russian trans., 48), reading HRAM for HRAT in error. Here, as in *SP*, fo. 118b, and *JT*, I, 752–3 (*SGK*, 144; *CC*, 260), he appears as the son of Baiju, a son of Chaghadai's son Mö'etügen, although some mss. of *JT* make Baiju Chaghadai's own son. In contrast, *JT*, II, 1109 (*DzhT*, III, 152; *CC*, 384 and n.1), suggests that Böjei himself (whose name there reads as 'Mochi') was Chaghadai's grandson, and Kamola, 'Untangling the Chaghadaids', 75–6, shows that this was the original version, which Rashīd al-Dīn subsequently amended. The amended version is followed in *SP*, which *MA* merely copied; see Quinn, '*Mu'izz al-Ansāb*', 234–5.
90. Aubin, 'L'ethnogénèse', 83 (repr. in his *Études*, 267). To the sources he cites, add *Ta'rīkh-i shāhī-yi Qarākhitā'iyyān*, ed. Muḥammad Ibrāhīm Bāstānī-Pārīzī (Tehran, 2535 shāhanshāhī/1977), 248–50.
91. Jackson, 'The Mongols of Central Asia', 93. On Abagha's campaign, see Aubin, 'L'ethnogénèse', 85, and for the date, n.4 ibid. (repr. in his *Études*, 269 and n.111).

92. *JT*, II, 772, 1109–10, 1210–11 (*SGK*, 153–4; *DzhT*, III, 153, 252; *CC*, 268, 384, 417). Pelliot, *Notes on Marco Polo*, I, 189–90. Martinez, 'Some notes', 224–5. Arom, '"In-*ger*" and "outer" diplomacy', 302. The detailed analysis in Grupper, 'A Barulas family narrative', 53–9, fails to distinguish clearly the Ilkhanid Qara'unas from those who remained in present-day Afghanistan; in reality his article deals only with the noyans appointed to command the former.
93. *JT*, I, 160, 178 (*DzhT*, I, part 1, 398, 456–7; *CC*, 61, 67): in the Bādghīs district. Ibid., I, 195 (*DzhT*, I, part 1, 509; *CC*, 72): the '*tümen* of Qara'unas'. Ibid., II, 1131, 1144–5 (*DzhT*, III, 175, 190; *CC*, 391, 395): wintering in Baghdad and spending the summer in Siyāh Kūh. Ibid., II, 1136, 1137 (*DzhT*, III, 180, 181; *CC*, 392, 393): a Qara'unas division under Nawrūz in 1284. Ibid., II, 1147 (*DzhT*, III, 193; *CC*, 396). Ibid., II, 1222, 1224, 1225, 1228–9, 1242 (*DzhT*, III, 264, 267, 271, 284; *CC*, 422, 423, 424–5, 432): in Khurāsān during Ghazan's governorship of the province; this last group was very probably the force under Buqa whom Ghazan, as Ilkhan, stationed in ʿIrāq-i ʿAjam (see later and n. 101).
94. On these Ilkhanid Qara'unas, see Aubin, 'L'ethnogénèse', 76–7, 87–90 (repr. in his *Études*, 261, 270–3); Jackson, 'The Mongols of Central Asia', 93–4. Shimo, 'The Qarāūnās', presents a good deal of evidence for the subsequent history of these troops, though some of his assumptions should be treated with caution. There is a convenient summary of their history in May, 'The Ilkhanate and Afghanistan', 292–4.
95. May, 'The Ilkhanate and Afghanistan', 289.
96. *JT*, I, 754, 758, 772, and II, 1109, 1211 (*SGK*, 139, 142, 154; *DzhT*, III, 153, 252; *CC*, 261, 262, 268, 384, 417): in the last of these references, they are expressly said to have attacked Fārs.
97. Qara'unas: ibid., II, 1211 (*DzhT*, III, 252; *CC*, 418). Negüderis: ibid., II, 1108–9 (*DzhT*, III, 152; *CC*, 383–4).
98. Waṣṣāf (1853), 198–9, 201–3 (*GW*, II, 118–20, 126–7, 129). Ibid. (1853), 527, line 13/(2009), 306, he alludes to attacks on India by the Negüderi Mongols.
99. Ibid. (1853), 510, lines 15–17/(2009), 268 (*GW*, IV, 296–7).
100. Ibid. (1853), 511, line 9, and 513, lines 3–4/(2009), 269, 273 (*GW*, IV, 298, 303).
101. Sayfī (1944), 431–4, 438/(2004), 454–6, 459. *JT*, II, 1288 (*DzhT*, III, 330; *CC*, 449). For this episode, see Aubin, 'L'ethnogénèse', 88–9 (repr. in his *Études*, 272–3).
102. Kutubī, *Ta'rīkh-i āl-i Muẓaffar*, 7–8. Compare also Faryūmadī, *Dhayl-i Majma' al-ansāb*, 318.
103. Kutubī, *Ta'rīkh-i āl-i Muẓaffar*, 9–11. See also HA, *Jughrāfiyya*, ed. Sajjādī, II, 202.
104. On the usage in India, see the sources cited in Jackson, *The Delhi Sultanate*, 328 (appendix III).
105. So Manz, *The Rise and Rule*, 161 (appendix A). May, 'The Ilkhanate and Afghanistan', 289, 295. Bosworth, *The History of the Saffarids of Sistan*, 420–2 (though at 423 he adds that the two names began to be used synonymously from the 1270s). Aubin, 'L'ethnogénèse', 84–5 (repr. in his *Études*, 268), sees them as interchangeable; Pelliot, *Notes on Marco Polo*, I, 194, considered this a possibility.

106. Though Aubin, 'L'ethnogénèse', 68–9 (repr. in his *Études*, 254-5), tends to accept it; compare also idem, 'Le khanat de Čaġatai', 17.
107. MP, I, 159 (tr. Ricci, 43; tr. Latham, 35; tr. Kinoshita, 30). This, at any rate, is the assumption of Pelliot, *Notes on Marco Polo*, I, 189, 196.
108. IB, III, 201 (tr. Gibb, 648–9). Aubin, 'L'ethnogénèse', 93 (repr. in his *Études*, 276–7).
109. On Tughluq's origins, see Jackson, *The Delhi Sultanate*, 178, André Wink, *Al-Hind. The Making of the Indo-Islamic World*, III: *Indo-Islamic Society 14th–15th Centuries* (Leiden and Boston, MA, 2004), 130–1; Sunil Kumar, 'Trans-regional contacts and relationships: Turks, Mongols, and the Delhi Sultanate in the thirteenth and fourteenth centuries', in Ismail K. Poonawala (ed.), *Turks in the Indian Subcontinent, Central and West Asia. The Turkish Presence in the Islamic World* (Oxford, 2017), 161–90 (here 176–7); and Michael Hope, 'The Mongols in South Asia', in May and Hope (eds), *The Mongol World*, 890–906 (here 896). For a fuller discussion, see R.C. Jauhri, 'Ghiyāthu'd-Dīn Tughluq – his original name and descent', in Horst Krüger (ed.), *Kunwar Mohammad Ashraf. An Indian Scholar and Revolutionary 1905–1962* (Berlin, 1966), 62–6.
110. *Masālik*, text, 39 (German trans., 117). Hayton of Gorighos, *La Flor des estoires de la terre d'Orient*, ed. Ch. Dulaurier, in *Recueil des Historiens des Croisades. Documents arméniens*, II (Paris, 1906), French text, 214, 215 (contemporary Latin trans. by Nicolas Faucon at 335). For these and other figures, see Biran, *Qaidu*, 85–6. Spuler, *Die Goldene Horde*, 376, sets the maximum size of the Golden Horde army at 60,000, which in my opinion is too low.
111. *Masālik*, text, 39–40 (German trans., 117–18); see also ibid., text, 67 (trans., 136), for another comment about the inadequacy of the inhabitants of the Golden Horde for war.
112. *JT*, II, 1062–3 (*DzhT*, III, 104; *CC*, 368). al-Yūnīnī, *Dhayl Mir'āt al-zamān* (Hyderabad, A.P., 1374–80/1954–61), II, 363/ed. Jarrākh, XVIII, 5, gives more detail but dates its construction in 665/1267. For *sübe/sibe*, see p. 556, n. 45.
113. *JT*, I, 758 (*SGK*, 142; *CC*, 262).
114. Ibid., II, 1163 (*DzhT*, III, 207; *CC*, 402).
115. Yasa'ur: ibid., I, 606–7 (*CC*, 212), and II, 1226 (a more detailed text in *DzhT*, III, 578; *CC*, 423–4). Sarban: Waṣṣāf (1853), 509, line 25–510, line 2/(2009), 266 (*GW*, IV, 295). This detail is not found in the Rawshan and Mūsawī edn; but see Jahn edn, 26, and *DzhT*, III, 577 (*CC*, 424). The name is variously spelled YSAWR, YASA'WR and YYSWR. The southward expansion of the Central Asian Mongols is discussed in Kempiners, 'Vaṣṣāf's *Tajziyat al-amṣār*', 180–4.
116. Very briefly recounted in *JT*, II, 1226; but see *DzhT*, III, 268, 577–8 (*CC*, 423–4). For his defection to Qaidu, see Biran, *Qaidu*, 57–9.
117. Waṣṣāf (1853), 314, lines 8–10 (*GW*, III, 134–5, where the phrasing is misunderstood) and 20; and see also ibid., 253, lines 11–12, *ba-ṭaraf-i Sīstān paywasta būd wa-bar lashgar-i Nikūdār ḥākim shuda būd* (*GW*, II, 243). For this use of 'Sīstān', see Aubin, 'L'ethnogénèse', 91 (repr. in his *Études*, 274).
118. Landa, 'New light on early Mongol Islamisation', 94–6. Coins minted in Badakhshān in 690/1291 and 691/1292 already bear Du'a's distinctive mark (*tamgha*), cp: Petrov, 'Badakhshan', 499–501.

119. Pelliot, *Notes on Marco Polo*, I, 64–5, citing *Yuanshi*, chap. 9.
120. *JT*, II, 957 (*SGK*, 329; *CC*, 332).
121. Sayfī (1944), 629–30/(2004), 635–6. Petrov, 'Khronologiia', 302–3, dates its subjection to Köpek's reign (*c.* 1320–1326).
122. *Masālik*, text, 38 (German trans., 116); though earlier, text, 46 (trans., 123), the kingdom is described as independent of other rulers.
123. See now Michael Hope, 'The "Nawrūz King": The rebellion of Amir Nawrūz in Khurasan (688–694/1289–94) and its implications for the Ilkhan polity at the end of the thirteenth century', *BSOAS* 78 (2015), 451–73.
124. For clarification of the corrupt text in *JT*, see Aubin, 'L'ethnogénèse', 84 and n.2 (repr. in his *Études*, 267–8 and n.103), and Kempiners, 'Vaṣṣāf's *Tajziyat al-amṣār*', 182–3.
125. Waṣṣāf (1853), 368, lines 1–2 (*GW*, III, 262–3). Aubin, 'L'ethnogénèse', 92 (repr. in his *Études*, 275).
126. *JT*, I, 758 (*SGK*, 142; *CC*, 262). Qāshānī, *Ta'rīkh-i Uljāytū Sulṭān*, 201. Waṣṣāf (1853), 367, line 25 (*GW*, III, 262). For Bīnī-yi Gāw, see n.86.
127. *SP*, fo. 118b; Taraghai was his son by a different wife, however. For Qutlugh Temür, see Aubin, 'L'ethnogénèse', 82 and n.3 (repr. in his *Études*, 266 and n.96); Fakhr al-Dīn Abū Sulaymān Dā'ūd b. Abī l-Faḍl Banākatī, *Rawḍat ūlī l-albāb fī ma'rifat al-tawārīkh wa l-ansāb*, ed. Jaʿfar Shiʿār (Tehran, 1348 shamsī/1969), 398; also p. 573 n.119. Qāshānī, *Ta'rīkh-i Uljāytū Sulṭān*, 36, calls Taraghai 'amir of Qutlugh Khwāja's *orda*'; and see also next note. The Ilkhanid sources make Qutlugh Temür the father of Eltüzmish, who married successively the Ilkhans Abagha, Gaikhatu and Öljeitü. The first of these marriages presumably dates from Abagha's expedition to eastern Khurāsān in 677–8/1278–9. On Tigīnābād, see Clifford Edmund Bosworth, *The Later Ghaznavids: Splendour and Decay. The Dynasty in Afghanistan and Northern India 1040–1186* (Edinburgh, 1977), 149–51, who judges that it 'must have lain very close to Qandahār'.
128. For an overview of Chaghadayid attacks on India, see Hope, 'The Mongols in South Asia', 893–4.
129. Waṣṣāf (1853), 510, line 6/(2009), 267, *ki lashgar-i Qutlugh Khwājarā mīdānist* (*GW*, IV, 296, unaccountably renders this as 'welcher das Heer Qotlogh Chodschas kannte').
130. On these two invasions, see Jackson, *The Delhi Sultanate*, 221–4.
131. Waṣṣāf (1853), 368, lines 2–3 (*GW*, III, 263). *JT*, I, 628, 758 (*SGK*, 25, 142; *CC*, 218, 262).
132. Waṣṣāf (1853), 368, line 3 (*GW*, III, 263); ibid., 368–71 (*GW*, III, 263–70), with the wrong year, 699, for the attack on southern Iran. *JT*, II, 1109 (*DzhT*, III, 152; *CC*, 384), briefly mentions the invasion of Fārs.
133. Waṣṣāf (1853), 454, line 13/(2009), 138 (*GW*, IV, 150). For stimulating observations on the Mongol attacks on India, see Wink, *Al-Hind*, III, 119–21.
134. Waṣṣāf (1853), 510, lines 3–4, and 517, line 5/(2009), 267, 283 (*GW*, IV, 295–6, 312).
135. Ibid. (1853), 517, lines 6–7/(2009), 283 (*GW*, IV, 312).
136. Jackson, 'The Mongols of Central Asia', 96. For Hashtnaghar, 25km N.W. of Peshawar, see IB, tr. Gibb, 591, n.212.
137. IB, III, 202 (tr. Gibb, 649). For Tughluq and the Mongols, see Jackson, *The Delhi Sultanate*, 229, 231.

138. Qāshānī, *Ta'rīkh-i Uljāytū Sulṭān*, 149–50. For It-qul, see *SP*, fo. 120a; *MA*, fo. 32b (Īt-qūlī), ed. Vokhidov, text, 66 (Russian trans., 51, spelling the first element Аят). He had accompanied Taraghai's forces in 705/1305: Waṣṣāf (1853), 510, lines 9–10/(2009), 267 (*GW*, IV, 296).
139. Qāshānī, *Ta'rīkh-i Uljāytū Sulṭān*, 201; another account of this incident, clearly from a different source, is given at 152. Ms. Ayasofya 3019, fos 66b, 88b, seems to support the reading LKMYR of the printed text.
140. Waṣṣāf (1853), 368, line 10 (*GW*, III, 263). For Abachi's earlier attacks on Herat and Kirmān, see Aubin, 'L'ethnogénèse', 88 (repr. in his *Études*, 272); Jackson, 'The Mongols of Central Asia', 96.
141. For the Chaghadayid campaign, see Qāshānī, *Ta'rīkh-i Uljāytū Sulṭān*, 208–11; it is also described more briefly ibid., 153 and 164.
142. Waṣṣāf (1853), 528/(2009), 308. Jackson, *The Delhi Sultanate*, 225.
143. His turbulent career in Khurāsān is discussed in Katō, 'Kebek and Yasawr', 104–11, and Mahendrarajah, *A History of Herat*, 105–11; compare also L.V. Stroieva, 'Bor'ba kochevoi i osedloi znati v chagataiskom gosudarstve v pervoi polovine XIV v.", in *Pamiati akademika Ignatiia Iulianovicha Krachkovskogo. Sbornik statei* (Leningrad, 1958), 206–20 (here 211–15). For his dealings with Sīstān, see Bosworth, *The History of the Saffarids of Sistan*, 437–8.
144. *JT*, I, 300 (*CC*, 104–5).
145. Qāshānī, *Ta'rīkh-i Uljāytū Sulṭān*, 150. See Claus-Peter Haase, 'Von der "Pax Mongolica" zum Timuridenreich', in Stephan Conermann and Jan Kusber (eds), *Die Mongolen in Asien und Europa* (Frankfurt am Main, 1997), 139–60 (here 157). Trepavlov, 'Sopravitel'stvo v mongol'skoi imperii', 260, sees the situation under Esen Buqa as possibly a condominium; he ignores the arrangements in Du'a's reign, as also the joint reigns of Khalīl Sulṭān and Qazan Sulṭān later.
146. *TR*, I (text), 245, II (trans.), 190–1. Ḥaydar here also infers that Du'a was a Muslim because his father Baraq had converted.
147. Qāshānī, *Ta'rīkh-i Uljāytū Sulṭān*, 54.
148. Ibid., 210: the text, following ms. Ayasofya 3019, fo. 93a, reads 'SNKWK for 'SYKWL.
149. Biran, 'Rulers and city life', 271. On the Chaghadayids' oscillation between two distinct geographical orientations in the early fourteenth century, see Dardess, *Conquerors and Confucians*, 27–8.
150. HA, *Jughrāfiyya* (in the section on Transoxiana), Bodleian ms. Fraser 155, fo. 172a.
151. Yazdī, *ZN* (1972), fo. 80a/(2008), I, 215.
152. Mentioned only in al-ʿAynī, *'Iqd al-jumān*: *SMIZO*, I, text, 494 (Russian trans., 524–5).
153. HA, *Jughrāfiyya*, BL ms. Or. 1577, fo. 294b. These details are not found in HA's other works, and his source is unknown. A Mongol inroad in the early 720s is mentioned by Baranī and ʿIṣāmī (though without naming Tarmashirin): see Jackson, *The Delhi Sultanate*, 231.
154. Ḥamd-Allāh Mustawfī Qazwīnī, *Ta'rīkh-i guzīda*, 617. Idem, *Ẓafar-nāma*, II, 1463, line 20–1464, line 9; hence HA, *Dhayl-i Jāmiʿ al-tawārīkh*, 167–8, although in his *Jughrāfiyya*, BL ms. Or. 1577, fos 294b–295a, he supplies a slightly fuller account.

155. Thus according to the earlier recension of Baranī's *Ta'rīkh-i Fīrūzshāhī*: RRL, Persian ms. 2053, 288; Bodleian mss. Elliot 353, fo. 192a, and S. Digby Or. 54, fo. 161a. It was followed by Muḥammad Bihāmadkhānī (writing in 842/1438–9), *Ta'rīkh-i Muḥammadī*, BL ms. Or. 137, fo. 400b (on this author, see *PL*, I, 90).
156. IB, III, 28–30 (tr. Gibb, 555).
157. Ibid., III, 41–2 (tr. Gibb, 561).
158. Compare Naṭanzī (1957), 262/(2004), 206. Manz, *The Rise and Rule*, 34.
159. Liu, 'War and peace', 348–50. For the remarks that follow, see also Hope, 'The Middle Empire', 307–8.
160. Biran, 'Rulers and city life', 271.
161. al-Dhahabī, *Ta'rīkh al-Islām*, LIII, 329. al-Ṣafadī, *al-Wāfī bi l-wafayāt*, X, 382. Idem, *A'yān al-'aṣr*, I, 523.
162. HA, *Jughrāfiyya*, BL ms. Or. 1577, fo. 308a.
163. 'Iṣāmī, *Futūḥ al-salāṭīn*, 423–4. For the date of Muḥammad's accession, usually given as 725, see above, p. 138 and p. 530n.190.
164. IB, II, 373, and III, 90 (tr. Gibb, 478, 591).
165. See Jackson, *The Delhi Sultanate*, 232, and for the authenticity of the invasion, which was long in doubt, idem, 'The Mongols and the Delhi Sultanate in the reign of Muḥammad Tughluq (1325–1351)', *CAJ* 19 (1975), 118–57 (here 119–26). In addition to the sources there discussed, see al-Jazarī, *Ḥawādith al-zamān*, II, 377, who dates the attack at the beginning of 730/in the winter of 1329–30. For the alleged bribe, see Hope, 'The Mongols in South Asia', 894.
166. For what follows, see generally Jackson, 'The Mongols and the Delhi Sultanate', 147–51; Aubin, 'Le khanat de Čaġatai', 22; Iqtidar Husain Siddiqui, 'Sultan Muḥammad bin Tughluq's foreign policy: A reappraisal', *Islamic Culture* 62 (1988), 1–22 (here 17–19); Jackson, *The Delhi Sultanate*, 233–4; and Hope, 'The Mongols in South Asia', 897–8.
167. Jalāl al-Dīn Yūsuf-i Ahl, *Farā'id-i Ghiyāthī*, SK ms. Fâtih 4012, fos 456a–457b. This document is cited (but with slightly different folio numbering) by Aubin, 'Le khanat de Čaġatai', 22.
168. IB, III, 120–1, 374–5, 393–5 (tr. Gibb, 606, 735, 743–4), for their names. On the Sultan's generosity to some of these figures, see Baranī, *Ta'rīkh-i Fīrūzshāhī*, 461 (tr. Zilli, 284).
169. IB, III, 43, 46 (tr. Gibb, 562, 564). The mss. of IB spell the son's name as BŠAY, but the form in *MA*, fo. 32a, ed. Vokhidov, text, 65 (Russian trans., 50), is possibly BAŠAYTY (*Pashaitai, 'man of the Pashai'?). Jackson, *The Delhi Sultanate*, 234; for the Pashai, a tribe living roughly N. of Kabul, see Pelliot, *Notes on Marco Polo*, II, 799–800. Baranī, *Ta'rīkh-i Fīrūzshāhī*, 533–4, mentions that by the time of Muḥammad b. Tughluq's death in 1351 Nawrūz had spent some years in the Delhi Sultanate, enjoying the Sultan's patronage (cf. Zilli trans., 327, omitting 'Nauroz' in error and calling him simply 'Kargan'). His stay in the Sultanate is also mentioned in the account of events following Muḥammad's death given in *ZT*, I, 235.
170. Baranī, *Ta'rīkh-i Fīrūzshāhī*, 499 (tr. Zilli, 307); compare also ibid., 462 (tr. Zilli, 284).
171. IB, III, 46 (tr. Gibb, 564).
172. In his first recension: Bodleian ms. S. Digby Or. 54, fo. 166a; the text in ms. Elliot 353, fo. 199b, omits *az īn sūī* and reads *wa-banda* for *parwarda*.

173. Aubin, 'Le khanat de Čaġatai', 32. For the 'overlordship', see IB, III, 74 (tr. Gibb, 580). Muʿizz al-Dīn's letter to Sultan Muḥammad is found in Yūsuf-i Ahl, *Farā'id-i Ghiyāthī*, ed. Mu'ayyad, I, 182–5.
174. Naṭanzī (1957), 197/(2004), 162.
175. Bihāmadkhānī, fo. 328b.
176. Baranī, *Ta'rīkh-i Fīrūzshāhī*, 524 (tr. Zilli, 321, reading 'Farghan'); compare also 533 (tr. Zilli, 327). In the first recension the figure appears as 3,000 or 4,000: Bodleian mss. Elliot 353, fo. 207b, and S. Digby Or. 54, fo. 171a. Bihāmadkhānī, fo. 405a, has merely 'a few thousand'. *ZT*, I, 235, supplies no figure.
177. Baranī, *Ta'rīkh-i Fīrūzshāhī*, 533–7 (tr. Zilli, 327–30).
178. Yazdī, *ZN* (1957), I, 29–30/(2008), I, 258. Naṭanzī (1957), 262/(2004), 206.
179. Shāmī, *ZN*, I, 14; compare Yazdī, *ZN* (1957), I, 29/(2008), I, 257; Naṭanzī (1957), 197, 200, 261/(2004), 162, 164, 205. Manz, 'The ulus Chaghatay', 83.
180. Khwāfī (1962), III, 66/(2007), II, 931, *s.a.* 744/1343–4; but as Aubin, 'Le khanate de Čaġatai', 29, suggests, this can only have been the date of the first attack. For the battle in which the Apardī amirs were killed, see Faryūmadī, *Dhayl-i Majmaʿ al-ansāb*, 322.
181. IB, III, 50–1, 64 (tr. Gibb, 566–7, 574). For Muʿizz al-Dīn's assumption of the style of sultan and Qazaghan's campaign against Herat, see Yazdī, *ZN* (1957), I, 24–8/(2008), I, 252–6; Aubin, 'Le khanat de Čaġatai', 29–36; Jackson, 'The Mongols and the Delhi Sultanate', 154–5; Potter, 'The Kart dynasty of Herat', 50–1.
182. HA, *Ta'rīkh-i salāṭīn-i Kart*, 185–7 (also in *CO*, text, 43–5). Faryūmadī, *Dhayl-i Majmaʿ al-ansāb*, 320–1; but his claim that Muʿizz al-Dīn did receive Chaghadayid assistance is evidently mistaken: see Aubin, 'Le khanat de Čaġatai', 36. Mahendrarajah, *The Sufi Saint of Jam*, 64–5.
183. Aubin, 'Le khanate de Čaġatai', 36. Potter, 'The Kart dynasty of Herat', 51.
184. Yazdī, *ZN* (1957), I, 31/(2008), I, 260.
185. Naṭanzī (1957), 197/(2004), 162.
186. Ibid. (1957), 204/(2004), 167, *qarāʿūnāsān ki parwarda-yi ān khānwāda būdand*; hence HA's addenda in Shāmī, *ZN*, II, 12.
187. Shāmī, *ZN*, I, 47, 50; and see also 43. Naṭanzī (1957), 243, 247, 270–1, 283, 284/(2004), 193, 196, 212, 220. Yazdī, *ZN* (1957), I, 96, 106–7, 120–1, 127–8/(2008), I, 332, 345, 361, 369. See too *ZT*, I, 417 (also in HA's additions to Shāmī, *ZN*, II, 12).
188. Shāmī, *ZN*, I, 15. But Yazdī, *ZN* (1957), I, 32/(2008), I, 261, says that Balkh was at this time held by Öljei Bugha of the Süldüs.
189. Naṭanzī (1957), 210/(2004), 170, followed by *ZT*, I, 325–6 (also in Shāmī, *ZN*, II, 15). Compare also Shāmī, *ZN*, I, 19; Yazdī, *ZN* (1957), I, 45/(2008), I, 275.
190. Yazdī, *ZN* (1957), I, 37/(2008), I, 267.
191. Ibid. (1957), I, 53, 55/(2008), I, 285, 287.
192. Naṭanzī (1957), 232/(2004), 185–6.
193. IB, III, 40–1 (tr. Gibb, 560–1).
194. Naṭanzī (1957), 201–2/(2004), 165, gives the most detailed version. Yazdī, *ZN* (1957), I, 29/(2008), I, 257. Khwāfī (1962), II, 80/(2007), II, 944 (tr. Iusupova, 79), places this in 754/1353–4. Qazaghan apparently objected to his son's action.
195. Yazdī, *ZN* (1957), I, 30/(2008), I, 259. Compare also Shāmī, *ZN*, I, 52. Manz, *The Rise and Rule*, 44.

196. Shāmī, *ZN*, I, 15. HA, *Jughrāfiyya*, BL ms. Or. 1577, fo. 308a, calls him ruler of 'Mā warā' al-nahr and Balkh'. IA (1979), 6/(1986), 45 (*TGA*, 3–4), calls Balkh his residence (*takht mulkihi*).
197. Shāmī, *ZN*, I, 51–2. Yazdī, *ZN* (1957), I, 131/(2008), I, 372–3. Manz, 'The ulus Chaghatay', 94–5, and *The Rise and Rule*, 54–5. However, Gronke, 'The Persian court between palace and tent', 18, suggests that the objection was to a fixed capital per se rather than to its location.
198. Aubin, 'Le khanat de Čaġatai', 19. Manz, *The Rise and Rule*, 58.
199. Manz, *The Rise and Rule*, 160 (appendix A). Bernardini, 'The Mongol puppet lords', 174–5.
200. Bernardini, *Mémoire et propagande*, 61–2, and 65–9 on the stance of the later Timurid historians Mīr-Khwānd and Khwānd-Amīr.
201. Manz, *The Rise and Rule*, 161, (appendix A); see also ibid., 43.
202. Ando, *Timuridische Emire*, 62–4.

8: TIMUR'S FOREBEARS AND THE ELITE OF THE CHAGHADAYID REALM

1. *JT*, I, 606 (*CC*, 211–12).
2. *SP*, fo. 117b (where the second element in Buqa's name appears as DWQLAMD [?]). For Möge, see also *JT*, I, 72 (*DzhT*, I, part 1, 149; *CC*, 30); at I, 606, 762, the name is given as 'Möngke' (cf. *SGK*, 145; *CC*, 212, 265).
3. For Timur's ancestry as given in the Timurid sources, see John E. Woods, 'Timur's genealogy', in Michael M. Mazzaoui and Vera B. Moreen (eds), *Intellectual Studies on Islam. Essays Written in Honor of Martin B. Dickson* (Salt Lake City, UT, 1990), 85–125 (here 91–9); and for his immediate family, Woods, *The Timurid Dynasty*, 17.
4. Only IA (1979), 3/(1986), 39 (*TGA*, 1), specifies the village, which lies 13 km S.W. of Kish: M.E. Masson and G.A. Pugachenkova, 'Shakhri Siabz pri Timure i Ulug-Beke', tr. J.M. Rogers as 'Shahr-i Sabz from Tīmūr to Ūlūgh Beg – I', *Iran* 16 (1978), 103–26, and '. . . – II', *Iran* 18 (1980), 121–43 (here '. . . – I', 109).
5. On the date of Taraghai's death, see V.V. Bartol'd, 'O pogrebenii Timura', in his *Sochineniia*, II, part 2, 423–54, tr. J.M. Rogers, 'V.V. Bartol'd's article *O pogrebenii Timura* ("The burial of Tīmūr")', *Iran* 12 (1974), 65–87 (here 67 and n.7).
6. Mentioned by Yazdī, *ZN* (1957), I, 8/(2008), I, 234. For the conflicting testimony regarding *Tekine Khatun, see Woods, 'Timur's genealogy', 97.
7. John of Sulṭāniyya, *Mémoire*, ed. Moranvillé, 447.
8. Compare Manz, 'Tamerlane and the symbolism', 116–17, on his possible efforts to downplay his father's status; and see also p. 389.
9. IA (1979), 7, *min jihat al-nisā'*/(1986), 45 (*TGA*, 4, 'without a break to Jenghizkhan through females' is misleading); the same phrase appears in Ibn Qāḍī Shuhba, *Ta'rīkh*, IV, 429. al-Maqrīzī, *Durar al-'uqūd*, I, 507, and Ibn Taghrībirdī, *al-Manhal*, IV, 104, simply make Timur's mother a descendant of Chinggis Khan. Hodgson, *The Venture of Islam*, II, 429, suggested that Timur 'may have had . . . Chingizid connections at least in a maternal line'.
10. *MA*, fo. 96b, ed. Vokhidov, text, 190 (Russian trans., 117). Woods, 'Timur's genealogy', 97. Ando, *Timuridische Emire*, 117, n.50, correcting Manz, *The Rise and Rule*, 165. HA, in his additions to Shāmī, *ZN*, II, 12, calls Ḥājjī Maḥmūdshāh the son of Taibuqa.

11. Yazdī, *ZN* (1957), I, 351/(2008), I, 631.
12. Shāmī, *ZN*, I, 21. Yazdī, *ZN* (1957), I, 54/(2008), I, 286–7. Karl Jahn, 'Timur und die Frauen', *Anzeiger der Österreichischen Akademie der Wissenschaften, phil.-hist. Klasse*, 111 (1974), 515–29 (here 517). For Qutlugh Terken's husbands, see *MA*, fo. 95a, ed. Vokhidov, text, 187 (Russian trans., 115).
13. Shāmī, *ZN*, I, 90. Yazdī, *ZN* (1957), I, 260/(2008), I, 529–30. Priscilla P. Soucek, 'Tīmūrid women: A cultural perspective', in Gavin R.G. Hambly (ed.), *Women in the Medieval Islamic World. Power, Patronage and Piety* (New York, 1998), 199–226 (here 201–2). For her tomb, see Muḥammad b. ʿAbd al-Jalīl Samarqandī, *Qandiyya*, in Īraj Afshār (ed.), *Qandiyya wa-samariyya. Dū risāla dar ta'rīkh-i mazārāt-u jughrāfiyyā-yi Samarqand* (Tehran, 1367 sh./1988), 165; on this work, which apparently dates from the fifteenth century in the form that has come down to us, see Barthold, *Turkestan*[3], 15–16.
14. *MA*, fo. 95a, ed. Vokhidov, text, 187 (Russian trans., 115). *ZT*, I, 42. Woods, *The Timurid Dynasty*, 19.
15. Yazdī, *ZN* (1957), I, 161–2/(2008), I, 407. For *tovachi*, see *TMEN*, I, 260–4 (no. 133, 'Truppeninspektor'); Manz, *The Rise and Rule*, 173–4.
16. Shāmī writes of two brothers of Timur, Ṣiddīq, who appears among his adherents in the mid-1360s, and Amīr ʿAlī, who took part in the campaign in Khurāsān in 782/1380–1: Ṣiddīq: Shāmī, *ZN*, I, 22. ʿAlī: ibid., I, 82, 88. But in the corresponding passages Sharaf al-Dīn Yazdī calls Ṣiddīq Barlās a descendant of Qarachar's son Ilder (and hence a distant relative), and makes Amīr ʿAlī the son of Mu'ayyad Arlāt by Timur's sister: Yazdī, *ZN* (1957), I, 58, 230/(2008), I, 289, 493.
17. See Woods, *The Timurid Dynasty*, 12. Bartol'd, 'O pogrebenii Timura', 424 (tr. Rogers, 67), questioned whether Timur's grandfather *Borogul had been a Muslim. An Aligarh ms. of *MA* states that Ailangir (see p. 232), *Borogul's father, was the first of Timur's ancestors to embrace Islam: Ando, *Timuridische Emire*, 70–1. But this ms. is very late (mid-19th century): ibid., 18–19.
18. Yazdī, *ZN* (1972), fo. 83a/(2008), I, 223; see also (1957), I, 475–6/(2008), I, 756. Yazdī gives the name as Kulār. On Shams al-Dīn Kulāl, see Bartol'd, 'O pogrebenii Timura', 425–6 (tr. Rogers, 67–9 and nn.13 and 24); Jürgen Paul, 'Scheiche und Herrscher im Khanat Čaġatay', *Der Islam* 67 (1990), 278–321 (here 291–9), arguing that this man is to be distinguished from Amīr Kulāl, with whom Bartol'd identified him.
19. Hans R. Roemer, 'Zur Herkunft Timurs', in Bernardini (ed.), *La civiltà timuride come fenomeno internazionale*, I, 5–8. Compare also the older verdicts of Grousset, *The Empire of the Steppes*, 409 ('In fact, he was no Mongol, but a Turk'), and of Hodgson, *The Venture of Islam*, II, 428–9, 430.
20. TSM, ms. Hazine 2152. See Emel Esin, 'Ḫanlar Ulaḵi (The succession of kings): On the illustrated genealogy, with Uygur inscriptions, of Mongol and Temürid dynasties, at the Topkapı Library', in Heissig and Sagaster (eds.), *Gedanke und Wirkung*, 113–27 (here 116–24, but misreading ḤSYN as ČYN); and Anna Caiozzo, 'Propagande dynastique et célébrations princières, mythes et images à la cour timouride', *BEO* 60 (2011), 177–202 (here 180). The genealogy is also shown in Thackston (trans.), *A Century of Princes*, xvi.
21. Woods, 'Timur's genealogy', 85, 109–14. Binbaş, 'Structure and function of the genealogical tree', 509–14.
22. These details are found in Yazdī's *Muqaddima*, the prologue to his *Ta'rīkh-i Jahāngīr* (above, p. 29): Yazdī, *ZN* (1972), fos 24a–25a/(2008), I, 64–6. Woods,

'Timur's genealogy', 91; and on the development of the story, Manz, 'Family and ruler', 66–7. For this paragraph and that following, see Biran, *Chinggis Khan*, 122–3, 125.

23. Yazdī, *ZN* (1972), fos 28a, 28b, 29a, 29b/(2008), I, 75, 76–7, 78, 80.
24. Ibid. (1972), fos 26b–27a/(2008), I, 71. Woods, 'Timur's genealogy', 92, raises important questions about Yazdī's reliability concerning Sughu.
25. Yazdī, *ZN* (1972), fo. 33a/(2008), I, 91.
26. Ibid. (1972), fos 61b, 62a, 75a/(2008), I, 168–9, 170, 200–1. Woods, 'Timur's genealogy', 92–3.
27. Yazdī, *ZN* (1972), fo. 75b/(2008), I, 202. Compare also the version in *MA*, fo. 81a–b, ed. Vokhidov, text, 159–60 (Russian trans., 104), and for an English rendering of this passage, Subtelny, *Timurids in Transition*, 19.
28. Yazdī, *ZN* (1972), fo. 76b/(2008), I, 205. Yazdī's account of this revolt is based on *TJG*, I, 85–90 (*HWC*, 109–15), where Qarachar, however, is mentioned nowhere: Binbaş, *Intellectual Networks*, 207, n.31. See, however, p. 232, on his son Ilder.
29. Yazdī, *ZN* (1972), fo. 81a, lines 15–18/(2008), I, 218. Woods, 'Timur's genealogy', 95.
30. Yazdī, *ZN* (1957), I, 9/(2008), I, 235–6.
31. Ibid. (1972), fos 22b, 23a, 24a, 83b, and (1957), II, 518/(2008), I, 60, 61, 63, 224, and II, 1337. Compare also (1972), fo. 7b/(2008), I, 20, for a less specific allusion to their common ancestry.
32. *MA*, fos 6b–7a, 79a, 81a, 82a–b, 94a, 95a, ed. Vokhidov, text, 14–15, 155, 159, 161, 185, 187 (Russian trans., 26–7, 103–5, 114, 115). *ZT*, I, 35, 36.
33. See Rudi P. Lindner, 'What was a nomadic tribe?', *CSSH* 24 (1982), 689–711 (here 696–701); Peter B. Golden, 'Ethnogenesis in the tribal zone: The shaping of the Turks', *AEMA* 16 (2008–9), 73–112 (esp. 74–5, 104–5), and repr. in Golden, *Studies on the Peoples and Cultures of the Eurasian Steppes*, ed. Cătălin Hriban (Bucharest, 2011), 17–63 (here 19–20, 54–5). But such fictions could be dispensed with: Paul, 'The state and the military', 28.
34. *JT*, I, 245, 247 (*CC*, 88, 89).
35. SH, §§ 45–6 (tr. De Rachewiltz, I, 9). The differing testimony of these sources is reviewed in Woods, 'Timur's genealogy', 88–91.
36. As Woods points out (ibid., 90), SH, § 120 (tr. De Rachewiltz, I, 47), is the only pre-Timurid source to mention Sughu Sechen.
37. *JT*, I, 201 (*DzhT*, I, part 1, 530–1; *CC*, 74). Manz, *The Rise and Rule*, 156.
38. *SP*, fo. 127b; Qachulai's descendants are listed at fo. 100a–b. Woods, 'Timur's genealogy', 90–1.
39. Eiji Mano, 'Amir Timūr Kürägän – The Timurid genealogy and Timur's position', *Tōyōshi Kenkyū* 34, no. 4 (March 1976), English abstract at 4–5, suggested that the genealogy is genuine but that it was far less important to Timur than it would be to his descendants. I regret that the Japanese text of this article is inaccessible to me.
40. Ibm Fatḥ-Allāh al-Baghdādī, *al-Ta'rīkh al-Ghiyāthī*, 169, 170, respectively.
41. As Ibn Khaldūn pointed out elsewhere: *Kitāb al-'Ibar*, V, 1117; Van den Bent, 'None of the kings', 177.
42. Ibn Khaldūn, *Kitāb al-'Ibar*, V, 1033, 1179; the printed text regularly reads *Jafaṭāī* for *Jaqaṭāī*.
43. Ibid., V, 1081–2.

44. Ibid., V, 1129.
45. IA (1979), 4, 6–7/(1986), 42, 45 (cf. *TGA*, 1–2, with 'smith', and translating *ṭā'ifat awshāb* as 'a mixed horde', and 4). This author unaccountably calls Taraghai's father 'BΓAY (Abaghai?). For later enhancement of Taraghai's status, see Sela, *The Legendary Biographies of Tamerlane*, 58.
46. Shāmī, *ZN*, I, 27.
47. Clavijo (1859), 125–6/(1928), 210. John of Sulṭāniyya, *Mémoire*, ed. Moranvillé, 441.
48. Roemer, 'Zur Herkunft Timurs', 6.
49. *JT*, I, 589 (*CC*, 205).
50. SH, § 243 (tr. De Rachewiltz, I, 167); of the two commanders other than Qarachar, Möngke must be the Möge named by Rashīd al-Dīn, but Idoqudai does not appear on the list in *JT* or *SP*. Compare SH, § 202 (tr. I, 133), where Qarachar is simply listed among the 95 commanders of 1,000. Kököchös belonged to the Ba'arin tribe: SH, § 120 (tr. De Rachewiltz, I, 47).
51. Naṭanzī (1957), 103/(2004), 84.
52. Shāmī, *ZN*, I, 10, 12–14, 58.
53. *MA*, fo. 81a, ed. Vokhidov, text, 159 (Russian trans., 104). Manz, 'Tamerlane and the symbolism', 111; Subtelny, *Timurids in Transition*, 21–2. For the *möchelge*, see Subtelny, 'The binding pledge (*möchälgä*): A Chinggisid practice and its survival in Safavid Iran', in Colin P. Mitchell (ed.), *New Perspectives on Safavid Iran, Empire and Society* (London and New York, 2011), 9–29.
54. For what follows, see Grupper, 'A Barulas family narrative', 21–33; also Subtelny, *Timurids in Transition*, 18–22, and her 'Tamerlane and his descendants', 171–2.
55. Assuming that he is the Buluqan mentioned in SH, § 202 (tr. De Rachewiltz, I, 167), as a commander of 1,000.
56. Grupper, 'A Barulas family narrative', 36, 79–81. But see now Atwood, '*Ulus* emirs', esp. 158–9.
57. Grupper, 'A Barulas family narrative', 35.
58. Ibid., 37; and see also the concluding remarks at 79–80.
59. Subtelny, *Timurids in Transition*, 21–2; and also compare her 'Tamerlane and his descendants', 171–2. On the *yarghuchi*, see Florence Hodous, 'Jarqu and jarquchin', in May and Hope (eds), *The Mongol World*, 331–40.
60. *TR*, I (text), 34, II (trans.), 30.
61. Ibid., I (text), 249, II (trans.), 194. For *tüzük*, see *TMEN*, II, 613 (no. 963: 'Regel, Vorschrift').
62. Subtelny, *Timurids in Transition*, 22–4; also her 'Tamerlane and his descendants', 172.
63. For examples from both categories, see *JT*, I, 73–5 (*DzhT*, I, part 1, 152–7; *CC*, 30–1).
64. Atwood, '*Ulus* emirs', 147–50, 154–6.
65. For the descendants of Qarachar's five sons (other than Timur's progeny), see *MA*, fos 82a–95a, ed. Vokhidov, text, 161–87 (Russian trans., 105–15), and *ZT*, I, 37–44. They are surveyed by Ando, *Timuridische Emire*, 68–83.
66. For a succinct introduction to the problems, see Manz, *The Rise and Rule*, 156–7.
67. Yazdī, *ZN* (1972), fos 77b–78a/(2008), I, 208–9.

68. *JT*, I, 606 (*CC*, 211–12, rendering the name as 'Echig'); compare also ibid., I, 201 (*DzhT*, I, part 1, 531; *CC*, 74). And see the account in Woods, 'Timur's genealogy', 94; Ando, *Timuridische Emire*, 69.
69. Woods, 'Timur's genealogy', 94.
70. Yazdī, *ZN* (1972), fos 79b, 83a/(2008), I, 213, 222. On this, see the comments of Woods, 'Timur's genealogy', 94–5.
71. *TJG*, I, 89, if we take the variant reading 'YLDR in place of 'YLDZ as adopted by Qazwīnī and followed in *HWC*, 114. For Ilder, see *MA*, fo. 82a, ed. Vokhidov, text, 161 (Russian trans., 105); Woods, *The Timurid Dynasty*, 9.
72. This name defies transcription. Waṣṣāf (1853) is inconsistent, offering TYLAY and NAMYLH, but the autograph İstanbul ms. Nuruosmaniye 2740/1–2 (old numbering: 3207), fo. 195a, has NMBLAY (cf. the garbled form in *GW*, IV, 295), and NAMBLH at fos 196a, 201a, 206a; Waṣṣāf (2009) accordingly settles for NAMBLH. He was a grandson of Qarachar: *MA*, fo. 88a, ed. Vokhidov, text, 173 (Russian trans., 108), where his name is given as NYMWLY, but it appears as TYMWLY at fo. 90a, ed. Vokhidov, text, 177 (but not in the Russian trans., 110); *ZT*, I, 39, has TYMWLY. Yazdī, *ZN* (1957), I, 31/(2008), I, 260, spells the name NMWLH. *Temülei was still alive in the winter of 1302–3: Qāshānī, *Ta'rīkh-i Uljāytū Sulṭān*, 18 (reading TMWLA, as does the ms., fo. 9b √).
73. Waṣṣāf (1853), 513, 517/(2009), 274, 283 (*GW*, IV, 303, 312).
74. Though *Ashitan, another officer of Du'a mentioned in this context, is perhaps identical with a Barlās kinsman of Qarachar's who bore that name: ibid. (1853), 516/(2009), 280 (*GW*, IV, 309–10); see *MA*, fo. 79a, ed. Vokhidov, text, 155 (Russian trans., 103).
75. *MA*, fo. 88a, ed. Vokhidov, text, 173 (Russian trans., 108); and for Ḥājjī Barlās's ancestry, see also Yazdī, *ZN* (1957), I, 31/(2008), I, 260; Ando, *Timuridische Emire*, 75–6 and table at 279.
76. We also encounter the term *tümen-i kalān*: Yazdī, *ZN* (1957), II, 66/(2008), I, 914.
77. *MA*, fos 88a (*ming*), 89a (*tümen*), ed. Vokhidov, text, 173, 175 (Russian trans., 108, 109). Manz, *The Rise and Rule*, 31. Woods, 'Timur's genealogy', 96. For HA's phrase (*ab^{an} 'an jadd*), see *ZT*, I, 320 (also his additions to Shāmī, *ZN*, II, 13). Ando, *Timuridische Emire*, 75–6, discusses these terms.
78. Manz, *The Rise and Rule*, n.42 at 180, suggests that terms like *ulugh ming* reflect the proximity of our sources to the Barlās tradition and that they treat the other tribes from the vantage point of outsiders.
79. Shāmī, *ZN*, I, 15. Yazdī, *ZN* (1957), I, 31–2/(2008), I, 261. In the same vein is the description of Kish as Timur's 'hereditary tümen', which Subtelny, *Timurids in Transition*, 22, appears to accept. Ando, *Timuridische Emire*, 75, is rightly sceptical.
80. Manz, *The Rise and Rule*, 45, and 'Tamerlane and the symbolism', 116–17.
81. Yazdī, *ZN* (1957), I, 7, 476, 566, and II, 141/(2008), I, 234, 756, 843, 985; also 'august father' (*pidar-i sa'īd*) in (1957), II, 419/(2008), II, 1252.
82. Ibid. (1972), fo. 83a/(2008), I, 223; for his friendship with the pious, see also (1957), I, 7/(2008), I, 234.
83. Ibid. (1957), II, 518–19/(2008), II, 1338. Woods, 'Timur's genealogy', 96.
84. Shāmī, *ZN*, I, 16, 18–19. Bernardini, 'La prise du pouvoir par Tamerlan', 140–1.
85. Yazdī, *ZN*, (1957), I, 45–6/(2008), I, 277.

86. Ibid. (1957), I, 29/(2008), I, 258. On the Orona'ut, see Paul Pelliot and Louis Hambis, *Histoire des campagnes de Gengis Khan. Cheng-wu Ts'in-tcheng-lou*, vol. I only published (Leiden, 1951), 73–4. IB, III, 29, also names a certain *Toqbugha (or possibly Toqtogha › Toqto'a; tr. Gibb, 555, 'Taqbughā') as Tarmashirin's lieutenant (*nā'ib*), though from the context this officer may simply have been the khan's second-in-command for his *orda* at Qarshī rather than viceroy for the entire ulus.
87. *TR*, I (text), 9, 33–4, II (trans.), 7–8, 29. On Manghalai Sübe, see above, p. 203 and p. 556 n. 45.
88. *TR*, I (text), 34, 91, II (trans.), 30, 73–4.
89. Ibid., I (text), 241, II (trans.), 188.
90. *JT*, I, 206–7 (*DzhT*, I, part 1, 549; *CC*, 77); more briefly in *SP*, fo. 117b.
91. See Pishchulina, *Iugo-vostochnyi Kazakhstan*, 44–5; Kim, 'The early history of the Moghul nomads', 300–1.
92. It may be significant that the earliest Dughlāt amir known to have married into the Chaghadayid royal line is Shams al-Dīn, who held the office of chief amir (*amīr al-umarā*; *āqā ūlughī*) in the mid-1360s and was a brother of the usurper Qamar al-Dīn: *MA*, fo. 33a, ed. Vokhidov, text, 67 (Russian trans., 51). His rank is specified by Naṭanzī (1957), 125/(2004), 102; for the phrase *āqā ūlughī*, see *TMEN*, I, 135. But whether the office or the marriage antedated Qamar al-Dīn's hegemony, we cannot know.
93. *TR*, I (text), 9–10, II (trans.), 7–8. For his dubious antecedents, see DeWeese, 'Islamization in the Mongol empire', 132; Jackson, *The Mongols and the Islamic World*, 358. But see also p. 127 above.
94. *TR*, I (text), 28, 31–2, II (trans.), 20, 28. Naṭanzī (1957), 130–1/(2004), 106, a near-contemporary, makes the kingmaker on this occasion Mīrak Āqā, whom he calls the atabeg of the ulus and Khudāydād's father (but whose name suspiciously resembles that of Khudāydād's mother, as given in Ḥaydar's version of events); and compare also ibid. (1957), 418/(2004), 305. *ZT*, I, 522 (and see HA's addenda to Shāmī, ZN, II, 39), calls Khudāydād's mother Amīra Āqā. Both Naṭanzī (1957), 115, 130/(2004), 93, 106, and Yazdī, *ZN* (1957), I, 337/(2008), I, 617, seem to accept Khiḍr Khwāja's paternity as authentic.
95. On the opposition party, see Kim, 'The early history of the Moghul nomads', esp. 307–13; and see also his 'The rise and fall of the Hami kingdom (ca. 1389–1513)', in *Land Routes of the Silk Roads* (*10 shi shi ji qian de si chou zhi lu he dong xi wen hua jiao liu*) (Beijing, 1996), 89–95 (here 90–2). Gunashiri[n], a descendant of Alughu's son Chübei, subsequently appears as prince of Hami (Qāmul): Morris Rossabi, 'Ming foreign policy: The case of Hami', in Sabine Dabringhaus and Roderich Ptak (eds, with Richard Teschke), *China and Her Neighbours. Borders, Visions of the Other, Foreign Policy 10th to 19th Century* (Wiesbaden, 1997), 79–97 (here 83, calling him 'Bunyashiri' in error), and repr. in Rossabi, *From Yuan to Modern China and Mongolia. The Writings of Morris Rossabi* (Leiden and Boston, MA, 2014), 19–37 (here 23); and Ralph Kauz, *Politik und Handel zwischen Ming und Timuriden. China, Iran und Zentralasien im Spätmittelalter* (Wiesbaden, 2005), 32–3. Robinson, *Ming China and Its Allies*, 165, sees Gunashiri[n]'s candidacy as a response to the threat from Timur.
96. For these various privileges, see *TR*, I (text), 33–4, II (trans.), 28–31.
97. Schamiloglu, 'The *Umdet ül-ahbar*'. For a later source, designed to provide the upstart khans of Khokand with a Timurid pedigree, see p. 439.

98. Uli Schamiloglu, 'The *Qaraçı* beys of the later Golden Horde: Notes on the organisation of the Mongol world empire', *AEMA* 4 (1984), 283–97. But see Atwood, '*Ulus* emirs'.
99. Schamiloglu, 'The *Umdet ül-ahbar*', 91–2.
100. For another analogy – with the role attributed by an early nineteenth-century history of the Khans of Khiva to their Qongqurat (Qongrat) ancestors in Jochi's ulus – see Yuri Bregel, 'Tribal tradition and dynastic history: The early rulers of the Qongrats according to Munis', *Asian and African Studies* 16 (1982), 357–98 (esp. 395–6); İsenbike Togan, 'The Qongrat in history', in Pfeiffer and Quinn (eds), *History and Historiography of Post-Mongol Central Asia*, 61–83 (here 79–80).
101. *SP*, fo. 127b.
102. SH, §§ 187, 219 (tr. De Rachewiltz, I, 108–9, 150; and see his commentary at 294–5). *TJG*, I, 27–8 (*HWC*, 36–8). Compare *JT*, I, 384 (*CC*, 131). It should be noted, however, that ibid., I, 172 (*DzhT*, I, part 1, 436; *CC*, 65), Qishliq Tarkhan is ascribed to the Oyirat Kilungghut, not to the Süldüs, and in *SP*, fo. 117b, Qishliq of the Süldüs is expressly distinguished from Qishliq Tarkhan. See the discussion in Ando, *Timuridische Emire*, 118.
103. Yazdī, *ZN* (1957), I, 177/(2008), I, 426; see also ibid. (1972), fo. 28b/(2008), I, 77. Manz, *The Rise and Rule*, n.31 at 186. But compare *SP*, as cited in the previous note.
104. *JT*, II, 942 (*SGK*, 313; *CC*, 327). ʿIṣāmī, *Futūḥ al-salāṭīn*, 318, calls him *sar-āhang-i ān kishwar*. Jackson, *The Delhi Sultanate*, 227–8.
105. *JT*, I, 606, 762, and II, 1077, 1080–1 (*SGK*, 145; *DzhT*, III, 118, 122; *CC*, 211–12, 265 [with Yesün in error], 373, 375); Waṣṣāf (1853), 71, 76 (*GW*, I, text, 142, 151–2, trans., 135, 144–5). He is not to be confused with earlier commanders of the same name, such as the Yasa'ur who took part in Chinggis Khan's seven-year expedition and later operated in north-western Iran under Chormaghun, heading an incursion into northern Syria in 1244, or the Yasa'ur who accompanied Hülegü to Iran. He must also be distinguished from his maternal grandson, the Chaghadayid prince of this name (d. 720/1320).
106. *JT*, II, 1163 (*DzhT*, III, 207; *CC*, 402).
107. Ibid., I, 606–7 (*CC*, 212), and II, 1226 (more fully in *DzhT*, III, 578; *CC*, 423). Waṣṣāf (1853), 314, line 10 (*GW*, III, 135, omits Yasa'ur's name).
108. Sayfī (1944), 409/(2004), 433. *Pace* Wing, *The Jalayirids*, 42, Yasa'ur was not captured by Ilkhanid forces: this was the fate of one of his sons.
109. *JT*, I, 607 (*CC*, 212).
110. Qāshānī, *Ta'rīkh-i Uljāytū Sulṭān*, 35–6, 153, 208–10, 211; for his activities after Prince Yasa'ur's departure, 214–15, 217; and for his death, 226. Compare also Waṣṣāf (1853), 513, 515–16, 518, 519/(2009), 274, 275, 279–81, 285–6 (*GW*, IV, 308, 309, 310, 314, 315, 316). Biran, *Qaidu*, 75, 83, identifies him with another commander, named Jangqi, who appears, however, to be a different man.
111. Qāshānī, *Ta'rīkh-i Uljāytū Sulṭān*, 36. It is noteworthy that at one point in 705/1305 he and his nephew, Prince Yasa'ur, took refuge in Khujand: Waṣṣāf (1853), 515/(2009), 280 (*GW*, IV, 309).
112. See *JT*, I, 67 (*DzhT*, I, part 1, 134–5; *CC*, 28).
113. Changshi's brothers: Qāshānī, *Ta'rīkh-i Uljāytū Sulṭān*, 208, 215. Orus Buqa: ibid., 39, where he is instrumental in the capture of one of Chapar's brothers.

114. *SP*, fos 126a (where Yasa'ur appears as 'Yeke Yesügür of the Jalayir tribe'), 127b. For Jalayirtai's marriage, see also *MA*, fo. 43b, ed. Vokhidov, text, 88 (Russian trans., 60).
115. *SP*, fo. 119b; these details are omitted in *MA*. Ando, *Timuridische Emire*, 109.
116. *JT*, II, 942 (*SGK*, 313; *CC*, 327). Il-Qutluq's husband is named as Ḥasan of the Süldüs in *SP*, fo. 137b (where it is not specified, however, that he was Köpek's son), but not named in *JT*.
117. *JT*, II, 1215 (*DzhT*, III, 256; *CC*, 419).
118. *SP*, fo. 127b. *MA*, fo. 42b, ed. Vokhidov, text, 86 (Russian trans., 59, muddles the names). He headed an attack on the Delhi Sultanate in *c.*705/1305: Jackson, *The Delhi Sultanate*, 227.
119. *SP*, fo. 118b. Banākatī, *Rawḍa*, 398. Qāshānī, *Ta'rīkh-i Uljāytū Sulṭān*, 7 (where the name of her mother Yesünjin appears as BBSWNḤṢ and Baiju's as MANQW; ms. Ayasofya 3019, fo. 4b, also has corrupt readings). Qutlugh Temür's son Taraghai, possibly the person of that name who was later Qutlugh Khwāja's lieutenant, is likewise styled Güregen. Qutlugh Temür had submitted to Alughu in 1260 and later took part in Baraq's invasion of Iran: Waṣṣāf (1853), 12, lines 17–21 (*GW*, I, text, 23–4, trans., 25); *JT*, II, 1077–8 (*DzhT*, III, 119; *CC*, 373–4); and see also above, p. 213 and p. 562 n.127.
120. Yazdī, *ZN* (1957), I, 155/(2008), I, 400.
121. Ibid. (1957), I, 172/(2008), I, 420; for Mūsā's tribe (*oimaq*), see (1957), I, 100/(2008), I, 337.
122. Ibid. (1957), I, 87/(2008), I, 323.
123. Ibid. (1957), I, 155/(2008), I, 400. Manz, *The Rise and Rule*, 158, suggests that these two princesses were probably the same person.
124. The only other one named, Ködege of the Dörben tribe, took as his wife a daughter of Khan Alughu: *SP*, fo. 122a; *MA*, fo. 37a, ed. Vokhidov, text, 75 (here spelled KWKH; he and his wife are omitted from the Russian trans., 54).
125. As Manz, *The Rise and Rule*, 157, points out.
126. See Jackson, *The Mongols and the Islamic World*, 243.
127. Yazdī, *ZN* (1957), I, 25/(2008), I, 253. ḤA, *Ta'rīkh-i salāṭīn-i Kart*, 180 (also in *CO*, text, 39). Aubin, 'Le khanat de Čaġatai', 35.
128. IB, III, 48–50 (tr. Gibb, 565–6); for their meeting, see ibid., III, 57 (tr. Gibb, 570).
129. Bosworth, 'The political and dynastic history of the Iranian world', 184. On the sayyids of Tirmidh generally, see W. Barthold, 'Tirmidh', *EI*², X, 543.
130. IB, III, 50 (tr. Gibb, 566).
131. Yazdī, *ZN* (1957), II, 140, 419/(2008), I, 984, and II, 1251.
132. Ibid. (1957), I, 157, 179, and II, 98, 396/(2008), I, 402, 428, 943, and II, 1229.
133. Jamāl al-Qarshī, *al-Mulḥaqāt bi l-Ṣurāḥ*, Ar. text, 177–8 (Russian trans., 130); also extract ed. in *Turkestan*[1], I, 140.
134. Chekhovich (ed.), *Bukharskie dokumenty*, text, 55–6 (Russian trans., 135–6). See also, for a slightly earlier period, A.K. Arends, A.B. Khalidov and O.D. Chekhovich (eds), *Bukharskii vakf XIII v.* (Moscow, 1979), facsimile of Pers. trans., plate 22 (Russian trans., 77–8). For the family, see C.E. Bosworth, 'Āl-e Borhān', *EIr*, I, 753–4.
135. *TJG*, I, 86, 88 (*HWC*, 110, 112). C.E. Bosworth, 'Ṣadr, I. In Transoxiana', *EI*², VIII, 748–9. Biran, 'The Mamluks and Mongol Central Asia', 381.
136. IB, III, 27 (tr. Gibb, 554). Biran, 'The Chaghadaids and Islam', 746. The *waqf-nāma*s are reproduced in Chekhovich (ed.), *Bukharskie dokumenty* (docs 1, 2 and 4).

137. IB, III, 30, 33 (tr. Gibb, 556, 557).
138. IB, III, 32 (tr. Gibb, 556). Qāshānī, *Ta'rīkh-i Uljāytū Sulṭān*, 213–14, claims that these towns were the only ones Yasa'ur spared (printed text to be corrected from SK Ayasofya ms. 3019, fo. 94b). But the sack of Bukhara, dated by implication early in Rajab 716 [late Sept. 1316], is mentioned by Aḥmad b. Maḥmūd Mu'īn al-fuqarā', *Ta'rīkh-i Mullāzāda*, ed. Aḥmad Gulchīn-i Ma'ānī as *Ta'rīkh-i Mullāzāda dar dhikr-i mazārāt-i Bukhārā*, 2nd edn (Tehran, 1370 shamsī/1991), 64 (also extract in *Turkestan*[1], I, 171).
139. IA (1979), 5–6/(1986), 43–4 (*TGA*, 2–3). Paul, 'Scheiche und Herrscher', 297–8, evidently sees the two men as identical.
140. On which see V.V. Bartol'd, 'Narodnoe dvizhenie v Samarkande v 1365 g.' (1907), tr. J.M. Rogers, 'Narodnoye dvizheniye v Samarkande v 1365 g. ("A popular uprising in Samarqand in 1365")', *Iran* 19 (1981), 21–31. The earliest sources to describe this movement are Shāmī, *ZN*, I, 32 (very briefly), and Yazdī, *ZN* (1957), I, 84, 86/(2008), I, 319, 321–2.
141. Paul, 'Mongol aristocrats and beyliks in Anatolia', 109 (including the phrase quoted). For the term *mulūk al-ṭawā'if*, see above, p. 127.
142. Naṭanzī (1957), 113, 197/(2004), 91, 162. *ZT*, I, 182–3 (also in Shāmī, *ZN*, II, 6). Bernardini, 'The Mongol puppet lords', 170, 172.
143. Yazdī, *ZN* (1957), I, 31, 38/(2008), I, 260, 268.
144. Sari Bugha of the Jalāyir appears heading 'the Qipchāq people (*qawm*)' in 766/1364–5: Yazdī, *ZN* (1957), I, 77/(2008), I, 313; see Manz, *The Rise and Rule*, 76, 120, 163.
145. Ando, *Timuridische Emire*, 62. Manz, *The Rise and Rule*, 32.
146. Ando, *Timuridische Emire*, 85–6.
147. Shāmī, *ZN*, I, 15. Naṭanzī (1957), 204/(2004), 167. Yazdī, *ZN* (1957), I, 31–2/(2008), I, 261. The sources are in agreement, except that according to Shāmī, Shabūrghān had been seized by Muḥammad Khwāja Apardī; since Yazdī confirms that he belonged to the Naiman, he was probably identical with Naṭanzī's Ḥamīd Khwāja. On the Apardī, see Ando, *Timuridische Emire*, 57–9.
148. Naṭanzī (1957), 273/(2004), 213.
149. Faryūmadī, *Dhayl-i Majma' al-ansāb*, 320.
150. Manz, *The Rise and Rule*, 160. I have tentatively read as BYST the variant forms in the editions of Yazdī's *ZN*, which are BYGT and TBYT or TYBT. The Besüt were associated with the Kabul region: Manz, *The Rise and Rule*, 157–8. A Besüt noyan named Orus had been active in the Herat and Bādghīs region on behalf of the Ilkhan Abagha: *JT*, I, 209 (*DzhT*, I, part 1, 557–9; *CC*, 77–8). Aubin, 'Le khanat de Čaġatai', 18, n.7, and Manz (*loc. cit.*) are noncommittal regarding the tribal name, but Ando, *Timuridische Emire*, 54, reads it as 'Tubayt', while conceding that this form does not occur elsewhere.
151. Naṭanzī (1957), 117/(2004), 96. For Bayrāmshāh, see Shāmī, *ZN*, I, 62; Yazdī, *ZN* (1957), I, 164/(2008), I, 410; Ando, *Timuridische Emire*, 60.
152. Yazdī, *ZN* (1957), I, 195/(2008), I, 450. See Ando, *Timuridische Emire*, 110, 169.
153. Manz, 'The ulus Chaghatay', 84 and n.11, and *The Rise and Rule*, 155.
154. Yazdī, *ZN* (1957), I, 147/(2008), I, 392.
155. Manz, 'The Ulus Chaghatay', 79, 85–6, and *The Rise and Rule*, 36–40.
156. Naṭanzī (1957), 204/(2004), 167. *ZT*, I, 317 (also in Shāmī, *ZN*, II, 12). If the rank of *amīr al-umarā'* is in question here, the allusion may have been to Du'a's chief amir, Köpek of the Süldüs (see earlier).

157. Yazdī, *ZN* (1957), I, 89, 119–20/(2008), I, 325–6, 359.
158. Ibid. (1957), I, 29–30/(2008), I, 258. Naṭanzī (1957), 262/(2004), 206.
159. Manz, 'The ulus Chaghatay', 86–7. See also her remarks in *The Rise and Rule*, 41–2, 63; Fletcher, 'The Mongols: Ecological and social perspectives', 27. *Mutatis mutandis*, this doubtless applies equally well, at an earlier date, to the installation and replacement of khans.
160. See Paul, 'Mongol aristocrats and beyliks in Anatolia', 115–21; also Paul, 'Zerfall und Bestehen', 727–8. Golden, *An Introduction*, 304–5. For the Nawrūzīs, see Muʿīn al-Dīn Yazdī, *Mawāhib-i ilāhī*, 207; Kutubī, *Ta'rīkh-i āl-i Muẓaffar*, 32.
161. As suggested in Jackson, *The Mongols and the Islamic World*, 402–3.
162. See, for example, Barthold, *Zwölf Vorlesungen*, 218–19 (= Bartol'd, *Sochineniia*, V, 172); Manz, *The Rise and Rule*, 164, and *Nomads in the Middle East*, 147; Katō, 'Kebek and Yasawr', 109; Ando, *Timuridische Emire*, 117; Nagel, *Timur der Eroberer*, 98 (wrongly calling Yasa'ur a son of Du'a); and Lee, *Qazaqlïq*, 63–4.
163. Yazdī, *ZN* (1957), I, 121/(2008), I, 361. Manz, 'The ulus Chaghatay', 84 and n.9, and *The Rise and Rule*, 155. Ando, *Timuridische Emire*, 57.
164. IA (1979), 7/(1986), 47 (*TGA*, 4).
165. *JT*, I, 166 (*DzhT*, I, part 1, 416; *CC*, 63). For the Orona'ut, see earlier and n. 86.
166. As Atwood, '*Ulus* emirs', 158–9, appears to assume.
167. Shāmī, *ZN*, I, 255. Yazdī, *ZN* (1957), I, 53, 162, 559, 563/(2008), I, 285, 407, 835, 839 (TMWK in the latter two places); elsewhere he omits the surname, as does Shāmī, *ẒN*, I, 21, 23, 24. On Temüge, see Ando, *Timuridische Emire*, 89–90. The term Qauchin is discussed in Manz, *The Rise and Rule*, 161–3.
168. Yazdī, *ZN* (1957), I, 462–3, 573/(2008), I, 742–3, 850.
169. *TR*, I (text), 246, II (trans.), 192.
170. *TMEN*, I, 423 (no. 295, 'alt, ursprünglich; Gardetruppe, bestehend aus alterprobten Kriegern'), citing the passage from Shāmī below, n. 178. Compare Atwood, '*Ulus* emirs', 159 ('the old ones'), and in *EMME*, 541, where he defines the *qauchin* as 'local soldiery created a century earlier under the Mongol census'.
171. Shāmī, *ZN*, I, 134. Yazdī, *ZN* (1957), I, 436/(2008), I, 715. For Tu. *boi*, see *TMEN*, II, 358–61 (no. 812, 'spezielle Leibgarden [wahrscheinlich solche, die dem eigenen Stamme des Herrschers angehörten]').
172. Beatrice F. Manz, 'The office of *darugha* under Tamerlane', in Joseph Fletcher, Richard Nelson Frye, Yuan-chu Lam and Omeljan Pritsak (eds, with Carolyn I. Cross), *Niġuča Bičig. An Anniversary Volume in Honor of Francis Woodman Cleaves* (Cambridge, MA, 1985 = *JTS* 9), 59–69 (here 67, n.54). This is also her conclusion in *The Rise and Rule*, 163 (and cf. 36). Thackston, in *TR*, II, 192, n.2, infers that 'the *qauchin* were originally bodyguards to the khaqan'.
173. Atwood, '*Ulus* emirs', 152–3. In *EMME*, 541, he calls the *qauchin* 'local soldiery' and distinguishes them from guard regiments.
174. A point made by Melville, 'The *keshig* in Iran', 161.
175. This obscure group is discussed by Ando, *Timuridische Emire*, 88 ff. To be added to the references given there is Salmānī, *Shams al-ḥusn*, text, fo. 162b (abridged German trans., 118).

176. Naṭanzī (1957), 107/(2004), 87. Barthold, *Zwölf Vorlesungen*, 218 (= Bartol'd, *Sochineniia*, V, 172).
177. Shāmī, *ZN*, I, 30, here speaking of the 'dependants (*tawābi'*) of Emperor Köpek'. Yazdī, *ZN* (1957), I, 83, 462, and II, 25/(2008), I, 319, 742, 871. Manz, *The Rise and Rule*, 34, 49–50, 83. Yangi was based at Balkh at the time of Tarmashirin's overthrow: IB, III, 42 (tr. Gibb, 562).
178. Shāmī, *ZN*, I, 194: *bā qūshūn-i khʷud ki az qāwchīnān-i bandagī-yi ḥaḍrat būdand*. See also Manz, *The Rise and Rule*, 163, citing HA.
179. Shāmī, *ZN*, I, 30. Yazdī, *ZN* (1957), I, 83/(2008), I, 319.
180. Manz, *The Rise and Rule*, 155.
181. An important distinction drawn by Manz, ibid., 43 ff.
182. As Manz points out, ibid., 44.

9: THE MAKING OF THE GREAT AMIR AND A NEW RULING CADRE

1. Yazdī, *ZN* (1957), II, 410–11/(2008), II, 1243.
2. Marozzi, *Tamerlane*, 206.
3. Manz, *The Rise and Rule*, 19.
4. Beatrice F. Manz, 'Administration and the delegation of authority in Temür's dominions', *CAJ* 20 (1976), 191–207 (here 196). Compare also Manz, *The Rise and Rule*, 18, 118–27, 167–75.
5. *Ta'rīf* (1951), 382/(2008), 255 (*IKT*, 47).
6. IA (1979), 315/(1986), 451 (*TGA*, 295): close to 80 (at his death). John of Sulṭāniyya, *Mémoire*, ed. Moranvillé, 463: 75 'or thereabouts' (in 1404); compare *Chronographia regum Francorum*, 213: aged 75 (in 1402–3).
7. al-Maqrīzī, *Durar al-'uqūd*, I, 501, 507; hence Ibn Taghrībirdī, *al-Manhal al-ṣāfī*, IV, 103. Ibn Ḥajar, *Inbā' al-ghumr*, ed. Ḥabashī, II, 299/ed. Khān, V, 225, says that he was 79. See generally Ito, 'Al-Maqrīzī's biography of Tīmūr', 312–13, 323.
8. Abū l-Walīd Muḥammad b. Maḥmūd Ibn al-Shiḥna, *Rawḍat al-manāẓir fī 'ilm al-awā'il wa l-awākhir* [printed in the margin of Ibn al-Athīr, *al-Kāmil fīl-ta'rīkh* (Būlāq, 1290/1873), IX], 218. IA (1979), 141/(1986), 216 (*TGA*, 129).
9. Mignanelli (1764), 138b/(2013), 332 (tr. in Fischel, 'A new Latin source', 227). John of Sulṭāniyya, *Mémoire*, ed. Moranvillé, 463, gives his age as 75; hence *Chronographia regum Francorum*, III, 213. Giorgio Stella, *Annales Genuenses* [*c.* 1405], ed. Giovanna Petti Balbi, *RIS*, n.s., XVII, part 2 (Bologna, 1975), 260, thought that Timur was around 70 when he attacked Syria and the Ottomans.
10. IA (1979), 314/(1986), 450–1 (cf. *TGA*, 295). Most of this description is reproduced (somewhat differently) by Roux, *Tamerlan*, 163.
11. John of Sulṭāniyya, *Mémoire*, ed. Moranvillé, 463. Compare *Chronographia regum Francorum*, III, 213. For all the inadequacy of these likenesses, any one of them is at least equal to the single contemporary description available for Chinggis Khan, by Zhao Gong, an envoy from the Song to the Mongol general Muqali in 1221, who personally never met Chinggis Khan but says in his *Mengda beilu*: 'he is of noble bearing, with a broad forehead and long whiskers, and cuts a heroic, robust figure': Christopher P. Atwood (trans. and ed., with Lynn Struve), *The Rise of the Mongols. Five Chinese Sources* (Indianapolis, IN, 2021), 73.

12. IA (1979), 4, 9–10/(1986), 42, 49 (*TGA*, 2, 6). Clavijo (1859), 77–8, 125–6/(1928), 137, 210–12. John of Sulṭāniyya, *Mémoire*, ed. Moranvillé, 441–2. Mignanelli (1764), 138b/(2013), 332–3 (tr. in Fischel, 'A new Latin source', 227–8).
13. *Patriarshaia ili Nikonovskaia letopis'*, in *PSRL*, XI, 158; tr. Serge A. and Betty J. Zenkovsky, *The Nikonian Chronicle*, IV. *From the Year 1382 to the Year 1425* (Princeton, NJ, 1988), 94. This text also stresses his low origins.
14. IA (1979), 6/(1986), 44 (*TGA*, 3).
15. See Lee, *Qazaqlïq*, 66–70, and 'The political vagabondage', esp. 61–2, 66–8.
16. See Ando, *Timuridische Emire*, 272. For the significance of the warband in Inner Asian polities, see Gommans, 'The warband'.
17. *Ta'rīf* (1951), 382/(2008), 255 (*IKT*, 47). Compare also John of Sulṭāniyya, *Mémoire*, ed. Moranvillé, 461, *et se delicte moult en argumens et questions*. For examples, see Yazdī, *ZN* (1957), II, 268, 396/(2008), II, 1105, 1229.
18. IA (1979), 319/(1986), 455 (*TGA*, 299). Ibn Qāḍī Shuhba, *Ta'rīkh*, IV, 182 (the context is a Persian translation of Ibn Khaldūn's description of the Maghrib); at IV, 438, Ibn Qāḍī Shuhba understands Ibn ʿArabshāh's statement to mean that Timur was illiterate and could neither read nor write. This is also the view of Roemer, 'Tīmūr in Iran', 44. Kehren, *Tamerlan*, 171, discusses the problem, suggesting that Timur may have received some education from sufi friends of his father while growing up in Kish. Roux, *Tamerlan*, 182, believes that 'illiteracy', in this context, meant simply that Timur lacked a knowledge of Arabic.
19. Only *ZT*, I, 319, mentions Bāyazīd's role (and see HA's additions to Shāmī, *ZN*, II, 12).
20. Shāmī, *ZN*, I, 16. Yazdī, *ZN* (1957), I, 36/(2008), I, 265. For Mo. *ghajarji*, see *TMEN*, I, 376–7 (no. 253: 'Wegführer: derjenige, der einem Expeditionsheer in einem fremden Lande das Gelände erklärt . . .').
21. Shāmī, *ZN*, I, 16, thus expresses the grant; see also Naṭanzī (1957), 117–18 (referring to the '*hazāra*' of Kish), 205–6/(2004), 96, 168. On Timur's submission, see Bernardini, 'La prise du pouvoir par Tamerlan', 140–1. The account of Timur's rise to power in the following paragraphs is based on Manz, *The Rise and Rule*, 45–57.
22. Shāmī, *ZN*, I, 17. Yazdī, *ZN* (1957), I, 42/(2008), I, 272. Both authors use the phrase *dar masnad-i ḥukūmat mutamakkin*, which can hardly signify merely the headship of the Jalāyir tribe.
23. Shāmī, *ZN*, I, 18. Yazdī, *ZN* (1957), I, 45/(2008), I, 275.
24. Shāmī, *ZN*, I, 19. Yazdī, *ZN* (1957), I, 47/(2008), I, 279.
25. Shāmī, *ZN*, I, 21–2. Yazdī, *ZN* (1957), I, 55–7/(2008), I, 287–9. Manz, *The Rise and Rule*, 48.
26. See Mahendrarajah, *A History of Herat*, 157–61.
27. Shāmī, *ZN*, I, 46, 49. Yazdī, *ZN* (1957), I, 121, 124/(2008), I, 362, 365. Compare also Naṭanzī (1957), 250/(2004), 195.
28. Shāmī, *ZN*, I, 47–51. Yazdī, *ZN* (1957), I, 122, 125–9/(2008), I, 363, 366–71. Shāmī, *ZN*, I, 46–7, and Naṭanzī (1957), 250/(2004), 195, indicate that Timur was offended by the failure of Bahrām to send him supplies or otherwise treat him with respect.
29. Bernardini, 'La prise du pouvoir par Tamerlan', 142; and compare also his *Mémoire et propagande*, 61–2. For earlier occurrences of the term Jata, see above, p. 206.

30. Shāmī, *ZN*, I, 32. See Bartol'd, 'Narodnoe dvizhenie', tr. Rogers.
31. See Michele Bernardini, 'Il colpo di Stato di Timur a Balḫ nel 1370', *OM* 85 (2005 = n.s., 24), 309–25.
32. Shāmī, *ZN*, I, 18–19. Yazdī, *ZN* (1957), I, 45/(2008), I, 275. On the pattern of shifting alliances, see Manz, *The Rise and Rule*, 47, 64.
33. Bernardini, 'La prise du pouvoir par Tamerlan', 141–2, 143–4. *Pace* Bernardini, the sources do sometimes employ the vocabulary of sworn compacts: for two examples of Timur and Ḥusayn renewing their 'sworn agreement' (*'ahd-u paymān*), see Shāmī, *ZN*, I, 25–6, 50–1.
34. E.g., Shāmī, *ZN*, I, 51.
35. Ibid., I, 57, 58.
36. Manz, *The Rise and Rule*, 81 and n.45 at 187; and for more detail, Ando, *Timuridische Emire*, 76–7.
37. Yazdī, *ZN* (1957), I, 189/(2008), I, 442.
38. Shāmī, *ZN*, I, 35. Yazdī, *ZN* (1957), I, 90/(2008), I, 326.
39. Shāmī, *ZN*, I, 56. Yazdī, *ZN* (1957), I, 143/(2008), I, 387. *ZT*, I, 439 (see also HA's additions in Shāmī, *ZN*, II, 27), gives a fuller explanation.
40. Manz, *The Rise and Rule*, 165.
41. Shāmī, *ZN*, I, 57.
42. Yazdī, *ZN* (1957), I, 203, 225, 241, and II, 402–3/(2008), I, 461, 488, 507, and II, 1235.
43. Manz, *The Rise and Rule*, 59–60; and for the Arlāt chiefs, Ando, *Timuridische Emire*, 60. The principal sources are Shāmī, *ZN*, I, 61–4; Yazdī, *ZN* (1957), I, 163–9, 171–3/(2008), I, 409–15, 417–21; and Naṭanzī (1957), 292–5/(2004), 227–9.
44. Yazdī, *ZN* (1957), I, 327/(2008), I, 605.
45. Manz, *The Rise and Rule*, 155 (appendix A).
46. Yazdī, *ZN* (1957), I, 177–8, 462/(2008), I, 426, 742.
47. Ibid. (1957), I, 354, and II, 159/(2008), I, 635, and II, 1005. Ando, *Timuridische Emire*, 262. *Malash accompanied the prince to Shīrāz in 795/1393: Yazdī, *ZN* (1957), I, 441/(2008), I, 720.
48. Manz, *The Rise and Rule*, 54.
49. Shāmī, *ZN*, I, 66–7. Yazdī, *ZN* (1957), I, 178, 181/(2008), I, 427, 430.
50. Yazdī, *ZN* (1957), I, 181, 320/(2008), I, 430–1, 595. *ZT*, II, 670 (also in HA's additions to Shāmī, *ZN*, II, 63).
51. Manz, *The Rise and Rule*, 49–50, 79, 133 and n.9 at 198.
52. Yazdī, *ZN* (1957), I, 192–3/(2008), I, 446–7. Shāmī, *ZN*, I, 70, 71, is much briefer and omits the execution of Bāyazīd's sons. The account of the revolt in Naṭanzī (1957), 414–16/(2004), 302–3, differs somewhat.
53. Yazdī, *ZN* (1957), I, 196–7/(2008), I, 451–2. Shāmī, *ZN*, I, 71, does not refer to the dispersal of the Jalāyir.
54. Manz, *The Rise and Rule*, 76, 82.
55. Yazdī, *ZN* (1957), I, 202/(2008), I, 458–9.
56. Ando, *Timuridische Emire*, 111. Manz, *The Rise and Rule*, 62.
57. Shāmī, *ZN*, I, 110. Yazdī, *ZN* (1957), I, 324–7/(2008), I, 602–5. Manz, *The Rise and Rule*, 78–9.
58. Manz, *The Rise and Rule*, 88–9, 128–9, 144–5; but for a possible exception, the rising of Pīr ʿAlī Tāz, which may have had a tribal basis, see ibid., 133–4.

59. Beckwith, *Empires of the Silk Road*, identifies such bands of sworn followers by the term *comitatus*: for this and other, earlier examples, see ibid., 12–23.
60. We might tentatively identify the BLKWT of the text with the tribe named Belgünüt in SH, § 42, on which see Pelliot and Hambis, *Histoire des campagnes de Gengis Khan*, 398; Lajos Bese, 'On some ethnic names in 13th century Inner-Asia', *AOH* 42 (1988), 17–42 (here 20). But compare the view of Ando, *Timuridische Emire*, 103.
61. Manz, *The Rise and Rule*, 74–5; and also compare 45–6, 57. Ando, *Timuridische Emire*, 65, gives a slightly longer list and ibid., 84, 89–90 and 101–2, 103–4, identifies the respective tribal affiliations of Shaykh ʿAlī, Aq Temür, Khiṭāy, Ilchi Bahādur and Taban; for *Eyegu Temur (whom he calls 'Īkū Tīmūr'), see ibid., 105–6.
62. Shāmī, *ZN*, I, 46, 69. Yazdī, *ZN* (1957), I, 118–19, 189/(2008), I, 357, 359, 442. For his allegiance to Amīr Ḥusayn, see also Naṭanzī (1957), 245–7/(2004), 194–5.
63. Temüge: Shāmī, *ZN*, I, 21, 23, 24; for the relationship, see Yazdī, *ZN* (1957), I, 161–2, 225/(2008), I, 407, 488. Mubashshir: Shāmī, *ZN*, I, 38, 66.
64. Shāmī, *ZN*, I, 38. For Sari Bugha, see Manz, *The Rise and Rule*, 75.
65. Salmānī, *Shams al-ḥusn*, text, fo. 108b (German trans., 80–1). But as Manz, *Power, Politics and Religion*, 36, n.74, points out, this author was 'fond of ascribing slave status to Temür's emirs'. And he certainly takes the opportunity to impugn the moral character of Üch Qara and his family.
66. Shāmī, *ZN*, I, 29. Yazdī, *ZN* (1957), I, 80/(2008), I, 315.
67. Shāmī, *ZN*, I, 38–9. Yazdī, *ZN* (1957), I, 161–2/(2008), I, 407.
68. Manz, *The Rise and Rule*, 119–20.
69. *MA*, fo. 91a, ed. Vokhidov, text, 179 (Russian trans., 111, 112). Ando, *Timuridische Emire*, 279.
70. Yazdī, *ZN* (1957), I, 41/(2008), I, 270.
71. Shabūrghān: ibid. (1957), I, 168/(2008), I, 414; Qunduz etc.: ibid. (1957), I, 176/(2008), I, 424. Shāmī, *ZN*, I, 63. Manz, *The Rise and Rule*, 58.
72. For a survey of amirs from the Barlās, see Ando, *Timuridische Emire*, 68–87.
73. *MA*, fo. 96a, ed. Vokhidov, text, 189 (Russian trans., 117).
74. Yazdī, *ZN* (1957), II, 154/(2008), II, 998.
75. Ibid. (1957), I, 320/(2008), I, 594. Manz, *The Rise and Rule*, 79. Ando, *Timuridische Emire*, 71.
76. Both listed by Yazdī, *ZN* (1957), I, 225/(2008), I, 488. On Jahāngīr and his descendants, see Ando, *Timuridische Emire*, 77.
77. Yazdī, *ZN* (1957), I, 275/(2008), I, 545. Shāmī, *ZN*, I, 110, does not mention his tribal affiliation. See Ando, *Timuridische Emire*, 83.
78. Shāmī, *ZN*, I, 144, 203. Yazdī, *ZN* (1957), I, 467, and II, 122/(2008), I, 747, 966.
79. Yazdī, *ZN* (1957), I, 560–1/(2008), I, 836. Shāmī, *ZN*, I, 166, omitting his tribal affiliation.
80. Yazdī, *ZN* (1957), II, 412/(2008), II, 1244.
81. Ibid. (1957), I, 232/(2008), I, 498.
82. Ibid. (1957), II, 167, 416/(2008), II, 1010–11, 1249.
83. Ibid. (1957), I, 304, 313, 441, 473, 577, and II, 272/(2008), I, 578, 587, 720, 754, 854, and II, 1109. The relationships are found also in *ZT*, I, 42. For the two former amirs, see Ando, *Timuridische Emire*, 83; for Nūr Malik, ibid., 132.

84. Yazdī, *ZN* (1957), I, 191/(2008), I, 444. See further Ando, *Timuridische Emire*, 86–7.
85. For what follows, see Yazdī, *ZN* (1957), I, 161–2/(2008), I, 407.
86. See Manz, *The Rise and Rule*, 169.
87. On this term, see ibid., 120; *TMEN*, II, 366–77 (no. 817: 'Held. . .').
88. Yazdī, *ZN* (1957), I, 193/(2008), I, 447.
89. Ibid. (1957), I, 364, 389/(2008), I, 645, 667. Manz, *The Rise and Rule*, 82.
90. Yazdī, *ZN* (1957), I, 240/(2008), I, 505.
91. For ʿAbbās's sons, see Ando, *Timuridische Emire*, 99–101.
92. Ibid., 95, and for two others, Sayf al-Mulūk and ʿAbd al-Ṣamad, among Timur's officers, see Yazdī, *ZN* (1957), I, 261/(2008), I, 530.
93. Yazdī, *ZN* (1957), I, 317/(2008), I, 592.
94. Ibid. (1957), I, 173/(2008), I, 421. Manz, *The Rise and Rule*, 60.
95. Yazdī, *ZN* (1957), I, 237, 325/(2008), I, 502, 602.
96. Manz, *The Rise and Rule*, 122–3. Temüge: see Yazdī, *ZN* (1957), I, 441, 559/(2008), I, 720, 835, here spelling the name TMWK. Jahāngīr: see *MA*, fo. 88b, ed. Vokhidov, text, 173 (Russian trans., 108).
97. Yazdī, *ZN* (1957), I, 161/(2008), I, 407.
98. Ibid. (1957), I, 176/(2008), I, 424.
99. Ibid. (1957), I, 194, 196/(2008), I, 450, 451. Shāmī, *ZN*, I, 71, describes him at this time as commander (*ḥākim*) of the citadel of Samarkand.
100. Yazdī, *ZN* (1957), I, 206/(2008), I, 464.
101. Ibid. (1957), I, 287/(2008), I, 559.
102. See generally Manz, *The Rise and Rule*, 121–2.
103. Yazdī, *ZN* (1957), I, 350/(2008), I, 630. *MA*, fo. 115b, ed. Vokhidov, text, 222 (Russian trans., 135). Manz, *The Rise and Rule*, 78, and *Power, Politics and Religion*, 22.
104. Manz, *Power, Politics and Religion*, 22, 38–9, 43–4. Woods, *The Timurid Dynasty*, 20, 21.
105. Manz, *The Rise and Rule*, n.31 at 186. Woods, *The Timurid Dynasty*, 23, 34.
106. See Ando, *Timuridische Emire*, 74, 109, and Manz, *The Rise and Rule*, 123–4.
107. For examples in Shāhrukh's establishment, notably from the families of Shaykh ʿAlī Bahādur, Dā'ūd Dughlāt and Ḥājjī Sayf al-Dīn, see Manz, *Power, Politics and Religion*, 22–3, 38–9.
108. There is a survey of Chekü's family in Ando, *Timuridische Emire*, 78–83, with a table at 280.
109. Yazdī, *ZN* (1957), I, 275/(2008), I, 545.
110. Shāmī, *ZN*, I, 115–17, 160–2. Yazdī, *ZN* (1957), I, 370, 378, 387, 535, 542/(2008), I, 650, 658, 666, 810, 816. Ando, *Timuridische Emire*, 80–1.
111. Yazdī, *ZN* (1957), II, 450/(2008), II, 1277.
112. Ibid. (1957), I, 573, and II, 66, 77, 257, 268/(2008), I, 850, 914, 924, and II, 1093, 1106.
113. *MA*, fo. 92a, ed. Vokhidov, text, 181 (Russian trans., 112). Manz, *The Rise and Rule*, 81, seems to imply that Jahānshāh did not retain command of the Qara'unas troops for the whole of Timur's lifetime. For Miḍrāb, see Manz, *Power, Politics and Religion*, 43, 114.
114. Yazdī, *ZN* (1957), I, 441, 499, 533, and II, 304/(2008), I, 720, 779, 809, and II, 1139.

115. Ibid. (1957), I, 441/(2008), I, 720. *MA*, fo. 91a, ed. Vokhidov, text, 179 (Russian trans., 111).
116. *MA*, fos 91a, 92a, ed. Vokhidov, text, 179, 181 (Russian trans., 112).
117. Clavijo (1859), 128/(1928), 213. But Ando, *Timuridische Emire*, 80–2, doubts whether the two men held the office of chief amir in succession or even exclusively, pointing to the prominent status of Dā'ūd Dughlāt and his son Sulaymānshāh.
118. For what follows, see the succinct survey of his career ibid., 111–13.
119. Shāmī, *ZN*, I, 171–2. Yazdī, *ZN* (1957), II, 33–4/(2008), I, 879–80.
120. Shāmī, *ZN*, I, 241. Yazdī, *ZN* (1957), II, 260, 263/(2008), II, 1096, 1099.
121. Shāmī, *ZN*, I, 255, 267. Yazdī, *ZN* (1957), II, 303–4, 310, 336/(2008), II, 1138, 1144, 1169.
122. Shāmī, *ZN*, I, 123. Yazdī, *ZN* (1957), I, 363, 383, 388, 441, and II, 17, 153, 159, 250/(2008), I, 644, 662, 667, 720, 863, and II, 997, 1003, 1086. Brief notice in Ando, *Timuridische Emire*, 116. He is to be distinguished from a homonymous amir who fought for Timur in Anatolia: Shāmī, *ZN*, I, 255.
123. Yazdī, *ZN* (1957), I, 315/(2008), I, 589. Compare Shāmī, *ZN*, I, 105.
124. Yazdī, *ZN* (1957), II, 137/(2008), I, 981. For the former, see A.D.H. Bivar, 'Naghar and Īryāb: Two little-known Islamic sites of the north-west frontier of Afghanistan and Pakistan', *Iran* 24 (1986), 131–8.
125. Shāmī, *ZN*, I, 67. Yazdī, *ZN* (1957), I, 179, and II, 278/(2008), I, 428, and II, 1116.
126. Shāmī, *ZN*, I, 69. Yazdī, *ZN* (1957), I, 189, 191/(2008), I, 443, 444.
127. Shāmī, *ZN*, I, 76. Yazdī, *ZN* (1957), I, 207/(2008), I, 466.
128. Yazdī, *ZN* (1957), I, 313/(2008), I, 587.
129. Shāmī, *ZN*, I, 91. Yazdī, *ZN* (1957), I, 262/(2008), I, 532.
130. Shāmī, *ZN*, I, 99. Yazdī, *ZN* (1957), I, 288/(2008), I, 560.
131. Shāmī, *ZN*, I, 122. Yazdī, *ZN* (1957), I, 377–8/(2008), I, 657–8.
132. Shāmī, *ZN*, I, 80–1. Yazdī, *ZN* (1957), I, 219/(2008), I, 481.
133. Yazdī, *ZN* (1957), I, 313/(2008), I, 587.
134. Ibid. (1957), I, 287, 320/(2008), I, 559, 595.
135. Ibid. (1957), II, 329/(2008), II, 1162.
136. Ibid. (1957), I, 544/(2008), I, 819.
137. Shāmī, *ZN*, I, 71–2. Yazdī, *ZN* (1957), I, 196–7/(2008), I, 451–2.
138. Yazdī, *ZN* (1957), I, 202/(2008), I, 459. I cannot see why Manz, *The Rise and Rule*, 76, dates this appointment in 781–2/1379–80. For a sketch of Sari Bugha's career, see Ando, *Timuridische Emire*, 110–11.
139. See Manz, *The Rise and Rule*, 49, 64.
140. Yazdī, *ZN* (1957), I, 207/(2008), I, 465.
141. Ibid. (1957), I, 284/(2008), I, 556. Compare Shāmī, *ZN*, I, 97.
142. Zayn al-Dīn (1990), text, 501 (Russian trans., 133)/(1993), 122. Wing, *The Jalayirids*, 157.
143. IA (1979), 175, 232/(1986), 293, 372 (*TGA*, 161, 213).
144. Yazdī, *ZN*, (1957), I, 199/(2008), I, 455.
145. *MA*, fo. 97a, ed. Vokhidov, text, 191 (Russian trans., 118).
146. Manz, *The Rise and Rule*, 111, 168 (appendix C). Manz, 'Administration and the delegation of authority', 138. For Jalāl-i Islām as a *bitikchi*, see Yazdī, *ZN* (1957), II, 94/(2008), I, 938. Both men are listed in *MA*, fo. 97a, ed. Vokhidov, text, 191 (Russian trans., 118, where Ṭabasī is misread as Ṭalabī).

147. Manz, *The Rise and Rule*, 113–18.
148. Yazdī, *ZN* (1957), II, 421/(2008), II, 1255.
149. Ibid. (1957), I, 565, 569–70/(2008), I, 843, 846.
150. Shāmī, *ZN*, I, 287–8. Yazdī, *ZN* (1957), II, 387–9/(2008), II, 1220–2. See Aubin, 'Comment Tamerlan', 90.
151. Yazdī, *ZN* (1957), II, 418/(2008), II, 1251.
152. Manz, *The Rise and Rule*, 115. Clavijo (1859), 149–50/(1928), 249–50: the two translations differ regarding the nature of the offence.
153. We are told that he was sixteen at that date and forty at his death in Rabīʿ I 796/Jan.–Feb. 1394: Shāmī, *ZN*, I, 58; Yazdī, *ZN* (1957), I, 149, 474/(2008), I, 395, 755; Naṭanzī (1957), 273–4/(2004), 213–14. Manz, *The Rise and Rule*, n.24 at 185, is not convinced that he was the eldest; but compare Woods, *The Timurid Dynasty*, 14, n.34.
154. Yazdī, *ZN* (1957), I, 196/(2008), I, 452.
155. Ibid. (1957), I, 388/(2008), I, 667.
156. Ibid. (1957), I, 113/(2008), I, 352.
157. Shāmī, *ZN*, I, 69–70. Yazdī, *ZN* (1957), I, 189–90/(2008), I, 442–3.
158. Shāmī, *ZN*, I, 71, 73. Yazdī, *ZN* (1957), I, 196, 199–201/(2008), I, 452, 455–7.
159. Yazdī, *ZN* (1957), I, 225/(2008), I, 488. For a brief biography, see Beatrice F. Manz, 'Mīrān<u>sh</u>āh b. Tīmūr', *EI*[2], VII, 105.
160. Yazdī, *ZN* (1957), I, 445/(2008), I, 724.
161. Ibid. (1957), I, 558–9/(2008), I, 834.
162. Shāmī, *ZN*, I, 132–4.
163. Yazdī, *ZN* (1957), I, 573/(2008), I, 849; Shāmī, *ZN*, I, 167, is briefer. For Shāhrukh's birth, see Yazdī, *ZN* (1957), I, 210–12/(2008), I, 469–72; and for an overview of his career, see Beatrice F. Manz, '<u>Sh</u>āh Ru<u>kh</u> b. Tīmūr', *EI*[2], IX, 197–8.
164. See Manz, *Power, Politics and Religion*, 17, n.7.
165. Shāmī, *ZN*, I, 119.
166. The date in Yazdī, *ZN* (1957), II, 351/(2008), II, 1183, and in *ZT*, II, 986 (also in HA's additions to Shāmī, *ZN*, II, 181).
167. Yazdī, *ZN* (1957), I, 401/(2008), I, 679. *ZT*, III, 54, adds Balkh, Ṭukhāristān and Qatlān (Khuttalān) to the list.
168. Yazdī, *ZN* (1957), I, 475/(2008), I, 755.
169. Ibid. (1957), II, 367/(2008), II, 1197–8.
170. Ibid. (1957), II, 153/(2008), II, 997; for his age, see ibid. (1957), II, 159/(2008), II, 1003.
171. Ibid. (1957), II, 399/(2008), II, 1232.
172. Ibid. (1957), II, 321/(2008), II, 1154.
173. Ibid. (1957), II, 386/(2008), II, 1219.
174. Ibid. (1957), II, 368–9/(2008), II, 1199.
175. Ibid. (1957), II, 393, 395, 402/(2008), II, 1225–6, 1227, 1235.
176. HA, *Dhayl-i Ẓafar-nāma*, ed. Tauer, 'Continuation du Ẓafarnāma', 434.
177. Yazdī, *ZN* (1957), II, 449/(2008), II, 1276. Manz, *The Rise and Rule*, 87. Shāmī completed his history too early to record these grants.
178. Yazdī, *ZN* (1957), I, 516/(2008), I, 793.
179. Ibid. (1957), II, 21, 141/(2008), I, 867, 985.
180. Ibid. (1957), II, 153/(2008), II, 997.
181. Ibid. (1957), II, 272–3, 321/(2008), II, 1110, 1154.

182. Ibid. (1957), I, 200–2, 242–3, 260–1/(2008), I, 456–8, 508–9, 529–30.
183. Manz, 'Family and ruler', 62, and her *Power, Politics and Religion*, 10–11; and see below.
184. Shāmī, *ZN*, I, 191. Yazdī, *ZN* (1957), II, 85/(2008), I, 931–2.
185. See Woods, *The Timurid Dynasty* (esp. 20, 29, 33, 43, for the wives of Timur's sons).
186. Clavijo (1859), 95–6/(1928), 162–3.
187. The fullest account is in Yazdī, *ZN* (1957), II, 147–8, 150–1, 155–7/(2008), II, 991, 994–5, 1000–1. Clavijo (1859), 95–6/(1928), 162–4, also provides details. As noticed earlier (p. 33), Shāmī, in the service of ʿUmar b. Amīrānshāh, does not allude to the episode.
188. Yazdī, *ZN* (1957), II, 167–8/(2008), II, 1011–12.
189. Ibid. (1957), II, 159–61, 275/(2008), II, 1003–5, 1113. Soucek, 'Eskandar b. ʿOmar Šayx', 77–8.
190. See Broadbridge, 'Spy or rebel?', esp. 30–2, 40.
191. Yazdī, *ZN* (1957), II, 482/(2008), II, 1306. See also *ZT*, III, 11.
192. Manz, *The Rise and Rule*, 114.
193. Broadbridge, 'Spy or rebel?', 35–9. See also Beatrice F. Manz, 'Temür and the early Timurids to *c.* 1450', in *CHIA*, 182–98 (here 186).
194. Woods, *The Timurid Dynasty*, 17. Binbaş, *Intellectual Networks*, 232.
195. *MA*, fo. 44a, ed. Vokhidov, text, 89 (Russian trans., 60). Woods, *The Timurid Dynasty*, 33.
196. Woods, 'Turco-Iranica II', 332–5; Binbaş, *Intellectual Networks*, 175–8. Timur himself referred to him as Güregen in the *fatḥ-nāma* from Syria in 1401: *Safīna*, BN ms. arabe 3423, fo. 399b. According to Manz, 'Tamerlane and the symbolism', 110, n.17, Amīrānshāh was apparently the only prince to use the title. He was certainly the only one so titled in the genealogical work of Ḥusayn b. ʿAlīshāh: Woods, 'Timur's genealogy', 112. Although Binbaş, *Intellectual Networks*, 177, ascribes this to the marriage to Khānzāda, her previous husband Jahāngīr had not assumed the title, as far as we know.
197. 1394: Gottfried Herrmann, 'Zur Intitulatio timuridischer Urkunden', in Wolfgang Voigt (ed.), *XVIII. Deutscher Orientalistentag vom 1. bis 5. Oktober 1972 in Lübeck. Vorträge*, *ZDMG* Supplement II (Wiesbaden, 1974), 498–521 (here 504). 1396: Woods, 'Turco-Iranica II'. For Amīrānshāh's marriages, see Woods, *The Timurid Dynasty*, 33; and for the practice of naming Timur, Muḥammad Sulṭān and Sulṭān Maḥmūd Khan in the khutba and on the coinage by this date, see p. 343.
198. Matsui, Watabe and Ono, 'A Turkic–Persian decree of Timurid Mīrān Šāh', esp. 55–7.
199. Binbaş, *Intellectual Networks*, 177–8.
200. See Brack, *An Afterlife for the Khan*, 115–17.
201. Yazdī, *ZN* (1957), I, 225/(2008), I, 488.
202. Ibid. (1957), I, 401/(2008), I, 679.
203. Ibid. (1957), I, 573–4/(2008), I, 850.
204. Ibid. (1957), I, 441/(2008), I, 720; for Mo. *tūsqāl*, see *TMEN*, I, 268–9 (no. 137: 'Schutz, Geleit, Geleitschutz').
205. Naṭanzī (1957), 420/(2004), 306–7. Manz, 'Administration and the delegation of authority', 204.
206. Clavijo (1859), 188/(1928), 317.

207. Manz, 'Administration and the delegation of authority', 193–4.
208. Manz, *The Rise and Rule*, 84–8. Compare also her 'Administration and the delegation of authority', 194, 195.
209. Yazdī, *ZN* (1957), II, 402–3/(2008), II, 1235.
210. Ibid. (1957), II, 416–17/(2008), II, 1249.
211. Hope, 'The *atābak*s in the Mongol empire', esp. 326–41; see also above, p. 113 and p. 516n.11. In the same vein, Manz, 'Administration and the delegation of authority', 192, speaks of such amirs being appointed 'more or less as guardians'.
212. Yazdī, *ZN* (1957), I, 463/(2008), I, 743.
213. Ibid. (1957), I, 515/(2008), I, 792.
214. Ibid. (1957), II, 161/(2008), II, 1005. Soucek, 'Eskandar b. ʿOmar Šayx', 78.
215. Timur's wives are listed in Woods, *The Timurid Dynasty*, 17–18. On their status, see Soucek, 'Tīmūrid women'; also the brief remarks by Laura Parodi, 'L'eredità mongola e altaica nell'Asia centrale islamica', in Gabriella Airaldi et al. (eds), *I Mongoli dal Pacifico al Mediterraneo* (Genoa, 2004), 241–58 (here 241–2).
216. On Sarai Mulk Khanim, see Soucek, 'Tīmūrid women', 202–6. Tümen Āghā may likewise have had Chaghadayid blood. Her mother, Mūsā's wife Ārzū Mulk Āghā, was a daughter of Bāyazīd Jalāyir and sister of ʿAlī Darwīsh: Yazdī, *ZN* (1957), I, 87, 105/(2008), I, 323, 342. Bāyazīd's wives are known to have included a daughter of Tarmashirin (above, p. 238), who was certainly ʿAlī Darwīsh's mother, but we are not told explicitly that Ārzū Mulk Āghā was born of this same marriage.
217. Shāmī, *ZN*, I, 129, 136. Yazdī, *ZN* (1957), I, 406, 407–8, 414 ff., 444, 449, 487, 494, 518, 522–3, 566, and II, 139–40, 360, 409–10, 480/(2008), I, 684, 686, 693 ff., 723, 728, 768, 774, 794, 799–800, 843, 983–4, and II, 1191, 1242–3, 1304. For the titles, see Jahn, 'Timur und die Frauen', 520–1.
218. Clavijo (1859), 141, 166/(1928), 234, 280–1. On her status, see Soucek, 'Tīmūrid women', 202–3; Jahn, 'Timur und die Frauen', 527, and further remarks at 522–3.
219. Jahn, 'Timur und die Frauen', 521. Judith Pfeiffer, '"Not every head that wears a crown deserves to rule": Women in Il-Khanid political life and court culture', in Rachel Ward (ed.), *Court and Craft. A Masterpiece from Northern Iraq* (London, 2014), 23–9 (here 26). On the other hand, the important roles of khatuns and imperial princesses are not in doubt: see generally Broadbridge, *Women and the Making of the Mongol Empire*.
220. Her father was Ḥājjī Beg of the Erkenüt, on whom see Shāmī, *ZN*, I, 15; Yazdī, *ZN* (1957), I, 33, 79, 124/(2008), I, 262, 314, 365.
221. Clavijo (1859), 154, 155/(1928), 258, 259. For the thirteenth century, see WR, 40, 52 (*MFW*, 89, 100).
222. Pfeiffer, '"Not every head"', 23. Bruno De Nicola, 'Elite women in the Mongol empire', in May and Hope (eds), *The Mongol World*, 422–39 (esp. 423–9).
223. See generally De Nicola, *Women in Mongol Iran*, chap. 1.
224. Lambton, *Continuity and Change*, 289–90, 293–4. Pfeiffer, '"Not every head"', 25. De Nicola, *Women in Mongol Iran*, chaps 3 and 4.
225. Examples in Soucek, 'Tīmūrid women', 202, 203.
226. Lambton, *Continuity and Change*, 289–90. De Nicola, 'Elite women in the Mongol empire', 424, 427, and *Women in Mongol Iran*, 98–9.

227. See Clavijo's account of the festivities, esp. (1859), 149, 159/(1928), 248, 267. Yazdī, *ZN* (1957), II, 422/(2008), II, 1256, terms this occasion a quriltai.
228. Yazdī, *ZN* (1957), II, 476–8/(2008), II, 1301–3.
229. Jahn, 'Timur und die Frauen', 526 and n.41.
230. Shāmī, *ZN*, I, 129. Yazdī, *ZN* (1957), I, 418/(2008), I, 697.
231. Shāmī, *ZN*, I, 102. Yazdī, *ZN* (1957), I, 301, and II, 269–70/(2008), I, 574–5, and II, 1107. For some of the journeys of the two khanims, see Barthold, *Four Studies*, II, 45–6 (= Bartol'd, *Sochineniia*, II, part 2, 64–5).
232. Yazdī, *ZN* (1957), I, 260–1/(2008), I, 529–30. Shāmī, *ZN*, I, 90, simply mentions her death.
233. Yazdī, *ZN* (1957), II, 94/(2008), I, 938.
234. See Beatrice F. Manz, 'Women in Timurid domestic politics', in Guity Nashat and Lois Beck (eds), *Women in Iran from the Rise of Islam to 1800* (Urbana and Chicago, IL, 2003), 121–39 (here 130–1), and Broadbridge, 'Spy or rebel?', 36–9.
235. Listed in Woods, *The Timurid Dynasty*, 18–19.
236. Sarai Mulk: Yazdī, *ZN* (1957), II, 421, 448, 449/(2008), II, 1255, 1275, 1276; for what is known of her *madrasa*, see Soucek, 'Tīmūrid women', 206–10. Tümen Āghā: Shāmī, I, 211; *RN* (1915), 203/(2000), 185 (*DPT*, 188); Yazdī, *ZN* (1957), II, 143, 145/(2008), I, 986, 988–9.
237. Shāmī, I, 90. Yazdī, *ZN* (1957), I, 260/(2008), I, 529. Soucek, 'Tīmūrid women', 201–2.
238. Shāmī, *ZN*, I, 150, 157. Yazdī, *ZN* (1957), I, 481, 505/(2008), I, 762, 784.
239. Yazdī, *ZN* (1957), I, 278/(2008), I, 549. For other infants entrusted to her, see Soucek, 'Tīmūrid women', 204.
240. Woods, *The Timurid Dynasty*, 29, 43. On this general point, see Manz, 'Women in Timurid domestic politics', 126.
241. Yazdī, *ZN* (1957), I, 515/(2008), I, 792. Binbaş, *Intellectual Networks*, 43.
242. Yazdī, *ZN* (1957), II, 151/(2008), II, 995. Soucek, 'Tīmūrid women', 211.
243. On these two episodes, see Yazdī, *ZN* (1957), II, 406, 454/(2008), II, 1239, 1280–1, respectively. Soucek, 'Tīmūrid women', 204–5. Although Clavijo (1928), 247, reads that Khānzāda had restored Amīrānshāh to Timur's favour, I can find no grounds for this statement in the Castilian text; it is omitted from the (1859) trans., 148.
244. Clavijo (1859), 148/(1928), 247–8. For an outline of her career, see Soucek, 'Tīmūrid women', 210–13.
245. As Manz, *The Rise and Rule*, 66–7, emphasises.

10: THE FORGING OF AN EMPIRE: A CAREER OF CONQUEST

1. For good, succinct surveys of Timur's campaigns, see Manz, *The Rise and Rule*, 69–73, and Subtelny, 'Tamerlane and his descendants', 174–8; a more detailed account of those in Iran is given by Roemer, 'Tīmūr in Iran'.
2. *TR*, I (text), 28, II (trans.), 20.
3. Although Shāmī, *ZN*, I, 65, says that when Timur obtained the leadership of the ulus Khwārazm had been under Ḥusayn Ṣūfī's rule for five years, and Yazdī, *ZN* (1957), I, 173/(2008), I, 422, for five or six years. Ḥusayn may in fact have been governor of the province since late Jumādā II 743/Nov. 1342: see DeWeese, 'Mapping Khwārazmian connections', 73.

4. Naṭanzī (1957), 427/(2004), 311, is more explicit in this regard than at 300–1/233; see also *ZT*, I, 465 (and HA's additions in Shāmī, *ZN*, II, 31–2), referring to the *kharāj*. Compare Shāmī, *ZN*, I, 65, and Yazdī, *ZN* (1957), I, 173, 324/(2008), I, 422, 601. Nagel, *Timur der Eroberer*, 142. Manz, 'Temür and the early Timurids', 184, sees Timur's claim as baseless, and Woods, 'The rise of Tīmūrid historiography', 104, dismisses it as an ingenious fabrication by Naṭanzī to justify the Khwārazm campaign. But compare p. 63 above, on precisely such allocations of revenue.
5. In the abridged later recension of his *Majma' al-ansāb*, BL ms. Add. 16696, fo. 107b, though not in the version composed in 738/1337.
6. These successive campaigns are described by Shāmī, *ZN*, I, 66–8, 71–2, and Yazdī, *ZN* (1957), I, 175–88/(2008), I, 423–39.
7. Shāmī, *ZN*, I, 79–81. Yazdī, *ZN* (1957), I, 214–21/(2008), I, 475–83.
8. Shāmī, *ZN*, I, 107–8: the year can be inferred from the fact that the titular khan Soyurghatmish died after Timur had left for Khwārazm and that Sulṭān Maḥmūd was enthroned on Timur's return: ibid., I, 110–11. The dates are supplied by Yazdī, *ZN* (1957), I, 322–4/(2008), I, 600–1.
9. The campaigns in Mughūlistān are surveyed by Barthold, *Four Studies*, I, 140–3 (Russian text in Bartol'd, *Sochineniia*, II, part 1, 81–4).
10. Shāmī, *ZN*, I, 69–70, dating the campaign in 777/1375 (the Year of the Hare). Yazdī, *ZN* (1957), I, 188–90/(2008), I, 441–4.
11. Shāmī, *ZN*, I, 72–4. Yazdī, *ZN* (1957), I, 197–9/(2008), I, 453–5.
12. Shāmī, *ZN*, I, 74, is very brief. Yazdī, *ZN* (1957), I, 203/(2008), I, 461–2.
13. Yazdī, *ZN* (1957), I, 261/(2008), I, 530–1.
14. Ibid. (1957), I, 354–5/(2008), I, 635–6.
15. *TR*, I (text), 31, II (trans.), 27–8.
16. *RN* (1915), 17/(2000), 22 (*DPT*, 30).
17. Shāmī, *ZN*, I, 106–7. Yazdī, *ZN* (1957), I, 318/(2008), I, 593.
18. Yazdī, *ZN* (1957), I, 342–3, 347/(2008), I, 622–3, 627.
19. Shāmī, *ZN*, I, 115. Yazdī, *ZN* (1957), I, 341, 342, 345, 347, 354, 355/(2008), I, 621, 622, 625, 627, 635, 636.
20. Yazdī, *ZN* (1957), II, 159–61/(2008), II, 1003–5.
21. For Farghāna, see Naṭanzī (1957), 296/(2004), 229; *ZT*, I, 461 (also in Shāmī, *ZN*, II, 30).
22. Yazdī, *ZN* (1957), I, 189–90/(2008), I, 443.
23. Ibid. (1957), I, 191/(2008), I, 444. Sālār Oghlan, a nephew of Du'a, had held Tashkent as his appanage: *MA*, fo. 31b, ed. Vokhidov, text, 64 (Russian trans., 49).
24. Buyan Temür: Yazdī, *ZN* (1957), I, 342, 441, 577, and II, 159, 161/(2008), I, 622, 720, 853, and II, 1003, 1005 (the third of these references reads erroneously 'Buyan Temür *and* Bekichuk' in both editions). Quṭb al-Dīn, Qamar al-Dīn's brother: ibid. (1957), I, 463/(2008), I, 742. Manz, *The Rise and Rule*, 102.
25. Shāmī, *ZN*, I, 64, with the year 773 and with Örüng Temür as Timur's lieutenant (but mentioning Köpek Temür's subsequent disaffection); and HA's additions ibid., II, 30–1. Yazdī, *ZN* (1957), I, 169–72/(2008), I, 417–18. Naṭanzī (1957), 296–8/(2004), 229–31. The sources do not support the assertion by Nagel, *Timur der Eroberer*, 136–7, 147, that Köpek Temür was installed as khan; he seems, rather, to have been merely Timur's lieutenant, appointed 'to

govern and maintain order' (*ba-ḍabṭ-u nasq*). For the chronology of the first two campaigns against Mughūlistān and the first Khwārazm expedition, see Aubin, 'Le khanat de Čaġatai', 49, n.149.

26. Shāmī, *ZN*, I, 117; with the earlier date added by HA, ibid., II, 75. Yazdī, *ZN* (1957), I, 348/(2008), I, 628, gives the later date.
27. Yazdī, *ZN* (1957), II, 159/(2008), II, 1003.
28. Ibid. (1957), II, 17/(2008), I, 863; and compare also *RN* (1915), 45a (with the date 800/1398; not in *RN* (2000)), and Shāmī, *ZN*, I, 170. IA (1979), 49/(1986), 102–3 (*TGA*, 47). For irrigation works, see Manz, *The Rise and Rule*, 116.
29. Yazdī, *ZN* (1957), II, 256/(2008), II, 1092.
30. IA (1979), 245–6/(1986), 384 (*TGA*, 225).
31. Salmānī, *Shams al-ḥusn*, text, fo. 23a–b (German trans., 22).
32. Yazdī, *ZN* (1957), II, 449/(2008), II, 1276. Salmānī, *Shams al-ḥuṣn*, text, fo. 23a–b (abridged German trans., 22), speaks of this as the grant of the (entire) Mughūl territory. Manz, *The Rise and Rule*, 87.
33. Yazdī, *ZN* (1957), I, 203–9, 212–14/(2008), I, 461–8, 473–4. Shāmī, *ZN*, I, 74–8, is briefer and says nothing of Timur's grant of the whole ulus. Both authors call Mamai 'Mamāq'. The date 778 given by these sources is one year too early, and is corrected by Safargaliev, *Raspad*, 141–2.
34. Shāmī, *ZN*, I, 78. Yazdī, *ZN* (1957), I, 213/(2008), I, 474.
35. Ibn Qāḍī Shuhba, *Ta'rīkh*, I, 139, 155. al-Maqrīzī, *al-Sulūk*, III, part 2, 524, 531. Broadbridge, *Kingship and Ideology*, 172.
36. Ilnur Mirgaleev, 'The reign of Khan Toqtamysh', in *HT*, III, 738.
37. For what follows, see ibid., 738–43; Spuler, *Die Goldene Horde*, 129–35.
38. I.M. Mirgaleev, 'Bek Bulat: From a military commander to a rebel', *ZOO* 4 (2016), no. 4, 784–9. Beg Bolod is possibly the 'Pūlād' who appears in *MA*, fo. 28a, ed. Vokhidov, text, 57 (Russian trans., 46), as a descendant of Toqa Temür. Toqtamish later executed him.
39. Shāmī, *ZN*, I, 161. Yazdī, *ZN* (1957), I, 542/(2008), I, 817. See Crummey, *The Formation of Muscovy*, 64.
40. Yazdī, *ZN* (1957), I, 552/(2008), I, 826. Manz, 'Mongol history rewritten', 140–1.
41. In 780/1378–9, 781/1379–80 and 787/1385–6: Yazdī, *ZN* (1957), I, 215–16, 221, 286/(2008), I, 476–7, 483, 557.
42. Martin, *Treasure of the Land of Darkness*, 33–4.
43. F. Thiriet (ed.), *Régestes des déliberations du Sénat de Venise concernant la Romanie*, I: *1329–1399* (Paris and The Hague, 1958), 217 (no. 930), and for the absence of restoration attempts, ibid., II: *1400–1430* (Paris and The Hague, 1959), 96–7 (no. 1403). Refortification of the town began only in 1419, when it had been subjected to two more assaults, by khans of the Golden Horde: Bernard Doumerc, 'Les Vénitiens à La Tana au XVᵉ siècle', *Le Moyen Age* 94 (1988), 363–79 (here 365); M.E. Martin, 'Venetian Tana in the later fourteenth and early fifteenth centuries', *Byzantinische Forschungen* 11 (1987), 375–9 (here 376–7), arguing that the decline of Tana has been overstated. See now Nicola Di Cosmo and Lorenzo Pubblici, *Venezia e i Mongoli. Commercio e diplomazia sulle vie della seta nel medioevo (secoli XIII–XV)* (Rome, 2022), 156–60, 162, 169–73.
44. Barbaro, *Viaggi*, § 52, ed. and tr. Skrzhinskaia, *Barbaro i Kontarini o Rossii*, text, 132 (Russian trans., 157); tr. Thomas, in Stanley of Alderley (ed.), *Travels to Tana and Persia*, 31.

45. Yazdī, *ZN* (1957), I, 538/(2008), I, 813. See Safargaliev, *Raspad*, 176; Pochekaev, *Tsari ordynaskie*, 218; Khakimov et al. (eds), *The Golden Horde in World History*, 696.
46. Spuler, *Die Goldene Horde*, 136–54. Vásáry, 'The Jochid realm', 85. Frank, 'The western steppe', 238–40. Pochekaev, *Tsari ordynskie*, chap. 13. For Temür Qutlugh's ancestry, see p. 611 n. 100.
47. Spuler, *Die Goldene Horde*, 141. Frank, 'The western steppe', 238, 239–40. *Patriarshaia ili Nikonovskaia letopis'*, in *PSRL*, XI, 198 (tr. Zenkovsky, IV, 156), dates Toqtamish's death in Jan. 6914 [1407]. For his last years, see DeWeese, 'Toḳtami<u>sh</u>', *EI*[2], X, 563. Favereau, *The Horde*, 288, erroneously places his death in the same year as Timur's.
48. Yazdī, *ZN* (1957), I, 541, 553/(2008), I, 815, 829.
49. IA (1979), 90–1/(1986), 148 (*TGA*, 85). See Spuler, *Die Goldene Horde*, 137; Aurel Decei, 'Établissement de Aktav de la Horde d'Or dans l'empire ottoman, au temps de Yildirim Bayezid', in *Zeki Velidi Togan'a armağan* (Istanbul, 1950–5), 77–92, skilfully reconstructing their movements by means of details taken from Shāmī, Yazdī and the Byzantine chronicler Chalkokondyles; Jackson, *The Mongols and the West*, 186.
50. Martin, *Treasure of the Land of Darkness*, 33.
51. Shāmī, *ZN*, I, 212–13. Yazdī, *ZN* (1957), II, 158/(2008), II, 1002.
52. Faryūmadī, *Dhayl-i Majma' al-ansāb*, 330. Aubin, 'Le khanat de Čaġatai', 48.
53. *RN* (1915), 20/(2000), 26 (*DPT*, 33).
54. Shāmī, *ZN*, I, 43. Yazdī, *ZN* (1957), I, 113/(2008), I, 351–2.
55. Yazdī, *ZN* (1957), I, 130/(2008), I, 371. On Muʿizz al-Dīn's interventions, see Aubin, 'Le khanat de Čaġatai', 19–20; for Kirmān, ibid., 26, and p. 178 above.
56. Shivan Mahendrarajah, 'Tamerlane's conquest of Herat and the "politics of notables"', *StIr* 46 (2017), 49–76. See also Mahendrarajah, 'A revised history of Mongol, Kart, and Timurid patronage', 117–18, and *A History of Herat*, 168–70. Jāmī's letters are found in in Yūsuf-i Ahl, *Farā'id-i Ghiyāthī*, ed. Mu'ayyad, I, 173–81, and II, 556–9.
57. Yazdī, *ZN* (1957), I, 228/(2008), I, 491.
58. Ibid. (1957), I, 241, 258–9/(2008), I, 507, 525, 527.
59. Mahendrarajah, *A History of Herat*, 171.
60. Aubin, 'La fin de l'état sarbadâr', 104–6 (repr. in his *Études*, 318–20).
61. Paul, 'Zerfall und Bestehen', 714.
62. Yazdī, *ZN* (1957), I, 223–4, 226/(2008), I, 486, 489.
63. *RN* (1915), 23/(2000), 31 (*DPT*, 36).
64. Yazdī, *ZN* (1957), I, 290/(2008), I, 562.
65. Bosworth, *The History of the Saffarids of Sistan*, 448–52. The main Timurid sources are Shāmī, *ZN*, I, 91–3, and Yazdī, *ZN* (1957), I, 262–72/(2008), I, 531–42. For the perspective from Sīstān, see Sīstānī, *Iḥyā' al-mulūk*, ed. Sutūda, 103–6; and for Ibn ʿArabshāh's testimony, p. 331 and p. 604 n. 157.
66. Shāmī, *ZN*, I, 131, 145. Yazdī, *ZN* (1957), I, 428, 469/(2008), I, 707, 749. Aubin, 'La fin de l'état sarbadâr', 112, 114 (repr. in his *Études*, 325, 327). Roemer, 'Tīmūr in Iran', 50.
67. Shāmī, *ZN*, I, 101. Yazdī, *ZN* (1957), I, 297/(2008), I, 570.
68. IA (1979), 34/(1986), 84–5 (*TGA*, 32–3). On Timur's dealings with the Muzaffarids, see Roemer, 'The Jalayirids, Muzaffarids and Sarbadārs', 16, and 'Tīmūr in Iran', 59–63.

69. The date given by Yazdī, *ZN* (1957), I, 314/(2008), I, 589. *RN* (1915), 30/(2000), 39 (*DPT*, 43–4), has Sunday 5th/17 Nov. 1387. See Aubin, 'Comment Tamerlan', n.9 at 101–2.
70. Yazdī, *ZN* (1957), I, 316/(2008), I, 590–1.
71. Kutubī, *Ta'rīkh-i āl-i Muẓaffar*, 111–12.
72. Ibid., 113–16.
73. Ibid., 117.
74. Ibid., 118. Yazdī, *ZN* (1957), I, 424–5/(2008), I, 704.
75. Kutubī, *Ta'rīkh-i āl-i Muẓaffar*, 119–20. Yazdī, *ZN* (1957), I, 425–7/(2008), I, 705–7.
76. For his activities, see Kutubī, *Ta'rīkh-i āl-i Muẓaffar*, 120–6. For the final battle, *RN* (1915), 35–7/(2000), 47–9 (*DPT*, 51–2); Shāmī, *ZN*, I, 132–4, gives a different account.
77. So according to Yazdī, *ZN* (1957), I, 441/(2008), I, 719–20, with the date as Mon. 23 Jumādā II/6 May 1393 for their execution; Shāmī, *ZN*, I, 135, supplies Tues. 12 Jumādā II/25 April (actually a Friday), corrected by HA (ibid., II, 106) to 12 Rajab/25 May; Kutubī, *Ta'rīkh-i āl-i Muẓaffar*, 127, has the first third of Rajab. Roemer, 'Tīmūr in Iran', 63, settles on 10 Rajab/22 May (a Thursday).
78. See the discussion of the expedition in Aubin, 'Les princes d'Ormuz', 111–13. Naṭanzī (1957), 19/(2004), 23, was concerned, of course, to contrast the submissiveness of Hurmuz towards his own patron, Iskandar b. 'Umar Shaykh.
79. Zayn al-Dīn (1990), text, 498–9 (Russian trans., 129–30)/(1993), 113–15. Ibn Fatḥ-Allāh al-Baghdādī, *al-Ta'rīkh al-Ghiyāthī*, 104–5.
80. Shāmī, *ZN*, I, 103, 104. Yazdī, *ZN* (1957), I, 303, 306/(2008), I, 577, 580.
81. See Wing, *The Jalayirids*, 157–8.
82. Michele Bernardini, 'The army of Timur during the Battle of Ankara', in Franz and Holzwarth (eds), *Nomad Military Power*, 209–32 (here 215, 220). Malaṭya: Yazdī, *ZN* (1957), II, 198/(2008), II, 1039. For Timur's relations with the Āq-Qūyūnlū, see Manz, *The Rise and Rule*, 103; and Patrick Wing, 'Submission, defiance, and the rules of politics on the Mamluk Sultanate's Anatolian frontier', *JRAS*, 3rd series, 25 (2015), 377–88 (here 378).
83. Shāmī, *ZN*, I, 139. Woods, 'The rise of Tīmūrid historiography', 85.
84. For Timur's treatment of Baghdad in 1401, see Jean Aubin, 'Tamerlan à Baġdād', *Arabica* 9 (1962), 303–9 (here 307–9).
85. Sulṭān Aḥmad's last years and the end of the dynasty are surveyed by Wing, *The Jalayirids*, 165–75. On the rulers in Khūzistān, see also Yıldız, 'Post-Mongol pastoral polities in eastern Anatolia', 35–6.
86. Jackson, *The Delhi Sultanate*, 228–9.
87. Yazdī, *ZN* (1957), I, 55/(2008), I, 287.
88. Ḥusayn: Shāmī, *ZN*, I, 31; Naṭanzī (1957), 227/(2004), 182. Yazdī, *ZN* (1957), I, 82/(2008), I, 318. His sons: ibid. (1957), I, 154/(2008), I, 399.
89. Yazdī, *ZN* (1957), I, 330/(2008), I, 607.
90. Bihāmadkhānī, BL ms. Or. 137, fo. 442b; partial trans. by Muhammad Zaki, *Tarikh-i-Muhammadi by Muhammad Bihamad Khani* (Aligarh, 1972), 60.
91. Ibid., fos 422b–423a (tr. Zaki, 32–3).
92. Ibid., fo. 432b (tr. Zaki, 47). Sirhindī, *Ta'rīkh-i Mubārakshāhī*, 160–1. For a survey of conditions in the Sultanate prior to Timur's invasion, see Simon

Digby, *War-Horse and Elephant in the Delhi Sultanate. A Study of Military Supplies* (Oxford and Delhi, 1971), 74–80; Gavin R.G. Hambly, 'The twilight of Tughluqid Delhi: Conflicting strategies in a disintegrating imperium', in R.E. Frykenberg (ed.), *Delhi through the Ages. Essays in Urban History, Culture and Society* (Oxford and Delhi, 1986), 45–62 (here 47–52).

93. *Ta'rīf* (1951), 364, *thumma ḍṭaraba mulūk al-Hind wa staṣarakha khārij*[un] *minhum bi l-amīr Tamur*/(2008), 238.
94. Shāmī, *ZN*, I, 187–8. IA (1979), 101/(1986), 162–3 (*TGA*, 95); hence Ibn Taghrībirdī, *al-Nujūm al-zāhira*, XII, 261–2 (tr. Popper, II, 58).
95. *RN* (1915), 43–4/(2000), 57–8 (*DPT*, 60). Yazdī, *ZN* (1957), II, 19/(2008), I, 865–6. Sirhindī, *Ta'rīkh-i Mubārakshāhī*, 162–3, according to whom Multān surrendered on 19 Ramaḍān (below).
96. *RN* (1915), 43/(2000), 57 (*DPT*, 59–60). Yazdī, *ZN* (1957), I, 401, and II, 18–19/(2008), I, 679, 865, for the more specific list of territories.
97. Though Subtelny, 'Tamerlane and his descendants', 176, assumes that Timur had sent the prince into the Punjab.
98. See Anooshahr, *The Ghazi Sultans*, 118–20, where attention is drawn to the noticeable shift in emphasis between Timur's *fatḥ-nāma*, sent in 801/1399 to Pīr Muḥammad b. ʿUmar Shaykh (not named but erroneously described by Anooshahr as 'one of his sons'), and Shāmī's account; also pp. 371–2.
99. *RN* (1915), 107a, 107b–108b/(2000), 107 (*DPT*, 110). Yazdī, *ZN* (1957), II, 19/(2008), I, 866.
100. *RN* (1915), 45a. See more generally ibid. (1915), 44/(2000), 58 (*DPT*, 60); Shāmī, *ZN*, I, 170; Yazdī, *ZN* (1957), II, 19–20/(2008), I, 866. *ZT*, II, 825 (and see HA's additions to Shāmī, *ZN*, II, 136), writes simply of the rise to power of Hindus as a whole. On the status of the Sultans' Hindu subjects, compare Jackson, *The Delhi Sultanate*, chap. 14.
101. Sirhindī, *Ta'rīkh-i Mubārakshāhī*, 159–60. Hambly, 'The twilight of Tughluqid Delhi', 48–50.
102. There is an outline of these events in Aubin, 'Comment Tamerlan', 110–11.
103. Yazdī, *ZN* (1957), II, 92/(2008), I, 937. Delhi had last been conquered by the Ghurid Muʿizz al-Dīn Muḥammad b. Sām in 588/1192.
104. For a detailed survey of the campaign, see Kishori Saran Lal, *Twilight of the Sultanate. A Political, Social and Cultural History of the Sultanate of Delhi from the Invasion of Timur to the Conquest of Babur, 1398–1526*, revised edn (New Delhi, 1980), 16–40; more briefly, Digby, *War-Horse and Elephant*, 80–1, and Jackson, *The Delhi Sultanate*, 313. For a broader perspective, see the analysis in Wink, *Al-Hind*, III, 124–5.
105. Yazdī, *ZN* (1957), II, 130/(2008), I, 974–5.
106. Sirhindī, *Ta'rīkh-i Mubārakshāhī*, 166–7. See Habib, 'Timur in the political tradition and historiography of Mughal India', 299–300; Jackson, *The Delhi Sultanate*, 318–19; and Wink, *Al-Hind*, III, 134. Bihāmadkhānī, fo. 306b (tr. Zaki, 93), says merely that the governorship (*shaḥnagī-u amārat*) of Delhi was conferred on Khiḍr Khan after the sack, but does not specify by whom.
107. Wink, *Al-Hind*, III, 145.
108. IA (1979), 107/(1986), 169–70 (*TGA*, 100). *Ta'rīf* (1951), 365/(2008), 238, mentions only Barqūq's death in this context.
109. Broadbridge, *Kingship and Ideology*, 151–6.

110. Ibn al-Furāt, *Taʾrīkh al-duwal wa l-mulūk*, IX, part 2, 369, provides a fuller account than do Ibn Ḥijjī, I, 37 (speaking of only one spy), and al-Maqrīzī, *al-Sulūk*, III, part 2, 802, as quoted in Yosef, 'Cross-boundary hatred', 174.
111. al-Maqrīzī, *al-Sulūk*, III, part 2, 537. Ibn Qāḍī Shuhba, *Taʾrīkh*, I, 189.
112. For their relations, see Broadbridge, *Kingship and Ideology*, 172–3.
113. Yazdī, *ZN* (1957), II, 200/(2008), II, 1041; Shāmī, *ZN*, I, 221–2, is briefer.
114. Yazdī, *ZN* (1957), I, 471/(2008), I, 751.
115. Broadbridge, *Kingship and Ideology*, 188–9.
116. Shāmī, *ZN*, I, 274–5. Yazdī, *ZN* (1957), II, 356–7/(2008), II, 1187–8. Broadbridge, *Kingship and Ideology*, 192–7; also her 'Royal authority', 235–6.
117. U. Vermeulen, 'Timur Lang en Syrie: la correspondance entre le Mamlūk Farağ et le Mérinide Abū Saʿīd', in U. Vermeulen and D. De Smet (eds), *Egypt and Syria in the Fatimid, Ayyubid and Mamluk Eras*, II. *Proceedings of the 4th and 5th International Colloquium organized at the Katholieke Universiteit Leuven in May 1995 and 1996* (Leuven, 1998), 303–11. For Ibn Khaldūn's letter to the Moroccan Sultan, see above, p. 39.
118. Werner, *Die Geburt einer Großmacht*, 163–4, 174. Heath W. Lowry, *The Nature of the Early Ottoman State* (Albany, NY, 2003), 83, 86–7; also 148–50 (appendix I).
119. Ilnur Mirgaleev, 'Tatary Desht-i Kypchaka v perepiske Aksak Timura s Baiazidom', *ZOTs* 8 (2015), 299–303 (here 300).
120. Bernardini, 'The army of Timur', 214.
121. Michele Bernardini, 'Motahharten entre Timur et Bayezid: une position inconfortable dans les remous de l'histoire anatolienne', in Gilles Veinstein (ed.), *Syncrétismes et hérésies dans l'Orient seldjoukide et ottoman (XIVe–XVIIIe siècle). Actes du Colloque du Collège de France, octobre 2001*, Collection Turcica 9 (Paris, 2005), 199–211. Rhoads Murphey, 'Bayezid I's foreign policy plans and priorities: Power relations, statecraft, military conditions and diplomatic practice in Anatolia and the Balkans', in Chrissis and Carr (eds), *Contact and Conflict*, 177–215 (here 196, 199–200).
122. Broadbridge, 'Royal authority', 242–3.
123. For Timur's campaign of 1402, see Marie-Mathilde Alexandrescu-Dersca, *La Campagne de Timur en Anatolie (1402)*, 2nd edn (London, 1977), chaps 4–5; I follow her date for the battle, ibid., 116–19 (appendix III).
124. Ibid., 73–8. Murphey, 'Bayezid I's foreign policy plans', 194.
125. IA (1979), 194–6, 198–9/(1986), 320–2, 328 (*TGA*, 178–9, 182). Yazdī, *ZN* (1957), II, 358/(2008), II, 1189. Paul, 'Mongol aristocrats and beyliks in Anatolia', 125–6. Bernardini, 'The army of Timur', 215–16. For what little is known of these Qara Tatars, see Jürgen Paul, 'Khalīl Sulṭān and the "Westerners" (1405–1407)', *Turcica* 42 (2010), 11–45 (here 16–20).
126. Yazdī, *ZN* (1957), II, 315–16, 330, 350/(2008), II, 1148–9, 1163, 1182. On the cage, see Marcus Milwright and Evanthia Baboula, 'Bayezid's cage: A re-examination of a venerable academic controversy', *JRAS*, 3rd series, 21 (2011), 239–60: ibid., 258–9, they suggest that the tale derived from a misreading of Ibn ʿArabshāh's account (as does Marozzi, *Tamerlane*, 335–7); but we might note that it is found also in Rus′ sources, which cannot have been indebted to Ibn ʿArabshāh.
127. Yazdī, *ZN* (1957), II, 349/(2008), II, 1181–2. Compare Shāmī, *ZN*, I, 271, who says only that during Bayezid's final illness Timur had renowned

physicians attend to him. Marozzi, *Tamerlane*, 358, sees the tears for Bayezid as having 'something of the crocodile' about them; but Roux, *Tamerlan*, 178, takes Yazdī's testimony at face value.

128. Dimitris J. Kastritsis, *The Sons of Bayezid. Empire Building and Representation in the Ottoman Civil War of 1402–1413* (Leiden and Boston, MA, 2007), 44–50. For Meḥmed, see also Colin Heywood, 'A mid-fifteenth century Byzantine and Ottoman coin hoard from Rumeli: The Ottoman component (a preliminary report)', in Hillenbrand (ed.), *Studies in Honour of Clifford Edmund Bosworth*, II, 109–23 (here 113); repr. in Heywood, *Ottomanica and Meta-Ottomanica*, 141–53 (here 144).
129. J. Delaville Le Roulx, *Les Hospitaliers à Rhodes (1310–1421)* (London, 1974), 283–6. Jürgen Sarnowsky, 'Die Johanniter und Smyrna 1344–1402 (Teil I)', *Römische Quartalschrift* 86 (1991), 215–51 (here 232–3).
130. Anthony Luttrell, 'The crisis in the Bosphorus following the battle near Ankara in 1402', in Rosario Villari (ed.), *Controllo degli stretti e insediamenti militari nel Mediterraneo* (Rome and Bari, 2002), 155–66 (here 159–60).
131. For their turbulent relationship with Timur, see W.E.D. Allen, *A History of the Georgian People from the Beginning down to the Russian Conquest in the Nineteenth Century* (London, 1932), 123–5.
132. Timur to John (VII), 15 May 1402, in Alexandrescu-Dersca, *La Campagne de Timur*, 123 (annexe 1). William Miller, *Trebizond. The Last Greek Empire of the Byzantine Era 1204–1461*, new edn (Chicago, IL, 1969), 71–2. Shukurov, *Velikie Komniny i vostok*, 271.
133. Clavijo (1859), 61/(1928), 111. For his role as intermediary, see Shukurov, *Velikie Komniny i vostok*, 269–71.
134. Byzantine dealings with Timur are discussed in John W. Barker, *Manuel II Palaeologus 1391–1425. A Study in Late Byzantine Statesmanship* (New Brunswick, NJ, 1969), 504–8. On the reaction of Byzantine authors, and of Manuel himself, to Bayezid's defeat, see now also Siren Çelik, *Manuel II Palaiologos (1350–1425). A Byzantine Emperor in a Time of Tumult* (Cambridge, 2021), 246–9.
135. Clavijo (1859), 24/(1928), 52.
136. Shāmī, *ZN*, I, 264; also compare ibid., I, 279, where Timur informs the Georgian king of this. Yazdī, *ZN* (1957), II, 331/(2008), II, 1164–5. Timur to John VII, in Alexandrescu-Dersca, *La Campagne de Timur*, 123–4 (annexe 1).
137. *Chronique du Religieux de Saint-Denys, contenant le règne de Charles VI, de 1380 à 1422*, ed. Louis François Bellaguet, 6 vols (Paris, 1839–52), III, 50.
138. Thus HA, *Dhayl-i Ẓafar-nāma*, ed. Tauer, 443.
139. Yazdī, *ZN* (1957), II, 328/(2008), II, 1161–2. Shāmī, *ZN*, I, 204, mentions only his submission.
140. Shāmī, *ZN*, I, 217. Yazdī, *ZN* (1957), II, 182–3/(2008), II, 1025. Shukurov, *Velikie Komniny i vostok*, 270, suggests that this probably occurred around the time of the first capture of Sivas in Sept. 1400; he discusses the alleged 'son of Murad' ibid., n.36.
141. Stella, *Annales Genuenses*, 260. Felicitas Schmieder, *Europa und die Fremden. Die Mongolen im Urteil des Abendlandes vom 13. bis in das 15. Jahrhundert*, Beiträge zur Geschichte und Quellenkunde des Mittelalters 16 (Sigmaringen, 1994), 185, n.588, regards this as apocryphal; as Michel Balard, *La Romanie génoise (XIIe–début du XVe siècle)* (Genoa, 1978), I, 101, points out, it is

confirmed by no other source. For the despatch of tribute, see Clavijo (1859), 76/(1928), 135.

142. Shāmī, *ZN*, I, 268–9. Yazdī, *ZN* (1957), II, 343, 344/(2008), II, 1175–6, 1177. Alexandrescu-Dersca, *La Campagne de Timur*, 90.

143. Venetian report dated 10 Sept. 1401, in N. Iorga, 'Notes et extraits pour servir à l'histoire des croisades au XVe siècle', *Revue de l'Orient Latin* 4 (1896), 25–118, 226–320, 503–622 (here 245); also in George T. Dennis (ed.), 'Three reports from Crete on the situation in Romania, 1401–1402', *Studi Veneziani* 12 (1970), 243–65 (here 245; trans. at 253), and repr. in Dennis, *Byzantium and the Franks 1350–1420* (London, 1982).

144. So according to Clavijo (1859), 76/(1928), 135.

145. Gerardo Sagredo, 12 Oct. 1402, in Alexandrescu-Dersca, *La Campagne de Timur*, 131–2 (annexe 3). Clavijo (1859), 77/(1928), 136, includes the Byzantines in this *volte-face*. See also Balard, *La Romanie génoise*, I, 102.

146. F. Thiriet (ed.), *Délibérations des assemblées vénitiennes concernant la Romanie*, II (Paris and The Hague, 1971), 95 (no. 1017).

147. See the analysis in Kedar, *Merchants in Crisis*, 129–30.

148. Clavijo (1859), 77/(1928), 136. For Smyrna, see Andreas de Redusiis de Quero, *Chronicon Tarvisinum*, col. 801.

149. Relations between Timur and Western Europe are surveyed in Knobler, 'The rise of Tīmūr'; Schmieder, *Europa und die Fremden*, 180–7; and Jackson, *The Mongols and the West*, 239–43.

150. Amīrānshāh, in his letter of 805/1403 to European monarchs, mentions having sent Archbishop John to Venice and Genoa: Baron Silvestre de Sacy, 'Mémoire sur une correspondance inédite de Tamerlan avec Charles VI', *Mémoires de l'Institut Royal de France. Académie des Inscriptions et Belles-Lettres* 6 (1822), 470–522 (here 479). In his reply to Timur's letter, Henry IV too refers to this earlier visit by Archbishop John on Amīrānshāh's behalf: Sir Henry Ellis (ed.), *Original Letters Illustrative of English History*, 3rd series, I (London, 1846), 56. The date when Amīrānshāh despatched the envoys can be inferred from their presence in Venice in late March 1401: Luttrell, 'Timur's Dominican envoy', n.7 at 210.

151. John calls his companion Francis *Ssathru, but Alexandrescu-Dersca, *La Campagne de Timur*, 39, n.4, has shown that this was a separate person, called 'Sandron' in the Italian version of Timur's letter to John VII; he had accompanied Francis on Timur's first embassy to Constantinople in 1401 (referred to at p. 305 and n.143 above): ibid., 123 (annexe 1); Iorga, 'Notes et extraits', 245.

152. *Chronographia regum Francorum*, III, 205–6, giving the date of John's arrival in Paris. Henry IV to Timur, in Ellis (ed.), *Original Letters*, 56–8. Compare also *Chronique du Religieux de Saint-Denys*, ed. Bellaguet, III, 134. Charles VI's reply is dated 15 June 1403: De Sacy, 'Mémoire sur une correspondance inédite', 522.

153. A. Soudavar, 'The concepts of "*al-aqdamo aṣaḥḥ*" and "*yaqin-e sābeq*", and the problem of semi-fakes', *StIr* 28 (1999), 255–73 (here 256–60), has highlighted suspect features of the letter from Timur to the French King, which paid scant regard to Timurid diplomatic conventions and was written in flawed Persian and on inferior paper, and argued that it was a forgery, most probably by John himself, who does not seem to have returned to Timur's

court. If this is true (and Soudavar's reservations deserve to be noted), it is nevertheless highly incongruous that, whereas this letter speaks only of trade with the west, the Latin translation voices a desire for military alliance and refers to Bayezid as the mutual enemy: Timur to Charles VI, in De Sacy, 'Mémoire sur une correspondance inédite', 473 (Pers. text), 479 (Latin trans.); compare also Amīrānshāh's letter, ibid., 480, with Charles VI's reply to Timur, 522. Why John should have tampered with the translation of a letter when he had fabricated the original remains to be explained.

154. Clavijo (1859), 4–5/(1928), 24–5.
155. Yazdī, *ZN* (1957), II, 421–2, 443, 449/(2008), II, 1255–6, 1271, 1276.
156. Clavijo (1859), 166–9/(1928), 280–5.
157. Ibid. (1859), 133–4/(1928), 221, 222–3. Papas and Toutant, *L'Asie centrale de Tamerlan*, 95, suggest that Timur's letter to Charles VI reflected a lower degree of esteem than he expressed for the Castilian king.
158. *Chronographia regum Francorum*, III, 206, 211. Luttrell, 'Timur's Dominican envoy', 220–1.
159. John of Sulṭāniyya, *Mémoire*, ed. Moranvillé, 462; hence *Chronographia regum Francorum*, III, 216.
160. Timur to Barqūq, as cited by Shāmī, I, 221, and Yazdī, *ZN* (1957), I, 458/(2008), I, 738; the relevant passage from the latter is cited in translation by Wing, *The Jalayirids*, 162.
161. Timur to Charles VI, in De Sacy, 'Mémoire sur une correspondance inédite', 473 (Pers. text), 474 (Latin trans.); also 479 (Latin trans.). Amīrānshāh to Charles VI, ibid., 480. Henry IV to Timur, in Ellis (ed.), *Original Letters*, 57, refers to Timur's desire that merchants pass freely between their respective dominions. The theme recurs in a letter from Martin I of Aragon to Timur, 1 April 1404: Antoni Rubió i Lluch (ed.), *Diplomatari de l'Orient Català (1301–1409)* (Barcelona, 1947), 700.
162. John of Sulṭāniyya, *Mémoire*, ed. Moranvillé, 463–4.
163. Diplomatic exchanges are surveyed by Kauz, *Politik und Handel*, 55–75 (also 24–5), and Robinson, *In the Shadow of the Mongol Empire*, 259–63. Zsombor Rajkai, 'Early fifteenth-century Sino-Central Asian relations: The Timurids and Ming China', in Zsombor Rajkai and Ildikó Bellér-Hann (eds), *Frontiers and Boundaries. Encounters on China's Margins*, AF 156 (Wiesbaden, 2012), 87–105, reviews earlier literature and analyses the gulf between Chinese imperial theory and reality.
164. For a translation of the text inserted in the *Mingshi*, see Bretschneider, *Mediaeval Researches*, II, 258–60.
165. Clavijo (1859), 133–4, 172–3/(1928), 222–3, 290–1. Kauz, *Politik und Handel*, 68–9.
166. Shih-shan Henry Tsai, *Perpetual Happiness. The Ming Emperor Yongle* (Seattle, WA, and London, 2001), 188.
167. Shāmī, *ZN*, I, 213. Yazdī, *ZN* (1972), fo. 65b/(2008), I, 179. Clavijo (1859), 135/(1928), 223. See *TMEN*, II, 585–7 (no. 945); *DTS*, 575, *s.v.* 'toŋuz', *dikaia svin'ia*. I owe my understanding of the pun to the kindness of Professor Hans Van Ess.
168. Edward L. Dreyer, *Early Ming China. A Political History 1355–1435* (Stanford, CA, 1982), 71–6, 140–3, 173–5. Morris Rossabi, 'The Ming and Inner Asia', in Denis Twitchett and Frederick W. Mote (eds), *CHC*, VIII: *The Ming*

Dynasty, 1368–1644, Part 2 (Cambridge, 1998), 221–71 (here 224–8). Robinson, *In the Shadow of the Mongol Empire*, 81, 163–4.

169. See David M. Robinson, 'The Ming court and the legacy of the Yuan Mongols', in Robinson (ed.), *Culture, Courtiers, and Competition. The Ming Court (1368–1644)* (Cambridge, MA, 2008), 365–421 (here 368–70 and passim); Robinson, *In the Shadow of the Mongol Empire*, passim.
170. David M. Robinson, 'Controlling memory and movement: The early Ming court and the changing Chinggisid world', in Biran (ed.), *Mobility Transformations and Cultural Exchange*, 503–24 (here 512–13, 518); Robinson, *In the Shadow of the Mongol Empire*, 259, 265–9, and *Ming China and Its Allies*, 165. On Gunashiri[n], see p. 236 and p. 571 n.95.
171. Shāmī, *ZN*, I, 213; it may be significant that in the corresponding passage Yazdī, *ZN* (1957), II, 158/(2008), II, 1002, says nothing of such a massacre. See Kauz, *Politik und Handel*, 68.
172. *RN* (1915), 45a/not in *RN* (2000); hence Shāmī, *ZN*, I, 170. These authors claim that Muḥammad Sulṭān's activities in Mughūlistān were a prelude to this campaign, but omit any link between the change of plan and Pīr Muḥammad's activities in India: the texts have *khitāī-u* xTn, but Khotan reads oddly in this context. I suspect that the diacritical points are misplaced and that the intended reading is čyn, i.e. *Chīn* (southern China). Yazdī, *ZN* (1957), II, 19/(2008), I, 866. al-Maqrīzī, *Durar al-ʿuqūd*, I, 545, was under the impression that Timur first conceived of attacking China during the Anatolian campaign.
173. Yazdī, *ZN* (1957), II, 402/(2008), II, 1234.
174. The date supplied by Salmānī, *Shams al-ḥusn*, text, fo. 34a–b (German trans., 28). *ZT*, I, 33 (and HA's additions to Shāmī, ZN, II, 204), has the 16th, but later, II, 1034, gives mid-Shaʿbān and (in a verse) the 17th. IA (1979), 254/(1986), 393 (*TGA*, 233), gives 17 Shaʿbān; al-Maqrīzī, *Durar al-ʿuqūd*, I, 547, the 19th: see the brief discussion in Ito, 'Al-Maqrīzī's biography of Tīmūr', 311, n.18. The date in the anonymous synoptic account is 14 Shaʿbān [15 Feb.]: Thackston (ed.), *Album Prefaces*, 90.
175. Salmānī, *Shams al-ḥusn*, text, fos 23a–25a, 27a (German trans., 22–3, 24).
176. Yazdī, *ZN* (1957), II, 477–84/(2008), II, 1301–8. Salmānī, *Shams al-ḥuṣn*, fos 27a–b, 31b, 41a–43b (German trans., 24–5, 26, 30–2). Bartol'd, 'O pogrebenii Timura', 443 (tr. Rogers, 80).
177. *TR*, I (text), 32–3, II (trans.), 29.
178. Ḥaydar incorrectly places Khiḍr Khwāja's death after Timur's elsewhere in his narrative too: ibid., I (text), 32, 33, II (trans.), 28–9.
179. Millward, 'Eastern Central Asia', 263.
180. The *Mingshi lu* speak of an imperial order of 24 March 1405 to meet the forthcoming attack. I owe this detail to an as yet unpublished paper by Professor Ralph Kauz, 'Timur's death and the subsequent crisis of his empire', read at the conference 'The Great Chinggisid Crisis: History, Context, Aftermath', in Bonn on 12 May 2023. Compare also Bretschneider, *Mediaeval Researches*, II, 261.
181. *ZT*, III, 460; this letter is also reproduced in Nawāʾī (ed.), *Asnād*, 131–2. See further Robinson, *Ming China and Its Allies*, 44–5.
182. al-Maqrīzī, *al-Sulūk*, IV, part 1, 26.
183. Yazdī, *ZN* (1957), II, 402/(2008), II, 1235.

184. Morgan, 'The empire of Tamerlane', 235. Manz, 'The empire of Tamerlane as an adaptation', 287.
185. See the remarks of Simon Digby, 'After Timur left: North India in the fifteenth century', in Francesca Orsini and Samira Sheikh (eds), *After Timur Left. Culture and Circulation in Fifteenth-Century North India* (Oxford and New Delhi, 2014), 47–59 (here 48–9).
186. For both Luristān and Anatolia, among other instances, see Manz, *The Rise and Rule*, 91–2.
187. Goto, 'Tīmūr and local dynasties', 74–5.
188. *ZT*, II, 591 (also in HA's additions to Shāmī, *ZN*, II, 50). HA, *Ta'rīkh-i salāṭīn-i Kart*, 214 (= *CO*, text, 68).
189. *RN* (1915), 18, 42/(2000), 23, 55 (*DPT*, 30, 57). For Toqtamish's dominions, see also Yazdī, *ZN* (1957), I, 541–2/(2008), I, 815–16.
190. Yazdī, *ZN* (1957), I, 225/(2008), I, 488.
191. Ibid. (1957), I, 360–1, 551, 553/(2008), I, 642, 825–7.
192. See ibid. (1957), I, 373, 383, 531/(2008), I, 653, 663, 807, and *ZT*, II, 729 (also HA's additions in Shāmī, *ZN*, II, 93), for infantry (*piyāda*, *piyādagān*) on the two Qipchaq campaigns; Shāmī, *ZN*, I, 252, and Yazdī, *ZN* (1957), I, 362, 375, 486/(2008), I, 643–4, 655, 767, for references to horse-armour (the first two in the context of the Qipchaq expeditions).
193. *TR*, I (text), 50, II (trans.), 42–3.
194. Martin, *Treasure of the Land of Darkness*, 33–4.
195. As Grousset supposed in *The Empire of the Steppes*, 300.
196. John of Sulṭāniyya, *Mémoire*, ed. Moranvillé, 454; hence *Chronographia regum Francorum*, III, 220.
197. IA (1979), 36–7/(1986), 87–8 (*TGA*, 34–5).
198. *ZT*, I, 19 (and in HA's addenda to Shāmī, *ZN*, II, 195), asserts that Timur's subordinates (*bandagān-i dawlat*) were never worsted in any campaign.

11: THE FORGING OF AN EMPIRE: THE FUNCTION AND CONDUCT OF WAR

1. Golden, *Central Asia in World History*, 96. Morgan, *The Mongols*, 176–7.
2. Christian, *A History of Russia, Central Asia and Mongolia*, II, 57.
3. Baumer, *The History of Central Asia*, III, 279.
4. Aubin, 'Comment Tamerlan', 102–3, with full references.
5. *ZT*, II, 748 (also in HA's additions to Shāmī, *ZN*, II, 101).
6. Shāmī, *ZN*, I, 168. Yazdī, *ZN* (1957), I, 579/(2008), I, 854. Aubin, 'Les princes d'Ormuz', 113.
7. Yazdī, *ZN* (1957), II, 398/(2008), II, 1230–1. Yukako Goto, 'Tīmūr and local dynasties in Iran', in Jeremiás (ed.), *Irano-Turkic Cultural Contacts*, 67–77 (here 73). I have assumed that the unit was the heavier *mann* (approximately 3kg) in use in Iran from the second half of the fourteenth century: see Walther Hinz, 'Ein orientalisches Handelsunternehmen im 15. Jahrhundert', *Die Welt des Orients* 1 (1947–52), 314–40 (here 325–6).
8. Clavijo (1859), 107/(1928), 181.
9. Yazdī, *ZN* (1957), I, 312/(2008), I, 586. Examples in Aubin, 'Comment Tamerlan', 97–104. For 'horseshoe money', see *TJG*, II, 147 (*HWC*, 415 and n.14).

10. Shāmī, *ZN*, I, 150. Yazdī, *ZN* (1957), I, 482–3/(2008), I, 763.
11. Ibn Qāḍī Shuhba, *Ta'rīkh*, I, 475.
12. Yazdī, *ZN* (1957), II, 95, 143/(2008), I, 939, 987.
13. Mignanelli (1764), 136a–138a/(2013), 322–31 (tr. in Fischel, 'A new Latin source', 217–25), a picture corroborated by Mamlūk sources (see later). Timur's treatment of Damascus is also examined in Aubin, 'Comment Tamerlan', 100, 106–7 and *passim*.
14. al-Maqrīzī, *al-Sulūk*, III, part 3, 1039–46; summarised in Stefan Heidemann, 'Tīmūr's campmint during the siege of Damascus in 803/1401', in Rika Gyselen and Maria Szuppe (eds), *Matériaux pour l'histoire économique du monde iranien*, StIr cahier 21 (Paris, 1999), 179–206 (here 182–5).
15. Yazdī, *ZN* (1957), 243/(2008), II, 1081. *ZT*, II, 926, is briefer. Heidemann, 'Tīmūr's campmint', 190–6.
16. Aubin, 'Comment Tamerlan', 97, asserts categorically that there were *no* exceptions to this rule.
17. Zayn al-Dīn (1990), text, 500 (Russian trans., 132)/(1993), 118.
18. *ZT*, I, 522; see also HA's additions to Shāmī, *ZN*, II, 39–40.
19. Yazdī, *ZN* (1957), I, 254/(2008), I, 521.
20. Ibid. (1957), II, 405/(2008), II, 1238.
21. For examples, see Aubin, 'Comment Tamerlan', 104–5.
22. *ZT*, II, 988–9; compare Shāmī, *ZN*, I, 275–6 (also HA's additions ibid., *ZN*, II, 182).
23. Baumer, *The History of Central Asia*, III, 279, regards the adornment of Samarkand, and Kish and Bukhara to a lesser extent, as Timur's 'only long-term goal'.
24. Thus Clavijo (1859), 120, 170–1/(1928), 202, 287–8, renders this figure as the total population of the city. For the development of Samarkand under Timur, see Schamiloglu, 'Beautés du mélange', 200–1.
25. Clavijo (1859), 171, 172/(1928), 287–8, 290. Yazdī, *ZN* (1957), I, 290, 320, 442, 456, and II, 242/(2008), I, 562, 597, 720–1, 735, 1080. Those from Fārs and Iraq, at least, were accompanied by their households. See also IA (1979), 175–7/(1986), 293–5 (*TGA*, 161–2), on Damascus.
26. Clavijo (1859), 171, 174/(1928), 288, 293.
27. Yazdī, *ZN* (1957), II, 144/(2008), I, 988.
28. IA (1979), 176/(1986), 293 (*TGA*, 161).
29. Yazdī, *ZN* (1957), I, 220, 237/(2008), I, 482, 502. *ZT*, II, 32, remarks on Timur's policy of removing skilled personnel to Samarkand and Kish (also in HA's additions to Shāmī, *ZN*, II, 203).
30. HA, *Jughrāfiyya*, Bodleian ms. Fraser 155, fo. 171b.
31. Yazdī, *ZN* (1957), I, 190, 346/(2008), I, 443, 627.
32. Ibid. (1957), I, 394/(2008), I, 673. Shāmī, *ZN*, I, 125.
33. Yazdī, *ZN* (1957), I, 542/(2008), I, 816.
34. Ibid. (1957), I, 358/(2008), I, 640.
35. Ibid. (1957), I, 304, 423, 447, 471, and II, 197/(2008), I, 578, 702, 725, 751, and II, 1038.
36. Ibid. (1957), II, 250–1, 252/(2008), II, 1087, 1088–9.
37. Beatrice F. Manz, 'Temür and the problem of a conqueror's legacy', *JRAS*, 3rd series, 8 (1998), 21–41 (here 28).
38. *Fatḥ-nāma* for Syria, in *Safīna*, BN ms. arabe 3423, fo. 400a.

39. al-Maqrīzī, *Durar al-'uqūd*, I, 507.
40. IA (1979), 187/(1986), 312 (*TGA*, 171–2).
41. An important point made by Kim, 'The early history of the Moghul nomads', 299, and by May, *The Mongol Empire*, 344.
42. Shāmī, *ZN*, I, 213. Yazdī, *ZN* (1957), II, 158–9/(2008), II, 1002–3. The date 799 [1396–7] given for Khiḍr Khwāja's death (after a reign of thirty years, which is erroneous in any case) by Naṭanzī (1957), 131/(2004), 107, is probably less trustworthy.
43. Though it is mentioned by IA (1979), 101/(1986), 162–3 (*TGA*, 95).
44. Wing, *The Jalayirids*, 160, 163. In addition to the references given there, see al-Maqrīzī, *Durar al-'uqūd*, I, 234 (Tabriz), 235 (Baghdad); Ibn Qāḍī Shuhba, *Ta'rīkh*, I, 473.
45. There is a discussion of the army, its weaponry etc., in Ashrafyan, 'Central Asia under Timur', 325–8.
46. Mignanelli (1764), 134/(2013), 316 (tr. in Fischel, 'A new Latin source', 210). Élodie Vigouroux, 'Comment Tamerlan a pris Alep en 803/1400', *Annales Islamologiques* 55 (2021), 303–25, n. 70; https://doi.org/10.4000/anisl.10223.
47. *RN* (1915), 36/(2000), 47–8 (*DPT*, 51).
48. Yazdī, *ZN* (1957), I, 336–7/(2008), I, 616. The classic description of the Mongol hunt is found in *TJG*, I, 19–20 (*HWC*, 27–8). On the *nerge* (or *jerge*), see *TMEN*, I, 291–3 (no. 161); and for the deployment in Mongol warfare, see *TJG*, III, 10, 53–4 (*HWC*, 554, 585); Timothy May, *The Mongol Art of War. Chinggis Khan and the Mongol Military System* (Barnsley, 2007), 46.
49. Yazdī, *ZN* (1957), II, 312/(2008), II, 1146. Compare also Alexandrescu-Dersca, *La Campagne de Timur*, 75.
50. See Lal, *Twilight of the Sultanate*, 27.
51. Yazdī, *ZN* (1957), II, 79–80/(2008), I, 926. IA (1979), 103–5/(1986), 165–7 (*TGA*, 97–8). Clavijo (1859), 153/(1928), 255. Digby, *War-Horse and Elephant*, 80–1, follows Yazdī.
52. John of Sulṭāniyya, *Mémoire*, ed. Moranvillé, 450, 454–5; hence *Chronographia regum Francorum*, III, 209, 221. *Ta'rīf* (1951), 382/(2008), 255 (*IKT*, 46). *Chronique du Religieux de Saint-Denys*, ed. Bellaguet, III, 46, credits Timur with forces totalling 1,100,000. Dennis, 'Three reports from Crete', 245 (mistrans. as '70,000' at 254). Schiltberger's figures are to be found in Johan Schiltberger, *Reisebuch*, tr. J. Buchan Telfer, *The Bondage and Travels of Johann Schiltberger, a Native of Bavaria, in Europe, Asia, and Africa, 1396–1427*, HS, 1st series, 58 (London, 1879), 20, 21 and 28, respectively (Bernardini, 'The army of Timur', 218, reproduces the figure for the Ankara campaign as 160,000). For a discussion of these and other totals, see Roux, *Tamerlan*, 296–7; inflated estimates of the size of Timur's army at Ankara are cited in Alexandrescu-Dersca, *La Campagne de Timur*, 112–13 (appendix I).
53. Ibn al-Furāt, *Ta'rīkh al-duwal wa l-mulūk*, IX, part 2, 370. Ibn Qāḍī Shuhba, *Ta'rīkh*, I, 507.
54. Ibn al-Shiḥna, 210; hence IA (1979), 136/(1986), 211–12 (*TGA*, 125).
55. Mignanelli (1764), 138b/(2013), 332 (tr. in Fischel, 'A new Latin source', 227).
56. Yazdī, *ZN* (1957), II, 450/(2008), II, 1277.
57. Ankara: *Chronique du Religieux de Saint-Denys*, xxiii, 10, ed. Bellaguet, III, 48. Damascus: Andreas de Redusiis de Quero, *Chronicon Tarvisinum* [down to

1428], in *RIS*, XIX (Milan, 1731), coll. 735–866 (here col. 800: the figure is misinterpreted as 1,100,000). Inscription: N.N. Poppe, 'Karasakpaiskaia nadpis' Timura', *Gosudarstvennyi Érmitazh. Trudy Otdela Vostoka/Travaux du Département Oriental* 2 (Leningrad, 1940), 185–7.

58. May, *The Mongol Art of War*, 27, sets the average size of the tümen at 60 per cent of full strength; Atwood, in *EMME*, 541, at 40 per cent.
59. Shāmī, *ZN*, I, 179. Yazdī, *ZN* (1957), II, 47–8/(2008), I, 895–6. For other references to the 'troops (*sipāh*, *lashgar*) of Khurāsān', see ibid. (1957), II, 38, 118, 153, 174, 378, 415/(2008), I, 884, 963, and II, 996, 1017, 1210, 1248; and for the 'people of Khurāsān and Sīstān' at the siege of the Damascus citadel, (1957), II, 241/(2008), II, 1079. Forces from the cities and towns are discussed in Manz, 'Nomad and settled'; for infantry in Timur's armies, see also Manz, *The Rise and Rule*, 98–9.
60. Yazdī, *ZN* (1957), II, 300/(2008), II, 1135.
61. Ibid. (1957), I, 547, and II, 375/(2008), I, 820, and II, 1207: the spelling of this tribal name varies.
62. Ibid. (1957), II, 417/(2008), II, 1250.
63. Ibid. (1957), II, 304/(2008), II, 1138. Bernardini, 'The army of Timur', 215, 220. For the Shīrwānshāh, see further Manz, *The Rise and Rule*, 93.
64. See, for example, those identified by Bernardini, 'The army of Timur', 219–20, as fighting for him at Ankara; also, in the context of the invasion of Syria, Michele Bernardini, 'Niẓām al-Dīn Shāmī's description of the Syrian campaign of Tīmūr', in Bauden and Dekkiche (eds), *Mamluk Cairo, a Crossroads for Embassies*, 381–409 (here 392–3), citing IA. For other examples, see Manz, *The Rise and Rule*, 93.
65. Yazdī, *ZN* (1957), I, 473, 559, and II, 222, 241, 304/(2008), I, 754, 835, and II, 1060–1, 1079, 1139. See also Shāmī, *ZN*, I, 228, 255; Naṭanzī (1957), 360/(2004), 268, 312; Sīstānī, *Iḥyā' al-mulūk*, 106; Bosworth, *The History of the Saffarids*, 452.
66. Yazdī, *ZN* (1957), II, 205/(2008), II, 1046.
67. Ibid. (1957), II, 450/(2008), II, 1277. See also the more general reference to the forces led by Khalīl Sulṭān after Timur's death as 'Turks, Tājīks, 'Irāqīs and Rūmīs': ibid. (1957), II, 484/(2008), II, 1308; Paul, 'Khalīl Sulṭān and the "Westerners"', 25, n.66.
68. Lal, *Twilight of the Sultanate*, 28.
69. Shāmī, *ZN*, I, 189–90. *RN* (1915), 115/(2000), 112 (*DPT*, 115). Yazdī, *ZN* (1957), II, 78/(2008), I, 925, gives 40,000 foot.
70. Shāmī, *ZN*, I, 191. *RN* (1915), 119/(2000), 114 (*DPT*, 117).
71. Alexandrescu-Dersca, *La Campagne de Timur*, 68; the likely figures are given ibid., 112–15 (appendices I and II).
72. Yazdī, *ZN* (1957), I, 385/(2008), I, 664. Clavijo (1859), 176/(1928), 296.
73. Clavijo (1859), 175–6/(1928), 296, 298.
74. See the admirable précis in Roux, *Tamerlan*, 185–7.
75. IA (1979), 315, 348/(1986), 451, 479 (*TGA*, 295, 322). On this, compare the comments of Manz, *The Rise and Rule*, 74.
76. Yazdī, *ZN* (1957), I, 372–3, 374/(2008), I, 653, 654.
77. Shāmī, *ZN*, I, 188. The context is the engagement outside Delhi. Cf. also *RN* (1915), 108b/(2000), 107 (*DPT*, 110–11), and Yazdī, *ZN* (1957), II, 71/(2008), I, 919.

78. Yazdī, *ZN* (1957), I, 381/(2008), I, 661. In his account of this battle, Naṭanzī (1957), 348/(2004), 261, gives the number of divisions (*ghūl*s) as 9.
79. *TR*, I (text), 32, II (trans.), 29. He claims to be citing Yazdī, but I can find no passage with these precise details in *ZN*.
80. *ZT*, II, 729 (and in HA's additions to Shāmī, *ZN*, II, 93). For *tutmaj*, 'noodles', see Buell and Anderson, *A Soup for the Qan*, appendix II, 625–6.
81. Yazdī, *ZN* (1957), I, 361/(2008), I, 642. For Tu. *bulmaq*/*bulamagh*, see *TMEN*, II, 321–3 (no. 770: 'eine Art dünnflüssiger Mehlbrei'); Buell and Anderson, *A Soup for the Qan*, appendix II, 625 (*bulamïq*/*bulgamac*: 'thin porridge, flour soup').
82. Clavijo (1859), 113/(1928), 191.
83. See, for example, ibid. (1859), 97/(1928), 165. Aubin, 'Comment Tamerlan', 103–4.
84. *TR*, I (text), 32, II (trans.), 29; and see n.79 above.
85. Shāmī, *ZN*, I, 95. Yazdī, *ZN* (1957), I, 279, 373/(2008), I, 550, 653. John of Sulṭāniyya, *Mémoire*, ed. Moranvillé, 453, appears to allude to such an ordinance; hence *Chronographia regum Francorum*, III, 219.
86. IA (1979), 177/(1986), 295 (*TGA*, 162). Compare also the brief remark on the execution of those who disobeyed orders, in John of Sulṭāniyya, *Mémoire*, ed. Moranvillé, 453; hence *Chronographia regum Francorum*, III, 219.
87. al-Maqrīzī, *Durar al-ʿuqūd*, I, 555.
88. Yazdī, *ZN* (1957), II, 275/(2008), II, 1113. Soucek, 'Eskandar b. ʿOmar Šayx', 78.
89. Yazdī, *ZN* (1957), I, 342, 417, and II, 420/(2008), I, 622, 696, and II, 1254.
90. *ZT*, II, 952; and see HA's additions to Shāmī, *ZN*, II, 175. Aubin, 'Comment Tamerlan', 86 and n.4.
91. Yazdī, *ZN* (1957), I, 349/(2008), I, 629; according to Barthold, *Four Studies*, I, 143 (= Bartol'd, *Sochineniia*, II, part 1, 83), this journey usually took caravans two months. See the general comment of John of Sulṭāniyya, *Mémoire*, ed. Moranvillé, 454; hence *Chronographia regum Francorum*, III, 220.
92. Aubin, 'Tamerlan à Baġdād', 303.
93. For example, Yazdī, *ZN* (1957), I, 206–7, 551/(2008), I, 465, 825. The expedition to Jata in 776/1375, and later the China campaign, had to be postponed because of extreme winter conditions, however: ibid. (1957), I, 188–9, and II, 452, 457–8/(2008), I, 441–2, and II, 1279–80, 1283.
94. IA (1979), 356–7/(1986), 485–6 (*TGA*, 328–30).
95. Shāmī, *ZN*, I, 222. Yazdī, *ZN* (1957), II, 203, 223/(2008), II, 1044, 1062. The troops were given twenty days to rest following the surrender of Ḥamā: ibid. (1957), II, 222/(2008), II, 1061. See further Manz, *The Rise and Rule*, 73.
96. Shāmī, *ZN*, I, 141. HA's additions ibid., II, 75. Yazdī, *ZN* (1957), I, 341, and II, 198, 221, 324/(2008), I, 621, and II 1039, 1060, 1157. For the distribution of the plunder from Aleppo, see also Shāmī, *ZN*, I, 228, and the *fatḥ-nāma* for Syria, in *Safīna*, BN ms. arabe 3423, fo. 400a, cited (as 400b) by Aubin, 'Comment Tamerlan', 108. See earlier for Delhi and livestock.
97. Shāmī, *ZN*, I, 193 (with '100 or more', as opposed to 150). *RN* (1915), 127/(2000), 121–2 (*DPT*, 124). Yazdī, *ZN* (1957), II, 95/(2008), I, 939. Aubin, 'Comment Tamerlan', 106.
98. Yazdī, *ZN* (1957), I, 553/(2008), I, 826–7.
99. Shāmī, *ZN*, I, 202; and compare also 200. Yazdī, *ZN* (1957), II, 119/(2008), I, 964.

100. Clavijo (1859), 90–2, 105–6/(1928), 155–8, 177–80. See Silverstein, *Postal Systems*, 162–3.
101. Yazdī, *ZN* (1957), I, 317/(2008), I, 591–2.
102. See *ZT*, I, 27–8 (also HA's additions to Shāmī, *ZN*, II, 200–1).
103. Astarābādī, *Bazm-u razm*, 449. Bernardini, 'The army of Timur', 212.
104. IA (1979), 320–1/(1986), 456: some of the terms are opaque and my renderings here are tentative (cf. *TGA*, 300–1), while this author's customary rhyming prose no doubt trumps a penchant for accuracy. Roemer, 'Tīmūr in Iran', 51–2, specifies dervishes and *qalandar*s. See also Ibn Ḥajar, *Inbā' al-ghumr*, ed. Ḥabashī, II, 303–4/ed. Khān, V, 236.
105. Yazdī, *ZN* (2008), I, 878 (not in 1957 edn).
106. Clavijo (1859), 173–4/(1928), 292.
107. IA (1979), 213–14/(1986), 351–2 (*TGA*, 196–7).
108. *Ta'rīf* (1951), 370, 374/(2008), 243, 246 (*IKT*, 35, 38); for the language of the report, see above, p. 557n.63. According to al-Maqrīzī, *Durar al-'uqūd*, II, 397, Ibn Khaldūn was required to describe the localities between Egypt and the Maghrib: their deserts and water supplies, the Arab tribes and the distances involved. IA (1979), 317–18/(1986), 453–4 (*TGA*, 297), alleges that Timur was merely trying to test Ibn Khaldūn's knowledge, but in his *Fākihat al-khulafā'*, ed. al-Najjār, 366/ed. al-Buḥayrī, 357, this author invests the commission with a strategic purpose.
109. Rafael Valencia, 'Ibn Jaldún y Tamerlán', in Jesús Viguera Molins (ed.), *Ibn Jaldún: El Mediterráneo en el siglo XIV. Auge y declive de los Imperios*, 2 vols (Seville, 2006), I: *Estudios*, 178–81 (here 179). Muhsin J. al-Musawi, *The Medieval Islamic Republic of Letters. Arabic Knowledge Construction* (Notre Dame, IN, 2015), 29 (suggesting designs even on Spain). Dale, *The Orange Trees of Marrakesh*, 149.
110. Roux, *Tamerlan*, 187.
111. Yazdī, *ZN* (1957), I, 469/(2008), I, 749. More generally, see IA (1979), 323–4/(1986), 458–9 (*TGA*, 302–3).
112. al-Maqrīzī, *Durar al-'uqūd*, I, 552–3. For an example, see IA (1979), 59–60/(1986), 113–14 (*TGA*, 56).
113. Clavijo (1859), 176/(1928), 297–8.
114. Vigouroux, 'Comment Tamerlan a pris Alep', n. 159; https://doi.org/10.4000/anisl.10223.
115. Digby, *War-Horse and Elephant*, 81. He was misled by Naṭanzī (1957), 372/(2004), 275–6, who seems to say that the elephants carried stone from India for the construction of Timur's mosque at Samarkand; as Digby points out, 'there is no sign of Indian carved stone or marble' on the mosque.
116. Yazdī, *ZN* (1957), II, 139, 143, 144/(2008), I, 983, 986–7, 988. *ZT*, I, 22. For elephants at the quriltai of 1404, see Yazdī, *ZN* (1957), II, 436/(2008), II, 1266. Schiltberger, 26, has Timur withdraw from India with 100 elephants.
117. Yazdī, *ZN* (1957), II, 91–2/(2008), I, 936, for the list of towns.
118. Clavijo (1859), 157–8/(1928), 264–5. The Delhi Sultans had used elephants armed in this fashion to execute criminals also: IB, III, 223, 330–1, 354 (tr. Gibb, 661, 715–16, 726). More generally, see Digby, *War-Horse and Elephant*, 50–4.
119. Shāmī, *ZN*, I, 226, 255, 294. IA (1979), 154/(1986), 248 (*TGA*, 142). Elephants at Aleppo, Damascus and Ankara: see also Yazdī, *ZN* (1957), II,

213, 216, 235, 305/(2008), II, 1054, 1055, 1073, 1140; Alexandrescu-Dersca, *La Campagne de Timur*, 73, for Ankara.

120. Schiltberger, 21. *Chronographia regum Francorum*, III, 200. John of Sulṭāniyya, *Mémoire*, ed. Moranvillé, 450; this figure was copied into *Chronographia regum Francorum*, III, 209.
121. Yazdī, *ZN* (1957), II, 459/(2008), II, 1285.
122. See Digby, *War-Horse and Elephant*, 20–2.
123. Clavijo (1859), 158/(1928), 265–6.
124. Yazdī, *ZN* (1957), II, 256/(2008), II, 1093.
125. Clavijo (1859), 171/(1928), 288.
126. Ibn Zunbul, cited in David Ayalon, *Gunpowder and Firearms in the Mamluk Kingdom. A Challenge to a Mediaeval Society*, 2nd edn (London and Totowa, NJ, 1978), n.245 at 128. But compare Robert Irwin, 'Gunpowder and firearms in the Mamluk Sultanate reconsidered', in Michael Winter and Amalia Levanoni (eds), *The Mamluks in Egyptian and Syrian Politics and Society*, MM 51 (Leiden, 2004), 117–39 (here 132–9). Evidence indicates that the Ottomans had begun to employ guns no earlier than 1422: Kelly DeVries, 'Gunpowder weapons at the siege of Constantinople, 1453', in Yaacov Lev (ed.), *War and Society in the Eastern Mediterranean, 7th–15th Centuries*, MM 9 (Leiden, 1997), 343–62 (here 353–4). The translation in Clavijo (1928), 288, where Timur is said to have carried off from Turkey 'their gun-smiths who make the arquebus', is inaccurate and tendentious. Compare (1859), 171 ('archers'); the Castilian original reads *vallesteros* (crossbowmen).
127. Tonio Andrade, *The Gunpowder Age. China, Military Innovation, and the Rise of the West in World History* (Princeton, NJ, 2016), chap. 3 (esp. 44–7). Iqtidar Alam Khan, 'Coming of gunpowder to the Islamic world and north India: Spotlight on the role of the Mongols', *JAH* 30 (1996), 27–45 (here 35–9). Thomas T. Allsen, 'The circulation of military technology in the Mongolian empire', in Di Cosmo (ed.), *Warfare in Inner Asian History*, 265–93. Stephen G. Haw, 'The Mongol empire – the first "Gunpowder Empire"?', *JRAS*, 3rd series, 23 (2013), 449–61.
128. Reuven Amitai, 'Armies and their economic basis in Iran and the surrounding lands, *c.*1000–1500', in *NCHI*, III, 539–60 (here 556).
129. Shāmī, *ZN*, I, 215, 267. Damascus: *Ta'rīf* (1951), 374/(2008), 246 (*IKT*, 38), though it has been proposed that *nufūṭ* here (translated by Fischel as 'naphtha guns') refers to cannon: Cheddadi, in (2008), n.7 at 270. Ankara: Shāmī, *ZN*, I, 255; though *ZT*, II, 961 (see also HA's additions to Shāmī, *ZN*, II, 177), reproducing this passage, substitutes *kamān-i ra'd* for *naft-andāzī*. In his index to Shāmī's *ZN*, Tauer translates *kamān-i ra'd* as 'grande balista, canon'. On the term *kamān-i ra'd*, see further Iqtidar Alam Khan, *Gunpowder and Firearms. Warfare in Medieval India* (Oxford and New Delhi, 2004), 42. For naphtha, see V. Christides, 'Nafṭ. 2. In the mediaeval Byzantine and Arab-Islamic worlds', *EI*[2], VII, 884–6.
130. The root is Ar. R'D, 'to thunder'. Ayalon, *Gunpowder and Firearms*, 18, lists *rawā'id*, the plural of *ra'āda*, among the terms used in connection with gunpowder.
131. Kutubī, *Ta'rīkh-i āl-i Muẓaffar*, 34.
132. Naṭanzī (1957), 305, 381/(2004), 236, 281. *TMEN*, III, 428, renders *ra'd* in the first of these passages as 'Geschütze'.

133. Shāmī, *ZN*, I, 155. Yazdī, *ZN* (1957), I, 493/(2008), I, 773.
134. Yazdī, *ZN* (1957), I, 412/(2008), I, 690.
135. *ZT*, II, 703 (and see HA's additions in Shāmī, *ZN*, II, 79).
136. Yazdī, *ZN* (1957), II, 239, 339, 408/(2008), II, 1077, 1172, 1174, 1240–1. At Damascus, however, *ZT*, II, 922, mentions the use of *ra'd* only by the garrison of the citadel.
137. Yazdī, *ZN* (1957), II, 219, 290/(2008), II, 1058, 1127.
138. Shāmī, *ZN*, I, 190. *RN* (1915), 115/(2000), 112 (*DPT*, 115, with the interpretation 'guns'). Yazdī, *ZN* (1957), II, 78/(2008), I, 925. Digby, *War-Horse and Elephant*, 80, translates as 'throwers of explosive grenades'.
139. Shāmī, *ZN*, I, 227, 231, 234. *ZT*, II, 977 (also in HA's additions to Shāmī, *ZN*, II, 179).
140. Yazdī, *ZN* (1957), II, 229/(2008), II, 1068.
141. Ibid. (1957), I, 254, 306, 461, and II, 194/(2008), I, 520, 579, 741, and II, 1036. In the Georgian campaign of 802/1400, we read of 'catapults, trebuchets and other instruments of war' (*manjanīq-u 'arrāda-u dīgar asbāb-i jang*): ibid. (1957), II, 178/(2008), II, 1021. Similarly, only 'scaling-ladders, trebuchets and the like' (*nardubānhā-u 'arrādahā-u naẓā'ir-i ān*) are mentioned in connection with Prince Iskandar's siege of Āqsū in 802/1399: ibid. (1957), II, 159/(2008), II, 1003.
142. Ibid. (1957), I, 578, and II, 240/(2008), II, 853, 1078.
143. Tāj al-Dīn Ḥasan Ibn Shihāb Yazdī, *Jāmi' al-tawārīkh-i Ḥasanī*, ed. Ḥusayn Mudarrisī Ṭabāṭabā'ī and Īraj Afshār (Karachi, 1987), 27, 42. Manz, *Power, Politics and Religion*, translates as 'cannoneers' (124) and 'missile throwers' (125).
144. Irwin, 'Gunpowder and firearms', 120, 126–7. See also Ayalon, *Gunpowder and Firearms*, 28–9, and Rhoads Murphey, *Ottoman Warfare, 1500–1700* (London, 1999), 13–16.
145. Timur: Roemer, 'Tīmūr in Iran', 54; Murphey, 'Bayezid I's foreign policy plans', 198. Bayezid: ibid., 185–94.
146. See the discussion in Aubin, 'Comment Tamerlan', 95–8; Roemer, 'Tīmūr in Iran', 55–7.
147. Shāmī, *ZN*, I, 265–6. Yazdī, *ZN* (1957), I, 561, and II, 255, 365–6/(2008), I, 837, and II, 1091, 1196. Their dealings are surveyed in Murphey, 'Bayezid I's foreign policy plans', 197–8.
148. See Larry V. Clark, 'The theme of revenge in the *Secret History of the Mongols*', in Clark and Draghi (eds.), *Aspects of Altaic Civilization, II*, 33–57; Roberte Hamayon, 'Mérite de l'offensé vengeur, plaisir du rival vainqueur', in Raymond Verdier (ed.), *La Vengeance. Études d'ethnologie, d'histoire et de philosophie, II. Vengeance et pouvoir dans quelques sociétés extra-occidentales* (Paris, 1980), 107–40; and Florence Hodous, 'The impact of the Mongol vengeance system on sedentary peoples', in *Old Tibet and Its Neighbours* (Wiesbaden, 2018 = *CAJ* 61), 163–80; also above, pp. 58–9.
149. Yazdī, *ZN* (1957), I, 271/(2008), I, 541.
150. Ibid. (1957), I, 239/(2008), I, 505. For the brothers' death, see ibid. (1957), I, 44/(2008), I, 274.
151. Shāmī, *ZN*, I, 147–8. Yazdī, *ZN* (1957), I, 474/(2008), I, 755.
152. Shāmī, *ZN*, I, 183.
153. Details in Aubin, 'Comment Tamerlan', 112–13; on Ṭūs and Shahr-i Sīstān, see also 116–17.

154. Yazdī, *ZN* (1957), I, 562–3/(2008), I, 838–9. See Aubin, 'Comment Tamerlan', 113–14.
155. Andreas de Redusiis de Quero, *Chronicon Tarvisinum*, col. 804.
156. al-Maqrīzī, *al-Sulūk*, III, part 3, 1046–8. Ibn Taghrībirdī, *al-Nujūm al-zāhira*, XII, 239–43 (tr. Popper, II, 46–9).
157. Shahr-i Sīstān: IA (1979), 25/(1986), 72 (*TGA*, 23). Takrīt: ibid. (1979), 69/(1986), 124 (*TGA*, 65). Awnīk: ibid. (1979), 73/(1986), 129 (*TGA*, 69). Aleppo citadel: Ibn al-Shiḥna, 212, whence IA (1979), 138/(1986), 214 (*TGA*, 127). Āmid: Astarābādī, *Bazm-u razm*, 454–5. Sivas: below.
158. See Jackson, *The Mongols and the Islamic World*, 163–4.
159. Clavijo (1859), 75/(1928), 133. John of Sulṭāniyya, *Mémoire*, ed. Moranvillé, 454; hence *Chronographia regum Francorum*, 220. Schiltberger, 20. Compare too IA (1979), 126/(1986), 193–4 (*TGA*, 116–17); more briefly, Ibn al-Shiḥna, 210; Budge, *The Chronography of Gregory Abû'l Faraj*, II, appendices, xxxii. For the investment of Sivas, see Alexandrescu-Dersca, *La Campagne de Timur*, 42–5. As to who and how many were buried, see further n. 162.
160. See Roux, *Tamerlan*, 193–5, for examples.
161. Aubin, 'Comment Tamerlan', 120. Roux, *Tamerlan*, 210.
162. 3,000: Ibn al-Shiḥna, 210–11; IA (1979), 126/(1986), 194 (*TGA*, 117); Ibn Ḥijjī, I, 451; and Ibn Ḥajar, *Inbā' al-ghumr*, ed. Ḥabashī, II, 133/ed. Muḥammad ʿAbd al-Muʿīd Khān, IV (repr. Beirut, 1406/1986), 189–90. 4,000: Shāmī, *ZN*, I, 219, and Yazdī, *ZN* (1957), II, 196/(2008), II, 1037 (both saying that the majority of the garrison were Armenians); and Tʿovma Metsobetʿsi, tr. Bedrosian, 53. 5,000: Schiltberger, 20. Clavijo (1859), 75/(1928), 133, and a garbled anonymous Syriac piece, in Budge, *The Chronography of Gregory Abû'l Faraj*, II, appendices, xxxii, mention only the city's chief men as the victims.
163. John of Sulṭāniyya, *Mémoire*, ed. Moranvillé, 454; hence *Chronographia regum Francorum*, 220.
164. Shāmī, *ZN*, I, 188. *RN* (1915), 110b/(2000), 108 (*DPT*, 111–12). Yazdī, *ZN* (1957), II, 72/(2008), II, 920. For the likely number, see Lal, *Twilight of the Sultanate*, 319–20 (appendix A).
165. Ibn Taghrībirdī, *al-Nujūm al-zāhira*, XII, 266 (tr. Popper, II, 60), citing a mamluk officer who had been a captive of Timur; he also quotes a figure of 90,000 from al-Maqrīzī (see *Durar al-ʿuqūd*, I, 531), who may have taken it from IA (1979), 183/(1986), 305 (*TGA*, 168). Naṭanzī (1957), 382/(2004), 282, supplies the impossible figure of 50 tümens (500,000).
166. For Mongol counts of the dead by these means, see Jackson, *The Mongols and the Islamic World*, 171.
167. Zirih: Yazdī, *ZN* (1957), I, 264/(2008), I, 534. Isfahan: Shāmī, *ZN*, I, 105; Yazdī, *ZN* (1957), I, 314/(2008), I, 588. Takrīt: Shāmī, *ZN*, I, 143–4. Delhi (without Timur's authorisation): Shāmī, *ZN*, I, 193; *RN* (1915), 128/(2000), 122 (*DPT*, 124); Yazdī, *ZN* (1957), II, 95/(2008), I, 940. Aleppo, Baghdad and Smyrna: IA (1979), 136, 184, 209/(1986), 209, 305, 347 (*TGA*, 125, 168, 192); for Baghdad, see also Ibn Ḥijjī, I, 503; and for Smyrna, Doukas, *Historia Turco-Byzantina* [to 1462], tr. Harry J. Magoulias, *Decline and Fall of Byzantium to the Ottoman Turks* (Detroit, MI, 1975), 98. Other examples in Aubin, 'Comment Tamerlan', 116, 119.

168. *ZT*, II, 667 (also in Shāmī, *ZN*, II, 62, cited by Aubin, 'Comment Tamerlan', 115, and by Nagel, *Timur der Eroberer*, 174). The figure of 70,000 appears in Shāmī, *ZN*, I, 105, and Yazdī, *ZN* (1957), I, 314/(2008), I, 588. For an account of this incident, see Aubin, 'Comment Tamerlan', 114–15.
169. al-Maqrīzī, *al-Sulūk*, III, part 3, 1034. Ibn Taghrībirdī, *al-Nujūm al-zāhira*, XII, 225 (Popper's trans., II, 39, renders *bārazat*[an] as 'protruding'). Aubin, 'Comment Tamerlan', 119. Vigouroux, 'Comment Tamerlan a pris Alep', nn.116–121. Nagel, *Timur der Eroberer*, 328. John of Sulṭāniyya, *Mémoire*, 456, relates this detail to the tower of heads at Baghdad. Doukas, tr. Magoulias, 98.
170. Yazdī, *ZN* (1957), I, 314/(2008), I, 588. Compare the conduct of Timur's troops at Baghdad, who, when ordered each to bring him two heads, resorted to cutting off the heads of women, Syrians etc.: IA (1979), 183/(1986), 305 (*TGA*, 168).
171. Ṭūs: *ZT*, II, 711–12 (and see HA's additions to Shāmī, *ZN*, II, 88). Herat: Yazdī, *ZN* (1957), I, 259/(2008), I, 526–7. See Roux, *Tamerlan*, 204; Manz, 'Unacceptable violence', 97.
172. HA, *Ta'rīkh-i salāṭīn-i Kart*, 179, cited from *CO*, text, 38, in Aubin, 'Comment Tamerlan', 118–19; see above, p. 181.
173. Muzaffarids: Aubin, 'Comment Tamerlan', 119, n.7, citing HA. ʿAlā' al-Dīn Khaljī: Jackson, *The Delhi Sultanate*, 230–1.
174. Manz, 'Unacceptable violence', 79–80, 96–101.
175. Shāmī, *ZN*, I, 192. *RN* (1915), 126/(2000), 121 (*DPT*, 123). Yazdī, *ZN* (1957), II, 93/(2008), I, 938.
176. Yazdī, *ZN* (1957), II, 245, *bī qaṣd-u ikhtiyār-i kasī*, 246/(2008), II, 1083, 1084. More detail at pp. 379–80.
177. Shāmī, *ZN*, I, 235–7.
178. Ibn al-Shiḥna, 225–7. Compare also IA (1979), 142–3/(1986), 219 (*TGA*, 131).
179. This seems to be implied in *ZT*, II, 712 (also in HA's additions to Shāmī, *ZN*, II, 88).
180. *CO*, text, 10; for Abū Bakr, see above, p. 334. On Isfizār and other atrocities, see Aubin, 'Comment Tamerlan', 83; more generally, Manz, 'Tamerlane and the symbolism', 118–19, and 'Unacceptable violence', 97–8.
181. Doukas, tr. Magoulias, 89–90. Alexandrescu-Dersca, *La Campagne de Timur*, 45.
182. Shāmī, *ZN*, I, 91; ibid., I, 219, he uses the same term in relation to Sivas. Compare also Yazdī, *ZN* (1957), I, 263, and II, 196/(2008), I, 533, and II, 1037.
183. Jackson, *The Mongols and the Islamic World*, 158 (Bāmiyān and Nishapur), 264–5 (Mosul).
184. See the remarks of Barthold, *Four Studies*, II, 39–40 (= Bartol'd, 'Ulugbek', in his *Sochineniia*, II, part 2, 60); also Morgan, *The Mongols*, 81, 176, and *Medieval Persia*, 86; and Roemer, 'Tīmūr in Iran', 55.
185. Aubin, 'Comment Tamerlan', 121, 122, respectively, for these quotations.
186. On which see Jackson, *The Mongols and the Islamic World*, 176–80.
187. Yazdī, *ZN* (1957), II, 451/(2008), II, 1278.
188. Ibid. (1957), I, 324/(2008), I, 601.
189. Ibid. (1957), II, 31/(2008), I, 877.

190. HA, *Jughrāfiyya*, partial edn and trans. by Dorothea Krawulsky, *Ḫorāsān zur Timuridenzeit nach dem Tārīḫ-e Ḥāfeẓ-e Abrū (verf. 817–823h.) des Nūrallāh 'Abdallāh b. Luṭfallāh al-Ḫvāfī genannt Ḥāfeẓ-e Abrū*, 2 vols (Wiesbaden, 1982–4), I (text), 32, II (trans.), 30–1; partial edn by Ghulām-riḍā Warhrām, *Jughrāfiyya-yi ta'rīkhī-yi Khurāsān* (Tehran, 1370 sh./1991), 22.
191. Yazdī, *ZN* (1957), II, 385/(2008), II, 1218. On Timur's concern to extend agriculture and repopulate devastated regions, see Ismail Aka, 'The agricultural and commercial activities of the Timurids in the first half of the 15th century', in Bernardini (ed.), *La civiltà Timuride*, I, 9–21 (here 10–12); more briefly, Papas and Toutant, *l'Asie centrale de Tamerlan*, 114, 122–4.
192. Aubin, 'Comment Tamerlan', 94. See also Papas and Toutant, *L'Asie centrale de Tamerlan*, 118.
193. Sīstānī, *Iḥyā' al-mulūk*, 106. Bosworth, *The History of the Saffarids*, 452.
194. Yazdī, *ZN* (1957), I, 473/(2008), I, 754.
195. Shāmī, *ZN*, I, 289, 291. Yazdī, *ZN* (1957), II, 384–7/(2008), II, 1218–20.
196. Clavijo (1859), 186; and compare (1928), 312.
197. Yazdī, *ZN* (1957), II, 407/(2008), II, 1240.
198. Ibid. (1957), II, 368–9, 393/(2008), II, 1199, 1225. More briefly, Shāmī, *ZN*, I, 278, 290. For these and other examples, see Aubin, 'Comment Tamerlan', 92–3.

12: THE *QARACHU* WARLORD AND THE IMPERIAL CHINGGISIDS

1. Woods, 'Timur's genealogy', 99–109, is the fundamental starting point for any discussion. A slightly earlier draft of part of this chapter appeared as 'Tamerlane and the Chinggisids', in Dunlop (ed.), *The Mongol Empire in Global History and Art History*, 73–96.
2. *TR*, I (text), 40, II (trans.), 35.
3. Naṭanzī (1957), 206/(2004), 168: my rendering differs slightly from that in Woods, 'Timur's genealogy', 101. Compare also *ZT*, I, 319–20, and HA's additions in Shāmī, *ZN*, II, 12–13.
4. Astarābādī, *Bazm-u razm*, 460.
5. They appear in *MA*, fos 43b–44a, ed. Vokhidov, text, 88–9 (Russian trans., 60). Binbaş, 'The Timurids and the Mongol empire', 938 and n.13 at 947, draws attention to a coin minted in Samarkand in 1398 that names as khan 'Sulṭān Aḥmad b. Jalāl al-Dīn Soyurghatmish', who is mentioned in no other source. I suspect that the inscription is erroneous and should read 'Sulṭān Maḥmūd'.
6. Shāmī, *ZN*, I, 58. *ZT*, I, 441–2 (also in HA's additions to Shāmī, *ZN*, II, 27).
7. See Jackson, *The Mongols and the Islamic World*, 98–9.
8. Manz, 'Tamerlane and the symbolism', 112, and 'Temür and the problem', 23, 25. Morgan, 'The empire of Tamerlane', 236–7. In the view of Soucek, *A History of Inner Asia*, 125, the choice of Ögödeyids was symptomatic of 'the purely formal value' of the expedient; but other interpretations are possible.
9. Binbaş, 'The Timurids and the Mongol empire', 938: he argues that the two khans were therefore not 'puppet khans' but 'pillars of the constitutional organization of Timur's empire'.
10. *TJG*, III, 38, 69–70 (*HWC*, 573, 595).
11. Though Soyurghatmish was not descended from Qaidu. There may have been few or no surviving descendants of Qaidu in S.W. Asia, to judge at least from the absence of later generations of his line from the tables in *MA*, fos 44b–45a,

ed. Vokhidov, 90–1 (Russian trans., 60–1). Several of his progeny, headed by Chapar, had taken refuge with the Yuan in the early fourteenth century.

12. Bernardini, 'The Mongol puppet lords', 174–5. Compare also Haase, 'Von der "Pax Mongolica" zum Timuridenreich', 160.
13. As Manz, 'Temür and the problem', 23, points out. For the date of Ilyās Khwāja's death, see p. 128 and p. 525n. 123.
14. So Manz, 'Tamerlane and the symbolism', 112–13.
15. *ZT*, I, 184, 210; see also HA's additions in Shāmī, *ZN*, II, 7.
16. Schamiloglu, 'Beautés du mélange', 197.
17. Yazdī, *ZN* (1957), I, 73–4/(2008), I, 307, *az wahm-i āsīb-i taghallubāt-i rūzgār*. For Dorji's murder, see ibid. (1972), fo. 81a/(2008), I, 217.
18. Naṭanzī (1957), 199/(2004), 163–4.
19. Yazdī, *ZN* (1957), I, 25, 26/(2008), I, 253, 254. HA, *Ta'rīkh-i salāṭīn-i Kart*, 182 (also in *CO*, text, 41).
20. Yazdī, *ZN* (1957), I, 30/(2008), I, 259.
21. Bernardini, 'The Mongol puppet lords', 171.
22. Yazdī, *ZN* (1957), I, 120, 123, 124/(2008), I, 361, 363, 365.
23. Naṭanzī (1957), 129, 260/(2004), 104–5, 204–5. Bernardini, 'The Mongol puppet lords', 173. The chronology is markedly confused. The date 765 for Kābul Shāh's enthronement is given by Yazdī, *ZN* (1957), I, 73–4/(2008), I, 307; Naṭanzī (1957), 221/(2004), 178, supplies mid-Rajab 761/the beginning of June 1360, which is probably too early. In addition, the narrative sources make ʿĀdil Sulṭān Kābul Shāh's successor, whereas the numismatic evidence clearly indicates the reverse or even that they ruled concurrently, with ʿĀdil Sulṭān's coins struck in 767/1365–6 and those of Kābul Shāh ranging from that date to 769/1367–8: Petrov, 'Khronologiia', 317.
24. Shāmī, *ZN*, I, 55. Yazdī, *ZN* (1957), I, 138, 142/(2008), I, 380, 385. Naṭanzī (1957), 260/(2004), 206.
25. Yazdī, *ZN* (1957), I, 151/(2008), I, 396. Roux, *Tamerlan*, 70, is in error here; he assumes that Ḥusayn's khan was still Kābul Shāh, whom he further describes as 'tout dévoué à feu l'émir Husaïn'.
26. Shāmī, *ZN*, I, 60. Yazdī, *ZN* (1957), I, 154/(2008), I, 399. Although neither author names the slain khan here, Naṭanzī (1957), 114, 129/(2004), 93, 104–5, makes it clear that it was ʿĀdil Sulṭān.
27. IA (1979), 16, *fī asrihi ka l-ḥimār fī l-ṭīn*/(1986), 57 (cf. *TGA*, 13, 'like a centipede in mud'). Ibn Ḥijjī, II, 587; hence Ibn Ḥajar, *Inbā' al-ghumr*, ed. Ḥabashī, II, 254/ed. Khān, V, 125, and Ibn Qāḍī Shuhba, *Ta'rīkh*, IV, 336.
28. John of Sulṭāniyya, *Mémoire*, ed. Moranvillé, 445.
29. *TR*, I (text), 45, II (trans.), 39 (Ḥaydar is likewise in error in asserting here that Soyurghatmish died in Iraq); compare ibid., I (text), 52, II (trans.), 44, for the quotation from Abū Saʿīd.
30. *Chronographia regum Francorum*, III, 209–10.
31. Shāmī, *ZN*, I, 38 (twice). See also *ZT*, I, 398, 399, where he is described as one of the commanders (*sardārān*) and as a great amir.
32. Shāmī, *ZN*, I, 57. Naṭanzī (1957), 272, 282/(2004), 213, 219. Compare also Yazdī, *ZN* (1957), I, 98, 100, 144/(2008), I, 334, 337, 390.
33. Shāmī, *ZN*, I, 67. Naṭanzī (1957), 315/(2004), 242. Yazdī, *ZN* (1957), I, 251/(2008), I, 518. HA's additions in Shāmī, *ZN*, II, 33. Bernardini, 'The Mongol puppet lords', 173.

34. Naṭanzī (1957), 340/(2004), 256; ibid. (1957), 129/(2004), 105, he dates this in 786 [1384–5]. *ZT*, II, 681 (and see HA's additions to Shāmī, *ZN*, II, 69). Shāmī, *ZN*, I, 110–11, and Yazdī, *ZN* (1957), I, 330/(2008), I, 608, do not say explicitly that the khan had been left behind, but place his death during Timur's absence in Khwārazm.
35. *RN* (1915), 53b/(2000), 65 (*DPT*, 68).
36. Yazdī, *ZN* (1957), I, 345/(2008), I, 625; and compare also ibid. (1957), I, 366, 381–2/(2008), I, 646, 661, and Shāmī, *ZN*, I, 123. For Tu. *bashlamishi*, see *TMEN*, II, 247–8 (no. 700).
37. Against Toqtamish: Naṭanzī (1957), 348/(2004), 261; Shāmī, *ZN*, I, 123, 161; Yazdī, *ZN* (1957), I, 366/(2008), I, 646. Baṣra: Ibn al-Furāt, IX, part 2, 348; al-ʿAynī, *'Iqd al-jumān*, ed. Shukrī, *al-Sulṭān Barqūq*, 368 (incorrectly stating that the prince, whom he calls here Timur's son, was captured and the khan killed, though at 440, *ad annum* 800, the khan is mentioned as still the nominal sovereign). India: *RN* (1915), 99/(2000), 99–100 (*DPT*, 102); Shāmī, *ZN*, I, 185, 186; Yazdī, *ZN* (1957), II, 34, 65–6/(2008), I, 881, 913–14. Syria and Baghdad: Ibn Ḥijjī, II, 587; Ibn Qāḍī Shuhba, *Ta'rīkh*, IV, 336; Yazdī, *ZN* (1957), II, 213, 232, 257, 266/(2008), II, 1053, 1071, 1093–4, 1103.
38. Yazdī, *ZN* (1957), II, 314/(2008), II, 1147. Iakubovskii, 'Timur', 71. Alexandrescu-Dersca, *La Campagne de Timur*, 79; to the sources listed there, add Naṭanzī (1957), 115/(2004), 93. Clavijo (1859), 164/(1928), 275, however, gives the credit for Bayezid's capture to Timur's grandson and heir-apparent, Muḥammad Sulṭān. Shāmī, *ZN*, I, 258, says simply that Bayezid was captured by Timur's troops. Sulṭān Maḥmūd's military activity is noticed by Bernardini, 'The Mongol puppet lords', 174.
39. Shāmī, *ZN*, I, 111.
40. *ZT*, II, 681.
41. Naṭanzī (1957), 129–30/(2004), 105. Woods, 'Timur's genealogy', 105–6, linked the delay with inhibitions about attacking the legitimate Chinggisid Toqtamish. The number of years is surely exaggerated; and see next note.
42. A.O. Bragin, P.N. Petrov and A.M. Kamyshev, 'Klad serebrianykh monet nachala XV v. iz Kashgar-Kyshtaka Kyrgyzstane', *NZO* 4 (2014), 107–13. *ZT*, II, 682, says expressly that Sulṭān Maḥmūd was enthroned in the latter part of 790. I am assuming here that the date supplied by Shāmī for Soyurghatmish's death is correct and that 786 [1384–5], as given by Naṭanzī, is wrong.
43. Naṭanzī (1957), 114/(2004), 93, *tarbiyat farmūd*. *Ta'rīf* (1951), 364, *kafalahū*, 382, *kafala ṣāḥib al-takht*/(2008), 237, 255 (the second of these references tr. in *IKT*, 46); hence, presumably, al-Maqrīzī, *Durar al-'uqūd*, I, 498.
44. *Ta'rīf* (1951), 373/(2008), 245 (*IKT*, 37).
45. The year given by Naṭanzī (1957), 130/(2004), 105, and by Ibn Ḥijjī, II, 587, followed by Ibn Ḥajar, *Inbā' al-ghumr*, ed. Ḥabashī, II, 254/ed. Khān, V, 125, Ibn Qāḍī Shuhba, *Ta'rīkh*, IV, 336, and Ibn Taghrībirdī, *al-Nujūm al-zāhira*, XIII, 32 (tr. Popper, II, 114–15). Yazdī, *ZN* (1957), II, 332/(2008), II, 1165, appears to place the event between the beginning of Rabīʿ I/end of Sept. and Timur's attack on Smyrna early in Jumādā I/Dec. 1402. News of the khan's demise (along with that of Bayezid, it seems) was brought to Damascus in late Dhū l-Qaʿda 805/mid-June 1403 by Timur's ambassador as he returned from the Egyptian Sultan's court: Ibn Ḥijjī, II, 586. *Shajarat al-atrāk*, fo. 116b, mistakenly has Sulṭān Maḥmūd reigning until after Timur's death.

46. Yazdī, *ZN* (1957), II, 332/(2008), II, 1165. Iakubovskii, 'Timur', 71, commented on the good relations between the two men.
47. *Ta'rīf* (1951), 372–3/(2008), 245 (*IKT*, 37).
48. *RN* (1915), 53b/(2000), 65 (*DPT*, 68). Compare also Timur to Bayezid for other, still more far-sought and grandiloquent titles: Sarī ʿAbd-Allāh Efendi, *Munsha'āt*, in Zeki Velidi Togan, 'Timur's Osteuropapolitik', *ZDMG* 108 n.F., 33 (1958), 279–98 (here 296); these lines are translated in Woods, 'Timur's genealogy', 106.
49. As Naṭanzī (1957), 130/(2004), 105, expressly says.
50. Shāmī, *ZN*, I, 111.
51. See Herrmann, 'Zur Intitulatio timuridischer Urkunden', 504–5; also the evidence collected in Woods, 'Turco-Iranica II', 332–3.
52. Ibn Ḥijjī, II, 587; and compare Ibn Qāḍī Shuhba, *Ta'rīkh*, IV, 336.
53. Ibn al-Furāt, *Ta'rīkh al-duwal wa l-mulūk*, IX, part 1, ed. Costi K. Zurayk (Beirut, 1936), 7, 9, 12 and passim. Bernardini, *Mémoire et propagande*, 52, and 'The Mongol puppet lords', 173.
54. Ibn al-Furāt, IX, part 2, 343, 348 (with a false report of Sulṭān Maḥmūd's death).
55. Shāmī, *ZN*, I, 118.
56. Cited by Woods, 'Timur's genealogy', 105.
57. Shāmī, *ZN*, I, 97. Goto, 'Tīmūr and local dynasties', 74.
58. Aubin, 'Comment Tamerlan', 99.
59. IA (1979), 94, 129, 207–8/(1986), 152, 197–8, 343 (*TGA*, 88–9, 119, 190). Ibn Taghrībirdī, *al-Nujūm al-zāhira*, XII, 269 (tr. Popper, II, 62), mentions that the Qaramanid amir received similar instructions. For coins of Tahartan at Arzinjān that name Sulṭān Maḥmūd, see İlker Evrim Binbaş, 'Did the Hurufis mint coins? Articulation of sacral kingship in an Aqquyunlu coin hoard from Erzincan', in Peacock and Yıldız (eds), *Islamic Literature and Intellectual Life*, 137–70 (here 148, n.48).
60. *RN* (1915), 124/(2000), 119 (*DPT*, 121); more explicitly in Shāmī, *ZN*, I, 192, as cited in Woods, 'The rise of Tīmūrid historiography', 104, and 'Turco-Iranica II', 333.
61. al-Maqrīzī, *al-Sulūk*, III, part 3, 1048, and Ibn Taghrībirdī, *al-Nujūm al-zāhira*, XII, 242 (tr. Popper, II, 48), omit the recital of Timur's own name and call the heir-apparent his son in error. Heidemann, 'Tīmūr's campmint', 194, 199–200.
62. Herrmann, 'Zur Intitulatio timuridischer Urkunden', 505, 508.
63. Shāmī, *ZN*, I, 274.
64. Ibn Ḥijjī, II, 587; hence Ibn Ḥajar, *Inbā' al-ghumr*, ed. Ḥabashī, II, 254/ed. Khān, V, 125, Ibn Qāḍī Shuhba, *Ta'rīkh*, IV, 336, and Ibn Taghrībirdī, *al-Nujūm al-zāhira*, XIII, 32 (tr. Popper, II, 114–15).
65. Naṭanzī (1957), 130/(2004), 105. Abū Saʿīd appears in *MA*, fo. 44a, ed. Vokhidov, text, 89 (Russian trans., 60).
66. Naṭanzī (1957), 125/(2004), 102.
67. See the discussion in Herrmann, 'Zur Intitulatio timuridischer Urkunden', 509–10.
68. Naṭanzī (1957), 130/(2004), 105.
69. Davidovich, *Klady*, 267; Linda Komaroff, 'The epigraphy of Timurid coinage: Some preliminary remarks', *ANSMN* 31 (1986), 207–32 (here 211, n.9).

70. Woods, 'Timur's genealogy', n.75 at 121. Herrmann, 'Zur Intitulatio timuridischer Urkunden', 510, cites a document reproduced in HA's continuation of Shāmī's *ZN*. But it was no longer fashionable to mention the nominal khan by the time HA wrote (see later); and since we lack the original text of the document, we cannot know whether he 'doctored' it.
71. For Woods, 'Timur's genealogy', 114, the action of Timur's grandson Khalīl Sulṭān in enthroning a khan in 807/1405 (see later) supports the assumption that Timur had ruled independently during the previous three years. Roux, *Tamerlan*, 174, assumes that Timur did not replace Sulṭān Maḥmūd because he no longer judged it advantageous to 'hide behind the [khan's] shadow'.
72. *ZT*, III, 12. Komaroff, 'The epigraphy of Timurid coinage', 216 and n.21. Manz, *Power, Politics and Religion*, 20. For Muḥammad Jahāngīr's birth in the winter of 799/1396–7, see Yazdī, *ZN* (1957), I, 570/(2008), I, 847.
73. *ZT*, III, 44. Binbaş, *Intellectual Networks*, 252. R.Iu. Pochekaev, 'Pravovoe nasledie mongol'skoi imperii v gosudarstve Timuridov (po dannym letopisei, numizmaticheskogo i aktogo materiala)', in V.P. Nikonorov (ed.), *Tsentral'naia Aziia ot Akhemenidov do Timuridov. Arkheologiia, istoriia, étnologia, kul'tura. Materialy mezhdunarodnoi nauchnoi konferentsii, posviashchennoi 100-letiiu so dnia rozhdeniia Aleksandra Markovicha Belenitskogo, Sankt-Peterburg, 2–5 noiabria 2004 goda* (St Petersburg, 2005), 291–4 (here 291).
74. Manz, *Power, Politics and Religion*, 25.
75. Ibid., 10; also Manz, 'Mongol history rewritten', 143, and 'Temür and the early Timurids', 196. Sheila S. Blair, 'Timurid signs of sovereignty', in Bernardini (ed.), *La civiltà Timuride come fenomeno internazionale*, II, 551–76 (here 559). Denise Aigle, 'Epilogue: The Mongol empire after Genghis Khan', in her *The Mongol Empire between Myth and Reality*, 306–22 (here 312).
76. Komaroff, 'The epigraphy of Timurid coinage', 217–18. Binbaş, *Intellectual Networks*, 260. For the concept of *khilāfat*, see above, pp. 103–4.
77. *TR*, I (text), 52, II (trans.), 44. The claim is made through the mouth of the Timurid sovereign Abū Saʿīd (d. 873/1469).
78. See, for example, Komaroff, 'The epigraphy of Timurid coinage', 216–21. Manz, 'Temür and the early Temürids', 194, is rightly sceptical about the retention of Chinggisid khans.
79. But see Beatrice F. Manz, 'Ulugh Beg, Transoxiana and Turco-Mongolian tradition', in Markus Ritter, Ralph Kauz and Birgitt Hoffmann (eds), *Iran und iranisch geprägte Kulturen. Studien zum 65. Geburtstag von Bert G. Fragner* (Wiesbaden, 2008), 20–7.
80. *TR*, I (text), 45–6, II (trans.), 39. See Woods, 'Timur's genealogy', 116; Beatrice F. Manz, 'Ulugh Beg', *EI*², X, 813; Manz, 'Ulugh Beg, Transoxiana and Turco-Mongolian tradition', 21; and her 'Temür and the early Timurids', 194. The date was offered by Barthold, *Four Studies*, II, 86, 104 (= Bartol'd, *Sochineniia*, II, part 2, 98, 113), who accepted Ḥaydar's testimony.
81. He appears as Sātuq in *MA*, fo. 33b, ed. Vokhidov, text, 68 (Russian trans., 51), and under the form STQ in *TGNN*, text, 190 (fo. 82b). He is possibly identical with a fugitive Chaghadayid prince, called Sāriq Oghlan in *ZT*, IV, 747–8, 877–8, who in Rajab 823/July 1420 had arrived in Samarkand with Shīr Muḥammad, another of Ways Khan's rivals (see next note), and had been detained there.

82. For Shīr Muḥammad's departure and his elevation as khan in Jata, see *ZT*, IV, 748, 878.
83. *TR*, I (text), 51–2, 127, II (trans.), 44, 102.
84. Barthold, *Four Studies*, II, 86, 138 (= Bartol'd, *Sochineniia*, II, part 2, 99, 158). Manz, *Power, Politics and Religion*, 266.
85. Khwānd-Amīr, *Ḥabīb al-siyar*, III, 33 (tr. Thackston, 360).
86. For example, Salmānī, *Shams al-ḥusn*, text, fos 7b, 31a–b, 33b, 34b (abridged German trans., 17, 26, 28). Yazdī, *ZN* (1972), fo. 83a, and (1957), I, 573/(2008), I, 224, 849.
87. *MA*, fo. 2a–b, ed. Vokhidov, text, 3–4 (Russian trans., 18, 20). Woods, *The Timurid Dynasty*, 3.
88. Woods, 'The rise of Tīmūrid historiography', 104–5. Manz, 'Tamerlane's career and its uses', 7.
89. Yazdī, *ZN* (1957), I, 155–9/(2008), I, 400–5. Compare the treatment in Shāmī, *ZN*, I, 58, 61.
90. Yazdī, *ZN* (1957), I, 285/(2008), I, 557.
91. Ibid. (1957), II, 92, 239/(2008), I, 936–7, and II, 1077, respectively.
92. Ibid. (1957), II, 356/(2008), II, 1187.
93. Ibid. (1957), I, 366/(2008), I, 646–7.
94. Ibid. (1957), I, 458/(2008), I, 737–8; there is a translation in Wing, *The Jalayirids*, 162. Compare the text given in Shāmī, *ZN*, I, 221. This is the letter quoted later (and see n. 117).
95. Yazdī, *ZN* (1957), I, 149, 330, and II, 332/(2008), I, 394, 608, and II, 1165.
96. Both princes: Naṭanzī (1957), 159/(2004), 128–9. Luqmān: Yazdī, *ZN* (1957), I, 282, 285/(2008), I, 553, 557. Pīr Pādishāh: Shāmī, *ZN*, I, 127; Yazdī, *ZN* (1957), I, 409/(2008), I, 687–8.
97. Yazdī, *ZN* (1957), I, 538/(2008), I, 813.
98. Clavijo (1859), 177/(1928), 299–300; for the son, see (1859), 133/(1928), 221. Timur was hosting an embassy from Toqtamish early in Sept. 1404: ibid. (1859), 130/(1928), 217.
99. Yazdī, *ZN* (1957), II, 459/(2008), II, 1285–6.
100. Shāmī, *ZN*, I, 107, 113, 124–5. Yazdī, *ZN* (1957), I, 333, 335, 357, 392, 394/(2008), I, 612, 614, 639, 671, 672. I have adopted the spelling suggested by the forms in Naṭanzī (1957), 342 (KLAJH), 364 (KNAČH)/(2004), 257, 271, of which the latter passed into *ZT*, II, 676 (where it is vocalized KUNAJH; cf. HA's additions to Shāmī, *ZN*, II, 70). Kunacha was fifth in descent from Toqa Temür and was the uncle of Temür Qutlugh and of another future khan, Shadibeg: *MA*, fo. 27b, ed. Vokhidov, text, 56 (Russian trans., 46); *TGNN*, fo. 73b (tr. in Ibragimov, *Materialy*, 40). But Yazdī, *ZN* (1957), I, 357/(2008), I, 639, makes Temür Qutlugh the son of Temür Malik Khan (i.e. a grandson of Orus) and hence from a different branch of the Toqatemürid line.
101. Pochekaev, *Tsari ordynskie*, 218.
102. Shāmī, *ZN*, I, 125, 159. Yazdī, *ZN* (1957), I, 394, 398/(2008), I, 672, 676. Elsewhere, however, Kunacha is listed among Toqtamish's commanders in the battle on the Terek in 797/1395: ibid. (1957), I, 533, 534/(2008), I, 808, 810. This may be an error.
103. Shāmī, *ZN*, I, 115, 139–40, 142, 152, 156, 172, 174. Naṭanzī (1957), 356, 362, 367, 431/(2004), 266, 269, 273, 314. Yazdī, *ZN* (1957), I, 342, 452–5, 459, 462, 487, 500, and II, 23, 26–8, 30, 34, 166/(2008), I, 622, 730–4, 739, 742, 768,

780, 869, 873–4, 876, 880–1, and II, 1010. For Ibaj as a son of Ordu Melik, see *TGNN*, text, 174 (fo. 75b; tr. in Ibragimov, *Materialy*, 43, with Имадж in error), and as a grandson, *MA*, fo. 27a, ed. Vokhidov, text, 55 (Russian trans., 44). Burhān Oghlan's relationship to other Jochids is not made clear.

104. Bash Temür: Yazdī, *ZN* (1957), II, 304, 423, 459/(2008), II, 1139, 1257, 1285; *ZT*, II, 960. On him, see *MA*, fo. 27b, ed. Vokhidov, text, 56 (Russian trans., 45); Reva, 'Saiid-Akhmad I i Giias ad-Din I', table at 55; for the descent of the Crimean khans, see ibid., and Frank, 'The western steppe', 256. The other prince, whose name is spelled YARQ, ibid. (1957), II, 137/(2008), I, 981, is probably the Toqatimurid (a cousin of Toqtamish's father) who appears as YARWQ in *MA*, fo. 25b, ed. Vokhidov, text, 52 (omitted in the Russian trans.).
105. There is some confusion here. *RN* (1915), 57/(2000), 68 (*DPT*, 71), Shāmī, *ZN*, I, 172, and HA's additions ibid., II, 138 (also in *ZT*, II, 830), call Tāīzī Oghlan an 'envoy from Khiṭā'. But the more detailed account in Yazdī, *ZN* (1957), II, 33/(2008), I, 879, makes it clear that he was a refugee prince who had rebelled against the Qaghan. For his recent attendance on Timur, see ibid. (1957), II, 423, 459/(2008), II, 1257, 1285.
106. Shāmī, *ZN*, I, 13. For the identification of Öljei Temür with Bunyashiri[n], see Louis Hambis, *Documents sur l'histoire des Mongols à l'époque des Ming*, Bibliothèque de l'Institut des Hautes Études Chinoises 21 (Paris, 1969), xxv; Honda, 'On the genealogy of the early Northern Yüan', 239.
107. Yazdī, *ZN* (1972), fo. 65b/(2008), I, 179: for the sense of the phrase *ūrā shūnqār kardand* used here by Yazdī, see *TMEN*, I, 360, and III, 275.
108. Bunyashiri[n]: Hambis, *Documents sur l'histoire des Mongols*, 20–2 (at 21, Öljei Temür is given as the name of one of Bunyashiri[n]'s Mongol officers). Tāīzī as an Ögödeyid: Yazdī, *ZN* (1957), II, 459/(2008), II, 1285. Khwānd-Amīr, *Ḥabīb al-siyar*, III, 74 (tr. Thackston, 41), cites Yazdī regarding Tāīzī and appears to identify him with Öljei Temür (whose name Thackston transcribes as 'Elchi-Temür'). Hookham, *Tamburlaine*, 269, distinguished the two men. Others see them as identical: Honda, 'On the genealogy of the early Northern Yüan', 243–4; Shiro Ando, 'Zum timuridischen Staatswesen: Eine Interpretation des Miniaturentwurfs in Diez A. Fol. 74', in Rudolf Veselý and Eduard Gombár (eds), *Ẓafar Nāme. Memorial Volume of Felix Tauer* (Prague, 1996), 17–33 (here 18–19); and Manz (see next note).
109. Manz, 'Ulugh Beg, Transoxiana and Turco-Mongolian tradition', 23 and n.20, and 'Temür and the early Timurids', 187, n.14 (on both occasions calling Öljei Temür 'Öljeitü').
110. Shāmī, *ZN*, I, 13.
111. Kauz, *Politik und Handel*, 76. Manz, 'The empire of Tamerlane as an adaptation', 287.
112. Nagel, *Timur der Eroberer*, 411. Barthold, too, was doubtful: *Four Studies*, II, 50–1 (= Bartol'd, *Sochineniia*, II, part 2, 69).
113. Honda, 'On the genealogy of the early Northern Yüan', 243. Veit, 'The eastern steppe', 162. Rossabi, 'The Ming and Inner Asia', 227–30. Robinson, *In the Shadow of the Mongol Empire*, 263–4. The stay in Beshbaligh is clear from a letter written to him there by the Ming Emperor Yongle in 1408 and preserved in the *Mingshi*: see Robinson, *Ming China and Its Allies*, 30–2, 36–7.
114. Yazdī, *ZN* (1957), II, 459/(2008), II, 1285. A nephew of the fourteenth-century khan ʿAbdal (ʿAbd-Allāh), Chekire is omitted from *MA*, appearing

only in *TGNN*, fo. 74a (tr. in Ibragimov, *Materialy*, 41). For a sketch of his career, see Khakimov et al. (eds), *The Golden Horde in World History*, 708; also p. 434 and p. 641n. 84.

115. For what follows, see Ando, 'Zum timuridischen Staatswesen', 17–22; and for his dating, 27. On the variant forms of Chekire's name, see Ando, 'Die timuridische Historiographie II', 225.
116. For Yādgār and Ajashirin, see respectively *MA*, fos 28a, 37b, ed. Vokhidov, text, 57, 76 (Russian trans., 46, where Yādgār is made a son of Alghui in error, and 54, where Ajashirin's name appears as Абāшӣрӣн). Ajashirin is not to be confused with another Mongol prince of that name (a descendant of Chinggis Khan's brother Temüge Otchigin) active in the Ming empire in 1388–9.
117. Timur to Barqūq, cited in Shāmī, *ZN*, I, 221. Reproducing this letter, Yazdī, *ZN* (1957), I, 458/(2008), I, 737–8, omits any mention of Chinggis Khan's descendant: see earlier and n. 94.
118. Astarābādī, *Bazm-u razm*, 460.
119. Timur to Bayezid, in Sarī ʿAbd-Allāh Efendi, *Munsha'āt*: Togan, 'Timur's Osteuropapolitik', 295–6; also quoted in translation by Woods, 'Timur's genealogy', 106.
120. Timur to Barqūq, in Nawā'ī (ed.), *Asnād*, 76, 77. The former passage is translated in Woods, 'Timur's genealogy', 107, where the letter is dated to the mid-1390s; for this version, see Broadbridge, *Kingship and Ideology*, 178–9 and n.53.
121. Nawā'ī (ed.), *Asnād*, 76–7. For the sporadic diplomatic contact between the Chaghadayids and the Mamlūk empire, see Biran, 'Diplomatic and chancellery practices', 376–7, and her comment in 'The Mamluks and Mongol Central Asia', 371 and n.19.
122. Yazdī, *ZN* (1972), fo. 75a/(2008), I, 200.
123. Ibid. (1957), I, 285/(2008), I, 557.
124. Herrmann, 'Zur Intitulatio timuridischer Urkunden', 504, 508–9. In view of Sulṭān Maḥmūd's evident sovereignty in Timur's Iranian conquests, the statement by Manz, 'Mongol history rewritten', 141, that Timur's nominees included 'a pretender to the Ilkhanid throne' (signifying Luqmān), is misleading.
125. Timur to Bayezid, in Sarī ʿAbd-Allāh Efendi, *Munsha'āt*: Togan, 'Timur's Osteuropapolitik', 296; partly quoted in translation by Woods, 'Timur's genealogy', 106. The conquered territories are listed as 'the Māzandarānāt, the Gīlānāt, Kurdistan, Lūristān, Shūlistān, Khūzistān, Fārs, the two Iraqs, Hurmuz, Kirmān, Kīch and Makrān, Diyār Bakr and Azerbaijan'.
126. Compare the different formulation by Manz, *Nomads in the Middle East*, 149: 'With three Chinggisid khans as protégés, Temür aimed at a symbolic restoration of the Mongol Empire, with himself at its center.'
127. Khan: Yazdī, *ZN* (1957), II, 9/(2008), I, 855, but styling him merely 'Oghlan' immediately below. Lesser titles: ibid. (1957), I, 344, 345, 346 (but cf. the verse ibid., where he is called the khan of Jata), and II, 158/(2008), I, 624, 625, 626, and II, 1002. Khiḍr Khwāja's governorship was seemingly on behalf of Timur rather than of the conqueror's nominal sovereign (whose existence Yazdī frequently ignores, as we have seen).
128. Shāmī, *ZN*, I, 13. Yazdī, *ZN* (1972), fo. 65b/(2008), I, 178–9.
129. IA (1979), 328/(1986), 463 (*TGA*, 307).

130. Timur to Bayezid, in Sarī ʿAbd-Allāh Efendi, *Munsha'āt*: Togan, 'Timur's Osteuropapolitik', 296. Shāmī, *ZN*, I, 118, 171, 274; simply *Pādishāh* at I, 123, 223. See also later and n. 134.
131. *RN* (1915), 53b–54b/(2000), 65–6 (*DPT*, 68–9).
132. Shāmī, *ZN*, I, 186, and *RN* (1915), 124/(2000), 119 (*DPT*, 121).
133. Shāmī, *ZN*, I, 171.
134. Ibid., I, 10; and see also I, 12, where they are again said to have been promoted to sovereignty (*salṭanat*) over Iran and Turan. There is a translation of the first passage in Lewis, *Islam*, I, 103.
135. Timur to Barqūq, in Nawā'ī (ed.), *Asnād*, 76; cited in translation by Woods, 'Timur's genealogy', 107.
136. Yazdī, *ZN* (1957), I, 11–12/(2008), I, 238; passage translated in Bernardini, *Mémoire et propagande*, 64–5. For Ghazan, cf. *JT*, II, 1210 (*DzhT*, III, 251–2; *CC*, 417).
137. Qarā Yūsuf to Bayezid, in Nawā'ī (ed.), *Asnād*, 87.
138. Timur to Bayezid, ibid., 99, cited by Woods, 'Timur's genealogy', 100; see further ibid., 109, for an interpretation.
139. Barqūq to Timur: IA (1979), 98/(1986), 157 (*TGA*, 92). For the sources that preserve this letter, see William M. Brinner, 'Some Ayyūbid and Mamlūk documents from non-archival sources', *Israel Oriental Studies* 2 (1972), 117–43 (here 123–4). The phrase *al-ḥaḍrat al-īlkhāniyya* is absent from the version given in al-Maqrīzī, *al-Sulūk*, III, part 2, 805, and *al-īlkhāniyya* appears as *al-khāniyya* in the corresponding section of Ibn Taghrībirdī, *al-Nujūm al-zāhira*, XII, 51 (cf. Popper trans., I, 142 and n.18). But see Muḥammad b. Muḥammad Ibn Ṣaṣrā, *al-Durrat al-muḍī'a fī l-dawlat al-Ẓ āhiriyya*, ed. and tr. William M. Brinner, *A Chronicle of Damascus 1389–1397 by Muḥammad ibn Muḥammad ibn Ṣaṣrā*, 2 vols (Berkeley and Los Angeles, 1963), I (trans.), 198, II (Ar. text), 147, and the apparatus in Brinner, 'Some Ayyūbid and Mamlūk documents', 136, n.4; also Broadbridge, *Kingship and Ideology*, 181.
140. Denise Aigle, 'Hülegü's letters to the last Ayyubid ruler of Syria: The construction of a model', in Aigle, *The Mongol Empire between Myth and Reality*, 199–218 (here 213–15). Brinner, 'Some Ayyūbid and Mamlūk documents', esp. 122, 126 (though he confuses this embassy with an earlier one, as Broadbridge, *Kingship and Ideology*, 181, n.70, points out).
141. Broadbridge, *Kingship and Ideology*, 182. Aigle, 'Hülegü's letters to the last Ayyubid ruler', 214.
142. Brinner, 'Some Ayyūbid and Mamlūk documents', 122. Broadbridge, *Kingship and Ideology*, 182–3.
143. Manz, 'Tamerlane and the symbolism', n.33 at 113–14, was the first to raise this question. See also Nagel, *Timur der Eroberer*, 175–6, and Bernardini, *Mémoire et propagande*, 53–5.
144. Yazdī, *ZN* (1957), I, 8/(2008), I, 234. So too he gives Timur's age at his 'enthronement' in 771/1370 as 34 solar years and his age at death as 71: ibid. (1957), I, 158, and II, 469/(2008), I, 403, and II, 1295. *ZT*, I, 8, 44, gives the same birth date (also HA's additions in Shāmī, *ZN*, II, 187, 205). See Naindeep Singh Chann, 'Lord of the Auspicious Conjunction: Origins of the *Ṣāḥib-Qirān*', *Iran and the Caucasus* 13 (2009), 93–110 (here 98).
145. Manz, 'Tamerlane and the symbolism', n.33 at 113–14.

146. As Broadbridge, *Kingship and Ideology*, 169, 178–9, 181, particularly emphasizes.
147. Manz, 'Mongol history rewritten', 135.
148. *Ta'rīf* (1951), 381/(2008), 254 (*IKT*, 45); earlier, (1951), 361/(2008), 236, Ibn Khaldūn says merely that Chinggis Khan set Tolui on 'the throne of Khurāsān'. Ibn ʿArabshāh, *Fākihat al-khulafāʾ*, ed. al-Najjār, 582, 587/ed. al-Buḥayrī, 565, 569.
149. These and Timur's other marriages are listed by Woods, *The Timurid Dynasty*, 17–18.
150. Shāmī, *ZN*, I, 70. Yazdī, *ZN* (1957), I, 190–1/(2008), I, 443–4. Naṭanzī (1957), 414/(2004), 302. For her parentage, cf. *MA*, fo. 33a, ed. Vokhidov, text, 67 (Russian trans., 51). She was not the only wife of Timur to bear the name Dilshād Āghā.
151. John of Sulṭāniyya, *Mémoire*, ed. Moranvillé, 444 (mistakenly making him the son of the khan Timur had slain when assuming control of the ulus); hence *Chronographia regum Francorum*, III, 208. Mignanelli (1764), 138b/(2013), 333 (tr. in Fischel, 'A new Latin source', 228). *Ta'rīf* (1951), 363–4 (naming the khan as 'Sāṭilmish'), 373, 382 (where the details are still more muddled, the wife herself being erroneously called 'Ṣurghatmish')/(2008), 237, 245, 255 (and see Cheddadi's index *s.v.* 'Satlamash'); the latter two references are tr. in *IKT*, 37, 46. Ibn Khaldūn, *Kitāb al-'Ibar*, V, 1142, appears to preserve a distorted reference to this marriage, confusing Soyurghatmish with Toqtamish (and cf. also ibid., V, 1129); hence Ibn Ḥajar, *Inbāʾ al-ghumr*, ed. Ḥabashī, II, 254, 301/ed. Khān, V, 125, 231, where Sulṭān Maḥmūd is called 'Maḥmūd Khān al-Ṭuqtamishī' and his father is called Toqtamish. Ibn Ḥijjī, II, 587, calls Sulṭān Maḥmūd Timur's son-in-law (*ṣihr*). But in fact he married a daughter of ʿUmar Shaykh: Naṭanzī (1957), 114/(2004), 93, and *MA*, fo. 101b, ed. Vokhidov, text, 198 (Russian trans., 121, incorrectly reads that her mother was the wife of Sulṭān Maḥmūd Khan); see also Naṭanzī (1957), 130/(2004), 105, and Woods, *The Timurid Dynasty*, 28.
152. Woods, *The Timurid Dynasty*, 20, 43, and 'The rise of Tīmūrid historiography', 93. Her father is commonly confused with the eastern Chaghadayid khan Khiḍr Khwāja (d. 1399): for example by Aubin, 'Le mécénat timouride', 76 (repr. in Aubin, *Études*, 159), and by Soucek, 'Eskandar b. ʿOmar Šayx', 74, 77, and 'Eskandar Solṭān', *EIr*, VIII, 603. *MA*, fo. 31b, ed. Vokhidov, text, 64 (Russian trans., 49–50), gives her correct genealogy. For ʿUmar Shaykh as Timur's eldest son, see p. 270 and p. 582 n. 153.
153. *MA*, fo. 44a, ed. Vokhidov, text, 89 (Russian trans., 60). Woods, *The Timurid Dynasty*, 33.
154. Yazdī, *ZN* (1957), I, 120/(2008), I, 360. Compare Shāmī, *ZN*, I, 47, where the marriage is mentioned but Ruqiyya's maternal ancestry is not given.
155. Woods, *The Timurid Dynasty*, 29. For the marriage, see Shāmī, *ZN*, I, 67–8, and Yazdī, *ZN* (1957), I, 180–8/(2008), I, 428–39.
156. Clavijo (1859), 148; the rendering in (1928), 247–8, 'descended from a prince who was the forefather of Timur', distorts the sense and is highly tendentious.
157. *MA*, fos 33a, 113b–114b, 119a, ed. Vokhidov, text, 67, 220–1, 228 (Russian trans., 52, 134–5, 137), where her father is variously called Sulṭān Malik and Muḥammad Oghlan; Woods, *The Timurid Dynasty*, 29, adopts the latter name. For his title Güregen, see Timur's *fatḥ-nāma* for Rūm, in *Safīna*, BN ms. arabe 3423, fos 400b, 401a.

158. Further examples in Manz, 'Women in Timurid domestic politics', 122–3. Binbaş, *Intellectual Networks*, 283, on the other hand, writes of 'a certain devaluation of marriage to Chinggisid princesses' consequent upon the dismantling of Chinggisid prestige after Timur's death.
159. Manz, 'Women in Timurid domestic politics', 130, and *Power, Politics and Religion*, 16–17.
160. Manz, 'Women in Timurid domestic politics', 123, 130. Beatrice F. Manz, 'Ulug͟h Beg', *EI*[2], X, 812–14 (here 812).
161. *MA*, fo. 44a, ed. Vokhidov, text, 89 (Russian trans., 60).
162. Khwānd-Amīr, *Ḥabīb al-siyar*, IV, 113–14 (tr. Thackston, 404).
163. *Taʿrīf* (1951), 382, *muttaṣil al-nasab maʿahū ilā Jaqaṭāī fī ābāʾ* .... *wa-hādhā Tamur ... huwa ibn ʿammihim*/(2008), 255 (*IKT*, 46). For Ibn Khaldūn's contradictory statements regarding Timur's ancestry, see above, p. 228.
164. Clavijo's remark that Timur's father was 'of the line (*linaje*) of the aforesaid Chaghatays' is immaterial here, since the context strongly suggests that he meant the Chaghatays *grosso modo* and not the ruling dynasty: see the Castilian text, ed. Francisco López Estrada (Madrid, 1943), 150. Compare Clavijo (1859), 125, 'of a lineage called Zagatay', and the still more misleading trans. in (1928), 210, 'allied by blood to the line of Chagatay'; and for Clavijo's somewhat wide-ranging definition of the term Chaghatay, ibid. (1859), 69/(1928), 122. Manz, 'The development and meaning of Chaghatay identity', 36–7.
165. Shāmī, *ZN*, I, 10, 58.
166. Woods, 'Timur's genealogy', 99 and Table 3 at 100.
167. Manz, 'Tamerlane and the symbolism', 106. For the title itself, see J.H. Kramers and C.E. Bosworth, 'Sulṭān', *EI*[2], IX, 849–51.
168. Poppe, 'Karasakpaiskaia nadpis′ Timura', 185–6. The rendering in Thomas W. Lentz and Glenn D. Lowry, *Timur and the Princely Vision. Persian Art and Culture in the Fifteenth Century* (Los Angeles, 1989), 25, omits the word 'Beg'.
169. Golombek, 'Tamerlane, Scourge of God', 55–6. See also Naṭanzī's use of the term *Sulṭān-i g͟hāzī*, as quoted at p. 362.

13: MUSLIM SULTAN AND HOLY WARRIOR: FAITH, PROPAGANDA AND POSTURE

1. Manz, 'Family and ruler', 57–68. See also pp. 32–3 above.
2. Manz, 'Tamerlane and the symbolism', 109–10.
3. Clavijo (1859), 162/(1928), 272.
4. For example, Shāmī, *ZN*, I, 41, 166, 257; Yazdī, *ZN* (1957), I, 385, 562, and II, 307, 403/(2008), I, 664, 837–8, and II, 1142, 1236.
5. Yazdī, *ZN* (1957), I, 292/(2008), I, 564; compare also (1957), I, 500, and II, 161–2/(2008), I, 780, and II, 1006. The word used here is *g͟hazā*, which strictly speaking denotes 'raiding' (though the target is most frequently the infidel) rather than 'holy war' (*jihād*): Michael Bonner, *Jihad in Islamic History: Doctrines and Practice* (Princeton, NJ, 2006), 2; I. Mélikoff, 'G͟hāzī', *EI*[2], II, 1043–5; T.M. Johnstone, 'G͟hazw', ibid., 1055–6. But Yazdī seems to use the two terms interchangeably and sometimes in conjunction; so also, though less frequently, does Shāmī.
6. Shāmī, *ZN*, I, 170.
7. Yazdī, *ZN* (1957), II, 457/(2008), II, 1284.

8. Shāmī, *ZN*, I, 170–1. Yazdī, *ZN* (1957), II, 21, 76/(2008), I, 866, 867, 923. *RN* (1915), 43–4, 45a–46a; and compare (2000), 58–9 (*DPT*, 60). Aubin, 'Comment Tamerlan', 90, is sceptical. For the motives behind Timur's invasion of India, see above, pp. 298–9.
9. Yazdī, *ZN* (1957), II, 23/(2008), I, 869.
10. Shāmī, *ZN*, I, 196. Yazdī, *ZN* (1957), II, 103–4/(2008), I, 948.
11. Yazdī, *ZN* (1957), II, 120/(2008), I, 964.
12. Shāmī, *ZN*, I, 204. Yazdī, *ZN* (1957), II, 41/(2008), I, 887. Lal, *Twilight of the Sultanate*, 38–9.
13. For Timur's campaigns against the Ās and various other non-Muslim populations, in 797/1395, see Yazdī, *ZN* (1957), I, 545–50, 554–7/(2008), I, 819–23, 830–2. On the Kaitak, see Jean Richard, 'Les missionnaires latins chez les Kaïtak du Daghestan (XIVe–XVe siècles)', in *TDPKV*, III, 606–11 (here 607–8); repr. in Richard, *Les Relations entre l'Orient et l'Occident au Moyen Age. Études et documents* (London, 1977).
14. For example, Shāmī, *ZN*, I, 285–6, and Timur's *fatḥ-nāma* on the capture of Delhi, addressed to his grandson Pīr Muḥammad b. ʿUmar Shaykh, in Nawāʾī (ed.), *Asnād*, 69; for the date of the *fatḥ-nāma*, in BN ms. arabe 3423, 20 Rajab 801/28 March 1399, which differs slightly from that in Nawāʾī's version, see Aubin, 'Comment Tamerlan', 90 and n.3.
15. Hailed with enthusiasm by Yazdī, *ZN* (1957), II, 164/(2008), II, 1008.
16. For the Jews of Bursa, see John of Sulṭāniyya, *Mémoire*, ed. Moranvillé, 456; and for those of Aleppo, Mignanelli (1764), 135a–b/(2013), 318–20 (tr. in Fischel, 'A new Latin source', 213–14). Michael Shterenshis, *Tamerlane and the Jews* (London, 2002), 97–8, dismisses these accounts as emanating from Christian writers and reflecting their anti-Jewish prejudice; and certainly they distort the details and conflict one with another. It is noteworthy that the fate of the Damascus Jews was reported by a merchant in Beirut and transmitted in a letter from Rhodes, dated 1 May 1401, to a merchant of the Datini Company resident in Montpellier: I owe this information to the kindness of Dr. Lorenzo Pubblici (email communication of 15 May 2023).
17. Roux, *Tamerlan*, 314.
18. Eaton, *India in the Persianate Age*, 105–8, 120, 122–3. Jackson, *The Delhi Sultanate*, 319–20. See Digby, 'After Timur left', 50.
19. Klaus-Peter Matschke, *Die Schlacht bei Ankara und das Schicksal von Byzanz. Studien zur spätbyzantinischen Geschichte zwischen 1402 und 1422* (Weimar, 1981), 9–39. Lindner, 'Anatolia, 1300–1451', 130–2.
20. Martin, *Medieval Russia,* 224–5, 241–2.
21. Naṭanzī (1957), 202/(2004), 165–6.
22. Yazdī, *ZN* (1957), II, 125–6/(2008), I, 970.
23. Shāmī, *ZN*, I, 267. Yazdī, *ZN* (1957), II, 336/(2008), II, 1169–70.
24. As recounted by Shāmī, *ZN*, I, 101, and Yazdī, *ZN* (1957), I, 296–7/(2008), I, 569–70. Roux, *Tamerlan*, 315, proposes that such conversions cannot be taken seriously.
25. Yazdī, *ZN* (1957), II, 366/(2008), II, 1197.
26. *RN* (1915), 20/(2000), 26: *az mulūk-i islām ba-kamāl-i musulmānī . . . . bar sar āmada būd* (*DPT*, 33).
27. Shāmī, *ZN*, I, 162. Yazdī, *ZN* (1957), I, 544/(2008), I, 818. For the fate of Christians in Tana, compare Michele Bernardini, 'Tamerlano, i Genovesi e il

favolosa Axalla', in Michele Bernardini, Clara Borrelli, Anna Cerbo and Encarnación Sánchez García (eds), *Europa e Islam tra i secoli XIV et XVI*, 2 vols (Naples, 2002), I, 391–426 (here 397).
28. Yazdī, *ZN* (1957), II, 69/(2008), I, 916.
29. Ibid. (1957), II, 196, 198/(2008), II, 1037, 1039.
30. Astarābādī, *Bazm-u razm*, 450.
31. Ibid., 17, 19, 22, 448, 455 (*kafara-yi mughūl-u ẓalama-yi chaghatāī-u tātār*). On this author's depiction of Timur and the Chaghatays, see Bernardini, *Mémoire et propagande*, 80–9; also his 'The army of Timur', 212.
32. IA (1979), 4/(1986), 42–3 (*TGA*, 2).
33. Ibid. (1979), 348/(1986), 479 (*TGA*, 322). Subtelny, *Timurids in Transition*, 13.
34. For Burhān al-Dīn, see Astarābādī, *Bazm-u razm*, 451, 457–8 (citing Burhān al-Dīn's letter to Barqūq); Broadbridge, *Kingship and Ideology*, 174; for Barqūq's various accusations, ibid., 184–5; and for Bayezid, Mirgaleev, 'Tatary Desht-i Kypchaka', 301.
35. Ibn al-Furāt, *Ta'rīkh al-duwal wa l-mulūk*, IX, part 2, 362. Ibn Qāḍī Shuhba, *Ta'rīkh*, I, 503. al-Maqrīzī, *al-Sulūk*, III, part 2, 797. See Broadbridge, *Kingship and Ideology*, 177–8; also Behrens-Abouseif, *Practising Diplomacy*, 70–1.
36. IA (1979), 99/(1986), 158 (*TGA*, 93).
37. Or 'that you are liars'. Ibid. (1979), 98, *qad za'amtum annanā kafara fa-qad thubita 'indanā annakum fajara*/(1986), 157 (*TGA*, 92, has 'you are wicked'). Compare the version of this letter in Ibn Ṣaṣrā, *al-Durrat al-muḍī'a*, ed. and tr. Brinner, II (Ar. text), 147 (and Brinner's trans. in I, 197), and al-Maqrīzī, *al-Sulūk*, III, part 2, 804, where the wording differs slightly, the last phrase reading *al-kafara al-fajara*; also Brinner, 'Some Ayyūbid and Mamlūk documents', 133.
38. Drory, 'Maqrīzī in *Durar al-'uqūd*', 394–9.
39. IA (1979), 240/(1986), 380 (*TGA*, 220).
40. Broadbridge, 'Royal authority', 235–6.
41. al-Maqrīzī, *al-Sulūk*, IV, part 1, 26.
42. al-Maqrīzī, *Durar al-'uqūd*, I, 559. See the comment of Drory, 'Maqrīzī in *Durar al-'uqūd*', 401.
43. But note his use of the term *al-ṭāghiya* ('tyrant') to describe Timur in *Durar al-'uqūd*, III, 31.
44. Ibid., II, 403. Broadbridge, 'Royal authority', 234. Rabbat, 'Who was al-Maqrīzī?', 11.
45. Ito, 'Al-Maqrīzī's biography of Tīmūr', 315. See *Ta'rīf* (1951), 383/(2008), 255 (*IKT*, 47). IA (1979), 128/(1986), 196 (*TGA*, 118), had been content to say simply that fortune favoured Timur and that God's will drove him on.
46. Ibn Qāḍī Shuhba, *Ta'rīkh*, IV, 429, *ra's al-mufsidīn wa-mukharrib bilād al-muslimīn wa-sāfik dimā' al-muwaḥḥidīn*.
47. For example, Ibn Ḥijjī, I, 45, 48, 58; hence Ibn Qāḍī Shuhba, *Ta'rīkh*, I, 507, 513; and see also Ibn Ḥajar, *Inbā' al-ghumr*, ed. Ḥabashī, II, 299/ed. Khān, V, 225. This is ironic, given Timur's devotion to the memory of the Caliph ʿAlī (see later), whom the Kharijites had opposed: see G. Levi della Vida, 'Khāridjites', *EI*[2], IV, 1074–7.
48. Ibn Qāḍī Shuhba, *Ta'rīkh*, I, 512. For the significance of the term, see T. Fahd, 'Ṭāghūt, 1.', *EI*[2], X, 93–4.
49. *ṭāghiya*: Ibn Taghrībirdī, *al-Manhal al-ṣāfī*, IV, 103; also at III, 348; idem, *al-Nujūm al-zāhira*, XIII, 160 (tr. Popper, II, 203). *al-makhdhūl* ('the forsaken'): Ibn Taghrībirdī, *al-Manhal al-ṣāfī*, II, 140.

50. For example, Ibn Taghrībirdī, *al-Manhal al-ṣāfī*, IV, 130, 138.
51. Ibn Taghrībirdī, *al-Nujūm al-zāhira*, XIII, 161, *halaka ilā la'nati llāh wa-sukhṭihi* (tr. Popper, II, 204).
52. Ibn Taghrībirdī, *al-Manhal al-ṣāfī*, IV, 138.
53. Mignanelli (1764), 138b/(2013), 332 (tr. in Fischel, 'A new Latin source', 227).
54. But for evidence that Juwaynī himself shared this view of Chinggis Khan, see *TJG*, I, 1 (*HWC*, 3).
55. Brinner, 'Some Ayyūbid and Mamlūk documents', 128. Compare also Timur to Barqūq, in Nawā'ī (ed.), *Asnād*, 75–6; Ibn Ṣaṣrā, *al-Durrat al-muḍī'a*, ed. and tr. Brinner, II (Ar. text), 147 (and Brinner's trans. in I, 196); IA (1979), 98/(1986), 155–6 (*TGA*, 91).
56. Shāmī, *ZN*, I, 228. Yazdī, *ZN* (1957), II, 220–1/(2008), II, 1059.
57. See Aubin, 'Comment Tamerlan', 87.
58. Yazdī, *ZN* (1957), I, 271/(2008), I, 541.
59. Shāmī, *ZN*, I, 97. Yazdī, *ZN* (1957), I, 286/(2008), I, 557. Zayn al-Dīn (1990), text, 499 (Russian trans., 131)/(1993), 117.
60. Barbaro, *Viaggi*, §§ 13–14, ed. and tr. Skrzhinskaia, *Barbaro i Kontarini o Rossii*, text, 117 (Russian trans., 140–1); tr. Thomas, in Stanley of Alderley (ed.), *Travels to Tana and Persia*, 8–9. Clavijo (1859), 177/(1928), 300. For Edigü's role, see DeWeese, *Islamization and Native Religion*, 339–42.
61. IA (1979), 78/(1986), 135 (*TGA*, 73). Barbaro, *Viaggi*, § 26, ed. and tr. Skrzhinskaia, *Barbaro i Kontarini o Rossii*, text, 122 (Russian trans., 146); tr. Thomas, in Stanley of Alderley (ed.), *Travels to Tana and Persia*, 16.
62. Yazdī, *ZN* (1957), I, 528/(2008), I, 804–5. See R. Wixman, 'Ḳaytaḳ', *EI*², IV, 846–7.
63. Yazdī, *ZN*, (1957), I, 331/(2008), I, 611. The passage is quoted in Bernardini, 'Tamerlano, i Genovesi e il favoloso Axalla', 392.
64. Timur to Bayezid, in Sarī ʿAbd-Allāh Efendi, *Munsha'āt*: Togan, 'Timur's Osteuropapolitik', 294; and compare ibid., 280–1, 284; also below and n.90. For Mamai's recruitment of these elements, see *Patriarshaia ili Nikonovskaia letopis'*, in *PSRL*, XI, 47 (tr. Zenkovsky, III, 267).
65. Timur to the Muzaffarid Shāh Yaḥyā, in Nawā'ī (ed.), *Asnād*, 20; Timur to Bayezid, ibid., 109. For these and other references, see Manz, 'Tamerlane and the symbolism', 111–12, and 'Temür and the problem', 23, 25–6.
66. Ibn al-Shiḥna, 213–15. Hence IA (1979), 139–40/(1986), 214–15 (*TGA*, 127–8).
67. IA (1979), 130/(1986), 198 (*TGA*, 119).
68. *Ta'rīf* (1951), 374–6/(2008), 247–9 (*IKT*, 39–41). On this episode, see Hassan, *Longing for the Lost Caliphate*, 125–6.
69. Sarī ʿAbd-Allāh Efendi, *Munsha'āt*, in Togan, 'Timurs Osteuropapolitik', 298.
70. On the vicissitudes of al-Mutawakkil's career and his burgeoning popularity, see Hassan, *Longing for the Lost Caliphate*, 89–93; more briefly, Broadbridge, *Kingship and Ideology*, 150, 171 and n.12. For the functions of the later Caliphs in general, compare Banister, *The Abbasid Caliphate of Cairo*.
71. Yazdī, *ZN* (1957), II, 41/(2008), I, 887.
72. Hassan, *Longing for the Lost Caliphate*, 97. Broadbridge, *Kingship and Ideology*, 150, 175. Ibn Khaldūn, *Kitāb al-'Ibar*, III, 1113, was aware of princes in India having done so. Chief among them were the Delhi Sultans Muḥammad b. Tughluq and his successor Fīrūz Shāh. The idea of obtaining endorsement

from the Caliph would even be mooted at the court of one of Timur's grandsons (above, p. 345).

73. Clavijo (1859), 123–5/(1928), 207–10. On the fortifications at Samarkand, see HA, *Jughrāfiyya*, Bodleian ms. Fraser 155, fo.169b. For his buildings, see Lentz and Lowry, *Timur and the Princely Vision*, 29, 34–6; Golombek, 'Tamerlane, Scourge of God', 34–53; for those in Kish, see Yazdī, *ZN* (1957), I, 221–2, 566 (Aqsarai)/(2008), I, 483–4, 843; and M.E. Masson and G.A. Pugachenkova, 'Shakhri Siabz pri Timure i Ulug Beke', *Trudy Sredneaziatskogo Gosudarstvennogo Universiteta* 49 (1953), 17–96, and tr. J.M. Rogers as 'Shakhri Syabz pri Timure i Ulug Beke ("Shahr-i Sabz from Tīmūr to Ūlūgh Beg")', *Iran* 16 (1978), 103–26, and 18 (1980), 121–43. The standard work is Lisa Golombek and Donald Wilber, *The Timurid Architecture of Iran and Turan*, 2 vols (Princeton, NJ, 1988), I, 254–63, 271–8, 281, 284–8.
74. See Lentz and Lowry, *Timur and the Princely Vision*, 36, 42–3; Elena Paskaleva, 'The Bibi Khanum mosque in Samarqand: Its Mongol and Timurid architecture', *The Silk Road* 10 (2012), 81–98.
75. Samarqandī, *Qandiyya*, 165–6.
76. Samarkand: Yazdī, *ZN* (1957), I, 416/(2008), I, 695. Jām: Mahendrarajah, *The Sufi Saint of Jam*, 109.
77. A. Azfar Moin, 'Sovereign violence: Temple destruction in India and shrine desecration in Iran and Central Asia', *CSSH* 57 (2015), 467–96 (quotation at 480).
78. For the buildings of Timur's wives, see Lentz and Lowry, *Timur and the Princely Vision*, 41. Soucek, 'Tīmūrid women', 210, raises the question whether the architectural patronage of Sarai Mulk Khanim, and that of other Timurid women, 'should be viewed as a personal venture, or as part of the larger corpus of imperial monuments'.
79. Golombek, 'Tamerlane, Scourge of God', 51–7. See also her 'Discourses of an imaginary arts council in fifteenth-century Iran', in Golombek and Subtelny (eds), *Timurid Art and Culture*, 1–17 (here 1–6).
80. Yazdī, *ZN* (1957), II, 421/(2008), II, 1255. Morgan, 'The empire of Tamerlane', 237.
81. V. Minorsky (trans.), *Calligraphers and Painters. A Treatise by Qāḍī Aḥmad, son of Mīr-Munshī (circa A.H. 1015/A.D. 1606)* (Washington, DC, 1959), 64; cited in Lentz and Lowry, *Timur and the Princely Vision*, 45. For the cubit, see W. Hinz, 'Dhirāʿ', *EI*[2], II, 231–2. On the anecdotes relating to building work, retailed by Clavijo and by Ibn ʿArabshāh, see Golombek, 'Tamerlane, Scourge of God', 52.
82. Manz, 'Mongol history rewritten and relived', 145, citing Mamlūk sources as utilised in Aḥmad Darrāg, *L'Égypte sous le règne de Barsbay, 825–41/1422–38* (Damascus, 1961), 162.
83. For Maḥmūd's posthumous reputation, see, for example, IB, III, 88 (tr. Gibb, 589–90); C.E. Bosworth, 'Maḥmūd of Ghazna in contemporary eyes and in later Persian literature', *Iran* 4 (1966), 85–92 (esp. 87–90), and repr. in Bosworth, *The Medieval History of Iran, Afghanistan and Central Asia* (London, 1977); and Charles Melville, 'The royal image in Mongol Iran', in Lynette Mitchell and Charles Melville (eds), *Every Inch a King. Comparative Studies on Kings and Kingship in the Ancient and Medieval Worlds* (Leiden, 2013), 343–69 (here 355–6). On Maḥmūd as a model for Timur, see Bernardini, *Mémoire et propagande*, 90.

84. *RN* (1915), 43/(2000), 57 (*DPT*, 59–60). Yazdī, *ZN* (1957), I, 401/(2008), I, 679. See Roemer, 'Tīmūr in Iran', 70, 94. In much the same way, the Iranian territory Timur allotted to his son Amīrānshāh in 798/1396 (and to Muḥammad Sulṭān in 803/1401 and Amīrānshāh's son ʿUmar in 806/1403) would be described as 'the throne of Hülegü', but only later, by Yazdī, *ZN* (1957), I, 445, and II, 250, 395, 402/(2008), I, 724, and II, 1086, 1227, 1235; Manz, 'Mongol history rewritten', 140, n.22.
85. *RN* (1915), 26/(2000), 34–5 (*DPT*, 39). His references to Maḥmūd of Ghazna are discussed by Bernardini, *Mémoire et propagande*, 95–100; see ibid., 99–100, for Ghiyāth al-Dīn's allusion to ʿUtbī's work.
86. Shāmī, *ZN*, I, 283. Yazdī, *ZN* (1957), II, 377, 383–4/(2008), II, 1210, 1216–17.
87. Yazdī, *ZN* (1972), fo. 3b/(2008), I, 9. See Binbaş, *Intellectual Networks*, 254–7, for Yazdī's linkage of Timur with Alexander (the passage in question is quoted at 255). Naṭanzī (1957), 215/(2004), 276, similarly has Timur's victories obliterating those of Alexander; hence *ZT*, I, 11 (and see HA's additions to Shāmī, *ZN*, II, 190).
88. On which see Baer, *The Ottomans. Khans, Caesars and Caliphs*, 52–3.
89. Timur to Bayezid, in Nawāʾī (ed.), *Asnād*, 96, 105–6, 121. Timur to Bayezid, in Sarī ʿAbd-Allāh Efendi, *Munshaʾāt*: Togan, 'Timur's Osteuropapolitik', 294; compare also 280–1, 284. Timur to Bayezid, in Yazdī, *ZN* (1957), II, 188/(2008), II, 1030. See further Shāmī, *ZN*, I, 218, 258; Yazdī, *ZN* (1957), II, 280, 286, 296, 315/(2008), II, 1117–18, 1123, 1132, 1148.
90. Timur to Bayezid, in Sarī ʿAbd-Allāh Efendi, *Munshaʾāt*: Togan, 'Timur's Osteuropapolitik', 297; and see ibid., 284; also earlier and nn. 63–4.
91. Shāmī, *ZN*, I, 271. Yazdī, *ZN* (1957), II, 330, 349/(2008), II, 1163, 1182.
92. Alexandrescu-Dersca, *La Campagne de Timur*, 86 and n.4 (quoting Neşri).
93. Anooshahr, *The Ghazi Sultans*, 120–8. Bernardini, *Mémoire et propagande*, 89, however, sees Timur's stance as first influenced by the denunciations of Burhān al-Dīn of Sivas.
94. Bernardini, *Mémoire et propagande*, 151.
95. Kastritsis, 'The Alexander Romance and the rise of the Ottoman empire', 259–60.
96. Shāmī, *ZN*, I, 255; and compare 258. Yazdī, *ZN* (1957), II, 306/(2008), II, 1140–1. Both mention specifically *pisar-i *Las* ('Lazar's son') and his troops. Bernardini, 'The army of Timur', 219.
97. Yazdī, *ZN* (1957), II, 328/(2008), II, 1161.
98. Andreas de Redusiis de Quero, *Chronicon Tarvisinum*, col. 801. See Sarnowsky, 'Die Johanniter und Smyrna', 215, 232, and Kastritsis, *The Sons of Bayezid*, 45.
99. Shāmī, *ZN*, I, 267. Yazdī, *ZN* (1957), II, 335–6, 340–1/(2008), II, 1169, 1174: there is a translation of this passage in Kastritsis, *The Sons of Bayezid*, n.16 at 45–6. Compare *ZT*, II, 976 (also HA's additions to Shāmī, *ZN*, II, 179), stating that the Franks held the stronghold as if it were 'the Great Kaʿba'.
100. Bernardini, *Mémoire et propagande*, 79–80.
101. Yazdī, *ZN* (1957), II, 401–2/(2008), II, 1234.
102. Ibid. (1957), II, 445–7/(2008), II, 1272–4. Salmānī, *Shams al-ḥusn*, text, fo. 23b (abridged German trans., 22).
103. IA (1979), 342/(1986), 473 (*TGA*, 317).
104. Yazdī, *ZN* (1957), II, 443/(2008), II, 1271. But John of Sulṭāniyya, *Mémoire*, ed. Moranvillé, 452, claims that drinking wine was (generally?) prohibited at

Timur's headquarters, as was the presence of loose women; compare also *Chronographia regum Francorum*, III, 218.

105. As Marozzi, *Tamerlane*, 361, reasonably surmises. On the deterioration in Timur's health by 1404, see Clavijo (1859), 166–8/(1928), 280–2.
106. Luttrell, 'Timur's Dominican envoy', 211–15.
107. Andreas de Redusiis de Quero, *Chronicon Tarvisinum*, col. 803, where they are described (possibly in error) as Franciscans.
108. *Pace* Jean Dauvillier, 'La papauté, l'union des Eglises et les missions en Orient durant le Moyen Age: A propos d'un ouvrage récent', *Revue d'Histoire Ecclésiastique* 74 (1979), 640–51 (here 650).
109. Bernardini, 'Motahharten entre Timur et Bayezid', 207.
110. Jackson, *The Mongols and the West*, 211.
111. Budge, *The Chronography of Gregory Abû'l Faraj*, II, appendices, xxxi, xxxiii–xxxiv, xxxvii. Fiey, 'Sources syriaques sur Tamerlan', 18.
112. For all these contradictory details, see T'ovma Metsobets'i, tr. Bedrosian, 10, 26, 34, 38, 46–7.
113. Knobler, 'The rise of Tīmür', 342.
114. See Adam Knobler, 'Pseudo-conversions and patchwork pedigrees: The Christianization of Muslim princes and the diplomacy of Holy War', *JWH* 7 (1996), 181–97; also his *Mythology and Diplomacy in the Age of Exploration* (Leiden and Boston, MA, 2017), chap. 2.
115. David Morgan, 'Prester John and the Mongols', in Charles F. Beckingham and Bernard Hamilton (eds), *Prester John, the Mongols and the Ten Lost Tribes* (Aldershot, 1996), 159–70 (here 159–63).
116. Knobler, 'The rise of Tīmūr', 344, 348–9, and his *Mythology and Diplomacy*, 25. For the reports of Ghazan's capture of Jerusalem and his 'conversion', see Sylvia Schein, '*Gesta Dei per Mongolos* 1300: The genesis of a non-event', *English Historical Review* 94 (1979), 805–19.
117. Ibn Ḥijjī, II, 597–8. Ibn Qāḍī Shuhba, *Ta'rīkh*, IV, 340–2 (calling them Genoese and Cypriots). al-Maqrīzī, *al-Sulūk*, III, part 3, 1114–16.
118. Schmieder, *Europa und die Fremden*, 181–2. Jackson, *The Mongols and the West*, 243–7.
119. John of Sulṭāniyya, *Mémoire*, ed. Moranvillé, 451; and see 454 on the fate of the populace of Sivas (only the Greeks, allegedly, being spared), 455 on the burning of the qadis and 'ulama of Damascus, and 456 on the massacre at Baghdad and the alleged burning of the Jews of Bursa. See also John's *Libellus de notitia orbis*, Universitätsbibliothek Graz ms. 1221, fo. 88b, on Khurāsān: *non remansit in ea civitas vel villa quam non vastavit et trucidavit crudeliter* (passage omitted in Kern's abridged edn). *Chronographia regum Francorum*, III, 217.
120. John of Sulṭāniyya, *Mémoire*, ed. Moranvillé, 453. This phrase is omitted from the Latin translation: *Chronographia regum Francorum*, III, 219.
121. For an extremely terse allusion, see John of Sulṭāniyya, *Libellus de notitia orbis*, ed. Kern, 118: the context is Mosul.
122. Ibid., 112.
123. John of Sulṭāniyya, *Mémoire*, ed. Moranvillé, 462. *Chronographia regum Francorum*, III, 216. The two versions differ slightly, the French text applying Timur's hatred of sodomy to the Muslims; but this may represent a scribal confusion.

124. John of Sulṭāniyya, *Libellus de notitia orbis*, ed. Kern, 104.
125. *Chronographia regum Francorum*, III, 205 (citing John, though this detail is absent from the 'Mémoire'). For the possible basis of this rumour, see Jackson, *The Mongols and the West*, 244–5. Clavijo (1928), 25 (and see n.3 at 340; cf. (1859), iii–iv), refers to female captives formerly in Bayezid's possession whom Timur sent as a gift to the King of Castile.
126. Dietrich von Nyem, *De scismate libri tres*, ed. G. Erler (Leipzig, 1890), 171–2.
127. Ellis (ed.), *Original Letters*, 3rd series, I, 57, note f. Luttrell, 'Timur's Dominican envoy', 221.
128. John of Sulṭāniyya, *Libellus de notitia orbis*, ed. Kern, 121. For a discussion of John's attitude towards Amīrānshāh, see Binbaş, *Intellectual Networks*, 181–4.
129. John of Sulṭāniyya, *Mémoire*, ed. Moranvillé, 446. *Chronographia regum Francorum*, III, 213.
130. F.C. Hingeston (ed.), *Royal and Historical Letters during the Reign of Henry the Fourth, King of England and of France, and Lord of Ireland*, I: *A.D. 1399–1404*, Rolls Series 18 (London, 1860), 425–6 (no. cl).
131. As related by Clavijo (1859), 95–6/(1928), 162–3. Yazdī, *ZN* (1957), II, 148/(2008), II, 991, does not specify which buildings were demolished.
132. Tʿovma Metsobetsʿi, tr. Bedrosian, 56–7.
133. Ibid., 55; though at 56 he describes Amīrānshāh as 'an extremely merciful and benevolent ruler'.
134. John of Sulṭāniyya, *Libellus de notitia orbis*, Universitätsbibliothek Graz ms. 1221, fo. 57a (this passage is abridged in Kern's edn, 99).
135. WR, 304, 306 (*MFW*, 266–7; and see n.2 at 266). See Sanjian (trans.), *Colophons of Armenian Manuscripts*, 94; and see index *s.v.* 'Nerses'.
136. Luttrell, 'Timur's Dominican envoy', 218–19, 227.
137. Schmieder, *Europa und die Fremden*, 187. Bernardini, 'Tamerlano, i Genovesi', 404–5.
138. It does not appear that the west in the early fourteenth century knew of the conversion of Ghazan to Islam (1295) or that of his brother and successor, Öljeitü: Jackson, *The Mongols and the West*, 215.
139. Richard, *La Papauté et les missions d'Orient*, 253–4, and his 'Les missionnaires latins chez les Kaïtak', 608. For Boniface's authorisation of a crusade against Bayezid (1394), see Aziz Suryal Atiya, *The Crusade of Nicopolis* (London, 1934), 33–4.
140. See Margaret Meserve, 'Italian humanists and the problem of the crusade', in Norman Housley (ed.), *Crusading in the Fifteenth Century. Message and Impact* (Basingstoke, 2004), 13–38 (here 20).
141. Naṭanzī (1957), 151, 288/(2004), 122, 224; Yazdī, *ZN* (1957), I, 146/(2008), I, 391–2; Binbaş, *Intellectual Networks*, 282–3. Aubin, 'Comment Tamerlan', 99.
142. Clavijo (1859), 141–2, 166/(1928), 235, 279–80; in the latter place, however, Timur is shown as angrily rejecting the sayyids' intercession on behalf of those inhabitants of Samarkand whose property had been demolished for the construction of a new street.
143. Shāmī, *ZN*, I, 64–5. Naṭanzī (1957), 299/(2004), 232; though at (1957), 411/(2004), 299–300, he says that both Khwāndzāda and a fellow conspirator, Shaykh Abū l-Layth Samarqandī, were sent to Mecca. *ZT*, I, 463 (also in Shāmī, *ZN*, II, 31), has only Shaykh Abū l-Layth despatched there.

144. Shāmī, *ZN*, I, 128. Yazdī, *ZN* (1957), I, 413–14/(2008), I, 691–2.
145. Yazdī, *ZN* (1957), II, 398/(2008), II, 1230–1.
146. Ibid. (1957), I, 171/(2008), I, 420.
147. Yazdī, *ZN* (1957), I, 145/(2008), I, 390. Shāmī, *ZN*, I, 57, calls him simply a sayyid of Mecca.
148. al-Maqrīzī, *Durar al-'uqūd*, I, 455–6 (no. 363).
149. Ashirbek Muminov and Bakhtiyar Babadzhanov, 'Amīr Temur and Sayyid Baraka', *CAJ* 45 (2001), 28–62 (esp. 29–43).
150. Naṭanzī (1957), 282–3/(2004), 219–20. Shāmī, *ZN*, I, 57. Yazdī, *ZN* (1957), I, 145–6/(2008), I, 390–1. Manz, *The Rise and Rule*, 56. Nagel, *Timur der Eroberer*, 116–17, 141.
151. Shāmī, *ZN*, I, 123, 126. Yazdī, *ZN* (1957), I, 157, 260, 386, and II, 396/(2008), I, 402, 530, 665, and II, 1228. al-Maqrīzī, *Durar al-'uqūd*, I, 456. On Sayyid Baraka's role, see Paul, 'Scheiche und Herrscher', 302–5; also Devin DeWeese, 'Sayyid Baraka', *EI*[3] (2017), fasc. 1, 138–43.
152. Yazdī, *ZN* (1957), I, 386/(2008), I, 665. IA (1979), 8, 16–17/(1986), 48, 59–60 (*TGA*, 5, 14); and for Shams al-Dīn Fākhūrī, who appears to be identical with Shams al-Dīn Kulāl, see also (1979), 5–6/(1986), 43–4 (*TGA*, 2). Shāmī, *ZN*, I, 123–4, briefly mentions the prayers of Baraka and other sayyids present.
153. Yazdī, *ZN* (1957), I, 260–1/(2008), I, 529–30.
154. Ibid. (1957), II, 398–9/(2008), II, 1231–2.
155. Muminov and Babadzhanov, 'Amir Temur and Sayyid Baraka', 43–5. Compare also Bartol'd, 'O pogrebenii Timura', 448 (tr. Rogers, 83). The story is found in Yazdī, *ZN* (1957), I, 146, and II, 510–11/(2008), I, 391, and II, 1331.
156. For example, in the *fatḥ-nāma* sent to Pīr Muḥammad b. 'Umar Shaykh: Nawā'ī (ed.), *Asnād*, 69.
157. Ibn al-Shiḥna, 216–17, 221–2. Hence IA (1979), 140, 141–2, 159–60/(1986), 216, 217, 261 (*TGA*, 129, 130, 147). See L. Veccia Vaglieri, 'al-Ḥusayn b. 'Alī b. Abī Ṭālib', *EI*[2], III, 607–15.
158. Ibn al-Shiḥna, 216, 217. Hence IA (1979), 140, 141–2/(1986), 216, 217 (*TGA*, 129, 130).
159. Yazdī, *ZN* (1957), II, 243–4/(2008), II, 1082.
160. Ibn al-Dawādārī, *Kanz al-durar*, IX, 36. al-Yūnīnī, *Dhayl Mir'āt al-zamān*, ed. and tr. Guo, I (trans.), 163–4, II (text), 124/ed. Jarrākh, XXI, 124–5. Zetterstéen (ed.), *Beiträge zur Geschichte der Mamlūkensultane*, 78–9. Aigle, 'A religious response', 295.
161. Yazdī, *ZN* (1957), II, 244–5/(2008), II, 1082–3. The extent of the damage to the mosque is unclear: see Elodie Vigouroux, 'La Mosquée des Omeyyades de Damas après Tamerlan: Chronique d'une renaissance (1401–1430)', *BEO* 61 (2012), 123–59 (here 125–7). Note that both the city and the mosque had suffered considerable damage earlier, during Mamlūk in-fighting in 791/1389: Ira Marvin Lapidus, *Muslim Cities in the Later Middle Ages* (Cambridge, MA, 1967), 27–8; Lapidus believed that the destruction exceeded that done by Timur.
162. IA (1979), 171–2/(1986), 285 (*TGA*, 158). McChesney, 'A note', 210–11.
163. Naṭanzī (1957), 379, cited by Aubin, 'La fin de l'état sarbadâr', 115 (repr. in his *Études*, 327); (2004), 280. For their presence at the siege of the citadel, see Yazdī, *ZN* (1957), II, 241/(2008), II, 1079; and for their views, Kazuo Morimoto, 'An enigmatic genealogical chart of the Timurids: A testimony to

the dynasty's claim to Yasavi-ʿAlid legitimacy?', *Oriens* 44 (2016), 145–78 (here 169–70, citing Jean Calmard).

164. Mignanelli (1764), 136b–137a/(2013), 326 (tr. in Fischel, 'A new Latin source', 220); compare IA (1979), 159/(1986), 260 (*TGA*, 146).
165. Shāmī, *ZN*, I, 235–6. Bernardini, 'Niẓām al-Dīn Shāmī's description', 403–4.
166. IA (1979), 159–62/(1986), 261–5 (*TGA*, 147–9). For 'innovation', see J. Robson, 'Bidʿa', *EI*², I, 1199; the rendering at *TGA*, 149, is somewhat free.
167. *Taʿrīf* (1951), 382/(2008), 255 (*IKT*, 47).
168. Ibn al-Shiḥna, 218. Hence IA (1979), 140/(1986), 216 (*TGA*, 129).
169. This is possibly what underlies Ibn ʿArabshāh's slightly inapposite comparison of the status of the Chinggisids and that of the Quraysh tribe within Islamic society: IA (1979), 16/(1986), 56 (*TGA*, 13). Compare p. 100 above, for the analogy drawn in the Ilkhanid era.
170. A.A. Semenov, 'Nadpisi na nadgrobiiakh Tīmūra i ego potomkov v Gur-i Emire', *EV* 2 (1948), 49–62, and 3 (1949), 45–54. Binbaş, *Intellectual Networks*, 278–84.
171. Notably by Nūrbakhsh and the Ḥurūfīs: Markiewicz, *The Crisis of Kingship*, 165.
172. Dawlatshāh Samarqandī, *Tadhkirat al-shuʿarā* (892/1487), ed. Edward G. Browne (Leiden and London, 1901), 322/ed. Muḥammad ʿAbbāsī (Tehran, 1337 sh./1958), 360; extract tr. in Thackston (ed.), *A Century of Princes*, 15. On ʿAlī Zayn al-ʿĀbidīn, see S. Husain M. Jafri, *The Origins and Early Development of Shiʿa Islam* (London and New York, 1979), 237–46.
173. Morimoto, 'An enigmatic genealogical chart of the Timurids', esp. 162–70.
174. Denise Aigle, 'The transformation of a myth of origins, Genghis Khan and Timur', in Aigle, *The Mongol Empire between Myth and Reality*, 121–33 (esp. 131–2).
175. Moin, *The Millennial Sovereign*, 37–9.
176. Paul, 'Scheiche und Herrscher', 317–18.
177. Shaykhs associated with Timur are listed by Paul, ibid., 296–313.
178. There exists a wide literature on this subject. See most recently Lewisohn, 'Sufism in late Mongol and early Timurid Persia'.
179. IA (1979), 5–6, 8/(1986), 43–4, 48 (*TGA*, 2–3, 5).
180. Nāṣir al-Dīn: *RN* (1915), 110b/(2000), 108 (*DPT*, 111–12), with the figure of 10; Shāmī, *ZN*, I, 188, and Yazdī, *ZN* (1957), II, 72–3/(2008), I, 920, with 15; on this episode, see p. 332 above. Other ʿulama in the army before Delhi: *RN* (1915), 115/(2000), 112 (*DPT*, 115); Yazdī, *ZN* (1957), II, 79/(2008), I, 926.
181. Yazdī, *ZN* (1957), II, 209/(2008), II, 1050.
182. Ibid. (1957), I, 313, and II, 265–6/(2008), I, 587–8, and II, 1101, respectively. Baghdad: Shāmī, *ZN*, I, 241.
183. Shāmī, *ZN*, I, 179.
184. Turka: Binbaş, *Intellectual Networks*, 37–8. al-Jazarī: Binbaş, 'A Damascene eyewitness', 161; Abdurrahman Atcıl, 'Mobility of scholars and formation of a self-sustaining scholarly system in the lands of Rūm during the fifteenth century', in Peacock and Yıldız (eds), *Islamic Literature and Intellectual Life*, 315–32 (here 320); more briefly in McChesney, 'A note', 215–17.
185. *Taʿrīf* (1951), 382/(2008), 255 (*IKT*, 47). Compare also John of Sulṭāniyya, *Mémoire*, ed. Moranvillé, 461, *et se delicte moult en argumens et questions*. For examples, see Yazdī, *ZN* (1957), II, 268, 396/(2008), II, 1105, 1229.

186. al-Musawi, *The Medieval Islamic Republic of Letters*, 30–1. For the debates of the Mongol era, see Brack, 'Disenchanting Heaven', 26–8 (the phrase quoted is at 27); also George Lane, 'Intellectual jousting and the Chinggisid wisdom bazaars', in May (ed.), *The Mongols and Post-Mongol Asia*, 235–47.
187. *ZT*, I, 15.
188. *Ta'rīf* (1951), 372–3/(2008), 245–6 (*IKT*, 36–8: I have amended Fischel's rendering of the phrase *mā 'alaynā min al-ṭabarī*, while relying here on his interpretation, in *IKT*, n.107 at 87, of an especially problematic passage).
189. IA (1979), 157–8/(1986), 256–7 (*TGA*, 145).
190. Ibid. (1979), 175/(1986), 291–3 (*TGA*, 160–1). Ibn Ḥajar, *Inbāʾ al-ghumr*, ed. Ḥabashī, II, 150–1/ed. Khān, IV, 248, refers briefly to Ibn Mufliḥ's death in the Biqāʿ region towards the end of Shaʿbān 803/early April 1401. al-Maqrīzī, *al-Sulūk*, III, part 3, 1075, and *Durar al-'uqūd*, I, 125 (no. 43), and Ibn Taghrībirdī, *al-Nujūm al-zāhira*, XIII, 25 (tr. Popper, II, 111), and *al-Manhal al-ṣāfī*, I, 165, likewise date his death in that month.
191. Ibn Ḥajar, *Inbāʾ al-ghumr*, ed. Ḥabashī, II, 150/ed. Khān, IV, 248; hence Ibn Qāḍī Shuhba, *Taʾrīkh*, IV, 196–7. For Ibn Mufliḥ's efforts, see al-Maqrīzī, *al-Sulūk*, III, part 3, 1046–7; Drory, 'Maqrīzī in *Durar al-'uqūd*', 397.
192. Ibn Ḥijjī, I, 483–5, 487–8, 490–1; and 509–10 for those missing. Others are named by Ibn Ḥajar, *Inbāʾ al-ghumr*, ed. al-Ḥabashī, II, 167/ed. Khān, IV, 285, and by al-ʿAynī, *'Iqd al-jumān*, BN ms. arabe 1544, fo. 52a; IA (1979), 174–5/(1986), 293 (*TGA*, 160); Ibn Ḥajar, *Inbāʾ al-ghumr*, ed. al-Ḥabashī, II, 189/ed. Khān, IV, 329–30; Ibn Qāḍī Shuhba, *Taʾrīkh*, IV, 240; and al-Maqrīzī, *al-Sulūk*, III, part 3, 1071.
193. IA (1979), 174/(1986), 291–3 (*TGA*, 160), states that both al-Munāwī and al-Nābulusī drowned, but see later, n. 195. Both appear in the list in Ibn Qāḍī Shuhba, *Taʾrīkh*, IV, 183, of those removed from Damascus.
194. Ibn Ḥijjī, I, 499 (in Shawwāl). Ibn Qāḍī Shuhba, *Taʾrīkh*, IV, 234–5. al-Maqrīzī, *al-Sulūk*, III, part 3, 1073. Ibn Taghrībirdī, *al-Nujūm al-zāhira*, XIII, 25 (tr. Popper, II, 111). Ibn Taghrībirdī, *al-Manhal al-ṣāfī*, IX, 215–16 (no. 1990). al-Maqrīzī, *Durar al-'uqūd*, III, 31–2 (no. 914), gives a fuller account of al-Munāwī's treatment.
195. Ibn Ḥijjī, I, 515; hence Ibn Qāḍī Shuhba, *Taʾrīkh*, IV, 255. See al-Maqrīzī, *Durar al-'uqūd*, III, 324 (no. 1249), for his return and his death in Muḥarram 805/Aug. 1402; also Ibn Taghrībirdī, *al-Manhal al-ṣāfī*, IX, 280 (no. 2043), with 22 Muḥarram; more briefly, Ibn Ḥajar, *Inbāʾ al-ghumr*, ed. Ḥabashī, II, 250/ed. Khān, V, 116, 119; al-Maqrīzī, *al-Sulūk*, III, part 3, 1108, records merely the date of his death, as 12 Muḥarram [11 Aug.].
196. Ibn Ḥijjī, I, 505. Ibn Taghrībirdī, *al-Nujūm al-zāhira*, XIII, 21 (tr. Popper, II, 109), saying that he was Timur's prisoner; Ibn Ḥajar, *Inbāʾ al-ghumr*, ed. Ḥabashī, II, 166/ed. Khān, IV, 285, that he died after the ordeal (*maḥna*) of Timur; al-Maqrīzī, *al-Sulūk*, III, part 3, 1072, that he died when it was under way, though this conflicts with the dates given for his death, in Dhū l-Qaʿda or Dhū l-Ḥijja 803 [June or July 1401], by Ibn Ḥijjī, al-Maqrīzī, *Durar al-'uqūd*, II, 342 (no. 664), and Ibn Qāḍī Shuhba, *Taʾrīkh*, IV, 217.
197. Ibn Ḥajar, *Inbāʾ al-ghumr*, ed. al-Ḥabashī, 195/ed. Khān, IV, 345. Ibn Qāḍī Shuhba, *Taʾrīkh*, IV, 249–50. Shams al-Dīn Abū l-Khayr Muḥammad b. ʿAbd al-Raḥmān al-Sakhāwī, *al-Ḍawʾ al-lāmi' li-ahl al-qarn al-tāsi'*, ed. Ḥusām al-Dīn al-Qudsī, 12 vols (Cairo, 1353–5/1934–6), X, 190 (no. 796).

198. al-Maqrīzī, *al-Sulūk*, III, part 3, 1056.
199. He may have belonged to the same family as Shaykh ʿAlāʾ al-Dīn al-Nuʿmān b. Dawlatshāh al-Khwārazmī (d. 740/1339), whom Ibn Baṭṭūṭa had encountered at the headquarters of the Jochid khan Özbeg and who was just possibly identical with one of al-ʿUmarī's informants: IB, II, 449 (tr. Gibb, 516). *Masālik*, text, 77–80 (German trans., 143–5; see also Lech's introduction, 30–1). DeWeese, *Islamization and Native Religion*, 125–9. ʿAbd al-Jabbār's descent is given by Ibn Taghrībirdī, *al-Manhal al-ṣāfī*, VII, 143 (no. 1359); for his father's name, cf. *RN* (1915), 115/(2000), 112 (*DPT*, 115); Yazdī, *ZN* (1957), II, 79/(2008), I, 926.
200. IA (1979), 159–60/(1986), 261 (*TGA*, 147). *Taʿrīf* (1951), 369, 372, 375, 379/(2008), 242, 244, 247, 252 (*IKT*, 31, 36, 39, 43).
201. IA (1979), 159, 162/(1986), 261, 265 (*TGA*, 147, 149).
202. Ibn Taghrībirdī, *al-Manhal al-ṣāfī*, VII, 144. al-Sakhāwī, *al-Ḍawʾ al-lāmiʿ*, IV, 35 (no. 103). The latter quotes al-Maqrīzī, whose *Durar al-ʿuqūd* contains no notice on ʿAbd al-Jabbār, though al-Maqrīzī cites there (I, 551–3, 555) oral information from ʿAbd al-Jabbār via Ibn Khaldūn (see also ibid., I, 529). Ibn Ḥajar, *Inbāʾ al-ghumr*, ed. al-Ḥabashī, II, 244/ed. Khān, V, 103–4, supplies a different notice on ʿAbd al-Jabbār that stresses his learning.
203. Yazdī, *ZN* (1957), II, 335/(2008), II, 1168. al-Maqrīzī, *al-Sulūk*, III, part 3, 1109, dates his death in Dhū l-Qaʿda/May–June.
204. Manz, 'Tamerlane and the symbolism', 112. Aubin, 'Comment Tamerlan', 89.
205. Yazdī, *ZN* (1957), II, 157/(2008), 1001.
206. Heribert Horst, 'Tīmūr und Ḫōǧä ʿAlī: Ein Beitrag zur Geschichte der Ṣafawiden', *Akademie der Wissenschaften und der Literatur. Abhandlungen der geistes- und sozialwissenschaftlichen Klasse* (1958), no. 2, 26–39, 44, 47–8. See also Hans Robert Roemer, 'The Safavid period', in *CHI*, VI, 205–6; Paul, 'Scheiche und Herrscher', 299–301; Maria Szuppe, 'L'évolution de l'image de Timour et des Timourides dans l'historiographie safavide du XVIe au XVIIIe siècle', in Szuppe (ed.), *L'Héritage timouride*, 319–22.
207. IA (1979), 24/(1986), 70–1 (*TGA*, 22–3).
208. Yazdī, *ZN* (1957), I, 228, 229/(2008), I, 491, 492. Clavijo (1928), 139; (1859), 79, slightly obscures the sense.
209. *RN* (1915), 11/(2000), 13 (*DPT*, 23). Manz, 'Tamerlane and the symbolism', 117.
210. Mahendrarajah, *The Sufi Saint of Jam*, 45–7.
211. Yazdī, *ZN* (1957), II, 55/(2008), I, 903.
212. Shāmī, *ZN*, I, 211. Yazdī, *ZN* (1957), II, 143/(2008), I, 986. Tümen Āghā had built a *khānaqāh* in this complex: Lentz and Lowry, *Timur and the Princely Vision*, 41–2. For the popularity of the shrine in an earlier generation, see IB, III, 54 (tr. Gibb, 568), who includes Mongols among its many visitors.
213. Yazdī, *ZN* (1957), II, 141, 154–5/(2008), I, 985, and II, 997–9.
214. Ibid. (1957), II, 417–19/(2008), II, 1250–1.
215. Mignanelli (1764), 135b/(2013), 320 (tr. in Fischel, 'A new Latin source', 214). Compare also John of Sulṭāniyya, *Mémoire*, ed. Moranvillé, 461, and the Latin version in *Chronographia regum Francorum*, III, 210. Dietrich von Nyem, *De scismate*, 173, heard similar rumours, possibly from John, though he speaks of informants in the plural.
216. *Taʿrīf* (1951), 382/(2008), 255 (*IKT*, 47).

217. Yazdī, *ZN* (1957), I, 371, 407/(2008), I, 651, 686, respectively.
218. Shāmī, *ZN*, I, 188–9. *RN* (1915), 110a/(2000), 109 (*DPT*, 112). Yazdī, *ZN* (1957), II, 73–5, 86/(2008), I, 920–2, 932.
219. Yazdī, *ZN* (1957), II, 283–4, 451/(2008), II, 1121–2, 1278, respectively. For the decision to attack Rūm, see also Alexandrescu-Dersca, *La Campagne de Timur*, 52–3.
220. There is a discussion in Moin, *The Millennial Sovereign*, esp. 26–31. These expectations had spread to Jewish scholars also since the Mongol invasions: Moshe Idel, 'Mongol invasions and astrology: Two sources of apocalyptic elements in 13th century Kabbalah', in Aldina Quintana, Raquel Ibáñez-Sperber and Ram Ben-Shalom (eds), *Between Edom and Kedar. Studies in Memory of Yom Tov Assis* (Jerusalem, 5774/2014 = *Hispania Judaica Bulletin* 10, part 1), 145–68 (here 150–1); I owe this reference to the kindness of Dr Na'ama Arom.
221. Chann, 'Lord of the Auspicious Conjunction', 93–9.
222. Ibn Khaldūn, *al-Muqaddima*, tr. Rosenthal, II, 213.
223. Moin, *The Millennial Sovereign*, 39.
224. Bernardini, *Mémoire et propagande*, 55–6.
225. Ghazan: *JT*, II, 1348 (*DzhT*, III, 389; compare *CC*, 469, 'rulers who are born under felicitous conjunctions'); also Banākatī, *Rawḍa*, 468. Öljeitü: Qāshānī, *Ta'rīkh-i Uljāytū Sulṭān*, 19. See Brack, 'Theologies of auspicious kingship', 1160; 'Chinggisid pluralism and religious competition', 835–6; and *An Afterlife for the Khan*, 66–78.
226. Chinggis Khan: Jamāl al-Qarshī. *al-Mulḥaqāt bi l-Ṣurāḥ*, Ar. text, 162 (the phrase is obscured in the Russian trans., 118); *JT*, I, 288 (*CC*, 101). Ögödei (by implication): *TJG*, I, 190 (*HWC*, 234). Hülegü: *JT*, II, 1489 (*DzhT*, III, 520; cf. *CC*, 515, 'the star-blessed monarch'). Arghun: Broadbridge, *Kingship and Ideology*, 44. See also Markiewicz, *The Crisis of Kingship*, 169–70, and Brack, *An Afterlife for the Khan*, 67–8, and chap. 4, for Rashīd al-Dīn's exegesis of Öljeitü's unique qualities.
227. Matthew Melvin-Koushki, 'Early modern Islamicate empire: New forms of religiopolitical legitimacy', in Armando Salvatore et al. (eds), *The Wiley Blackwell History of Islam* (Hoboken, NJ, 2018), 353–75 (here 358).
228. Ibn Khaldūn, *al-Muqaddima*, tr. Rosenthal, II, 211–13; and see ibid., II, 196–7, regarding the credulity of the masses. Moin, *The Millennial Sovereign*, 28–9.
229. Thus strongly hinting at the application of the title of *Ṣāḥib-Qirān* to Timur also: Moin, *The Millennial Sovereign*, 27–8, 31. For the speech, see *Ta'rīf* (1951), 372–3/(2008), 244–5 (*IKT*, 36–7).
230. Subtelny, *Timurids in Transition*, 12. Moin, *The Millennial Sovereign*, 31–2, on the other hand, suggests that its public attribution may date only from after his death.

14: THE MONGOL EMPIRE RESURRECTED?

1. Morgan, *Medieval Persia*, 86. Gommans, 'The warband', 336–7. See further pp. 261–5 above.
2. For Timur's reminiscences, see IA (1979), 5–6, 8/(1986), 43–4, 47–8 (*TGA*, 2–3, 5); more briefly, John of Sulṭāniyya, *Mémoire*, ed. Moranvillé, 447.

3. Manz, 'Tamerlane and the symbolism', 115–17. See also Beatrice F. Manz, 'The legacy of Timur', *Asian Art* 2, part 2 (Spring 1989), 10–30 (here 26).
4. Robinson, *In the Shadow of the Mongol Empire*, 212–14; for Taizu's emphasis on his own lowly origins, see also ibid., 170, 194, 215, 232, 234.
5. Shāmī, *ZN*, I, 32–3, 55–6. Yazdī, *ZN* (1957), I, 141/(2008), I, 385. Bernardini, 'La prise du pouvoir par Tamerlan', 143–4.
6. Ong Khan: SH, §§ 152, 157, 177 (tr. De Rachewiltz, I, 75, 79, 99). Pelliot and Hambis (eds), *Histoire des campagnes de Gengis Khan*, 264–5. *JT*, I, 387–91 (*CC*, 133–4). Allsen, 'Preliminary remarks on redistribution', 36. A more apposite parallel with Ḥusayn would have been Temüjin's blood-brother, ally and later enemy, Jamuqa: Morgan, *Medieval Persia*, 85; on Jamuqa, see Ratchnevsky, *Genghis Khan*, 19–20, 37–9.
7. IA (1979), 3/(1986), 41 (*TGA*, 1). SH, § 59 (tr. De Rachewiltz, I, 13; and commentary at 321: the theme has a long pedigree among the Altaic peoples). Bernardini, *Mémoire et propagande*, 57–8. Note that on occasion the account of Timur's early life echoes that of Ghazan Khan: above, p. 355.
8. *RN* (1915), 72/(2000), 80 (*DPT*, 84). Yazdī, *ZN* (1957), II, 45/(2008), I, 893.
9. *RN* (1915), 133, 136/(2000), 126, 128 (*DPT*, 129, 131). Shāmī, *ZN*, I, 194. Yazdī, *ZN* (1957), II, 99–100/(2008), I, 944, 946. For Tarmashirin's siege of Mīrat, see ʿIṣāmī, *Futūḥ al-salāṭīn*, 463–5.
10. Yazdī, *ZN* (1957), I, 527/(2008), I, 803.
11. Ibid. (1972), fo. 82a/(2008), I, 221.
12. Ibid. (1957), II, 41/(2008), I, 887.
13. Ibid. (1972), fo. 82a–b/(2008), I, 221. There was some limited justification for this claim: see above, pp. 335–6.
14. *ZT*, I, 13–14 (also in HA's additions to Shāmī, *ZN*, II, 191): the statement is quoted by Manz, 'Family and ruler', 64, from the Istanbul ms. of HA's *Majmūʿa*.
15. Ibn al-Shiḥna, 215. Hence IA (1979), 140/(1986), 215 (*TGA*, 128).
16. IA (1979), 341–2/(1986), 472–3 (*TGA*, 317); cited in Polyakova, 'Timur as described by the 15th century court historiographers', 35. The speech is reproduced, with some modifications, in al-Maqrīzī, *Durar al-ʿuqūd*, I, 558, and abridged in Ibn Taghrībirdī, *al-Manhal al-ṣāfī*, IV, 138.
17. Manz, 'Tamerlane and the symbolism', 117, citing a letter to Barqūq in Nawāʾī (ed.), *Asnād*, 75.
18. For examples, see Yazdī, *ZN* (1957), I, 195, 208, 213, and II, 160/(2008), I, 451, 466, 474, and II, 1004.
19. Shāmī, *ZN*, I, 257.
20. Toqtamish: ibid., I, 102; Yazdī, *ZN* (1957), I, 300, 359/(2008), I, 574, 640. Faraj: Emmanuel Piloti, *De modo, progressu, ordine ac diligenti providentia habendis in passagio Christianorum pro conquesta Terre Sancte*, ed. and tr. P.-H. Dopp, *L'Égypte au commencement du quinzième siècle d'après le Traité d'Emmanuel Piloti de Crète* (Cairo, 1950), 120; but compare Broadbridge, *Kingship and Ideology*, 194, citing a letter from Timur to Bayezid. Henry III: Clavijo (1859), 133, 134, 165/(1928), 221, 222–3, 277 (at 223 *su fijo, quera su amigo* is rendered ambiguously as 'the good friend of Timur and his son'). See the comment of Manz, 'Tamerlane and the symbolism', 121.
21. Timur to Bayezid, in Sarī ʿAbd-Allāh Efendi, *Munshaʾāt*: Togan, 'Timur's Osteuropapolitik', 297; for the date, see Togan's reasoning, ibid., 280. Roemer, 'Tīmūr in Iran', 72. For Chinggis Khan and the Khwārazmshāh, see *TN*, II, 103 (tr. Raverty, 966).

22. Manz, *The Rise and Rule*, 87–8. See also her 'Tamerlane and the symbolism', 119; *Power, Politics and Religion*, 14; and 'Temür and the early Timurids', 188. Morgan, 'The empire of Tamerlane', 238.
23. See, for example, Jackson, *The Mongols and the West*, 235, and *The Mongols and the Islamic World*, 384.
24. *TR*, I (text), 107, II (trans.), 85. Jackson, *The Mongols and the Islamic World*, 183.
25. On this, see Jackson, 'From *ulus* to khanate', 33–4. Certainly, the Timurid historians Shāmī and Sharaf al-Dīn Yazdī are silent on these allocations, referring only to the domains of the four sons. Yazdī, *ZN* (1972), fo. 26b/(2008), I, 71, mentions Chinggis Khan's brothers simply as sons of Yesügei and adds that their progeny are numerous; Shāmī does not allude to the brothers at all.
26. The phrasing is that of Manz, *The Rise and Rule*, 87–8. See also Morgan, 'The empire of Tamerlane', 238.
27. Manz, *The Rise and Rule*, 87.
28. Shāmī, *ZN*, I, 12.
29. Yazdī, *ZN* (1957), I, 18, 225, and II, 422–3/(2008), I, 244–5, 488, and II, 1256–7.
30. For a parallel, see, for example, the comments on the insatiable ambition of the Delhi Sultan Muḥammad b. Tughluq by Baranī, *Ta'rīkh-i Fīrūzshāhī*, 458 (tr. Zilli, 281–2).
31. *RN* (1915), 45b, 132, 138, 165/(2000), 58, 125, 131, 155 (*DPT*, 61, 127, 134, 158). For allusions to Alexander the Great by Timurid authors, see above, p. 371.
32. Shāmī, *ZN*, I, 228. Yazdī, *ZN* (1957), II, 220–1/(2008), II, 1059.
33. IA (1979), 24/(1986), 71 (*TGA*, 22–3).
34. Ibn al-Shiḥna, 215. Hence IA (1979), 140/(1986), 215 (*TGA*, 128).
35. Nawā'ī (ed.), *Asnād*, 76, and *Safīna*, BN ms. arabe 3423, fo. 399b, respectively.
36. The phrase 'Iran and Turan' recurs relatively often in connection with Timur's dominions, though sometimes with 'and most of the lands of the four quarters [of the world]' added. See, for example, Shāmī, *ZN*, I, 9, 10, 12; *RN* (1915), 1/(2000), 1 (*DPT*, 12); Yazdī, *ZN* (1972), fo. 5a, and (1957), II, 243, 331, 387, 465, 468/(2008), I, 13, and II, 1081, 1164, 1220, 1291, 1293 (in the last two cases purportedly quoting Timur himself); Kutubī, *Ta'rīkh-i āl-i Muẓaffar*, 104; *MA*, fo. 81b, ed. Vokhidov, text, 160 (Russian trans., 105); Ibn Shihāb Yazdī, *Jāmi' al-tawārīkh-i Ḥasanī*, 13.
37. Such views abound in the secondary literature, including my own work: see Jackson, *The Mongols and the West*, 235, and *The Mongols and the Islamic World*, 11. For more nuanced formulations, see Manz, *The Rise and Rule*, 1–2, and Morgan, as quoted later, n. 45; also Roux, *Tamerlan*, 284 and esp. 312, 'Je ne crois plus maintenant que Timur ait véritablement voulu reconstituer l'empire gengiskhanide . . .'
38. Kim, 'Unity and continuity', 65, assumes that in planning to conquer China Timur was seeking to 'restore the unity of the empire'.
39. Timur to Barqūq, in Nawā'ī (ed.), *Asnād*, 77. Broadbridge, *Kingship and Ideology*, 179.
40. Nagel, *Timur der Eroberer*, 183.
41. Yazdī, *ZN* (1957), I, 286/(2008), I, 558. Shāmī, *ZN*, I, 98, says merely that Timur was distressed by the news.
42. Yazdī, *ZN* (1957), I, 522/(2008), I, 800.

43. Shāmī, *ZN*, I, 71–2. Yazdī, *ZN* (1957), I, 196/(2008), I, 452.
44. Shāmī, *ZN*, I, 221–2. Yazdī, *ZN* (1957), II, 199/(2008), II, 1040–1. Nagel, *Timur der Eroberer*, 322–3. Broadbridge, *Kingship and Ideology*, 180 and n.64.
45. Morgan, *Medieval Persia*, 88. See also his 'The empire of Tamerlane', 235.
46. Salmānī, *Shams al-ḥusn*, text, fo. 23a–b (German trans., 22).
47. Grousset, *The Empire of the Steppes*, chap. 11. The original French edition (entitled *L'Empire des steppes. Attila, Gengis-Khan, Tamerlan*) first appeared in 1939.
48. As pointed out by Manz: see *The Rise and Rule*, 1–2; 'Temür and the problem', 27–9; and *Nomads in the Middle East*, 149–50, 154. Di Cosmo, 'State formation and periodization', 35. Roux, *Tamerlan*, 284.
49. May, *The Mongol Empire*, 307. See also pp. 135–6 above. Mamai's authority in the western Jochid territories was of relatively recent origin.
50. Beatrice F. Manz, 'Tīmūr Lang', *EI*², X, 512, surmises that he had probably decided by the mid-1390s not to incorporate the steppe lands into his domain; see too her *Nomads in the Middle East*, 149. In 'Temür and the early Timurids', 186, she proposes that the decision dates from the first major campaign against Toqtamish (793/1391), in which Timur's forces suffered great hardships; compare also her 'Empire of Tamerlane', 287. Golden, *An Introduction*, 311, suggests that Timur made little attempt to recruit non-Chaghatay nomads into his forces; and see also his *Central Asia in World History*, 96.
51. Donald N. Wilber, 'The Timurid court: Life in gardens and tents', *Iran* 17 (1979), 127–33 (here 128), lists those years in which Timur spent time in Samarkand ('most of these stays were not more than a few months').
52. Yazdī, *ZN* (1957), I, 570–1/(2008), I, 846–8. See Wilber, 'The Timurid court'; Gronke, 'The Persian court between palace and tent', 18–19; O'Kane, 'From tents to pavilions', 250–1.
53. Examples (from the forces despatched with one of Timur's sons to garrison a province) in Yazdī, *ZN* (1957), I, 225, 573/(2008), I, 488, 850. Clavijo (1859), 112, 115–16/(1928), 190–1, 196. In 1405, for the expedition against Mughūlistān and China: Salmānī, *Shams al-ḥusn*, text, fo. 25a (German trans., 23). Manz, *The Rise and Rule*, 37. Yet Timur's decree, on the eve of his seven-year campaign, that his troops might bring their womenfolk should they wish, suggests that this might have been an exception among the major long-term expeditions: Clavijo (1859), 172/(1928), 290.
54. Manz, 'The empire of Tamerlane as an adaptation', 288.
55. See the comments of Christopher Mott, *The Formless Empire. A Short History of Diplomacy and Warfare in Central Asia* (Yardley, PA, 2015), 43, 46.
56. Thus Manz, 'Tamerlane and the symbolism', 106, 112.
57. Shaykh Uways: Timur to Barqūq, in Nawā'ī (ed.), *Asnād*, 77. IA (1979), 67/(1986), 122 (*TGA*, 63), had heard tell of this ruler's virtues; see also Faryūmadī, *Dhayl-i Majma' al-ansāb*, 330–1. Fīrūz Shāh: Timur's *fatḥ-nāma* on the capture of Delhi, in Nawā'ī (ed.), *Asnād*, 69–70.
58. *Fatḥ-nāma*, in Nawā'ī (ed.), *Asnād*, 70. Timur to Barqūq, ibid., 75–6. Timur to Bayezid, ibid., 109.
59. Shāmī, *ZN*, I, 98. Yazdī, *ZN* (1957), I, 288/(2008), I, 560.
60. Yazdī, *ZN* (1957), I, 302–3, 467/(2008), I, 576–7, 747.
61. Shāmī, *ZN*, I, 141–2. Yazdī, *ZN* (1957), I, 458–67/(2008), I, 738–46. *ZT*, II, 770, adds that they harassed pilgrims.
62. Clavijo (1859), 81/(1928), 142.

63. Yazdī, *ZN* (1957), II, 64/(2008), I, 911–12.
64. Ibid. (1957), I, 456/(2008), I, 734–5.
65. HA, *Dhayl-i Zafar-nāma*, ed. Tauer, 435.
66. Clavijo (1859), 122/(1928), 204–5.
67. Shāmī, *ZN*, I, 9; quoted in A.K.S. Lambton, 'Early Timurid theories of state: Ḥāfiẓ Abrū and Niẓām al-Dīn Šāmī', in *Mélanges offerts à Henri Laoust*, II (Damascus, 1978 = *BEO* 30), 1–9 (here 8–9).
68. John of Sulṭāniyya, *Mémoire*, ed. Moranvillé, 459–60; *Chronographia regum Francorum*, III, 211, 212.
69. This was certainly the case in China: Atwood (trans.), *The Rise of the Mongols*, 147; and compare also 111.
70. See, for example, Yazdī, *ZN* (1957), I, 456, 468/(2008), I, 734–5, 748. The point is well made by Aubin, 'Comment Tamerlan', 91.
71. Fīrūz Shāh's slaves: Timur's *fatḥ-nāma*, in Safīna, BN ms. arabe 3423, fo. 391b (also in Nawā'ī [ed.], *Asnād*, 70, as cited by Aubin, 'Comment Tamerlan', 90). Qarā Yūsuf: Timur to Bayezid, in Nawā'ī (ed.), *Asnād*, 109; Yazdī, *ZN*, (1957), II, 280/(2008), II, 1117–18; Shāmī, *ZN*, I, 248, 249, 293. Hindu tribes: ibid., I, 175, 176. Afghans: *RN* (1915), 53, 58/(2000), 65, 68 (*DPT*, 68, 72); Yazdī, *ZN* (1957), I, 273, and II, 36, 38/(2008), I, 543, 882, 885. Lurs: Yazdī, *ZN* (1957), I, 288, 421, 562/(2008), I, 560–1, 700, 837. Kurds: Shāmī, *ZN*, I, 144; Yazdī, *ZN* (1957), I, 456 (and cf. also 458), and II, 267/(2008), I, 734 (and cf. also 738), and II, 1103. Kurds and Lurs together: Timur to Bayezid, in Sarī ʿAbd-Allāh Efendi, *Munsha'āt*: Togan, 'Timur's Osteuropapolitik', 295. Takrīt: Shāmī, *ZN*, I, 144; Yazdī, *ZN* (1957), I, 464/(2008), 744. Elements in Darband: ibid. (1957), I, 448/(2008), I, 727. More generally, see *RN* (1915), 26–7/(2000), 35–6 (*DPT*, 39–40); Shāmī, *ZN*, I, 263; Yazdī, *ZN* (1957), II, 446/(2008), II, 1272–3 (*qāṭiʿān-i ṭarīq*); also Manz, 'Tamerlane and the symbolism', 111 (with examples in n.24).
72. Timur to Bayezid, in Sarī ʿAbd-Allāh Efendi, *Munsha'āt*: Togan, 'Timur's Osteuropapolitik', 295.
73. Shāmī, *ZN*, I, 221, and Yazdī, *ZN* (1957), I, 458/(2008), I, 737. Compare also ibid. (1957), I, 225/(2008), I, 488, *ba-Īrān-zamīn dar har mamlakatī ṭā'ifa'ī khurūj karda būdand*, and (1957), I, 215, 286/(2008), I, 476, 558. For *mulūk al-ṭawā'if*, see above, p. 127.
74. For coins on which the Jalayirid ruler is styled Sultan, see Rabino, 'Coins of the Jalā'ir', 105–6.
75. Yūsuf-i Ahl, *Farā'id-i Ghiyāthī*, I, 147; compare also I, 183–4, for the same argument, and *Farā'id-i Ghiyāthī*, ms. Fâtih 4012, fo. 447a–b. Aubin, 'Le khanat de Čağatai', 31, 32–3.
76. Ḥusayn Ṣūfī: *RN* (1915), 19/(2000), 23–4 (*DPT*, 31). Mughūls: ibid. (1915), 17/(2000), 22 (*DPT*, 29–30).
77. On Ilkhanid disdain for the Mamlūk Sultans as slaves, see Broadbridge, *Kingship and Ideology*, 13, 29–30, 33–4, 74–5, 79; Amitai, *Holy War and Rapprochement*, 50. For the Mamlūks as runaways, see Charles J. Halperin, 'The Kipchak connection: The Ilkhans, the Mamluks and Ayn Jalut', *BSOAS* 63 (2000), 229–45.
78. For Barqūq's rise to power, see Petry, *The Mamluk Sultanate*, 23–5; and for Timur's attitude, Yazdī, *ZN* (1957), II, 201–2/(2008), II, 1042–3, as cited in translation by Bernardini, 'Niẓām al-Dīn Shāmī's description', 386–7. Barqūq had not in fact murdered his master to ascend the throne, as Timur claimed.

79. Broadbridge, *Kingship and Ideology*, 170, 174, 179–80, 188, 194.
80. Timur's *fatḥ-nāma* for Delhi, in Nawā'ī (ed.), *Asnād*, 70.
81. For example, *RN* (1915), 38–9/(2000), 50, 52; Sarī ʿAbd-Allāh Efendi, *Munsha'āt*, in Togan, 'Timur's Osteuropapolitik', 298; *fatḥ-nāma* for Syria, in *Safīna*, BN ms. arabe 2423, fo. 398a.
82. Binbaş, 'The Timurids and the Mongol empire', 945–7.
83. Yazdī, *ZN* (1957), II, 399/(2008), II, 1232.
84. Shāmī, *ZN*, I, 144, 237, 293.
85. Manz, 'The office of *darugha* under Tamerlane', 59–69.
86. Subtelny, 'Tamerlane and his descendants', 178–9.
87. Shāmī, *ZN*, I, 107, 122–3. Yazdī, *ZN* (1957), I, 322, 379–80/(2008), I, 599, 659. Ando, *Timuridische Emire*, 118, n.51. For this and other institutions inherited from the Mongols, see Binbaş, 'The Timurids and the Mongol empire', 941.
88. *ZT*, I, 211 (also HA's additions in Shāmī, *ZN*, II, 10).
89. Manz, *The Rise and Rule*, 171 (appendix C).
90. Reuven Amitai, 'Turko-Mongolian nomads and the *iqṭāʿ* system in the Islamic Middle East (ca. 1000–1400 AD)', in Khazanov and Wink (eds), *Nomads in the Sedentary World*, 152–71 (here 164).
91. A copious literature exists on this institution: I.P. Petrushevskii, 'K istorii instituta soiurgala', *Sovetskoe Vostokovedenie* 6 (1949), 227–46, and tr. August N. Samie and John E. Woods, 'On the history of the institution of the *Soyūrghāl*', *JESHO* 64 (2021), 1035–71; *TMEN*, I, 351–3 (no. 228: 'erbliches steuerfreies Lehen'); Ann K.S. Lambton, 'Soyūrg͟hāl', *EI*[2], IX, 731–4; Manz, 'Administration and the delegation of authority', 202–3; D.T. Potts, *Nomadism in Iran from Antiquity to the Modern Era* (Oxford, 2014), 211–12; Fragner, 'Social and internal economic affairs', 504 ff.; Binbaş, 'The Timurids and the Mongol empire', 941. For other usages of the term, see Halil İnalcık, 'Autonomous enclaves in Islamic states', in Pfeiffer and Quinn (eds), *History and Historiography of Post-Mongol Central Asia*, 112–34 (here 119–24).
92. Hope, *Power, Politics, and Tradition*, 196.
93. For Ghazan's knowledge of the Yasa, see *JT*, I, 29, and II, 1210 (*DzhT*, I, part 1, 55, and III, 251; *CC*, 11, 417). Jackson, *The Mongols and the Islamic World*, 375–6.
94. See the comments of Manz, 'Mongol history rewritten and relived', 143.
95. Golden, *An Introduction*, 302. Golden, 'The Türk imperial tradition', 36–8. Roman Iu. Pochekaev, '*Törü*: Ancient Turkic law "privatised" by Chinggis Khan and his descendants', *Inner Asia* 18 (2016), 182–95.
96. *TMEN*, I, 264–7 (no. 134: 'Recht, Gesetz, Gewohnheitsrecht'). Golden, 'The Türk imperial tradition', 38. Vásáry, '*Yāsā* and *Sharīʿa*', 72–3.
97. See the discussion in Subtelny, *Timurids in Transition*, 15–17 (with examples at n.22); and more briefly, 'Tamerlane and his descendants', 172–3.
98. The formulation in Papas and Toutant, *L'Asie centrale de Tamerlan*, 105.
99. Like Rashīd al-Dīn, Timurid writers use *yāsāq* more often than not as part of the phrase *ba-yāsā[q] rasānīdan*, 'to execute, put to death'. We also encounter *yasāqiyān*, meaning '[auxiliary] soldiers': Shāmī, *ZN*, I, 291. Yazdī, *ZN* (1957), I, 485/(2008), I, 765; compare also Naṭanzī (1957), 323, 394/(2004), 247, 289. *TMEN*, IV, 78–9, translates simply as 'Soldaten', 'Hilfstruppensoldaten'. Clearly *yasa[q]* and its derivatives had acquired a broad range of associations.

100. Naṭanzī (1957), 318–19/(2004), 244. See above, p. 119, for the probable significance of this.
101. Yazdī, *ZN* (1957), I, 526/(2008), I, 802.
102. *ZT*, III, 44. See Woods, 'Timur's genealogy', 115; Pochekaev, 'Pravovoe nasledie', 291.
103. Naṭanzī (1957), 99/(2004), 80. Vásáry, '*Yāsā* and *Sharī'a*', 73.
104. Naṭanzī (1957), 104–5/(2004), 85.
105. Shāmī, *ZN*, I, 58.
106. As narrated by Naṭanzī, BL ms. Or. 1566, fo. 231b (not in the selections ed. by Aubin or Istakhrī), and Yazdī, *ZN* (1972), fo. 61b/(2008), I, 169. See above, p. 338.
107. For example, Naṭanzī (1957), 323, 341, 346, 369/(2004), 247, 257, 260, 274.
108. Ibid. (1957), 64/(2004), 57.
109. Shāmī, *ZN*, I, 188. *RN* (1915), 108b/(2000), 107 (*DPT*, 110–11). Yazdī, *ZN* (1957), II, 71/(2008), I, 919.
110. Naṭanzī (1957), 275/(2004), 215. *ZT*, I, 8, 34 (also in HA's additions to Shāmī, *ZN*, II, 188, 204).
111. Shāmī, *ZN*, I, 9, 98.
112. Ibid., I, 230.
113. Ibid., I, 147. Yazdī, *ZN* (1957), I, 472/(2008), I, 751.
114. Nawā'ī (ed.), *Asnād*, 164; cited in İlker Evrim Binbaş, 'Timurid experimentation with eschatological absolutism: Mīrzā Iskandar, Shāh Ni'matullāh Walī, and Sayyid Sharīf Jurjānī in 815/1412', in Orkhan Mir-Kasimov (ed.), *Unity in Diversity. Mysticism, Messianism and the Construction of Religious Authority in Islam*, IHC 105 (Leiden and Boston, MA, 2014), 277–303 (here 280).
115. Naṭanzī (1957), 382/(2004), 282.
116. Ibid. (1957), 291/(2004), 226.
117. Yazdī, *ZN* (1957), II, 436/(2008), II, 1266.
118. Bābur, *Bābur-nāma*, tr. Beveridge, 298–9/tr. Thackston, 224.
119. Naṭanzī (1957), 222/(2004), 178.
120. Ibid. (1957), 402/(2004), 294.
121. Ibid. (1957), 93 (calling Temür Malik 'Temür Beg'), 125/(2004), 77, 101–2. For the first of these references, see Vásáry, '*Yāsā* and *Sharī'a*', 73.
122. Naṭanzī (1957), 204/(2004), 167.
123. Ibid. (1957), 275/(2004), 215.
124. Yazdī, *ZN* (1957), I, 47/(2008), I, 279, *bar qarār namānd*: there is a clear parallel with the usage in SH, § 189, on which see p. 500n. 107.
125. Yazdī, *ZN* (1957), II, 151/(2008), II, 995. In this sense the word is by no means confined to the post-Chinggisid context. Yazdī says that one of the grandsons of Oghuz Khan governed the troops in accordance with his father's and grandfather's regime (*yāsāq*) and that Chinggis Khan's grandfather Bartan Baghatur 'renewed' the rule (*yāsāq*) of his father Qabul Khan: Yazdī, *ZN* (1972), fos 20b, 26a/(2008), I, 54, 69.
126. Vásáry, '*Yāsā* and *Sharī'a*', 67–8. See also the important points made by Binbaş, 'The Timurids and the Mongol empire', 942–3.
127. *TR*, I (text), 43, II (trans.), 38 (slightly modified). As Manz, 'Ulugh Beg, Transoxiana and Turco-Mongolian tradition', 21, points out, the tale itself is most probably apocryphal.

128. It should be noted that a great many of the pages listed under *yāsāq* in the index to the Ṣādiq and Nawā'ī edition (II, 1916) do not in fact contain the term but refer, rather, to a command (e.g. *yarligh*).
129. Woods, 'The rise of Tīmūrid historiography', 98–9.
130. Vásáry, '*Yāsā* and *Sharī'a*', 73. On Naṭanzī's informants, see above, p. 29 and pp. 483–4n. 42.
131. Bartol'd, 'O pogrebenii Timura', in his *Sochineniia*, II, part 2, 445, 446, 448 (tr. Rogers, 81, 82, 83).
132. *ZT*, III, 467. The Persian text of Shāhrukh's letter, which is longer than the Arabic version, is reproduced from Samarqandī's *Maṭla' al-sa'dayn* (and hence with minor differences) in Nawā'ī (ed.), *Asnād*, 133–5.
133. Jalāl al-Dīn Muḥammad Qāyinī, *Naṣā'iḥ-i Shāhrukhī*, Österreichische Nationalbibliothek, Vienna, ms. A.F. 112, fo. 2a–b. On Qāyinī and his work, see Maria Eva Subtelny, 'The Sunni revival under Shāh-Rukh and its promoters: A study of the connection between ideology and higher learning in Timurid Iran', in *Proceedings of the 27th Meeting of Haneda Memorial Hall. Symposium on Central Asia and Iran, August 30, 1993* (Kyoto, [1994]), 14–23 (here 17–21); Maria Eva Subtelny and Anas B. Khalidov, 'The curriculum of Islamic higher learning in Timurid Iran in the light of the Sunni revival under Shāh-Rukh', *JAOS* 115 (1995), 210–36 (here 217 ff.); also Subtelny, *Timurids in Transition*, 107–10, and Binbaş, *Intellectual Networks*, 263.
134. Woods, 'Timur's genealogy', 115, citing a document in Yūsuf-i Ahl, *Farā'id-i Ghiyāthī*.
135. Binbaş, *Intellectual Networks*, 262–4, 265. Waṣṣāf (1853), 539, had used it of Rashīd al-Dīn. But see p. 194 and p. 553n. 162, for its possible application to the Muzaffarid Mubāriz al-Dīn Muḥammad in the mid-fourteenth century. On '*mujaddid* kingship', see Brack, *An Afterlife for the Khan*, 93–5.
136. Manz, 'Mongol history rewritten', 143–5. Aigle, 'Epilogue. The Mongol empire after Genghis Khan', 312. In his letter to Yongle, Shāhrukh is given the title 'Sultan of Islam'.
137. Subtelny, 'The Sunni revival'. Subtelny and Khalidov, 'The curriculum', 211–12. On the suppression of wine-drinking, see Rossabi, 'A translation of Ch'en Ch'eng's *Hsi-yü*', 51.
138. Manz, 'Temür and the problem', 34–8; also her 'Family and ruler', 65–6.
139. Shāmī, *ZN*, I, 16. Yazdī, *ZN* (1957), I, 36/(2008), I, 266.
140. Brack, 'Theologies of auspicious kingship', 1146, 1148, 1161–4, 1169–70. Brack, 'A Mongol Mahdī in medieval Anatolia', 627. Brack, *An Afterlife for the Khan*, passim.
141. Qāyinī, *Naṣā'iḥ-i Shāhrukhī*, fos. 199a–b, 200a; at fo. 200a–b, he urges that pious foundations (*awqāf*) be free of such imposts. See Subtelny, 'The Sunni revival', 20, and *Timurids in Transition*, 109, 161.
142. Binbaş, *Intellectual Networks*, 264–5.
143. Faḍl-Allāh b. Rūzbihān Khunjī, *Ta'rīkh-i 'ālam-ārā-yi Amīnī*, ed. John E. Woods (London, 1992), text, 355–6; I have followed the translation given by Subtelny, *Timurids in Transition*, 25. For Qāḍī 'Īsā's reforms, see Vladimir Minorsky, 'The Aq-Qoyunlu and land reforms', *BSOAS* 17 (1955), 449–62; repr. in Minorsky, *Iranica. Twenty Articles* (Tehran, 1964), 228–41; Woods, *The Aqquyunlu*, 144–5. See generally the remarks of Manz, 'Temür and the problem', 38.

144. *ZT*, III, 467; and for Yongle's letter claiming Timur as a loyal vassal, ibid., III, 460. See Brack, 'Theologies of auspicious kingship', 1143–6. On Shāhrukh's relations with the Ming, see Chap. 15.
145. Morgan, 'The Great *Yāsā* of Chingiz Khān', 173–6; repr. in Hawting (ed.), *Muslims, Mongols and Crusaders*, 208–11. For a survey of the operation of the *yarghu* under the Ilkhans, see also Spuler, *Die Mongolen in Iran*, 316–20.
146. Yazdī, *ZN* (1957), I, 321–2/(2008), I, 599.
147. Ibid. (1957), I, 11/(2008), I, 238.
148. Shāmī, *ZN*, I, 33.
149. Yazdī, *ZN* (1957), II, 161, 275/(2008), II, 1005, 1113.
150. Ibid. (1957), II, 165–6, 191/(2008), II, 1009–10, 1033, respectively.
151. See Manz, *The Rise and Rule*, 169, 171–2. Yazdī, *ZN* (1957), II, 165–6, 191/(2008), II, 1009, 1033, has the *dīwān-i buzurg* conducting the *yarghu*.
152. See A.K.S. Lambton, 'Yarghu', *EI*[2], XI, 284–6; Subtelny, *Timurids in Transition*, 24.
153. Shāmī, *ZN*, I, 67. Yazdī, *ZN* (1957), I, 181, 193/(2008), I, 430, 446.
154. Naṭanzī (1957), 299, 411/(2004), 232, 299–300.
155. Ṣā'in al-Dīn ʿAlī b. Muḥammad Ibn Turka Iṣfahānī, *Chahārdah risāla-yi fārsī*, ed. Sayyid ʿAlī Mūsā Bihbahānī and Sayyid Ibrāhīm Dībāchī (Tehran, 1351 sh./1972), 171, *ba-yamn-i 'āṭifat-i īn pādishāh-i dīn-parwar dar hīch jā nām-u nishān-i ū namānda*. See Subtelny, *Timurids in Transition*, 27, n.64; Binbaş, *Intellectual Networks*, 148–9, 264; and for Ibn Turka, ibid., 140–50.
156. Aigle, 'Epilogue. The Mongol empire after Genghis Khan', 313.
157. There is a particularly stimulating discussion in Binbaş, 'The Timurids and the Mongol empire', 943–4. See also Subtelny, *Timurids in Transition*, 25–7, 95, and Manz, 'Mongol history rewritten', 144–6. For an overview of adherence to, or abandonment of, Mongol law under Timur's successors, see Pochekaev, 'Pravovoe nasledie'.
158. Yazdī, *ZN* (1972), fo. 33a/(2008), I, 91. Compare *TJG*, I, 29 (*HWC*, 40); and for Juwaynī's work as a source for Yazdī's *Muqaddima*, see Binbaş, *Intellectual Networks*, 207. According to Lambton, 'Early Timurid theories of state', 5, n.19, 'in the Mongol period *siyāsat* would appear to be used mainly in the sense of coercive punishment and execution'; cf. also Christian Lange, *Justice, Punishment and the Medieval Muslim Imagination*, CSIC (Cambridge, 2008), 14, 42.
159. Yazdī, *ZN* (1972), fo. 75a/(2008), I, 201.
160. *TJG*, I, 161–2 (*HWC*, 204–5); the section is abridged in *JT*.
161. See the discussion in Binbaş, 'The Timurids and the Mongol empire', 941–2; also Subtelny, 'Tamerlane and his descendants', 173.
162. Astarābādī, *Bazm-u razm*, 451.
163. IA (1979), 20, 233, 319/(1986), 65, 373, 455 (*TGA*, 18, 214, 299).
164. Ibid. (1979), 255–6/(1986), 395 (cf. *TGA*, 234).
165. Ibid. (1979), 320/(1986), 455 (*TGA*, 299). Hence Ibn Q̲āḍī Shuhba, *Ta'rīkh*, IV, 438–9.
166. IA (1979), 320/(1986), 456 (*TGA*, 299). Subtelny, *Timurids in Transition*, 26.
167. Robert Irwin, 'What the partridge told the eagle: A neglected Arabic source on Chinggis Khan and the early history of the Mongols', in Amitai-Preiss and Morgan (eds), *The Mongol Empire and Its Legacy*, 5–11, and repr. in Irwin, *Mamlūks and Crusaders*. Irwin here used the 1832 edition of *Fākihat*

al-khulafā'. The section on Chinggis Khan's decrees is to be found in al-Najjār's edition at 550–3 and in al-Buḥayrī's at 534–7. See also Morgan, 'The "Great *Yasa* of Chinggis Khan" revisited', 306–7.

168. For example, Shāmī, *ZN*, I, 198, 279, 286; Yazdī, *ZN* (1957), II, 181, 343–4, 377, 383–4/(2008), II, 1024, 1176, 1211, 1216–17.
169. *JT*, II, 1307–8, 1348 (*DzhT*, III, 350–2, 389–90; *CC*, 456, 469). Amitai-Preiss, 'Ghazan, Islam and Mongol tradition', 9; repr. in Hawting (ed.), *Muslims, Mongols and Crusaders*, 261. Jackson, *The Mongols and the Islamic World*, 363–4.
170. Yazdī, *ZN* (1957), I, 437/(2008), I, 716. Aubin, 'Comment Tamerlan', 86–7.
171. Parodi, 'L'eredità mongola e altaica', 242; for the details, see Bartol'd, 'O pogrebenii Timura', 443–50 (tr. Rogers, 80–5).
172. John of Sulṭāniyya, *Mémoire*, ed. Moranvillé, 447, 462–3. *Chronographia regum Francorum*, III, 216–17.
173. IA (1979), 315/(1986), 451–2 (*TGA*, 295–6).
174. Where the ladder has fifty rungs: see Yūsuf Khāṣṣ Ḥājib, *Qutadghu Bilig*, tr. Robert Dankoff, *Wisdom of Royal Glory (Kutadgu Bilig). A Turko-Islamic Mirror for Princes* (Chicago, IL, and London, 1983), 236–7; Jean-Paul Roux, 'Quelques objets numineux des Turcs et des Mongols, 4. La coupe', *Turcica* 12 (1980), 40–65 (here 58–9), and repr. in Roux, *Études d'iconographie islamique* (Paris and Leuven, 1982), 101–2.
175. *JT*, I, 167 (*DzhT*, I, part 1, 420–1; *CC*, 63); there is a less specific reference to his miraculous powers at I, 571 (*CC*, 197). Hayton, *La Flor des estoires*, French text, 148, 152 (contemporary Latin trans., 284, 287).
176. Yazdī, *ZN* (1957), II, 107/(2008), I, 951.
177. Ibid. (1957), I, 69–9/(2008), I, 302; passage cited (from the 1887 edition) by Aubin, 'Comment Tamerlan', 88, n.4. For *khilāfat-i ṣūrī*, see Binbaş, *Intellectual Networks*, 257–9, 266–8.
178. David Ayalon, 'The Great *Yāsa* of Chingiz Khān: A re-examination (C_2)', *StIsl* 38 (1973), 107–56 (here 107–27); repr. in Ayalon, *Outsiders in the Lands of Islam*. Like *ba-yāsā rasānīdan* in the Mongol period, *siyāsat farmūdan* had come to mean 'to execute' since the twelfth century: Lange, *Justice, Punishment and the Medieval Muslim Imagination*, 42 and n.96.
179. *TR*, I (text), 167, II (trans.), 132.
180. Ron Sela, *Ritual and Authority in Central Asia. The Khan's Inauguration Ceremony*, PIA 37 (Bloomington, IN, 2003), 28–32. For other instances, taken from Uzbek practice, see McChesney, 'The Chinggisid restoration in Central Asia', 283–6.
181. R.D. McChesney, 'Zamzam water on a white felt carpet: Adapting Mongol ways in Muslim Central Asia, 1550–1650', in Michael Gervers and Wayne Schlepp (eds), *Religion, Customary Law, and Nomadic Technology*, TSCIA 4 (Toronto, 2000), 63–80.
182. Dale, *The Garden of the Eight Paradises*, 171, 209. Parodi, 'L'eredità mongola e altaica', 245.

15: AFTERMATH: TIMUR'S SUCCESSORS

1. And not just, therefore, news of Timur's death. Salmānī, *Shams al-ḥusn*, text, fo. 33a (German trans., 27). Yazdī, *ZN* (1957), II, 466, 473/(2008), II, 1291, 1298. The later account in Ja'farī *Ta'rīkh-i kabīr*, tr. Zaryab, 32, says that Timur died

the night following the nomination. Manz, *The Rise and Rule*, 128, and *Power, Politics and Religion*, 17, deduces that Timur made the decision on his deathbed.

2. Clavijo (1859), 152–3/(1928), 254–5. Pīr Muḥammad was then in Samarkand for the quriltai: Yazdī, *ZN* (1957), II, 426, 448/(2008), II, 1259–60, 1275.
3. Soucek, *A History of Inner Asia*, 127. Compare also Ashrafyan, 'Central Asia under Timur', 335.
4. Binbaş, 'The Timurids and the Mongol empire', 940.
5. See the remarks of Manz, 'The legacy of Timur', 23.
6. Woods, *The Timurid Dynasty*, 20 (no. 1.1), 23 (nos 1.3 and 1.4), 34 (nos 3.2 and 3.4), 35 (no. 3.5).
7. Clavijo (1859), 189–90/(1928), 317–20. Salmānī, *Shams al-ḥusn*, text, fo. 130b (German trans., 92). Jaʿfarī, *Taʾrīkh-i kabīr*, tr. Zaryab, 45.
8. I can only endorse here the judicious assessment of Manz, *The Rise and Rule*, 135, 145–6.
9. Salmānī, *Shams al-ḥusn*, text, fos 44b–45b (German trans., 33–4). Paul, 'Khalīl Sulṭān and the "Westerners"', 12–13.
10. Salmānī, *Shams al-ḥusn*, text, fos 47a–48a (German trans., 35). The date is given in *ZT*, III, 13. Jaʿfarī, *Taʾrīkh-i kabīr*, tr. Zaryab, 35, dates his enthronement on Wednesday 27 Ramaḍān [29 March], though this was in fact a Sunday.
11. Manz, *Power, Politics and Religion*, 21, and her 'Temür and the early Timurids', 189.
12. Salmānī, *Shams al-ḥusn*, text, fo. 76a (German trans., 55).
13. Ibid., editor's introduction, 12–13.
14. Ibid., text, fos 162b–164b (German trans., 117–20). See Yazdī, *ZN* (1957), II, 517/(2008), II, 1336; Jahn, 'Timur und die Frauen', 528.
15. Yazdī, *ZN* (1957), II, 454/(2008), II, 1281.
16. There is a long and detailed account of these events in Salmānī, *Shams al-ḥusn*, text, fos 76b–83b (German trans., 55–62), and another in *ZT*, III, 82–8, which gives the date (*sabʿ* appears as *tasʿ* in error in the printed text) of Khalīl Sulṭān's departure from Samarkand. Jaʿfarī, *Taʾrīkh-i kabīr*, tr. Zaryab, 38–9, 40, offers a much shorter version that ends with Sulṭān Ḥusayn's flight to Sulaymānshāh.
17. Though the marriage is not listed in Woods, 'Timur's genealogy', 30. For the coins, see Binbaş, 'The Timurids and the Mongol empire', n.19 at 948. Khān Sulṭān Khānīka was a granddaughter of Bayan Quli Khan and thus a Chinggisid (above, p. 358 and n. 157 at p. 615).
18. Salmānī, *Shams al-ḥusn*, text, fos 96b–97b (German trans., 72–3). *ZT*, III, 103, and Khwāfī (1962), III, 167/(2007), III, 1024 (tr. Iusupova, 135–6), give the date as 2 Ramaḍān [21 Feb.].
19. Salmānī, *Shams al-ḥusn*, text, fos 139a–141a (German trans., 100–1).
20. IA (1979), 303–4/(1986), 440–1 (*TGA*, 282–3), says so explicitly.
21. Paul, 'Khalīl Sulṭān and the "Westerners"', 16–25. More briefly, Manz, *The Rise and Rule*, 131–2.
22. Salmānī, *Shams al-ḥusn*, text, fo. 78a (German trans., 56), and *ZT*, III, 83, for the executions. For the other amirs, see Ando, *Timuridische Emire*, 81–2, 94–5, 100, 115, respectively.
23. Shāmī, *ZN*, I, 189, 190–1, 200, 234–6, 240, 250, 270, 284. Yazdī, *ZN* (1957), II, 224, 237, 286, 346, 380, 454, 459, 466/(2008), II, 1063, 1075, 1124, 1179, 1213, 1281, 1285–6, 1292.

24. Salmānī, *Shams al-ḥusn*, text, fo. 90a (German trans., 67).
25. Ibid., text, fos 131a–132b (German trans., 92–4), describes one military encounter, ending in Khalīl Sulṭān's defeat, at the beginning of 808/June–July 1405.
26. These events are surveyed in Manz, *The Rise and Rule*, 134–5; for the desertions, see 136.
27. Salmānī, *Shams al-ḥusn*, text, fo. 167b (German trans., 122).
28. Manz, *Power, Politics and Religion*, 24–5. A brief account in Jaʿfarī, *Ta'rīkh-i kabīr*, tr. Zaryab, 53–5.
29. For the fortunes of Amīrānshāh and his sons, see Manz, *The Rise and Rule*, 141–4.
30. John of Sulṭāniyya, *Mémoire*, 446; hence *Chronographia regum Francorum*, III, 213. Clavijo (1859), 188/(1928), 316. *ZT*, III, 44.
31. Salmānī, *Shams al-ḥusn*, text, fo. 64b (German trans., 46–7). *ZT*, III, 40–2, 60, 63.
32. Salmānī, *Shams al-ḥusn*, text, fos 64b, 84a, 139a–b (German trans., 46–7, 62–3, 101). Hans R. Roemer, 'The successors of Tīmūr', in *CHI*, VI, 98–146 (here 100), assumes that their aim was to assist Khalīl Sulṭān.
33. Clavijo (1859), 188/(1928), 316.
34. *ZT*, III, 43. Manz, *Power, Politics and Religion*, 29.
35. Salmānī, *Shams al-ḥusn*, text, fos 116b–123a (German trans., 86–9). The date of the allies' defeat is given by Jaʿfarī, *Ta'rīkh-i kabīr*, tr. Zaryab, 38. *ZT*, III, 72–7, 80, 126–8, 137–8, placing ʿUmar's arrival at Shāhrukh's court on 1 Rabīʿ I 809/16 Aug. 1406. HA, *Jughrāfiyya*, ed. Sajjādī, II, 322, 324–5.
36. Salmānī, *Shams al-ḥusn*, text, fos 125b–131a (German trans., 90–2). *ZT*, III, 150–4, 161–2. Jaʿfarī, *Ta'rīkh-i kabīr*, tr. Zaryab, 45, is briefer and supplies the year 810/1407–8.
37. Jaʿfarī, *Ta'rīkh-i kabīr*, tr. Zaryab, 39–40.
38. *ZT*, III, 178–9 (*ad annum* 809/1406–7); 174–7 for Iskandar's invasion of Kirmān. In a more detailed account of Iskandar's fortunes, Ibn Shihāb Yazdī, *Jāmiʿ al-tawārīkh-i Ḥasanī*, 15–17, says that he was freed on Shāhrukh's orders and returned to Shiraz, where he and Pīr Muḥammad were reconciled; the narrative then moves on fairly rapidly to Pīr Muḥammad's murder. The intervening events (including ʿUmar b. Amīrānshāh's request for aid and Abā Bakr's attack on Isfahan) are described ibid., 27–31. Ibn Shihāb was evidently confused by the fact that Iskandar mounted two distinct attempts to seize Kirmān. See Soucek, 'Eskandar b. ʿOmar Šayx', 79, for a brief chronological survey.
39. HA, *Jughrāfiyya*, ed. Sajjādī, II, 326–31. *ZT*, III, 177–83. Jaʿfarī, *Ta'rīkh-i kabīr*, tr. Zaryab, 45–7, dating these events in 810/1407–8.
40. Salmānī, *Shams al-ḥusn*, text, fos 149b–152b, 158b–159b (German trans., 108–10, 114, 116), in an otherwise detailed account, omits Abā Bakr's dealings with Pīr Muḥammad, as does *ZT*, III, 255–7. See Jaʿfarī, *Ta'rīkh-i kabīr*, tr. Zaryab, 47–8; and for Pīr Muḥammad's appeal for assistance, 46. Abā Bakr's activities in Kirmān are recounted in HA, *Jughrāfiyya*, ed. Sajjādī, III, 201–4, with dates; hence Aubin, *Deux sayyids de Bam*, 30–4. Bosworth, *The History of the Saffarids*, 455.
41. Shāhrukh's rise to supreme power is surveyed in Manz, *The Rise and Rule*, 128–47, and *Power, Politics and Religion*, 16–33.

42. Salmānī, *Shams al-ḥusn*, text, fo. 42b (German trans., 31).
43. Ibid., text, fo. 63a–b (reading with Roemer *khalaf* for ḴLQ; see German trans., 45 and n.2).
44. *ZT*, III, 8–9. Jaʿfarī, *Taʾrīkh-i kabīr*, tr. Zaryab, 35, 36, who claims that the amirs present in Khurāsān swore allegiance to Shāhrukh and that his name was inserted in the khutba and on the coinage there and in Iraq and Fārs, here seems to be following *ZT*; though earlier, at 32, he does mention Pīr Muḥammad's nomination.
45. *ZT*, III, 10–11.
46. Ibid., III, 44–5. Also compare HA, *Jughrāfiyya*, ed. Sajjādī, II, 321. Jaʿfarī, *Taʾrīkh-i kabīr*, tr. Zaryab, 36, asserts that Pīr Muḥammad struck coins in Shāhrukh's name. Manz, Power, *Politics and Religion*, 156, accepts HA's testimony. I am assuming that *buzurg*, 'great', still held the significance it had for the thirteenth-century Mongols: see above, p. 69.
47. *ZT*, III, 178. Jaʿfarī, *Taʾrīkh-i kabīr*, tr. Zaryab, 45. Ibn Shihāb Yazdī, *Jāmiʿ al-tawārīkh-i Ḥasanī*, 16.
48. As Manz, *Power, Politics and Religion*, 156, points out, Pīr Muḥammad was also married to a sister of Shāhrukh's chief wife Gawhar Shād.
49. Salmānī, *Shams al-ḥusn*, text, fos 82b, 84a (German trans., 61, 62).
50. Ibid., text, fos 72b–73a (German trans., 53). Shāhrukh's letter is further quoted at p. 432.
51. Jaʿfarī, *Taʾrīkh-i kabīr*, tr. Zaryab, 37, expressly links this ambition with Pīr Pādishāh's Chinggisid descent.
52. Salmānī, *Shams al-ḥusn*, text, fos 65a–b, 68a–69b (German trans., 47, 50). Aubin, 'La fin de l'état sarbadâr', 115–16 (repr. in his *Études*, 327–8).
53. Bosworth, *The History of the Saffarids*, 453–7.
54. A point made by Manz, *Power, Politics and Religion*, 24, and 'Temür and the early Timurids', 190; compare also her *The Rise and Rule*, 139–40.
55. These events are surveyed by Manz, *Power, Politics and Religion*, 26–8.
56. For Iskandar's wanderings, see *ZT*, III, 286–91.
57. Ibid., III, 341–2. Jaʿfarī, *Taʾrīkh-i kabīr*, tr. Zaryab, 50, supplies the date.
58. *ZT*, III, 223–4, 345–8. HA, *Jughrāfiyya*, ed. Sajjādī, II, 337–8. Brief details in Naṭanzī (1957), 183, 196/(2004), 151, 161. Jaʿfarī, *Taʾrīkh-i kabīr*, tr. Zaryab, 51–2, and Ibn Shihāb Yazdī, *Jāmiʿ al-tawārīkh-i Ḥasanī*, 19–21, recount only the attempt on Isfahan. Khwāfī (1962), III, 184, 197, describes this episode twice; compare (2007), III, 1049. Manz, *Power, Politics and Religion*, 160.
59. *ZT*, III, 395–9, 444–6. Ibn Shihāb Yazdī, *Jāmiʿ al-tawārīkh-i Ḥasanī*, 23–4. Soucek, 'Eskandar b. ʿOmar Šayx', 80–1.
60. Kirmān: Aubin, *Deux sayyids de Bam*, 35–6. Qum: *ZT*, III, 481, with the date; Jaʿfarī, *Taʾrīkh-i kabīr*, tr. Zaryab, 57–8, giving 816 [1413–14].
61. *ZT*, III, 49. Aubin, 'Le mécénat timouride à Chiraz', 76–7 (repr. in his *Études*, 159). For Iskandar's campaign on the eastern frontier, see above, p. 286, and Soucek, 'Eskandar b. ʿOmar Šayx', 76–8. Binbaş, *Intellectual Networks*, 197–8, views the phrase as symbolizing aspirations to sovereignty over Timur's empire as a whole, but in my opinion this divorces it from its context; see also his 'Timurid experimentation', 295–6 and n.54.
62. 'Anonymous synoptic account', 90.
63. Ibid., 90–1. Ibn Shihāb Yazdī, *Jāmiʿ al-tawārīkh-i Ḥasanī*, 24, speaks of the exchange of gifts between Sulṭān Aḥmad and Iskandar.

64. See Naṭanzī (1957), 433/(2004), 316, and Soucek, 'Eskandar b. ʿOmar Šayx', 76, on his terminology. For Iskandar's rise to power and his ideological programme, see Binbaş, *Intellectual Networks*, 189–98, and 'Timurid experimentation', esp. 290–300 (n.53 for the date when he assumed the title of sultan).
65. For Iskandar's downfall, see Soucek, 'Eskandar b. ʿOmar Šayx', 81–2. Jaʿfarī, *Ta'rīkh-i kabīr*, tr. Zaryab, 65, says that Rustam had him killed.
66. Jaʿfarī, *Ta'rīkh-i kabīr*, tr. Zaryab, 73, gives the date 6 Shawwāl 827 [1 Sept. 1424]. Khwāfī (1962), III, 257/(2007), III, 1108 (tr. Iusupova, 197), furnishes the alternative years 827 and 828 for his death.
67. *ZT*, III, 191–2.
68. Ibid., III, 353–4, 396–9, 436–7. The date of death is given also in *MA*, fo. 127a, ed. Vokhidov, text, 242 (Russian trans., 147).
69. *ZT*, III, 354.
70. Khwāfī (1962), III, 176/(2007), III, 1036 (tr. Iusupova, 142).
71. *ZT*, III, 301. Manz, *Power, Politics, and Religion*, 26.
72. *ZT*, III, 557–8. HA, *Jughrāfiyya*, ed. Sajjādī, II, 361. For his rebellion, see Manz, *Power, Politics and Religion*, 32, 132.
73. Jaʿfarī, *Ta'rīkh-i kabīr*, tr. Zaryab, 42, 43.
74. *ZT*, IV, 641–2.
75. Ibid., IV, 679–92. Jaʿfarī, *Ta'rīkh-i kabīr*, tr. Zaryab, 66, 69. Manz, *Power, Politics and Religion*, 33.
76. Stephen Dale, 'The later Timurids *c.* 1450–1526', in *CHIA*, 199–217 (here 204–5); see also his more general indictment ibid., 199–200. Compare also Soucek, as quoted earlier, n. 3.
77. Salmānī, *Shams al-ḥusn*, text, fos 70a–71a (German trans., 51).
78. Ibid., text, fos 74a–75a, 118b (German trans., 53–4, 87).
79. 'Anonymous synoptic account', 92.
80. Malika Dekkiche, 'New source, new debate: Re-evaluation of the Mamluk–Timurid struggle for religious supremacy in the Hijaz (Paris, BnF MS ar. 4440)', *MSR* 18 (2014–15), 247–71.
81. Binbaş, *Intellectual Networks*, 62–4.
82. Wing, 'Submission, defiance, and the rules of politics', 378–80.
83. Manz, *Power, Politics and Religion*, 28.
84. Schiltberger, 33–7. This testimony is not necessarily reliable. Chekire deserted Khalīl Sulṭān in 809/1406–7 in order to make for the Jochid lands, but seems to have turned back: Salmānī, *Shams al-ḥusn*, text, fo. 153a (German trans., 110). In 813/1410–11 he was in the service of the Timurid amir Shaykh Nūr al-Dīn: *ZT*, III, 367, 369. See Safargaliev, *Raspad*, 190–2; Frank, 'The western steppe', 239; Pochekaev, *Tsari ordynskie*, 225 ('Чокре'). He would become khan with Edigü's support: Naṭanzī (1957), 101–2/(2004), 82; *ZT*, III, 479 (suggesting that he was with Edigü by *c.* 815/1412–13), 635.
85. Baraq: *ZT*, IV, 704, 906–7. Shīr Muḥammad: ibid., IV, 748, 877–8. For Sātūq, see above, p. 346.
86. For relations with Baraq and Shīr Muḥammad, see Barthold, *Four Studies*, II, 89–101, 101–3 (= Bartol'd, *Sochineniia*, II, part 2, 101–11, 111–12), respectively; more briefly Manz, 'Temür and the early Timurids', 193–4.
87. Kauz, *Politik und Handel*, 82–3.
88. Robinson, *Ming China and Its Allies*, 35.

89. For Shāhrukh's dealings with the Ming generally, see Kauz, *Politik und Handel*, 93–143.
90. Ibid., 93, 95–9. Robinson, *Ming China and Its Allies*, 44.
91. Kauz, *Politik und Handel*, 136–41. Ghiyāth al-Dīn's account is found in Maitra (ed. and trans.), *A Persian Embassy to China*; for the Persian text, see also *ZT*, IV, 817–64.
92. See generally Ishtiyaq Ahmad Zilli, 'Relations of the Saiyyid [*sic*] Sultans of Delhi with the Timurids – a reappraisal', in Nazir Ahmad and Asloob Ahmed Ansari (eds), *Fakhruddin Ali Ahmed Memorial Volume* (New Delhi, 1994), 221–8. See also Jackson, *The Delhi Sultanate*, 322.
93. Bihāmadkhānī, fo. 312a (tr. Zaki, 95).
94. On the dynasty in general, see Beatrice F. Manz, 'Tīmūrids, 1. History', *EI*², X, 513–16.
95. A good, brief survey in J. Aubin, 'Abū Saʿīd b. Muḥammad b. Mīrān<u>sh</u>āh', *EI*², I, 147–8.
96. Manz, 'Family and ruler', 58.
97. For these various conflicts, see Roemer, 'The successors of Tīmūr', 102–17, and 'The Türkmen dynasties'.
98. Allsen, 'Eurasia after the Mongols', 163.
99. Stephen F. Dale, 'The legacy of the Timurids', *JRAS*, 3rd series, 8 (1998), 43–58 (here 44–51); repr. in Levi (ed.), *India and Central Asia*, 177–85. Lisa Balabanlilar, 'Lords of the Auspicious Conjunction: Turco-Mongol imperial identity on the subcontinent', *JWH* 18 (2007), 1–39, and her *Imperial Identity*, 44–6.
100. Dale, 'The legacy of the Timurids', 46–7; also in Levi (ed.), *India and Central Asia*, 180. Balabanlilar, *Imperial Identity*, 44–8. Moin, *The Millennial Sovereign*, 23–4. Eaton, *India in the Persianate Age*, 280, 285–6. More generally, see Richard C. Foltz, *Mughal India and Central Asia* (Oxford and Karachi, 1998), chap. 2.
101. Dale, 'The legacy of the Timurids', 43; also in Levi (ed.), *India and Central Asia*, 176.
102. Sholeh A. Quinn, 'Notes on Timurid legitimacy in three Safavid chronicles', *IrSt* 31 (1998), 149–58. Quinn, *Historical Writing during the Reign of Shah 'Abbas* (Salt Lake City, UT, 2000), 44–5, 49–52, 75, 86–9.
103. Ernest Tucker, 'Seeking a world empire: Nādir Shāh in Tīmūr's path', in Pfeiffer and Quinn (eds), *History and Historiography of Post-Mongol Central Asia*, 332–42. Tucker, *Nadir Shah's Quest for Legitimacy in Post-Safavid Iran* (Gainesville, FL, 2006), 68–75.
104. Cornell Fleischer, 'Royal authority, dynastic cyclism, and "Ibn Khaldûnism" in sixteenth-century Ottoman letters', in Bruce B. Lawrence (ed.), *Ibn Khaldun and Islamic Ideology* (Leiden, 1984), 46–68 (here 57). Dale, 'The legacy of the Timurids', 54–6; also in Levi (ed.), *India and Central Asia*, 189–90. See too Balabanlilar, *Imperial Identity*, 38–40.
105. Melville, 'Visualising Tamerlane', 101.
106. Levi, *The Rise and Fall of Khoqand*, 99–108. Timur K. Beisembiev, 'Farghana's contacts with India in the eighteenth and nineteenth centuries', in Scott C. Levi (ed.), *India and Central Asia. Commerce and Culture, 1500–1800* (Oxford and Delhi, 2007), 176–99 (here 264–5). Aftandil Erkinov, 'Les Timourides, modèles de légitimeté et les recueils poétiques de Kokand', in Francis Richard

and Maria Szuppe (eds), *Écrit et culture en Asie centrale et dans le monde turco-iranien, Xe–XIXe siècles*, StIr cahier 40 (Paris, 2009), 285–330. At one time it was believed that Bābur's maternal Chinggisid ancestry was equally central to the forging of the claim, but this notion has now been discredited: see A. Erkinov, 'Fabrication of legitimation in the Khoqand Khānate under the reign of ʿUmar-Khān (1225–1237/1810–1822): Palace manuscript of "Bakhtiyār-nāma" Daqāyiqī Samarqandī as a source for the legend of Āltūn Bīshīk', *MO* 19, no. 2 (Dec. 2013), 3–18.

107. John Darwin, *After Tamerlane. The Global History of Empire since 1405* (London and New York, 2007), 4.
108. Martin B. Dickson, 'Uzbek dynastic theory in the sixteenth century', in *TDPKV*, III, 208–16. McChesney, 'The Chinggisid restoration in Central Asia', 280–2.
109. On the split, see Bregel, 'Uzbeks, Qazaqs and Turkmens', 224–9.
110. See Peter C. Perdue, *China Marches West. The Qing Conquest of Central Eurasia* (Cambridge, MA, 2005), 54–9. For a good sketch of Oyirat history, see 'Oyirat', in *EMME*, 419–23. The fifteenth-century history is also dealt with by Christian, *A History of Russia, Central Asia and Mongolia*, II, 65–6.
111. See Perdue, *China Marches West*, 59–60, arguing against this view as espoused by Frederick Mote.
112. Veit, 'The eastern steppe', 167–70.
113. On the history of the Zunghar empire, see Nicola Di Cosmo, 'The Qing and Inner Asia: 1636–1800', in *CHIA*, 333–62 (here 344–53); idem, 'The extension of Ch'ing rule over Mongolia, Sinkiang, and Tibet, 1636–1800', in *CHC*, IX, part 2, 117–35; and Christian, *A History of Russia, Central Asia and Mongolia*, II, 186–92.
114. Di Cosmo, 'The Qing and Inner Asia', 334, prefers 'mixed'.
115. See Veit, 'The eastern steppe', 177–81; Pamela Kyle Crossley, *The Manchus* (Oxford, 1997), 75–80.
116. Qualifications to this view are expressed in David O. Morgan and Anthony Reid, 'Introduction: Islam in a plural Asia', in *NCHI*, III, 1–17 (here 16–17). For a restatement, see Anatoly M. Khazanov, 'The Eurasian steppe nomads in world military history', in Jürgen Paul (ed.), *Nomad Aristocrats in a World of Empires* (Wiesbaden, 2013), 187–207 (here 202–3).
117. The view of Stephen F. Dale: see his *The Garden of the Eight Paradises*, 329–30; 'The later Timurids', 215; and *Babur*, 128–9.
118. Irwin, 'Gunpowder and firearms'. Leslie Collins, 'The military organization and tactics of the Crimean Tatars during the sixteenth and seventeenth centuries', in V.J. Parry and M.E. Yapp (eds), *War, Technology and Society in the Middle East* (Oxford, 1975), 257–76.
119. Darwin, *After Tamerlane*, 5–6.
120. Whether in the sixteenth century 'Europe was becoming the world's engine' and 'all roads now led to Europe', as Peter Frankopan opines in *The Silk Roads. A New History of the World* (London and New York, 2015), 243, is debatable: for a very different verdict, see Darwin, *After Tamerlane*, esp. 73 ff., 93–9, 104–5.
121. Scott C. Levi, 'India, Russia and the eighteenth-century transformation of the Central Asian caravan trade', *JESHO* 42 (1999), 519–48 (esp. 522–32); repr. in Levi (ed.), *India and Central Asia*, 93–122 (esp. 95–104). See also

Morris Rossabi, 'The "decline" of the Central Asian caravan trade', in James D. Tracy (ed.), *The Rise of Merchant Empires. Long-Distance Trade in the Early Modern World, 1350–1750* (Cambridge, 1990), 351–70, and repr. in Rossabi, *From Yuan to Modern China*, 201–20; Millward, 'Eastern Central Asia', 266–7, 270–1; Allsen, 'Eurasia after the Mongols', 175.

122. David Christian, 'Silk Roads or Steppe Roads? The Silk Roads in world history', *JWH* 11 (2000), 1–26 (here 18–21).
123. Perdue, *China Marches West*, 10–11, sees the period 1680–1760 as 'tipping the balance against unfettered nomadism'.
124. Jos Gommans, 'Warhorse and post-nomadic empire in Asia, *c*. 1000–1800', *JGH* 2 (2007), 1–21. Allsen, 'Eurasia after the Mongols', 172–6.
125. Allsen, 'Eurasia after the Mongols', 180.

BIBLIOGRAPHY

PRIMARY SOURCES

Arabic and Persian

Aḥmad b. Ḥusayn b. ʿAlī Kātib, *Taʾrīkh-i jadīd-i Yazd*, ed. Īraj Afshār, 2nd edn (Tehran, 2537 shāhanshāhī/1978)

Ahrī, Abū Bakr Quṭbī, *Taʾrīkh-i Shaykh Uways*, facsimile edn (of Leiden ms. 2634) and trans. by J.B. Van Loon, *Taʾrīkh-i Shaikh Uwais. An Important Source for the History of Ādharbaijān in the Fourteenth Century* (The Hague, 1954)

Amīr Khusraw Dihlawī, *Khazāʾin al-futūḥ*, ed. Mohammad Wahid Mirza, Bibliotheca Indica (Calcutta, 1953)

Āmulī, Awliyāʾ-Allāh, *Taʾrīkh-i Rūyān*, ed. Manūchihr Sutūda (Tehran, 1348 shamsī/1969)

Āmulī, Shams al-Dīn Muḥammad b. Maḥmūd, *Nafāʾis al-funūn fī ʿarāʾis al-ʿuyūn*, ed. Mīrzā Abū l-Ḥasan Shaʿrānī and Sayyid Ibrāhīm Miyānajī, 3 vols (Tehran, 1377–9/1958–60)

Anonymous, *Akhbār-i Mughūlān dar anbāna-yi Quṭb*, ed. Īraj Afshār (Qum, 1389 shamsī/2009); trans. George Lane, *The Mongols in Iran. Quṭb al-Dīn Shīrāzī's Akhbār-i Moghūlān* (London and New York, 2018)

Anonymous, *Dhayl-i Jāmiʿ al-tawārīkh*, BL ms. Or. 2885

Anonymous, *Dhayl-i Taʾrīkh-i guzīda*, ed. Osamu Otsuka (from BN ms. Supplément persan 172, fos 334b–344b), 'Research on the continuations of the *Tārīkh-i Guzīda* with a special reference to the newly discovered "continuation" concerning Jalayerid history', *Ajia Afurika gengo bunka kenkyū (Journal of Asian and African Studies)* (Tokyo), 85 (March 2013), text at 192–205

Anonymous, *jung* or *safīna* (literary anthology), BN ms. arabe 3423 (includes texts of three of Timur's *fatḥ-nāmas*)

Anonymous, *Muʿizz al-ansāb fī shajarat al-ansāb*, BN ms. Anc. fonds persan 67; facsimile edn and Russian trans. by Sh.Kh. Vokhidov, *Muʿizz al-ansāb (Proslavliaiushchee genealogii)*, in *IKPI*, III (Almaty, 2006) [the folio numbering in this edition differs slightly from that in the ms., which is followed in the present book]

Anonymous, *Shajarat al-atrāk*, Harvard University, Houghton Library, Persian ms. 6F; extract trans. (as *Ta'rīkh-i arba' ulūs*) by M.Kh. Abuseitova, in *IKPI*, V, 88–112

Anonymous, 'Synoptic account of the Timurid house', ed. and trans. in Wheeler M. Thackston (ed.), *Album Prefaces and Other Documents on the History of Calligraphers and Painters*, Studies and Sources in Islamic Art and Architecture. Supplements to Muqarnas 10 (Leiden, Boston, MA, and Cologne, 2001), 88–98

Anonymous, *Ta'rīkh-i shāhī-yi Qarākhitā'iyyān*, ed. Muḥammad Ibrāhīm Bāstānī-Pārīzī (Tehran, 2535 shāhanshāhī/1977)

Anonymous, *Ta'rīkh-i Sīstān*, ed. Malik al-Shuʿarā Bahār (Tehran, 1314 shamsī/1935)

Āqsarā'ī, Karīm al-Dīn Maḥmūd b. Muḥammad, *Musāmarat al-akhbār*, ed. Osman Turan as *Müsâmeret l-ahbâr. Mogollar zamanında Türkiye Selçukluları tarihi* (Ankara, 1944)

Arends, A.K.; Khalidov, A.B.; and Chekhovich, O.D. (eds), *Bukharskii vakf XIII v.* (Moscow, 1979)

Astarābādī, ʿAzīz b. Ardashīr, *Bazm-u razm*, ed. Kilisli Rıfat Beg, with introduction by Mehmet Fuat Köprülüzade (Istanbul, 1928)

al-ʿAynī, Badr al-Dīn Abū Muḥammad Maḥmūd b. Aḥmad, *'Iqd al-jumān fī ta'rīkh ahl al-zamān*, partial edn by Aymān ʿUmar Shukrī, *Al-Sulṭān Barqūq mu'assis Dawlat al-mamālīk al-jarākisa 784–801 H./1382–1398 min khilāl makhṭūṭ 'Iqd al-jumān fī ta'rīkh ahl al-zamān li-Badr al-'Aynī* (Cairo, 2002); also BN ms. arabe 1544

Bābur, Ẓahīr al-Dīn Muḥammad, *Bābur-nāma*, trans. Annette S. Beveridge, *The Bābur-nāma in English* (London, 1921–2; reprinted in 1 vol., 1969); trans. Wheeler M. Thackston, *The Baburnama. The Memoirs of Babur, Prince and Emperor* (New York, 2002)

Banākatī, Fakhr al-Dīn Abū Sulaymān Dā'ūd b. Abī l-Faḍl, *Rawḍat ūlī l-albāb fī ma'rifat al-tawārīkh wa l-ansāb*, ed. Jaʿfar Shiʿār (Tehran, 1348 shamsī/1969)

Baranī, Ḍiyā' al-Dīn, *Ta'rīkh-i Fīrūzshāhī*, ed. Saiyid Ahmad Khán, Bibliotheca Indica (Calcutta, 1862); trans. Ishtiyaq Ahmad Zilli (Delhi, 2015)

Baranī, Ḍiyā' al-Dīn, *Ta'rīkh-i Fīrūzshāhī*, earlier recension: RRL, Persian ms. 2053; Bodleian Library, mss. Elliot 353 and S. Digby Or. 54

Bāybars al-Manṣūrī al-Dawādār, Rukn al-Dīn, *Zubdat al-fikra fī ta'rīkh al-hijra*, ed. D.S. Richards, BI 42 (Beirut, 1998)

Bihāmadkhānī, Muḥammad, *Ta'rīkh-i Muḥammadī*, BL ms. Or. 137; partial trans. by Muhammad Zaki, *Tarikh-i-Muhammadi by Muhammad Bihamad Khani* (Aligarh, 1972)

al-Birzālī, ʿAlam al-Dīn Abū Muḥammad al-Qāsim b. Muḥammad, *al-Muqtafā li-ta'rīkh al-shaykh Shihāb al-Dīn Abū Shāma*, ed. ʿUmar ʿAbd al-Salām Tadmurī, 4 vols (Ṣaydā, 1427/2006)

Bukhārī, Ṣalāḥ al-Dīn b. Mubārak, *Anīs al-ṭālibīn wa-'uddat al-sālikīn*, ed. Tawfīq Subḥānī (Tehran, 1371 shamsī/1992)

Chekhovich, O.D. (ed.), *Bukharskie dokumenty XIV veka* (Tashkent, 1965)

Dawlatshāh Samarqandī, *Tadhkirat al-shu'arā*, ed. Edward G. Browne (Leiden and London, 1901); also ed. Muḥammad ʿAbbāsī (Tehran, 1337 shamsī/1958)

al-Dhahabī, Shams al-Dīn Abū ʿAbd-Allāh Muḥammad b. ʿUthmān, *Siyar a'lām*

al-nubalā', XXIII, ed. Bashshār ʿAwwād Maʿrūf and Muḥyī Halāl al-Sirḥān (Beirut, 1405/1985)
al-Dhahabī, Shams al-Dīn Abū ʿAbd-Allāh Muḥammad b. ʿUthmān, *Ta'rīkh al-Islām wa-wafayāt al-mashāhīr wa l-aʿlām*, ed. ʿUmar ʿAbd al-Salām Tadmurī, 53 vols (Beirut, 1415–24/1995–2004)
Falak ʿAlā-yi Tabrīzī (ʿAbd-Allāh b. ʿAlī), *Saʿādat-nāma*, ed. and trans. Mirkamal Nabipour (Göttingen, 1973)
Faryūmadī, Ghiyāth al-Dīn, *Dhayl-i Majmaʿ al-ansāb*, ed. Mīr Hāshim Muḥaddith (Tehran, 1363 shamsī/1984) [with Shabānkāra'ī's *Majmaʿ al-ansāb*; see below]
Ḥāfiẓ-i Abrū (Shihāb al-Dīn ʿAbd-Allāh b. Luṭf-Allāh Khwāfī), *Cinq opuscules de Ḥāfiẓ-i Abrū concernant l'histoire de l'Iran au temps de Tamerlan*, ed. Felix Tauer, Archiv Orientální Supplementa 5 (Prague, 1959)
Ḥāfiẓ-i Abrū (Shihāb al-Dīn ʿAbd-Allāh b. Luṭf-Allāh Khwāfī), *Dhayl-i Jāmiʿ al-tawārīkh*, ed. Khān-bābā Bayānī, 2nd edn (Tehran, 1350 shamsī/1971)
Ḥāfiẓ-i Abrū (Shihāb al-Dīn ʿAbd-Allāh b. Luṭf-Allāh Khwāfī), *Dhayl-i Ẓafar-nāma*, ed. Felix Tauer, 'Continuation du Ẓafarnāma de Niẓāmuddīn Šāmī par Ḥāfiẓ-i Abrū', *Archiv Orientální* 6 (1934), 429–65
Ḥāfiẓ-i Abrū (Shihāb al-Dīn ʿAbd-Allāh b. Luṭf-Allāh Khwāfī), *Jughrāfiyya*, partial edn and trans. by Dorothea Krawulsky, *Ḫorāsān zur Timuridenzeit nach dem Tārīḫ-e Ḥāfeẓ-e Abrū (verf. 817–823) des Nūrallāh ʿAbdallāh b. Luṭfallāh al-Ḫvāfī*, 2 vols, Beihefte zum Tübinger Atlas des Vorderen Orients, Reihe B, 46 (Wiesbaden, 1982–4); partial edn by Ghulām-riḍā Warhrām, *Jughrāfiyya-yi ta'rīkhī-yi Khurāsān* (Tehran, 1370 shamsī/1991); partial edn by Ṣādiq Sajjādī, 3 vols (Tehran, 1377–8 shamsī/1997–9); BL ms. Or. 1577 [Iran]; Bodleian ms. Fraser 155, fos 168b–173a [part of Transoxiana]
Ḥāfiẓ-i Abrū (Shihāb al-Dīn ʿAbd-Allāh b. Luṭf-Allāh Khwāfī), *Majmūʿa*, BN ms. supplément person 2046
Ḥāfiẓ-i Abrū (Shihāb al-Dīn ʿAbd-Allāh b. Luṭf-Allāh Khwāfī), *Ta'rīkh-i salāṭīn-i Kart*, ed. Mīr Hāshim Muḥaddith (Tehran, 1389 shamsī/2010); also ed. Tauer in *Cinq opuscules de Ḥāfiẓ-i Abrū* [above], 31–72
Ḥāfiẓ-i Abrū (Shihāb al-Dīn ʿAbd-Allāh b. Luṭf-Allāh Khwāfī), *Zubdat al-tawārīkh*, ed. Sayyid Ḥājj Kamāl Sayyid Jawādī, 4 vols (I and II: Tehran, 1380 shamsī/2001–2; III and IV: Tehran, 1372 shamsī/1993 [when printed as I and II], reprinted [as III and IV] 1380); extracts in Maitra [see secondary literature] and in Shāmī, *Ẓafar-nāma*, ed. Tauer [below], II
Ḥamd-Allāh Mustawfī Qazwīnī, *Dhayl-i Ta'rīkh-i guzīda*, ed. V.Z. Piriiev (Baku, 1978); trans. M.D. Kazimov and V.Z. Piriiev (Baku, 1986)
Ḥamd-Allāh Mustawfī Qazwīnī, *Nuzhat al-qulūb*, partial edn and trans. by Guy Le Strange, *The Geographical Part of the Nuzhat al-qulūb*, 2 vols, GMS 23 (Leiden and London, 1915–19), I (text), II (trans.); partial edn by Muḥammad Dabīr-Siyāqī (Tehran, 1336 shamsī/1958)
Ḥamd-Allāh Mustawfī Qazwīnī, *Ta'rīkh-i guzīda*, ed. ʿAbd al-Ḥusayn Nawā'ī (Tehran, 1339 shamsī/1960)
Ḥamd-Allāh Mustawfī Qazwīnī, *Ẓafar-nāma*, facsimile edn (of BL ms. Or. 2833) by Naṣr-Allāh Pūrjawādī and Nuṣrat-Allāh Rastagār, *Ẓafarnāma von Ḥamdallāh Mustaufī und Šāhnāma von Abu'l-Qāsim Firdausī*, 2 vols (Tehran, 1377 shamsī, and Vienna, 1999); partial trans. by Leonard J. Ward, 'The Ẓafar-Nāmah of Ḥamdallāh Mustaufī and the Il-Khān Dynasty of Iran', unpublished Ph.D. thesis, University of Manchester, 1983, 3 vols [years 650 to 735/1252–3 to 1334–5]

Ḥaydar Dughlāt, Mīrzā, *Ta'rīkh-i Rashīdī*, ed. and trans. Wheeler M. Thackston, *Mirza Haydar Dughlat's Tarikh-i-Rashidi. A History of the Khans of Moghulistan*, 2 vols (Cambridge, MA, 1996)

Hilālī, ʿAlā-yi Qazwīnī (ʿAlī b. al-Ḥusayn b. ʿAlī), *Manāhij al-ṭālibīn fī maʿārif al-ṣādiqīn*, BL ms. IO Islamic 1660

Ibn Abī l-Faḍā'il, al-Mufaḍḍal, *al-Nahj al-sadīd wa l-durr al-farīd fī mā baʿd ta'rīkh Ibn al-ʿAmīd*; partial edn and trans. by Edgar Blochet, 'Moufazzal Ibn Abil-Fazaïl. Histoire des Sultans Mamlouks', part 1, *Patrologia Orientalis* 12 (1919), 343–550; part 2, ibid., 14 (1920), 375–672; part 3, ibid., 20 (1929), 3–270 [years 658–716/1260–1316]

Ibn Abī l-Ḥadīd (ʿIzz al-Dīn Abū Ḥāmid ʿAbd al-Ḥamīd b. Hibat-Allāh al-Madā'inī), *Sharḥ Nahj al-bilāgha*, partial edn and trans. by Moktar Djebli, *Les Invasions mongoles en Orient vécues par un savant médiéval arabe* (Paris, 1995)

Ibn ʿArabshāh, Aḥmad b. Muḥammad, *ʿAjā'ib al-maqdūr fī nawā'ib Tīmūr*, ed. ʿAlī Muḥammad ʿUmar (Cairo, 1399/1979); ed. Aḥmad Fā'iz al-Ḥimṣī (Beirut, 1407/1986–7); trans. J.H. Sanders, *Tamerlane or Timur, the Great Amir* (London, 1935)

Ibn ʿArabshāh, Aḥmad b. Muḥammad, *Fākihat al-khulafā' wa-mufākahat al-ẓurafā'*, ed. Muḥammad Rajab al-Najjār (al-Kuwayt, 1997); ed. Ayman ʿAbd al-Jābir al-Buḥayrī (Cairo, 1421/2001)

Ibn Baṭṭūṭa, Shams al-Dīn Abū ʿAbd-Allāh Muḥammad b. ʿAbd-Allāh al-Lawātī al-Ṭanjī, *Tuḥfat al-nuẓẓār fī gharā'ib al-amṣār*, ed. Ch. Defrémery and B.S. Sanguinetti, 4 vols (Paris, 1853–8); trans. H.A.R. Gibb and C.F. Beckingham, *The Travels of Ibn Baṭṭūṭa A.D. 1325–1354*, 4 vols with continuous pagination and index volume, HS, 2nd series, 110, 117, 141, 178 and 190 (Cambridge, 1958–2000)

Ibn al-Dawādārī, Abū Bakr b. ʿAbd-Allāh b. Aybak, *Kanz al-durar wa-jāmiʿ al-ghurar*, VIII, ed. Ulrich Haarmann, *Der Bericht über die frühen Mamluken*, QGIA 1h (Cairo, 1391/1971); IX, ed. Hans R. Roemer, *Der Bericht über den Sultan al-Malik an-Nāṣir Muḥammad ibn Qala'un*, QGIA 1i (Cairo, 1379/1960)

Ibn Faḍl-Allāh al-ʿUmarī, Shihāb al-Dīn Aḥmad, *Masālik al-abṣār fī mamālik al-amṣār*, partial edn and trans. by Klaus Lech, *Das mongolische Weltreich. Al-ʿUmarī's Darstellung der mongolischen Reiche in seinem Werk* Masālik al-abṣār fī mamālik al-amṣār, AF 22 (Wiesbaden, 1968); partial edn by Otto Spies, *Ibn Faḍlallāh al-ʿOmarī's Bericht über Indien in seinem Werke* Masālik al-abṣār fī mamālik al-amṣār, SOL 14 (Leipzig, 1943), and trans. Iqtidar Husain Siddiqi and Qazi Muhammad Ahmad, *A Fourteenth Century Arab Account of India under Sultan Muhammad bin Tughluq* (Aligarh, [1972])

Ibn Faḍl-Allāh al-ʿUmarī, Shihāb al-Dīn Aḥmad, *al-Taʿrīf bi l-muṣṭalaḥ al-sharīf* (Cairo, 1312/1894); new edn by Samīr al-Durūbī, 2 vols (al-Karak, 1992)

Ibn Fatḥ-Allāh al-Baghdādī, ʿAbd-Allāh, *al-Ta'rīkh al-Ghiyāthī*, partial edn by Ṭāriq Nāfiʿ al-Ḥamdānī (Baghdad, 1975)

Ibn al-Furāt, Nāṣir al-Dīn Muḥammad b. ʿAbd al-Raḥīm, *Ta'rīkh al-duwal wa l-mulūk*, IX, part 1, ed. Costi K. Zurayk, *The History of Ibn al-Furāt* (Beirut, 1936), and part 2, ed. Costi K. Zurayk and Nedjla Izzeddin (Beirut, 1938) [years 789–99/1387–97]

Ibn Ḥajar al-ʿAsqalānī, Shihāb al-Dīn Abū l-Faḍl Aḥmad b. ʿAlī, *Badhl al-māʿūn fī faḍl al-ṭāʿūn*, ed. Aḥmad ʿIṣām ʿAbd al-Qādir al-Kātib (al-Riyāḍ, 1411/1991)

Ibn Ḥajar al-ʿAsqalānī, Shihāb al-Dīn Abū l-Faḍl Aḥmad b. ʿAlī, *al-Durar al-kāmina fī aʿyān al-miʾa al-thāmina*, 2nd edn, 6 vols (Hyderabad, A.P., 1392–6/1972–6)

Ibn Ḥajar al-ʿAsqalānī, Shihāb al-Dīn Abū l-Faḍl Aḥmad b. ʿAlī, *Inbāʾ al-ghumr bi-ibnāʾ al-ʿumr fī l-taʾrīkh*, ed. Ḥasan Ḥabashī, 3 vols (Cairo, 1389–92/1969–72); also ed. Muḥammad ʿAbd al-Muʿīd Khān, 9 vols (Hyderabad, A.P., 1387–96/1967–76); III–IV, 2nd edn (Beirut, 1406/1986)

Ibn Ḥijjī, Shihāb al-Dīn Abū l-ʿAbbās Aḥmad, *Taʾrīkh*, ed. Abū Yaḥyā ʿAbd-Allāh al-Kandarī, 2 vols (Beirut, 1424/2003)

Ibn Isfandiyār, *Taʾrīkh-i Ṭabaristān*, abridged trans. by Edward G. Browne, GMS 2 (Leiden and London, 1905)

Ibn al-Jawzī, ʿAbd al-Raḥmān, *al-Muntaẓam fī taʾrīkh al-mulūk wa l-umam*, ed. F. Krenkow, 10 vols (Hyderabad, Deccan, 1357–9/1938–40)

Ibn Kathīr, ʿImād al-Dīn Abū l-Fidāʾ Ismāʿīl b. ʿUmar, *al-Bidāya wa l-nihāya fī l-taʾrīkh*, 14 vols (Cairo, 1351/1932–[no final date])

Ibn Khaldūn, Walī al-Dīn ʿAbd al-Raḥmān b. Muḥammad, *Kitāb al-ʿibar wa-dīwān al-mubtadaʾ wa l-khabar fī ayyām al-ʿarab wa l-ʿajam wa l-barbar wa-man ʿāṣarahum min dhawī l-sulṭān al-akbar*, ed. Yūsuf Asʿad Dāghir, *Taʾrīkh al-ʿallāma Ibn Khaldūn*, 7 vols (Beirut, 1956–61)

Ibn Khaldūn, Walī al-Dīn ʿAbd al-Raḥmān b. Muḥammad, *al-Muqaddima*, trans. Franz Rosenthal, *Ibn Khaldûn. The Muqaddimah. An Introduction to History*, 2nd edn, 3 vols (Princeton, NJ, 1967; reprinted London and Henley, 1986)

Ibn Khaldūn, Walī al-Dīn ʿAbd al-Raḥmān b. Muḥammad, *al-Taʿrīf bi-Ibn Khaldūn wa-riḥlatuhu gharb^{an} wa-sharq^{an}*, ed. Muḥammad ibn Tāwīt al-Ṭanjī (Cairo, 1370/1951); ed. and trans. Abdesselam Cheddadi, *Ibn Khaldûn. Autobiographie* (Algiers, 2008); partial trans. and commentary in Fischel, *Ibn Khaldûn and Tamerlane* [see secondary literature below], 29–120

Ibn al-Khaṭīb (Abū ʿAbd-Allāh Muḥammad b. ʿAbd-Allāh al-Salmānī), *Muqniʿat al-sāʾil ʿan al-maraḍ al-hāʾil*, ed. and trans. M.J. Müller, 'Ibnulkhatīb's Bericht über die Pest', *Sitzungsberichte der königlich bayerischen Akademie der Wissenschaften, philosophisch-philologische Classe* (1863), part 2, 1–34; reprinted in Fuat Sezgin (ed., with M. Amawi, D. Bischoff and E. Neubauer), *Beiträge zur Geschichte der arabisch-islamischen Medizin. Aufsätze*, I (Frankfurt am Main, 1987), 559–92

Ibn Khātima, Abū Jaʿfar Aḥmad, *Taḥṣīl al-gharaḍ al-ḥāṣid fī tafṣīl al-maraḍ al-wāfid*, trans. Taha Dīnānah, 'Die Schrift von Abī [sic] Jaʿfar Aḥmed ibn ʿAlī ibn Muḥammed ibn ʿAlī ibn Ḥātimah aus Almeriah über die Pest', *Archiv für Geschichte der Medizin* 19 (1927), 27–81

Ibn Qāḍī Shuhba, Taqī al-Dīn Abū Bakr b. Aḥmad, *Taʾrīkh*, ed. ʿAdnān Darwīsh, 4 vols (Damascus, 1977–97)

Ibn Ṣaṣrā, Muḥammad b. Muḥammad, *al-Durrat al-muḍīʾa fī l-dawlat al-Ẓāhiriyya*, ed. and trans. William M. Brinner, *A Chronicle of Damascus 1389–1397 by Muḥammad ibn Muḥammad ibn Ṣaṣrā*, 2 vols (Berkeley and Los Angeles, 1963)

Ibn Shihāb Yazdī, Tāj al-Dīn Ḥasan, *Jāmiʿ al-tawārīkh-i Ḥasanī*, ed. Ḥusayn Mudarrisī Ṭabāṭabāʾī and Īraj Afshār (Karachi, 1987)

Ibn al-Shiḥna, Abū l-Walīd Muḥammad b. Maḥmūd, *Rawḍat al-manāẓir fī ʿilm al-awāʾil wa l-awākhir*, printed in the margin of Ibn al-Athīr, *al-Kāmil fī l-taʾrīkh* (Būlāq, 1290/1873), IX

Ibn Taghrībirdī, Abū l-Maḥāsin Yūsuf, *al-Manhal al-ṣāfī wa l-mustawfī baʿd al-Wāfī*, ed. Muḥammad Muḥammad Amīn, Saʿīd ʿAbd al-Fattāḥ ʿĀshūr et al., 9 vols so far (Cairo, 1984–1423/2002)

Ibn Taghrībirdī, Abū l-Maḥāsin Yūsuf, *al-Nujūm al-zāhira fī mulūk Miṣr wa l-Qāhira*, 16 vols (Cairo, 1348–92/1929–72); trans. William Popper, *History of Egypt 1382–1469 A.D.*, 8 vols, University of California Publications in Semitic Philology 13–14, 17–19, 22–24 (Berkeley and Los Angeles, CA, 1954–63)

Ibn Turka Iṣfahānī, Ṣā'in al-Dīn ʿAlī b. Muḥammad, *Chahārdah risāla-yi fārsī*, ed. Sayyid ʿAlī Mūsā Bihbahānī and Sayyid Ibrāhīm Dībāchī (Tehran, 1351 shamsī/1972)

Ibn al-Wardī, Zayn al-Dīn Abū Ḥafṣ ʿUmar b. Muẓaffar, *Risālat al-naba' ʿan al-wabā'*, trans. Michael Dols, 'Ibn al-Wardī's *Risālah al-naba' ʿan al-waba' [sic]*: A translation of a major source for the history of the Black Death in the Middle East', in Dickran K. Kouymjian (ed.), *Near Eastern Numismatics, Iconography, Epigraphy and History. Studies in Honor of George C. Miles* (Beirut, 1974), 443–55

Ibn al-Wardī, Zayn al-Dīn Abū Ḥafṣ ʿUmar b. Muẓaffar, *Tatimmat al-Mukhtaṣar fī akhbār al-bashar*, ed. Aḥmad Rifʿat al-Badrāwī, 2 vols (Beirut, 1389/1970)

Ibn Yamīn Faryūmadī, *Dīwān-i ashʿār*, ed. Ḥusayn ʿAlī Bāstānī-Rād ([Tehran, 1344 shamsī/1965])

Ibragimov, S.K. (ed.), *Materialy po istorii kazakhskikh khanstv XV–XVIII vekov (izvlecheniia iz persidskikh i tiurkskikh sochinenii)* (Alma-Ata, 1969)

ʿIṣāmī, ʿAbd al-Malik, *Futūḥ al-salāṭīn*, ed. A.S. Usha (Madras, 1948)

Jaʿfarī, Jaʿfar b. Muḥammad Ḥusaynī, *Ta'rīkh-i kabīr*, partial trans. by Abbas Zaryab, 'Der Bericht über die Nachfolger Timurs aus dem Ta'rīḫ-i kabīr des Ǧaʿfarī ibn Muḥammad al-Ḥusainī', unpublished doctoral dissertation, Johannes Gutenberg-Universität Mainz, 1960

Jaʿfarī, Jaʿfar b. Muḥammad Ḥusaynī, *Ta'rīkh-i Yazd*, ed. Īraj Afshār (Tehran, 1338 shamsī/1960)

Jamāl al-Qarshī (Abū l-Faḍl Muḥammad b. ʿUmar b. Khālid), *al-Mulḥaqāt bi l-Ṣurāḥ*, ed. and trans. Sh.Kh. Vokhidov and B.B. Aminov, in *IKPI*, I (Almaty, 2005); extracts also ed. in V.V. Bartol'd, *Turkestan v épokhu mongol'skogo nashestviia*, I. *Teksty* (St Petersburg, 1898), 128–52

al-Jazarī, Shams al-Dīn Abū ʿAbd-Allāh Muḥammad b. Ibrāhīm, *Ḥawādith al-zamān wa-anbā'ihi wa-wafayāt al-akābir wa l-aʿyān min abnā'ihi*, ed. ʿUmar ʿAbd al-Salām Tadmurī, 3 vols (Ṣaydā, 1419/1998) [years 689–699/1290 to 1299–1300 and 725–738/1325 to 1337–8]

Juwaynī, ʿAlā' al-Dīn ʿAṭā Malik, *Ta'rīkh-i jahān-gushā*, ed. Mīrzā Muḥammad Qazwīni, 3 vols, GMS, n.s. 16 (Leiden and London, 1912–37); trans. John A. Boyle, *The History of the World-Conqueror*, 2 vols with continuous pagination (Manchester, 1958; reprinted in 1 vol. with introduction by David Morgan, 1997)

Jūzjānī, Minhāj al-Dīn Abū ʿUmar ʿUthmān b. Sirāj al-Dīn, *Ṭabaqāt-i Nāṣirī*, ed. ʿAbd al-Ḥayy Ḥabībī, 2nd edn, 2 vols (Kabul, 1342–3 shamsī/1963–4); trans. Henry G. Raverty, *Ṭabaḳāt-i Nāṣirī. A General History of the Muhammadan Dynasties of Asia*, 2 vols with continuous pagination, Bibliotheca Indica (Calcutta, 1872–81)

Khunjī, Faḍl-Allāh b. Rūzbihān, *Ta'rīkh-i ʿālam-ārā-yi Amīnī*, ed. John E. Woods, with abridged trans. by V. Minorsky (London, 1992)

Khwāfī, Faṣīḥ al-Dīn Aḥmad b. Jalāl al-Dīn Muḥammad, *Mujmal-i Faṣīḥī*, ed. Maḥmūd Farrukh, 2 vols in 3 parts (Mashhad, 1339–41 shamsī/1960–2); ed.

Sayyid Muḥsin Nājī Naṣrābādī, 3 vols, with continuous pagination (Tehran, 1386 shamsī/2007–8); trans. D.Iu. Iusupova (Tashkent, 1980) [years 700–845/ 1301–2 to 1441–2 only]

Khwānd-Amīr (Ghiyāth al-Dīn b. Humām al-Dīn Muḥammad Ḥusaynī), *Ḥabīb al-siyar fī akhbār afrād al-bashar*, ed. Jalāl Humā'ī, 4 vols (Tehran, 1333 shamsī/1954); trans. Wheeler M. Thackston, *Classical Writings of the Medieval Islamic World. Persian Histories of the Mongol Dynasties*, II (London and New York, 2012)

Khwārazmī (or Bukhārī), ʿAlā' al-Dīn ʿAlīshāh b. Muḥammad, *Ashjār-u athmār*, Glasgow University Library ms. Hunter 174 (T.8.6); Cambridge University Library ms. Browne Coll. O.8

Kutubī, Maḥmūd, *Ta'rīkh-i āl-i Muẓaffar*, ed. ʿAbd al-Ḥusayn Nawā'ī (Tehran, 1335 shamsī/1956)

Lewis, B. (trans. and ed.), *Islam from the Prophet Muhammad to the Capture of Constantinople*, 2 vols (London and Basingstoke, 1974)

al-Maqrīzī, Taqī al-Dīn Aḥmad b. ʿAlī, *Durar al-ʿuqūd al-farīda fī tarājim aʿyān al-mufīda*, ed. Maḥmūd al-Jalīlī, 4 vols (Beirut, 1423/2002)

al-Maqrīzī, Taqī al-Dīn Aḥmad b. ʿAlī, *al-Sulūk li-maʿrifat duwal al-mulūk*, ed. Muṣṭafā Ziyāda and Saʿīd ʿAbd al-Fattāḥ ʿĀshūr, 4 vols in 12 parts (Cairo, 1934–72)

Marʿashī, Sayyid Ẓahīr al-Dīn, *Ta'rīkh-i Ṭabaristān-u Rūyān-u Māzandarān*, ed. Muḥammad Ḥusayn Tasbīḥī (Tehran, 1345 shamsī/1966)

Mīr-Khwānd (Mīr Muḥammad b. Sayyid Burhān al-Dīn Khwānd Shāh), *Ta'rīkh Rawḍat al-ṣafā*, 10 vols (Tehran, 1338–9 shamsī/1959–60)

al-Mufaḍḍal Ibn Abī l-Faḍā'il, *al-Nahj al-sadīd wa l-durr al-farīd*, partial edn. by Edgar Blochet, 'Moufazzal Ibn Abil-Fazaïl. Histoire des Sultans Mamlouks', *Patrologia Orientalis* 12 (1919), 343–550; 14 (1920), 373–672; and 20 (1929), 1–270

Muʿīn al-fuqarā' (Aḥmad b. Maḥmūd), *Kitāb-i Mullāzāda*, ed. Aḥmad Gulchīn-i Maʿānī as *Ta'rīkh-i Mullāzāda dar dhikr-i mazārāt-i Bukhārā*, 2nd edn (Tehran, 1370 shamsī/1991)

Naṭanzī, Muʿīn al-Dīn, *Muntakhab al-tawārīkh*, partial edn by Jean Aubin, *Extraits du Muntakhab al-tavarikh-i Mu'ini (Anonyme d'Iskandar)* (Tehran, 1336 shamsī/1957); partial edn by Parwīn Istakhrī (Tehran, 1383 shamsī/2004); also BL ms. Or. 1566 and BN ms. Supplément persan 1651

Nawā'ī, ʿAbd al-Ḥusayn (ed.), *Asnād-u mukātabāt-i ta'rīkhī-yi Īrān az Taymūr tā Shāh Ismāʿīl* (Tehran, 1341 shamsī/1962)

al-Nuwayrī, Shihāb al-Dīn Aḥmad b. ʿAbd al-Wahhāb, *Nihāyat al-arab fī funūn al-adab*, XXVII, ed. Saʿīd ʿĀshūr with Muḥammad Muṣṭafā Ziyāda and Fu'ād ʿAbd al-Muʿṭī al-Ṣayyād (Cairo, 1405/1985)

al-Qalqashandī, Shihāb al-Dīn Abū l-ʿAbbās Aḥmad b. ʿAlī, *Ṣubḥ al-aʿshā fī ṣināʿat al-inshā'*, ed. Muḥammad Ḥusayn Shams al-Dīn (Beirut, 1987), 15 vols

Qaraṭāy al-ʿIzzī al-Khaznadārī, *Ta'rīkh majmūʿ al-nawādir mimmā jarā li l-awā'il wa l-awākhir*, ed. Horst Hein and Muḥammad al-Ḥuğayrī, BI 46 (Beirut and Berlin, 2005)

Qāshānī, Jamāl al-Dīn Abū l-Qāsim ʿAbd-Allāh b. ʿAlī, *Ta'rīkh-i Uljāytū Sulṭān*, ed. Mahin Hambly (Tehran, 1348 shamsī/1969); also SK ms. Ayasofya 3019, part 2 [photocopy in SOAS Library]

Qāyinī, Jalāl al-Dīn Abū Muḥammad b. Najm al-Dīn Muḥammad, *Naṣā'iḥ-i Shāhrukhī*, Österreichische Nationalbibliothek, Vienna, ms. A.F. 112

Rashīd al-Dīn Faḍl-Allāh Hamadānī, *Jāmi' al-tawārīkh*, Part I: *Ta'rīkh-i mubārak-i Ghāzānī*, ed. Muḥammad Rawshan and Muṣṭafā Mūsawī, 4 vols, with continuous pagination (Tehran, 1373 shamsī/1994); trans. Wheeler M. Thackston, *Classical Writings of the Medieval Islamic World. Persian Histories of the Mongol Dynasties*, III (London and New York, 2012). Partial edns: by A.A. Romaskevich et al., *Dzhāmī' at-tavārīkh*, I, part 1 (Moscow, 1965); by A.A. Alizade ('Abd al-Karīm 'Alī-ughlī 'Alīzāda), *Dzhāmi' at-tavārīkh*, II, part 1 (Moscow, 1980); by A.A. Alizade, *Dzhāmī-at-tavārīkh*, III (Baku, 1957). Partial edn and trans. of III by Étienne Quatremère, *Raschid-eldin. Histoire des Mongols de la Perse* (Paris, 1836; reprinted Amsterdam, 1970). Partial trans. of II by John A. Boyle, *The Successors of Genghis Khan* (New York, 1971)

Rashīd al-Dīn Faḍl-Allāh Hamadānī, *Shu'ab-i panjgāna*, TSM ms. III Ahmet 2937

al-Ṣafadī, Ṣalāḥ al-Dīn Khalīl b. Aybak, *A'yān al-'aṣr wa-a'wān al-naṣr*, ed. Fāliḥ Aḥmad al-Bakkūr, 4 vols (Beirut, 1419/1998)

al-Ṣafadī, Ṣalāḥ al-Dīn Khalīl b. Aybak, *al-Wāfī bi l-wafayāt*, ed. Helmut Ritter et al., *Das biographische Lexikon des Ṣalāḥaddīn Ḫalīl b. Aybak aṣ-Ṣafadī*, 32 vols, BI 6 (Istanbul, Leipzig, Wiesbaden and Beirut, 1931–2013)

al-Sakhāwī, Shams al-Dīn Abū l-Khayr Muḥammad b. 'Abd al-Raḥmān, *al-Ḍaw' al-lāmi' li-ahl al-qarn al-tāsi'*, ed. Ḥusām al-Dīn al-Qudsī, 12 vols (Cairo, 1353–5/1934–6)

Salmānī, Tāj al-Dīn, *Shams al-ḥusn*, facsimile edn (of Istanbul ms. Lala Ismail Efendi 304) and abridged trans. by Hans R. Roemer, *Šams al-Ḥusn, eine Chronik vom Tode Timurs bis zum Jahre 1409 von Tāǧ as-Salmānī*, VOK 8 (Wiesbaden, 1956)

Samarqandī, Muḥammad b. 'Abd al-Jalīl, *Qandiyya*, 16th-century Persian trans., in Īraj Afshār (ed.), *Qandiyya wa-Samariyya. Dū risāla dar ta'rīkh-i mazārāt-u jughrāfiyya-yi Samarqand* (Tehran, 1367 shamsī/1988–9)

Sayfī (Sayf b. Muḥammad b. Ya'qūb al-Harawī), *Ta'rīkh-nāma-yi Harāt*, ed. Muḥammad Zubayr aṣ-Ṣiddíqí (Calcutta, 1944); ed. Ghulām-riḍā Ṭabāṭabā'ī Majd (Tehran, 1383 shamsī/2004)

Shabānkāra'ī, Muḥammad b. 'Alī, *Majma' al-ansāb*, ed. Mīr Hāshim Muḥaddith (Tehran, 1363 shamsī/1984) [with Faryūmadī's *Dhayl*]

Shabānkāra'ī, Muḥammad b. 'Alī, *Majma' al-ansāb*, third recension: BN ms. Supplément persan 1278; abridged version: BL ms. Add. 16696

Shāmī, Niẓām al-Dīn, *Ẓafar-nāma*, ed. Felix Tauer, *Histoire des conquêtes de Tamerlan intitulée Ẓafarnāma par Niẓāmuddīn Šāmī, avec des additions empruntées au Zubdatu-t-tawārīḫ-i Bāysunġurī de Ḥāfiẓ-i Abrū*, 2 vols, Monografie Archívu Orientálního 5 (Prague, 1937–56)

al-Shujā'ī, Shams al-Dīn, *Ta'rīkh al-Malik al-Nāṣir Muḥammad b. Qalāwūn al-Ṣāliḥī wa-awlādihi*, ed. and trans. Barbara Schäfer, 2 vols, QGIA 2a–b (Wiesbaden, 1977–85)

Sirhindī, Yaḥyā b. Aḥmad, *Ta'rīkh-i Mubārakshāhī*, ed. S.M. Hidayat Husain, Bibliotheca Indica (Calcutta, 1931)

Sīstānī, Malik Shāh Ḥusayn, *Iḥyā' al-mulūk*, ed. Manūchihr Sutūda (Tehran, 1344 shamsī/1966) al-Suyūṭī, Jalāl al-Dīn Abū l-Faḍl ʿAbd al-Raḥmān, *Mā rawāhu l-wāʿūn fī akhbār al-ṭāʿūn*, BL ms. Or. 3053

Thackston, W.M. (trans. and ed.), *A Century of Princes. Sources on Timurid History and Art* (Cambridge, MA, 1989)

Tizengauzen (Tiesenhausen), V.G., Frhr. von (ed. and trans), *Sbornik materialov, otnosiashchikhsia k istorii Zolotoi Ordy*, 2 vols, I. *izvlecheniia iz sochinenii arabskikh* (St Petersburg, 1884); II. *izvlecheniia iz persidskikh sochinenii*, ed. A.A. Romaskevich and S.L. Volyn (Moscow and Leningrad, 1941)

Waṣṣāf (Shihāb al-Dīn ʿAbd-Allāh b. Faḍl-Allāh Shīrāzī), *Tajziyat al-amṣār wa-tazjiyat al-aʿṣār*, in 5 parts, lithograph edn by Muḥammad Mahdī Iṣfahānī (Bombay, 1269/1853); ed. and trans. Joseph Frhr. von Hammer-Purgstall, *Geschichte Wassaf's*, I (Vienna, 1856); *Geschichte Wassafs*, II–IV, trans. Joseph Frhr. von Hammer-Purgstall and ed. Sibylla Wentker, with Elisabeth and Klaus Wundsam (Vienna, 2010–16); new edition of Part 4 (based on an autograph ms.) by ʿAlī-Riḍā Ḥājjiyān Nizhād, *Ta'rīkh-i Waṣṣāf al-Ḥaḍrat*, IV (Tehran, 1388 shamsī/2009); also Istanbul ms. Nuruosmaniye 2740/1–2 (old numbering: 3207)

Yazdī, Ghiyāth al-Dīn ʿAlī, *Rūz-nāma-yi ghazawāt-i Hind*, ed. L.A. Zimin, *Dnevnik pokhoda Timura v Indiiu Giias-ad-dina Ali*, with introduction by V.V. Bartol'd (Petrograd, 1915); ed. Īraj Afshār as *Saʿādat Nāma yā rūz-nāma-yi ghazawāt-i Hindūstān dar sālhā-yi 800–801 hijrī* (Tehran and Karachi, 1379 shamsī/2000); trans. A.A. Semenov, *Giiāṡaddīn 'Alī. Dnevnik pokhoda Tīmūra v Indiiu* (Moscow, 1958)

Yazdī, Muʿīn al-Dīn b. Jalāl al-Dīn Muḥammad Muʿallim, *Mawāhib-i ilāhī dar ta'rīkh-i āl-i Muẓaffar*, partial edn by Saʿīd Nafīsī (Tehran, 1326 shamsī/1947); BL ms. Add. 7632

Yazdī, Sharaf al-Dīn ʿAlī, *Ẓafar-nāma*, ed. Muḥammad ʿAbbāsī, 2 vols (Tehran, 1336 shamsī/1957); facsimile edn (of Gosudarstvennyi Institut Vostokovedeniia, Tashkent, ms. 4472) by A. Urunbaev (Tashkent, 1972) [here cited for the *Muqaddima*]; ed. Saʿīd Mīr Muḥammad Ṣādiq and ʿAbd al-Ḥusayn Nawā'ī, 2 vols with continuous pagination (Tehran, 1387 shamsī/2008) [the entire work]

al-Yūnīnī, Quṭb al-Dīn Abū l-Fatḥ Mūsā b. Muḥammad, *Dhayl Mir'āt al-zamān*, complete edn by ʿAbbās Hānī Jarrākh, in Sibṭ Ibn al-Jawzī, *Mir'āt al-zamān*, and al-Yūnīnī, *Dhayl Mir'āt al-zamān* (Beirut, 1434/2013), XVI–XXII; partial edns: 4 vols (Hyderabad, A.P., 1374–80/1954–61) [down to the year 686/1287]; ed. and trans. Li Guo, *Early Mamluk Syrian Historiography. Al-Yūnīnī's* Dhayl Mir'āt al-Zamān, IHC 21, 2 vols (Leiden, Boston, MA, and Cologne, 1998) [years 697–701/1297–8 to 1301–2]

Yūsuf-i Ahl, Jalāl al-Dīn, *Farā'id-i Ghiyāthī*, partial edn by Ḥishmat Mu'ayyad, 2 vols (Tehran, 2536 shāhanshāhī/1977 and 1358 shamsī/1979); also Süleymaniye Kütüphanesi, Istanbul, ms. Fâtih 4012

al-Yūsufī, ʿImād al-Dīn Mūsā b. Muḥammad b. Yaḥyā, *Nuzhat al-nāẓir fī sīrat al-Malik al-Nāṣir*, ed. Aḥmad Ḥuṭayṭ (Beirut, 1406/1986)

Zayn al-Dīn b. Ḥamd-Allāh Mustawfī Qazwīnī, *Dhayl-i Ta'rīkh-i guzīda*, ed. Īraj Afshār (Tehran, 1372 shamsī/1993); facsimile edn and trans. by M.D. Kazimov and V.Z. Piriiev (Baku, 1990)

Zetterstéen, K.V. (ed.), *Beiträge zur Geschichte der Mamlūkensultane in den Jahren 690–741 der Hiǵra nach arabischen Handschriften* (Leiden, 1919)

Mongolian

Anonymous, *Mongghol'un niucha tobcha'an*, trans. Igor de Rachewiltz, *The Secret History of the Mongols. A Mongolian Epic Chronicle of the Thirteenth Century*, 3 vols, BIAL 7 (Leiden and Boston, MA, 2004–13)

Mostaert, A., and Cleaves, Francis W. (eds), 'Trois documents mongols des archives secrètes vaticanes', *HJAS* 15 (1952), 419–506

Mostaert, A., and Cleaves, Francis W. (eds), *Les Lettres de 1289 et 1305 des ilkhan Aryun et Öljeitü à Philippe le Bel*, Harvard-Yenching Institute, Scripta Mongolica Monograph series 1 (Cambridge, MA, 1962)

Chinese

Atwood, Christopher P. (trans. and ed., with Lynn Struve), *The Rise of the Mongols. Five Chinese Sources* (Indianapolis, IN, 2021)

Bretschneider, E. (trans. and ed.), *Mediaeval Researches from Eastern Asiatic Sources. Fragments towards the Knowledge of the Geography and History of Central and Western Asia from the 13th to the 17th Century*, 2 vols (London, 1888; reprinted 1910)

Franke, H. (trans.), *Beiträge zur Kulturgeschichte Chinas unter der Mongolenherrschaft. Das* Shan-kü sin-hua *des Yang Yü*, AKM 32/2 (Wiesbaden, 1956)

Hambis, Louis *Documents sur l'histoire des Mongols à l'époque des Ming*, Bibliothèque de l'Institut des Hautes Études Chinoises 21 (Paris, 1969)

Pelliot, Paul, and Hambis, Louis (ed. and trans.), *Histoire des campagnes de Gengis Khan. Cheng-wou Ts'in-tcheng lou*, I [only] (Leiden, 1951)

Quanheng, *Gengshen waishi*, trans. Helmut Schulte-Uffelage, *Das Keng-shen Wai-shih. Eine Quelle zur späten Mongolenzeit*, Ostasiatische Forschungen: Monographien 2 (Berlin, 1963)

Song Lian et al., *Yuanshi*, chaps 98–99, ed. and trans. in Hsiao, *The Military Establishment of the Yuan Dynasty*, 65–124

Song Lian et al., *Yuanshi*, chap. 107, ed. and trans. Louis Hambis (with supplementary notes by Paul Pelliot), *Le Chapitre CVII du Yuan che. Les généalogies impériales mongoles dans l'histoire chinoise officielle de la dynastie mongole*, Supplement to *TP* 38 (Leiden, 1945)

Song Lian et al., *Yuanshi*, chap. 108, ed. and trans. Louis Hambis, *Le Chapitre CVIII du Yuan che. Les fiefs attribués aux membres de la famille impériale et aux ministres de la cour mongole d'après l'histoire chinoise officielle de la dynastie mongole*, Monographies du *TP* 3 (Leiden, 1954)

See also Rossabi, 'A translation of Ch'en Ch'eng's *Hsi-yü fan-kuo chih*' [secondary literature below]

Turkish

Anonymous, *Tawārīkh-i guzīda-yi nuṣrat-nāma*, BL ms. Or. 3222; facsimile edn (of this ms.) by A.M. Akramov (Tashkent, 1967); partial trans. in Ibragimov (ed.), *Materialy po istorii kazakhskikh khanstv XV–XVIII vekov*, 9–43

Abū l-Ghāzī Bahādur Khān, *Shajarat al-atrāk*, ed. and trans. Petr I. Desmaisons, *Histoire des Mongols et des Tatares par Aboul-Ghâzî Béhâdour Khân* (St Petersburg, 1871–4; reprinted Amsterdam, 1970)

Bābur, Ẓahīr al-Dīn Muḥammad, *Bābur-nāma*, trans. Annette S. Beveridge, *The Bābur-nāma in English* (London, 1922; reprinted 1969); trans. Wheeler M.

Thackston, *The Baburnama. Memoirs of Babur, Prince and Emperor* (New York, 2002)
Ötemish Ḥājjī, *Chingīz-nāma*, ed. and transcribed by Takushi Kawaguchi, Hiroyuki Nagamine and Mutsumi Sugahara, *Ötämiš Ḥājī. Čingīz-nāma* (Tokyo, 2008)
Yūsuf Khāṣṣ Ḥājib, *Qutadghu Bilig*, trans. Robert Dankoff, *Wisdom of Royal Glory (Kutadgu Bilig). A Turko-Islamic Mirror for Princes* (Chicago, IL, and London, 1983)

Tibetan

'Gos lo-tsā-ba gŽon-nu-dpal, *Debther sṅon-po*, trans. George N. Roerich, *The Blue Annals*, 2 vols (Calcutta, 1949; reprinted in 1 vol., Delhi, 1979)

Latin and Old French

Anonymous, *Chronica XXIV generalium ordinis Minorum*, in *Analecta Franciscana*, III (Quaracchi, 1897)
Anonymous, 'Chronicon Dubnicense', in Flórián Mátyás (ed.), *Historiae Hungaricae fontes domestici*, III (Leipzig, 1884), 1–212
Anonymous, *Chronicon Estense*, ed. Giulio Bertoni and Emilio Paolo Vicini, in *RIS*, n.s., XV, part 3 (Città di Castello, 1908)
Anonymous, *Chronographia regum Francorum*, ed. H. Moranvillé, 3 vols (Paris, 1891–7)
Anonymous, *Chronique du Religieux de Saint-Denys contenant le règne de Charles VI, de 1380 à 1422*, ed. Louis F. Bellaguet, 6 vols (Paris, 1839–52)
Anonymous, *De statu, conditione ac regimine magni canis*, ed. Christine Gadrat, '*De statu, conditione ac regimine magni canis*: l'original latin du «Livre de l'estat du grant can» et la question de l'auteur', *BEC* 165 (2007), 355–71; 14th-century French translation, ed. M. Jacquet, 'Le Livre du Grant Caan, extrait d'un manuscrit de la Bibliothèque du Roi', *JA* 6 (1830), 57–72, and trans. in Yule, *Cathay and the Way Thither*, III, 89–103
Anonymous, treatise on commerce, ed. in Bautier, 'Les relations économiques des Occidentaux' [see secondary literature below], 311–20 (Appendice I)
Andreas de Redusiis de Quero, *Chronicon Tarvisinum*, in *RIS*, XIX (Milan, 1731), coll. 735–866
Barbaro, Giosafa, *Viaggi*, ed. and trans. in E.Ch. Skrzhinskaia, *Barbaro i Kontarini o Rossii. K istorii italo-russkikh sviazei v XV v.* (Leningrad, 1971), Italian text, 113–36, Russian trans. and commentary, 136–87; trans. William Thomas, in Henry Edward John Stanley, Baron Stanley of Alderley (ed.), *Travels to Tana and Persia by Josafa Barbaro and Ambrogio Contarini*, HS, 1st series, [49a] (London, 1873)
Bartolomeo da Pisa, *De conformitate vitae beati Francisci ad vitam domini Iesu*, in *Analecta Franciscana*, IV (Quaracchi, 1906)
Bergdolt, K. (ed. and trans.), *Die Pest 1348 in Italien. Fünfzig zeitgenössische Quellen* (Heidelberg, 1989)
Clavijo, Ruy Gonzalez de, *Embajada a Tamorlán*, ed. Francisco López Estrada (Madrid, 1943); trans. Clements R. Markham, *Narrative of the Embassy of Ruy González de Clavijo to the Court of Timour, at Samarcand, A.D. 1403–6*, HS, 1st series, [26] (London, 1859); trans. Guy Le Strange, *Clavijo. Embassy to Tamerlane 1403–1406* (London, 1928)

'Corpus chronicorum Bononiensium, III', ed. Albano Sorbelli, in *RIS*, new series, XVIII, part 1, II (Città di Castello and Bologna, 1905–40)

Dennis, George T. (ed.), 'Three reports from Crete on the situation in Romania, 1401–1402', *Studi Veneziani* 12 (1970), 243–65; reprinted in Dennis, *Byzantium and the Franks 1350–1420* (London, 1982)

Dietrich von Nyem, *De scismate libri tres*, ed. G. Erler (Leipzig, 1890)

Dörrie, H. (ed.), 'Drei Texte zur Geschichte der Ungarn und Mongolen: Die Missionsreisen des fr. Julianus O.P. ins Uralgebiet (1234/5) und nach Rußland (1237) und der Bericht des Erzbischofs Peter über die Tartaren', *Nachrichten der Akademie der Wissenschaften in Göttingen, phil.-hist. Klasse* (1956), no. 6, 125–202

Ellis, Sir Henry (ed.), *Original Letters Illustrative of English History*, 3rd series, I (London, 1846)

František of Prague, *Chronica Pragensis*, ed. as 'Kronika Františka Pražského', in Josef Emler (ed.), *Prameny dějin českých. Fontes rerum Bohemicarum*, IV (Prague, 1884), 347–456; new edn by Jana Zachová, *Chronicon Francisci Pragensis/ Kronika Františka Pražského*, Prameny dějin českých/Fontes rerum Bohemicarum, nová řada, I (Prague, 1997)

Gabriele de' Mussi, *De morbo*, ed. A.G. Tononi, 'La peste dell'anno 1348', *Giornale Ligustico di Archeologia, Storia e Letteratura* 11 (1884), 139–52; trans. in Horrox, *The Black Death* [see secondary literature below], 14–26

Geoffrey Le Baker, *Chronicon*, trans. David Preest, *The Chronicle of Geoffrey le Baker of Swinbrook* (Woodbridge, 2012); also extract trans. in Horrox, *The Black Death*, 80–2

Giorgio Stella, *Annales Genuenses*, ed. Giovanna Petti Balbi, in *RIS*, new series, XVII, part 2 (Bologna, 1975)

Hingeston, F.C. (ed.), *Royal and Historical Letters during the Reign of Henry the Fourth, King of England and of France, and Lord of Ireland*, I: *A.D. 1399–1404*, Rolls Series 18 (London, 1860)

John, Archbishop of Sulṭāniyya, *Libellus de notitia orbis*, Universitätsbibliothek Graz ms. 1221, fos 41a–127a; partial edn by Anton Kern, 'Der 'Libellus de notitia orbis' Iohannes' III. (de Galonifontibus?) O.P. Erzbischofs von Sultanyeh [*sic*]', *AFP* 8 (1938), 82–123

John, Archbishop of Sulṭāniyya, *Mémoire*, ed. H. Moranvillé, 'Mémoire sur Tamerlan et sa cour par un Dominicain, en 1403', *BEC* 55 (1894), 441–64

Knighton, Henry, *Chronica de eventibus Angliae a tempore regis Edgari usque mortem regis Ricardi Secundi*, partial edn by G.H. Martin, *Knighton's Chronicle 1337–1396*, Oxford Medieval Texts (Oxford, 1995)

Marco Polo, *Le devisement du monde*, ed. Philippe Ménard et al., 6 vols (Geneva, 2001–9); trans. Aldo Ricci, *The Travels of Marco Polo* (London, 1931); trans. Ronald Latham, *Marco Polo. The Travels* (Harmondsworth, 1958); trans. Sharon Kinoshita, *Marco Polo. The Description of the World* (Indianapolis, IN, 2016)

Marignolli, John of, 'Relatio', in Van den Wyngaert (ed.), *Sinica Franciscana*, I, 513–60; excerpts ed. in Irene Malfatto, 'Le digressioni sull'Oriente nel *Chronicon Bohemorum* di Giovanni de' Marignolli' (Firenze, 2013), http://ecodicibus.sismelfirenze.it/index.php/iohannes-de-marignollis-chronicon-bohemorum-excerpta-de-rebus-orientalibus;dc; partial trans. in Yule, *Cathay and the Way Thither*, III, 209–69

Matthew Paris, *Chronica Majora*, ed. Henry Richards Luard, 7 vols, Rolls Series 57 (London, 1872–83)

Mignanelli, Beltramo di, *De ruina Damasci*, ed. Étienne Baluze as 'Vita Tamerlani', in *Miscellanea novo ordine digesta et non paucis ineditis monumentis opportunisque animadversionibus aucta*, new edn by J.D. Mansi (Lucca, 1764), IV, 134–40; ed. in Helmy, *Tra Siena, l'Oriente e la Curia* [see secondary literature below], 315–40; partial trans. by Walter J. Fischel, 'A new Latin source on Tamerlane's conquest of Damascus (1400/1401) (B. de Mignanelli's "Vita Tamerlani" 1416)', *Oriens* 9 (1956), 201–32

Paschal de Vittoria, 'Epistola', in Van den Wyngaert (ed.), *Sinica Franciscana*, I, 501–6; trans. in Yule, *Cathay and the Way Thither*, III, 81–8

Pegolotti, Francesco Balducci, *La pratica della mercatura*, ed. Allan Evans (Cambridge, MA, 1936)

Piloti, Emmanuel, *De modo, progressu, ordine ac diligenti providentia habendis in passagio Christianorum pro conquesta Terre Sancte*, ed. and trans. P.-H. Dopp, *L'Égypte au commencement du quinzième siècle d'après le Traité d'Emmanuel Piloti de Crète (Incipit 1420)* (Cairo, 1950)

Plano Carpini, John of (Giovanni del Pian di Carpine), *Ystoria Mongalorum quos nos Tartaros appellamus*, ed. Enrico Menestò et al., *Giovanni di Pian di Carpine. Storia dei Mongoli* (Spoleto, 1989); trans. in Christopher Dawson (ed.), *The Mongol Mission. Narratives and Letters of the Franciscan Missionaries in Mongolia and China in the Thirteenth and Fourteenth Centuries* (London, 1955), 1–72

Rafaino Caresini, *Chronica*, ed. Ester Pastorello, 'Raphayni de Caresinis cancellarii Venetiarum Chronica', in *RIS*, new series, XII, part 2 (Bologna, 1938–58)

Riccoldo da Montecroce, *Liber peregrinationis*, ed. and trans. René Kappler in *Riccold de Montecroce. Pérégrination en Terre Sainte et au Proche Orient. . . . Lettres sur la chute de Saint-Jean d'Acre* (Paris, 1997), 33–205; trans. in Rita George-Tvrtković, *A Christian Pilgrim in Medieval Iraq. Riccoldo da Montecroce's Encounter with Islam* (Turnhout, 2012), Appendix B, 175–227

Rubió i Lluch, Antoni (ed.), *Diplomatari de l'Orient Català (1301–1409)* (Barcelona, 1947)

Rubruck, William of, *Itinerarium*, ed. Paolo Chiesa, *Guglielmo di Rubruk. Viaggio in Mongolia* ([Milan], 2011); also in Van den Wyngaert (ed.), *Sinica Franciscana*, I, 164–332; trans. and ed. Peter Jackson with David Morgan, *The Mission of Friar William of Rubruck. His Journey to the Court of the Great Khan Möngke 1253–1255*, HS, 2nd series, 173 (London, 1990)

Schiltberger, Johann, *Reisebuch*, trans. J. Buchan Telfer (with notes by P. Bruun), *The Bondage and Travels of Johann Schiltberger, a Native of Bavaria, in Europe, Asia, and Africa, 1396–1427*, HS, 1st series, 58 (London, 1879)

Simon of Saint-Quentin, *Historia Tartarorum* [excerpted from Vincent of Beauvais, *Speculum historiale*], ed. Jean Richard, *Simon de Saint-Quentin. Histoire des Tartares*, Documents relatifs à l'histoire des Croisades 8 (Paris, 1965)

'Tartar Relation', ed. George D. Painter et al., in *The Vinland Map and the Tartar Relation*, new edn (New Haven, CT, and London, 1995)

Thiriet, F. (ed.), *Délibérations des assemblées vénitiennes concernant la Romanie*, II: *1364–1463*, D&R 11 (Paris and the Hague, 1971)

Thiriet, F. (ed.), *Régestes des délibérations du Sénat de Venise concernant la Romanie*, I: *1329–1399*; II: *1400–1430*, D&R 1–2 (Paris and The Hague, 1958–9)

Van den Wyngaert, A. (ed.), *Sinica Franciscana*, I. *Itinera et relationes Fratrum Minorum saeculi XIII et XIV* (Quaracchi-Firenze, 1929)

Villani, Giovanni, *Nuova cronica*, ed. Giuseppe Porta, 3 vols (Parma, 1990–1)

Villani, Matteo, *Cronica*, ed. Giuseppe Porta, 2 vols (Parma, 1995)
Yule, H. (trans. and ed.), *Cathay and the Way Thither; Being a Collection of Medieval Notices of China*, new edn by Henri Cordier, 4 vols, HS, 2nd series, 33, 37, 38 and 41 (London, 1913–16)

Syriac

Bar Hebraeus, Gregory Abū l-Faraj, *Maktheᵉbānut zabnē*, ed. and trans. E.A. Wallis Budge, *The Chronography of Gregory Abu'l-Faraj Son of Aaron the Physician Commonly Known as Bar Hebraeus*, 2 vols (Oxford and London, 1932), I (trans.); II (text), appendices, xxx–liii, contains translations of Syriac fragments relating to Timur and the Timurids

Greek

Doukas, *Historia Turco-Byzantina*, trans. Harry J. Magoulias, *Decline and Fall of Byzantium to the Ottoman Turks* (Detroit, MI, 1975)
Gregoras, Nikephoros, *Rhomaïkē historia*, trans. Jan L. Van Dieten, *Nikephoros Gregoras. Rhomäische Geschichte*, 6 vols in 7 parts, Bibliothek der griechischen Literatur 24 (Stuttgart, 1973–2007)
Panaretos, Michaēl, *Peri tōn tēs Trapezountos basileōn*, ed. and trans. Scott Kennedy, in *Two Works on Trebizond. Michael Panaretos. Bessarion* (Cambridge, MA, 2019), 2–57
Schreiner, P. (ed.), *Die byzantinischen Kleinchroniken*, 3 vols, Corpus Fontium Historiae Byzantinae, XII, 1–3 (Vienna, 1975–9)
see also Bartsocas [secondary literature below]

Russian

Ermolinskaia letopis', in *PSRL*, XXIII (St Petersburg, 1910)
Moskovskii letopisnyi svod kontsa XV veka, in *PSRL*, XXV (Moscow and Leningrad, 1949)
Patriarshaia ili Nikonovskaia letopis', in *PSRL*, X (St Petersburg, 1885; reprinted Moscow, 1962), and XI (St Petersburg, 1897; reprinted Moscow, 1965); trans. Serge A. and Betty Jean Zenkovsky, *The Nikonian Chronicle*, III: *From the Year 1241 to the Year 1381* (Princeton, NJ, 1986)
Pskovskie letopisi, ed. A. Nasonov, I (Moscow and Leningrad, 1941; reprinted The Hague, 1967)
Troitskaia letopis', ed. M.D. Priselkov (Moscow, 1950)

Caucasian

Galstian, A.G. (trans.), *Armianskike istochniki o mongolakh* (Moscow, 1962)
Hayton of Gorighos, *La Flor des estoires de la terre d'Orient*, ed. Ch. Kohler, in *Recueil des Historiens des Croisades. Documents arméniens*, II (Paris, 1906), Old French text, 111–253, contemporary Latin translation (by Nicolas Faucon), 255–363
Kirakos Ganjakets'i, *Patmut'iwn Hayots'*, trans. Robert Bedrosian, *Kirakos Ganjakets'i's History of the Armenians* (New York, 1986); trans. L.A. Khanlarian, *Kirakos Gandzaketsi. Istoriia Armenii*, Pamiatniki Pis'mennosti Vostoka 53 (Moscow, 1976)
Sanjian, A.K. (trans. and ed.), *Colophons of Armenian Manuscripts, 1301–1480. A Source for Middle Eastern History* (Cambridge, MA, 1969)

Step'anos Orbelian, *Patmut'iwn nahangin Sisakan*, trans. M.-F. Brosset, *Histoire de la Siounie*, 2 vols (St Petersburg, 1864–6)

T'ovma Metsobet'si, *Patmut'iwn lank-T'amuray ew yajordats' iwrots'*, trans. Robert Bedrosian, *T'ovma Metsobet'si's History of Tamerlane and His Successors* (New York, 1987)

Vardan Arewelts'i, *Hawak'umn patmut'ean*, trans. Robert W. Thomson, 'The historical compilation of Vardan Arewelc'i', *Dumbarton Oaks Papers* 34 (1989), 125–226

SECONDARY LITERATURE

This section contains only those works that appear more than once in the notes. Each author's works are listed in chronological order of publication.

Abu-Lughod, Janet L., *Before European Hegemony. The World System A.D. 1250–1350* (Oxford, 1989)

Abu-Lughod, Janet Lippman, 'The world system in the thirteenth century: Dead-end or precursor?', in Michael Adas (ed.), *Islamic and European Expansion. The Forging of a Global Order* (Philadelphia, PA, 1993), 75–102

Adshead, S.A.M., *Central Asia in World History* (Basingstoke, 1993)

Aerke, Kristiaan, 'Au miroir des peurs occidentales', in Fourniau (ed.), *Samarcande 1400–1500*, 55–71

Aigle, Denise, 'Loi mongole *vs* loi islamique. Entre mythe et réalité', *AHSS* 59 (2004), 971–96; revised and trans. as 'Mongol law *versus* Islamic law: Myth and reality', in Aigle, *The Mongol Empire between Myth and Reality*, 134–56

Aigle, Denise, 'Le Grand *Jasaq* de Gengis-Khan, l'empire, la culture mongole et le *Shari'a*', *JESHO* 47 (2004), 31–79

Aigle, Denise, *The Mongol Empire between Myth and Reality. Studies in Anthropological History* (Leiden and Boston, MA, 2015)

Aigle, Denise, 'The historical *taqwīm* in Muslim East', in Aigle, *The Mongol Empire between Myth and Reality*, 89–104

Aigle, Denise, 'Hülegü's letters to the last Ayyubid ruler of Syria: The construction of a model', in Aigle, *The Mongol Empire between Myth and Reality*, 199–218

Aigle, Denise, 'A religious response to Ghazan Khan's invasions of Syria: The three "Anti-Mongol" *fatwā*s of Ibn Taymiyya', in Aigle, *The Mongol Empire between Myth and Reality*, 283–305

Aigle, Denise, 'Epilogue. The Mongol empire after Genghis Khan', in Aigle, *The Mongol Empire between Myth and Reality*, 306–22

Aigle, Denise (ed.), *L'Iran face à la domination mongole*, Bibliothèque Iranienne 45 (Tehran, 1997)

Akasoy, Anna; Burnett, Charles; and Yoeli-Tlalim, Ronit (eds), *Rashīd al-Dīn. Agent and Mediator of Cultural Exchanges in Ilkhanid Iran*, Warburg Institute Colloquia 24 (London and Turin, 2013)

Akopyan, Alexander V., and Mosanef, Farbod, 'Between Jūjīds [*sic*] and Jalāyirids: The coinage of the Chopānids, Akhījūq and their contemporaries, 754–759/1353–1358', *Der Islam* 92 (2015), 197–246

Album, Stephen, 'Power and legitimacy: The coinage of Mubāriz al-Dīn Muḥammad ibn al-Muẓaffar at Yazd and Kirman', *Le Monde Iranien et l'Islam* 2 (1974), 157–71

Album, Stephen, 'Studies in Ilkhanid history and numismatics, I. A late Ilkhanid hoard (743/1342)', *StIr* 13 (1984), 49–116

Alexander, John T., *Bubonic Plague in Early Modern Russia. Public Health and Urban Disaster* (Oxford, 2003)

Alexandrescu-Dersca, Marie-Mathilde, *La Campagne de Timur en Anatolie (1402)* (1942); 2nd edn (London, 1977)

Allsen, Thomas T., 'The Yüan dynasty and the Uighurs of Turfan in the 13th century', in Morris Rossabi (ed.), *China among Equals. The Middle Kingdom and Its Neighbors, 10th–14th Centuries* (Berkeley and Los Angeles, CA, 1983), 243–80

Allsen, Thomas T., 'The Princes of the Left Hand: An introduction to the history of the *ulus* of Orda in the thirteenth and early fourteenth centuries', *AEMA* 5 (1985–7), 5–40

Allsen, Thomas T., *Mongol Imperialism. The Policies of the Grand Qan Möngke in China, Russia, and the Islamic Lands, 1251–1259* (Berkeley and Los Angeles, CA, 1987)

Allsen, Thomas T., 'Changing forms of legitimation in Mongol Iran', in Gary Seaman and Daniel Marks (eds), *Rulers from the Steppe. State Formation on the Eurasian Periphery* (Los Angeles, CA, 1991), 223–41

Allsen, Thomas T., 'The rise of the Mongolian empire and Mongolian rule in north China', in *CHC*, VI, 321–413

Allsen, Thomas T., 'Spiritual geography and political legitimacy in the eastern steppe', in Henri J.M. Claessen and Jarich G. Oosten (eds), *Ideology and the Formation of Early States*, Studies in Human Society 11 (Leiden, 1996), 116–35

Allsen, Thomas T., *Commodity and Exchange in the Mongol Empire. A Cultural History of Islamic Textiles*, CSIC (Cambridge, 1997)

Allsen, Thomas T., *Culture and Conquest in Mongol Eurasia*, CSIC (Cambridge, 2001)

Allsen, Thomas T., 'Sharing out the empire: Apportioned lands under the Mongols', in Khazanov and Wink (eds), *Nomads in the Sedentary World*, 172–90

Allsen, Thomas T., 'Eurasia after the Mongols', in *CWH*, VI, part 1, 159–81

Amitai, Reuven, *The Mongols in the Islamic Lands. Studies in the History of the Ilkhanate* (Aldershot and Burlington, VT, 2007)

Amitai, Reuven, '*Im Westen nichts Neues*? Re-examining Hülegü's offensive into the Jazira and Northern Syria in light of recent research', in Krämer, Schmidt and Singer (eds), *Historicizing the 'Beyond'*, 83–96

Amitai, Reuven, *Holy War and Rapprochement. Studies in the Relationship between the Mamluk Sultanate and the Mongol Ilkhanate (1260–1335)* (Turnhout, 2013)

Amitai, Reuven, 'Ibn Khaldūn on the Mongols and their military might', in Franz and Holzwarth (eds), *Nomad Military Power in Iran and Adjacent Areas in the Islamic Period*, 193–208

Amitai, Reuven, 'Political legitimation in the Ilkhanate: More thoughts on the Mongol imperial ideology, the introduction of Muslim justifications, and the revival of Iranian ideals', in May, Dashdondog and Atwood (eds), *New Approaches to Ilkhanid History*, 209–48

Amitai, Reuven, and Biran, Michal (eds), *Mongols, Turks, and Others. Eurasian Nomads and the Sedentary World*, BIAL 11 (Leiden and Boston, MA, 2005)

Amitai, Reuven, and Biran, Michal (eds), *Nomads as Agents of Cultural Change. The Mongols and Their Eurasian Predecessors* (Honolulu, HI, 2015)

Amitai, Reuven, and Conermann, Stephan (eds), *The Mamluk Sultanate from the Perspective of Regional and World History. Economic, Social and Cultural*

Development in an Era of Increasing International Interaction and Competition (Göttingen, 2019)

Amitai-Preiss, Reuven, 'Ghazan, Islam and Mongol tradition: A view from the Mamluk Sultanate', *BSOAS* 59 (1996), 1–10; reprinted in Hawting (ed.), *Muslims, Mongols and Crusaders*, 253–62, and in Amitai, *The Mongols in the Islamic Lands*

Amitai-Preiss, Reuven, 'Sufis and shamans: Some remarks on the Islamization of the Mongols in the Ilkhanate', *JESHO* 42 (1999), 27–46; reprinted in Amitai, *The Mongols in the Islamic Lands*

Amitai-Preiss, Reuven, and Morgan, David O. (eds), *The Mongol Empire and Its Legacy*, IHC 24 (Leiden, Boston, MA, and Köln, 1999)

Ando Shiro, *Timuridische Emire nach dem Mu'izz al-ansāb. Untersuchung zur Stammesaristokratie Zentralasiens im 14. und 15. Jahrhundert*, IU 153 (Berlin, 1992)

Ando Shiro, 'Die timuridische Historiographie II – Šaraf al-dīn ʿAlī Yazdī', *StIr* 24 (1995), 219–46

Ando Shiro, 'Zum timuridischen Staatswesen: eine Interpretation des Miniaturentwurfs in Diez A. Fol. 74', in Rudolf Veselý and Eduard Gombár (eds), *Ẓafar Nāme. Memorial Volume of Felix Tauer* (Prague, 1996), 17–33

Anooshahr, Ali, *The Ghazi Sultans and the Frontiers of Islam. A Comparative Study of the Late Medieval and Early Modern Periods* (London and New York, 2009)

Arom, Na'ama O., '"In-*ger*" and "outer" diplomacy – Ilkhanid contacts with the Mongols and the outside world, 1260–1282', in Fiaschetti (ed.), *Diplomacy in the Age of Mongol Globalization*, 286–309

Ashrafyan, K.Z., 'Central Asia under Timur from 1370 to the early fifteenth century', in *HCCA*, IV, part 1, 319–45

Atwood, Christopher P., 'Validation by holiness or sovereignty: Religious toleration as political theology in the Mongol world empire of the thirteenth century', *International History Review* 26 (2004), 237–56

Atwood, Christopher P., '*Ulus* emirs, *keshig* elders, signatures, and marriage partners: The evolution of a classic Mongol institution', in Sneath (ed.), *Imperial Statecraft*, 141–73

Atwood, Christopher P., 'Rashīd al-Dīn's Ghazanid Chronicle and its Mongolian sources', in May, Dashdondog and Atwood (eds), *New Approaches to Ilkhanid History*, 53–121

Atwood, Christopher P., *The Rise of the Mongols*: see above, primary sources: Chinese

Aubin, Jean, 'Les princes d'Ormuz du XIIIe au XVe siècle', *JA* 241 (1953), 77–138

Aubin, Jean, *Deux sayyids de Bam au XVe siècle. Contribution à l'histoire de l'Iran timouride*, Akademie der Wissenschaften und der Literatur: Abhandlungen der geistes- und sozialwissenschaftlichen Klasse 1956, no. 7 (Wiesbaden, 1956), 373–501 [references are to the pagination of the separatum]

Aubin, Jean, 'Le mécénat timouride à Chiraz', *StIsl* 8 (1957), 71–88; reprinted in Aubin, *Études sur l'Iran médiéval*, 155–68

Aubin, Jean, 'Tamerlan à Baġdād', *Arabica* 9 (1962), 303–9

Aubin, Jean, 'Comment Tamerlan prenait les villes', *StIsl* 19 (1963), 83–122

Aubin, Jean, 'L'ethnogénèse des Q̣araunas', *Turcica* 1 (1969), 65–94; reprinted in Aubin, *Études sur l'Iran médiéval*, 251–77

Aubin, Jean, 'La fin de l'état sarbadâr du Khorassan', *JA* 262 (1974), 95–118; reprinted in Aubin, *Études sur l'Iran médiéval*, 311–30

Aubin, Jean, 'Le khanat de Čaġatai et le Khorassan (1334–1380)', *Turcica* 8 (1976), part 2, 16–60

Aubin, Jean, 'Un chroniqueur méconnu, Šabānkāra'ī', *StIr* 10 (1981), 213–24; reprinted in Aubin, *Études sur l'Iran médiéval*, 143–54

Aubin, Jean, 'Le *quriltai* de Sultân-Maydân (1336)', *JA* 279 (1991), 175–97; reprinted in Aubin, *Études sur l'Iran médiéval*, 279–97

Aubin, Jean, *Études sur l'Iran médiéval, géographie historique et société*, ed. Denise Aigle, *StIr* Cahier 60 (Paris, 2018)

Ayalon, David, 'The Great *Yāsa* of Chingiz Khān: A re-examination (A)', *StIsl* 33 (1971), 99–140; '. . . . (B)', *StIsl* 34 (1971), 151–80; '. . . . (C_1)', *StIsl* 36 (1972), 113–58; '. . . . (C_2)', *StIsl* 38 (1973), 107–56; all reprinted in Ayalon, *Outsiders in the Lands of Islam*

Ayalon, David, *Gunpowder and Firearms in the Mamluk Kingdom. A Challenge to a Mediaeval Society* (1956), 2nd edn (London and Totowa, NJ, 1978)

Ayalon, David, *Outsiders in the Lands of Islam. Mamluks, Mongols and Eunuchs* (London, 1988)

Ayalon, Yaron, *Natural Disasters in the Ottoman Empire. Plague, Famine, and Other Misfortunes* (Cambridge, 2015)

Babaie, Sussan (ed.), *Iran after the Mongols*, The Idea of Iran 8 (London and New York, 2019)

Baer, Marc David, *The Ottomans. Khans, Caesars and Caliphs* (London, 2021)

Balabanlilar, Lisa, *Imperial Identity in the Mughal Empire. Memory and Dynastic Politics in Early Modern South and Central Asia* (London and New York, 2012)

Balard, Michel, *La Romanie génoise (XIIe–début du XVe siècle)*, Atti della Società Ligure di Storia Patria, n.s., 18, part 1, I (Genoa, 1978)

Banister, Mustafa, '"Nought remains to the Caliph but his title": Revisiting Abbasid authority in Mamluk Cairo', *MSR* 18 (2014–15), 219–45

Banister, Mustafa, The *Abbasid Caliphate of Cairo*, 1261–1517. *Out of the Shadows*, Edinburgh Studies in Classical Islamic History and Culture (Edinburgh, 2021)

Barker, Hannah, 'Laying the corpses to rest: Grain, embargoes and *Yersinia pestis* in the Black Sea, 1346–48', *Speculum* 96 (2021), 97–126

Barthold, W., *Zwölf Vorlesungen über die Geschichte der Türken Mittelasiens*, trans. and ed. Theodor Menzel (Berlin, 1935); Russian text, 'Dvenadtsat' lektsii po istorii turetskikh narodov Srednei Azii', in Bartol'd, *Sochineniia*, V, 17–192

Barthold, W., *Four Studies on the History of Central Asia*, trans. V. and T. Minorsky, 3 vols in 4 parts (Leiden, 1956–62); Russian texts in Bartol'd, *Sochineniia*, II, part 1, 21–106 ('Ocherk istorii Semirech'ia'), and part 2, 23–196 ('Ulugbek i ego vremia'), 197–260 ('Mir Ali-Shir i politicheskaia zhizn'')

Barthold, W., *Turkestan down to the Mongol Invasion*, 3rd edn with additional chapter trans. T. Minorsky, ed. C.E. Bosworth, GMS, n.s. 5 (London, 1968); Russian text in Bartol'd, *Sochineniia*, I, 43–759

Bartol'd, V.V., 'Narodnoe dvizhenie v Samarkande v 1365 g.' (1907), trans. J.M. Rogers, 'Narodnoye dvizheniye v Samarkande v 1365 g. ("A popular uprising in Samarqand in 1365")', *Iran* 19 (1981), 21–31

Bartol'd, V.V., 'O pogrebenii Timura', trans. J.M. Rogers, 'V.V. Bartol'd's article *O pogrebenii Timura* ("The burial of Tīmūr")', *Iran* 12 (1974), 65–87; original text reprinted in Bartol'd, *Sochineniia*, II, part 2, 423–54

Bartol'd, V.V., *Sochineniia*, general ed. B.G. Gafurov, 9 vols in 10 parts (Moscow, 1963–77)

Bartsocas, Christos S., 'Two fourteenth century Greek descriptions of the "Black Death"', *Journal of the History of Medicine and Allied Sciences* 21 (1966), 394–400

Bauden, Frédéric, and Dekkiche, Malika (eds), *Mamluk Cairo, a Crossroads for Embassies. Studies on Diplomacy and Diplomatics*, IHC 161 (Leiden and Boston, MA, 2019)

Baumer, Christoph, *The History of Central Asia*, III: *The Age of Islam and the Mongols* (London and New York, 2016)

Bautier, Robert-Henri, 'Les relations économiques des Occidentaux avec les pays d'Orient au Moyen Âge: points de vue et documents', in M. Mollat du Jourdain (ed.), *Sociétés et compagnies de commerce en Orient et dans l'Océan indien. Actes du VIIIe colloque international d'histoire maritime, Beyrouth 5–10 septembre 1966* (Paris, 1970), 263–331

Beckwith, Christopher I., *Empires of the Silk Road. A History of Central Eurasia from the Bronze Age to the Present* (Princeton, NJ, 2009)

Behrens-Abouseif, Doris, *Practising Diplomacy in the Mamluk Sultanate. Gifts and Material Culture in the Medieval Islamic World* (London and New York, 2014)

Belich, James, *The World the Plague Made. The Black Death and the Rise of Europe* (Princeton, NJ, and Oxford, 2022)

Benedictow, Ole J., *The Black Death 1346–1353. The Complete History* (Woodbridge, 2004)

Bernardini, Michele, 'Tamerlano, i Genovesi e il favoloso Axalla', in Michele Bernardini, Clara Borrelli, Anna Cerbo and Encarnación Sánchez García (eds), *Europa e Islam tra i secoli XIV e XVI / Europe and Islam between 14th and 16th Centuries*, 2 vols (Naples, 2002), I, 391–426

Bernardini, Michele, 'Motahharten entre Timur et Bayezid: une position inconfortable dans les remous de l'histoire anatolienne', in Gilles Veinstein (ed.), *Syncrétismes et hérésies dans l'Orient seldjoukide et ottoman (XIVe–XVIIIe siècle). Actes du Colloque du Collège de France, octobre 2001*, Collection Turcica 9 (Paris, 2005), 199–211

Bernardini, Michele, *Mémoire et propagande à l'époque timouride*, *StIr* Cahier 37 (Paris, 2008)

Bernardini, Michele, 'La prise du pouvoir par Tamerlan dans l'ulus Chaghatay', in Marie-France Auzépy and Guillaume Saint-Guillain (eds), *Oralité et lien social au Moyen Âge (Occident, Byzance, Islam). Parole donné, foi jurée, serment* (Paris, 2008), 137–45

Bernardini, Michele, 'The Mongol puppet lords and the Qarawnas', in Robert Hillenbrand, A.C.S. Peacock and Firuza Abdullaeva (eds), *Ferdowsi, the Mongols and the History of Iran: Art, Literature and Culture from Early Islam to Qajar Persia. Studies in Honour of Charles Melville* (London and New York, 2013), 169–76

Bernardini, Michele, 'Niẓām al-Dīn Shāmī's description of the Syrian campaign of Tīmūr', in Bauden and Dekkiche (eds), *Mamluk Cairo, a Crossroads for Embassies*, 381–409

Bernardini, Michele (ed.), *La civiltà Timuride come fenomeno internazionale*, 2 vols with continuous pagination (Rome, 1996 = *OM* 76/n.s. 15, part 2)

Binbaş, İlker Evrim, 'Structure and function of the genealogical tree in Islamic historiography (1200–1500)', in İlker Evrim Binbaş and Nurten Kılıç-Schubel (eds), *Horizons of the World. Festschrift for İsenbike Togan / Hudûdü'l-Âlem. İsenbike Togan'a Armağan* (Istanbul, 2011), 465–544

Binbaş, İlker Evrim, 'A Damascene eyewitness to the Battle of Nicopolis: Shams al-Dīn Ibn [*sic*] al-Jazarī (d. 833/1429)', in Chrissis and Carr (eds), *Contact and Conflict in Frankish Greece and the Aegean*, 153–75

Binbaş, İlker Evrim, 'Timurid experimentation with eschatological absolutism: Mīrzā Iskandar, Shāh Niʿmatullāh Walī, and Sayyid Sharīf Jurjānī in 815/1412', in Mir-Kasimov (ed.), *Unity in Diversity*, 277–303

Binbaş, İlker Evrim, *Intellectual Networks in Timurid Iran. Sharaf al-Dīn 'Alī Yazdī and the Islamicate Republic of Letters*, CSIC (Cambridge, 2016)

Binbaş, (İlker) Evrim, 'Condominial sovereignty and condominial messianism in the Timurid empire: Historiographical and numismatic evidence', *JESHO* 61 (2018), 172–202

Binbaş, (İlker) Evrim, 'The Timurids and the Mongol empire', in May and Hope (eds), *The Mongol World*, 936–52

Biraben, Jean-Noël, *Les Hommes et la peste en France et dans les pays européens et méditerranéans*, 2 vols, Civilisations et Sociétés 35 (Paris and The Hague, 1975–6)

Biran, Michal, *Qaidu and the Rise of the Independent Mongol State in Central Asia* (Richmond, Surrey, 1997)

Biran, Michal, 'The Chaghadaids and Islam: The conversion of Tarmashirin Khan (1331–34)', *JAOS* 122 (2002), 742–52

Biran, Michal, 'The Mongol transformation: From the steppe to Eurasian empire', in Johann P. Arnason and Björn Wittrock (eds), *Eurasian Transformations, Tenth to Thirteenth Centuries. Crystallizations, Divergences, Renaissances* (Leiden and Boston, MA, 2004 = *ME* 10), 339–61

Biran, Michal, *Chinggis Khan* (Oxford, 2007)

Biran, Michal, 'Culture and cross-cultural contacts in the Chaghadaid realm (1220–1370). Some preliminary notes', *Chronica* [Szeged] 7–8 (2007–8), 26–43

Biran, Michal, 'Diplomatic and chancellery practices in the Chagataid khanate: Some preliminary remarks', *OM* 88 (2008), 369–93

Biran, Michal, 'The Mongols in Central Asia from Chinggis Khan's invasion to the rise of Temür: The Ögödeid and Chaghadaid realms', in *CHIA*, 46–66

Biran, Michal, 'Rulers and city life in Mongol Central Asia (1220–1370)', in Durand-Guédy (ed.), *Turko-Mongol Rulers, Cities and City Life*, 257–83

Biran, Michal, 'The Mamluks and Mongol Central Asia: Political, economic and cultural aspects', in Amitai and Conermann (eds), *The Mamluk Sultanate from the Perspective of Regional and World History*, 367–89

Biran, Michal (ed.), *In the Service of the Khans. Elites in Transition in Mongol Eurasia* (Bern, 2017 = *AS* 71, part 4, 1051–1245)

Biran, Michal (ed.), *Mobility Transformations and Cultural Exchange in Mongol Eurasia* (Leiden and Boston, MA, 2019 = *JESHO* 62, nos 2–3)

Biran, Michal; Brack, Jonathan; and Fiaschetti, Francesca (eds), *Along the Silk Roads in Mongol Eurasia. Generals, Merchants, and Intellectuals* (Oakland, CA, 2020)

Biran, Michal, and Kim Hodong (eds), *The Cambridge History of the Mongol Empire*, 2 vols (Cambridge, 2023)

Bosworth, C.E., 'The political and dynastic history of the Iranian world (A.D. 1000–1217)', in *CHI*, V, 1–202

Bosworth, Clifford Edmund, *The History of the Saffarids of Sistan and the Maliks of Nimruz (247/861 to 949/1542–3)*, Columbia Lectures on Iranian Studies 8 (Costa Mesa, CA, and New York, 1994)
Boyle, J.A., 'Dynastic and political history of the Īlkhāns', in *CHI*, V, 303–421
Brack, Jonathan, 'Theologies of auspicious kingship: The Islamization of Chinggisid sacral kingship in the Islamic world', *CSSH* 60 (2018), 1143–71
Brack, Jonathan, 'A Mongol Mahdi in medieval Anatolia: Rebellion, reform, and divine right in the post-Mongol Islamic world', *JAOS* 139 (2019), 611–29
Brack, Jonathan, 'Disenchanting Heaven: Interfaith debate, sacral kingship, and conversion to Islam in the Mongol empire, 1260–1335', *Past and Present* 250 (2021), 11–53
Brack, Jonathan, 'Chinggisid pluralism and religious competition: Buddhists, Muslims, and the question of violence and sovereignty in Ilkhanid Iran', *Modern Asian Studies* 56 (2022), 815–39
Brack, Jonathan Z., *An Afterlife for the Khan. Muslims, Buddhists, and Sacred Kingship in Mongol Iran and Eurasia* (Oakland, CA, 2023)
Bregel, Yuri, 'Uzbeks, Qazaqs and Turkmens', in *CHIA*, 221–36
Brinner, William M., 'Some Ayyūbid and Mamlūk documents from non-archival sources', *Israel Oriental Studies* 2 (1972), 117–43
Broadbridge, Anne F., 'Royal authority, justice and order in society: The influence of Ibn Khaldūn on the writings of al-Maqrīzī and Ibn Taghrībirdī', *MSR* 7 (2003), part 2, 231–45
Broadbridge, Anne F., *Kingship and Ideology in the Islamic and Mongol Worlds*, CSIC (Cambridge, 2008)
Broadbridge, Anne F., 'Spy or rebel? The curious incident of the Temürid Sulṭān-Ḥusayn's defection to the Mamluks at Damascus in 803/1400–1', *MSR* 14 (2010), 29–42
Broadbridge, Anne F., 'Marriage, family and politics: The Ilkhanid-Oirat connection', in May (ed.), *The Mongols and Post-Mongol Asia*, 121–35
Broadbridge, Anne F., *Women and the Making of the Mongol Empire*, CSIC (Cambridge, 2018)
Buell, Paul D., 'Qubilai and the rats', *Sudhoffs Archiv* 96 (2012), no. 2, 127–44
Buell, Paul D., and Anderson, Eugene N., *A Soup for the Qan. Chinese Dietary Medicine of the Mongol Era as Seen in Hu Szu-hui's* Yin-shan Cheng-yao (London and New York, 2000)
Büssow, Johann; Durand-Guédy, David; and Paul, Jürgen (eds), *Nomads in the Political Field* (Rome, 2011 = *ES* 9, parts 1–2)
Campbell, Bruce M.S., *The Great Transition. Climate, Disease and Society in the Late-Medieval World* (Cambridge, 2016)
Chann, Naindeep Singh, 'Lord of the Auspicious Conjunction: Origins of the *Ṣāḥib-Qirān*', *Iran and the Caucasus* 13 (2009), 93–110
Chrissis, Nikolaos G., and Carr, Mike (eds), *Contact and Conflict in Frankish Greece and the Aegean, 1204–1453. Crusade, Religion and Trade between Latins, Greeks and Turks*, Crusades: Subsidia 5 (Farnham and Burlington, VT, 2014)
Christian, David, 'State formation in the Inner Eurasian steppes', in David Christian and Craig Benjamin (eds), *Worlds of the Silk Roads: Ancient and Modern. Proceedings from the Second Conference of the Australasian Society for Inner Asian Studies (A.S.I.A.S.) Macquarie University, September 21–22, 1996*, SRS 2 (Turnhout, 1999), 50–76

Christian, David, *A History of Russia, Central Asia and Mongolia*, II: *Inner Eurasia from the Mongol Empire to Today, 1260–2000* (Hoboken, NJ, and Chichester, 2018)

Clark, Larry V., and Draghi, Paul Alexander (eds), *Aspects of Altaic Civilization II: Proceedings of the XVIII PIAC, Bloomington, June 29–July 5, 1975*, IUUAS 134 (Bloomington, IN, 1978)

Cleaves, Francis Woodman, 'The rescript of Qubilai prohibiting the slaughtering of animals by slitting the throat', in *Richard Nelson Frye Festschrift I*, 67–89

Conermann, Stephan, *Die Beschreibung Indiens in der „Riḥla" des Ibn Baṭṭūṭa. Aspekte einer herrschaftssoziologischen Einordnung des Delhi-Sultanates unter Muḥammad Ibn Tuġluq*, IU 165 (Berlin, 1993)

Conrad, Lawrence I., 'Arabic plague chronologies and treatises: Social and historical factors in the formation of a literary genre', *StIsl* 54 (1981), 51–93

Cook, David, 'Apocalyptic incidents during the Mongol invasions', in Wolfram Brandes and Felicitas Schmieder (eds), *Endzeiten. Eschatologie in den monotheistischen Weltreligionen*, Millennium-Studien 16 (Berlin and New York, 2008), 293–312

Crummey, Robert O., *The Formation of Muscovy 1304–1613*, Longman's History of Russia (Harlow, 1987)

Cui Yujun et al., 'Historical variations in mutation rate in an epidemic pathogen, *Yersinia pestis*', *PNAS* 110, no. 2 (8 Jan. 2013), 577–82

Dale, Stephen, 'The later Timurids *c.*1450–1526', in *CHIA*, 199–217

Dale, Stephen, 'Autobiography and biography: The Turco–Mongol case: Bābur, Ḥaydar Mīrzā, Gulbadan Begim and Jahāngīr', in L. Marlow (ed.), *The Rhetoric of Biography. Narrating Lives in Persianate Societies* (Boston and Cambridge, MA, 2011), 89–105

Dale, Stephen F., *The Garden of the Eight Paradises. Bābur and the Culture of Empire in Central Asia, Afghanistan and India (1483–1530)*, BIAL 10 (Leiden and Boston, MA, 2004)

Dale, Stephen F., 'Ibn Khaldun, the Yüan and Îl-Khân dynasties', in Golden et al. (eds), *Festschrift for Thomas T. Allsen*, 43–52

Dale, Stephen Frederic, 'The legacy of the Timurids', *JRAS*, 3rd series, 8 (1998), 43–58; reprinted in Levi (ed.), *India and Central Asia. Commerce and Culture, 1500–1800*, 176–99

Dale, Stephen Frederic, *The Orange Trees of Marrakesh. Ibn Khaldun and the Science of Man* (Cambridge, MA, 2015)

Dale, Stephen Frederic, *Babur. Timurid Prince and Mughal Emperor, 1483–1530* (Cambridge and Delhi, 2018)

Dardess, John W., 'From Mongol empire to Yüan dynasty: Changing forms of imperial rule in Mongolia and Central Asia', *Monumenta Serica* 30 (1972–3), 117–65

Dardess, John W., *Conquerors and Confucians. Aspects of Political Change in Late Yüan China* (New York and London, 1973)

Darwin, John, *After Tamerlane. The Global History of Empire since 1405* (London and New York, 2007)

Davidovich, E.A., *Klady drevnikh i srednevekovykh monet Tadzhikistana* (Moscow, 1979)

De Nicola, Bruno, *Women in Mongol Iran. The* Khātūns, *1206–1335* (Edinburgh, 2017)

De Nicola, Bruno, 'Elite women in the Mongol empire', in May and Hope (eds), *The Mongol World*, 422–39

De Nicola, Bruno, and Melville, Charles (eds), *The Mongols' Middle East. Transformation and Continuity in Ilkhanid Iran*, IHC 127 (Leiden and Boston, MA, 2016)

De Rachewiltz, Igor, 'Some reflections on Činggis Qan's *ǰasay*', *East Asian History* 6 (Dec. 1993), 91–104

De Sacy, Baron Silvestre, 'Mémoire sur une correspondance inédite de Tamerlan avec Charles VI', *Mémoires de l'Institut Royal de France. Académie des Inscriptions et Belles-Lettres* 6 (1822), 470–522

Dechant, John, 'Depictions of the Islamization of the Mongols in the *Manāqib al-'ārifīn* and the foundation of the Mawlawī community', *Mawlana Rumi Review* 2 (2011), 135–64

DeWeese, Devin, *Islamization and Native Religion in the Golden Horde. Baba Tükles and Conversion to Islam in Historical and Epic Tradition* (University Park, PA, 1994)

DeWeese, Devin, 'Yasavī *šayḫs* in the Timurid era: Notes on the social and political role of communal sufi affiliations in the 14th and 15th centuries', in Bernardini (ed.), *La civiltà Timuride come fenomeno internazionale*, I, 173–88; reprinted in DeWeese, *Studies on Sufism in Central Asia* (Farnham and Burlington, VT, 2012)

DeWeese, Devin, 'Problems of Islamization in the Volga-Ural region: Traditions about Berke Khan', in Ali Çaksu and Radik Mukhammetshin (eds), *Proceedings of the International Symposium on Islamic Civilisation in the Volga-Ural Region, Kazan, 8–11 June 2001* (Istanbul, 2004), 3–13

DeWeese, Devin, 'Islamization in the Mongol empire', in *CHIA*, 120–34

DeWeese, Devin, 'Mapping Khwārazmian connections in the history of Sufi traditions: Local embeddedness, regional networks, and global ties of the Sufi communities of Khwārazm', *ES* 14 (2016), 37–97

Di Cosmo, Nicola, 'State formation and periodization in Inner Asian history', *JWH* 10 (1999), 1–40

Di Cosmo, Nicola, 'The Qing and Inner Asia: 1636–1800', in *CHIA*, 333–62

Digby, Simon, *War-Horse and Elephant in the Delhi Sultanate. A Study of Military Supplies* (Oxford and Delhi, 1971)

Digby, Simon, 'After Timur left: North India in the fifteenth century', in Francesca Orsini and Samira Sheikh (eds), *After Timur Left. Culture and Circulation in Fifteenth-Century North India* (Oxford and New Delhi, 2014), 47–59

Dols, Michael W., *The Black Death in the Middle East* (Princeton, NJ, 1977)

Drory, Joseph, 'Maqrīzī in *Durar al-'uqūd* with regard to Timur Leng', in U. Vermeulen, K. D'Hulster and J. Van Steenbergen (eds), *Egypt and Syria in the Fatimid, Ayyubid and Mamluk Eras*, VII. *Proceedings of the 16th, 17th and 18th International Colloquium Organized at Ghent University in May 2007, 2008 and 2009* (Leuven, Paris and Walpole, MA, 2013), 393–401

Dunlop, Anne (ed.), *The Mongol Empire in Global History and Art History*, I Tatti Research Series 5 (Firenze, 2023)

Dunn, Ross E., *The Adventures of Ibn Battuta. A Muslim Traveler of the Fourteenth Century*, 2nd edn, reprinted with new preface (Berkeley and Los Angeles, CA, 2012)

Durand-Guédy, David (ed.), *Turko–Mongol Rulers, Cities and City Life* (Leiden and Boston, MA, 2013)

Eaton, Richard M., *India in the Persianate Age, 1000–1765* (London, 2019)

Egorov, V.L., *Istoricheskaia geografiia Zolotoi Ordy v XIII–XIV vv.* (Moscow, 1985)

Ellenblum, Ronnie, *The Collapse of the Eastern Mediterranean. Climate Change and the Decline of the East, 950–1072* (Cambridge, 2012)

Elverskog, Johan, *Our Great Qing. The Mongols, Buddhism, and the State in Late Imperial China* (Honolulu, HI, 2006)

Elverskog, Johan, *Buddhism and Islam on the Silk Road* (Philadelphia, PA, 2010)

Fancy, Nahyan, and Green, Monica H., 'Plague and the fall of Baghdad (1258)', *Medical History* 65 (2021), 157–77

Favereau, Marie, 'The Mongol Peace and global medieval Eurasia', *Comparativ: Zeitschrift für Globalgeschichte und vergleichende Gesellschaftsforschung* 28 (2018), part 4, 49–70

Favereau, Marie, *The Horde. How the Mongols Changed the World* (Cambridge, MA, 2021)

Favereau, Marie (ed.), *La Horde d'Or et l'islamisation des steppes eurasiatiques / The Golden Horde and the Islamisation of the Eurasian Steppes* (Aix-en-Provence, 2018 = *REMMM* 143, part 1)

Fazlinejad, Ahmad, and Ahmadi, Farajollah, 'The Black Death in Iran, according to Iranian historical accounts from the fourteenth through fifteenth centuries', *JPS* 11 (2018), 56–71

Fiaschetti, Francesca (ed.), *Diplomacy in the Age of Mongol Globalization* (Leiden and Boston, MA, 2019 = *ES* 17, part 2)

Fiey, Jean Maurice, 'Sources syriaques sur Tamerlan', *Le Muséon* 101 (1988), 13–20

Fischel, Walter J., *Ibn Khaldūn and Tamerlane. Their Historic Meeting in Damascus, 1401 A.D. (803 A.H.): A Study Based on Arabic Manuscripts of Ibn Khaldūn's "Autobiography," with a Translation into English, and a Commentary* (Berkeley and Los Angeles, CA, 1952)

Fischel, Walter J., *Ibn Khaldūn in Egypt. His Public Functions and His Historical Research (1382–1406): A Study in Islamic Historiography* (Berkeley and Los Angeles, CA, 1967)

Fletcher, Joseph F., 'The Mongols: Ecological and social perspectives', *HJAS* 46 (1986), 11–50; reprinted in Fletcher, *Studies on Chinese and Islamic Inner Asia*, ed. Beatrice Forbes Manz (Aldershot and Brookfield, VT, 1995)

Fourniau, Vincent (ed.), *Samarcande 1400–1500. La Cité-oasis de Tamerlan. Cœur d'un Empire et d'une Renaissance* (Paris, 1995)

Fragner, Bert G., 'Social and internal economic affairs', in *CHI*, VI, 491–567

Fragner, Bert G., *Selected Writings*, ed. Velizar Sadovski and Antonio Panaino (with Sara Circassia and Bettina Hofleitner), Indo-Iranica, Series Purpurea 1–2 (Milan, 2009–10; reprinted in 1 vol., 2014)

Frank, Allen J., 'The western steppe: Volga-Ural region, Siberia and the Crimea', in *CHIA*, 237–59

Franke, Herbert, 'Zur Datierung der mongolischen Schreiben aus Turfan', *Oriens* 15 (1962), 399–410

Franke, Herbert, *From Tribal Chieftain to Universal Emperor and God. The Legitimation of the Yüan Dynasty* (Munich, 1978 = *Sitzungsberichte der bayerischen Akademie der Wissenschaften, philosophisch-historische Klasse*, 2)

Franz, Kurt, and Holzwarth, Wolfgang (eds), *Nomad Military Power in Iran and Adjacent Areas in the Islamic Period* (Wiesbaden, 2015)

Fromherz, Allen James, *Ibn Khaldun, Life and Times* (Edinburgh, 2010)

Gleave, Robert, and Kristó-Nagy, István T. (eds), *Violence in Islamic Thought from the Mongols to European Imperialism* (Edinburgh, 2018)

Golden, P.B.; Kovalev, R.K.; Martinez, A.P.; Skaff, J.; and Zimonyi, A. (eds), *Festschrift for Thomas T. Allsen in Celebration of His 75th Birthday* (Wiesbaden, 2015 = *AEMA* 21 [2014–15])

Golden, Peter B., 'Imperial ideology and the sources of political unity amongst the pre-Činggisid nomads of western Eurasia', *AEMA* 2 (1982), 37–76; reprinted in Golden, *Nomads and Their Neighbours in the Russian Steppe. Turks, Khazars and Qipchaqs* (Aldershot and Burlington, VT, 2003)

Golden, Peter B., *An Introduction to the History of the Turkic Peoples. Ethnogenesis and State-Formation in Medieval and Early Modern Eurasia and the Middle East*, Turcologica 9 (Wiesbaden, 1992)

Golden, Peter B., '"I will give the people unto thee": The Činggisid conquests and their aftermath in the Turkic world', *JRAS*, 3rd series, 10 (2000), 21–41

Golden, Peter B., 'The Türk imperial tradition in the pre-Chinggisid era', in Sneath (ed.), *Imperial Statecraft*, 23–61

Golden, Peter B., *Central Asia in World History* (Oxford, 2011)

Golombek, Lisa, 'Tamerlane, Scourge of God', *Asian Art* 2, part 2 (Spring 1989), 31–61

Golombek, Lisa, and Subtelny, Maria (eds), *Timurid Art and Culture. Iran and Central Asia in the Fifteenth Century*, Studies in Islamic Art and Architecture (Supplements to *Muqarnas*) 6 (Leiden, New York and Köln, 1992)

Gommans, Jos, 'The warband in the making of Eurasian empires', in Van Berkel and Duindam (eds), *Prince, Pen, and Sword. Eurasian Perspectives*, 297–383

Goto Yukako, 'Tīmūr and local dynasties in Iran', in Jeremiás (ed.), *Irano-Turkic Cultural Contacts in the 11th–17th Centuries*, 67–77

Green, Monica H., 'Editor's introduction to *Pandemic Disease in the Medieval World. Rethinking the Black Death*', 9–25

Green, Monica H., 'Taking pandemic seriously: Making the Black Death global', in Green (ed.), *Pandemic Disease in the Medieval World*, 27–61

Green, Monica H., 'The four Black Deaths', *American Historical Review* 125 (2020), 1601–31

Green, Monica H. (ed.), *Pandemic Disease in the Medieval World. Rethinking the Black Death* (Kalamazoo, MI, 2015 = *The Medieval Globe* 1 [Fall 2014])

Grigor'ev, A.P., 'Zolotoordynskie khany 60–70-kh godov XIV v.: khronologiia pravlenii', *Istoriografiia i Istochnikovedenie Istorii Stran Azii i Afriki* 7 (1983), 9–54

Gronke, Monika, 'The Persian court between palace and tent: From Timur to ʿAbbas I', in Golombek and Subtelny (eds), *Timurid Art and Culture*, 18–22

Grousset, René, *The Empire of the Steppes. A History of Central Asia*, trans. Naomi Walford (New Brunswick, NJ, 1970)

Grupper, Samuel M., 'A Barulas family narrative in the *Yuan Shih*: Some neglected prosopographical and institutional sources on Timurid origins', *AEMA* 8 (1992–4), 11–97

Haase, Claus-Peter, 'Von der "Pax Mongolica" zum Timuridenreich', in Stephan Conermann and Jan Kusber (eds), *Die Mongolen in Asien und Europa*, Kieler Werkstücke, Reihe F, 4 (Frankfurt am Main, 1997), 139–60

Habib, Irfan, 'Timur in the political tradition and historiography of Mughal India', in Szuppe (ed.), *L'Héritage Timouride*, 297–312

Hambly, Gavin R.G., 'The twilight of Tughluqid Delhi: Conflicting strategies in a disintegrating imperium', in R.E. Frykenberg (ed.), *Delhi through the Ages. Essays in Urban History, Culture and Society* (Oxford and Delhi, 1986), 45–62

Hassan, Mona, *Longing for the Lost Caliphate. A Transregional History* (Princeton, NJ, 2016)
Hautala, Roman, 'Comparing the islamisation of the Jochid and Hülegüid *uluses*', in Favereau (ed.), *La Horde d'Or et l'islamisation des steppes eurasiatiques*, 65–79
Hawting, G.R. (ed.), *Muslims, Mongols and Crusaders. An Anthology of Articles Published in the* Bulletin of the School of Oriental and African Studies (London and New York, 2005)
Heidemann, Stefan, 'Tīmūr's campmint during the siege of Damascus in 803/1401', in Rika Gyselen and Maria Szuppe (eds), *Matériaux pour l'histoire économique du monde iranien*, *StIr* cahier 21 (Paris, 1999), 179–206
Heissig, Walther, and Sagaster, Klaus (eds), *Gedanke und Wirkung. Festschrift zum 90. Geburtstag von Nikolaus Poppe*, AF 108 (Wiesbaden, 1989)
Helmy, Nelly Mahmoud, *Tra Siena, l'Oriente e la Curia. Beltramo di Leonardo Mignanelli e le sue opere* (Rome, 2013)
Herrmann, Gottfried, 'Zur Intitulatio timuridischer Urkunden', in Wolfgang Voigt (ed.), *XVIII. Deutscher Orientalistentag vom 1. bis 5. Oktober 1972 in Lübeck. Vorträge*, *ZDMG* Supplement II (Wiesbaden, 1974), 498–521
Heywood, Colin, *Ottomanica and Meta-Ottomanica. Studies in and around Ottoman History, 13th–18th Centuries* (Istanbul, 2013)
Hillenbrand, Carole (ed.), *Studies in Honour of Clifford Edmund Bosworth, II: The Sultan's Turret. Studies in Persian and Turkish Culture* (Leiden, 2000)
Hodgson, Marshall G.S., *The Venture of Islam. Conscience and History in a World Civilization*, 3 vols (Chicago, IL, 1974), II: *The Expansion of Islam in the Middle Periods*
Holzwarth, Wolfgang, 'Nomaden und Sesshafte in *turkī*-Quellen (narrative Quellen aus dem frühen 16. Jahrhundert)', in Bernhard Streck and Stefan Leder (eds), *Akkulturation und Selbstbehauptung*, Orientwissenschaftliche Hefte 4 (Halle, 2002), 147–65
Honda, M., 'On the genealogy of the early Northern Yüan', *UAJ* 30 (1958), 232–48
Hookham, Hilda, *Tamburlaine the Conqueror* (London, 1962)
Hope, Michael, *Power, Politics, and Tradition in the Mongol Empire and the Īlkhānate of Iran* (Oxford, 2016)
Hope, Michael, 'Some remarks about the use of the term '*īlkhān*' in the historical sources and modern historiography', *CAJ* 60 (2017), 273–99
Hope, Michael, '"The Pillars of State": Some notes on the *Qarachu Begs* and the *kešikten* in the Īl-Khānate (1256–1335)', *JRAS*, 3rd series, 27 (2017), 181–99
Hope, Michael, 'The *atābaks* in the Mongol empire and the Ilkhanate of Iran (602–736/1206–1335)', in May, Dashdondog and Atwood (eds), *New Approaches to Ilkhanid History*, 321–45
Hope, Michael, 'The political configuration of late Ilkhanid Iran: A case study of the Chubanid Amirate (738–758/1337–1357)', *Iran*, DOI: 10.1080/05786967.2021.1889930 [published online 19 Feb. 2021]
Hope, Michael, 'The Middle Empire', in May and Hope (eds), *The Mongol World*, 298–316
Hope, Michael, 'The Mongols in South Asia', in May and Hope (eds), *The Mongol World*, 890–906
Horrox, Rosemary (trans. and ed.), *The Black Death* (Manchester, 1994)
Hymes, Robert, 'Epilogue: A hypothesis on the East Asian beginnings of the *Yersinia pestis* polytomy', in Green (ed.), *Pandemic Disease in the Medieval World*, 285–308

Iakubovskii, AIu., 'Timur (opyt kratkoi kharakteristiki)', *Voprosy Istorii* 8–9 (1946), 42–74

Iorga, N., 'Notes et extraits pour servir à l'histoire des croisades au XVe siècle', *Revue de l'Orient Latin* 4 (1896), 25–118, 226–320, 503–622

Irwin, Robert, *Mamlūks and Crusaders. Men of the Sword and Men of the Pen* (Farnham and Burlington, VT, 2010)

Irwin, Robert, *Ibn Khaldun. An Intellectual Biography* (Princeton, NJ, and Oxford, 2018)

Ito Takao, 'Al-Maqrīzī's biography of Tīmūr', *Arabica* 62 (2015), 308–27

Jackson, Peter, 'The Mongols and the Delhi Sultanate in the reign of Muḥammad Tughluq (1325–1351)', *CAJ* 19 (1975), 118–57; reprinted in Jackson, *Studies on the Mongol Empire*

Jackson, Peter, 'The dissolution of the Mongol empire', *CAJ* 22 (1978), 186–244; reprinted in Jackson, *Studies on the Mongol Empire*; Russian trans. as 'Raspad mongol'skoi imperii', *ZOTs* 10 (2017), 50–83

Jackson, Peter, *The Delhi Sultanate. A Political and Military History*, CSIC (Cambridge, 1999)

Jackson, Peter, 'From *ulus* to khanate: The making of the Mongol states, c. 1220–c. 1290', in Amitai-Preiss and Morgan (eds), *The Mongol Empire and Its Legacy*, 12–38; reprinted in Jackson, *Studies on the Mongol Empire*

Jackson, Peter, 'The Mongols and the faith of the conquered', in Amitai and Biran (eds), *Mongols, Turks, and Others*, 245–90; reprinted in Jackson, *Studies on the Mongol Empire*

Jackson, Peter, *Studies on the Mongol Empire and Early Muslim India* (Farnham and Burlington, VT, 2009)

Jackson, Peter, *The Mongols and the Islamic World. From Conquest to Conversion* (New Haven, CT, and London, 2017)

Jackson, Peter, *The Mongols and the West, 1221–1410* (2005); 2nd edn (London and New York, 2018)

Jackson, Peter, 'The Mongols of Central Asia and the Qaraunas', *Iran* 56 (2018), 91–103

Jahn, Karl, 'Timur und die Frauen', *Anzeiger der Österreichischen Akademie der Wissenschaften, phil.-hist. Klasse*, 111 (1974), 515–29

Jeremiás, Éva M. (ed.), *Irano-Turkic Cultural Contacts in the 11th–17th Centuries* (Piliscsaba, [2002] 2003)

Kamola, Stefan, *Making Mongol History. Rashid al-Din and the Jami' al-Tawarikh*, Edinburgh Studies in Classical Islamic History and Culture (Edinburgh, 2019)

Kamola, Stefan, 'Untangling the Chaghadaids: Why we should and should not trust Rashīd al-Dīn', *CAJ* 62 (2019), 69–90

Kara, György, 'Mediaeval Mongol documents from Khara Khoto and East Turkestan in the St. Petersburg branch of the Institute of Oriental Studies', *MO* 9 (2003), part 2, 3–40

Karpov, S.P., 'Nachalo smuty v Zolotoi Orde i perevorot Navruza', *ZOO* 6 (2018), 528–36

Kastritsis, Dimitris, 'The Alexander Romance and the rise of the Ottoman empire', in Peacock and Yıldız (eds), *Islamic Literature and Intellectual Life in Fourteenth- and Fifteenth-Century Anatolia*, 243–83

Kastritsis, Dimitris J., *The Sons of Bayezid. Empire Building and Representation in the Ottoman Civil War of 1402–1413* (Leiden and Boston, MA, 2007)

Katō Kazuhide, 'Kebek and Yasawr – the establishment of the Chaghatai khanate', *MTB* 49 (1991), 97–118

Kauz, Ralph, *Politik und Handel zwischen Ming und Timuriden. China, Iran und Zentralasien im Spätmittelalter* (Wiesbaden, 2005)

Kedar, Benjamin Z., *Merchants in Crisis. Genoese and Venetian Men of Affairs and the Fourteenth-Century Depression* (New Haven, CT, and London, 1976)

Kehren, Lucien, *Tamerlan. L'Empire du Seigneur de fer* (Neuchâtel, 1978)

Kempiners, Russell G., Jr, 'Vaṣṣāf's *Tajziyat al-amṣār wa Tazjiyat al-a'ṣār* as a source for the history of the Chaghadayid khanate', *JAH* 22 (1988), 160–87

Khakimov, Rafael; Trepavlov, Vadim; and Favereau, Marie (eds), *The Golden Horde in World History* (Oxford and Kazan´, 2017)

Khazanov, Anatoly M., and Wink, André (eds), *Nomads in the Sedentary World* (Richmond, Surrey, 2001)

Kim Hodong, 'The early history of the Moghul nomads: The legacy of the Chaghatai khanate', in Amitai-Preiss and Morgan (eds), *The Mongol Empire and Its Legacy*, 290–318

Kim Hodong, 'Unity and continuity of the Mongol empire', *Mongolica* 18 (39) (2006), 57–65

Kim Hodong, 'The unity of the Mongol empire and continental exchanges over Eurasia', *Journal of Central Eurasian Studies* 1 (2009), 15–42

Kim Hodong, 'Was "Da Yuan" a Chinese dynasty?', *JSYS* 45 (2015), 279–305

Kim Hodong, 'Formation and changes of *ulus*es in the Mongol empire', in Biran (ed.), *Mobility Transformations and Cultural Exchange in Mongol Eurasia*, 269–317

Knobler, Adam, 'The rise of Tīmūr and Western diplomatic response, 1390–1405', *JRAS*, 3rd series, 5 (1995), 341–9

Knobler, Adam, 'Timur the (Terrible/Tartar) trope: A case of repositioning in popular literature and history', *ME* 7 (2001), 101–12

Knobler, Adam, *Mythology and Diplomacy in the Age of Exploration* (Leiden and Boston, MA, 2017)

Komaroff, Linda, 'The epigraphy of Timurid coinage: Some preliminary remarks', *ANSMN* 31 (1986), 207–32

Komaroff, Linda (ed.), *Beyond the Legacy of Genghis Khan*, IHC 64 (Leiden and Boston, MA, 2006)

Krawulsky, Dorothea, *Mongolen und Ilkhâne – Ideologie und Geschichte* (Beirut, 1989); revised version trans. as *The Mongol Īlkhāns and Their Vizier Rashīd al-Dīn* (Frankfurt am Main, 2011)

Kuroda Akinobu, 'The Eurasian silver century, 1276–1359: Commensurability and multiplicity', *JGH* 4 (2009), 245–69

Lal, Kishori Saran, *Twilight of the Sultanate. A Political, Social and Cultural History of the Sultanate of Delhi from the Invasion of Timur to the Conquest of Babur, 1398–1526*, revised edn (New Delhi, 1980)

Lambton, A.K.S., 'Early Timurid theories of state: Ḥāfiẓ Abrū and Niẓām al-Dīn Šāmī', in *Mélanges offerts à Henri Laoust*, II (Damascus, 1978 = *BEO* 30), 1–9

Lambton, Ann K.S., *Continuity and Change in Medieval Persia. Aspects of Administrative, Economic and Social History, 11th–14th Century* (London, 1988)

Landa, Ishayahu, 'New light on early Mongol Islamisation: The case of Arghun Aqa's family', *JRAS*, 3rd series, 28 (2018), 77–100

Landa, Ishayahu, 'The Islamization of the Mongols', in May and Hope (eds), *The Mongol World*, 642–61

Lane, George, *Early Mongol Rule in Thirteenth-Century Iran. A Persian Renaissance* (London and New York, 2003)
Lange, Christian, *Justice, Punishment and the Medieval Muslim Imagination*, CSIC (Cambridge, 2008)
Langer, Lawrence N., 'The Black Death in Russia: Its effects upon urban labor', *Russian History* 2 (1975), 53–67
Le Roy Ladurie, Emmanuel, 'A concept: The unification of the globe by disease (fourteenth to seventeenth centuries)', in his *The Mind and Method of the Historian*, trans. Siân and Ben Reynolds (Brighton and Chicago, IL, 1981), 28–83
Lee, Joo-Yup, Qazaqlïq, *or* Ambitious Brigandage, *and the Formation of the Qazaqs. State and Identity in Post-Mongol Central Eurasia*, Studies in Persian Cultural History 8 (Leiden and Boston, MA, 2016)
Lee, Joo-Yup, 'The political vagabondage of the Chinggisid and Timurid contenders to the throne and others in post-Mongol Central Asia and the Qipchaq steppe: A comprehensive study of *qazaqlïq*, or the *qazaq* way of life', *CAJ* 60 (2017), 59–95
Lee, Joo-Yup, 'Some remarks on the Turkicisation of the Mongols in post-Mongol Central Asia and the Qipchaq steppe', *AOH* 71 (2018), 121–44
Lentz, Thomas W., and Lowry, Glenn D., *Timur and the Princely Vision. Persian Art and Culture in the Fifteenth Century* (Los Angeles, 1989)
Lev, Yaacov (ed.), *War and Society in the Eastern Mediterranean, 7th–15th Centuries*, MM 9 (Leiden, New York and Köln, 1997)
Levi, Scott C., *The Rise and Fall of Khoqand, 1709–1876. Central Asia in the Global Age* (Pittsburgh, PA, 2017)
Levi, Scott C. (ed.), *India and Central Asia. Commerce and Culture, 1500–1800* (Oxford and Delhi, 2007)
Lewisohn, Leonard, 'Sufism in late Mongol and early Timurid Persia, from ʿAlaʾ al-Dawla Simnānī (d. 736/1326 [*sic*]) to Shāh Qāsim Anvār (d. 837/1434)', in Babaie (ed.), *Iran after the Mongols*, 177–209
Lindner, Rudi Paul, 'Anatolia, 1300–1451', in *CHT*, 102–37
Little, Donald P., 'Historiography of the Ayyūbid and Mamlūk epochs', in *CHE*, 412–44
Liu Yingsheng, 'War and peace between the Yuan dynasty and the Chaghadaid khanate', in Amitai and Biran (eds), *Mongols, Turks, and Others*, 339–58
Luttrell, Anthony, 'Timur's Dominican envoy', in Colin Heywood and Colin Imber (eds), *Studies in Ottoman History in Honour of Professor V.L. Ménage* (Istanbul, 1994), 209–29
Mahendrarajah, Shivan, 'The Sarbadars of Sabzavar: Re-examining their "Shiʿa" roots and alleged goal to "destroy Khurasanian Sunnism"', *Journal of Shiʿa Islamic Studies* 5 (2012), 379–402
Mahendrarajah, Shivan, 'A revised history of Mongol, Kart, and Timurid patronage of the shrine of Shaykh al-Islam Ahmad-i Jam', *Iran* 54 (2016), part 2, 107–28
Mahendrarajah, Shivan, 'The Iranian interlude: From Mongol decline to Timur's invasion', in Babaie (ed.), *Iran after the Mongols*, 159–76
Mahendrarajah, Shivan, *The Sufi Saint of Jam. History, Religion, and Politics of a Sunni Shrine in Shiʿi Iran*, CSIC (Cambridge, 2021)
Mahendrarajah, Shivan, *A History of Herat from Chingiz Khan to Tamerlane, Edinburgh Studies in Classical Islamic History and Culture* (Edinburgh, 2022)

Maitra, K.M. (ed. and trans.), *A Persian Embassy to China* (Lahore, 1934; repr. New York, 1970)
Manz, Beatrice F. (ed.), *Central Asia in Historical Perspective* (Boulder, CO, San Francisco and Oxford, 1994)
Manz, Beatrice Forbes, 'Administration and the delegation of authority in Temür's dominions', *CAJ* 20 (1976), 191–207
Manz, Beatrice Forbes, 'The ulus Chaghatay before and after Temür's rise to power: The transformation from tribal confederation to army of conquest', *CAJ* 27 (1983), 79–100
Manz, Beatrice Forbes, 'The office of *darugha* under Tamerlane', in Joseph Fletcher, Richard Nelson Frye, Yuan-chu Lam and Omeljan Pritsak (eds, with Carolyn I. Cross), *Niğuča Bičig. An Anniversary Volume in Honor of Francis Woodman Cleaves* (Cambridge, MA, 1985 = *JTS* 9), 59–69
Manz, Beatrice Forbes, 'Tamerlane and the symbolism of sovereignty', *IrSt* 21 (1988), nos 1–2, 105–22
Manz, Beatrice Forbes, *The Rise and Rule of Tamerlane*, CSIC (Cambridge, 1989)
Manz, Beatrice Forbes, 'The legacy of Timur', *Asian Art* 2, part 2 (Spring 1989), 10–30
Manz, Beatrice Forbes, 'The development and meaning of Chaghatay identity', in Jo-Ann Gross (ed.), *Muslims in Central Asia. Expressions of Identity and Change* (Durham, NC, and London, 1992), 29–45
Manz, Beatrice Forbes, 'Military manpower in late Mongol and Timurid Iran', in Szuppe (ed.), *L'Héritage Timouride*, 43–55
Manz, Beatrice Forbes, 'Temür and the problem of a conqueror's legacy', *JRAS*, 3rd series, 8 (1998), 21–41
Manz, Beatrice Forbes, 'Mongol history rewritten and relived', in Aigle (ed.), *Figures mythiques des mondes musulmans* (Aix-en-Provence, 2000 = *REMMM* 89–90), 129–49
Manz, Beatrice Forbes, 'Family and ruler in Timurid historiography', in Devin DeWeese (ed.), *Studies on Central Asian History in Honor of Yuri Bregel*, IUUAS 167 (Bloomington, IN, 2001), 57–78
Manz, Beatrice Forbes, 'Tamerlane's career and its uses', *JWH* 13 (2002), 1–25
Manz, Beatrice Forbes, 'Women in Timurid domestic politics', in Guity Nashat and Lois Beck (eds), *Women in Iran from the Rise of Islam to 1800* (Urbana and Chicago, IL, 2003), 121–39
Manz, Beatrice Forbes, 'Nomad and settled in the Timurid military', in Amitai and Biran (eds), *Mongols, Turks, and Others*, 425–57
Manz, Beatrice Forbes, *Power, Politics and Religion in Timurid Iran*, CSIC (Cambridge, 2007)
Manz, Beatrice Forbes, 'Johannes Schiltberger and other outside sources on the Timurids', in Encarnación Sánchez García, Pablo Martín Asuero and Michele Bernardini (eds), *España y el Oriente islámico entre los siglos XV y XVI (Imperio Ottomano, Persia y Asia central. Actas del congreso Università degli Studi di Napoli 'l'Orientale' Nápoles 30 de septiembre-2 de octubre de 2004)* (Istanbul, 2007), 53–62
Manz, Beatrice Forbes, 'Ulugh Beg, Transoxiana and Turco-Mongolian tradition', in Markus Ritter, Ralph Kauz and Birgitt Hoffmann (eds), *Iran und iranisch geprägte Kulturen. Studien zum 65. Geburtstag von Bert G. Fragner* (Wiesbaden, 2008), 20–7
Manz, Beatrice Forbes, 'Temür and the early Timurids to *c.* 1450', in *CHIA*, 182–98

Manz, Beatrice Forbes, 'The rule of the infidels: The Mongols and the Islamic world', in *NCHI*, III, 128–68
Manz, Beatrice Forbes, 'Nomads and regional armies in the Middle East', in Franz and Holzwarth (eds), *Nomad Military Power in Iran and Adjacent Areas*, 1–27
Manz, Beatrice Forbes, 'The empire of Tamerlane as an adaptation of the Mongol empire: An answer to David Morgan, "The empire of Tamerlane: An unsuccessful re-run of the Mongol empire?"', in May (ed.), *The Mongols and Post-Mongol Asia*, 281–91
Manz, Beatrice Forbes, 'Unacceptable violence as legitimation in Mongol and Timurid Iran', in Gleave and Kristó-Nagy (eds), *Violence in Islamic Thought from the Mongols to European Imperialism*, 79–103
Manz, Beatrice Forbes, 'Iranian elites under the Timurids', in Van Steenbergen (ed.), *Trajectories of State Formation across Fifteenth-Century Islamic West-Asia*, 257–82
Manz, Beatrice Forbes, *Nomads in the Middle East* (Cambridge, 2021)
Markiewicz, Christopher, *The Crisis of Kingship in Late Medieval Islam. Persian Emigres and the Making of Ottoman Sovereignty*, CSIC (Cambridge, 2019)
Marozzi, Justin, *Tamerlane. Sword of Islam, Conqueror of the World* (Hammersmith, 2004)
Martin, Janet, *Treasure of the Land of Darkness. The Fur Trade and Its Significance for Medieval Russia* (Cambridge, 1986)
Martin, Janet, *Medieval Russia 980–1584*, 2nd edn (Cambridge, 2007)
Martinez, A.P., 'Some notes on the Īl-xānid army', *AEMA* 6 (1986 [1988]), 129–242
Martinez, A.P., 'Bullionistic imperialism: The Īl-Xānid mint's exploitation of the Rūm-Saljūqid currency, 654–695 H./1256–1296 A.D.', in *Tibor Halasi-Kun Memorial Volume* (Wiesbaden, 1994 = *Archivum Ottomanicum* 13 [1993–4]), 169–276
Martinez, A.P., 'The Eurasian overland and Pontic trades in the thirteenth and fourteenth centuries with special reference to their impact on the Golden Horde, the West, and Russia, and to the evidence in archival material and mint outputs', *AEMA* 16 (2008–9), 127–221
Martinez, A.P., 'Institutional development, revenues and trade', in *CHIA*, 89–108
Masson, M.E., and Pugachenkova, G.A., 'Shakhri Siabz pri Timure i Ulug Beke', *Trudy Sredneaziatskogo Gosudarstvennogo Universiteta* 49 (1953), 17–96; trans. J.M. Rogers as 'Shakhri Syabz pri Timure i Ulug Beke ("Shahr-i Sabz from Tīmūr to Ūlūgh Beg") – I', *Iran* 16 (1978), 103–26, and '. . . – II', *Iran* 18 (1980), 121–43
Massoud, Sami G., *The Chronicles and Annalistic Sources of the Early Mamluk Circassian Period*, IHC 67 (Leiden and Boston, MA, 2007)
Matsui Dai, 'Taxation systems as seen in the Uigur and Mongol documents from Turfan: An overview', *Transactions of the International Conference of Eastern Studies* 50 (2005), 67–82
Matsui Dai, 'An Uigur decree of tax exemption in the name of Duwa-Khan', *Šinžlex Uxvany Akademiin Mebee* [*Proceedings of the Mongolian Academy of Sciences*] (2007), no. 4, 60–8
Matsui Dai, 'A Mongolian decree from the Chaghataid Khanate discovered at Dunhuang', in Peter Zieme (ed.), *Aspects of Research into Central Asian Buddhism. In Memoriam Kōgi Kudara*, SRS 16 (Turnhout, 2008), 159–78

Matsui Dai, '*Dumdadu Mongγol Ulus* "The Middle Mongolian Empire"', in Rybatzki et al. (eds), *The Early Mongols. Language, Culture and History*, 111–19
Matsui Dai, Watabe Ryoko and Ono Hiroshi, 'A Turkic-Persian decree of Timurid Mīrān Šāh of 800 AH/1398 CE', *Orient* 50 (2015), 53–75
May, Timothy, 'Nökhöd to noyad: Chinggis Khan's social revolution', *Mongolica* 19 (40) (2006), 296–308
May, Timothy, *The Mongol Conquests in World History* (London, 2012)
May, Timothy, *The Mongol Empire* (Edinburgh, 2018)
May, Timothy, 'The Mongols as the Scourge of God in the Islamic world', in Gleave and Kristó-Nagy (eds), *Violence in Islamic Thought from the Mongols to European Imperialism*, 32–57
May, Timothy, 'The Ilkhanate and Afghanistan', in May, Dashdondog and Atwood (eds), *New Approaches to Ilkhanid History*, 272–320
May, Timothy (ed.), *The Mongols and Post-Mongol Asia. Studies in Honour of David O. Morgan* (Cambridge, 2016 = *JRAS*, 3rd series, 26, parts 1–2)
May, Timothy; Dashdondog Bayarsaikhan; and Atwood, Christopher P. (eds), *New Approaches to Ilkhanid History*, BIAL 39 (Leiden and Boston, MA, 2020)
May, Timothy, and Hope, Michael (eds), *The Mongol World* (London and New York, 2022)
McChesney, R.D., 'A note on the life and works of Ibn ʿArabshāh', in Pfeiffer and Quinn (eds), *History and Historiography of Post-Mongol Central Asia and the Middle East*, 205–49
McChesney, R.D., 'The Chinggisid restoration in Central Asia: 1500–1785', in *CHIA*, 277–302
McNeill, William H., *Plagues and Peoples* (Oxford, 1977)
Melville, Charles, '*Pādishāh-i Islām*: The conversion of Sultan Maḥmūd Ghāzān Khān', in Melville (ed.), *Persian and Islamic Studies in Honour of P.W. Avery* (Cambridge, 1990 = *Pembroke Papers* 1), 159–77
Melville, Charles, 'Ḥamd Allāh Mustawfī's *Ẓafarnāmah* and the historiography of the late Ilkhanid period', in Kambiz Eslami (ed.), *Iran and Iranian Studies. Essays in Honor of Iraj Afshar* (Princeton, NJ, 1998), 1–12
Melville, Charles, *The Fall of Amir Chupan and the Decline of the Ilkhanate, 1327–37. A Decade of Discord in Mongol Iran*, PIA 30 (Bloomington, IN, 1999)
Melville, Charles, 'The Caspian provinces: A world apart. Three local histories of Mazandaran', *IrSt* 33 (2000), 45–91
Melville, Charles, 'The *keshig* in Iran: The survival of the royal Mongol household', in Komaroff (ed.), *Beyond the Legacy of Genghis Khan*, 135–64
Melville, Charles, 'The end of the Ilkhanate and after: Observations on the collapse of the Mongol world empire', in De Nicola and Melville (eds), *The Mongols' Middle East*, 309–35
Melville, Charles, 'Concepts of government and state formation in Mongol Iran', in Babaie (ed.), *Iran after the Mongols*, 33–54
Melville, Charles, 'Visualising Tamerlane: History and its image', *Iran* 57 (2019), 83–106
Melville, Charles (ed.), *The Timurid Century*, The Idea of Iran 9 (London and New York, 2020)
Melvin-Koushki, Matthew, 'Early modern Islamicate empire: New forms of religiopolitical legitimacy', in Armando Salvatore et al. (eds), *The Wiley Blackwell History of Islam* (Hoboken, NJ, 2018), 353–75

Millward, James, 'Eastern Central Asia (Xinjiang): 1300–1800', in *CHIA*, 260–76
Mir-Kasimov, Orkhan (ed.), *Unity in Diversity. Mysticism, Messianism, and the Construction of Religious Authority in Islam*, IHC 105 (Leiden and Boston, MA, 2014)
Mirgaleev, Ilnur, 'Tatary Desht-i Kypchaka v perepiske Aksak Timura s Baiazidom', *ZOTs* 8 (2015), 299–303
Mirgaleev, Ilnur, 'The Time of Troubles in the 1360s and 1370s', in Khakimov et al. (eds), *The Golden Horde in World History*, 689–92
Moin, A. Azfar, *The Millennial Sovereign. Sacred Kingship and Sainthood in Islam* (New York, 2012)
Morgan, David O., 'Persian historians on the Mongols', in D.O. Morgan (ed.), *Medieval Historical Writing in the Christian and Islamic Worlds* (London, 1982), 109–24
Morgan, David O., 'Who ran the Mongol empire?', *JRAS* (1982), 124–36
Morgan, David O., 'The "Great *Yāsā* of Chingiz Khān" and Mongol law in the Īlkhānate', *BSOAS* 49 (1986), 163–76; reprinted in Hawting (ed.), *Muslims, Mongols and Crusaders*, 198–211
Morgan, David O., 'The empire of Tamerlane: An unsuccessful re-run of the Mongol empire?', in J.R. Maddicott and D.M. Palliser (eds), *The Medieval State. Essays Presented to James Campbell* (London and Rio Grande, 2000), 233–41
Morgan, David O., 'The Mongols in Iran: A reappraisal', *Iran* 42 (2004), 131–6
Morgan, David O., 'The "Great *Yasa* of Chinggis Khan" revisited', in Amitai and Biran (eds), *Mongols, Turks, and Others*, 291–308
Morgan, David O., *The Mongols* (1986); 2nd edn (Oxford, 2007)
Morgan, David O., 'The decline and fall of the Mongol Empire', *JRAS*, 3rd series, 19 (2009), 427–37
Morgan, David O., *Medieval Persia 1040–1797* (1988); 2nd edn (London and New York, 2016)
Morgan, David O., 'The Mongols in Iran, 1219–1256', in David O. Morgan and Sarah Stewart (eds), *The Coming of the Mongols*, The Idea of Iran 7 (London and New York, 2018), 45–53
Morimoto Kazuo, 'An enigmatic genealogical chart of the Timurids: A testimony to the dynasty's claim to Yasavi-ʿAlid legitimacy?', *Oriens* 44 (2016), 145–78
Mukminova, R.G., 'The Timurid states in the fifteenth and sixteenth centuries', in *HCCA*, IV, part 1, 347–63
Müller, Claudius C., and Pleiger, Henriette (eds), *Dschingis Khan und seine Erben. Das Weltreich der Mongolen* (Munich, [2005])
Muminov, Ashirbek, and Babadzhanov, Bakhtiyar, 'Amīr Temur and Sayyid Baraka' (trans. Sean Pollock), *CAJ* 45 (2001), 28–62
Munkh-Erdene, Lhamsuren, 'Where did the Mongol empire come from? Medieval Mongol ideas of people, state and empire', *Inner Asia* 13 (2011), 211–37
Munkh-Erdene, Lhamsuren, 'Political order in pre-modern Eurasia: Imperial incorporation and the hereditary divisional system', *JRAS*, 3rd series, 26 (2016), 633–55
Munkh-Erdene, Lhamsuren, 'The rise of the Chinggisid dynasty: Pre-modern Eurasian political order and culture at a glance', *International Journal of Asian Studies* 15 (2018), 39–84
Murphey, Rhoads, 'Bayezid I's foreign policy plans and priorities: Power relations, statecraft, military conditions and diplomatic practice in Anatolia and the

Balkans', in Chrissis and Carr (eds), *Contact and Conflict in Frankish Greece and the Aegean*, 177–215

al-Musawi, Muhsin J., *The Medieval Islamic Republic of Letters. Arabic Knowledge Construction* (Notre Dame, IN, 2015)

Nagel, Tilman, *Timur der Eroberer und die islamische Welt des späten Mittelalters* (Munich, 1993)

Norris, John, 'East or west? The geographic origin of the Black Death', *BHM* 51 (1977), 1–24

Oberling, Pierre (ed., with Geraldine Cecilia Butash), *Turks, Hungarians and Kipchaks. A Festschrift in Honor of Tibor Halasi-Kun* (Cambridge, MA, 1984 = *JTS* 8)

O'Kane, Bernard, 'From tents to pavilions: Royal mobility and Persian palace design', *Ars Orientalis* 23 (1993), 249–68

Pachkalov, A.V., 'K voprosu ob imennykh monet Mamaia', *NZO* 2 (2012), 117–19

Papas, Alexandre, and Toutant, Marc, *L'Asie centrale de Tamerlan* (Paris, 2022)

Parodi, Laura Emilia, 'L'eredità mongola e altaica nell'Asia centrale islamica', in Gabriella Airaldi, Paola Mortari Vergara Caffarelli and Laura Emilia Parodi (eds), *I Mongoli dal Pacifico al Mediterraneo. Atti del Convegno Internazionale Genova, Palazzo Doria Spinola, 7–8 maggio 2002* (Genoa, 2004), 241–58

Paul, Jürgen, 'Scheiche und Herrscher im khanat Čaġatay', *Der Islam* 67 (1990), 278–321

Paul, Jürgen, 'The state and the military – a nomadic perspective', in Irene Schneider (ed.), *Militär und Staatlichkeit. Beiträge des Kolloquiums am 29. und 30.04.2002*, Orientwissenschaftliche Hefte 12 (Halle, 2003), 25–68

Paul, Jürgen, 'Perspectives nomades. État et structures militaires', *AHSS* 59 (2004), nos 5–6, 1069–93

Paul, Jürgen, 'Khalīl Sulṭān and the "Westerners" (1405–1407)', *Turcica* 42 (2010), 11–45

Paul, Jürgen, 'Mongol aristocrats and beyliks in Anatolia: A study of Astarābādī's *Bazm va Razm*', in Büssow, Durand-Guédy and Paul (eds), *Nomads in the Political Field*, 105–58

Paul, Jürgen, 'Zerfall und Bestehen: Die Ǧaun-i Qurban im 14. Jahrhundert', *AS* 65 (2011), 695–733

Peacock, A.C.S., 'Islamisation in Anatolia and the Golden Horde: Some remarks on travelling scholars and texts', in Favereau (ed.), *La Horde d'Or et l'islamisation des steppes eurasiatiques*, 151–63

Peacock, A.C.S., *Islam, Literature and Society in Mongol Anatolia*, CSIC (Cambridge, 2019)

Peacock, A.C.S. (ed.), *Islamisation. Comparative Perspectives from History* (Edinburgh, 2017)

Peacock, A.C.S., and Yıldız, Sara Nur (eds), *Islamic Literature and Intellectual Life in Fourteenth- and Fifteenth-Century Anatolia*, Istanbuler Texte und Studien 34 (Würzburg, 2016)

Pelliot, Paul, 'Les Mongols et la papauté', *Revue de l'Orient Chrétien* 23 (1922–3), 3–30; 24 (1924), 225–335; and 28 (1931–2), 3–84

Pelliot, Paul, *Notes on Marco Polo*, 3 vols (Paris, 1959–73)

Perdue, Peter C., *China Marches West. The Qing Conquest of Central Eurasia* (Cambridge, MA, 2005)

Petrov, P.N., 'Badakhshan XIII–XIV vv. pod vlast'iu mongol'skikh khanov', *Zapiski Vostochnogo Otdeleniia Rossiiskogo Arkheologicheskogo Obshchestva*, n.s. 2 (2006), 496–540

Petrov, P.N., 'Khronologiia pravleniia khanov v Chagataiskom gosudarstve v 1271–1368 gg. (po materialam numizmaticheskikh pamiatnikov)', in S.G. Kliashtornyi, T.I. Sultanov and V.V. Trepavlov (eds), *Istoriia i kul'tura tiurkskikh narodov Rossii i sopredel'nykh stran* (Moscow 2009 = *TS* 2007–8), 294–319

Petry, Carl F., *The Mamluk Sultanate. A History* (Cambridge, 2022)

Petry, Carl F. (ed.), *The Cambridge History of Egypt*, I: *Islamic Egypt, 640–1517* (Cambridge, 1998)

Pfeiffer, Judith, 'Conversion versions: Sultan Öljeitü's conversion to Shiᶜism (709/1309) in Muslim narrative sources', *MS* 22 (1999), 35–67

Pfeiffer, Judith, 'Reflections on a "double rapprochement": Conversion to Islam among the Mongol elite during the early Ilkhanate', in Komaroff (ed.), *Beyond the Legacy of Genghis Khan*, 369–89

Pfeiffer, Judith, 'The canonization of cultural memory: Ghāzān Khan, Rashīd al-Dīn, and the construction of the Mongol past', in Akasoy, Burnett and Yoeli-Tlalim (eds), *Rashīd al-Dīn. Agent and Mediator of Cultural Exchanges in Ilkhanid Iran*, 57–70

Pfeiffer, Judith, 'Confessional ambiguity vs. confessional polarization: Politics and the negotiation of religious boundaries in the Ilkhanate', in Pfeiffer (ed.), *Politics, Patronage and the Transmission of Knowledge*, 129–68

Pfeiffer, Judith, '"Not every head that wears a crown deserves to rule": Women in Il-Khanid political life and court culture', in Rachel Ward (ed.), *Court and Craft. A Masterpiece from Northern Iraq* (London, 2014), 23–9

Pfeiffer, Judith (ed.), *Politics, Patronage and the Transmission of Knowledge in 13th–15th Century Tabriz* (Leiden and Boston, MA, 2014)

Pfeiffer, Judith, and Quinn, Sholeh A. (eds, with Ernest Tucker), *History and Historiography of Post-Mongol Central Asia and the Middle East. Studies in Honor of John E. Woods* (Wiesbaden, 2006)

Pishchulina, K.A., *Iugo-vostochnyi Kazakhstan v seredine XIV–nachale XVI vekov (voprosy politicheskoi i sotsial'no-ékonomicheskoi istorii)* (Alma-Ata, 1977)

Pochekaev, R.Iu., 'Pravovoe nasledie mongol'skoi imperii v gosudarstve Timuridov (po dannym letopisei, numizmaticheskogo i aktogo materiala)', in V.P. Nikonorov (ed.), *Tsentral'naia Aziia ot Akhemenidov do Timuridov. Arkheologiia, istoriia, étnologia, kul'tura. Materialy mezhdunarodnoi nauchnoi konferentsii, posviashchennoi 100-letiiu so dnia rozhdeniia Aleksandra Markovicha Belenitskogo, Sankt-Peterburg, 2–5 noiabria 2004 goda* (St Petersburg, 2005), 291–4

Pochekaev, R.Iu., 'Svedeniia o Zolotoi Orde v «Knige o Velikom Khane»', *TS* (2006 [2007]), 260–73

Pochekaev, R.Iu., 'K voprosu o perekhode vlasti v gosudarstvakh Chingizidov (4). Zolotaia Orda v 1358–1362 gg.: dinasticheskii krizis i fenomen samovanstva', *ZOTs* 2 (2009), 39–49

Pochekaev, R.Iu., *Tsari ordynskie. Biografii khanov i pravitelei Zolotoi Ordy*, 2nd edn (St Petersburg, 2012)

Pochekaev, R.Iu, 'Chinggis Khan's Great Yasa in the Mongol empire and Chinggisid states of the 13th–14th centuries: Legal code or ideal "law and order"?', *ZOO* 4 (2016), no. 4, 724–33

Pochekaev, Roman Iu., '*Törü*; Ancient Turkic law "privatised" by Chinggis Khan and his descendants', *Inner Asia* 18 (2016), 182–95

Polyakova, E.A., 'Timur as described by the 15th century court historiographers', *IrSt* 21 (1988), nos 1–2, 31–44

Poonawala, Ismail K. (ed.), *Turks in the Indian Subcontinent, Central and West Asia. The Turkish Presence in the Islamic World* (Oxford and Delhi, 2017)

Poppe, N.N., 'Karasakpaiskaia nadpis' Timura', *Gosudarstvennyi Érmitazh. Trudy Otdela Vostoka/Travaux du Département Oriental* 2 (Leningrad, 1940), 185–7

Potter, Lawrence Goddard, 'The Kart dynasty of Herat: Religion and politics in medieval Iran', unpublished PhD thesis, Columbia University, 1992

Qiu Yihao, 'Independent ruler, indefinable role: Understanding the history of the Golden Horde from the perspectives of the Yuan dynasty', in Favereau (ed.), *La Horde d'Or et l'islamisation des steppes eurasiatiques*, 29–48

Quinn, Sholeh A., 'The *Mu'izz al-Ansāb* and the *Shu'ab-i Panjgānah* as sources for the Chaghatayid period of history: A comparative analysis', *CAJ* 33 (1989), 229–53

Rabbat, Nasser, 'Who was al-Maqrīzī? A biographical sketch', *MSR* 7 (2003), part 2, 1–19

Rabino, H.L., 'Coins of the Jalā'ir, Ḳarā Ḳoyūnlū, Musha'sha' and Āḳ Ḳoyūnlū dynasties', *Numismatic Chronicle*, 6th series, 10 (1950), 94–139

Ratchnevsky, Paul, *Genghis Khan. His Life and Legacy*, trans. Thomas Nivison Haining (Oxford, 1991)

Reva, R.Iu., 'Saiid-Akhmad I i Giias ad-Din I (istoriografiia otkrytiia, genealogiia, novoobnaruzhennye monetnye vypuski)', *NZO* 4 (2014), 48–60

Richard, Jean, 'Les missionnaires latins chez les Kaïtak du Daghestan (XIVe–XVe siècles)', in *TDPKV*, III, 606–11; reprinted in Richard, *Les Relations entre l'Orient et l'Occident au Moyen Age. Études et documents* (London, 1977)

Richard, Jean, *La Papauté et les missions d'Orient au Moyen Age (XIIIe–XVe siècles)* (Rome, 1977)

Richard Nelson Frye Festschrift I: Essays Presented to Richard Nelson Frye on His Seventieth Birthday by His Colleagues and Students (Cambridge, MA, 1992 = *JTS* 16)

Robinson, Chase F., *Islamic Civilization in Thirty Lives. The First 1,000 Years* ([London, 2018])

Robinson, David M., *In the Shadow of the Mongol Empire. Ming China and Eurasia* (Cambridge, 2020)

Robinson, David M., *Ming China and Its Allies. Imperial Rule in Eurasia* (Cambridge, 2020)

Roemer, Hans Robert, 'The Jalayirids, Muzaffarids and Sarbadārs', in *CHI*, VI, 1–41

Roemer, Hans Robert, 'Tīmūr in Iran', in *CHI*, VI, 42–97

Roemer, Hans Robert, 'The successors of Tīmūr', in *CHI*, VI, 98–146

Roemer, Hans Robert, 'The Türkmen dynasties', in *CHI*, VI, 147–88

Roemer, Hans Robert, 'Zur Herkunft Timurs', in Bernardini (ed.), *La civiltà Timuride come fenomeno internazionale*, I, 5–8

Rossabi, Morris, 'A translation of Ch'en Ch'eng's *Hsi-yü fan-kuo chih*', *Ming Studies* 17 (1983), 49–59

Rossabi, Morris, 'The Ming and Inner Asia', in *CHI*, VIII, part 2, 221–71

Rossabi, Morris, *From Yuan to Modern China and Mongolia. The Writings of Morris Rossabi* (Leiden and Boston, MA, 2014)

Rossabi, Morris (ed.), *How Mongolia Matters. War, Law, and Society*, BIAL 36 (Leiden and Boston, MA, 2017)

Roux, Jean-Paul, 'Recherches des survivances pré-islamiques dans les textes turcs musulmans: le «*Bābur-Nāme*»', *JA* 256 (1968), 247–61

Roux, Jean-Paul, *Tamerlan* (Paris, 1991)
Roxburgh, David J., 'The Timurids and Turkmen', in Roxburgh (ed.), *Turks. A Journey of a Thousand Years, 600–1600* (London, 2005), 190–260
Rybatzki, Volker; Pozzi, Alessandra; Geier, Peter W.; and Krueger, John R. (eds), *The Early Mongols: Language, Culture and History. Studies in Honor of Igor de Rachewiltz on the Occasion of His 80th Birthday*, IUUAS 173 (Bloomington, IN, 2009)
Safargaliev, M.G., *Raspad Zolotoi Ordy* (Saransk, 1960)
Sarnowsky, Jürgen, 'Die Johanniter und Smyrna 1344–1402 (Teil I)', *Römische Quartalschrift* 86 (1991), 215–51
Schamiloglu, Uli, 'The *Umdet ül-ahbar* and the Turkic narrative sources for the Golden Horde and the later Golden Horde', in Hasan B. Paksoy (ed.), *Central Asian Monuments* (Istanbul, 1992), 81–93
Schamiloglu, Uli, 'Preliminary remarks on the role of disease in the history of the Golden Horde', *Central Asian Survey* 12 (1993), 447–57
Schamiloglu, Uli, 'Beautés du mélange', in Fourniau (ed.), *Samarcande 1400–1500*, 191–204
Schmieder, Felicitas, *Europa und die Fremden. Die Mongolen im Urteil des Abendlandes vom 13. bis in das 15. Jahrhundert*, Beiträge zur Geschichte und Quellenkunde des Mittelalters 16 (Sigmaringen, 1994)
Sela, Ron, *The Legendary Biographies of Tamerlane. Islam and Heroic Apocrypha in Central Asia*, CSIC (Cambridge, 2011)
Sela, Ron, 'Rashīd al-Dīn's historiographical legacy in the Muslim world', in Akasoy, Burnett and Yoeli-Tlalim (eds), *Rashīd al-Dīn. Agent and Mediator of Cultural Exchanges in Ilkhanid Iran*, 213–22
Shim Hosung, 'The postal roads of the Great Khans in Central Asia under the Mongol-Yuan empire', *JSYS* 44 (2014), 405–69
Shimo Hirotoshi, 'The Qarāūnās in the historical materials of the Īlkhanate', *MTB* 35 (1977), 131–81
Shukurov, R.M., *Velikie Komniny i vostok (1204–1461)* (St Petersburg, 2001)
Silverstein, Adam J., *Postal Systems in the Pre-Modern Islamic World*, CSIC (Cambridge, 2007)
Sinor, Denis (ed.), *Aspects of Altaic Civilization III. Proceedings of the Thirtieth Meeting of the Permanent International Altaistic Conference, Indiana University, Bloomington, Indiana June 19–25, 1987*, IUUAS 145 (Bloomington, IN, 1990)
Slavin, Philip, 'Death by the lake: Mortality crisis in early fourteenth-century Central Asia', *Journal of Interdisciplinary History* 50, no. 1 (Summer 2019), 59–90
Slavin, Philip, 'A rise and fall of a Chaghadaid community: Demographic growth and crisis in "late-medieval" Semirech'ye (Zhetysu), *circa* 1248–1345', *JRAS*, 3rd series, 33 (2023), 513–44
Smith, John Masson, Jr, *The History of the Sarbadār Dynasty 1336–1381 A.D. and Its Sources* (The Hague and Paris, 1970)
Smith, John Masson, Jr, 'Mongol society and military in the Middle East: Antecedents and adaptations', in Lev (ed.), *War and Society in the Eastern Mediterranean*, 249–66
Sneath, David (ed.), *Imperial Statecraft. Political Forms and Techniques of Governance in Inner Asia, Sixth–Twentieth Centuries*, SEA 26 (Bellingham, WA, 2006)

Soucek, Priscilla P., 'Eskandar b. ʿOmar Šayx b. Timur: A biography', in Bernardini, (ed.), *La civiltà Timuride come fenomeno internazionale*, I, 73–87
Soucek, Priscilla P., 'Tīmūrid women: A cultural perspective', in Gavin R.G. Hambly (ed.), *Women in the Medieval Islamic World. Power, Patronage and Piety* (New York, 1998), 199–226
Soucek, Svat, *A History of Inner Asia* (Cambridge, 2000)
Spuler, Bertold, *Die Goldene Horde. Die Mongolen in Rußland 1223–1502*, 2nd edn (Wiesbaden, 1965)
Spuler, Bertold, *Die Mongolen in Iran. Politik, Verwaltung und Kultur der Ilchanzeit 1220–1350*, 4th edn (Leiden, 1985)
Strathern, Alan, 'Global patterns of ruler conversion to Islam and the logic of empirical religiosity', in Peacock (ed.), *Islamisation. Comparative Perspectives from History*, 21–55
Subtelny, Maria Eva, 'The Sunni revival under Shāh-Rukh and its promoters: A study of the connection between ideology and higher learning in Timurid Iran', in *Proceedings of the 27th Meeting of Haneda Memorial Hall. Symposium on Central Asia and Iran, August 30, 1993* (Kyoto, [1994]), 14–23
Subtelny, Maria Eva, 'The Timurid legacy: A reaffirmation and a reassessment', in Szuppe (ed.), *L'Héritage Timouride*, 9–19
Subtelny, Maria E., *Timurids in Transition. Turko-Persian Politics and Acculturation in Medieval Iran*, BIAL 19 (Leiden and Boston, MA, 2007)
Subtelny, Maria E., 'Tamerlane and his descendants: From paladins to patrons', in *NCHI*, III, 169–200
Subtelny, Maria Eva, and Khalidov, Anas B., 'The curriculum of Islamic higher learning in Timurid Iran in the light of the Sunni revival under Shāh-Rukh', *JAOS* 115 (1995), 210–36
Sultanov, T.I., '*Muʿizz al-ansāb* and spurious Chingīzids', *MO* 2, no. 3 (Sept. 1996), 3–7
Sussman, George D., 'Was the Black Death in India and China?', *BHM* 85 (2011), 319–55
Szuppe, Maria, 'Historiography, v. Timurid period', *EIr*, XII, 356–63
Szuppe, Maria (ed.), *L'Héritage Timouride. Iran-Asie Centrale-Inde, XVe–XVIIIe siècles* (Tashkent and Aix-en-Provence, 1997 = *CAC* 3–4)
Togan, İsenbike, *Flexibility and Limitation in Steppe Formations. The Kerait Khanate and Chinggis Khan* (Leiden, New York and Cologne, 1998)
Togan, İsenbike, 'Variations in the perception of jasagh', in D.A. Alimova (ed.), *Markazii Osiyo tarikhi zamonavii medievistika talkinida (Professor Roziia Mukminova khotirasiga bagishlanadi) / History of Central Asia in Modern Medieval Studies (In Memoriam of Professor Roziya Mukminova)* (Tashkent, 2013), 67–101
Togan, Zeki Velidi, 'Timurs Osteuropapolitik', *ZDMG* 108/n.s. 33 (1958), 279–98
Trepavlov, V.V., 'Sopravitel'stvo v mongol'skoi imperii (XIII v.)', *AEMA* 7 (1987–91), 249–78
Uskenbay, Kanat, 'Left Wing of the Ulus of Jochi in the 13– the beginning of the 15th centuries', in Khakimov et al. (eds), *The Golden Horde in World History*, 203–12
Usmanov, Mirkasym, and Khakimov, Rafael (eds), *The History of the Tatars. Since Ancient Times*, III: *The Ulus of Jochi (Golden Horde), 13th Century–Mid-15th Century* (Kazan´, 2017)

Van Berkel, Maaike, and Duindam, Jeroen (eds), *Prince, Pen, and Sword. Eurasian Perspectives* (Leiden, 2018)

Van Den Bent, Josephine, '"None of the kings on Earth is their equal in *'aṣabiyya*": The Mongols in Ibn Khaldūn's works', *Al-Masāq* 28 (2016), 171–86

Van Steenbergen, Jo (ed.), *Trajectories of State Formation across Fifteenth-Century Islamic West-Asia. Eurasian Parallels, Connections and Divergences*, Rulers and Elites: Comparative Studies in Governance 18 (Leiden and Boston, MA, 2020)

Varlık, Nükhet, *Plague and Empire in the Early Modern Mediterranean World. The Ottoman Experience, 1347–1600* (Cambridge, 2015)

Varvarovskii, Iu.E., *Ulus Dzhuchi v 60–70-e gody XIV veka* (Kazan, 2008)

Vásáry, István, *Turks, Tatars and Russians in the 13th–16th Centuries* (Aldershot and Burlington, VT, 2007)

Vásáry, István, 'The Jochid realm: The western steppe and Eastern Europe', in *CHIA*, 67–85

Vásáry, István, 'The beginnings of coinage in the Blue Horde', *AOH* 62 (2009), 371–85

Vásáry, István, '*Yāsā* and *Sharī'a*: Islamic attitudes towards the Mongol law in the Turco-Mongolian world (from the Golden Horde to Timur's time)', in Gleave and Kristó-Nagy (eds), *Violence in Islamic Thought from the Mongols to European Imperialism*, 58–78

Veit, Veronika, 'The eastern steppe: Mongol regimes after the Yuan (1368–1636)', in *CHIA*, 157–81

Vernadsky, George, *The Mongols and Russia*, A History of Russia, III (New Haven, CT, 1953)

Vigouroux, Élodie, 'Comment Tamerlan a pris Alep en 800/1403', *Annales Islamologiques* 55 (2021), 303–25; https://doi.org/10.4000/anisl.10223

Voegelin, Eric, 'The Mongol orders of submission to European powers, 1245–1255', *Byzantion* 15 (1940–1), 378–413; revised version in Ellis Sandoz (ed.), *Collected Works of Eric Voegelin*, X: *1940–1952* (Columbia, MO, 2000), 76–125

Von Glahn, Richard, *Fountain of Fortune. Money and Monetary Policy in China, 1000–1700* (Berkeley and Los Angeles, CA, 1996)

Weiers, Michael (ed., with Veronika Veit and Walther Heissig), *Die Mongolen. Beiträge zu ihrer Geschichte und Kultur* (Darmstadt, 1986)

Werner, Ernst, *Die Geburt einer Großmacht – Die Osmanen (1300–1481). Ein Beitrag zur Genesis des türkischen Feudalismus*, Forschungen zur mittelalterlichen Geschichte 32 (Vienna, Cologne and Graz, 1985)

Wiet, G., 'La grande peste Noire en Syrie et en Égypte', in *Études d'orientalisme dédiées à la mémoire de Lévi-Provençal* (Paris, 1962), I, 367–84

Wilber, Donald N., 'The Timurid court: Life in gardens and tents', *Iran* 17 (1979), 127–33

Wilkens, Jens, 'Buddhism in the West Uyghur kingdom and beyond', in Carmen Meinert (ed.), *Transfer of Buddhism across Central Asian Networks (7th to 13th Centuries)* (Leiden and Boston, MA, 2016), 191–249

Wing, Patrick, 'Submission, defiance, and the rules of politics on the Mamluk Sultanate's Anatolian frontier', *JRAS*, 3rd series, 25 (2015), 377–88

Wing, Patrick, *The Jalayirids. Dynastic State Formation in the Mongol Middle East* (Edinburgh, 2016)

Wink, André, *Al-Hind. The Making of the Indo-Islamic World*, III: *Indo-Islamic Society 14th–15th Centuries* (Leiden and Boston, MA, 2004)

Woods, John E., 'Turco-Iranica II: Notes on a Timurid decree of 1396/798', *JNES* 43 (1984), 331–7

Woods, John E., 'The rise of Tīmūrid historiography', *JNES* 46 (1987), no. 2, 81–108

Woods, John E., *The Timurid Dynasty*, PIA 14 (Bloomington, IN, 1990)

Woods, John E., 'Timur's genealogy', in Michael M. Mazzaoui and Vera B. Moreen (eds), *Intellectual Studies on Islam. Essays Written in Honor of Martin B. Dickson* (Salt Lake City, UT, 1990), 85–125

Woods, John E., *The Aqquyunlu. Clan, Confederation, Empire*, revised and expanded edn (Salt Lake City, UT, 1999)

Yavari, Neguin; Potter, Lawrence G.; and Oppenheim, Jean-Marc Ran (eds), *Views from the Edge. Essays in Honor of Richard W. Bulliet* (New York, 2004)

Yıldız, Sara Nur, 'Post-Mongol pastoral polities in eastern Anatolia during the late Middle Ages', in Deniz Beyazit (ed.), *At the Crossroads of Empires. 14th–15th Century Eastern Anatolia. Proceedings of the International Symposium Held in Istanbul, 4th–6th May 2007* (Paris, 2012), 27–48

Yosef, Koby, 'Cross-boundary hatred: (Changing) attitudes towards Mongol and "Christian" *mamlūks* in the Mamluk Sultanate', in Amitai and Conermann (eds), *The Mamluk Sultanate from the Perspective of Regional and World History*, 149–214

Zakrzewski, Daniel, 'An idea of Iran on Mongol foundations: Territory, dynasties and Tabriz as royal city (seventh/thirteenth to ninth/fifteenth century)', in Melville (ed.), *The Timurid Century*, 45–76

INDEX

Abā Bakr, Dughlāt amir, 106
Abā Bakr b. Amīrānshāh, Timurid prince, 32, 264, 274, 278, 281, 297, 336, 418, 423–6, 431, 433–4, 639; his appanage, 272
Abachi, Negüderi chief, 214, 563
Abagha, Ilkhan, 23, 72, 78, 81, 87, 91, 170, 192, 208–9, 211, 232, 559, 562, 574
Abarqūh, 179, 329, 549
ʿAbbās, Timurid amir, 261, 264, 266; his progeny, 263, 580
ʿAbbās I, Safawid Shah, 438
ʿAbbasid Caliph/Caliphate, ʿAbbasids, 10, 55, 64, 86, 100, 103, 119, 194, 239, 368–9; ʿAbbasid revolution, 96; ʿAbbasid Caliphs in Cairo, 78, 96, 103, 113, 119, 178, 180, 193–4, 302, 340, 345, 405, 444, 519; *see also* Caliph, Caliphate
ʿAbd al-Ghaffār Qirimī, late Jochid author, 236
ʿAbd al-Jabbār b. al-Nuʿmān Khwārazmī, imam, 327, 368–9, 384, 627
ʿAbd al-Laṭīf b. Ulugh Beg, Timurid Sultan, 347
ʿAbd al-Malik Ibn al-Takrītī, Timurid amir, 268
ʿAbd al-Razzāq, Sarbadār leader, 186, 551
ʿAbd al-Ṣamad b. Ḥājjī Sayf al-Dīn, 580
ʿAbd-Allāh, Chaghadayid prince and Negüderi chief, 209
ʿAbd-Allāh (ʿAbdal), Jochid khan, 121–3, 521–2, 612
ʿAbd-Allāh, Uzbek khan, 414
ʿAbd-Allāh b. Maʾulai, Ilkhanid amir, 185
ʿAbd-Allāh b. Qazaghan, Qaraʾunas amir, 127, 219–21, 243, 254, 284, 337, 339–40, 364
ʿAbd-Allāh Anṣārī, ancestor of the Injuid dynasty, 172
al-Ābilī, Muḥammad b. Ibrāhīm, 40
Abīward, 184
Abkhazians, 150
Abū Bakr, Khurāsānī amir, 189, 334
Abū Bakr, the first Caliph, 380
Abū Isḥāq b. Khiḍr Yasāʾūrī, Chaghadayid amir, 258
Abū l-Ghāzī Bahādur Khan, ruler of Khiva and historian, 48
Abū l-Khayr, Uzbek khan, 19, 121, 436–8
Abū Saʿīd, Ilkhan, 23–5, 34, 70, 81, 83, 105, 112–14, 124, 130, 132–3, 135–7, 142–3, 167–9, 173, 178,

191–3, 214, 216, 352, 356, 444, 516, 526, 529, 552
Abū Saʿīd, son of Sulṭān Maḥmūd Khan, 344, 609
Abū Saʿīd, Timurid Sultan, 312, 341, 346, 436, 607, 610
Abulustān, 318
ʿĀdil Āqā (Ṣāriq ʿĀdil), Jalayirid amir, 174–6, 267–8, 296
ʿĀdil Sulṭān, Chaghadayid khan, 340, 607
ʿĀdilshāh Jalāyir, Chaghadayid amir, 257, 259–60, 267, 270, 396
Adshead, Samuel, 146
Aegean Sea, 305
Afghanistan, 3, 7, 16, 58, 63, 136, 198–9, 208, 210, 218, 246, 260, 316
Afghans, 400, 632
Āghā Beki, daughter of Muḥammad Sulṭān b. Jahāngīr, 358
Āghā Beki, daughter of Timur, 264, 273; married to Muḥammad Beg b. Mūsā, 274
Agra, 438
ahl al-bayt, descendants of the Prophet, 100, 379; Timur's devotion to, 377–81
ahl al-dhimma ('Protected Peoples'), 87–8, 105, 108
Aḥmedī, Ottoman chronicler, 41, 372
Ahrī, Abū Bakr, Jalayirid chronicler, 26, 126, 137, 155, 169
Aigle, Denise, 356
Ailangir, ancestor of Timur, 232, 567
ʿAjā'ib al-maqdūr, *see* Ibn ʿArabshāh
Ajashirin, Chaghadayid prince, 351, 613
Ajodhan, 385
Akhbār-i Mughūlān, 75
Akhīchuq, Mongol amir and ruler of Azerbaijan, 173, 179, 549
Akhsīkat, 235, 273, 287
Akshehir, 271, 305
Āl-i Burhān dynasty, 240
ʿAlā' al-Dawla Simnānī, 511
ʿAlā' al-Dīn ʿAlī Beg b. Muḥammad, ruler of Sivas, 156, 177
ʿAlā' al-Dīn Khaljī, Sultan of Delhi, 81, 207, 210, 213–14, 333
ʿAlā' al-Dīn Muḥammad b. Tekish, Khwārazmshāh, 58, 239, 391
ʿAlā' al-Dīn Sikandar Shāh, Sultan of Delhi, 298
ʿAlā' al-Mulk Khudāwandzāda, 239
Alan Qo'a, ancestress of Chinggis Khan, 57, 380–1
Alans (Ās), 363, 368
Alatagh, 87, 116
Aleppo, 27, 39, 42, 76, 150, 153, 252, 301, 309, 318–19, 321, 325, 327, 329, 331–2, 334, 363, 367–8, 379–80, 382, 391, 394, 423, 600–1, 604, 617
Alexander the Great, 8, 101, 239, 383; Timur compared with, 371, 394, 621
Alexandria, 145, 375
ʿAlī b. Abī Ṭālib, fourth Caliph, 333, 379–81, 386; descendants of, 381; Timur's devotion to, 379–81, 618; *see also ahl al-bayt*; sayyids
ʿAlī Beg, amir of the Jā'ūn-i Qurbān, 185, 255, 330
ʿAlī Beg, Chaghadayid amir, 238
ʿAlī Beg, ruler of Sivas, *see* ʿAlā al-Dīn ʿAlī Beg
ʿAlī Darwīsh b. Bāyazīd Jalāyir, Chaghadayid amir, 238, 259, 584
ʿAlī Ke'ün, brother of the Ilkhan Taghai Temür, 186, 518, 551
ʿAlī Pādishāh, Ilkhanid amir, 114–15, 117, 130–1, 134
ʿAlī Sulṭān, (Ögödeyid) khan of Chaghadai's ulus, 94, 125, 144, 200, 227, 524
ʿAlī Yasā'ūrī, Chaghadayid amir, 258, 267
ʿAlī Zayn al-ʿĀbidīn, fourth Shīʿī Imam, 381, 625
ʿAlī-yi Mu'ayyad, Najm al-Dīn, Sarbadār ruler, 175, 187–91, 267, 292–3, 551
ʿAlī-yi Ramaḍān, Ilkhanid amir, 185, 189
ʿĀlim Shaykh, brother of Timur, 224
Alinjaq, 328
Allāhdād, Timurid amir, 326
Allāhdād, Timurid amir and brother of Ḥājjī Sayf al-Dīn, 421

Allsen, Thomas T., 64, 147, 437, 443
Almaligh, 62, 94, 125–6, 151, 199–200, 239
Altai mountains, 351
Altan Khan, ruler of the Khalkha Mongols, 440
altan urugh ('Golden Lineage'), 14, 68, 73, 100, 119, 130, 337, 380
Altun Bahādur, Chaghadayid amir, 217
Alughu, Chaghadayid khan, 75, 78, 80, 232, 284, 573; his progeny, 80, 102, 571
Alughui Temür, Ögödeyid prince, 134, 138, 528
amān, *see māl-i amānī*
Amasya, 304
Ambaghai, Mongol khan, 57–8
Āmid, 176, 297, 331, 604
Amīr ʿAlī b. Mu'ayyad Arlāt, Timurid amir, 567
Amīr Ḥusayn, Qara'unas amir, ally and later rival of Timur, 133, 135, 182, 185, 198, 200, 205, 219–21, 238, 241, 254–60, 262, 267, 278, 284, 291, 298, 330, 337, 339–41, 357, 378, 389, 406, 409, 445, 578–9, 589, 607; his sister (wife of Timur), 254, 256; his sons, 298, 589
Amīr Khusraw Dihlawī, poet, 207
Amīr Walī, Mongol ruler in Astarābād, 25, 31, 118, 156, 168–9, 171, 174–6, 180, 183–4, 188–90, 195, 291–2, 318, 550, 554
Amīrak Aḥmad b. ʿUmar Shaykh, grandson of Timur, 264, 418, 431
Amīrānshāh, son of Timur, 32, 42, 45, 205, 281, 291, 306, 320, 329, 333–4, 342, 352, 374, 376, 412, 415, 423–4, 426–7, 432–3, 583, 585, 593–4, 621, 639; governor of Khurāsān, 270, 276, 291–2; transferred to Azerbaijan, 270, 277; marriage to a daughter of the khan Soyurghatmish, 275, 358; his descendants, 32, 272, 418, 431, 436; his alleged insanity, 33, 274, 276; insubordination of, 275–6, 406; regarded by some as Timur's heir, 274, 423; his amirs, 410
amīrzāda, title, 337, 360
Amitai, Reuven, 97, 99
Amū-daryā, 2, 4, 80, 202, 422, 427; *see also* Oxus
Āmul, 155, 187, 311
Āmulī, Awliyā'-Allāh, 167
Āmulī, Shams al-Dīn Muḥammad, encyclopaedist, 124, 131
Ananda, Prince of Anxi, Toluid, 95, 98
Anatolia (Rūm), 2, 3, 4, 9, 25, 38, 55, 64, 74, 77–8, 96, 115, 117–18, 136, 149–50, 159, 168, 170–1, 176–8, 193, 242, 244, 271–2, 301, 309–10, 316, 319, 322, 327, 342–4, 384, 421, 445, 536, 596; *see also* Seljuq Sultanate
Anbarjī, Ilkhanid prince, 526
anda (blood-brother), 57
Andalusia, 40
Andarāb, 219
Andijān, 73, 202, 235, 270, 272–3, 285, 287, 292, 316, 431
Andkhūd (or Andkhūy), 212, 216, 218–19, 243, 379
Ando, Shira, 233, 242, 260–1
Andrea Biglia, 377
Ankara, 304; battle of (1402), 35, 46, 265–6, 272, 303, 305–6, 320–3, 327–8, 341, 372, 374, 376, 391, 438, 598–9, 601–2
Annam, 78
al-Anṣārī, Mūsā b. Muḥammad, qadi of Aleppo, 384
Anūshīrwān, Ilkhan, 116, 131, 192, 518, 526–7
Anūshīrwān b. Aq Bugha, Timurid amir, 266
Apaq, Timurid amir, 269
Apardī Mongols, 181, 218, 246, 258–60, 262; amirs of, 242–4, 257–9, 291, 565
Āq-Qūyūnlū dynasty, 176–7, 296, 319, 322, 409, 434, 436, 589
Aq Bugha Naiman, Timurid amir, 261, 263–4
Aq Buqa, Jochid envoy, 498
Aq Temür Bahādur, Timurid amir, 260–1, 263, 266, 579
Aqsarai palace, 369

Āqsū, 127, 203, 235, 286, 603
Aqsulat, 350
Aqtau, Jochid amir, 290
Arabs, 38, 40, 53, 56, 110, 118, 168, 178, 192, 316, 601
ʿArabshāh, Jochid khan, 121–2, 521
Aratna, Ilkhanid amir, 117–18, 156, 169, 171, 176–7; his dynasty, 177, 300, 303
Araxes (Aras), River, 336
Ardabīl, 384
Arghandāb (Hilmand River), 213
Arghun, Ilkhan, 91, 101, 106–7, 112–13, 134, 136, 168–9, 209, 386, 529, 628
Arghun Aqa, Mongol administrator, 67, 78, 92, 98–9
Arghūnshāh, Ilkhanid amir and leader of the Jaʾūn-i Qurbān, 115, 182, 184–5
Arghūnshāh, Timurid amir, 419, 421–2
Arhang, 126, 218, 242
Arigh Böke, Mongol Qaghan, 75–6, 508; descendants of, 80, 112, 114, 134, 238, 515
Arjīsh, 374, 376
Arlāt, tribe, 169, 181, 243–4, 246, 258; chiefs, 578
Armenia, Armenians, 46, 150, 160, 272, 336, 363–4, 376–7, 419, 604
Arpa, Ilkhan, 80, 114, 116, 130, 134, 137, 172, 527, 529
Arrān, 75, 79, 175, 211, 269, 272, 288, 294, 419
Arslan Khan, Qarluq ruler, 58, 68
Artuqid dynasty, 117, 301, 330
Aruq, Ilkhanid amir, 515
Arzinjān (Erzincan), 118, 178, 296, 303, 322, 374, 609
Ārzū Mulk Āghā, 584
Ās, 617; *see also* Alans
ʿ*aṣabiyya* ('group solidarity'), 40–1, 84
Ascelin, papal envoy, 494
*Ashitan, Chaghadayid amir, 570
Āshpara, 273, 287, 326
Ashraf (or Malik Ashraf), Chobanid amir, 116–18, 120, 129, 131, 135–6, 144, 155, 159, 169, 172–3, 192, 541
Assassins (Ismāʿīlīs), 64
Astarābād, 31, 118, 155, 170, 180, 183, 188, 293, 348, 352, 426, 551
Astarābādī, ʿAzīz b. Ardashīr, 42, 171, 176, 338, 351, 364–5, 411
Astrakhan, 122, 145, 289, 325; Khanate of, 121
Asutai, Chaghadayid prince, 504
atabeg (*atābak*, guardian of a young prince), atabegate, 113, 275, 278, 287, 343, 516
Atbāsh, 235, 285
*Atlamish, Timurid amir, 301–2, 397
Attila, 68
Atwood, Christopher, 23, 90, 231
Aubin, Jean, 26–7, 131, 182, 193, 198, 208, 223, 295, 332, 335
Awghānī Mongols, 66, 170, 244
Awnīk, 328, 331, 604
ʿAyn Jālūt, battle of (1260), 76, 78, 170
al-ʿAynī, Badr al-Dīn, Mamlūk chronicler, 43
Ayyubid dynasty, 64
Azāq (Azov), 122–3, 364, 520; *see also* Tana
Azerbaijan, 3, 33, 75, 79, 116–18, 120, 132, 135, 144, 155–6, 160, 169, 172–3, 175, 179, 192–3, 195, 211, 270, 272, 280, 288–9, 293–4, 306, 310, 316–17, 322, 329, 345, 348, 352, 395–6, 402, 423–4, 430, 432–3, 436, 452, 613
ʿAzīz Shaykh (ʿAzīz Baba?), Jochid khan, 121, 520

Baʾarin, tribe, 569
Bābā Sangū, shaykh, 384
Bābur, Ẓahīr al-Dīn Muḥammad, Timurid prince and first Mughul Emperor in India, 11–12, 19, 48, 202, 204, 406, 414, 437–40, 442, 451, 643; memoirs of (*Bābur-nāma*), 11–12, 49
Badakhshān, 78, 126, 212, 216, 219, 254, 291, 322, 561; maliks or shahs of, 128, 212, 239, 431
Bādghīs, 211, 237, 560, 574
Badīʿ al-Zamān, Timurid prince, 406

Baghdad, 10, 23–4, 27, 42, 55, 103, 115–18, 131, 147–9, 154–6, 159, 173–6, 193–4, 266, 268, 270, 274, 281, 293–4, 296–7, 302, 310, 324–5, 327–8, 336, 352, 365–6, 382–3, 405, 423, 541, 560, 589, 604–5, 608, 622, 625; Timur's treatment of, 296–7, 315, 331–2
Baghdād Khatun, chief wife of the Ilkhan Abū Sa'īd, 114
Baghlān, 219, 262, 265, 299
Bagrat V, king of Georgia, 296, 304, 364
bahādur ('champion'), 263
Bahrain, 193
Bahrām Jalāyir, Chaghadayid amir, 238, 243, 255–7, 298, 577
Bāī, 203, 286
Baidu, Ilkhan, 97, 108, 114, 130, 514
Baidughan, Dughlāt amir, 235
Baiju, Chaghadayid prince, 238, 559
Baiju, Mongol general, 64, 74, 92
Baikal, Lake, 57
Bākharz, 264
Bākharzī, Sayf al-Dīn Sa'īd b. al-Muṭ ahhar, shaykh, 98, 104, 200, 240–1, 509, 511
bakhshī (Buddhist monk), 137; (scribe), 268
Bākū, 270
Ba'labakk, 39, 301
bālish (silver ingot), 141
Balkans, 304–5, 371, 453
Balkh, 182, 211–12, 215–16, 219–20, 237, 242, 246, 259, 262, 322, 340, 347, 420–1, 430, 565–6, 576, 582
Bāmiyān, 63, 216, 334, 487
Banākatī, Fakhr al-Dīn, 24,
Bar Hebraeus, Christian author, continuator of, 108
Bārambāy, quasi-tribal group in Anatolia, 244
Baraq, Chaghadayid khan, 80, 208, 237–8, 240, 353, 358, 405, 559, 563, 573; adoption of Islam, 93
Baraq, Jochid khan, 434, 641
Barbaro, Giosafa, 145, 289, 367–8
Barchinlighkent (Bārchin), 522, 538
Barda'a, 272
Barlās tribe, 1, 30–1, 231, 236, 244, 262–4; amirs of, 223, 232–5, 237–8, 242, 246–7, 251, 254, 262–3, 445, 579; territory of, in Transoxiana, 223–4, 242, 257; *see also* Barulas; *ulugh ming*
Barqūq, al-Ẓāhir, Mamlūk Sultan, 35, 300–1, 307, 310, 319, 321, 348, 351, 356, 361, 365, 367–9, 394–5, 397, 401, 590, 618, 632
Barsbay, Mamlūk Sultan, 433
Bartan Baghatur, Chinggis Khan's grandfather, 634
Barthold, W., 5
Barulas, tribe, 65, 69, 227–8, 359, 498; noyans of, under the Yuan, 230–1; *see also* Barlās
Bash (or Tash) Temür, Jochid prince, 349–50, 612
Bāshtīn, 186
basqaq (Mongol governor or 'resident'), 66–7
Baṣra, 272, 341, 608
Batu, khan of the Golden Horde, 62, 64, 72, 74, 89, 92–3, 98, 104, 158, 412, 509; his descendants, 77, 112, 121, 444, 516, 520; his ulus, 114, 132
Baumer, Christoph, 314
Bavaria, 46
Bawandid dynasty, 155
Bayan, khan of the Blue Horde, 134, 212
Bayan Quli, Chaghadayid khan, 126–7, 200, 219, 339–40, 358, 524, 638
Bāyazīd Jalāyir, Chaghadayid amir, 238, 242–3, 254–5, 259, 267, 577–8, 584
Baybars, Mamlūk Sultan, 78, 81, 96, 103–4
Baybars al-Manṣūrī, Mamlūk chronicler, 93, 487
Bayezid I, Ottoman Sultan, 2, 6, 35, 44, 45–6, 171, 177–8, 290, 301–4, 318, 320, 322–4, 330, 342, 351, 353, 361, 363, 369, 371–3, 375–7, 382, 391–2, 438, 450, 591–2, 608, 618; sons of, 304, 310, 363; his wife, 372

Bayhaq, 116
Baylaqān, 269, 272, 336
Bāyqarā b. ʿUmar Shaykh, 430–1
Bayrām Khwāja, Qarā-Qūyūnlū chief, 177
Bayrāmshāh Arlāt, Chaghadayid amir, 243, 258, 574
Bāysunghur b. Shāhrukh, grandson of Timur, 30, 47, 431
Bazarchi, Jochid khan, 121, 134, 519, 521
Bedouins, 399
Beg Bolod, Jochid prince, 289, 587
Behesni, 322
Beirut, 145, 617
Bekichuk, Mughūl amir, 255, 275, 287
*Belgüt (Belgünüt?), tribe, 261, 579
Belich, James, 158
Benedictow, Ole J., 143, 145, 151
Bengal, 141, 363, 440
Berbers, 38, 40
Berdibeg, khan of the Golden Horde, 120–1, 123, 133, 173, 491, 519–20
Berdibeg b. Sari Bugha, Timurid amir, 266
Berke, son of Jochi and khan of the Golden Horde, 74, 76, 78, 81, 88, 92, 96, 104–5, 206; his adoption of Islam, 91, 98, 510
Bernardini, Michele, 6, 13, 220, 257, 339, 372, 374
Beshbaligh, 56, 58–9, 78, 128, 350, 612
'Bessermens', 150, 538
Besüt, tribe, 183, 574
*beylik*s, in Anatolia, 171, 176, 178
Bezhdezh, 150, 160
Bhatner, 299
Bibi Khanim Mosque, 360, 369–70
Bihāmadkhānī, Muḥammad, Indian chronicler, 41, 217, 298, 435
bilig (saying, adage, particularly of a Mongol ruler), 73
Binbān, 208
Binbaş, İlker Evrim, 30
Bīnī-yi Gāw, 208, 210, 213, 559, 562
Biran, Michal, 27
al-Birzālī, Mamlūk author, 109
Bisṭām, 385
bitikchi (scribe), 268
Black Death, 15, 26, 138, 143, 145–61 passim, 535, 539–40
Black Sea, 144, 149
Blue Annals, Tibetan chronicle, 105, 161
Blue Horde, 62–3, 77, 112, 122–3, 134, 160, 216, 264, 267, 285, 287–8, 348, 396, 406, 434, 436, 444, 449
Bo'al, son of Jochi, 521
bodhisattva, 512
Bodonchar, ancestor of Chinggis Khan, 57, 227, 381
Böjei, Chaghadayid prince, 208–9, 213, 559
Bolad, 532
Bolod (Pūlād) Temür, Jochid khan, 122, 521
Bolodchi (Pūlādchī), Dughlāt amir, 127, 201, 236
Boniface IX, Pope, 377
Borjighid, clan, 57, 68, 122
Borogul, Timur's grandfather, 233–4, 567
Boroldai, Chaghadayid amir, 201, 215, 218; his *tümen*/troops, 216, 258, 260, 262
Börte, Chinggis Khan's chief wife, 61, 75, 392
Bosphorus, 304
Brack, Jonathan, 103, 408
Broadbridge, Anne, 275, 356
Buddhism, Buddhists, 3, 18, 89, 92, 95, 99–100, 102–3, 105, 128, 137, 202, 205, 236, 512–13; in Iran, 87, 91, 105
Buell, Paul, 67, 152
Bukhara, 4, 62, 78, 86, 91, 98, 199–200, 216, 227, 240–1, 262, 285, 288, 341, 352, 367, 597
Būlar, 536; *see also* Bulghār
Bulgaria, kingdom of, 178, 303, 371
Bulghār, 62, 122, 289, 521
bulmaq, porridge (?), 323–4, 600
Bulughan Khatun, 106
Bulughan Qalja, Yuan noyan, 230
Bunyashirin, *see* Öljei Temür; Tāīzī Oghlan
Buqa, Ilkhanid amir, 83, 113

Buqa, Qara'unas commander, 210, 560
Buqa 'Dūqalāt', 223, 235
Burhān Oghlan, Jochid prince, 349, 612
Burhān al-Dīn, Qadi, ruler of Sivas, 42, 177, 256, 300–1, 303, 332, 343, 351, 365, 411, 618, 621
Büri, Chaghadayid prince, 528
Burqan Qaldun, mountain, 72, 498
Bursa, 303, 363, 382, 617, 622
Burūjird, 272; *see also* Wurūjird
Burunduq b. Jahānshāh, Timurid amir, 265, 321, 421
Bust, 214, 293
Buyan Süldüs, Chaghadayid amir, 219, 221, 242–3, 247, 254–5, 406
Buyan Temür b. Aq Bugha, Timurid amir, 258, 263, 266
Buyan Temür b. Bekichuk, Timurid amir, 275, 278, 287, 586
Buyantu, Qaghan, 72
Buyur Nor, 57
Buzan, Chaghadayid khan, 105, 107, 124–6, 220, 267, 339, 514, 523
Byzantine Empire, Byzantium, 9, 178, 303–5, 363, 371, 543, 592–3; Byzantine authors, 374, 592

Caesar, 383
Cairo, 36–7, 43, 78, 96, 103, 301–3, 326, 368, 378, 401, 434
Caliph, Caliphate, 40, 86, 96, 103, 105, 109, 119, 194, 368–9, 413, 452; *see also* ʿAbbasid, Umayyad
cannon, 602; *see also* gunpowder; *raʿd*
Caresini, Rafaino, Venetian chancellor, 149
Carpathian mountains, 77
Casimir III, king of Poland, 160
Caspian Sea, 59
Castile, king of, 40, 594, 623; *see also* Henry III
'Cathay', 55, 149–50, 537
Caucasus, 3, 76, 79, 96, 211, 296
Chaghadai, second son of Chinggis Khan, 3, 4, 62–3, 88, 198, 226, 229–30, 232, 235, 285, 351–2, 392, 394, 559; his alleged antipathy towards Muslims, 88, 92; his enforcement of the Yasa, 198, 410–11; his chief noyans, 223
Chaghadai 'the Lesser', Mongol amir, 223
Chaghadayid khanate, ulus of Chaghadai, Chaghadayids, 3, 14–16, 22, 26–7, 30, 62, 65–6, 74, 77, 78–83, 102, 105, 112–13, 120, 124–9, 132–5, 137–9, 151, 157, 159, 161, 171, 181, 195, 198–221, 225–6, 229–47, 285, 297, 313, 336, 338, 351–3, 355, 357, 359, 395, 399, 421, 441, 444–6, 451–2, 544; silver currency of, 143, 315; division into two khanates, 126–9; shadow khans in Transoxiana, 127, 338–44; *see also Imperium Medium*
Chaghatay Turkic, 11
Chaghatays, 5, 12, 27, 39, 42, 45–6, 202, 205–6, 266, 268–9, 284–7, 295–7, 302–3, 309, 311, 315, 317–18, 320–2, 328–9, 331, 334–5, 342–3, 348, 353, 365, 374–5, 380, 413–14, 446, 448, 616, 618
chakravartin, 18, 102
Chalkokondyles, Byzantine chronicler, 588
Changshi, Chaghadayid khan, 124–5, 137, 144, 201, 523
Changshi Güregen, Chaghadayid amir, 237–8, 572
Chapar, son of Qaidu, Mongol khan, 77, 80, 82, 85, 209, 211, 213, 246, 298, 572, 607
Charles VI, king of France, 306, 593–4
Chechektü, 269
Chekire (or Chinggis Oghlan), Jochid khan, 350, 434, 612–13, 641
Chekü Barlās, Chaghadayid amir, 258, 261–5; his descendants, 580
Chenab, River, 390
chess, played by Timur, 9, 30, 349
China, 3, 18, 21, 23, 41, 55, 57, 61, 64, 69, 74, 87, 91, 110–13, 138, 140, 144–5, 147, 149, 151–4, 200, 287, 293, 306, 429, 434–5, 533, 536,

538–40, 543, 632; *see also* Jin; Liao; Ming; Qing; Song; Tang; Yuan
Chinggis Khan, 1–6, 8, 10–11, 13–17, 30, 34, 86, 101–2, 108–9, 226–31, 235, 319, 321, 330, 332–4, 367, 375, 381–2, 386, 390–3, 398–9, 410, 413, 416–17, 432, 445–6, 450–1, 484, 628–9; modern biographies of, 5; his rise to power, 57–63; administrative measures, 64–8; his decrees, 64, 71, 89, 92, 95, 138, 324, 405, 409, 499, 517, 637; *see also* Yasa; his emphasis on unity, 84–5; and different faiths, 89–90; his allocations of territory and troops to his sons and other kinsfolk, 61–2, 77, 79, 223, 233, 351–2, 392, 630
Chinggis Oghlan, *see* Chekire
Chinggisid dynasty, Chinggisids, 14, 16–17, 19, 23, 63, 72, 79–80, 90, 92, 95, 99, 105–6, 122, 130, 135, 167–9, 173, 206, 229, 276, 279, 281, 308, 337–8, 344–8, 350–4, 357–9, 380, 392–3, 395, 398–9, 401–2, 407–9, 411, 414, 417, 426, 434, 437–8, 441, 446–50, 452–3, 511, 625; charisma of, 136, 169; sovereignty confined to, 135, 337; Timurid marriage links with, 136, 274, 357–8, 447; *see also altan urugh*
Chios (Sāquz), 305
Chirchik, River, 256
Choban, Ilkhanid amir, 83, 113, 172, 291, 552
Choban, Qara'unas amir, 185
Chobanid dynasty, 116–17, 120, 123, 144, 169, 172, 187, 193
Cholpan Mulk Āghā, wife of Timur, 279–80
Chormaghun, Mongol general, 63–4, 207
Christendom, Christian Europe, 8, 35, 140; Western Christendom, 307
Christian, David, 68, 313
Christians, 87–8, 91, 94, 105, 513; Christian merchants, 143; *see also* Greek, Monophysite, Nestorian
Chronographia regum Francorum, French royal chronicle, 45, 328
Chübei, Chaghadayid prince, 571
Circassians, 368, 401
Clavijo, Ruy Gonzalez de, 11, 45, 84, 202, 205, 229, 253, 265, 269, 274, 277, 280–1, 289, 304–7, 316–17, 320, 322–3, 325, 327–8, 331, 336, 349, 358, 361, 368–9, 384, 399, 416, 423–4, 537, 620
Clement VI, Pope, 157
climate, in Asia, 145–6, 159, 448
Confucians, Confucius, 102
conjunction astrology, 40, 386
Constantine, Georgian prince, 364
Constantinople, 47, 303–5, 593
Crete, 320
Crimea, 3, 71, 122, 149–51, 154, 157, 303; khans, khanate of, 121, 236, 349, 612
Crimean Tatars, 442
Crossley, Pamela, 18
Cui Yujun, 147
Cypriots, 622

Dadu, *see* Khanbaligh
Daghestan, 363, 368
al-Dajjāl ('Antichrist'), 37
Dalai Lama, 441
Dale, Stephen, 12, 44, 432, 438
Damascus, 11, 12, 35–7, 39, 46, 76, 105, 159, 266, 275, 297, 302, 309, 317, 321, 324, 326, 328–9, 343, 347, 363, 367–8, 379–80, 383, 601, 608, 622; Timur's treatment of, 315–16, 331, 333–4, 379–80, 383–4, 597, 624
Damāwand, 336
Dāmghān, 183, 187
Danishmandcha, (Ögödeyid) khan of Chaghadai's ulus, 83, 126–7, 338–40, 524
Danube, River, 290
Daoists, 89
Daqūqā, 526
Darband, 289, 400, 429, 632

Dardess, John, 76
darugha, *darughachi* (Mongol or Timurid governor), 66–7, 262–4, 402
Darwin, John, 439, 442
Darwīsh ʿAzīz, radical preacher, 187–9
Dā'ūd, Chaghadayid amir, 232–3
Dā'ūd Dughlāt, Timurid amir, 261, 264, 581; his descendants, 580
Dā'ūd Khwāja, Chaghadayid prince, 214
Dawlatshāh, late Timurid author, 381
Dawlatshāh Bakhshī, Timurid amir, 263
Dayan Khan, ruler of the Khalkha Mongols, 440
De Rachewiltz, Igor, 72, 101, 404
Deccan, 141, 300
Delhi, 4, 27, 41, 91, 213–14, 216–17, 273, 280, 298, 300, 315, 322, 325, 332–4, 343, 347, 353, 382, 390, 399, 431, 435, 438, 590, 604; battle outside (1398), 299, 320, 329, 385, 446, 599
Delhi, Sultan/Sultanate of, 2, 22, 107, 111, 117, 141, 153, 297, 310, 319, 326–7, 363, 390, 401, 435, 438, 484, 564, 573, 601, 619
Deopalpur, 330
dervishes, 116, 186, 188–9, 200, 297, 384, 524, 601
al-Dhahabī, Mamlūk author, 98, 131
Dhayl-i Ta'rīkh-i guzīda, as continuation of Ḥamd-Allāh's *Ẓafar-nāma*, 25; anonymous, 26, 169, 172; *see also* Ḥamd-Allāh, Zayn al-Dīn
dhimmīs, *see ahl al-dhimma*
Di Cosmo, Nicola, 56
Dietrich von Nyem, 376
Diez Album, 351
Dihistān, 184
Dilshād Āghā, wife of Timur, 273, 280, 357, 378, 614
Dilshād Khatun, wife of Ilkhan Abū Saʿīd and Shaykh Ḥasan, 114–15, 169
dīwān, 265, 315
dīwān-i aʿlā (finance ministry), 263
dīwān-i buzurg (supreme council), 263, 410, 636
Diyār Bakr, 117, 176, 272, 296, 309, 318, 327, 551, 613
Dīzak, 422
Dnieper, River, 392
Doab, 299
Dolbin, D.A., 160
Dominicans, 99, 157, 374
Don, River, 45, 140, 149, 151, 538
Dörben, tribe, 573
Dorji, Chaghadayid prince, 125, 339, 523, 607
Doukas, Byzantine chronicler, 46, 332
Du'a, Chaghadayid khan, 73, 77–8, 80–2, 85, 112, 125, 127, 133, 205, 109, 211–13, 215, 232–3, 237–8, 240, 244, 246–7, 298, 340, 353, 561, 563, 570, 586; his descendants, 112, 126–7, 528
Dughlāt tribe, 49, 264; amirs of, 128, 223 ('Dūqalāt), 224, 230, 235–7; lands of, 129, 235
Dukhtui, Chaghadayid amir, 127
Dulghadir (Dhū l-Qadr), Türkmen dynasty, 176
Dumdadu Mongghol Ulus, 79, 353; *see also* Chaghadayid khanate; *Imperium Medium*
Durr Sulṭān Āghā, concubine of Timur, 279
Dūst Muḥammad, Mughūl khan, 106, 513

Ebülün, Yuan noyan, 230
Edigü, Jochid amir, 44, 124, 289–90, 349, 368, 405, 434, 445, 486, 523, 619, 641
Edigü Barlās, Timurid governor of Kirmān, 170, 263, 265, 295, 425
Edirne, 304
Egypt, 22, 35, 39, 46, 55, 117, 137, 140–3, 149, 153–4, 301, 303, 310, 326, 353, 384, 601; sultan of, 515; *see also* Mamlūk Sultanate
Elburz mountains, 64, 321
elephants, 320; acquired and deployed by Timur, 327–8, 601

Elgei, Mongol commander and ancestor of the Jalayirids, 65, 173
Eljigidei, Chaghadayid khan, 83, 215, 308, 350; 'people' or 'troops of Eljigidei', 245, 261
Ellenblum, Ronnie, 147
Eltüzmish, wife of the Ilkhans Abagha, Gaikhatu and Öljeitü, 562
Emil, River, 62
Emil Khwāja, Chaghadayid prince, 127
Engke Tura, Mughūl amir, 555
England, 45, 152, 306, 375; king of, 361; *see also* Henry IV
Erdeni Baatur Khongtaiji, ruler of the Oyirat/Zunghars, 441
Erkenüt, tribe, 584
Erzurum, 176, 296, 384
Esen Buqa (I), Chaghadayid khan, 80, 127, 213–16, 245, 525, 563
Esen Buqa (II), Mughūl khan, 346, 554
Esen Tayishi, Oyirat leader, 337, 440
Ethiopia, 157
Euphrates, River, 42, 76–7, 320
Europe, 8, 17; *see also* Christendom; Franks; Latin Christendom; Western Christians
Eyegü Temür, Timurid amir, 261, 266, 579

Fakhr al-Dawla Ḥasan, king of Āmul, 155, 541
Fanākat (Shāhrukhiyya), 335
Fancy, Nahyan, 544
faqīrs, 99, 200; *see also* sufis
Farā'id-i Ghiyāthī, 34
Faraj, al-Nāṣir, Mamlūk Sultan, 35, 301–2, 310, 315, 343, 348, 353, 366, 368, 383, 391, 629
Farghāna, 19, 28, 73, 202, 215, 236, 238, 259, 270, 272, 274, 276, 286, 310, 358, 397, 427–8, 437, 439
Fārs, 24, 28–9, 32, 66, 118, 168, 172, 192, 194, 209, 213–14, 266, 270–2, 277, 293, 295, 317, 322, 345, 352, 428–31, 436, 452, 483, 555, 560, 562, 597, 613, 640
Fāryāb, 212
Faryūmadī, Ghiyāth al-Dīn, 25–6, 132, 135, 155, 159, 167, 173, 177, 183, 187–8, 193, 243
Fatḥābād, 200, 241
fatwā, 96, 108
Fez, 40
Firdawsī, 2, 25, 192
Firishta, Mughul chronicler, 210, 300
Fīrūz Shāh, Sultan of Delhi, 218, 298, 399, 401, 619, 631; his heirs and successors, 298–9, 400; his slave officers, 400–1, 632
Fīrūzābād, 299
Fīrūzkūh, 329
Fletcher, Joseph, 73, 133
France, 45, 304, 306; king of, 361; *see also* Charles VI; Louis IX; Philip IV
Francis, Dominican friar, 305–6, 374, 376, 593
Franciscans, 82, 94, 200
Franke, Herbert, 95
Franks, 23, 45, 100, 305, 329, 368, 372, 375–7, 433, 621
friars, 21; *see also* Dominicans; Franciscans
fur trade, 122, 397

Gabriele de' Mussi, 149–50, 161
Gaikhatu, Ilkhan, 116, 515, 562
Galdan, ruler of the Oyirat/Zunghars, 441
Galicia (Halicz), 160
Ganges, River, 10, 216, 453
Gansu, 151, 161, 236, 351
Gasparini, Francesco, 6
Gawhar Shād, wife of Shāhrukh, 264, 273, 436, 640
Genoa, Genoese, 123, 140, 144, 148, 305, 320, 376, 593, 622; *see also* Kaffa
Georgia, kingdom of, Georgians, 46, 63, 75, 272, 293, 296, 321, 328, 336, 363, 371, 375, 412, 419, 603; king of, 592
Gerasimov, M.M., 6
gerege (tablet of authority), 84
ghajarji, 254, 577
Gharchistān, 212

ghazā, *ghazw* (holy war), 362, 616
al-Ghazālī, 407
Ghazan Maḥmūd, Ilkhan, 23–4, 34, 76, 79, 82, 84–5, 87, 91, 95, 101–2, 105–8, 113, 119, 130–1, 133, 143, 168, 184, 193, 212, 279, 300, 354–5, 370–1, 379, 383, 386, 404, 407–8, 412–13, 450, 528, 537, 551, 560, 622, 628, 633; adoption of Islam, 94, 96–7, 99–100, 104, 109, 510–11; his relations with the Christian West, 375, 623
Ghazan (II), Ilkhan, 118, 348, 518
ghāzī (Muslim holy warrior), 305, 372–3
Ghāzī Malik, 210; *see also* Ghiyāth al-Dīn Tughluq
Ghazna, 63, 76, 201, 208–9, 213–15, 219, 271, 276, 299, 352, 371, 416, 487
Ghaznawid dynasty, 55, 386; *see also* Maḥmūd of Ghazna; Yaminid dynasty
Ghiyāth al-Dīn b. Rashīd al-Dīn, Ilkhanid wazir, 25, 114, 134–5
Ghiyāth al-Dīn Dāmghānī, Sultan of Maʿbar, 154
Ghiyāth al-Dīn Maḥmūd Shāh, Sultan of Delhi, 298–300, 320
Ghiyāth al-Dīn Muḥammad b. Aratna, ruler of Sivas, 177
Ghiyāth al-Dīn Naqqāsh, Timurid envoy to the Ming, 202, 435, 642
Ghiyāth al-Dīn Pīr ʿAlī, Kartid Sultan of Herat, 169, 182–3, 189–91, 291–2, 405
Ghiyāth al-Dīn Tarkhān, Timurid amir, 237, 261, 264, 273–4
Ghiyāth al-Dīn Tughluq, Sultan of Delhi, 210, 214, 217, 562; his Qara'unas origins, 111, 210, 217
ghulām, *see* mamluk
Ghūr, 22, 209, 212, 311
Ghurid dynasty, 58
Ghuriyān, River, 335
Gibbon, Edward, 9, 478
Gil-Khandān, 336
Gīlān, 168, 184, 270, 293, 322, 343; 'Gīlānāt', 314, 613
Giorgi VII, king of Georgia, 304, 364
Golden, Peter B., 313
Golden Horde, 3, 15, 19, 106, 118, 143, 157, 172, 211, 236, 289, 397, 561, 587; *see also* Jochids, Qipchaq Khanate
Granada, 36, 538
'Great Amirs', 113–14, 340, 445
Great Schism, 8
'Great Troubles' (in the Qipchaq Khanate), 120, 127, 132, 288, 519
Greek Christians, Greeks, 332, 364, 622
Green, Monica, 147, 544
Gregoras, Nikephoros, Byzantine chronicler, 149
Grousset, René, 397
Grupper, Samuel, 230, 233, 235
Güchülüg, Naiman prince and gür-khan of the Qara Khitai, 58, 507
Guillaume Adam, archbishop of Sulṭ āniyya, 99
Gujarat, 217, 363
Gulf, *see* Persian Gulf
Gülichi, Mongol Qaghan (Northern Yuan), 112, 350
Gunashiri[n], Chaghadayid prince of Hami, 236, 308, 571, 595
gunpowder, 328–30, 442
Gūr-i Mīr, Timur's mausoleum, 309, 369, 379–80
güregen (imperial son-in-law), 68, 229, 357
Gür-khan, title of the Qara Khitai ruler, 56, 58
Gurziwān, 243
Güyüg, Mongol Qaghan, 21, 61–2, 64, 70–1, 74, 338, 494
Güzel Ḥiṣār, 384

Ḥabash ʿAmīd, chief minister to Chaghadai, 88
ḥadīth, *see* traditions of the Prophet
Ḥāfiẓ, poet, 179
Ḥāfiẓ-i Abrū, 11, 12, 25, 28, 30–4, 47, 132, 156, 170, 200, 206, 215–16, 224, 227, 233, 314, 316, 323–4, 329, 335, 339, 342, 356, 359, 361, 390, 403, 405, 407, 423, 425, 430,

435; his continuation of Rashīd al-Dīn's *Jāmiʿ al-tawārīkh*, 30; continuation of Shāmī's *Ẓafar-nāma*, 27–8, 31, 272; his *jughrafiyya*, 31; his *Majmūʿa*, 31, 629; his *Zubdat al-tawārīkh*, 31, 224, 227, 359, 407, 435
Hafsid Caliphate, 35,
Ḥājjī, Ilkhanid amir, 184
Ḥājjī Barlās, Chaghadayid amir, 221, 229, 233–4, 242, 254–5, 257, 262, 330, 337, 570
Ḥājjī Beg, Mughūl amir, 584
Ḥājjī Beg b. Sari Bugha, Timurid amir, 266
Ḥājjī Cherkes, Jochid amir, 122
Ḥājjī Ke'ün, Ilkhanid prince, 117, 518
Ḥājjī Maḥmūdshāh Yasā'ūrī, Chaghadayid amir, 224, 254, 257–8, 261, 263, 566
Ḥājjī Muḥammad, envoy from Timur to Castile, 306
Ḥājjī Sayf al-Dīn, Timurid amir, 191, 261, 264, 281, 326, 421; his progeny, 263, 580
Ḥamā, 39, 301, 331, 600
Hamadān, 79, 175, 271–2, 423, 430
Ḥamd-Allāh Mustawfī Qazwīnī, 24–5, 33, 97, 107, 142, 202, 482; his *Nuzhat al-qulūb*, 142, 202; his *Ta'rīkh-i guzīda*, 25–6, 33, 482; his *Ẓafar-nāma*, 25, 33
Hami (Qāmul), 80, 200, 308, 351, 571
Ḥamīd, Chaghadayid amir, 229
Ḥamuwayī, Saʿd al-Dīn, 99
Ḥamuwayī, Ṣadr al-Dīn, 99
Ḥamza b. Mūsā, Chaghadayid amir, 258
Ḥanafī school of Islamic law, 90, 368, 383
Ḥanbalī school of Islamic law, 108, 380
Handel, George Frideric, 6
Hardwar, 300
Harī Malik, Timurid amir, 266
Ḥasan, Jochid amir, 521
Ḥasan b. Shaykh Uways, Jalayirid prince, 174
Ḥasan (*-i Kūchak*), Chobanid amir, 116, 132, 144, 169, 172
Ḥasan b. Choban, 215
Ḥasan b. Köpek, Chaghadayid amir, 238, 573
Ḥasan Baṣrī, amir of the Jā'ūn-i Qurbān, 185, 189
Ḥasan Dāmghānī, Sarbadār ruler, 187, 190
Ḥasan Jūrī, radical preacher, 186–8
Hashtnaghar, 214, 216, 562
al-Hawwārī, shaykh, 104
Ḥaydar Dughlāt, Mīrzā, 26, 48–9, 77, 91, 94–5, 97, 106, 124, 126–7, 129, 199, 201–4, 206–7, 215, 230–1, 235–6, 245, 286, 309, 312, 323–4, 337, 341, 346, 392, 406, 414; his account of his ancestors, 235–6
Ḥaydar Qaṣṣāb, Sarbadār ruler, 187
Hayton of Gorighos, chronicler, 22, 211, 413
Hazār Sutūn palace, Delhi, 280
Hazaraspid dynasty, 168
heads, towers constructed of, 332–4
Heaven, mandate of, 41, 101
Hebei, 539
Henry III, King of Castile, 45, 306, 391, 629
Henry IV, King of England, 306, 376, 593–4
Herat, 17, 25, 31, 33–4, 66, 75, 80, 118–19, 124, 126, 129, 136, 155–6, 158, 170, 181–4, 187–9, 213, 219, 239, 247, 269–70, 291, 317, 329, 331, 333, 339, 345–6, 352, 399, 406, 408, 410, 419–20, 424, 426, 429, 431–2, 435, 439, 447, 482, 548, 559, 563, 565, 574, 605; malik of, 170, 210, 214, 395, 544; *see also* Kartid dynasty
Hijaz, 27, 191, 272, 370, 378
Hilālī, ʿAlā-yi Qazwīnī, Muzaffarid author, 26, 179, 193–4
Hilmand, River, 219, 367
Ḥimṣ, 39, 301
Hindu Kush, 77, 219, 363
Hindus, 299–300, 332, 362, 632; position of, in the Delhi Sultanate, 299, 364, 590; 'Hindus', for Indians generally, 322, 333
Hindūstān, 213, 318, 352; *see also* India

Ḥiṣār-i Shādmān, 219, 242, 259, 421
Ḥiya Taghai, Ilkhanid amir, 184–5
Hodgson, Marshall, 9
hoi-yin irgen ('forest tribes'), 57
holy war, 96, 104, 202, 305, 308, 350, 362–3, 368, 371–3, 395, 412; *see also jihād*
Hongwu, *see* Taizu
Hookham, Hilda, 6–8
Hope, Michael, 278
'horseshoe money' (*naʿl-i bahā*), 314–15, 596
Hospitallers of St John, 304–5, 363, 373, 412; *see also* Smyrna
Hülegü, Mongol prince and founder of the Ilkhanate, 23, 64–5, 72, 74–5, 78, 81, 87, 96, 103, 112, 170, 173, 193, 207, 300, 351–2, 354, 356–7, 367, 386, 572, 628; descendants of, 130, 354, 357; 'ulus of', as Timurid appanage, 272, 277, 402, 621
Hung Taiji, Manchu chief and founder of the Qing, 441
Hungary, 64, 92; king of, 61
Huns, 68
hunt, 320, 402; *see also nerge*
Hurmuz, 140, 193, 213, 272, 295, 314, 329, 589, 613
Ḥurūfīs, 408, 625
Ḥusām al-Dīn Yāghī, shaykh, 94, 241, 508
Ḥusayn, Ilkhanid amir and father of Shaykh Ḥasan, 173, 498
al-Ḥusayn b. ʿAlī, grandson of the Prophet, 239, 379–80
Ḥusayn b. ʿAlīshāh, Timurid author, 30, 225, 359, 583
Ḥusayn Barlās, Timurid amir, 261, 263, 266
Ḥusayn Ṣūfī, ruler of Khwārazm, 259, 284–5, 585, 632
Ḥuwayza, 264
Hymes, Ronald, 147

Iakubovskii, A.Iu., 5
Ibaj Oghlan, Jochid prince, 349, 612
ʿIbar, *see* Ibn Khaldūn
Ibn Abī Ḥajala, author of plague treatise, 542
Ibn ʿArabshāh, Aḥmad b. Muḥammad, 11, 35–8, 42, 44, 151, 171, 224, 228, 241, 244–5, 252–3, 292, 302, 315, 318, 320–1, 324, 326–7, 332, 340, 354, 356–7, 359, 361, 366, 368, 378–9, 382–3, 389, 391, 394, 406, 411, 591, 620; his *Fākihat al-khulafāʾ*, 36, 357, 412; his *ʿAjāʾib al-maqdūr*, 36–7, 42, 48, 412; use of, by Mamlūk authors, 44; his attitude towards Timur, 36–7, 49, 256, 323, 362, 365, 413
Ibn Bādīs, Abū ʿAlī, Maghribī preacher, 40
Ibn Baṭṭūṭa, Moroccan traveller, 22, 93, 105, 107, 109, 111, 117, 124, 126, 130, 136–7, 152, 158, 170, 188, 200–1, 204, 208, 210, 214–18, 220, 235, 239–42, 627; his itinerary, 152–4, 524, 540; his alleged visit to China, 22, 481, 533
Ibn Duqmāq, Mamlūk chronicler, 42
Ibn Faḍl-Allāh al-ʿUmarī, Mamlūk encyclopaedist, 22, 27, 75, 79, 82–3, 93, 97, 125, 129–30, 133, 136, 143, 198–9, 201, 204, 211–12, 627; his *Masālik al-abṣār*, 22, 38; his *Taʿrīf*, 22, 130
Ibn Fatḥ-Allāh al-Baghdādī, ʿAbd-Allāh, late 15th-century chronicler, 48, 130; *see also al-Taʾrīkh al-Ghiyāthī*
Ibn al-Furāt, Mamlūk chronicler, 42, 343
Ibn al-Fuwaṭī, Ilkhanid author, 104
Ibn Ḥajar al-ʿAsqalānī, Mamlūk author, 43–4, 366, 383, 490; his plague treatise, 148
Ibn al-Ḥakīm, Niẓām al-Dīn Yaḥyā, 129–30
Ibn Ḥijjī, Mamlūk chronicler, 42–4, 341, 343, 366
Ibn Juzayy, 22
Ibn al-Kafrī, Taqī al-Dīn ʿAbd-Allāh, Qadi, 383
Ibn Kathīr, Damascene chronicler, 154
Ibn Khaldūn, 12, 35–41, 43–4, 49, 84, 148, 199, 205, 228, 252–3, 298, 320, 324, 327, 342, 357, 383–6, 451, 601, 627; his encounters with

Timur, 37–41, 43–4, 253, 302, 383, 488; his *ʿIbar*, 38–40, 487; his *Muqaddima*, 38, 40, 148; his *Taʿrīf*, 38–9, 357, 366; *see also ʿaṣabiyya*
Ibn Khallikān, Mamlūk author, 43
Ibn al-Khaṭīb, author of plague treatise, 152–3
Ibn Khātima, author of plague treatise, 152–3, 161, 544
Ibn Mufliḥ, Taqī al-Dīn Ibrāhīm, Qadi, 331, 380, 383, 626
Ibn Qāḍī Shuhba, Mamlūk chronicler, 42–4, 366, 487
Ibn Ṣaṣrā, Mamlūk chronicler, 42, 356
Ibn Shākir al-Kutubī, Mamlūk chronicler, 544
Ibn Shihāb Yazdī, Tāj al-Dīn Ḥasan, Timurid chronicler, 47, 329, 492
Ibn al-Shiḥna, Zayn al-Dīn Muḥ ammad, Mamlūk author, 36, 42, 252, 321, 334, 368, 379–80, 391, 394
Ibn Taghrībirdī, Abū l-Maḥāsin Yūsuf, Mamlūk author, 43–4, 366–7; his *Manhal*, 44, 366–7; his *Nujūm*, 43, 367
Ibn Taymiyya, 108–9, 379, 383, 412
Ibn Turka Iṣfahānī, Ṣāʾin al-Dīn ʿAlī b. Muḥammad, 382, 410, 636
Ibn al-Wardī, Aleppan chronicler and author of treatise on plague, 149–50, 153–4, 157, 161
Ibn Yamīn, poet, 527
Ibrāhīm Lodi, Sultan of Delhi, 437
Ibrāhīm Sulṭān b. Shāhrukh, grandson of Timur, 28–9, 33, 280–1, 309, 393, 484; his appanages, 273, 287, 430–1
ʿĪd, observance of, 362
idolators, idolatry, 87, 362
Idoqudai, Mongol noyan, 569
iduq-qut, title of the Uighur ruler, 58, 66, 78, 128
Igdir, 399
Iḥyāʾ al-mulūk, chronicle of Sīstān, 292
Ijil, ancestor of Timur, 232
Il-Qutluq, Mongol princess, 238, 573
ilchi, envoy, messenger, 70, 84, 306, 325
Ilchi Bahādur, Timurid amir, 261, 263, 266, 579
Ilder, Mongol noyan, 232, 567, 570
Ili, River, 62, 266, 286
Ilkhanate, Ilkhanid dynasty, Ilkhans, 3, 11, 15–16, 23–5, 34, 75–83, 87, 97, 103, 111–19, 122, 128–9, 131–5, 142–3, 167–70, 172–3, 178, 181, 185, 191–5, 199, 208, 211, 231, 234, 237, 241, 278, 295, 300, 310, 325, 340, 352, 354, 360, 372, 390, 395, 399, 410, 414, 444–5, 613, 636; foundation of, 74–8, 85, 115, 354, 392; collapse of Ilkhanate, 114–18, 356
Ilyās Khwāja, Chaghadayid khan, 128, 135, 234, 241, 255–6, 284, 339, 406, 525, 529, 607
Ilyās Yasāʾūrī, Chaghadayid amir, 258
ʿImād al-Dīn Masʿūd, nephew of ʿAlī-yi Muʾayyad, 268, 293, 297
Imperium Medium, *Imperium de Medio* (Chaghadayid khanate), 79, 144, 150; *see also Dumdadu Monggol Ulus*; 'Medes'
India, 9–11, 23–4, 35, 48, 55, 85, 107, 125–6, 137, 140, 142, 153–4, 157, 193, 213–15, 237, 240, 265–6, 297–300, 309–10, 317, 325, 539–40, 560, 562, 601, 619; as term embracing China and Central Asia, 149–50, 536–7; 'Upper India', 149, 537
Indian Ocean, 154, 442
Indus, River, 207–8, 217–18, 271, 299, 371, 390, 540
injü, personal estates of ruler, 172, 209, 245
Injuid dynasty, 118–19, 168, 172
Innocent IV, Pope, 21, 61
Iran, 3, 9, 16–17, 38, 41, 55, 64, 72, 74, 76–7, 85, 87, 124, 132, 136, 140, 150, 160; idea of, 192–5
'Iran and Turan', as Timur's dominions, 394, 630
'Iranian interlude', 168, 192
Iraq (ʿIrāq-i ʿArab), 63–4, 75, 77, 111, 114, 116–17, 136, 156, 171, 173, 175, 272, 279, 309–10, 317, 322,

399–400, 402, 421, 597, 640; 'the two Iraqs', 613
ʿIrāq-i ʿAjam ('Persian Iraq'), 153, 175–6, 179, 192, 194, 210, 270, 272, 293, 295, 424–5, 430, 432, 436, 560
Iron Gates, 400
Irtysh, River, 57, 62, 286
Irwin, Robert, 6, 442
Īryāb, 266
İsa Beg, son of Bayezid, 304
Isfahan, 32, 90, 118, 156, 172, 174, 178–81, 266, 293–5, 315, 322, 331–3, 382, 423–5, 428–30, 436, 546, 549, 604, 639–40
Isfandiyār, ruler of Sinope, 343
Isfizār, 334
Iskandar b. ʿUmar Shaykh, grandson of Timur, 28–9, 32–3, 272, 274–5, 278, 286–7, 324, 410, 418, 423–4, 426–31, 484, 589, 603, 639–40; as rival to Shāhrukh, 428–30, 641
Islam, acceptance of, by Mongols, 92, 95–7; its adoption by Chinggisid princes, 91, 93–6; mediators of, 97–9; impulses behind Islamisation, 99–103; limitations of Islamic observance, 104–9; objections to Islamisation, 109–10
Islamic law, *see* Sharīʿa, schools of, 109–10
Ismāʿīl, Shah and founder of the Safawid dynasty, 437
Ismāʿīl Barlās, Timurid amir, 262
Ismāʿīlīs, 64
Issyk Köl, 62, 215
It-Qul, Chaghadayid prince, 214, 563
ʿIzz al-Dīn, king of Sīstān, 255

Jaʿfar Beg, Mongol amir, 185–6
Jaʿfarī (Jaʿfar b. Muḥammad Ḥusaynī), late Timurid historian, 47, 179, 194, 422, 424, 553
Jahān Temür, Ilkhan, 116–17, 119, 517
Jahāngīr, Mughul Emperor in India, 11
Jahāngīr, son of Timur, 32, 255, 260, 270, 273, 275, 280, 285, 317, 412, 415, 418, 450, 552, 583; his marriage, 285, 358; his descendants, 32–3, 271, 418, 422, 427, 436
Jahāngīr Barlās, Timurid amir, 262, 264, 579–80
Jahānshāh b. Qarā Yūsuf, Qarā-Qūyūnlū chief, 433, 436
Jahānshāh Barlās, Timurid amir, 258, 260, 265, 278, 580
Jājarm, 186
Jalāl-i Islām Ṭabasī, finance minister to Timur, 268, 581
Jalāl al-Dawla Iskandar, *ustundār* of Rūyān, 171, 190, 552
Jalāl al-Dīn, last Khwārazmshāh, 59, 63, 390, 487
Jalāl al-Dīn Rūmī, 101
Jalayir (Jalāyir) tribe, 65; in Transoxiana, 65, 223, 237–8, 242–4, 246–7, 257, 259–61, 264, 267, 577; amirs of, 32, 65, 223, 237–8, 247
Jalayirid dynasty, Jalayirids, 25, 33–4, 48, 65, 117, 129, 156, 168–9, 171 173–9, 190, 193, 195, 267, 270, 293, 302, 310, 318, 346, 355, 395, 399, 401, 403, 432–3, 448–9, 632; as heirs of the Ilkhans, 169, 193, 295
Jalayirtai, Chaghadayid amir, 237–8, 573
Jām, 182, 385, 424; shaykhs of, 34, 182, 291
Jamāl al-Qarshī, 26, 48, 240
Jāmī, Muʿīn al-Dīn Muḥammad, Kartid wazir, 182–3, 291, 385, 588
Jāmī, Raḍī' al-Dīn, 182; his invitation to Timur, 182
Jāmī, Shaykh Aḥmad, 182, 385
Jāmī, Shaykh Quṭb al-Dīn, 182
Jāmiʿ al-tawārīkh, *see* Rashīd al-Dīn Faḍl-Allāh
Jammu, 300, 363; raja of, 364
Jamuqa, Mongol leader, 629
Janibeg, khan of the Golden Horde, 79, 83, 118, 120–1, 124, 126, 133, 135, 137, 143–4, 148–9, 157, 160, 288, 396, 520, 522, 540; his conquest of Azerbaijan, 118, 120, 172

János of Eger, 157
Japan, 503
Jata, 113, 124, 127, 159, 206–7, 255–7, 260, 266, 270, 273, 276, 285–7, 290, 311–12, 324, 339, 411, 434, 523, 558, 577, 600, 611, 613; *see also* Mughūlistān, Mughūls
Jats, tribe (in the Punjab), 210, 400
Jā'ūn-i Qurbān Mongols, 31, 66, 118, 170, 184–7, 189–90, 244, 255, 292–3, 316, 320, 330, 421
Jaunpur, 363
al-Jazarī, Shams al-Dīn Muḥammad, 36, 382
Jazīra, 96, 117, 171, 301, 310
Jebe, Mongol general, 59
Jerusalem, 46, 375, 622
Jews, Judaism, 23, 40, 87, 90, 94, 99, 101, 105, 108, 363, 508, 617, 622, 628
jihād (holy war), 2, 104, 362, 616
Jimgim, son of Qubilai, 133
Jin dynasty, Jin China, 55–9, 61, 63, 89, 141, 147, 321
jizya, the Islamic poll-tax, 87, 105, 108, 299, 305, 362, 373, 409
Jochi, eldest son of Chinggis Khan, 3, 19, 62, 392
Jochi Qasar, brother of Chinggis Khan, 72, 517; descendants of, 71–2, 80, 115, 134, 517
Jochid territories, Jochids, 3, 26, 48, 62, 67, 74–5, 79, 99, 112, 118, 126, 132, 152, 159, 171, 173, 206, 208, 211, 216, 220, 311, 322, 352, 354, 368, 398, 411, 434, 449, 544; *see also* Golden Horde; Qipchaq Khanate; Orda, ulus of; Blue Horde
John, Dominican friar and archbishop of Sulṭāniyya, 11, 45, 49, 150, 224, 229, 252–3, 306–7, 312, 320, 328, 331–2, 341, 400, 423, 451, 593–4, 627; his view of Timur, 374–7; his *Libellus de notitia orbis*, 45, 375–6; his *Mémoire*, 45, 307, 341, 375–6; Latin translation of *Mémoire*, 45, 622
John VII, Byzantine co-Emperor, 304, 306, 592–3
Juki, brother of Timur, 224
Juki, Chaghadayid prince, 126, 524
Julian, Dominican Friar, 61, 68, 538
Junābād, 185
Junayd-i Boroldai, Timurid amir, 277
Jupiter, 40, 252, 356, 386
Jurchen, 55, 64, 441; *see also* Jin dynasty; Manchus
Jurjān, 186
Jurma'ī Mongols, 66, 136, 170, 244
Jurjānī, ʿAlī (al-Sayyid al-sharīf), 36
Juwayn, 330
Juwaynī, ʿAlā' al-Dīn ʿAṭā Malik, 22–3, 33, 62, 69, 84, 86, 88–9, 92, 101–2, 104, 141, 367, 410–11, 636
Juwaynī, Bahā' al-Dīn, 98
Juwaynī, Shams al-Dīn, 23
Jūzjān, 212
Jūzjānī, Minhāj al-Dīn, 22, 86, 88, 91–2, 104

Kaʿba, 371, 434
Kabul, 19, 215, 219, 262, 271, 276, 299, 349, 371, 416, 427, 431, 437–8, 440, 452, 564, 574
Kābul (or Qabūl) Shāh, Chaghadayid khan, 132, 200, 255, 339–40, 525, 607
Kaffa, 123, 140, 143–4, 148, 155, 157, 368
Kaitak (Qāytāgh), 363, 368, 377, 617
Kalāt, 156, 184
Kalpi, 41, 363
Kālpūsh, 423
Kamākh, 329
Kangxi, Qing Emperor of China, 441
Karābī, Yaḥyā Sarbadār ruler, 185, 187, 189–90
Karābī, Ẓahīr al-Dīn, Sarbadār ruler, 188
Karasakpai inscription, 360, 452
Karbalā, 42, 379
Karimov, Islam, 19
Karma-pa Lama Rol-pa'i rDo-rje, 105
Kartid (or Kurtid) dynasty, 31, 66, 80, 118, 124, 129, 156, 168, 170, 181–3, 185–6, 194, 267, 270, 302, 311, 314, 318, 364, 395, 399, 446, 546
Kāsān, 235

Kāshān, 167, 179, 316
Kāshghar, 48, 128, 203, 207, 235, 239, 273, 287, 310, 316, 397, 434
Kashgharia, 199, 428, 441
Kashmir, 87, 363; Sultan of, 310
Kasimov, Khanate of, 236
Kastamonu, 343
Kastritsis, Dimitris, 41
Kāt, 63, 285
Katak, 91, 202
Kator, 362
Kaykhusraw, amir of Khuttalān, 128, 242, 255–7, 259–60, 267, 273, 358, 410
Kayqubād, amir of Khuttalān, 267
Kayserı, 118, 159, 177
Kazakhstan, Kazakhs, 3, 150, 206, 321, 440
Kazan, Khanate of, 121, 236
Ked-buqa, Mongol general, 76, 170
Kehren, Lucien, 7
Kenjek, 143
Kereyits, tribe, 57, 65, 226; Christians among, 88; Kereyits in Mughūlistān, 287
Kerülen, River, 57, 62
keshig (guard), 64–5, 84, 230–1, 244, 246, 496
ke'ün (prince), 114, 131
Khaidarov, T.F., 160
Khalaj, tribe, 69, 316
Khalīl Sulṭān b. Amīrānshāh, grandson of Timur, 28, 32, 43, 106, 226, 272, 278, 280–1, 345, 351, 358, 418, 423–8, 430–1, 434–5, 447, 599, 610, 638–9, 641; in power in Samarkand, 418–22
Khalīl Sulṭān, Chaghadayid khan, 124–6, 134, 137, 200, 218, 239, 244, 252, 523–4, 563
Khaljī Sultans of Delhi, 142, 280
Khalkha Mongols, 440–1
Khalkāl, 292
Khān Sulṭān Khānīka, wife of Muḥammad Sulṭān b. Jahāngīr, 420–1, 638
khānaqāh, 281, 370, 627
Khanbaligh (Dadu; modern Beijing), 77, 152, 504, 533
Khandesh, 363
Khānzāda, Sevin Beg, wife successively of Jahāngīr and Amīrānshāh, 270, 274–5, 281, 358, 406, 418, 583, 585
kharāj, land tax (or tribute), 193, 269, 299, 373, 409, 586
Kharijites, 366, 618
Khazars, 53, 113
Khiḍr, Chaghadayid prince, 358
Khiḍr, Jochid khan, 121–3, 160, 519–21
Khiḍr Khan, founder of the Sayyid dynasty, 300, 431, 435, 590
Khiḍr Khan, son of the Delhi Sultan ʿAlāʾ al-Dīn Khaljī, 214
Khiḍr Khwāja, Mughūl khan, 128–9, 202, 236, 279, 286, 309, 319, 324, 353, 357, 434–5, 571, 595, 598, 613
Khiḍr Yasāʾūrī, Chaghadayid amir, 242, 254–5, 258
khilāfat, 103–4, 194, 413, 610, 637; *see also* Caliph
Khitā(y) (northern China), 69, 159, 354, 539, 612
Khiṭāy Bahādur Qipchaq, Timurid amir, 261, 263, 266, 579
Khiva, 48, 63, 285; khanate/khans of, 437, 572
Khokand, khanate, khans of, 439, 571
Khokhars, tribe, 300, 326
Khotan, 203, 235, 239, 273, 286–7
Khudāydād, Dughlāt amir, 236, 406–7, 571; his mother, 571
Khudāydād Ḥusaynī, Timurid amir, 263, 287, 418, 422, 427
Khujand, 199, 238, 241–2, 256, 572
Khulm, 243
Khunjī, Faḍl-Allāh Rūzbihān, 409
Khurāsān, 16, 19, 23, 25, 31, 40, 58, 60, 75–6, 80, 93, 99, 115–16, 118–19, 132, 135, 138, 159, 167, 169–70, 173, 178, 183–4, 188, 190–2, 198, 205, 208–10, 212, 214, 242, 244, 253–6, 265, 270–1, 290–3, 309, 316, 321–2, 336, 379, 409, 421, 423–5, 429, 432, 436–7, 439, 448, 452, 537, 551, 562–3, 599, 614, 640

Khurāsānīs, 205, 315
Khurāshā, 330
Khurmātū, 270, 330
Khurramābād, 179
Khusraw Anūshīrwān, Sasanian king, 192, 383
Khuttalān, 219, 242, 258, 260, 582; *tümen* of, 259
Khūzistān, 117, 175, 264, 297, 589, 613
Khwāf, 154, 178, 211, 384
Khwāfī, Faṣīḥ al-Dīn (or Faṣīḥ-i), 47, 151
Khwāja ʿAlī, shaykh at Ardabīl, 384
Khwāja ʿAlī Apardī, Chaghadayid amir, 258
Khwāja Masʿūd b. Yaḥyā Simnānī, finance minister to Timur, 268
Khwāja Mīrjān, Jalayirid governor of Baghdad, 173
Khwāja Ilghār, Timur's birthplace, 223
Khwāja Yūsuf, Timurid amir, 421
Khwāja Yūsuf Apardī, Chaghadayid amir, 258
Khwānd-Amīr (Ghiyāth al-Dīn b. Humām al-Dīn), 48, 347, 359, 508, 566
Khwārazm, Khwarazmians, 59–60, 62–3, 122, 128–9, 150, 220, 258–60, 264, 266, 284–5, 287–8, 290, 310, 313–14, 317, 322, 336, 341, 396, 399, 434, 437, 585–7, 608
Khwārazmshāhs, 55, 58–9, 61, 63, 279, 321, 629
Kildibeg, Jochid khan, 121–2, 520
Kim, Hodong, 61, 81
Kirmān, 25, 66, 98, 118, 136, 168, 170, 172, 178–9, 181, 189, 209, 213, 244, 265, 272, 291, 293–5, 329, 424–5, 428, 432, 436, 548, 563, 588, 613, 639
Kish, 15, 18, 199, 215, 225, 233–4, 241–2, 262, 317, 340, 385, 395, 398, 422, 566, 570, 577, 597; Timur's buildings in, 369, 620; *tümen* of, 223, 233–4, 254–5; *see also* Shahr-i Sabz, *ulugh ming*
Kīsh (Qays), 140, 193, 429
Kishm, 212
Kitans, tribe, 55, 59–60, 64; *see also* Liao dynasty
Knights Hospitallers, *see* Hospitallers
Ködege, Mongol amir, 573
Kök Türks, *see* Türks
kökeltash (foster-brother), 98
Kököchös, Mongol noyan, 229, 569
Könchek, Chaghadayid khan, 215
Konya, 176
Köpek, Chaghadayid amir, 237–8, 247, 573–4
Köpek, Chaghadayid khan, 72, 83, 126, 137, 143, 199, 204, 214–16, 235, 241, 245–6, 502, 504, 562; '*tümen*' or 'people of Köpek Khan', 245, 576
Köpek Temür, Mughūl amir, 200, 287, 586
Korea, 77
Koryŏ (Korea), kingdom of, 67, 141
Kūcha (Kūsān), 203, 207
Kūh-i Kiyā, 548
Kulikovo Pol´e, battle of (1380), 132
Kulnā, Jochid khan, 121, 519
Külün Nor, 57
Kunacha, Jochid prince, 349, 611
Kura, River, 211
Kurdistan, 272, 613
Kurds, 168, 314, 400, 632
Kurramān, 208
Kūsān, 235, 286; *see also* Kūcha
Kutāhiya, 325
Kutubī, Maḥmūd, historian of the Muzaffarids, 26, 156, 176, 180, 193, 294, 553
Kyrgyzstan, 3, 147, 151–2, 154
Kyushu, 78

Labnasagut, 87
Lahore, 208
*Lakchir, Negüderi chief, 214
'Land of Darkness', 149
Landa, Ishayahu, 97
Latin Christendom, Christians, Latin West, 9, 17, 81
Lazar, Serbian prince, 372
Le Baker, Geoffrey, English chronicler, 152

Le Roy Ladurie, Emmanuel, 146
levirate marriage, 69, 106, 412, 451, 513
Liao dynasty, 55–6, 59, 145
Liaoyang, 114
Lighdan, khan of the Chakhar Mongols, 441
lingchi (command of a regional khan), 83, 504
Lithuania, Lithuanians, 289, 364, 372
Loni, 364
Lop Nor, 91, 202
'Lord of the Auspicious Conjunction', *see Ṣāḥib-Qirān*
Louis I, King of Hungary, 157, 160
Louis IX, King of France, 21, 493
Luqmān, Ilkhanid prince and ruler of Astarābād, 183, 291, 293, 348, 352, 611, 613
Luristān, Lurs, 178, 266, 274, 293, 400, 430, 596, 613, 632; Greater (Lur-i Buzurg), 168, 311; Lesser, 272, 399, 405
Luṭf-Allāh b. Masʿūd, Sarbadār ruler, 187, 551

Maʿbar, 153–4, 363, 536, 540
madrasa, 280, 370, 585
Maghrib, 38, 40, 43, 205, 601; *see also* Morocco
Māhāna, 314
Maḥbūbī, family, 240
Mahdī, the, 102, 186, 386, 408, 429
Mahendrarajah, Shivan, 188, 385
Maḥmūd, Oyirat chief, 350, 440
Maḥmūd of Ghazna, 215, 371, 446, 620–1; 'throne' of, as Timurid appanage, 271, 371
Maḥmūd Khwārazmī, 373, 391
Maḥmūd Shāh, Sultan of Delhi, *see* Ghiyāth al-Dīn Maḥmūd Shāh
Mākhān, 182, 185
Makrān, 429, 613
māl-i amānī ('security payment', indemnity), 269, 314, 325, 382
Malabar, 536
*Malash Apardī, Chaghadayid amir, 259, 578
Malaṭiya, 296, 301, 325, 364
Maldives, 154
Mali, sultan of, 532
Malik Ashraf, *see* Ashraf
Malik Bāqir, Kartid ruler of Herat, 182, 189
Malik Shāh Ḥusayn, king and historian of Sīstān, 292
Malikat Āghā, Chaghadayid princess and wife of ʿUmar Shaykh, 358, 418
Mālikī school of Islamic law, 36,
Mallū Khan, Delhi amir, 298, 320
Malwa, 363
Mamai, Jochid amir and kingmaker, 114, 122–3, 132, 135, 160, 288, 368, 445, 449, 491, 522, 587, 619
Mamlūk Sultan/Sultanate, Mamlūks, 2, 6, 11, 22, 34–6, 55, 75, 78, 81–2, 96, 100, 113, 118, 137, 142, 145, 275, 288–9, 293, 297, 300–2, 324, 327–8, 340, 356, 365, 369, 375, 396, 401, 433–4, 533, 542, 557, 632
Mamlūk sources, 22, 27, 42–4, 63, 117, 152, 169, 216, 319, 331, 343, 365, 384, 523, 597, 620
mamluks (*ghulāms*, Turkish slaves), 55, 501
Manchuria, 3, 53, 55, 60–1, 69, 77, 441
Manchus, 18, 112, 441, 443; *see also* Qing dynasty
Manghalai Sübe, 203, 235, 556
Manichaeans, 508
Manuel II Palaeologus, Byzantine Emperor, 304, 592
Manuel III Comnenus, Emperor of Trebizond, 304
Manz, Beatrice Forbes, 6, 71, 220–1, 233, 242–6, 251, 260–1, 267, 269, 318, 350, 389, 398, 408, 436, 449
al-Maqrīzī, Taqī al-Dīn Aḥmad, Mamlūk author, 37, 39, 42–4, 49, 152, 159, 252, 309–10, 316, 318–19, 324, 365–7, 378, 384, 413, 518; his *Sulūk*, 43, 316, 365–6; his *Durar al-ʿuqūd*, 39, 43–4, 366–7; his view of Timur, 366, 618
Marāgha, 79, 115, 547

Marʿash, 176
Marʿashī, Ẓahīr al-Dīn, 206
Marʿashī Sayyids, *see* Sayyid rulers of Māzandarān
Marco Polo, 21–2, 73, 141, 207–8, 210–11
Mārdīn, 96, 117, 272, 297, 301, 315, 330
Marignolli, John of, papal envoy, 140, 144, 152, 536, 539
Marinid Sultan, 39, 302; *see also* Morocco, sultan of
Marlowe, Christopher, 1, 6, 9
  his *Tamburlaine the Great*, 1, 9
Marozzi, Justin, 7–8
'Marshes of Maeotis', 149
Martin I, king of Aragon, 594
Marūchaq, 212
Marwārīd, ʿAbd-Allāh, 34
Mashhad, 185, 188
Masʿūd, Wajīh al-Dīn, Sarbadār ruler, 186–8, 190, 552
Masʿūd Beg, Chaghadayid finance minister, 67, 78, 143, 240
Mā warā' al-nahr, 1, 205, 322, 409; *see also* Transoxiana
Ma'ulai, Ilkhanid amir, 379, 551
May, Timothy, 66, 73, 113, 398, 402
Maybud, 178, 210
Maydānī, Badr al-Dīn, shaykh, 241
Māzandarān, 116, 118, 155, 167–8, 170, 180, 183–4, 187, 189–90, 271, 278–9, 290, 292–3, 296, 311, 314, 318, 322, 347, 352, 421, 424, 426, 432; 'Māzandarānāt', 613
Māzandarānī, ʿAbd-Allāh b. Muḥ ammad, 34
Mazīd Barlās, Timurid amir, 262
McChesney, Robert, 135
McNeill, William, 158
Mecca, 369, 378, 414, 429, 433, 623
'Medes', 79, 150, 161, 537; *see also* *Imperium Medium*
Medieval Climate Anomaly, 145
Medina, 369, 378, 429, 434
Mediterranean Sea, 10, 149, 154
Meḥmed I, Ottoman Sultan, 304, 405, 592
Meḥmed II, Ottoman Sultan, 171, 547
'Mekrit' (Bekrin?), 322
Melik, son of Ögödei, 80, 338, 528
Melville, Charles, 97, 129, 135
Mengü Temür, Chaghadayid amir, 238
Mengü Temür, khan of the Golden Horde, 93
Mengü Temür, son of Hülegü, 115
Merkit, 57
Merovingians, 113
Merv, 211–12, 216, 237, 437
messianic movements, 408; *see also* Ḥurūfīs
Metsopʿ, 374; *see also* Tʿovma
Michaēl Panaretos, continuator of, 46
Miḍrāb Barlās, Timurid amir, 265, 580
Mignanelli, Beltramo di, 46, 49, 252–3, 315–16, 319, 321, 367, 380, 385
Mihrabanid dynasty, 168
Ming annals, *see Mingshi*
Ming dynasty, Ming China, Ming Emperor, 2, 3, 21, 114, 200, 230, 279, 287, 307–9, 312, 326, 350, 363, 373, 389, 395–6, 408, 434–5, 439–41, 444, 446–7, 513, 642
Ming Temür, ancestor of the Shibanid Uzbek khans, 121, 520
mingghan, military unit of a thousand, 64
Mingli Bugha, Chaghadayid amir, 259
Mingshi, 307, 350, 555, 594–5, 612
Mīr-Khwānd, late Timurid chronicler, 47, 566
Mīrat (Meerut), 216, 300, 362, 390, 629
'Mirrors for Princes', 35, 407, 412
Mīrzā Ḥaydar, *see* Ḥaydar Dughlāt
Miyāna, 179
möchelge (written oath), 229, 323, 569
Mö'etügen, son of Chaghadai, 559
Möge, Chaghadayid amir, 223, 237, 566
Mohi, battle of (1241), 320
Möngke, Mongol Qaghan, 64, 67, 74–6, 89, 93, 95, 99–100, 352, 500
Mongol law/custom/tradition, 2, 4, 14–15, 36, 69, 101, 110, 119, 169, 345–6, 398, 403–4, 408, 411, 413; *see also Töre*; *Yasa*; *yusūn*/*yūsūn*

Mongolia, 3, 53, 55, 57, 61, 72, 75, 77, 83, 91, 112, 127, 207, 308, 350, 417, 440, 539
Mongolian language, 205, 557
Mongolian Republic, 18
Mongols, passim; rise of, 56–64; mission of world-conquest, 60–1; Great Mongol People/State, 60–1, 64–73; conflict among, 73–6; emergence of autonomous states, 76–81
Monophysite Christians, 108
Mordvins, tribe, 521
Morgan, David O., 61, 66, 69, 109, 155, 313, 397
Morocco, 36, 39, 302, 326, 386; sultan of, 320, 326, 515, 591; *see also* Maghrib; Marinid Sultan
Morton, Alexander, 23
Moscow, Muscovites, 122, 132, 289, 364, 368; *see also* Muscovy
Mosul, 176–7, 334, 622
mu'adhdhin, 93, 108
Muʿāwiya, Umayyad Caliph, 379
Mu'ayyad Arlāt, Timurid amir, 261
Mubārak Khwāja, khan of the Blue Horde, 123, 522
Mubārak Shāh, Chaghadayid khan, 93, 208, 232, 238; adoption of Islam, 93
Mubārak Shāh b. Khiḍr Khan, Sayyid Sultan of Delhi, 41
Mubāriz al-Dīn Muḥammad b. al-Muẓaffar, founder of the Muzaffarid dynasty, 118–19, 169–70, 172–3, 178–9, 194, 210, 519, 546–9, 635; his receipt of title of Sultan from the Caliph, 178–9, 193–4, 553
Mubashshir, Timurid amir, 261, 579
Mūghān, 175
Mughul Empire, 11, 48, 437–9
Mughūlistān, Mughūls, 32, 49, 85, 113, 126–8, 135, 146, 161, 182, 192, 199, 201–4, 206, 220, 231, 234, 236, 241, 254–7, 266–7, 274, 279, 284–7, 290, 308–9, 311–13, 317–18, 324, 339, 346, 350, 353, 396–9, 408, 422, 427–9, 434–5, 438–9, 444–6, 556–8, 586–7; viewed as infidels, 201–2, 367, 555; *see also* Jata
Muḥammad, Ilkhan, 115–16, 130–1, 526–7
Muḥammad, Mughūl khan, 95, 201, 346, 422, 555
Muḥammad b. al-Ḥanafiyya, 381
Muḥammad b. Bolod (Pūlād), Chaghadayid khan, 125–6, 524
Muḥammad b. Mubārak Shāh, Sayyid Sultan of Delhi, 435
Muḥammad b. Sulṭānshāh Khurāsānī, Timurid amir, 267
Muḥammad b. Tughluq, Sultan of Delhi, 138, 142, 153, 216–18, 298, 530, 540, 564–5, 619, 630
Muḥammad Beg b. Arghunshāh, amir of the Jā'ūn-i Qurbān, 185, 190
Muḥammad Beg b. Mūsā, Chaghadayid amir, 258; married to Timur's daughter Āghā Beki, 274
Muḥammad Bulaq, Jochid khan, 123, 132, 522
Muḥammad Burunduq, Timurid amir, 414
Muḥammad Darwīsh b. Bāyazīd Jalāyir, 259
Muḥammad Ḥaydar, Dughlāt amir, 106
Muḥammad Jahāngīr b. Muḥammad Sulṭān, Timurid prince and khan in Samarkand, 345, 358, 419, 422, 427, 430, 610
Muḥammad Khwāja Apardī, Qara'unas amir, 185, 243–4, 257, 574
Muḥammad Mīraka b. Shīr Bahrām, amir of Khuttalān, 259–60
Muḥammad Shībānī, Uzbek khan, 19, 48, 204, 437, 439
Muḥammad Sulṭān b. Jahāngīr, grandson and heir-apparent of Timur, 264, 271, 273–5, 281, 295, 314, 329, 341, 343, 345, 358, 370, 393, 400, 409, 415–16, 419, 429, 449, 583, 595, 608, 621; his sons, 280
Muḥammad Taraghai, 315; *see also* Ulugh Beg

Muʿizz al-ansāb, Timurid genealogical work, 31, 48, 121, 127, 224–5, 227, 229–30, 232–4, 238, 262, 265, 268, 339, 347
Muʿizz al-Dīn Muḥammad b. Sām, Ghurid Sultan, 590
Muʿizz al-Dīn Pīr Ḥusayn Muḥ ammad, Kartid Sultan of Herat, 119, 126, 135–6, 169–71, 181–7, 189, 194, 217–18, 255, 291, 333, 364, 401, 550, 553, 565, 588
mujaddid ('Renewer'), 34, 407–8, 429, 553, 635
mukūs, uncanonical taxes, 143, 532
Multān, 208, 210, 214, 298–300, 431, 515, 590
mulūk al-ṭawāʾif ('factional princes'), 127–8, 191, 219, 242, 254, 326, 373, 401, 574
al-Munāwī, Ṣadr al-Dīn, Qadi, 37, 39, 383, 626
Mūnk, 126, 218, 243
Muqali, Mongol general, 576
Murād, Timurid amir, 267
Murad I, Ottoman Sultan, 171, 302, 373
Murād Khwāja, Jochid khan, 121–2, 521
Murghāb, River, 335, 424
Mūsā, Chaghadayid amir, 238, 242, 258, 261, 274, 278, 526, 573, 584
Mūsā, Ilkhan, 114–15, 117, 130–1, 134
Musāfir Kābulī, Timurid officer, 330
Muscovy, 439, 442–3; *see also* Moscow
Mūsh, 177
al-Muʿtaḍid bi-llāh, ʿAbbasid Caliph in Cairo, 119, 193, 519
al-Mutawakkil ʿalā Allāh, ʿAbbasid Caliph in Cairo, 368–9, 619
Muẓaffar Kāshī, Muzaffarid amir, 181, 294
Muzaffarid dynasty, Muzaffarids, 26, 28, 31, 48, 118–19, 156, 168, 170, 172, 174–6, 178–81, 189, 193, 195, 210, 266, 270, 272, 293, 296, 302, 311, 314, 318, 333, 399, 405, 432–3, 447–8; as heirs of the Ilkhans, 193
al-Nābulusī, Shams al-Dīn Muḥ ammad b. Aḥmad, Qadi, 380, 383, 626
Nādir Shāh Afshār, Shah of Iran, 438
Nagel, Tilman, 6, 350
Naiman, tribe, 57–8, 60, 65; Christians among, 88; Naimans in Transoxiana, 243, 258, 574; *see also* Apardī
Nakhchiwān, 45; bishop of, 374, 491
Nakhchiwānī, Muḥammad b. Hindūshāh, 34, 169
Nakhshab, 199, 215, 378
Naliqo'a, Chaghadayid khan, 98, 528
naphtha, 327–9, 602
Naples, 160
Naqachu, Mongol commander, 114
Naqshband, Bahāʾ al-Dīn, shaykh, 200, 240, 524
Naqshbandiyya, shaykhs, 240
Naruchatʹ, 521
Nasā, 183–4
Naṣāʾiḥ-i Shāhrukhī, 407; *see also* Qāyinī
Nāṣir al-Dīn Maḥmūd, Sultan of Delhi, 22
Nāṣir al-Dīn Muḥammad Shāh, Sultan of Delhi, 298, 396
Nāṣir al-Dīn Nuṣrat Shāh, Sultan of Delhi, 299
Naṣīr al-Dīn ʿUmar, Qadi, 27–8, 31–2, 382
al-Nāṣir Muḥammad, Mamlūk Sultan, 117, 137, 352
al-Nāṣir Yūsuf, last Ayyubid ruler of Syria, 356, 367
Naṭanzī, Muʿīn al-Dīn, Timurid chronicler, 28–9, 31–3, 63, 125–6, 129, 184, 201, 206, 217, 219–20, 224, 243, 245, 254, 276, 295, 328, 337, 340, 342, 344, 362, 364, 378, 404–7, 428–9, 483; his *Muntakhab al-tawārīkh*, 28, 33, 361
naṣṣ (designation of a successor), 429
Nawrūz b. Arghun Aqa, Ilkhanid amir, 97–9, 104–5, 113, 184, 212, 237, 291, 546, 560
Nawrūz, Jochid khan, 121, 519–21

Nawrūz Güregen, son-in-law of Tarmashirin, 217–18, 564
Nawrūzī Mongols, 170, 184, 244, 575
Nebuchadnezzar, 383
Negüder, Mongol commander, 76, 208–9, 559
Negüderi Mongols, Negüderis, 63, 66, 79, 170, 208–10, 212–14, 244, 367, 546, 559–60; *see also* Qara'unas
nerge (encircling tactic), 320, 598
Nerses the Great, Saint, 377
Nestorian Christianity, Christians, 88, 91, 374, 509, 523; cemeteries of, in Kyrgyzstan, 147, 151, 160
New Sarai, 122, 520–1
Nicopolis, battle of (1396), 45–6, 178, 375
Nigār Āghā, concubine of Timur, 279
Nihāwand, 262, 272
Nikruz, Ilkhanid amir, 545
Nishapur, 170, 182, 184, 186, 190–1, 293, 314, 334
Noghai, Jochid khan, 77
nökör (sworn follower), 57, 65, 259–60
nomads, nomadism, 4, 5, 7, 40–1, 56, 60, 198–9, 202–4, 206–8, 227, 311–12, 397–8, 442–3; and plague, 157–60; and resistance to urbanisation, 72–3, 136, 203
Norris, John, 143, 145, 151
Northern Yuan dynasty, 112–13, 132, 312, 344, 349, 354, 395, 440–1, 447
noyan, commander, general, 64
Nūr Malik Barlās, Timurid amir, 263, 579
Nūrbaksh, messianic leader, 625
al-Nuwayrī, Mamlūk chronicler and encyclopaedist, 487

Oghuz, 53, 55, 59, 147
Oghuz Khan, 634
Ögödei, Mongol Qaghan, son and successor of Chinggis Khan, 59–60, 62–3, 67, 70–1, 74, 76, 88, 90–2, 141, 338, 386, 392, 405, 417, 447, 487, 628; descendants of; *see also* Ögödeyids
Ögödeyids, 74, 77–8, 80, 112–13, 125–6, 134, 238, 350, 355, 395, 405, 446–7, 528; Ögödeyid origins of Timur's khans, 78, 80, 338, 345, 606
Öljei Bugha Süldüs, Chaghadayid amir, 242–3, 259, 565
Öljei Temür, Mongol Qaghan (Northern Yuan), 349–50, 354, 396, 612; *see also* Bunyashirin, Tāīzī Oghlan
Öljeitü Apardī, Chaghadayid amir, 242–4, 257–8, 523
Öljeitü Khudābanda, Ilkhan, 23–4, 72–3, 81–3, 98, 101–2, 105, 109, 133, 137, 168, 173, 184, 214, 274, 276, 386, 511, 523, 562, 623, 628; his adoption of Twelver Shiʿism, 100
Öljetei, Ilkhanid princess, 169
Ong Khan (Toghril), khan of the Kereyits, 57, 75, 226, 389
Önggüts, 57–8, 65; Christians among, 88
Onon, River, 57, 62
Orda, son of Jochi, 62–3; ulus of, 72, 77, 123, 487; descendants of, 112–13, 123; *see also* Blue Horde
orda (encampment), 65, 150, 158, 339
Ordos, 57
Ordu Buqa, Ilkhanid amir, 545
Ordu Melik, Jochid khan, 121–2, 612
'Ornach', 150, 538; *see also* Ürgench
Orona'ut, tribe, 218, 244, 571, 575
Orqon, River, 57, 60, 397
Orthodox Caliphs, 188
Örtü Bora, Dughlāt amir, 235–6
Örüng Temür, Mughūl amir, 586
Orus, Jochid khan, 123, 264, 266, 287–9, 317, 348–9, 396, 434, 522–3, 611
Orus, Ilkhanid amir, 574
Orus Buqa, Chaghadayid amir, 238, 572
Ötemish Ḥājjī, late Jochid chronicler, 48, 123
ötügen-yish (sacred precinct of the Türks), 60, 494
Ottoman sources, 41–2, 489

Ottoman Sultanate, Ottomans, 2, 6, 8, 9, 34–5, 45–7, 118, 171, 176–8, 293, 297, 300, 302–5, 310, 319, 328, 363, 365, 371–2, 374–7, 396, 405, 433, 438–9, 450, 543, 548, 602
Oxus, River, 2, 4, 10, 59, 75, 191, 207–8, 211–12, 214–15, 218–20, 232, 234, 237, 242, 246–7, 253, 255, 400; *see also* Amū-daryā
Oyirat, tribe, 57, 65, 171, 184, 207, 440–1, 643
Oyiratai Ghazan, Ilkhanid amir, 184
Özbeg, khan of the Golden Horde, 79, 106, 110–11, 114, 118, 120–1, 133, 137, 149–50, 158, 206, 270–1, 288, 345, 358, 519, 521, 523, 528, 558, 627; adoption of Islam, 93, 95

Pādishāh-i Islām, title assumed by the Ilkhan Ghazan, 96, 102, 354, 370; by other rulers, 119, 193; ascribed to Timur's nominal khans, 342–3, 351, 354, 370, 407; assumed by Shāhrukh, 346, 407
Pʻags-pa Lama, 102
paiza (tablet of authority), 84; *see also gerege*
Pamir, mountains, 58
Panipat, battle of (1526), 437, 442
Panjdih, 212
Paris, 306–7, 593
Parwān, 201
Paschal de Vittoria, Franciscan, 144
Pashai, tribe, 564
Paul, Jürgen, 184, 421
Pax Mongolica, 140
Pāykand, 242
Pegolotti, Francesco Balducci, Florentine banker, 141, 144, 151
Pera, 305, 376
Persian Gulf, 140, 153, 156, 295, 553
Persian Iraq, 153; *see also* ʿIrāq-i ʿAjam
Peshawar, 214, 216
Peter, Rus´ prelate, 538
Pfeiffer, Judith, 24,
Philip IV, King of France, 82
Phocaea (Fūcha), 305
Pīr ʿAlī Tāz Süldüs, 259, 420–1, 431, 578
Pīr Bādik, Jalayirid amir, 175, 193
Pīr Ḥusayn, Chobanid ruler, 178, 548
Pīr Ḥusayn Barlās, Timurid amir, 262
Pīr Muḥammad b. Jahāngīr, grandson and heir-apparent of Timur, 33, 271, 299, 308, 345, 393, 416, 418–21, 425–7, 450, 595, 638, 640; governor of Ghazna etc., 276–7, 371
Pīr Muḥammad b. ʿUmar Shaykh, grandson of Timur, 264, 345, 405, 410, 418, 423–4, 426–8, 519, 553, 590, 617, 639; governor of Fārs, 271–2, 274–5, 278
Pīr Pādishāh b. Luqmān, ruler of Astarābād, 322, 348, 426, 611, 640
plague, 15, 146–61 passim, 171, 448–9, 504, 530, 533–6, 538–42, 544; *see also* Black Death
Plano Carpini, John of, papal envoy, 21, 58, 61, 70, 404
Pochekaev, Roman Iu., 123
Poe, Edgar Allan, 6
Poland, Poles, 64, 372, 442
Pontic/Pontic-Caspian steppes, 136, 140, 149, 151, 160, 312; *see also* Qipchaq steppe
postal relay system, 67, 69, 82; *see also yam*
Prester John, 377
Prophet Muḥammad, 86, 103; his descendants, *see ahl al-bayt*; sayyids
Punjab, 2, 79, 211, 216–17, 310, 330, 332, 363, 446

Qabul Khan, ancestor of Chinggis Khan, 225, 359, 634
Qachulai, Mongol prince, 225–7, 359, 568
Qadan, son of Ögödei, 80, 238
Qadaq Khatun, Timur's stepmother, 224
Qāḍī ʿĪsā, Āq-Qūyūnlū finance minister, 409, 635
Qaghan (Khāqān), 3, 53, 59–60, 67, 71, 78, 81–3, 111–12, 133, 152, 200,

231, 308, 338, 344, 349, 356, 417, 440, 444, 447, 504–5, 536; title appropriated by regional khans, 83, and by post-Mongol rulers, 302, 346; *see also* Arigh Böke; Buyantu; Gülichi; Güyüg; Möngke; Ögödei; Öljei Temür; Qoshila; Qubilai; Temür; Toghan Temür; Toghus Temür; Yesün Temür
Qaghanbeg, Jochid khan, 521
Qaidu, Mongol khan, 27, 73, 77–82, 209, 211–12, 232, 237, 240, 246, 338, 502, 508, 561; his descendants, 606–7
Qaidu b. Pīr Muḥammad b. Jahāngīr, 430–1
qalan, *qalānāt* (unspecified) taxation, 67, 409
qalandar, 200, 339, 601
Qalʿat al-Rūm, 318
Qalāwūn, Mamlūk Sultan, 94, 401
Qāliqūṭ, 154
Qalmāq (western Mongolia), 127, 207, 309, 349–50, 440
al-Qalqashandī, Shihāb al-Dīn, 35,
Qamar al-Dīn, Dughlāt amir, 114, 128, 135, 267, 270, 276, 284–6, 311, 318, 339, 353, 396, 401, 555, 571
Qandahār, 262, 271, 299, 371, 416, 431, 562
Qandiyya, 370
Qara Hülegü, Chaghadayid khan, 229
Qara Khitai empire, Qara Khitayans, 56, 58, 60, 86
Qarā Muḥammad, Qarā-Qūyūnlū chief, 177, 296–7
Qara Noghai, khan of the Blue Horde, 123
Qarā-Qūyūnlū, Türkmen dynasty, 117, 175–7, 277, 296–7, 397, 399, 424, 431, 433, 436
Qara Tatars, 171, 303, 316, 322, 421, 591
Qarā Yulūk ʿUthmān, Āq-Qūyūnlū chief, 296, 322
Qarā Yūsuf, Qarā-Qūyūnlū chief, 297, 301, 355, 400, 423–4, 428, 632
Qarābāgh, 156, 336, 379
Qarachar, Chaghadayid amir and ancestor of Timur, 223, 225–31, 233–5, 359, 445, 567–70;
his descendants, 225, 231–5, 569
qarachu (commoner), 14, 68, 71, 113, 133, 135, 336–7, 353, 398, 403, 440, 452
Qarakhanid dynasty, Qarakhanids, 26, 55–6, 58, 86, 381
Qarākhwāja (Qaraqocho), 128, 200, 202, 286
Qaraman, Qaramanid dynasty, 159, 176–7, 305, 609
Qaraqorum, 60, 63, 72–3, 81, 90–1, 397
Qaratal (Qaratau?), 288
Qara'unas Mongols, 66, 170, 181, 185, 190, 198, 208, 211, 213–14, 216–19, 246, 254–5, 262, 291, 298, 333, 544, 559–60, 580; regarded as Turks, 208, 221; Qara'unas amirs as effective rulers of the western regions of Chaghadai's ulus, 218–21, 247, 339–40, 444–5; as a nickname for the Mongols in those regions, 207, 211; corps of, in Ilkhanid Iran, 209–10, 560; *see also* Negüderis; Qazaghan
Qarluqs, tribe, 53, 55, 69, 204, 207, 556
Qarshī, 72, 199, 215–16, 235, 571; river, 421
Qartamīn, 374, 376
Qāshānī, Jamāl al-Dīn, Ilkhanid chronicler, 24–5, 27, 33, 109, 213, 233–4, 386
Qashqa-daryā, 5
Qauchin, alleged tribe, 244–6, 575; ʿAlī Qauchin, 245; Temüge Qauchin, 245
qauchin, 244–5, 264
Qayaligh, 62
Qāyinī, Jalāl al-Dīn Abū Muḥammad, 35, 403, 407–10, 635
Qayrawān, 140
Qays, *see* Kīsh
Qazaghan, Qara'unas amir, 119, 126–7, 135, 181–2, 200, 217–21, 239, 242–4, 247, 252, 254, 265, 291,

337–40, 364, 395, 399, 403, 524, 544, 565
Qazan Sulṭān, Chaghadayid khan, 125–7, 134, 159, 200, 217–18, 238, 242, 244, 252, 256, 267, 278, 289, 339, 351, 357, 524, 563
qazaq, *qazaqliq*, 206, 253, 558
Qazwīn, 171, 179, 190, 547, 552
Qianlong, Qing Emperor of China, 441
Qing dynasty, 18, 439, 441–3; *see also* Manchus
Qinghai-Tibet plateau, 147
Qipchaq/Qangli, 53, 58–9, 64, 69–70, 136, 204; Qipchaq slaves, trade in, 76, 401, 501; Qipchaq steppe, 32, 70, 104, 133, 146, 160, 192, 211, 265–6, 285, 303, 310–11, 316–17, 319, 323–4, 327, 343, 360, 394, 434, 447; Qipchaq, tribe, in Transoxiana, 242
Qipchaq Khanate (White Horde or Golden Horde), 3, 9, 15, 77, 79, 85, 95, 112, 120–4, 133–5, 137, 141, 150, 152, 154–5, 160–1, 172, 288, 290, 312, 317–19, 346, 348, 363–4, 396–7, 405, 434, 444, 449; *see also* Jochids, 'Great Troubles'
Qirghiz (Kirghiz), 53, 57
Qirim, 289
Qishliq, Chaghadayid amir, 223, 237, 572
Qiyat, tribe, 68, 122, 498
Qobuq, River, 62
qol-un ulus ('ulus of the centre'), 63, 417
Qongqurat, tribe, 122, 213, 238, 284, 496, 572; *see also* Ṣūfī dynasty
Qonichi, khan of the Blue Horde, 134
qorchi (quiver-bearer), 402
Qoshila, Mongol Qaghan, 83, 308, 350, 508
Qoyurichaq, Jochid khan, 289, 349, 353–4, 434
Quanzhou, 152
qubchur, poll-tax, 67, 84, 87, 89, 403
Qubilai, Mongol Qaghan, 23, 64, 70, 72, 74–8, 81, 87–8, 102, 110, 141, 231, 392, 508
Quetta, 559
Quhandiz, 274, 336
Quhistān, 170–1, 184, 316
Quli, son of Orda, 63
Qum, 167, 179, 316, 428, 431
Qumārī Inaq Qauchin, 261
Qumārshāh Barlās, Timurid amir, 262
Qūmis, 184
Qundurcha, River, battle of (1391), 270, 289, 317, 322–3, 349, 378
Qunduz, 219, 262, 265, 299, 579
Quraysh, 625
quriltai, 69–70, 73, 80, 84, 109, 135, 255–6, 258, 279, 306, 373, 406
Qurumshi, Yuan noyan, 230
Qutadghu bilig, Turkic epic, 413
Quṭb al-Dīn (I), king of Sīstān, 292–3
Quṭb al-Dīn (II), king of Sīstān, 426
Quṭb al-Dīn Dughlāt, Mughūl amir, 586
Quṭb al-Dīn Muḥammad, king of Sīstān, 155
Qutham b. ʿAbbās, 385
Qutlugh Khwāja, Chaghadayid prince, 212–15, 233, 298, 562
Qutlugh Temür, Qara'unas amir, 213, 238, 562, 573
Qutlugh Temür b. Boroldai, Qara'unas amir, 218, 244
Qutlugh Terken Āghā, sister of Timur, 224, 273, 280–1, 370, 378, 567
Qutlughkhanid dynasty, 98, 178
Qutlughshāh, Ilkhanid amir, 108–10, 514–15
quṭṭāʿ al-ṭarīq ('highway robbers'), 366, 400
Qutuqdur, Mongol commander, 65

raʿd, 328–9, 603; *kamān-i raʿd*, 329, 602; *see also* gunpowder
al-Raḥba, 301
Ramaḍān, observance of, 108, 362
Ramaḍān Khwāja, Timurid amir, 266
Rashīd al-Dīn Faḍl-Allāh, 22–4, 30, 33–4, 69–70, 72, 74–5, 78–9, 81, 84, 88, 95, 98, 101–3, 107–10, 207–12, 214, 223, 225, 227, 229, 234, 236–7, 244, 355, 359, 386, 404, 413, 511, 559, 633;

'correspondence' of, 23; his *Jāmi' al-tawārīkh*, 22–4, 27, 30, 33, 65, 223, 227, 232, 236–7; his *Shu'ab-i panjgāna*, 23, 27, 31, 213, 227, 237
Rayy, 167, 171, 183–4, 190, 270–2, 352, 430, 508
religions, categories of: immanentist, 88–9, 100; transcendental, 89
Roemer, Hans Robert, 191, 225, 229
Roux, Jean-Paul, 7, 326, 363
Rubruck, William of, 21, 60, 74, 89, 95, 104, 141, 158, 377, 509
Rūd-i Garm, 548
Rukn al-Dīn, Suhrawardī shaykh, 515
Rūm, 176, 272, 304, 310, 326, 628; *see also* Anatolia
Rumeli, Ottoman province, 304
Ruqiyya Khānīka, daughter of Kaykhusraw of Khuttalān, 358, 615
Rus', 64, 158, 160, 363, 368, 532, 538, 544; princes, principalities, 122, 506; Rus' chronicles, 26, 120, 122, 124, 132, 135, 150, 155, 160, 253, 289, 519, 538, 591
Russians, 442–3
Rustam b. Mūsā, Chaghadayid amir, 258, 277
Rustam b. 'Umar Shaykh, grandson of Timur, 264, 272, 274, 278, 322, 423–4, 427–8, 430, 641
Rustamdār, 187
Rūyān, 171, 190
Rūz-nāma, *see* Yazdī, Ghiyāth al-Dīn 'Alī

Sabzawār, 116, 175, 186, 189–90, 263, 266, 292, 426
Sa'd al-Dawla, Ilkhanid wazir, 101, 386
Sa'd-i Waqqāṣ b. Muḥammad Sulṭān, 431
ṣadr, office of, 240
al-Ṣafadī, Khalīl b. Aybak, 22, 43; his *A'yān al-'aṣr*, 22; his *Wāfī*, 22
Safawid dynasty, Safawids, 9, 48, 384, 437–40
Ṣafī al-Dīn, ancestor of the Safawid dynasty, 384
Ṣāḥib-Qirān ('Lord of the Auspicious Conjunction'), 18, 292; title applied to Timur, 251, 356, 386–7, 429, 628; applied to earlier Mongol rulers, 386, 628
Sa'īd Barlās, Timurid amir, 262, 274, 278
Saint-Denis, chronicler of, 321
Sālār Oghlan, Chaghadayid prince, 586
Sali Sarai, 126, 218, 243
Salmānī, Tāj al-Dīn, Timurid chronicler, 28, 32, 106, 201, 261, 287, 308, 347, 373, 416, 419–23, 425–6, 432
Samalas volcano, 145
Samarkand, 4, 5, 11, 17, 20, 36–7, 45, 62, 78, 159, 195, 216, 219–20, 224, 226, 240–2, 252, 254–5, 258, 260, 264, 267, 269–70, 273, 279–80, 285, 287, 290, 292–3, 302, 309, 316, 324–5, 338–9, 342, 344, 346, 351, 366, 379, 385, 398, 409, 417–20, 422–3, 437, 439, 483, 544, 558, 580, 597, 601, 606, 610, 631, 638; Timur's efforts to enlarge and embellish the city, 316–17, 395; his buildings in, 369–70, 620
Samarqandī, Kamāl al-Dīn 'Abd al-Razzāq, Timurid chronicler, 47, 155
Samarqandī, Mawlānāzāda, 241
Samos, 305
Sangān, 211
Sāniz, Dughlāt amir, 106
Sanjar, Seljuq Sultan, 56, 385
Saqsīn, 62
Sar-i Pul, 242
Sarai, 72, 121–3, 150, 287–9, 325, 521, 538, 544
Sarai Mulk Khanim, Chaghadayid princess and chief wife of Timur, 238, 256, 258, 278–81, 357, 370, 584–5, 620
Saraichik, 289, 538
Sarakhs, 130, 183, 189, 292
Sārang Khan, Delhi amir and governor of Multān, 298–9

Sarbadār dynasty, Sarbadārs, in Khurāsān, 25, 31, 116, 118, 156, 159, 168, 170–1, 181, 183–91, 193–4, 218, 292, 294, 318–20, 334, 379, 401, 426, 433, 448, 518, 527, 543, 554;
sarbadārs in Samarkand, 241, 256
Sarban, son of Qaidu, 209, 212–13
Sari Bugha, Timurid amir, 260–1, 263, 265, 267, 270, 396, 574, 579, 581
Sāriq Oghlan, Mughūl prince, 610
Sarsatī, 299
Sartaq, khan of the Golden Horde, 89
Sasanian empire, 53, 192
Satibeg, Ilkhanid princess, 114, 116–17, 132
Satilmish Beg, Mongol amir in Quhistān, 185, 190
Sātūq, Chaghadayid prince, 346, 434, 641
Saturn, 40, 252, 356, 386
Sāwa, 179, 187, 316, 433
Ṣawrān or Ṣabrān, 263, 288, 419
Sayf al-Dīn, *see* Ḥājjī Sayf al-Dīn
Sayf al-Mulūk b. Ḥājjī Sayf al-Dīn, 580
Sayfal Barlās, Timurid amir, 262
Sayfī, historian of Herat, 31, 33, 75, 210, 482, 502
Ṣayin Temür, Timurid amir, 267
Sayrām, 268, 273, 287
Sayyid dynasty, in Delhi, 41, 300, 435
Sayyid rulers of Māzandarān, 314, 343, 378
Sayyid Aḥmad b. ʿUmar Shaykh, 431
Sayyid ʿAlī Kiyā, ruler of Gīlān, 343
Sayyid Riḍā Kiyā, ruler of Gīlān, 378
Sayyid Baraka, 370, 378–9, 623
Sayyid Muḥammad Mīrzā, Dughlāt amir, 106
sayyids, 118, 217, 239–40, 377, 382; *see also* Ahl al-bayt, Tirmidh
Schamiloglu, Uli, 157
Schiltberger, Johan, 46, 320, 327, 350, 361, 434
Scorpio, 386
Scythians, 397
Secret History of the Mongols, 10, 21, 56, 58–9, 227, 229, 359, 390
Selenga, River, 57
Seljuqs, Seljuq Sultans, 55–6, 86, 105, 147, 177, 269, 279, 343, 360, 386, 513, 516; Seljuq Sultanate of Anatolia (Rūm), 64, 141, 170, 176, 528
Semirech'e, 199, 203
Serbia, Serbs, 177, 303, 372
Sevinch, Ilkhanid amir, 113
Sevinch Qutlugh Āghā, Chaghadayid princess, 238
Sevinchek, Timurid governor of Fārs, 265, 278, 336
Shaanxi, 153
Shabānkāra, 118, 168, 178
Shabānkāra'ī, Muḥammad b. ʿAlī, 25, 75, 82, 101, 115, 131, 137, 285, 357, 482, 501
Shabūrghān, 211–12, 216, 218–19, 237, 243, 258, 262–3, 431, 574, 579
Shād Mulk, wife of Khalīl Sulṭān, 281, 420
Shadibeg, Jochid khan, 290, 611
Shāfiʿī school of Islamic law, 39, 90, 383
Shāh-i Shāhān, Tāj al-Dīn, king of Sīstān, 293, 322, 336, 426
Shāh-i Shujāʿ b. Muḥammad b. Muẓaffar, Muzaffarid ruler, 26, 119, 174–6, 179–81, 189, 193, 293–4, 336, 369, 549, 553; his receipt of title of Sultan from the Caliph, 180, 194
Shāh Jahān, Mughul Emperor in India, 438
Shāh Maḥmūd b. Muḥammad b. Muẓaffar, Muzaffarid ruler, 174, 179–80, 549
Shāh Malik, Timurid amir, 28, 420–2, 425, 427, 434
Shāh Malik Barlās, Timurid amir, 263
Shāh Manṣūr, Muzaffarid ruler, 28, 44, 175, 179–81, 183, 265, 294–5, 320, 412
Shāh Yaḥyā, Muzaffarid ruler, 179–81, 189, 294, 619
Shāh-nāma, 2, 25, 192; *see also* Firdawsī
shahāda, the profession of the Islamic faith, 93, 96, 104, 108

Shahr-i Sabz, 18, 20, 233; *see also* Kish
Shahr-i Sīstān, 293, 331, 603–4
Shāhrukh, Timurid Sultan, 17, 28–34, 41, 43, 47, 205, 264–5, 273, 278, 297, 300, 309, 345–7, 358, 365, 379, 393, 403, 405, 412, 414–15, 417–18, 420–30, 432–3, 483, 492, 555, 580, 582, 635–6, 639–40, 642; governor of Khurāsān, 271–2, 276; his paramountcy, 430–5; his alleged reversion to Islamic norms, 34–5, 407–12, 429, 451; his sons, 273, 431–2
Shāhrukhiyya (formerly Fanākat), 335
Shajarat al-atrāk, 47
Shakkī, 423
shamans, 89, 99; 'shamanism', 88–9, 95
Shamʿ-i Jahān, Mughūl khan, 435
Shāmī, Niẓām al-Dīn (Niẓām-i), biographer of Timur, 11, 12, 27–9, 31–3, 120, 127, 133, 201, 205, 233–4, 245, 254, 256, 296, 299, 301, 305, 317, 322–3, 328–9, 333–4, 341–3, 347, 349–50, 354–5, 359, 362, 364, 367, 372, 380, 386, 391, 393, 400, 405, 407–8, 412, 447, 616, 630; his *Ẓafar-nāma*, 347, 361
Shams al-Dīn Almālighī, Timurid envoy, 405
Shams al-Dīn b. ʿAbbās, Timurid amir, 421
Shams al-Dīn Dughlāt, Mughūl amir, 357, 571
Shams al-Dīn Fākhūrī, 241 378, 623
Shams al-Dīn Kulāl, shaykh, 225, 234, 369, 382, 385, 567
Shams al-Dīn Muḥammad, Kartid prince, 169, 183, 189, 292
Shanūzān, 266
Sharaf al-Dīn Maḥmūdshāh 'Īnjū', Ilkhanid official and ancestor of the Injuid dynasty, 114, 172
Sharaf al-Dīn al-Muẓaffar, 178
Sharīʿa, 15, 41, 87, 110, 119, 136, 143, 194, 407–9, 411, 429; clash with Mongol institutions and customs, 87–8, 406–7, 409, 451
Shāsh, 202, 239; *see also* Tashkent
Shāsmān, 334
Shaykh Abū Isḥāq Īnjū, ruler of Fārs, 119, 172, 178–9, 189
Shaykh ʿAlāʾ al-Dīn al-Nuʿmān b. Dawlatshāh al-Khwārazmī, 627
Shaykh ʿAlī, Jalayirid prince, 174–5
Shaykh ʿAlī Bahādur Barlās, Timurid amir, 261, 263, 579; his progeny, 580
Shaykh ʿAlī Qūshchī, Ilkhanid amir, 115
Shaykh ʿAlī-yi Hindū, Ilkhanid amir, 183
Shaykh Bāyazīd Bisṭāmī, 385
Shaykh Farīd al-Dīn, shrine of, 385
Shaykh Ḥasan, Timurid amir, 266
Shaykh Ḥasan (*-i Buzurg*), founder of the Jalayirid dynasty, 70, 115–19, 132, 155, 169, 171–3, 177, 498, 519, 541, 545, 553
Shaykh Ibrāhīm, Shīrwānshāh, 322, 423
Shaykh Muḥammad b. Buyan Süldüs, Chaghadayid amir, 257, 259–60, 410
Shaykh Nūr al-Dīn b. Sari Bugha, Timurid amir, 265–6, 281, 418, 420, 422, 425, 427, 641
Shaykh Temür, Timurid amir, 263
Shaykh Uways, Jalayirid ruler, 34, 156, 169, 173–4, 177, 179–80, 183, 355, 395, 399, 428, 545, 547, 550, 631
Shaykhā, Khokhar chief, 326
Shaykhiyya, radical dervishes, 186, 188
Shiban, son of Jochi, 62; descendants of, 112, 121, 436–7, 520–1
Shidebala, Mongol Qaghan, 504
Shihāb al-Dīn Ibn al-ʿIzz, 490
Shīʿī Muslims, 100, 187, 379–80
Shim, Hosung, 83
Shīr Bahrām, 259
Shīr Muḥammad, Mughūl khan, 346, 434, 610–11, 641
Shiraz, 29, 119, 172, 174, 176, 178–81, 189, 265, 269, 271, 274, 294–5, 318, 320, 325, 423–4, 428, 430, 549

Shīrāzī, Mawlānā ʿIzz al-Dīn, physician, 342
Shirgha, son of Qarachar, 262
Shīrīn Bīka Āghā, Timur's sister, 370
Shīrwān, 270, 289, 293
Shīrwānshāh (ruler of Shīrwān), 173, 599
Shuʿab-i panjgāna, *see* Rashīd al-Dīn
al-Shujāʿī, Mamlūk chronicler, 117, 131–2, 518
Shūlistān, 613
Shūshtar, 175, 179–81, 193, 293–4, 318
Siberia, 57, 77, 124, 149, 290, 397, 442
Sibṭ Ibn al-Jawzī, Ayyubid chronicler, 544
Sicily, 149
Ṣiddīq Barlās, Timurid amir, 567
Sighnāq, 123, 288, 434, 523
'Silk Roads', 76, 140, 308, 397
Simnān, 171, 183, 187, 190
Simon of Saint-Quentin, 92
Sind, 150, 208, 213, 277, 299, 308
Sinope, 343
Sīr-daryā (River Jaxartes), 4, 77, 123, 146, 150, 216, 263, 287, 308, 422, 425, 434, 453, 538
Sirhindī, Yaḥyā b. Aḥmad, Indian chronicler, 41, 300
Sīrjān, 294, 322
Sīstān, 155–6, 168, 181, 209, 271, 292–3, 311, 318, 322, 330, 336, 425, 549, 563, 588, 599; kings of, 314; in the narrow sense of Ghūr and Gharchistān, 212, 561
Sitataśastra, Buddhist treatise, 161
Sivas, 42, 46, 118, 156, 177–8, 300, 303, 320, 329, 364, 592, 604, 622; Timur's treatment of, 331–2, 334
Siwālik, 362
Siwnikʿ, 328
Siyāh Kūh, 560
Slavin, Philip, 151
Smyrna (Izmir), 266, 304–5, 329, 332–3, 363–4, 373, 412, 593, 604
Song dynasty, Song empire, 63–4, 70, 78, 141, 147, 531
Sönit, tribe, 223
Sorqaqtani, wife of Tolui, 91, 98
Soucek, Svat, 416
Soudavar, Abolala, 593–4
Soviets, Soviet Union, 6, 18, 19
soyurghal, grant of land or privilege, 205, 403, 431, 633
Soyurghatmish, brother of Timur, 224
Soyurghatmish, (Ögödeyid) khan of Chaghadai's ulus, 133, 256, 275, 338, 340–4, 347–8, 353–4, 357–8, 405, 418, 490, 586, 606–8, 615
Soyurghatmish b. Shāhrukh, 431
Spain, 423, 601
Stalin, Joseph, 6
Stepan Lazarovich, prince of Serbia, 303
Strathern, Alan, 100
Sübe'edei, Mongol general, 59, 64
Subtelny, Maria, 230–1, 386–7, 404
sufis, 98–101, 200, 240–1, 370, 381; *see also faqīr*s
Ṣūfī dynasty, in Khwārazm, 122, 129, 270, 285, 358, 396
Sughu Sechen, father of Qarachar, 226–7, 568
Suhrawardī, sufis, 225
Sulaymān, Ilkhan, 116–17, 119, 130–1, 187, 517, 527
Sulaymānshāh b. Dā'ūd Dughlāt, Timurid amir, 264, 420, 581, 638
Süldüs tribe, 65, 113; in Transoxiana, 65, 223, 237–8, 242–4, 247, 259–60; amirs of, 32, 113, 223, 237–8, 246, 257; *īl* and *tümen* of, 259, 263
Süleyman, son of Bayezid, 304
Sulṭān Abū Isḥāq, Muzaffarid prince, 294
Sulṭān Aḥmad, Mughūl khan, 204
Sulṭān Aḥmad, Jalayirid ruler, 42, 44, 174–7, 184, 288, 292, 296–7, 301, 303, 319, 369, 397, 400, 423, 429, 545, 589, 640
Sulṭān Aḥmad, Muzaffarid ruler, 179–81, 294
Sulṭān ʿAlī b. ʿImād al-Dīn Masʿūd, Sarbadār rebel, 426
Sulṭān Bāyazīd, Jalayirid prince, 174–6
Sulṭān Ḥusayn, Jalayirid ruler, 174–6, 183–4

Sulṭān Ḥusayn b. Muḥammad Beg, maternal grandson of Timur, 274–5, 309, 419–22, 426, 558, 638
Sulṭān Ḥusayn Bāyqarā, Timurid Sultan, 17, 34, 359, 410, 414, 436, 485; his sons, 437
Sulṭān Maḥmūd, (Ögödeyid) khan of Chaghadai's ulus, 275, 338, 340–4, 347–8, 351–5, 358, 399, 447, 450, 583, 586, 608–10, 613, 615; as Timur's stepson, 357
Sulṭān Maḥmūd b. Kaykhusraw, 259
Sulṭān Maḥmūd b. Shāh Walad, Jalayirid ruler, 297
Sulṭān Muḥammad, Muzaffarid prince, 294
Sulṭān Muʿtaṣim, Muzaffarid prince, 428
Sulṭān Saʿīd, Mughūl khan, 203, 206
Sulṭān Shiblī, Muzaffarid prince, 295
Sulṭān Uways, Muzaffarid prince, 180
Sulṭān Walad, shaykh, 101
Sulṭāniyya, 72–3, 116, 156, 173–6, 180, 193, 195, 267, 274, 279, 288, 295–6, 376, 395, 423;
  ecclesiastical province of, 161, 542; archbishop of, 99, 157; *see also* John
Sunnī Islam, Sunnī Muslims, 100, 188
Sura (Sara), River, 544
al-Suyūṭī, author of plague treatise, 148
synoptic account of Timur, 28, 32, 428–9, 433, 595
Syria, Syrians, 2, 4, 9, 35–7, 42–3, 55, 63–4, 67, 76, 78, 82, 96, 100, 108, 137, 140, 143, 145, 148–9, 153, 272, 289, 293, 297, 300–1, 310, 316, 324–5, 327, 333, 353, 375, 419, 428, 433, 445, 572, 599, 608
Syriac sources, 374, 376

Taban Qauchin, Timurid amir, 261, 263, 266, 579
al-Ṭabarī, early Islamic historian, 383
Tabriz, 79, 115, 131, 155–6, 169–70, 173–5, 179–80, 183, 193, 268, 288, 294–7, 325, 367, 547, 549, 553; as political heart of Iran, 173, 193, 553
Taftāzān, 167
Taghai, Jochid amir, 521
Taghai Bugha Barlās, Timurid amir, 261–2
Taghai Temür, Ilkhan, 25, 31, 80, 115–19, 130–2, 134–5, 155–6, 158–9, 168–71, 182–4, 186–9, 192, 206, 291, 348, 352, 426, 518, 527, 550, 553; his sons, 541
Ṭahartan (or Muṭahhartan), ruler of Arzinjān, 296, 303, 322, 609
Taidula, Jochid khatun, 120
Tāīzī Oghlan (Bunyashirin), Ögödeyid prince, 344, 349–51, 396, 612; identical with Öljei Temür, 349–50
Taizu (the Hongwu Emperor), founder of the Ming dynasty, 111, 307–8, 319, 363, 389, 629
Tāj al-Dīn ʿAlī Chishumī, Sarbadār ruler, 187
Tājīks, 4, 69, 135, 168–70, 177, 182, 204–5, 239, 268, 410, 599; in Timur's service, 268–9, 311, 323
Tajikistan, 3
Takht-i Sulaymān, 192, 553
Takrīt, 297, 329, 331–2, 399–400, 604, 632
Talās, 143, 199, 215, 239, 273, 287
*Talikhān, 184
Ṭāliqān, 212, 216
*Talmīna, 382
tamgha, commercial tax, 67, 84, 87, 90, 403, 409, 451
tamghachi, 403
tamma (frontier forces), 66–7, 78, 92, 207, 209, 244
Tana, 45, 140, 144–5, 151, 157, 289, 331, 363, 374–5, 587, 617
Tang dynasty, 57
Tangut, son of Jochi, 121
Tangut empire, 63; *see also* Xi Xia
'tanistry', 73
Tārābī, Maḥmūd, rebel against Mongols, 227, 232, 240
Taraghai, Chaghadayid amir, 209, 213, 298, 562–3, 573
Taraghai, Timur's father, 94, 223–5, 228–9, 233–4, 566, 569

Ṭarāz, *see* Talās
Ta'rīkh-i arba' a ulūs, 47, 77
al-Ta'rīkh al-Ghiyāthī, 48, 227
Ta'rīkh-i guzīda, *see* Ḥamd-Allāh Mustawfī
Ta'rīkh-i mubārak-i Ghāzānī, 24–5,
Ta'rīkh-i Yamīnī, 371; *see also* 'Utbī
Tarim, River, 203, 286 (Tārim), 441
tarkhan (*darqan*), one of privileged status, 65, 235, 237
Tarmashirin, Chaghadayid khan, 83, 94–5, 107, 109, 111–12, 124–5, 138, 143, 201, 203–5, 215–18, 220, 224, 236, 238, 241, 252, 297, 351, 353, 390, 450, 513, 523, 571, 584, 629; his adoption of Islam, 93, 97, 137; his offspring, 107, 217, 564
Ṭārum, 210
Tashkent, 256, 273, 287, 293, 586; *see also* Shāsh
Tatar Tongga, Uighur scribe, 60
Tatars, 2, 57, 64
ṭā' ūn (generally 'plague'), 148, 154
Tawārīkh-i guzīda Nuṣrat-nāma, 48, 121
Ṭāyaqān, 212, 258 ('Ṭāyikhān')
Tayichi'ut, tribe, 238, 242, 258, 274
Tāyyabād, 384
Teb-Tenggeri (Kököchü), Mongol shaman, 59, 102, 413
Tegüder, Chaghadayid prince, 78, 232, 559
Tegüder-Aḥmad, Ilkhan, 23, 94, 98, 107, 109, 209, 514; adoption of Islam, 93–4, 96, 104
*Tekine Khatun, Timur's mother, 224, 566
Temüge Otchigin, brother of Chinggis Khan, 70, 417, 517
Temüge Qauchin, Timurid amir, 261, 264, 579–80
Temüjin, 1, 56–7, 59, 88, 226, 253, 261, 389–90; *see also* Chinggis Khan
*Temülei, Chaghadayid amir, 232–3, 570
Temür, Mongol Qaghan, 77, 82, 85, 212–13
Temür, Negüderi chief, 214
Temür Khwāja, Jochid khan, 121–2, 521
Temür Khwāja b. Aq Khwāja, Timurid amir, 263, 421
Temür Malik, khan of the Blue Horde, 288, 406, 611
Temür Qutlugh, Jochid khan, 289–90, 319, 349, 351, 353–4, 588, 611
Temür Shāh, Chaghadayid khan, 127, 525
Temürtash, Timurid amir, 263–4
Tenggeri ('Heaven'), 59–60, 101, 367, 391
Tengiz Buqa, Jochid amir, 123
Terek, River, battle on the (1395), 289, 323, 611
Tian Shan, 147, 203
Tibet, 3, 87, 147
Tigīnābād, 213–14, 562
Tilang (Telingana), 153–4
Tilenchi Arlāt, Chaghadayid amir, 243, 258
Timur, 1–5, 7–10, 63, 69, 73, 79, 100, 103, 113, 119, 128, 135–6, 160–1, 189–90; modern studies of, 6–7; primary sources on, 11–13, 27–49; his *fatḥ-nāma*s, 34–5, 485; his correspondence, 34–5; alleged 'memoirs', 11–12, 479
  date of birth, 252, 356, 576; appearance, 6, 252–3; fictive ancestry, 31, 225–9, 359; degree of literacy, 253, 557, 577; early career and rise to power, 182, 185, 220–1, 254–7; as head of Chaghadai's ulus, 257–60; status as *güregen*, 357; wives, 278–81; *see also* Sarai Mulk Khanim, Tümen Āghā; his khans, 30, 78, 80, 85, 133, 338–44, 352–5; *see also* Soyurghatmish, Sulṭān Maḥ mūd; his lieutenants, 261–9; building projects, 8, 36–7, 46, 369–70; as heir of the Ilkhans, 276, 355–6, 614; emulation of Chinggis Khan, 388–9; alleged supernatural gifts, 412–13; death and burial, 5–6, 308–9, 369–70, 380–1, 412, 438; legacy, 9–10,

437–9; compared with Chinggis Khan, 2, 4, 8, 389–99, 416–17
campaigns: against Khwārazm, 285; in Khurāsān and Sīstān, 290–3; in southern Iran, 293–5; against the Jalayirids and Qarā-Qūyūnlū, 295–7; in the Qipchaq steppe, 287–9; against Jata (Mughūlistān), 200, 285–7; in India, 298–300; in Syria, 301–2; against the Ottomans, 302–4, 310; preparations for, and purpose of, the abortive campaign against Ming China, 265, 287, 307–9, 321, 323–4, 350, 373, 395
war aims, 313–18, 393–401; supposed intention to restore the Mongol empire, 338, 393–9; generalship and tactics, 319–20, 323–5, 327–8; strength of his armies, 320–3, 327–30; intelligence network, 301, 325–7; plunder acquired by, 313–18, 325; atrocities, 330–5; efforts to rehabilitate the conquered lands, 335–6
Timurid dynasty, Timurids, 7, 11, 14, 17–19, 31, 48, 85, 106, 136, 168, 202, 265, 270–8, 297, 300, 321, 341, 345–7, 350, 352, 359, 406, 408–9, 415–40, 449; Timurids with Chinggisid ancestry, 271, 345, 358, 415–17, 419–20, 428
Timurid historians/sources, 12, 22, 26, 41, 47–9, 62, 120, 124, 126–7, 145, 201, 205–6, 219–20, 223–4, 229–30, 233–4, 236, 242, 245–6, 252–3, 257, 278, 289, 292, 304, 308, 316, 318, 322, 332–3, 350–1, 354, 367, 373, 381, 386. 389–91, 394, 398, 403–5, 413, 444–5, 447
Tinibeg, khan of the Golden Horde, 120, 481, 522
Tirmidh, 125–6, 215, 239–40, 264; qadi of, 217; sayyids of, 239–40, 377, 410
Töde Mengü, khan of the Golden Horde, 93, 96; adoption of Islam, 93
Toghan, Oyirat chief, 440
Toghan Temür, Mongol Qaghan, 111, 138
Toghmaq, 318, *see* Qipchaq steppe
Toghril, *see* Ong Khan
Toghus Temür, Qaghan (Northern Yuan), 307
Töle Buqa, khan of the Golden Horde, 93
Tolui, fourth son of Chinggis Khan, 3, 62, 74–5, 91, 357, 392, 487, 614; descendants of, *see* Toluids
Toluids, 30, 62, 74, 83, 112, 115, 131, 484, 500; transfer of imperial dignity to, 74, 77, 80, 85, 338, 356
Tonguz Khan, nickname for the first Ming Emperor, 307
Toqa Temür, son of Jochi, 62; descendants of, 112, 121, 123, 440, 522–3, 587, 611–12
*Toqbugha, Chaghadayid amir, 571
Toqtamish, khan of the Golden Horde, 12, 44, 79, 121–4, 132, 160, 259, 262, 265–6, 271, 285, 287–90, 293, 311–12, 316–17, 319, 321–3, 325, 327, 341, 343, 348–50, 354, 360, 364, 367–8, 372, 390–2, 395–6, 405, 409, 447, 449, 490–1, 519, 522, 587–8, 596, 608, 611, 629, 631; his sons, 206, 290, 611
Toqtaqaya, khan of the Blue Horde, 288
Toqto'a, khan of the Golden Horde, 93, 211
Töre, 14, 17, 36, 119, 229, 231, 337, 404–8, 411–12, 414, 429; *see also* Yasa
tovachi, inspector of troops, 224, 263, 321, 323
T'ovma Metsobets'i (Thomas of Metsop'), Armenian chronicler, 46, 374, 376
Toynbee, Arnold, 478
trade, Timur's concern for, 290, 307, 335–6, 594
traditions (*ḥadīth*) of the Prophet, 86
Transcaucasus, 92, 348
Transoxiana, 1, 3–5, 10, 17, 19, 27–9, 35, 53, 58–9, 65–6, 85, 113, 125–6,

128, 131, 146, 150, 161, 170–1, 182, 199–202, 205, 208, 214–15, 223, 225, 232, 234–5, 238, 254–5, 257, 264, 267–73, 281, 286, 288–91, 293–4, 298, 313–14, 316, 336–7, 339, 344–7, 353, 358, 365, 381, 388, 393, 395–6, 398–400, 406, 415, 417, 421–2, 426–7, 430–1, 434, 436–9, 444–5, 447, 449, 483; *see also* Mā warā' al-nahr
Transylvania, 143
Trebizond, 156–7
Tsewang Arabdan, ruler of the Oyirat/Zunghars, 441
'Tsunami strategy', 66, 402
Tughluq Temür, Chaghadayid khan, 48–9, 125, 127–9, 201, 204, 219, 230, 234, 236, 254–5, 257, 259, 267, 286, 337, 406, 445, 525; his adoption of Islam, 94–5, 97, 105
Tughluqid dynasty, Tughluqids, in Delhi, 354; *see also* Fīrūz Shāh, Ghiyāth al-Dīn Tughluq, Muḥ ammad b. Tughluq
Tükel b. Yādgār Barlās, Timurid amir, 277
Tükel Buqa, amir of the Jā'ūn-i Qurbān, 184
Tükel Khanim, Chaghadayid princess and wife of Timur, 279, 357
Tükel Qutlugh, Ögödeyid prince, 131, 526
Ṭukhāristān, 345, 430, 582
Tülek, Dughlāt amir, 201
Tulunbeg, Jochid princess and wife of Mamai, 123
Tümen, Negüderi amir, 219
tümen, military unit of ten thousand/district capable of raising that number, 64, 209, 212, 230, 232, 266, 276, 321, 341, 367, 604
Tümen Āghā, wife of Timur, 278–81, 420, 584–5, 627
Tümenei, Mongol khan and ancestor of Chinggis Khan, 225–9, 236; alleged compact of, 226–7
Tunis, Tunisia, 35–6, 140
Turan, 2, 195, 269, 311, 355, 360, 394, 452, 614, 630
Turbat-i Shaykh Jām, 370
*Turchiyan, Chaghadayid amir, 223, 237
Turfan, 202, 205; Turfan expeditions, 83
Turkān, Arlāt chief, 259
Turkestan, 3, 93, 140, 144, 237, 246, 316, 322, 354
Turkish language, 4, 59, 204–5, 225, 253, 384
Turkistān (Yasi), 202
Turkmenistan, 3, 55, 246
Türkmens, 9, 69, 117, 168, 171, 175–8, 207, 318; *see also* Āq-Qūyūnlū, Qarā-Qūyūnlū
Turks, 3–4, 40, 48, 55, 60, 67, 86, 92, 135, 153, 161, 204, 206, 208, 240, 245, 268, 304, 311, 323, 390, 509, 599; Mongols regarded as, 40, 69, 86, 204, 546, 557; assimilation with Mongols, 92, 136, 204, 225, 529
Türk empire, Türks (Kök Türks), 53, 59–60, 68, 72, 397, 404
Turshīz, 316, 329
Ṭūs, 118, 167, 170, 184–5, 187, 331, 333, 603, 605
tutmaj, noodles, 323, 600
Twelve Imams, 100, 188
Twelver Shiʿism, Twelver Shīʿīs, 100, 186; *see also* Öljeitü

Üch, 203, 286
Üch Qara, Timurid amir, 261, 579
Uchch, 298
Ügek, 289
Uighur empire, 53, 59–60
Uighur script, 60, 169, 205, 226–7, 253
Uighuristan, Uighurs, 56, 58–60, 66–7, 69, 78, 87, 91, 104, 128, 200, 204–5, 207
  Uighur scribes, 12
ʿulama, 106–7, 217, 241, 269, 368, 379–80, 382, 411
Ulugh Beg (Muḥammad Taraghai) b. Shāhrukh, Timurid Sultan, 5, 17, 28, 47, 77, 94, 280, 346–7, 358, 393, 406–7, 421–2, 427, 431, 434–6; his appanage, 273, 287;

ulugh ming ('the great thousand' of Kish) or *ulugh tümen*, 233, 257, 570
ulus, 3, 61
ʿUmar b. ʿAbbās, Timurid amir, 266
ʿUmar b. Amīrānshāh, Timurid prince, 27, 32–3, 273, 400, 418, 423–4, 431, 583, 621, 639; his appanage, 272–3, 277, 310
ʿUmar Shaykh, son of Timur, 32–3, 259, 270, 275–7, 287, 316, 330, 412, 423, 429, 615; made governor of Andijān, 270; transferred to Fārs, 270, 276–7, 295; marriage to a Chaghadayid princess, 358; his descendants, 32–3, 359, 418, 423–4, 427–31, 436, 485
al-ʿUmarī, *see* Ibn Faḍl-Allāh al-ʿUmarī
Umayyad Mosque, 39, 302, 379
Umayyad Caliphate, Umayyads, 100, 333, 379–80
Ural, River, 121, 144, 151, 323
Ürgench, 150–1, 220, 285, 317, 328, 335, 364, 538
Uriyangqats, tribe, 57
Ūrūn Sulṭān Khānīka, Ögödeyid princess, 358, 418
Ürüngtash (Uz Temür?), Jochid prince, 522–3
ʿushr (tithe), 403, 409
ʿUtbī, Ghaznawid author, 371, 621
ʿUthmān b. ʿAbbās, Timurid amir, 267, 278
Utrār, 58, 125, 151, 308–9, 349
Uways, *see* Shaykh Uways
Uways b. Edigü Barlās, Timurid governor of Kirmān, 425
Uzbekistan, 3, 7, 18–19
Uzbek khans, Uzbeks, 19, 48, 121, 206, 436–9, 637
Ūzkand, 235, 285, 358, 427–8, 431
Uzun Ḥasan, Āq-Qūyūnlū Sultan, 436

Vajrapāṇi, 18
Van, 329
Vardapet Yovhannēs, 374
Vásáry, István, 120, 406
Venetians, Venice, 45, 140, 144–5, 289, 305, 320, 331, 363, 374, 593; *see also* Tana
Villani, Giovanni, Florentine chronicler, 157
Villani, Matteo, Florentine chronicler, 149
Virgin Mary, 289
Vivaldi, Antonio, 6, 19
Vladimir, Grand Prince of, 122
Volga, River, 3, 53, 72, 123, 157, 544
Volga Bulgars, Volga Bulgaria, 64, 536; language of, 157
Voltaire, 8

wabā' ('pestilence'), 148, 154, 541
waqf (pl. *awqāf*., pious foundations), 94, 98, 240, 378, 635
Wāqwāq, 531
'War of the Straits' (1350–5), 144
Wāsiṭ, 272
Waṣṣāf, Ilkhanid chronicler, 24, 27, 29, 70–1, 96, 104, 109, 136, 140, 198, 209, 212–13, 233–4
Ways (Uways), Mughūl khan, 206, 337, 346, 434, 440, 610
Weiers, Michael, 102
Western Christians, 45, 76
Woods, John, 232–3
Wurūjird, 549; *see also* Burūjird

Xi Liao, *see* Qara-Khitai
Xi Xia (Tangut) empire, 147
xingsheng, 'joint satellite administration', 67–8, 78
Xinjiang, 2, 3, 441

Yādgār Barlās, Timurid amir, 262
Yādgār Oghlan, Jochid prince, 351, 613
Yaḥyā, Timurid amir, 278
Yājūj and Mājūj (Gog and Magog), 37
yam, postal relay system, 67–8, 84, 325
Yaminid (or Ghaznawid) dynasty, 55, 371
Yangi, Chaghadayid prince, 246, 576
Yangī, 273, 287; Yangī-Talās, 199; *see also* Talās
Yangikent, 538
Yaʿqūb, Āq-Qūyūnlū Sultan, 409

yarghu, tribunal, 84, 87, 231, 259, 409–11, 451, 636; *yarghuchi*, 230–1
Yārkand, 48, 203, 215, 235, 286
yarligh (command), restricted to the Qaghan, 83; of other monarchs, 343; *see also lingchi*
Yaruq, Jochid prince, 349
Yasa/'Chinggis Khan's Yasa', 14–15, 17, 36, 69–72, 84–5, 109–10, 119, 136–7, 198–9, 201, 229, 231, 337, 403–4, 406–7, 409–11, 451, 554, 633
*yasa*s, *yāsāq*, 71–2, 84–5, 87–9, 138, 323–4, 345, 404–6, 411, 506, 515, 633–5; 'Great Book of *yasa*s', 69–70
Yasa'ur (Ulugh Yasa'ur), Chaghadayid amir, 211, 237–8, 244, 247, 572–3
Yasa'ur, Chaghadayid prince, 81, 125–6, 134, 214–15, 238, 241, 244, 524, 572
Yasa'ur, Mongol amir, 572
Yasā'ūrī Mongols, 66, 244, 257–9
Yasawī, Shaykh Aḥmad, 356; his tomb, 369
Yasi (Turkistān), 369
Yayiq, *see* Ural, River
Yazd, 28, 47, 118, 156, 168, 172, 175, 178–81, 189, 210, 264, 293, 328–9, 331, 424, 426, 428
Yazdī, Ghiyāth al-Dīn ʿAlī, Timurid chronicler, 11, 27–8, 31–2, 199, 201, 291–2, 299, 311, 320, 322, 347, 354–5, 362, 364, 371, 384, 390, 621; his *Rūz-nāma*, 28, 342, 347, 361
Yazdī, Muʿīn al-Dīn, Muzaffarid chronicler, 26, 31, 156, 193
Yazdī, Sharaf al-Dīn ʿAlī, Timurid chronicler, 11, 12, 29–30, 32–4, 47–9, 103–4, 120, 125, 127, 135, 191, 200–3, 219, 224–7, 232–5, 245, 251, 262–3, 267, 272–3, 275–6, 287–90, 298–9, 301–3, 305–6, 311, 315, 317, 320, 322–4, 328–9, 333, 335, 342, 347–50, 353–6, 359, 364, 367, 370–3, 378, 382, 390, 405–6, 408–11, 413, 416, 450, 616, 630; his historical works, 29–30; his *Muqaddima*, 29–30, 47, 227, 234, 359, 523, 636; his *Ẓafar-nāma*, 29–30, 227, 361, 485
Yazīd, Umayyad Caliph, 379
yengelik, 513; *see also* levirate marriage
Yersinia pestis (plague bacillus), 147, 534–6
Yesü Buqa, Chaghadayid amir, 238
Yesü Möngke, Chaghadayid khan, 80
Yesüder, Mongol Qaghan (Northern Yuan), 515
Yesügei, father of Chinggis Khan, 57, 226, 630
Yesün Temür, Chaghadayid khan, 125, 144, 357–8, 504, 523
Yesün Temür, Mongol Qaghan, 82
Yesünjin, Chaghadayid princess, 213, 238, 573
*Yesünte Möngke, son of Qarachar, 232, 235
Yeti-su, 199
Yongle, Emperor of China, 307, 309, 407–9, 612, 635–6
Yoshmut, son of Hülegü, 116
Yuan dynasty, Yuan empire, 3, 15, 18, 22–3, 63, 77, 79–80, 82–4, 102, 111, 134, 137, 141, 504, 607; *see also* Northern Yuan
Yuanshi, 21, 81, 230–1
Yugra people, 149
Yul Qutlugh, secretary, 268
*Yula Temür, Ilkhanid amir, 514
Yüldüz, 199, 215, 310, 324; River, 286
Yunnan, 536
Yūnus, Mughūl khan, 48, 201–3, 346, 438
yurtchi (quartermaster), 402
Yūsuf b. Sulaymānshāh, Timurid amir, 264
Yūsuf Barlās, Timurid amir, 262
Yūsuf Ṣūfī, ruler of Khwārazm, 285
Yūsuf-i Ahl, 34
al-Yūsufī, Mamlūk chronicler, 117, 152, 518
yusūn/*yūsūn* (custom), 70–2, 110, 405–6, 515
yut, 159

Zāb, River, 383
Ẓafār, 154
Ẓafar-nāma, 26; continuations of, 26; *see also* Ḥāfiẓ-i Abrū, Ḥ amd-Allāh Mustawfī Qazwīnī
al-Ẓāhir ʿĪsā, sultan of Mārdīn, 330
zakāt, Islamic alms tax, 105, 108, 409
Zamzam, 414
Zanjīr Sarai, palace, 289
Zāwa, battle of (1342), 181, 187, 518
Zayn al-ʿĀbidīn ʿAlī, Muzaffarid ruler, 181, 294–5, 428
Zayn al-Dīn b. Ḥamd-Allāh Mustawfī, Jalayirid chronicler, 26, 33, 131, 155–6, 183, 367
Zayn al-Dīn Khwāfī, shaykh, 378, 384, 394
Zayton, *see* Quanzhou
Zhao Gong, Song envoy to the Mongols, 576
Zhongdu, 57
Zhu Di, 435; *see also* Yongle
Zhu Yuanzhang, *see* Taizu
Zinda Ḥasham, Chaghadayid amir, 243, 257–8, 262, 291
Zīrak Barlās, Timurid amir, 265
Zirih, 332, 604
Zoroastrians, 508
Zunghars, Zungharia, 62, 207, 441–2, 532, 643